DC HAS WHAT YOU'RE LO

Can't find those rare, expensive back issues of your favorite DC Comics and Vertigo titles?

Many of our most famous sagas are available in affordable, convenient trade paperback collections. To find them, just ask your local comics retailer.

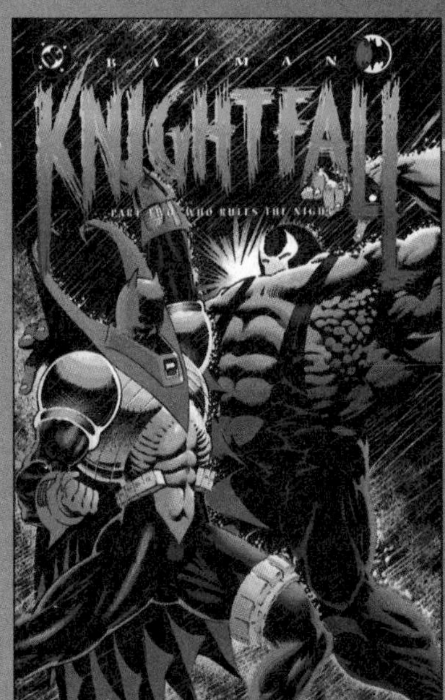

WORTH READING! WORTH KEEPING!

All Vertigo titles are suggested for mature readers.

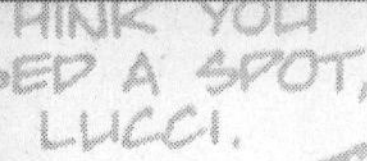

1996 COMIC BOOK PRICE GUIDE ANNUAL

2ND EDITION

The Wizard 1996 Comic Book Price Guide Annual (2nd Edition)
is an original publication published by Wizard Press.

Wizard Press
151 Wells Avenue
Congers, NY 10920
914.268.3594
WizardTGTC@aol.com

Distributed to the book trade by Prima Publishing
3875 Atherton Road
Rocklin, CA 95765-3716

Please direct all inquiries concerning editorial information to Wizard 1996 Comic Book Price Guide Annual Editorial Department, 151 Wells Avenue, Congers, NY 10920-2064.

CONTENTS

EDITOR-IN-CHIEF Patrick McCallum
EDITOR Brian Cunningham
SENIOR MANAGING EDITOR Joe Yanarella
MANAGING EDITOR Scott Gramling
CONTRIBUTING EDITOR Marc Wilkofsky
COPY EDITOR Andrew Kardon
PRICE GUIDE DIRECTOR Stephen Shamus
SENIOR PRICE GUIDE EDITOR Jon Warren
PRICE GUIDE EDITOR Bob Marshall
ASSISTANT PRICE GUIDE EDITOR Phil Colligan
ADMINISTRATIVE ASSISTANT Mercedes Cabo

ART DIRECTOR Brad "Bearsby" Fountain
DESIGNERS Matt Tierney, Arlene So
ART ASSISTANT Daniel Reilly, Ken Bell
HERO FOR ALL CAL RIPKEN JR.

CONTRIBUTING WRITERS

Paul J. Grant, Kurt Jackson, Bill Liebowitz, John Marsland, Marc Shapiro and Craig Shutt

SPIDER-MAN COVER ART Peter Scanlan

WIZARD PRESS
PRESIDENT/PUBLISHER Gareb S. Shamus
EXECUTIVE VP Fred Pierce
VP FINANCE Edward L. DuPré
EXECUTIVE ASSISTANT Martha Scheidegger
PRODUCTION DIRECTOR Douglas Goldstein
PROMOTIONS & PUBLICITY MANAGER Jim McLauchlin
PROMOTIONS & PUBLICITY COORDINATOR Kathy Newman
DIR. OF CIRCULATION & DISTRIBUTION Paul Rolnick
CIRCULATION MANAGER Kate Torpey
CIRCULATION ANALYST Jen Winheim
ACCOUNTING MANAGER Raka Raychaudhuri
FINANCIAL ANALYST Jeff Petrik
DIRECT SALES MANAGER Marty Stever
ONLINE EDITOR Buddy Scalera

CUSTOMER SERVICE Maria Capello @ (914) 268-3594

FULL PAGE INC. ADVERTISING
GROUP ADVERTISING DIRECTOR Michael C. Roberts
MANAGER, SPECIAL PROJECTS Alison James
MIDWEST/WEST ACCOUNTS MANAGER Karen Lee James
EASTERN ACCOUNTS MANAGER Jason Kelley
ADVERTISING COORDINATOR Karen Evora
SALES ASSISTANT Elizabeth Almond
EAST: PH: (914) 268-3907 **FAX:** (914) 268-5386

PREFACE

8 WORDS BEFORE YOU BEGIN
A word (or two) on collecting comics
by Harlan Ellison

CONTEST

14 WIN AN OLD MUTANT
Wanna win an *X-Men* #1...you know, the original Stan 'n' Jack masterpiece from 1963? All you haveta to do is answer a few questions....

SMART COLLECTING

16 START ME UP!
Looking to start a collection of comic books? Let us get you rolling.
by the *Wizard* staff

24 COMICS 101
Everything you were afraid to know about comics but wanted to ask
by Bill Liebowitz

30 KA-CHING!
Helpful hints on how to buy and sell your comics
by Kurt Jackson

32 PACK IT IN
The best way to make sure your comics last forever
by Kurt Jackson

BEYOND THE COMICS

34 PLUG IN!
Wizard's introduction and guide to comics in cyberspace
by Buddy Scalera

40 BIG BUSINESS
Comics make their presence felt in today's mass-merchandising world
by John Marsland

44 LONG STRANGE TRIP
A review of 1995 proves that when it comes to comics, anything is possible
by Marc Shapiro

MOVERS & SHAKERS

55 MILESTONES
Landmark books that have made comic history
by Jon Warren and Marc Wikofsky

62 CREATIVE JUICES
Meet the masterminds behind the comics
by Marc Shapiro

CLOSER LOOK

72 ANATOMY OF A COMIC BOOK
Ever stop to think what *really* makes up a comic book?

74 GRADE SCHOOL
A lesson on how to grade your comic books

PRICE GUIDE

80 COMIC BOOK PRICE GUIDE
More comic book price listings than you could ever want to know

287 CONVENTION CALENDAR
Pack the party van...time for a road trip!

288 RESOURCE PAGE
How to get in touch with your favorite companies

Words Before You Begin

BY HARLAN ELLISON

Upon the eventual death, in 1923, of George Edward Stanhope Molyneux Herbert, 5th Earl of Carnarvon, co-discoverer (with archaeologist Howard Carter) of the ages-lost tomb of Tutankhamun in the Valley of the Kings, it was softly and gently whispered that a great many more artifacts than had been catalogued, had in fact been unearthed in that astonishing Egyptian necropolis. It was bruited through the international museum underground in "Chinese Whispers" that Lord Carnarvon had, er, uh, well, *excluded* more than a few of the choicest pieces. His death, only a year after the opening of the tomb, with all the attendant nonsense mythology about The Curse of the Pharaohs (it was a mosquito bite), served to damp the rumors. Even though "new" icons kept turning up.

Albert L. Ortega

Decades later, on the occasion of reburbishing the ancestral manse of the Carnarvons, a carpenter assigned the task of ripping out mildew-reeking baseboards and watersoaked panelling, prised open a decrepit section of wall in an upstairs gallery and found himself staring at a series of large, dust-thick, cobwebbed chambers that had lain hidden and unknown, lost and unopened, since the untimely demise of the 5th Earl. Racked and shelved, billeted and closeted, stashed and secreted, in glass cases and reliquaries, mounted on walls and still nesting in crates full of excelsior, stacked in niches and arrayed in Victorian armoires, were hundreds of unknown artifacts: "finger rings of blue faience decorated with the cartouche of Tutankhamun's throne name, Nebkheperura; slender silver nails withdrawn from the second coffin of the King, and two royal nails, in solid gold, from the third coffin; an elegant broad collar of blue faience beads; a solid-gold ring; the fragmentary handle of a golden fan or scepter inlaid masterfully with pieces of carnelian, lapis lazuli and green feldspar set into a series of horizontal chevrons..." and on and on.

Carnarvon and Carter, in secret, had stolen back into the newly-opened tomb and had desported themselves as had tomb-robbers throughout the centuries. They had spirited away and hidden—knowing no public display could *ever* be made of their possessions lest they be disgraced and likely even be criminally charged—the collectibles that cried out to them, "Take me! You want me, you must have me! I'm yours if only you'll take me up, and take me away!" And so they did. Two of the most famous men in the annals of archaeology risked *everything* to possess the rare, the special, the incalculably treasurable, the unique. They robbed, they looted, they pilfered, they took demented and criminal risk...to own that which no one else owned.

They were collectors.

H.G. Wells was a collector of military miniatures. He made whole rooms in his home useless for human congress because they were filled with mock battles posed by thousands of lead soldiers massed in phalanxes and battalions and hollow squares. He got daily mailings from all over the world, from fans and enthusiasts, of zouaves and paratroopers and dragoons and Horse Guards; and when he lay dying in 1946, he held a tiny toy soldier; and when his nurse fussed over him, as his last moment arrived, he said, "Go away. I'm all right." He was a collector.

The Romanovs collected Fabergé eggs; Andy Warhol filled warehouses with collections of cookie jars, salt and pepper shakers, wind-up toys, greeting cards; the actor Robert Culp collects *Big Little Books* from the '30s and '40s; Jay Leno has a collection of rare cars so large he has to lease half a dozen airplane hangar-sized storage facilities; in the world of comic book moguls, avid collectors Mike Richardson, Steve Geppi, Russ Cochran and Denis Kitchen all have collections worth millions of dollars. They are all collectors.

I was considering ponying up the king's ransom to buy *Hit Comics* #5 from 1940, with that incredible Lou Fine cover, when an urchin in rollerblades sallied up beside me, took one look, and asked, "How much's that worth?" I looked down at him. "It's worth all the jewels and essences of Araby to me, kiddo." He looked up at me, sneered and said, "Is it gonna sell for more than the first issue of *Spawn*?"

This is a sickness. It is a need for the laying on of hands. It is a never-diminishing fever that possesses otherwise decent and normal men and women and children.

I have seen a comic book collector, desirous of obtaining an issue of *Pep Comics* from the mid-'40s from another archivist who could not bear to part with it, go mad with lust. I have seen him hire thugs and pistoleros and, after kicking in the front door of the archivist's home, have seen him and his vile horde slaughter the residents of that house, to the last child and puppy and guppy, simply to possess that one perfect 10¢ periodical.

I have seen sensible, sensitive and sensual women, driven by the need to complete their run of Wm. Moulton Marsten *Wonder Woman* comics, seduce and poison magazine dealers who had priced the rarities beyond normal means. New horrors! New horrors!

To own the unique. To sit in the wee steamy hours wearing nothing but thin latex gloves, turning the pages of a Street & Smith *Shadow Comic* with most excellent drawings by Bob Powell. To gaze at the rarest of the rare. To sell one's spouse and offspring into harems and whorehouses in the oil duchys of the Mideast, to obtain the funds to buy a mint copy of *Captain Marvel Adventures* #1. To be able to say, all glassy-eyed and short of breath, to the postal person or random Federal Express messenger, "Would you like to see my collection?" To be a fine collector. Is this not Life at the Top?

If the truth be known, I hate these damned price guides. They are hand-maiden to the grossing-out of the American Kid Comic Buying Constituency. Kids don't go into a comic book shop and look about in wonder these days. They don't enter the shop like Ali Baba whipping a fast open-sesame on a blank wall and gaining entrance to the cave of miracles. They don't enter the holiest of holies, the little shoppe of comix, with eyes all bugged and filled with bounty. They don't save their pennies to buy that one special comic they just *gotta* have.

Today, or actually a few months ago, a ratty little weasel of a kid was standing next to me as I was considering ponying up the king's ransom to buy *Hit Comics* #5 from 1940, with that incredible Lou Fine cover, when an urchin in rollerblades sallied up beside me, took one look, and asked, "How much's that worth?" I looked down at him. "It's worth all the jewels and essences of Araby to me, kiddo." He looked up at me, sneered and said, "Is it gonna sell for more than the first issue of *Spawn*?"

Fortunately, I was able to stomp the little piss-ant to death before he was able to extrude his pods and open his shell and spread his demonseed to the wind. Bill and Sharon and Tony at Golden Apple helped me swab up the green slime. Hoping you are the same.

The point being:

I really *really* don't like these price guide things. All they do is leach the joy out of comic book reading and collecting, and turn innocent kids into clone-children of Reaganomics, pukey li'l greedheads who don't know a good story from a pimple on the butt. Price guides tell them that the value of a creative item is not inherently in the item itself, it's in the dubious market value. And as we all know, those who sell rare and old and valuable comics are uniformly twisted, demented, aberrant toads only recently escaped from institutions of moral turpitude or asylums for the terminally boring. Also, they don't stand close enough to their toothbrushes in the morning.

GET BITTEN BY THE BUG
THE SENSATIONAL SPIDER-MAN
#0
48 pages by
DAN JURGENS
+
KLAUS JANSON
SHIPPING IN NOVEMBER
MARVEL
TM & © MARVEL ENTERTAINMENT GROUP, INC. ALL RIGHTS RESERVED

So here I am, having been pressed into service to write yet another introduction or preface or whatever, to yet another price guide for yet another year. And I'm taking money for it, so that tells you a lot more than you need to know about *me*.

What you *might* find interesting about me, is that I dwell beneath the cloak of madness that is collecting, the same as many of you. I collect military miniatures and art deco furniture; *Big Little Books* and postal first day covers; pewter figurines and rare glass like Lalique and Muller Fréres and Correia; collectible comic art drinking glasses and pocket watches; first edition books and wind-up toys; trading cards and the film scores of Ennio Morricone. But most of all, I collect comics. Hundreds of comics. Thousands of comics. *Tens* of thousands of comics. Been collecting them since I bought (or got, or stole) my first one, *New York World's Fair Comics* in 1939. And I still have all of them.

Price Guides like this one are nifty and spiffy and max cool and imperial, not because they tell you some treasure in your attic is worth eighty gazillion bucks, but because they show you the history and timeline of the existence of this purely American-born art-form. It may have prices in it, but the delight is for your eyes; not your wallet.

My mother respected my hobbies. She never threw mine out. And so, when I consult last year's *Wizard Comic Book Price Guide Annual*, I discover to my horror and great sadness that the 1939 comic bearing its price tag of 15¢ (it was, I believe, the first 15¢ comic in an era when *all* comics—except *Nickel Comics*—cost a mere ten cents) (15¢ was a fortune in them days) now goes for $12,000 in mint condition and $3025 in very good condition. My copy is somewhere between those two. And my copy of the 1940 *New York World's Fair Comics* (which then became, for one issue, *World's Best Comics* and thereafter spent its existence as the DC anthology *World's Finest Comics*) can be obtained in mint condition for a mere $7000.

Now do you understand why I hate these price guide things? It's sorrowful enough to dwell beneath the cloak of collector lunacy, to want, to need, to hunger for physical possessions. It's an obsession that can never be sated. One can never own enough, or have enough, or be content enough...merely to *stop*. It's bad enough to be trapped in a habit pattern like that.

But it's infinitely worse to consider what those dear, lovely and rare artifacts are *worth*.

I own a Hannes Bok painting. Someone asked me if I'd sell it for ten grand. I bought it for a *lot* less than that. I said no. How about fifteen g's? No. Then maybe twenty, twenty-five, my last offer is thirty, whaddaya say? I say no. Not in a million years. Not if I had no money to buy shoes. I didn't buy that spectacular Bok painting to make a goddam *profit* off it, you pinhead! I bought it to look at it, to marvel at it, to *enjoy* it. I am a collector.

And here I am, a collector, a lover of comics from the age of five, now sixty-one years old editing a comic that bears my name every month, and I *still* love comics. As rotten as so many of them are these days, as expensive as they've become, as much space as they take up cataloguing and bagging and storing them...I *still* love them. The feel of them, the look of them, the moments when they're so good you wish they could be on display in the Guggenheim, and the knowledge that even though kids will continue to be corrupted by price guides and hustlers trying to separate them from their dollars with lies about "rarity" and "hot collectible"...still, they are a joy unparalleled. The comic book. It's there to be read. To be enjoyed. To hell with how valuable it is. To hell with ego-drenched creators who go along with grub-hungry publishers who issue alternate covers and metallic editions and holographic specials and create all the artificial "collectibles" that drive you nuts. To hell with them. They aren't comic book lovers, or readers, or even collectors. They're Home Shopping Nitwit hustlers, and to hell with them.

Price Guides like this one are nifty and spiffy and max cool and imperial, not because they tell you some treasure in your attic is worth eighty gazillion bucks, but because they show you the history and timeline of the existence of this purely American-born art-form. It may have prices in it, but the delight is for your eyes; not your wallet.

And now, you'll have to excuse me, the black-hooded thugs from the Comic Inquisition are here to drag my sorry carcass away to be tortured, for having written such heretical crap.

According to the New York Times, multiple award-winning author HARLAN ELLISON has "the spellbinding quality of a great nonstop talker, with a cultural warehouse for a mind." He appears as Commentator every week on the USA Network's "Sci-Fi Buzz" TV program; his 65th book, "The City of the Edge of Forever" (featuring the original teleplay of his famous Star Trek script) has just been released; he is one of a mere handful of great talents to win the coveted Lifetime Achievement Award of the World Fantasy Convention; last year he was included in The Best American Short Stories; and he is the co-editor and guiding intelligence behind the ongoing Dark Horse comic Harlan Ellison's Dream Corridor. He is a really sweet guy.\

MaxiMage™

LIEFELD
EXTREME
STUDIOS

Win an old mutant

Hey, you. Yeah, you! This is the **WIZARD** Price Guide Annual, so just like any issue of our swell Wizard magazine, we've gotta run a monster kick-butt contest. And here she be. All you haveta do is answer a few questions, and you could win the...

GRAND PRIZE (1):

X-Men #1!

No, we ain't talkin' that modern-day, Johnny-Come-Lately 1991 version. We're talking the original—the Stan 'n' Jack masterpiece from 1963! Ooogala ooogala ooogala!

If you're good, maybe we'll even throw in a bag to keep it in.

Mouth drooling and various body parts all tingly? Good.

HERE'S HOW TO PLAY:

Just take a gander at these here X-Men trivia questions, answer them on the official X-Men entry form below, and mail the whole enchilada off to:

X-Men #1 Contest
c/o Wizard Press
P.O. Box 118
Congers NY 10920-0118

Deadline is July 1, 1996

X-MEN TRIVIA:

1) Who penciled the *X-Men and the Micronauts* limited series?

2) Which evil "Age of Apocalypse" X-Man crossed back into our world in *X-Men Prime*?

3) What was the title of the X-Men African famine relief benefit comic?

4) Which three X-Men starred in solo stories in *Bizarre Adventures #27*?

5) How are Professor X and the Juggernaut related?

6) Sabretooth first appeared in the pages of which issue of *The Uncanny X-Men*?

7) What is the alter ego of the X-Men villain Sauron?

8) Which comic featured Dazzler's first appearance?

9) Which two X-Men once had roller skates as part of their costume?

10) Which issue of *The Uncanny X-Men* featured the first appearance of Gambit?

Whoa! Whoever wins also gets to *swivel* over at the Beast's house!*

No purchase necessary. Contest is open to anyone except employees of Wizard Press and those of you bored enough to read tiny legal type. What, the TV remote is out of reach and this was the last thing in the book left to read? Print your name, date of birth, address, city, state, zip and telephone number with area code, along with your answers to the 10 questions, on the official entry form, a standard postcard or a 3-by-5-inch index card. Enter as many times as you like. Mail each entry separately to: X-Men #1 Contest, c/o Wizard Press, P.O. Box 118, Congers, NY 10920-0118. No mechanical reproductions of completed forms are accepted. All entries become property of Wizard Press and none will be returned. All taxes (federal, state and local, if any) will be the responsibility of the prize winner. No cash equivalent or substitute prize will be offered. Prize is awarded in the name of the contest winner and is not transferable. Offer void where prohibited, regulated or restricted by law in a manner inconsistent with the purposes and rules hereof. Hey, wanna know how to tell if you're a mutant? Go eat seven bacon double cheeseburgers, four large fries and three glasses of Strawberry Quik, and then skip rope for 20 minutes. If you don't projectile-vomit your entire digestive tract onto your neighbor's lawn, you're not normal. **All entries must be received at contest headquarters by July 1, 1996.** Wizard Press is not responsible for lost, late, misdirected or mutilated entries. Odds of winning will be determined by the number of valid entries received prior to the closing date of the contest. Prize winner will be selected by random drawing among all properly completed entries by Wizard Press. Drawing will take place on July 15, 1996.

* The Beast is actually a fictional character with a fictional house, so there'll be no swiveling.

For the winner's name, available after July 15, 1996, send a self-addressed stamped envelope to: X-Men #1 Contest Winner, c/o Wizard Press, P.O. Box 118, Congers, NY 10920-0118.

UNCANNY LEGAL TEXT

OFFICIAL X-MEN #1 ENTRY FORM

ANSWERS

1) ____________________

2) ____________________

3) ____________________

4) ____________________

5) ____________________

6) ____________________

7) ____________________

8) ____________________

9) ____________________

10) ____________________

Answer alla them correctly and maybe you could win this **FABULOUS** prize!

____
Name

____
Date of Birth

____
Address

____
City

____
State Zip

____
Phone Number (with area code)

Start Me Up!

Looking to start a collection of comic books? Let us get you rolling.

BY THE WIZARD STAFF

OK, you want to start collecting comic books, but don't know where to start. Hey, no problem. What we've done here is broken down the types of comics into 10 specific genres and recommended five comic series for each, followed by a brief capsule of what the book's all about.

And with that said, we're off…

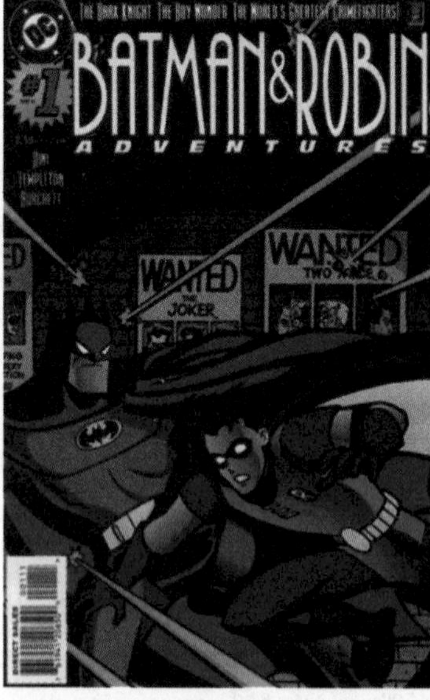

SUPERHERO

BATMAN & ROBIN ADVENTURES

Published monthly by DC Comics

Don't be fooled by the cartoony look. Though an outgrowth of the Fox-TV animated cartoon, this series brings out the best in both heroes. Action-packed with great stories and dynamic art, this series can be enjoyed by both kids and adults. If you're looking for a darker version of Batman, check out the "regular" Batman titles such as the monthly *Batman, Detective Comics* and *Batman: Shadow of the Bat.*

GEN^{13}

Published monthly by Image Comics

Follow the misadventures of five superpowered teens on the run from a secret government agency. Fun, light-hearted stuff in tune with today's teens.

ASTRO CITY

Published monthly by Image Comics

A realistic look at superheroes and the problems they face (and cause). Fans of both Golden Age and present day heroes can easily get into this series.

GREEN LANTERN

Published monthly by DC Comics

Readers learn how to be a superhero right along with Kyle Rayner, who recently gained the single most powerful weapon in the universe: Green Lantern's power ring.

UNTOLD TALES OF SPIDER-MAN

Published monthly by Marvel Comics

The most light-hearted and enjoyable of all the Spider-Man books published by Marvel, *Untold Tales* chronicle the early, "untold" tales of a young, inexperienced Spider-Man.

FEMALE HEROES

CATWOMAN

Published monthly by DC Comics

The feline *femme fatale* who's both Batman's love interest and nemesis is Gotham City's most notorious cat burgular. But she has a moral code that forces her to stand in the way of Gotham's more murderous villains. A tough, take-no-crap antiheroine who steals from the rich...and keeps it.

WONDER WOMAN

Published monthly by DC Comics

After learning how violent the world can be, the Amazon known as Wonder Woman has dropped her peaceful ways to become a crimefighter with a healthy combo of brains, power and attitude.

GHOST

Published monthly by Dark Horse Comics

When Elisa Cameron, a dedicated reporter in the city of Arcadia, was killed, she became one of today's most hard-hitting heroines: Ghost. Along with her superior skills at using two powerful guns, she can both fly and teleport from place to place. Having forgotten who she was, she'll need these powers as she tries to track down her killer and rediscover her life amidst some thrilling adventures.

MANTRA

Published monthly by Malibu Comics

What do you do when you're a fairly normal young woman who's suddenly thrown into a life of tremendous power and reponsibility? Ask Lauren, who now possesses the ancient power of Mantra, and is learning to cope with being a superheroine.

SHI

Published bimonthly by Crusade Entertainment

Though beautiful and smart, gallery curator Ana Ishikawa is also a fierce vigilante living in Manhattan. She balances improving her social life while taking on formidable foes. The series is often educational with references to Japanese history and culture.

RELATIONSHIPS

LOVE & ROCKETS

Published quarterly by Fantagraphics Books

This slice-of-life series presents the dramatic lives of several characters who live in two fictional towns (one a suburb of Los Angeles, the other in Central America). With heavy doses of Latino culture, the series shows bisexuality, family relations and alternative music. For mature readers.

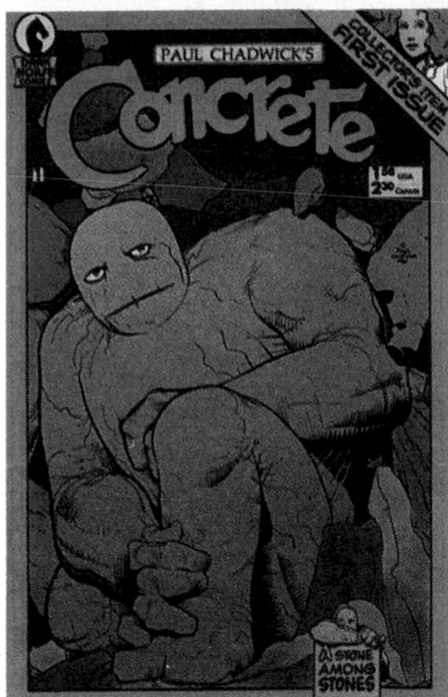

CONCRETE

Published sporadically in mini-series format by Dark Horse Comics

Congressional speechwriter Ronald Lithgow's got it tough. Y'see, he was abducted by aliens and had his brain put in an body made of a concrete-like substance. Life's been a little difficult ever since.

HEPCATS

Published sporadically in graphic novel format by Double Diamond Press

Though drawn with "funny animal" heads on human bodies, these down-to-earth stories deal with human problems like child abuse, suicide and getting a girlfriend. For mature readers.

STRANGERS IN PARADISE

Published bimonthly by Abstract Studios

In a zany tale of relationships, the neurotic Francine is gaining weight because of a break-up with a boyfriend. Meanwhile, her roommate Katchoo hates men, but is in love with Francine. David, the nicest guy in the world, is in love with Katchoo, who, in turn, is starting to have feelings for him. Watch these people sort it all out in this involving comic. For mature readers.

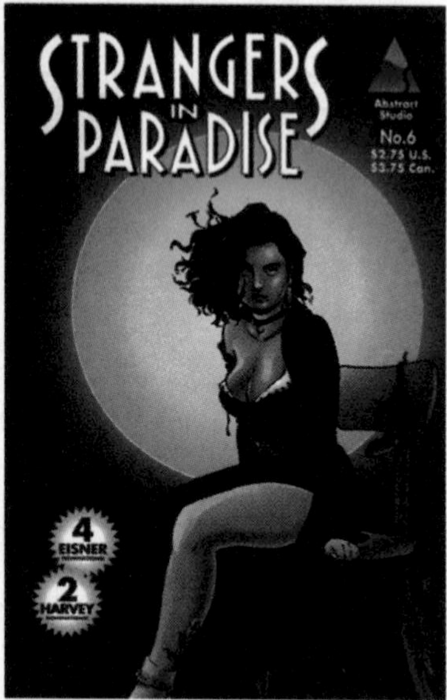

OMAHA THE CAT DANCER

Published bimonthly by Fantagraphics Books

Populated by humanoid animals in a real-world setting, Omaha is a feline exotic dancer whose chief enemy is Senator Bonner, and who must face everyday problems ranging from facing down annoying detectives to how to have good sex. Adult material, folks.

WESTERN

ZORRO

Resumes monthly schedule in Fall '96 by Topps Comics

Set in California during Spanish rule in the 1820s, Zorro, the "black fox," pits his wits and unbreakable sword against the corrupt forces of Capitan Monasterio and a rogues gallery of exotic, pulp-fictionish villains.

JONAH HEX: TWO-GUN MOJO

A five-issue mini-series published by DC/Vertigo in 1993

Wild Bill Hickok comes back from the dead with an undead army, and only Jonah Hex can stop him. Also check out its sequel *Jonah Hex: Riders of the Worm and Such* mini-series.

THE LONE RANGER AND TONTO

A four-issue mini-series published by Topps Comics in 1994

In the wild west of the 1880s, the Lone Ranger and Tonto end their long-standing partnership over a mistake the Ranger regrets. The Ranger must ponder if he can regain his friendship while halting a mad alien killer.

TUROK: DINOSAUR HUNTER

Published monthly by Acclaim Comics

A Kiowa Apache from the old west is thrown through time, landing in present-day times, and must try and fit in with present-day society (while also hunting down monstrous, time-displaced creatures).

BLUEBERRY

A five-volume series of Graphic Novels published by Epic/Marvel Comics in 1989

Mike Donovan was a rogue Confederate soldier who changed his name to Blueberry and joined the Union army. With the Civil War over, this adventure has Blueberry on a hunt to recover Jefferson Davis' hidden treasure that could potentially revive the old Confederacy and start another civil war.

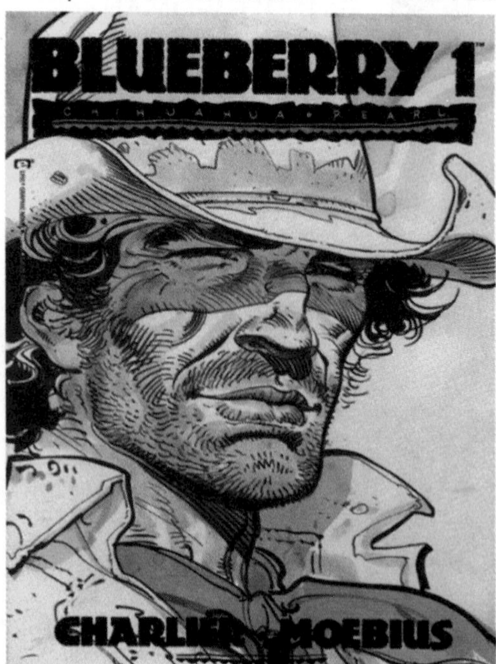

SCIENCE-FICTION

STAR WARS BOOKS

Published sporadically as mini-series by Dark Horse Comics

Spinning off concepts and storylines from the popular Star Wars movie trilogy, these series chronicle the further adventures of Han, Luke, Leia and other familiar (and some new) faces.

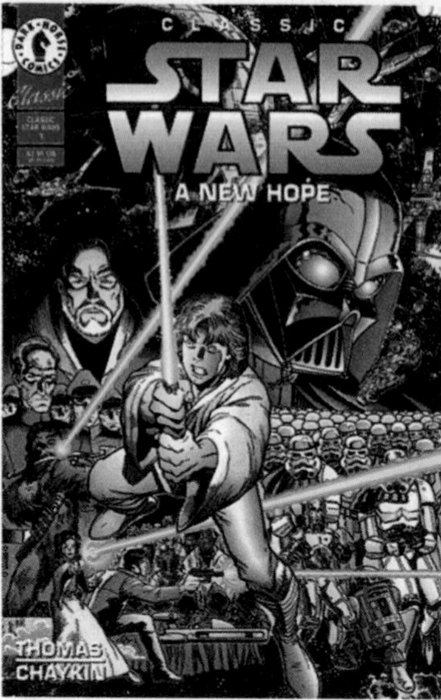

ALIENS BOOKS

Published sporadically as mini-series by Dark Horse Comics

Further tales of the struggles against the acid-blooded killing machines made famous by the three Alien movies.

BATTLESTAR GALACTICA

Published monthly by Maximum Press

Based on the late '70s TV series, follow a "rag-tag fugitive fleet" as they search for the fabled planet Earth, all the while dodging the evil, inhuman Cylon Empire.

LEGION OF SUPER-HEROES & LEGIONNAIRES

Published monthly by DC Comics

Set in the 30th Century, a team of young heroes from a handful of worlds uses its various powers and technology to fend off all threats to the galaxy.

MAGNUS: ROBOT FIGHTER

Published by Acclaim Comics; formerly a monthly ongoing title, it will resume as a mini-series in Spring '96

Raised by a robot in the distant future, Magnus' lot in life is to destroy deadly robots who have gained independant thought, and have turned murderous to their human masters.

HORROR

THE SPECTRE

Published monthly by DC Comics

As the physical embodiment of the wrath of God, the Spectre (who inhabits the body of Jim Corrigan, a dead police officer), is a spirit of vengeance who acts as judge, jury and highly creative executioner to those who commit evil.

HELLBLAZER

Published monthly by Vertigo/DC

Thrust into the role of supernatural specialist, the mysterious John Constantine finds himself in such intriguing situations from trying to outwit the devil to having someone else pick up his bar tab. For mature readers.

PREACHER

Published monthly by Vertigo/DC

Reverend Jesse Custer has learned that God has abondoned Heaven, and, along with his ex-sweetie Tulip and an Irish vampire named Cassidy, sets off on a quest across the world to find Him. For mature readers.

THE X-FILES

Published monthly by Topps Comics

Based on the Fox-TV series, join FBI agents Scully and Mulder as they attempt to find the truths behind unexplained phenomena.

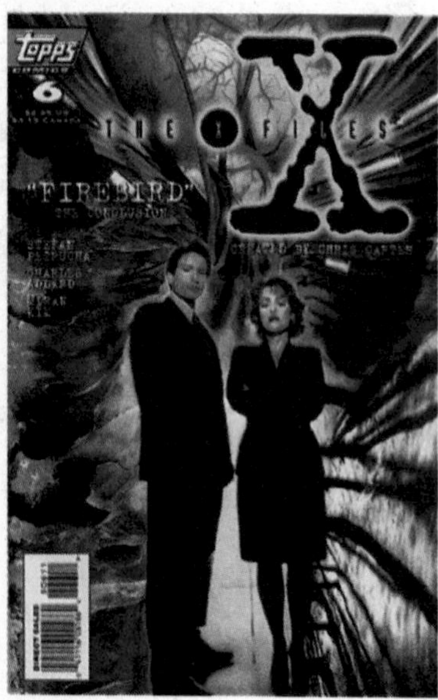

RUNE

Published monthly by Malibu

Rune is a horrific energy vampire, an alien who absorbs energy from living beings to reverse a disease that was killing him. Now "The Dark God" has discovered that he can only feed on superpowered people, so superheroes beware!

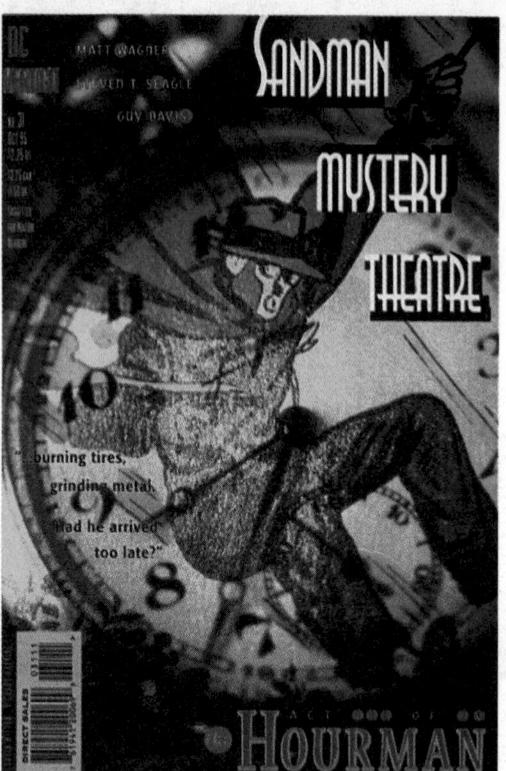

CRIME

SANDMAN MYSTERY THEATRE

Published monthly by DC/Vertigo

Set in New York City in the late '30s, Wesley Dodds has nightmares which foretell of hideous crimes which he must stop as the Sandman. For mature readers.

SIN CITY BOOKS

Available in single-issue format or trade paperbacks published by Dark Horse Comics

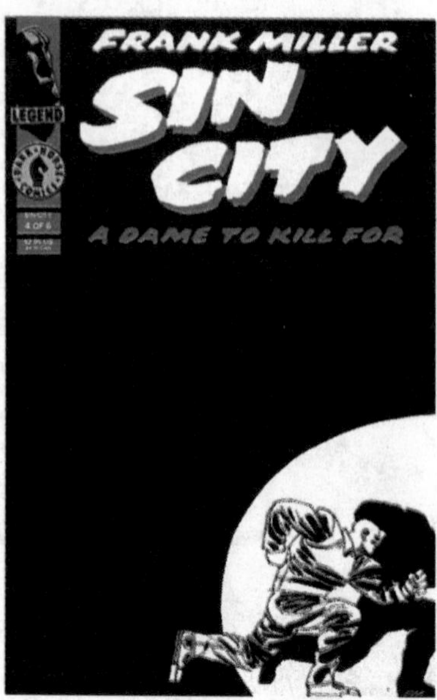

A hard-boiled string of *noir* stories which hit hard and fast. Individual stories include the original *Sin City*, *Sin City: A Dame to Kill For*, *Sin City: The Babe Wore Red*, *Sin City: The Big Fat Kill*, and *Sin City: Silent Night*. Not for children.

$TRAY BULLETS

Published bimonthly by El Capitán

A book of stand-alone stories, yet part of a larger storyline. A stark, visceral look at how crime can affect different phases of normal life. For mature readers.

X

Published monthly by Dark Horse Comics

If you break X's law in the city of Arcadia once, you become marked. Cross this mysterious enforcer twice, and you're dead.

KANE

Published bimonthly by Dancing Elephant Press

Detective Kane is a good cop with a bad rep, and he's trying to take the city of New Eden back from mob lord Oscar Darke. But it's tough when his own police force shuns him because Kane once shot his corrupt partner in self-defense. Rough stuff.

HUMOR

BONE

Published bimonthly by Image Comics

Three cartoonish cousins (Fone Bone, Phoney Bone and Smiley Bone) get run out of their hometown and stumble into a valley where its inhabitants are both friendly, like the Great Red Dragon and Gran'ma Ben, as well as the very unpleasent quiche-eating Rat Creatures.

GROO

Published monthly by Image Comics

A hapless barbarian with a fondness for cheese dip and eviscerations wanders through a fantasy medieval setting, doing battle with...everything.

MILK & CHEESE

Published sporadically by Slave Labor Press

One's a carton of hate! The other's a wedge of spite! They're dairy products gone bad, and they're not for those who're easily offended or can't take vomit jokes. Violent stuff.

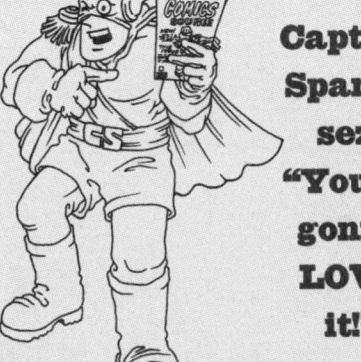

THE TICK

Published sporadically by New England Comics

A satirical look at superheroes starring a dim-witted, nigh-invulnerable champion of justice called the Tick, and co-starring Sewer-Urchin, American Maid, Man-Eating Cow and other...heroes.

SCUD, THE DISPOSABLE ASSASSIN

Published approximately bimonthly by Fireman Press

A disposable assassin hired through a vending machine learns that if his target dies he'll self-destruct, and must now do everything in his power to keep that target alive.

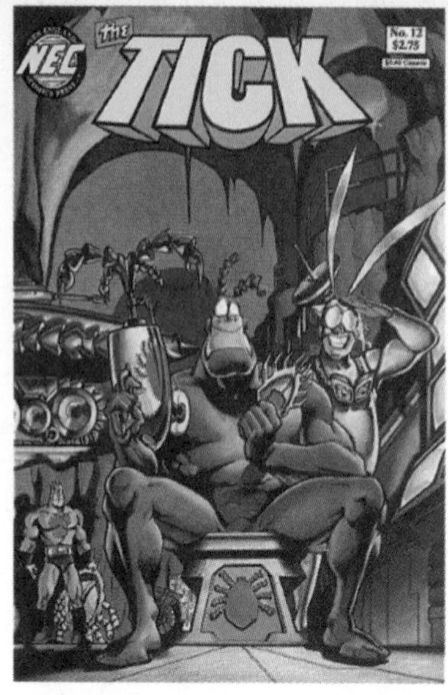

FANTASY

ELFQUEST BOOKS

Published monthly by WaRP Graphics

Follow the lives of the elven Wolfriders as they seek to find their place in the World of Two Moons, and unlock the secrets of their past. Available in individual issues or graphic novel collections titled *Elfquest*, *Elfquest: Hidden Years*, *Elfquest: New Blood* and *Elfquest: Shards*.

THE BOOKS OF MAGIC

Published monthly by DC/Vertigo

Fourteen-year-old Timothy Hunter has the potential to be the world's greatest sorcerer. Only problem is, he's unsure how this whole "magic" thing actually works. And it doesn't help much that his evil future self is trying to sabotage him, and it could prove more than he can handle.

CONAN BOOKS

Published monthly by Marvel Comics

The adventures of a wandering barbarian in a sword 'n' sorcery world, living by his wits and his ability to halve people, are chronicled in two books every month: *Conan* and *Conan the Savage*.

DR. STRANGE

Published monthly by Marvel Comics

The Marvel Universe's most powerful sorcerer protects our world and does battle with supernatural foes that would put the kibosh on a "regular" superhero.

POISON ELVES

Published monthly by Sirius Entertainment

Armed with a magical gun that has limitless ammunition, Lusiphur is an elf with an attitude who embarks on different adventures as an assassin in order to make his mark and his money.

KIDS

DISNEY COMICS

Published on a monthly basis by Gladstone/Disney Comics

The further comic adventures of Mickey Mouse, Donald Duck, Goofy and all your favorite Walt Disney characters.

ARCHIE BOOKS

Published on a monthly basis by Archie Comics

Old-fashioned fun is the key throughout all of the Archie books, starring Archie, Jughead, Betty, Veronica, Reggie, Moose and the gang.

ANIMANIACS

Published monthly by DC Comics

You can read about the adventures of TV's weirdest, wildest cartoon trio—Yakko, Wakko and Dot—in this incredibly funny comic book series. Features brand-new stories about these nutty little guys and their pals.

SPIDER-MAN ADVENTURES

Published monthly by Marvel Comics

If you love Spidey's Saturday morning cartoon, this comic book series is perfect for you because it offers stories straight from the cartoon! Action-packed reading for Spider-fans.

GARGOYLES

Published monthly by Marvel Comics

When not turned to stone in the daylight, the purple-skinned Goliath leads his fellow team of good-hearted gargoyles as they try to cope with society and evil gargoyles.

So that's that. If you want to know more about these comic book series or others that look cool, visit your local comic book store and ask someone who works there. Explain what it is you're looking for in a comic, and they'll be able to point you in the right direction.

Then grab your stack of comics, a box of Ritz Bits peanut butter sandwiches and a cold Yoo-Hoo, and go to town!

BY BILL LIEBOWITZ PHOTOS BY HARRY PETERSON

COMICS 101

Everything you were afraid to know about comics but wanted to ask

The comics industry is a huge and wondrous place to be. There are heroes, villains and mutants everywhere. Men fly. Women bend steel in their bare hands. And a teensy little spider can change one boy's life. But the comics world can also be a scary place in that at times you can get quite overwhelmed, especially if you're a newcomer to the field. That's why the following, containing some of the most frequently asked questions about comics, should help you get a firm grasp on the wonderful world of comic collecting.

LOOK DEEP INTO MY ARMPITS. WHAT DO YOU SEE?
C'MON, THIS IS COSTING ME 40 BUCKS!

Q: I'm just starting. What should I do?
A: Read as much as you can about the hobby and the books currently being published. Many publishers and comic book stores have newsletters, catalogs and/or hotlines to keep you informed. Other good sources of information are comics magazines and newspapers which contain articles on trends, news and prices for the industry. (*Wizard* is a good example.) You can also check out distributor catalogs (Diamond Comics Distributors' *Previews* and Heroes World's *Mega Marvel*), which are monthly books that give information on upcoming comics from certain publishers. Other than that, you should get plenty of bags, backing boards and boxes for storage (See **"Pack It In"** on page 32), a good reading light and some free time.

Q: What should I collect?
A: Books that you like. This hobby should primarily be enjoyable. Take it slowly at first and ask a lot of questions. Don't give up on a new title just because you didn't like the last issue. Give it a chance. Sample different stuff. If you can't afford to, then borrow some books from your friends. You might find that you like a certain character, artist or writer. Talk to friends or store employees; if you can explain what you like or dislike, they can steer you toward (or away from) similar items. For a more in-depth answer, see page 16 for our **"Start Me Up!"** feature.

Q: What does "Golden Age," "Silver Age" and "Modern Age" mean?
A: These terms refer to broad time periods in the history of comics publishing. The Golden Age (1938-1954) was an innocent

time when superheroes like Superman and Batman fought Lex Luthor and the Joker. Good and evil were clear cut and well defined. The Silver Age (1955-1970) introduced a whole new crop of heroes like Spider-Man, The Fantastic Four, the new Flash, the new Green Lantern and many, many others. Stories dealt much more with heroes' personal problems and the characters themselves had much more depth. The Modern Age (1971-present) contains much darker characters like Marvel's The Punisher and Ghost Rider, and even anti-heroes like DC's Deathstroke. As the Modern Age continues, "real world" themes pop up as many stories are for a more mature audience focusing on societal problems like alcoholism, abortion and prejudice.

Q: What's a "crossover"?
A: A storyline that crosses over from one title to another. Marvel's six-part "Fatal Attractions" crossover began in *X-Factor* #92 continued in a number of different comic book issues and eventually concluded in *Excalibur* #71. Crossovers can also include more than one company such as the 1976 comic that starred both DC Comics' Superman and Marvel's Spider-Man.

Q: What's a "mini-series" or "limited series"?
A: A finite series with a predetermined number of issues. They are generally used to introduce new characters (Marvel's *Longshot*), spotlight characters that don't have their own series (Marvel's *Gambit*), or tell some major company event (DC's *Zero Hour*). Sometimes really long mini-series (like 12 issues) are called "maxi-series."

Q: What's a "graphic novel"?
A: Usually a large self-contained original story which is presented in either a normal comic book size or slightly larger format than that. They generally deal with more serious and mature themes, and contain an important story such as Marvel's first graphic novel which featured the death of a major character, namely the original Captain Marvel.

Q: What's a "one-shot"?
A: A one-issue comic book that stands on its own and has no issue of the same title continuing after it. It tells a special story or continues an ongoing storyline from another comic book. It's different from a graphic novel because a one-shot is usually a standard comic book with twice the amount of pages.

Q: What's an "annual"?
A: A one-shot that comes out once a year and usually has more pages than the standard monthly comic. They generally come out in the summer and sometimes feature a number of stories by a variety of writers and artists.

Q: What's a "trade paperback"?
A: A compilation of previously released comics which generally doesn't contain any new material. Trade paperbacks (or "TPBs") usually collect a popular storyline or crossover like DC's "Batman: Year One" (which originally ran from *Batman* #404 to #407) or a complete mini-series like Marvel's four-issue *Wolverine*. TPBs usually have thicker covers which feature new artwork.

Q: What's an "alternate cover"?
A: An alternate cover is a comic book with two (or more) different covers available for purchase. Sometimes the alternate cover has some special feature (it glows in the dark, has a high-tech hologram on it or sports a nifty metallic cover paper), which gives it a higher cover price. These alternate covers are also known as "enhanced" or "collector's editions," and can even be referred to as "gimmick covers" because collectors are led to believe that they should give special attention to these comics. Also, an alternate cover is sometimes rarer than the normal cover and can have a higher cover price if it's enhanced; since it's harder to find, it's collectibility and value may increase.

Q: What is a "back-issue"?
A: Any issue of a series that is not the most recent issue, or a comic that is more than a month old.

Q: What is an "indicia"?
A: The small print usually found at the bottom of the first page of a comic that contains all sorts of legal text, along with a mailing address and a subscription rate.

Q: What's a "second (third, fourth) printing" or a "reprint"?
A: These are all just additional copies of a comic. They contain the same exact story as the original, but are printed at a later date. You can tell what printing you have by looking in the indicia for either the exact words "second printing" or a decreasing list of numbers like: 10 9 8 7 6 5 4 3 2 1 (with the last number telling you exactly which printing it is; a "1" is first printing, etc.). Some companies will even print a Roman numeral on an issue's cover telling you which printing it is.

Q: What's a "direct market edition"?
A: Basically, it's a comic book bought from a comic book shop rather than from a "newsstand" such as your local drug store, Waldenbooks or Kmart. Direct market editions come out at least two weeks earlier than newsstand editions because comic stores order from one distributor while Waldenbooks has to go through two. The only other difference between a direct mar-

Collect books that you like. This hobby should be fun. Don't give up on a titie just because you didn't like the last issue.

HMMM... SHALL I ORDER THE CHOCOLATE TOFU OR THE BACON TRUFFLES?
"AQUAMAN." IS THIS A GOOD READ? HELLO? ARE YOU THINKING ABOUT FOOD AGAIN?

ket and newsstand edition of a comic is that it actually says "direct market" on the cover of an issue in the white UPC box.

Q: What does the term "small press" mean?
A: The "small press" refers to an expanding group of small comic publishers (like El Cápitan, Aardvark-Vanaheim and Coppervale Press) whose comics have a smaller print run than the high profile comic publishers like Marvel, DC or Image.

Q: What's a "fanboy"?
A: A slang term for a super-enthusiastic comic collector who sometimes becomes fanatical with a particular comic book series, artist, writer or character.

Most comics have a letters page that will indicate where to write to the editors, artists and writers. You can get a good listing of addresses on page 288.

Q: How can I contact my favorite artist?
A: Most comics have a letters page that will indicate where to write to the editors, artists and writers. Also, every comic has an indicia in it, listing a company's mailing address. You can get a good listing of addresses and even some phone numbers on this book's Resource Page located on page 288.

Q: I'm looking for a book I saw a while ago that had a blue guy and some blonde girl on the cover. Do you still have it?
A: If you are looking for a particular issue, you need to be *very* clear and know more than just a vague description of the cover. Think hard, and see if you can't remember the name of the book, the lead character or even the publisher. Retailers are there to help, but they need a certain amount of information to successfully do so.

Q: Should I open a polybagged comic?
A: Hmm...that's a loaded question. If a polybagged comic increases in value and is removed from the polybag it came in, the comic will be considered by many to be "damaged goods" if you ever planned on selling it. The reason being the comic is not in its original package. The problem with this line of thinking is that almost all polybags are of fairly low quality, and will begin to deteriorate after several years and may even damage the comic inside it. Our suggestion? Carefully slit open the top of the polybag and store it, the comic and anything else that may have come in the bag (i.e., trading cards, posters, etc.), in an acid-free comic bag and backboard. That way you'll be able to read it and keep all the comic's original components together.

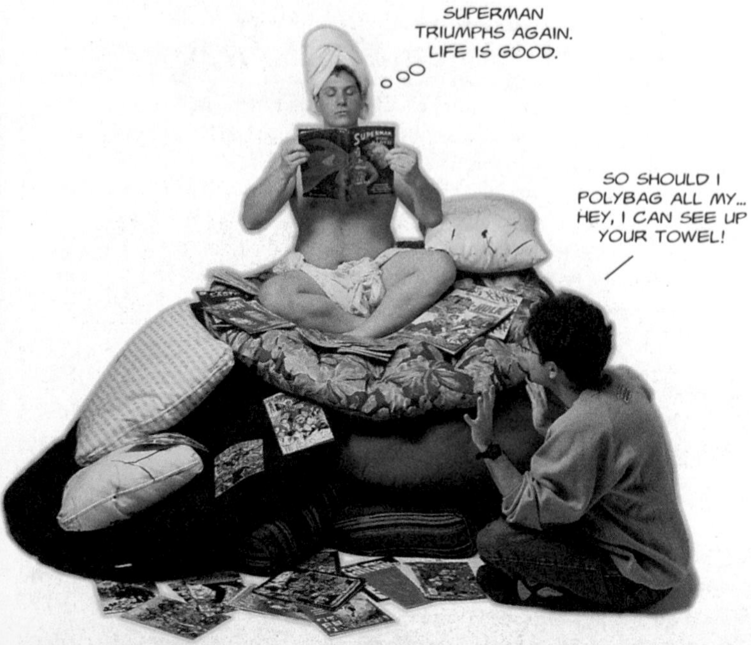
SUPERMAN TRIUMPHS AGAIN. LIFE IS GOOD.
SO SHOULD I POLYBAG ALL MY... HEY, I CAN SEE UP YOUR TOWEL!

Q: What are the most expensive comics?
A: The three most expensive comics that first come to mind are *Action Comics* #1 (1938, the first appearance of Superman) at $125,000, *Detective Comics* #27 (1939, the first appearance of Batman) at $125,000 and *Marvel Comics* #1 (1939, the first Marvel comic, the first appearance of the original Human Torch and the origin of Sub-Mariner) at $70,000.

Q: What is a price guide?
A: An extensive listing of comic books and the prices people should expect to pay for them. Be aware that, just as the name says, it is merely a guide. These prices are not set in stone, and are quite negotiable. Different areas of the country (or even in the same city) will often have very different prices for the same titles.

Q: The price guide says that *Spider-Man #1* is worth $15,750, but this copy is priced at $3. What's the deal?
A: The expensive book is *The **Amazing** Spider-Man #1*, published in 1963. The other one is *Spider-Man #1*, from 1990. It's a completely different issue. Be very careful of these differences. Also, be careful of reprints, mini-series and annuals. In general, retailers don't make these kinds of mistakes, but there are plenty of horror stories where people payed a lot of money for common reprints.

Q: Why do comics go up in value?
A: It's a good question, but there's no clear-cut answer. The factors that can cause a comic to go up in value often vary. Factors include the book's rarity, the first issue of a series, any major changes to the status quo of the series (i.e., the death of a character, the marriage of two characters, a major change in a character's power, a new costume, etc.), appearance of a popular character, a popular character's first appearance.

Q: This comic is listed for $10 in the price guide. How come my local store's got it for $20?!
A: Price guides are not bibles, and don't take into account regional variations in supply and demand, and popularity. Especially for hot books (comics that are in very high demand). Remember that guides have to be researched, formulated, printed and distributed. A lot can change in that two to six week period.

Q: What can I buy now that will go up in value in the future?
A: We suggest that you only buy what you like to read. However, comics can go up in

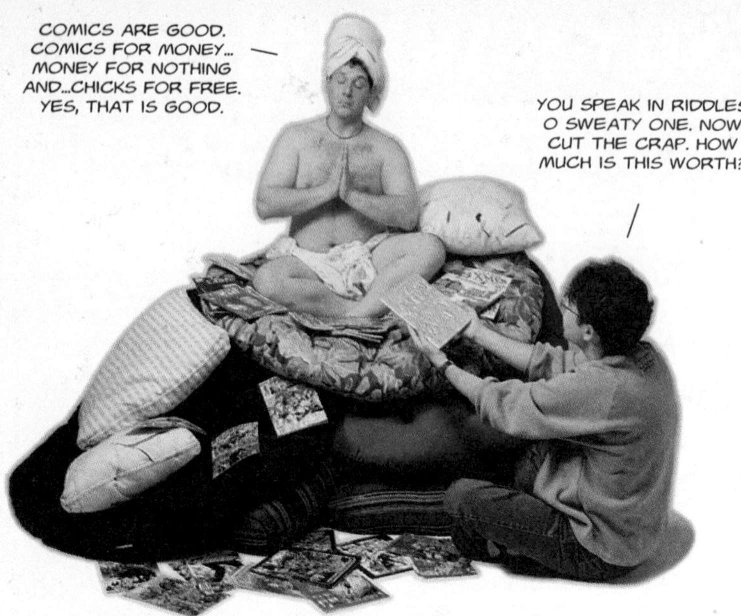
COMICS ARE GOOD.
COMICS FOR MONEY...
MONEY FOR NOTHING
AND...CHICKS FOR FREE.
YES, THAT IS GOOD.
YOU SPEAK IN RIDDLES
O SWEATY ONE. NOW
CUT THE CRAP. HOW
MUCH IS THIS WORTH?

value for a number of reasons: supply and demand, perceived value, introduction of new characters, major plot developments, a popular artist, etc. Just remember that a comic is not really worth $10, but there might be someone who's willing to *pay* $10 for it. Therefore the worth of the comic, and your ability to sell it, really depend on a number of factors including luck, timing and perceived value by the buyer. But if you're buying a comic to read it then any price increase or decrease shouldn't matter at all.

Q: I really liked this comic book. What else would I like?

A: You need to realize just why you liked it. Was it the character, art, writing or even the shiny cover? There are over 500 regularly issued titles that come out every month, and a good story and sales person can usually steer you in the right direction if you give them enough to go on. For more information check out the **"Start Me Up!"** feature on page 16.

Q: Are signed comics worth more?

A: Yes and no. As a rule of thumb, a comic that's worth about $5 to $10, will sell for more if it's autographed by the penciler, creator and possibly even the writer. If you get an autograph on a book that's worth more than that you run the risk of defacing it, and perhaps decreasing its value. But more importantly, an autograph on a book is most special to the person who got it. Many artists like to personalize their signatures for their fans. It shows that the fan cares about the artist, and doesn't intend to re-sell the book. Most comic book creators enjoy being appreciated for their work rather than for the value of their signatures.

Q: What are comic book conventions?

A: Conventions are like big comic book carnivals. There are tons of comic book retailers selling all sorts of comics (old and new), as well as comic companies showing previews of upcoming releases and giving away free pins, posters and even comics! You can meet writers and artists to whom you can talk and get autographs from. For a listing of some 1996 comic book shows see page 287.

Q: If I buy an issue of a comic book series, how will I know when the next one's coming out?

A: Most comics are published once a month. One way to check is to scan the indicia of the comic, as it'll usually state the publishing schedule of a book. Otherwise ask your retailer.

Q: It's been over two months since the last issue of my favorite comic book came out. Isn't the new one due soon?

A: There are many reasons a comic is delivered late to your local store, including printing problems, losing art, contract problems and even injury to a creator. Please write to the publisher and/or artist and tell them how disappointed you are that your favorite books are always late. This lateness hurts everybody.

Q: My husband (boyfriend, sister, dentist, etc.) is a big Batman fan. What do you recommend as a gift for a special occasion?

A: There are all sorts of goodies available at comic stores such as hardcovers, video tapes, posters and T-shirts related to popular comic characters. Try to get something a little out of the ordinary that your friend may enjoy. With Batman, there are a number of great books available like *The Dark Knight Returns*, *The Greatest Batman Stories Ever Told* and *The Complete Frank Miller Batman*. You also might want to get a gift certificate from a comic book store and have your friend pick out exactly what he or she wants.

So there you have it. Some basic questions and some basic answers for all you comic collectors out there. It may seem a little confusing at first, but if you stick with it and ask tons of questions you can get a lot more out of collecting than you think. The bottom line is to just have fun.

Bill Liebowitz is the owner of Golden Apple comic shop in Los Angeles. Wizard's own Buddy Scalera and Marc Wilkofsky are the two goofballs in the photos.

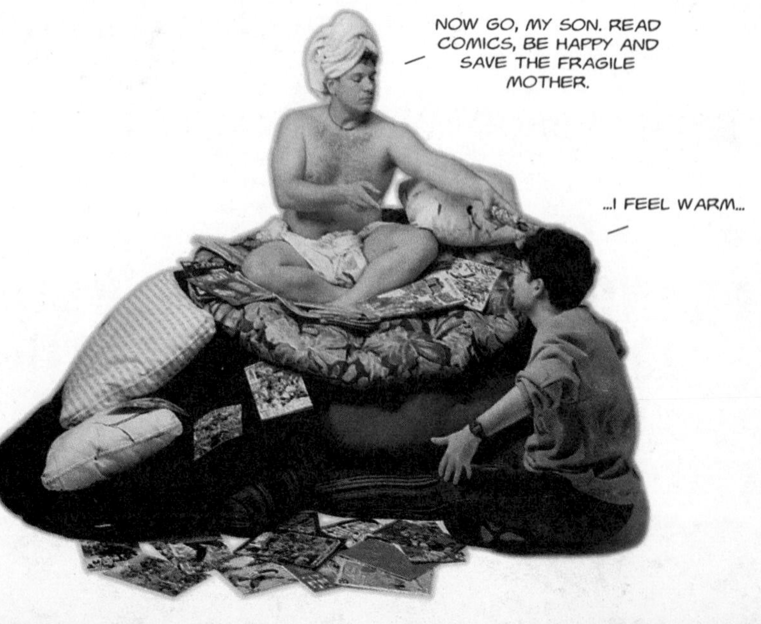
NOW GO, MY SON. READ
COMICS, BE HAPPY AND
SAVE THE FRAGILE
MOTHER.
...I FEEL WARM...

PACIFIC COMIC EXCHANGE, INC

P.O. BOX 34849, Los Angeles, CA 90034 ❖ 337 S. Robertson Blvd. Suite 203, Beverly Hills, CA 90211 ❖ Tel: (310) 836-7234 (PCEI) FAX: (310) 836-7127 Modem: (310) 836-3076

***Instructions** (Please read before ordering)* :The following books are currently listed on the Exchange and are available for sale at the prices specified. All prices are "negotiable" and subject to change without notice. All orders are subject to a 10% buyers commission. The grade listed is the CGSA grade (see diagram below). Books may be returned (must be undamaged) if not satisfied and we are notified within 5 days of receipt by telephone . Payment can be made by money order or check and is due within 5 business days of order. Shipping and handling is $10.00 (includes insurance). A full list of all books is free with any purchase. The PCE monthly listing report contains all current bid and ask prices and recent sales and is available by annual subscription ($45 U.S.). All payments should be mailed to post office box.
a: Appearance Grade, d: Double Cover, t: Trimmed Book, R: Restored (C: Color Touch, S: Slight (e.g. tear sealed, cleaned, etc), L: Light, M: Moderate, E: Extensive),
PgQ: Page Quality (0.0, 1, 2, 2.5, 3: White; 3.3: Near White; 3.5: Off-White; 4: Beige or Cream Color, Blank: Not-Rated). Page Quality follows the CGSA grade.
P: Pedigree (AL:Allentown, BM:Bethlehem, BW:Biljo White, C8:Circle 8, CA:Cosmic Airplane, CC:Carson City, CH:Chicago, CT:Court Case, DV:Denver, FC:File Copy, GA:Gaines File Copy, JS:Jerry Siegel, LA:Larson, MA:Murphy Anderson, MH:Mile High, MV:Mohawk Valley, OV:Overstreet, PA:Pennsylvania, SF:San Francisco, WM:White Mountain)
California residents please add 8 1/4% sales tax. **• Prices may be NEGOTIABLE •**

Consignments Accepted Immediately!

CGSA / M	NM/M	NM	VFN/NM	VFN	FN/VFN	FN	VG/FN	VG	G/VG	G	Fr	Pr
100.99.98.97.96.95.94.93.92.91	90	88.85.80.75	70	65.60.55	50	45.40.35	30	25.20	15	10	6	3
PgQ 0 1 2 2.5	3	3.3 4	5	6	6.5	7	7.5	8	8.5	9	9.5	10

Jerry Siegel's Typewriter
1st & Only Portable Typewriter
1938 Royal $65,000

DC Action Comics 4
Scarce
VG/FN 30 (5.5) $5,500

DC Action Comics 5
Scarce
FN-- 32 (5.0) $7,000

DC All Star Comics 20
Mile High / White Pages
NM/M 90 (1.0) $6,000

FOX All Top Comics 8
B. Beetle & Phantom Lady Begin
NM 80 (2.5) $2,600

DC All-American Comics 61
Origin/1st App Solomon Grundy
VF/VF+ 63 (4.5) $3,000

TIM All Winners Comics 1
VFN 60 (4.5) $9,500

MVL Amazing Fantasy 15
Origin/1st App Spider-Man
VF+ 65 (3.3) $17,500

FWCT America's Greatest 1
Mile High / White Pages
NM+ 85 (2.0) $7,000

DC Batman 1
Origin Batman/1st App Joker
VG/FN 30 (3.3) $18,000

DC Batman 5
1st App Of Batmobile
NM 80 (3.3) $7,500

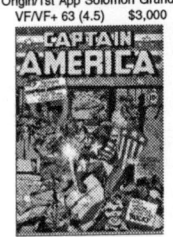

TIM Captain America Comics 1
Origin / 1st App Capt America
VG+ 25 (5.0) $10,000

TIM Captain America 4
Murphy Anderson Collection
FN+ 45 (5.5) $3,750

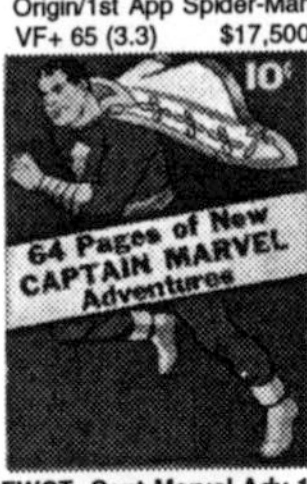

FWCT Capt Marvel Adv 1
Captain Marvel by Jack Kirby
E aVG+ 25 (4.5) $4,000

DC Detective 31
Mod. Restore/Classic Batman-C
M aVG+ 25 (5.0) $4,500

TIM Human Torch 2 (1)
(#1) Intro/Origin Toro
VG+ 25 (3.5) $5,000

MVL Incredible Hulk 1
Origin/1st App Hulk
VFN+ 65 (4.0) $6,500

DC More Fun Comics 54
Lt. Restore By S. Ciccone
L aVFN 60 (4.0) $4,200

DC More Fun Comics 101
Origin/1st App Superboy
FN/VFN 50 (4.0) $5,000

DC New Adventure 24
Mile High
VFN/NM 70 (3.3) $5,000

DC New Book Of Comics 2
Mile High
NM 80 (2.0) $15,000

DC New Comics 8
Scarce
VFN+ 65 (5.0) $3,000

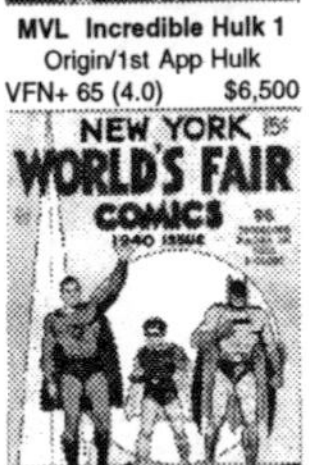

DC New York World's Fair 40
Superman,Batman & Robin-C
VFN 60 (4.5) $9,000

FOX Phantom Lady 17
Ovst. Copy/Classic Bondage-C
VFN+ 65 (3.5) $5,750

DC Showcase 4
Origin/1st App SA Flash
NM 80 (4.0) $40,000

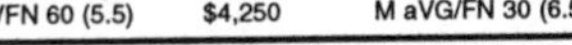

DC Showcase 14
Mohawk Valley/4th App SA Flash
VFN 60 (5.5) $4,250

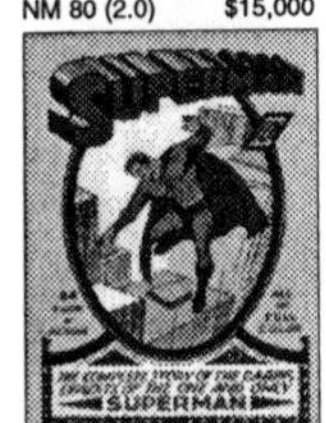

DC Superman 1
Origin Superman
M aVG/FN 30 (6.5) $20,000

DC Superman 1
Mod. Restored By W. Sarill
M aFN+ 45 (5.5) $25,000

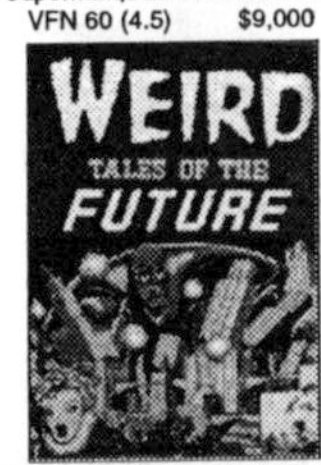

SPM Weird Tales Of Future 2
Wolverton C/A
VFN/NM 70 (4.5) $1,500

FWCT Whiz Comics 25
1st App Captain Marvel Jr.
FN 35 (5.0) $3,000

Sept, 1995

Ka-ChinG!

Helpful Hints on How to Buy and Sell Your Comics

BY KURT JACKSON

Comic fans are freaks. It's a known fact. But they're also a collection of freaks. Fans of all ages, shapes and sizes can join in on the fun of searching for ways to enhance their comic book collections.

Some fans will spend $125,000 for the first appearance of Batman in *Detective Comics* #27 or even $200 for a copy of *Avengers* #5 (Hey, it's got the first appearance of the Lava Men!). On the other hand, there are thousands of eager fans willing to wade through dozens of five-for-a-dollar comic boxes just to stock up on some reading material. Chances are, if you're a fan, you fit somewhere in the middle.

Regardless of the category in which you fall, you're going to find yourself thumbing through back issue bins at your local comic shop looking for those elusive comics you need to complete your run of *Iron Man* or *Spawn*. Unfortunately, you'll also be frantically fumbling through your wallet for an extra $5 or $10 that you hope is hidden somewhere in there. You can pray to Odin, Crom, Hera or even the Mighty Stan Lee, but you ain't gonna find that cash.

Have no fear, because one way to afford the comics you want is to sell off the comics you don't. You might have 15 copies of *Punisher* #1. So, why not sell off those extra 14 copies, and buy some comics that you need? Or you might have a couple copies of *Action Comics #1* or *Amazing Fantasy #15* that you think have been taking up a lot of extra space in your collection; so why not junk 'em? You can even sell off your entire collection or that 50-issue run of *Wonder Woman* you don't read anymore. The most important thing is to be prepared.

So take this advice to heart as you venture forth into the wacky world of comics commerce.

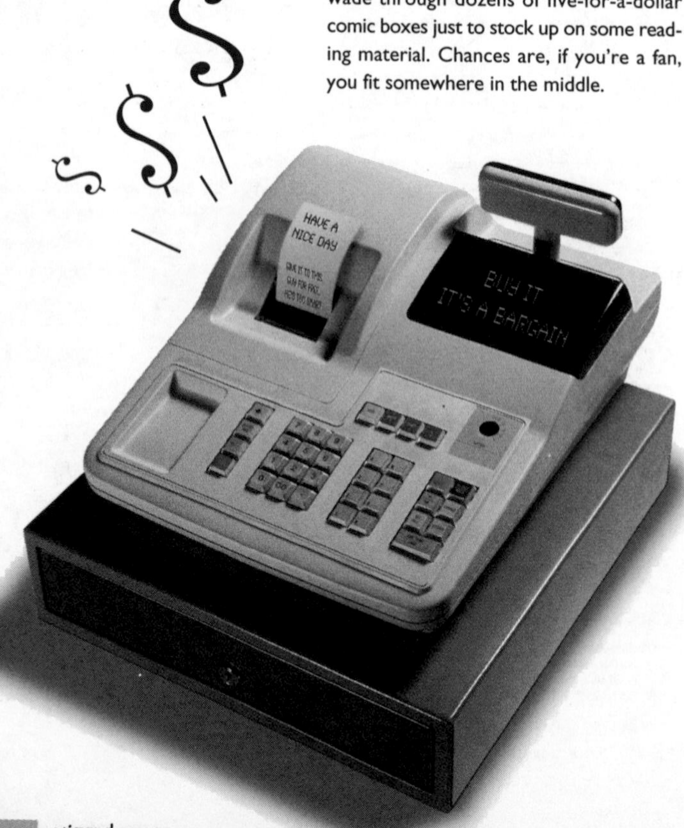

Screw the college fund. How about blowin' a cool $125,000 on the first Batman? Think your parents' heads would explode?

BUYING

It sounds pretty basic, but the first thing you really need to do is decide exactly what it is you want. In comics, that means more than just a title and issue number. Prices are determined by condition (see page 74) and availability.

If you're the type of person who thinks a book has to be in mint condition, be prepared to pay top dollar and spend a long time searching. And you'd better know what "top dollar" *really* means before you go out on your quest. Check a price guide and know what the current market value is. That doesn't mean you have to pay that price; after all, a price guide is just a "guide." It is, however, a solid starting point for negotiations.

If you just want to get a readable copy, you might get lucky and find it in an ol' bargain bin at your local comics shop. Hustle on down there right now and take a look. Go on, we'll wait. And if you don't see the book you want, ask. Retailers sometimes have tons of goodies in the back room.

Once you finally find a copy, make sure you know what you're getting, especially if you're paying big bucks. You should be allowed to look at a book before buying it. Open it up and make sure no pages are missing, no coupons are clipped out and nobody's kid brother has drawn a self portrait in the margins.

Obviously, if you're buying a comic book through a mail order service, there's just no way you can check the condition. And just like in any other industry, there are certain mail order companies that will rip you off. The majority of them, however, are quite reputable. The most important thing to do with a mail order service is find out whether you can return an issue you're unhappy with. Don't be afraid to ask. And if it doesn't feel right, don't do it.

make sure you know what you're getting. Open the book up and make sure no pages are missing, no coupons are clipped out and nobody's little brother has drawn a self portrait in the margins.

If you're buying a book for investment purposes and the condition is just too good to be true, ask if the comic has been restored. This is when a beat-up comic is fixed to look like its original state. There are some amazing techniques available for removing stains, brightening covers and replacing staples. A restored comic may look great, but it's worth a lot less than its unrestored counterpart.

Also be sure that you're getting a first printing. You can usually tell by looking inside the front cover or on the bottom of the first page. At the end of the indicia (that's where all that really small legal text is), it should say "second printing." It will rarely say "first printing," so if you can't find any mention of a print number, you most likely have a first print. Certain companies may also put Roman numerals on the front cover by the issue number, telling you exactly what printing it is. The values on subsequent printings are generally much lower than first printings, so be careful.

And most of all, don't allow yourself to be pressured. If you've reached your limit or feel uncomfortable with the way negotiations have gone, walk away. There will be other times and other comics. And hey, you may just find that very same issue in better condition *and* at a better price. That's the whole fun of collecting!

SELLING

There are basically two ways to sell your comics. You can do it yourself through some long and hard work, or you can sell everything at once to a comics retailer or a convention dealer.

The latter course is the fastest and simplest. You'll probably even come out no worse in the long run if you just let everything go for one big price. Sure, the buyer is getting that sought after *X-Men* #1 as part of the deal, but he's also taking *Micronauts* #26-#48, which are now worth less than free Pepsi refills. If you want to avoid the hassle, and you can get a reasonable price (shop things around, by the way, don't just take the very first offer), this is the way to go.

Be aware, however, that most reputable stores will limit their purchases. Be prepared to sell quality books for 25 percent to 40 percent of their retail value, and about 10 cents to 25 cents for all other books, especially those in bulk. At first this may seem like you're getting ripped off, but you're really not. You have to remember that retailers are not going to pay you guide prices for books, especially if they're selling their copies at guide price. Selling comics is a business, and retailers have a lot of expenses to pay including rent, salaries and other costs that go along with running a business.

don't get greedy. No matter what the guides or your friends say, a comic is worth only what somebody is willing to pay for it.

On the other hand, you can get a nicer profit if you have the time, stamina and energy to sell your books yourself. Run some ads in the right places (like the weekly *Comics' Buyers Guide* and other comic publications, along with the Internet—see "**Plug In!**" on page 34) and price your books a little under guide. Be aware that you've got to factor in costs for advertising, postage and other expenses, not to mention that you'll be spending a lot of time on this. It's certainly a lot easier to sell your books to a comic shop. In either case, be sure your comics are well presented, bagged and look like they've been cared for.

Finally, don't get greedy. No matter what the guides or your friends say, a comic is worth only what somebody is willing to pay for it. Keep this in mind: If you ask $20 for a comic that you only paid $1 for, and you finally settle on a price of $5, that's still a 500 percent profit.

Just remember that comic collecting is mainly a hobby. Comics are tons of fun to read and only some people can make a successful business out of it.

So if you happen to sell your comics, consider yourself pretty lucky. On top of a profit, no matter how small, you hopefully took the time to read and enjoy your comics somewhere along the way.

Kurt Jackson, who doesn't really exist, prefers "Chicago Hope" to "ER." Go figure.

Pack it in

The Best Way to Make Sure Your Comics Last Forever

BY KURT JACKSON

There are two types of comic book readers. After savoring a particularly exciting adventure of his favorite superhero and closing the book, one has a this-book-will-always-mean-something-to-me reaction ("Man, that issue was something else!"). Meanwhile, the other typically has a this-book-is-going-to-mean-something-to-*others* reaction ("Gee, I'd better keep this book safe so I can sell it later!").

Both types of reader places some worth upon this important comic and wishes to keep it in good condition. The latter person is concerned about how to keep it in the same fine shape it was when he bought it, so he can sell it for hopefully big bucks sometime in the future. The former person is concerned that his pleasure of the comic will become diminished when years after first enjoying it, he opens up the treasured book to find it unreadable because it's falling apart.

So no matter which type of comic reader you are, careful and correct storage of your books is important because it ensures that your collection will stay in good condition.

Basically, your purpose is to preserve each individual comic in a state as close to the way it was when it first rolled off the presses as you can (assuming it was in perfect condition at that point). In order to do that, you want to protect it from anything that might harm that original state, including light, heat and other outside forces that might cause it to deteriorate or discolor.

It's not an easy job, but somebody's got to do it. Since they're your comics, you're elected.

Store your comics standing up vertically in boxes. Most retailers sell special comics boxes designed for this purpose.

HERE'S WHAT YOU CAN DO TO PRESERVE YOUR COMICS:

• Store your comics standing up vertically in boxes large enough so that they are taller than the tops of the comics. There are special comics boxes designed for this purpose, which are sold for about $4 each by most retailers or are available by mail direct from the manufacturers (look for advertisements in comic books themselves, *Wizard* or another of your favorite comics publications). If you store your books in a box that does not cover them completely, chances are the comics will bend and crease at the point where the box ends. Also, remember to fill each box tightly from front to back with comics (or find material to pack firmly between the first book and the inside front of the box), so that the books won't bend or slip.

• Store your comics in Mylar (or plastic film) comics bags if you're planning to keep them an extended period of time. Less expensive plastic bags, made from polypropylene or polyethylene, are also fine, but these tend to deteriorate after five years or so. Keep your eye out for any discoloration or breakdown in your storage bags and replace them, because the chemical resulting from the bag's deterioration can be harmful to your comics. There are different-sized bags for Silver Age and Modern Age comics—since comics have gotten slightly smaller since the Silver Age (1955-1970)—so be sure to pick up the right ones for your books. Each comic should have an acid-free cardboard backing board in its bag. Specially designed bags and boards, like storage boxes, are available from your retailer or direct, in various grades and prices. Oh, and please—one comic per bag, folks; don't stuff 10 of them into one bag.

• For more expensive comics, a Mylar bag is actually strong and cost-effective enough for collectors with low budgets. If using these bags for your better issues, it's best to place a set of them together in one box. There are several more expensive storage products out there, of course, including the Showcase Sealer (two thick blocks of plastic you can slip your book into and screw together). Several collectors increase their feelings of security by keeping a valuable book in a rented safety deposit box at a bank. You might not want to show off your *Sandman* #1 in an armoire at home, since one of the key factors in storing costly books is keeping them out of light. Speaking of that...

• All the elements—light, air, moisture, etc.—are the deadly enemies of paper products. Your comics should be stored in a cool, dark and dry place where there are no extreme temperature changes during the year (attic and basement storage is generally not a good idea). You might want to consider a dehumidifier for the area in which your boxes are stored if you live in a humid climate. And light can be a serious problem; every time paper is exposed to light, at least some minimal damage is done. Unless you've a good reason for taking one of your treasured comics out of its protected environment (to read it, for example, which is always worth whatever risks involved), don't do it.

• Mice, insects and other happy little vermin, no matter how cute they might look in the pages of your stash of Disney titles, can be horribly destructive forces. They just love to nest in comfy piles of paper, munching away on their surroundings to their heart's content. Be sure that the place you choose for storage is clean and secure. Also do everything in your power to keep whatever pets you have away from your books; cats can mercilessly scratch up a book faster than a speeding bullet.

• Since there will be times when you'll want to find a given issue, you should store your books according to a system that works for you: alphabetically, by title, by character, whatever. If you can't find that *She-Hulk* #50 when you want it, it's likely that you'll go a little crazy and possibly do more harm to your collection during a frantic search than all the elements and rodents mentioned above could wreak in a year. It's only common sense to arrange and store your collection in an orderly fashion. And you can be as creative as you want: Nobody else need be able to deal with your system, but you'd better be able to. (See the feature elsewhere in this book on systems you can use to file your comics.)

• Beware of small children. Little Cousin Louie might, in his loving mother's eyes, "just love those nice comic books," but he could just as well be interested in eating them. Try to explain to family and friends that your collection is important and valuable to you, and that it should be respected. If that doesn't work and family pressure persists, you can head down to the comics shop and pick up a selection of the cheapest books you can find in the back issue boxes. Throw those at the little rugrat as soon as he appears at your door and everybody will be just bubbling over about how generous you are.

Beware of small children. Little Cousin Louie could be more interested in eating comics than he is in reading them.

A FEW THINGS YOU DEFINITELY SHOULDN'T DO:

• When we recommend that you keep your comics safely bagged, that does not mean that you should be sealing them up with heavy tape. You'll never get those bags open without a serious struggle, ruining the bag (and possibly the comic). Normal transparent tape is fine and some comics bags are self-sealing, the best option of all. Above all, if you must use tape, be very careful, or suffer the ripped-cover consequences.

• For heaven's sake, don't get careless. Once you've gone through the time and effort of setting up your storage system, the last thing you want to do is rip or bend a cover while putting a comic into its bag or taking it out, or wrinkle an issue because you're not paying attention.

• Do not eat or drink near your treasured comics. Trust us on this one: No matter how long it's been since you inadvertently knocked over a glass of milk, it will happen if you spread out your lunch on the same table as your favorite books. *The Bible* tells us there's a time for everything. *The Bible* doesn't lie.

While it appears that there are many rules to correctly and effectively protecting your comics, there's one rule listed above that you truly shouldn't forget. Make sure you set up a filing system that will let you lay hands on the book you want when you want it. Because the most important aspect of collecting comics is going through a box of them whenever you feel like it, picking out a standout issue, and starting to read.

Kurt Jackson is a freelance writer who lives in parts unknown. His neighbors are Mr. Wrestling I and Mr. Wrestling II

PLUG IN!

Wizard's Introduction and Guide to Comics in Cyberspace

BY BUDDY SCALERA

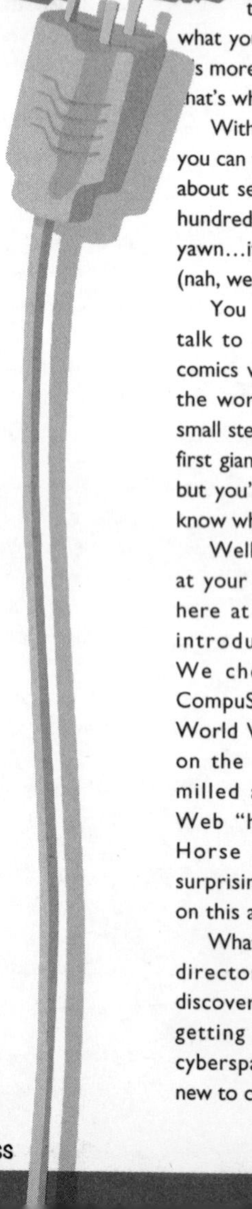

Here's how it happens: you hear about it in school or at work. You see it on TV and read about it in the paper. You get curious, you try it, you get hooked. No, it's not what you're thinking. It's cyberspace, and 's more addictive than any drug. At least, hat's what you've heard.

With just a computer and a modem, you can tap deep into reference databases about sewing, woodworking, politics and hundreds of other important subjects... yawn...if you're into that type of thing. (nah, we're not either).

You want to download free software, talk to comic professionals and trade comics with people on the other side of the world. You want to take that first small step into the digital domain and that first giant leap into online comic fandom, but you're a little intimidated. You don't know where to start.

Well, comic fans, cower no longer at your computer keyboard. Your pals here at *Wizard* have provided a brief introduction to getting online. We checked out America Online, CompuServe, eWorld, Prodigy and the World Wide Web. We met comic fans on the other side of the world. We milled around on the World Wide Web "home pages" set up by Dark Horse and Todd McFarlane. (Not surprising, we had hours of fun working on this article.)

What follows is a sort of yellow-pages directory of cool places that we discovered. It also gives some tips for getting started if you're new to cyberspace. And, hey, who really isn't new to cyberspace?

THE BASICS

To get started, you'll need an IBM-compatible or Macintosh computer, a modem and a phone line. Plug everything in and fire up the software of your choice (we'll get to that later). The type of computer you are using is secondary to the modem you choose. Modems are rated according to their speed. You can get a cheap modem that runs at 2400 baud, which—without getting too technical—is how fast your modem is "talking" with other modems. This speed is pretty slow and not recommended. How come? Well, slow modems cost you money in the long run because online services charge by the hour. Yeah, you may save a few bucks in the beginning, but in the end you will definitely suffer and regret it.

We recommend buying a modem that operates at 14,400 baud or higher. If you've got the cashola, get yourself a 28,800 baud speed modem. It'll save you time and aggravation in the long run. Don't say we didn't warn ya.

GENERAL TIPS

Be patient: You ain't gonna learn how to do it all right away. There are many tricks that you'll pick up as you go. If you're feeling somewhat dazed and confused online, just get the FAQs if the forum has them available. These funky lifesavers are files that contain helpful hints for new users. Quite literally, they stand for Frequently Asked Questions. Reading FAQs saves you valuable online time, which translates into more fun for your money.

FAQs usually can be found in downloadable libraries or in welcome screens. It's smart to download FAQs and read them before progressing any further.

Look, listen and learn. It's easy to become overwhelmed by the hugeness of the online world. Read what's on the bulletin boards (places packed with tons of information on a wide range of topics) before you jump in with your guns-a-blazin'. You don't want to be labeled as a newbie (a newcomer to an area) your first time out.

Learn the Lingo: Many users "speak" with little emoticons or netspeak when in an online "chat room," where you can communicate directly with others. It's important to learn how to use these abbreviations to effectively communicate online (see sidebar). For example, use <G> when you want to show someone that you are grinning. You may even learn to use little pictures like :), which is just a smiley face on its side. It's all part of learning the online language.

COOL PLACES TO VISIT ONLINE

America Online

ATTRACTIONS:

Keyword: DC
Keyword: Comics or Wizard
Keyword: Scifi

One of the distinct disadvantages America Online (AOL) has from its competition

You get curious, you try it, you get hooked. Cyberspace is more addicting than any drug.

over at CompuServe, is that it has limited chat rooms. Chat rooms are places you can visit, where anywhere from 2 to 100 (or more) people can hang out and talk to each other about all sorts of things (preferably comic books in a comic chat room). DC Comics has two and Wizard World has only one. Most of the time, though, users just argue about what they are going to discuss.

DC Comics is an active and popular forum on AOL. DC's forum is both lively and remarkably interactive. It hosts chat rooms with many popular DC creators including John Byrne and others.

Everything that you ever wanted to know about DC Comics is there for the taking. It's comprehensive and interactive.

DC's forum on America Online is smooth and well organized. DC fans can easily become addicted to the depth of information available here. DC allows users to download hundreds of covers from graphic novels and comic books. There's also information for *Mad Magazine*, Vertigo, Milestone and Paradox Press.

One of the most interesting areas is the DC Comics Virtual Fiction area, which allows users to help develop a serialized weekly adventure featuring a DC character. DC's major drawback is its inability to adequately serve the interests of Marvel, Image and other independent readers. Of course, that brings you to, yours truly, Wizard World online which covers DC, along with any other publisher. Wizard World is the official online home of both *Wizard: The Guide to Comics* and *InQuest: The Guide to Collectible Card Games.*

Each month, *Wizard* uploads most of its news articles, features and columns. Not everything from the magazine appears online, and not everything that's online will appear in the magazine. You can also access *Wizard* and *InQuest*'s price guides as well as talk to the price guide editors any time you want. In fact, many of *Wizard*'s editors—including Publisher Gareb Shamus—are on Wizard World.

Wizard World is the new kid on the block at America Online, but has already developed a dedicated following, most likely due to the variety in the chat rooms and downloadable material (like artwork, photos and stories).

ADVANTAGES: Wizard and DC have established forums that cater to both general and specific interests. The combined draw of both forums is helping to attract many top name creators including Tom Lyle, Richard Pini, Walter Simonson, John Cleary, David Campiti, Bernard Chang, Beau Smith, Andy Kubert, Bill Tucci and many others.

DISADVANTAGES: Every forum comes with its own icons and backgrounds that must be downloaded to your computer the first time you enter the forum. Wizard World is relatively new and not all of the forum's interactive features and events are available to the public.

AMERICA ONLINE
800-754-4400

America Online is home to Wizard and DC because of its advanced software interface. Graphics and text are combined for a package that is visually appealing and easy to use.

CompuServe

ATTRACTIONS:

GO: Comics
GO: Compub

It may not be the first and it certainly ain't the prettiest, but no one can dispute the fact that CompuServe is one of the great granddaddies of the

Compuserve offers megabytes of information and conversation with none of the flashy graphics.

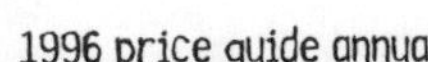

eWorld looks great, but for comic fans, it's missing a hook. No major publishers have staked out a home on it yet

With just a computer and a modem, you can tap deep into reference databases about hundreds of important subjects.

online services for comic fans. The heavily trafficked Comic Book & Animation forum is an extremely popular and useful forum.

It's packed solid with bulletin boards, software and chat rooms. CompuServe is amazingly addictive and can help your buttocks grow a few sizes every day. Unlike its competition on competing services, CompuServe doesn't limit users to just a few chat rooms; there are at least 20 rooms in the forum. Most of the conversation is lively, interesting and extremely friendly. CompuServe is most famous for its large base of professional artists and writers. It is not uncommon to bump into creators like James Robinson, Neil Gaiman, Kurt Busiek and many, many others.

The Comics and Animation forum has a little sister forum called the Comics Publishers forum. It's a much less-frequented forum that mainly houses folders allowing you to send mail to independent publishers. The Marvel, DC and Wizard folders are present, but little action is seen in them. The folders are a pipeline to many independent publishers.

ADVANTAGES: CompuServe's comic book forums cater to an older audience that enjoys discussing industry issues. The forum is well established and has many interesting events. Both forums feature hundreds of useful downloadable files catering to every related interest.

DISADVANTAGES: The CompuServe system is not really set up for graphics, making it seem a little bland. There's not a lot of art to download, and forums can't offer up much more than talk.

COMPUSERVE
800-848-8199

eWorld

ATTRACTIONS:
Shortcut: SF

When it comes to raw potential, no one comes close to eWorld. Not even Bo Jackson. The graphics and interface are smooth and enjoyable to use.

Yet, unlike multi-sport Bo, eWorld seems content on serving a teeny tiny population of online users: Macintosh owners. Except...*except*, there's no one there using it. Sometimes when you log on, you wonder if anyone else is on with you. Chat rooms are uninhabited and the bulletin boards are relatively unused. eWorld is like outer space: nobody can hear you scream...because nobody is there.

You've got to wonder if comic books are one of eWorld's dirty little secrets. The comic discussion area is so deeply tucked away in the Science Fiction area, that you'd almost think eWorld is trying to hide something. There are some spirited discussions about comics, but not nearly enough active participants to make eWorld an appealing hangout for someone primarily interested in comics. There is a helpful folder called "creative sources," that links fans and aspiring pros. However, there's really not all that much traffic on there to justify getting an account.

ADVANTAGES: If you're a Macintosh lover, this place was built for you. Cool sounds and a smooth interface make this place an absolute pleasure to explore.

DISADVANTAGES: It's lonely. This service is so new that it's barely inhabited yet. Imagine Disney World with no one to play with except the ride operators.

eWORLD
800-775-4556

Prodigy

ATTRACTIONS:
Jump: Comics
Jump: Tekno

If they gave awards out for most improved online service, Prodigy would win. Problem is: it just isn't enough; at least as far as comic fans are concerned. Prodigy's two main attractions are the Comics Bulletin Board and the Tekno•Comix forum. The Comics BB is just plain vanilla in an industry that wants Ben & Jerry's Chunky Monkey.

Prodigy has made a home for Techno Comix's interactive forum. The system has a lot to offer, but has lost a lot of ground to other services with better content and interface.

The Tekno forum is about as much fun as wearing your mom's heels to play hoops. It does take an ambitious stab at creating an exciting community for comics readers, though. Of course, like the DC Comics forum on America Online, the Tekno forum is geared toward specific comic readers.

On Prodigy, you're in luck if you read *Mullkon Empire* and *Mike Danger*. If you read the *X-Men* or *Spawn*, you can go pound salt. One of the more interesting features of the Tekno forum is an ongoing online comic book called Neuro Jack that you can read right on your monitor. It's a clever idea that needs better graphics and writing for it to catch on with mainstream readers.

ADVANTAGES: Lots of people. Several fun topics and chat rooms. Some of the graphics and interfaces are really intense. Prodigy has stepped up to the plate with a large bat and lots of improvements. Just when everybody had counted them out, Prodigy proved they're still in the game.

DISADVANTAGES: Prodigy sometimes seems like a big dinosaur compared to its competition. Some of the graphics and interfaces are kind of lame.

PRODIGY
800-776-3449

World Wide Web

The World Wide Web (WWW or Web) is like nothing else you've ever experienced. It is simultaneously wonderful and boring as hell. It's sometimes a great research tool and other times electronic junk mail.

With the Web, you have to learn as you go. The Web is still free of charge, but you need to have access to a pay service in order to use it. Each of the major services including America Online, CompuServe, eWorld, GEnie and Prodigy offer entrance ramps to the Internet and the Web. The WWW is composed of many linked "home pages" that serve varied interests. Of course, there are numerous cool comic book Web pages. (We won't even try to go into the history of the Web or the Internet because it's way too long, boring and confusing.)

To get around on the Web, you can usually just click on search words and travel through different "links" that will take you to new places. Sometimes you will want to go somewhere specific. To get there you will need to know the "URL address," which is one of those ridiculously long code addresses like http://www.blah.blah.blah. Don't be intimidated, you'll get used to these long addresses. Hey, you remembered y=mx+b, didn't you?

ATTRACTIONS:
Here are some of the cool places that we found on the Web. Incidentally, the WWW is not really an official corporate entity, so any of these pages can be here today and gone tomorrow. Some of the areas are set up by publishers to help further promote their products. Others are established by fellow fans just for sheer enjoyment.

If you are new to the WWW, we recommend you check out some of the pages that provide listings of links before you try memorizing long URL addresses. These listings are extremely helpful to the new user. Two of our favorites are http://www.yahoo.com/Entertainment/Comics/ and http://www.bluefin.net/~donlisk/. We liked these pages of links because they lead us to many other cool pages, and of course, more links.

Due to spatial constraints, we can only print a few of our favorites; there are just too damn many to list. However, we will

WWW pages allow ordinary people to produce their own "electronic fanzines."

NETSPEAK!

i n t e r n e t j a r g o n

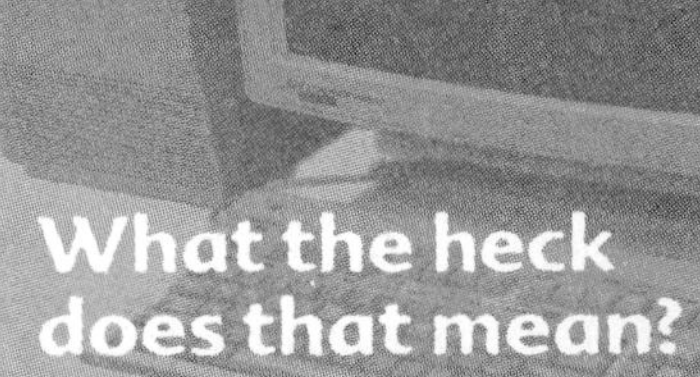

What the heck does that mean?

USER 1: She was so funny that I was <ROFL>!

USER 2: <G>, yeah. She makes me :-D

SAY WHAT? You catch all of that? If you're new to being online, that little conversation probably went right over your head.

What that little snippet contained was portions of "netspeak" and "emoticons," online languages that allow people to express themselves quickly on the keyboard. People use these symbols to spice up conversations and keep everything moving. Learning the lingo can help you communicate better with your online peers.

Here's a few of the most common emotions that you'll see online:

<G> = Grinning
<J> = Joking
<LOL> = Laughing out loud
BTW = By the way
OTOH = On the other hand
??? = What?
:) = Smiley face
:-D = Laughing
:-0 = Uh oh
:-@ = Screaming
;-) = Winking
<ROFL> = Rolling on the floor laughing

be providing updated link information and comprehensive Web listings in the Wizard World forum of America Online. Also, if you find something really cool that's not listed in Wizard World, be sure to drop us an e-mail so that we can include it in our directory.

BATMAN

Batman fans will find lots of truly innovative pages dedicated to the Dark Knight. Try out Wayne Manor at http://www.books.com/batman/batman1.htm and a nifty little Batman web page at http://syzygy.math.ufl.edu/%7ewdn/comics/batman/. (By the way, the heavily advertised http://www.riddler.com has nothing to do with Batman comics.)

COMIC SKETCHES CENTRAL

Comic Sketches Central at http://underground.net/~koganuts/Galleries/comics01.html is one of those neato fan pages with a non-corporate attitude. This is a neat place to see original art that may or may not have been published.

DARK HORSE

Dark Horse fans have no reason not to find out Dark Horse's newest projects, when they go to the Dark Horse Web site at http://www.dhorse.com/~dhc/. Not only is this site easy to use, it is a prime example of just how good these sites can be. The Dark Horse site is easily one of the finest areas online for comic fans with a specific interest. Don't miss it or Marv'll be all over yer butt.

SMASH

Smash, located at http://smash.cs.com, is billing itself as a cyber magazine. It provides a variety of information for comic-minded Web surfers. Smash offers a little bit of news, transcripts of interviews, a few reviews and other stuff. It's a cool place to visit and offers several good links.

SPAWN

Just before we went to press with this article we were thinking that we hadn't seen very much stuff on Spawn. There was a little bit of info at http://www.cris.com/~dspiral/sp.shtml, but not enough to satisfy the Violator's hunger. At the last moment, we cracked a secret code and discovered the not-yet-released official Spawn page at http://www.mcfarlane.com. We saw the page in its final stages of development. Trust us, it's one of the coolest pages on the Web. If we're lying, you can sew up our faces with a shoe lace.

TOO MUCH COFFEE MAN

Shannon Wheeler has his own snappy little cozy coffee-centric area at http://college.antioch.edu/~pbradley/tmcm/. Come and pray to the Java God and hope that he doesn't drive a nail through your hand or make you work retail.

X-MEN

As you would probably guess, there are a lot of bytes dedicated to Marvel's mutants. To list all the places would waste a lot of ink. We'd rather point you to the Uncanny X-Page at http://www.students.uiuc.edu/~m-blase/x-page.html. It's a great place to start for students of the atom. Not only is it incredibly well organized and fun to use, but it has great links to many other X-Men related hot spots on the Web.

ADVANTAGES: The Web is a wide open field for developers and fans. There is no censorship. It's available through all of the major services discussed here.

DISADVANTAGES: It's unregulated, so many areas do not function properly or are a waste of time. Some of the areas are just big advertisements and this costs you money because, remember, you're paying by the hour for these online services. Not all of the areas have links to bulletin boards and chat rooms, which can get pretty dull. There's also a much higher chance of getting a virus on your computer from downloadable files.

What's to Come

Well, that about covers it for the brief overview of getting online. As you get online yourself, you'll see that the magnitude of the online world is far larger than what we could cover in a single magazine article.

We also only touched on three of the most popular online services, one smaller service and some of the WWW. Trust us, there is so much more out there. The Web is developing at a dizzying pace and new pages pop up every day.

As this article goes to press, Windows 95 has just been launched, and with it, the new heavy on the block, Microsoft Network. Due to time constraints and the newness of the network, we decided that it would not be fair to Microsoft Network to judge the system so early. There is definitely stuff out there for comic book fans, but the bulletin boards are still in their infancy. It's not a far stretch, however, to predict that the Microsoft Network will soon begin to assert its hugeness online.

We hope you picked up a few pointers from our introduction. We also hope that you understand that this is far from a comprehensive listing of what's online for comic fans. We'd need an entire book just to touch on everything that's available.

If you have any questions or comments, we welcome them at our e-mail address WizardTGTC@aol.com. C'ya in cyberspace.

Buddy Scalera is the Wizard Press Online Editor and the host of Wizard World on America Online. He shares an office with an inflatable bison. Don't ask.

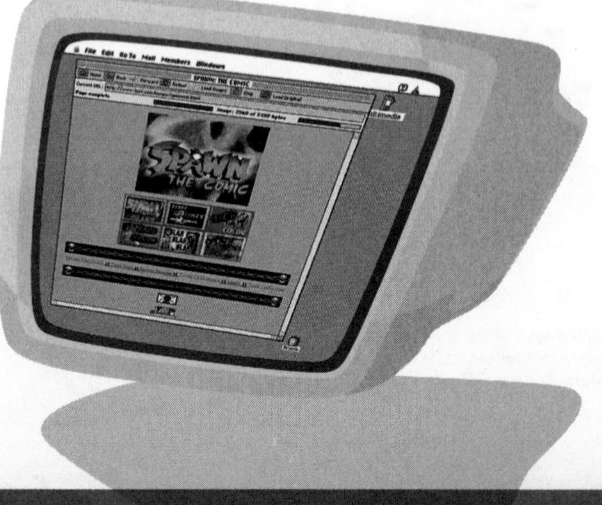

Some WWW pages are fan-designed sites and others are official home pages. Dark Horse and Spawn pages are among the most exciting and innovative official home pages on the internet.

Big Business

Comics make their presence felt in today's mass-merchandising world

BY JOHN MARSLAND

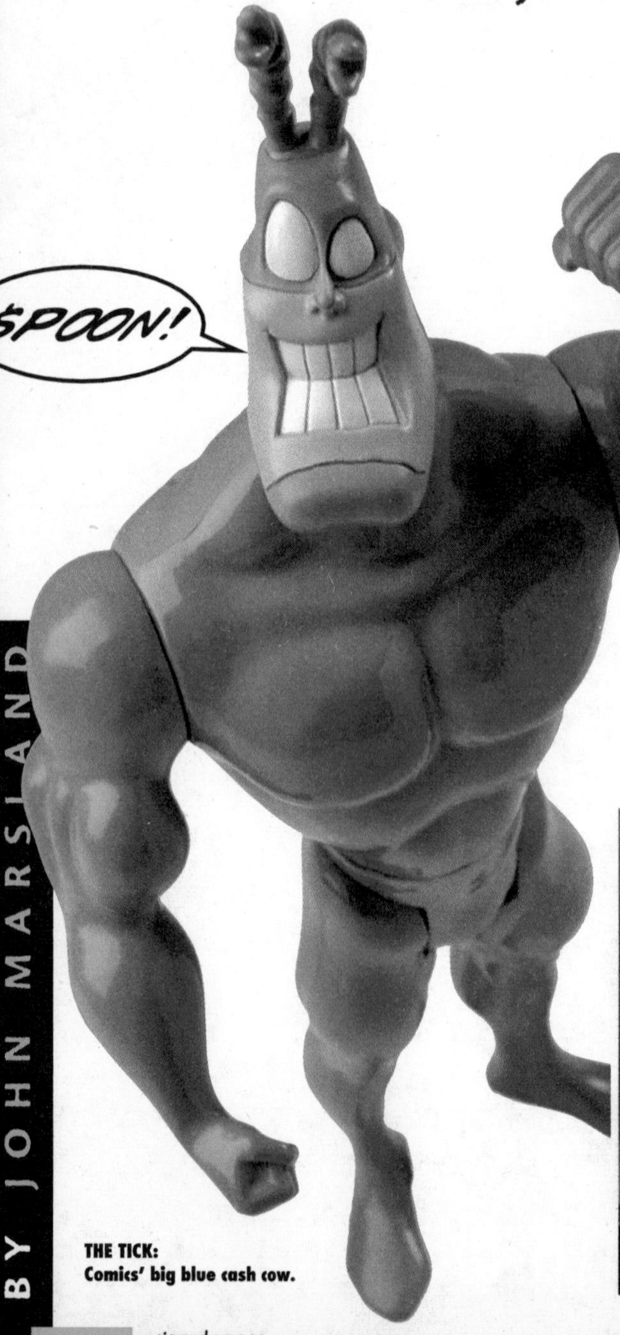

The secret world of comic books isn't so secret anymore.

Funny what a four-pack of pizza-munching turtles and a $251-million grossing movie about a guy in a cape can do to wake up mainstream America.

When the Teenage Mutant Ninja Turtles jumped off the pages of a comic book in 1987 to appear in a television series and a movie (1990), it signaled a wakeup call to capitalists. As in, there's gold in them there pages. Turtle power represented green, as in cash.

Others point to the original *Batman* film in 1989, which merged starpower like Jack Nicholson and Micheal Keaton with kiddie books, on its way to becoming the ninth-highest grossing film of all time.

No matter who blazed the path, comic books represent big business these days.

From big-budget films—up to 15 projects were in the works in 1995—to video games to toys to animation to trading cards to fast food tie-ins to youth-targeted merchandise, comic book-related paraphernalia represents a multi-billion dollar industry.

Holy cash cow, Batman.

But why? How did comics evolve from 10-cent books stuffed in your closet that mom invariably tossed out into the gross national product of a small country?

Simple, say industry insiders, its time had come.

"The Turtles proved to everyone that if you market it properly, you can create a multi-million dollar industry," says Ron Antonette, a spokesman at Golin Harris, which distributes the Playmates line of Turtles toys.

THE TICK: Comics' big blue cash cow.

And the Fab Four proved it in Hollywood. If you can make it there, you can make it anywhere.

"In Hollywood, nothing succeeds like success," says Dave Davis, a film analyst for Paul Kagen and Associates, an L.A.-based media research firm. "When there is success in one genre, the natural tendency is for everyone to jump on the bandwagon and try to repeat that success."

"There is a new respect for comics and the people who read them," adds Chuck Russell, who directed *The Mask*, based on a comic published by Dark Horse Comics. "It's not just kids reading comics anymore, but people into their adulthood."

The success of the Turtles and Batman fueled more comic-related projects. And more comic-related projects meant more hype and licensing opportunities for the natural offshoots of big-budget films, such as licensed video games, animation, toys, cards and related merchandise—from knapsacks to lunch boxes to mugs to piggy banks, the list goes on and on.

So where should we start? How about with movies, where *Batman* and the *Teenage Mutant Ninja Turtles* (three Turtles films grossed more than $250 million) began the feeding frenzy.

Movies

We will always remember 1995 as the year of the comic book film. The third installment of the Batman series, *Batman Forever*, survived the loss of former Batman Michael Keaton and raced out of the Batcave, grossing an all-time best $52.8 million its first weekend. After the first three Batman films grossed more than $600 million, plans for a fourth Batman are already in the works for a summer '97 release, with director Joel Schumacher already signed on and Julia Roberts slated as the villainess Poison Ivy. Schumacher has publicly stated that he wants Val Kilmer and Chris O'Donnell to reprise their roles as Batman and Robin. "I've heard both Val and Chris say that they'd do another one if I directed it," Schumacher was quoted as saying.

But Batman had to slug it out at the box office with other comic book projects over the past 18 months.

• Sly Stallone weighed in with *Judge Dredd*, based on the futuristic British comic book about a near-lawless society that featured Stallone as judge and jury. The verdict: Stallone found guilty on all charges of a flop.

• Jim Carrey sparkled as *The Mask*, on the way to grossing $120 million dollars for donning the green-faced, morphing mask made famous by Dark Horse Comics.

• *The Crow* became better known for the movie set marred by the tragic death of Brandon Lee, but the film based on a Kitchen Sink Press comic of the same name grossed more than $100 million.

• Macaulay Culkin cashed in as *Richie Rich*, the good-hearted kid with a wallet of gold.

• Lori Petty shaved her head to star in *Tank Girl*, but it was hair-today, gone tomorrow for the futuristic, sci-fi film.

The list goes on and on: *Casper the Friendly Ghost*, *Mighty Morphin Power Rangers*, etc.

And coming down the pike are more comic-based projects: from James Cameron's Spider-Man film to Wesley Snipes as Luke Cage to the Fantastic Four.

"Comic books are a great breeding ground," says Harvey Comics Entertainment, Inc.'s chairman Jeffrey Montgomery. "To launch a comic book costs less than $50,000. If it hits, it's worth billions."

And it doesn't just end with film grosses. Films based on comics are the perfect vehicle for related merchandise.

"It's a natural cross-fertilization in terms of toys and marketing," says syndicated entertainment reporter Stephen Shaefer.

Ah yes, the toys.

Hollywood has become infatuated with comic-based films like *Batman, The Mask, The Crow* and *Teenage Mutant Ninja Turtles*.

Toys

In the world of toys, licensed products rank among the top properties, accounting for $17 billion worth of merchandise sold in 1994. And comic book properties play a key role among licensed products. Bat-merchandise alone has generated nearly $3 billion in sales since the first film in 1989. And *Batman Forever* was no different, with 125 licensees (many marketing multiple products) cranking out the Bat-stuff. For the actors in the films, being immortalized on a toy can be equally lucrative, as much as 15 percent of merchandise revenues.

"It's kind of like getting an award," Sylvester Stallone was quoted as saying. "It's amazing because you grow up playing with toys and you look at that and go, 'Not bad.' You want to carry it around as a badge of honor — you are a toy. But I don't dwell on it; I don't think, 'Will this next movie produce a kite?' "

The Mighty Morphin Power Rangers cooled off slightly from the sizzling sales recorded in 1994, but when you consider that the Power Rangers were selling three toys for every one Teenage Mutant Ninja Turtle-related toy purchased during its heyday, it's still quite impressive.

Also flooding toy stores during '95 were toys based on Casper, The Mask, Cyberforce, Spawn, WildC.A.T.s, Youngblood, Star Wars, industry staple G.I. Joe, the ever-popular Star Trek characters, hot newcomer The Tick and a host of Marvel characters, including the X-Men, Spider-Man, Iron Man and the Fantastic Four.

SPAWN: Part of the '95 toy flood.

Animation

Animation exploded in 1995 and one thing was clear: Cartoons aren't just for kids anymore. While Disney continued to churn out hits with *Pocahontas* following up on the success of *The Lion King*, MTV became a player in animation, unveiling adult-oriented cartoons such as *The Maxx* (based on the Image comic book). And comic-based cartoons continued to fill TV schedules with *The Adventures of Batman and Robin*, the *Marvel Action Hour* (consisting of Iron Man and the Fantastic Four), *Spider-Man*, *Teenage Mutant Ninja Turtles*, *The Tick*, *WildC.A.T.s* and *X-Men*. Debuting in the fall of '95 were *Savage Dragon* and an updated Felix the Cat cartoon. In the planning stages are cartoons based on Codename: Stryke Force, Cyberforce, Zen Intergalactic Ninja, Superman (Sept. '96) and Youngblood. Todd McFarlane's Spawn is scheduled to appear in an HBO cartoon.

MTV's *The Maxx*.

"If you wanted to do a cartoon, and you were looking for source material, what would be more natural," *Marvel Action Hour* host Stan Lee has said publicly. "What makes a good comic strip usually will make good animation, and vice versa."

"Five years ago, you couldn't sell a comic book to the networks," says Bruce Timm, producer/director of *The Adventures of Batman and Robin*. "At the time, comedy was what kids wanted. Now, superhero shows seem to be what people want."

And it's not strictly targeted at kids. Sam Kieth's *The Maxx* on MTV weaves a surrealistic tale about a hero trapped in two worlds. Definitely not kid stuff. The success of *The Maxx* and other animated shows such as *Beavis and Butt-Head* has convinced MTV to create its own animation department, with more than 100 employees.

"Animation is not just Saturday morning kid stuff anymore," says MTV senior vice president Abby Terkuhle.

Additionally, *Elfquest*, based on Richard and Wendy Pini's comic about a tribe of elves trying to find their place in the World of Two Moons, is in the production stages for a feature film but a release date not yet scheduled.

Video games

The video game industry went through a major shakeup in 1995 as old game-playing systems became passé and hi-tech, more powerful ones lept to the forefront. There were a few problems, however. Like the price tag. The new gaming systems (Sony Playstation, Sega Saturn, Nintendo Ultra 64-bit) cost upwards of $400, a significant jump from past hardware systems. Mix in the threat of games played on personal computers and CD-ROMs, and video game companies are concerned about an industry that generated $10 billion worldwide in 1994, or roughly double the size of the movie industry's annual gross receipts.

Licensed properties represented a significant portion of the video game market, with films such as *Mighty Morphin Power Rangers*, *Judge Dredd* and *Batman Forever* becoming games.

Other comic-based properties included X-Men, The Adventures of Batman & Robin, Prime, Green Lantern, WildC.A.T.s, Spider-Man, Lobo, Justice League Task Force and Punisher.

VIDEO GAMES: The king of the merchandising hill.

A unique entry into the world of video was Comix Zone, the first truly interactive comic book from Sega. The video game revolved around a comic artist stuck in his own comic book world and featured full comic book pages with graphics from real comic book artists.

Fast Food Promotions

Fast food chains hopped on the superhero express in '95, turning to comic characters to help promote and increase those billions and billions served. After Hollywood discovered the films (*Batman Forever, The Mask, Casper, Mighty Morphin Power Rangers*) and television shows (*The Tick, Spider-Man, X-Men*), fast food restaurants quickly followed suit.

"It was a real superhero summer for us," says McDonald's spokesman Steve Bender.

McDonald's sponsored a Spider-Man promotion in May followed by the Gotham Glassware Collection to coincide with Batman Forever in June, capped by a Mighty Morphin Power Ranger Happy Meal deal in July.

So fast food chains have discovered the power of comic characters, cartoons and action figures. But why now?

"A lot of big entertainment properties lend themselves to action figures and related merchandise—natural product tie-ins for movies and TV series," says Karen Raugust, executive editor of *The Licensing Letter*.

And, as frequently happens in the advertising and promotional business, other fast food chains followed suit.

"In the toy business, action figures is one of the fastest-growing categories," adds Raugust. "Since there is demand for more action figures, the fast food outlets naturally want to capitalize. With so many high-visibility movies competing, the comic merchandise tie-ins aren't enough to differentiate the chains from each other, so you have significantly higher advertising expenditures, particularly for TV, with the licensed characters getting the great additional exposure."

Among the promotions were:

- Taco Bell sponsored a pair of six-week promotions: a "specTICKular" cross promotion with the Fox Saturday morning animated series, *The Tick*, and four different Kid's Meal premiums based on *The Mask*.
- While Casper the Friendly Ghost celebrated his 40th birthday with a major-motion picture, Pizza Hut chipped in with four collectible, glow-in-the-dark hand puppets.
- Hardee's/Roy Rogers turned to the comic world's hottest group, the X-Men, for a four-week promotion. Included were a Beast action figure on a Glider, X-Men tattoos, Pogs, trading cards, and two different sets of two mini-comics. Also created were four combination "X-Men and its enemies" figures on pedestal bases that fit together like a puzzle to make a "battlefield."

BELOW: Comic-based cards—losing steam. BOTTOM RIGHT: Cereals have a new surprise inside.

Trading cards

The sale of entertainment cards experienced a downward turn—reflecting the comic industry—because of a variety of factors: a market flooded with sets both in terms of variety and volume, the high prices of sets and competition from collectible card games.

What '95 was noted for in terms of card sets was variants and gimmicks—chromium, metal, oversized cards, etc. The enhancements in turn drove up the price of card sets.

Comic-based card sets continued to pour in with Fleer and SkyBox putting out some of the higher profile properties. Among Fleer's highlights were sets based on Casper and Batman, Ultra Spider-Man, Marvel Metal, Marvel Masterpieces and Ultra X-Men. Skybox scored with sets based on Pocahontas, DC Villains, DC Legends and a variety of Star Trek properties. December also saw a DC versus Marvel/Marvel vs. DC card set based on the comic crossovers.

Other characters immortalized in card sets this year were Lady Death, Evil Ernie, Shi, Cyberforce, Vampirella, Gen[13], Groo, Prophet, The Tick, Youngblood, Dawn, Spawn and Bone.

Collectible card games were a success story, boosted by the phemenonal sales of Magic: The Gathering. Fleer joined the collectible card wars with Fleer OverPower, featuring Marvel superheroes such as the X-Men, Spider-Man, Fantastic Four and Captain America.

Merchandise

Aside from the usual assortment of lunchboxes, knapsacks and clothing paraphernalia, food products jumped into the superhero business. There were Spider-Man and the X-Men featured on Chef Boyardee pasta, Batman on a box of Corn Pops and Apple Jacks offered an exclusive Star Wars 12-page comic offer. Ralston-Purina even unveiled a new Spider-Man cereal.

SO WHAT HAVE WE LEARNED?

Hollywood is infatuated with comic books right now so the revenues will continue to roll in. The hype, exposure and marketing are all in place. But what happens when the films stop coming, when comic-based projects go the way of the western or the musical?

Will the toys still sell? Will the cartoons still be made? Will McDonald's and Burger King still run comic promotions?

Only time will tell if comics will stay ingrained in the mainstream or will return to its secret society, cult-like status. One thing is for sure, however, comics are currently enjoying a place in the mainstream—and reaping the revenues that go along with it—like never before.

John Marsland likes to watch the Batman films while wearing his superhero Underoos. (With additional reporting by John Seals)

Long, Strange Trip

A review of 1995 proves that when it comes to comics, anything is possible

BY MARC SHAPIRO

What a long, strange trip it's been. Lyric courtesy of The Grateful Dead. And a dead-on description of the comic industry in the year just concluded. Companies merged with other companies. Companies formed exclusive distribution deals. Retailers bitched. But, at the heart of the maelstrom, creative artists and writers, oblivious to the corporate gas, remained hard at work creating new and dynamic characters, rejuvenating grizzled veterans and, on a regular basis, taking these characters from the paneled page to the small and large live-action and animated screen. While the likes of Marvel and DC continued their steady parade of heroes and heroines, the real pulse lay with the independents who broke new ground with the tide of Bad Girls, effective movies, TV adaptations and a steady stream of unorthodox superheroes.

Adding to the growth spurt of comics was the fact that Hollywood sat up and took notice in a big way. *Batman: Forever*, *Tank Girl* and *Judge Dredd* packed movie houses to varying degrees while the animated likes of Spider-Man, X-Men and WildC.A.T.s swooped down on Saturday Mornings. The toys? The cards? Comics were *everywhere* in 1995. Look out '96! The long, strange trip will continue!

Lady Death, at right, demonstrates why the Bad Girl trend is so gosh-darned popular these days.

LADY DEATH

The pioneer babe of the current Bad Girl craze continued to flex her scantily clad muscles in the past year. This feisty, white-skinned female used to be a "good" little girl named Hope, until her dad made some deals with the devil and she took on the horned one herself. Now, as the Queen of the Endless Graveyard, she's banished from Earth until the very last human being is killed. Her *Between Heaven and Hell* mini-series brought her to new heights of popularity. Artistically, Lady Death remained a treat for the eyes as hellish color combos grabbed and hung on to the Lady's luscious curves and obvious assets. Writer/creator Brian Pulido and the folks at Chaos! continue to be true to their vision and the result is one of the toughest and most entertaining trips to hell to emerge from the comics underground in years.

GEN^{13}

Few fights, regular clothes (if any!), lots of dialogue and a bunch of superpowered teenagers. Everybody loved the adventures of this genetically engineered team consisting of the powerful Fairchild, the fire-controllin' Burnout, the levitatin' Freefall, the rain-handlin' Rainmaker and the molecular-rearrangin' Grunge. This year's run of Gen-adventures, complete with such enticing and successful gimmicks as the Pulp Fiction and Do it Yourself variant covers, continues to exemplify the new hero spirit abroad in the comic book landscape. The book continues to project a slick toughness in the pages while the character relationships, crisp dialogue and confrontations ring truer than true. *Gen^{13}* never lets you forget it's a comic book but you're also quite aware that there's a good dose o' reality emerged throughout.

BATMAN FOREVER

This much anticipated third film installment of The Caped Crusader proved to be a box office success despite mixed critical reviews. Val Kilmer played Bruce Wayne/Batman as a much more humane—if occasionally invisible—lead. Jim Carrey and Tommy Lee Jones were appropriately villainous as The Riddler and Two-Face, while Chris O'Donnell as Robin proved the film's story and character highpoints. The Bat cause in 1995 was also helped by the continuing and wide-ranging comic book adventures. New entries into the Bat universe, *Batman: Gotham Nights 2*, *Batman: Jazz* and *Batman: Two-Face—Crime and Punishment* mixed stylistically with such ongoing titles as *Batman Chronicles*, *Detective Comics* and *Batman*.

THE MAXX

No less exciting was the rags-to-riches rise of the unorthodox Maxx from near obscurity to animated stardom on MTV. This buck-toothed purple hero spends his time protecting a social worker named Julie who also happens to be the Jungle Queen in a different reality known as the Outback. Unfortunately, neither the readers nor the Maxx know which reality is real. The first season's episodes proved an entertaining and largely literate translation of the Image books and won the critical hearts and audience minds. Capping the first season plaudits found "The Maxx" taking its notoriety overseas and winning top honors at a prestigious animation festival in France. "The Maxx" was recently greenlighted for another season on MTV, proving once again that the world of comics and television is ripe to embrace something totally different.

AT RIGHT: **MTV's The Maxx**
BOTTOM: **Comics' hottest teens, GEN^{13}**

X-MEN

The X-Men franchise survived the late '94 scare involving the cancellation of some of the more than 22 market-friendly titles to be a major force in the Marvel Universe. *X-Men: Omega* was one of the more potent entries in the X-race with its atmospheric and quite literate conclusion to the "Age of Apocalypse" storyline which involved a drastically altered cast of mutants in a time-altered future. Following hot on the heels was *X-Men: Prime* which brought the fighting team back to real time with some slight alterations in character profiles. Eleven X-Men titles, one shots and continuing series and reprint collections, regularly graced the Top 100 list and made the most of a continued interest in taking the time-honored title on new and improved trips.

THE TICK

He's the big-headed, huge-bodied, blue, humorous hero who, in 1995, became one of the most recognizable non-traditional crimefighters on the planet. This naïve (and nigh-invulnerable) character pulls no punches as he pokes fun at the entire comics industry. The underground interest generated by Ben Edlund's first dozen issues of the New England Comics series aroused interest in Hollywood and a successful animated series that made a reasonably good translation from paneled page to the small screen animated stage. The show is successfully running through its second season and so will assure a ready market for the second generation of Tick comics and a number of Tick toys and other merchandising off-shoots which took on a life of their own this past year. The bottom line is that The Tick phenomenon just happened.

BONE

Everybody and their girlfriends loved following the adventures of those adorable li'l Bone cousins as they avoided the nasty yet stupid, stupid Rat Creatures and tried to find their way back home to Boneville. The continued success of *Bone* in 1995 has been two-fold. When any self-published effort reaches issue #20 (which *Bone* did in October) it's cause for celebration. But Jeff Smith gets extra brownie points for continuing the high quality of this series while continually getting these suckers out on time. Image smelled the Bone and collared Smith and *Bone* for its own stable. But Smith cautions against tagging him with the label of sell-out. According to the terms of the Image distribution deal, Smith will have final say on what is written and drawn in the Bone world. Which means the quality control will continue and *Bone* will thrive and prosper.

Continued on page 48

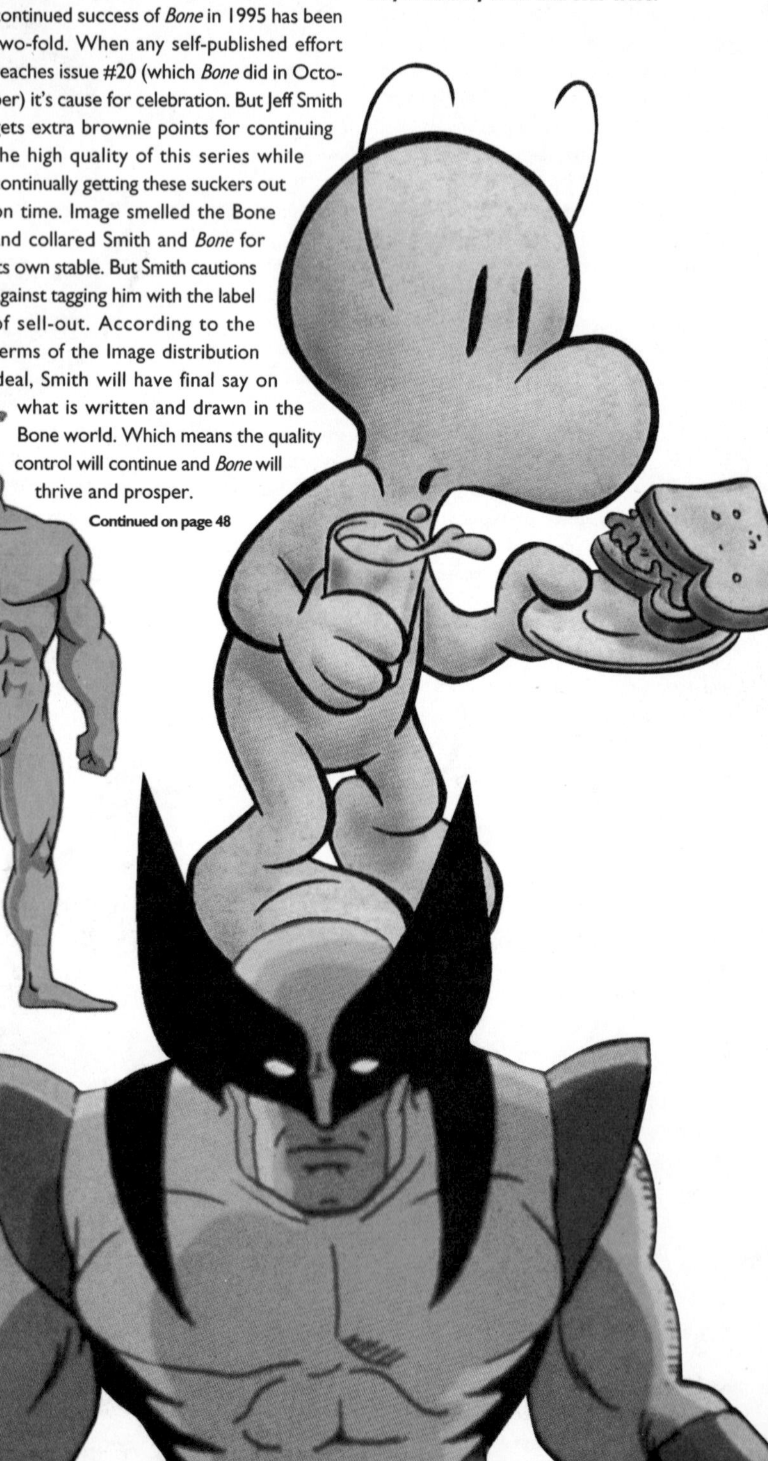

The Tick (below left) stayed mighty, while Fone Bone (below) gained a new "image."

Opposite page (top to bottom): X-Files, Shi, Preacher, Crow and Star Wars.

Wolverine (right) and the X-Men survived mass-cancellation and an altered reality.

Five Books To Watch In '96

THE X-FILES

Lost in the wake of the insane speculative frenzy behind this popular title is the fact that the stories, not to mention the cover art, have been some of the best in the business. Any fear that *X-Files*, creatively, might be running out of gas was put to rest with the release of *X-Files Annual* #1 which featured one of the best stories to date. Read these books for the story and art, and don't bother with the idea that these books are someday going to put your kid through college.

SHI

This could be the frontrunner of the Bad Girls brigade in '96, especially if the movie deal comes through. Besides all of the blood and death filling this series, readers were enticed to tons of historical facts and philosophy. Creator Bill Tucci should avoid too many crossovers, however, as they tend to slow down the release of Shi's regular book. Besides, Shi on her own is more than enough.

PREACHER

This hysterical, yet sickingly horrific title from the folks at Vertigo may seem like a bit of a stretch, but anybody who latched onto *Preacher* from the beginning knows what's what. The tale centers around a preacher with the power to command people with his voice and his journey in search of God who has abandoned his heavenly post. The wit and intelligence may be dark, but they're definitely there. Get hip to what you've missed.

THE CROW

There will be a number of new Crow series in '96—the first of which is the three-issue mini-series *The Crow: Dead Time*, plotted by Crow creator James O'Barr and beginning in January—and they will kick major league butt. Adding to the Crow mania will be the movie release of *The Crow: City of Angels* which, despite the loss of Brandon Lee, will prove to be a superior sequel. You heard it here first.

STAR WARS

The always expanding Star Wars universe of books will continue its high quality, imaginative ways throughout the year and make a lot of sparks in light of the recent resurgence of interest in the next Star Wars film trilogy due to be released before the end of the century. These books, currently being produced by Dark Horse Comics, have never been less than very good and that trend should keep on keeping on.

While Judge Dredd (below) bombed, Tetsuo from *Akira* (right) ravaged the anime front.

JUDGE DREDD

Easily the most dramatic development in the comics-to-film race in 1995 was the failure, on a very loud scale, of the film version of Judge Dredd, the superhero who moonlights as judge, jury and executioner. Why it failed was anybody's guess. The England-spawned Judge might've been too obscure for U.S. comic audiences (although it's been reported that more cutting-edge readers turned out in droves). But the bottom line is that Sly Stallone's best acting stint since *Rocky*, in Hollywood's questionable hands, was all flash and special effects splash without a whole lot of story and heart—the very things that make the comics work. Adding insult to injury, U.S. filmmakers also managed to mangle *Tank Girl*. Filmmakers beware! This is not as easy as it looks.

MANGA AND ANIME '95

Manga (Japanese comics) continued to explode in America as Dark Horse released plenty of fan-favorites such as *Oh My Goddess!*, *Ghost in the Shell* and *Dirty Pair*. This popular artistic style has spilled over into mainstream comics to influence such artists as *Uncanny X-Men*'s Joe Madureira and *Gen[13]*'s J. Scott Campbell in a style known as "American Manga." The anime (Japanese animation) front was also quite hectic as *Akira* continued to be one of the hottest adventures on the anime scene throughout the year, and a number of new and newly released titles offered alternatives in this ever-expanding genre. *Giant Robo* proved to be good, clean fun, while the extremely over-the-top *Devil Man* (complete with a Verotik comic tie-in) pushed the bounds of violence and decency to a fantastic level. Other recent titles well worth your viewing time are *Record of Lodoss War* and *Black Magic M-66*

SPIDER-MAN

The Clone Saga, as well as the aftermath of Doctor Octopus and Aunt May's deaths, made picking up any of the numerous Spider-Man titles during the year a fun yet confusing ride. There were surprises and secrets aplenty in the Clone Saga books and, regardless of how good or bad the storylines may have been received, fans certainly seemed to take notice. At a time when a lot of veteran characters were beginning to crack at the seams, Spider-Man was at the tip of everyone's tongue.

Marc Shapiro likes to jungle boogie

Love it or hate it, Spider-Man's recent clone saga has got people talking about the web-slinger.

milestones

Landmark books that have made comic history

Comic books have had a long, widespread history, shaped by a huge number of books, characters and events. Each type of character that you see in your favorite comics today—from superhero to western hero to Bad Girl—and every form of comic—from mini-series to self-published series to variant cover edition—had its start somewhere. While a few of these introductions are fairly well-known by comic fans and collectors, many aren't exactly common knowledge.

What was the first superhero team? (It wasn't the X-Men, folks.) When did the first company crossover book strike the stands? And what issue really got the enormous Bad Girl trend hopping? The following pages display these and many other milestone events that hit the comic industry through the years.

FIRST COMIC BOOK

Funnies on Parade (1933)

Published by Eastern Color Printing of Waterbury, Conn., *Funnies on Parade* was the first comic book in the standard format we know so well today. The book was a giveaway, a promotional item distributed by the company Procter & Gamble to its soap customers. Based on the success of the F.O.P. promotion, other sponsors were approached by the printing company, and eventually the idea dawned on Eastern Color to slap a 10-cent cover price on a comic and sell it on the newsstands.

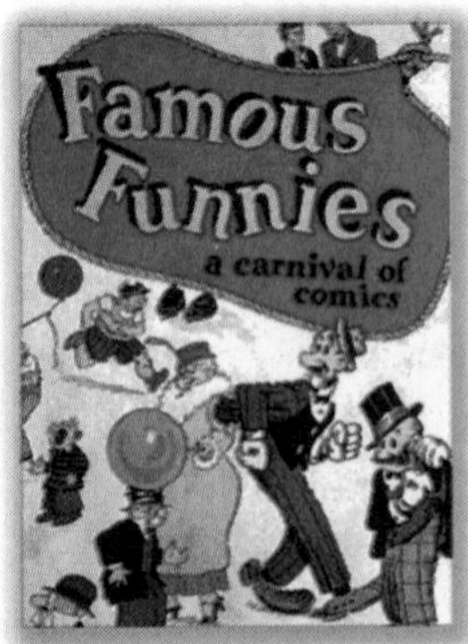

FIRST COMIC SOLD ON THE STANDS AND FIRST COMIC BOOK SERIES

Famous Funnies #1 (1934)

The inventor of the four-color, modern comic was Harry I. Wildenberg, a sales manager for Eastern Color. Wildenberg convinced Eastern Color and American News Company to distribute 200,000 copies of a 64-page color comic with a cover price of 10 cents. The comic sold 90 percent of the copies distributed, a minor miracle in the middle of the Depression. Who knows what would have become of the concept of four-color comics magazines had *Famous Funnies* #1 flopped on the stands?

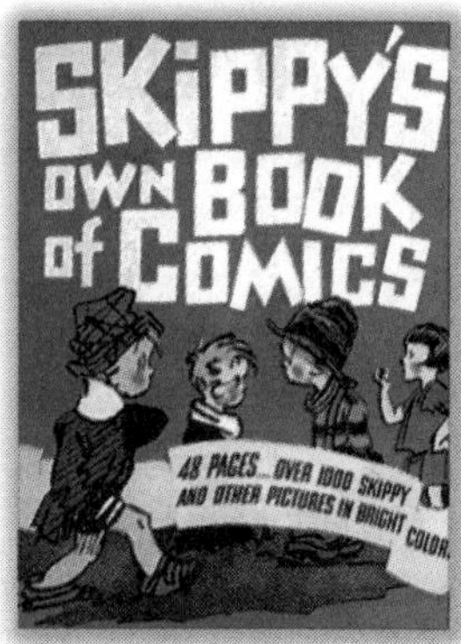

FIRST COMIC DEVOTED TO A SINGLE CHARACTER

Skippy #1 (1934)

Skippy was a popular radio character of the 1930s. Not until *Superman* #1, four years later, would a comic book series be devoted to a single character; in this case a superhero.

FIRST COMIC DEVOTED TO WESTERN THEME

Western Picture Stories #1 (Feb. 1937)

The 1930s entertainment mediums were dominated by cowboy heroes. The movies had Tom Mix, the radio had The Lone Ranger, and comics readers would soon have more western cowboy comics than they could read in a month. *WPS* #1 was the first to recognize the ready-made market for western heroes.

FIRST DC COMIC

New Fun Comics #1 (Feb. 1935)

DC's entry into the comic book publishing world was the first to feature an anthology format of all-original material. Prior to this book's release, comics had been reprints of newspaper funnies.

FIRST MOVIE TIE-IN COMIC AND FIRST MOVIE ADAPTATION

Mickey Mouse Magazine (vol. 3) #3 (Jan. 1938)

The idea of comic books based on movies was a natural. This issue featured the first part of a serialization of Disney's *Snow White and the Seven Dwarfs.*

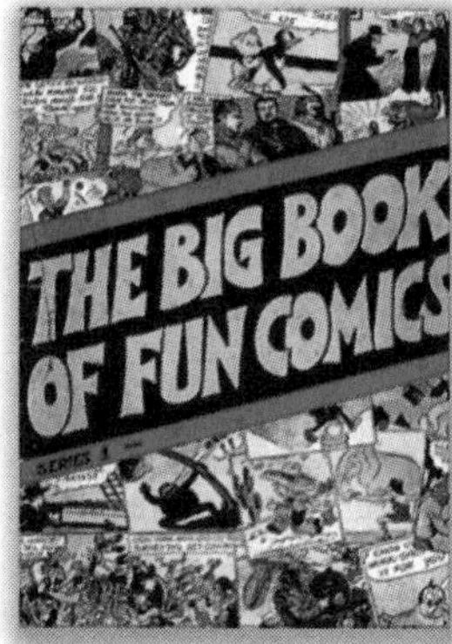

FIRST ANNUAL

Big Book of Fun Comics #1 (Spring 1936)

The idea of repackaging stories from prior issues into a giant-sized extravaganza issue was tested for the first time with the release of this comic, which featured reprints of *New Fun* #1-#5.

FIRST SUPERHERO

Action Comics #1 (June 1938)

With this book, Jerry Siegel and Joe Shuster brought Superman down to Earth and into the world of comic books, beginning the long-running era of superheroes. Over 55 years later, the still-popular Last Son of Krypton stars in five regular titles.

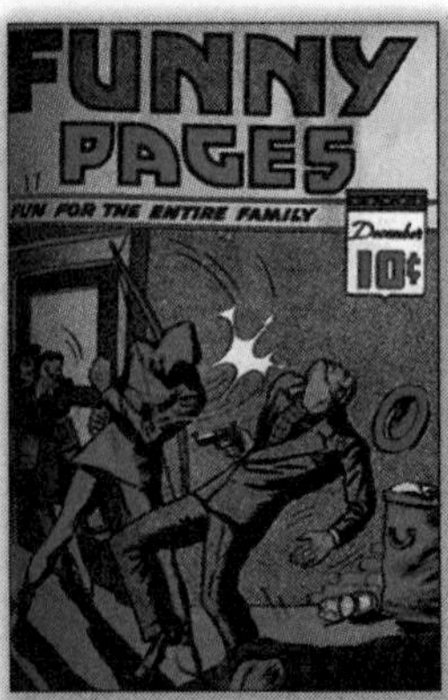

FIRST APPEARANCE OF THE ARROW

Funny Pages (vol. 2) #10 (Sept. 1938)

A mysterious archer in a red suit and cowl, the Arrow was the first non-superpowered costumed hero to appear in comics, beating Batman in *Detective Comics* #27 by eight months.

FIRST MARVEL COMIC BOOK

Marvel Comics #1 (Nov. 1939)

Marvel established two superheroes in its inaugural issue, the Human Torch and Sub-Mariner. Human Torch makes his debut, while Sub-Mariner's origin is retold from the story that first appeared in *Motion Pictures Funnies Weekly.*

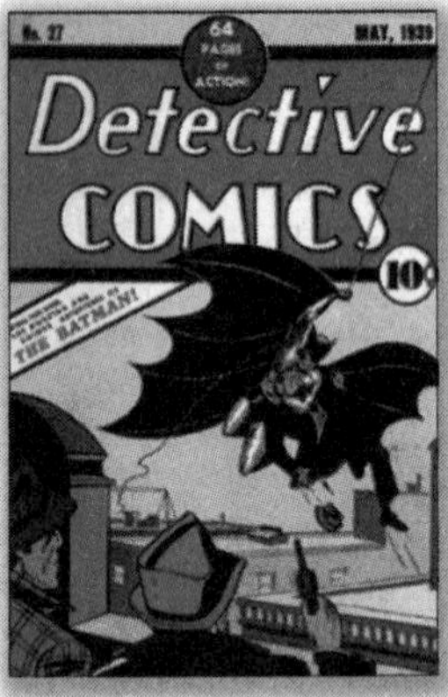

FIRST BATMAN

Detective Comics #27 (May 1939)

Batman debuts and sets the comics-reading public on its Bat-ears. DC's second substantial newsstand success, #27 is also important because it helped entrench the concept of successful superhero comics. This super-rare issue from May 1939 is one of the world's most valuable comics, with a current market value in the $150,000 range!

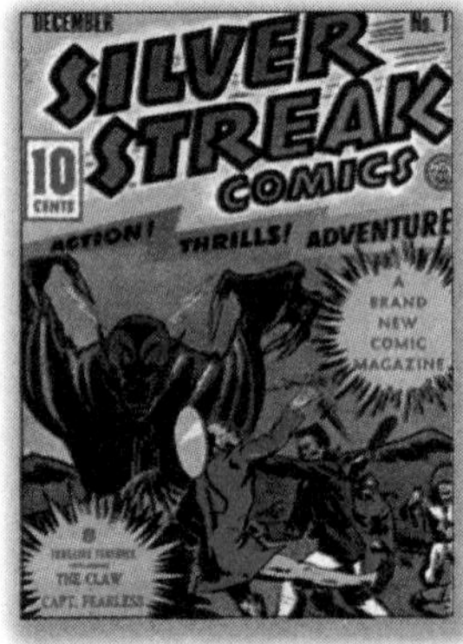

FIRST SUPERVILLAIN (THE CLAW)

Silver Streak #1 (Dec. 1939)

Comic book readers of the early days soon tired of superheroes beating up on everyday criminals. The Claw was an adversary worthy of a superhero. Standing 100 feet tall, and looking like a Fu Manchu mutant with long fangs, the Claw went about causing destruction and mayhem. The superhero to bring him down, the original Daredevil (who shouldn't be confused with today's DD), wouldn't be introduced until five issues later.

FIRST SERIES DEVOTED TO A SINGLE SUPERHERO

Superman #1 (Summer 1939)

While *Action Comics*, which introduced Superman, was shared by the Man of Steel with other characters, Superman won his own title, and the first of its kind. The series lives on today as *Adventures of Superman.*

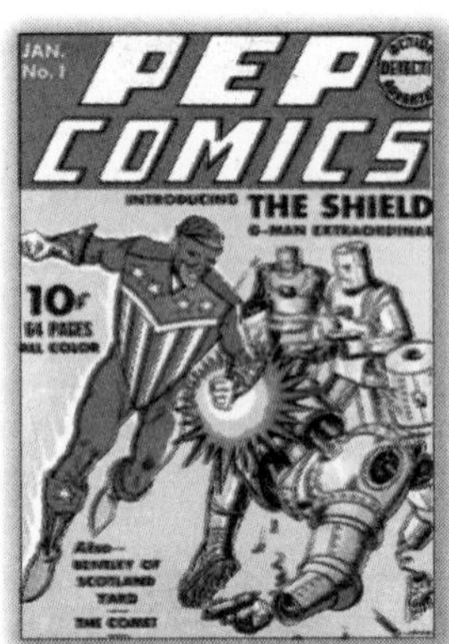

FIRST PATRIOTIC SUPERHERO (THE SHIELD)

Pep Comics #1 (Jan. 1940)

The Shield, by legendary writer/artist team of Joe Simon and Jack Kirby, was the first of many superheroes to appeal to America's patriotism during the WWII years. A year later, Simon & Kirby would render another patriotic hero, Captain America, who lives on to this day as one of the most well-loved characters the two created.

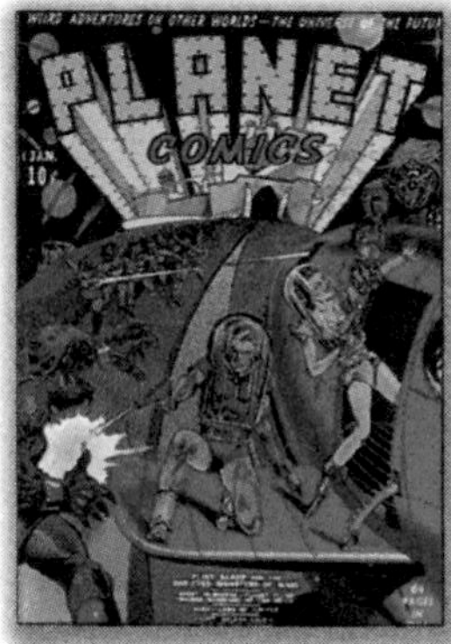

FIRST COMIC DEVOTED TO SCI-FI

Planet Comics #1 (Jan. 1940)

Fiction House was a major publisher in the pulp fiction field prior to entering comics. One of the company's more popular titles was *Planet Stories. Planet Comics* would follow a similar theme of otherworldly stories in the comic book format and make history doing it, by being the first comic series devoted to the science fiction genre, which was massively popular back in the '30s and '40s.

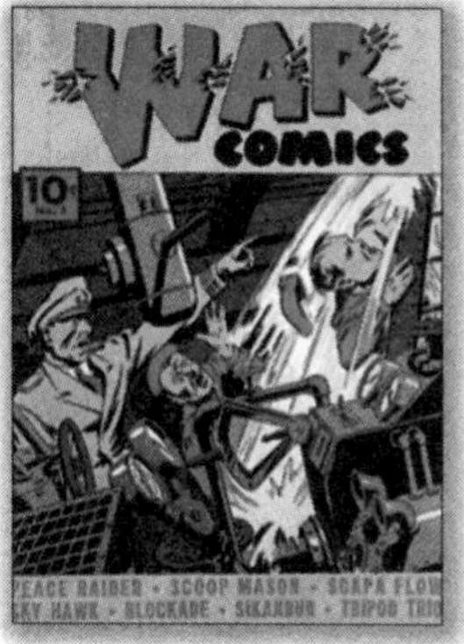

FIRST COMIC TO REFLECT WORLD WAR II CONCERNS

War Comics #1 (May 1940)

This comic, released prior to the U.S.'s entrance into WWII, was the first to recognize the market for war comics at a time that the public was concerned about impending war. A flood of comics reflecting patriotism and U.S. military victory would hit the stands over the next four years. Being first does not always guarantee success, however—*War Comics* lasted only four issues.

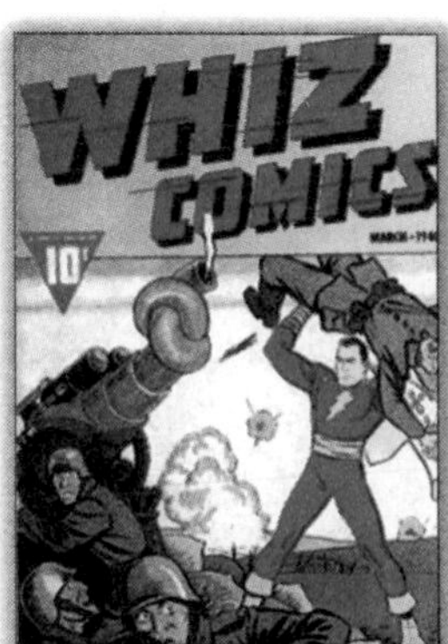

DEBUT OF CAPTAIN MARVEL

Whiz Comics #2 (Feb. 1940)

This series introduced the hero Captain Marvel. His title *Captain Marvel Adventures* became the all-time most successful superhero series, with over two million copies sold per issue, which were published every two weeks.

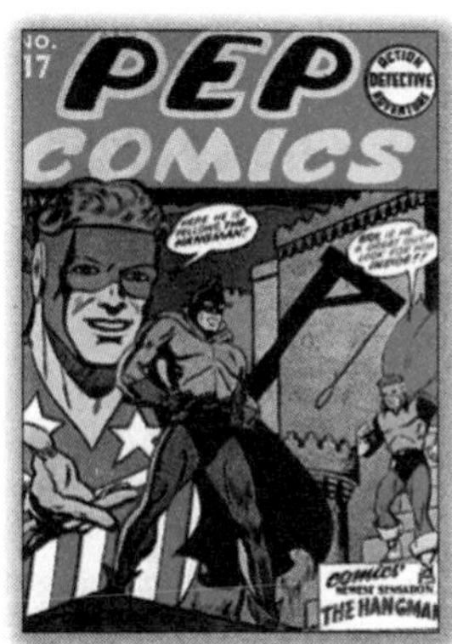

FIRST TIME A SUPERHERO ACTUALLY DIES (THE COMET)

Pep Comics #17 (July 1941)

The Comet, created by Jack Cole, first appeared in *Pep Comics* #1. He wore a brightly-colored costume and was frequently seen whizzing across the sky. In issue #17, the Comet is gunned down by gangsters. His brother vows to avenge his brother's death, and thus becomes the Hangman. The Hangman became the lead feature of *Pep.*

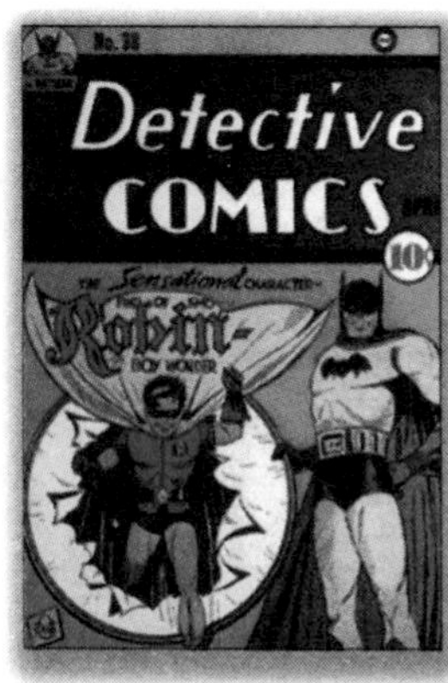

FIRST SIDEKICK IN COMICS (ROBIN)

Detective Comics #38 (Apr. 1940)

Everyone needs a little help—even superheroes—and young Dick Grayson proved to be not only a fine crimefighting assistant to Batman, but a hugely popular character.

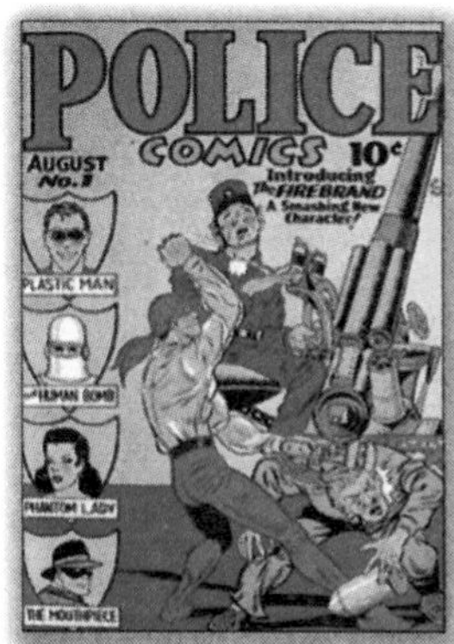

FIRST "BAD GIRL" IN COMICS (PHANTOM LADY)

Police Comics #1 (Aug. 1941)

Phantom Lady began as a minor backup story in *Police Comics.* Her adventures were tame, but the same could not be said for her costume, a revealing halter and tight, short pants. Her early adventures reflected the patriotism of the day, featuring PL beating up on Nazis and Japanese soldiers. A new incarnation of the heroine appeared in one of DC's *Starman* series (1988-92).

FIRST CHRISTMAS (OR HOLIDAY-RELATED) COMIC

X-Mas Comics #1 (Nov. 1941)

Fawcett Publications was the first to figure out that around Christmastime, comic books with pictures of Santa Claus on them would sell like hotcakes. They repackaged some leftover unbound issues from some of their other comics, wrapped a smiling Santa Claus cover on each one, and slapped a 50-cent cover price (for 324 pages) on it. They sold like hotcakes, as expected.

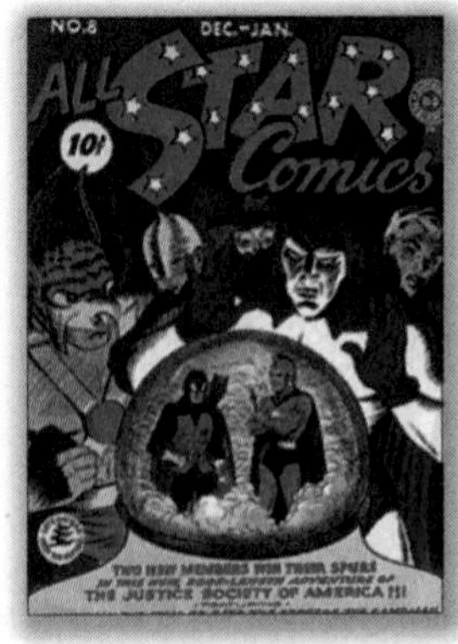

DC'S FIRST FEMALE SUPERHERO (WONDER WOMAN)

All Star #8 (Dec. 1941-Jan. 1942)

DC's first superheroine is still the most recognized, after over 50 years of up-and-down history in her own title. Starting as a "secretary" for the Justice Society, she became a central figure in this book, scoring the only solo cover in its run.

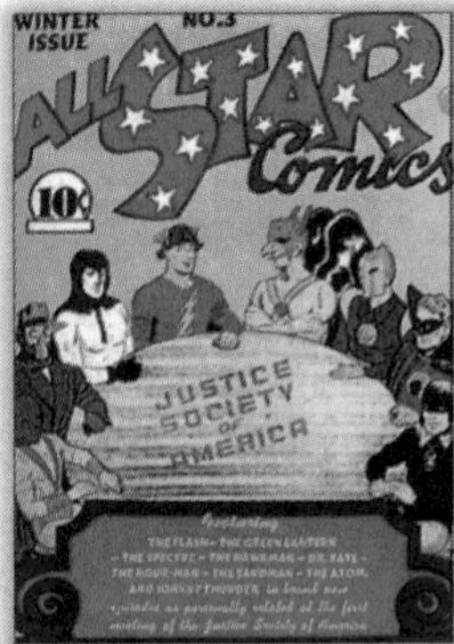

FIRST SUPERHERO TEAM (JUSTICE SOCIETY)

All Star #3 (Winter 1940-41)

The Justice Society of America formed in this issue, banding a group of superheroes together against forces over evil for the first time. The powerful superteam included Hawkman, Hourman and Flash, and gained several new members over the years.

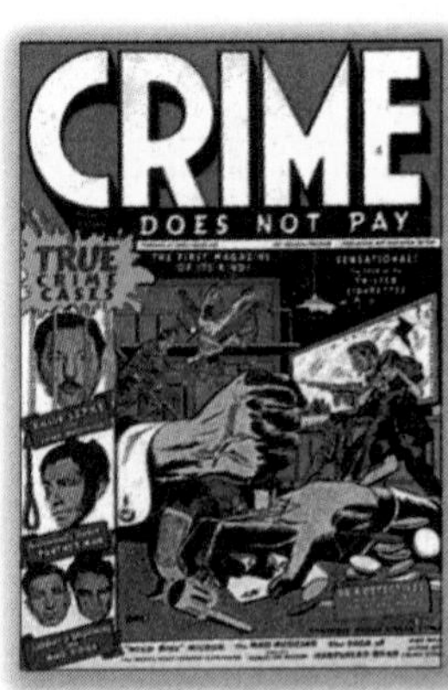

FIRST COMIC DEVOTED TO CRIME THEME, FIRST COMIC AIMED AT AN ADULT AUDIENCE

Crime Does Not Pay #22 (June 1942)

After WWII, superhero comics experienced a slump in popularity, and publishers began looking for new subject matter to regain their market share. Many "discovered" crime as a theme, spawning a rash of crime comics in the late '40s.

FIRST COMIC DEVOTED TO TEENAGE HUMOR

Pep Comics #22 (Archie, Dec. 1941)

Everything's Archie...the always-hip gang of teens debuted here. Archie and his fun-loving pals Jughead, Betty, Veronica and Reggie gave young comic book readers someone to relate to on a regular basis.

FIRST COMIC SERIES DEVOTED TO A FEMALE STAR

Wonder Woman #1 (Summer 1942)

William Moulton Marston's star-spangled superheroine soared into her own series, the first comic book title starring a woman, let alone a heroine.

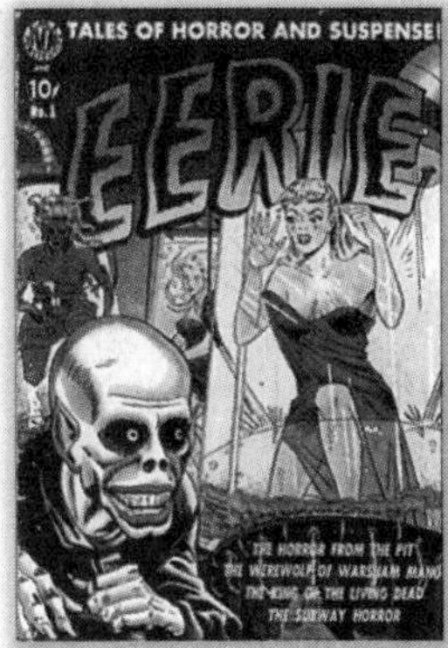

FIRST HORROR COMIC

Eerie Comics #1
(Avon, Jan. 1947)

The horror genre had been popular in other mediums—movies, radio and books—for years, so it was only a matter of time before comics would pick up on this genre. Targeted at adults, *Eerie Comics* #1 stands as another example of the post-war search for new markets for comics.

FIRST COMIC BASED ON A TV SHOW

Howdy Doody #1 (Jan. 1950)

Buffalo Bob and Howdy Doody were the first children's TV sensations, launching a licensing empire that included toys and games of all kinds, and the first comics licensed from a television series.

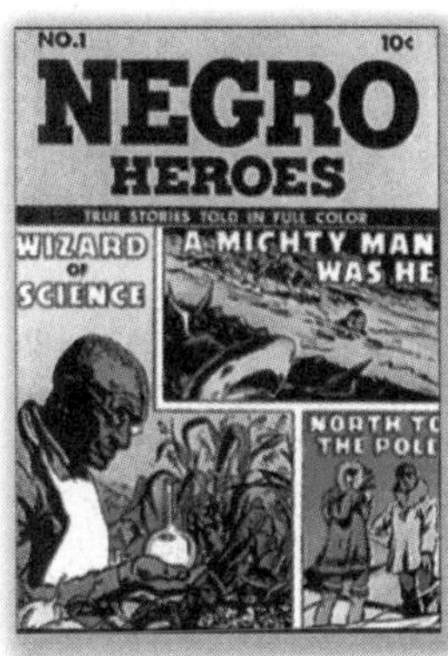

FIRST COMIC DEVOTED TO AN ALL-BLACK AUDIENCE

Negro Heroes #1
(Spring 1947)

After WWII, publishers began seeking new markets for comics. This comic was published by a black-owned publishing company in an attempt to reach an all-black audience. Later, *All-Negro Comics* and *Negro Romances* would attempt to reach the same market.

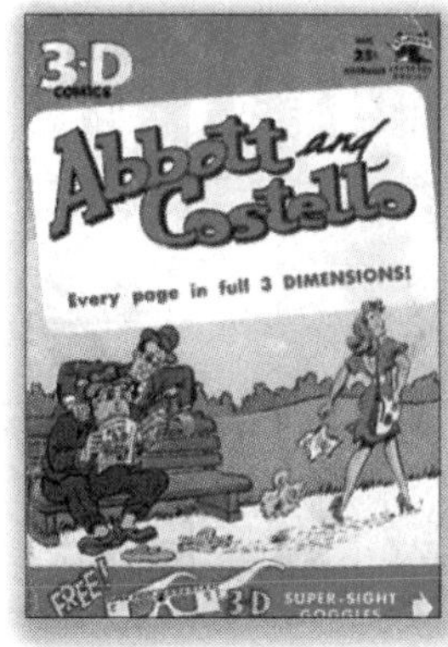

FIRST 3-D COMIC

Three Dimension Comics #1
(Sept. 1953)

When 3-D movies started hitting the screens in 1953, comic book publishers saw 3-D comics (Glasses included!) as a way to cash in on the trend; this was the first such publication.

BEGINS THE FIRST COMIC SERIES DEVOTED TO ROMANCE THEME

Young Romance #1
(Sept. 1947)

It finally dawned on publishers that they were reaching only half of the youth market, the boys, with superhero comics. Prize Publications was the first publisher to recognize the potentially lucrative market for comics targeted at teenage girls. Issue #1, besides being a landmark issue as the first issue in this series, is also highly sought after by collectors for its beautiful art by Jack Kirby and Joe Simon.

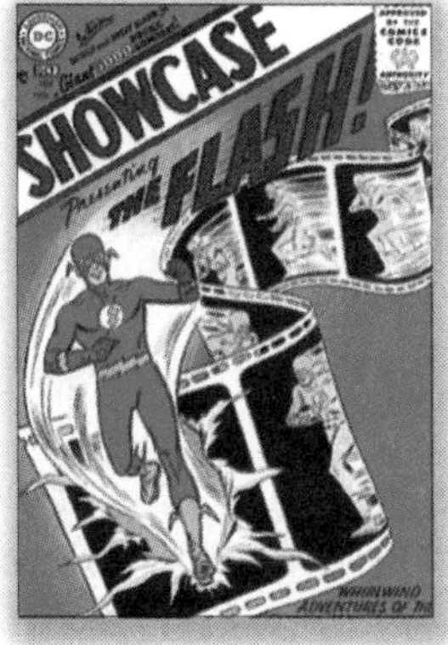

INTRODUCTION OF THE SILVER AGE

Showcase #4 (Oct. 1956)

This book, which introduced the new Flash (a.k.a. Barry Allen), is known by collectors as the launcher of the Silver Age of comics. This age spawned brand-new heroes and several different types of comics. Without the tremendous response to this comic on the newsstands, the renaissance of superheroes may not have occurred. Based on the demand for this issue, DC decided to get back into the superhero game by releasing a host of new superhero characters.

DEBUT OF THE JUSTICE LEAGUE OF AMERICA

The Brave and the Bold #28 (Feb./March 1960)

The first superteam of the Silver Age, the Justice League of America was initially made up of seven heroes: Aquaman, Green Lantern, Martian Manhunter, Wonder Woman, Flash, Superman and Batman. After the understandably popular team was awarded its own ongoing series in late 1960, major heroes like Green Arrow, the Atom and Hawkman soon joined the JLA.

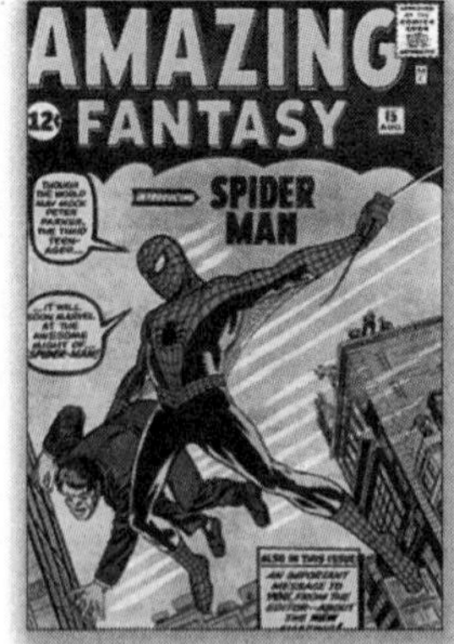

FIRST SPIDER-MAN

Amazing Fantasy #15 (Aug. 1962)

One of the most intriguing aspects of the new hero this book introduced was his humanity: Peter Parker was an average teenager who became a superhero thanks to the bite of a radioactive spider, and whose personal problems didn't disappear when he donned the blue-and-red costume. Added to that were his large, well-developed supporting cast and nefarious rogues gallery. Those are some of the many reasons Spider-Man has garnered immense fame in his 30-plus years.

BROUGHT EARTH-2 TO SILVER AGE COMICS

The Flash #123 (Sept. 1961)

In this historic issue, it was revealed that the Golden Age heroes like the Flash (Jay Garrick) and Starman were denizens of another Earth in a separate dimension, called Earth-2. Here, the Jay Garrick Flash met the Barry Allen Flash for the first time. Earth-2 was later melded into Earth-1 during DC's *Crisis on Infinite Earths* maxi-series in 1985, along with its heroes.

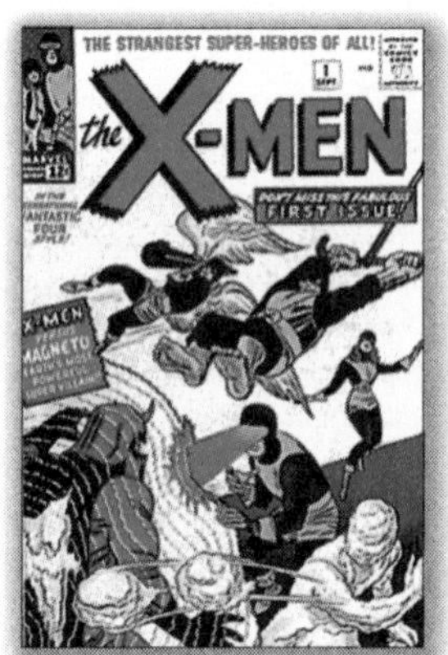

FIRST MUTANT TEAM COMIC

X-Men #1 (vol. 1, Sept. 1963)

Probably the most popular superhero team on the planet, the X-Men were born over 30 years ago in this innovative book. This series has seen numerous exciting stories and talented creators over the years, and is now under the name of *The Uncanny X-Men*.

FIRST MARVEL SILVER AGE SUPERHERO COMIC

Fantastic Four #1 (Nov. 1961)

Marvel's first superteam premiered in the company's first Silver Age comic starring superheroes. When Reed Richards, Ben Grimm, Sue Storm and her brother Johnny were bombarded by cosmic rays on an experimental space expedition, a popular and highly influential force in comics was born.

CAPTAIN AMERICA ENTERS SILVER AGE

The Avengers #4 (Mar.-Apr. 1964)

This book's major claim to fame is the reintroduction of Captain America into comics. Cap had been the best-selling character in Marvel's stable in the early days. Another interesting landmark in this issue is the first death of a sidekick. In a flashback, Bucky bites the dust for good in this issue.

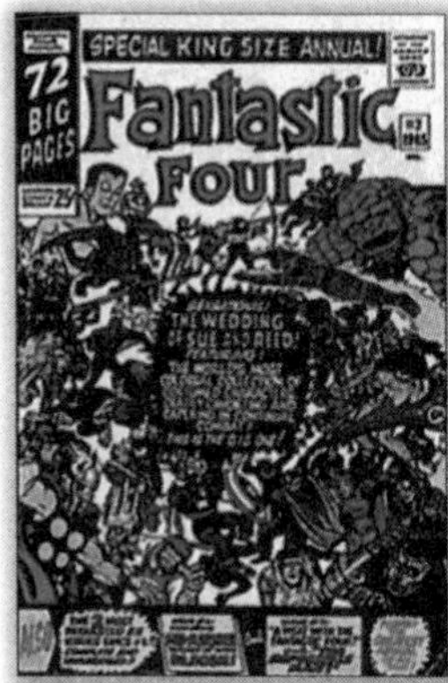

FIRST MAJOR SUPERHERO WEDDING

Fantastic Four Annual #3 (1965)

Reed Richards and Sue Storm make history by becoming the first superheroes to tie the knot, with the lot of the Marvel Universe looking onward.

FIRST USE OF DRUGS IN A MAINSTREAM COMIC

The Amazing Spider-Man #96 (May 1971)

This is the first part of a three-issue story in which Harry Osborn (son of the Green Goblin) takes drugs, believing they will help him to forget his troubles, and then critically overdoses on them. This was the first time drug abuse was portrayed in a widely circulated, popular comic book. While these issues were not approved by the Comics Code Authority, the first Code-approved "drug issues" in comics were 1971's *Green Lantern/Green Arrow* #85-#86, in which GA's ward Speedy reveals his habit.

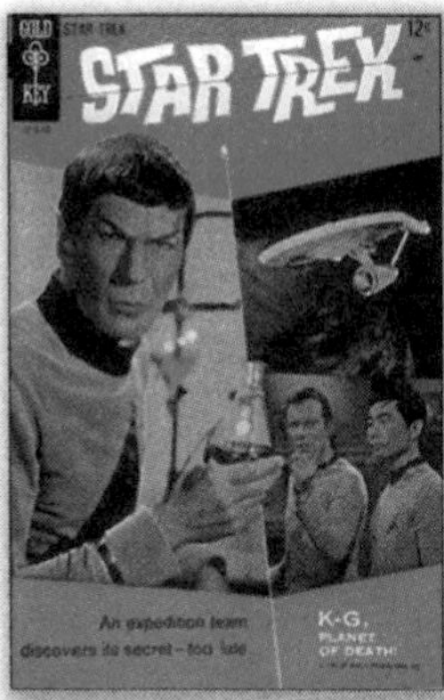

FIRST "STAR TREK" COMIC

Star Trek #1 (July 1967, Gold Key)

Before "The Next Generation" and "Voyager" came the original TV series of "Star Trek," in which Captain Kirk and his stalwart crew traveled to places no one had gone before. Suddenly, these characters wound up in the comic book universe, where brand-new adventures were told by creators who perfectly captured the characterizations and excitement of the show. Today, DC's *Star Trek* and *Star Trek: The Next Generation* titles join Malibu's *Deep Space Nine* in the fight to keep Trekkies satisfied.

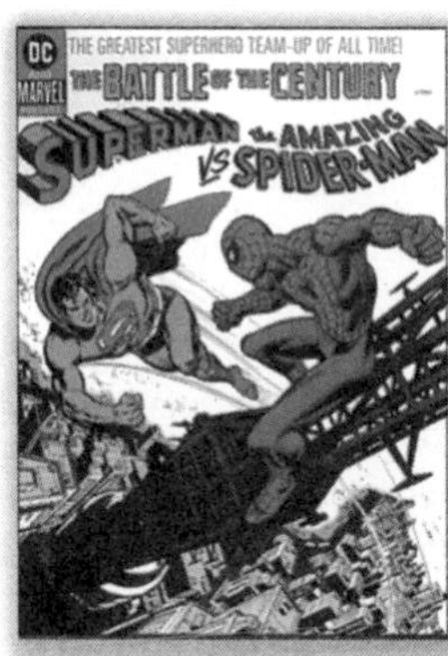

FIRST COMPANY CROSSOVER BOOK

Superman vs. Spider-Man (1976)

This one-shot tabloid-sized edition did something unimaginable at the time: It brought together the two major heroes from DC and Marvel for one literally huge story. Several similar crossovers, between these two companies (*Batman vs. The Incredible Hulk, Batman/Spider-Man*), and between others (*Shadowhawk/Vampirella, Spawn/Batman*) followed.

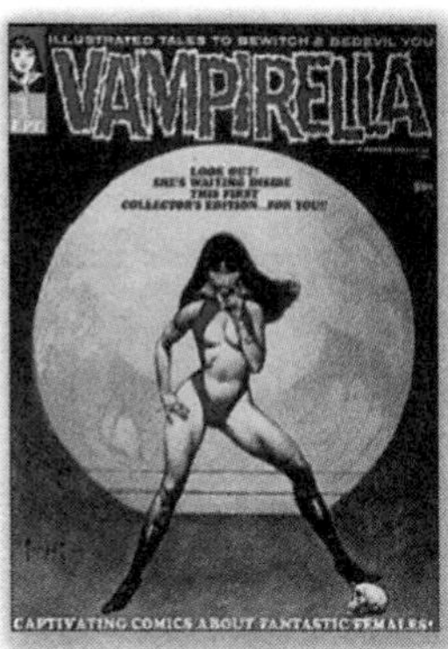

FIRST MODERN "BAD GIRL" BOOK

Vampirella #1 (Warren, Sept. 1969)

The modern-day furor over Bad Girls has its roots in the very first Modern Age Bad Girl appearance, *Vampirella* #1. Vampirella began as a satire, and switched to a "serious" Bad Girl beginning with issue #8. Harris Comics now publishes her monthly adventures in *Vengeance of Vampirella.*

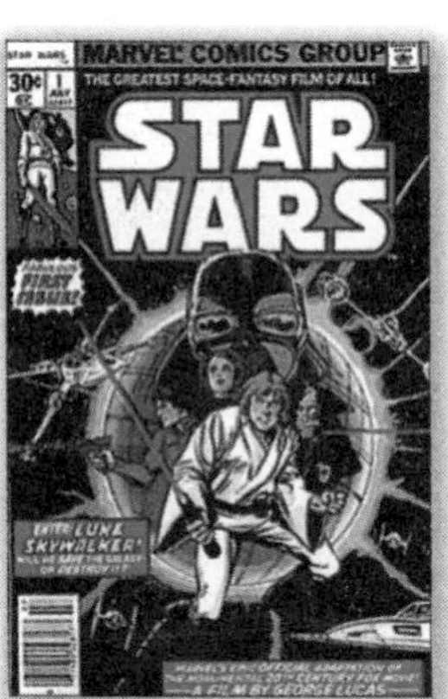

FIRST "STAR WARS" COMIC

Star Wars #1 (July 1977, Marvel)

The adventures of Luke, Leia, Han and that nutty pair of droids jumped from the big screen to the comic panels the same year the first "Star Wars" movie was released. This issue began a six-issue, high-quality adaptation of the movie, and began a fairly successful 107-issue comic book series. Dark Horse currently continues the battle with several popular titles.

FIRST MAJOR INDEPENDENT COMIC

Cerebus #1 (Dec. 1977)

Who would've thought an aardvark—make that a *barbarian* aardvark—would win over the hearts of so many fans, and become a huge cult favorite? Dave Sim's satirical series became popular enough for Sim to mandate it being 300 issues in length; the title just passed its 200th issue landmark.

FIRST DIRECT SALES BOOK

Dazzler #1 (Mar. 1981)

After her debut in *The Uncanny X-Men* #130, Marvel gave the light-blasting heroine Dazzler her own book, a book that only comic book stores received in the new direct-from-distributors program. While that program still exists today, Alison Blaire's series, alas, does not.

FIRST COMIC BOOK MINI-SERIES

World of Krypton #1 (July 1979)

Using a mini-series format, this look into Superman's homeworld initiated an explosion of limited series that presented single important stories, from *Batman: The Dark Knight Returns* to *Hawkworld* to *Marvels*.

DEATH OF ELEKTRA

Daredevil #181 (Apr. 1982)

While this shocking book is seen as a milestone by followers of Frank Miller's work, along with Daredevil and—of course—Elektra fans, even people who aren't interested in any of that see this issue as important, in its no-holds-barred telling of a heated battle (between Bullseye and Elektra, Daredevil's former lover) and a vicious death.

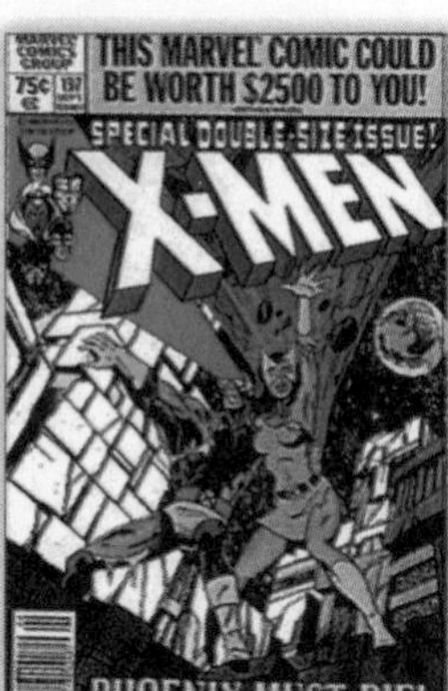

JEAN GREY DIES

Uncanny X-Men #137 (Sept. 1980)

A milestone in any longtime X-fan's mind, this issue had Jean Grey, accused of destroying a planet of aliens during her furious time as Dark Phoenix, die during the battle for her life. It was revealed later (in *Fantastic Four* #286) that the Phoenix force had placed the true Jean in an undersea cocoon when it took over a "clone" of her body. The psionically gifted mutant battles with the X-Men today.

FIRST SUPERTEAM COMPANY CROSSOVER BOOK

Marvel & DC Present X-Men/Teen Titans (1982):

It took DC and Marvel six years to do it after the success of *Superman/Spider-Man*, but they finally brought together their two hottest superteams (at the time, both the X-Men and Titans ruled the popularity charts) for this one-shot, in which the teams battled the forces of DC's Darkseid and Marvel's Dark Phoenix. *X-Men/Teen Titans* paved the way for books like *Avengers/UltraForce* and the huge *Marvel vs. DC* series.

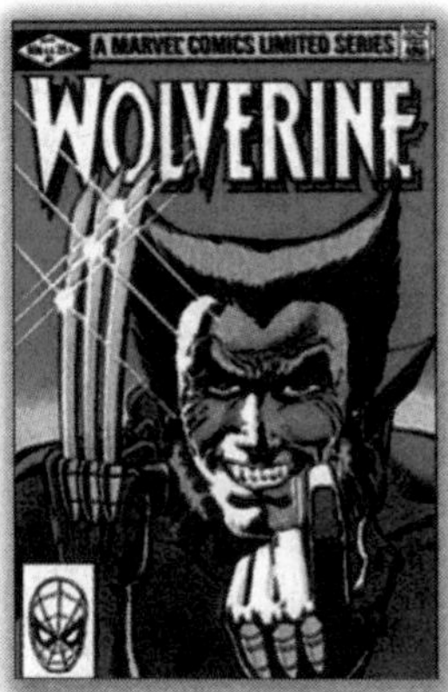

FIRST X-MAN TO GET HIS OWN SERIES

Wolverine (mini-series) #1 (Sept. 1982)

Writer Chris Claremont joined artist Frank Miller in creating a four-issue mini-series that related the background of the most popular X-character in history, Wolverine. From a look at his experiences in Japan to a glimpse into his past, readers learned more about Logan, the first of many X-Men to score their own mini-series, later including Gambit, Rogue and Bishop.

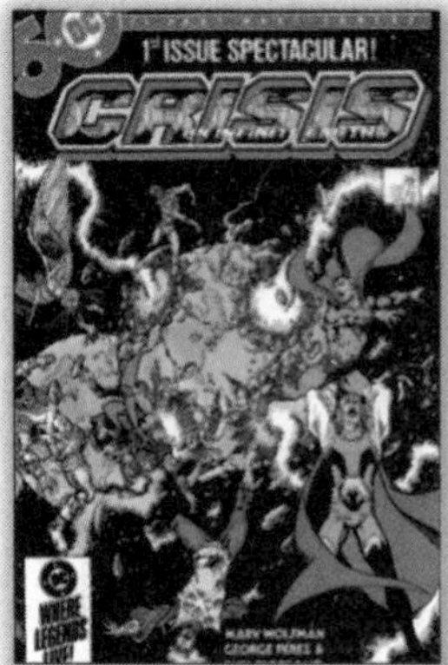

HISTORY-MAKING DC SERIES

Crisis on Infinite Earths #1 (Apr. 1985)

In an attempt to totally revamp DC Comics' superhero universe and clean up the convoluted continuity of its 50-year history, the company published this major 12-issue series. It included the merging of several of DC's Earths (including Earth-1 and Earth-2), the death of cornerstone heroes like Supergirl and Flash, the introduction of heroes like Captain Atom, Blue Beetle and Captain Marvel into the main DC Universe, and the birth of many heroes like the new Flash (a.k.a. Wally West).

MOST FINANCIALLY SUCCESSFUL INDEPENDENT SERIES BEGAN; LAUNCHED BLACK-AND-WHITE BOOM

Teenage Mutant Ninja Turtles #1 (1984)

The cartoon! The movies! The video games! The cereal! The toys! When Kevin Eastman and Peter Laird created this heroic quartet of anthropomorphic turtles, they had no idea how insanely popular their team would become. After years of multimedia licensing, the Turtles have lost their heat, but may regain some of it with their latest Archie comics.

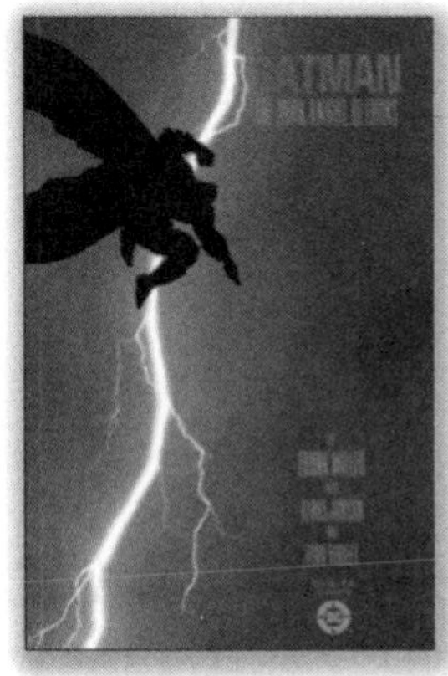

MAJOR COMIC BOOK MINI-SERIES

Batman: The Dark Knight Returns #1 (Mar. 1986)

One of the most important and influential series in comic book history, Frank Miller's *The Dark Knight Returns* took Batman into a possible future and opened the eyes of many fans (and non-fans) about the potential of comic books. It was covered in magazines like *Rolling Stone* and *Spin*, and some college professors have this book on their course lists.

MARVEL'S FIRST MAJOR CROSSOVER SERIES

Secret Wars #1 (May 1984)

This issue began Marvel's first major crossover series within the company. For the first time, many of Marvel's titles had crossover issues containing stories that were connected to this 12-issue epic. The *Secret Wars* story itself—where Marvel's most popular heroes and villains do battle—wasn't as important as two of its numerous results: a number of similar intracompany crossovers of all sizes, and the creation of Spider-Man's controversial black costume.

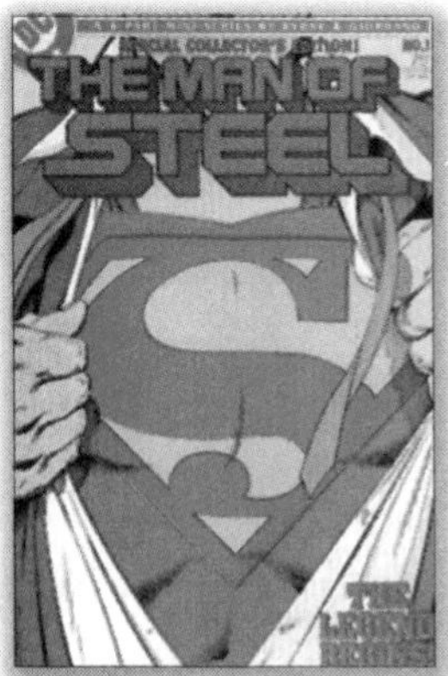

FIRST VARIANT COVER BOOK

The Man of Steel #1 (June 1986)

The initial issue of John Byrne's revamp of Superman gave the industry something highly unprecedented and unexpected—the publication of two versions of one issue, with different covers—and much copied afterwards. The success of promotions like the several editions of 1990's *Spider-Man* #1 and 1991's *X-Men* #1 spawned an tremendously intense trend of publishers releasing books with variant cover editions, coming to a head with Image's whopping 13 editions of *Gen*[13] (ongoing series) #1 in 1995.

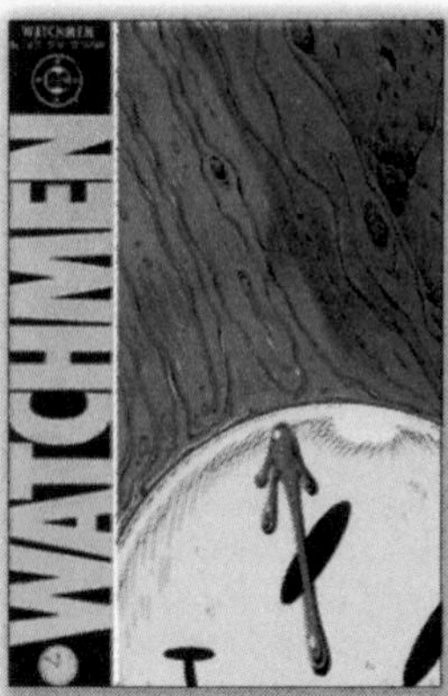

MAJOR COMIC BOOK MINI-SERIES

Watchmen #1 (Sept. 1986)

This innovative 12-issue series—by writer Alan Moore and artist Dave Gibbons—asked the question "What if there really were superheroes in the world?" and totally redefined the way many people looked at superhero comics. Using the intrinsic aspects of classic literature—including irony, flashbacks and foreshadowing—and very detailed artwork, Moore and Gibbons produced a both enjoyable and believable epic that demonstrated the high potential of comics.

SERIES THAT CHANGED THE SELF-PUBLISHING WORLD

Bone #1 (July 1991)

Jeff Smith's hilarious and highly innovative series featuring funny-looking creatures in a wild world not only influenced the mainstream audience to look for good, non-superhero material, but also made a lasting mark on the self-publishing world. The series' success inspired many creators to venture into publishing their own works, giving the comic world much more variety, including books like Terry Moore's *Strangers in Paradise* and Paul Pope's *THB*.

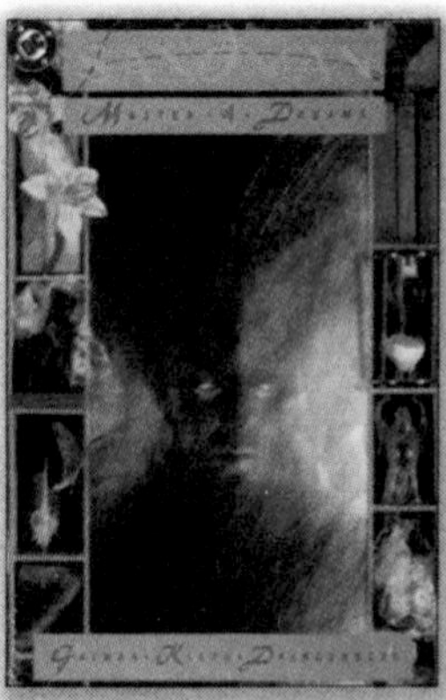

BEGINNING OF AN IMPORTANT DC SERIES

The Sandman #1 (Jan. 1989)

There are few comic book titles which can claim to have brought as many new readers of all ages to the comic world as *Sandman* did. Neil Gaiman's masterpiece—inspired by DC Comics characters but going a step above them—offered new worlds to comic fans, and characters that quickly became beloved, like Morpheus and Death. *Sandman* #19 won the World of Fantasy award for Best Short Story in 1991, making it the first comic to do so. This series firmly established the fact that comics are absolutely not just for kids.

FIRST IMAGE BOOK

Youngblood #1 (Apr. 1992)

Rob Liefeld, one of the seven creators who left Marvel Comics in 1992 and formed Image Comics, was the first to release his creation to the public: a superteam with engaging characters. Instant hits like Todd McFarlane's *Spawn* and Jim Lee's *WildC.A.T.s* soon followed.

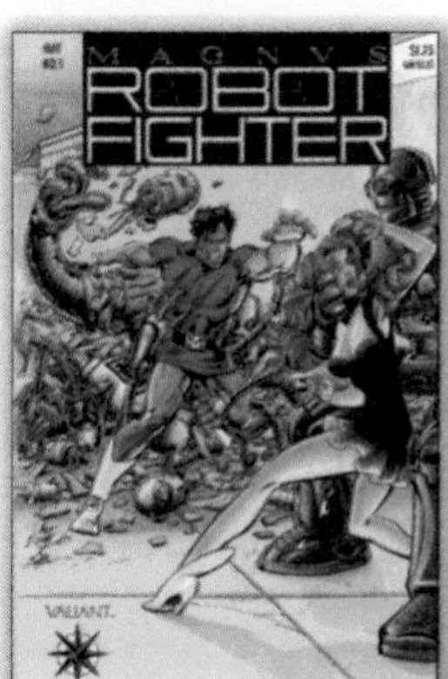

FIRST VALIANT SUPERHERO COMIC

Magnus, Robot Fighter #1 (May 1991)

Valiant Comics, after a failed attempt at producing Nintendo comics, brought three heroes "back to life" in their own titles. The first was Magnus, Robot Fighter, followed soon by Solar, and later, Turok. While these heroic figures from the 1960s and '70s benefited from Valiant's fresh take on them, the company's brand-new books like *X-O Manowar*, *Shadowman* and *Harbinger* truly increased the Valiant fanship.

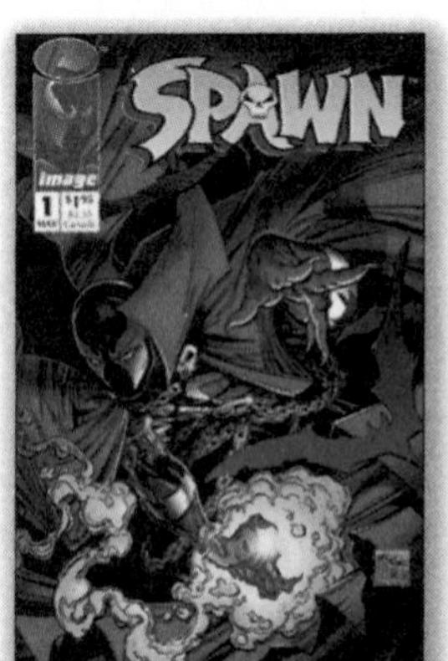

FIRST SPAWN BOOK

Spawn #1 (May 1992)

Practically from the moment Todd McFarlane introduced his Image Comics title to an eager fanship, *Spawn* became a consistent best-seller, and continues to be one today. *Spawn* initially proved Image could do well in the market.

THE DEATH OF SUPERMAN

Superman #75 (Jan. 1993)

This issue, in which the monstrous Doomsday killed Superman, arguably brought more people into the comic world than any other book in history, thanks to massive media coverage. Everyone wanted to see how the Man of Steel could be vanquished, producing a very hot book in the market. And when Superman returned, his books stayed popular.

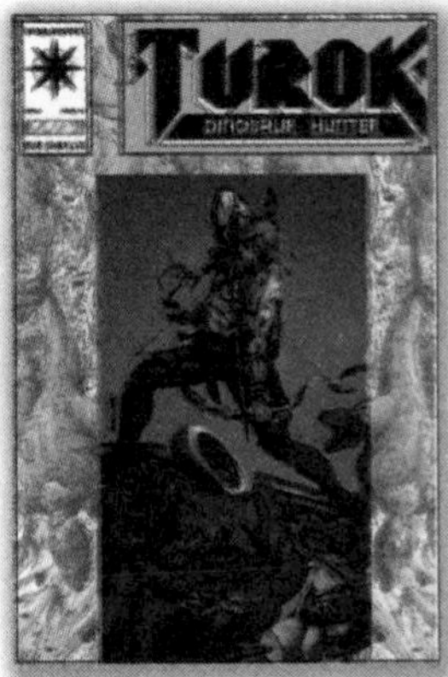

FIRST BOOK WITH A CHROMIUM COVER

Turok: Dinosaur Hunter #1 (Valiant, July 1993)

Valiant was the first comic company to latch onto a new process by which images could be printed on a shiny piece of metal. Its entry into the Chromium cover world was *Turok* #1, which didn't have a full Chromium cover but was still different. It appears several companies know that the look of their books' covers is worth the high price of Chromium, and it has become widely used in the industry.

VERTIGO IMPRINT FOR DC BEGINS

The Sandman #46 (and others, Feb. 1993)

After having significant success with "Suggested for Mature Readers" titles like *Green Arrow* and *Swamp Thing*, DC placed several of these titles—including *Sandman* and *Animal Man*—under a new all-mature imprint called Vertigo. Vertigo has been entertaining readers for nearly three years.

BOOK THAT SPARKED THE BAD GIRL TREND

Lady Death (mini-series) #1 (Jan. 1994)

Although Harris Comics' publication of a brand-new *Vampirella* series opened collectors' eyes, when Chaos! Comics produced a mini-series starring the female antiheroine from Eternity's *Evil Ernie* mini-series, the market went wild for books with female characters. Books like *Shi* and *Lady Rawhide* soon fueled this fiery "Bad Girl" trend.

FIRST MILESTONE MEDIA BOOK

Hardware #1 (Apr. 1993)

This book, starring a high-tech-powered hero, launched DC Comics' imprint of multicultural comics. These comics featured characters of many races and backgrounds, including Hispanic, Korean and black heroes. Currently in its third year, Milestone now publishes several titles about and for people from a variety of cultural backgrounds, including the popular *Icon, Static, Blood Syndicate* and *Xombi*, along with the new *Heroes*.

POSSIBLY THE BIGGEST TV ADAPTATION BOOK EVER

The X-Files #1 (Jan. 1995)

Thanks to its awe-inspiring sales figures and increasing number of fans, *The X-Files*—which adapts the popular TV show about two FBI agents searching for unexplained phenomena—may become the biggest TV adaptation in comic book history.

Marc Wilkofsky and Jon Warren hopped in a time machine to research this baby. Judging by their wardrobes, they have yet to return to present day.

Creative Juices

Meet the masterminds behind the comics

BY MARC SHAPIRO

Photos by Albert L. Ortega, Joseph Schuyler, Gabe Palacio, Carlo Allegri, Jim McHugh, Jim Gund, Craig Molenhouse, Jon Gip and DC Comics

ART ADAMS

Occupation: Writer, artist
Place of Birth: Holyoke, Massachusetts
Career Highlights: Marvel's *New Mutants, Uncanny X-Men*. Dark Horse's *Godzilla*. Comico's *Gumby*.
Did You Know: Art Adams made pizzas before landing a job in comics. He also has an extensive toy collection.

NEAL ADAMS

Occupation: Writer, artist
Place of Birth: Governor's Island, New York
Career Highlights: DC's *Batman, Detective Comics, Brave and the Bold, Green Lantern/Green Arrow*. Marvel's *X-Men* (vol. 1).
Did You Know: Adams' major influence is famed artist Norman Rockwell. He also founded Continuity Associates.

MIKE ALLRED

Occupation: Writer, artist
Place of Birth: Oregon
Career Highlights: Created Madman and currently writes and draws Dark Horse's *Madman Comics*.
Did You Know: As a reporter for American Forces radio, Allred was at the Berlin Wall when it came down.

SERGIO ARAGONÉS

Occupation: Writer, artist
Place of Birth: Spain
Career Highlights: EC's *Mad Magazine*. Created Groo.
Did You Know: Aragonés once worked as a mime and a clown, and studied at the feet of famed mime Marcel Marceau.

MARK BAGLEY

Occupation: Artist
Place of Birth: Frankfurt, Germany
Career Highlights: Marvel's *Amazing Spider-Man, The New Warriors*.
Did You Know: Bagley broke into the Marvel ranks by entering and winning a contest in the company's *Official Marvel Try-Out Book* contest.

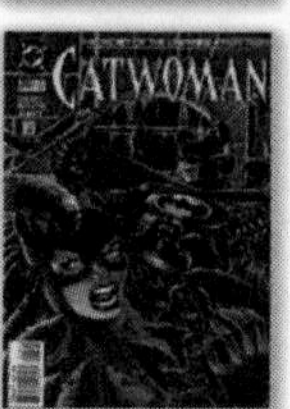

JIM BALENT

Occupation: Artist
Place of Birth: Wilkes Barre, Pennsylvania
Career Highlights: DC's *Catwoman* and *Green Lantern Corps Quarterly*.
Did You Know: At one time, Balent paid the rent as a grave digger.

SIMON BISLEY

Occupation: Artist
Place of Birth: England
Career Highlights: DC's *Lobo* mini-series, *Batman/Judge Dredd* crossover, covers for *Doom Patrol*. Verotik's *Death Dealer*.
Did You Know: Bisley was an art school dropout.

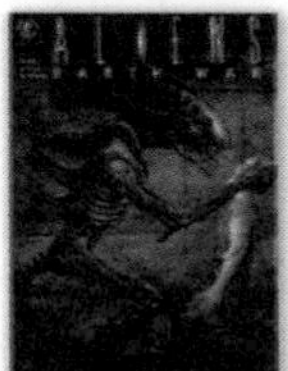

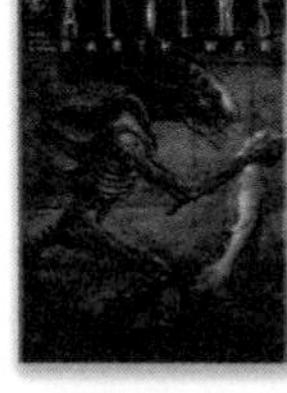

JOHN BOLTON

Occupation: Artist
Place of Birth: London, England
Career Highlights: Marvel's *King Kull*, *Classic X-Men*. Vertigo's *Books of Magic* (mini-series) #1. DC's *Batman: Man-Bat*.
Did You Know: Bolton's London home is decorated with *Hellraiser* and *Nightbreed* masks (courtesy of Clive Barker), and animal skulls with light bulbs poking out of their eye sockets.

JOHN BYRNE

Occupation: Writer, artist
Place of Birth: West Bromwich, Staffordshire, England
Career Highlights: Marvel's *Uncanny X-Men*, *Fantastic Four*. DC's *Superman*, *Wonder Woman*. Dark Horse's *Next Men* and *Danger Unlimited*.
Did You Know: Byrne's Alberta College of Art end of term project, a comic book, was so impressive that the school printed 500 copies.

J. SCOTT CAMPBELL

Occupation: Artist
Place of Birth: Aurora, Colorado
Career Highlights: Image's *Gen*[13], *WildC.A.T.s Sourcebook*, *StormWatch* #0.
Did You Know: Campbell responded to a talent search headed by Image co-founder Jim Lee, and got a call from Lee a week later to do some work.

GREG CAPULLO

Occupation: Artist
Place of Birth: Schenectady, New York
Career Highlights: Image's *Spawn*. Marvel's *X-Force*.
Did You Know: Capullo made big bucks in advertising before Marvel gave him work.

TRAVIS CHAREST

Occupation: Artist
Place of Birth: Edmonton, Canada
Career Highlights: Image's *WildC.A.T.s*. Marvel's *Hulk Annual*. DC's *Darkstars*.
Did You Know: Charest grew up on a farm, isolated from comics, so he wasn't a big comic book fan as a kid.

HOWARD CHAYKIN

Occupation: Writer, artist
Place of Birth: Newark, New Jersey
Career Highlights: Created First's *American Flagg!*. Did the comic book adaptation of *Star Wars* for Marvel.
Did You Know: Chaykin wrote scripts for the "Flash" television series and served as Executive Script Consultant for the TV series "Viper."

DENYS COWAN

Occupation: Artist
Place of Birth: New York City, New York
Career Highlights: Co-founder of the Milestone Media imprint of DC Comics. Helped revamp Marvel's Deathlok. Worked on *Detective Comics* #500.
Did You Know: Cowan has been a comic book professional since age 14.

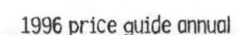

ROGER CRUZ

Occupation: Artist
Place of Birth: Sao Paolo, Brazil
Career Highlights: Marvel's *X-Men: Alpha* and *Omega*, *The Uncanny X-Men*.
Did You Know: Cruz's first name is really Rogerio.

ALAN DAVIS

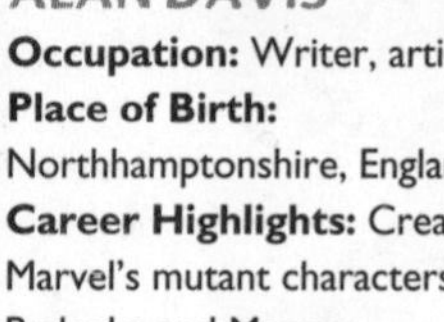

Occupation: Writer, artist
Place of Birth: Northhamptonshire, England
Career Highlights: Created Marvel's mutant characters Psylocke and Meggan. Co-created *Excalibur*.
Did You Know: Davis teamed up with writer Alan Moore on *2000 A.D.*'s "D.R. and Quinch" back-up stories.

MIKE DEODATO JR.

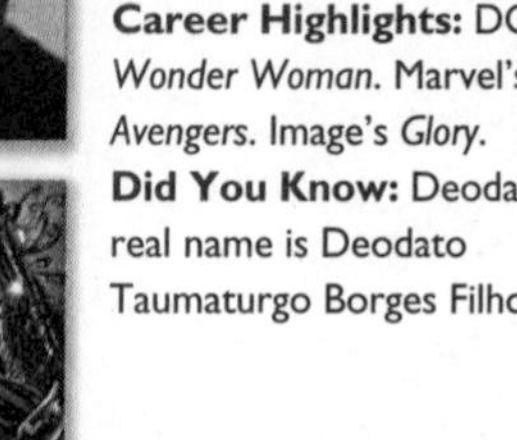

Occupation: Artist
Place of Birth: Campina Grande, Brazil
Career Highlights: DC's *Wonder Woman*. Marvel's *Avengers*. Image's *Glory*.
Did You Know: Deodato's real name is Deodato Taumaturgo Borges Filho.

COLLEEN DORAN

Occupation: Writer, artist
Place of Birth: Cincinnati, Ohio
Career Highlights: Created *A Distant Soil*. Formed Aria Press, which now publishes *A Distant Soil*.
Did You Know: Doran began working as an advertising illustrator at age 15.

KEVIN EASTMAN

Occupation: Writer, artist
Place of Birth: Portland, Maine
Career Highlights: Co-created *Teenage Mutant Ninja Turtles* with Peter Laird.
Did You Know: Eastman opened the Words and Pictures Museum in Boston in 1991.

WILL EISNER

Occupation: Writer, artist
Place of Birth: New York City, New York
Career Highlights: Created The Spirit. Created Quality's Blackhawk, Doll Man and other characters.
Did You Know: Eisner created what many consider the first comic book graphic novel with *Contract With God* published in 1978.

NEIL GAIMAN

Occupation: Writer
Place of Birth: England
Career Highlights: Co-created DC's *Sandman*. DC's *Black Orchid*, *Books of Magic* (mini-series).
Did You Know: Gaiman wrote the *Angela* mini-series for Image Comics to please his son Mikey.

WILLIAM GAINES

Occupation: Publisher, writer
Place of Birth: New York City, New York
Career Highlights: Founding the classic EC horror comics line, along with co-creating its *Mad Magazine* with Harvey Kurtzman.
Did You Know: Gaines was originally going to be a chemistry professor.

DAVE GIBBONS

Occupation: Writer, artist
Place of Birth: England
Career Highlights: DC's *Watchmen* and *Green Lantern*. Dark Horse's *Give Me Liberty*, *Martha Washington Goes to War*.
Did You Know: Gibbons was one of the first British artists to be recruited by DC in the early '80s; he worked on *Green Lantern*.

KEITH GIFFEN

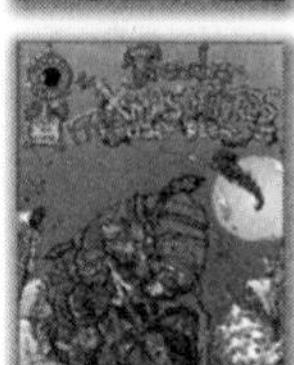

Occupation: Writer, artist
Place of Birth: Queens, New York.
Career Highlights: DC's *Legion of Super-Heroes, Justice League of America*. Acclaim's *Magnus, Robot Fighter*.
Did You Know: Giffen once sold vacuum cleaners and worked as a repo man to pay the bills.

MIKE GRELL

Occupation: Writer, artist
Place of Birth: Iron Mountain, Michigan
Career Highlights: Created *Warlord* for DC, *Jon Sable* for First, and *Shaman's Tears* for Image. He has had long runs on DC's *Green Arrow* and *Green Lantern*.
Did You Know: Grell originally intended a career in architecture before the comics bug bit.

TOM GRUMMETT

Occupation: Artist
Place of Birth: Saskatoon, Canada
Career Highlights: A long run on DC's *Adventures of Superman* (including the "Death Of Superman" storyline), *Robin*, *Superman: The Man of Tomorrow*.
Did You Know: Because of his renditions of Robin, Superboy and The New Titans, Grummett became known as a "teen artist."

ADAM HUGHES

Occupation: Artist
Place of Birth: New Jersey
Career Highlights: Dark Horse's *Ghost*. DC's *Justice League America* and *Star Trek: Debt of Honor*. Covers for Harris' *Vampirella*.
Did You Know: Hughes was fired from his job building electrical transformers. He also spent some time working in a comic book shop.

DAN JURGENS

Occupation: Writer, artist
Place of Birth: Ortonville, Minnesota.
Career Highlights: Wrote and penciled DC's *Superman* #75 (the issue in which he "died"), *Zero Hour*, *Superman/Doomsday*. Marvel's *Sensational Spider-Man*. Acclaim's *Solar, Man of the Atom*.
Did You Know: Jurgens created the visuals to Doomsday, the monster that killed Superman.

BOB KANE

Occupation: Artist
Place of Birth: New York City, New York
Career Highlights: Created Batman.
Did You Know: During the early development of Batman, Bob Kane referred to the character as Bird Man and the character had bird wings.

GIL KANE

Occupation: Artist
Place of Birth: Riga, Latvia
Career Highlights: DC's *Green Lantern*, *Atom*. Marvel's *Amazing Spider-Man*, *Captain Marvel*, *Daredevil*, *Captain America*.
Did You Know: Gil Kane once used *American Flagg!* creator Howard Chaykin as an assistant.

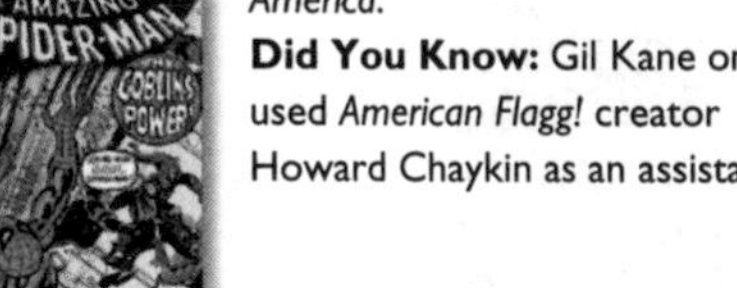

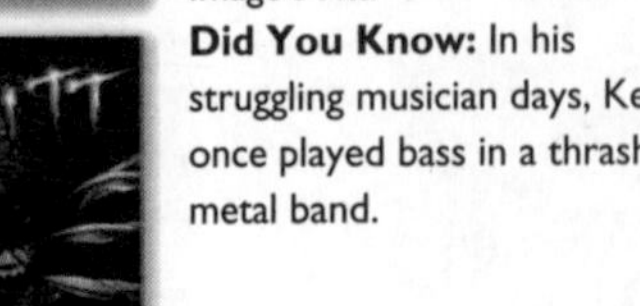

DALE KEOWN

Occupation: Artist
Place of Birth: Grande Prairie, Alberta, Canada.
Career Highlights: Marvel's *The Incredible Hulk*. Creator of Image's *Pitt*.
Did You Know: In his struggling musician days, Keown once played bass in a thrash metal band.

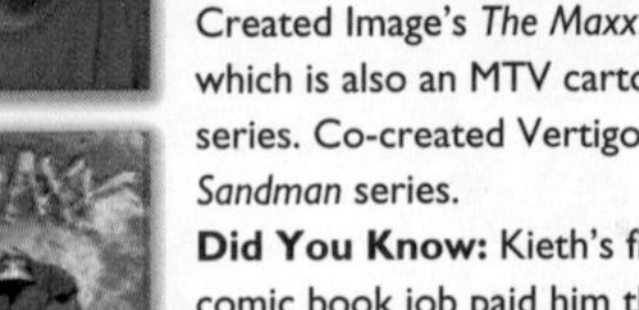

SAM KIETH

Occupation: Writer, artist
Place of Birth: Sacramento, California
Career Highlights: Created Image's *The Maxx*, which is also an MTV cartoon series. Co-created Vertigo's *Sandman* series.
Did You Know: Kieth's first comic book job paid him the princely sum of $10 a page.

JACK KIRBY

Occupation: Writer, artist
Place of Birth: New York City, New York
Career Highlights: Co-created Marvel's *Captain America, The Fantastic Four, Incredible Hulk, X-Men, The Mighty Thor, The Avengers* and a host of others.
Did You Know: Jack Kirby's real name is Jacob Kurtzberg.

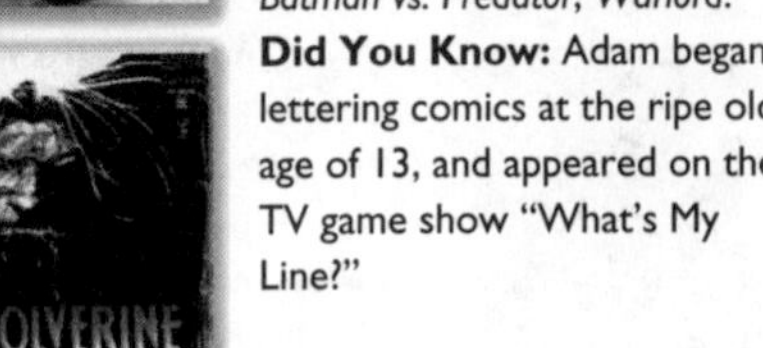

ADAM KUBERT

Occupation: Artist
Place of Birth: Boonton, New Jersey
Career Highlights: Marvel's *Wolverine* and *Ghost Rider*. DC's *Batman vs. Predator, Warlord.*
Did You Know: Adam began lettering comics at the ripe old age of 13, and appeared on the TV game show "What's My Line?"

ANDY KUBERT

Occupation: Artist
Place of Birth: Boonton, New Jersey.
Career Highlights: Marvel's *X-Men, Savage Sword of Conan.* DC's *Sgt. Rock, Adam Strange, Doc Savage, Warlord.*
Did You Know: Andy, before becoming a comic artist, was all set to work in his father's school as an administrator.

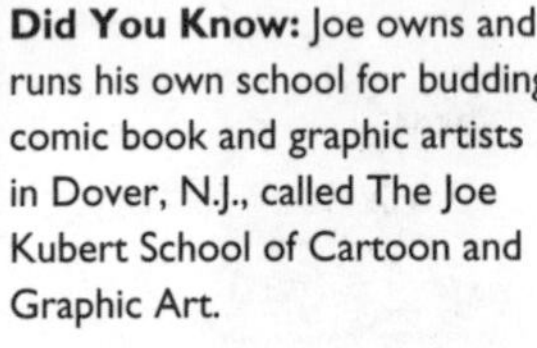

JOE KUBERT

Occupation: Artist
Place of Birth: Brooklyn, New York.
Career Highlights: DC's *Hawkman, Sgt. Rock, Flash, Star Spangled War Stories.* Marvel's *Ghost Rider.*
Did You Know: Joe owns and runs his own school for budding comic book and graphic artists in Dover, N.J., called The Joe Kubert School of Cartoon and Graphic Art.

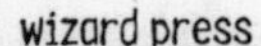

DAVID LAPHAM

Occupation: Writer, artist
Place of Birth: Lakewood, New Jersey
Career Highlights: Co-created Defiant's *Plasm* and Valiant's *Shadowman*. Self-publishes *Stray Bullets*.
Did You Know: Lapham spent a lot of time in Baltimore, Md., where much of his *Stray Bullets* stories are set.

ERIK LARSEN

Occupation: Writer, artist
Place of Birth: Minneapolis, Minnesota
Career Highlights: *Amazing Spider-Man, Spider-Man, Savage Dragon, Doom Patrol, Punisher.*
Did You Know: Erik Larsen was one of the original seven artists who formed Image. He also was the artist who took over *Amazing Spider-Man* and *Spider-Man* from Todd McFarlane.

BOB LAYTON

Occupation: Writer, artist
Place of Birth: Indianapolis, Indiana
Career Highlights: Co-plotted Marvel's *Iron Man* alcoholism storyline. Co-creator of Marvel's *X-Factor* and creator of Acclaim's *X-O Manowar*.
Did You Know: Bob Layton's first work appeared in a number of '70s fanzines including *Witzend*.

JAE LEE

Occupation: Artist
Place of Birth: South Korea
Career Highlights: Marvel's *Namor*. Image's *Hellshock*, *Youngblood: Strikefile*, *WildC.A.T.s Trilogy*.
Did You Know: Jae Lee left art school because he got bored and was discovered by comics at the tender age of 18.

JIM LEE

Occupation: Writer, artist
Place of Birth: South Korea
Career Highlights: Marvel's *Uncanny X-Men*, *X-Men*. Created Image's *WildC.A.T.s* and *Gen[13]*.
Did You Know: Jim Lee's favorite breakfast cereal is a bowl of granola.

STAN LEE

Occupation: Writer
Place of Birth: New York City, New York
Career Highlights: Co-created *Spider-Man*, *The Fantastic Four*, *The Incredible Hulk*, *The Mighty Thor*, *Silver Surfer*, *Daredevil* and others.
Did You Know: During his stint as Marvel editor, art director and head writer, Lee would often script five comic books in a week.

ROB LIEFELD

Occupation: Writer, artist
Place of Birth: Orange County, California
Career Highlights: Co-founded Image Comics and created its flagship title, *Youngblood*. Created Marvel's *X-Force*.
Did You Know: Liefeld is fond of fast food, particularly the chicken burrito at Taco Bell.

RON LIM

Occupation: Artist
Place of Birth: Marysville, California
Career Highlights: Marvel's *Silver Surfer*, *The Infinity Gauntlet*, *Captain America*.
Did You Know: Lim's favorite characters are the original Fantastic Four.

JOE MADUREIRA

Occupation: Artist
Place of Birth: Queens, New York
Career Highlights: Marvel's *Uncanny X-Men*, *The Astonishing X-Men*.
Did You Know: Madureira was a working pro before he graduated from high school.

DAVID MAZZUCCHELLI

Occupation: Writer, artist
Place of Birth: Providence, Rhode Island
Career Highlights: DC's *Batman: Year One*. Marvel's *Daredevil*.
Did You Know: Mazzucchelli enjoys the grunt work of selecting paper, inks and design of the artwork for printers while producing *Rubber Blanket*.

DWAYNE McDUFFIE

Occupation: Writer
Place of Birth: Detroit, Michigan
Career Highlights: Marvel's *Iron Man*, *Avengers*, *Hellraiser*, *Captain Marvel*. Milestone Media's *Icon* and *Hardware*.
Did You Know: McDuffie co-founded Milestone Media, and became its editor-in-chief.

TODD McFARLANE

Occupation: Writer, artist
Place of Birth: Calgary, Canada
Career Highlights: Created *Spawn*. Lengthy runs on *The Incredible Hulk* and *Amazing Spider-Man*. Helped launch *Spider-Man*.
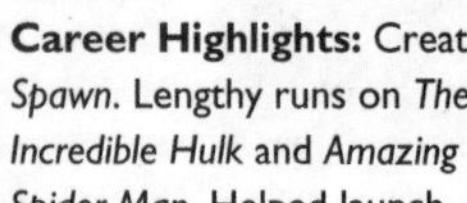
Did You Know: McFarlane's massive collectibles collection includes Babe Ruth's baseball cleats and Madonna's bustier.

MIKE MIGNOLA

Occupation: Writer, artist
Place of Birth: Berkeley, California
Career Highlights: Dark Horse's *Hellboy*. Topps' adaptation of Bram Stoker's *Dracula* movie. DC's *Batman: Gotham by Gaslight*.
Did You Know: Mignola first drew Hellboy as a sketch at a comic book convention.

FRANK MILLER

Occupation: Writer, artist
Place of Birth: Maryland
Career Highlights: DC's *Batman: The Dark Knight Returns*, *Batman: Year One*, *Ronin*. Dark Horse's *Sin City*. Marvel's *Daredevil*, *Daredevil: Man Without Fear*.
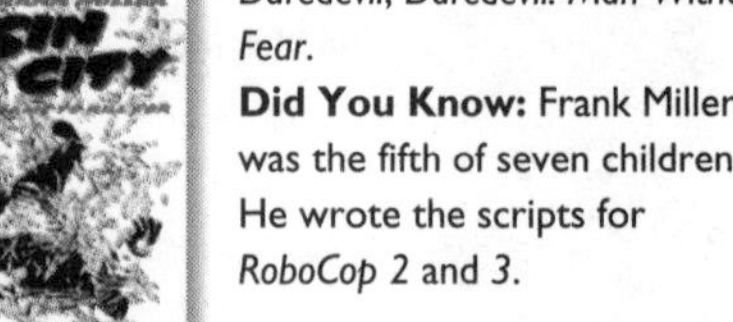
Did You Know: Frank Miller was the fifth of seven children. He wrote the scripts for *RoboCop 2* and *3*.

DENNIS O'NEIL

Occupation: Writer
Place of Birth: St. Louis, Missouri
Career Highlights: DC's *Batman*, *Detective Comics*, *Green Lantern/Green Arrow*. Marvel's *Daredevil*.
Did You Know: O'Neil received the princely sum of $4 a page for writing "Children of Doom" for *Charlton Premiere Comics* #2.

JERRY ORDWAY

Occupation: Writer, artist
Place of Birth: Milwaukee, Wisconsin
Career Highlights: DC's *Superman*, *Adventures of Superman*, *The Power of Shazam!*. Image's *WildStar: Sky Zero*.
Did You Know: Ordway spent seven years either drawing and/or writing various Superman titles.

JOHN OSTRANDER

Occupation: Writer
Place of Birth: Chicago, Illinois
Career Highlights: First's *Grimjack*. DC's *The Spectre* and *Suicide Squad*.
Did You Know: Ostrander served as an usher at a Beatles concert.

GEORGE PÉREZ

Occupation: Writer, artist
Place of Birth: Bronx, New York
Career Highlights: Co-created DC's *New Teen Titans*. DC's *Crisis on Infinite Earths*. Marvel's *Avengers*. Malibu's *UltraForce*.
Did You Know: Pérez broke into comics as an art assistant to Rich Buckler.

WENDY PINI

Occupation: Writer, artist
Place of Birth: San Francisco, California
Career Highlights: Formed WaRP Graphics with husband Richard, and co-created *Elfquest* with him.
Did You Know: Pini met her husband, WaRP publisher Richard Pini, by corresponding with him through a *Silver Surfer* letter column.

STEPHEN PLATT

Occupation: Artist
Place of Birth: Manchester, England
Career Highlights: Marvel's *Moon Knight*. Image's *Prophet*.
Did You Know: Platt's first Moon Knight work for *Marvel Comics Presents* has never been published.

WHILCE PORTACIO

Occupation: Writer, artist
Place of Birth: The Philippines
Career Highlights: Created Image's *WetWorks*. Penciled and co-plotted Marvel's *Uncanny X-Men, The Punisher, Alpha Flight, X-Factor*.
Did You Know: Portacio was originally a co-founder of Image Comics but dropped out for personal reasons.

BRIAN PULIDO

Occupation: Writer
Place of Birth: Newark, N.J.
Career Highlights: Formed Chaos! Comics and successfully publishes *Evil Ernie* and *Lady Death*.
Did You Know: Pulido was the first assistant director on the movie *Tougher Than Leather*, starring the rap group Run D.M.C.

JOE QUESADA

Occupation: Writer, artist
Place of Birth: New York City, New York
Career Highlights: Co-founded Event Comics for the purpose of publishing his creation *Ash*. Co-created DC's Azrael. Designed DC's new Ray.
Did You Know: Quesada once worked as a toy salesman. He researched *Ash* by hanging out with real New York firefighters.

JOHN ROMITA JR.

Occupation: Artist
Place of Birth: Brooklyn, New York
Career Highlights: Marvel's *Iron Man, Uncanny X Men, The Punisher*.
Did You Know: Romita Jr. used to draw on the covers of his Catholic grammar school books.

JOHN ROMITA SR.

Occupation: Artist
Place of Birth: Brooklyn, New York
Career Highlights: Marvel's *Captain America*. Co-created *The Punisher*. Worked on *Amazing Spider-Man* from 1966 to 1973.
Did You Know: Romita Sr. started out with a goal of being a magazine illustrator instead of a comic book artist.

ALEX ROSS

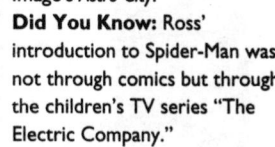

Occupation: Artist
Place of Birth: Portland, Oregon
Career Highlights: Marvel's *Marvels*. DC's *Kingdom Come* and *Sandman Mystery Theatre Annual* #1. Covers to Image's *Astro City*.
Did You Know: Ross' introduction to Spider-Man was not through comics but through the children's TV series "The Electric Company."

BART SEARS

Occupation: Artist
Place of Birth: Syracuse, New York
Career Highlights: DC's *Justice League Europe*. Acclaim's *X-O Manowar*. Image's *Violator*.
Did You Know: Sears dropped out of The Joe Kubert School of Cartoon and Graphic Art after one year because he was "sick of sitting at a table and drawing."

JIM SHOOTER

Occupation: Writer
Place of Birth: Pittsburgh, Pennsylvania
Career Highlights: Editor-in-chief at Marvel, Valiant, Defiant.
Did You Know: Shooter turned comic book pro as a writer at the ripe old age of 13.

JOE SHUSTER

Occupation: Artist
Place of Birth: Toronto, Canada
Career Highlights: Co-created Superman with Jerry Siegel.
Did You Know: Shuster and Siegel were paid $130 for the first Superman story. Shuster's last published work, a Superman pinup, appeared in 1983's *Action Comics* #554.

JERRY SIEGEL

Occupation: Writer
Place of Birth: Cleveland, Ohio
Career Highlights: Co-created DC's Superman, The Spectre, Legion of Super-Heroes and Adam Strange.
Did You Know: The last comic work Siegel has done appeared in early '70s *X-Men*, *Human Torch* and *Ka-Zar* books.

BILL SIENKIEWICZ

Occupation: Writer, artist
Place of Birth: Blakley, Pennsylvania
Career Highlights: Marvel's *Moon Knight, Stray Toasters, The New Mutants, Daredevil: Love and War, Elektra: Assassin.*
Did You Know: Sienkiewicz made his living installing television antennas before walking into the Marvel offices without an appointment and landing the *Moon Knight* job.

MARC SILVESTRI

Occupation: Artist
Place of Birth: Palm Beach, Florida
Career Highlights: Co-founded Image Comics to create *Cyberforce*. Marvel's *Uncanny X-Men, Wolverine.*
Did You Know: Silvestri's musical tastes run from Stone Temple Pilots and Nine Inch Nails to Bach and Beethoven.

DAVE SIM

Occupation: Writer, artist
Place of Birth: Hamilton, Ontario, Canada
Career Highlights: Created *Cerebus*, one of the longest running independent comics.
Did You Know: The title character Cerebus was actually misspelled by Sim, as the character was supposed to be known as "Cerberus."

WALT SIMONSON

Occupation: Writer, artist
Place of Birth: Knoxville, Tennessee
Career Highlights: Marvel's *Thor, X-Factor*. Dark Horse's *RoboCop vs. Terminator.*
Did You Know: Walt Simonson has a degree in geology and was originally going to be a paleontologist.

Albert L. Ortega, Joseph Schuyler, Gabe Palacio, Carlo Allegri, Jim McHugh, Jim Gund, Craig Molenhouse, Jon Gip, DC Comics

JEFF SMITH

Occupation: Writer, artist
Place of Birth: Columbus, Ohio
Career Highlights: After refusing lucrative syndication offers, Smith decided to form Cartoon Books and self-publish *Bone.*
Did You Know: The idea for the Bone characters came to Smith while in kindergarten.

ROGER STERN

Occupation: Writer
Place of Birth: Noblesville, Indiana
Career Highlights: DC's *Action Comics, Superman.* Marvel's *Avengers, Dr. Strange* and *Amazing Spider-Man.*
Did You Know: Stern's novel *The Death and Life of Superman* spent several weeks on the national book charts.

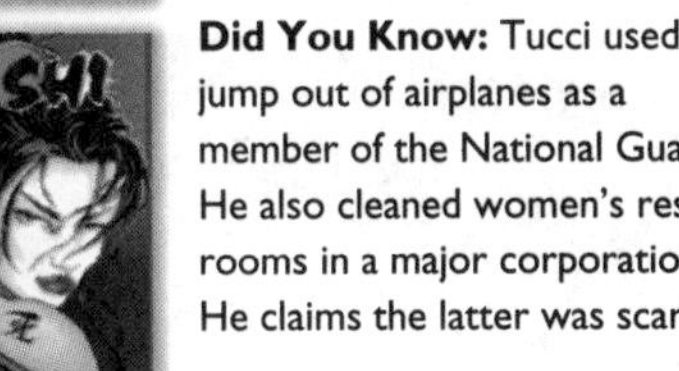

BILL TUCCI

Occupation: Writer, artist
Place of Birth: Long Island, New York
Career Highlights: Created *Shi.* Formed his own company Crusade Comics.
Did You Know: Tucci used to jump out of airplanes as a member of the National Guard. He also cleaned women's rest rooms in a major corporation. He claims the latter was scarier.

CHARLES VESS

Occupation: Artist
Place of Birth: Lynchburg, Virginia
Career Highlights: Marvel's *Spider-Man: Spirits of the Earth* graphic novel. Vertigo's *Books of Magic* (mini-series) #3, and covers for the ongoing series.
Did You Know: Vess drew Vertigo's *Sandman* #19 which won the World Fantasy Award for Best Short Story.

MATT WAGNER

Occupation: Writer, artist
Place of Birth: Lewistown, Pennsylvania
Career Highlights: *Sandman Mystery Theatre, Grendel, Batman/Grendel.*
Did You Know: Wagner's two-issue *Batman/Grendel* crossover was completed three-and-a-half years before it saw print in 1993.

BARRY WINDSOR-SMITH

Occupation: Writer, artist
Place of Birth: London, England
Career Highlights: Marvel's *Conan the Barbarian.* Co-created Malibu's *Rune,* along with Valiant's *Archer and Armstrong.*
Did You Know: Windsor-Smith dropped out of comics in the mid-'70s for 10 years to found Gorblimey Press which turned out portfolios and posters.

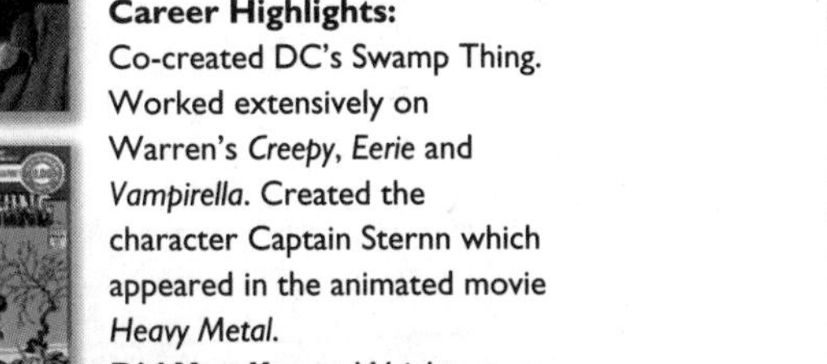

BERNIE WRIGHTSON

Occupation: Artist
Place of Birth: Baltimore, Maryland
Career Highlights: Co-created DC's Swamp Thing. Worked extensively on Warren's *Creepy, Eerie* and *Vampirella.* Created the character Captain Sternn which appeared in the animated movie *Heavy Metal.*
Did You Know: Wrightson, as a child, kept *Haunt of Fear* #27 under his mattress for a year and a half.

MIKE ZECK

Occupation: Artist
Place of Birth: Greenville, Pennsylvania
Career Highlights: Marvel's *Secret Wars* maxi-series, the first *Punisher* mini-series.
Did You Know: Zeck designed Spider-Man's black costume, which the web-slinger wore in the mid-'80s.

Marc Shapiro is a fun chap.

Anatomy of A comic book

Ever stop to think what really makes up a comic book?

Sure, comics sport a lot of cool drawings of mutants beating the crap out of each other. But have you ever taken a really close look at a comic book? You know, like all the little codes and words and seals and stuff?

Well, we're here to make sure you take that closer look. We're taking you step by step through the anatomy of a comic book:

TITLE
The title of the book is featured prominently in the upper third of the front cover.

PUBLISHER
The publisher of a book. Usually appears in a box in one of the upper corners of the front covers.

CORNER BOX
Many publishers depict the comic's main character or characters in a box in the upper left-hand corner of the cover.

PRICE
The suggested retail price of a "new" comic. If the comic is meant for international distribution, foreign prices (usually Canada and United Kingdom) are printed below the U.S. price. It appears near the top left or top right corner, under the publisher's name and near the cover price.

ISSUE NUMBER
Indicates how many editions of a periodical have been published. Comic books are usually identified by the title followed by the issue number, which most often appears near the top left or top right corner of the front cover, under the publisher's name and near the cover price.

COVER DATE
Normally between one and two months after the comic's release to indicate to retailers and vendors when the comic should be removed from the shelves, it appears near the top left or top right corner, under the publisher's name and near the cover price.

CCA SEAL
Signifying Comics Code Authority approval of the book upon which it appears, it is located near one of the upper corners of the front cover.

UPC
The Universal Product Code identifies to a laser scanner the product upon which it appears. The UPC appears on books distributed to newsstands. Until recently, the UPC box on direct-market copies would be blank or contain art; now, many publishers are including the code on direct-market issues along with a notation that the copy is a direct-market item. The trend should continue as more comics retailers computerize their stores. The UPC usually appears on the lower left- or lower right-hand corner of the front cover.

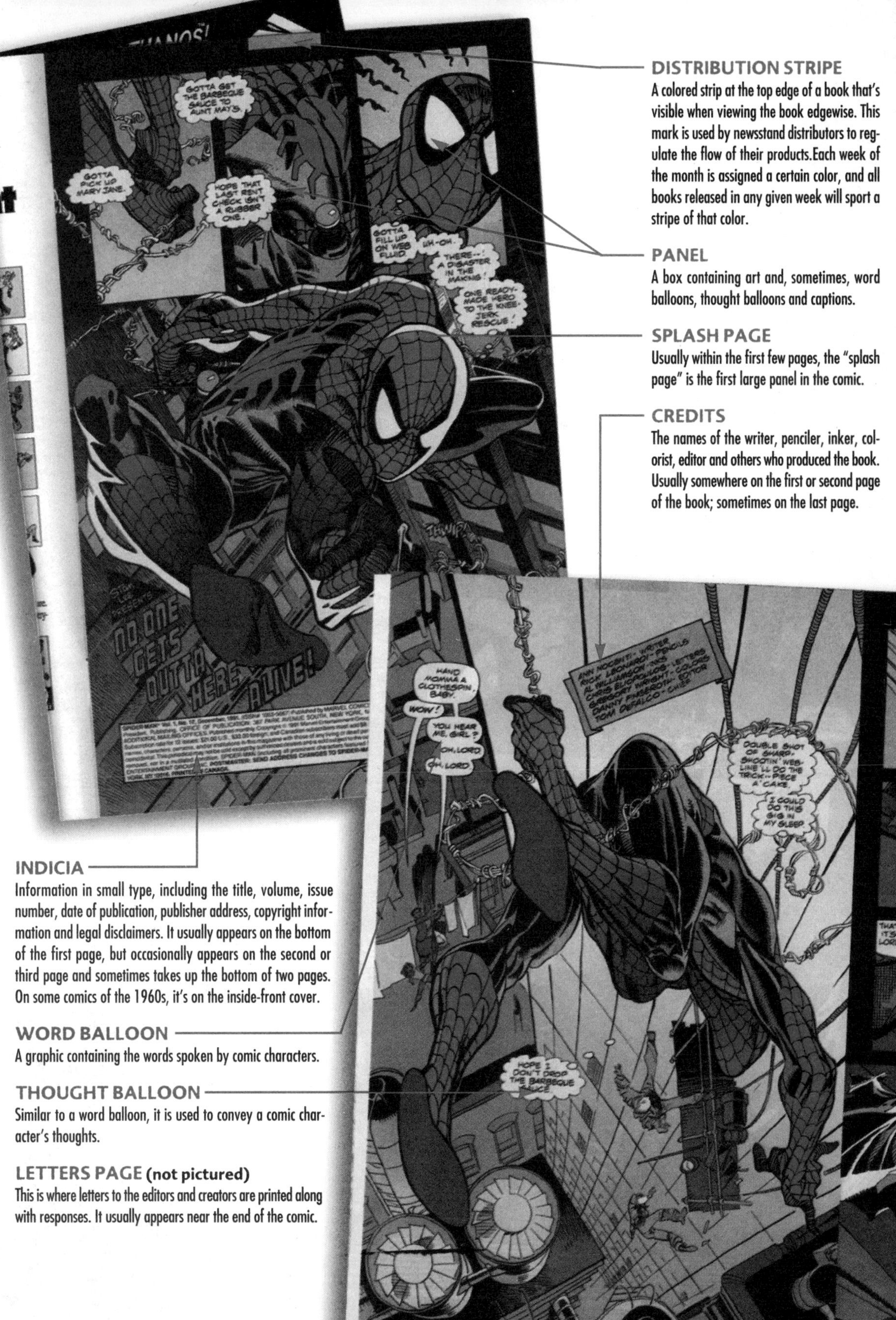

DISTRIBUTION STRIPE
A colored strip at the top edge of a book that's visible when viewing the book edgewise. This mark is used by newsstand distributors to regulate the flow of their products.Each week of the month is assigned a certain color, and all books released in any given week will sport a stripe of that color.

PANEL
A box containing art and, sometimes, word balloons, thought balloons and captions.

SPLASH PAGE
Usually within the first few pages, the "splash page" is the first large panel in the comic.

CREDITS
The names of the writer, penciler, inker, colorist, editor and others who produced the book. Usually somewhere on the first or second page of the book; sometimes on the last page.

INDICIA
Information in small type, including the title, volume, issue number, date of publication, publisher address, copyright information and legal disclaimers. It usually appears on the bottom of the first page, but occasionally appears on the second or third page and sometimes takes up the bottom of two pages. On some comics of the 1960s, it's on the inside-front cover.

WORD BALLOON
A graphic containing the words spoken by comic characters.

THOUGHT BALLOON
Similar to a word balloon, it is used to convey a comic character's thoughts.

LETTERS PAGE (not pictured)
This is where letters to the editors and creators are printed along with responses. It usually appears near the end of the comic.

Grade School

How to grade your comic books

Your comics might not be worth the paper they're printed on.

Now don't get me wrong. They could be the best stories this side of the Mississippi and feature milestones in the annals of comic history, but if they look like they've seen the business end of a love-starved Doberman, they won't be worth their cover price.

Y'see, since collecting comic books is a high-octane hobby fueled by millions of fans across the globe, it's become something of a science to properly grade a comic's condition. Collectors want comics in perfect condition, and if they can't get a flawless gem, they want something pretty darn close. And that's where different condition grades for comics come in. There are Mint, perfect condition books that command premium prices. The same book in Very Fine condition will feature a substantially smaller price tag and that same book in Poor condition will be lucky if its price tag breaks a buck. Heck, the list of comic book grades and the values attached to them is as long as your arm.

"But how am I supposed to know what condition my books are in?" Hey, don't sweat it. Grading your comics ain't as scary as it

MINT (M)

This is a Mint comic book. Unlike me, there's nothing wrong with it. Me, I've got hemorrhoids.

Mint books CANNOT contain any flaw, regardless of how minute. No nicks, dings or creases. Colors are crystal clear and vibrant, the cover is nice and glossy and even the stupid staples are perfect.

Keep in mind that few comics are actually Mint, even the newest issue of a title. Why? After going through the huge, soulless machines that slap 'em together, then being stuffed into boxes, bounced around by delivery vans, crammed on to shelves by store owners and then thumbed-through by fans like yourself, just be thankful they're still in one piece.

Grade Value: 125%-150% of NM guide. Mint Silver and Golden Age books sometimes sell at multiples of the guide prices (like a Mint GA comic might go for three times its price in NM).

PERFECTAMUNDO

NEAR MINT (NM)

Oy, this is a good book. Just about Mint, in fact. It has one, maybe two, minor—and I do mean MINOR—flaws. Upon close inspection you'll notice the most teeny li'l thing wrong with it. A very small crease on the spine, a teeny miscolored dot, a slightly whitened corner or minor fraying by the staple are things to look for. Gloss and color are vibrant.

Most collectors are more than happy with a book in this condition, so unless you're some weird anal type, a Near Mint book will make any collection proud.

Grade Value: 100% of NM guide

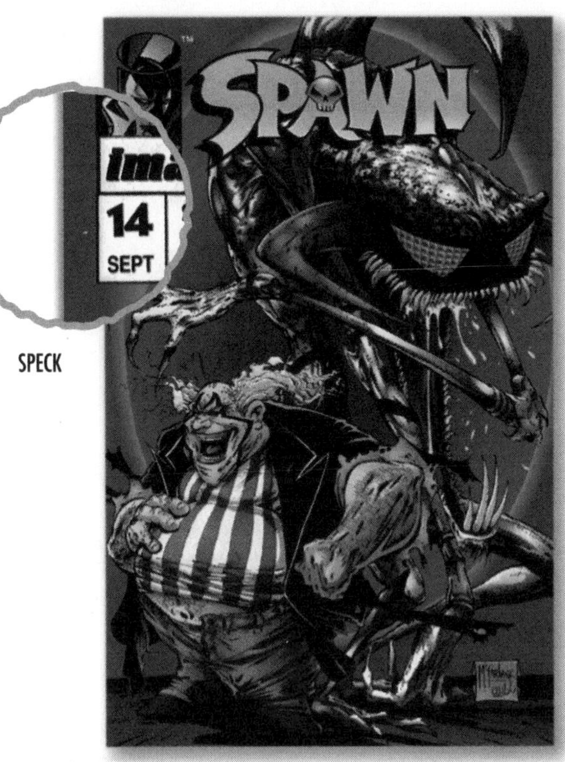

SOLID

VERY FINE (VF)

Hey, look familiar? It should. The most commonly traded books are usually in Very Fine condition, since, like I said earlier, comics get handled a lot. Betcha most collections feature more Very Fine books than any other condition.

That's not to say Very Fine books suck. Quite the contrary. They are clean and sharp in every way, and may even pass for NM on first glance. Closer inspection reveals some flaws, though, like a small crease or two on the spine, a small spot or two on the cover, and possibly a slight frayed corner or three. Darn good condition!

Grade Value: 70% of NM guide

GOOD

FINE (F)

Heeey...still pretty sharp. Fine comics are pretty neat, but most collectors begin to turn their noses up at these. Why? A lot of it has something to do with the more noticeable defects that begin to show up. Like what? Glad you asked. A book in Fine condition features small creases on corners and multiple creases on the spine, chipping, flaking and scuff marks, discolorations and soft, rounded corners.

But hey, if nothing else, it's a good way to pick up older, more expensive comics without emptying your wallet!

Grade Value:
40% of NM guide

ADD TO THE EQUATION

Aside from the more obvious flaws covered in the main article, there exist other defects that will affect a book's value and grade.

FADING: Unless stored someplace where light can't get to 'em, the colors on a comic's cover will begin to fade. Even if a book is otherwise Mint, a faded cover, depending on the severity of the discoloration, will easily knock it down a grade or two.

PAGE QUALITY: Unless properly stored and cared for, interior pages may turn yellow or brown, and will begin to get crumbly and frayed about the edges. Depending on the severity of the deterioration and how many pages are affected, this can really lower a book's condition. If your book's cover looks high-grade but you have crumbly, discolored pages inside, that'll knock it down at least a whole grade.

RESTORED COMICS: Since most old, highly desirable comics aren't in the best of shape, someone came up with the idea to restore comic books, as most collectors want their books in tip-top shape. Just like piecing a junked '57 Chevy back together and getting her up and running,

VERY GOOD (VG)

Ooooh...not pretty. As you can see, a Very Good comic isn't, well, very good. Think this condition is popular among collectors? Well, it's not.

Y'see, the books that find themselves in this condition have to suffer through multiple, more pronounced creases on the corners and spine, more severe cover flaking, plus rounded and almost dented corners. You'll also notice that li'l tears are beginning to pop up.

Very Good is the "normal" condition for books over 30 years old.

Grade Value:
100% of VG guide

restored comics are books that were once in a lesser condition (F, VG, etc.) and, using modern technology, were pieced back together to look like high-grade books (VF and up). Creases were filled in, tears were mended and stains were removed; even missing sections of the book may have been replaced from other copies of the same book.

As far as grading goes, a VG book restored to the point where it looks NM is no longer truly VG, nor is it valued at an NM price. It is, however, now higher than a VG grade and worth more. How much so? It depends on the book. If it's a rare book where few copies exist in high grade, even the prices of restored books can approach (perhaps even match) guide values. If this book that can already be found in high grades, and multiple restored copies are available on the market, that greatly reduces the chances of the restored book increasing in value.

Restored comics are currently not as sought-after as non-restored comics, though they are growing in popularity and acceptance. Also remember that a retailer MUST

GOOD, FAIR OR POOR (G), (FA) OR (P)

Aaaaahhhhh!! It's an abomination in the face of God!

Oh, wait, it's just a comic that's been beat to hell. Sheesh, where do I start with this thing? Let's see...major creases crisscrossing the cover (try and say that three times fast), whole chunks torn from the book, stains, scuff marks and flaking running rampant, writing on the cover...geez, I could go on forever. Let's just say that books in this condition really aren't all that collectible, and are usually nothing more than reading copies or gap-fillers in extensive collections.

These grades suck.

Grade Values:
Good: 5%-10% of NM guide
Fair: 3%-5% of NM guide
Poor: 1% of NM guide

And those are the basics. As you get better acquainted with the subtleties of grading and how the various defects combine to alter a book's condition, you'll grow past what we taught you here. You'll learn that there are more condition grades that fall between those listed in these pages. Grades like Fine/Very Fine, which is not quite as good as Very Fine, but certainly better (and sells for more) than a book in Fine. Or Near Mint/Mint, which is flawless with the exception of a minuscule, virtually non-existent flaw that carries a price tag way over Near Mint values (and is the closest to a true Mint book you'll ever find, in some people's minds).

And that is that. Now go bug a relative for cash and buy some back issues.

ADD TO THE EQUATION...cont.

tell you if a book is restored when you inquire about purchasing it.

POLYBAGS: What to do about comics that come sealed in plastic polybags? Carefully open the top of the bag with a pair of scissors. Make your cut straight; don't make your bag a jagged mess. Then store it, along with anything that may have come inside the bag (like a card), on the opposite side of the backing board you keep in your comic bag. As long as you keep the bag and whatever came in it in good shape, the whole package will be considered to be in the same condition the comic is in.

INSERTS: Manufacturers of stuff like temporary tattoos, stickers and the like have found that a large majority of their audience really digs comics, and have occasionally inserted sample products into them. They're usually slipped right in and stapled with the comic pages.

Now, even though these aren't really part of the actual comic, if you remove an insert from the comic, you knock the grade of your book down at least one full grade. So be careful! •

About the Price guide

The **WIZARD** price guide contains the most accurate and up-to-minute comic book prices available on the planet. To ensure that our values are as timely as possible, we constantly communicate with our ever-expanding network of comic book retailers and regularly send scouts to check prices in stores and at shows throughout the country.

HOW TO USE THE PRICE GUIDE

It's easy, and best of all, you can learn at home. The price guide is arranged alphabetically by title. Listings for trade paperbacks, annuals, one-shots and graphic novels are found after the regular listing for a title, and are likewise listed alphabetically.

PRICING YOUR COMICS

The first price listed in this guide (the lower price) is for books in Very Good (VG) condition. The second price listed (the higher price) is for comics in Near Mint (NM) condition. When your comic isn't in either of these two conditions, you compute the price based on the percentages shown below. (For details on grading comics, see page 74.) Keep in mind this is only a guide, and percentages can vary depending on several factors, including age, supply and demand for the various grades, retailer location, local availability of a title and its current popularity.

MINT (M) 125-150% of NM price. Comics after 1970 in Mint should be priced at the Near Mint price, since Mint copies are not unusual for comics after 1970.

NEAR MINT (NM) 100% of NM price

VERY FINE (VF) 70% of NM price (75-80% for pre-1970 books)

FINE-VERY FINE (FVF) 50% of NM price

FINE (FN) 40% of NM price

VERY GOOD (VG) 100% of VG price

GOOD (G) 5%-10% of NM price

FAIR (FR) 3%-5% of NM price

POOR (P) 1% of NM price

REFERENCES

1st:	First Appearance of	M:	Married
anniv:	Anniversary issue	O:	Origin
B:	Begin stories with	p:	part #
C:	Cameo that pre-dates 1st	PF:	Prestige Format
cvr:	Cover	Q:	Quits
D:	Death/Destruction of	R:	Return of
GN:	Graphic Novel	SC:	Softcover
HC:	Hardcover	sz:	Size
IR:	Identity revealed	TPB:	Trade Paperback
J:	Joins	w/:	With
L:	Last story with	w/o:	Without

A-1 COMICS
ME (1944-1948)

1 ... 25.00 80.00
2 Kerry Drake. ... 17.00 55.00
3 ... 9.00 27.00
4 Texas Slim And Dirty Dalton. ... 9.00 27.00
5-6 ... 9.00 27.00
7 The Corsair. ... 9.00 27.00
8 Rodeo Ryan. ... 9.00 27.00
9 Texas Slim. ... 9.00 27.00
10 The Masquerader. ... 9.00 27.00
11-12 Teena. ... 9.00 27.00
13 Guns Of Fact And Fiction. ... 35.00 110.00
15 Teena. For other A-1 issues, see individual cover titles. ... 9.00 27.00

AARDWOLF
AARDWOLF (1994)

1-3 ... .75 2.95
1A Certificate edition (limited, signed, includes art print). ... 5.00 15.95

ABBIE AN' SLATS
ST. JOHN (1947)

1 From Treasury Of Comics series. ... 23.00 75.00
4 From Treasury Of Comics series. (9/47) 13.00 40.00

ABBIE AN' SLATS
UNITED FEATURES (1948)

1 ... 31.00 100.00
2 ... 16.00 50.00
3-4 ... 13.00 40.00

ABBOTT AND COSTELLO
CHARLTON (1968-1971)

1 ... 10.00 33.00
2 ... 5.00 16.00
3-12 ... 4.00 11.00
13-22 ... 2.25 8.75

ABBOTT AND COSTELLO
ST. JOHN (1948-1956)

1 ... 85.00 270.00
2 ... 40.00 130.00
3 ... 25.00 80.00
4-7 ... 25.00 80.00
8 (8/49) ... 17.00 55.00
9 ... 17.00 55.00
10 Art: Joe Kubert (Son of Sinbad story). 25.00 80.00
11 (10/50) ... 17.00 55.00
12 Same cover art as #1. ... 17.00 55.00
13-14 ... 14.00 44.00
15 (12/52) ... 14.00 44.00
16-24 ... 14.00 44.00
25-36 ... 10.00 33.00
37-40 ... 9.00 27.00
3-D#1 With glasses. (11/53) ... 70.00 220.00

ABRAHAM LINCOLN LIFE STORY
DELL (1958)

1 25 cent Dell Giant. ... 11.00 36.00

ABSENT-MINDED PROFESSOR, THE
DELL FOUR COLOR SERIES (1961)

1199 Disney movie photo cover (Fred MacMurray). (4/61) ... 16.00 50.00

ABSOLUTE VERTIGO
DC (1995)

1 Sampling of Vertigo projects. ... .30 1.00

ABSOLUTE ZERO
ANTARCTIC PRESS (1995-CURRENT)

1 ... 1.00 3.50

ABYSS, THE
DARK HORSE (1989)

1 Movie tie-in. ... .75 2.00
2 ... .75 2.00

ACE COMICS
DAVID MCKAY (1937-1949)

1 Starring Tex Thorne, Believe It Or Not, Blondie. ... 500.00 1900.00
2 Starring Believe It Or Not, Tex Thorne, Blondie. ... 200.00 650.00
3 Starring Ripley's Believe It Or Not. ... 135.00 440.00
4-5 Starring Ripley's Believe It Or Not. 95.00 300.00
6 Starring Tex Thorne, Believe It Or Not, Blondie. ... 95.00 300.00
7-10 ... 75.00 240.00
11 Begin: The Phantom. ... 95.00 300.00
12-25 ... 70.00 220.00
26 1st & Origin: Prince Valiant. ... 150.00 490.00
27-37 ... 60.00 190.00
38-48 ... 40.00 130.00
49-60 ... 35.00 110.00
61-81 ... 28.00 90.00
82-99 ... 20.00 65.00
100 ... 23.00 75.00
101-134 ... 15.00 49.00
135 Begin: The Lone Ranger. ... 17.00 55.00
136-140 ... 14.00 44.00
141-151 ... 10.00 33.00

ACES HIGH
EC (1955)

1 "New Direction." ... 35.00 110.00
2-3 ... 25.00 80.00
4-5 ... 20.00 65.00

ACME NOVELTY LIBRARY
FANTAGRAPHICS (1994)

1 1: Jimmy Corrigan. ... 1.50 5.00
2 Quimby The Mouse (b&w tabloid). ... 1.25 4.00
3 Digest size. ... 1.00 3.95
4 Tabloid size, Sparky's Best Comics. ... 1.25 4.95

ACTION ADVENTURE COMICS
GILMORE (1955)

2 Previous title: Real Adventure Comics #1. 7.00 20.00
3-4 ... 7.00 20.00

ACTION COMICS
DC (1938-CURRENT)

0 (8/94) ... .75 2.25
1 1st & Origin Superman, 1st Lois Lane. ... 50000.00 175000.00
2 Origin story, pt. 2. Superman not on cover. ... 6100.00 24000.00
3 ... 2300.00 9000.00
4-5 ... 1300.00 5000.00
6 1st Jimmy Olsen. ... 1300.00 5000.00
7 2nd Superman cover. ... 2300.00 9000.00
8 (1/39) ... 1000.00 3900.00
9 ... 1000.00 3900.00
10 3rd Superman cover. ... 1300.00 5000.00
11 ... 700.00 2600.00
12 Superman inset on cover. ... 700.00 2600.00
13 4th Superman cover. ... 1000.00 3900.00
14 Superman inset on cover. ... 500.00 1900.00
15 5th Superman cover. ... 900.00 3200.00
16 Begin: Superman inset upper left corner (runs through #127). ... 500.00 1900.00
17 6th Superman cover. ... 700.00 2600.00
18 ... 400.00 1500.00
19 Begin: Superman covers. ... 700.00 2600.00
20 1st Superman costume variant (S left off). (1/40) ... 500.00 1900.00
21-22 ... 400.00 1300.00
23 1st Luthor, 1st Daily Planet. ... 1600.00 6000.00
24-31 ... 300.00 975.00
32 (1/41) ... 240.00 775.00
33 Origin: Mr. America. ... 220.00 700.00
34-36 ... 220.00 700.00
37 Origin: Congo Bill. ... 250.00 825.00
38-41 ... 220.00 700.00
42 1st & Origin Vigilante. ... 300.00 975.00
43 ... 220.00 700.00
44 (1/42) ... 200.00 650.00
45 (2/42) ... 200.00 650.00
46 Superman Battles The Domino. ... 200.00 650.00
47 "Superman Tangles with Luthor in the Startling Adventure of the Powerstone" 1st Luthor cover. (4/42) 240.00 775.00
48 ... 200.00 650.00
49 Vs. The Puzzler in "The Wizard Of Chance!" ... 200.00 650.00
50 ... 200.00 650.00
51 1st Prankster in "The Foolproof Plot!" (8/42) ... 220.00 725.00
52 ... 220.00 700.00
53-55 ... 200.00 650.00
56 "Design For Doom!" (1/43) ... 155.00 500.00
57 The Prankster in "Crime's Comedy King!" ... 155.00 500.00
58-63 ... 155.00 500.00
64 1st Toyman in "The Terrible Toyman" (9/43) ... 180.00 575.00
65 "Million-Dollar Marathon" ... 155.00 500.00
66-67 ... 155.00 500.00
68 (1/44) ... 140.00 450.00
69 The Prankster. ... 120.00 390.00
70 ... 120.00 390.00
71 "Valentine Villany" ... 120.00 390.00
72-73 ... 120.00 390.00
74 "The Courtship Of Adelbert Dribble" 120.00 390.00
75 "Aesop's Modern Fables" ... 120.00 390.00
76 ... 120.00 390.00
77 "Another Superman vs. Prankster Adventure" ... 120.00 390.00
78 "The Chef Of Bohemia" ... 120.00 390.00
79 ... 120.00 390.00
80 "Back By Popular Demand to Plague Superman! The Imp of Imps—Mr. Mxyztplk!" (1/45) ... 200.00 650.00
80A Special Edition-U.S. Navy giveaway. 200.00 650.00
81 ... 120.00 390.00
81A Special Edition-U.S. Navy giveaway. 120.00 390.00
82 ... 120.00 390.00
83 "Introducing Hocus and Pocus, Magicians By Accident!" ... 130.00 420.00
84 ... 120.00 390.00
84A Special Edition-U.S Navy giveaway. 120.00 390.00
85-87 ... 120.00 390.00
88 Hocus and Pocus. ... 120.00 390.00
89 "The King Of Color" ... 120.00 390.00
90-91 ... 120.00 390.00
92 (1/46) ... 110.00 350.00
93-94 ... 110.00 350.00
95 The Prankster in "The Laughing-Stock Of Metropolis!" (4/46) ... 110.00 350.00
96 ... 110.00 350.00
97 Hocus and Pocus. ... 110.00 350.00
98 ... 110.00 350.00
99 1st small Superman inset. ... 120.00 390.00
100 "The Sleuth Who Never Failed!" 200.00 650.00
101 "Superman Covers Atom Bomb Test! Atomic explosion cover. (10/46) ... 110.00 350.00
102 "Mr. Mxyztplk And His Wonderful Lamp!" ... 110.00 350.00
103 ... 110.00 350.00
104 "Superman vs. Prankster in Candytown, U.S.A." (1/47) ... 110.00 350.00
105 "His Lordship, Clark Kent" ... 100.00 320.00
106-108 ... 100.00 320.00
109 Superman vs. Prankster in "The Man Who Robbed The Mint!" ... 100.00 320.00
110 "The Mother Goose Crimes!" ... 100.00 320.00
111 "Cameras In The Clouds!" ... 100.00 320.00
112 Mr. Mxyztplk in "The Cross-Country Chess Crimes!" ... 100.00 320.00
113 "Just An Ordinary Guy?" ... 100.00 320.00
114 Superman in search of an honest man. ... 100.00 320.00
115 "The Wish That Came True!" ... 100.00 320.00
116 Wolfingham in "The Wizard Of Winter" (1/48) ... 90.00 290.00
117 "Featuring A Superman Christmas Adventure!" (2/48) ... 90.00 290.00
118 ... 90.00 290.00
119 "Clark Kent Tries To Become Superman For A Day!" ... 90.00 290.00
120 "Superman becomes Super Stuntman!" ... 90.00 290.00
121 "Superman Vs. Atlas!" ... 90.00 290.00
122 "The Super Sideshow!" ... 90.00 290.00
123 ... 90.00 290.00
124 "A Superman Of Doom!" ... 90.00 290.00
125 ... 90.00 290.00
126 "Superman On Television!" (11/48) ... 90.00 290.00
127 "Superman Meets Radio's Ralph Edwards in Truth Or Consequences!" Begin: Tommy Tomorrow. (12/48) ... 120.00 390.00
128 "The Adventure Of Little Red" (1/49) ... 90.00 290.00
129 "Lois Lane, Cavegirl!" ... 90.00 290.00
130 "Superman And The Mermaid" Movie tie-in starring Ann Blyth. (3/49) ... 90.00 290.00
131 "Luthor Makes Superman Vanish Into The 4th Dimension!" ... 90.00 290.00
132 ... 90.00 290.00
133 "The World's Most Perfect Girl" ... 90.00 290.00
134 "Superman Becomes A Super-Cowboy!" ... 90.00 290.00
135-136 ... 90.00 290.00
137 "Looks Like This Is A Job For Lois Lane!" ... 90.00 290.00
138-140 ... 90.00 290.00
141 "Luthor's Secret Weapon!" (2/50) 90.00 290.00
142 ... 90.00 290.00
143 "The Bride Of Superman" ... 90.00 290.00
144-147 ... 90.00 290.00
148 "Superman, Indian Chief!" ... 90.00 290.00
149 "The Courtship On Krypton!" ... 90.00 290.00
150 ... 90.00 290.00
151 "Luthor, The Prankster, and Mr. Mxyzptlk Declare War On The Man Of Steel!" ... 80.00 260.00
152 (1/51) ... 80.00 260.00
153 "The 100 Deaths Of Clark Kent!" 80.00 260.00
154 "Miss Robinson Crusoe" ... 80.00 260.00
155 "The Cover Girl Mystery!" ... 80.00 260.00
156 "The Girl Of Steel!" ... 80.00 260.00
157 "The Superman Who Couldn't Fly!" 80.00 260.00
158 "The Kid From Krypton!" Origin retold: Superman. (7/51) ... 80.00 260.00
159 "The Man Who Owned Superman!" 80.00 260.00
160 "Meet Superman's Aunt Minerva!" 80.00 260.00
161 "Exit Superman!" ... 80.00 260.00
162 "Superman Vs. It!" ... 80.00 260.00
163 "The Girl of Tomorrow" ... 80.00 260.00
164 "Superman's Hall Of Trophies!" (1/52) ... 80.00 260.00
165 "The Man Who Conquered Superman!" ... 80.00 260.00

ACE COMICS #102

ACTION COMICS #36

ACTION COMICS #44

ACTION COMICS #69

ACTION COMICS #78

ACTION COMICS #82

ACTION COMICS #141

ACTION COMICS #144

FAMOUS · FIRSTS

ACTION COMICS #252

After readers approved of a one-shot story featuring a "Supergirl," Kara Zor-El crash-lands on Earth and joins her cousin Superman. Her existence is kept secret as Superman's "secret weapon" until *Action* #285.

166 "The Three Scoops Of Death!"	80.00	260.00
167 "The Machines Of Crime!"	80.00	260.00
168 "The Menace From Planet Z!"	80.00	260.00
169 "Clark Kent, Caveman!"	80.00	260.00
170 "The Mad Artist Of Metropolis"	80.00	260.00
171 "The Secrets Of Superman!"	80.00	260.00
172 "Lois Lane, Witch!"	80.00	260.00
173 "Superman's Invulnerable Foe!"	80.00	260.00
174 "The Man Who Shackled Superman!"	80.00	260.00
175 "The Five Against Superman!"	80.00	260.00
176 "Muscles For Money!" (1/53)	80.00	260.00
177 "The Anti-Superman Weapon"	80.00	260.00
178 "The Sandman Of Crime!"	80.00	260.00
179 "Supermanor!"	80.00	260.00
180 "The Super Telethon!"	80.00	260.00
181 "The New Superman!"	80.00	260.00
182 "The Return Of Planet Krypton!"	80.00	260.00
183 "The Perfect Plot To Kill Superman!"	80.00	260.00
184 "The Covered Wagon Of Doom!"	80.00	260.00
185	80.00	260.00
186 "The Haunted Superman!"	80.00	260.00
187 "Superman's New Super-Powers!"	80.00	260.00
188 "The Spectral Superman!" (1/54)	80.00	260.00
189 "Clark Kent's New Father And Mother!"	80.00	260.00
190 "The Boy Who Saved Superman's Life!"	80.00	260.00
191 "Calling Doctor Superman!"	80.00	260.00
192 "The Man Who Sped Up Superman!"	80.00	260.00
193 "Beware Of Superman-Everything He Touches Turns To Gold!"	80.00	260.00
194 "The Return Of The Outlaws From Krypton!"	80.00	260.00
195 "Lois Lane—Wanted!"	80.00	260.00
196 "The Adventures Of Mental-Man!"	80.00	260.00
197 "The Stolen S-Shirts!"	80.00	260.00
198 "The Six Lives Of Lois Lane!" End: Vigilante.	80.00	260.00
199 "The Phantom Superman!"	80.00	260.00
200 "The Test Of A Warrior!" (1/55)	80.00	260.00
201 "The Challenge Of Stoneman!"	80.00	260.00
202 "Lois Lane's X-Ray Vision!" 1st Code Approved issue. (3/55)	80.00	260.00
203 "The International Daily Planet!"	55.00	175.00
204 "The Man Who Could Make Superman Do Anything!"	55.00	175.00
205 "Sergeant Superman!"	55.00	175.00
206 "Superman Marries Lois Lane!"	55.00	175.00
207 "The Four Superman Medals!"	55.00	175.00
208 "The Magic Of Mr. Mxyzptlk!"	55.00	175.00
209 "The Man Who Was Mightier Than Superman!"	55.00	175.00
210 "Welcome To Superman Land!"	55.00	175.00
211 "The Superman Spectaculars!"	55.00	175.00
212 "The Superman Calendar!" (1/56)	55.00	175.00
213 "Paul Paxton Alias Superman!"	55.00	175.00
214 (3/56)	55.00	175.00
215 "The Superman Of Tomorrow!"	55.00	175.00
216 "The Super-Menace Of Metropolis!"	55.00	175.00
217 "The Amazing Super-Baby!"	55.00	175.00
218 "The Super-Ape From Krypton!"	55.00	175.00
219 "Superman's Treasure Hoard!"	55.00	175.00
220 "The Inter-Planetary Olympics!"	55.00	175.00
221 "Superman's New Super-Power!"	55.00	175.00
222 "Duplicate Superman!"	55.00	175.00
223 "The First Superman Of Krypton!"	55.00	175.00
224 "The Secret Of Superman Island!" (1/57)	55.00	175.00
225 "The Death of Superman!"	55.00	175.00
226 "The Invulnerable Enemy!"	55.00	175.00
227 "The Man With Triple X-Ray Eyes!"	55.00	175.00
228 "Superman's Super-Skyscraper!"	55.00	175.00
229 "The Superman Satellite!"	55.00	175.00
230 "Superman Loses His Powers!"	55.00	175.00
231-234	55.00	175.00
235 "The Super-Prisoner Of Amazon Island!"	55.00	175.00
236 (1/58)	55.00	175.00
237-239	55.00	175.00
240 "The Superman Sphinx"	55.00	175.00
241 App: Batman.	65.00	200.00
242 1st & Origin: Brainiac in "The Super-Duel In Space!" (7/58)	260.00	850.00
243-244	35.00	110.00
245 "The Shrinking Superman" (10/58)	35.00	110.00
246-247	35.00	110.00
248 Congorilla. (1/59)	35.00	110.00
249	35.00	110.00
250 "The Eye Of Metropolis!"	35.00	110.00
251	35.00	110.00
252 1st & Origin: Supergirl in "The Supergirl From Krypton!" (5/59)	310.00	1000.00
253 "The War Between Jimmy Olsen And Superman!" 2nd: Supergirl.	65.00	200.00
254 1st: Bizarro in "The Battle With Bizarro!" (7/59)	70.00	225.00
255 1st: Bizarro Lois in "The Bride Of Bizarro!" (8/59)	40.00	125.00
256-260	23.00	75.00
261	26.00	85.00
262 App: Supergirl.	23.00	75.00
263 Origin: Bizarro World.	23.00	75.00
264-266	16.00	50.00
267 App: Legion, 1st: Chameleon Boy, Invisible Kid, Colossal Boy.	95.00	300.00
268-269	16.00	50.00
270 App: Batman.	16.00	50.00
271 App: Luthor.	16.00	50.00
272-274	16.00	50.00
275 App: Brainiac.	16.00	50.00
276 App: Legion.	40.00	125.00
277-282	16.00	50.00
283 Legion of Super-Villains.	31.00	100.00
284 App: Mon-El. 1st: 12 cent cover.	16.00	50.00
285 App: Supergirl.	16.00	50.00
286	8.00	25.00
287 App: Legion.	8.00	25.00
288 App: Mon-El.	8.00	25.00
289 App: Legion.	8.00	25.00
290 App: Legion, Phantom Girl.	8.00	25.00
291	7.00	20.00
292 Comet the Superhorse.	7.00	20.00
293 Origin: Comet (Superhorse).	17.00	55.00
294-295	7.00	20.00
296 (1/63)	7.00	20.00
297-299 App: Mon-El.	7.00	20.00
300	13.00	40.00
301-303	4.00	12.00
304 1st & Origin: Black Flame.	5.00	15.00
305-308	5.00	15.00
309 App: Legion, Batman.	7.00	20.00
310-313	5.00	15.00
314 App: Justice League.	5.00	15.00
315-320	5.00	15.00
321-333	2.75	10.00
334 80 Pg. Giant #G-20.	8.00	25.00
335-340	2.75	10.00
341-343	2.00	7.00
344 App: Batman.	2.00	7.00
345-346	2.00	7.00
347 80 Pg. Giant #G-33.	5.00	16.00
348-349	2.00	7.00
350 App: Batman.	2.00	7.00
351-359	2.00	7.00
360 80 Pg. Giant #G-45, app: Supergirl.	5.00	16.00
361-364	1.75	6.00
365 App: Legion.	1.75	6.00
366-369	1.75	6.00
370 New facts about Superman.	1.75	6.00
371-372	1.75	6.00
373 80 page Giant (#G-57), app: Supergirl.	5.00	16.00
374-375	1.75	6.00
376 End: Supergirl.	1.75	6.00
377 Begin: Legion Of Super Heroes.	1.75	6.00
378-383	1.75	6.00
384-391	1.50	5.00
392 End: Legion.	1.50	5.00
393-410	1.50	5.00
411 Origin: Eclipso.	1.75	6.00
412	1.25	4.00
413 Begin: Metamorpho.	1.25	4.00
414-417	1.25	4.00
418 End: Metamorpho.	1.25	4.00
419 1st Human Target.	1.75	6.00
420-424	1.25	4.00
425 Art: Neal Adams. Begin: Atom.	5.00	15.00
426-436	1.25	4.00
437 100 Page Giant.	2.25	8.00
438-439	1.25	4.00
440 1st Mike Grell art on Green Arrow.	1.75	6.00
441	1.50	5.00
442	1.00	3.00
443 100 Page Giant.	2.25	8.00
444-499	1.00	3.00
500 Superman life story.	1.25	4.00
501-551	.75	2.00

552-553 App: Animal Man. 1.75 6.00
554 1.00 3.00
555-582 .75 2.00
583 Alan Moore. 1.75 6.00
584 1.00 3.00
585-597 .75 2.00
598 1st: Checkmate. 1.00 3.00
599 .75 2.00
600 50th Anniversary issue. 2.00 7.00
601-644 .50 1.75
645 1st: Maxima. 1.00 3.00
646-659 .50 1.75
660 Death: Lex Luthor. 1.25 4.00
661 .50 1.75
662 1.00 3.00
663-666 .50 1.50
667 Giant size. .50 1.50
668-670 .50 1.50
671 1st: Lex Luthor II. .50 1.50
672-678 .50 1.50
679-682 .50 1.25
683 Cameo: Doomsday 1.00 3.00
684 Doomsday, pt. 4. 1.00 3.00
685 Funeral For A Friend, pt. 2. 1.00 3.00
686 Funeral For A Friend, pt. 6. .75 2.00
687 Deluxe edition. Reign Of The Supermen, pt. 1. .75 2.50
687A Newstand edition. .50 1.50
688 Reign Of The Supermen, pt. 5. .75 2.50
689 Reign Of The Supermen, pt. 9. Return: real Superman. .75 2.00
690-691 Reign, pt. 13. .75 2.00
692-699 .50 1.50
700 Double size. .75 2.50
701-709 .50 1.50
710-711 .75 2.00
712-713 .50 1.95

ACTION COMICS ANNUAL
DC (1987-CURRENT)
1 Art: Art Adams. 2.00 7.00
2 .75 2.50
3 .75 2.00
4 App: Eclipso. .75 2.50
5 .75 2.50
6 Elseworlds story. (1994) .75 2.95

ACTION COMICS THEATRE GIVEAWAY
DC (1947)
NO# "Free Souvenir Edition" 32 pages "In Honor Of Columbia's Thrilling New Movie Serial 'The Vigilante'." 600.00 2000.00

ACTUAL CONFESSIONS
MARVEL(ATLAS) (1952)
13-14 7.00 20.00

ACTUAL ROMANCES
MARVEL (1949-1950)
1 10.00 30.00
2 7.00 20.00

ADAM STRANGE
DC (MINI-SERIES) (1990)
1-3 1.25 4.00

ADAM-12
GOLD KEY (1973-1976)
1 TV tie-in with photo covers on all issues. 7.00 20.00
2 4.00 12.00
3-10 2.75 10.00

ADDAMS FAMILY
GOLD KEY (1974-1975)
1 Hanna-Barbera TV cartoon. 12.00 38.00
2 9.00 27.00
3 7.00 22.00

ADLAI STEVENSON
DELL (1966)
1 Dell Giant. Photo cover, biography. 10.00 30.00

ADOLESCENT RADIOACTIVE BLACK BELT HAMSTERS
ECLIPSE (1986-1989)
1 .75 2.00
2-9 .30 1.00

ADVANCED DUNGEONS AND DRAGONS
DC (1988-1990)
1-ANNUAL 1 1.00 3.00
2-6 .75 2.00
7-36 .30 1.00

ADVENTURE BOUND
DELL FOUR COLOR SERIES (1949)
239 (8/49) 10.00 30.00

ADVENTURE COMICS
DC (1938-1983)
32 Previous title: New Adventure Comics. 400.00 1500.00
33-39 300.00 975.00
40 "Starting this issue: The daring exploits of The Sandman!" Begin: Sandman. (7/39) This Sandman story was intended to be the 1st appearance and introduction, but the 1939 New York World's Fair issue was released first. 8800.00 35000.00
41 Sandman story. 700.00 2600.00
42 Sandman cover & story. 900.00 3200.00
43 Sandman story. 700.00 2600.00
44 Sandman cover & story. 900.00 3200.00
45 400.00 1500.00
46-47 Sandman cover & story. 900.00 3200.00
48 "Introducing In This Issue: The Hour-Man!" (3/40) 1st: Hour-Man. 5100.00 20000.00
49 400.00 1300.00
50 Hour-Man cover. 400.00 1300.00
51 Sandman cover & story. 500.00 1900.00
52 Hour-Man cover and story. 310.00 1000.00
53 "The Hour-Man Presents Minute Man Martin and the Minute Men of America!" (8/40) 310.00 1000.00
54 Hour-Man cover. 310.00 1000.00
55-56 Hour-Man cover. 300.00 975.00
57-59 Hour-Man. 300.00 975.00
60 Sandman cover & story. 500.00 1900.00
61 1st: Starman. (4/41) 2100.00 8000.00
62-65 310.00 1000.00
66 1st & Origin: Shining Knight. (7/41) 400.00 1500.00
67-68 300.00 975.00
69 1st Sandy. 400.00 1300.00
70 (1/42) 280.00 900.00
71 1st Miracle Ray. 310.00 1000.00
72 1st Sandman by Simon & Kirby. (3/42) 1900.00 7500.00
73 Begin & Origin: Manhunter. 2400.00 9500.00
74 400.00 1500.00
75 Sandman in "Villain For Valhalla!" 400.00 1300.00
76-78 400.00 1300.00
79 "Manhunter Stalks Nazi Raiders in Cobras Of The Deep!" 400.00 1300.00
80 Last Manhunter by Simon & Kirby. 300.00 1100.00
81 310.00 1000.00
82 (1/43) 310.00 1000.00
83 310.00 1000.00
84 280.00 900.00
85 "Sandman invades The Amazing Dreams Of Gentleman Jack!" 280.00 900.00
86-90 280.00 900.00
91 Last Sandman by Simon & Kirby. 280.00 900.00
92 Last Manhunter. 200.00 650.00
93 Sandman in "Sleep For Sale" 155.00 500.00
94-97 155.00 500.00
98 Sandman in "Hero Of Dreams" 155.00 500.00
99 155.00 500.00
100 280.00 900.00
101 155.00 500.00
102 Last Sandman, Starman. 180.00 575.00
103 "Now starring Superboy and featuring Green Arrow, Johnny Quick, Shining Knight, Aquaman!" (4/46) 700.00 2600.00
104 310.00 1000.00
105-108 200.00 650.00
109-111 155.00 500.00
112 (1/47) 155.00 500.00
113-118 130.00 420.00
119 "Superboy Meets Girl!" 130.00 420.00
120 130.00 420.00
121 "Stamps! Coins! Autographs! Superboy Collects Them All in The Great Hobby Contest!" (10/47) 130.00 420.00
122 "Superboy-Super-Magician" 130.00 420.00
123 "Tug Of War—Superboy Vs. Jumbo" 130.00 420.00
124 (1/48) 130.00 420.00
125 130.00 420.00
126 120.00 390.00
127 "Super-Bellboy" 120.00 390.00
128 "How Clark Kent Met Lois Lane!" (5/48) 140.00 450.00
129-130 120.00 390.00
131 "The Million Dollar Athlete" 120.00 390.00
132 "Super Cowboy!" 120.00 390.00
133 "Superboy's Report Card" 120.00 390.00
134-135 120.00 390.00
136 (1/49) 120.00 390.00
137 "The Treasure Of Tondimo" 120.00 390.00
138 "Superboy Tours Around The World In 80 Minutes" 120.00 390.00
139 120.00 390.00
140 "Six Superboys On The Moon" 120.00 390.00
141 "Superboy Without His Super-Powers!" 100.00 320.00
142 Origin retold: Shining Knight. 120.00 390.00
143-147 100.00 320.00
148 (1/50) 100.00 320.00
149 100.00 320.00
150-151 Frazetta. 120.00 390.00
152 "Superboy Hunts For A Job" 100.00 320.00
153 Frazetta. 120.00 390.00
154 100.00 320.00
155 Frazetta. 120.00 390.00
156 100.00 320.00
157 "The Worst Boy In Smallville!" Frazetta art on Shining Knight story. 120.00 390.00
158 100.00 320.00
159 "Superboy, Millionaire" Frazetta art on Shining Knight story. 120.00 390.00
160 (1/51) 100.00 320.00
161 Frazetta. 120.00 390.00
162 "The Super-Coach Of Smallville High!" 100.00 320.00
163 "Superboy's Phoney Father!" Frazetta art on Shining Knight story. (4/51) 120.00 390.00
164 "Superboy Discovers The Secrets Of A Lost Indian Tribe!" 100.00 320.00
165 "Superboy's School For Stunment!" 100.00 320.00
166 "The Town That Stole Superboy!" End: Shining Knight. 100.00 320.00
167 "Lana Lang, Super-Girl" (8/51) 80.00 260.00
168 "The Boy Who Outsmarted Superboy!" 80.00 260.00
169 "Clark Kent's Private Butler" 70.00 230.00
170 "Lana Lang's Big Crush!" 70.00 230.00
171 "Superboy's Toughest Tasks!" 70.00 230.00
172 "The Laws That Backfired!" (1/52) 70.00 230.00
173 "Superboy's School Of Hard Knocks!" 70.00 230.00
174 "The New Lana Lang!" 70.00 230.00
175 "The Duel Of The Superboys!" 70.00 230.00
176 "Superboy's New Parents!" 70.00 230.00
177 "Superboy Against Ben Hur in The Hot-Rod Chariot Race!" 70.00 230.00
178 "The Boy In The Lead Mask!" 70.00 230.00
179 "The World's Whackiest Inventors!" 70.00 230.00
180 "The Grand Prize Of The Underworld!" 70.00 230.00
181 "Mask For A Hero!" 70.00 230.00
182 "The Super-Hick From Smallville!" 70.00 230.00
183 "Superboy And Cleopatra!" 70.00 230.00
184 "The Shutterbugs Of Smallville!" (1/53) 70.00 230.00
185 "The Mythical Monsters!" 70.00 230.00
186 70.00 230.00
187 "The 25th Century Superboy!" 70.00 230.00
188 "The Bullfighter From Smallville!" 70.00 230.00
189 "The Girl of Steel!" 70.00 230.00
190 70.00 230.00
191 "The Two Clark Kents!" 70.00 230.00
192 "The Coronation of Queen Lana Lang!" 70.00 230.00
193 "Superboy's Lost Costume" 70.00 230.00
194 "The Super-Charged Superboy!" 70.00 230.00
195 "Lana Lang's Romance On Mars!" 70.00 230.00
196 "Superboy Vs. Kingorilla!" (1/54) 70.00 230.00
197 "Superboy Battles Juvenile Gangs!" 70.00 230.00
198 "The Super-Carnival From Space!" 70.00 230.00
199 "Superboy Meets Superlad!" 70.00 230.00
200 "Superboy And The Apes!" 130.00 420.00
201 "Safari In Smallville!" 90.00 290.00
202 "Superboy City, U.S.A." 90.00 290.00
203 "Uncle Superboy!" 90.00 290.00
204 "The Super-Brat Of Smallville!" 90.00 290.00
205 "The Journey Of The Second Superboy!" 90.00 290.00
206 "The Impossible Creatures!" 90.00 290.00
207 "Smallville's Worst Athlete!" 90.00 290.00
208 "The Rip Van Winkle Of Smallville!" (1/55) 90.00 290.00
209 "Superboy Week!" 90.00 290.00
210 1st: Krypto in "The Superdog From Krypton!" (3/55) 600.00 2350.00
211 "Superboy's Most Amazing Dream!" 70.00 225.00
212 "Superboy's Robot Twin!" 70.00 225.00
213 "The Junior Jury Of Smallville!" 70.00 225.00
214 2nd: Krypto in "The Dog Of Steel!" (7/55) 155.00 520.00
215 "The Super-Hobby Of Superboy!" 55.00 175.00
216 "The Wizard City!" 55.00 175.00
217 "Superboy's Farewell To Smallville!" 55.00 175.00
218 "The Two Worlds Of Superboy!" 55.00 175.00
219 "The Gorilla With X-Ray Eyes!" 55.00 175.00
220 3rd: Krypto in "The Greatest Show On Earth!" (1/56) 55.00 175.00
221 "The Babe Of Steel!" 55.00 175.00
222 "Superboy's Repeat Performances!" 55.00 175.00
223 "Superboy as Hercules Junior!" 55.00 175.00
224 "Pa Kent, Superman!" 55.00 175.00
225 "The Bird With Super-Powers!" 55.00 175.00
226 "Superboy's Super-Rival!" 55.00 175.00
227 "The Good Samaritan Of Smallville!" 55.00 175.00
228 "Clark Kent's Bodyguard!" 55.00 175.00
229 "The End Of The Kent Family!" 55.00 175.00
230 "The Secret Of The Flying Horse!" 55.00 175.00
231 "The Super-Feats Of Super-Baby!" 55.00 175.00
232 "The House Where Superboy Was Born!" (1/57) 55.00 175.00

ACTION COMICS #358

ACTION COMICS #397

ADAM STRANGE #1

ADVENTURE COMICS #45

ADVENTURE COMICS #239

ADVENTURE COMICS #270

ADVENTURE INTO MYSTERY #2

ADVENTURES INTO DARKNESS #5

233 "Joe Smith, Man Of Steel!" 55.00 175.00
234 "The 1001 Rides Of Superboy!" 55.00 175.00
235 "The Confession Of Superboy!" ... 55.00 175.00
236 "Clark Kent's Super-Dad!" 55.00 175.00
237 "The Robot War Of Smallville!" ... 50.00 150.00
238 "The Secret Past Of Superboy's Father!" 50.00 150.00
239 Krypto in "The Super-Tricks Of The Dog Of Steel!" 50.00 150.00
240 "The Super-Teacher From Krypton!" 50.00 150.00
241 "The Super-Outlaw Of Smallville!" 50.00 150.00
242 "The Kid From Krypton!" 50.00 150.00
243 "The Super-Toys From Krypton!" 50.00 150.00
244 "The Poorest Family In Smallville!" (1/58) 50.00 150.00
245 "The Mystery Of Monster X" ... 50.00 150.00
246 "The Girl Who Trapped Superboy!" 50.00 150.00
247 1st & Origin: Legion in "The Legion Of Super-Heroes!" (4/58). 1000.00 3700.00
248 App: Green Arrow. 35.00 110.00
249 "Superboy's Lost Costume!" App: Green Arrow 35.00 110.00
250 "The Hunter From The Future!" App: Green Arrow 35.00 110.00
251 "Superboy's Last Day!" App: Green Arrow. 35.00 110.00
252 "The Super-Sentry Of Smallville!" App: Green Arrow 35.00 110.00
253 "Superboy Meets Robin!" (10/58) 50.00 150.00
254 "I Was A Teen-Age Superboy!" App: Green Arrow. 31.00 100.00
255 "The Splitting Of Superboy!" App: Green Arrow 31.00 100.00
256 "The Kryptonite Dragnet!" Origin retold: Green Arrow. (1/59) 140.00 450.00
257 "Superboy Meets The First Two Super-Men!" App: Green Arrow, Aquaman. 31.00 100.00
258 "Superboy Meets The Young Green Arrow!" App: Green Arrow, Aquaman. 31.00 100.00
259 "The Blind Boy Of Steel!" 28.00 90.00
260 "The Kent's Second Super-Son!" also Origin retold: Aquaman in "How Aquaman Got His Powers!" (5/59) 155.00 500.00
261 "Lois Lane Meets Superboy!" App: Green Arrow, Aquaman. 22.00 70.00
262 "The Colossal Super-Dog!" also 1st & Origin: Speedy in "How Green Arrow Met Speedy!" 28.00 90.00
263 "The Great Superboy Double-Cross!" 22.00 70.00
264 "The Helpless Hero!" 22.00 70.00
265 "The First Superman Robot!" ... 22.00 70.00
266 "The Super-Pranks Of Superdog!" 22.00 70.00
267 "Prisoner Of The Super-Heroes!" 2nd: Legion Of Super Heroes. 190.00 600.00
268 "The Week Clark Kent Lost His Memory!" (1/60) 22.00 70.00
269 "Superdog's Mean Master!" also 1st & Origin: Aqualad. "Aquaman Teams Up With Aqua-Boy!" (2/60) 50.00 160.00
270 "The Stolen Identities!" Begin: Congorilla. 22.00 70.00
271 ...... 50.00 150.00
272-274 ...... 16.00 50.00
275 "The Origin Of The Superman-Batman Team!" (8/60) 40.00 130.00
276-281 ...... 16.00 50.00
282 Origin: Star Boy. 40.00 125.00
283 1st: Phantom Zone. 29.00 95.00
284 App: Aquaman. 16.00 50.00
285 1st: Bizarro World. 28.00 90.00
286 1st: Bizarro Mr. Mxyzptlk. 28.00 90.00
287 1st: Bizarro Jimmy Olsen, Perry White. 17.00 55.00
288-289 ...... 16.00 50.00
290 1st & Origin: Sun Boy. "The Secret Of The Seventh Super-Hero!" 35.00 110.00
291 1st 12 cent cover price. 11.00 35.00
292 1st: Bizarro Lana Lang, Lucy Lane. 13.00 40.00
293 1st: Bizarro Luthor, app: Mon-El. 22.00 70.00
294 1st: Bizarro Marilyn Monroe, John F. Kennedy. 22.00 70.00
295-298 ...... 11.00 35.00
299 1st: Gold Kryptonite. 13.00 40.00
300 Begin: "Tales Of The Legion Of Super-Heroes!" 100.00 325.00
301 1st & Origin: Bouncing Boy. 28.00 90.00
302-305 ...... 19.00 60.00
306 1st: Legion Of Substitute Heroes. 16.00 50.00
307 1st: Element Lad. "The Secret Power Of The Mystery Super-Hero!" 16.00 50.00
308 1st: Lightning Lass. "The Strange Return Of Lightning Lad!" 16.00 50.00
309-310 App: Legion. 16.00 50.00
311-315 ...... 11.00 35.00
316 Origins retold: All members of the Legion Of Super-Heroes. 11.00 35.00
317-320 ...... 11.00 35.00
321 1st: Time Trapper. 11.00 35.00
322-326 ...... 8.00 25.00
327 1st & Origin: Lone Wolf. 8.00 25.00
328-330 ...... 8.00 25.00
331-340 ...... 7.00 20.00
341 ...... 5.00 15.00
342-345 ...... 4.00 12.00
346 1st: Karate Kid, Ferro Lad, Projectra. 4.00 12.00
347-351 ...... 4.00 11.00
352 ...... 2.75 10.00
353 Death: Ferro Lad, Sun-Eater. 4.00 13.00
354-360 ...... 2.50 9.00
361-364 ...... 2.00 7.00
365 1st: Shadow Lass. 2.25 8.00
366-370 ...... 2.00 7.00
371 ...... 2.25 8.00
372 ...... 2.00 7.00
373-374 ...... 1.75 6.00
375 ...... 2.00 7.00
376-380 ...... 1.50 5.00
381 Begin: Supergirl. 1.25 4.00
382-389 ...... 1.00 3.00
390 80 pg. Giant #G-69. ...... 4.00 12.00
391-399 ...... 1.00 3.00
400 35th anniversary issue. 1.00 3.50
401-402 ...... 1.00 3.00
403 80 Pg. Giant #G-81. ...... 4.00 12.00
404-411 ...... .75 2.00
412 App: Animal Man. 1.75 6.00
413 App: Hawkman. ...... .75 2.00
414-415 App: Animal Man. 1.00 3.00
416 DC 100 Page Super Spectacular #10. 1.50 5.50
417-419 ...... .75 2.00
420-421 App: Animal Man. 1.25 4.00
422-424 ...... .75 2.00
425 Begin: New Look. ...... .75 2.00
426 ...... .75 2.00
427 1st: Black Canary. ...... .75 2.00
428 App: Black Canary. 2.75 10.00
429 App: Black Canary. 1.75 6.00
430 App: Black Canary. ...... .50 1.50
431 Begin: Spectre. ...... .50 1.50
432-439 ...... .50 1.50
440 New Origin: Spectre. ...... .50 1.50
441-460 ...... .50 1.50
461 Begin: Justice Society Of America, app: Earth-2 Batman. 1.75 6.00
462 Death: Earth-2 Batman. 1.75 6.00
463-466 ...... .50 1.50
467 Starman by Steve Ditko. ...... .50 1.50
468 ...... .50 1.50
469-470 Origin: Starman. ...... .50 1.50
471-478 ...... .50 1.50
479 Begin: Dial H For Hero. ...... .50 1.50
480-489 ...... .50 1.50
490 End: Dial H For Hero. ...... .50 1.50
491 Begin: 100 Pg. Digest Size. ...... .50 1.50
492-503 ...... .50 1.50

ADVENTURE ILLUSTRATED

NEW MEDIA (1981) MAGAZINE

1-2 ...... .75 2.95

ADVENTURE INTO FEAR

MARVEL (1972-1975)

10 Begin: Man-Thing. Previous title: Fear. 2.25 8.00
11-12 ...... 1.00 3.50
13-18 ...... .75 2.25
19 1st: Howard The Duck. End: Man-Thing. 5.00 15.00
20 Begin: Morbius..The Living Vampire. 5.00 14.00
21-22 ...... 2.00 7.00
23-30 ...... 1.50 5.00
31 End: Morbius. 1.50 5.00

ADVENTURE INTO MYSTERY

MARVEL(ATLAS) (1956-1957)

1 Art: Bob Powell. 55.00 180.00
2 ...... 28.00 90.00
3 ...... 23.00 75.00
4 Art: Williamson & Powell. 28.00 90.00
5-8 ...... 19.00 60.00

ADVENTURE IS MY CAREER

STREET & SMITH (1944)

NO# 40.00 125.00

ADVENTURERS, THE

AIRCEL (1986-1987)

1 ...... .75 2.00
2-10 ...... .50 1.50

ADVENTURES

SEE ADVENTURES IN ROMANCE #1, SPECTACULAR ADVENTURES #2

-

ADVENTURES IN 3-D

HARVEY (1953-1954)

1 Art: Bob Powell. 35.00 110.00
1A Giveaway with Odell's Hair Trainer. 40.00 130.00
2 Art: Bob Powell. 25.00 80.00

ADVENTURES IN PARADISE

DELL FOUR COLOR SERIES (1962)

1301 (2/62) 13.00 40.00

ADVENTURES IN ROMANCE

ST. JOHN (1949)

1 Title changes to Spectacular Adventures #2. ...... 40.00 125.00

ADVENTURES IN WONDERLAND

JR. READERS GUILD (1955-1956)

1 ...... 13.00 40.00
2-5 ...... 10.00 30.00

ADVENTURES INSIDE THE ATOM

GIVEAWAY (1948)

NO# Stamped "American Museum Of Atomic Energy, Oak Ridge, Tennessee." 13.00 40.00

ADVENTURES INTO DARKNESS

STANDARD (1952-1954)

5 ...... 40.00 120.00
6-12 ...... 22.00 70.00
13 Cannibalism. 28.00 90.00
14 ...... 22.00 70.00

ADVENTURES INTO TERROR

MARVEL(ATLAS) (1950-1954)

1 (#43) 80.00 250.00
2 (#44) 50.00 160.00
3 ...... 40.00 120.00
4 ...... 31.00 100.00
5 Cover: Wolverton. 40.00 120.00
6 ...... 28.00 90.00
7 "Where Monsters Dwell!" by Wolverton. 85.00 280.00
8 ...... 28.00 90.00
9-10 Art: Krigstein. 28.00 90.00
11 ...... 19.00 60.00
12 Art: Krigstein. 28.00 90.00
13-24 ...... 19.00 60.00
25 Art: Matt Fox. 28.00 90.00
26-31 ...... 16.00 50.00

ADVENTURES INTO THE UNKNOWN

ACG (1948-1967)

1 ...... 250.00 825.00
2 ...... 130.00 420.00
3 Art: Feldstein. 110.00 360.00
4-6 ...... 95.00 300.00
7-8 ...... 75.00 240.00
9-10 ...... 55.00 180.00
11 ...... 40.00 120.00
12 ...... 28.00 90.00
13 Giant Tyrannosaurus cover. Lead story: "The Vampire Swoops" (10-11/50). 28.00 90.00
14-26 ...... 28.00 90.00
27 Art: Williamson/Krenkel. 45.00 140.00
28-40 ...... 19.00 60.00
41-50 ...... 15.00 48.00
51 Begin: 3-D effect. 50.00 150.00
52-57 ...... 50.00 150.00
58 End: 3-D effect. 50.00 150.00
59 ...... 19.00 60.00
60-61 ...... 15.00 48.00
62 1st Code Approved issue. 19.00 60.00
63-75 ...... 11.00 36.00
76-99 ...... 10.00 30.00
100 ...... 13.00 42.00
101-128 ...... 8.00 24.00
129 1st 12 cent cover price. 8.00 24.00
130-153 ...... 6.00 18.00
154 Origin: Nemesis. 8.00 24.00
155 Begin: Nemesis. 6.00 18.00
156-167 ...... 5.00 14.00
168 Art: Steve Ditko. 8.00 24.00
169 ...... 5.00 14.00
170 End: Nemesis. 5.00 14.00
171-174 ...... 4.00 12.00

ADVENTURES INTO WEIRD WORLDS

MARVEL(ATLAS) (1952-1954)

1 ...... 80.00 250.00
2 ...... 50.00 150.00
3-4 ...... 45.00 140.00
5 ...... 50.00 150.00
6 ...... 40.00 120.00
7 ...... 50.00 150.00
8-12 ...... 40.00 120.00
13-24 ...... 28.00 90.00
25-26 ...... 19.00 60.00
27 "The Dwarf Of Horrormoor!" Classic cover 40.00 120.00
28-30 ...... 19.00 60.00

ADVENTURES OF AARON

CHIASMUS (1994)

1 ...... .75 2.50

ADVENTURES OF ALAN LADD
DC (1949-1951)
1 Begin photo covers. 135.00 440.00
2 .... 70.00 220.00
3-5 .... 50.00 160.00
6 End photo covers. 50.00 160.00
7-9 .... 40.00 130.00

ADVENTURES OF ALICE, THE
CIVIL SERVICE (1945-1946)
1 ...In Wonderland. 16.00 50.00
2 ...Through The Magic Looking Glass. 11.00 35.00
3 ...At Monkey Island. 11.00 35.00

ADVENTURES OF BIG BOY, THE (GIVEAWAY)
MARVEL(TIMELY) (1956-CURRENT)
1 Two cover versions exist (different Big Boy on each, same background). 80.00 250.00
2 .... 40.00 125.00
3-6 .... 13.00 40.00
7-12 .... 8.00 25.00
13-24 .... 5.00 15.00
25-50 .... 2.75 10.00
51-100 .... 1.75 6.00
101-150 .... 1.00 3.00
151-200 .... .50 1.50
201-300 .... .20 .75
301-425 .... .20 .40

ADVENTURES OF BOB HOPE
DC (1950-1968)
1 Begin photo covers. 280.00 900.00
2-3 .... 140.00 460.00
4 End photo covers. 140.00 460.00
5-6 .... 70.00 230.00
7-12 .... 45.00 140.00
13-31 .... 26.00 85.00
32 1st Code Approved issue. 20.00 65.00
33-50 .... 17.00 55.00
51-75 .... 11.00 34.00
76-94 .... 7.00 23.00
95 1st: Monster issue. 7.00 23.00
96-100 .... 7.00 23.00
101-105 .... 4.00 11.00
106-109 Neal Adams. 13.00 40.00

ADVENTURES OF CAPTAIN AMERICA
MARVEL (1991-1992)
1-4 .... 1.25 4.95

ADVENTURES OF CHRISSIE CLAUS
HEROIC (1991)
1-2 .... .50 1.50

ADVENTURES OF CYCLOPS AND PHOENIX
MARVEL (1994)
1-4 .... 1.25 4.00

ADVENTURES OF DEAN MARTIN & JERRY LEWIS
DC (1952-1957)
1 .... 180.00 575.00
2 .... 105.00 340.00
3-6 .... 55.00 170.00
7-12 .... 35.00 110.00
13-19 .... 25.00 80.00
20 1st Code Approved issue. 20.00 65.00
21-24 .... 17.00 55.00
25-30 .... 14.00 46.00
31-36 .... 13.00 40.00
37-39 .... 11.00 34.00
40 With #41 changes to Adventures Of Jerry Lewis. 11.00 34.00

ADVENTURES OF HOMER COBB, THE
SBP (1947)
1 .... 31.00 100.00

ADVENTURES OF HOMER GHOST
MARVEL(ATLAS) (1957)
1 .... 11.00 36.00
2 .... 8.00 24.00

ADVENTURES OF JERRY LEWIS
DC (1957-1971)
41 Previous title: Adventures Of Dean Martin & Jerry Lewis. 9.00 28.00
42-50 .... 9.00 28.00
51-67 .... 7.00 23.00
68 Photo cover. 10.00 32.00
69-73 .... 7.00 23.00
74 Photo cover. 10.00 32.00
75 .... 7.00 23.00
76-91 .... 6.00 17.00
92 App: Superman. 7.00 23.00
93-96 .... 6.00 17.00
97 Batman & Joker cover and story. ... 11.00 34.00
98-100 .... 6.00 17.00
101 Neal Adams. 7.00 23.00
102 App: The Beatles. 9.00 28.00
103-104 Neal Adams. 7.00 23.00
105 App: Superman. 9.00 28.00
106-111 .... 4.00 11.00
112 App: Flash. 7.00 23.00
113-116 .... 2.50 9.00
117 App: Wonder Woman. 4.00 11.00
118-124 .... 2.50 9.00

ADVENTURES OF JESUS (UNDERGROUND)
GILBERT SHELTON (1962)
1 Art: Gilbert Shelton, Frank Stack. 1st Underground comic. 14 pages,stapled, white photocopies. ... 800.00 3000.00

ADVENTURES OF LITTLE ORPHAN ANNIE COMICS, THE
GIVEAWAY (1940-1942)
1 Orphan Annie And The Kidnappers. ... 7.00 20.00
2 Orphan Annie And The Rescue. 7.00 20.00
3 Orphan Annie And Mr. Gudge. 7.00 20.00

ADVENTURES OF MANUEL PACIFICO, TUNA FISHERMAN
GIVEAWAY (1951)
1 .... 7.00 20.00

ADVENTURES OF MIGHTY MOUSE
ST. JOHN (1951-1955)
1 "The Visitor From Outer Space". ... 55.00 180.00
2 .... 40.00 120.00
3-6 .... 28.00 90.00
7-12 .... 22.00 70.00
13-18 .... 16.00 50.00

ADVENTURES OF MIGHTY MOUSE
ST. JOHN/PINES/DELL/GOLD KEY (1955-1963)
126 Previous Title: Paul Terry's Comics. 6.00 18.00
127-128 .... 5.00 14.00
129 Begin Pines publishing. 5.00 14.00
130-143 .... 5.00 14.00
144 Begin Dell publishing. 4.00 12.00
145-155 .... 4.00 12.00
156 Begin Gold Key publishing. 2.50 9.50
157-160 .... 2.50 9.50

ADVENTURES OF OZZIE AND HARRIET, THE
DC (1949-1950)
1 TV tie-in. 135.00 440.00
2 .... 85.00 270.00
3-5 .... 70.00 220.00

ADVENTURES OF PATORUZU, THE
GREEN (1946)
NO# 8.00 25.00

ADVENTURES OF PINKY LEE, THE
MARVEL(ATLAS) (1955)
1 TV tie-in. 55.00 180.00
2 .... 40.00 120.00

ADVENTURES OF PIPSQUEAK, THE
ARCHIE (1959-1960)
34 Previous title: Pat The Brat. 7.00 20.00
35-39 .... 5.00 15.00

ADVENTURES OF REX THE WONDER DOG
DC (1952-1959)
1 (1-2/52) 270.00 875.00
2 "Outwits The King Of Beasts On Peril Island!" 155.00 500.00
3 .... 115.00 370.00
4 "The Battle Of Suicide Forest!" ... 115.00 370.00
5 "Wanted, One P.O.W.!" 80.00 250.00
6 "Rex The Ghost Fighter!" 80.00 250.00
7 "Battle Trail!" (1-2/53) 55.00 180.00
8 "Island Fortress!" 55.00 180.00
9 .... 55.00 180.00
10 "The Secret Of The Lost River!" ... 55.00 180.00
11 "Rex-Dinosaur Destroyer!" Dinosaur cover. 55.00 180.00
12 "The Terror Of Tornado Town!" ... 55.00 180.00
13 "African Man Hunt!" (1-2/54) ... 40.00 120.00
14 "The Eagle Hunter!" 40.00 120.00
15 "The Frozen Terror!" 40.00 120.00
16 "The Floating Big Top!" 40.00 120.00
17 "Sir Rex, Four-Footed Knight!" ... 40.00 120.00
18 "The Secret Of The Vanishing Island!" 40.00 120.00
19 "The Gold Stampede!" 28.00 90.00
20 1st Code Approved issue. 40.00 120.00
21-30 .... 28.00 90.00
31-46 .... 19.00 60.00

ADVENTURES OF ROBIN HOOD, THE
GOLD KEY (1974-1975)
1 (#90291-403) Disney cartoon tie-in. 1.00 3.00
2-7 .... 1.00 3.00

ADVENTURES OF ROBIN HOOD
ME (1957)
6 Previous title: Robin Hood. Richard Greene TV photo cover. 19.00 60.00
7 Richard Greene TV photo cover. 19.00 60.00
8 Richard Greene TV photo cover. 16.00 50.00

ADVENTURES OF SLIM AND SPUD
PRAIRIE FARMER (1924)
1924 Measures 9-3/4" x 4". Cardboard cover, strip reprint book. 31.00 100.00

ADVENTURES OF SUPERBOY
SEE SUPERBOY

ADVENTURES OF SUPERMAN
DC (1987-CURRENT)
0 .... .75 2.00
424 Previous title: Superman. .... .75 2.00
425-435 .... .50 1.50
436 Begin: John Byrne art. .... .50 1.50
437-454 .... .50 1.50
455 1st Eradicator. 1.25 4.00
456-462 .... .50 1.50
463 Superman/Flash race. .... .75 2.50
464 App: Lobo. 1.25 4.00
465 .... .50 1.50
466 1st Cyborg Superman. 1.50 5.00
467-495 .... .50 1.50
496 Doomsday. 1.00 3.00
497 Doomsday Battle. 1.50 5.00
498 Funeral For A Friend, pt. 1. ...... 1.25 4.00
499 Funeral For A Friend, pt. 5. ...... .75 2.50
500 1st new Supermen. 1.00 3.50
500A Newsstand edition. .... .75 2.50
500B Platinum edition. 7.00 20.00
501 Reign Of The Supermen, pt. 4. ... .75 2.50
501A Newstand edition. .... .50 1.50
502-504 .... .75 2.00
505 Holographic foil cover. 1.00 3.00
505A Newstand edition. .... .75 2.00
506-523 .... .75 2.00
524-525 .... .75 2.00
526-527 .... .75 2.00

ADVENTURES OF SUPERMAN ANNUAL
DC (1987-CURRENT)
1 .... .75 2.50
2 App: Lobo. 1.50 5.00
3 .... .75 2.00
4-5 .... .75 2.50
6 Elseworlds story. (1994) .... .75 2.95
7 .... 1.00 3.95

ADVENTURES OF THE DOVER BOYS
ARCHIE (1950)
1 .... 11.00 35.00
2 .... 10.00 30.00

ADVENTURES OF THE FLY
RADIO(ARCHIE) (1959-1965)
1 Origin: The Fly (8/59). "The Fly Battles Spider Spry!" by Simon/Kirby (came out 3 years before Amazing Fantasy #15) 115.00 380.00
2 Art: Simon & Kirby. 70.00 220.00
3 Origin retold. Art: Powell. 40.00 130.00
4 .... 29.00 95.00
5-6 .... 20.00 65.00
7 1st: Black Hood (Silver Age). 20.00 65.00
8 1st: The Hood (Silver Age). 20.00 65.00
9-12 .... 20.00 65.00
13 .... 14.00 44.00
14 1st & Origin: Fly Girl. 20.00 65.00
15-16 .... 13.00 40.00
17 1st 12 cent cover price. 13.00 40.00
18-24 .... 13.00 40.00
25-31 .... 9.00 28.00

ADVENTURES OF THE JAGUAR
RADIO(ARCHIE) (1961-1963)
1 1st & Origin: The Jaguar. 45.00 140.00
2 .... 25.00 80.00
3 .... 22.00 70.00
4 1st 12 cent cover price. 17.00 55.00
5-6 .... 17.00 55.00
7-8 .... 15.00 49.00
9-12 .... 14.00 44.00
13-15 .... 10.00 33.00

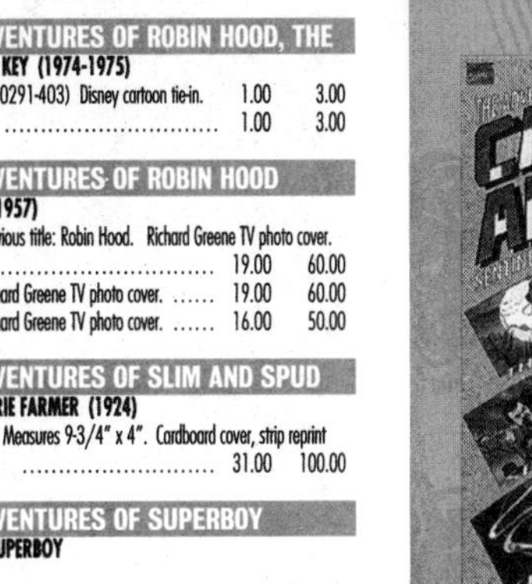

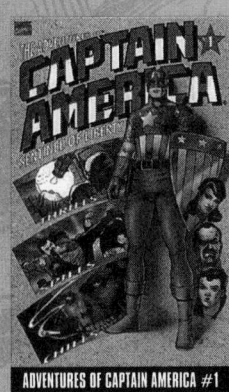

ADVENTURES OF CAPTAIN AMERICA #1

ADVENTURES OF CYCLOPS & PHOENIX #3

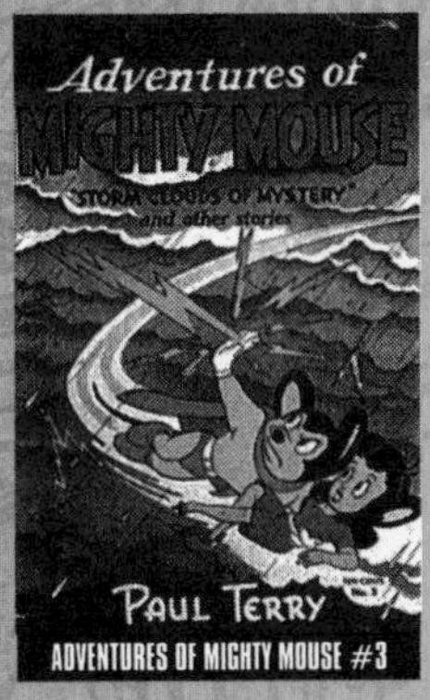

ADVENTURES OF MIGHTY MOUSE #3

ADVENTURES OF SUPERMAN #497

AGENT LIBERTY #1

AIRBOY #27

AKIRA #29

ALARMING TALES #2

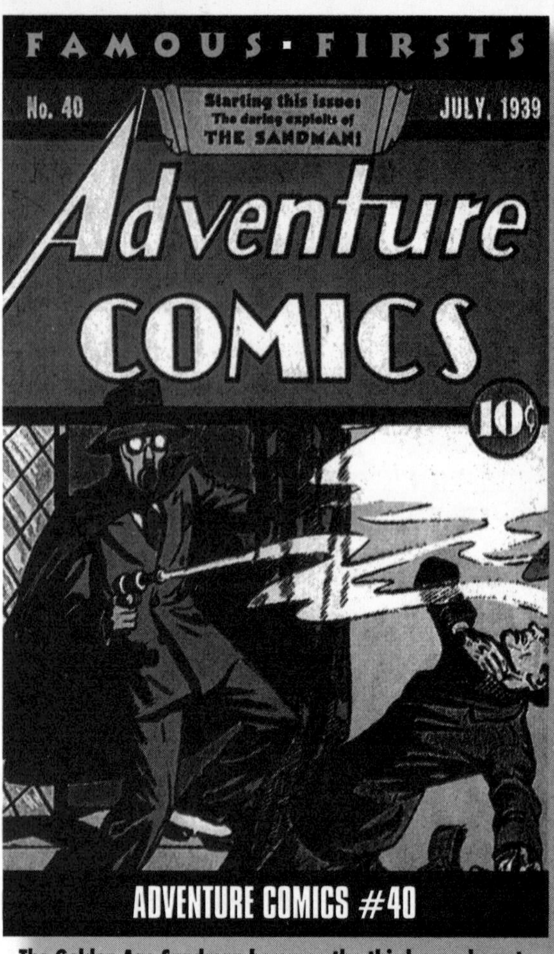

ADVENTURE COMICS #40

The Golden Age Sandman becomes the third superhero to be cover-featured by DC (after Superman and Batman). He's soon followed by Hourman (in #48) and Starman (in #64). Wesley (Sandman) Dodds still adventures today.

ADVENTURES OF THE OUTSIDERS
DC (1986-1987)
33 Previous title: Batman & The Outsiders. .50 1.25
34-46 .... .50 1.25

ADVENTURES OF THE SUPER MARIO BROTHERS
VALIANT (1990-1991)
1-8 .... .75 2.00

ADVENTURES OF THE THING
MARVEL (1992)
1-4 .... .50 1.50

ADVENTURES OF TINKER BELL, THE
DELL FOUR COLOR SERIES (1958-1959)
896 Disney. (4/58) 10.00 30.00
982 "New...". (4/59) 11.00 35.00

ADVENTURES OF TOM-TOM, THE
ME (1947)
3 Christmas Issue. Previous title: Tom-Tom The Jungle Boy.
.... 8.00 25.00

ADVENTURES ON THE PLANET OF THE APES
MARVEL (1975-1976)
1 Movie tie-in. Cover: Jim Starlin. 1.00 3.50
2 .... .75 2.50
3-5 .... .75 2.00
6 Cover: Starlin. .... .75 2.00
7-11 .... .75 2.00

AFRICA (A-1 SERIES)
ME (1955)
1 (A-1 #137). 10.00 30.00

AFRICAN LION, THE
DELL FOUR COLOR SERIES (1955)
665 Disney movie tie-in. (11/55) ... 11.00 35.00

AFTER DARK
STERLING (1955)
6-8 .... 13.00 40.00

AFTER HOURS
WARREN (1957-1958)
1 1st Warren magazine. Although not a comic-related magazine, this title is listed for its importance as the first Warren magazine and for issue #4, the Famous Monsters prototype, which spawned all of the Warren horror mags. 31.00 100.00
2 Betty Page. 40.00 125.00
3 .... 23.00 75.00
4 Famous Monsters prototype. This issue received such a large volume of fan mail that Warren decided to launch a magazine devoted to horror monsters, thus was born Famous Monsters Of Filmland. 250.00 800.00

AGE OF REPTILES
DARK HORSE (1993-1994)
1-4 .... .75 2.50

AGENT LIBERTY
DC (1991)
1 .... .75 2.00

AGENT THREE ZERO
GALAXINOVELS (1993)
1 Art: Stephen Platt. 1.75 6.00
2-3 .... 1.00 3.95

AGENTS OF LAW
DARK HORSE (1995-CURRENT)
1-5 .... .75 2.50

AGGIE MACK
DELL FOUR COLOR SERIES (1962)
1335 (4/62) 10.00 30.00

AGGIE MACK
SUPERIOR (1948-1949)
1 Art: Feldstein. 25.00 80.00
2-3 Cover: Kamen. 17.00 55.00
4 Cover: Kamen. Art: Feldstein. 17.00 55.00
5-8 Cover: Kamen. 17.00 55.00

AIR ACE COMICS
STREET & SMITH (1944-1947)
V2#1 Previous title: Bill Barnes, America's Air Ace Comics.
.... 35.00 110.00
V2#2-V2#6 .... 17.00 55.00
V2#7 Art: Bob Powell. 20.00 65.00
V2#8-V2#12 .... 14.00 44.00
V3#1-V3#6 .... 14.00 44.00
V3#7 Classic Bob Powell cover. 26.00 85.00
V3#8 Bob Powell art & cover. 20.00 65.00

AIR FIGHTERS COMICS
HILLMAN (1941-1945)
V1#1 .... 260.00 850.00
V1#2 Origin: Airboy. 500.00 1700.00
V1#3 1st & Origin: Heap. 280.00 900.00
V1#4 .... 180.00 575.00
V1#5-V1#7 .... 140.00 460.00
V1#8-V1#12 .... 105.00 340.00
V2#1 .... 85.00 280.00
V2#2 Airboy meets Valkyrie. 125.00 400.00
V2#3-V2#4 .... 85.00 280.00
V2#5 Classic cover. 105.00 340.00
V2#6-V2#9 .... 85.00 280.00
V2#10 Title changes to Airboy Comics with V2#11.
.... 85.00 280.00

AIRBOY
ECLIPSE (1986-1989)
1-50 .... .30 1.00

AIRBOY COMICS
HILLMAN (1945-1953)
V2#11 Previous title: Air Fighters Comics (12/45).
.... 105.00 340.00
V2#12 .... 70.00 230.00
V3#1-V3#5 .... 55.00 170.00
V3#6 "An American Legend!" 55.00 170.00
V3#7-V3#12 .... 55.00 170.00
V4#1-V4#3 .... 45.00 140.00
V4#4 Cover by Simon & Kirby. 55.00 170.00
V4#5-V4#12 .... 45.00 140.00
V5#1-V5#9 .... 26.00 85.00
V5#10 .... 26.00 85.00
V5#11-V5#12 .... 25.00 80.00
V6#1-V8#12 .... 20.00 65.00
V9#1-V10#1 .... 17.00 55.00

AKIRA
MARVEL(EPIC) (1988-1994)
1 .... 5.00 15.00
2 .... 2.50 9.00
3-17 .... 1.75 6.00
18-33 .... 1.50 5.00

AL CAPP'S DOGPATCH
TOBY PRESS (1949)
1 (#71) 40.00 125.00
2-4 .... 31.00 100.00

AL CAPP'S SHMOO COMICS
TOBY PRESS (1949-1950)
1 .... 65.00 200.00
2 .... 31.00 100.00
3 .... 50.00 150.00
4 1st & Origin: Super Shmoo. 50.00 150.00
5 .... 50.00 150.00

AL CAPP'S WOLF GAL
TOBY (1951)
1-2 .... 50.00 150.00

ALARMING ADVENTURES
HARVEY (1962-1963)
1 Art: Williamson & Crandall. 13.00 42.00
2 Art: Williamson & Crandall. 10.00 30.00
3 Art: Williamson. 10.00 30.00

ALARMING TALES
HARVEY (1957-1958)
1 Art: Jack Kirby. 28.00 90.00
2-3 Art: Jack Kirby. 22.00 70.00
4 Art: Kirby, Powell. 25.00 80.00
5 Art: Kirby, Williamson. 22.00 70.00
6 Art: Jack Kirby. 19.00 60.00

ALBEDO
THOUGHTS & IMAGES (1983-1989)
0 Yellow cover, print run: 50. .... 16.00 50.00
0A White cover, print run: 450. ...... 12.00 37.50
0B Blue cover, print run: 500. .... 8.00 25.00
0B (2ND) Blue cover, 2nd printing. Print run: 1000.
.... 4.00 12.00
0 (3RD) 3rd printing. .... .50 1.50
0 (4TH) 4th printing. .... .30 1.00
1 Dark red cover. 1st: Usagi Yojimbo. 5.00 15.00
1A Lighter red cover. 4.00 12.00
2 .... 2.75 10.00
3-14 .... .75 2.00

ALBERT THE ALLIGATOR AND POGO POSSUM
DELL FOUR COLOR SERIES (1946-1947)
105 Art: Walt Kelly. 190.00 600.00
148 Art: Walt Kelly. 145.00 475.00

ALEX
FANTAGRAPHICS (1994)
1-4 .... .75 2.95

ALEXANDER THE GREAT
DELL FOUR COLOR SERIES (1956)
688 Movie photo cover. (5/56) ... 16.00 50.00

ALF
MARVEL (1988-1992)
1 TV tie-in. .... .30 1.00
2-49 .... .30 1.00
50 Double size final issue. .... .50 1.75
ANNUAL 1-ANNUAL 3 .... .75 2.00

ALGIE
TIMOR (1953-1954)
1 .... 8.00 25.00
1 (2ND) Reprint, Accepted publications. 2.75 10.00
2-3 .... 5.00 15.00

ALICE
ZIFF-DAVIS (1952)
10-11 .... 16.00 50.00

ALICE AT MONKEY ISLAND
SEE THE ADVENTURES OF ALICE

ALICE COOPER: LAST TEMPTATION OF ALICE
MARVEL (1994)
1-3 .... 1.25 4.95

ALICE IN WONDERLAND
DELL FOUR COLOR SERIES (1951)
331 Disney. (5/51) 23.00 75.00
341 "Unbirthday Party With...". (7/51) 19.00 60.00

ALICE IN WONDERLAND
GOLD KEY (1965)
10144-503 Disney movie tie-in. 6.00 18.00

ALIEN 3
DARK HORSE (1992)
1 Movie adaptation. .... .75 2.50
2-3 .... .75 2.50

ALIEN LEGION
MARVEL (EPIC) (1984-1987)
1-2 .... 1.00 3.00
3-6 .... .75 2.50
7-20 .... .50 1.75

ALIEN LEGION
MARVEL (EPIC) (1987-1990)
1-2 .... .50 1.50
3-18 .... .75 2.00

ALIEN LEGION: ON THE EDGE
MARVEL (1990-1991)
1-4 .... 1.25 4.95

ALIEN LEGION: ONE PLANET AT A TIME
MARVEL (1993)
1-3 .... 1.25 4.95

ALIEN LEGION: TENANTS OF HELL
MARVEL (1991)
1-2 .... 1.25 4.95

ALIEN NATION
DC (1988)
1 Movie adaptation. 1.00 3.00

ALIEN: THE ILLUSTRATED STORY
HMB (1980)
NO# Movie adaptation. 1.75 6.00

ALIEN WORLDS
PACIFIC/ECLIPSE (1982-1985)
1 .... 1.25 4.00
2-7 .... 1.00 3.00
8-9 .... .75 2.00

ALIENS
DARK HORSE (1988-1989)
TPB Reprints issues #1-6. .... 4.00 11.95
1 .... 8.00 25.00
1 (2ND) 2nd printing. 1.00 3.00
1 (3RD) 3rd printing. .... .50 1.50
1 (4TH) 4th printing. .... .50 1.50
2 .... 5.00 15.00
2 (2ND) 2nd printing. .... .50 1.50
2 (3RD) 3rd printing. .... .50 1.50
3 .... 2.00 7.00
3 (2ND) 2nd printing. .... .50 1.50
4 .... 2.00 7.00
5-6 .... 1.50 5.00

ALIENS
DARK HORSE (1989-1990) COLOR MINI-SERIES
1 .... 2.00 7.00
2 .... 1.25 4.00
3-4 .... 1.00 3.00

ALIENS, THE
GOLD KEY (1967)
1 Magnus reprints. 7.00 20.00
2 Reprints: Magnus #1. .... 2.75 10.00

ALIENS: BERSERKER
DARK HORSE (1995)
1-4 .... .75 2.50

ALIENS: COLONIAL MARINES
DARK HORSE (1993-1994)
1-10 .... .75 2.50

ALIENS: EARTH ANGEL
DARK HORSE (1994)
1 .... .75 2.95
1A Hardcover limited edition. 6.00 19.95

ALIENS: EARTH WAR
DARK HORSE (1990)
1 .... 2.25 8.00
1 (2ND) 2nd printing. .... .75 2.50
2 .... 2.00 7.00
3-4 .... 1.75 6.00
TPB Signed & numbered Hardcover. ... 18.00 59.95

ALIENS: GENOCIDE
DARK HORSE (1991-1992)
1 .... 1.00 3.00
2-4 .... .75 2.50
TPB Reprints issues #1-4. .... 5.00 13.95

ALIENS: HIVE
DARK HORSE (1992)
1 .... 1.00 3.00
2-4 .... .75 2.00
TPB Reprints issues #1-4. .... 5.00 13.95

ALIENS: LABYRINTH
DARK HORSE (1993-1994)
1-4 .... .75 2.00
TPB Reprints issues #1-4. .... 6.00 17.95

ALIENS: MONDO PEST
DARK HORSE (1995)
1 One shot (reprints stories from Dark Horse Comics).
.... .75 2.95

ALIENS: MUSIC OF THE SPEARS
DARK HORSE (1994)
1-4 .... .75 2.50

ALIENS: NEWT'S TALE
DARK HORSE
1-2 .... 1.25 4.95

ALIENS: ROGUE
DARK HORSE (1993)
1-4 .... .75 2.50
TPB Reprints issues #1-4. .... 5.00 14.95

ALIENS: SACRIFICE
DARK HORSE (1993)
1 .... 1.25 4.95

ALIENS: STRONGHOLD
DARK HORSE (1994)
1-4 .... .75 2.50

ALIENS VS PREDATOR
DARK HORSE (1990)
0 Reprints issues #34-36 from DHP. ... 4.00 12.00
1 .... 2.25 8.00
1 (2ND) 2nd printing. .... .75 2.00
2-4 .... 1.50 5.00
HC Hardcover Limited Edition (1000 copies), with slipcase.
.... 24.00 79.95
TPB Reprints issues #1-4. .... 6.00 19.95

ALIENS VS PREDATOR: DUEL
DARK HORSE (1995)
1-2 .... .75 2.50

ALIENS VS PREDATOR: WAR
DARK HORSE (1995)
0 Reprints serial from Dark Horse Insider plus new material.
.... .75 2.50
1-3 .... .75 2.50

ALIENS/PREDATOR: THE DEADLIEST OF THE SPECIES
DARK HORSE (1993-1994)
1 .... 1.00 3.00
2-11 .... .75 2.00
12 .... .75 2.50

ALL AMERICAN ATHLETE COTTON WOODS
DELL FOUR COLOR SERIES (1957)
837 (9/57) 13.00 40.00

ALL AMERICAN COMICS
DC (1939-1948)
1 Anthology series. "Introducing Red, White and Blue!" (4/39)
.... 1000.00 3700.00
2 Begin: Ripley's Believe It Or Not. ... 310.00 1000.00
3 .... 270.00 875.00
4 .... 230.00 750.00
5-6 .... 190.00 625.00
7 "C. H. Claude's A Thousand Years A Minute!"
.... 190.00 625.00
8 Begin: Gary Concord, Ultra Man. ... 310.00 1000.00
9 .... 190.00 625.00
10 Christmas cover. (1/40) 190.00 625.00
11 Ultra Man. 230.00 750.00
12 Red, White and Blue. 190.00 625.00
13 "The Infra-Red Destroyers!" 190.00 625.00
14 Hop Harrigan. 190.00 625.00
15 Gary Concord, Ultra Man (6/40). 230.00 750.00
16 1st & Origin: Green Lantern. (7/40)
.... 13800.00 55000.00
17 .... 2300.00 9000.00
18 .... 1400.00 5500.00
19 1st & Origin: The Atom (10/40) 2300.00 9000.00
20 Begin: The Atom in costume. 700.00 2500.00
21 .... 400.00 1200.00
22 (1/41) 400.00 1200.00
23 .... 400.00 1200.00
24 .... 400.00 1500.00
25 1st & Origin: Dr. Midnite. 1600.00 6000.00
26 1st & Origin: Sargon, The Sorcerer. 500.00 1800.00
27 1st: Doiby Dickles. "Introducing Doiby Dickles, Right-Hand Man To The Green Lantern!" 700.00 2500.00
28-30 .... 280.00 925.00
31 "The Adventure Of The Underfed Orphans!"
.... 190.00 625.00
32-33 .... 190.00 625.00
34 (1/42) 190.00 625.00
35 Doiby learns Lantern's secret identity. 210.00 675.00
36-37 .... 190.00 625.00
38 "Green Lantern Vs. A Modern Napoleon"
.... 190.00 625.00
39-40 .... 190.00 625.00
41-43 .... 170.00 550.00
44 "I Accuse The Green Lantern!" ... 170.00 550.00
45 .... 170.00 550.00
46 "The Riddle Of Dickles Manor!" (1/43)
.... 170.00 550.00
47 Hop Harrigan cover. "Hop Harrigan Meets The Enemy"
.... 170.00 550.00
48 .... 170.00 550.00
49 "The Saga Of Doiby Dickles Cab!" 170.00 550.00
50 .... 170.00 550.00
51 "Murder Under The Stars!" 155.00 500.00
52 "Introducing The Silhouette!" ... 155.00 500.00
53 "Green Lantern Delivers The Mail!" 155.00 500.00
54 .... 155.00 500.00
55 "The Riddle Of The Runaway Trolley!" (1/44)
.... 155.00 500.00
56 "Green Lantern and the Reforming of Elegant Esmond!"
.... 155.00 500.00
57 "Green Lantern and the Mystery of the Melancholy Men!"
.... 155.00 500.00

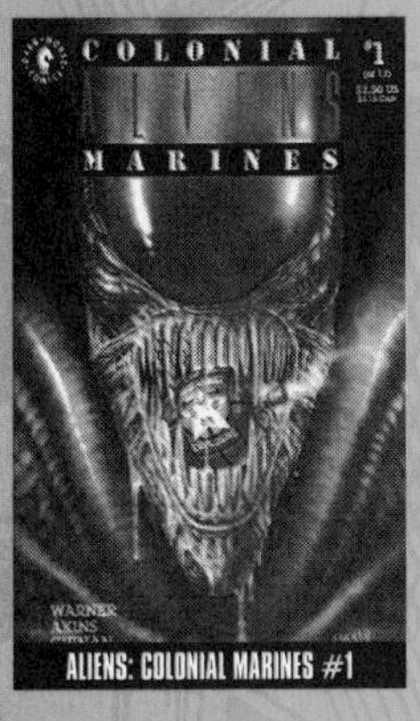

ALIENS: COLONIAL MARINES #1

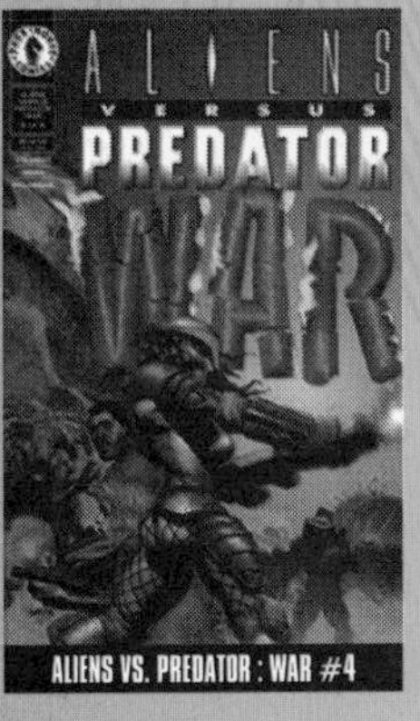

ALIENS VS. PREDATOR : WAR #4

ALL AMERICAN COMICS #16

ALL AMERICAN COMICS #52

ALL AMERICAN MEN OF WAR #9

ALL AMERICAN MEN OF WAR #41

ALL AMERICAN MEN OF WAR #127

ALL HERO COMICS #1

58 .... 155.00 500.00
59 "The Story Of The Man Who Could Not Tell The Truth!" 155.00 500.00
60 .... 155.00 500.00
61 1st & Origin: Solomon Grundy in "Fights Never Cry!" (10/44) 800.00 3000.00
62 "Da Distrik Attoiney" 130.00 430.00
63 "The Garrulous Mr. Gabb!" 130.00 430.00
64 "Green Lantern and A Bag Of Assorted Nuts!" 130.00 430.00
65 "Green Lantern and the Man Who Lost Wednesday!" 130.00 430.00
66 "Green Lantern and the Soles Of Manhattan!" 130.00 430.00
67 "King Shark Comes Back!" 130.00 430.00
68 "Green Lantern Meets Napoleon and Joe Safeen" 130.00 430.00
69 "Green Lantern and the Backwards Man!" 130.00 430.00
70 "Green Lantern and the Tale Of Cooley The Leprechaun!" (1/45) 130.00 430.00
71 "Doiby Dickles, The Human Bomb" 130.00 430.00
72 "Rumors Of The Round Table" End: The Atom. 130.00 430.00
73 "Mountain Music Mayhem!" 115.00 370.00
74 .... 115.00 370.00
75 "Adventure In A Planetarium!" 115.00 370.00
76 "Spring Time For Doiby" 115.00 370.00
77 Hop Harrigan cover. 115.00 370.00
78 .... 115.00 370.00
79 Mutt & Jeff cover. 115.00 370.00
80 .... 115.00 370.00
81 (1/46) 115.00 370.00
82 .... 115.00 370.00
83 Mutt & Jeff cover. 115.00 370.00
84 "The Adventure of the Man With Two Faces!" 115.00 370.00
85 .... 115.00 370.00
86 "The Crime Of The Month Club!" 115.00 370.00
87 "The Strange Case Of Professor Nobody" 115.00 370.00
88 "Canvas Of Crime!" 115.00 370.00
89 1st & Origin: Harlequin. (9/46) 155.00 500.00
90 1st & Origin: Icicle in "Introducing The Icicle, the Coldest Criminal In History!" 130.00 430.00
91 "The Wedding Of The Harlequin!" 115.00 370.00
92 "The Icicle Goes South." 115.00 370.00
93 "The Double-Crossing Decoy!" (1/47) 115.00 370.00
94 .... 115.00 370.00
95 "The Unmasking Of The Harlequin!" 115.00 370.00
96 "Streak (the Wonder Dog) and Green Lantern Solve The Mystery of the Emerald Necklace!" 115.00 370.00
97 "The Country Fair Crimes!" 115.00 370.00
98 "The End Of Sports!" 115.00 370.00
99 "Nest Of Terror!" 115.00 370.00
100 "Introducing the Sensational New Fighting Western Team, Johnny Thunder and Black Lightning!" Johnny Thunder cover. Green Lantern in "Gotham's Golden Jubilee!" 115.00 370.00
101 "Masquerade At Mesa City!" 115.00 370.00
102 Johnny Thunder in "The Bridge Of Peril!" (10/47) Title changes to All American Western with #103. .... 115.00 370.00

ALL AMERICAN MEN OF WAR
DC (1952-1966)

1 (#127) Previous title: All American Western. 170.00 560.00
2 (#128) (10-11/52) 120.00 390.00
2 (12-1/53) 100.00 325.00
3-6 .... 95.00 310.00
7-12 .... 70.00 225.00
13-18 .... 60.00 200.00
19 1st: Code Approved issue. 70.00 225.00
20-30 .... 45.00 140.00
31-42 .... 35.00 115.00
43-54 .... 25.00 85.00
55-66 .... 20.00 70.00
67 1st: Gunner & Sarge. 35.00 110.00
68-72 .... 19.00 60.00
73-81 .... 14.00 45.00
82 Begin: Johnny Cloud. 13.00 40.00
83-88 .... 9.00 27.50
89 1st 12 cent cover price. 9.00 27.50
90-108 .... 9.00 27.50
109-117 .... 4.00 13.00

ALL AMERICAN WESTERN
DC (1948-1952)

103 Previous title: All American Comics. Begin: Johnny Thunder. 110.00 360.00
104-105 Art: Joe Kubert. 75.00 240.00
106 .... 50.00 150.00
107 Art: Kubert. 75.00 240.00
108-110 .... 40.00 120.00
111 Art: Kubert. 50.00 150.00
112 .... 40.00 120.00
113 Cover: Alex Toth. 55.00 180.00
114-116 Art: Kubert. 50.00 150.00
117-120 .... 40.00 120.00
121 Art: Kubert. 50.00 150.00
122-126 .... 40.00 120.00

ALL COMICS
CHICAGO NITE LIFE (1945)

1 .... 23.00 75.00

ALL FAMOUS CRIME
STAR (1950-1951)

4 1st issue. Cover: L.B. Cole. 14.00 44.00
5 Cover: L.B. Cole. 17.00 55.00
8 Cover: L.B. Cole. (5/51) 14.00 44.00
9 Cover: L.B. Cole. 25.00 80.00
10 Cover: L.B. Cole. 10.00 33.00

ALL FAMOUS POLICE CASES
STAR (1952-1954)

6 Cover: L.B. Cole on all issues. 14.00 44.00
7 Art: Kubert. 14.00 44.00
8 .... 10.00 33.00
9-16 .... 7.00 22.00

ALL FLASH QUARTERLY
DC (1941-1948)

1 Origin retold: The Flash (see Flash Comics #1 for 1st app). (Summer/41) 2100.00 8000.00
2 .... 400.00 1500.00
3 .... 310.00 1000.00
4 (Spring/42) 310.00 1000.00
5 .... 280.00 900.00
6 "Now A Bi-Monthly!" (9-10/42) 280.00 900.00
7 "The House Of Horror!" 200.00 650.00
8 "The Flash and the Formula To Fairyland!" (1-2/43) 200.00 650.00
9 "Adventure of the Stolen Telescope!" and "Adventure of the Magic Mirror!" 200.00 650.00
10 "The Case Of The Curious Cat!" 200.00 650.00
11 "Troubles Come In Doubles!" 200.00 650.00
12 "The Three Dimwits Discover A Vanishing Vitamin!" 1st & Origin: The Thinker. Back to quarterly frequency. 220.00 700.00
13 "Muscleman, The Djinn and The Flash!" 155.00 500.00
14 App: Green Lantern. 200.00 650.00
15-16 .... 155.00 500.00
17 "The Flash And The Adventure Of The 4-In-1 Criminal!" 155.00 500.00
18 "The Hotel Of Missing Men!" 155.00 500.00
19 "The Adventure Of The Mummy Case and the Wooden Man!" 155.00 500.00
20 .... 155.00 500.00
21 "The Fastest Man Alive Vs. The Slowest Man Alive!" 155.00 500.00
22 Begin: Bi-Monthly. 155.00 500.00
23 "A World With Two Futures!" 155.00 500.00
24 "3 Court Clowns Get Caught!" 155.00 500.00
25 "The Flash Goes Jitterbug!" 140.00 450.00
26-28 .... 140.00 450.00
29 "The Thousand-Year-Old Terror!" 140.00 450.00
30 "Anything Can Happen!" 140.00 450.00
31 "The Planet Of Sport!" 140.00 450.00
32 1st & Origin: The Fiddler. 1st: Star Sapphire. (1-2/47) 200.00 650.00

ALL FOR LOVE
PRIZE (1957-1959)

1 .... 7.00 20.00
2-6 .... 5.00 15.00
7 (Vol.2 #1) 2.75 10.00
8 (Vol.2 #2) 2.75 10.00
9 (Vol.2 #3) 2.75 10.00
10 (Vol.2 #4) 2.75 10.00
11 (Vol.2 #5) 2.75 10.00
12 (Vol.2 #6) 2.75 10.00
13 (Vol.3 #1) 2.75 10.00
14 (Vol.3 #2) 2.75 10.00
15 (Vol.3 #3) 2.75 10.00
16 (Vol.3 #4) 2.75 10.00

ALL FUNNY COMICS
DC (1943-1948)

1 1st: Genius Jones. 1st: Buzzy. 120.00 390.00
2 .... 60.00 190.00
3 .... 40.00 130.00
4-6 .... 29.00 95.00
7-9 .... 23.00 75.00
10-12 .... 20.00 65.00
13-15 .... 16.00 50.00
16 Super Heroes special issue. 80.00 260.00
17-23 .... 16.00 50.00

ALL GOOD COMICS
FOX (1946)

1 10 cent cover price. 23.00 75.00

ALL GOOD COMICS
R.W. VOIGHT (1944)

1 128 pages. 25 cent cover price. 50.00 150.00

ALL GOOD COMICS
ST. JOHN (1949)

NO# 256 pages. 50 cent cover price. 125.00 400.00

ALL GREAT COMICS
FOX (1946)

1 One-shot Fox giant. 22.00 70.00

ALL GREAT COMICS
FOX (1947)

13 Origin Dagar, Desert Hawk. 55.00 175.00

ALL GREAT COMICS
WILLIAM H. WISE (1944)

NO# 128 pages., contains Green Mask, Joan Mason & others. 55.00 175.00

ALL GREAT JUNGLE ADVENTURES
FOX (1949)

NO# 132 page Fox Giant. 28.00 90.00

ALL HERO COMICS
FAWCETT (1943)

1 App: Captain Midnight, Golden Arrow, Captain Marvel, Jr., Ibis The Invincible, Spy Smasher, Lance O'Casey. 280.00 900.00

ALL HUMOR COMICS
QUALITY (1946-1949)

1 .... 28.00 90.00
2 .... 15.00 48.00
3-5 .... 11.00 36.00
6-16 .... 8.00 24.00
17 .... 10.00 30.00

ALL LOVE ROMANCES
ACE (1949-1950)

26 Previous title: Ernie Comics. 10.00 30.00
27 L.B. Cole art. 11.00 35.00
28-32 .... 7.00 20.00

ALL NEGRO COMICS
ALL-NEGRO PRESS (1947)

1 15 cent cover price. 400.00 1200.00

ALL NEW COLLECTOR EDITION
DC (1978-1979)

C-53 Rudolph The Red-nosed Reindeer. .... .30 1.00
C-54 Superman Vs. Wonder Woman. .... .75 2.00
C-55 Superboy & The Legion Of Super-Heroes. .75 2.00
C-56 Superman Vs. Muhammad Ali. .... .75 2.00
C-58 Superman Vs. Shazam. .... .75 2.00
C-60 Rudolph's Summer Fun. .... .30 1.00
C-61 Superman. .... .75 2.00
C-62 Superman The Movie. 1.00 3.00

ALL NEW COMICS
HARVEY (1943-1947)

1 ("Short Story" in title on 1st 3 issues). 220.00 700.00
2 Origin: Scarlet Phantom. Art: Kubert. 110.00 360.00
3 .... 95.00 300.00
4-5 .... 75.00 240.00
6 App: Black Cat. 95.00 300.00
7 App: Black Cat. Art: Kubert & Powell. 95.00 300.00
8-9 Cover: Schomburg. 95.00 300.00
10 App: The Zebra. 75.00 240.00
11 App: Men In Black. 85.00 270.00
12 Art: Kubert. 85.00 270.00
13 Art: Simon & Kirby (Stuntman story). Cover & App: Green Hornet. 95.00 300.00
14 Art: Bob Powell (on The Man In Black story). App: The Green Hornet. 95.00 300.00
15 Sent to subscribers to fulfill final issue. (B&W, 5.5"x8.5"). App: Black Cat, Joe Palooka. 75.00 240.00

ALL OUT WAR
DC (1979-1980)

1 .... 1.00 3.00
2-6 .... .75 2.00

ALL PICTURE ADVENTURE
ST. JOHN (1952)

1 100 pages. War. 40.00 125.00
2 100 pages. Horror. 65.00 200.00

ALL PICTURE ALL TRUE LOVE STORY
ST. JOHN (1952)

1 100 pages. Art: Matt Baker. 85.00 275.00

ALL PICTURE COMEDY CARNIVAL
ST. JOHN (1952)

1 100 pages. 65.00 200.00

ALL ROMANCES
ACE (1949-1950)
1 .... 13.00 40.00
2 .... 7.00 20.00
3-6 .... 5.00 15.00

ALL SELECT COMICS
MARVEL(TIMELY) (1943-1946)
1 Begin: Captain America, Sub-Mariner, Human Torch anthology series. 900.00 3500.00
2 App: Red Skull. 400.00 1200.00
3 App: The Whizzer. 270.00 875.00
4 .... 190.00 625.00
5 End: Sub-Mariner. 190.00 625.00
6 App: The Destroyer. 190.00 625.00
7-9 .... 155.00 500.00
10 App: Sub-Mariner. 170.00 550.00
11 1st: Blonde Phantom. 230.00 750.00

ALL SPORTS COMICS
HILLMAN (1949)
2 Previous title: Real Sports Comics. ... 50.00 150.00
3 Title changes to All Time Sports Comics with #4. .... 40.00 125.00

ALL STAR ARCHIVES
DC (1992)
NO# Deluxe Hardcover reprints G.A. All Star Comics #3-6. .... 15.00 49.95

ALL STAR COMICS
DC (1940-1951)
1 Begin: The Flash, Hawkman, Hour-Man, Sandman, Spectre anthology series. (Summer/40) ... 2600.00 10000.00
2 Begin: Green Lantern series. 1000.00 3900.00
3 1st & Origin: The Justice Society Of America, the first Super Hero team. Begin: Dr. Fate, The Atom, JSA series. (Winter/40-41) 6300.00 25000.00
4 (3-4/41) 900.00 3300.00
5 1st: Hawkgirl (6/41). 800.00 2900.00
6 "The Justice Society Initiates Johnny Thunder!" 500.00 1900.00
7 "The JSA Raises $1,000,000 For War Orphans!" App: Batman, Flash, Superman. End: The Hour Man. 600.00 2300.00
8 1st & Origin: Wonder Woman (origin concludes in Sensation Comics #1). Starman, Dr, Midnite join JSA. 1st female Super-Hero. (12-1/42) 3600.00 14000.00
9 .... 500.00 1800.00
10 "500 Years Into The Future With The JSA!" App: Flash, Green Lantern. New costume: Sandman. 500.00 1900.00
11 "The JSA Joins The War On Japan!" Begin: Wonder Woman series. 400.00 1500.00
12 "The JSA Pursues Victory For America and Democracy!" Wonder Woman joins JSA. 400.00 1500.00
13 "Shanghaied Into Space!" 400.00 1500.00
14 "Food For Starving Patriots!" (12-1/43) 400.00 1500.00
15 "The Story Of The Man Who Created Images!" 1st & Origin: Brain Wave. 400.00 1500.00
16 "The Justice Society Fights For A United America!" 310.00 1000.00
17 "The Brain Wave Goes Berserk!" 310.00 1000.00
18 "Insects Turn To Crime!" 310.00 1000.00
19 "Crimes Set To Music" 310.00 1000.00
20 "A Movie That Changed A Man's Life!" 310.00 1000.00
21 "The Man Who Relived His Life!" App: Spectre, Atom, Dr. Fate. 310.00 1000.00
22 "A Cure For The World!" Patriotic cover. 310.00 1000.00
23 End: Spectre, Starman. (Winter/44) 310.00 1000.00
24 "This Is Our Enemy!" App: Flash, Green Lantern. Begin: Hawkman by Joe Kubert. 300.00 1100.00
25 "The Forgotten Crime!" Begin: Flash, Green Lantern. 310.00 1000.00
26 "The Mystery Of The Metal Menace!" on cover but story is titled "Vampires Of The Void!" on the inside. 280.00 900.00
27 "A Place In The World" 280.00 900.00
28 "The Paintings That Walked The Earth!" 240.00 775.00
29 "The Man Who Knows Too Much!" 240.00 775.00
30 "Dreams Of Madness!" 240.00 775.00
31 "The JSA Battles The Globe-Being From Space!" 240.00 775.00
32 "The Return Of The Psycho-Pirate" (12-1/47) 240.00 775.00
33 "The Revenge Of Solomon Grundy!" App: Solomon Grundy. Classic issue. 400.00 1500.00
34 "The Wiles Of The Wizard!" 200.00 650.00
35 "The Day That Dropped Out Of Time!" 200.00 650.00
36 "Superman and Batman Guest Star!" App: Batman, Superman in JSA story. 400.00 1500.00
37 1st: Injustice Society in "The Injustice Of The World!" End: Hawkman by Kubert. 280.00 900.00
38 "The JSA Battles History's Crime Wave!" (12-1/48) Begin: Black Canary. 310.00 1000.00
39 "Invasion From Fairyland!" 200.00 650.00
40 "Tackles The Problem Of Juvenile Delinquency!" 200.00 650.00
41 "The Case Of The Patriotic Crimes!" Black Canary joins JSA. 180.00 575.00
42 "The Man Who Hated Science!" New Costume: The Atom, Hawkman. 200.00 650.00
43 "The Secret Of The Golden Universe!" 200.00 650.00
44 "Evil Star Over Hollywood!" (12-1/49) 200.00 650.00
45 "The Case Of The Cosmic Criminals!" 200.00 650.00
46 "The Adventure Of The Invisible Band!" 200.00 650.00
47 "The Ghost Of Billy The Kid!" ... 200.00 650.00
48 "The Strange Lives Of Edmund Blake!" 200.00 650.00
49 "The Invasion Of The Fire People!" 200.00 650.00
50 "The Prophecy Of Peril!" (12-1/50) Art: Frank Frazetta (1 story). 240.00 775.00
51 "Invaders From The World Below!" 240.00 775.00
52 "The Secret Conquest Of The Earth!" 240.00 775.00
53 "The Gun That Dropped Through Time!" 240.00 775.00
54 "Under The Big Top!" 240.00 775.00
55 "The Man Who Conquered The Solar System!" 240.00 775.00
56 "The Day The World Ended!" (12-1/51) 240.00 775.00
57 "The Mystery Of The Vanishing Detective!" Title changes to All Star Western with #58. Final Golden Age appearances of Dr. Midnite, Flash and Green Lantern. (2-3/51) 300.00 975.00

ALL STAR COMICS
DC (1976-1978)
58-74 .... .30 1.00

ALL STAR SQUADRON
DC (1981-1987)
1 Origin: Golden Age Atom, Dr. Midnite, Hawkman, Robotman. .... .75 2.00
2-24 .... .30 1.00
25 1st: Infinity, Inc. .... .75 2.00
26-40 .... .30 1.00
41 Origin: Starman. .... .30 1.00
42-46 .... .30 1.00
47 Art: Todd McFarlane. Origin: Dr. Fate. 1.00 3.00
48-49 .... .30 1.00
50 Crossover: Crisis. Double size. ...... .75 2.50
51-67 .... .30 1.00

ALL STAR SQUADRON ANNUAL
DC (1982-1984)
1 .... .75 2.00
2 .... 1.00 3.00
3 .... .75 2.00

ALL STAR WESTERN
DC (1951-1961)
58 Previous title: All Star Comics. 95.00 300.00
59-60 .... 40.00 120.00
61-64 Art: Alex Toth. 45.00 140.00
65-66 .... 40.00 120.00
67 Begin: Johnny Thunder by Gil Kane. 50.00 150.00
68-81 .... 22.00 70.00
82 1st: Code Approved issue. 20.00 65.00
83-98 .... 15.00 48.00
99 Reprint: Jimmy Wakely #4 by Frank Frazetta. 19.00 60.00
100 .... 15.00 48.00
101-107 .... 11.00 36.00
108 Origin: Johnny Thunder. 40.00 120.00
109-119 .... 11.00 36.00

ALL STAR WESTERN
DC (1970-1972)
1 .... 2.75 10.00
2-9 .... 1.25 4.00
10 1st: Jonah Hex. 28.00 90.00
11 2nd:Jonah Hex. 13.00 40.00

ALL SURPRISE
MARVEL(TIMELY) (1943-1947)
1 Begin: Super Rabbit. 40.00 120.00
2 .... 15.00 48.00
3-5 .... 10.00 30.00
6-12 .... 8.00 24.00

ALL TEEN COMICS
MARVEL (TIMELY) (1947)
20 Previous title: All Winners Comics. Title changes to Teen Comics with #21. .... 19.00 60.00

ALL TIME SPORTS COMICS
HILLMAN (1949)
4 Previous title: All Sports Comics. ... 25.00 80.00
5-7 .... 19.00 60.00

ALL TOP COMICS
FOX (1946-1949)
1 Cosmo Cat. 31.00 100.00
2 .... 13.00 40.00
3-7 .... 10.00 30.00
8 Begin: Rulah, Blue Beetle, Phantom Lady, Jo-Jo. 190.00 600.00
9 .... 110.00 360.00
10 .... 130.00 420.00
11-13 .... 95.00 300.00
14 Classic issue. 145.00 480.00
15-17 .... 95.00 300.00
18 App: Dagar. 75.00 240.00

ALL TOP COMICS
WISE (1944)
NO# 128 pages. 50.00 150.00

ALL TRUE ALL PICTURE POLICE CASES
ST. JOHN (1952)
1 100 pages. 65.00 200.00

ALL TRUE CRIME
MARVEL(ATLAS) (1948-1952)
26 Previous title: Official True Crime Cases. 28.00 90.00
27 .... 19.00 60.00
28-52 .... 8.00 24.00

ALL TRUE DETECTIVE CASES
AVON (1954)
1 .... 20.00 65.00
2 .... 17.00 55.00
3 .... 7.00 23.00
4 Art: Jack Kamen. 17.00 55.00

ALL TRUE ROMANCE
ARTFUL/COMIC MEDIA (1951-1958)
1 .... 17.00 55.00
2-5 .... 11.00 34.00
6 Art: Wallace Wood. 26.00 85.00
7 (9/52) 11.00 34.00
7A (11/52) 14.00 46.00
8-34 .... 6.00 17.00

ALL WESTERN WINNERS
MARVEL(TIMELY) (1948-1949)
2 Previous title: All Winners Comics. 1st & Origin: Black Rider. 100.00 330.00
3 .... 50.00 160.00
4 Title changes to Western Winners with #5. .... 60.00 190.00

ALL WINNERS COMICS
MARVEL(TIMELY) (1941-1946)
1 Captain America & Bucky (Simon & Kirby), Human Torch & Toro, Sub-Mariner, The Angel, Black Marvel. 1900.00 7500.00
2 "Carnival Of Death!" (Fall/41). ... 600.00 2000.00
3 .... 300.00 1100.00
4 Classic Schomburg cover. 400.00 1500.00
5 .... 240.00 775.00
6 .... 310.00 1000.00
7-10 .... 240.00 775.00
11 .... 155.00 500.00
12 App: Red Skull. 180.00 575.00
13 .... 155.00 500.00
14-16 No Human Torch. 140.00 450.00
17-18 .... 155.00 500.00
19 1st & Origin: All Winners Squad. (Fall/46) 600.00 2000.00
21 "The Riddle Of The Demented Dwarf!" (Winter/46) Title changes to All Teen Comics with #20. 600.00 2000.00

ALL WINNERS COMICS
MARVEL(TIMELY) (1948)
1 Title changes to All Western Winners with #2. Features Blonde Phantom, Human Torch, Captain America, Sub-Mariner 310.00 1000.00

ALL YOUR COMICS
FOX (1946)
1 .... 16.00 50.00

ALLEY OOP
ARGO (1955-1956)
1 .... 16.00 50.00
2 .... 10.00 30.00
3 .... 7.00 20.00

ALLEY OOP
DELL (1962)
1-2 .... 10.00 30.00

ALLEY OOP
DELL FOUR COLOR SERIES (1942)
3 .... 115.00 375.00

ALL STAR COMICS #4

ALL STAR COMICS #26

ALL TOP COMICS #8

ALL WINNERS COMICS #6

ALPHA FLIGHT #1

AMAZING ADVENTURES #11

AMAZING ADVENTURES #18

AMAZING FANTASY #15

FAMOUS • FIRSTS

AMAZING SPIDER-MAN #1

Stan Lee and Steve Ditko's blend of soap opera and superheroism makes Spider-Man a star. Six months after his first appearance in *Amazing Fantasy* #15, Spidey gets his own comic and crosses over with The Fantastic Four!

ALLEY OOP
STANDARD (1947-1949)

10	25.00	80.00
11-16	16.00	50.00
17-18 Cover: Schomburg.	25.00	80.00

ALMANAC OF CRIME
FOX (1949-1950)

NO# 148 pages.	20.00	65.00
1 132 pages.	17.00	55.00

ALPHA FLIGHT
MARVEL (1983-1994)

1 Origin: Alpha Flight. Cameo: Wolverine and Nightcrawler.	.60	2.00
2-11	.50	1.50
12 Double size.	.50	1.50
13 App: Wolverine.	.60	2.00
14-16	.50	1.50
17 Crossover: X-Men.	.75	2.00
18-27	.50	1.50
28 End: John Byrne art.	.50	1.50
29-32	.50	1.50
33 App: X-Men.	.60	2.00
34 Origin: Wolverine.	.60	2.00
35-49	.50	1.50
50 Double size.	.50	1.50
51 App: Wolverine. 1st: Jim Lee art.	1.75	6.00
52-53	1.00	3.00
54-62	.75	2.00
63-74	.50	1.50
75 Double size.	.75	2.50
76-86	.50	1.50
87-90 App: Wolverine.	1.25	4.00
91-105	.50	1.50
106 Northstar discloses orientation.	1.00	3.00
106 (2ND) 2nd printing.	.50	1.75
107-119	.50	1.75
120	.75	2.25
121-129	.50	1.75
130	.75	2.25

ALPHA FLIGHT ANNUAL
MARVEL (1986-1987)

1 (1986)	.75	2.50
2 (1987)	.75	2.00

ALPHA FLIGHT ORIGIN SPECIAL
MARVEL (1992)

1 Wolverine. (1992)	.75	2.50

ALPHA FLIGHT SPECIAL
MARVEL (1991)

1-4	.50	1.50

ALVIN
DELL (1962-1973)

1 (#12-021-212) TV cartoon tie-in.	19.00	60.00
2	10.00	30.00
3-28	8.00	25.00

AMAZING ADULT FANTASY
MARVEL (1961-1962)

7 Previous title: Amazing Adventures. Cover & art: Steve Ditko (in all issues).	125.00	425.00
8	95.00	325.00
9 1st 12 cent cover price.	85.00	300.00
10-13	85.00	280.00
14 Professor X prototype (7/62). "The Man In The Sky!" Five page story by Ditko/Lee. Peter Parker prototype (see Tad Carter in same story). Title changes to Amazing Fantasy with #15.	110.00	375.00

AMAZING ADVENTURE FUNNIES
CENTAUR (1940)

1 Contents of both issues are reprinted from earlier Centaur titles.	310.00	1000.00
2	250.00	800.00

AMAZING ADVENTURES
MARVEL (1961)

1 Begin: Ditko/Kirby art. 1st & Origin: Dr. Droom (Marvel's 1st Silver Age superhero). Kirby covers on all issues.	310.00	1100.00
2	140.00	475.00
3-5	125.00	425.00
6 Death: Dr. Droom. Title changes to: Amazing Adult Fantasy with #7.	125.00	425.00

AMAZING ADVENTURES
MARVEL (1970-1976)

1 Begin: The Inhumans And The Black Widow.	6.00	18.00
2-4	2.75	10.00
5-8	2.25	8.00
9 Black Bolt And The Inhumans. App: Magneto.	1.75	6.00
10 Black Bolt And The Inhumans. App: Magneto, End: Inhumans.	1.75	6.00
11 Begin: The (New) Beast.	5.00	15.00
12 App: Iron Man.	2.50	9.00
13	2.50	9.00
14 App: Iron Man. (1/73)	2.50	9.00
15 App: X-Men.	2.50	9.00
16	2.50	9.00
17 App: X-Men. Origin: The Beast.	2.50	9.00
18 Begin: War Of The Worlds. 1st & Origin: Killraven, Art: Neal Adams.	5.00	15.00
19-39	1.50	5.00

AMAZING ADVENTURES
MARVEL (1979-1981)

1 Reprints X-Men #1 & 38.	.75	2.00
2 Reprints X-Men #39.	.75	2.00
3 Reprints X-Men #40.	.75	2.00
4 Reprints X-Men #41.	.75	2.00
5 Reprints X-Men #42.	.75	2.00
6 Reprints X-Men #43.	.75	2.00
7 Reprints X-Men #44.	.75	2.00
8 Reprints X-Men #45.	.75	2.00
9 Reprints X-Men #46.	.75	2.00
10 Reprints X-Men #47.	.75	2.00
11 Reprints X-Men #48.	.75	2.00
12 Reprints X-Men #6.	.75	2.00
13 Reprints X-Men #7.	.75	2.00
14 Reprints X-Men #8.	.75	2.00

AMAZING ADVENTURES
ZIFF-DAVIS (1950-1952)

1 Cover: Schomburg.	85.00	280.00
2-5	40.00	130.00
6 Art: Krigstein.	55.00	170.00

AMAZING COMICS
MARVEL(TIMELY) (1944)

1 Featuring The Young Allies. Cover: Schomburg. Title changes to: Complete Comics with #2.	310.00	1000.00

AMAZING DETECTIVE CASES
MARVEL(ATLAS) (1950-1952)

3	29.00	95.00
4-10	20.00	65.00
11	23.00	75.00
12 Art: Krigstein.	28.00	90.00
13 Art: Bill Everett.	31.00	100.00
14	23.00	75.00

AMAZING FANTASY
MARVEL (1962)

15 Art: Steve Ditko. Cover: Kirby/Ditko. 1st & Origin: Spider-Man. 1st: Aunt May. 1st & Death: Uncle Ben. Lead story: "Spider-Man!", story continued in Amazing Spider-Man #1.	5500.00	22000.00

AMAZING GHOST STORIES
ST. JOHN (1954-1955)

14 Cover: Matt Baker. Previous title: Nightmare.	28.00	90.00
15 Cover: Baker. Art: Powell.	20.00	65.00
16 Cover: Baker.	20.00	65.00

AMAZING HIGH ADVENTURE
MARVEL (1984-1986)

1-4	.75	2.00

AMAZING MAN COMICS
CENTAUR (1939-1942)

5 Previous title: Western Picture Stories 4? 1st & Origin: Amazing Man. Begin: Bill Everett art. Cat Man by Mills, Iron Skull by Carlos Burgos.	3800.00	15000.00
6	800.00	3000.00
7	400.00	1400.00
8-10	400.00	1200.00
11 Costume: Amazing Man. End: Everett art.	400.00	1200.00
12	250.00	800.00
13	220.00	700.00

14-22 190.00 600.00
23 1st & Origin: Amazing Kid. 190.00 600.00
24 190.00 600.00
25-26 Art: Wolverton (1 story). 250.00 800.00

AMAZING MYSTERIES

MARVEL (1949-1950)
32 App: The Witness. 115.00 370.00
33 50.00 150.00
34 Photo cover. 50.00 150.00
35 Photo cover, "Decoy For The Hot-Seat!" 50.00 150.00

AMAZING MYSTERY FUNNIES

CENTAUR (1938-1940)
1 Cover: Bill Everett. 800.00 2800.00
2 1st: Bill Everett story art. 400.00 1500.00
3 220.00 700.00
4 (#3 on indicia). (12/38) 190.00 600.00
5 (V2#1) 155.00 500.00
6 (V2#2) Classic cover. 155.00 500.00
7 (V2#3) 155.00 500.00
8 (V2#4) 155.00 500.00
9 (V2#5) Classic cover: Bill Everett. 230.00 750.00
10 (V2#6) 155.00 500.00
11 (V2#7) 1st & Begin: Fantom Of The Fair. 700.00 2500.00
12 (V2#8) 1st & Origin: Speed Centaur. 250.00 800.00
13 (V2#9) 155.00 500.00
14 (V2#10) 155.00 500.00
15 (V2#11) Bill Everett biography. 170.00 550.00
16 (V2#12) 1st: Space Patrol by Basil Wolverton. 400.00 1500.00
17 (V3#1) 155.00 500.00
18 Fantom Of The Fair. 155.00 500.00
19 Space Patrol by Wolverton. 250.00 800.00
20 190.00 600.00
21-24 Space Patrol by Wolverton. 250.00 800.00

AMAZING SAINTS

LOGOS (1974)
NO# .30 1.00

AMAZING SPIDER-MAN

MARVEL (1963-CURRENT)
1 1st: J.Jonah Jameson. 1st: Chameleon. "Spider-Man, Part 2" story continued from Amazing Fantasy #15. (3/63) 4000.00 16000.00
1A Golden Record set (1966), 33-1/3 record album still sealed with Amazing Spider-Man #1 reprint (identical to original but without cover price and original ads). 65.00 200.00
1B Golden Record reprint, removed from original 33-1/3 record album, identical to Amazing Spider-Man #1 but without cover price and original ads. 26.00 85.00
2 1st: Vulture. "The Vulture!" 1st: Tinkerer. "The Terrible Tinkerer!" Issues 1-38 are all by Ditko/Lee. 600.00 2300.00
3 1st & Origin: Dr. Octopus in "Spider-Man Versus Doctor Octopus!" 400.00 1400.00
4 1st & Origin: Sandman. "Nothing Can Stop...The Sandman!" 300.00 1150.00
5 App: Dr. Doom, Fantastic Four. "Marked For Destruction By Dr. Doom!" 310.00 1000.00
6 1st & Origin: The Lizard. "Face-To-Face With...The Lizard!" 280.00 900.00
7 2nd: Vulture. "The Vultures Return!" 200.00 650.00
8 App: Human Torch. 210.00 675.00
9 1st & Origin: Electro. "The Man Called Electro!" 220.00 700.00
10 1st: Enforcers. "The Enforcers!" 170.00 550.00
11 2nd: Dr. Octopus. "Return Of Doctor Octopus!" 130.00 425.00
12 App: Dr. Octopus. "Unmasked By Dr. Octopus!" 115.00 375.00
13 1st & Origin: Mysterio. 130.00 425.00
14 1st: The Green Goblin in "The Green Goblin!" (7/64) 400.00 1250.00
15 1st & Origin: Kraven. "Kraven The Hunter!" 115.00 375.00
16 App: Daredevil. "Spidey Battles Daredevil!" 95.00 300.00
17 2nd: Green Goblin. "The Return Of The Green Goblin!" 140.00 450.00
18 App: Sandman, 1st: Ned Leeds. "The End Of Spider-Man!" 85.00 280.00
19 App: Sandman. "Spidey Strikes Back!" 80.00 250.00
20 1st & Origin Mac Gargan as The Scorpion. "The Coming Of The Scorpion!" 85.00 275.00
21 App: The Beetle, Human Torch. "Where Flies The Beetle...!" 55.00 175.00
22 App: Ringmaster, 1st: Princess Python. "The Clown And His Masters Of Menace!" 55.00 175.00
23 App: Green Goblin. "The Goblin And The Gangsters!" 80.00 250.00
24 App: Mysterio. "Spider-Man Goes Mad!" 55.00 175.00
25 1st: Mary Jane (face hidden), 1st: Spencer Smythe. "Captured By J.Jonah Jameson!" 55.00 175.00
26 1st: Crime Master. "The Man In The Crime-Master's Mask!" 65.00 200.00
27 App: Green Goblin. "Bring Back My Goblin To Me!" 65.00 200.00
28 1st & Origin: Molten Man. "The Molten Man!" 95.00 300.00
29 App: Scorpion. "Never Step On A Scorpion!" 40.00 130.00
30 1st: Cat Burglar. "The Claws Of The Cat!" 40.00 130.00
31 1st: Gwen Stacy, 1st: Harry Osborne. "If This Be My Destiny...!" 45.00 140.00
32 App: Dr. Octopus. "Man On A Rampage!" 31.00 100.00
33 "The Final Chapter!" App: Dr. Octopus. 31.00 100.00
34 App: Kraven. "The Thrill Of The Hunt!" 31.00 100.00
35 App: Molten Man. "The Molten Man Regrets...!" 31.00 100.00
36 1st: Looter. "When Falls The Meteor!" 31.00 100.00
37 1st: Mendel Stromm. "Once Upon A Time, There Was A Robot...!" 31.00 100.00
38 2nd: Mary Jane (face hidden). "Just A Guy Named Joe!" 31.00 100.00
39 App: Green Goblin. 50.00 160.00
40 Origin: Green Goblin. "The End Of The Green Goblin!" by Romita/Lee. 80.00 250.00
41 1st: Rhino. "The Horns Of The Rhino!" by Romita/Lee. 40.00 125.00
42 1st: Mary Jane (full appearance). "The Birth Of A Super-Hero!" by Romita/Lee. 35.00 110.00
43 2nd: Rhino. "Rhino On The Rampage!" by Romita/Lee. 23.00 75.00
44 2nd: Lizard. "Where Crawls The Lizard!" by Romita/Lee. 23.00 75.00
45 App: Lizard. "Spidey Smashes Out!" 20.00 65.00
46 1st: Shocker. "The Sinister Shocker!" by Romita/Lee. 20.00 65.00
47 App: Kraven. 20.00 65.00
48 1st & Origin: Vulture II. 20.00 65.00
49 App: Kraven, Vulture. 20.00 65.00
50 1st: Kingpin. "Spider-Man No More!" 105.00 350.00
51 App: Kingpin, 1st:Joseph "Robbie" Robinson. 35.00 115.00
52 App: Kingpin. "To Die A Hero!" by Romita/Lee. 19.00 60.00
53 App: Dr. Octopus. "Enter: Dr. Octopus!" by Romita/Lee. 16.00 50.00
54 App: Dr. Octopus. "The Tentacles And The Trap!" by Romita/Lee. 16.00 50.00
55 App: Dr. Octopus. "Doc Ock Wins!" by Romita/Lee. 16.00 50.00
56 1st: Captain George Stacy, App: Dr. Octopus. "Disaster!" by Romita/Lee. 17.00 55.00
57 App: Ka-Zar. "The Coming Of Ka-Zar!" by Romita/Lee. 14.00 45.00
58 App: Ka-Zar. "To Kill A Spider-Man!" by Romita/Lee. 14.00 45.00
59 App: Kingpin. "The Brand Of The Brainwasher!" by Romita/Lee. 16.00 50.00
60 App: Kingpin. "O, Bitter Victory!" by Romita/Lee. 16.00 50.00
61 App: Kingpin. "What A Tangled Web We Weave...!" by Romita/Lee. 16.00 50.00
62-67 13.00 40.00
68 App: Kingpin. "Crisis On The Campus!" by Romita/Lee. 14.00 45.00
69 App: Kingpin. "Mission: Crush The Kingpin!" by Romita/Lee. 14.00 45.00
70 1st: Vanessa Fisk, App: Kingpin. "Spider-Man Wanted!" by Romita/Lee. 14.00 45.00
71 App: Quicksilver. 13.00 40.00
72 App: Shocker. "Rocked By The Shocker!" by Romita/Lee. 13.00 40.00
73 1st: Man Mountain Marko, Silvermane. 13.00 40.00
74 App: Silvermane, Maggia. 13.00 40.00
75 Death: Silvermane, App: Lizard. "Death Without Warning!" by Romita/Lee. 10.00 32.00
76 App: Lizard. 10.00 32.00
77 App: Human Torch, Lizard. 10.00 32.00
78 1st: Prowler. 10.00 32.00
79 App: Prowler. "To Prowl No More!" by Mooney/Lee. 10.00 32.00
80 App: Chameleon. 10.00 32.00
81-82 10.00 32.00
83 1st: Richard Fisk (as The Schemer). "The Coming Of The Schemer!" by Romita-Demeo/Lee. 11.00 36.00
84-86 10.00 32.00
87 11.00 35.00
88-89 10.00 32.00
90 Death: Capt. Stacy. 16.00 50.00
91 1st: Sam Bullit. "To Smash The Spider!" by Kane/Lee. 10.00 32.00
92 10.00 32.00
93 App: The Prowler. "The Lady And The Prowler!" by Romita/Lee. 10.00 32.00
94 Origin retold: Spider-Man. 17.00 55.00
95 8.00 25.00

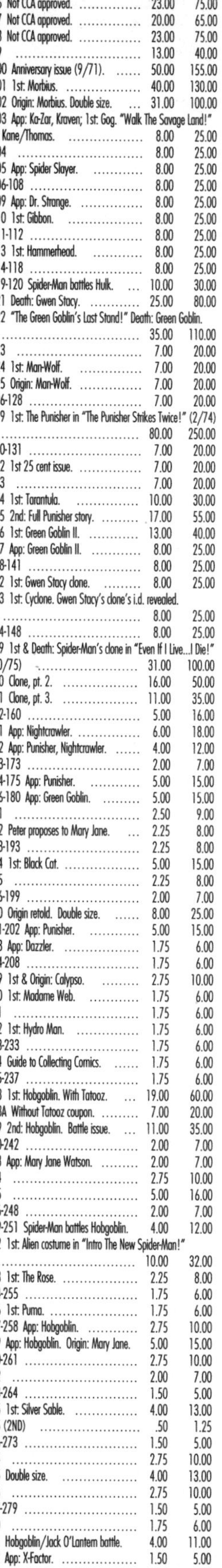

96 Not CCA approved. 23.00 75.00
97 Not CCA approved. 20.00 65.00
98 Not CCA approved. 23.00 75.00
99 13.00 40.00
100 Anniversary issue (9/71). 50.00 155.00
101 1st: Morbius. 40.00 130.00
102 Origin: Morbius. Double size. 31.00 100.00
103 App: Ka-Zar, Kraven; 1st: Gog. "Walk The Savage Land!" by Kane/Thomas. 8.00 25.00
104 8.00 25.00
105 App: Spider Slayer. 8.00 25.00
106-108 8.00 25.00
109 App: Dr. Strange. 8.00 25.00
110 1st: Gibbon. 8.00 25.00
111-112 8.00 25.00
113 1st: Hammerhead. 8.00 25.00
114-118 8.00 25.00
119-120 Spider-Man battles Hulk. 10.00 30.00
121 Death: Gwen Stacy. 25.00 80.00
122 "The Green Goblin's Last Stand!" Death: Green Goblin. 35.00 110.00
123 7.00 20.00
124 1st: Man-Wolf. 7.00 20.00
125 Origin: Man-Wolf. 7.00 20.00
126-128 7.00 20.00
129 1st: The Punisher in "The Punisher Strikes Twice!" (2/74) 80.00 250.00
130-131 7.00 20.00
132 1st 25 cent issue. 7.00 20.00
133 7.00 20.00
134 1st: Tarantula. 10.00 30.00
135 2nd: Full Punisher story. 17.00 55.00
136 1st: Green Goblin II. 13.00 40.00
137 App: Green Goblin II. 8.00 25.00
138-141 8.00 25.00
142 1st: Gwen Stacy clone. 8.00 25.00
143 1st: Cyclone. Gwen Stacy's clone's i.d. revealed. 8.00 25.00
144-148 8.00 25.00
149 1st & Death: Spider-Man's clone in "Even If I Live...I Die!" (10/75) 31.00 100.00
150 Clone, pt. 2. 16.00 50.00
151 Clone, pt. 3. 11.00 35.00
152-160 5.00 16.00
161 App: Nightcrawler. 6.00 18.00
162 App: Punisher, Nightcrawler. 4.00 12.00
163-173 2.00 7.00
174-175 App: Punisher. 5.00 15.00
176-180 App: Green Goblin. 5.00 15.00
181 2.50 9.00
182 Peter proposes to Mary Jane. 2.25 8.00
183-193 2.25 8.00
194 1st: Black Cat. 5.00 15.00
195 2.25 8.00
196-199 2.00 7.00
200 Origin retold. Double size. 8.00 25.00
201-202 App: Punisher. 5.00 15.00
203 App: Dazzler. 1.75 6.00
204-208 1.75 6.00
209 1st & Origin: Calypso. 2.75 10.00
210 1st: Madame Web. 1.75 6.00
211 1.75 6.00
212 1st: Hydro Man. 1.75 6.00
213-233 1.75 6.00
234 Guide to Collecting Comics. 1.75 6.00
235-237 1.75 6.00
238 1st: Hobgoblin. With Tatooz. 19.00 60.00
238A Without Tatooz coupon. 7.00 20.00
239 2nd: Hobgoblin. Battle issue. 11.00 35.00
240-242 2.00 7.00
243 App: Mary Jane Watson. 2.00 7.00
244 2.75 10.00
245 5.00 16.00
246-248 2.00 7.00
249-251 Spider-Man battles Hobgoblin. 4.00 12.00
252 1st: Alien costume in "Intro The New Spider-Man!" 10.00 32.00
253 1st: The Rose. 2.25 8.00
254-255 1.75 6.00
256 1st: Puma. 1.75 6.00
257-258 App: Hobgoblin. 2.75 10.00
259 App: Hobgoblin. Origin: Mary Jane. 5.00 15.00
260-261 2.75 10.00
262 2.00 7.00
263-264 1.50 5.00
265 1st: Silver Sable. 4.00 13.00
265 (2ND) .50 1.25
266-273 1.50 5.00
274 2.75 10.00
275 Double size. 4.00 13.00
276 2.75 10.00
277-279 1.50 5.00
280 1.75 6.00
281 Hobgoblin/Jack O'Lantern battle. 4.00 11.00
282 App: X-Factor. 1.50 5.00
283 1.50 5.00
284 Begin: Gang War. App: Hobgoblin. 2.25 8.00
285 App: Punisher. 5.00 16.00

AMAZING SPIDER-MAN #1

AMAZING SPIDER-MAN #97

AMAZING SPIDER-MAN #252

AMAZING SPIDER-MAN #260

AMAZING SPIDER-MAN ANNUAL #2

AMAZING X-MEN #1

AMERICAN FLAGG! #22

AMERICA'S BEST TV COMICS #1

286-287 App: Hobgoblin. 2.00 7.00
288 End: Gang War. App: Hobgoblin. 2.25 8.00
289 Death: Ned Leeds. Double size. 7.00 20.00
290 Peter proposes to Mary Jane. 1.50 5.00
291-292 1.50 5.00
293 2.75 10.00
294 Death: Kraven. 2.75 10.00
295-297 1.50 5.00
298 1st: Todd McFarlane art on Spider-Man. Cameo: Venom. 11.00 36.00
299 1st: Venom in costume (cameo). 10.00 30.00
300 1st & Origin:Venom (1st full story). Double size 25th Anniversary issue. 23.00 75.00
301-303 5.00 15.00
304 2.75 10.00
305 5.00 15.00
306-311 2.75 10.00
312 Green Goblin battles Hobgoblin. 7.00 22.00
313-314 2.75 10.00
315-317 App: Venom. 6.00 18.00
318-320 2.75 10.00
321-322 2.00 7.50
323 2.50 9.00
324 Cover only: McFarlane. App: Sabretooth. 2.50 9.00
325 2.00 7.00
326 1.75 6.00
327 1.25 4.00
328 End: McFarlane. App: Hulk. 2.25 8.00
329 1.25 4.00
330-331 App: Punisher. 1.75 6.00
332-333 App: Venom. 2.25 8.00
334-336 1.00 3.00
337 App: Hobgoblin. 1.00 3.00
338-343 1.00 3.00
344 1st: Cletus Kasady who later becomes Carnage. 2.75 10.00
345 Venom costume infects Cletus Kasady. 4.00 12.00
346-347 App: Venom. 2.25 8.00
348 App: Avengers. 1.00 3.00
349 1.00 3.00
350 Spider-Man battles Dr. Doom. Double size. 1.00 3.00
351-356 1.00 3.00
357-358 App: Punisher. 1.00 3.00
359 2.00 7.00
360 1st: Carnage (cameo). 2.25 8.00
361 1st: Carnage (full). Origin: Cletus Kasady. 6.00 17.00
361 (2ND) .50 1.25
362 App: Carnage & Venom. 4.00 11.00
362 (2ND) .50 1.25
363 App: Carnage & Venom. 2.75 10.00
364 .75 2.00
365 30th Anniversary. Double size. 2.25 8.00
366-368 .50 1.75
369 App: Green Goblin II. .50 1.75
370-372 .50 1.75
373 App: Venom. .75 2.50
374 App: Venom. 1.00 3.50
375 Hologram cover. Double size. 1.75 6.00
376-377 .50 1.50
378 Maximum Carnage. .75 2.50
379 .75 2.50
380 .50 1.50
381-382 App: Hulk. .50 1.25
383-385 .50 1.25
386 Lifetheft, pt.1. 1.50 5.50
387 Lifetheft, pt.2. 1.75 6.00
388 Lifetheft, pt.3. Double size. Collector's edition. Parent's secret. 1.25 4.50
388A Newsstand edition. 1.00 3.00
389 .50 1.50
390 1.00 3.00
390A Newsstand edition. .50 1.50
391-393 .50 1.50
394 Spidey & clone. Foil-stamped covers. 1.25 4.50
394A Newsstand edition. .75 2.50
395-396 .50 1.50
397 Double size. .75 2.25
398-399 .50 1.50
400 Death: Aunt May. Double size. Die-cut enhanced cover. 1.75 7.00
400A Regular edition. 1.00 3.50
400B White cover. 8.00 25.00
401-405 .50 1.50

AMAZING SPIDER-MAN ANNUAL
MARVEL (1964-CURRENT)
1 Origin retold: Spider-Man. 1st: Sinister Six. "The Sinister Six!" 135.00 475.00
2 "The Wondrous Worlds Of Doctor Strange!" plus reprints #1, 2, 5. (1965) 70.00 225.00
3 Reprints #11, 12. (1966) 23.00 75.00
4 "The Web And The Flame!" new story: Spider-Man battles Human Torch. (1967) 23.00 75.00
5 New Story: The Parents Of Peter Parker! (1968) 25.00 80.00
6 Reprints 1st story Annual #1. (1969) 9.00 28.00
7 Reprints #1, 2. (1970) 8.00 24.00
8 Reprints. (1971) 8.00 24.00
9 Reprints. (1973) 7.00 20.00
10 Origin: Human Fly. 5.00 14.00
11 5.00 14.00
12 Reprints #119, 120. 5.00 14.00
13 5.00 14.00
14 Cover/Art: Frank Miller. 5.00 14.00
15 Cover/Art: Miller. App: Punisher. 6.00 18.00
16 1st & Origin: New Captain Marvel. 1.75 6.00
17-19 1.75 6.00
20 (1986) 1.75 6.00
21 Wedding issue. Spider-Man cover. 5.00 15.00
21A Wedding issue. Tuxedo cover. 6.00 17.00
22 Evolutionary War. 2.25 8.00
23 Atlantis Attacks. 2.25 8.00
24 1.00 3.50
25 Art: Ditko (6 pages). App: Venom. 1.00 3.00
26 App: Venom. 1.00 3.00
27-28 1.00 3.00

AMAZING SPIDER-MAN: CHAOS IN CALGARY
MARVEL (1990)
4 .75 2.00

AMAZING SPIDER-MAN: DOUBLE TROUBLE
MARVEL (1990)
2 .75 2.00

AMAZING SPIDER-MAN GIVEAWAYS
MARVEL
1A Aim Toothpaste. .75 2.00
1B Chicago Tribune (6/8/80). w/ The Hulk, 20 pages. 1.50 5.00
1C Acme & Dingo Children's Boots (1980). 1.00 3.00
1D 7-11 Stores. Includes Captain America, Incredible Hulk, Spider-Woman (1981). 1.00 3.00
1E National Committee For The Prevention Of Child Abuse. (1984) w/ Power Pack. .30 1.00

AMAZING SPIDER-MAN: HIT AND RUN
MARVEL (1990)
3 .75 2.00

AMAZING SPIDER-MAN MARVEL MILESTONE
MARVEL (1994)
1 Reprints: #149. Metallic ink cover. .75 2.95
2 Reprints #3. Metallic ink cover. .75 2.95

AMAZING SPIDER-MAN: SKATING ON THIN ICE
MARVEL (1990)
1 .75 2.00

AMAZING SPIDER-MAN SUPER SIZE SPECIAL
MARVEL (1995)
1 1.25 4.50

AMAZING WILLIE MAYS, THE
FFP (1954)
NO# 110.00 350.00

AMAZING X-MEN, THE
MARVEL (1995)
1 Deluxe edition. Previous title: X-Men (2nd series). 1.50 7.50
2 1.00 3.00
3-4 .75 2.75

AMERICA IN ACTION
DELL (1942)
NO# 68 pages. 31.00 100.00

AMERICA IN ACTION
MAYFLOWER HOUSE (1945)
1 19.00 60.00

AMERICA VS. THE JUSTICE SOCIETY
DC (1985)
1 Double size. .75 2.00
2-4 .30 1.00
SPECIAL .75 2.00

AMERICA'S BEST COMICS
STANDARD (1942-1949)
1 Begin: Capt. Future, Doc Strange. 270.00 875.00
2 115.00 370.00
3 Begin: Pyroman. 115.00 370.00
4 85.00 280.00
5 End: Capt. Future. 85.00 280.00
6 65.00 210.00
7 Hitler, Mussolini. 80.00 250.00
8 55.00 180.00
9 Begin: Fighting Yank. 80.00 250.00
10 Patriotic cover. 55.00 180.00
11-21 40.00 120.00
22 Capt. Future. 40.00 130.00
23 Begin: Miss Masque. 50.00 150.00
24 40.00 120.00
25 End: Fighting Yank. 40.00 120.00
26 40.00 120.00
27 Doc Strange. 40.00 120.00
28 40.00 120.00
29 End: Pyroman. 40.00 120.00
30-31 40.00 120.00

AMERICA'S BEST TV COMICS
ABC TELEVISION NETWORK (1967) ONE SHOT
NO# Includes: Fantastic Four, Casper, Spider-Man, Journey To The Center Of The Earth, and others. Giant-size. 16.00 50.00

AMERICA'S BIGGEST COMICS BOOK
WILLIAM H. WISE (1944)
NO# 196 page one-shot. Includes Silver Knight, Zudo, Sea Scribe, Little Oliver, Barnaby Beep, Thunderhoof, Jocko and Socko. 65.00 200.00

AMERICA'S FUNNIEST COMICS
WILLIAM H. WISE (1944)
NO# 80 pages. 50.00 150.00

AMERICA'S GREATEST COMICS
FAWCETT (1941-1943)
1 Begin: Bulletman, Capt. Marvel, Spy Smasher. 500.00 1800.00
2 220.00 700.00
3 190.00 600.00
4-5 145.00 480.00
6-7 130.00 420.00
8 145.00 480.00

AMERICAN, THE
DARK HORSE (1987-1989)
1 1.50 5.00
2 1.00 3.00
3-9 .75 2.00

AMERICAN AIR FORCES
FLYING CADET (1944-1945)
1 10.00 30.00
2-4 7.00 20.00

AMERICAN AIR FORCES (A-1 SERIES)
ME (1951-1954)
5 (A-1 #45). 7.00 20.00
6 (A-1 #54). 7.00 20.00
7 (A-1 #58). 7.00 20.00
8 (A-1 #65). 7.00 20.00
9 (A-1 #67). 7.00 20.00
10 (A-1 #74). 7.00 20.00
11 (A-1 #79). 7.00 20.00
12 (A-1 #91). 7.00 20.00

AMERICAN FLAGG
FIRST (1983-1988)
1-50 .50 1.50
SPECIAL 1 (1986) .75 2.75

AMERICAN FLAGG
FIRST (1988-1989)
1-5 .75 2.00
6 Elvis photo cover. 1.75 6.00
7-12 .75 2.00

AMERICAN FREAK: A TALE OF THE UN-MEN
DC (1994)
1-5 .50 1.95

AMERICAN GRAPHICS
HS (1954, 1957)
1 "The Maid Of The Mist" and "The Last Of The Eries." 10.00 30.00
2 "The War Of 1812." 7.00 20.00

AMERICAN LIBRARY
DAVID MCKAY (1944-1945)
1 See Thirty Seconds Over Tokyo.
2 See Guadalcanal Diary.
3 Look To The Mountain. 16.00 50.00
4 The Case Of The Crooked Candle. 16.00 50.00
5 Duel In The Sun. Movie tie-in. 20.00 65.00
6 Wingate's Raiders. 16.00 50.00

AMERICAN SPLENDOR
HARVEY PEKAR (1976-1990)
1 All are magazine size. 7.00 20.00

2-5 2.75 10.00
6-12 1.50 5.00
13-15 1.25 4.00
16 (Tundra published, 1991) 1.25 4.00
17 (Dark Horse, 1993) 1.50 5.00

AMERICAN SPLENDOR SPECIAL: A STEP OUT OF THE NEST
DARK HORSE (1994)
NO# .75 2.95

AMERICAN SPLENDOR: WINDFALL
DARK HORSE (1995)
1-2 1.00 3.95

AMETHYST
DC (1983-1984)
1 .30 1.00
1A 35 cent test cover. 2.75 10.00
2 .30 1.00
2A 35 cent test cover. 2.75 10.00
3-12 .30 1.00
ANNUAL 1 (1984) .30 1.00

AMETHYST
DC (1985-1986)
1-16 .30 1.00

AMETHYST
DC (1987-1988)
1-4 .30 1.00

ANCHORS ANDREWS
ST. JOHN (1953)
1 Art: Matt Baker (9 pgs.). 25.00 80.00
2-4 (...The Salt Water Daffy). 7.00 20.00

ANDREW VACHSS' BLUE BELLE
DARK HORSE (1994)
1 1.00 3.95

ANDREW VACHSS' UNDERGROUND
DARK HORSE (1994)
1-4 1.00 3.95

ANDY BURNETT
DELL FOUR COLOR SERIES (1957)
865 TV photo cover. (12/57) 19.00 60.00

ANDY COMICS
ACE (1948)
20 Previous title: Scream Comics. 8.00 25.00
21 Title changes to Ernie Comics with #22. 8.00 25.00

ANDY DEVINE WESTERN
FAWCETT (1950-1951)
1 Photo cover. 100.00 330.00
2 Photo cover. 70.00 220.00

ANDY GRIFFITH SHOW, THE
DELL FOUR COLOR SERIES (1962)
1252 TV photo cover. (1/62) 80.00 250.00
1341 TV photo cover. (4/62) 65.00 200.00

ANDY HARDY COMICS
DELL (1952-1954)
1 (#389) From the 4-Color Series. (4/52) 10.00 30.00
2 (#447) From the 4-Color Series. (1/53) 5.00 15.00
3 (#480) From the 4-Color Series. (7/53) 5.00 15.00
4 (#515) From the 4-Color Series. (11/53) 5.00 15.00
5-6 5.00 15.00

ANDY PANDA
DELL (1952-1962)
16-56 1.75 6.00

ANDY PANDA
DELL FOUR COLOR SERIES (1943-1952)
25 95.00 300.00
54 65.00 200.00
85 "The Mad Dog Mystery" 40.00 125.00
130 "The City Of Ice" 19.00 60.00
154 "The Ghost Of Captain Kidd" 19.00 60.00
198 "The Mighty Mites" 19.00 60.00
216 "And The Police Pup" 13.00 40.00
240 13.00 40.00
258 "And The Balloon Race" 13.00 40.00
280 "The Isle Of Mechanical Men" 13.00 40.00
297 "The Haunted Inn" 13.00 40.00
326 8.00 25.00
345 "Scotland Yard" 8.00 25.00
358 8.00 25.00
383 (3/52) 5.00 15.00
409 (7/52) 5.00 15.00

ANGEL
DELL (1954-1958)
1 (#576) From the 4-Color Series. (8/54) 7.00 20.00
2-16 2.25 8.00

ANGEL AND THE APE
DC (1968-1969)
1 7.00 22.00
2-6 4.00 11.00

ANGEL AND THE APE
DC (1991)
1-4 .30 1.00

ANGELA
IMAGE (1994-1995)
1 Mini-series. 2.00 7.50
2 2.00 7.50
3 1.75 6.00

ANGRY CHRIST COMICS
SIRIUS (1994)
TPB Reprints Cry For Dawn stories. 7.00 22.00

ANIMA
DC (1994)
0 .50 1.95
1-5 .50 1.75
6-13 .50 1.95
14 .75 2.25

ANIMAL ADVENTURES
TIMOR (1953-1954)
1 2.75 10.00
2 2.00 6.00

ANIMAL ANTICS
DC (1946-1949)
1 Begin: Raccoon Kids. 85.00 270.00
2 40.00 130.00
3-6 31.00 100.00
7-12 23.00 75.00
13-22 20.00 65.00
23 Title changes to Movie Town Animal Antics with #24. 20.00 65.00

ANIMAL COMICS
DELL (1941-1948)
1 1st: Pogo. Art: Walt Kelly. 200.00 650.00
2 85.00 270.00
3 70.00 220.00
4 No Pogo. 35.00 110.00
5 70.00 220.00
6-7 No Pogo. 35.00 110.00
8-12 40.00 130.00
13-18 26.00 85.00
19-24 20.00 65.00
25-30 14.00 44.00

ANIMAL CRACKERS
GREEN (1959)
9 2.75 10.00

ANIMAL FABLES
EC (1946-1947)
1 65.00 200.00
2 Begin: Aesop's Fables. 40.00 125.00
3-6 31.00 100.00
7 Origin: Moon Girl. 190.00 600.00

ANIMAL FAIR
FAWCETT (1946-1947)
1 35.00 110.00
2 25.00 80.00
3-6 17.00 55.00
7-11 11.00 34.00

ANIMAL FUN 3-D
PREMIER (1953)
1 (With glasses.) 55.00 180.00

ANIMAL MAN
DC (1988-CURRENT)
1 2.25 8.00
2 1.50 5.00
3-5 1.00 3.00
6-11 .60 2.00
12-22 .60 2.00
23-40 .60 2.00
41-49 .50 1.75
50 Double size. .75 2.95
51-55 .50 1.75
56 Double size. 1.00 3.50
57-59 .50 1.75
60-82 .50 1.95
83-84 .75 2.25
ANNUAL 1 Children's Crusade. 1.25 4.00

ANIMAL MYSTIC
CRY FOR DAWN/SIRIUS (1993-CURRENT)
1 Art: Dark One. 10.00 30.00
1A Limited, signed & numbered edition, with 8 new pages & alternate cover. 20.00 80.00
1 (2ND) 2nd printing. New cover. 1.00 3.00
2 Intro: Klor. 10.00 30.00
2 (2ND) 2nd printing. New cover. .75 2.50
3 2.25 8.00

ANIMAL WORLD, THE
DELL FOUR COLOR SERIES (1956)
713 (8/56) 11.00 35.00

ANIMATED COMICS
EC (1947)
1 180.00 575.00

ANIMATED FUNNY COMIC-TUNES
MARVEL(TIMELY) (1944-1946)
16 19.00 60.00
17 13.00 43.00
18-19 12.00 37.00
20-21 10.00 31.00
22 12.00 37.00
23 Art: Harvey Kurtzman. 13.00 43.00

ANIMATED MOVIE-TUNES COMICS
MARVEL (TIMELY) (1945-1946)
1 31.00 100.00
2 Title changes to Movie Tunes with #3. 25.00 80.00

ANNETTE
DELL FOUR COLOR SERIES (1958-1960)
905 Disney TV photo cover. (5/58) 50.00 150.00
1100 "...Life Story" Disney TV photo cover. (5/60) 50.00 150.00

ANNEX
MARVEL (1994)
1-4 .50 1.75

ANNIE
MARVEL (1982)
1 Movie tie-in. .30 1.00
2 .30 1.00

ANNIE OAKLEY
MARVEL(TIMELY) (1948-1956)
1 App: Hedy Devine. 75.00 240.00
2 40.00 120.00
3-4 28.00 90.00
5 (1955) 19.00 60.00
6-8 15.00 48.00
9 Art: Williamson (one story). 19.00 60.00
10 15.00 48.00
11 Cover: Severin. 16.00 50.00

ANNIE OAKLEY AND TAGG
DELL (1952-1959)
1 (#438) From the 4-Color Series. TV tie-in. (11/52) 31.00 100.00
2 (#481) "And Tagg" From the 4-Color Series. (8/53) 17.00 55.00
3 (#575) "And Tagg" From the 4-Color Series. (8/54) 17.00 55.00
4-10 13.00 40.00
11-18 10.00 30.00

ANNIE OAKLEY AND TAGG
GOLD KEY (1965)
1 Photo cover. 7.00 20.00

ANTHRO
DC (1968-1969)
1 11.00 34.00
2-5 7.00 23.00
6 Cover & Art: Wallace Wood. 7.00 23.00

APACHE
FICTION HOUSE (1951)
1 Cover: Matt Baker. 25.00 80.00

APACHE KID
MARVEL(ATLAS) (1950-1956)
1 (#53) 40.00 130.00
2 25.00 80.00
3-6 17.00 55.00
7-12 10.00 33.00
13-19 7.00 22.00

APACHE TRAIL
AMERICA'S BEST (1957-1958)
1 8.00 25.00
2-4 5.00 15.00

ANGELA #1

ANIMAL MAN #34

ANNEX #3

ANNIE OAKLEY #4

AQUAMAN #6

AQUAMAN: TIME & TIDE #1

ARCHER & ARMSTRONG #8

ARCHER & ARMSTRONG #11

FAMOUS • FIRSTS

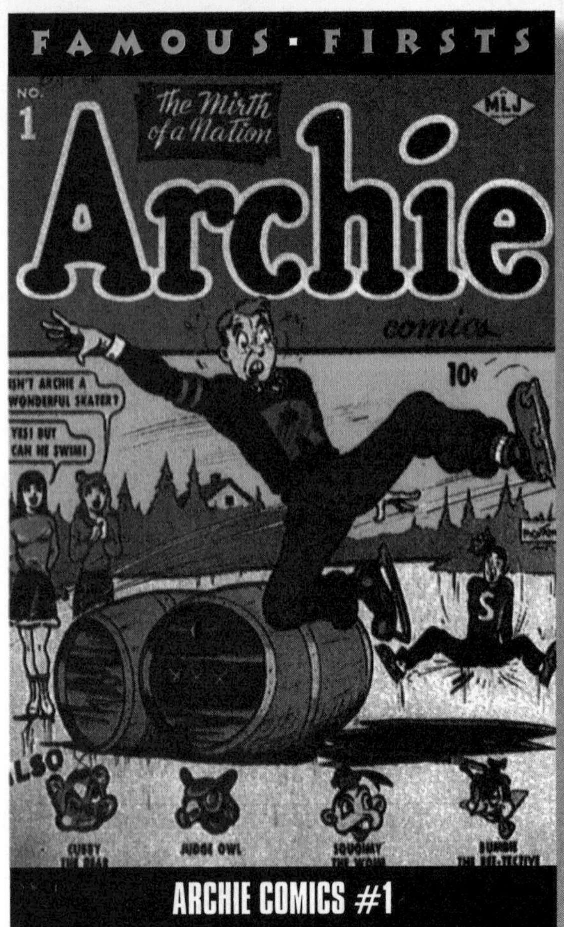

ARCHIE COMICS #1

Introduced in *Pep Comics* #22, Archie Andrews got his own comic in 1942, the first of many in the Archie Empire. It features a new "secret origin" for how Archie met Veronica, plus a Who's Who page describing the gang.

APOCALYPSE STRIKE FILES
MARVEL (1995)

1 One shot.	.75	2.50

APPLESEED (BOOK 1)
ECLIPSE (1988-1989)

1 1st: Briareos.	5.00	14.00
2-3	2.00	7.00
4-5	1.50	5.00

APPLESEED (BOOK 2)
ECLIPSE (1989)

1	1.00	3.50
2-5	1.00	3.00

APPLESEED (BOOK 3)
ECLIPSE (1989-1990)

1	1.00	3.00
2-5	1.00	3.50

APPLESEED (BOOK 4)
ECLIPSE (1991)

1-5	1.00	3.50

APPLESEED DATA BOOK
DARK HORSE (1995)

1	2.75	10.00
2	1.00	3.50

APPROVED COMICS
SEE INDIVIDUAL TITLES.

- THE HAWK, INVISIBLE BOY, WILD BOY OF THE CONGO, KID COWBOY, FLYBOY, DARING ADVENTURES, CRIME ON THE RUN, WESTERN BANDIT TRAILS, FIGHTIN' MARINES, NORTHWEST MOUNTIES.

AQUAMAN
DC (1962-1978)

1 1st: Quisp.	145.00	475.00
2	55.00	180.00
3	40.00	125.00
4-6	26.00	85.00
7-10	20.00	64.00
11 1st: Mera.	20.00	64.00
12	20.00	64.00
13-17	11.00	36.00
18 App: JLA.	11.00	36.00
19-20	11.00	36.00
21-25	10.00	30.00
26 Huntress.	10.00	30.00
27-29	10.00	30.00
30 App: Batman, Superman.	10.00	30.00
31-32	7.00	20.00
33 1st: Aquagirl.	13.00	40.00
34-40	7.00	20.00
41-47	4.00	12.00
48 Origin retold.	5.00	16.00
49	4.00	12.00
50-52 Art: Neal Adams. Deadman.	8.00	25.00
53-55	1.75	6.00
56 1st: Crusader. (1971)	1.75	6.00
57 (1977)	1.75	6.00
58 Origin retold.	1.75	6.00
59-63	1.75	6.00

AQUAMAN
DC (1986)

1 Mini-series.	1.25	4.00
2-4	.75	2.50

AQUAMAN
DC (1989)

1 Mini-series.	.75	2.50
2-5	.50	1.50

AQUAMAN
DC (1991-1992)

1	.75	2.00
2-3	.30	1.25
4-6	.30	1.25
7-8	.30	1.25
9-11	.30	1.25
12-13	.30	1.25

AQUAMAN
DC (1994-CURRENT)

0	.75	2.50
1-2	1.00	3.50
3-8	.75	2.50
9-12	.50	1.75
ANNUAL 1 (1995)	1.00	3.50

AQUAMAN SPECIAL
DC (1988)

1	.75	2.00

AQUAMAN: TIME & TIDE
DC (1993-1994)

1 New origin: Aquaman.	.75	2.50
2	.75	2.00
3-4	.50	1.50

AQUANAUTS, THE
DELL FOUR COLOR SERIES (1961)

1197 TV photo cover. (4/61)	19.00	60.00

ARABIAN NIGHTS
UNIVERSAL (1942)

NO# Movie giveaway (4 pages). From the Cinema Comics Herald series.	16.00	50.00

ARACHNIS
MUSHROOM (1995)

1 Mini-series.	.75	2.50

ARACHNOPHOBIA
HOLLYWOOD (1990)

1A 64 page graphic novel; Adapts movie.	2.25	8.00
1B Comic book edition.	1.00	3.00

ARAK
DC (1981-1985)

1 Origin: Arak.	.30	1.00
2-11	.30	1.00
12 Origin: Valda.	.30	1.00
13-49	.30	1.00
50 Double size.	.30	1.00
ANNUAL 1	.30	1.00

ARCANA
DC (1993)

ANNUAL 1 Children's Crusade.	1.00	3.95

ARCHER AND ARMSTRONG
VALIANT (1992-1994)

0 1st: Armstrong. 1st & origin: Archer.	1.50	5.00
0A Gold logo version.	5.00	15.00
1	1.25	4.00
2 2nd: Turok.	1.00	3.00
3-7	.75	2.00
8 1st: Ivar, Time Walker. Combined with Eternal Warrior #8.	1.00	3.00
9-25	.75	2.25
26 Combined with Eternal Warrior #26.	.75	2.75

ARCHIE AND ME
ARCHIE (1964-1987)

1	35.00	115.00
2	20.00	65.00
3-6	10.00	30.00
7-9	6.00	18.00
10-12	5.00	15.00
13-24	2.25	8.00
25-36	1.75	6.00
37-42	1.00	3.00
43 Begin: Giant size.	1.25	4.00
44-62	1.25	4.00
63 End: Giant size.	1.25	4.00
64-161	.30	1.00

ARCHIE AS PUREHEART THE POWERFUL
ARCHIE (1966-1967)

1	14.00	45.00
2	10.00	30.00
3	8.00	25.00
4-6 Capt. Pureheart.	8.00	25.00

ARCHIE AT RIVERDALE HIGH
ARCHIE (1972-1987)

1	10.00	33.00
2	7.00	22.00
3-6	4.00	13.00
7-12	2.00	7.50
13-24	1.25	4.25
25-36	1.00	3.25
37-50	.75	2.00

51-88 .30 1.00
89 4th: Cheryl Blossom. .75 2.00
90-113 .30 1.00

ARCHIE COMICS

ARCHIE (1942-CURRENT)

1 Cover & art: Bob Montana. 2nd: Veronica. See Pep #22 for 1st Archie. 1800.00 7000.00
2 500.00 1600.00
3 400.00 1200.00
4-5 230.00 750.00
6 170.00 550.00
7-8 155.00 500.00
9 "Archie The Caveman." 155.00 500.00
10 155.00 500.00
11-12 115.00 375.00
13-20 110.00 350.00
21-24 85.00 275.00
25-30 70.00 225.00
31-36 65.00 210.00
37-50 40.00 120.00
51-60 23.00 75.00
61-70 17.00 55.00
71-80 14.00 45.00
81-93 11.00 35.00
94 1st: Coach Kleets. 14.00 45.00
95-99 11.00 35.00
100 13.00 40.00
101-110 7.00 22.00
111-120 6.00 18.00
121-123 4.00 12.00
124 1st 12 cent cover. 4.00 12.00
125-130 4.00 12.00
131-132 2.50 9.00
133 1st: Cricket O'Dell. 2.50 9.00
134-140 2.50 9.00
141-150 2.25 8.00
151-160 2.00 7.00
161-170 1.75 6.00
171-180 1.25 4.75
181-200 1.00 3.50
201-225 1.00 3.00
226-300 .75 2.25
301-406 .50 1.50
407 With trading card. .50 1.50
408-425 .50 1.50

ARCHIE COMICS ANNUAL

ARCHIE (1950-1975)

1 (1950) 250.00 800.00
2 155.00 500.00
3-4 95.00 300.00
5 (1954) 80.00 250.00
6 80.00 250.00
7-10 55.00 180.00
11-13 22.00 70.00
14 (1964) 22.00 70.00
15 22.00 70.00
16-17 11.00 35.00
18-19 8.00 25.00
20 (1970) 6.00 18.00
21 6.00 18.00
22-25 4.00 12.00
26 (1975) 4.00 12.00

ARCHIE GIANT SERIES

ARCHIE (1960-1992)

7 Katy Keene Holiday Fun. 60.00 185.00
8 Betty And Veronica Summer Fun. 60.00 185.00
9 The World Of Jughead. 60.00 185.00
10 Archie's Christmas Stocking. 60.00 185.00
11 Betty And Veronica Spectacular. 50.00 150.00
12 Katy Keene Holiday Fun. 40.00 120.00
13 Betty And Veronica Summer Fun. 50.00 150.00
14 The World Of Jughead. 40.00 120.00
15 Archie's Christmas Stocking. 35.00 110.00
16 Betty And Veronica Spectacular. 50.00 150.00
17 Archie's Jokes. 35.00 110.00
18 Betty And Veronica Summer Fun. 50.00 150.00
19 The World Of Jughead. 31.00 100.00
20 Archie's Christmas Stocking. 31.00 100.00
21 Betty And Veronica Spectacular. 25.00 80.00
22 Archie's Jokes. 25.00 80.00
23 Betty And Veronica Summer Fun. 25.00 80.00
24 The World Of Jughead. 25.00 80.00
25 Archie's Christmas Stocking. 22.00 70.00
26 Betty And Veronica Spectacular. 22.00 70.00
27 Archie's Jokes. 22.00 70.00
28 Betty And Veronica Summer Fun. 22.00 70.00
29 Around The World With Archie. 22.00 70.00
30 The World Of Jughead. 19.00 60.00
31 Archie's Christmas Stocking. 19.00 60.00
32 Betty And Veronica Spectacular. 19.00 60.00
33 Archie's Jokes. 19.00 60.00
34 Betty And Veronica Summer Fun. 19.00 60.00
35 Around The World With Archie. 19.00 60.00
136-141 11.00 36.00
142 Archie's Super Hero Special. Origin: Capt. Pureheart. 15.00 48.00
143-147 6.00 18.00
148 World Of Archie. 6.00 18.00
149-158 6.00 18.00
159 (1/69) 4.00 12.00
160-167 4.00 12.00
168 Betty And Veronica Christmas Spectacular. 4.00 12.00
169 Archie's Christmas Love-In. 4.00 12.00
170 Jughead's Eat-Out Comic. 4.00 12.00
171-202 4.00 12.00
203 (12/72) 1.75 6.00
204-218 1.75 6.00
219 Li'l Jinx Christmas Bag. 1.75 6.00
220-225 1.75 6.00
226-251 1.00 3.50
452-500 .75 2.25
501-572 .30 1.00
573 Archie At Riverdale High. .30 1.00
574-575 .30 1.00
576 Pep. .30 1.00
577-602 .30 1.00
603 Archie And Me. .30 1.00
604-630 .30 1.00
631 .50 1.50
632 Betty And Veronica Spectacular. .50 1.50

ARCHIE MEETS THE PUNISHER

ARCHIE/MARVEL (1994)

1 1.00 3.00

ARCHIE'S CHRISTMAS STOCKING

ARCHIE (1954-1959)

1 (1954), Giant edition. 220.00 700.00
2 (1955), Giant edition. 125.00 410.00
3 (1956), Giant edition. 95.00 300.00
4 (1957), Giant edition. 95.00 300.00
5 (1958), Giant edition. 95.00 300.00
6 (1959), Giant edition. 95.00 300.00

ARCHIE'S GIRLS, BETTY AND VERONICA

ARCHIE (1950-1987)

1 280.00 900.00
2 145.00 480.00
3-5 100.00 330.00
6 Art: Dan DeCarlo (his 1st). 100.00 330.00
7-12 55.00 180.00
13-24 40.00 120.00
25-36 28.00 90.00
37-48 22.00 70.00
49-60 19.00 60.00
61-72 15.00 48.00
73 1st 12 cent cover. 11.00 36.00
74 11.00 36.00
75 Deal with devil issue. 31.00 100.00
76-84 11.00 36.00
85-99 8.00 24.00
100 10.00 30.00
101-110 6.00 18.00
111-130 4.00 12.00
131-140 2.25 8.25
141-150 1.75 6.00
151-170 1.25 4.75
171-190 1.25 4.00
191-200 1.00 3.50
201-220 .75 2.25
221-250 .50 1.75
251-319 .50 1.50
320 1st: Cheryl Blossom. 1.00 3.50
321 .50 1.50
322 5th: Cheryl Blossom (1st: introduction to Archie Andrews). 1.00 3.50
323-347 .50 1.50

ARCHIE'S GIRLS, BETTY AND VERONICA ANNUAL

ARCHIE (1953-1960)

1 (1953) 160.00 510.00
2 (1954) 75.00 240.00
3 (1955) 50.00 150.00
4 (1956) 50.00 150.00
5 (1957) 50.00 150.00
6 (1958) 50.00 150.00
7 (1959) 40.00 120.00
8 (1960) 40.00 120.00

ARCHIE'S JOKE BOOK

ARCHIE (1953-1982)

1 (No#) 160.00 525.00
2 Cover: Bob Montana. 95.00 300.00
3 #4-14 do not exist. 65.00 210.00
15 50.00 150.00
16 1st Code Approved issue. 50.00 150.00
17-24 50.00 150.00
25-36 29.00 95.00
37-40 19.00 60.00
41 Art: Neal Adams (his first). 40.00 120.00
42-47 19.00 60.00
48 Art: Neal Adams. 19.00 60.00
49-58 11.00 36.00
59 1st 12 cent cover. 11.00 36.00
60 11.00 36.00
61-72 8.00 24.00
73-84 6.00 18.00
85-99 4.00 12.00
100 5.00 14.00
101-108 2.50 9.50
109-120 1.75 6.00
121-132 1.00 3.50
133-150 .75 2.25
151-250 .50 1.75
251-288 .30 1.00

ARCHIE'S MADHOUSE

ARCHIE (1959-1968)

1 70.00 220.00
2 35.00 110.00
3-6 25.00 80.00
7-12 17.00 55.00
13-17 10.00 33.00
18-21 7.00 22.00
22 1st: Sabrina. 17.00 55.00
23-24 7.00 22.00
25-34 4.00 11.00
35 Beatles. 5.00 16.00
36 4.00 11.00
37-48 1.50 5.50
49-66 .75 2.00
ANNUAL 1 (1962) 14.00 44.00
ANNUAL 2 (1964) 7.00 22.00
ANNUAL 3 (1965) 5.00 16.00
ANNUAL 4 (1966) 4.00 11.00
ANNUAL 5 (1967) 4.00 11.00
ANNUAL 6 (1968) 4.00 11.00

ARCHIE'S MECHANICS

ARCHIE (1954)

1 190.00 600.00
2 110.00 360.00
3 95.00 300.00

ARCHIE'S PAL, JUGHEAD

ARCHIE (1949-1965)

1 1st: Moose. 230.00 750.00
2 100.00 330.00
3-6 75.00 240.00
7-12 40.00 130.00
13-24 35.00 110.00
25-40 17.00 55.00
41-50 14.00 44.00
51-60 12.00 38.00
61-70 9.00 27.00
71-79 7.00 22.00
80 1st 12 cent cover. 7.00 22.00
81-90 5.00 16.00
91-100 4.00 11.00
101-120 2.25 8.75

ARCHIE'S PAL JUGHEAD ANNUAL

ARCHIE (1953-1960)

1 115.00 380.00
2 70.00 220.00
3-6 50.00 160.00
7-8 35.00 110.00

ARCHIE'S PALS 'N' GALS

ARCHIE (1952-1991)

1 Issues #1-83 are giant size. 145.00 480.00
2 75.00 240.00
3-5 55.00 180.00
6-10 40.00 120.00
11-20 22.00 70.00
21-28 11.00 36.00
29 Beatles parody. 15.00 48.00
30-40 10.00 30.00
41-50 6.00 18.00
51-60 4.00 12.00
61-70 2.50 9.50
71-80 2.00 7.00
81-90 1.25 4.75
91-100 1.00 3.50
101-110 .75 2.25
111-130 .50 1.75
131-160 .30 1.00
161 3rd: Cheryl Blossom. .75 2.25
162-224 .30 1.00

ARCHIE'S RIVAL REGGIE

ARCHIE (1950-1954)

1 160.00 525.00
2 75.00 240.00
3-6 55.00 170.00
7-12 40.00 120.00
13 28.00 90.00
14 Title changes to Reggie with #15. 28.00 90.00

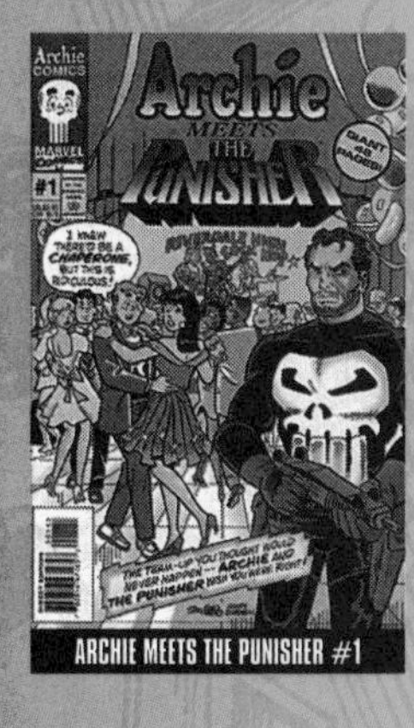

ARCHIE MEETS THE PUNISHER #1

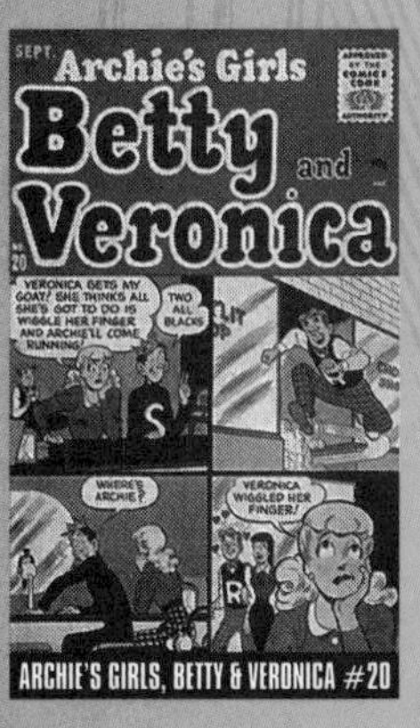

ARCHIE'S GIRLS, BETTY & VERONICA #20

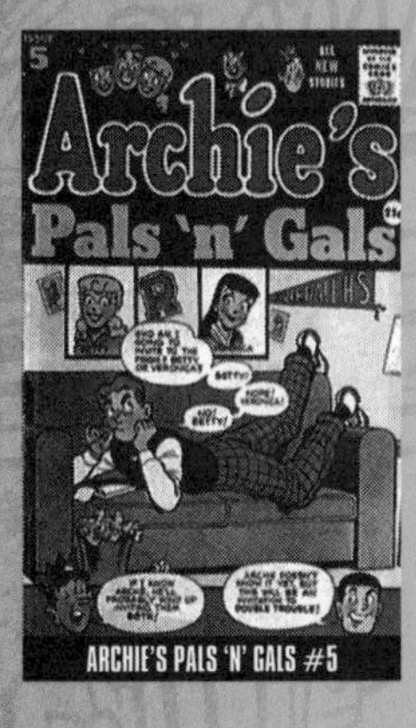

ARCHIE'S PALS 'N' GALS #5

ARCHIE'S RIVAL, REGGIE #12

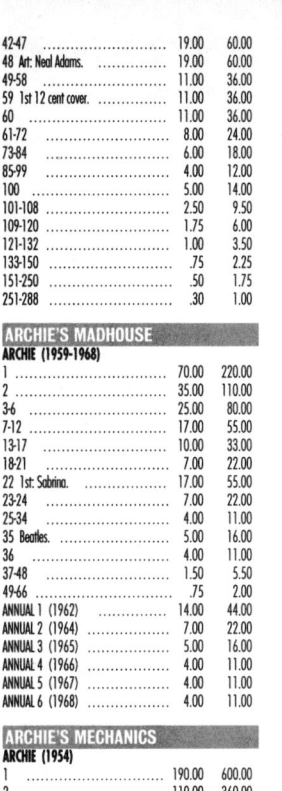

ARGUS #2

ARMAGEDDON 2001 #1

ASH #1

THE ASTONISHING X-MEN #1

ARCHIE'S TV LAUGH-OUT
ARCHIE (1969-1986)
1 Issues #1-23 are giant size. 12.00 38.00
2 ...... 5.00 16.00
3-6 ...... 2.25 8.75
7-12 ...... 1.75 6.50
13-24 ...... 1.50 5.50
25-40 ...... 1.00 3.25
41-60 ...... .75 2.00
61-70 ...... .50 1.50
71-105 ...... .30 1.00

ARGOSY COMIC BOOK PRICE GUIDE
ARGOSY (1965)
NO# 1st: Comic Book price guide. 40 pages offset, no illustrations, staple bound softcover. ... 230.00 750.00

ARGUS
DC (1995-CURRENT)
1 ...... .75 2.00
2-5 ...... .50 1.75

ARION
DC (1982-1985)
1-35 ...... .30 1.00

ARION THE IMMORTAL
DC (1992)
1-6 ...... .30 1.00

ARISTOCATS, THE
GOLD KEY (1971)
30045-103 Movie tie-in. With poster. 14.00 45.00

ARIZONA KID
MARVEL(ATLAS) (1951-1952)
1 ...... 25.00 80.00
2-3 ...... 14.00 44.00
4-6 ...... 12.00 38.00

ARMAGEDDON 2001
DC (1991)
1 1st & origin: Waverider. 1st: Monarch. 1.00 3.00
1 (2ND) 2nd printing (silver). ...... .50 1.50
1 (3RD) 3rd printing (silver). ...... .50 1.50
2 ...... .50 1.50

ARMAGEDDON: INFERNO
DC (1992)
1-3 ...... .30 1.00
4 ...... .50 1.50

ARMAGEDDON: THE ALIEN AGENDA
DC (1991-1992)
1-4 ...... .30 1.00

ARMOR
CONTINUITY (1985-1992)
1 (The Revengers featuring Armor and Silver Streak inside). ...... .75 2.50
2-18 ...... .75 2.50

ARMOR
CONTINUITY (1993-1994)
1 Deathwatch 2000, pt.3. ...... .75 2.50
2 Deathwatch 2000, pt.9. ...... .75 2.50
3 Deathwatch 2000, pt.15. ...... .75 2.50
4-6 Rise Of Magic. ...... .75 2.50
7-12 ...... .75 2.50

ARMORINES
VALIANT (1994-1995)
0 From X-O #25. ...... .75 2.00
1-12 ...... .75 2.25

ARMY AND NAVY COMICS
STREET & SMITH (1941-1942)
1 Begin: Nick Carter. 85.00 280.00
2 ...... 45.00 140.00
3-4 ...... 26.00 85.00
5 App: Supersnipe. 70.00 230.00

ARMY AT WAR
DC (1978)
1 ...... 1.00 3.00

AROUND THE BLOCK WITH DUNC AND LOO
DELL (1961-1963)
1 ...... 16.00 50.00
2-8 ...... 8.00 25.00

AROUND THE WORLD IN 80 DAYS
DELL FOUR COLOR SERIES (1957)
784 Movie photo cover. (2/57) ... 16.00 50.00

AROUND THE WORLD UNDER THE SEA
DELL (1966)
12-030-612 Movie tie-in. 7.00 20.00

ARRGH!
MARVEL (1974-1975)
1 ...... 1.25 4.00
2 ...... .75 2.00
3-5 ...... .50 1.50

ARROW, THE
CENTAUR (1940-1941)
1 Reprints Arrow stories from Funny Pages V3#1, V3#3. ...... 400.00 1500.00
2 Reprints Arrow stories from Funny Pages V3#4, V3#5; one new Arrow story by Bob Lubbers. 220.00 700.00
3 (10/41) Contains two new Arrow stories; identity revealed as Ralph Payne. Origin: The Human Meteor. 310.00 1000.00

ARROWHEAD
MARVEL(ATLAS) (1954)
1 ...... 23.00 75.00
2-3 ...... 13.00 40.00

ASH
EVENT (1994-CURRENT)
1 1st: Ash. 5.00 15.00
1A Connoisseur's Kit. Signed & numbered, bagged with Kid Death litho. (1995) 10.00 30.00
2 ...... 2.75 10.00
3 ...... 1.25 4.00
4 ...... .75 2.50

ASTER
ENTITY (1994-1995)
0 ...... 1.25 4.00
1 ...... 1.25 4.50
1 (GOLD) 4.00 12.00
1B Signed & limited edition. 9.00 29.95
2-3 ...... 1.00 3.25
3A Variant cover. 2.00 7.50
4 ...... 1.00 3.00
TPB Reprints issues #1-4, plus pin-ups. 4.00 12.95

ASTER: THE LAST CELESTIAL KNIGHT
ENTITY (1995-CURRENT)
1 ...... 1.00 3.75

ASTONISHING
MARVEL(ATLAS) (1951-1957)
3 Previous title: Marvel Boy. 145.00 480.00
4-5 Marvel Boy. 110.00 360.00
6-12 ...... 40.00 120.00
13-14 Art: Krigstein. 40.00 130.00
15 ...... 40.00 120.00
16 Art: Krigstein. 40.00 130.00
17-18 ...... 29.00 95.00
19 Art: Krigstein. 40.00 120.00
20 ...... 29.00 95.00
21-22 ...... 22.00 70.00
23 ...... 25.00 80.00
24-25 ...... 22.00 70.00
26-29 ...... 19.00 60.00
30 ...... 22.00 70.00
31-32 ...... 19.00 60.00
33 "Once A Werewolf" (6/54). 19.00 60.00
34-37 ...... 19.00 60.00
38 1st Code Approved issue. 15.00 48.00
39-44 ...... 11.00 36.00
45 Art: Krigstein. 13.00 42.00
46 ...... 11.00 36.00
47 Art: Krigstein. 13.00 42.00
48-52 ...... 11.00 36.00
53 Art: Steve Ditko. 15.00 48.00
54-61 ...... 11.00 36.00
62 Art: Bob Powell. 13.00 42.00
63 ...... 11.00 36.00

ASTONISHING TALES
MARVEL (1970-1976)
1 Begin: Ka-Zar and Dr. Doom. 7.00 20.00
2 ...... 4.00 12.00
3-6 ...... 6.00 17.00
7 ...... 4.00 12.00
8 End: Dr. Doom. 25 cent, double size. 4.00 12.00
9 ...... 1.25 4.00
10 ...... 2.25 8.00
11 Origin retold: Ka-Zar. 2.25 8.00
12 Art: Neal Adams. Man Thing. 2.25 8.00
13-19 ...... 1.00 3.00
20 End: Ka-Zar. 1.00 3.00
21 Begin: It! The Living Colossus. 1.00 3.00
22-23 ...... 1.00 3.00
24 End: It! 1.00 3.00
25 1st: Deathlok The Demolisher. ... 10.00 30.00
26 1st: Warwolf. 2.25 8.00
27 Origin: Deathlok. 2.25 8.00
28 ...... 2.25 8.00
29 Origin: Guardians Of The Galaxy (no Deathlok). 2.25 8.00
30 ...... 2.25 8.00
31 Backup: Reprint Silver Surfer #3. ... 2.25 8.00
32-35 ...... 2.25 8.00
36 1st: Godwulf. 2.25 8.00

ASTONISHING X-MEN, THE
MARVEL (1995)
1 ...... 1.50 5.00
2-3 ...... 1.00 3.00
4 ...... .75 2.50
TPB "The Ultimate Astonishing X-Men", reprints #1-4. ...... 2.25 8.95

ASTRO BOY
GOLD KEY (1965)
1 1st: Astro Boy. TV tie-in. 95.00 310.00

ATARI FORCE
DC (1984-1986)
1-20 ...... .30 1.00
SPECIAL (1986) ...... .30 1.00

A-TEAM, THE
MARVEL (1984)
1 TV tie-in. ...... .75 2.00
2-3 ...... .50 1.50

ATLANTIS CHRONICLES, THE
DC (1990)
1-6 ...... 1.00 3.00
7 New Origin: Aquaman. 1.00 3.00

ATLANTIS, THE LOST CONTINENT
DELL FOUR COLOR SERIES (1961)
1188 Movie photo cover. (5/61) ... 26.00 85.00

ATLAS
DARK HORSE (1994)
1-4 ...... .75 2.50

ATOM, THE
DC (1962-1968)
1 1st: Plant Master. "Master Of The Plant World!" See Showcase #34 for 1st appearance The Atom. 210.00 675.00
2 ...... 70.00 230.00
3 1st & Origin: Chronos. 55.00 170.00
4 ...... 35.00 110.00
5-6 ...... 31.00 100.00
7 App: Hawkman. 65.00 210.00
8 App: Justice League. 25.00 80.00
9-10 ...... 25.00 80.00
11-15 ...... 17.00 55.00
16-20 ...... 13.00 40.00
21-28 ...... 10.00 30.00
29 App: Golden Age Atom. 25.00 100.00
30 ...... 10.00 30.00
31 App: Hawkman. 10.00 30.00
32-35 ...... 10.00 30.00
36 App: Golden Age Atom. 13.00 40.00
37 ...... 10.00 30.00
38 Title changes to Atom And Hawkman with #39. ...... 10.00 30.00

ATOM AGE COMBAT
FAGO (1959)
1 Cover & art: Dick Ayers (all issues). 35.00 110.00
2-3 ...... 26.00 85.00

ATOM AGE COMBAT
ST. JOHN (1952-1953)
1 ...... 65.00 200.00
2 ...... 35.00 110.00
3 ...... 26.00 85.00
4 ...... 35.00 110.00
5 ...... 26.00 85.00

ATOM AND HAWKMAN
DC (1968-1969)
39 Previous title: The Atom. 8.00 25.00
40-43 ...... 8.00 25.00
44 1st 15 cent cover price. 8.00 25.00
45 ...... 8.00 25.00

ATOM ANT
GOLD KEY (1966)
10170-601 (#1). TV tie-in. 55.00 175.00

ATOM SPECIAL, THE
DC (1993)
1 ...... .75 2.50
2 ...... .75 2.95

ATOM THE CAT
CHARLTON (1957-1959)
9 Previous title: Tom Cat. 16.00 50.00
10 60 pgs. 10.00 30.00
11 100 pgs. 16.00 50.00
12 .... 10.00 30.00
13-17 .... 7.00 20.00

ATOMAN
SPARK (1946)
1 1st & Origin: Atoman. 70.00 230.00
2 .... 55.00 170.00

ATOMIC ATTACK!
YOUTHFUL (1953)
5 "I'll Fight In Tomorrow's War" 55.00 170.00
6 "PW Riot At Koje!" 31.00 100.00
7 "The Commandos' Last Raid!" 31.00 100.00
8 "Expedition 'Meat Chopper'" 31.00 100.00

ATOMIC BOMB
BARTIS (1948)
1 .... 70.00 230.00

ATOMIC BUNNY
CHARLTON (1958-1959)
12 Previous title: Atomic Rabbit. 17.00 55.00
13-19 .... 17.00 55.00

ATOMIC COMICS
DANIELS (1946)
1 App: Rocketman. 50.00 150.00

ATOMIC COMICS
GREEN (1946)
1 Art: Siegel & Shuster (Radio Squad). 190.00 600.00
2 Art: Matt Baker (Kid Kane). 85.00 275.00
3 .... 55.00 175.00
4 Cover: Matt Baker. 80.00 250.00

ATOMIC MOUSE
CHARLTON (1953-1963)
1 1st & Origin: Atomic Mouse. 35.00 110.00
2 .... 15.00 50.00
3-12 .... 10.00 33.00
13-24 .... 7.00 22.00
25 .... 5.00 16.00
26 Double size. 17.00 55.00
27-36 .... 5.00 16.00
37-48 .... 4.00 11.00
49-54 .... 2.25 8.75

ATOMIC RABBIT
CHARLTON (1955-1958)
1 1st & Origin: Atomic Rabbit. 29.00 95.00
2 .... 15.00 48.00
3-10 .... 11.00 36.00
11 Title changes to Atomic Bunny with #12.
.... 19.00 60.00

ATOMIC SPY CASES
AVON (1950)
1 .... 40.00 120.00

ATOMIC THUNDERBOLT, THE
REGOR (1946)
1 .... 95.00 300.00
2 .... 65.00 200.00

ATOMIC WAR!
ACE (1952-1953)
1 "The Sneak Attack" (11/52). ... 100.00 330.00
2-4 .... 70.00 220.00

ATTACK
CHARLTON (1958-1959)
54 100 pages. 16.00 50.00
55-60 .... 7.00 20.00

ATTACK!
YOUTHFUL/TROJAN (1952-1953)
1 .... 26.00 85.00
2-3 .... 14.00 44.00
4 Art: Krenkel. 17.00 55.00
5 (1/53) 10.00 33.00
6-8 .... 10.00 33.00

ATTACK ON PLANET MARS
AVON (1951)
1 .... 125.00 400.00

AUTHENTIC POLICE CASES
ST. JOHN (1948-1955)
1 .... 35.00 110.00
2 App: Lady Satan. 26.00 85.00
3 SOTI. 50.00 160.00
4-5 .... 23.00 75.00
6 Cover: Matt Baker. SOTI. 50.00 160.00
7 Art: Jack Cole. 25.00 80.00
8 Art: Matt Baker. 20.00 65.00
9-14 .... 20.00 65.00
15 Cover: Matt Baker. 23.00 75.00
16 .... 14.00 44.00
17 Cover: Matt Baker. 15.00 50.00
18 .... 14.00 44.00
19 Cover: Matt Baker. 15.00 50.00
20-21 .... 10.00 33.00
22 Cover: Matt Baker. 12.00 38.00
23 .... 9.00 27.00
24-28 100 pages. 35.00 110.00
29-30 .... 9.00 27.00
31-38 Cover: Matt Baker. 12.00 38.00

AV IN 3-D
AARDVARK (1984)
1 App: Cerebus. 1.00 3.00

AVENGELYNE
MAXIMUM PRESS (1995-CURRENT)
1 1st: Avengelyne. Chromium cover. ... 1.75 6.50
1A Newsstand edition. .... .75 2.50
1B Holochrome cover (limited to 200). 8.00 25.00
2 Polybagged with card. 1.00 3.50
3 .... .75 2.50

AVENGER, THE (A-1 SERIES)
ME (1955)
1 (A-1 #129). Origin: The Avenger. ... 40.00 130.00
2 (A-1 #131). 35.00 110.00
3 (A-1 #133). 35.00 110.00
4 (A-1 #138). 40.00 130.00

AVENGERS
MARVEL (1963-CURRENT)
1 Debut & Origin: Avengers in "The Coming Of The Avengers!" by Kirby/Lee. 500.00 1950.00
2 1st: Space Phantom. "The Space Phantom!" by Kirby/Lee. 160.00 525.00
3 "The Hulk And Sub-Mariner Vs. The Avengers!" by Kirby/Lee. 110.00 350.00
4 Debut & Origin: Silver Age Captain America in "Captain America Lives Again!" by Kirby/Lee. ... 400.00 1400.00
4A Golden Record set, 33-1/3 record album still sealed with reprint comic (identical to Avengers 4 but without cover price and ads). 35.00 110.00
4B Golden Record reprint, removed from record album set, identical to Avengers 4 but without cover price and original ads. 20.00 65.00
5 1st: Lava Men. "Invasion Of The Lava Men!" by Kirby/Lee. 65.00 200.00
6 1st: Masters Of Evil, Origin: Baron Zemo. "Zemo, And His Masters Of Evil!" by Kirby/Lee. 50.00 150.00
7 App: Enchantress, Executioner. "Their Darkest Hour!" by Kirby/Lee. 50.00 150.00
8 1st & Origin: Kang. "Kang, The Conqueror!" by Kirby/Lee. 50.00 150.00
9 1st & Death: Wonder Man. "The Coming Of The...Wonder Man!" by Heck/Lee. 50.00 150.00
10 1st: Immortus. "The Avengers Break Up!" by Heck/Lee. 50.00 150.00
11 Spider-Man app. 55.00 190.00
12 App: Mole Man. "This Hostage Earth!" by Heck/Lee. 28.00 90.00
13 1st: Count Nefaria. 1st: Maggia. "The Castle Of Count Nefaria!" by Heck/Lee. 28.00 90.00
14 1st: Ogor. "Even Avengers Can Die!" 20.00 65.00
15 Death: Baron Zemo. "Now, By My Hand, Shall Die A Villain!" by Heck/Lee. 20.00 65.00
16 New line-up. "The Old Order Changeth!" by Ayers/Lee. 25.00 80.00
17 1st: Minotaur. "Four Against The Minotaur!" by Heck/Lee. 16.00 50.00
18 App: Commissar. "When The Commissar Commands!" by Heck/Lee. 16.00 50.00
19 1st & Origin: Swordsman. Origin: Hawkeye. "The Coming Of...The Swordsman!" by Heck/Lee. ... 16.00 50.00
20 "Vengeance Is Ours!" 10.00 35.00
21 1st: Power Man. "The Bitter Taste Of Defeat!" by Heck/Lee. 10.00 35.00
22 "The Road Back!" 10.00 35.00
23 "Once An Avenger...!" 10.00 35.00
24 App: Kang. "From The Ashes Of Defeat!" by Heck/Lee. 10.00 35.00
25 App: Dr. Doom. "Enter...Dr. Doom!" 14.00 45.00
26 "The Voice Of The Wasp!" 8.00 25.00
27 "Four Against The Flood-Tide!" ... 8.00 25.00
28 Giant Man becomes Goliath in "Among Us Walks A...Goliath!" 8.00 25.00
29 "This Power Unleashed!" 8.00 25.00
30 "Frenzy In A Far-Off Land!" 8.00 25.00
31 "Never Bug A Giant!" 8.00 25.00
32 "The Sign Of The Serpent!" 8.00 25.00
33 "To Smash A Serpent!" 8.00 25.00
34 "The Living Laser!" 8.00 25.00
35 "The Light That Failed!" 8.00 25.00
36 "The Ultroids Attack!" 9.00 30.00
37 "To Conquer A Colossus!" 8.00 25.00
38 "In Our Midst...An Immortal!" 8.00 25.00
39 "The Torment And The Triumph!" ... 8.00 25.00
40 "Suddenly...The Sub-Mariner!" ... 8.00 25.00
41 "Let Sleeping Dragons Lie!" 5.00 15.00
42 "The Plan And The Power!" 5.00 15.00
43 Red Guardian. "Color Him...The Red Guardian!" 5.00 15.00
44 Red Guardian. 5.00 15.00
45 "Blitzkrieg In Central Park!" 5.00 15.00
46 "The Agony And The Anthill!" 5.00 15.00
47 "Magneto Walks The Earth!" 6.00 20.00
48 1st & Origin: Black Knight. "The Black Knight Lives Again!" 7.00 20.00
49 "Mine Is The Power!" 5.00 15.00
50 "To Tame A Titan!" (3/68) 5.00 15.00
51 .... 5.00 15.00
52 Joins: Black Panther. 8.00 25.00
53 X-Men. 10.00 30.00
54 "...And Deliver Us From...The Masters Of Evil!" 5.00 15.00
55 "Mayhem Over Manhattan!" 5.00 15.00
56 "Death Be Not Proud!" 5.00 15.00
57 1st: The Vision. "Behold...The Vision!" 19.00 60.00
58 Origin: The Vision. "Even An Android Can Cry!" 13.00 40.00
59 "His Name Is...Yellowjacket!" 7.00 20.00
60 "'Til Death Do Us Part!" 7.00 20.00
61 "Some Say The World Will End In Fire...Some Say In Ice!" 4.00 12.00
62 "The Monarch And The Man-Ape!" 4.00 12.00
63 "And In This Corner...Goliath!" ... 4.00 12.00
64 "Like A Death Ray From The Sky!" 4.00 12.00
65 "The Swordsman Strikes!" 4.00 12.00
66 1st 15 cent cover price. Art: Barry Smith. "The Great Betrayal!" 4.00 12.00
67 Art: Barry Smith. "Die, Avengers...Die!" 4.00 12.00
68-69 .... 4.00 12.00
70 "Enter: The Squadron Sinister!" ... 4.00 12.00
71 1st: Invaders. 1st: Nighthawk. "The Final Battle!" 7.00 20.00
72 "Did You Hear The One About Scorpio?" 4.00 12.00
73 "The Sons Of The Serpent Strike!" 4.00 12.00
74 "Death Is The Hunter!" 4.00 12.00
75 .... 4.00 12.00
76 "The Day The Earth Exploded!" ... 4.00 12.00
77 "For Hire: The Avengers!" 4.00 12.00
78 .... 4.00 12.00
79 "Lo! The Lethal Legion!" 4.00 12.00
80 "The Coming Of Red Wolf!" 4.00 12.00
81 "When A Legend Dies!" 4.00 12.00
82 App: Daredevil. "Avengers Assemble!" 4.00 12.00
83 .... 5.00 16.00
84-86 .... 4.00 12.00
87 Origin: Black Panther. "Look Homeward, Avenger!" 8.00 25.00
88 "The Summons Of Psyklop!" 2.75 10.00
89 "The Only Good Alien...Is A Dead Alien!" 2.75 10.00
90 "Death Lies Waiting...At The Top Of The World!" 2.75 10.00
91 "Take One Giant Step...Backward!" 2.75 10.00
92 "...For All Things Must End!" 2.75 10.00
93 Art: Neal Adams. Double size. "This Beach-Head Earth!" 16.00 50.00
94 Art: Neal Adams. "Behold The Mandroids!" 10.00 30.00
95 Art: Neal Adams. "Something Inhuman This Way Comes..!" 9.00 28.00
96 Art: Neal Adams. "The Andromeda Swarm!" 9.00 28.00
97 "Godhood's End!" 5.00 15.00
98 Art: Barry Smith. "The Coming Of War-Hawk!" 7.00 20.00
99 Art: Barry Smith. "Hercules!...Whom The Gods Would Destroy!" 7.00 20.00
100 Art: Barry Smith. Anniversary issue. (6/72) 17.00 55.00
101-106 .... 2.50 9.00
107 Art: Jim Starlin. 2.50 9.00
108-109 .... 2.50 9.00
110-111 App: X-Men. 5.00 16.00
112 1st: Mantis. 5.00 16.00
113-115 .... 2.00 7.00
116 Silver Surfer. 5.00 16.00
117-118 Silver Surfer. 2.00 7.00
119-122 .... 2.00 7.00
123 Origin: Mantis. 2.00 7.00
124 .... 2.00 7.00
125 App: Thanos. 4.00 12.00
126-127 .... 2.75 10.00
128-132 .... 2.25 8.00
133-143 .... 1.75 6.00
144 1st & Origin: Hellcat. 1.75 6.00
145-163 .... 1.75 6.00
164-166 Art: John Byrne. 1.75 6.00
167-180 .... 1.50 5.00
181 Begin: Byrne art. 1.75 6.00
182-190 .... 1.75 6.00

AVENGERS #4

AVENGERS #6

AVENGERS #172

AVENGERS #181

a b c d e f g h i j k l m n o p q r s t u v w x y z

AVENGERS #314

AVENGERS #387

AVENGERS ANNUAL #7

AZRAEL #1

FAMOUS · FIRSTS

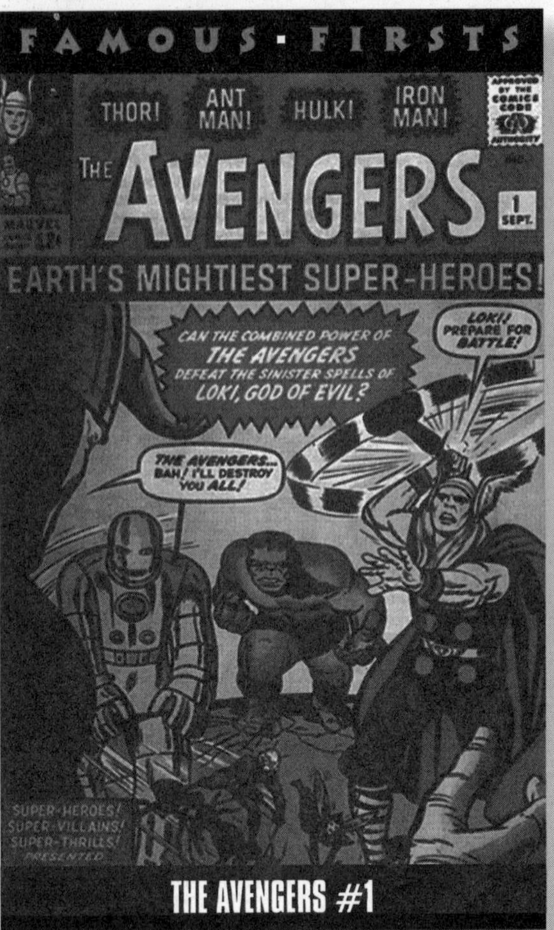

THE AVENGERS #1

Loki manipulates The Hulk into fighting Iron Man, Thor, Ant-Man and The Wasp. They finally figure it out, defeat Loki, and assemble as The Avengers! The Hulk leaves in #3 and Captain America joins in #4.

191 End: Byrne art. 1.75 6.00
192-199 .... 1.50 5.00
200 Double-sized anniversary issue. ... 1.50 5.00
201-213 .... 1.00 3.00
214 Ghost Rider. 1.25 4.00
215-216 Silver Surfer. 1.00 3.00
217-229 .... 1.00 3.00
230-235 .... .75 2.50
236-237 .... 1.25 4.00
238 .... .75 2.50
239 .... 1.00 3.00
240-249 .... .75 2.50
250 .... 1.25 4.50
251-262 .... .75 2.50
263 1st: X-Factor. Story continues in Fantastic Four 286.
.... 1.75 6.50
264 .... 1.00 3.00
265-270 .... .75 2.00
271-272 .... 1.00 3.00
273-299 .... .75 2.00
300 Joins: Thor. Double size. 1.25 4.00
301-304 .... .75 2.00
305 .... 1.00 3.00
306-312 .... .75 2.00
313 .... 1.50 5.00
314-315 Spider-Man. 1.00 3.50
316-318 Spider-Man. 1.00 3.00
319-325 .... .75 2.00
326 1st: Rage. 1.75 6.00
327 Origin: Rage. .... .75 2.00
328 .... 1.00 3.00
329-346 .... .50 1.75
347 Double size. .... .50 1.75
348-349 .... .50 1.75
350 Double size. .... .75 2.50
351-359 .... .50 1.25
360 30th anniversary issue. 1.25 4.00
361-362 .... .50 1.25
363 Silver foil cover. 1.00 3.50
364 .... .50 1.25
365 .... .75 2.00
366 Gold foil embossed cover. 1.25 4.50
367 .... .75 2.00
368 Bloodties pt.1 (X-Men). 1.25 4.00
369 .... 1.00 3.25
370-372 .... .50 1.25
373 .... .50 1.75
374 .... .50 1.50
375 .... 1.00 3.00
375A Posterless version. .... .75 2.00
376-379 .... .50 1.50
379A (Avengers Double Feature #1) flip book with Giant-Man #1. .... .75 2.50
380 .... .50 1.50
380A (Avengers Double Feature #2) flip book with Giant-Man #2. .... .75 2.50
381 .... .50 1.50
381A (Avengers Double Feature #3) flip book with Giant-Man #3. .... .75 2.50
382 .... .50 1.50
382A (Avengers Double Feature #4) flip book with Giant-Man #4. .... .75 2.50
383 .... .50 1.50
384-385 .... .75 2.50
386 .... .50 1.50
387-390 .... .75 2.50

AVENGERS, THE
SEE JOHN STEED, EMMA PEEL

AVENGERS ANNUAL, THE
MARVEL (1967-CURRENT)
1 King-Size Special. (1967) 14.00 45.00
2 King-Size Special. (1968) 8.00 25.00
3 King Size Special. Reprints Avengers #4 & Tales Of Suspense #66-68. (1969) 5.00 15.00
4 King-Size Special. Reprints Avengers #5-6. (1971)
.... 4.00 12.00
5 Special. "Along Came A Spider-Man!" Reprints Avengers #8, 11. (1972) 4.00 12.00
6 (1976) 2.75 10.00
7 Cover/Art: Jim Starlin. Death: Warlock. App: Thanos. (1977) 4.00 12.00
8 (1978) 1.50 5.00
9 (1979) 1.50 5.00
10 1st: Rogue. (1981) 7.00 22.00
11 (1982) 1.00 3.50
12 (1983) 1.00 3.50
13 (1984) 1.25 4.00
14 (1985) 1.00 3.50
15 (1986) 1.00 3.50
16 (1987) 1.00 3.75
17 Evolutionary War. (1988) 1.25 4.00
18 Atlantis Attacks. (1989) 1.00 3.50
19 (1990) 1.25 4.00
20 (1991) .... .75 2.00
21 (1992) .... .75 2.25
22 1st: Bloodwraith. Polybagged with card. (1993)
.... .75 2.95
23 (1994) .... .75 2.95

AVENGERS KING-SIZE SPECIAL
SEE AVENGERS ANNUAL

AVENGERS MARVEL MILESTONE
MARVEL (1994)
1 Reprints: Avengers #1. .... .75 2.95
2 Reprints: Avengers #16. .... .75 2.95
3 Reprints: Avengers #4. Metallic ink cover. .75 2.95

AVENGERS SPOTLIGHT
MARVEL (1989-1991)
21 Cover & art: John Byrne. Previous title: Solo Avengers.
.... .30 1.00
22-40 .... .30 1.00

AVENGERS STRIKE FILE
MARVEL (1993)
1 .... .50 1.75

AVENGERS: THE CROSSING
MARVEL (1995)
1 Chromium cover. 1.25 4.95

AVENGERS: THE TERMINATRIX OBJECTIVE
MARVEL (1993-1994)
1 Holographix foil cover. .... .75 2.50
2-4 .... .50 1.25

AVENGERS WEST COAST
MARVEL (1989-1993)
47 Previous title: West Coast Avengers. .30 1.00
48-49 .... .30 1.00
50 .... 1.00 3.50
51-74 .... .30 1.00
75 App: Fantastic Four. Double size. ... .50 1.50
76-86 .... .30 1.00
87-88 Wolverine. .... .30 1.00
89-99 .... .30 1.00
100 Red foil embossed. 1.00 3.00
101 X-Men. 2.00 7.00
102 .... 1.00 3.00
ANNUAL 4 Atlantis Attacks. (1989) ... .75 2.00
ANNUAL 5 Subterranean Wars. (1990) .75 2.00
ANNUAL 6 (1991) .... .75 2.00
ANNUAL 7 (1992) .... .75 2.00
ANNUAL 8 1st: Raptor. Polybagged with card. (1993)
.... .75 2.00

AVIATION ADVENTURES & MODEL BUILDING
PMI (1946-1947)
16 Previous title: True Aviation Picture Stories.
.... 7.00 20.00
17 .... 7.00 20.00

AVIATION CADETS
STREET & SMITH (1943)
NO# 25.00 80.00

AWFUL OSCAR
MARVEL (1949)
11 Previous title: Oscar Comics. 11.00 35.00
12 .... 11.00 35.00

AXA
ECLIPSE (1987)
1-2 .... .75 2.00

AZRAEL
DC (1994-CURRENT)
1 .... 1.50 5.50
2 .... 1.25 4.50
3-5 .... .75 3.00
6-8 .... .50 2.25

BABE
DARK HORSE (1994)
1 1st: Babe. Cover & art: John Byrne. .... .75 2.50
2-4 .... .75 2.50

BABE
PRIZE (1948-1950)
1 Cover & art: Boody Rogers in all. 25.00 80.00
2 .... 14.00 44.00
3-4 .... 10.00 33.00
5-6 .... 9.00 27.00
7-11 .... 7.00 22.00

BABE 2
DARK HORSE (1995)
1 Cover & art: John Byrne. .... .75 2.50
2 .... .75 2.50

BABE RUTH SPORTS COMICS
HARVEY (1949-1951)
1 Cover/Art: Bob Powell in all issues. 55.00 180.00
2 .... 50.00 150.00
3 Cover/Story: Joe DiMaggio. 50.00 150.00
4 Cover/Story: Bob Feller. 50.00 150.00
5-7 .... 22.00 70.00
8 Cover/Story: Yogi Berra. 50.00 150.00
9 Cover/Story: Stan Musial. 50.00 150.00
10-11 .... 22.00 70.00

BABES IN TOYLAND
DELL FOUR COLOR SERIES (1962)
1282 Movie photo cover (Annette Funicello). (1/62)
.... 25.00 80.00

BABY HUEY AND PAPA
HARVEY (1962-1968)
1 .... 19.00 60.00
2 .... 10.00 30.00
3-6 .... 7.00 20.00
7-12 .... 4.00 12.00
13-24 .... 2.25 8.00
25-30 .... 1.75 6.00

BABY HUEY DUCKLAND
HARVEY (1962-1966)
1 All issues are 25 cent Giants. 13.00 40.00
2 .... 8.00 25.00
3-6 .... 7.00 20.00
7-12 .... 5.00 15.00
13-15 .... 2.75 10.00

BABY HUEY, THE BABY GIANT
HARVEY (1956-1990)
1 .... 50.00 150.00
2 .... 23.00 75.00
3 .... 20.00 65.00
4-6 .... 13.00 40.00
7-12 .... 10.00 30.00
13-24 .... 7.00 20.00
25-36 .... 5.00 15.00
37-60 .... 2.75 10.00
61-79 .... 2.25 8.00
80 Begin: Giant size editions. 2.75 10.00
81-96 .... 2.75 10.00
97 End: Giant size editions. 2.75 10.00
98-100 .... 1.00 3.00

BABY SNOOTS
GOLD KEY (1970-1975)
1 .... 2.75 10.00
2 .... 1.50 5.00
3-12 .... 1.25 4.00
13-22 .... 1.00 3.00

BABYLON 5
DC (1994-CURRENT)
1 TV tie-in. 1.25 4.00
2-5 .... .50 1.95
6-8 .... .75 2.50

BACHELOR FATHER
DELL (1962)
1 (#1332) From the 4-Color Series. TV tie-in. (4/62)
.... 16.00 50.00
2 .... 10.00 30.00

BACHELOR'S DIARY
AVON (1949)
1 .... 50.00 150.00

BACKLASH
IMAGE (1994-CURRENT)
1 .... 1.00 4.00
1A alternate cover: white outer cover. 1.00 4.00
2 .... .75 2.50
3-7 .... .75 2.50
8 With cards. .... .75 2.50
8A Newstand edition. No cards. .... .50 1.95

9-10 .... .75 2.50

BAD MEN OF THE WEST
AVON (1951)
1 128 pg. Giant. 55.00 175.00

BAD MEN OF TOMBSTONE
AVON (1950)
NO# 22.00 70.00

BADGE OF JUSTICE
CHARLTON (1955)
22 .... 10.00 30.00
23 .... 8.00 25.00

BADGER, THE
CAPITOL/FIRST (1983-1991)
1 .... 1.75 6.00
2-4 .... 1.25 4.00
5 Begin First publication. 1.25 4.00
6 .... 1.25 4.00
7-30 .... 1.00 3.00
31-49 .... 1.00 3.00
50 .... 1.50 5.00
51 .... 1.00 3.00
52-54 Art: Tim Vigil. 1.75 6.00
55-70 .... 1.00 3.00

BADGER GOES BERSERK
FIRST (1989)
1-4 .... 1.00 3.00

BADGER: SHATTERED MIRRORS
DARK HORSE (1994)
1-4 .... .75 2.50

BADGER: ZEN POP FUNNY-ANIMAL VERSION
DARK HORSE (1994)
1-2 .... .75 2.50

BADMEN OF THE WEST (A-1 SERIES)
ME (1954)
1 (A-1 #100). 26.00 85.00
2 (A-1 #120). 20.00 65.00

BADROCK
IMAGE (1995-CURRENT)
1A Inked by Todd McFarlane. .... .75 2.50
1B Inked by Stephen Platt. .... .75 2.50
1C Inked by Dan Fraga. .... .50 1.75
2-3 .... .50 1.75
ANNUAL 1 (1995) .... .75 2.95

BADROCK & COMPANY
IMAGE (1994-1995)
1 Cover: Rob Liefeld. .... .75 2.50
2-6 .... .75 2.50

BAFFLING MYSTERIES
ACE (1951-1955)
5 .... 45.00 140.00
6-9 .... 29.00 95.00
10 Crypt Keeper swipe. 40.00 120.00
11-12 .... 29.00 95.00
13-24 .... 23.00 75.00
25-26 Reprint. 15.00 48.00

BALDER THE BRAVE
MARVEL (1985-1986)
1-4 .... .20 .75

BALLISTIC
IMAGE (1995-CURRENT)
1 .... .75 2.50

BALTIMORE COLTS
GIVEAWAY (1950)
NO# Cover: Will Eisner. 95.00 300.00

BAMBI
DELL (1956)
3 Disney movie tie-in. Reprints Bambi #186 (from the 4-Color series). 11.00 35.00

BAMBI
DELL FOUR COLOR SERIES (1942-1948)
12 .... 115.00 375.00
30 "...Children" 110.00 350.00
186 Disney movie tie-in. 25.00 80.00

BAMBI
GOLD KEY (1963)
10087-309 Disney movie tie-in. 7.00 20.00

BAMBI
GOLD KEY (1966)
10087-607 Disney movie tie-in. 5.00 15.00

BAMM-BAMM AND PEBBLES FLINTSTONE
GOLD KEY (1964)
10127-410 TV tie-in. 16.00 50.00

BANANA SPLITS, THE
GOLD KEY (1969-1971)
1 TV Photo cover. 7.00 20.00
2-8 .... 2.75 10.00

BANG-UP COMICS
PROGRESSIVE (1941-1942)
1 (12/41) 140.00 460.00
2 (3/42) 85.00 280.00
3 (Summer/42) 85.00 280.00

BANNER COMICS
ACE MAGAZINE (1941-1942)
3 1st: Captain Courageous. (9/41) 180.00 575.00
4 Patriotic cover. (11/41) 130.00 430.00
5 Title changes to Captain Courageous Comics with #6. (1/42)
.... 125.00 400.00

BAR SINISTER
ACCLAIM/WINDJAMMER (1995-CURRENT)
1-4 .... .75 2.50

BARB WIRE
DARK HORSE (1994-1995)
1 .... 1.00 4.50
2-4 .... .75 2.50
5-9 .... .75 2.50

BARBI TWINS ADVENTURES
TOPPS (1995-CURRENT)
1 Razor app. 1.25 4.00

BARBIE
MARVEL (1991-CURRENT)
1-55 .... .30 1.00

BARBIE & KEN
DELL (1962-1964)
1 (01-053-207). 80.00 250.00
2-5 .... 55.00 175.00

BARBIE FASHION
MARVEL (1991-CURRENT)
1-55 .... .30 1.00

BARKER, THE
QUALITY (1946-1949)
1 .... 19.00 60.00
2 .... 10.00 30.00
3-12 .... 7.00 20.00
13-14 .... 5.00 15.00
15 Art: Jack Cole. 8.00 25.00

BARNABUS: SINS OF HONOR
CAP-UP (1992)
1-2 .... .75 2.00

BARNEY BAXTER
DELL FOUR COLOR SERIES (1943)
20 .... 50.00 150.00

BARNEY GOOGLE AND SNUFFY SMITH
CHARLTON (1970-1971)
1 .... 2.75 10.00
2-6 .... 1.25 4.00

BARNEY GOOGLE AND SNUFFY SMITH
DELL FOUR COLOR SERIES (1944)
40 .... 50.00 150.00

BARNEY GOOGLE AND SNUFFY SMITH
SEE LARGE FEATURE COMICS (SERIES II) #11.

BARNEY GOOGLE AND SNUFFY SMITH
TOBY (1951-1952)
1 .... 13.00 40.00
2-4 .... 7.00 20.00

BARNEY GOOGLE AND SPARK PLUG
CUPPLES & LEON (1923-1928)
1 .... 50.00 150.00
2-6 .... 31.00 100.00

BARNYARD COMICS
STANDARD (1944-1957)
1 .... 23.00 75.00
2 .... 10.00 30.00
3-6 .... 8.00 25.00

BABE #2 (DARK HORSE)

BARB WIRE #1

THE BARKER #2

BARNYARD COMICS #4

BARTMAN #6

7-12 .... 7.00 20.00
13-15 Frazetta illustrations. 8.00 25.00
16 .... 5.00 15.00
17-27 Frazetta illustrations. 8.00 25.00
28 .... 5.00 15.00
29 Art: Frazetta illustrations. 13.00 40.00
30-31 .... 5.00 15.00

BARTMAN
BONGO (1993-CURRENT)
1 Silver foil cover. 1.25 4.50
2 .... .75 2.25
3 With card. .... .75 2.25
4-6 .... .75 2.25

BASEBALL COMICS
WILL EISNER (1949)
1 Cover/Art: Will Eisner. 85.00 275.00

BASEBALL HEROES
FAWCETT (1952)
1 Babe Ruth photo cover. 155.00 500.00

BASEBALL THRILLS
ZIFF DAVIS (1951-1952)
1 (#10 on cover). Bob Feller. 80.00 250.00
2 Babe Ruth. 50.00 150.00
3 Joe DiMaggio. 50.00 150.00

BATGIRL SPECIAL #1

BASIL THE ROYAL CAT
ST. JOHN (1953)
1 .... 8.00 25.00
2 .... 4.00 12.00
3-4 .... 2.75 10.00

BASIL WOLVERTON'S GATEWAY TO HORROR
DARK HORSE (1988)
1 Reprints. .... .50 1.75

BASIL WOLVERTON'S PLANET OF TERROR
DARK HORSE (1987)
1 Reprints. .... .50 1.75

BAT LASH
DC (1968-1969)
1 .... 5.00 16.00
2 .... 2.25 8.75
3-7 .... 1.75 6.50

BAT MASTERSON
DELL (1959-1962)
1 (#1013) From the 4-Color Series. TV photo cover. (8/59) 20.00 65.00
2 Photo covers on all. 10.00 30.00
3-6 .... 8.00 25.00
7-9 .... 7.00 20.00

BATMAN #0

BATGIRL SPECIAL
DC (1988)
1 One shot. 1.75 6.00

BATMAN
DC (1940-CURRENT)
0 (8/94) .... .75 2.50
1 Origin retold: Batman. 1st: Joker. 1st: The Cat (Catwoman). (Spring/40) 12600.00 50000.00
2 2nd: Joker. 2nd: Catwoman. 1900.00 7500.00
3 1st: Catwoman in costume. 1400.00 5500.00
4 4th: Joker. 1200.00 4500.00
5 Joker story, "The Riddle of the Missing Card" by Bob Kane. 1st: Batmobile. (Spring/41) 900.00 3200.00
6-7 .... 600.00 2300.00
8 Infinity cover. 600.00 2300.00
9-10 .... 600.00 2300.00
11 1st Joker cover. 700.00 2600.00
12 "Anniversary Issue" 500.00 1900.00
13 .... 500.00 1900.00
14 2nd: Penguin. 1st Penguin cover. 600.00 2000.00
15 App: The Catwoman in "Your Face Is Your Fortune" (2-3/43) by Robinson. 500.00 1900.00
16 "Someone Learns The Secret Identities Of Batman and Robin—Who Can He Be?" 1st & Origin: Alfred. (4-5/43) 1100.00 4000.00
17 App: Penguin. (6-7/43) 300.00 1100.00
18 "Insure The Fourth Of July!" 300.00 1100.00
19 "Batman Makes A Deadline!" 300.00 1100.00
20 (1-2/44) 300.00 1100.00
21 Penguin. 310.00 1000.00
22 1st: Alfred solo story, "The Adventures Of Alfred!" (4-5/44) 300.00 1100.00
23 2nd Joker cover. 400.00 1200.00
24 "It Happened In Rome!" 310.00 1000.00
25 1st Joker/Penguin teamup, 1st super-villain teamup in comics. (10-11/44) 400.00 1600.00
26 (1-2/45) 310.00 1000.00
27 Christmas cover, "Season Greetings From Batman and Robin!" 300.00 1100.00
28 "Shadow City!" (4-5/45). 280.00 925.00
29-31 .... 280.00 925.00
32 "The Three Musketeers!" (1-2/46) Origin retold: Robin. 300.00 975.00
33 .... 240.00 775.00
34 "Marathon Of Menace!" 240.00 775.00
35 "Dick Grayson, Author!" App:Catwoman. 250.00 825.00
36 "Sir Batman and Robin in King Arthur's Court!" App:Penguin. 250.00 825.00
37 "The Joker Steals Batman's Thunder!" 280.00 900.00
38 Penguin (1-2/47) 250.00 825.00
39 "Catwoman vs. Batman!" 240.00 775.00
40 The Joker in "The 13 Club" 280.00 900.00
41 "Batman, Interplanetary Policeman!" 250.00 825.00
42 "The Partners In Peril Face The Steel-Clawed Fury of The Catwoman!" (2nd Catwoman cover). 240.00 775.00
43 The Penguin. 250.00 825.00
44 Joker cover, story "Gamble With Doom!" (12-1/48) 280.00 900.00
45 "A Batman and Robin Christmas Adventure" App:Catwoman. 200.00 650.00
46 "Batman and Robin Battle Mutiny In The Big House!" 180.00 575.00
47 Lead story: "Fashions in Crime!", 1st detailed Origin: Batman in last story "The Origin Of Batman!" (6-7/48) 1100.00 4000.00
48 "The 1000 Secrets Of The Batcave" (8-9/48) 220.00 700.00
49 1st: Mad Hatter. The Joker in "Batman's Arabian Knights!" 280.00 900.00
50 "The Return Of Two-Face!" (1-2/49) 180.00 575.00
51 "The Wonderful Mr. Wimble" 170.00 550.00
52 The Joker (4-5/49). 200.00 650.00
53 The Joker. 180.00 575.00
54 .... 170.00 550.00
55 The Joker in "The Case Of The 48 Jokers!" 200.00 650.00
56 "Ride, Bat-Hombre, Ride!" (1-2/50) 170.00 550.00
57 "Giant 1950 Pin-Up Calendar!" ... 170.00 550.00
58 "The Penguin's State-Bird Crimes!" 170.00 550.00
59 "Batman In The Future" 1st: Deadshot. 180.00 575.00
60 .... 170.00 550.00
61 "The Origin Of Batplane II!" (10-11/50) 180.00 575.00
62 Origin: Catwoman in "The Secret Life Of The Catwoman!" (1-2/51) 240.00 775.00
63 "The Origin Of Killer Moth!" 145.00 480.00
64 .... 130.00 420.00
65 Catwoman in "The Empress Of The Underworld!" 130.00 420.00
66 "The Joker's Comedy Of Errors!" 145.00 480.00
67 "The Mystery Rope!" 130.00 420.00
68 "The New Crimes Of Two-Face!" (12-1/52) 140.00 450.00
69 Catwoman in "The King Of Cats!" 140.00 450.00
70 "The Robot Cop Of Gotham City!" 130.00 420.00
71 "The Jail Of Heroes!" 130.00 420.00
72 "The Jungle Batman!" 130.00 420.00
73 "The Joker's Utility Belt!" (10-11/52). 170.00 550.00
74 "The Movie That Killed Batman!" (1-2/53) 120.00 390.00
75 "The Gorilla Boss Of Gotham City!" 120.00 390.00
76 "The Danger Club" 120.00 390.00
77 "The Crime Predictor!" 120.00 390.00
78 "Batman Of The Mounties!" 120.00 390.00
79 "The Bride Of Batman!" 120.00 390.00
80 "Machines Of Menace!" (1/54) 140.00 450.00
81 "Two-Face Strikes Again!" 140.00 450.00
82 "The Flying Batman!" 120.00 390.00
83 "The Testing Of Batman!" 120.00 390.00
84 "The Sleeping Beauties Of Gotham City!" 120.00 390.00
85 "The Costume Of Doom!" 120.00 390.00
86 "Batman-Indian Chief!" 120.00 390.00
87 "Batman Falls In Love!" 120.00 390.00
88 "The Son Of Batman!" 120.00 390.00
89 "Bruce Wayne's Aunt Agatha!" (2/55) 120.00 390.00
90 "The Adventures Of Batboy!" 1st Code Approved issue. 130.00 420.00
91 "The Living Batplane!" (4/55) 130.00 420.00
92 1st: Bat-Hound in "Ace, The Bat-Hound!" 145.00 480.00
93 "The Mystery Of The Sky Museum!" 120.00 390.00
94 "The Ballad Of Batman!" 120.00 390.00
95-96 "Third Alarm For Batman!" ... 120.00 390.00
97 2nd: Bat-Hound in "The Return Of Bat-Hound!" (2/56) 130.00 420.00
98 "The Secret Of The Batmobile!" plus "The Return Of Mr. Future!" 120.00 390.00
99 "The Phantom of The Bat-Cave!" 120.00 390.00
100 "Batmantown, U.S.A.," "The Hunters Of Gotham City," "The Great Batman Contest." (6/56) 500.00 1600.00
101 "The Great Bat-Cape Hunt!" 85.00 280.00
102 "Caveman At Large!" 85.00 280.00
103 "Bat-Hound, Movie Star!" 85.00 280.00
104 "The Creature From 20,000 Fathoms!" 85.00 280.00
105 2nd: Batwoman in "The Challenge Of Batwoman!" (2/57) 110.00 360.00
106 "The Batman Puppet!" 85.00 280.00
107 "The Grown-Up Boy Wonder!" ... 85.00 280.00
108 "The Career Of Batman Jones!" 85.00 280.00
109 "The 1,001 Inventions Of Batman!" 85.00 280.00
110 "The Phantom Batman!" 80.00 250.00
111 "The Armored Batman!" 65.00 200.00
112 "Am I Really Batman?" 65.00 200.00
113 "Batman-Superman Of Planet X!" (2/58) 65.00 200.00
114 "The Bat-Ape!" 65.00 200.00
115 "The Batman In The Bottle!" ... 65.00 200.00
116 "The Winged Bat-People!" 65.00 200.00
117 "Manhunt In Outer Space!" 65.00 200.00
118 "The Merman Batman!" 65.00 200.00
119 "Rip Van Batman!" 65.00 200.00
120 "The Airborne Batman!" 65.00 200.00
121 "The Ice Crimes Of Mr. Zero!" (2/59) 40.00 130.00
122 "The Marriage Of Batman And Batwoman!" 40.00 130.00
123 "The Fugitive Batman!" 45.00 140.00
124 "The Mystery Seeds From Space!" 40.00 130.00
125 "King Batman The First!" 40.00 130.00
126 "The Menace Of The Firefly!" ... 40.00 130.00
127 Batman battles Thor in "The Hammer Of Thor!" (10/60) 50.00 150.00
128 "The Interplanetary Batman!" ... 40.00 130.00
129 "The Web Of The Spinner!" Origin retold: Robin. (2/60) 65.00 200.00
130 "The Hand From Nowhere!" App: Lex Luthor. 40.00 130.00
131 "The Second Batman and Robin Team!" 28.00 90.00
132 "Lair Of The Sea Fox!" 28.00 90.00
133 "Batwoman's Publicity Agent!" ... 28.00 90.00
134 "The Rainbow Creature!" 28.00 90.00
135 "Menace Of The Sky Creature!" 28.00 90.00
136 "Challenge of the Joker!" 40.00 125.00
137 "Robin's New Boss!" (2/61) ... 28.00 90.00
138 "Secret Of The Sea Beast!" 28.00 90.00
139 "Batman, Robin and Batwoman Meet Batgirl!" 29.00 95.00
140 "The Eighth Wonder Of Space!" 29.00 95.00
141-143 .... 28.00 90.00
144 1st 12 cent cover price. App: Joker. 28.00 90.00
145 Joker. 40.00 120.00
146-147 .... 23.00 75.00
148 .... 40.00 120.00
149 .... 55.00 175.00
150 "Robin, The Super Boy Wonder!" 55.00 175.00
151 .... 19.00 60.00
152 Joker. 16.00 50.00
153-154 .... 16.00 50.00
155 1st: Silver Age Penguin. 80.00 255.00
156-158 .... 16.00 50.00
159 Joker. 19.00 60.00
160-162 .... 16.00 50.00
163 Joker. 19.00 60.00
164-168 .... 16.00 50.00
169 2nd: Silver Age Penguin. 31.00 100.00
170 .... 16.00 50.00
171 1st: Silver Age Riddler (5/65). ... 90.00 285.00
172-175 .... 11.00 35.00
176 80 Page Giant #G-17. .... 17.00 55.00
177-178 .... 11.00 35.00
179 2nd: S.A. Riddler. 23.00 75.00
180 .... 11.00 35.00
181 1st: Poison Ivy. 30.00 90.00
182 80 Page Giant #G-24. .... 16.00 50.00
183 .... 15.00 50.00
184 .... 11.00 35.00
185 80 Page Giant #G-27. .... 11.00 35.00
186 .... 11.00 35.00
187 80 Page Giant #G-30. .... 16.00 50.00
188 .... 7.00 20.00
189 1st: Silver Age Scarecrow. 25.00 80.00
190 Penguin. 8.00 25.00
191-192 .... 7.00 20.00
193 80 Page Giant #G-37. .... 10.00 30.00
194-196 .... 7.00 20.00
197 Silver Age Catwoman. 13.00 40.00
198 80 Page Giant #G-43. .... 17.00 55.00
199 .... 7.00 20.00
200 Origin retold: Batman & Robin (3/68). 31.00 100.00
201 Joker. 7.00 20.00
202 .... 7.00 20.00
203 80 Page Giant #G-49. "Secrets of the Batcave." 8.00 25.00
204-207 .... 5.00 14.00
208 80 Page Giant #G-55. .... 8.00 25.00

BATMAN #200

209 5.00 14.00
210 5.00 16.00
211-212 5.00 14.00
213 80 Page Giant #G-61. 30th Anniversary issue. 11.00 35.00
214 1st 15 cent issue. 4.00 12.00
215-216 4.00 12.00
217 5.00 16.00
218 80 Page Giant #G-67 (1-2/70). 5.00 16.00
219 Art: Neal Adams. 7.00 22.00
220-221 4.00 12.00
222 Beatles. 8.00 25.00
223 80 Page Giant #G-73. 8.00 25.00
224-227 4.00 12.00
228 80 Page Giant #G-79. 8.00 25.00
229-231 4.00 12.00
232 1st: Ra's Al Ghul. Art: Neal Adams. 13.00 40.00
233 80 Page Giant #G-85. 8.00 25.00
234 1st: Silver Age Two-Face. 25.00 80.00
235-236 4.00 12.00
237 Art: Neal Adams. 10.00 33.00
238 DC 100 Page Super Spectacular #8. 4.00 12.00
239-242 4.00 12.00
243-245 Art: Neal Adams. 7.00 22.00
246-250 4.00 12.00
251 Joker cover & story by Neal Adams (9/73). 11.00 36.00
252-253 4.00 12.00
254 100 pages. 4.00 12.00
255 Art: Neal Adams. 100 pages. 5.00 15.00
256-257 100 pages. 4.00 12.00
258 100 pages. Joker. 4.00 12.00
259 100 pages. 4.00 12.00
260 100 pages. Joker. 8.00 24.00
261 100 pages. 4.00 12.00
262 2.00 7.00
263 2.75 10.00
264-285 2.00 7.00
286 Joker. 2.25 8.00
287-290 2.00 7.00
291 Joker. 2.00 7.00
292-293 2.00 7.00
294 Joker. 2.00 7.00
295-299 2.00 7.00
300 Double size. 2.75 10.00
301-312 2.00 7.00
313-314 2.25 8.00
315-320 2.00 7.00
321 Joker. 2.25 8.00
322-327 2.00 7.00
328-329 2.25 8.00
330-338 2.00 7.00
339 2.75 10.00
340-352 1.75 6.00
353 Joker. 2.25 8.00
354-356 1.75 6.00
357 1st: Jason Todd. 2.00 7.00
358 1.75 6.00
359 Joker. 2.25 8.00
360-365 1.75 6.00
366 1st: Jason Todd in Robin costume. 7.00 22.00
367 1.75 6.00
368 1st: New Robin (Jason Todd). 6.00 18.00
369-370 1.75 6.00
371-399 1.50 5.00
400 Double size. 7.00 20.00
401-403 1.50 5.00
404 Begin: Year 1. 1st: New Catwoman. 5.00 16.00
405-406 1.75 6.00
407 End: Year 1. 1.75 6.00
408-409 1.75 6.00
410 2.25 8.00
411 1.50 5.00
412-415 1.25 4.00
416 1.75 6.00
417 Begin: Ten Nights Of The Beast. 5.00 14.00
418-419 4.00 13.00
420 End: Ten Nights Of The Beast. 4.00 12.00
421-425 1.25 4.00
426 Begin: "Death in the Family." 2.75 10.00
427 "Death In The Family", part 2. 2.25 8.00
427A "Death In The Family", part 2. w/o phone number. 2.00 7.00
428 "Death In The Family", part 3. Death: Robin. 2.25 8.00
429 "Death In The Family", part 4. 1.50 5.00
430 1.50 5.00
431-432 1.00 3.00
433 Begin: Many Deaths Of The Batman. 1.25 4.00
434 1.25 4.00
435 End: Many Deaths Of The Batman. 1.25 4.00
436 Begin: Year 3. 1st: Timothy Drake. 1.75 6.00
436 (2ND) 2nd printing. .50 1.25
437-438 1.00 3.00
439 End: Year 3. 1.00 3.00
440-441 1.00 3.00
442 1st: Timothy Drake in Robin costume. 1.75 6.00
443-454 .75 2.00
455-456 .50 1.75
457 Timothy Drake becomes Robin. 1.75 6.00
457 (2ND) 2nd printing. .30 1.00
458-459 .50 1.75
460-461 Catwoman. .75 2.00
462-464 .50 1.50
465 .75 2.50
466-482 .50 1.50
483-487 .50 1.25
488 Azrael. 4.00 12.00
489 App: Bane. 1st: Azrael in costume. 2.75 10.00
490 App: Azrael, Bane. 2.50 9.00
491 2.25 8.00
492 Knightfall pt.1 2.75 10.00
492A Platinum edition. 7.00 20.00
493 Knightfall pt.3 1.75 6.00
494 Knightfall pt.5 1.25 4.00
495 Knightfall pt.7 1.25 4.00
496 Knightfall pt.9 1.25 4.00
497 Knightfall, pt.11 (Bane breaks Batman's back). 1.75 6.00
497 (2ND) 2nd printing. .75 2.00
497A Newsstand edition. 1.00 3.00
497C Platinum version (COUNTERFEIT-not published by DC). NO VALUE!
498 Knightfall pt.15 1.00 3.00
499 Knightfall pt.17 .75 2.50
500 Knightfall pt.19 (Double size). 1.50 5.00
500A Newsstand edition. 1.00 3.00
501-508 .75 2.00
509 1.00 3.50
510 .75 2.50
511 .75 2.00
512 .75 2.50
513-514 .75 2.00
515 Embossed cover. .75 2.50
515A Regular cover. .50 1.50
516-518 .75 2.00
519-522 .50 1.95

BATMAN (KELLOGG'S POPTARTS)

DC (1966)

NO# Six different giveaways. 7.00 20.00

BATMAN ADVENTURES

DC (1992-CURRENT)

1 TV cartoon tie-in. 1.75 6.00
2 Catwoman. 1.25 4.00
3 Joker. 1.00 3.50
4-5 1.00 3.00
6 .75 2.50
7 Polybagged with trading card. 2.25 8.00
7A Without card. .75 2.50
8-24 .75 2.00
25 Double size. .75 2.50
26-31 .75 2.00
32-35 .50 1.75
ANNUAL 1 (1994) .75 2.95
ANNUAL 2 (1995) 1.00 3.50
SPECIAL 1 Holiday one shot. (1994) .75 2.95
TPB VOL 1 Reprints issues #1-6. 1.50 5.95
TPB VOL 2 Reprints issues #7-12. 1.50 5.95

BATMAN ADVENTURES: MAD LOVE

DC (1993)

NO# Soft cover book format. 2.25 8.00
NO# (2ND) 2nd printing (Prestige format). 1.25 4.95

BATMAN AND DRACULA: RED RAIN

DC (1991)

GN Hardcover ($24.95 cover price). 16.00 50.00
TPB Softcover ($9.95 cover price). 2.50 9.95

BATMAN AND THE OUTSIDERS

DC (1983-1986)

1 .75 2.00
2-31 .30 1.00
32 Batman quits. Title changes to Adventures Of The Outsiders with #33. .30 1.00
ANNUAL 1-ANNUAL 2 .50 1.50

BATMAN ANIMATED MOVIE

DC (1993)

1 Mask Of The Phantasm movie adaptation, prestige format. 1.25 4.95
1A Standard format. .75 2.95

BATMAN ANNUAL

DC (1961-CURRENT)

1 (1961) 100.00 350.00
2 (Winter/61) 60.00 200.00
3 Cover/Story: Joker. (Summer/62) 40.00 125.00
4 (Winter/62) 23.00 75.00
5 (Summer/63) 23.00 75.00
6 (Winter/63) 17.00 55.00
7 (7/64) 17.00 55.00
8 (1982) 2.00 7.00
9 (1985) 1.75 6.00
10 (1986) 1.75 6.00
11 (1987) 2.00 7.00
12 (1988) 1.25 4.00
13 (1989) 1.50 5.00
14 Origin: Two-Face. (1990) 1.75 6.00
15 (1991) 1.25 4.75
15 (2ND) 2nd printing. .75 2.00
16 (1992) .75 2.50
17 1st: Decimator. Bloodlines, pt 8. (1993) .75 2.50
18 Elseworlds story. (1994) .75 2.95
19 Year One; Scarecrow. (1995) 1.00 3.95

BATMAN: ARCHIVES

DC (1990-1991)

1 Hardcover. Reprints Detective Comics #27-50. 12.00 39.95
2 Hardcover. 12.00 39.95
3 Hardcover. Reprints Detective Comics #71-86. 12.00 39.95

BATMAN: ARKHAM ASYLUM

DC (1989)

HC Hardcover graphic novel ($24.95 cover). 8.00 25.00
TPB Trade Paperback version of Hardcover ($14.95 cover). 5.00 15.00

BATMAN: CATWOMAN DEFIANT

DC (1992)

NO# 1.25 4.95

BATMAN: DARK KNIGHT RETURNS

DC (1986)

1 8.00 25.00
1 (2ND) 2nd printing. 1.00 3.00
1 (3RD) 3rd printing. 1.00 3.00
2 4.00 12.00
2 (2ND) 2nd printing (determined only by comparing inside front cover with facing page-if both are the same light gray shade then the book is a 1st printing, if the facing page is slightly darker then it is a 2nd printing). 1.00 3.00
2 (3RD) 3rd printing. 1.00 3.00
3 2.00 7.00
3 (2ND) 2nd printing. 1.00 3.00
4 1.50 5.00
HC 14.00 45.00
LIMITED Limited Edition hardcover. Edition of 3950. Signed and numbered. 85.00 275.00
PROOF Hardcover Press Proof (limited to 50 copies). 400.00 1200.00
TPB Softcover. 4.00 12.95

BATMAN: DEATH IN THE FAMILY

DC (1988)

TPB Softcover, reprints issues #426-429. 1.50 5.00

BATMAN FAMILY

DC (1975-1978)

1 2.75 10.00
2-5 1.50 5.00
6 1.50 5.50
7-8 1.00 3.50
9-10 1.50 5.00
11 Begin: New stories. 1.50 5.00
12-14 1.50 5.00
15-16 1.25 4.00
17 Double size. 1.50 5.00
18-20 1.25 4.00

BATMAN: FEATURING TWO-FACE & THE RIDDLER

DC (1995)

TPB Reprints. 4.00 12.95

BATMAN FOREVER

DC (1995)

1 Movie adaptation. 1.00 3.95
1A Prestige format. 1.50 5.95

BATMAN: FROM THE 1930S TO THE 1970S

DC (1971)

NO# Hardcover book, with dustjacket. First edition. 16.00 50.00

BATMAN: FULL CIRCLE

DC (1991)

1 1st: Reaper II. 1.50 5.95

BATMAN GALLERY

DC (1992)

1 .75 2.95

BATMAN: GOTHAM BY GASLIGHT

DC (1989)

NO# Squarebound. 1.50 5.00

BATMAN: GOTHAM NIGHTS

DC (1992)

1 Batman. .50 1.25
2-4 .50 1.25

BATMAN #488

BATMAN ADVENTURES #25

BATMAN: DARK KNIGHT RETURNS #1

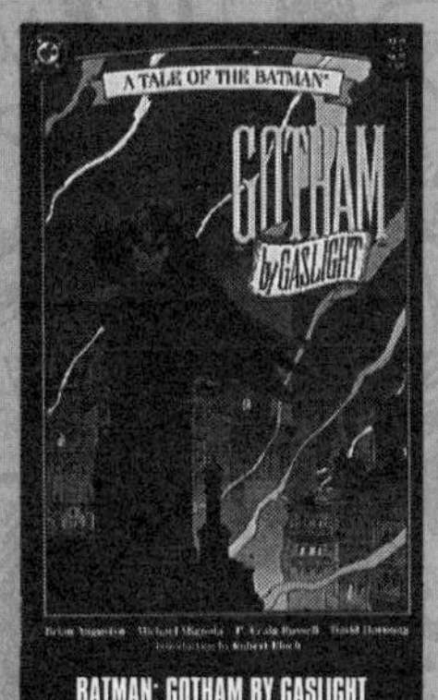

BATMAN: GOTHAM BY GASLIGHT

BATMAN: JAZZ #1

BATMAN: L. OF THE DARK KNIGHT #69

BATMAN: THE KILLING JOKE

BATMAN: VENGEANCE OF BANE #1

FAMOUS • FIRSTS

No. 1
SPRING ISSUE
BATMAN
ALL BRAND NEW ADVENTURES OF THE BATMAN AND ROBIN, THE BOY WONDER!

BATMAN #1

Introduced in *Detective Comics* #27, the Dark Knight got his own comic less than a year later. It debuts his perennial arch-nemesis, The Joker. It also shows Batman machine-gunning some crooks.

BATMAN: GOTHAM NIGHTS 2
DC (1995)
1-4 .50 1.95

BATMAN: HOLY TERROR
DC (1991)
NO# Elseworlds story. 1.25 4.95

BATMAN: IN DARKEST KNIGHT
DC (1994)
NO# Elseworlds story. 1.25 4.95

BATMAN: JAZZ
DC (1995)
1-3 .75 2.50

BATMAN: LEGENDS OF THE DARK KNIGHT
DC (1989-CURRENT)
0 (8/94) 1.00 3.00
1 4 different cover variations exist (yellow, blue, orange, pink). 1.50 5.00
2-4 .75 2.50
5-10 .75 2.00
11 1.50 5.00
12-13 1.25 4.00
14-15 1.00 3.00
16-20 2.25 8.00
21-49 .75 2.00
50 Embossed gold foil cover. 1.50 5.00
51-62 .75 2.00
63 1.00 3.00
64-75 .50 1.95
ANNUAL 1 App: Joker. (1991) 1.00 3.00
ANNUAL 2 (1992) 1.00 3.00
ANNUAL 3 (1993) 1.00 3.00
ANNUAL 4 Elseworlds story. (1994) 1.00 3.00
ANNUAL 5 (1995) 1.00 3.95
SPECIAL 1 Halloween edition. App: Scarecrow. (1993) 2.00 7.00
SPECIAL 2 Madness. Halloween edition. (1994) 1.25 4.95

BATMAN: MASTER OF THE FUTURE
DC (1991)
NO# Elseworlds story. 1.50 5.95

BATMAN: MITEFALL
DC (1995)
1 1.25 4.95

BATMAN: MOVIE ADAPTATION
DC (1989)
1A Regular. .75 2.50
1B Deluxe. 1.25 4.95

BATMAN: PENGUIN TRIUMPHANT
DC (1992)
NO# 1.25 4.95

BATMAN RECORD ALBUM/COMIC
DC (1966)
1A Record and comic still sealed. 65.00 200.00
1B Comic only. 10.00 30.00

BATMAN RETURNS: MOVIE ADAPTATION
DC (1992)
1A Regular size. 1.00 3.95
1B Deluxe size. 1.50 5.95

BATMAN: RUN, RIDDLER, RUN
DC (1992)
1-3 1.25 4.95

BATMAN: SEDUCTION OF THE GUN
DC (1993)
1 .75 2.50

BATMAN: SHADOW OF THE BAT
SEE SHADOW OF THE BAT

BATMAN: SON OF THE DEMON
DC (1987)
1A Hardcover. 14.00 45.00
1B Limited signed and numbered hardcover. 31.00 100.00
SC Softcover. 2.50 9.95

BATMAN: SWORD OF AZRAEL
DC (1992-1993)
1 1st: Azrael. 7.00 20.00
2 4.00 12.00
3-4 3.00 10.00
TPB Reprints issues #1-4. 3.00 10.00
TPB (GOLD) 10.00 30.00

BATMAN: TALES OF THE DEMON
DC (1991)
TPB 6.00 17.95

BATMAN: THE BLUE, THE GREY, & THE BAT
DC (1992)
NO# Elseworlds story. 1.50 5.95

BATMAN: THE COMPLETE FRANK MILLER
DC
HC Leather Bound. 10.00 30.00
HC (2ND) 2nd printing. 10.00 30.00

BATMAN: THE CULT
DC (1988)
1 1st: Deacon Blackfire. 2.75 10.00
2-3 2.25 8.00
4 2.00 7.00
TPB Trade paperback. 5.00 14.95

BATMAN: THE KILLING JOKE
DC (1988)
1-SHOT Joker shoots Batgirl 4.00 12.00
1-SHOT–A 2nd print 2.25 7.00
1-SHOT–B 3rd print 1.50 5.00
1-SHOT–C-F 4th-7th print 1.00......3.00

BATMAN: THE POISON TOMORROW
DC (1992)
NO# 1.50 5.95

BATMAN: TWO-FACE STRIKES TWICE
DC (1993)
1-2 1.25 4.95

BATMAN: VENGEANCE OF BANE
DC (1993)
1 1st: Bane. 7.00 20.00
1 (2ND) 2nd printing. 2.00 7.50

BATMAN VERSUS PREDATOR
DC/DARK HORSE (1991-1992)
1 Prestige format, Batman cover. 1.75 6.00
1A Prestige format, Predator cover. 1.75 6.00
1B Newsstand version. .50 1.95
2 1.50 5.50
2A Newsstand version. .50 1.95
3 1.25 4.95
3A Newsstand version. .50 1.95
TPB Softcover, reprints #1-3. 1.50 5.95

BATMAN VS PREDATOR II: BLOODMATCH
DC/DARK HORSE (1994-1995)
1-4 .75 2.50

BATMAN/GRENDEL
DC (1993)
1 Continues as Grendel/Batman #2. 1.25 4.95

BATMAN/HOUDINI: THE DEVIL'S WORKSHOP
DC (1993)
NO# Elseworlds story. 1.50 5.95

BATMAN/JUDGE DREDD: JUDGMENT ON GOTHAM
DC/FLEETWAY (1991)
1A 1st printing. 2.00 7.00
1B 2nd printing. 1.50 5.95

BATMAN/JUDGE DREDD: THE ULTIMATE RIDDLE
DC/FLEETWAY-QUALITY (1995)
1 1.25 4.95

BATMAN/JUDGE DREDD: VENDETTA IN GOTHAM
DC/FLEETWAY-QUALITY
1 1.25 4.95

BATMAN/PUNISHER: LAKE OF FIRE
DC/MARVEL (1994)
NO# ... 1.25 4.95

BATMAN-SPAWN: WAR DEVIL
DC (1994)
NO# Spawn in Gotham City. Crossover with SPAWN-BATMAN: RED SCARE. ... 1.50 5.25

BATTLE
MARVEL(ATLAS) (1951-1960)
1 ... 26.00 85.00
2 ... 14.00 44.00
3-6 ... 10.00 33.00
7-12 ... 9.00 27.00
13-20 ... 7.00 22.00
21 Art: Krigstein. ... 9.00 27.00
22 ... 7.00 22.00
23 Art: Krigstein. ... 9.00 27.00
24 ... 7.00 22.00
25-35 ... 5.00 16.00
36 Art: Bill Everett. ... 7.00 22.00
37 Art: Kubert. ... 7.00 22.00
38 1st Code Approved issue. ... 5.00 16.00
39-48 ... 5.00 16.00
49 Art: Jack Davis. ... 7.00 22.00
50-54 ... 5.00 16.00
55 Art: Al Williamson. ... 7.00 22.00
56-62 ... 5.00 16.00
63 Art: Steve Ditko. ... 10.00 33.00
64-66 Art: Jack Kirby. ... 10.00 33.00
67 Art: Crandall/Kirby/Williamson. ... 10.00 33.00
68 Art: Kirby/Ditko/Williamson. ... 10.00 33.00
69 Art: Jack Kirby. ... 10.00 33.00
70 Art: Kirby/Ditko. ... 10.00 33.00

BATTLE ACTION
MARVEL(ATLAS) (1952-1957)
1 ... 23.00 75.00
2 ... 14.00 44.00
3-6 ... 10.00 33.00
7 ... 7.00 22.00
8 Art: Krigstein. ... 10.00 33.00
9-15 ... 7.00 22.00
16 1st Code Approved issue. ... 7.00 22.00
17-30 ... 5.00 16.00

BATTLE ANGEL ALITA (PART 1)
VIZ (1992)
1 ... 2.75 10.00
2 ... 2.25 8.00
3-6 ... 1.50 5.00
7-9 ... .75 2.75

BATTLE ANGEL ALITA (PART 2)
VIZ (1993)
1-7 ... .75 2.75

BATTLE ANGEL ALITA (PART 3)
VIZ (1993-1994)
1-5 ... .75 2.75
6 Scarce. ... 1.50 5.00
7-13 ... .75 2.75

BATTLE ANGEL ALITA (PART 4)
VIZ (1994-CURRENT)
1-7 ... .75 2.75

BATTLE ATTACK
STANMOR (1952-1955)
1 ... 10.00 30.00
2 ... 5.00 15.00
3-8 ... 2.75 10.00

BATTLE BRADY
MARVEL(ATLAS) (1953)
10 Previous title: Men In Action. ... 13.00 40.00
11 ... 10.00 30.00
12-14 ... 7.00 20.00

BATTLE CLASSICS
DC (1978)
1 ... .75 2.00

BATTLE CRY
STANMOR (1952-1955)
1 ... 11.00 35.00
2 ... 7.00 20.00
3 ... 2.75 10.00
4 E.C. swipe. ... 10.00 30.00
5-12 ... 2.75 10.00
13-20 ... 2.25 8.00

BATTLE FIRE
STANMOR (1952-1955)
1 ... 7.00 20.00
2 ... 2.75 10.00
3-7 ... 2.25 8.00

BATTLE FOR A THREE DIMENSIONAL WORLD
3D COSMIC (1983)
501 Fold-out poster. ... 1.00 3.00
502 Variant of #501. ... 1.00 3.00

BATTLE GROUND
MARVEL(ATLAS) (1954-1957)
1 ... 25.00 80.00
2 ... 14.00 44.00
3-4 ... 9.00 27.00
5 1st Code Approved issue. ... 9.00 27.00
6 ... 9.00 27.00
7-8 ... 5.00 16.00
9 Art: Krigstein. ... 7.00 22.00
10 ... 5.00 16.00
11 Art: Al Williamson. ... 9.00 27.00
12 ... 5.00 16.00
13 Art: Al Williamson. ... 10.00 33.00
14 Art: Jack Kirby. ... 10.00 33.00
15-17 ... 5.00 16.00
18 Art: Al Williamson. ... 10.00 33.00
19-20 ... 5.00 16.00

BATTLE OF THE BULGE
DELL (1966)
12-056-606 Movie tie-in. ... 7.00 22.00

BATTLE REPORT
AJAX-FARRELL (1952-1953)
1 ... 8.00 25.00
2 ... 7.00 20.00
3-6 ... 5.00 15.00

BATTLE SQUADRON
STANMOR (1955)
1 ... 8.00 25.00
2 ... 7.00 20.00
3-5 ... 5.00 15.00

BATTLE STORIES
FAWCETT (1952-1953)
1 ... 17.00 55.00
2 ... 9.00 27.00
3-11 ... 6.00 19.00

BATTLEFIELD
MARVEL(ATLAS) (1952-1953)
1 ... 25.00 80.00
2 ... 13.00 40.00
3-6 ... 10.00 30.00
7-11 ... 7.00 20.00

BATTLEFIELD ACTION
CHARLTON (1957-1984)
16 Previous title: Foreign Intrigue. ... 7.00 20.00
17-20 ... 5.00 15.00
21-40 ... 2.75 10.00
41-65 ... 1.50 5.00
66 (1966) ... 1.50 5.00
67 (1983) ... .30 1.00
68-89 ... .30 1.00

BATTLEFRONT
MARVEL(ATLAS) (1952-1957)
1 ... 26.00 85.00
2 ... 14.00 44.00
3-5 ... 10.00 33.00
6-10 Combat Kelly. ... 12.00 38.00
11-24 ... 7.00 22.00
25-28 ... 5.00 16.00
29 1st Code Approved issue. ... 5.00 16.00
30-36 ... 5.00 16.00
37-39 ... 4.00 13.00
40 Art: Al Williamson. ... 7.00 22.00
41 ... 4.00 13.00
42 Art: Al Williamson. ... 7.00 22.00
43-47 ... 4.00 13.00
48 Art: Reed Crandall. ... 7.00 22.00

BATTLEFRONT
STANDARD (1952)
5 ... 16.00 50.00

BATTLESTAR GALACTICA
MARVEL (1979-1980)
1 TV tie-in. ... 1.25 4.00
2-5 ... 1.00 3.00
6 Original stories. ... .50 1.50
7-23 ... .50 1.50

BATTLESTAR GALACTICA
MAXIMUM (1995-CURRENT)
1 ... .75 2.50

BATTLESTONE
IMAGE (1994)
1-2 ... .75 2.50

BATTLETIDE
MARVEL (1992-1993)
1-4 ... .50 1.75

BATTLETIDE II
MARVEL (1993)
1 ... .75 2.95
2-8 ... .50 1.75

BEACH BLANKET BINGO
DELL (1965)
12-058-509 Movie photo cover (Annette Funicello). ... 16.00 50.00

BEANBAGS
ZIFF-DAVIS (1951-1952)
1 ... 13.00 40.00
2 ... 10.00 30.00

BEANIE THE MEANIE
FAGO (1958-1959)
1 ... 8.00 25.00
2-3 ... 5.00 15.00

BEANY AND CECIL
DELL (1962-1963)
1 (#01-057-209). ... 23.00 75.00
2-5 ... 16.00 50.00

BEANY AND CECIL
DELL FOUR COLOR SERIES (1952-1955)
368 (1/52) ... 50.00 150.00
414 "Horse-Fly Hubbub" (8/52) ... 40.00 125.00
448 (1/53) ... 35.00 110.00
477 (6/53) ... 35.00 110.00
530 (1/54) ... 35.00 110.00
570 (7/54) ... 35.00 110.00
635 (6/55) ... 35.00 110.00

BEAR COUNTRY
DELL FOUR COLOR SERIES (1956)
758 Disney movie tie-in. (12/56) ... 11.00 35.00

B.E.A.S.T.I.E.S.
AXIS (1993)
1-3 ... .50 1.95

BEATLES, THE
DELL (1964)
1 Stories and color pin-ups. ... 125.00 400.00

BEATLES EXPERIENCE
REVOLUTIONARY (1991)
ANNUAL 1 ... .75 2.50

BEAUTIFUL STORIES FOR UGLY CHILDREN
DC (PIRANHA) (1989-1994)
1-30 ... .75 2.00

BEAUTY AND THE BEAST
INNOVATION (1993)
1 Newsstand edition. ... .75 2.50
1A Deluxe edition. ... 1.00 3.95
2-7 ... .75 2.50

BEAUTY AND THE BEAST
MARVEL (1985)
1-4 ... .75 2.00

BEAUTY AND THE BEAST: PORTRAIT OF LOVE
FIRST (1989)
1 TV tie in. ... 1.75 6.00
2 Title changes to ...: Night Of Beauty. ... 1.75 6.00

BEAVER VALLEY
DELL FOUR COLOR SERIES (1955)
625 Disney movie tie-in. (4/55) ... 7.00 20.00

BEAVIS & BUTT-HEAD
MARVEL (1994-CURRENT)
1 MTV tie in. ... 1.50 5.00
2 ... 1.00 3.00
3 ... .75 2.00
4-19 ... .50 1.95
TPB VOL 1 Greatest Hits. Reprints issues #1-4. ... 4.00 12.95
TPB VOL 2 Trashcan Edition. Reprints issues #5-8. ... 4.00 12.95
TPB VOL 3 Holidazed And Confused. Reprints issues #10-14. ... 4.00 12.95

BEDTIME STORY
COLUMBIA (1941)
NO# Movie giveaway (4 pages). From the Cinema Comics Herald series. ... 16.00 50.00

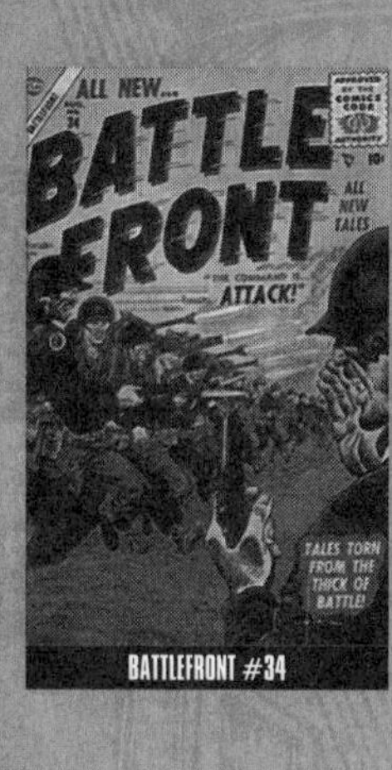

BATTLEFRONT #34

BATTLEFRONT #37

BATTLESTONE #2

BEAVIS & BUTT-HEAD #7

BEST OF BRAVE & THE BOLD #6

BEYOND #1

BIG 3 COMICS #4

BIG 3 COMICS #7

BEE-29, THE BOMBARDIER
NEAL (1945)

1	16.00	50.00

BEEP BEEP THE ROAD RUNNER
DELL (1958-1962)

1 (#918) From the 4-Color Series. (7/58)	22.00	70.00
2 (#1008) From the 4-Color Series. (7/59)	16.00	50.00
3 (#1046) From the 4-Color Series. (11/59)	13.00	40.00
4-14	8.00	25.00

BEEP BEEP THE ROADRUNNER
GOLD KEY (1966-1974)

1	8.00	25.00
2	5.00	15.00
3-6	4.00	12.00
7-18	2.75	10.00
19 With poster.	7.00	20.00
20-24	2.75	10.00
25-36	2.25	8.00
37-60	1.50	5.00
61-105	.75	2.00

BEETLE BAILEY
DELL (1953-1980)

1 (#469) From the 4-Color Series. (5/53)	19.00	60.00
2 (#521) From the 4-Color Series. (12/53)	10.00	30.00
3 (#552) From the 4-Color Series. (4/54)	10.00	30.00
4 (#622) From the 4-Color Series. (4/55)	8.00	25.00
5-12	8.00	25.00
13-24	6.00	18.00
25-38	2.75	10.00
39-60	1.50	5.00
61-100	1.00	3.00
101-132	.50	1.50

BEHIND PRISON BARS
REALISTIC (1952)

1 "Murder At Newgate Prison!"	31.00	100.00

BEN AND ME
DELL FOUR COLOR SERIES (1954)

539 (3/54)	5.00	15.00

BEN BOWIE AND HIS MOUNTAIN MEN
DELL (1953-1959)

1 (#443) From the 4-Color Series. (1/53)	16.00	50.00
2 (#513) From the 4-Color Series. (11/53)	10.00	30.00
3 (#557) From the 4-Color Series. (5/54)	8.00	25.00
4 (#599) From the 4-Color Series. (11/54)	7.00	20.00
5 (#626) From the 4-Color Series. (5/55)	7.00	20.00
6 (#657) From the 4-Color Series. (11/55)	7.00	20.00
7-12	5.00	15.00
13-17	2.75	10.00

BEN CASEY
DELL (1962-1965)

1 (#12-063-207). TV photo cover.	8.00	25.00
2 TV photo cover.	5.00	15.00
3-6	4.00	12.00
7-10	2.75	10.00

BEN CASEY FILM STORY
GOLD KEY (1962)

30009-211 All TV photos, no story.	10.00	30.00

BEN ISRAEL
LOGOS (1974)

NO#	.30	1.00

BENEATH THE PLANET OF THE APES
GOLD KEY (1970)

30044-012 Movie photo cover. With poster.	11.00	35.00

BEN-HUR
DELL FOUR COLOR SERIES (1959)

1052 Movie tie-in. (11/59)	19.00	60.00

BEOWULF
DC (1975-1976)

1	.50	1.50
2-6	.30	1.00

BERNIE WRIGHTSON MASTER OF THE MACABRE
PACIFIC (1983-1984)

1-5	.50	1.50

BERRYS, THE
ARGO (1956)

1	7.00	20.00

BEST COMICS
BETTER (1939-1940)

1 Oblong format. 1st: Red Mask. (11/39)	110.00	360.00
2 (12/39)	75.00	240.00
3 (1/40)	75.00	240.00
4 (2/40)	75.00	240.00

BEST FROM BOY'S LIFE
GILBERTON (1957-1958)

1	12.00	37.00
2	6.00	18.00
3-5	4.00	12.00

BEST LOVE
MARVEL (1949-1950)

33 Photo covers on all issues.	13.00	40.00
34-36	10.00	30.00

BEST OF BUGS BUNNY, THE
GOLD KEY (1966,1968)

1 Giant size.	10.00	30.00
2 Giant size. (10/68)	7.00	20.00

BEST OF DENNIS THE MENACE, THE
HALLDEN/FAWCETT (1959-1961)

1	8.00	25.00
2-3	5.00	15.00
4 Surprise Package.	5.00	15.00
5	5.00	15.00

BEST OF DONALD DUCK
GOLD KEY (1965)

1 (10166-511) Reprints 4C-223 by Barks.	8.00	25.00

BEST OF DONALD DUCK AND UNCLE SCROOGE
GOLD KEY (1964-1967)

1 (30022-411) Barks reprints.	10.00	30.00
2 (30022-709) Reprints 4-Color #256 "Luck Of The North."	8.00	25.00

BEST OF THE BRAVE AND THE BOLD
DC (1988)

1-6	.75	2.50

BEST OF THE WEST (A-1 SERIES)
ME (1951-1954)

1 (A-1 #42). Begin: Ghost Rider, Straight Arrow, Durango Kid.	70.00	220.00
2 (A-1 #46).	26.00	85.00
3 (A-1 #52).	20.00	65.00
4 (A-1 #59).	20.00	65.00
5 (A-1 #66).	20.00	65.00
6 (A-1 #70).	20.00	65.00
7 (A-1 #76).	17.00	55.00
8 (A-1 #81).	17.00	55.00
9 (A-1 #85).	17.00	55.00
10 (A-1 #87).	17.00	55.00
11 (A-1 #97).	17.00	55.00
12 (A-1 #103).	17.00	55.00

BEST OF UNCLE SCROOGE AND DONALD DUCK
GOLD KEY (1966)

1 (30030-611) Barks reprints.	10.00	30.00

BEST ROMANCE
STANDARD (1952)

5 Photo cover.	10.00	30.00
6-7	5.00	15.00

BEST WESTERN
MARVEL (1949)

58	25.00	80.00
59 Title changes to Western Outlaws And Sheriffs with issue #60.	25.00	80.00

BETTY AND HER STEADY
AVON (1950)

2 Previous title: Going Steady With Betty.	10.00	33.00

BETTY AND ME
ARCHIE (1965-1982)

1	25.00	80.00
2	10.00	33.00
3-6	7.00	22.00
7-12	4.00	11.00
13-35	1.50	5.50
36 Begin: Giant size issues.	1.50	5.50
37-54	1.00	3.25
55 End: Giant size issues.	1.00	3.25
56-60	1.00	3.25
61-100	.75	2.00
101-200	.30	1.00

BETTY BETZ' DOLLFACE
DELL FOUR COLOR SERIES (1951)

309 "And Her Gang" (1/51)	13.00	40.00

BEVERLY HILLBILLIES
DELL (1963-1971)

1 All have TV photo covers except #10.	35.00	110.00
2	20.00	65.00
3-6	16.00	50.00
7-9	13.00	40.00
10	7.00	23.00
11-12	13.00	40.00
13-18	9.00	28.00
19-21	7.00	23.00

BEWARE
MARVEL (1973-1974)

1	1.25	4.00
2-7	.75	2.00
8 Title changes to Tomb of Darkness with #9.	.75	2.00

BEWARE
TROJAN (1953-1955)

1 (#13)	40.00	130.00
2 (#14)	26.00	85.00
3 (#15)-4 (#16)	22.00	70.00
5 (9/53)	20.00	65.00
6 SOTI	55.00	170.00
7-9	22.00	70.00
10 Cover: Frank Frazetta.	70.00	220.00
11	35.00	110.00
12-15	22.00	70.00

BEWARE
YOUTHFUL (1952)

10 Previous title: Fantastic.	40.00	130.00
11	29.00	95.00
12 SOTI Title changes to Chilling Tales with #13.	35.00	110.00

BEWARE TERROR TALES
FAWCETT (1952-1953)

1 Art: Bob Powell.	40.00	130.00
2 Art: Bob Powell.	26.00	85.00
3-7	22.00	70.00
8 Art: Bob Powell.	26.00	85.00

BEWARE THE CREEPER
DC (1968-1969)

1 Cover/Art: Steve Ditko.	13.00	40.00
2-5 Cover/Art: Steve Ditko.	7.00	20.00
6 Art: Steve Ditko.	7.00	20.00

BEWITCHED
DELL (1965-1969)

1 TV tie-in. All have photo covers except for #2, 14.	25.00	80.00
2	9.00	27.00
3-13	12.00	38.00
14	5.00	16.00

BEYOND
ACE (1950-1955)

1	50.00	160.00
2	25.00	80.00
3-6	22.00	70.00
7-12	19.00	60.00
13-24	15.00	50.00
25-26	12.00	38.00
27 SOTI	15.00	50.00
28-30	12.00	38.00

BEYOND THE GRAVE
CHARLTON (1975-1984)

1	1.50	5.00
2	1.00	3.00
3-6	.75	2.00
7 Begin: Reprints.	.30	1.00
8-17	.30	1.00

BIBLE TALES FOR YOUNG FOLK
MARVEL(ATLAS) (1953-1954)

1	26.00	85.00
2	20.00	65.00
3	14.00	44.00
4 Title variation "...Young People"	14.00	44.00
5	14.00	44.00

BIG 3 COMICS
FOX (1940-1942)

1 Begin: Blue Beetle, Flame, Samson.	290.00	950.00
2	145.00	480.00
3-4	130.00	420.00
5-6	110.00	360.00
7	95.00	300.00

BIG ALL AMERICAN COMIC BOOK
DC (1944)
NO# 128 pages, contains Flash, Wonder Woman, Green Lantern, Hawkman and others. (12/44) 2800.00 11000.00

BIG BOOK OF FUN COMICS
DC (1936)
NO# Reprints: New Fun #1-5. ...... 2600.00 10000.00

BIG BOOK ROMANCES
FAWCETT (1950)
1 .... 55.00 180.00

BIG CHIEF WAHOO
EASTERN (1942-1945)
1 .... 40.00 125.00
2 .... 19.00 60.00
3-4 .... 16.00 50.00
5-8 .... 13.00 40.00
9-12 .... 11.00 35.00
13-16 .... 10.00 30.00
17-20 .... 8.00 25.00
21-23 .... 7.00 20.00

BIG CIRCUS, THE
DELL FOUR COLOR SERIES (1959)
1036 Movie tie-in. (8/59) 11.00 35.00

BIG COUNTRY, THE
DELL FOUR COLOR SERIES (1958)
946 Movie photo cover. (8/58) ... 16.00 50.00

BIG GUY AND RUSTY THE BOY ROBOT, THE
DARK HORSE (1995)
1 Over-sized format (9" x 12.5"). ... 1.25 6.00
2 .... 1.25 4.95

BIG JIM'S P.A.C.K.
MARVEL (1970'S)
NO# Given away with Big Jim doll. ... 1.00 3.00

BIG JON AND SPARKIE
ZIFF-DAVIS (1952)
3 Previous title: Sparkie. 31.00 100.00
4 .... 25.00 80.00

BIG LAND, THE
DELL FOUR COLOR SERIES (1957)
812 Movie photo cover (Alan Ladd). (8/57)
.... 23.00 75.00

BIG RED
GOLD KEY (1962-1965)
10026-211 Disney movie photo cover. 7.00 20.00
10026-503 Reprint. Disney movie photo cover.
.... 2.75 10.00

BIG SHOT COMICS
COLUMBIA (1940-1949)
1 .... 200.00 650.00
2 .... 85.00 270.00
3-6 .... 70.00 220.00
7-12 .... 50.00 160.00
13 .... 40.00 130.00
14 1st & Origin: Sparky Watts. 60.00 190.00
15 Origin: The Cloak. 70.00 220.00
16-24 .... 40.00 130.00
25-30 .... 35.00 110.00
31-40 .... 26.00 85.00
41-60 .... 20.00 65.00
61-72 .... 15.00 50.00
73-84 .... 12.00 38.00
85-96 .... 9.00 27.00
97-99 .... 7.00 22.00
100 .... 12.00 38.00
101-104 .... 7.00 22.00

BIG TEX
TOBY (1953)
1 .... 11.00 35.00

BIG TOP COMICS, THE
TOBY (1951)
1 Classic clown cover. 10.00 30.00
2 .... 7.00 20.00

BIG TOWN
DC (1951-1958)
1 Radio/TV tie-in. 115.00 370.00
2 .... 55.00 170.00
3-4 .... 35.00 110.00
5-6 .... 28.00 90.00
7-9 .... 25.00 80.00
10-12 .... 17.00 55.00
13-24 .... 14.00 46.00
25-31 .... 13.00 40.00
32 1st Code Approved issue. 11.00 34.00
33-36 .... 11.00 34.00
37-48 .... 9.00 28.00
49-50 .... 7.00 23.00

BIG VALLEY, THE
DELL (1966-1969)
1 TV photo cover on all issues except #6. 13.00 40.00
2 .... 7.00 20.00
3-5 .... 6.00 18.00
6 Reprints #1. .... 2.75 10.00

BILL BARNES, AMERICA'S AIR ACE COMICS
STREET & SMITH (1940-1943)
1 "The Adventures Of Bill Barnes Comics" on issue #1 only.
.... 135.00 440.00
2 .... 70.00 220.00
3-6 .... 50.00 160.00
7-11 .... 40.00 130.00
12 Title changes to Air Ace with V2#1. 40.00 130.00

BILL BATTLE, THE ONE MAN ARMY
FAWCETT (1952-1953)
1 .... 10.00 30.00
2 .... 5.00 16.00
3-4 .... 4.00 11.00

BILL BOYD WESTERN
FAWCETT (1950-1952)
1 All have photo covers except #2. ... 70.00 220.00
2 .... 25.00 80.00
3 .... 40.00 130.00
4-6 .... 35.00 110.00
7-12 .... 23.00 75.00
13-23 .... 20.00 65.00

BILL BUMLIN
ST. JOHN (1947)
3 From the Treasury Of Comics series. (8/47)
.... 13.00 40.00

BILL ELLIOTT COMICS
SEE WILD BILL ELLIOTT (FOUR-COLOR SERIES)

BILL STERN'S SPORTS BOOK
ZIFF-DAVIS (1951-1952)
1 .... 35.00 110.00
2 .... 17.00 55.00
V2#2 Double size. 25.00 80.00

BILL THE GALACTIC HERO
TOPPS (1994)
1-3 .... 1.25 4.95

BILLY AND BUGGY BEAR
I.W.
10 (1964) 1.50 5.00
1 Reprints. 1.50 5.00

BILLY BUCKSKIN WESTERN
MARVEL(ATLAS) (1955-1956)
1 Cover: Maneely. 20.00 65.00
2-3 .... 11.00 35.00

BILLY BUNNY
EXCELLENT (1954)
1 .... 13.00 40.00
2 .... 8.00 25.00
3-4 .... 7.00 20.00
5 Title changes to Black Cobra with #6. 7.00 20.00

BILLY BUNNY'S CHRISTMAS FROLICS
FARRELL (1952)
1 100 page giant. 16.00 50.00

BILLY THE KID
BONEYARD (1993)
1 .... .30 1.00

BILLY THE KID
CHARLTON (1957-1983)
9 Previous title: The Masked Raider. ... 11.00 35.00
10 .... 8.00 25.00
11 Double size. Origin: Billy The Kid. ... 10.00 30.00
12-20 .... 7.00 20.00
21-30 .... 5.00 15.00
31-40 .... 2.75 10.00
41-60 .... 1.75 6.00
61-70 .... 1.25 4.00
71-80 .... .75 2.00
81-100 .... .30 1.00
101-153 .... .20 .50

BILLY THE KID ADVENTURE MAGAZINE
TOBY (1950-1955)
1 .... 40.00 130.00
2 .... 20.00 65.00
3 Art: Al Williamson/Frank Frazetta. ... 40.00 130.00
4-5 .... 14.00 44.00
6 Partial Frazetta art. 20.00 65.00
7-12 .... 10.00 33.00
13-24 .... 7.00 22.00
25-30 .... 5.00 16.00

BILLY THE KID AND OSCAR
FAWCETT (1945-1946)
1 .... 23.00 75.00
2-3 .... 16.00 50.00

BILLY WEST
STANDARD (1949-1952)
1 .... 8.00 25.00
2 .... 4.00 12.00
3-6 .... 2.25 8.00
7-8 Cover: Alex Schomburg. 5.00 15.00
9-10 .... 2.25 8.00

BINGO
ST. JOHN (1951)
1 The Monkey Doodle Boy. 10.00 30.00

BINGO COMICS
HOWARD (1945)
1 .... 13.00 40.00

BINGO, THE MONKEY DOODLE BOY
ST. JOHN (1953)
1 .... 8.00 25.00

BINKY
DC (1970-1971)
72 Previous title: Leave It To Binky. ... 1.75 6.00
73-81 .... 1.75 6.00

BINKY'S BUDDIES
DC (1969-1970)
1 .... 4.00 12.00
2 .... 2.00 7.00
3-6 .... 1.75 6.00
7-12 .... 1.25 4.75

BIONIC WOMAN
CHARLTON (1977-1978)
1 TV tie-in. .... .75 2.00
2-5 .... .30 1.00

BIRDLAND
EROS (1993)
1 .... .75 2.00

BIRTH OF THE DEFIANT UNIVERSE
DEFIANT (1993)
1 Preview edition. Signed & numbered. 8.00 25.00

BISHOP
MARVEL (1994-1995)
1 Foil stamped cover. 1.00 3.50
2 Foil stamped cover. .... .75 2.95
3-4 .... .75 2.95

BISLEY'S SCRAPBOOK
ATOMEKA (1993)
1 .... .75 2.50

BIZARRE ADVENTURES
MARVEL (1981-1983) MAGAZINE
25 Lethal Ladies. .... .75 2.00
26 King Kull. .... .75 2.00
27 Secret Lives Of The X-Men (Phoenix, Nightcrawler, and Iceman). 1.00 3.00
28 Unlikely Heroes (includes Elektra by Frank Miller).
.... .50 1.50
29 Great Horror. .... .50 1.50
30 After Tomorrow. .... .50 1.50
31 The Violence Stops. .... .50 1.50
32 "Thor and other gods..." .... .50 1.50
33 Alternate Gods. .... .50 1.50
34 Howard The Duck. 1.00 3.00

BIZARRE HEROES
FIASCO (1994-CURRENT)
0 Reprints Kitchen Sink issue. .... .75 2.95
1 .... 1.25 4.00
2-11 .... .75 2.95

BIZARRE HEROES
KITCHEN SINK (1990)
NO# One shot. 1.50 5.00

BIG ALL-AMERICAN COMIC BOOK

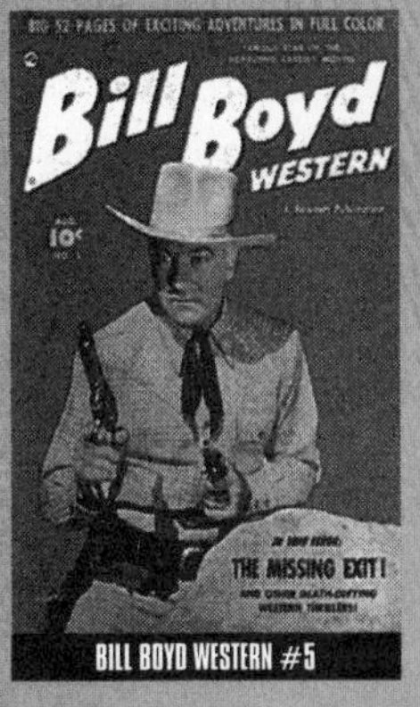

BILL BOYD WESTERN #5

BILLY THE KID & OSCAR #3

BIZARRE ADVENTURES #27

a
b
c
d
e
f
g
h
i
j
k
l
m
n
o
p
q
r
s
t
u
v
w
x
y
z

BLACK CANARY #1

BLACK CONDOR #11

BLACK FLAG #1

BLACK LIGHTNING #7 (2ND SERIES)

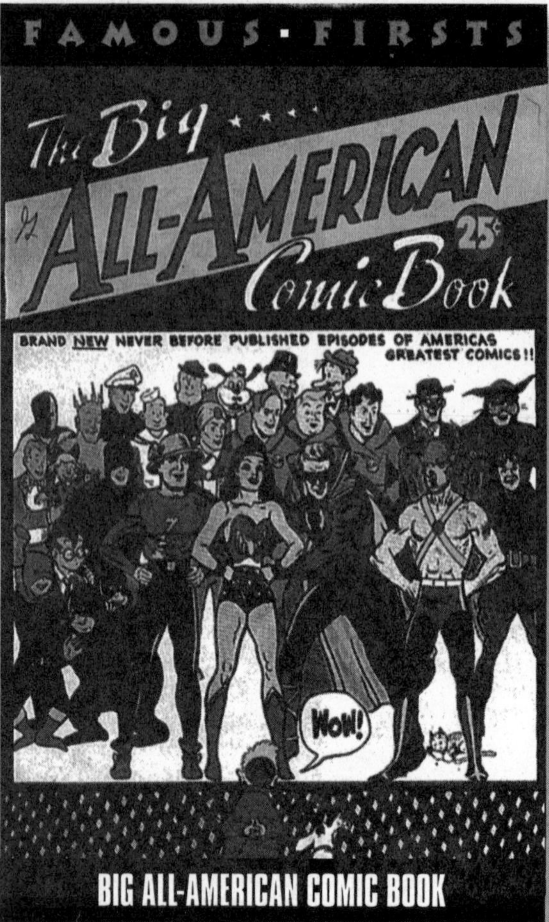

BIG ALL-AMERICAN COMIC BOOK

"Big" doesn't begin to describe this 132-page 25-cent comic! Sold during Christmas 1944, the book features all-new stories of The Flash, Wonder Woman, Green Lantern, The Atom and others.

BLACK AXE
MARVEL UK (1993-1994)
1-13 .... .50 1.75

BLACK BEAUTY
DELL FOUR COLOR SERIES (1952)
440 (12/52) 10.00 30.00

BLACK CANARY
DC (1991-1992)
1 Mini-series. .... .30 1.00
2-4 .... .30 1.00

BLACK CANARY
DC (1993-1994)
1-12 .... .30 1.00

BLACK CAT
MARVEL (1994)
1-4 .... .50 1.50

BLACK CAT COMICS
HARVEY (1946-1951)
1 .... 105.00 340.00
2 Art: Joe Kubert. 55.00 170.00
3-4 .... 31.00 100.00
5-6 The Scarlet Arrow by Bob Powell. 45.00 140.00
7 .... 31.00 100.00
8 Art: Joe Simon/Jack Kirby. 45.00 140.00
9 .... 35.00 110.00
10-12 .... 28.00 90.00
13-24 .... 25.00 80.00
25-26 .... 20.00 65.00
27 SOTI 28.00 90.00
28-29 .... 20.00 65.00

BLACK CAT MYSTERY
HARVEY (1951-1963)
30 .... 17.00 55.00
31-35 .... 16.00 50.00
36 SOTI 26.00 85.00
37-38 .... 14.00 46.00
39 SOTI 26.00 85.00
40-44 .... 14.00 46.00
45 "Colorama" by Bob Powell. 28.00 90.00
46-49 .... 17.00 55.00
50 Classic cover. 26.00 85.00
51 .... 17.00 55.00
52 Reprint #34. .... 11.00 34.00
53 Reprint #35. .... 11.00 34.00
54 .... 17.00 55.00
55 1st Code Approved issue. 14.00 46.00
56 .... 14.00 46.00
57 Cover: Jack Kirby. 14.00 46.00
58-59 Cover/Art: Jack Kirby. 17.00 55.00
60 Art: Jack Kirby. 14.00 46.00
61 Reprints #45. .... 13.00 40.00
62 .... 11.00 34.00
63-65 Giant reprints. 14.00 46.00

BLACK COBRA
AJAX (1954-1955)
1 .... 25.00 80.00
2 (#6 in indicia). 17.00 55.00
3 .... 17.00 55.00

BLACK CONDOR
DC (1992-1993)
1-12 .... .30 1.00

BLACK DIAMOND WESTERN
LEV GLEASON (1949-1956)
9 .... 23.00 75.00
10 .... 16.00 50.00
11-12 .... 14.00 45.00
13-15 .... 11.00 35.00
16 Begin: Bing Bang Buster by Wolverton. 19.00 60.00
17-27 .... 19.00 60.00
28 End: Bing Bang Buster. 19.00 60.00
29-36 .... 8.00 25.00
37-50 .... 7.00 20.00
51-52 3-D effect. 19.00 60.00
53-60 .... 5.00 15.00

BLACK ENCHANTRESS
HEROIC (1994)
1 Ash-can edition, limited to 500 signed copies.
.... 5.00 15.00

BLACK FLAG
IMAGE (1994)
NO# Preview edition. .... .50 1.95

BLACK FLAG
MAXIMUM (1995-CURRENT)
0 .... .75 2.50
1-6 .... .75 2.50

BLACK FURY
CHARLTON (1955-1966)
1 .... 7.00 20.00
2 .... 2.75 10.00
3-6 .... 2.25 8.00
7-15 .... 2.00 7.00
16-18 Art: Steve Ditko. 7.00 20.00
19-24 .... 1.50 5.00
25-36 .... 1.25 4.00
37-57 .... 1.00 3.00

BLACK GOLIATH
MARVEL (1976)
1 .... 1.50 5.00
2 .... 1.25 4.00
3-5 .... 1.00 3.00

BLACK HOOD COMICS
MLJ (1944-1946)
9 Begin: The Hangman. 155.00 500.00
10 .... 115.00 370.00
11 No Hangman. 40.00 120.00
12-19 .... 80.00 250.00

BLACK JACK
CHARLTON (1957-1959)
20-30 .... 4.00 12.00

BLACK KNIGHT
MARVEL (1990)
1 Mini-series. .... .50 1.50
2-4 .... .50 1.50

BLACK KNIGHT
MARVEL(ATLAS) (1955-1956)
1 .... 170.00 550.00
2 .... 100.00 330.00
3-5 .... 95.00 300.00

BLACK KNIGHT, THE
TOBY (1953)
1 .... 35.00 110.00

BLACK LIGHTNING
DC (1977-1978)
1 .... 1.00 3.00
2 .... .75 2.00
3-11 .... .30 1.00

BLACK LIGHTNING
DC (1994-CURRENT)
1-4 .... .50 1.95
5 .... .75 2.25

BLACK MAGIC
CRESTWOOD (1950-1961)
V1#1 Art: Joe Simon/Jack Kirby. 155.00 500.00
V1#2 Art: Joe Simon/Jack Kirby. 80.00 250.00
V1#3-V2#1 Art: Joe Simon/Jack Kirby. 55.00 170.00
V2#2-V2#3 .... 28.00 90.00
V2#4-V2#5 Art: Joe Simon/Jack Kirby. 40.00 130.00
V2#6 .... 28.00 90.00
V2#7 Art: Joe Simon/Jack Kirby. 35.00 110.00
V2#8 .... 28.00 90.00
V2#9 .... 28.00 90.00
V2#10 (#16). 28.00 90.00
V2#11 .... 28.00 90.00
V2#12 Art: Joe Simon/Jack Kirby. 35.00 110.00
V3#1-V3#3 Art: Joe Simon/Jack Kirby. 35.00 110.00
V3#4 (#22 on cover). "The Monsters On The Lake!" (3/53).
Art: Joe Simon/Jack Kirby. 35.00 110.00
V3#5-V4#2 Art: Joe Simon/Jack Kirby. 35.00 110.00
V4#3 Art: Joe Simon/Jack Kirby, Steve Ditko. 1st Ditko art in comics (10-12/53). 140.00 460.00
V4#4 Art: Joe Simon/Jack Kirby, Steve Ditko.
.... 55.00 170.00
V4#5 (#29) Art: Joe Simon/Jack Kirby, Steve Ditko.
.... 45.00 140.00
V4#6 Art: Joe Simon/Jack Kirby. 28.00 90.00

V5#1 (#31) Art: Joe Simon/Jack Kirby. 28.00 90.00
V5#2-V5#3 Art: Joe Simon/Jack Kirby. 28.00 90.00
V6#1 (#34). 14.00 46.00
V6#2-V6#3 14.00 46.00
V6#4-V6#6 13.00 40.00
V7#1-V7#6 11.00 34.00
V8#1 Art: Bob Powell. 13.00 40.00
V8#2 Art: Steve Ditko, Bob Powell. 20.00 65.00
V8#3 11.00 34.00
V8#4-V8#5 Art: Bob Powell. 13.00 40.00

BLACK MAGIC
DC (1973-1975)
1 Reprints: Simon & Kirby stories. .75 2.00
2-9 .50 1.50

BLACK MASK
DC (1993)
1-3 1.25 4.95

BLACK ORCHID
DC (1988-1989)
1 Origin: Black Orchid. 1.75 6.50
2 App: Batman. 2.25 8.00
3 1.75 6.00
TPB Reprints issues #1-3. 5.00 14.95

BLACK ORCHID
DC (1993-CURRENT)
1 .75 2.50
1A Platinum edition. 5.00 15.00
2-3 .75 2.00
4 1st: Nick. .50 1.95
5-20 .50 1.95
21-22 .75 2.25
ANNUAL 1 Children's Crusade. 1.00 3.95

BLACK PANTHER
MARVEL (1977-1979)
1 2.75 10.00
2 1.50 5.00
3-10 1.25 4.00
11-13 1.00 3.00
14-15 App: Avengers. 1.00 3.00

BLACK PANTHER
MARVEL (1988)
1 Mini-series. .50 1.50
2-4 .50 1.50

BLACK PANTHER: PANTHER'S PREY
MARVEL (1991)
1-4 1.25 4.95

BLACK PHANTOM (A-1 SERIES)
ME (1954)
1 (A-1 #122). App: Ghost Rider. 70.00 225.00

BLACK RIDER
MARVEL(ATLAS) (1950-1953)
8 80.00 250.00
9 40.00 130.00
10 Origin: Black Rider. 55.00 170.00
11-14 29.00 95.00
15-18 25.00 80.00
19 Begin: Two Gun Kid. 29.00 95.00
20-22 29.00 95.00
23 End: Two Gun Kid. 29.00 95.00
24-25 17.00 55.00
26 Kid Colt. 20.00 65.00
27 Kid Colt. Title changes to Western Tales Of The Black Rider with #28. 20.00 65.00

BLACK RIDER RIDES AGAIN!
MARVEL(ATLAS) (1957)
1 "Treachery At Hangman's Bridge!" 45.00 140.00

BLACK SABBATH
MALIBU (1994)
1 1.00 3.95

BLACK SWAN COMICS
MLJ (1945)
1 Reprint: Black Hood #14. 31.00 100.00

BLACK TERROR
STANDARD (1942-1949)
1 Begin: Black Terror. 290.00 950.00
2 Begin: Alex Schomburg covers. 145.00 480.00
3 110.00 360.00
4-6 85.00 270.00
7-12 65.00 210.00
13-24 55.00 180.00
25-27 50.00 150.00

BLACKBEARD'S GHOST
GOLD KEY (1968)
10222-806 Disney movie photo cover. 7.00 20.00

BLACKHAWK
DC (1988)
1-3 1.00 3.50

BLACKHAWK
DC (1989-1990)
1-6 .50 1.50
7 Double size. Reprint: Military #1. .50 1.50
8-16 .50 1.50
ANNUAL 1 1.00 3.00

BLACKHAWK COMICS
QUALITY/DC (1944-1984)
9 "Bait For A Death Trap!" (Winter/44) Previous title: Uncle Sam Comics. 500.00 1700.00
10 (1946) 180.00 575.00
11-12 125.00 400.00
13 105.00 340.00
14 Art: Bill Ward. 125.00 400.00
15-19 105.00 340.00
20 Art: Bill Ward. 115.00 370.00
21-24 95.00 310.00
25-30 70.00 230.00
31 Art: Jack Cole. App: Chop Chop. 80.00 250.00
32-36 70.00 230.00
37-50 55.00 170.00
51-60 45.00 140.00
61-70 35.00 110.00
71 Origin retold: Blackhawk. 45.00 140.00
72-80 35.00 110.00
81-86 31.00 100.00
87 1st Code Approved issue (4/55). 31.00 100.00
88-99 28.00 90.00
100 Anniversary issue. 40.00 120.00
101-107 28.00 90.00
108 1st DC published issue. 105.00 340.00
109-112 35.00 110.00
113-120 31.00 100.00
121-136 26.00 85.00
137-145 17.00 55.00
146-160 14.00 46.00
161-163 13.00 40.00
164 Origin retold: Blackhawk. 13.00 40.00
165-166 13.00 40.00
167 1st 12 cent cover price. 14.00 46.00
168-170 10.00 30.00
171-180 7.00 20.00
181-190 2.75 10.00
191 2.25 8.00
192-197 1.75 6.00
198 Origin retold: Blackhawk. 1.75 6.00
199-202 1.75 6.00
203 Origin: Chop Chop (12/64). 2.75 10.00
204-242 1.75 6.00
243 (1968) 1.75 6.00
244 (1976) 1.00 3.00
245-250 1.00 3.00
251 Origin retold: Blackhawk. .50 1.50
252-272 .50 1.50
273 1.00 3.00

BLACKHAWK INDIAN TOMAHAWK WAR, THE
AVON (1951)
NO# 23.00 75.00

BLACKHAWK SPECIAL
DC (1992)
1 1.00 3.50

BLACKMAIL TERROR
HARVEY (1952)
2 From Harvey Comics Library series. App: Dick Tracy, Sparkle Plenty by Chester Gould. 23.00 75.00

BLACKRAY
GALAXINOVELS (1993)
1 Polybagged with poster & card. 1.00 3.95

BLACKSTONE, MASTER MAGICIAN
STREET & SMITH (1946)
1 35.00 110.00
2 20.00 65.00
3 17.00 55.00

BLACKSTONE THE MAGICIAN
MARVEL (1948)
2 Blonde Phantom. 110.00 360.00
3 Blonde Phantom. 75.00 240.00
4 Blonde Phantom. 85.00 270.00

BLACKSTONE THE MAGICIAN FIGHTS CRIME
EC (1947) ONE-SHOT
1 1st Happy Houlihans. 105.00 340.00

BLACKWATCH
HEROIC (1993)
1 1.00 3.95

BLACKWULF
MARVEL (1994-CURRENT)
1 1st: Blackwulf. .30 1.00
2-12 .30 1.00

BLADE RUNNER
MARVEL (1982)
1 Movie Adaptation. .30 1.00
2 .30 1.00

BLADE, THE VAMPIRE HUNTER
MARVEL (1994-CURRENT)
1 Foil-stamped cover. .30 1.00
2-12 .30 1.00

BLAKE'S 7
MARVEL (1994)
SPECIAL Summer. TV tie in. Double size. 1.50 5.95
YEARBOOK 2.00 7.95

BLAST-OFF
HARVEY (1965)
1 Cover: Jack Kirby. The 3 Rocketeers. 8.00 24.00

BLAZE
MARVEL (1994-CURRENT)
1 Embossed foil-stamped cover. .75 2.95
2-11 .50 1.95

BLAZE CARSON
MARVEL (1948-1949)
1 35.00 110.00
2 20.00 65.00
3 Used in NY State Legislative Commission's investigation of comic books. 35.00 110.00
4 Two Gun Kid. 26.00 85.00
5 17.00 55.00

BLAZE: LEGACY OF BLOOD
MARVEL (1993-1994)
1 .50 1.95
2-4 .50 1.75

BLAZE THE WONDER COLLIE
MARVEL (1949-1950)
2 "Blaze-Son Of Fury!" Photo cover. 40.00 130.00
3 "The Adventure Of The Lonely Boy!" Photo cover. (2/50) 40.00 125.00

BLAZING COMBAT
APPLE (1980)
1 Reprints original Warren title. 1.25 4.50
2 1.25 4.50

BLAZING COMBAT
WARREN (1965-1966) MAGAZINE
1 Cover: Frank Frazetta (on all issues). 19.00 60.00
2 8.00 24.00
3-4 6.00 18.00

BLAZING COMICS
ENWIL (1944-1945)
1 50.00 160.00
2 25.00 80.00
3 Art: Dick Briefer. 35.00 110.00
4-6 20.00 65.00

BLAZING SIXGUNS
AVON (1952)
1 Cover & Art: Kinstler. 23.00 75.00

BLAZING SIXGUNS
I.W. (1964)
1 Reprints original series. 2.75 10.00

BLAZING WEST
ACG (1948-1952)
1 23.00 75.00
2 10.00 30.00
3-6 8.00 25.00
7-13 7.00 20.00
14 1st & Origin: The Hooded Horseman. 16.00 50.00
15-19 5.00 15.00
20 Title changes to The Hooded Horseman with #21. 5.00 15.00

BLITZKRIEG
DC (1976)
1-5 .50 1.50

BLONDE PHANTOM
MARVEL (1946-1949)
12 Previous title: All Select Comics. 220.00 700.00
13-15 App: Sub-Mariner. 155.00 500.00

BLACK PANTHER: PANTHER'S PREY #1

BLADE, THE VAMPIRE HUNTER #8

BLAZE #9

BLAZING COMICS #4

a b c d e f g h i j k l m n o p q r s t u v w x y z

BLOODSHOT #1

BLOODSTRIKE #9

BLUE BEETLE #5 (DC)

BLUE DEVIL #23

16 Captain America story (6 pages). 190.00 625.00
17-22 App: Sub-Mariner. 155.00 500.00

BLONDIE AND DAGWOOD FAMILY
HARVEY (1963-1965)
1 4.00 12.00
2-4 2.25 8.00

BLONDIE COMICS
MCKAY/HARVEY/KING/CHARLTON (1947-1976)
1 40.00 125.00
2 19.00 60.00
3-6 10.00 30.00
7-15 7.00 20.00
16 Begin: Harvey publication. 5.00 15.00
17-24 5.00 15.00
25-40 2.75 10.00
41-70 2.25 8.00
71-100 2.00 7.00
101-150 1.25 4.00
151-163 .75 2.50
164 Begin: King publication. .75 2.50
165-176 .75 2.50
177 Begin: Charlton publication. .75 2.50
178-200 .75 2.50
201-222 .50 1.50

BLOOD AND GLORY
MARVEL (1992)
1 Captain America & The Punisher. 1.50 5.95
2-3 1.50 5.95

BLOOD AND ROSES: SEARCH FOR THE TIME STONE
SKY (1994)
1-2 .75 2.50

BLOOD IS THE HARVEST
CATECHETICAL GUILD (1950)
NO# 155.00 500.00

BLOOD PACK
DC (1995)
1-4 .50 1.50

BLOOD SYNDICATE
DC (1993-CURRENT)
1 Polybagged with card. 1.00 3.50
1A Newsstand version. .75 2.00
2-9 .50 1.50
10 .75 2.50
11-17 .50 1.50
18-24 .50 1.75
25 Double-size. .75 2.95
26-27 .50 1.75
28 .75 2.50
29 .30 1.00
30 .75 2.50

BLOODBATH
DC (1993)
1 End of Bloodlines story. 1.00 3.50
2 1.00 3.50

BLOODFIRE
LIGHTNING (1993-CURRENT)
0 1.00 3.50
1A Platinum edition. 7.00 20.00
1 1st: Bloodfire. Foil-stamped cover. 2.25 8.00
2 Origin: Bloodfire. 1.50 5.50
3 1.25 4.75
4 1.25 4.50
5 Polybagged with card. 1.00 3.75
6-12 .75 2.95

BLOODSHOT
VALIANT (1992-CURRENT)
0 Origin: Bloodshot. Chromium cover. 1.00 3.00
0A Gold edition. 2.75 10.00
1 1st chromium cover on comics. 1.50 5.00
2-5 .75 2.00
6 1st: Ninjak. 1.00 3.00
7-39 .75 2.00
YEARBOOK 1 1.00 3.95

BLOODSTRIKE
IMAGE (1993-CURRENT)
1 1st: Bloodstrike. .75 2.95
2-12 .50 1.95
13-14 .75 2.50
15 .50 1.95
16 .75 2.50
17 .50 1.95
18-22 .75 2.50
25 .50 1.95

BLOODSTRIKE: ASSASSIN
IMAGE (1995-CURRENT)
1-2 .75 2.50

BLOODTHIRST: THE NIGHTFALL CONSPIRACY
ALPHA (1994)
1-2 .75 2.50

BLOODWULF
IMAGE (1995)
1-4 .75 2.50

BLUE BEETLE
CHARLTON (1955)
18 Previous title: The Thing. 28.00 90.00
19 22.00 70.00
20 23.00 75.00
21 22.00 70.00

BLUE BEETLE
CHARLTON (1964-1966)
V2#1 Origin: Blue Beetle (Dan Garrett). 17.00 55.00
V2#2 14.00 46.00
V2#3-V2#5 13.00 40.00
V3#50-V3#54 11.00 34.00

BLUE BEETLE
CHARLTON (1967-1968)
1 Begin: The Question by Steve Ditko. 28.00 90.00
2 Origin: Blue Beetle. 19.00 60.00
3-4 11.00 36.00
5 End: The Question. 11.00 36.00

BLUE BEETLE
DC (1986-1988)
1 Origin retold: Blue Beetle. .30 1.00
2-4 .30 1.00
5-7 The Question. .30 1.00
8-19 .30 1.00
20 App: Justice League. .30 1.00
21-22 Millenium. .30 1.00
23-24 .30 1.00

BLUE BEETLE, THE
FOX (1939-1950)
1 Origin: Blue Beetle. 600.00 2000.00
2 270.00 875.00
3 190.00 625.00
4 130.00 430.00
5 115.00 370.00
6 Origin retold: Blue Beetle. 105.00 340.00
7-8 95.00 310.00
9-11 80.00 250.00
12 App: Black Fury. 85.00 270.00
13 1st & Begin: V Man. 95.00 310.00
14-20 65.00 200.00
21-33 50.00 160.00
34-38 55.00 180.00
39-40 40.00 120.00
41-46 28.00 90.00
47 Begin: Matt Baker/Jack Kamen cover&art. 130.00 430.00
48 115.00 370.00
49-50 105.00 340.00
51 95.00 310.00
52-53 80.00 250.00
54 SOTI 85.00 280.00
55 80.00 250.00
56 SOTI 85.00 280.00
57 End: Jack Kamen art. 80.00 250.00
58-60 Art: Baker. 20.00 65.00

BLUE BOLT
NOVELTY PRESS (1940-1949)
V1#1 Origin: Blue Bolt. 400.00 1400.00
V1#2 220.00 700.00
V1#3 Art: Simon/Kirby. 190.00 600.00
V1#4 Art: Simon/Kirby. 145.00 480.00
V1#5 Art: Simon/Kirby/Everett. 160.00 525.00
V1#6 Art: Simon/Kirby. 145.00 480.00
V1#7 Art: Simon/Kirby. 160.00 525.00
V1#8-V1#9 Art: Simon/Kirby. 145.00 480.00
V1#10 Art: Simon/Kirby. 145.00 480.00
V1#11-V1#12 110.00 360.00
V2#1 40.00 120.00
V2#2 28.00 90.00
V2#3-V2#6 22.00 70.00
V2#7-V2#12 19.00 60.00
V3#1-V3#12 15.00 48.00
V4#1-V4#6 11.00 36.00
V4#7-V4#12 10.00 30.00
V5#1-V9#7 6.00 18.00
V9#8 No Blue Bolt. 4.00 12.00
V9#9 -V10#1 6.00 18.00

BLUE BOLT
STAR (1949-1953)
102-104 31.00 100.00
105 Origin retold: Blue Bolt. 70.00 230.00
106 Begin: Simon & Kirby. 55.00 170.00
107-110 55.00 170.00
111-119 Weird Tales. 55.00 170.00

BLUE CIRCLE COMICS
RURAL HOME (1944-1945)
1 1st: Blue Circle. 23.00 75.00
2 13.00 40.00
3-5 10.00 30.00

BLUE DEVIL
DC (1984-1986)
1-16 .30 1.00
17-19 Crisis. .30 1.00
20-31 .30 1.00
ANNUAL 1 (1985) .30 1.00

BLUE LILY
DARK HORSE (1993-1994)
1-3 1.00 3.95

BLUE PHANTOM, THE
DELL (1962)
01-066-208 Civil War tribute. 5.00 15.00

BLUE RIBBON COMICS
MLJ (1939-1942)
1 500.00 1700.00
2 230.00 750.00
3 Art: Jack Cole. 190.00 625.00
4 155.00 500.00
5-6 115.00 370.00
7 (11/40). 115.00 370.00
8 115.00 370.00
9 1st & Origin: Mr. Justice (2/41). 400.00 1500.00
10-15 Mr. Justice. 155.00 500.00
16 1st & Origin: Captain Flag (9/41). 280.00 925.00
17 Captain Flag, Mr. Justice. 155.00 500.00
18-21 Captain Flag. 130.00 430.00
22 Origin retold: Mr. Justice. 155.00 500.00

BLUE RIBBON COMICS (2ND SERIES)
SEE INDIVIDUAL TITLES.
- HECKLE AND JECKLE, DIARY SECRETS, TEENAGE DIARY SECRETS, DINKY COMICS.

BLUE STREAK COMICS, THE
HOLYOKE (1944-1945)
8 From the Holyoke One-Shot series. 19.00 60.00

BLYTHE
DELL FOUR COLOR SERIES (1960)
1072 (2/60) 10.00 30.00

BO
CHARLTON (1955)
1 11.00 35.00
2 7.00 20.00
3 Title changes to Tom Cat with #4. 7.00 20.00

BOB COLT
FAWCETT (1950-1952)
1 Movie photo cover. 70.00 220.00
2 Photo covers on all issues. 35.00 110.00
3-6 28.00 90.00
7-10 25.00 80.00

BOB MARLEY: TALE OF THE TUFF GONG
MARVEL (1994)
1-3 1.50 5.95

BOB, SON OF BATTLE
DELL FOUR COLOR SERIES (1956)
729 (11/56) 7.00 20.00

BOB STEELE WESTERN
FAWCETT (1950-1952)
1 Photo covers on all. 85.00 270.00
2 50.00 160.00
3-6 35.00 110.00
7-10 28.00 90.00

BOB SWIFT
FAWCETT (1951-1952)
1 Cover: Norman Saunders. 9.00 27.00
2 5.00 16.00
3-5 4.00 11.00

BOB, THE GALACTIC BUM
DC (1994-1995)
1-4 .50 1.95

BOBBY BENSON'S B-BAR-B RIDERS
ME (1950-1953)
1 Art: Bob Powell. 50.00 160.00
2 Art: Bob Powell. 25.00 80.00
3-6 Art: Bob Powell. 17.00 55.00
7-8 Art: Bob Powell. 14.00 44.00
9 Cover: Frank Frazetta. Art: Bob Powell. 40.00 130.00
10 Art: Bob Powell. 14.00 44.00
11 Cover: Frank Frazetta. Art: Bob Powell. 40.00 130.00
12 Art: Bob Powell. 14.00 44.00
13 Cover: Frank Frazetta. Ghost Rider. 50.00 160.00
14 "The Ghost Bell of Terror Valley!" Ghost Rider. 20.00 65.00
15 Ghost Rider. 20.00 65.00
16 Photo cover. 17.00 55.00
17-19 14.00 44.00

BOBBY BENSON'S B-BAR-B RIDERS (A-1 SERIES)
ME (1953)
20 (A-1 #88). 14.00 45.00

BOBBY GETS HEP
BELL TELEPHONE (1946)
NO# 8 page giveaway, newsprint (early use of the word "groovy", more typically associated with the 1960's). 10.00 30.00

BOBBY SHERMAN
CHARLTON (1972)
1 TV tie-in. 8.00 25.00
2 5.00 15.00
3 2.75 10.00
4 5.00 15.00
5-7 2.75 10.00

BOLD STORIES
KIRBY (1950)
1 (3/50) Art: Wallace Wood. 95.00 300.00
2 (5/50) 95.00 300.00
3 (7/50) 95.00 300.00

BOMBA, THE JUNGLE BOY
DC (1967-1968)
1 1st: Bomba. 5.00 15.00
2 4.00 12.00
3-7 2.25 8.00

BOMBARDIER
RKO (1943)
NO# Movie giveaway (4 pages). From the Cinema Comics Herald series. 16.00 50.00

BOMBAST
TOPPS (1993)
1 Polybagged with card. .75 2.95

BOMBER COMICS
ELLIOT (1944)
1 App: Wonder Boy. 55.00 170.00
2-4 35.00 110.00

BON VOYAGE
DELL (1962)
12-068-212 Disney movie photo cover (Fred MacMurray). 7.00 20.00

BONANZA
DELL FOUR COLOR SERIES (1960-1962)
1110 TV photo cover. (6/60) 65.00 200.00
1221 TV photo cover. (8/61) 50.00 160.00
1283 TV photo cover. (1/62) 45.00 135.00

BONANZA
GOLD KEY (1962-1970)
12-070-207 35.00 110.00
12-070-210 28.00 90.00
1 TV photo covers on all issues. 29.00 95.00
2 20.00 65.00
3-6 14.00 44.00
7-12 10.00 30.00
13-24 7.00 22.00
25-37 5.00 16.00

BONE
CARTOON BOOKS (1991-CURRENT)
1 1st:Fone Bone, 1st:Phoney Bone, 1st:Smiley Bone. 70.00 225.00
1 (2ND) 2nd printing. 6.00 18.00
1 (3RD) 3rd printing. 2.75 10.00
1 (4TH) 4th printing. 1.50 5.00
1 (5TH) 5th printing. 1.00 3.25
2 Fone Bone meets Thorn. 40.00 120.00
2 (2ND) 2.75 10.00
3 1st: Gran'ma Ben. Fone & Phoney reunited. 25.00 80.00
3 (2ND) 2.25 8.00
4 The Rat Creatures attack. 19.00 60.00
5 Rescued by the dragon. 16.00 50.00
6 Hooded stranger wants Phoney's soul. 16.00 50.00
7 At the fair. 11.00 35.00
8 The map's secret. 10.00 30.00
9 Captured by rat creatures. 4.00 12.00
10 The Great Cow Race. 2.25 8.00
11-13 1.25 4.50
13 1/2 Wizard mail-away. 2.75 10.00
13 1/2 A Gold version. 7.00 20.00
14-20 .75 2.95
TPB VOL 1 The Collected Adventures. Reprints issues #1-6. 4.00 12.95
TPB VOL 2 The Collected Adventures. Reprints issues #7-12. 4.00 12.95
TPB VOL 3 The Collected Adventures. Reprints #13-18. 4.00 12.95

BONGO AND LUMPJAW
DELL FOUR COLOR SERIES (1956-1958)
706 (6/56) 7.00 20.00
886 (3/58) 7.00 20.00

BOOF
IMAGE (1994)
1-3 .50 1.95

BOOF AND THE BRUISE CREW
IMAGE (1994)
1-3 .50 1.95

BOOK OF COMICS
WILLIAM H. WISE (1944)
NO# 128 pages, 25 cent cover price. Includes Captain "V" and others. 55.00 175.00

BOOK OF THE DEAD
MARVEL (1993-CURRENT)
1-6 .50 1.75

BOOK OF THE NIGHT
DARK HORSE (1987)
1-2 .75 2.00

BOOKS OF MAGIC
DC (1990-1991)
1 2.50 9.00
2 2.75 10.00
3 2.25 8.00
4 1.75 6.00
TPB Reprints issues #1-4. 6.00 19.95

BOOKS OF MAGIC
DC (1994-CURRENT)
1 1.50 6.00
2 1.00 4.50
3 1.00 4.00
4 App: Death. 1.25 4.50
5-12 .75 2.50
13-16 .75 2.50
TPB Bindings. Reprints issues #1-4 (regular series). 4.00 12.95

BOOSTER GOLD
DC (1986-1988)
1-25 .20 .50

BOOTS AND HER BUDDIES
STANDARD (1948-1949)
5 19.00 60.00
6 13.00 40.00
7 17.00 55.00
8 13.00 40.00
9 Art: Frazetta (2 pages). 31.00 100.00

BOOTS AND SADDLES
DELL FOUR COLOR SERIES (1958-1960)
919 TV photo cover. (7/58) 17.00 55.00
1029 TV photo cover. (9/59) 11.00 35.00
1116 TV photo cover. (8/60) 11.00 35.00

BOOTS AND SADDLES
METROPOLITAN (1950)
1 Giveaway (5.25 x 8.5, bound at top). 7.00 20.00

BORIS KARLOFF TALES OF MYSTERY
GOLD KEY (1963-1980)
3 TV tie-in series. Previous title: Boris Karloff Thriller. 7.00 20.00
4-8 5.00 15.00
9 Art: Wallace Wood. 5.00 15.00
10 5.00 15.00
11 Art: Al Williamson. 5.00 15.00
12 5.00 15.00
13-14 2.75 10.00
15 Art: Reed Crandall 4.00 12.00
16-20 2.75 10.00
21 "The Screaming Skull!" by Jeff Jones. 5.00 15.00
22-36 2.00 7.00
37-60 1.50 5.00
61-80 1.00 3.00
81-97 .75 2.00
DIGEST (1970) 2.75 10.00

BORIS KARLOFF THRILLER
GOLD KEY (1962-1963)
1 TV photo cover. 13.00 40.00
2 Title changes to Boris Karloff Tales Of Mystery with #3. 9.00 28.00

BORIS THE BEAR
DARK HORSE (1987-1988)
1-20 .20 .50

BOUNCER, THE
FOX (1944-1945)
10 31.00 100.00
11 Origin: The Bouncer. 26.00 85.00
12-14 20.00 65.00

BOY AND THE PIRATES, THE
DELL FOUR COLOR SERIES (1960)
1117 Movie photo cover. (6/60) 13.00 40.00

BOY COMICS
LEV GLEASON (1942-1956)
3 Previous title: Captain Battle. 300.00 1100.00
4 Hitler, Mussolini, Tojo cover. (6/42) 140.00 460.00
5 (8/42) 105.00 340.00
6 Origin: Iron Jaw. "Son Of Iron Jaw Battles Crimebuster!" (10/42) 270.00 875.00
7 Hitler, Mussolini, Tojo cover. (12/42) 85.00 280.00
8 Death: Iron Jaw. (2/43) 105.00 340.00
9 Intro: He-She. (4/43) 85.00 280.00
10 Return of Iron Jaw. (6/43) 140.00 460.00
11-14 65.00 200.00
15 Death: Iron Jaw. 80.00 250.00
16 35.00 110.00
17 Patriotic cover. 45.00 140.00
18-24 35.00 110.00
25-29 25.00 80.00
30 Origin retold: Crimebuster. 45.00 140.00
31-36 19.00 60.00
37-42 16.00 50.00
43 Title changes to Boy Illustories (12/48) 16.00 50.00
44-48 16.00 50.00
49-59 14.00 46.00
60 Return of Iron Jaw. 16.00 50.00
61 14.00 46.00
62 Death explained: Iron Jaw. 16.00 50.00
63-70 13.00 40.00
71-90 11.00 34.00
91-107 9.00 28.00
108 Title changes back to Boy Comics. 9.00 28.00
109-119 9.00 28.00

BOY COMMANDOS
DC (1942-1949)
1 Cover/Art: Simon & Kirby (issues 1-8). 800.00 3000.00
2 280.00 900.00
3 190.00 600.00
4-5 110.00 360.00
6 190.00 600.00
7-8 110.00 360.00
9 Cover: Simon & Kirby. 75.00 240.00
10 75.00 240.00
11-18 55.00 180.00
19-22 50.00 150.00
23 Cover/Art: Simon & Kirby. 55.00 180.00
24-35 31.00 100.00
36 The Atomobile. 40.00 120.00

BOY COMMANDOS
DC (1973)
1 Reprints: Golden Age Simon & Kirby. 1.00 3.00
2 Reprints. 1.00 3.00

BOY DETECTIVE
AVON (1951-1952)
1 23.00 75.00
2 10.00 30.00
3 Cover: Raymond Kinstler. 10.00 30.00
4 Cover/Art: Raymond Kinstler. 25.00 80.00

BOY EXPLORERS COMICS
HARVEY (1946)
1 Cover/Art: Simon & Kirby. This series was Simon and Kirby's first collaboration after their return from World War II. 110.00 360.00
2 Scarce black & white issue. 145.00 480.00

BOY ILLUSTORIES
SEE BOY COMICS

BOOSTER GOLD #7

BOY COMICS #15

BOY COMMANDOS #14

BOY DETECTIVE #4

BOYS RANCH #1

THE BRAIN #1

BRAVE AND THE BOLD #30

BRAVE AND THE BOLD #35

FAMOUS • FIRSTS

BRAVE AND THE BOLD #28

DC's greatest heroes are introduced when the Justice League of America battle an alien starfish. Already teammates at the time of this adventure, they tell how they formed in issue #9 of *Justice League of America*.

BOY MEETS GIRL
LEV GLEASON (1950-1952)

1 .... 7.00 20.00
2 .... 2.75 10.00
3-12 .... 2.00 7.00
13-24 .... 1.50 5.00

BOYS' RANCH
HARVEY (1950-1951)

1 Cover/Art: Simon & Kirby. Begin: The Kid Cowboys. 85.00 270.00
2-4 Cover/Art: Simon & Kirby. 70.00 220.00
5-6 Cover: Simon & Kirby. 29.00 95.00

BOZO THE CLOWN
DELL (1951-1952)

2-7 .... 19.00 60.00

BOZO THE CLOWN
DELL FOUR COLOR SERIES (1950-1954)

285 "And His Minikin Circus" (7/50) 31.00 100.00
464 "Bozo The Capitol Clown" (4/53) 20.00 65.00
508 (10/53) 20.00 65.00
551 (4/54) 20.00 65.00
594 (10/54) 20.00 65.00

BRADY BUNCH, THE
GOLD KEY (1970)

1 TV tie-in. 9.00 27.00
2 .... 7.00 22.00

BRADY BUNCH KITE FUN BOOK, THE
WHITMAN (1976)

1976 .... 8.00 25.00

BRAIN, THE
ME (1958-1959)

1 .... 7.00 20.00
2 .... 4.00 12.00
3-7 .... 2.25 8.00

BRAIN BOY
DELL (1962-1963)

1 (#1330) From the 4-Color Series. Origin: Brain Boy. (4/62) 16.00 50.00
2-6 .... 7.00 20.00

BRAM STOKER'S DRACULA
SEE DRACULA (BRAM STOKER'S...)

BRAT PACK
KING HELL/TUNDRA (1990-1991)

1 1st: Dr. Blasphemy. 1.50 5.00
1 (2ND) 2nd printing. .... .75 2.95
2-5 .... .75 2.95
TPB Reprints issues #1-5 (with new ending). 4.00 13.00

BRATS BIZARRE
MARVEL (1994)

1-4 .... .75 2.50

BRAVE AND THE BOLD
DC (1955-1983)

1 Begin: The Golden Gladiator, The Viking Prince, The Silent Knight. 500.00 1750.00
2 App: The Viking Prince, The Silent Knight, The Golden Gladiator. 170.00 550.00
3 App: The Viking Prince, The Silent Knight, The Golden Gladiator. 100.00 325.00
4 App: The Viking Prince, The Silent Knight, The Golden Gladiator. "The Robber Baron Of Forest Perilous!" 100.00 325.00
5 Begin: Robin Hood, App: The Silent Knight, The Viking Prince. 100.00 325.00
6 App: Robin Hood, The Silent Knight, The Golden Gladiator. 80.00 260.00
7 App: Robin Hood, The Silent Knight. "Duel Of The Double Identities!" 80.00 260.00
8 App: Robin Hood, The Silent Knight, The Golden Gladiator. 80.00 260.00
9-10 App: Robin Hood, The Silent Knight, The Viking Prince. 80.00 260.00
11-12 App: Robin Hood, The Silent Knight, The Viking Prince. 70.00 220.00
13-14 App: Robin Hood, The Viking Prince, The Silent Knight. 65.00 200.00
15 App: The Silent Knight, Robin Hood, The Viking Prince. 65.00 200.00
16 App: The Viking Prince, The Silent Knight. 65.00 200.00
17-18 App: The Silent Knight, The Viking Prince. 65.00 200.00
19 App: The Viking Prince, The Silent Knight. 65.00 200.00
20 App: The Silent Knight, The Viking Prince. 65.00 200.00
21 App: The Viking Prince, The Silent Knight. 65.00 200.00
22 Last: Silent Knight. App: The Viking Prince. 65.00 200.00
23 Origin: The Viking Prince. 80.00 260.00
24 Last: Viking Prince. "The Trail Of The Black Falcon!" & "Curse Of The Dragon's Moon!" by Kubert. 65.00 200.00
25 1st: Suicide Squad. 165.00 525.00
26-27 Suicide Squad. 75.00 240.00
28 1st: Justice League Of America. "Starro The Conqueror!" Origin: Snapper Carr. 1100.00 4300.00
29 2nd: Justice League. 500.00 1650.00
30 3rd: Justice League in "The Case Of The Stolen Super-Powers!" 400.00 1450.00
31 1st: Cave Carson. 80.00 250.00
32-33 Cave Carson. 35.00 110.00
34 1st & Origin: Hawkman & Byth. "Creature Of A Thousand Shapes!" 400.00 1600.00
35 Hawkman. 130.00 425.00
36 App: Hawkman, Origin: Shadow Thief. "The Shadow-Thief Of Midway City!" 100.00 330.00
37 Suicide Squad. 50.00 160.00
38 Suicide Squad. 50.00 150.00
39 Suicide Squad. 1st 12 cent cover price. 50.00 150.00
40-41 Cave Carson Inside Earth. 28.00 90.00
42 Hawkman. 75.00 240.00
43 Origin retold: Hawkman. "Masked Marauders Of Earth!" by Kubert. 85.00 275.00
44 Hawkman in "The Men Who Moved The World!" 65.00 200.00
45-49 Strange Sports Stories. 11.00 35.00
50 The Green Arrow & Martian Manhunter. 31.00 100.00
51 Aquaman & Hawkman. Pre-Hawkman #1. .... 50.00 150.00
52 Sgt. Rock, Haunted Tank, Johnny Cloud, & Mlle. Marie. 26.00 85.00
53 Atom & The Flash. 11.00 35.00
54 App: Kid Flash, Robin & Aqualad; 1st & Origin: Teen Titans (6-7/64). 55.00 180.00
55 Metal Men & The Atom. 7.00 22.00
56 The Flash & Martian Manhunter. 7.00 22.00
57 1st & Origin: Metamorpho. 31.00 100.00
58 Metamorpho. 13.00 40.00
59 Batman & Green Lantern. 16.00 50.00
60 Teen Titans. 19.00 60.00
61 Origin: Starman & Black Canary. 16.00 50.00
62 Origin continued: Starman & Black Canary. 16.00 50.00
63 Supergirl & Wonder Woman. 5.00 15.00
64 Batman vs. Eclipso. 16.00 50.00
65 The Flash & The Doom Patrol. 5.00 15.00
66 Metamorpho & Metal Men. 4.00 12.00
67 Batman & The Flash. 8.00 25.00
68 Batman & Metamorpho. 14.00 45.00
69 Batman & Green Lantern. 7.00 20.00
70 Batman & Hawkman. 7.00 20.00
71 Batman & Green Arrow. 7.00 20.00
72 The Flash & The Spectre. 5.00 15.00
73 Aquaman & The Atom. 5.00 15.00
74 Batman & The Metal Men. 5.00 15.00
75 Batman & The Spectre. 5.00 15.00
76 Batman & Plastic Man. 5.00 15.00
77 Batman & The Atom. 5.00 15.00
78 Batman & Wonder Woman & Batgirl. 5.00 15.00
79 Batman & Deadman. Art: Neal Adams. 10.00 32.00
80 Batman & The Creeper. Art: Neal Adams. 9.00 28.00
81 Batman & The Flash. Art: Neal Adams. 8.00 25.00
82 Batman & Aquaman. Art: Neal Adams. 8.00 25.00
83 Batman & The Teen Titans. Art: Neal Adams. 13.00 40.00
84 Batman & Sgt Rock. Art: Neal Adams. 8.00 25.00
85 Batman & Green Arrow. Art: Neal Adams. 8.00 25.00
86 Batman & Deadman. Art: Neal Adams. 8.00 25.00
87 Batman & Wonder Woman. 5.00 15.00
88 Batman & Wildcat. 5.00 15.00
89 Batman & Phantom Stranger. 5.00 15.00
90 Batman & Adam Strange. 5.00 15.00

91 Batman & Black Canary. 5.00 15.00
92 Batman & Bat Squad. 5.00 15.00
93 Batman & The House of Mystery. Art: Neal Adams. 8.00 26.00
94 Batman & The Teen Titans. 2.75 10.00
95 Batman & Plastic Man. 2.75 10.00
96 Batman & Sgt. Rock. 2.75 10.00
97 Batman & Wildcat. App: Deadman. 2.75 10.00
98 Batman & The Phantom Stranger. 2.75 10.00
99 Batman & The Flash. 2.75 10.00
100 Batman-Green Lantern-Green Arrow-Black Canary-Robin; Deadman. 9.00 28.00
101 Batman-Metamorpho; Viking Prince. 1.50 5.00
102 Batman & The Teen Titans. Art: Neal Adams. 2.75 10.00
103 Batman & The Metal Men. 1.50 5.00
104 Batman & Deadman. 1.50 5.00
105 Batman & Wonder Woman. 1.50 5.00
106 Batman & Green Arrow. 1.50 5.00
107 Batman & Black Canary. 1.50 5.00
108 Batman & Sgt. Rock. 1.50 5.00
109 Batman & The Demon. 1.50 5.00
110 Batman & Wildcat. 1.50 5.00
111 Batman & The Joker. 4.00 12.00
112 Batman & Mr. Miracle. 100 page issue. 2.25 8.00
113 Batman & The Metal Men. 100 page issue. 2.25 8.00
114 Batman & Aquaman. 100 page issue. 2.25 8.00
115 Batman & The Atom. Origin retold: Viking Prince. 100 page issue. 2.25 8.00
116 Batman & The Spectre. 100 page issue. 2.25 8.00
117 Batman & Sgt. Rock. 100 page issue. 2.25 8.00
118 Batman & Wildcat & The Joker. 4.00 12.00
119 Batman & Man-Bat. 1.25 4.00
120 Batman & Kamandi. 1.25 4.00
121 Batman & The Metal Men. 1.25 4.00
122 Batman & The Swamp Thing. 1.25 4.00
123 Batman & Plastic Man. 1.25 4.00
124 Batman & Sgt. Rock. 1.25 4.00
125 Batman & The Flash. 1.25 4.00
126 Batman & Aquaman. 1.25 4.00
127 Batman & Wildcat. 1.25 4.00
128 Batman & Mr. Miracle. 1.25 4.00
129-130 Batman & Green Arrow. 4.00 12.00
131 Batman & Wonder Woman. 1.25 4.00
132 Batman & Kung Fu Fighter. 1.25 4.00
133 Batman & Deadman. 1.25 4.00
134 Batman & Green Lantern. 1.25 4.00
135 Batman & The Metal Men. 1.25 4.00
136 Batman & Green Arrow & The Metal Men. 1.25 4.00
137 Batman & The Demon. 1.25 4.00
138 Batman & Mr. Miracle. 1.25 4.00
139 Batman & Hawkman. 1.25 4.00
140 Batman & Wonder Woman. 1.25 4.00
141 Batman & Black Canary. 2.75 10.00
142 Batman & Aquaman. 1.25 4.00
143 Batman & The Creeper. 1.25 4.00
144 Batman & Green Arrow. 1.25 4.00
145 Batman & The Phantom Stranger. 1.25 4.00
146 Batman & The Unknown Soldier. 1.25 4.00
147 Batman & Supergirl. 1.25 4.00
148 Batman & Plastic Man. 1.25 4.00
149 Batman & The Teen Titans. 1.25 4.00
150 Batman & Superman. 1.25 4.00
151 Batman & The Flash. 1.25 4.00
152 Batman & The Atom. 1.25 4.00
153 Batman & The Red Tornado. 1.25 4.00
154 Batman & Metamorpho. 1.25 4.00
155 Batman & Green Lantern. 1.25 4.00
156 Batman & Doctor Fate. 1.25 4.00
157 Batman & Kamandi. 1.25 4.00
158 Batman & Wonder Woman. 1.25 4.00
159 Batman & Ra's Al Ghul. 1.25 4.00
160 Batman & Supergirl. 1.25 4.00
161 Batman & Adam Strange. 1.25 4.00
162 Batman & Sgt. Rock. 1.25 4.00
163 Batman & Black Lightning. 1.25 4.00
164 Batman & Hawkman. 1.25 4.00
165 Batman & Man-Bat. 1.25 4.00
166 Batman & Black Canary. 1.25 4.00
167 Batman & Blackhawk. 1.25 4.00
168 Batman & Green Arrow. 1.25 4.00
169 Batman & Zatanna. 1.25 4.00
170 Batman & Nemesis. 1.25 4.00
171 Batman & Scalphunter. 1.25 4.00
172 Batman & Firestorm. 1.25 4.00
173 Batman & Guardians Of The Universe. 1.25 4.00
174 Batman & Green Lantern. 1.25 4.00
175 Batman & Lois Lane. 1.25 4.00
176 Batman & The Swamp Thing. 1.25 4.00
177 Batman & The Elongated Man. 1.25 4.00
178 Batman & The Creeper. 1.25 4.00
179 Batman & The Legion Of Super Heroes. 1.25 4.00
180 Batman & The Spectre. 1.25 4.00
181 Batman & Hawk And The Dove. 1.25 4.00
182 Batman & Robin. 1.25 4.00
183 Batman & The Riddler. 1.25 4.00
184 Batman & The Huntress. 1.25 4.00
185 Batman & Green Arrow. 1.25 4.00
186 Batman & Hawkman. 1.25 4.00
187 Batman & Metal Men. 1.25 4.00
188-189 Batman & Rose And The Thorn. 1.25 4.00
190 Batman & Adam Strange. 1.25 4.00
191 Batman & The Joker. 2.50 9.00
192 Batman & Superboy. 1.25 4.00
193 Batman & Nemesis. 1.25 4.00
194 Batman & The Flash. 1.25 4.00
195 Batman & The Vampire. 1.25 4.00
196 Batman & Ragman. 1.25 4.00
197 Batman & Catwoman. 1.25 4.00
198 Batman & The Karate Kid. 1.25 4.00
199 Batman & The Spectre. 1.25 4.00
200 Earth One and Earth Two Batman team-up; Intro/1st app. Batman & The Outsiders. 2.25 8.00

BRAVE AND THE BOLD, THE
DC (1991-1992)
1-6 .50 1.75

BRAVE EAGLE
DELL FOUR COLOR SERIES (1956-1958)
705 TV photo cover. (5/56) 11.00 35.00
770 TV photo cover. (2/57) 8.00 25.00
816 TV photo cover. (7/57) 8.00 25.00
879 TV photo cover. (2/58) 8.00 25.00
929 TV photo cover. (8/58) 7.00 20.00

BRAVE ONE, THE
DELL FOUR COLOR SERIES (1957)
773 (2/57) 11.00 35.00

BRAVURA PREVIEW BOOK 1995
MALIBU (1994)
1 .50 1.50

BREAK THE CHAIN
MARVEL (1994)
1 Includes audio cassette. 1.75 6.99

BREAK THRU
MALIBU (1993-1994)
1 1.00 3.00
1A Ultra limited foil edition. 2.75 10.00
2 .75 2.50

BREATHTAKER
DC (1990)
1-4 1.50 5.00

BREED
MALIBU (1994)
1 1.00 3.50
1A Newsstand edition (variant cover). .75 2.95
2-6 .75 2.75
TPB Reprints issues #1-6. 4.00 12.95

BREED II
MALIBU (1994-1995)
1-6 .75 2.95

BRENDA LEE'S LIFE STORY
DELL (1962)
01-078-209 Photo cover. 19.00 60.00

BRENDA STARR
CHARLTON (1955)
13-15 31.00 100.00

BRENDA STARR
SUPERIOR (1947-1949)
1 (#13) 115.00 380.00
2 (#14) Cover: Kamen. 100.00 330.00
3 85.00 270.00
4 SOTI 100.00 330.00
5-12 70.00 220.00

BRENDA STARR REPORTER
DELL (1963)
1 23.00 75.00

BRER RABBIT
DELL FOUR COLOR SERIES (1946-1949)
129 "Uncle Remus And His Tales Of...". Walt Disney movie tie-in (Song Of The South). 50.00 150.00
208 "Does It Again!". Disney. 23.00 75.00

BRER RABBIT OUTWITS BRER FOX
DISNEY (1947)
X3 Cheerios Premium. 2.75 10.00

BRER RABBIT'S SECRET
DISNEY (1947)
Y2 Cheerios Premium. 2.75 10.00

BRICK BRADFORD
KING (1948-1949)
5 19.00 60.00
6-8 16.00 50.00

BRIDES ROMANCES
QUALITY (1953-1956)
1 13.00 40.00
2 7.00 20.00
3-12 5.00 15.00
13-23 2.75 10.00

BRIGADE
IMAGE (1992-1993)
1 1st: Brigade. 1.25 4.00
1A Gold edition. 2.75 10.00
1B Signed Gold edition. 5.00 15.00
2 With coupon. 1.00 3.00
2A Without coupon. .30 1.00
3 .50 1.95
4 .75 2.50

BRIGADE
IMAGE (1993-CURRENT)
0 (7/95) .50 1.95
1 .50 1.95
2 Mirri-cote cover. .75 2.95
3-10 .50 1.95
11-12 .75 2.50
13-15 .50 1.95
16-22 .75 2.50
25-26 (shipped after #10) .50 1.95
SOURCEBOOK .75 2.95

BRINGING UP FATHER
CUPPLES & LEON (1919-1934)
BIG BOOK 1 (1926) Hardcover book. 95.00 300.00
BIG BOOK 2 (1929) Hardcover book. 65.00 200.00
1 65.00 200.00
2 (1920) 50.00 150.00
3-6 40.00 125.00
7-26 31.00 100.00

BRINGING UP FATHER
DELL FOUR COLOR SERIES (1944)
37 50.00 150.00

BRINGING UP FATHER
SEE LARGE FEATURE COMICS (SERIES II) #9.

BRINKE OF ETERNITY
CHAOS! (1994)
1 .75 2.75

BROADWAY HOLLYWOOD BLACKOUTS
STANHALL (1954)
1 10.00 30.00
2-3 7.00 20.00

BROADWAY ROMANCES
QUALITY (1950)
1 31.00 100.00
2 19.00 60.00
3-5 13.00 40.00

BROKEN ARROW
DELL FOUR COLOR SERIES (1957-1958)
855 TV photo cover. (11/57) 11.00 35.00
947 TV photo cover. (11/58) 11.00 35.00

BRONCO BILL
STANDARD (1948-1950)
5 13.00 40.00
6-12 7.00 20.00
13-16 4.00 12.00

BROTHER POWER THE GEEK
DC (1968)
1 Origin: Brother Power. 10.00 30.00
2 7.00 22.00

BROWNIES, THE
DELL FOUR COLOR SERIES (1948-1954)
192 (6/48) 31.00 100.00
244 (9/49) 25.00 80.00
293 (9/50) 22.00 70.00
337 (6/51) 8.00 25.00
365 (12/51) 8.00 25.00
398 (5/52) 8.00 25.00
436 (11/52) 7.00 20.00
482 (7/53) 7.00 20.00
522 (12/53) 7.00 20.00
605 (12/54) 5.00 15.00

BRUCE GENTRY
STANDARD (1948-1949)
1 40.00 125.00

BRAVE AND THE BOLD #184

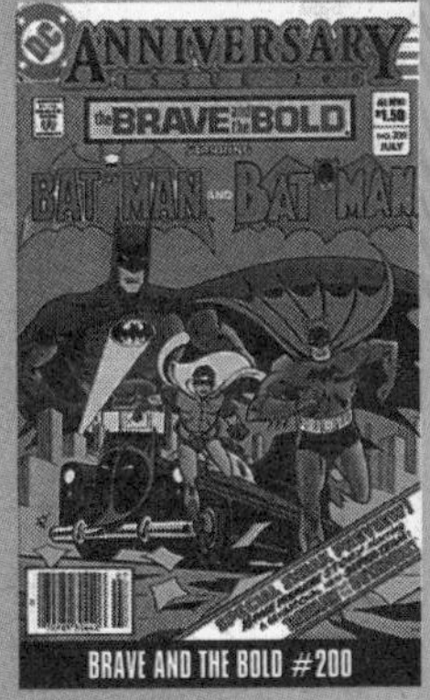

BRAVE AND THE BOLD #200

BRIGADE (MINI-SERIES) #4

BRUCE GENTRY #1

BRUTE & BABE: MAEL'S RAGE #1

BUCK ROGERS #9

BUFFALO BILL PICTURE STORIES #1

BUGS BUNNY VACATION FUNNIES #2

2 31.00 100.00
3 28.00 90.00
4-5 22.00 70.00
6 19.00 60.00
7-8 16.00 50.00

BRUCE LEE
MALIBU (1994)
1-6 .75 2.95

BRUTE, THE
ATLAS(SEABOARD) (1975)
1 1st & Origin: The Brute. .75 2.00
2-3 .75 2.00

BRUTE & BABE: CHAKALL, SHE SLAVE FROM BEYOND
OMINOUS (1994)
1 .75 2.00

BRUTE & BABE: MAEL'S RAGE
OMINOUS (1994)
1 .75 2.50

BRUTE & BABE: MONUMENT SET: IT BEGINS...
OMINOUS (1994)
1 Set of unstapled comic pages. 1.00 3.95

BRUTE & BABE: MONUMENT SET II: DEATH OF PHEROS
OMINOUS (1994)
1 Set of unstapled comic pages. 1.25 4.95

BRUTE & BABE: OMEN
OMINOUS (1994)
1 .75 2.50

BUCCANEER
I.W.
1 Reprints Quality series. 7.00 20.00

BUCCANEERS, THE
DELL FOUR COLOR SERIES (1957)
800 TV photo cover. (5/57) 16.00 50.00

BUCCANEERS
QUALITY (1950-1951)
12 Super Reprint (1964) 2.25 8.75
19 Previous title: Kid Eternity. 70.00 220.00
20-21 50.00 160.00
22-23 40.00 130.00
24-26 29.00 95.00
27 Cover & art: Reed Crandall. 40.00 130.00

BUCK JONES
DELL (1950-1952)
1 (#299) "And The Iron Horse Trail." From the 4-Color Series. (10/50) 28.00 90.00
2 (4/51) 10.00 30.00
3-8 7.00 20.00

BUCK JONES
DELL FOUR COLOR SERIES (1953-1957)
460 (4/53) 8.00 25.00
500 (10/53) 7.00 20.00
546 (4/54) 8.00 25.00
589 (10/54) 5.00 15.00
652 (10/55) 5.00 15.00
733 (10/56) 5.00 15.00
850 (10/57) 5.00 15.00

BUCK ROGERS
FAMOUS FUNNIES (1940-1943)
1 250.00 800.00
2 155.00 500.00
3-4 125.00 400.00
5-6 95.00 300.00

BUCK ROGERS
GOLD KEY (1964-1982)
1 (10128-410). 7.00 20.00

BUCK ROGERS
TOBY (1951)
9 Art: Murphy Anderson. 31.00 100.00
100-101 31.00 100.00

BUCKAROO BANZAI
MARVEL (1984-1985)
1 Movie Adaptation. .75 2.00
2 .75 2.00

BUCKSKIN
DELL FOUR COLOR SERIES (1959-1960)
1011 TV photo cover. (7/59) 22.00 70.00
1107 TV photo cover. (6/60) 16.00 50.00

BUCKY BUG AND THE CANNIBAL KING
DISNEY (1947)
W2 Cheerios Premium. 2.75 10.00

BUDDIES IN THE U.S. ARMY
AVON (1952-1953)
1 10.00 30.00
2 7.00 20.00

BUFFALO BEE
DELL FOUR COLOR SERIES (1958-1959)
957 (12/58) 19.00 60.00
1002 (6/59) 13.00 40.00
1061 (12/59) 10.00 30.00

BUFFALO BILL
YOUTHFUL (1950-1951)
2 10.00 30.00
3-6 7.00 20.00
7-9 5.00 15.00

BUFFALO BILL JR.
DELL (1956-1959)
1 (#673) From the 4-Color Series. TV photo covers on all issues. (1/56) 16.00 50.00
2 (#742) From the 4-Color Series. (9/56) 10.00 30.00
3 (#766) From the 4-Color Series. (2/57) 8.00 25.00
4 (#798) From the 4-Color Series. (5/57) 8.00 25.00
5 (#828) From the 4-Color Series. (8/57) 8.00 25.00
6 (#856) From the 4-Color Series. (11/57) 8.00 25.00
7-13 7.00 20.00

BUFFALO BILL PICTURE STORIES
STREET & SMITH (1949)
1 Art: Bob Powell. 13.00 40.00
2 Art: Bob Powell. 10.00 30.00

BUGHOUSE
AJAX (1954)
1 16.00 50.00
2-4 10.00 30.00

BUGS BUNNY
DC (1990)
1 Mini-series. .30 1.00
2-3 .30 1.00

BUGS BUNNY
DELL FOUR COLOR SERIES (1943-1959)
33 "Public Nuisance No. 1" 125.00 400.00
51 "Finds The Lost Treasure" 65.00 200.00
88 "...Great Adventure" 50.00 150.00
123 "Dangerous Venture" 25.00 80.00
142 "And The Haunted Mountains" 25.00 80.00
164 "Finds The Frozen Kingdom" 22.00 70.00
187 "And The Dreadful Dragon" 22.00 70.00
200 "Super Sleuth" 19.00 60.00
217 "Court Jester" 23.00 75.00
233 "Sleepwalking Sleuth" 23.00 75.00
250 "Diamond Daze" 23.00 75.00
266 "On The Isle Of Hercules" 19.00 60.00
274 "Hare-Brained Reporter" 19.00 60.00
281 "The Great Circus Mystery" 19.00 60.00
289 "Indian Trouble" 19.00 60.00
298 "Sheik For A Day" 19.00 60.00
307 "Lumberjack Jackrabbit" 16.00 50.00
317 "Hair Today, Gone Tomorrow" 16.00 50.00
327 "And The Rajah's Elephant" 16.00 50.00
338 "And The Rocking Horse Thieves" 16.00 50.00
347 "The Frigid Hare" 16.00 50.00
355 "Hot-Rod Hare" 16.00 50.00
366 "Uncle Buckskin Comes To Town" 16.00 50.00
376 "The Magic Sneeze" 16.00 50.00
393 16.00 50.00
407 "The Foreign-Legion Hare" 11.00 35.00
420 "The Mysterious Buckaroo" 11.00 35.00
432 "And The Rabbit Olympics" 11.00 35.00
838 "...Life Story Album" 8.00 25.00
1064 "Merry Christmas" 10.00 30.00

BUGS BUNNY
DELL/GOLD KEY (1952-1983)
28 7.00 20.00
29-36 5.00 15.00
37-50 4.00 12.00
51-85 2.50 9.00
86-88 Double size. 8.00 25.00
89-120 1.75 6.00
121-150 1.25 4.00
151-170 .75 2.00
171-200 .50 1.50
201-245 .30 1.00

BUGS BUNNY
SEE LARGE FEATURE COMICS (SERIES II) #8.

BUGS BUNNY'S ALBUM
DELL FOUR COLOR SERIES (1953-1956)
498 (9/53) 8.00 25.00
585 (9/54) 7.00 20.00
647 (9/55) 7.00 20.00
724 (9/56) 5.00 15.00

BUGS BUNNY'S CHRISTMAS FUNNIES
DELL (1950-1958)
1 Giant 116 page edition. 70.00 220.00
2 50.00 160.00
3-5 40.00 130.00
6 Title variation: "...Christmas Party." Dell Giant. 40.00 130.00
7-9 35.00 110.00

BUGS BUNNY'S COUNTY FAIR
DELL (1957)
1 Dell Giant. 31.00 100.00

BUGS BUNNY'S HALLOWEEN FUN TRICK'N'TREAT
DELL (1956)
4 Dell Giant. Previous title: "Bugs Bunny's Trick'N'Treat Halloween Fun." 25.00 80.00

BUGS BUNNY'S HALLOWEEN PARADE
DELL (1953-1954)
1 Giant edition. 31.00 100.00
2 Giant edition. 25.00 80.00

BUGS BUNNY'S TRICK'N'TREAT HALLOWEEN FUN
DELL (1955)
3 Dell Giant. Previous title: Bugs Bunny's Halloween Parade. Title changes to Bugs Bunny's Halloween Fun Trick'N'Treat with #4. 25.00 80.00

BUGS BUNNY'S VACATION FUNNIES
DELL (1951-1959)
1 65.00 200.00
2 50.00 150.00
3-6 31.00 100.00
7-9 25.00 80.00

BULLETMAN
FAWCETT (1941-1946)
1 500.00 1800.00
2 250.00 825.00
3 190.00 600.00
4-6 145.00 480.00
7-12 130.00 420.00
13-16 110.00 360.00

BULLS EYE
CHARLTON (1954-1955)
1 Cover: Simon & Kirby (all issues). 70.00 220.00
2 85.00 270.00
3-5 70.00 220.00
6 50.00 160.00
7 70.00 220.00

BULLS EYE COMICS
CHESLER (1944)
11 70.00 220.00

BULLWHIP GRIFFIN
GOLD KEY (1967)
10181-706 Disney movie photo cover. 7.00 20.00

BULLWINKLE
GOLD KEY (1962-1980)
1 (11/62) 35.00 110.00
2 (2/63) 26.00 85.00
3 (4/72) 5.00 16.00
4-11 5.00 16.00
12 (6/76) 1.75 6.50
13-25 1.75 6.50
01-090-209 40.00 130.00
01-530-207 Mother Moose Nursery Poems. 26.00 85.00

BULLWINKLE AND ROCKY
DELL FOUR COLOR SERIES (1962)
1270 TV tie-in. (2/62) 50.00 150.00

BURIAL OF THE RATS
COSMIC (1995)
1 .75 2.50

BURKE'S LAW
DELL (1964-1965)
1 TV photo covers on all issues. 8.00 25.00

2-3 .... 5.00 15.00

BUSTER BROWN COMICS
BROWN SHOE (1945-1959)
1 Radio tie-in. All issues giveaways. ... 50.00 150.00
2 .... 22.00 70.00
3-6 .... 19.00 60.00
7-12 .... 16.00 50.00
13-24 .... 13.00 40.00
25-29 .... 10.00 30.00
30-32 Art: Crandall. 19.00 60.00
33-43 .... 7.00 20.00

BUSTER BROWN GOES TO MARS
BROWN SHOE (1958)
NO# Giveaway. 11.00 35.00

BUSTER CRABBE
FAMOUS FUNNIES (1951-1953)
1 "The Arrow Of Death!" TV tie-in series. 50.00 160.00
2 .... 40.00 130.00
3 .... 29.00 95.00
4 Cover & 1 pg. art: Frank Frazetta. ... 70.00 220.00
5 Cover: Frank Frazetta (7/52). Scarce. 135.00 440.00
6-12 .... 14.00 44.00

BUSTER CRABBE
LEV GLEASON (1953)
1 .... 19.00 60.00
2-3 Art: Alex Toth. 22.00 70.00
4 .... 16.00 50.00

BUTCH CASSIDY
AVON (1951)
1 "And The Wild Bunch" 22.00 70.00

BUTCHER
DC (1990)
1-5 .... .50 1.50

BUZ SAWYER
STANDARD (1948)
1 .... 22.00 70.00
2 .... 13.00 40.00
3 .... 10.00 30.00

BUZZY
DC (1944-1958)
1 .... 60.00 190.00
2 .... 26.00 85.00
3-6 .... 20.00 65.00
7-12 .... 14.00 44.00
13-24 .... 10.00 33.00
25-36 .... 7.00 22.00
37-48 .... 5.00 16.00
49-62 .... 4.00 13.00
63 1st Code Approved issue. 4.00 11.00
64-77 .... 2.25 8.75

CABLE
MARVEL (1992)
1 .... 1.00 3.50
2 .... .75 2.50

CABLE
MARVEL (1993-1994)
1 .... 1.25 4.00
2-5 .... .75 2.00
6-8 .... .75 2.50
9-15 .... .75 2.00
16 Prismatic foil-stamped cover. Double size.
.... 1.75 6.00
16A Regular cover. .... .75 2.50
17 Deluxe edition (glossy stock paper). .50 1.95
17A Regular edition. .... .50 1.50
18 Deluxe edition. .... .50 1.95
18A Regular edition. .... .50 1.50
19 Deluxe edition. .... .50 1.95
19A Regular edition. .... .50 1.50
20 Deluxe edition, with card. 1.00 3.00
20A Regular edition. .... .50 1.50
21-23 .... .50 1.95

CADET GRAY OF WEST POINT
DELL (1958)
1 .... 8.00 25.00

CADILLACS AND DINOSAURS
MARVEL(EPIC) (1990-1991)
1 Reprints Xenozoic Tales .... .75 2.50
2-6 .... .75 2.50

CADILLACS AND DINOSAURS
TOPPS (1994)
1 Vol. 2 in indicia. Foil enhanced cover by William Stout..
.... .75 2.95
1A Newsstand edition. .... .75 2.50
2 .... .75 2.50
2A Newsstand edition. .... .75 2.50
3 .... .75 2.50
3A Newsstand edition. .... .75 2.50

CADILLACS AND DINOSAURS 3-D
KITCHEN SINK (1992)
1 Reprints: stories from Xenozoic Tales #6,7. 1.00 3.95

CADILLACS AND DINOSAURS: MAN EATER!
TOPPS (1994)
1 Both newsstand and direct versions exist. .75 2.50
2-3 .... .75 2.50

CADILLACS AND DINOSAURS: THE WILD ONES
TOPPS (1994-1995)
1 Cover: Linsner (all issues). 1.25 4.00
2-3 .... 1.25 4.00

CAGE
MARVEL (1992-1993)
1 .... .50 1.50
2-11 .... .50 1.25
12 App: Iron Fist. .... .50 1.75
13-20 .... .50 1.25

CAGES
TUNDRA (1991-1992)
1 .... 2.25 8.00
2-4 .... 1.75 6.00
5-10 .... 1.25 4.00

CAIN
HARRIS (1993-1994)
1 Polybagged w/card. 1.00 3.50
2 .... .75 2.95

CAIN/VAMPIRELLA
HARRIS (1994)
1 Flip book. 1.75 6.95

CALIBER PRESENTS
CALIBER (1989-1990)
1 1st: The Crow. 35.00 110.00
2 Art: Tim Vigil. 4.00 12.00
3-14 .... .75 2.00
15 Crow #5 preview. 8.00 25.00
16-24 .... .75 2.00
CHRISTMAS App: The Crow. 7.00 22.00
SUMMER 1 .... 1.00 3.95

CALLING ALL BOYS
PMI (1946-1948)
1 .... 10.00 30.00
2 .... 5.00 15.00
3-6 .... 2.75 10.00
7-9 .... 2.25 8.00
10 Photo cover (Gary Cooper). 7.00 20.00
11 .... 2.25 8.00
12 Photo cover (Bob Hope). 7.00 20.00
13 Photo cover (Bing Crosby). 7.00 20.00
14-17 .... 2.25 8.00

CALLING ALL GIRLS
PMI (1941-1949)
1 .... 10.00 30.00
2 .... 7.00 20.00
3 Photo cover (Shirley Temple). 7.00 20.00
4-12 .... 5.00 15.00
13-24 .... 2.75 10.00
25-40 .... 2.25 8.00
41-51 .... 1.75 6.00
52-89 .... 1.50 5.00

CALLING ALL KIDS
PMI (1945-1949)
1 .... 10.00 30.00
2 .... 5.00 15.00
3-12 .... 2.75 10.00
13-26 .... 1.75 6.00

CALVIN AND THE COLONEL
DELL (1962)
1 (#1354) From the 4-Color Series. TV tie-in. (4/62)
.... 13.00 40.00
2 .... 7.00 20.00

CAMELOT 3000
DC (1982-1984)
1-12 .... .50 1.50

CAMERA COMICS
U.S. CAMERA (1944-1946)
1 (10/44) 19.00 60.00
2 .... 13.00 40.00
3 .... 10.00 30.00
4-9 .... 7.00 20.00

CAMP COMICS
DELL (1942)
1 Art: Walt Kelly in all issues. Photo cover on all issues. (2/42)
.... 70.00 220.00
2 (3/42) 50.00 160.00
3 (4/42) 70.00 220.00

CAMPUS LOVES
QUALITY (1949-1950)
1 Cover/Art: Bill Ward. (12/49) ... 35.00 110.00
2 Cover/Art: Bill Ward. (2/50) 23.00 75.00
3 Photo cover. (4/50) 10.00 33.00
4 Photo cover. (6/50) 10.00 33.00
5 Photo cover. (8/50) 10.00 33.00

CAMPUS ROMANCES
AVON (1949-1950)
1 .... 25.00 80.00
2-3 .... 19.00 60.00

CANADIAN HEROES
- (1945)
V5#6 .... 7.00 20.00

CANADIAN ROCK SPECIAL
REVOLUTIONARY (1993)
1 Featuring Rush. .... .75 2.50

CANCELLED COMIC CAVALCADE
DC (1978)
1 Xeroxed unpublished material bound and published (35 copies) for copyright registration. Art: Black Lightning #12; Claw #13,14; The Deserted #1; Doorway To Nightmare #6; Firestorm #6; The Green Team #2,3. Cover: Black Lightning #13.
.... 310.00 1000.00
2 Art: Kamandi #60,61; Prez #5; Shade #9; Showcase #105,106; Vixen #1. Covers: Battle Classics #3; Demand Classics #1,2; Dynamic Classics #3; Mr. Miracle #26; Our Army At War #2; Ragman #6; Weird Mystery #25,26; Western Classics #1,2. .... 250.00 800.00

CANDID TALES
ANC (1950)
NO# Art: Wallace Wood. 80.00 250.00

CANDY
QUALITY (1947-1956)
1 .... 19.00 60.00
2 .... 13.00 40.00
3-12 .... 8.00 25.00
13-24 .... 7.00 20.00
25-36 .... 5.00 15.00
37-64 .... 4.00 12.00

CANDY COMICS
WILLIAM H. WISE (1944-1945)
1 Art: Basil Wolverton in all issues. ... 40.00 125.00
2-3 .... 40.00 125.00

CANNONBALL COMICS
RURAL (1945)
1 Begin: Crash Kid, Crime Crusader. (2/45)
.... 70.00 220.00
2 (3/45) 55.00 170.00

CANTEEN KATE
ST. JOHN (1952)
1 Cover/Art: Matt Baker. (6/52) ... 70.00 220.00
2 Cover/Art: Matt Baker. "Lucky Leathernecks!"
.... 60.00 190.00
3 Cover/Art: Matt Baker. (11/52) ... 70.00 220.00

CAPT. STORM
DC (1964-1967)
1 Origin: Capt. Storm. 8.00 25.00
2 .... 6.00 18.00
3 Art: Joe Kubert. 5.00 14.00
4-5 .... 5.00 14.00
6 Art: Joe Kubert. 5.00 14.00
7-12 .... 2.50 9.75
13 Art: Joe Kubert. 2.50 9.75
14-18 .... 2.50 9.75

CAPTAIN 3-D
HARVEY (1953)
1 Art: Jack Kirby, Steve Ditko. Ditko's 2nd published work. (12/53) (Warehouse find in late 1980s) 26.00 85.00

CAPTAIN ACTION
DC (1968-1969)
1 Origin: Captain Action. 16.00 50.00
2-5 .... 9.00 27.00

CAPTAIN ACTION AND ACTION BOY
IDEAL TOY (1967)
NO# Giveaway, 32 pages. 1st: Captain Action in comics.
.... 25.00 80.00

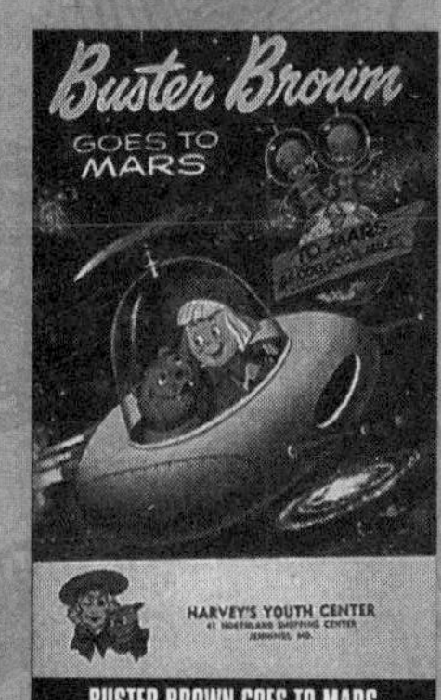

BUSTER BROWN GOES TO MARS

CABLE #20

CAIN #1

CANNONBALL COMICS #1

CAPTAIN AERO #15

CAPTAIN AMERICA #100

CAPTAIN AMERICA #241

CAPTAIN AMERICA ANNUAL #11

CAPTAIN AMERICA COMICS #1

The origin and first appearance of one of comics' first patriotic heroes, Captain America, is told in this issue, which also introduces The Red Skull. Cap adventured into the 1950s and was later revived during the 1960s.

CAPTAIN AERO

HOLYOKE (1941-1946)

1 (12/41)	210.00	675.00
2 (2/42)	105.00	340.00
3 Alias X. (#9 inside front cover).	85.00	280.00
4 Origin: The Gargoyle.	85.00	280.00
5 Art: Joe Kubert.	85.00	280.00
6 Miss Victory.	85.00	280.00
7-11 Miss Victory.	70.00	230.00
12-14	45.00	140.00
15 Miss Victory.	55.00	170.00
16	26.00	85.00
17 (10-44) #'s 18-20 don't exist.	26.00	85.00
21 Cover: L.B. Cole. (12/44)	25.00	80.00
22-24 Cover: L.B. Cole.	25.00	80.00
25 Cover: L.B. Cole.	31.00	100.00
26 Cover: L.B. Cole.	25.00	80.00

CAPTAIN AMERICA

MARVEL (1968-CURRENT)

ASHCAN	.20	.75
100 Lead story: "This Monster Un-Masked!" (4/68) Previous title: Tales Of Suspense.	65.00	250.00
101	23.00	75.00
102-108	13.00	40.00
109 Origin retold: Captain America.	17.00	55.00
110 Cover & art: Jim Steranko.	17.00	55.00
111 Cover & Art: Jim Steranko.	17.00	55.00
112 Origin retold: Captain America.	8.00	25.00
113 Cover & Art: Jim Steranko.	17.00	55.00
114-115	7.00	20.00
116 1st 15 cent cover price.	6.00	18.00
117 1st: Falcon.	20.00	65.00
118 2nd: Falcon.	5.00	16.00
119-121	5.00	16.00
122-136	4.00	12.00
137-138 Spider-Man.	5.00	15.00
139-140	2.75	10.00
141-142	1.75	6.00
143 Double size.	1.75	6.00
144 1st 20 cent cover price.	2.75	10.00
145-153	1.75	6.00
154 1st: Jack Monroe.	2.00	7.00
155 Origin: Jack Monroe.	1.75	6.00
156-171	1.75	6.00
172-175 X-Men.	5.00	15.00
176 "Captain America Must Die!" by Buscema. (8/74)	1.75	6.00
177-179	1.75	6.00
180 1st & Origin: Nomad.	2.75	10.00
181-185	1.75	6.00
186 Origin: The Falcon.	1.75	6.00
187-200	1.75	6.00
201-215	1.25	4.00
216 Reprint: Strange Tales #114.	1.25	4.00
217-229	1.25	4.00
230 Captain America battles The Hulk.	1.25	4.00
231-240	1.25	4.00
241 App: Punisher. Scarce without printer's crease.	10.00	30.00
242-246	1.25	4.00
247-248 Art: John Byrne.	1.25	4.00
249 Art:John Byrne.	1.25	4.00
250-254 Art: John Byrne.	1.25	4.00
255 Art: John Byrne.	1.00	3.00
256-260	1.00	3.00
261 1st: Nomad II.	1.50	5.00
262-264	1.00	3.00
265-266 Spider-Man.	1.00	3.00
267-281	1.00	3.00
282 New Nomad.	2.50	9.00
282 (2ND) 2nd printing.	.50	1.75
283 Origin: New Nomad.	1.25	4.00
284-285	1.00	3.00
286-288 Deathlok.	1.50	5.00
289-322	1.00	3.00
323 1st: new Super Patriot.	1.00	3.00
324-331	1.00	3.00
332 Quits: Captain America (Steve Rogers).	4.00	12.00
333 1st: Johnny Walker as Captain America II.	2.75	10.00
334 1st: new Bucky.	1.00	3.00
335 1st: Watch Dogs.	1.00	3.00
336 Return of Steve Rogers.	1.00	3.00
337 1st: Steve Rogers as The Captain.	1.00	3.00
338 Death: Professor Power.	1.00	3.00
339 Fall Of The Mutants.	1.00	3.00
340-343	1.00	3.00
344 Double size.	1.00	3.00
345-349	1.00	3.00
350 Double size. Return: Steve Rogers.	1.75	6.00
351-372	.75	2.00
373 Bulls-eye.	.75	2.00
374-382	.75	2.00
383	1.75	6.00
384-399	.75	2.00
400	1.00	3.00
401-404	.50	1.50
405-419	.50	1.25
420 Polybagged with Dirt Magazine.	.75	2.95
420A Without Dirt magazine.	.50	1.25
421-424	.50	1.25
425 Embossed foil cover.	1.00	3.50
425A Newsstand edition.	1.00	3.50
426	.50	1.25
427-443	.50	1.50

CAPTAIN AMERICA ANNUAL

MARVEL (1971-CURRENT)

1 King-Size Special. Origin retold: Captain America (reprints Tales Of Suspense #59, 61, 62.	7.00	20.00
2 Special. "The Final Sleep!"	2.75	10.00
3 (1976)	1.75	6.00
4 Cover/Art: Jack Kirby. App: Magneto. (1977)	1.75	6.00
5 (1981)	1.75	6.00
6 (1982)	.75	2.50
7 (1983)	.75	2.50
8 Cover: Mike Zeck. App: Wolverine. (1986)	8.00	25.00
9 1st: new Nomad. (1990)	1.75	6.00
10 (1991)	1.00	3.00
11 (1992)	.75	2.25
12 Bagged with trading card. (1993)	.75	2.95
13 (1994)	.75	2.95

CAPTAIN AMERICA CLASSIC YEARS

MARVEL

HC Hardcover.	7.00	25.00

CAPTAIN AMERICA COMICS

MARVEL(TIMELY) (1941-1954)

1 1st & Origin: Captain America, Bucky by Joe Simon & Jack Kirby.	12600.00	50000.00
2	1900.00	7500.00
3 1st Stan Lee work for Marvel. (5/41)	1800.00	7000.00
4	1000.00	3600.00
5	900.00	3200.00
6	700.00	2600.00
7	900.00	3200.00
8-9	600.00	2300.00
10 End: Simon & Kirby art. (1/42)	600.00	2300.00
11	500.00	1600.00
12	400.00	1500.00
13	600.00	2200.00
14-15	400.00	1500.00
16	500.00	1900.00
17	400.00	1400.00
18-19 Human Torch.	300.00	1100.00
20 App: Sub-Mariner. (11/42)	300.00	1100.00
21-22	300.00	1100.00
22A 128 pages, black & white (cover is from Captain America Comics #22, contents are from Marvel Mystery #33 and Captain America Comics #18).	1900.00	7500.00
23-27	300.00	1100.00
28	300.00	975.00
29	280.00	900.00
30 (9/43)	280.00	900.00
31-36	280.00	900.00
37 App: Red Skull.	300.00	975.00
38-39	240.00	775.00
40 (7/44)	240.00	775.00
41-48	240.00	775.00
49	220.00	700.00
50 (10/45)	220.00	700.00
51 "Mystery Of The Atomic Boomerang!"	220.00	700.00
52-58	220.00	700.00
59 Origin retold: Captain America. (11/46)	400.00	1400.00
60 Battling "The Human Fly!".	220.00	700.00
61 Red Skull.	300.00	1100.00
62-65	220.00	700.00
66	280.00	900.00
67-69	240.00	775.00
70 Science fiction theme.	240.00	775.00
71 "Trapped By The Trickster!" (3/49)	240.00	775.00

72-73 ... 240.00 775.00
74 Captain America Weird Tales. (10/49)
... 1900.00 7500.00
75 Captain America Weird Tales. (2/50) 500.00 1750.00
76 (5/54) ... 155.00 500.00
77 (7/54) ... 155.00 500.00
78 (9/54) ... 155.00 500.00

CAPTAIN AMERICA GIVEAWAYS
...FIGHTS IN THE WAR AGAINST DRUGS. MARVEL
1A ... .30 1.00

CAPTAIN AMERICA MARVEL MILESTONE
MARVEL (1995)
NO# One shot. Reprint. ... 1.00 3.95

CAPTAIN AMERICA SPECIAL
SEE CAPTAIN AMERICA ANNUAL

CAPTAIN AMERICA SPECIAL EDITION
MARVEL (1984)
1-2 Reprint. ... .75 2.75

CAPTAIN AMERICA: THE MEDUSA EFFECT
MARVEL (1995)
NO# One shot. ... .75 2.95

CAPTAIN AND THE KIDS, THE
DELL FOUR COLOR SERIES (1958)
881 (2/58) ... 7.00 20.00

CAPTAIN AND THE KIDS, THE
UNITED FEATURES (1949-1953)
1A 50th Anniversary issue (1948). ... 10.00 30.00
1B Special Issue (Summer/48). ... 8.00 25.00
1C Special Issue (Fall/48). ... 8.00 25.00
16 ... 13.00 40.00
17 ... 10.00 30.00
18-19 ... 8.00 25.00
20-21 ... 7.00 20.00
22 ... 6.00 18.00
23-24 ... 5.00 15.00
25-32 ... 2.75 10.00

CAPTAIN ATOM
CHARLTON (1965-1967)
78 Origin retold: Captain Atom. ... 20.00 65.00
79 1st: Dr. Specter. ... 12.00 38.00
80-82 ... 10.00 33.00
83 1st: Ted Kord as Blue Beetle. ... 12.00 38.00
84 1st: New Captain Atom. ... 12.00 38.00
85-89 ... 10.00 33.00

CAPTAIN ATOM
DC (1987-1991)
1 1st & Origin: New Captain Atom. ... .75 2.00
2-41 ... .30 1.00
42 App: Death. (6/90) ... .75 2.00
43-49 ... .30 1.00
50 Double size. ... .75 2.00
51-57 ... .30 1.00
ANNUAL 1 ($1.25 cp., 1988) ... .75 2.00
ANNUAL 2 ... .75 2.00

CAPTAIN ATOM
NATIONWIDE (1950-1951)
1 1st & origin: Captain Atom. 5"x7" 45.00 140.00
2 ... 26.00 85.00
3-7 ... 17.00 55.00

CAPTAIN BATTLE
COMIC HOUSE (1941)
1 Summer issue. Begin: Captain Battle from Silver Streak Comics. ... 220.00 700.00
2 Title changes to Boy Comics with issue #3.
... 145.00 480.00

CAPTAIN BATTLE
MP (1942-1943)
3 Origin retold: Silver Streak. ... 110.00 360.00
4-5 ... 65.00 210.00

CAPTAIN BATTLE, JR.
LEV GLEASON (1943-1944)
1 App: The Claw. "The Kidnap Flight To Berlin!"
... 190.00 600.00
2 Art: Basil Wolverton (Scoop Scuttle story).
... 145.00 480.00

CAPTAIN BRITAIN
MARVEL(INTERNATIONAL) (1976-1977)
1 Origin: Captain Britain. ... 1.75 6.00
2 Origin concludes. ... 1.25 4.00
3-6 ... 1.00 3.00
7-12 ... .75 2.50

13-15 ... .75 2.00
16-26 ... 1.00 3.00
27-39 ... .75 2.00

CAPTAIN BRITAIN CLASSICS
MARVEL (1995-CURRENT)
1 Reprints. ... .75 2.50

CAPTAIN CANUCK
COMELY (1975-1981)
1 ... 2.25 8.00
2-8 ... 1.00 3.00
9-12 ... .75 2.00
13-14 ... .50 1.50

CAPTAIN CARROT
DC (1982-1983)
1-20 ... .20 .75

CAPTAIN CONFEDERACY
STEELDRAGON (1986-1988)
1-12 ... .50 1.50

CAPTAIN COURAGEOUS COMICS
ACE MAGAZINE (1942)
6 1st & Origin: The Sword. Previous title: Banner Comics.
... 115.00 375.00

CAPTAIN DAVY JONES
DELL FOUR COLOR SERIES (1954)
598 (11/54) ... 7.00 20.00

CAPTAIN EASY
DELL FOUR COLOR SERIES (1946)
111 (6/46) ... 25.00 80.00

CAPTAIN EASY
STANDARD (1939-1949)
1(NO#) Sunday strip reprints. (1939) 95.00 300.00
10 ... 13.00 40.00
11-12 ... 11.00 35.00
13-17 ... 10.00 30.00

CAPTAIN FEARLESS COMICS
HOLYOKE (1941)
1 1st & Origin: Miss Victory. ... 135.00 440.00
2 ... 85.00 270.00

CAPTAIN FEARLESS COMICS
HOLYOKE (1945)
6 From the Holyoke One-Shot series. ... 17.00 55.00

CAPTAIN FLASH
STERLING (1954-1955)
1 Origin: Captain Flash. "The Beginning!" (11/54)
... 50.00 160.00
2 ... 35.00 110.00
3-4 ... 25.00 80.00

CAPTAIN FLEET
ZIFF-DAVIS (1952)
1 Cover: Norman Saunders. ... 22.00 70.00

CAPTAIN FLIGHT COMICS
FOUR STAR (1944-1947)
1 (No# on cover). ... 26.00 85.00
2 ... 14.00 44.00
3 ... 12.00 38.00
4 ... 10.00 33.00
5 Begin: Red Rocket. ... 14.00 44.00
6-7 ... 10.00 33.00
8 Begin: Black Cobra. ... 17.00 55.00
9-11 ... 17.00 55.00

CAPTAIN GALLANT
CHARLTON (1955-1956)
NO# Giveaway (non-Heinz version). ... 2.75 10.00
NO#A Giveaway (Heinz 57 ad on inside back cover). Large quantities surfaced in 1991. ... 1.75 6.00
1 TV tie-in. ... 10.00 30.00
2 ... 7.00 20.00
3-4 ... 5.00 15.00

CAPTAIN HOBBY COMICS
EXPORT (1948)
1 Canadian. ... 7.00 20.00

CAPTAIN HOOK AND PETER PAN
DELL FOUR COLOR SERIES (1953)
446 Disney movie tie-in. (1/53) ... 17.00 55.00

CAPTAIN JET
CM (1952)
1 ... 20.00 65.00
2 ... 17.00 55.00
3-5 ... 12.00 38.00

CAPTAIN JUSTICE
MARVEL (1988)
1-2 ... .30 1.00

CAPTAIN KANGAROO
DELL FOUR COLOR SERIES (1956-1958)
721 TV photo cover. (8/56) ... 40.00 120.00
780 TV photo cover. (3/57) ... 31.00 100.00
872 TV photo cover. (1/58) ... 31.00 100.00

CAPTAIN MARVEL
ARCHIE (1966)
1 Origin. ... 7.00 22.00
2 ... 4.00 13.00
3-4 ... 4.00 11.00

CAPTAIN MARVEL
MARVEL (1968-1979)
1 "Out Of The Holocaust...A Hero!" ... 25.00 80.00
2 ... 7.00 20.00
3-5 ... 6.00 15.00
6-11 ... 2.75 10.00
12-13 ... 2.25 8.00
14 Battles Iron Man. ... 2.25 8.00
15 1st 15 cent cover price. ... 2.00 7.00
16-20 ... 2.00 7.00
21 Battles Hulk. ... 2.00 7.00
22 1st 20 cent cover price. ... 2.00 7.00
23-24 ... 2.00 7.00
25 Begin: Jim Starlin cover/art. Begin: Thanos.
... 5.00 12.00
26 ... 7.00 18.00
27-28 ... 2.75 9.00
29-30 ... 2.25 8.00
31 Thanos. ... 2.25 8.00
32 ... 2.25 8.00
33 Thanos. ... 2.75 9.00
34 End: Jim Starlin art. ... 1.50 5.00
35 ... 1.25 4.00
36 Reprint: Marvel Super Heroes #12. 1.50 5.00
37-56 ... .75 2.50
57 Thanos. ... 1.00 3.00
58-62 ... .75 2.50

CAPTAIN MARVEL (ONE SHOT)
MARVEL (1989)
1 ... .75 2.50

CAPTAIN MARVEL ADVENTURES
FAWCETT (1941-1953)
1 (NO#) Art: Jack Kirby. ... 5400.00 21500.00
2 ... 700.00 2600.00
3 ... 400.00 1500.00
4 ... 310.00 1000.00
5 ... 280.00 900.00
6 ... 220.00 700.00
7 ... 190.00 600.00
8-12 ... 160.00 525.00
13-17 ... 145.00 480.00
18 1st & Origin: Mary Marvel. ... 220.00 700.00
19 ... 130.00 420.00
20-21 ... 100.00 330.00
22 Begin: new mystery serial "The Pearl of Peril!" 1st: Mr. Mind. ... 160.00 525.00
23 ... 100.00 330.00
24 "Captain Marvel Solves The Minneapolis Mystery".
... 100.00 330.00
25 ... 85.00 270.00
26 Patriotic Flag cover. (8/43) ... 110.00 360.00
27-29 ... 75.00 240.00
30 "The $40,000,000 Denver Plot!" 75.00 240.00
31-32 ... 75.00 240.00
33 Captain Marvel's "Adventure In Omaha!"
... 75.00 240.00
34 "Capt. Marvel Visits Oklahoma City." 75.00 240.00
35 Origin: Radar. "Captain Marvel Visits Indianapolis"
... 75.00 240.00
36 "Captain Marvel Travels To St. Louis, Missouri!"
... 75.00 240.00
37 Mary Marvel crossover. "Capt. Marvel Battles The Blockbusting Bubbles Of Cincinnati, Ohio." 75.00 240.00
38-40 ... 75.00 240.00
41 "Captain Marvel Visits Dayton, Ohio." 75.00 240.00
42 "Captain Marvel in St. Paul, Minn." (1/45)
... 75.00 240.00
43 1st: Uncle Marvel. ... 75.00 240.00
44-45 ... 75.00 240.00
46 End: Mr. Mind. ... 85.00 270.00
47-50 ... 55.00 180.00
51 "Captain Marvel Goes Western!" (1/46)
... 55.00 180.00
52-53 ... 55.00 180.00
54 Double size. ... 85.00 270.00
55-60 ... 50.00 150.00
61 Begin: Cult Of The Curse. ... 55.00 180.00
62-65 ... 50.00 160.00
66 End: Cult Of The Curse. ... 50.00 160.00
67-79 ... 40.00 120.00

CAPTAIN BATTLE #1

CAPTAIN MARVEL #1 (MARVEL)

CAPTAIN MARVEL #29 (MARVEL)

CAPTAIN MARVEL ADVENTURES #26

CAPTAIN MARVEL JR. #11

CAPTAIN SAVAGE #1

CASEY JONES SPECIAL #1

CASPER THE FRIENDLY GHOST #6

80 (1/48) 31.00 100.00
81-99 .... 31.00 100.00
100 Origin retold. Anniversary issue. 75.00 240.00
101-103 .... 29.00 95.00
104 (1/50) 29.00 95.00
105 (2/50) 29.00 95.00
106 "The Menace Of The Moon" ... 29.00 95.00
107-120 .... 29.00 95.00
121 Origin retold. 31.00 100.00
122-140 .... 28.00 90.00
141-149 .... 25.00 80.00
150 .... 50.00 150.00

CAPTAIN MARVEL ADVENTURES WHEATIES GIVEAWAY
FAWCETT (1945)
NO# Originally taped to cereal box, therefore copies without tape stains are rare. Contains "Captain Marvel and the Threads of Life." Small size. 155.00 500.00

CAPTAIN MARVEL AND THE GOOD HUMOR MAN
FAWCETT (1950)
1 Movie tie-in. 125.00 400.00

CAPTAIN MARVEL, JR.
FAWCETT (1942-1953)
1 See Whiz #25 for 1st appearance. 600.00 2000.00
2 .... 290.00 950.00
3 .... 190.00 600.00
4 .... 160.00 525.00
5 .... 145.00 480.00
6-12 .... 130.00 420.00
13-24 .... 100.00 330.00
25-36 .... 65.00 210.00
37-48 .... 50.00 150.00
49-60 .... 40.00 120.00
61-72 .... 29.00 95.00
73-99 .... 25.00 80.00
100 Anniversary issue. 28.00 90.00
101-114 .... 23.00 75.00
115 .... 29.00 95.00
116-119 .... 23.00 75.00

CAPTAIN MARVEL PAINT BOOK
SAMUEL LOWE (1943)
NO# Stories to read and color. 190.00 600.00

CAPTAIN MARVEL PRESENTS THE TERRIBLE 5
ARCHIE(RADIO) (1966)
1 .... 7.00 22.00

CAPTAIN MARVEL STORYBOOK
FAWCETT (1946-1948)
1 .... 130.00 420.00
2-4 .... 85.00 270.00

CAPTAIN MARVEL THRILL BOOK
FAWCETT (1941)
1 Color cover with black and white interiors. Reprints of stories from Special Edition Comics and Whiz. 500.00 1800.00

CAPTAIN MARVEL'S FUN BOOK
SAMUEL LOWE (1944)
NO# 65.00 200.00

CAPTAIN MIDNIGHT
FAWCETT (1942-1948)
1 Origin retold from 1st appearance in The Funnies #57. .... 400.00 1200.00
2 .... 190.00 625.00
3-6 .... 115.00 370.00
7-8 .... 95.00 310.00
9-11 Cover: Mac Raboy. 115.00 370.00
12 .... 95.00 310.00
13-16 .... 55.00 180.00
17-18 Cover: Mac Raboy. 95.00 310.00
19-24 .... 55.00 180.00
25-36 .... 40.00 120.00
37-50 .... 28.00 90.00
51-67 .... 23.00 75.00

CAPTAIN NICE
GOLD KEY (1967)
10211-711 TV photo cover. 11.00 35.00

CAPTAIN PLANET AND THE PLANETEERS
MARVEL (1991)
1-12 .... .20 .75

CAPTAIN POWER AND THE SOLDIERS OF THE FUTURE
CONTINUITY
1 TV tie-in. .... .75 2.00

CAPTAIN ROCKET
PLP (1951)
1 "The Graveyard Of The Rocketeers" (11/51) 70.00 225.00

CAPTAIN SAVAGE
MARVEL (1968-1970)
1 "The Last Banzai!" App: Sgt. Fury. ... 4.00 12.00
2 .... 2.25 8.00
3 .... 1.75 6.00
4-6 .... 1.50 5.00
7-19 .... 1.25 4.00

CAPTAIN SCIENCE
YOUTHFUL (1950-1951)
1 Origin: Captain Science. 145.00 480.00
2 .... 75.00 240.00
3 .... 65.00 210.00
4-5 Cover/Art: Wallace Wood. 110.00 360.00
6 .... 55.00 180.00
7 Title changes to Fantastic with #8. ... 55.00 180.00

CAPTAIN SINDBAD
GOLD KEY (1963)
10077-309 Movie photo cover. 10.00 30.00

CAPTAIN STEVE SAVAGE
AVON (1950-1953)
1 (No#) "...Over Korea!" 65.00 200.00
2 "...And His Jet Fighters" 13.00 40.00
3 "...And His Secret Super-Jet" 11.00 35.00
4 "...Fights The Red Raiders From Siang-Po!" 10.00 30.00
5 "...And The Rockets Of Death!" ... 10.00 30.00
6 "...Operation Destruction" 10.00 30.00
7 "...Flight To Kill!" 10.00 30.00
8 "...Battles The Red Mystery Jet" ... 10.00 30.00
9-11 .... 10.00 30.00
12 Art: Wood. 16.00 50.00
13 .... 10.00 30.00

CAPTAIN STEVE SAVAGE
AVON (1954-1956)
5 (9-10/54) 10.00 30.00
6 (11-12/54) Art: Wallace Wood. ... 16.00 50.00
7 (3/55) 8.00 25.00
8 (5-6/55) 8.00 25.00
9 (8-9/55) 8.00 25.00
10-11 .... 8.00 25.00
12 "The Last Stand Of Col. Kobari!" ... 8.00 25.00
13 "The Ghost Ship!" 8.00 25.00

CAPTAIN STONE COMICS
HOLYOKE (1944-1945)
10 From the Holyoke One-Shot series. 19.00 60.00

CAPTAIN THUNDER AND BLUE BOLT
HEROIC (1987-1988)
1 Origin: Blue Bolt. .... .75 2.50
2-10 .... .75 2.00

CAPTAIN THUNDER AND BLUE BOLT
HEROIC (1992)
1 .... .75 2.00
2 .... .50 1.50

CAPTAIN TOOTSIE AND THE SECRET LEGION
TOBY (1950)
1 "Rocket To The Planet Venus!" ... 50.00 150.00
2 "The Rocketeer Patrol!" 26.00 85.00

CAPTAIN VENTURE
GOLD KEY (1968-1969)
1 "...And The Land Beneath The Sea." 7.00 20.00
2 .... 5.00 15.00

CAPTAIN VICTORY AND THE GALACTIC RANGERS
PACIFIC (1981-1984)
1-13 .... .30 1.00
SPECIAL 1 (1983) .... .30 1.00

CAPTAIN VIDEO
FAWCETT (1951)
1 TV tie-in. 130.00 420.00
2 SOTI 110.00 360.00
3 .... 100.00 330.00
4 .... 95.00 300.00
5-6 .... 85.00 270.00

CAPTAIN WIZARD COMICS
RURAL HOME (1945)
1 One shot. 31.00 100.00

CAP-UP
CAP-UP (1972-1973)
1 .... 1.75 6.00

2-3 .... 1.00 3.00

CAR 54 WHERE ARE YOU?
DELL (1962-1963)
1 (#1257) From the 4-Color Series. TV photo covers on all issues. (3/62) 19.00 60.00
2 .... 10.00 30.00
3 .... 8.00 25.00
4-7 .... 7.00 20.00

CAR TOONS
MEGA (1960)
2 .... 1.50 5.00

CARAVAN KIDD PART 3
DARK HORSE (1994)
1-8 .... .75 2.50

CARDINAL MINDSZENTY
CATECHETICAL GUILD (1949)
NO# (The Truth Behind The Trial Of...) 13.00 40.00

CARE BEARS
MARVEL(STAR) (1985-1989)
1-20 .... .20 .50

CAREER GIRL ROMANCES
CHARLTON (1964-1973)
24-30 .... 1.00 3.00
31 .... 1.25 4.00
32 Elvis Presley. 7.00 20.00
33-48 .... 1.00 3.00
49-60 .... .75 2.00
61-78 .... .30 1.00

CARNIVAL COMICS
PSP (1945)
NO# "Animal Crackers" 16.00 50.00

CAROLINE KENNEDY
CHARLTON (1961)
NO# 13.00 40.00

CARTOON KIDS
MARVEL(ATLAS) (1956)
1 .... 10.00 30.00

CARVEL COMICS
CARVEL (1975-1976)
1-5 .... .30 1.00

CASEY JONES
DELL FOUR COLOR SERIES (1958)
915 TV photo cover. (7/58) 14.00 45.00

CASEY JONES AND RAPHAEL
MIRAGE (1994-1995)
1-5 .... .75 2.75

CASEY JONES SPECIAL
MIRAGE (1994)
1-2 .... .75 2.75

CASEY-CRIME PHOTOGRAPHER
MARVEL (1949-1950)
1 Photo covers on all issues. 20.00 65.00
2 .... 14.00 44.00
3-4 .... 10.00 33.00

CASPER AND NIGHTMARE
HARVEY (1964-1974)
6 Previous title: Nightmare And Casper. 2.75 10.00
7-10 .... 1.50 5.00
11-30 .... .75 2.00
31-46 .... .30 1.00

CASPER CAT
I.W. (1958)
1 .... 1.75 6.00

CASPER THE FRIENDLY GHOST
HARVEY (1990-1991)
254-260 .... .30 1.00

CASPER THE FRIENDLY GHOST
ST. JOHN/HARVEY (1949-1958)
1 1st: Casper The Friendly Ghost. 1st & Origin: Baby Huey. 125.00 400.00
2 .... 80.00 250.00
3-5 .... 65.00 200.00
6 Does not exist. Harvey Comics Hits #61 is actually issue #6 from this run.
7 .... 50.00 150.00
8 .... 28.00 90.00
9 .... 25.00 80.00
10 1st: Spooky. 28.00 90.00
11-18 .... 13.00 40.00
19 1st: Nightmare. 16.00 50.00

20 1st: Wendy The Witch. 23.00 75.00
21-36 11.00 35.00
37-48 10.00 30.00
49-60 7.00 20.00
61-69 5.00 15.00
70 Also see: The Friendly Ghost Casper. 5.00 15.00

CASPER'S GHOSTLAND
HARVEY (1958-1979)
1 23.00 75.00
2 13.00 40.00
3-6 10.00 30.00
7-12 8.00 25.00
13-24 7.00 20.00
25-48 4.00 12.00
49-61 2.75 10.00
62-72 2.25 8.00
73-98 1.50 5.00

CASTILIAN, THE
DELL (1964)
12-110-401 Movie tie-in. 5.00 15.00

CASTLE OF FRANKENSTEIN
GOTHIC CASTLE (1963-1974) MAGAZINE
1 12.00 38.00
2-8 7.00 22.00
9 Joker (Caesar Romero) photo cover. 9.00 27.00
10 Green Hornet photo cover. 9.00 27.00
11 Spock (Star Trek) photo cover. 12.00 38.00
12-13 7.00 22.00
14 Star Trek photo cover. 12.00 38.00
15-18 7.00 22.00
19 The World Of Ray Harryhausen, pt.1. 9.00 27.00
20 The World Of Ray Harryhausen, pt.2. 9.00 27.00
21-25 7.00 22.00
ANNUAL (1963) 7.00 22.00

CAT, THE
DELL (1966)
12-109-612 Movie tie-in. 5.00 15.00

CAT, THE
MARVEL (1972-1973)
1 1st & Origin: The Cat. 5.00 15.00
2-4 2.25 8.00

CATALYST: AGENTS OF CHANGE
DARK HORSE (1994-CURRENT)
1 .50 1.50
2-7 .75 2.00

CATFIGHT
LIGHTNING (1995)
1 1st: Catfight. 1.00 3.00
1 (GOLD) 1.50 5.95
1B Signed & numbered. 1.25 4.95

CATFIGHT: DREAM WARRIOR
LIGHTNING (1995-CURRENT)
1 .75 2.75

CATHOLIC COMICS
CATHOLIC (1946-1947)
1 31.00 100.00
2 16.00 50.00
3 13.00 40.00
4-13 11.00 35.00
14 (Vol.2 #1) 7.00 20.00
15 (Vol.2 #2) 7.00 20.00
16 (Vol.2 #3) 7.00 20.00
17 (Vol.2 #4) 7.00 20.00
18 (Vol.2 #5) 7.00 20.00
19 (Vol.2 #6) 7.00 20.00
20 (Vol.2 #7) 7.00 20.00
21 (Vol.2 #8) 7.00 20.00
22 (Vol.2 #9) 7.00 20.00
23 (Vol.2 #10) 7.00 20.00
24 (Vol.3 #1) 5.00 15.00
25 (Vol.3 #2) 5.00 15.00
26 (Vol.3 #3) 5.00 15.00
27 (Vol.3 #4) 5.00 15.00
28 (Vol.3 #5) 5.00 15.00
29 (Vol.3 #6) 5.00 15.00
30 (Vol.3 #7) 5.00 15.00
31 (Vol.3 #8) 5.00 15.00
32 (Vol.3 #9) 5.00 15.00
33 (Vol.3 #10) 5.00 15.00

CATHOLIC PICTORIAL
CATHOLIC GUILD (1947)
1 Rare. 65.00 200.00

CATMAN COMICS
HOLYOKE (1941-1946)
1 (V1#6) 310.00 1000.00
2 160.00 525.00
3-4 130.00 430.00
5 Begin: The Hood. Origin: Kitten. 125.00 400.00
6-7 100.00 330.00
8 Begin: Volton by Joe Kubert. 130.00 430.00
9 Begin: Phantom Falcon. 95.00 300.00
10-12 85.00 270.00
13-20 70.00 230.00
21-27 65.00 200.00
28 Cover & art: L. B. Cole. 85.00 270.00
29-32 65.00 200.00

CATWOMAN
DC (1989)
1 App: Bane. 4.00 12.00
2 2.25 8.00
3-4 1.75 6.00
TPB Her Sister's Keeper. Reprints issues #1-4. (1991) 2.50 9.95

CATWOMAN
DC (1993-CURRENT)
0 (8/94) 1.25 4.00
1 App: Bane. Embossed cover. 1.75 6.50
2-3 .75 2.50
4-11 .75 2.00
12 Bruce Wayne back in Batman costume. 1.25 4.50
13-20 .75 2.00
21-24 .75 2.00
ANNUAL 1 Elseworlds story. (1994) .75 2.95
ANNUAL 2 (1995) 1.00 3.95

CAUGHT
MARVEL(ATLAS) (1956-1957)
1 23.00 75.00
2-5 13.00 40.00

CAVALIER COMICS
NUGENT (1945)
2 Canadian. 16.00 50.00

CAVE GIRL (A-1 SERIES)
ME (1953-1954)
11 (A-1 #82), Origin: Cave Girl. 70.00 220.00
12 (A-1 #96). 40.00 130.00
13 (A-1 #116). 40.00 130.00
14 (A-1 #125). 40.00 130.00

CENTURY OF COMICS
EASTERN (1933)
NO# 100 pages of newspaper comic strip reprints. Generally regarded as the 3rd comic book in the modern format. 2400.00 9500.00

CEREBUS BI-WEEKLY
AARDVARK-VANAHEIM (1988-1989)
1 Reprints. .50 1.25
2-19 .50 1.25
20 1st: Milk & Cheese. (11/88) 1.00 3.00
21-25 .50 1.25

CEREBUS HIGH SOCIETY
AARDVARK-VANAHEIM (1986)
1 Reprints. .75 2.75
2-25 .75 2.00

CEREBUS JAM
AARDVARK-VANAHEIM (1985)
1 Art: Eisner. 1.25 4.00

CEREBUS THE AARDVARK
AARDVARK-VANAHEIM (1977-CURRENT)
0 Reprints. .75 2.25
1 1st: Cerebus. 95.00 310.00
1-C Counterfeit (spotty blacks) No value.
2 26.00 85.00
3 Origin: Red Sophia. 23.00 75.00
4 16.00 50.00
5-6 13.00 40.00
7-10 10.00 30.00
11 Origin: Captain Cockroach. 7.00 22.00
12 7.00 22.00
13-15 4.00 12.00
16-20 2.75 10.00
21 Scarce. 13.00 40.00
22 Scarce. No cover price. 4.00 12.00
23-30 2.75 10.00
31 Origin: Moonroach. 2.25 8.00
32-50 1.50 5.00
51 4.00 12.00
52 1.00 3.00
53 1st: Wolveroach. 1.75 6.00
54 1st: full Wolveroach. 2.25 8.00
55-56 Wolveroach. 1.75 6.00
57-60 1.25 4.00
61-62 App: Flaming Carrot. 1.75 6.00
63-103 1.00 3.00
104 App: Flaming Carrot. 1.00 3.00
105-150 1.00 3.00
151 .75 2.25
151 (2ND) 2nd printing. .75 2.25
152 .75 2.25
152 (2ND) 2nd printing. .75 2.25
153 .75 2.25
153 (2ND) 2nd printing. .75 2.25
154-160 .75 2.25
161 Bone backup story. 2.75 10.00
162-196 .75 2.25

CEREBUS WORLD TOUR BOOK "95
AARDVARK-VANAHEIM (1995)
1 Reprints. .75 2.95

CHAIN GANG WAR
DC (1993-1994)
1 Foil embossed cover. .75 2.00
2-4 .30 1.00
5 Foil embossed cover. .75 2.00
6 .75 2.00
7-12 .30 1.00

CHAINS OF CHAOS
HARRIS (1994-1995)
1 App: Vampirella. .75 2.95
2-3 .75 2.95

CHALLENGE OF THE UNKNOWN
ACE (1950)
6 31.00 100.00

CHALLENGE TO THE WORLD
CATECHETICAL GUILD (1950)
NO# The Story Of Fatima. 7.00 20.00

CHALLENGER, THE
TC COMICS (1945-1946)
1 (NO#) No date. Origin: The Challenger Club. 40.00 125.00
2-3 Art: Kubert. 31.00 100.00
4 31.00 100.00

CHALLENGERS OF THE UNKNOWN
DC (1958-1978)
1 "The Human Pets!" by Jack Kirby (Kirby art in issues 1-8). (5/58) See Showcase 6 for 1st app. 400.00 1500.00
2 "The Monster Maker!" 160.00 525.00
3 "The Invincible Challenger!" 130.00 425.00
4 "The Wizard Of Time!" 110.00 350.00
5 "Riddle Of The Star-Stone!" 110.00 350.00
6 "The Sorcerers Of Forbidden Valley!" 110.00 350.00
7 "The Isle Of No Return!" 110.00 350.00
8 "Prisoners Of Robot Planet!" 115.00 375.00
9-10 70.00 225.00
11-18 40.00 125.00
19-22 31.00 100.00
23 1st 12 cent cover price. 19.00 60.00
24-30 19.00 60.00
31 Origin retold. 23.00 75.00
32-40 11.00 35.00
41-60 5.00 15.00
61-68 2.75 10.00
69 1st 15 cent cover price. 2.00 7.00
70-73 2.00 7.00
74 Art: Neal Adams. Deadman. 7.00 20.00
75-77 1.75 6.00
78-80 1.25 4.00
81 1.00 3.00
82 Begin: Swamp Thing. 1.00 3.00
83-87 1.00 3.00

CHALLENGERS OF THE UNKNOWN
DC (1991)
1-6 .50 1.75
7 Art: Arthur Adams. .50 1.75
8 .50 1.75

CHAMBER OF CHILLS
HARVEY (1951-1954)
1 (#21) 50.00 150.00
2 (#22) 28.00 90.00
3 (#23) 31.00 100.00
4 (#24) 25.00 80.00
5 29.00 95.00
6 28.00 90.00
7 SOTI 25.00 80.00
8-10 23.00 75.00
11-15 19.00 60.00
16-20 15.00 48.00
21-25 11.00 36.00
26 Title changes to Chamber Of Clues with #27. 11.00 36.00

CHAMBER OF CHILLS
MARVEL (1972-1976)
1 1.25 4.00
2-25 .75 2.00

CATMAN COMICS #31

CATWOMAN #12

CEREBUS #189

CHALLENGERS OF THE UNKNOWN #8

THE CHAOS EFFECT ALPHA

CHAPEL #2

CHARLIE CHAN #9

CHEVAL NOIR #41

FAMOUS · FIRSTS

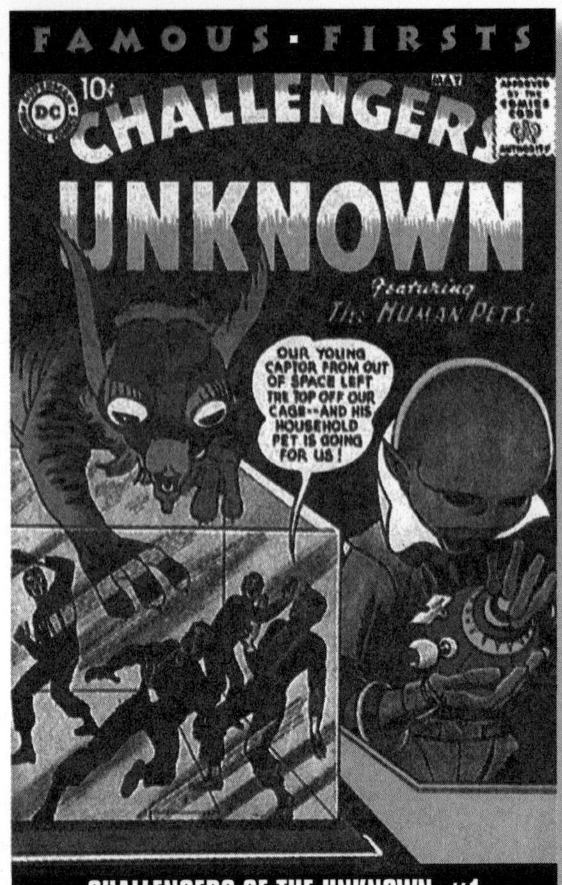

CHALLENGERS OF THE UNKNOWN #1

First appearing in *Showcase* #6, the Challengers are four guys who nearly die in a plane crash. They use this "borrowed time" to fight weird menaces. Challengers was created by Jack Kirby.

CHAMBER OF CLUES
HARVEY (1955)
27 Art: Bob Powell. Previous title: Chamber Of Chills.
.... 17.00 55.00
28 .... 10.00 33.00

CHAMBER OF DARKNESS
MARVEL (1969-1970)
1 .... 11.00 35.00
2 .... 4.00 13.00
3 Art: Barry Smith. 4.00 13.00
4 Art: Barry Smith. Conan prototype. 13.00 40.00
5-6 .... 2.00 7.00
7 1st Berni Wrightson work at Marvel. 5.00 16.00
8 Title changes to Monsters On The Prowl with #9.
.... 2.00 7.00

CHAMBER OF DARKNESS SPECIAL
MARVEL (1972)
1 Double size. 1.75 6.00

CHAMP COMICS
CHAMP (1940-1944)
11 Previous title: Champion Comics. ... 85.00 270.00
12 .... 85.00 270.00
13-15 .... 75.00 240.00
16-18 .... 65.00 210.00
19-29 .... 55.00 180.00

CHAMPION COMICS
WORTH (1939-1940)
2 Begin: The Champ, Neptina, Jungleman, Liberty Lads.
230.00 .... 750.00
3 .... 115.00 370.00
4 .... 105.00 340.00
5-7 .... 95.00 310.00
8 Cover: Joe Simon. (6/40) 85.00 280.00
9 .... 85.00 280.00
10 Title changes to Champ Comics with #11.
.... 85.00 280.00

CHAMPION SPORTS
DC (1973-1974)
1 .... .75 2.00
2-3 .... .50 1.50

CHAMPIONS
ECLIPSE (1986-1987)
1 1st: Flare. .... .75 2.00
2-6 .... .75 2.00

CHAMPIONS
HEROIC (1987-1988)
1-12 .... .50 1.25
ANNUAL 1 (1988) .... .50 1.25

CHAMPIONS, THE
MARVEL (1975-1978)
1 1st & Origin: Champions. 6.00 18.00
2-10 .... 2.75 10.00
11-15 Art: John Byrne. 4.00 12.00
16 .... 4.00 12.00
17 Art: John Byrne. 4.00 12.00

CHAMPIONS CLASSICS
HEROIC (1992-1994)
1 Champions V3 in indicia. .... .50 1.25
2-15 .... .50 1.25
ANNUAL 2 (1993) .... .50 1.25

CHAOS EFFECT, THE
VALIANT (1994)
ALPHA 1.00 3.00
ALPHA R Red version. 1.25 4.00
EPILOGUE 1-EPILOGUE 2 .... .75 2.95
OMEGA .... .75 2.25
OMEGA G Gold version. 2.25 8.00

CHAPEL
IMAGE (1995)
1 .... 1.00 3.50
1A Variant cover. 1.50 5.00
2 .... .75 2.50

CHARLIE CHAN
CRESTWOOD (1948-1956)
1 Cover: Simon & Kirby. 100.00 330.00
2 Cover: Simon & Kirby. 55.00 180.00
3 Cover/Art: Simon & Kirby. 75.00 240.00
4 Cover: Simon & Kirby. 55.00 180.00
5 Cover: Simon & Kirby. (3/49) ... 55.00 180.00
6 Cover: Simon & Kirby. (6/55) ... 40.00 120.00
7-8 .... 19.00 60.00
9 Title changes to Zaza The Mystic with #10.
.... 19.00 60.00

CHARLIE CHAPLIN
M.A. DONAHUE (1917)
316 "In The Movies" Art: Segar. (9.5 x 16, 18 pages)
.... 155.00 500.00
317 "Up In The Air" Art: Segar. 155.00 500.00
318 "In The Army" Art: Segar. 155.00 500.00
315 "Comic Capers" Art: Segar. ... 155.00 500.00

CHARLIE MCCARTHY
DELL (1949-1952)
1 .... 25.00 80.00
2-4 .... 16.00 50.00
5-9 .... 11.00 35.00

CHARLIE MCCARTHY
DELL FOUR COLOR SERIES (1947-1954)
171 "And The Twenty Thieves" (11/47) 40.00 125.00
196 "The Haunted Hide-Out" Photo (insert) cover. (9/48)
.... 31.00 100.00
445 (1/53) 11.00 35.00
478 (7/53) 10.00 30.00
527 (1/54) 8.00 25.00
571 (7/54) 7.00 20.00

CHARLTON PREMIERE
CHARLTON (1967-1968)
1-4 .... 1.00 3.00

CHECKMATE
DC (1988-1991)
1-33 .... .20 .50

CHECKMATE
GOLD KEY (1962)
1 TV photo cover. 10.00 30.00
2 TV photo cover. 7.00 20.00

CHEERIOS 3-D GIVEAWAYS
DISNEY (1954)
SET 1 #1 Donald Duck And Uncle Scrooge, "The Firefighters."
.... 19.00 60.00
SET 1 #2 Mickey Mouse And Goofy, "Pirate Plunder."
.... 19.00 60.00
SET 1 #3 Donald Duck's Nephews, "Fabulous Inventors."
.... 19.00 60.00
SET 1 #4 Mickey Mouse, "Secret Of The Ming Vase."
.... 19.00 60.00
SET 1 #5 Donald Duck With Huey, Dewey & Louie, "The Seafarers." 19.00 60.00
SET 1 #6 Mickey Mouse, "Moaning Mountain."
.... 19.00 60.00
SET 1 #7 Donald Duck, "Apache Gold." 19.00 60.00
SET 1 #8 Mickey Mouse, "Flight To Nowhere."
.... 19.00 60.00
SET 2 #1 Donald Duck, "Treasure Of Timbuktu."
.... 19.00 60.00
SET 2 #2 Mickey Mouse And Pluto, "Operation China."
.... 19.00 60.00
SET 2 #3 Donald Duck, "Magic Cows." 19.00 60.00
SET 2 #4 Mickey Mouse And Goofy, "Kid Kokonut."
.... 19.00 60.00
SET 2 #5 Donald Duck, "Mystery Ship." 19.00 60.00
SET 2 #6 Mickey Mouse, "Phantom Sheriff."
.... 19.00 60.00
SET 2 #7 Donald Duck, Circus Adventures. 19.00 60.00
SET 2 #8 Mickey Mouse, "Arctic Explorers. 19.00 60.00
SET 3 #1 Donald Duck, "Witch Hazel." 19.00 60.00
SET 3 #2 Mickey Mouse, "Darkest Africa." 19.00 60.00
SET 3 #3 Donald Duck And Uncle Scrooge, "Timber Trouble."
.... 19.00 60.00
SET 3 #4 Mickey Mouse, "Rajah's Rescue."
.... 19.00 60.00
SET 3 #5 Donald Duck, "Robot Reporter." 19.00 60.00
SET 3 #6 Mickey Mouse, "Slumbering Sleuth."
.... 19.00 60.00
SET 3 #7 Donald Duck, "Foreign Legion." 19.00 60.00
SET 3 #8 Mickey Mouse, "Airwalking Wonder."
.... 19.00 60.00

CHEVAL NOIR
DARK HORSE (1989-CURRENT)

1-8 ..... 1.00 3.50
9 ..... 1.25 4.50
10 ..... 1.00 3.50
11 ..... 1.25 4.50
12 ..... 1.25 4.00
13 ..... 1.25 4.50
14 ..... 1.50 5.00
15 ..... 1.25 4.50
16 ..... 1.00 3.75
17 ..... 1.25 4.50
18-19 ..... 1.25 4.00
20 ..... 1.25 4.50
21 ..... 1.25 4.00
22 ..... 1.25 4.50
23 ..... 1.25 4.00
24 ..... 1.00 3.75
25-26 ..... 1.25 4.00
27-50 ..... 1.00 3.00

CHEYENNE
DELL (1956-1962)

1 (#734) From the 4-Color Series. TV photo covers (Clint Walker) on all issues. (10/56) 31.00 100.00
2 (#772) From the 4-Color Series. (2/57) 16.00 50.00
3 (#803) From the 4-Color Series. (5/57) 16.00 50.00
4 ..... 13.00 40.00
5 ..... 11.00 35.00
6-12 ..... 10.00 30.00
13-25 ..... 8.00 25.00

CHEYENNE AUTUMN
DELL (1965)

12-112-506 Movie tie-in (photo inserts on cover). 10.00 30.00

CHEYENNE KID
CHARLTON (1957-1973)

8 Previous title: Wild Frontier. 7.00 20.00
9 ..... 5.00 15.00
10 Art: Al Williamson. Cover: Steve Ditko. 10.00 30.00
11 Art: Williamson. Double size. 8.00 25.00
12-17 ..... 5.00 15.00
18 Art: Williamson. 5.00 15.00
19-25 ..... 2.75 10.00
26-30 ..... 1.75 6.00
31-50 ..... 1.00 3.00
51-60 ..... .75 2.00
61-99 ..... .30 1.00

CHIAROSCURO: THE PRIVATE LIVES OF LEONARDO DA VINCI
DC (1995-CURRENT)

1 Vertigo mini-series. 1.25 4.25
2-3 ..... .75 3.00

CHIEF, THE
DELL (1950-1951)

1 (#290) From the 4-Color Series. (8/50) 11.00 35.00
2 Title changes to Indian Chief with #3. 7.00 20.00

CHIEF CRAZY HORSE
AVON (1950)

NO# "The Fetterman Massacre!" ... 23.00 75.00

CHIEF VICTORIO'S APACHE MASSACRE
AVON (1951)

NO# "The Bloody Ambush At Rincon!" Art: Frank Frazetta/Al Williamson. 50.00 150.00

CHILDREN'S BIG BOOK
DORENE (1945)

NO# 16.00 50.00

CHILDREN'S MENU FEATURING 2001: A SPACE ODYSSEY
HOWARD JOHNSON (1969)

NO# Giveaway. Movie tie-in. 13.00 40.00

CHILDRENS CRUSADE, THE
DC (1993)

1 Vertigo crossover book. 1.25 4.25
2 ..... 1.00 3.95

CHILI
MARVEL (1969-1973)

1 ..... 9.00 27.00
2 ..... 5.00 16.00
3-6 ..... 4.00 13.00
7-12 ..... 4.00 11.00
13-26 ..... 2.25 8.75
SPECIAL 4.00 11.00

CHILLING ADVENTURES IN SORCERY
RED CIRCLE (1972-1974)

1 ..... 1.50 5.00
2-4 ..... .75 2.00
5 Title changes to Sorcery with #6. ... .75 2.00

CHILLING TALES
YOUTHFUL (1952-1953)

13 (#1) Cover: Matt Fox. "The Screaming Skull" Previous title: Beware. 65.00 210.00
14 "The Ancient Mariner" (2/53) ... 40.00 120.00
15 (#14 on cover) (4/53) 45.00 140.00
16 ..... 31.00 100.00
17 ..... 40.00 120.00

CHILLY WILLY
DELL FOUR COLOR SERIES (1956-1962)

740 (10/56) 8.00 25.00
852 (2/58) 5.00 15.00
967 (2/59) 5.00 15.00
1017 (8/59) 5.00 15.00
1074 (2/60) 5.00 15.00
1122 (8/60) 7.00 20.00
1177 (3/61) 5.00 15.00
1212 (8/61) 7.00 20.00
1281 (3/62) 7.00 20.00

CHIP 'N' DALE
DELL (1953-1962)

1 (#517) From the 4-Color Series. (11/53) 10.00 30.00
2 (#581) From the 4-Color Series. (8/54) 5.00 15.00
3 (#636) From the 4-Color Series. 5.00 15.00
4-10 ..... 2.75 10.00
11-30 ..... 2.00 7.00

CHIP 'N' DALE
GOLD KEY (1967-1982)

1 ..... 2.75 10.00
2-12 ..... 1.75 6.00
13-40 ..... 1.25 4.00
41-83 ..... .75 2.00

CHITTY CHITTY BANG BANG
GOLD KEY (1969)

30038-902 Disney movie photo cover. With poster. 8.00 25.00

CHOICE COMICS
GREAT (1941-1942)

1 ..... 190.00 600.00
2 ..... 130.00 420.00
3 Movie tie-in: The Lost City. 190.00 600.00

CHRISTMAS CARNIVAL
ST. JOHN (1955)

2 Reprints Ziff-Davis issue. Same cover except title in white. 31.00 100.00

CHRISTMAS CARNIVAL
ZIFF-DAVIS (1952)

NO# Title in black. 50.00 150.00

CHRISTMAS IN DISNEYLAND
DELL (1957)

1 Dell Giant. Art: Carl Barks. 50.00 150.00

CHRISTMAS PARADE
DELL (1949-1957)

1 Dell Giant, Disney. Art: Carl Barks (25 pgs.) (11/49) 155.00 500.00
2 Art: Carl Barks (25 pgs.) 125.00 400.00
3-7 ..... 23.00 75.00
8 Art: Carl Barks (8 pgs.) 50.00 150.00
9 Art: Carl Barks (20 pgs.) 55.00 175.00

CHRISTMAS PARADE
GOLD KEY (1963-1978)

1 ..... 10.00 30.00
2-6 ..... 7.00 20.00
7 ..... 5.00 15.00
8 With pull-out poster intact. 7.00 20.00
9 ..... 5.00 15.00

CHRISTMAS STORIES
DELL FOUR COLOR SERIES (1958-1959)

959 (12/58) 7.00 20.00
1062 (12/59) 7.00 20.00

CHRISTMAS TREASURY, A
DELL (1954)

1 100 pg. Dell Giant. 31.00 100.00

CHRISTMAS WITH MOTHER GOOSE
DELL FOUR COLOR SERIES (1945-1949)

90 Art: Walt Kelly in all issues. 50.00 150.00
126 (11/46) 31.00 100.00
172 (11/47) 31.00 100.00
201 (11/48) 28.00 90.00
253 (11/49) 25.00 80.00

CHRISTOPHERS, THE
GUILD PRESS (1951)

NO# Giveaway of the Christopher Movement. 31.00 100.00

CHUCK NORRIS
MARVEL(STAR) (1987)

1 Art: Steve Ditko. ..... .30 1.00
2-3 ..... .30 1.00

CHUCK WAGON, THE
AVON (1950)

1 Cover/Art: Kinstler. 16.00 50.00

CHUCKLE, THE GIGGLY BOOK OF COMIC ANIMALS
R.B. LEFFINGWELL (1944)

1 130 pages. 31.00 100.00

CINDERELLA
DELL FOUR COLOR SERIES (1950-1957)

272 Disney. (4/50) 20.00 65.00
786 (3/57) 8.00 25.00

CINDERELLA
GOLD KEY (1965)

10152-508 Disney movie tie-in. 8.00 25.00

CINDERELLA LOVE
ZIFF-DAVIS/ST. JOHN (1950-1954)

1 (#10 on cover, 1950) 16.00 50.00
2 (#11 on cover, 1951) 10.00 30.00
3 (#12 on cover, 1951). 8.00 25.00
4-8 ..... 7.00 20.00
9 Art: Kinstler. 10.00 30.00
10 ..... 7.00 20.00
11-14 ..... 6.00 18.00
15 Cover: Matt Baker. 8.00 25.00
16-24 ..... 5.00 15.00
25 ..... 4.00 12.00
26-27 Cover: Matt Baker. 7.00 20.00
28 ..... 4.00 12.00
29 Cover: Matt Baker. 7.00 20.00

CINDY COMICS
MARVEL(TIMELY) (1947-1950)

27 ..... 22.00 70.00
28-31 ..... 15.00 48.00
32-40 ..... 10.00 30.00

CIRCUS BOY
DELL FOUR COLOR SERIES (1956-1957)

759 TV photo cover (Mickey Dolenz). (12/56) 25.00 80.00
785 TV photo cover (Mickey Dolenz). (4/57) 25.00 80.00
813 TV photo cover (Mickey Dolenz). (7/57) 25.00 80.00

CIRCUS COMICS
D.S. (1948)

1 Art: Frank Frazetta. 50.00 150.00

CIRCUS COMICS
FMP (1945)

1 Canadian. 10.00 30.00
2 ..... 7.00 20.00

CIRCUS OF FUN COMICS
A.W. NUGENT (1946-1947)

1 ..... 16.00 50.00
2-3 ..... 10.00 30.00

CIRCUS THE COMIC RIOT
GLOBE (1938)

1 (6/38) 500.00 1600.00
2 (7/38) 300.00 975.00
3 (8/38) 300.00 975.00

CIRCUS WORLD
DELL (1964)

12-115-411 Movie photo cover (John Wayne). 25.00 80.00

CISCO KID
DELL (1950-1958)

1 (#292) From the 4-Color Series. (9/50) 50.00 150.00
2 ..... 19.00 60.00
3-6 ..... 16.00 50.00
7-20 ..... 13.00 40.00
21-30 ..... 10.00 30.00
31-36 ..... 7.00 20.00
37-41 Movie photo cover. 23.00 75.00

CHILDREN'S BIG BOOK #1

CHRISTMAS CARNIVAL #2

CIRCUS OF FUN COMICS #2

THE CISCO KID #3

CLASSIC COMICS #3

CLASSIC COMICS #6

CLASSIC COMICS #13

CLASSIC COMICS #19

CISCO KID COMICS
B. BAILEY (1944)

1 .... 65.00 200.00

CITIZEN SMITH COMICS
HOLYOKE (1944-1945)

9 From the Holyoke One-Shot series. ... 19.00 60.00

CITY KNIGHTS, THE
ACCLAIM/WINDJAMMER (1995)

1-2 .... .75 2.50

CITY OF THE LIVING DEAD!
AVON (1952)

NO# Art: Hollingsworth. "The Glistening Death!"
.... 50.00 150.00

CLAIRE VOYANT
STANDARD (1946-1947)

1 (NO#) 70.00 220.00
2-3 .... 50.00 160.00
4 .... 70.00 220.00

CLASSIC COMICS
GILBERTON (1941-1947)

1 The Three Musketeers (1941). ... 1000.00 3800.00
1 (2ND) HRN #10. .... 70.00 220.00
1 (3RD) HRN #15. .... 35.00 110.00
1 (4TH) HRN #18 or #20. .... 26.00 85.00
1 (5TH) HRN #21. .... 23.00 75.00
1 (6TH) HRN #28. .... 20.00 65.00
1 (7TH) HRN #36. .... 9.00 27.00
1 (8TH) HRN #60. .... 6.00 19.00
1 (9TH) HRN #64. .... 5.00 16.00
1 (10TH) HRN #78. .... 5.00 16.00
1 (11TH) HRN #93. .... 5.00 16.00
1 (12TH) HRN #114. .... 4.00 11.00
1 (13TH) HRN #134. .... 4.00 11.00
1 (14TH) HRN #143. .... 4.00 11.00
1 (15TH) HRN #150. .... 4.00 11.00
1 (16TH) HRN #149. .... 1.25 4.25
1 (17TH) HRN #167. .... 1.25 4.25
1 (18TH) HRN #166. .... 1.25 4.25
1 (19TH) HRN #169. .... 1.25 4.25
2 Ivanhoe (1941). 300.00 1100.00
2 (2ND) HRN #10. .... 60.00 190.00
2 (3RD) HRN #15. .... 40.00 130.00
2 (4TH) HRN #18 or #20. .... 35.00 110.00
2 (5TH) HRN #21. .... 35.00 110.00
2 (6TH) HRN #28 (1946). 25.00 80.00
2 (7TH) HRN #36. .... 10.00 33.00
2 (8TH) HRN #60. .... 7.00 22.00
2 (9TH) HRN #64. .... 7.00 22.00
2 (10TH) HRN #78. .... 5.00 16.00
2 (11TH) HRN #89. .... 5.00 16.00
2 (12TH) HRN #106. .... 4.00 11.00
2 (13TH) HRN #121. .... 4.00 11.00
2 (14TH) HRN #136. .... 4.00 11.00
2 (15TH) HRN #142. .... 1.25 4.25
2 (16TH) HRN #153. .... 1.25 4.25
2 (17TH) HRN #149. .... 1.25 4.25
2 (18TH) HRN #167. .... 1.25 4.25
2 (19TH) HRN #166. .... 1.25 4.25
2 (20TH) HRN #169. .... 1.25 4.25
3 The Count of Monte Cristo (3/42). 270.00 875.00
3 (2ND) HRN #10. .... 60.00 190.00
3 (3RD) HRN #15. .... 40.00 130.00
3 (4TH) HRN #18 or #20. .... 35.00 110.00
3 (5TH) HRN #21. .... 25.00 80.00
3 (6TH) HRN #28 (1946). 22.00 70.00
3 (7TH) HRN #36. .... 10.00 33.00
3 (8TH) HRN #60. .... 7.00 22.00
3 (9TH) HRN #62. .... 7.00 22.00
3 (10TH) HRN #71. .... 7.00 22.00
3 (11TH) HRN #87. .... 5.00 16.00
3 (12TH) HRN #113. .... 4.00 11.00
3 (13TH) HRN #135. .... 4.00 11.00
3 (14TH) HRN #143. .... 1.25 4.25
3 (15TH) HRN #153. .... 1.25 4.25
3 (16TH) HRN #161. .... 1.25 4.25
3 (17TH) HRN #167. .... 1.25 4.25
3 (18TH) HRN #166. .... 1.25 4.25
3 (19TH) HRN #169. .... 1.25 4.25
4 The Last of the Mohicans (1942). 230.00 750.00
4 (2ND) HRN #12. .... 50.00 160.00
4 (3RD) HRN #15. .... 40.00 130.00
4 (4TH) HRN #20. .... 35.00 110.00
4 (5TH) HRN #21. .... 26.00 85.00
4 (6TH) HRN #28 (1946). 20.00 65.00
4 (7TH) HRN #36. .... 10.00 33.00
4 (8TH) HRN #60. .... 7.00 22.00
4 (9TH) HRN #64. .... 5.00 16.00
4 (10TH) HRN #78. .... 5.00 16.00
4 (11TH) HRN #89. .... 5.00 16.00
4 (12TH) HRN #117. .... 4.00 11.00
4 (13TH) HRN #135. .... 4.00 11.00
4 (14TH) HRN #141. .... 4.00 11.00
4 (15TH) HRN #150. .... 4.00 11.00
4 (16TH) HRN #161. .... 1.25 4.25
4 (17TH) HRN #167. .... 1.25 4.25
4 (18TH) HRN #166. .... 1.25 4.25
4 (19TH) HRN #169. .... 1.25 4.25
5 Moby Dick (1942). 270.00 875.00
5 (2ND) HRN #10. .... 55.00 170.00
5 (3RD) HRN #15. .... 35.00 110.00
5 (4TH) HRN #18 or #20. .... 35.00 110.00
5 (5TH) HRN #21. .... 35.00 110.00
5 (6TH) HRN #28 (1946). 20.00 65.00
5 (7TH) HRN #36. .... 10.00 33.00
5 (8TH) HRN #60. .... 7.00 22.00
5 (9TH) HRN #62. .... 7.00 22.00
5 (10TH) HRN #71. .... 5.00 16.00
5 (11TH) HRN #87. .... 5.00 16.00
5 (12TH) HRN #118. .... 4.00 11.00
5 (13TH) HRN #131. .... 4.00 11.00
5 (14TH) HRN #138. .... 1.25 4.25
5 (15TH) HRN #148. .... 1.25 4.25
5 (16TH) HRN #158. .... 1.25 4.25
5 (17TH) HRN #167. .... 1.25 4.25
5 (18TH) HRN #166. .... 1.25 4.25
5 (19TH) HRN #169. .... 1.25 4.25
6 A Tale of Two Cities (1942). 230.00 750.00
6 (2ND) HRN #14. .... 50.00 160.00
6 (3RD) HRN #18. .... 35.00 110.00
6 (4TH) HRN #20. .... 35.00 110.00
6 (5TH) HRN #28 (1946). 20.00 65.00
6 (6TH) HRN #51. .... 9.00 27.00
6 (7TH) HRN #64. .... 7.00 22.00
6 (8TH) HRN #78. .... 5.00 16.00
6 (9TH) HRN #89. .... 4.00 11.00
6 (10TH) HRN #117. .... 4.00 11.00
6 (11TH) HRN #132. .... 4.00 11.00
6 (12TH) HRN #140. .... 1.25 4.25
6 (13TH) HRN #147. .... 1.25 4.25
6 (14TH) HRN #152. .... 1.25 4.25
6 (15TH) HRN #153. .... 1.25 4.25
6 (16TH) HRN #149. .... 1.25 4.25
6 (17TH) HRN #167. .... 1.25 4.25
6 (18TH) HRN #166. .... 1.25 4.25
6 (19TH) HRN #169. .... 1.25 4.25
7 Robin Hood (1942). 200.00 650.00
7 (2ND) HRN #12. .... 50.00 160.00
7 (3RD) HRN #18. .... 40.00 120.00
7 (4TH) HRN #20. .... 35.00 110.00
7 (5TH) HRN #22. .... 26.00 85.00
7 (6TH) HRN #28. .... 20.00 65.00
7 (7TH) HRN #51. .... 9.00 27.00
7 (8TH) HRN #64. .... 7.00 22.00
7 (9TH) HRN #78. .... 5.00 16.00
7 (10TH) HRN #97. .... 5.00 16.00
7 (11TH) HRN #106. .... 4.00 11.00
7 (12TH) HRN #121. .... 4.00 11.00
7 (13TH) HRN #129. .... 4.00 11.00
7 (14TH) HRN #136. .... 4.00 11.00
7 (15TH) HRN #143. .... 1.25 4.25
7 (16TH) HRN #153. .... 1.25 4.25
7 (17TH) HRN #164. .... 1.25 4.25
7 (18TH) HRN #167. .... 1.25 4.25
7 (19TH) HRN #166. .... 1.25 4.25
7 (20TH) HRN #169. .... 1.25 4.25
8 Arabian Nights (1943). 500.00 1600.00
8 (2ND) HRN #17. .... 170.00 550.00
8 (3RD) HRN #20. .... 135.00 440.00
8 (4TH) HRN #28. .... 100.00 330.00
8 (5TH) HRN #51. .... 50.00 160.00
8 (6TH) HRN #64. .... 40.00 120.00
8 (7TH) HRN #78. .... 35.00 110.00
8 (8TH) HRN #164. .... 26.00 85.00
9 Les Miserables (3/43). 170.00 550.00
9 (2ND) HRN #14. .... 40.00 130.00
9 (3RD) HRN #18. .... 35.00 110.00
9 (4TH) HRN #20. .... 26.00 85.00
9 (5TH) HRN #28. .... 17.00 55.00
9 (6TH) HRN #51. .... 7.00 22.00
9 (7TH) HRN #71. .... 7.00 22.00
9 (8TH) HRN #87. .... 7.00 22.00
9 (9TH) HRN #161. .... 4.00 13.00
9 (10TH) HRN #167. .... 4.00 13.00
9 (11TH) HRN #166. .... 4.00 13.00
10 Robinson Crusoe (4/43). SOTI. ... 190.00 600.00
10 (2ND) HRN #14. .... 50.00 160.00
10 (3RD) HRN #18. .... 35.00 110.00
10 (4TH) HRN #20. .... 26.00 85.00
10 (5TH) HRN #28 (1946). 20.00 65.00
10 (6TH) HRN #51. .... 9.00 27.00
10 (7TH) HRN #64. .... 7.00 22.00
10 (8TH) HRN #78. .... 5.00 16.00
10 (9TH) HRN #97. .... 5.00 16.00
10 (10TH) HRN #114. .... 4.00 11.00
10 (11TH) HRN #130. .... 4.00 11.00
10 (12TH) HRN #140. .... 4.00 11.00
10 (13TH) HRN #153. .... 1.25 4.25
10 (14TH) HRN #164. .... 1.25 4.25
10 (15TH) HRN #167. .... 1.25 4.25
10 (16TH) HRN #166. .... 1.25 4.25
10 (17TH) HRN #169. .... 1.25 4.25
11 Don Quixote (5/43). 170.00 550.00
11 (2ND) HRN #18. .... 50.00 160.00
11 (3RD) HRN #21. .... 35.00 110.00
11 (4TH) HRN #28. .... 20.00 65.00
11 (5TH) HRN #110. .... 7.00 22.00
11 (6TH) HRN #156. .... 1.50 5.50
11 (7TH) HRN #165. .... 1.50 5.50
11 (8TH) HRN #167. .... 1.50 5.50
11 (9TH) HRN #166. .... 1.50 5.50
12 Rip Van Winkle and The Headless Horseman (6/43).
.... 170.00 550.00
12 (2ND) HRN #15. .... 50.00 160.00
12 (3RD) HRN #20. .... 35.00 110.00
12 (4TH) HRN #22. .... 26.00 85.00
12 (5TH) HRN #28. .... 20.00 65.00
12 (6TH) HRN #60. .... 9.00 27.00
12 (7TH) HRN #62. .... 7.00 22.00
12 (8TH) HRN #71. .... 5.00 16.00
12 (9TH) HRN #89. .... 5.00 16.00
12 (10TH) HRN #118. .... 4.00 11.00
12 (11TH) HRN #132. .... 4.00 11.00
12 (12TH) HRN #150. .... 4.00 11.00
12 (13TH) HRN #158. .... 1.25 4.25
12 (14TH) HRN #167. .... 1.25 4.25
12 (15TH) HRN #166. .... 1.25 4.25
12 (16TH) HRN #169. .... 1.25 4.25
13 Dr. Jekyll and Mr. Hyde (8/43). SOTI.
.... 270.00 875.00
13 (2ND) HRN #15. .... 50.00 160.00
13 (3RD) HRN #20. .... 35.00 110.00
13 (4TH) HRN #28. .... 26.00 85.00
13 (5TH) HRN #60. .... 9.00 27.00
13 (6TH) HRN #62. .... 7.00 22.00
13 (7TH) HRN #71. .... 5.00 16.00
13 (8TH) HRN #87. .... 5.00 16.00
13 (9TH) HRN #112. .... 5.00 16.00
13 (10TH) HRN #153. .... 1.25 4.25
13 (11TH) HRN #161. .... 1.25 4.25
13 (12TH) HRN #167. .... 1.25 4.25
13 (13TH) HRN #166. .... 1.25 4.25
13 (14TH) HRN #169. .... 1.25 4.25
14 Westward Ho! HRN #13 (9/43). 400.00 1300.00
14 (2ND) HRN #15. .... 135.00 440.00
14 (3RD) HRN #21. .... 100.00 330.00
14 (4TH) HRN #28. .... 85.00 270.00
14 (5TH) HRN #53. .... 70.00 220.00
15 Uncle Tom's Cabin. HRN #14 (11/43).
.... 135.00 440.00
15 (2ND) HRN #15. .... 50.00 160.00
15 (3RD) HRN #21. .... 40.00 130.00
15 (4TH) HRN #28. .... 25.00 80.00
15 (5TH) HRN #53. .... 10.00 33.00
15 (6TH) HRN #71. .... 7.00 22.00
15 (7TH) HRN #89. .... 7.00 22.00
15 (8TH) HRN #117. .... 4.00 11.00
15 (9TH) HRN #128. .... 4.00 11.00
15 (10TH) HRN #137. .... 1.25 4.25
15 (11TH) HRN #146. .... 1.25 4.25
15 (12TH) HRN #154. .... 1.25 4.25
15 (13TH) HRN #161. .... 1.25 4.25
15 (14TH) HRN #167. .... 1.25 4.25
15 (15TH) HRN #166. .... 1.25 4.25
15 (16TH) HRN #169. .... 1.25 4.25
16 Gullivers Travels. HRN #15 (12/43). 135.00 440.00
16 (2ND) HRN #18 or #20. .... 40.00 130.00
16 (3RD) HRN #22. .... 35.00 110.00
16 (4TH) HRN #28. .... 20.00 65.00
16 (5TH) HRN #60. .... 7.00 22.00
16 (6TH) HRN #62. .... 7.00 22.00
16 (7TH) HRN #78. .... 5.00 16.00
16 (8TH) HRN #89. .... 4.00 11.00
16 (9TH) HRN #155. .... 4.00 11.00
16 (10TH) HRN #165. .... 1.25 4.25
16 (11TH) HRN #167. .... 1.25 4.25
16 (12TH) HRN #166. .... 1.25 4.25
16 (13TH) HRN #169. .... 1.25 4.25
17 The Deerslayer. HRN #16 (1/44). 135.00 440.00
17 (2ND) HRN #18. .... 40.00 130.00
17 (3RD) HRN #22. .... 35.00 110.00
17 (4TH) HRN #28. .... 20.00 65.00
17 (5TH) HRN #60. .... 7.00 22.00
17 (6TH) HRN #64. .... 5.00 16.00
17 (7TH) HRN #85. .... 5.00 16.00
17 (8TH) HRN #118. .... 4.00 11.00
17 (9TH) HRN #132. .... 4.00 11.00
17 (10TH) HRN #167. .... 4.00 11.00
17 (11TH) HRN #166. .... 4.00 11.00
17 (12TH) HRN #169. .... 4.00 11.00
18 The Hunchback of Notre Dame. HRN #17 (3/44).
.... 170.00 550.00
18 (2ND) HRN #18 or #20. .... 40.00 130.00
18 (3RD) HRN #22. .... 35.00 110.00
18 (4TH) HRN #28. .... 25.00 80.00
18 (5TH) HRN #60. .... 9.00 27.00
18 (6TH) HRN #62. .... 5.00 16.00
18 (7TH) HRN #78. .... 5.00 16.00
18 (8TH) HRN #89. .... 5.00 16.00
18 (9TH) HRN #118. .... 5.00 16.00

18 (10TH) HRN #140. 5.00 16.00
18 (11TH) HRN #146. 5.00 16.00
18 (12TH) HRN #158. 5.00 16.00
18 (13TH) HRN #165. 1.25 4.25
18 (14TH) HRN #167. 1.25 4.25
18 (15TH) HRN #166. 1.25 4.25
18 (16TH) HRN #169. 1.25 4.25
19 Huckleberry Finn. HRN #18 (4/44). 100.00 330.00
19 (2ND) HRN #22. 35.00 110.00
19 (3RD) HRN #28. 20.00 65.00
19 (4TH) HRN #60. 7.00 22.00
19 (5TH) HRN #62. 7.00 22.00
19 (6TH) HRN #78. 5.00 16.00
19 (7TH) HRN #89. 5.00 16.00
19 (8TH) HRN #117. 4.00 11.00
19 (9TH) HRN #131. 4.00 11.00
19 (10TH) HRN #140. 1.25 4.25
19 (11TH) HRN #150. 1.25 4.25
19 (12TH) HRN #158. 1.25 4.25
19 (13TH) HRN #165. 1.25 4.25
19 (14TH) HRN #167. 1.25 4.25
19 (15TH) HRN #166. 1.25 4.25
19 (16TH) HRN #169. 1.25 4.25
20 The Corsican Brothers. HRN #20 (6/44). 125.00 410.00
20 (2ND) HRN #22. 40.00 130.00
20 (3RD) HRN #28. 35.00 110.00
20 (4TH) HRN #60. 20.00 65.00
20 (5TH) HRN #62. 17.00 55.00
20 (6TH) HRN #78. 14.00 44.00
20 (7TH) HRN #97. 10.00 33.00
21 3 Famous Mysteries. "Sherlock Holmes 'The Sign Of The 4'", "The Murders In The Rue Morgue", "The Flayed Hand." HRN #21 (7/44). 200.00 650.00
21 (2ND) HRN #22. 60.00 190.00
21 (3RD) HRN #30. 50.00 160.00
21 (4TH) HRN #62. 40.00 130.00
21 (5TH) HRN #70. 35.00 110.00
21 (6TH) HRN #85. 26.00 85.00
21 (7TH) HRN #114. 26.00 85.00
22 The Pathfinder. HRN #22 (10/44). 100.00 330.00
22 (2ND) HRN #30. 20.00 65.00
22 (3RD) HRN #60. 5.00 16.00
22 (4TH) HRN #70. 5.00 16.00
22 (5TH) HRN #85. 4.00 11.00
22 (6TH) HRN #118. 4.00 11.00
22 (7TH) HRN #132. 4.00 11.00
22 (8TH) HRN #146. 4.00 11.00
22 (9TH) HRN #167. 4.00 11.00
22 (10TH) HRN #166. 4.00 11.00
23 Oliver Twist. HRN #23 (7/45). 75.00 240.00
23 (2ND) HRN #30. 50.00 160.00
23 (3RD) HRN #60. 7.00 22.00
23 (4TH) HRN #62. 7.00 22.00
23 (5TH) HRN #71. 5.00 16.00
23 (6TH) HRN #85. 5.00 16.00
23 (7TH) HRN #94. 4.00 11.00
23 (8TH) HRN #118. 4.00 11.00
23 (9TH) HRN #136. 4.00 11.00
23 (10TH) HRN #150. 2.25 8.75
23 (11TH) HRN #164. 2.25 8.75
23 (12TH) HRN #167. 1.25 4.25
23 (13TH) HRN #166. 1.25 4.25
23 (14TH) HRN #169. 1.25 4.25
24 A Connecticut Yankee in King Arthur's Court (9/45). 75.00 240.00
24 (2ND) HRN #30. 20.00 65.00
24 (3RD) HRN #60. 7.00 22.00
24 (4TH) HRN #62. 7.00 22.00
24 (5TH) HRN #71. 5.00 16.00
24 (6TH) HRN #87. 5.00 16.00
24 (7TH) HRN #121. 4.00 11.00
24 (8TH) HRN #140. 4.00 11.00
24 (9TH) HRN #153. 4.00 11.00
24 (10TH) HRN #164. 1.25 4.25
24 (11TH) HRN #167. 1.25 4.25
24 (12TH) HRN #166. 1.25 4.25
24 (13TH) HRN #169. 1.25 4.25
25 Two Years Before the Mast (10/45). 75.00 240.00
25 (2ND) HRN #30. 25.00 80.00
25 (3RD) HRN #60. 9.00 27.00
25 (4TH) HRN #62. 7.00 22.00
25 (5TH) HRN #71. 5.00 16.00
25 (6TH) HRN #85. 5.00 16.00
25 (7TH) HRN #114. 4.00 11.00
25 (8TH) HRN #156. 4.00 11.00
25 (9TH) HRN #167. 1.25 4.25
25 (10TH) HRN #166. 1.25 4.25
25 (11TH) HRN #169. 1.25 4.25
26 Frankenstein. HRN #26 (12/45). 200.00 650.00
26 (2ND) HRN #30. 70.00 220.00
26 (3RD) HRN #60. 17.00 55.00
26 (4TH) HRN #62. 17.00 55.00
26 (5TH) HRN #71. 9.00 27.00
26 (6TH) HRN #82. 7.00 22.00
26 (7TH) HRN #117. 5.00 16.00
26 (8TH) HRN #146. 5.00 16.00
26 (9TH) HRN #152. 9.00 27.00
26 (10TH) HRN #153. 1.25 4.25
26 (11TH) HRN #160. 1.25 4.25
26 (12TH) HRN #165. 1.25 4.25
26 (13TH) HRN #167. 1.25 4.25
26 (14TH) HRN #166. 1.25 4.25
26 (15TH) HRN #169. 1.25 4.25
27 The Adventures of Marco Polo (4/46). 85.00 270.00
27 (2ND) HRN #30. 20.00 65.00
27 (3RD) HRN #70. 7.00 22.00
27 (4TH) HRN #87. 4.00 13.00
27 (5TH) HRN #117. 4.00 11.00
27 (6TH) HRN #154. 4.00 11.00
27 (7TH) HRN #165. 1.25 4.25
27 (8TH) HRN #167. 1.25 4.25
27 (9TH) HRN #169. 1.25 4.25
28 Michael Strogoff (6/46). 70.00 220.00
28 (2ND) HRN #51. 20.00 65.00
28 (3RD) HRN #115. 4.00 13.00
28 (4TH) HRN #155. 1.50 5.50
28 (5TH) HRN #167. 1.50 5.50
28 (6TH) HRN #169. 1.50 5.50
29 The Prince and the Pauper (7/46). 125.00 410.00
29 (2ND) HRN #60. 7.00 22.00
29 (3RD) HRN #62. 7.00 22.00
29 (4TH) HRN #71. 5.00 16.00
29 (5TH) HRN #93. 5.00 16.00
29 (6TH) HRN #114. 4.00 11.00
29 (7TH) HRN #128. 4.00 11.00
29 (8TH) HRN #138. 1.25 4.25
29 (9TH) HRN #150. 1.25 4.25
29 (10TH) HRN #164. 1.25 4.25
29 (11TH) HRN #167. 1.25 4.25
29 (12TH) HRN #166. 1.25 4.25
29 (13TH) HRN #169. 1.25 4.25
30 The Moonstone (9/46). 70.00 220.00
30 (2ND) HRN #60. 7.00 22.00
30 (3RD) HRN #70. 7.00 22.00
30 (4TH) HRN #155. Cover: L.B. Cole. 10.00 33.00
30 (5TH) HRN #165. Cover: L.B. Cole. 4.00 11.00
30 (6TH) HRN #167. Cover: L.B. Cole. 1.50 5.50
30 (7TH) HRN #166. Cover: L.B. Cole. 1.50 5.50
31 The Black Arrow (10/46). 60.00 190.00
31 (2ND) HRN #51. 7.00 22.00
31 (3RD) HRN #64. 5.00 16.00
31 (4TH) HRN #87. 4.00 11.00
31 (5TH) HRN #108. 4.00 11.00
31 (6TH) HRN #125. 4.00 11.00
31 (7TH) HRN #131. 4.00 11.00
31 (8TH) HRN #140. 1.25 4.25
31 (9TH) HRN #148. 1.25 4.25
31 (10TH) HRN #161. 1.25 4.25
31 (11TH) HRN #167. 1.25 4.25
31 (12TH) HRN #166. 1.25 4.25
32 Lorna Doone. Cover & art: Matt Baker. 85.00 270.00
32 (2ND) HRN #53 or #64. 10.00 33.00
32 (3RD) HRN #85. 7.00 22.00
32 (4TH) HRN #118. 4.00 13.00
32 (5TH) HRN #138. 4.00 11.00
32 (6TH) HRN #150. 1.25 4.25
32 (7TH) HRN #165. 1.25 4.25
32 (8TH) HRN #167. 1.25 4.25
32 (9TH) HRN #166. 1.25 4.25
33 The Adventures of Sherlock Holmes. HRN #33 (1/47). 250.00 825.00
33 (2ND) HRN #53. 85.00 270.00
33 (3RD) HRN #71. 50.00 160.00
33 (4TH) HRN #89. 40.00 130.00
34 Mysterious Island (2/47). Title changes to Classics Illustrated with #35. 70.00 220.00
34 (2ND) HRN #60. 7.00 22.00
34 (3RD) HRN #62. 7.00 22.00
34 (4TH) HRN #71. 7.00 22.00
34 (5TH) HRN #78. 5.00 16.00
34 (6TH) HRN #92. 4.00 11.00
34 (7TH) HRN #117. 2.25 8.75
34 (8TH) HRN #140. 2.25 8.75
34 (9TH) HRN #156. 1.25 4.25
34 (10TH) HRN #167. 1.25 4.25
34 (11TH) HRN #166. 1.25 4.25

CLASSIC STAR WARS

DARK HORSE (1992-1994)

1 Reprint: Daily strip. 2.25 8.00
2 1.00 3.00
3-20 .75 2.00
TPB VOL 1 Reprints issues #1-7. 5.00 15.95
TPB VOL 2 6.00 16.95

CLASSIC STAR WARS: A NEW HOPE

DARK HORSE (1994)

1-2 1.00 3.95

CLASSIC STAR WARS: RETURN OF THE JEDI

DARK HORSE (1994)

1 Reprint: Return Of The Jedi (Marvel). Bagged with card. 1.00 3.50
2 1.00 3.50

CLASSIC STAR WARS: THE EARLY ADVENTURES

DARK HORSE (1994-1995)

1 Art & story: Russ Manning (all issues). .75 2.50
2-9 .75 2.50

CLASSIC STAR WARS: THE EMPIRE STRIKES BACK

DARK HORSE (1994)

1 Reprint: The Empire Strikes Back (Marvel). 1.00 3.95
2 1.00 3.95

CLASSIC STAR WARS: THE VANDELHEIM MISSION

DARK HORSE (1995)

NO# One-shot. .75 2.50

CLASSIC X-MEN

MARVEL (1986-1990)

1 Reprints. 2.75 10.00
2 1.75 6.00
3-9 1.50 5.00
10 App: Sabretooth. 2.25 8.00
11 1.50 5.00
12 Origin: Magneto. 2.25 8.00
13-16 1.50 5.00
17 Wolverine. 2.00 7.00
18-25 1.50 5.00
26 Reprint: X-Men #120. 2.00 7.00
27 Reprint: X-Men #121. 1.00 3.00
28-34 1.00 3.00
35 Reprint X-Men #129. 1.00 3.00
36-38 1.00 3.00
39 New Wolverine story by Jim Lee. 2.75 10.00
40 .75 2.50
41-42 .75 2.00
43 Double size. .75 2.00
44 .75 2.00
45 Title changes to X-Men Classic with #46. .75 2.00

CLASSICS GIVEAWAYS

GILBERTON (1969)

1969 "A Christmas Adventure". 8.00 25.00

CLASSICS ILLUSTRATED

GILBERTON (1947-1971)

35 The Last Days Of Pompeii. (3/47) Previous title: Classic Comics. 70.00 220.00
35 (2ND) HRN #161. Art: Jack Kirby. 7.00 22.00
35 (3RD) HRN #167. 1.50 5.50
35 (4TH) HRN #169. 1.50 5.50
36 Typee. (4/47) 35.00 110.00
36 (2ND) HRN #64. 7.00 22.00
36 (3RD) HRN #155. 4.00 11.00
36 (4TH) HRN #167. 1.50 5.50
36 (5TH) HRN #169. 1.50 5.50
37 The Pioneers. HRN #37. (5/47) 35.00 110.00
37 (2ND) HRN #62. 20.00 65.00
37 (3RD) HRN #70. 4.00 13.00
37 (4TH) HRN #92. 4.00 11.00
37 (5TH) HRN #118. 4.00 11.00
37 (6TH) HRN #131. 4.00 11.00
37 (7TH) HRN #132. 4.00 11.00
37 (8TH) HRN #153. 1.75 6.50
37 (9TH) HRN #167. 1.25 4.25
37 (10TH) HRN #166. 1.25 4.25
38 Adventures of Cellini. (6/47) 50.00 160.00
38 (2ND) HRN #164. (12/63) 1.50 5.50
38 (3RD) HRN #167. 1.50 5.50
38 (4TH) HRN #169. 1.50 5.50
39 Jane Eyre. (7/47) 40.00 130.00
39 (2ND) HRN #60. 7.00 22.00
39 (3RD) HRN #62. 5.00 16.00
39 (4TH) HRN #71. 5.00 16.00
39 (5TH) HRN #92. 4.00 11.00
39 (6TH) HRN #118. 4.00 11.00
39 (7TH) HRN #142. 4.00 11.00
39 (8TH) HRN #154. 4.00 11.00
39 (9TH) HRN #165. 4.00 11.00
39 (10TH) HRN #167. 4.00 11.00
39 (11TH) HRN #166. 4.00 11.00
40 Mysteries. (8/47) 150.00 490.00
40 (2ND) HRN #62. 40.00 130.00
40 (3RD) HRN #75. 35.00 110.00
40 (4TH) HRN #92. 26.00 85.00
41 Twenty Years After. (9/47) 95.00 300.00
41 (2ND) HRN #62. 7.00 22.00
41 (3RD) HRN #78. 5.00 16.00
41 (4TH) HRN #156. 1.25 4.25
41 (5TH) HRN #167. 1.25 4.25
41 (6TH) HRN #169. 1.25 4.25
42 Swiss Family Robinson. HRN #42. (10/47) 35.00 110.00
42 (2ND) HRN #62. 7.00 22.00
42 (3RD) HRN #75. 4.00 13.00
42 (4TH) HRN #93. 4.00 11.00
42 (5TH) HRN #117. 4.00 11.00

CLASSIC COMICS #27

CLASSIC COMICS #32

CLASSIC STAR WARS #4

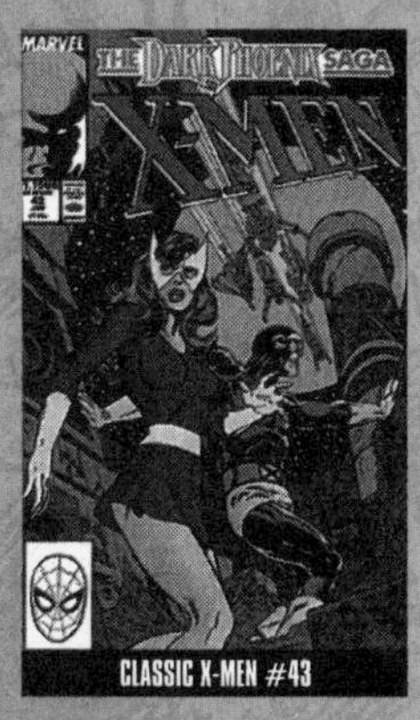

CLASSIC X-MEN #43

CLASSICS ILLUSTRATED #48

CLASSICS ILLUSTRATED #55

CLASSICS ILLUSTRATED #65

CLASSICS ILLUSTRATED #68

FAMOUS · FIRSTS

CLASSIC COMICS #1

Begun in 1941, *Classic Comics* brought literature to the funny books. Some 169 classics were published in the original series' run, starting with *The Three Musketeers*, *Ivanhoe*, and *The Count of Monte Cristo*.

42 (6TH) HRN #131. .... 4.00 11.00
42 (7TH) HRN #137. .... 4.00 11.00
42 (8TH) HRN #141. .... 4.00 11.00
42 (9TH) HRN #152. .... 4.00 11.00
42 (10TH) HRN #158. .... 1.25 4.25
42 (11TH) HRN #165. .... 1.25 4.25
42 (12TH) HRN #167. .... 1.25 4.25
42 (13TH) HRN #166. .... 1.25 4.25
42 (14TH) HRN #169. .... 1.25 4.25
43 Great Expectations. (11/47) SOTI 150.00 490.00
43 (2ND) HRN #62. .... 85.00 270.00
44 Mysteries of Paris. HRN #44. (12/47) 115.00 380.00
44 (2ND) HRN #62. .... 40.00 130.00
44 (3RD) HRN #78. .... 35.00 110.00
45 Tom Brown's School Days. HRN #44. (1/48) 20.00 65.00
45 (2ND) HRN #64. .... 7.00 22.00
45 (3RD) HRN #161. .... 4.00 11.00
45 (4TH) HRN #167. .... 1.50 5.50
45 (5TH) HRN #166. .... 1.50 5.50
46 Kidnapped. HRN #47. (4/48) ... 20.00 65.00
46 (2ND) HRN #62. .... 7.00 22.00
46 (3RD) HRN #78. .... 4.00 13.00
46 (4TH) HRN #87. .... 4.00 11.00
46 (5TH) HRN #118. .... 4.00 11.00
46 (6TH) HRN #131. .... 4.00 11.00
46 (7TH) HRN #140. .... 1.25 4.25
46 (8TH) HRN #150. .... 1.25 4.25
46 (9TH) HRN #164. .... 1.25 4.25
46 (10TH) HRN #167. .... 1.25 4.25
46 (11TH) HRN #166. .... 1.25 4.25
46 (12TH) HRN #169. .... 1.25 4.25
47 Twenty Thousand Leagues Under the Sea. HRN #47. (5/48) 17.00 55.00
47 (2ND) HRN #64. .... 7.00 22.00
47 (3RD) HRN #78. .... 4.00 13.00
47 (4TH) HRN #94. .... 4.00 11.00
47 (5TH) HRN #118. .... 4.00 11.00
47 (6TH) HRN #128. .... 4.00 11.00
47 (7TH) HRN #133. .... 4.00 11.00
47 (8TH) HRN #140. .... 1.25 4.25
47 (9TH) HRN #148. .... 1.25 4.25
47 (10TH) HRN #156. .... 1.25 4.25
47 (11TH) HRN #165. .... 1.25 4.25
47 (12TH) HRN #167. .... 1.25 4.25
47 (13TH) HRN #166. .... 1.25 4.25
47 (14TH) HRN #169. .... 1.25 4.25
48 David Copperfield. HRN #47. (6/48) 20.00 65.00
48 (2ND) HRN #64. .... 7.00 22.00
48 (3RD) HRN #87. .... 4.00 13.00
48 (4TH) HRN #121. .... 4.00 11.00
48 (5TH) HRN #130. .... 1.25 4.25
48 (6TH) HRN #140. .... 1.25 4.25
48 (7TH) HRN #148. .... 4.00 11.00
48 (8TH) HRN #156. .... 1.25 4.25
48 (9TH) HRN #167. .... 1.25 4.25
48 (10TH) HRN #166. .... 1.25 4.25
48 (11TH) HRN #169. .... 1.25 4.25
49 Alice in Wonderland. HRN #47. (7/48) 40.00 120.00
49 (2ND) HRN #64. .... 9.00 27.00
49 (3RD) HRN #85. .... 6.00 19.00
49 (4TH) HRN #155. .... 5.00 16.00
49 (5TH) HRN #165. .... 5.00 16.00
49 (6TH) HRN #167. .... 5.00 16.00
49 (7TH) HRN #166. .... 1.25 4.25
50 The Adventures of Tom Sawyer. HRN #51. (8/48) 22.00 70.00
50 (2ND) HRN #64. .... 5.00 16.00
50 (3RD) HRN #78. .... 4.00 11.00
50 (4TH) HRN #94. .... 4.00 11.00
50 (5TH) HRN #117. .... 4.00 11.00
50 (6TH) HRN #132. .... 4.00 11.00
50 (7TH) HRN #140. .... 4.00 11.00
50 (8TH) HRN #150. .... 4.00 11.00
50 (9TH) HRN #164. .... 4.00 11.00
50 (10TH) HRN #167. .... 1.25 4.25
50 (11TH) HRN #166. .... 1.25 4.25
50 (12TH) HRN #169. .... 1.25 4.25
51 The Spy. HRN #51. (9/48) ... 22.00 70.00
51 (2ND) HRN #89. .... 5.00 16.00
51 (3RD) HRN #121. .... 4.00 11.00
51 (4TH) HRN #139. .... 4.00 11.00
51 (5TH) HRN #156. .... 1.25 4.25
51 (6TH) HRN #167. .... 1.25 4.25
51 (7TH) HRN #166. .... 1.25 4.25
52 The House of the Seven Gables. HRN #53. (10/48) 20.00 65.00
52 (2ND) HRN #89. .... 5.00 16.00
52 (3RD) HRN #121. .... 4.00 11.00
52 (4TH) HRN #142. .... 4.00 11.00
52 (5TH) HRN #156. .... 1.25 4.25
52 (6TH) HRN #165. .... 1.25 4.25
52 (7TH) HRN #167. .... 1.25 4.25
52 (8TH) HRN #166. .... 1.25 4.25
52 (9TH) HRN #169. .... 1.25 4.25
53 A Christmas Carol. HRN #53. (11/48) 35.00 110.00
54 The Man in the Iron Mask. HRN #55. (12/48) 20.00 65.00
54 (2ND) HRN #93. .... 5.00 16.00
54 (3RD) HRN #111. .... 5.00 16.00
54 (4TH) HRN #142. .... 4.00 11.00
54 (5TH) HRN #154. .... 1.25 4.25
54 (6TH) HRN #165. .... 1.25 4.25
54 (7TH) HRN #167. .... 1.25 4.25
54 (8TH) HRN #166. .... 1.25 4.25
55 Silas Marner. HRN #55. (1/49) SOTI 20.00 65.00
55 (2ND) HRN #75. .... 7.00 22.00
55 (3RD) HRN #97. .... 4.00 11.00
55 (4TH) HRN #121. .... 4.00 11.00
55 (5TH) HRN #130. .... 1.25 4.25
55 (6TH) HRN #140. .... 1.25 4.25
55 (7TH) HRN #154. .... 1.25 4.25
55 (8TH) HRN #165. .... 1.25 4.25
55 (9TH) HRN #167. .... 1.25 4.25
55 (10TH) HRN #166. .... 1.25 4.25
56 The Toilers of the Sea. HRN #55. (2/49) 35.00 110.00
56 (2ND) HRN #165. .... 5.00 16.00
56 (3RD) HRN #167. .... 5.00 16.00
57 The Song of Hiawatha. HRN #55. (3/49) 20.00 65.00
57 (2ND) HRN #75. .... 5.00 16.00
57 (3RD) HRN #94. .... 5.00 16.00
57 (4TH) HRN #118. .... 4.00 11.00
57 (5TH) HRN #134. .... 4.00 11.00
57 (6TH) HRN #139. .... 1.25 4.25
57 (7TH) HRN #154. .... 1.25 4.25
57 (8TH) HRN #167. .... 1.25 4.25
57 (9TH) HRN #166. .... 1.25 4.25
58 The Prairie. HRN #60. (4/49) ... 20.00 65.00
58 (2ND) HRN #62. .... 10.00 33.00
58 (3RD) HRN #78. .... 5.00 16.00
58 (4TH) HRN #114. .... 4.00 11.00
58 (5TH) HRN #131. .... 4.00 11.00
58 (6TH) HRN #132. .... 4.00 11.00
58 (7TH) HRN #146. .... 4.00 11.00
58 (8TH) HRN #155. .... 1.25 4.25
58 (9TH) HRN #167. .... 1.25 4.25
58 (10TH) HRN #169. .... 1.25 4.25
59 Wuthering Heights. HRN #60. (5/49) 25.00 80.00
59 (2ND) HRN #85. .... 7.00 22.00
59 (3RD) HRN #156. .... 4.00 11.00
59 (4TH) HRN #167. .... 1.50 5.50
59 (5TH) HRN #169. .... 1.50 5.50
60 Black Beauty. HRN #62. (6/49) 20.00 65.00
60 (2ND) HRN #85. .... 7.00 22.00
60 (3RD) HRN #158. .... 5.00 16.00
60 (4TH) HRN #167. .... 4.00 11.00
60 (5TH) HRN #166. .... 4.00 11.00
61 The Woman in White. HRN #62. (7/49) 23.00 75.00
61 (2ND) HRN #156. .... 4.00 11.00
61 (3RD) HRN #167. .... 4.00 11.00
61 (4TH) HRN #166. .... 4.00 11.00
62 Western Stories. HRN #62. (8/49) 23.00 75.00
62 (2ND) HRN #89. .... 7.00 22.00
62 (3RD) HRN #121. .... 5.00 16.00
62 (4TH) HRN #137. .... 4.00 11.00
62 (5TH) HRN #152. .... 1.50 5.50
62 (6TH) HRN #167. .... 1.50 5.50
62 (7TH) HRN #166. .... 1.50 5.50
63 The Man Without a Country. HRN #62. (9/49) 23.00 75.00
63 (2ND) HRN #78. .... 7.00 22.00
63 (3RD) HRN #156. .... 5.00 16.00
63 (4TH) HRN #165. .... 1.25 4.25
63 (5TH) HRN #167. .... 1.25 4.25
63 (6TH) HRN #169. .... 1.25 4.25
64 Treasure Island. HRN #62. (10/49) 23.00 75.00
64 (2ND) HRN #82. .... 7.00 22.00
64 (3RD) HRN #117. .... 5.00 16.00
64 (4TH) HRN #131. .... 4.00 11.00
64 (5TH) HRN #138. .... 1.25 4.25

64 (6TH) HRN #146.	1.25	4.25
64 (7TH) HRN #158.	1.25	4.25
64 (8TH) HRN #165.	1.25	4.25
64 (9TH) HRN #167.	1.25	4.25
64 (10TH) HRN #166.	1.25	4.25
64 (11TH) HRN #169.	1.25	4.25
65 Benjamin Franklin. HRN #64. (11/49)	23.00	75.00
65 (2ND) HRN #131.	4.00	11.00
65 (3RD) HRN #154.	1.25	4.25
65 (4TH) HRN #167.	1.25	4.25
65 (5TH) HRN #169.	1.25	4.25
66 The Cloister and the Hearth. HRN #67. (12/49)	55.00	170.00
67 The Scottish Chiefs. HRN #67. (1/50)	23.00	75.00
67 (2ND) HRN #85.	7.00	22.00
67 (3RD) HRN #118.	4.00	11.00
67 (4TH) HRN #136.	4.00	11.00
67 (5TH) HRN #154.	1.75	6.50
67 (6TH) HRN #167.	1.75	6.50
68 Julius Caeser. HRN #70. (2/50) SOTI	23.00	75.00
68 (2ND) HRN #85.	7.00	22.00
68 (3RD) HRN #108.	5.00	16.00
68 (4TH) HRN #156.	5.00	16.00
68 (5TH) HRN #165.	5.00	16.00
68 (6TH) HRN #167.	1.25	4.25
68 (7TH) HRN #166.	1.25	4.25
68 (8TH) HRN #169.	1.25	4.25
69 Around the World in 80 Days. HRN #70. (3/50)	23.00	75.00
69 (2ND) HRN #87.	7.00	22.00
69 (3RD) HRN #125.	5.00	16.00
69 (4TH) HRN #136.	4.00	11.00
69 (5TH) HRN #146.	1.25	4.25
69 (6TH) HRN #152.	1.25	4.25
69 (7TH) HRN #164.	1.25	4.25
69 (8TH) HRN #167.	1.25	4.25
69 (9TH) HRN #166.	1.25	4.25
69 (10TH) HRN #169.	1.25	4.25
70 The Pilot. HRN #71. (4/50)	19.00	60.00
70 (2ND) HRN #92.	7.00	22.00
70 (3RD) HRN #125.	4.00	11.00
70 (4TH) HRN #156.	4.00	11.00
70 (5TH) HRN #167.	1.75	6.50
71 The Man Who Laughs. HRN #71. (5/50)	26.00	85.00
71 (2ND) HRN #165.	14.00	44.00
71 (3RD) HRN #167.	10.00	33.00
72 The Oregon Trail. HRN #73. (6/50)	19.00	60.00
72 (2ND) HRN #89.	7.00	22.00
72 (3RD) HRN #121.	5.00	16.00
72 (4TH) HRN #131.	4.00	11.00
72 (5TH) HRN #140.	1.25	4.25
72 (6TH) HRN #150.	1.25	4.25
72 (7TH) HRN #164.	1.25	4.25
72 (8TH) HRN #167.	1.25	4.25
72 (9TH) HRN #166.	1.25	4.25
73 The Black Tulip. HRN #75. (7/50)	50.00	160.00
74 Mr. Midshipman Easy. HRN #75. (8/50)	50.00	160.00
75 The Lady of the Lake. HRN #75. (9/50)	14.00	44.00
75 (2ND) HRN #85.	7.00	22.00
75 (3RD) HRN #118.	5.00	16.00
75 (4TH) HRN #139.	4.00	11.00
75 (5TH) HRN #154.	1.25	4.25
75 (6TH) HRN #165.	1.25	4.25
75 (7TH) HRN #167.	1.25	4.25
75 (8TH) HRN #169.	1.25	4.25
76 The Prisoner of Zenda. HRN #75. (10/50)	17.00	55.00
76 (2ND) HRN #85.	7.00	22.00
76 (3RD) HRN #111.	5.00	16.00
76 (4TH) HRN #128.	4.00	11.00
76 (5TH) HRN #152.	1.25	4.25
76 (6TH) HRN #165.	1.25	4.25
76 (7TH) HRN #167.	1.25	4.25
76 (8TH) HRN #169.	1.25	4.25
77 The Iliad. HRN #78. (11/50)	17.00	55.00
77 (2ND) HRN #87.	7.00	22.00
77 (3RD) HRN #121.	5.00	16.00
77 (4TH) HRN #139.	4.00	11.00
77 (5TH) HRN #150.	1.25	4.25
77 (6TH) HRN #165.	1.25	4.25
77 (7TH) HRN #167.	1.25	4.25
77 (8TH) HRN #166.	1.25	4.25
78 Joan of Arc. HRN #78. (12/50)	17.00	55.00
78 (2ND) HRN #87.	7.00	22.00
78 (3RD) HRN #113.	5.00	16.00
78 (4TH) HRN #128.	4.00	11.00
78 (5TH) HRN #140.	1.25	4.25
78 (6TH) HRN #150.	1.25	4.25
78 (7TH) HRN #159.	1.25	4.25
78 (8TH) HRN #167.	1.25	4.25
78 (9TH) HRN #166.	1.25	4.25
79 Cyrano de Bergerac. HRN #78. (1/51)	17.00	55.00
79 (2ND) HRN #85.	7.00	22.00
79 (3RD) HRN #118.	5.00	16.00
79 (4TH) HRN #133.	4.00	11.00
79 (5TH) HRN #156.	1.75	6.50
79 (6TH) HRN #167.	1.75	6.50
80 White Fang. HRN #79. (2/51)	17.00	55.00
80 (2ND) HRN #87.	7.00	22.00
80 (3RD) HRN #125.	5.00	16.00
80 (4TH) HRN #132.	4.00	11.00
80 (5TH) HRN #140.	1.25	4.25
80 (6TH) HRN #153.	1.25	4.25
80 (7TH) HRN #167.	1.25	4.25
80 (8TH) HRN #166.	1.25	4.25
80 (9TH) HRN #169.	1.25	4.25
81 The Odyssey. HRN #82. (3/51)	12.00	38.00
81 (2ND) HRN #167.	4.00	11.00
81 (3RD) HRN #169.	4.00	11.00
82 The Master of Ballantrae. HRN #82. (4/51)	12.00	38.00
82 (2ND) HRN #167.	4.00	11.00
82 (3RD) HRN #166.	4.00	11.00
83 The Jungle Book. HRN #85. (5/51)	12.00	38.00
83 (2ND) HRN #110.	1.25	4.25
83 (3RD) HRN #125.	1.25	4.25
83 (4TH) HRN #134.	1.25	4.25
83 (5TH) HRN #142.	1.25	4.25
83 (6TH) HRN #150.	1.25	4.25
83 (7TH) HRN #159.	1.25	4.25
83 (8TH) HRN #167.	1.25	4.25
83 (9TH) HRN #166.	1.25	4.25
84 The Gold Bug and Other Stories. HRN #85. (6/51)	26.00	85.00
84 (2ND) HRN #167.	9.00	27.00
85 The Sea Wolf. HRN #85. (7/51)	7.00	22.00
85 (2ND) HRN #121.	1.25	4.25
85 (3RD) HRN #132.	1.25	4.25
85 (4TH) HRN #141.	1.25	4.25
85 (5TH) HRN #161.	1.25	4.25
85 (6TH) HRN #167.	1.25	4.25
85 (7TH) HRN #169.	1.25	4.25
86 Under Two Flags. HRN #87. (8/51)	7.00	22.00
86 (2ND) HRN #117.	1.25	4.25
86 (3RD) HRN #139.	1.25	4.25
86 (4TH) HRN #158.	1.25	4.25
86 (5TH) HRN #167.	1.25	4.25
86 (7TH) HRN #169.	1.25	4.25
87 A Midsummer Night's Dream. HRN #87. (9/51)	7.00	22.00
87 (2ND) HRN #161.	1.25	4.25
87 (3RD) HRN #167.	1.25	4.25
87 (4TH) HRN #169.	1.25	4.25
88 Men of Iron. HRN #89. (10/51)	7.00	22.00
88 (2ND) HRN #154.	1.25	4.25
88 (3RD) HRN #167.	1.25	4.25
88 (4TH) HRN #166.	1.25	4.25
89 Crime and Punishment. HRN #89. (11/51)	7.00	22.00
89 (2ND) HRN #152.	1.25	4.25
89 (3RD) HRN #167.	1.25	4.25
89 (4TH) HRN #169.	1.25	4.25
90 Green Mansions. HRN #89. (12/51)	7.00	22.00
90 (2ND) HRN #148.	1.25	4.25
90 (3RD) HRN #165.	1.25	4.25
90 (4TH) HRN #167.	1.25	4.25
90 (5TH) HRN #169.	1.25	4.25
91 The Call of the Wild. HRN #92. (1/52)	7.00	22.00
91 (2ND) HRN #112.	1.25	4.25
91 (3RD) HRN #125.	1.25	4.25
91 (4TH) HRN #134.	1.25	4.25
91 (5TH) HRN #143.	1.25	4.25
91 (6TH) HRN #165.	1.25	4.25
91 (7TH) HRN #167.	1.25	4.25
91 (8TH) HRN #166.	1.25	4.25
91 (9TH) HRN #169.	1.25	4.25
92 The Courtship of Miles Standish. HRN #92. (2/52)	7.00	22.00
92 (2ND) HRN #165.	1.25	4.25
92 (3RD) HRN #167.	1.25	4.25
92 (4TH) HRN #166.	1.25	4.25
92 (5TH) HRN #169.	1.25	4.25
93 Pudd'nhead Wilson. HRN #94. (3/52)	7.00	22.00
93 (2ND) HRN #165.	1.25	4.25
93 (3RD) HRN #167.	1.25	4.25
93 (4TH) HRN #166.	1.25	4.25
94 David Balfour. HRN #94. (4/52)	7.00	22.00
94 (2ND) HRN #167.	1.25	4.25
94 (3RD) HRN #166.	1.25	4.25
95 All Quiet on the Western Front. HRN #96. (5/52)	7.00	22.00
95 (2ND) HRN #167.	4.00	11.00
96 Daniel Boone. HRN #97. (6/52)	7.00	22.00
96 (2ND) HRN #117.	1.25	4.25
96 (3RD) HRN #128.	1.25	4.25
96 (4TH) HRN #132.	1.25	4.25
96 (5TH) HRN #134.	1.25	4.25
96 (6TH) HRN #158.	1.25	4.25
96 (7TH) HRN #167.	1.25	4.25
96 (8TH) HRN #166.	1.25	4.25
97 King Solomon's Mines. HRN #96. (7/52)	7.00	22.00
97 (2ND) HRN #118.	1.25	4.25
97 (3RD) HRN #131.	1.25	4.25
97 (4TH) HRN #141.	1.25	4.25
97 (5TH) HRN #158.	1.25	4.25
97 (6TH) HRN #167.	1.25	4.25
97 (7TH) HRN #169.	1.25	4.25
98 The Red Badge of Courage. HRN #98. (8/52)	7.00	22.00
98 (2ND) HRN #118.	1.25	4.25
98 (3RD) HRN #132.	1.25	4.25
98 (4TH) HRN #142.	1.25	4.25
98 (5TH) HRN #152.	1.25	4.25
98 (6TH) HRN #161.	1.25	4.25
98 (7TH) HRN #167.	1.25	4.25
98 (8TH) HRN #166.	1.25	4.25
99 Hamlet. HRN #98. (9/52)	7.00	22.00
99 (2ND) HRN #121.	1.25	4.25
99 (3RD) HRN #141.	1.25	4.25
99 (4TH) HRN #158.	1.25	4.25
99 (5TH) HRN #167.	1.25	4.25
99 (6TH) HRN #166.	1.25	4.25
99 (7TH) HRN #169.	1.25	4.25
100 Mutiny on the Bounty. HRN #100. (10/52)	7.00	22.00
100 (2ND) HRN #117.	1.25	4.25
100 (3RD) HRN #132.	1.25	4.25
100 (4TH) HRN #142.	1.25	4.25
100 (5TH) HRN #155.	1.25	4.25
100 (6TH) HRN #167.	1.25	4.25
100 (7TH) HRN #169.	1.25	4.25
101 William Tell. HRN #101. (11/52)	7.00	22.00
101 (2ND) HRN #118.	1.25	4.25
101 (3RD) HRN #141.	1.25	4.25
101 (4TH) HRN #158.	1.25	4.25
101 (5TH) HRN #167.	1.25	4.25
101 (6TH) HRN #166.	1.25	4.25
101 (7TH) HRN #169.	1.25	4.25
102 The White Company. HRN #104. (12/52)	14.00	44.00
102 (2ND) HRN #165.	5.00	16.00
102 (3RD) HRN #167.	5.00	16.00
103 Men Against the Sea. HRN #104. (1/53)	7.00	22.00
103 (2ND) HRN #114.	1.25	4.25
103 (3RD) HRN #131.	1.25	4.25
103 (4TH) HRN #158.	1.25	4.25
103 (5TH) HRN #149.	1.25	4.25
103 (6TH) HRN #167.	1.25	4.25
104 Bring 'Em Back Alive. HRN #105. (2/53)	7.00	22.00
104 (2ND) HRN #118.	1.25	4.25
104 (3RD) HRN #133.	1.25	4.25
104 (4TH) HRN #150.	1.25	4.25
104 (5TH) HRN #158.	1.25	4.25
104 (6TH) HRN #167.	1.25	4.25
104 (7TH) HRN #169.	1.25	4.25
105 From the Earth to the Moon. HRN #106. (3/53)	7.00	22.00
105 (2ND) HRN #118.	1.25	4.25
105 (3RD) HRN #132.	1.25	4.25
105 (4TH) HRN #141.	1.25	4.25
105 (5TH) HRN #146.	1.25	4.25
105 (6TH) HRN #156.	1.25	4.25
105 (7TH) HRN #167.	1.25	4.25
105 (8TH) HRN #166.	1.25	4.25
105 (9TH) HRN #169.	1.25	4.25
106 Buffalo Bill. HRN #107. (4/53)	7.00	22.00
106 (2ND) HRN #118.	1.25	4.25
106 (3RD) HRN #132.	1.25	4.25
106 (4TH) HRN #142.	1.25	4.25
106 (5TH) HRN #161.	1.25	4.25
106 (6TH) HRN #167.	1.25	4.25
106 (7TH) HRN #166.	1.25	4.25
106 (8TH) HRN #169.	1.25	4.25
107 King of the Khyber Rifles. HRN #108. (5/53)	7.00	22.00
107 (2ND) HRN #118.	1.25	4.25
107 (3RD) HRN #146.	1.25	4.25
107 (4TH) HRN #158.	1.25	4.25
107 (5TH) HRN #167.	1.25	4.25
108 Knights of the Round Table. HRN #108. (6/53)	7.00	22.00
108 (2ND) HRN #117.	1.25	4.25
108 (3RD) HRN #165.	1.25	4.25
108 (4TH) HRN #167.	1.25	4.25
108 (5TH) HRN #166.	1.25	4.25
108 (6TH) HRN #169.	1.25	4.25
109 Pitcairn's Island. HRN #110. (7/53)	7.00	22.00
109 (2ND) HRN #165.	2.25	8.75
109 (3RD) HRN #167.	2.25	8.75
109 (4TH) HRN #166.	2.25	8.75

CLASSICS ILLUSTRATED #74

CLASSICS ILLUSTRATED #83

CLASSICS ILLUSTRATED #88

CLASSICS ILLUSTRATED #97

CLASSICS ILLUSTRATED #128

CLASSICS ILLUSTRATED #138

CLASSICS ILLUSTRATED #150

CLASSICS ILLUSTRATED #155

110 A Study in Scarlet. HRN #111. (8/53)
.... 28.00 90.00
110 (2ND) HRN #165. .... 14.00 44.00
111 The Talisman. HRN #112. (9/53) 12.00 38.00
111 (2ND) HRN #165. .... 1.75 6.50
111 (3RD) HRN #167. .... 1.75 6.50
111 (4TH) HRN #166. .... 1.75 6.50
112 The Adventures of Kit Carson. HRN #113. (10/53)
.... 12.00 38.00
112 (2ND) HRN #129. .... 1.25 4.25
112 (3RD) HRN #141. .... 1.25 4.25
112 (4TH) HRN #152. .... 1.25 4.25
112 (5TH) HRN #161. .... 1.25 4.25
112 (6TH) HRN #167. .... 1.25 4.25
112 (7TH) HRN #166. .... 1.25 4.25
113 The Forty-Five Guardsmen. HRN #114. (11/53)
.... 17.00 55.00
113 (2ND) HRN #166. .... 7.00 22.00
114 The Red Rover. HRN #115. (12/53)
.... 17.00 55.00
114 (2ND) HRN #166. (7/67) 7.00 22.00
115 How I Found Livingstone. HRN #116. (1/54)
.... 17.00 55.00
115 (2ND) HRN #167. .... 7.00 22.00
116 The Bottle Imp. HRN #117. (2/54) 17.00 55.00
116 (2ND) HRN #167. .... 7.00 22.00
117 Captains Courageous. HRN #118. (3/54)
.... 14.00 44.00
117 (2ND) HRN #167. .... 4.00 11.00
117 (3RD) HRN #169. .... 4.00 11.00
118 Rob Roy. HRN #119. (4/54) ... 17.00 55.00
118 (2ND) HRN #167. .... 7.00 22.00
119 Soldiers of Fortune. HRN #120. (5/54)
.... 17.00 55.00
119 (2ND) HRN #166. .... 4.00 11.00
119 (3RD) HRN #169. .... 2.25 8.75
120 The Hurricane. HRN #121. (6/54) 17.00 55.00
120 (2ND) HRN #166. (3/67) 7.00 22.00
121 Wild Bill Hickok. HRN #122. (7/54) 9.00 27.00
121 (2ND) HRN #132. .... 1.50 5.50
121 (3RD) HRN #141. .... 1.50 5.50
121 (4TH) HRN #154. .... 1.50 5.50
121 (5TH) HRN #167. .... 1.50 5.50
121 (6TH) HRN #166. .... 1.50 5.50
121 (7TH) HRN #169. .... 1.50 5.50
122 The Mutineers. HRN #123. (9/54) 7.00 22.00
122 (2ND) HRN #136. .... 1.50 5.50
122 (3RD) HRN #146. .... 1.50 5.50
122 (4TH) HRN #158. .... 1.50 5.50
122 (5TH) HRN #167. .... 1.50 5.50
122 (6TH) HRN #166. .... 1.50 5.50
123 Fang and Claw. HRN #124. (11/54)
.... 7.00 22.00
123 (2ND) HRN #133. .... 1.50 5.50
123 (3RD) HRN #143. .... 1.50 5.50
123 (4TH) HRN #154. .... 1.50 5.50
123 (5TH) HRN #167. .... 1.50 5.50
124 The War of the Worlds. HRN #125. (1/55)
.... 10.00 33.00
124 (2ND) HRN #131. .... 1.50 5.50
124 (3RD) HRN #141. .... 1.50 5.50
124 (4TH) HRN #148. .... 1.50 5.50
124 (5TH) HRN #156. .... 1.50 5.50
124 (6TH) HRN #165. .... 1.50 5.50
124 (7TH) HRN #167. .... 1.50 5.50
124 (8TH) HRN #166. .... 1.50 5.50
124 (9TH) HRN #169. .... 1.50 5.50
125 The Ox-Bow Incident. (3/55) ... 7.00 22.00
125 (2ND) HRN #143. .... 1.50 5.50
125 (3RD) HRN #152. .... 1.50 5.50
125 (4TH) HRN #149. .... 1.50 5.50
125 (5TH) HRN #167. .... 1.50 5.50
125 (6TH) HRN #166. .... 1.50 5.50
125 (7TH) HRN #169. .... 1.50 5.50
126 The Downfall. (5/55) 7.00 22.00
126 (2ND) HRN #167. .... 1.50 5.50
126 (3RD) HRN #166. .... 1.50 5.50
127 The King of the Mountains. HRN #128. (7/55)
.... 7.00 22.00
127 (2ND) HRN #167. .... 1.50 5.50
127 (3RD) HRN #166. .... 1.50 5.50
128 Macbeth. HRN #128. (9/55) ... 7.00 22.00
128 (2ND) HRN #143. .... 1.50 5.50
128 (3RD) HRN #158. .... 1.50 5.50
128 (4TH) HRN #167. .... 1.50 5.50
128 (5TH) HRN #166. .... 1.50 5.50
128 (6TH) HRN #169. .... 1.50 5.50
129 Davy Crockett. HRN #129. (11/55) 17.00 55.00
129 (2ND) HRN #167. .... 9.00 27.00
130 Caesar's Conquests. HRN #130. (1/56)
.... 7.00 22.00
130 (2ND) HRN #142. .... 1.50 5.50
130 (3RD) HRN #152. .... 1.50 5.50
130 (4TH) HRN #149. .... 1.50 5.50
130 (5TH) HRN #167. .... 1.50 5.50
131 The Covered Wagon. HRN #131. (3/56)
.... 7.00 22.00
131 (2ND) HRN #143. .... 1.50 5.50
131 (3RD) HRN #152. .... 1.50 5.50
131 (4TH) HRN #158. .... 1.50 5.50
131 (5TH) HRN #167. .... 1.50 5.50
131 (6TH) HRN #169. .... 1.50 5.50
132 The Dark Frigate. HRN #132. (5/56)
.... 7.00 22.00
132 (2ND) HRN #150. .... 1.50 5.50
132 (3RD) HRN #167. .... 1.50 5.50
132 (4TH) HRN #166. .... 1.50 5.50
133 The Time Machine. HRN #132. (7/56)
.... 10.00 33.00
133 (2ND) HRN #142. .... 1.50 5.50
133 (3RD) HRN #152. .... 1.50 5.50
133 (4TH) HRN #158. .... 1.50 5.50
133 (5TH) HRN #167. .... 1.50 5.50
133 (6TH) HRN #166. .... 1.50 5.50
133 (7TH) HRN #169. .... 1.50 5.50
134 Romeo and Juliet. HRN #134. (9/56)
.... 7.00 22.00
134 (2ND) HRN #161. .... 1.50 5.50
134 (3RD) HRN #167. .... 1.50 5.50
134 (4TH) HRN #166. .... 1.50 5.50
135 Waterloo. HRN #135. (11/56) 7.00 22.00
135 (2ND) HRN #153. .... 1.50 5.50
135 (3RD) HRN #167. .... 1.50 5.50
135 (4TH) HRN #166. .... 1.50 5.50
136 Lord Jim. HRN #136. (1/57) ... 7.00 22.00
136 (2ND) HRN #165. .... 1.50 5.50
136 (3RD) HRN #167. .... 1.50 5.50
136 (4TH) HRN #169. .... 1.50 5.50
137 The Little Savage. HRN #136. (3/57)
.... 7.00 22.00
137 (2ND) HRN #148. .... 1.50 5.50
137 (3RD) HRN #156. .... 1.50 5.50
137 (4TH) HRN #167. .... 1.50 5.50
137 (5TH) HRN #166. .... 1.50 5.50
137 (6TH) HRN #169. .... 1.50 5.50
138 A Journey to the Center of the Earth. HRN #136. (5/57)
.... 10.00 33.00
138 (2ND) HRN #146. .... 1.50 5.50
138 (3RD) HRN #156. .... 1.50 5.50
138 (4TH) HRN #158. .... 1.50 5.50
138 (5TH) HRN #167. .... 1.50 5.50
138 (6TH) HRN #166. .... 1.50 5.50
139 In the Reign of Terror. HRN #139. (7/57)
.... 7.00 22.00
139 (2ND) HRN #154. .... 1.50 5.50
139 (3RD) HRN #167. .... 1.50 5.50
139 (4TH) HRN #166. .... 1.50 5.50
140 On Jungle Trails. HRN #140. (9/57) 7.00 22.00
140 (2ND) HRN #150. .... 1.50 5.50
140 (3RD) HRN #160. .... 1.50 5.50
140 (4TH) HRN #167. .... 1.50 5.50
141 Castle Dangerous. HRN #141. (11/57)
.... 7.00 22.00
141 (2ND) HRN #152. .... 1.50 5.50
141 (3RD) HRN #167. .... 1.50 5.50
141 (4TH) HRN #166. .... 1.50 5.50
142 Abraham Lincoln. HRN #142. (1/58)
.... 7.00 22.00
142 (2ND) HRN #154. .... 1.50 5.50
142 (3RD) HRN #158. .... 1.50 5.50
142 (4TH) HRN #167. .... 1.50 5.50
142 (5TH) HRN #166. .... 1.50 5.50
142 (6TH) HRN #169. .... 1.50 5.50
143 Kim. HRN #143. (3/58) 7.00 22.00
143 (2ND) HRN #165. .... 1.50 5.50
143 (3RD) HRN #167. .... 1.50 5.50
143 (4TH) HRN #169. .... 1.50 5.50
144 The First Men in the Moon. HRN #143. (5/58)
.... 10.00 33.00
144 (2ND) HRN #152. .... 1.50 5.50
144 (3RD) HRN #153. .... 1.50 5.50
144 (4TH) HRN #161. .... 1.50 5.50
144 (5TH) HRN #167. .... 1.50 5.50
144 (6TH) HRN #166. .... 1.50 5.50
144 (7TH) HRN #169. .... 1.50 5.50
145 The Crisis. HRN #143. (7/58) ... 7.00 22.00
145 (2ND) HRN #156. .... 1.50 5.50
145 (3RD) HRN #167. .... 1.50 5.50
145 (4TH) HRN #166. .... 1.50 5.50
146 With Fire and Sword. HRN #143. (9/58)
.... 7.00 22.00
146 (2ND) HRN #156. .... 1.50 5.50
146 (3RD) HRN #167. .... 1.50 5.50
147 Ben-Hur. HRN #147. (11/58) 7.00 22.00
147 (2ND) HRN #152. .... 7.00 22.00
147 (3RD) HRN #153. .... 1.50 5.50
147 (4TH) HRN #158. .... 1.50 5.50
147 (5TH) HRN #167. .... 1.50 5.50
147 (6TH) HRN #166. .... 1.50 5.50
148 The Buccaneer. HRN #148. (1/59) 7.00 22.00
148 (2ND) HRN #568 (Classics Illustrated Junior).
.... 4.00 11.00
148 (3RD) HRN #167. .... 1.50 5.50
148 (4TH) HRN #169. .... 1.50 5.50
149 Off on a Comet. HRN #149. (3/59) 7.00 22.00
149 (2ND) HRN #155. .... 1.50 5.50
149 (3RD) HRN #149 (3/61). 1.50 5.50
149 (4TH) HRN #167. .... 1.50 5.50
149 (5TH) HRN #166. .... 1.50 5.50
150 The Virginian. HRN #150. (5/59) 12.00 38.00
150 (2ND) HRN #164. .... 4.00 11.00
150 (3RD) HRN #167. .... 4.00 11.00
151 Won by the Sword. HRN #150. (7/59)
.... 12.00 38.00
151 (2ND) HRN #164. .... 4.00 11.00
151 (3RD) HRN #167. .... 2.25 8.75
151 (4TH) HRN #166. .... 2.25 8.75
152 Wild Animals I Have Known. HRN #152. Cover & art: L.B. Cole. (9/59) 12.00 38.00
152 (2ND) HRN #149. .... 4.00 11.00
152 (3RD) HRN #167. .... 1.50 5.50
152 (4TH) HRN #169. .... 1.50 5.50
153 The Invisible Man. HRN #153. (11/59)
.... 10.00 33.00
153 (2ND) HRN #149. .... 1.50 5.50
153 (3RD) HRN #167. .... 1.50 5.50
153 (4TH) HRN #166. .... 1.50 5.50
153 (5TH) HRN #169. .... 1.50 5.50
154 The Conspiracy of Pontiac. HRN #154. (1/60)
.... 10.00 33.00
154 (2ND) HRN #167. .... 4.00 11.00
154 (3RD) HRN #166. .... 4.00 11.00
155 The Lion of the North. HRN #154. (3/60)
.... 10.00 33.00
155 (2ND) HRN #167. .... 4.00 11.00
155 (3RD) HRN #166. .... 4.00 11.00
156 The Conquest of Mexico. HRN #156. (5/60)
.... 10.00 33.00
156 (2ND) HRN #167. .... 1.50 5.50
156 (3RD) HRN #166. .... 1.50 5.50
156 (4TH) HRN #169. .... 1.50 5.50
157 Lives of the Hunted. HRN #156. (7/60)
.... 12.00 38.00
157 (2ND) HRN #167. .... 4.00 11.00
157 (3RD) HRN #166. .... 4.00 11.00
158 The Conspirators. HRN #156. (9/60)
.... 12.00 38.00
158 (2ND) HRN #167. .... 4.00 11.00
158 (3RD) HRN #166. .... 4.00 11.00
159 The Octopus. HRN #159. (11/60) 10.00 33.00
159 (2ND) HRN #167. .... 4.00 11.00
159 (3RD) HRN #166. .... 4.00 11.00
160 The Food of the Gods. HRN #159. (1/61)
.... 10.00 33.00
160 (2ND) HRN #167. .... 4.00 11.00
160 (3RD) HRN #166. .... 4.00 11.00
161 Cleopatra. HRN #161. (3/61) 10.00 33.00
161 (2ND) HRN #167. .... 4.00 11.00
161 (3RD) HRN #166. .... 4.00 11.00
162 Robur the Conqueror. HRN #162. (5/61)
.... 10.00 33.00
162 (2ND) HRN #167. .... 4.00 11.00
162 (3RD) HRN #166. .... 4.00 11.00
163 Master of the World. HRN #163. (7/61)
.... 10.00 33.00
163 (2ND) HRN #167. .... 4.00 11.00
163 (3RD) HRN #166. .... 4.00 11.00
164 The Cossack Chief. HRN #164. (No date)
.... 10.00 33.00
164 (2ND) HRN #167. .... 4.00 11.00
164 (3RD) HRN #166. .... 4.00 11.00
165 The Queen's Necklace. HRN #164. (1/62)
.... 10.00 33.00
165 (2ND) HRN #167. .... 4.00 11.00
165 (3RD) HRN #166. .... 4.00 11.00
166 Tigers and Traitors. HRN #165. (5/62)
.... 17.00 55.00
166 (2ND) HRN #167. .... 4.00 11.00
167 Faust. HRN #165. (8/62) ... 17.00 55.00
167 (2ND) HRN #167. .... 9.00 27.00
167 (3RD) HRN #166. .... 9.00 27.00
168 In Freedom's Cause. HRN #169. (Winter/69)
.... 17.00 55.00
169 Negro Americans - The Early Years. HRN #166.
.... 17.00 55.00
169 (2ND) HRN #169. .... 9.00 27.00

CLASSICS ILLUSTRATED EDUCATIONAL SERIES

GILBERTON (1951-1953)

NO# The Westinghouse Story. The Dreams Of A Man. (1953 giveaway) 16.00 50.00
1 Shelter Through The Ages. 15 cent cover price. (1951)
.... 16.00 50.00

CLASSICS ILLUSTRATED JR.

GILBERTON (1953-1971) PRICES ARE FOR ORIGINAL EDITIONS.

501 Snow White & the Seven Dwarfs. 16.00 50.00
502 The Ugly Duckling. 10.00 30.00
503 Cinderella. 7.00 20.00
504 The Pied Piper. 4.00 12.00
505 The Sleeping Beauty. 4.00 12.00
506 The Three Little Pigs. 4.00 12.00

507 Jack & the Beanstalk. 4.00 12.00
508 Goldilocks & the Three Bears. ... 4.00 12.00
509 Beauty and the Beast. 4.00 12.00
510 Little Red Riding Hood. 4.00 12.00
511 Puss-N-Boots. 2.75 10.00
512 Rumpelstiltskin. 2.75 10.00
513 Pinocchio. 2.75 10.00
514 The Steadfast Tin Soldier. 2.75 10.00
515 Johnny Appleseed. 2.75 10.00
516 Aladdin and His Lamp. 2.75 10.00
517 The Emperor's New Clothes. 2.75 10.00
518 The Golden Goose. 2.75 10.00
519 Paul Bunyan. 2.75 10.00
520 Thumbelina. 2.75 10.00
521 King of the Golden River. 2.75 10.00
522 The Nightingale. 2.75 10.00
523 The Gallant Tailor. 2.75 10.00
524 The Wild Swans. 2.75 10.00
525 The Little Mermaid. 2.75 10.00
526 The Frog Prince. 2.75 10.00
527 The Golden-Haired Giant. 2.75 10.00
528 The Penny Prince. 2.75 10.00
529 The Magic Servants. 2.75 10.00
530 The Golden Bird. 2.75 10.00
531 Rapunzel. 2.75 10.00
532 The Dancing Princesses. 2.75 10.00
533 The Magic Fountain. 2.75 10.00
534 The Golden Touch. 2.75 10.00
535 The Wizard of Oz. 2.75 10.00
536 The Chimney Sweep. 2.75 10.00
537 The Three Fairies. 2.75 10.00
538 Silly Hans. 2.75 10.00
539 The Enchanted Fish. 2.75 10.00
540 The Tinder-Box. 2.75 10.00
541 Snow White & Rose Red. 2.75 10.00
542 The Donkey's Tale. 2.75 10.00
543 The House in the Woods. 2.75 10.00
544 The Golden Fleece. 2.75 10.00
545 The Glass Mountain. 2.75 10.00
546 The Elves & the Shoemaker. 2.75 10.00
547 The Wishing Table. 2.75 10.00
548 The Magic Pitcher. 2.75 10.00
549 Simple Kate. 2.75 10.00
550 The Singing Donkey. 2.75 10.00
551 The Queen Bee. 2.75 10.00
552 The Three Little Dwarfs. 2.75 10.00
553 King Thrushbeard. 2.75 10.00
554 The Enchanted Deer. 2.75 10.00
555 The Three Golden Apples. 2.75 10.00
556 The Elf Mound. 2.75 10.00
557 Silly Willy. 2.75 10.00
558 The Magic Dish. 2.75 10.00
559 The Japanese Lantern. 2.75 10.00
560 The Doll Princess. 2.75 10.00
561 Hans Humdrum. 2.75 10.00
562 The Enchanted Pony. 2.75 10.00
563 The Wishing Well. 2.75 10.00
564 The Salt Mountain. 2.75 10.00
565 The Silly Princess. 2.75 10.00
566 Clumsy Hans. 2.75 10.00
567 The Bearskin Soldier. 2.75 10.00
568 The Happy Hedgehog. 2.75 10.00
569 The Three Giants. 2.75 10.00
570 The Pearl Princess. 2.75 10.00
571 How Fire Came to the Indians. ... 2.75 10.00
572 The Drummer Boy. 2.75 10.00
573 The Crystal Ball. 2.75 10.00
574 Brightboots. 2.75 10.00
575 The Fearless Prince. 2.75 10.00
576 The Princess Who Saw Everything. 2.75 10.00
577 The Runaway Dumpling. 2.75 10.00

CLASSICS ILLUSTRATED SPECIAL ISSUE
GILBERTON (1955-1962)
NO# The United Nations. 55.00 180.00
129 The Story Of Jesus. 8.00 24.00
132A The Story Of America. 8.00 24.00
135A The Ten Commandments. 8.00 24.00
138A Adventures In Science. 8.00 24.00
141A The Rough Rider. 8.00 24.00
144A Blazing The Trails West. 8.00 24.00
147A Crossing The Rockies. 8.00 24.00
150A Royal Canadian Mounted Police. 8.00 24.00
153A Men, Guns And Cattle. 8.00 24.00
156A The Atomic Age. 8.00 24.00
159A Rockets, Jets and Missiles. 8.00 24.00
162A The War Between the States. ... 8.00 24.00
165A To The Stars! 8.00 24.00
166A World War II. 8.00 24.00
167A Prehistoric World. 8.00 24.00

CLAW THE UNCONQUERED
DC (1975-1978)
1 1st: Claw. .... .75 2.00
2-8 .... .30 1.00
9 Origin: Claw. .... .30 1.00
10-12 .... .30 1.00

CLAY CODY GUNSLINGER
PINES (1957)
1 .... 8.00 25.00

CLEAN FUN STARRING SHOOGAFOOTS JONES
SPECIALTY (1945)
NO# 7.00 20.00

CLIMAX!
GILMOR (1955)
1 .... 13.00 40.00
2 .... 11.00 35.00

CLINT AND MAC
DELL FOUR COLOR SERIES (1958)
889 TV photo cover. (3/58) 23.00 75.00

CLOAK AND DAGGER
MARVEL (1983-1984)
1-4 .... .30 1.00

CLOAK AND DAGGER
MARVEL (1985-1987)
1-2 .... .50 1.50
3 Spider-Man. .... .50 1.50
4 Secret Wars II. .... .50 1.50
5 1st: Mayhem. .... .50 1.50
6-11 .... .50 1.50

CLOAK AND DAGGER
ZIFF-DAVIS (1952)
1 Cover: Norman Saunders. 26.00 85.00

CLOAK AND DAGGER (MUTANT MISADVENTURES)
MARVEL (1988-1991)
1 .... .75 2.50
2-8 .... .75 2.00
9 Double size. .... .75 2.50
10-18 .... .75 2.00
19 Double size. .... .75 2.50

CLOWN COMICS
HARVEY (1945-1946)
NO# 1st issue (Clown Comic Book). ... 10.00 30.00
2-3 .... 7.00 20.00

CLUB "16"
FAMOUS FUNNIES (1948)
1 .... 13.00 40.00
2-4 .... 8.00 25.00

CLUBHOUSE RASCALS
ME (1956)
1 .... 8.00 25.00
2 .... 5.00 15.00

CLUE COMICS
HILLMAN (1943-1947)
1 .... 125.00 400.00
2 .... 65.00 200.00
3-6 .... 40.00 125.00
7 .... 50.00 150.00
8-9 .... 31.00 100.00
10 1st & Origin: The Gun Master. 40.00 125.00
11 .... 31.00 100.00
12 Origin: Rockman. 40.00 125.00
V2#1-V2#2 Art: Simon & Kirby. 65.00 200.00
V2#3 Art: Simon & Kirby. Title changes to: Real Clue Crime Stories with V2#4. .... 65.00 200.00

CLUTCHING HAND, THE
ACG (1954)
1 .... 55.00 180.00

CLYDE BEATTY COMICS
COMMODORE (1953, 1956)
1 Movie photo cover. 50.00 150.00
1956 African Jungle Book. 13.00 40.00

CLYDE CRASHCUP
DELL (1963-1964)
1 .... 16.00 50.00
2-5 .... 8.00 25.00

C-M-O COMICS
CENTAUR (1942)
1 Contains Centaur costumed heroes. 190.00 600.00
2 .... 155.00 500.00

COCOMALT BIG BOOK OF COMICS
HARRY A. CHESLER (1938)
1 Giveaway. Rare. 400.00 1500.00

CODENAME: STRYKE FORCE
IMAGE/TOP COW (1994-CURRENT)
0 (5/95) .... .75 2.50
1 .... 1.00 3.00
1 (BLUE) 8.00 25.00
1 (GOLD) 6.00 17.00
2-5 .... .75 2.50
6-7 .... .50 1.95
8A With Cyblade poster by Bill Tucci. ... 1.50 5.00
8B With Shi poster by Marc Silvestri. ... 1.50 5.00
8C With Tempest poster by Billy Tan. ... 1.00 3.00
9-12 .... .50 1.95
13-14 .... .75 2.25
TPB Reprints 1st story arc. 2.50 9.95

CODENAME: FIREARM
MALIBU (1995)
0-3 .... .75 2.95

CODENAME: SPITFIRE
MARVEL (1987)
10 Previous title: Spitfire And The Troubleshooters. .... .30 1.00
11-13 .... .30 1.00

CODY OF THE PONY EXPRESS
CHARLTON (1955-1956)
8-10 .... 7.00 20.00

CODY OF THE PONY EXPRESS
FOX (1950-1951)
1 (9/50) 13.00 40.00
2 (11/50) 10.00 30.00
3 (1/51) 8.00 25.00

COLOSSAL COMICS
COLOSSAL (1944)
8 Scarce Canadian comic. 31.00 100.00

COLOSSAL FEATURES MAGAZINE
FOX (1950)
1 (#33 on cover) Cody Of The Pony Express, movie/serial tie-in. (5/50) 16.00 50.00
2 (#34 on cover) Cody Of The Pony Express, movie photo cover. (7/50) 16.00 50.00
3 (9/50) 13.00 40.00

COLOSSUS COMICS
SUN (1940)
1 .... 500.00 1600.00

COLOSSUS: GOD'S COUNTRY
MARVEL (1994)
1 Prestige format. 1.75 6.95

COLT .45
DELL (1958-1961)
1 (#924) From the 4-Color Series. TV photo cover. (8/58) 20.00 65.00
2 (#1004) From the 4-Color Series. TV photo cover. (6/59) 16.00 50.00
3 (#1058) From the 4-Color Series. TV photo cover. (11/59) 16.00 50.00
4 TV photo covers on all issues. 11.00 35.00
5-9 .... 11.00 35.00

COLUMBIA COMICS
WILLIAM H. WISE (1944)
1 Joe Palooka, Charlie Chan. 40.00 125.00

COMANCHE
DELL FOUR COLOR SERIES (1962)
1350 Movie photo cover (reprints "Tonka"). (3/62) 13.00 40.00

COMANCHEROS, THE
DELL FOUR COLOR SERIES (1962)
1300 Movie photo cover (John Wayne). 40.00 120.00

COMBAT
DELL (1961-1973)
1 .... 8.00 25.00
2-6 .... 4.00 12.00
7-12 .... 2.75 10.00
13-27 .... 2.25 8.00
28 Begin reprints. 1.50 5.00
29-40 .... 1.50 5.00

COMBAT
MARVEL(ATLAS) (1952-1953)
1 .... 23.00 75.00
2 Cover/Art: Russ Heath. 13.00 40.00
3-6 .... 10.00 30.00
7-11 .... 7.00 20.00

COMBAT CASEY
MARVEL(ATLAS) (1953-1957)
6 Previous title: War Combat. 14.00 44.00
7-10 .... 10.00 33.00
11-20 .... 7.00 22.00
21 1st Code Approved issue. 4.00 13.00

CLOAK AND DAGGER #10

CLOWN COMICS #2

CODENAME: STRYKE FORCE #4

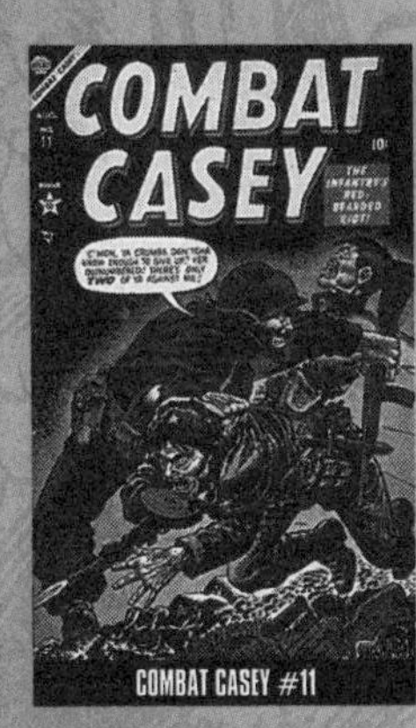

COMBAT CASEY #11

a b c d e f g h i j k l m n o p q r s t u v w x y z

a b c d e f g h i j k l m n o p q r s t u v w x y z

COMBAT KELLY #8

COMIC CALVALCADE #4

COMIC CALVALCADE #7

COMICS ON PARADE #9

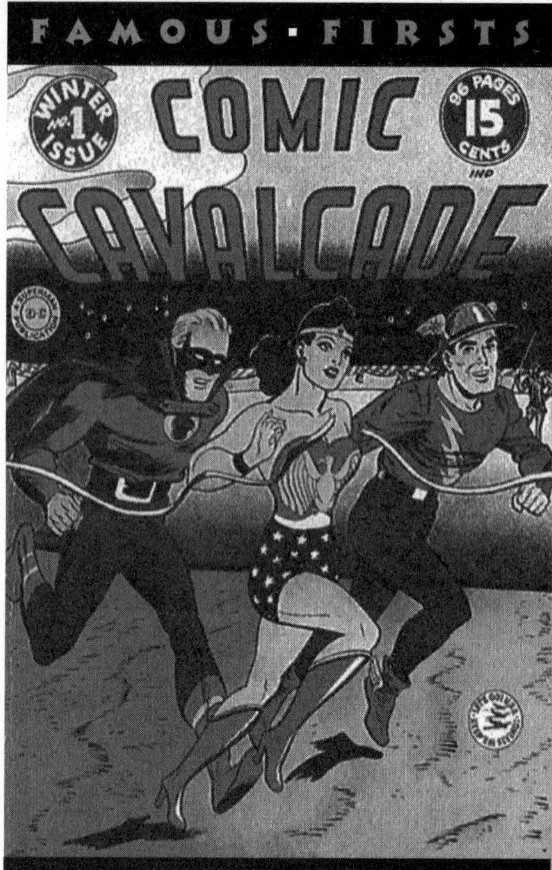

COMIC CAVALCADE #1

This comic combines three of DC's top characters—Green Lantern, Wonder Woman and The Flash—in one book (in separate adventures). Such a cavalcade of heroes needed 96 pages and a 15-cent price tag to cover it all.

22-30 .... 4.00 13.00
31-34 .... 4.00 11.00

COMBAT KELLY
MARVEL(ATLAS) (1951-1957)
1 1st: Combat Kelly. 35.00 110.00
2 .... 14.00 44.00
3-12 .... 10.00 33.00
13-24 .... 7.00 22.00
25-28 .... 5.00 16.00
29 1st Code Approved issue. 5.00 16.00
30-44 .... 5.00 16.00

COMBAT KELLY AND THE DEADLY DOZEN
MARVEL (1972-1973)
1 1st & Origin: new Combat Kelly. ... 1.25 4.00
2-9 .... .75 2.00

COMEDY COMICS
MARVEL(TIMELY) (1942-1946)
9 Previous title: Daring Mystery Comics. 400.00 1300.00
10 .... 280.00 900.00
11 .... 80.00 260.00
12-13 .... 40.00 130.00
14 1st & Origin: Super Rabbit. 80.00 260.00
15-20 .... 23.00 75.00
21-33 .... 20.00 65.00
34 Art: Wolverton. (Fall/46) Title changes to Margie Comics with #35. .... 40.00 130.00

COMEDY COMICS
MARVEL(TIMELY) (1948-1950)
1 .... 55.00 170.00
2 .... 26.00 85.00
3-5 .... 17.00 55.00
6-10 .... 11.00 34.00

COMIC ALBUM
DELL (1958-1962)
1 Donald Duck. 8.00 25.00
2 Bugs Bunny. 5.00 15.00
3 Donald Duck. 8.00 25.00
4 Tom & Jerry. 5.00 15.00
5 Woody Woodpecker. 5.00 15.00
6 Bugs Bunny. 5.00 15.00
7 Popeye. 5.00 15.00
8 Tom & Jerry. 5.00 15.00
9 Woody Woodpecker. 5.00 15.00
10 Bugs Bunny. 5.00 15.00
11 Popeye. 5.00 15.00
12 Tom & Jerry. 5.00 15.00
13 Woody Woodpecker. 5.00 15.00
14 Bugs Bunny. 5.00 15.00
15 Popeye. 5.00 15.00
16 Flintstones. 19.00 60.00
17 Space Mouse. 8.00 25.00
18 Three Stooges. Movie photo cover. 19.00 60.00

COMIC CAPERS
MARVEL(TIMELY) (1944-1946)
1 .... 31.00 100.00
2 .... 19.00 60.00
3-6 .... 16.00 50.00

COMIC CAVALCADE
DC (1942-1954)
1 Begin: Flash, Green Lantern, Wonder Woman.
.... 1300.00 5000.00
2 Begin: Mutt And Jeff. 400.00 1400.00
3 Begin: Sargon The Sorcerer. 290.00 950.00
4-6 .... 220.00 700.00
7 Lead story: Wonder Woman in "The Vulture's Nest!"
.... 190.00 600.00
8-12 .... 190.00 600.00
13 App: Solomon Grundy. 290.00 950.00
14-23 .... 160.00 525.00
24 App: Solomon Grundy. 220.00 700.00
25-28 .... 145.00 480.00
29 End: Flash, Green Lantern, Wonder Woman.
.... 145.00 480.00
30 Begin: Fox And The Crow. 75.00 240.00
31-36 .... 50.00 150.00
37-40 .... 40.00 120.00
41-50 .... 29.00 95.00
51-62 .... 45.00 140.00
63 .... 75.00 240.00

COMIC COMICS
FAWCETT (1946-1947)
1 Captain Kidd. 16.00 50.00
2 Art: Wolverton (4 pages). 25.00 80.00
3-10 Art: Wolverton. 25.00 80.00

COMIC LAND
FACT AND FICTION (1946)
1 .... 16.00 50.00

COMIC PAGES
CENTAUR (1939)
V3#4 Previous title: Funny Picture Stories. 155.00 500.00
V3#5-V3#6 .... 125.00 400.00

COMICS, THE
DELL (1937-1939)
1 1st: Tom Mix. 280.00 900.00
2 .... 140.00 460.00
3 Begin: Alley Oop series. 140.00 460.00
4-5 .... 125.00 400.00
6-11 .... 105.00 340.00

COMICS MAGAZINE, THE
COMICS MAGAZINE (1936)
1 Dr. Mystic by Siegel & Shuster (Superman prototype), story continues in More Fun Comics #14 as Dr. Occult whereupon character acquires cape, chest insignia, and flying ability. Title changes to Funny Pages with issue #2. 2600.00 10000.00

COMICS NOVEL
FAWCETT (1947)
1 Anarcho, Dictator of Death. 31.00 100.00

COMICS ON PARADE
UFS (1938-1955)
1 Begin: Tarzan, L'il Abner, etc. 500.00 1600.00
2 .... 170.00 550.00
3 .... 135.00 440.00
4-6 .... 100.00 330.00
7-12 .... 70.00 220.00
13-24 .... 50.00 160.00
25-28 .... 40.00 130.00
29 End: Tarzan. 40.00 130.00
30 Li'l Abner. 26.00 85.00
31 The Captain And The Kids. 26.00 85.00
32 Fritzi Ritz (with Nancy and Phil Fumble).
.... 26.00 85.00
33 Li'l Abner. 26.00 85.00
34 The Captain And The Kids. 26.00 85.00
35 Fritzi Ritz (with Nancy and Phil Fumble).
.... 26.00 85.00
36 Li'l Abner. 26.00 85.00
37 The Captain And The Kids. 26.00 85.00
38 Nancy and Fritzi Ritz. 26.00 85.00
39 Li'l Abner. 26.00 85.00
40 The Captain And The Kids. 26.00 85.00
41 Nancy and Fritzi Ritz. 17.00 55.00
42 Li'l Abner. 17.00 55.00
43 The Captain And The Kids. 17.00 55.00
44 Nancy and Fritzi Ritz. 17.00 55.00
45 Li'l Abner. 17.00 55.00
46 The Captain And The Kids. 17.00 55.00
47 Nancy and Fritzi Ritz. 17.00 55.00
48 Li'l Abner. 17.00 55.00
49 The Captain And The Kids. 17.00 55.00
50 Nancy and Fritzi Ritz. 17.00 55.00
51 Li'l Abner. 17.00 55.00
52 The Captain And The Kids. 17.00 55.00
53 Nancy and Fritzi Ritz. 17.00 55.00
54 Li'l Abner. 17.00 55.00
55 Nancy and Fritzi Ritz. 17.00 55.00
56 The Captain And The Kids. 17.00 55.00
57 Nancy and Fritzi Ritz. 17.00 55.00
58 Li'l Abner. 17.00 55.00
59 The Captain And The Kids. 17.00 55.00
60 Nancy and Fritzi Ritz. 17.00 55.00
61-70 Nancy and Fritzi Ritz. 14.00 44.00
71-76 Nancy. 14.00 44.00
77-80 Nancy and Sluggo. 14.00 44.00
81-104 Nancy and Sluggo. 10.00 33.00
SPECIAL The Captain And The Kids. (1948)
.... 11.00 35.00

COMICS READING LIBRARIES
KING
8 Prince Valiant. (1973) 5.00 15.00

16 Flash Gordon reprint. (1977) 5.00 15.00

COMICS REVUE
ST. JOHN (1947-1948)
1 Ella Cinders And Blackie. 5.00 15.00
2 Hap Hooper Comics. 5.00 15.00
3 Iron Vic. 5.00 15.00
4 Ella Cinders. 5.00 15.00
5 Gordo. 5.00 15.00

COMICS' GREATEST WORLD: ARCADIA
DARK HORSE (1993)
WEEK 1 "X" .75 2.00
WEEK 1A Platinum edition. 2.75 10.00
WEEK 2 "Pit Bulls" 1st: Pit Bulls. .50 1.50
WEEK 3 "Ghost" 1st: Ghost. 2.25 9.00
WEEK 4 "Monster" 1st: Monster. .50 1.50

COMICS' GREATEST WORLD: GOLDEN CITY
DARK HORSE (1993)
WEEK 1 "Rebel" 1st: Rebel. .50 1.25
WEEK 1A Gold edition. 2.75 10.00
WEEK 2 "Mecha" 1st: Mecha. .50 1.25
WEEK 3 "Titan" 1st: Titan. .50 1.25
WEEK 4 "Catalyst: Agents Of Change" 1st: Catalyst. .50 1.25

COMICS' GREATEST WORLD: STEEL HARBOR
DARK HORSE (1993)
WEEK 1 "Barb Wire" 1st: Barb Wire. 1.25 5.00
WEEK 2 "The Machine" .50 1.25
WEEK 3 "Wolf Gang" .50 1.25
WEEK 4 "Motorhead" .50 1.25

COMICS' GREATEST WORLD: VORTEX
DARK HORSE (1993)
WEEK 1 "Division 13" .30 1.00
WEEK 2 "Hero Zero" .30 1.00
WEEK 3 "King Tiger" .30 1.00
WEEK 4 "Out Of The Vortex" .30 1.00

COMICS' GREATEST WORLD: WILL TO POWER
DARK HORSE (1994)
WEEK 1-WEEK 9 .30 1.00

COMING OF APHRODITE, THE
HEROIC (1992)
GN 1.25 4.00

COMMANDER BATTLE ATOMIC SUB
ACG (1954-1955)
1 50.00 160.00
2 26.00 85.00
3 35.00 110.00
4-7 26.00 85.00

COMMANDO ADVENTURES
MARVEL(ATLAS) (1957)
1 17.00 55.00
2 12.00 38.00

COMPLETE BOOK OF COMICS AND FUNNIES
WILLIAM H. WISE (1945)
1 50.00 150.00

COMPLETE BOOK OF TRUE CRIME COMICS
WISE (1945)
NO# 132 pages. 95.00 300.00

COMPLETE COMICS
MARVEL(TIMELY) (1944)
2 Cover: Schomburg. Featuring The Young Allies. Previous title: Amazing Comics. 250.00 800.00

COMPLETE JUDGE ANDERSON
TITAN (1995)
TPB 7.00 22.00

COMPLETE JUDGE CALIGULA
TITAN (1995)
TPB 6.00 19.50

COMPLETE JUDGE CHILD QUEST
TITAN (1995)
TPB 8.00 24.00

COMPLETE JUDGE DREDD APOCALYPSE WAR
TITAN (1995)
TPB 8.00 24.00

COMPLETE JUDGE DREDD IN OZ
TITAN (1995)
TPB 8.00 24.50

COMPLETE JUDGE DREDD IN THE CURSED EARTH
TITAN (1994)
TPB 6.00 19.95

COMPLETE LOVE MAGAZINE
ACE (1951-1956)
1 (Vol.26 #2) 5.00 15.00
2 (Vol.26 #3) 5.00 15.00
3 (Vol.27 #1) 5.00 15.00
4-32 5.00 15.00

COMPLETE MYSTERY
MARVEL (1948-1949)
1 "Seven Dead Men." 75.00 240.00
2 "Jigsaw Of Doom!" 55.00 180.00
3 "Fear In The Night!" 55.00 180.00
4 "A Squealer Dies Fast!" Title changes to: True Complete Mystery with #5. 65.00 210.00

COMPLETE ROMANCE
AVON (1949)
1 "Women To Love" 50.00 150.00

CONAN
MARVEL (1995-CURRENT)
1-2 .75 2.95

CONAN CLASSIC
MARVEL (1994-CURRENT)
1-6 .50 1.50

CONAN SAGA
MARVEL (1987-CURRENT) MAGAZINE
1 1.50 5.00
2-3 1.25 4.00
4-10 1.00 3.50
11-35 1.00 3.00
36-57 .75 2.50
58-74 .75 2.25
75 1.00 3.95
76-91 .75 2.25

CONAN THE ADVENTURER
MARVEL (1994-1995)
1 Young Conan. .75 2.50
2-14 .50 1.50

CONAN THE BARBARIAN
MARVEL (1970-1994)
1 1st & Origin: Conan. "The Coming Of Conan!" by Barry Smith. 60.00 185.00
2 Art: Barry Smith. 20.00 65.00
3 Art: Barry Smith. Low distribution. 40.00 125.00
4-5 Art: Barry Smith. 17.00 55.00
6-9 Art: Barry Smith. 11.00 35.00
10-11 Art: Barry Smith. Double size. 14.00 45.00
12-13 Art: Barry Smith. 10.00 30.00
14-15 Art: Barry Smith. 13.00 40.00
16 Art: Barry Smith. Reprint: Savage Tales #1. 7.00 22.00
17-18 4.00 13.00
19-20 Art: Barry Smith. 7.00 22.00
21-22 Art: Barry Smith. 7.00 20.00
23 Art: Barry Smith. 1st: Red Sonja. 10.00 30.00
24 Art: Barry Smith. 1st full story: Red Sonja. 10.00 30.00
25 2.75 10.00
26 2.00 7.00
27-36 1.50 5.00
37 Cover/Art: Neal Adams. 2.00 7.00
38-43 1.00 3.00
44-45 1.50 5.00
46-57 1.00 3.00
58 1st: Belit. 1.00 3.00
59-80 .75 2.00
81-99 .50 1.50
100 Double size. .50 1.50
101-114 .50 1.50
115 Double size. 1.00 3.50
116-240 .50 1.50
241 1.75 6.00
242-255 .50 1.50
256-274 .50 1.25
275 Final issue. Double size. .75 2.50

CONAN THE BARBARIAN ANNUAL
MARVEL (1973-1993)
1 (King Size Special). (1973) 4.00 12.00
2 (1976) 1.00 3.50
3 (1977) .75 2.25
4 (1978) .50 1.75
5 (1979) .50 1.75
6 (1981) .50 1.75
7 (1982) .50 1.75
8 (1983) .50 1.75
9 (1984) .50 1.50
10-12 .50 1.50

CONAN THE BARBARIAN MOVIE SPECIAL
MARVEL (1982)
1-2 .50 1.50

CONAN THE BARBARIAN: RED NAILS
MARVEL (1989)
1 Art: Barry Windsor-Smith. 1.00 3.50

CONAN THE DESTROYER
MARVEL (1985)
1 Movie tie-in. .30 1.00
2 .30 1.00

CONAN THE KING
MARVEL (1984-1989)
20 Previous title: King Conan. .30 1.00
21-55 .30 1.00

CONAN THE SAVAGE
MARVEL (1995-CURRENT) MAGAZINE
1-2 .75 2.95

CONCRETE
DARK HORSE (1987-1989)
1 5.00 15.00
2 1.50 5.00
3 Origin: Concrete. 1.50 5.00
4 1.50 5.00
5-10 1.25 4.00

CONCRETE: EARTH DAY
DARK HORSE (1990)
1 1.75 6.00

CONCRETE: ECLECTICA
DARK HORSE (1993)
1 .75 2.50
2 .75 2.50

CONCRETE: FRAGILE CREATURES
DARK HORSE (1991-1992)
1-4 .75 2.50
TPB Reprints issues #1-4. 5.00 15.95

CONCRETE: KILLER SMILE
DARK HORSE (1994)
1-4 .75 2.95

CONCRETE: LAND AND SEA
DARK HORSE (1989)
1 1.00 3.00

CONCRETE: NEW LIFE
DARK HORSE (1989)
1 1.00 3.00

CONCRETE: THE COMPLETE SHORT STORIES 1986-1989
DARK HORSE (1994)
HC Hardcover Limited Edition (2000 copies). 12.00 39.95

CONFESSIONS ILLUSTRATED
EC (1956)
1 29.00 95.00
2 25.00 80.00

CONFESSIONS OF LOVE
ARTFUL (1950)
1 31.00 100.00
2 19.00 60.00

CONFESSIONS OF LOVE
STAR (1952-1953)
4 (3/53) 7.00 20.00
5 (5/53) 7.00 20.00
6 (8/53) Title changes to Confessions Of Romance with #7. 7.00 20.00
11 (#1) (7/52) 13.00 40.00
12 (9/52) 10.00 30.00
13 (11/52) 8.00 25.00
14 (1/53) 8.00 25.00

CONFESSIONS OF ROMANCE
STAR (1953-1954)
7 Previous title: Confessions Of Love. 13.00 40.00
8 8.00 25.00
9-11 10.00 30.00

CONFESSIONS OF THE LOVELORN
ACG (1954-1960)
52 Previous title: Lovelorn. 19.00 60.00

COMIC'S GREATEST WORLD: GOLDEN CITY WEEK 1

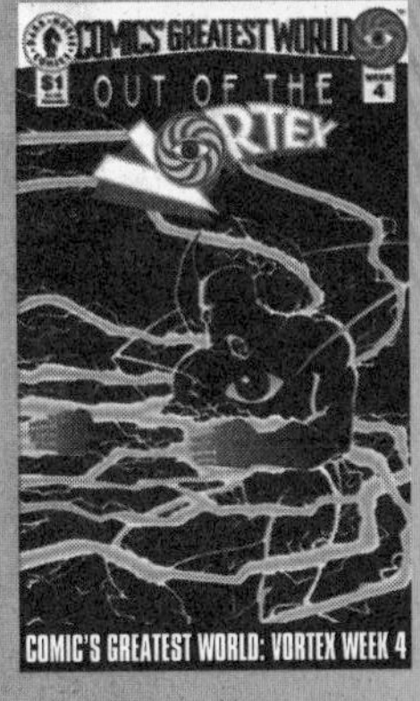

COMIC'S GREATEST WORLD: VORTEX WEEK 4

CONAN THE ADVENTURER #11

CONAN THE BARBARIAN ANNUAL #2

CONTEST OF CHAMPIONS #1

COO COO COMICS #28

COSMIC POWERS #1

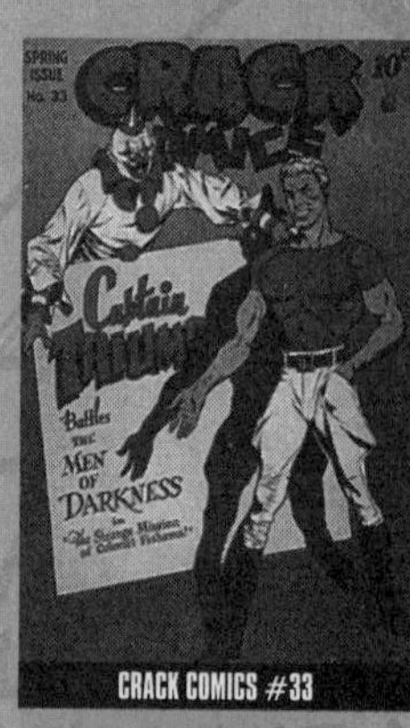

CRACK COMICS #33

53 7.00 20.00
54 16.00 50.00
55-56 7.00 20.00
57-114 2.25 8.00

CONGO BILL
DC (1954-1955)
1 "The Golden Gorilla!" and more. 190.00 600.00
2 "The River Of 1000 Crocodiles!" 145.00 480.00
3 "The Girl Who Loved Danger!" 110.00 360.00
4 "Hunter Of Jungle Sounds!" 110.00 360.00
5 "Bombo, Rogue Elephant!" 1st Code Approved issue. 95.00 300.00
6 "Gorilla City!" 75.00 240.00
7 "The Unarmed Safari!" 75.00 240.00

CONQUEROR, THE
DELL FOUR COLOR SERIES (1956)
690 Movie photo cover (John Wayne). (4/56) 40.00 125.00

CONQUEROR COMICS
ALBRECHT (1945)
NO# 23.00 75.00

CONQUEST
FAMOUS FUNNIES (1955)
1 11 Adventure Stories. 10.00 30.00

CONTACT COMICS
AVIATION (1944-1946)
1 (NO# on cover) (7/44). 50.00 150.00
2 31.00 100.00
3-4 28.00 90.00
5-6 25.00 80.00
7-12 22.00 70.00

CONTEST OF CHAMPIONS
MARVEL (1982)
1 1st Marvel mini-series. 1.75 6.00
2-3 1.75 6.00

CONTINUM
CONTINUM (1988)
1 1st: Dawn by Joe Linsner. 20.00 80.00

COO COO COMICS
STANDARD (1942-1952)
1 1st & Origin: Supermouse. 35.00 110.00
2 17.00 55.00
3-12 10.00 33.00
13-36 7.00 22.00
37-40 5.00 16.00
41 Art: Frazetta (2 pages). 20.00 65.00
42-48 5.00 16.00
49 3-D effect. 17.00 55.00
50-51 3-D effect. 14.00 44.00
52-62 4.00 11.00

COOKIE
ACG (1946-1955)
1 23.00 75.00
2 13.00 40.00
3-12 10.00 30.00
13-24 7.00 20.00
25-55 5.00 15.00

COOL CAT
PRIZE (1962)
V9#1-V9#2 7.00 20.00

COPPER CANYON
FAWCETT (1950)
NO# Movie photo cover (Ray Milland & Hedy Lamarr). From the Fawcett Movie Comic series. 28.00 90.00

CORKY AND WHITE SHADOW
DELL FOUR COLOR SERIES (1956)
707 (5/56) 10.00 30.00

COSMIC POWERS
MARVEL (1994)
1-6 .75 2.00

COSMIC POWERS UNLIMITED
MARVEL (1995-CURRENT)
1-2 1.00 3.95

COSMO CAT
FOX (1946-1947)
1 20.00 65.00
2 11.00 34.00
3 Origin: Cosmo Cat. 13.00 40.00
4-10 7.00 23.00

COSMO THE MERRY MARTIAN
ARCHIE (1958-1959)
1 28.00 90.00
2 15.00 48.00
3-6 11.00 36.00

COUNT OF MONTE CRISTO, THE
DELL FOUR COLOR SERIES (1957)
794 Movie tie-in. (4/57) 22.00 70.00

COUNTDOWN
DELL (1967)
12-150-710 Movie photo cover. 8.00 25.00

COURAGE COMICS
J. EDWARD SLAVIN (1945)
1-2 13.00 40.00
3 (#77 on cover). 13.00 40.00

COURTSHIP OF EDDIE'S FATHER
DELL (1970)
1 TV photo cover. 8.00 25.00
2 TV photo cover. 7.00 20.00

COUTOO
DARK HORSE (1994-CURRENT)
1 1st: Lieutenant Joe Kraft. 1.00 3.50

COVERED WAGONS, HO!
DELL FOUR COLOR SERIES (1957)
814 (7/57) 10.00 30.00

COW PUNCHER
AVON (1947-1949)
1 50.00 150.00
2 40.00 125.00
3-7 31.00 100.00

COW PUNCHER
REALISTIC (1953)
2 Art: Joe Kubert. 13.00 40.00

COWBOY ACTION
MARVEL(ATLAS) (1955-1956)
5 Previous title: Western Thrillers. 13.00 40.00
6-10 10.00 30.00
11 Title changes to Quick-Trigger Western with #12. 10.00 30.00

COWBOY COMICS
CENTAUR (1938)
13 Previous title: Star Ranger. 220.00 700.00
14 Title changes to Star Ranger Funnies with #15. 155.00 500.00

COWBOY LOVE
CHARLTON (1955)
28 Previous title: Romantic Story. 5.00 15.00
29-31 5.00 15.00

COWBOY LOVE
FAWCETT (1949-1950)
1 Photo cover, (Rocky Lane photo back cover). 26.00 85.00
2-4 Photo cover. 7.00 22.00
5 Photo cover (Bill Boyd). 10.00 33.00
6 Photo cover. 7.00 22.00
7 Photo cover. Art: Al Williamson. 10.00 33.00
8-11 Photo cover. 5.00 16.00

COWBOY ROMANCES
MARVEL(ATLAS) (1949-1950)
1 Photo cover. 25.00 80.00
2 Movie photo cover: Streets Of Laredo. 35.00 110.00
3 Photo cover. Title changes to Young Men with #4. 17.00 55.00

COWBOY WESTERN
CHARLTON (1954-1958)
49 Previous title: Cowboy Western Heroes. 8.00 25.00
50-66 8.00 25.00
67 Title changes to Wild Bill Hickok And Jingles with #68. 8.00 25.00

COWBOY WESTERN COMICS
CHARLTON (1948-1953)
17 Previous title: Jack-In-The-Box Comics. 20.00 65.00
18-19 Art: Joe Orlando. 12.00 38.00
20-23 9.00 27.00
24 Movie photo cover: Three Faces West. 17.00 55.00
25 Movie photo cover: Northwest Stampede. 17.00 55.00
26 Movie photo cover: Indian Scout. 17.00 55.00
27 Movie photo cover: Sunset Carson Rides Again. 100.00 330.00
28-29 Sunset Carson. 50.00 160.00
30 Movie photo cover: Deadline. 17.00 55.00
31-34 9.00 27.00
35-36 Sunset Carson. 50.00 160.00
37 20.00 65.00
38 9.00 27.00
39 (8/52) Title changes to Space Western Comics with #40. 9.00 27.00
46 (10/53) Previous title: Space Western Comics. Title changes to Cowboy Western Heroes with #47. 9.00 27.00

COWBOY WESTERN HEROES
CHARLTON (1953-1954)
47 Previous title: Cowboy Western Comics. 8.00 25.00
48 Title changes to Cowboy Western with #49. 8.00 25.00

COWBOYS 'N' INJUNS COMICS
ME (1946-1947)
1 16.00 50.00
2-5 10.00 30.00

COWBOYS AND INDIANS (A-1 SERIES)
ME (1949-1952)
6 (A-1 #23). 10.00 30.00
7 (A-1 #41). 7.00 20.00
8 (A-1 #48). 7.00 20.00

COWGIRL ROMANCES
FICTION HOUSE (1950-1952)
1 40.00 130.00
2 20.00 65.00
3-6 14.00 44.00
7-9 10.00 33.00
10 Art: Frazetta, Williamson, Kamen, Baker. 40.00 130.00
11-12 10.00 33.00

COWGIRL ROMANCES
MARVEL (1950)
28 Movie photo cover (Copper Canyon). 40.00 125.00

COYOTE
MARVEL(EPIC) (1983-1986)
1-10 .50 1.50
11 1st Todd McFarlane art at Marvel. 1.50 5.00
12-14 Art: McFarlane. .50 1.50
15-16 .50 1.50

CRACK COMICS
QUALITY (1940-1949)
1 Art: Lou Fine. 1st & Origin Black Condor. 700.00 2500.00
2 300.00 1100.00
3-6 230.00 750.00
7-12 155.00 500.00
13-18 115.00 370.00
19-23 95.00 310.00
24 End: Black Condor by Lou Fine. 95.00 310.00
25-26 80.00 250.00
27 1st & Origin: Captain Triumph. 190.00 625.00
28-30 55.00 180.00
31 End: Black Condor. 55.00 180.00
32-48 40.00 120.00
49-61 28.00 90.00
62 Title changes to Crack Western with #63. 28.00 90.00

CRACK WESTERN
QUALITY (1949-1953)
63 Previous title: Crack Comics. 25.00 80.00
64-65 Art: Reed Crandall. 26.00 85.00
66-69 22.00 70.00
70 1st & Origin: The Whip. 25.00 80.00
71 25.00 80.00
72 Photo cover (Tim Holt). 28.00 90.00
73 19.00 60.00
74-76 Reed Crandall art. 16.00 50.00
77 13.00 40.00
78-79 Reed Crandall art. 16.00 50.00
80 13.00 40.00
81 Reed Crandall art. 16.00 50.00
82 13.00 40.00
83 Reed Crandall art. 16.00 50.00
84 Reed Crandall art, Paul Gustavson cover. 20.00 65.00

CRACKAJACK FUNNIES
DELL (1938-1942)
1 280.00 900.00
2 125.00 400.00
3-4 110.00 350.00
5 80.00 250.00
6 65.00 200.00
7-8 50.00 150.00
9 1st & Begin: Red Ryder. 95.00 300.00
10-12 50.00 150.00
13-14 40.00 125.00
15 Begin: Tarzan by ERB. 65.00 200.00
16-24 55.00 175.00
25 1st & Begin: The Owl. 110.00 350.00
26-30 65.00 200.00
31 70.00 225.00

32-35 .... 50.00 150.00
36 End: Tarzan. 50.00 150.00
37-38 .... 40.00 125.00
39 1st & Begin: Andy Panda. 40.00 125.00
40-43 .... 31.00 100.00

CRACKED
MAJOR (1958-CURRENT) MAGAZINE
1 .... 19.00 60.00
2 .... 10.00 30.00
3-6 .... 7.00 22.00
7-12 .... 5.00 15.00
13-24 .... 4.00 12.00
25-40 .... 2.75 10.00
41-60 .... 2.25 8.00
61-90 .... 1.75 6.00
91-150 .... 1.00 3.00
151-200 .... .75 2.00
201-300 .... .50 1.50

CRASH COMICS
TEM (1940)
1 Intro: Strongman. Art: Simon & Kirby. (5/40) 400.00 1200.00
2 Art: Simon & Kirby. (6/40) 190.00 600.00
3 Art: Simon & Kirby. (7/40) 190.00 600.00
4 Art: Simon & Kirby. 1st & Origin: Catman. (9/40) 400.00 1200.00
5 Art: Simon & Kirby. App: Catman. Title changes to Catman Comics. (11/40) 125.00 400.00

CRASH DIVE
20TH CENTURY FOX (1943)
NO# Movie giveaway (4 pages). From the Cinema Comics Herald series. 16.00 50.00

CRASH RYAN
MARVEL (1984-1985)
1-4 .... .30 1.00

CRAZY!
MARVEL (1973)
1-3 .... .75 2.00

CRAZY
MARVEL (1973-1983) MAGAZINE
1 .... 1.50 5.00
2-57 .... .30 1.00
58 Super Special. .... .75 2.00
59-81 .... .30 1.00
82 Super Special. .... .75 2.00
83-94 .... .30 1.00

CRAZY
MARVEL(ATLAS) (1953-1954)
1 Cover/Art: Bill Everett. 35.00 110.00
2 .... 28.00 90.00
3-7 .... 25.00 80.00

CRAZY, MAN, CRAZY
CHARLTON (1956)
V3#1 Art: Wolverton, Ward, Ditko. ... 75.00 240.00

CRAZYMAN
CONTINUITY (1992)
1-3 .... .75 2.50

CREATURE, THE
DELL (1963-1964)
12-142-302 Movie tie-in. 10.00 30.00
12-142-410 Movie tie-in (reprint). ... 4.00 12.00

CREATURES OF THE ID
TUNDRA (1990)
1 1st: Frank Einstein (Madman). 2.75 10.00

CREATURES ON THE LOOSE
MARVEL (1971-1975)
10 Art: Berni Wrightson. 1st: King Kull. 9.00 28.00
11-37 .... 1.00 3.00

CREED
HALL OF HEROES (1994-1995)
1 1st: Creed. 6.00 20.00
2 .... 6.00 22.00

CREED
LIGHTNING (1995)
1 Mini-series. .... .75 3.00
1 (GOLD) 8.00 25.00

CREEPY
WARREN (1964-1985) MAGAZINE
1 Cover: Jack Davis. Art: Frank Frazetta (6 pages). 1st Warren magazine in comics format—see After Hours #1 for 1st Warren magazine. 25.00 85.00
2 .... 10.00 30.00
3-7 Cover: Frazetta. 6.00 18.00
8 .... 6.00 18.00
9 Cover: Frazetta. 1st: Berni Wrightson published work. 6.00 18.00
10 .... 6.00 18.00
11 Cover: Frazetta. 6.00 18.00
12 .... 6.00 18.00
13 .... 4.00 12.00
14 Art: Neal Adams. 8.00 25.00
15-16 Cover: Frazetta. 4.00 12.00
17-25 .... 4.00 12.00
26-40 .... 2.75 10.00
41-47 .... 2.00 7.00
48 1973 Annual. 5.00 15.00
49-54 .... 2.00 7.00
55 1974 Annual. 5.00 15.00
56-64 .... 2.00 7.00
65 1975 Annual. 5.00 15.00
66-143 .... 2.00 7.00
144 Double size. 2.00 7.00
145 .... 2.00 7.00
146 Double size. 2.50 9.00

CREEPY FEARBOOK
HARRIS (1993)
1 Re-intro: Vampirella. 8.00 25.00

CREEPY YEARBOOK
WARREN (1968-1972) MAGAZINE
1968 .... 5.00 15.00
1969-1970 .... 4.00 12.00
1971-1972 .... 2.75 10.00

CRIME AND JUSTICE
CHARLTON (1951-1955)
1 .... 31.00 100.00
2 .... 13.00 40.00
3-6 .... 10.00 30.00
7-8 .... 8.00 25.00
9 "Comics Vs. Crime!" 25.00 80.00
10-15 .... 10.00 30.00
16-17 .... 8.00 25.00
18 Art: Steve Ditko. 23.00 75.00
19-26 .... 7.00 20.00

CRIME AND PUNISHMENT
LEV GLEASON (1948-1955)
1 .... 40.00 120.00
2 .... 15.00 50.00
3 SOTI 20.00 65.00
4-6 .... 12.00 38.00
7-12 .... 9.00 27.00
13-24 .... 7.00 22.00
25-38 .... 5.00 16.00
39 "The Five Dopes." 10.00 33.00
40-44 .... 5.00 16.00
45 "Hophead Killer!" 10.00 33.00
46-58 .... 5.00 16.00
59 SOTI 26.00 85.00
60-65 .... 5.00 16.00
66 3-D effect. 50.00 160.00
67-68 3-D effect. 35.00 110.00
69 .... 10.00 33.00
70-74 .... 5.00 16.00

CRIME CAN'T WIN
MARVEL(ATLAS) (1950-1952)
1 (#41) 25.00 80.00
2 (#42) 12.00 38.00
3 (#43) 14.00 44.00
4-12 .... 10.00 33.00

CRIME CASES
MARVEL(ATLAS) (1950-1952)
1 (#24) 15.00 50.00
2 (#25)-4 (#27) 12.00 38.00
5-12 .... 10.00 33.00

CRIME CLINIC
ZIFF-DAVIS (1951-1952)
1 (#10) 26.00 85.00
2 (#11) 20.00 65.00
3 SOTI 23.00 75.00
4-5 .... 20.00 65.00

CRIME DETECTIVE COMICS
HILLMAN (1948-1953)
1 .... 26.00 85.00
2 .... 14.00 44.00
3-8 .... 10.00 33.00
9 SOTI 45.00 140.00
10-12 .... 10.00 33.00
13 (V2#1) 9.00 27.00
14 (V2#2) 9.00 27.00
15 (V2#3) 9.00 27.00
16 (V2#4) 9.00 27.00
17 (V2#5) 9.00 27.00
18 (V2#6) 9.00 27.00
19 (V2#7) 9.00 27.00
20 (V2#8) 9.00 27.00
21 (V2#9) 9.00 27.00
22 (V2#10) 9.00 27.00
23 (V2#11) 9.00 27.00
24 (V2#12) 9.00 27.00
25 (V3#1) 7.00 22.00
26 (V3#2) 7.00 22.00
27 (V3#3) 7.00 22.00
28 (V3#4) 7.00 22.00
29 (V3#5) 7.00 22.00
30 (V3#6) 7.00 22.00
31 (V3#7) 7.00 22.00
32 (V3#8) 7.00 22.00

CRIME DETECTOR
TIMOR (1954)
1 .... 16.00 50.00
2-4 .... 10.00 30.00
5 Art: Jay Disbrow. 16.00 50.00

CRIME DOES NOT PAY
LEV GLEASON (1942-1955)
22 (#23) #23 inside, actually #22 (Killer Lepke, Panther Man, Esposito Brothers on cover). Previous title: Silver Streak Comics. 300.00 1100.00
23 John Dillinger, Baby Face Nelson, John Hamilton on cover. 180.00 .... 575.00
24 1st: Mr. Crime. 180.00 575.00
25-30 .... 85.00 280.00
31-40 .... 55.00 170.00
41 1st & Origin: Mr. Common Sense. 35.00 110.00
42 .... 35.00 110.00
43-50 .... 26.00 85.00
51-75 .... 13.00 40.00
76-85 .... 11.00 34.00
86-100 .... 9.00 28.00
101-120 .... 7.00 23.00
121-130 .... 6.00 17.00
131-146 .... 4.00 11.00
ANNUAL 1 (1944) 125.00 400.00
ANNUAL 2 (1945-1948) 95.00 300.00
ANNUAL 3 (1949-1953) 95.00 300.00

CRIME EXPOSED
MARVEL(ATLAS) (1948-1952)
1 (6/48) 35.00 110.00
1A (12/50) 20.00 65.00
2 .... 17.00 55.00
3-6 .... 14.00 44.00
7-14 .... 10.00 33.00

CRIME FIGHTERS
MARVEL(ATLAS) (1954-1955)
11 .... 12.00 38.00
12-13 .... 10.00 33.00

CRIME FIGHTING DETECTIVE
STAR (1950-1952)
11 Previous title: Criminals On The Run. 12.00 38.00
12-13 .... 10.00 33.00
14 Reprint: Law Crime #2. .... 14.00 44.00
15-18 .... 10.00 33.00
19 Title changes to Shock Detective Cases with #20. .... 10.00 33.00

CRIME FILES
STANDARD (1952)
5 .... 31.00 100.00
6 .... 19.00 60.00

CRIME ILLUSTRATED
EC (1955)
1 .... 28.00 90.00
2 .... 22.00 70.00

CRIME INCORPORATED
SEE CRIMES INCORPORATED.

CRIME MACHINE, THE
SKYWALD (1971) MAGAZINE
1-2 .... 2.75 10.00

CRIME MUST LOSE!
MARVEL(ATLAS) (1950-1952)
4 .... 17.00 55.00
5-6 .... 14.00 44.00
7-12 .... 12.00 38.00

CRIME MUST PAY THE PENALTY!
ACE (1948-1955)
1 (#33) (2/48) 23.00 75.00
2 .... 16.00 50.00
3 .... 11.00 35.00
4-10 .... 8.00 25.00
11-24 .... 5.00 16.00
25-45 .... 4.00 12.00
46 Title changes to Penalty with #47. .... 4.00 12.00

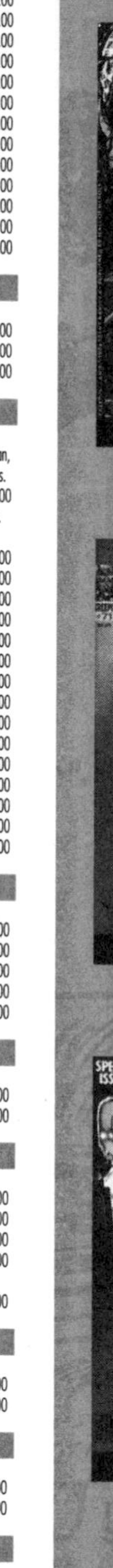

CREED #1 (HALL OF HEROES)

CREEPY #71

CREEPY #100

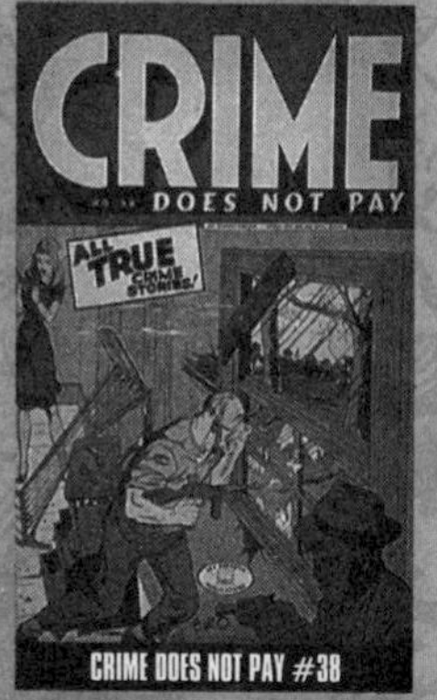

CRIME DOES NOT PAY #38

CRIME SUSPENSTORIES #16

CRISIS ON INFINITE EARTHS #8

CROSSOVER CLASSICS: MARVEL & DC TPB

THE CROW TPB

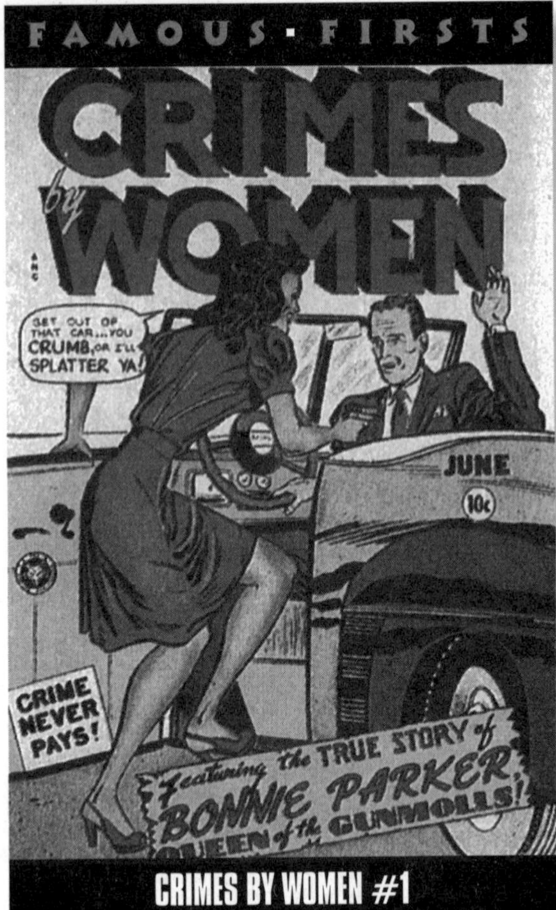

CRIMES BY WOMEN #1

A forerunner to today's Bad Girl books, this 1948 gem combined good girl art with crime stories and had parents swooning! It proved to be a favorite with doomsayers who thought comics were corrupting the young.

CRIME MYSTERIES
RIBAGE (1952-1954)

1	75.00	240.00
2	55.00	180.00
3	40.00	120.00
4 Classic gruesome cover.	75.00	240.00
5-9	29.00	95.00
10-12	25.00	80.00
13 1st Angelo Torres art in comics.	40.00	120.00
14	29.00	95.00
15 Gruesome acid-in-face cover.	40.00	120.00

CRIME ON THE RUN
ST. JOHN (1954)

8 From Approved Comics series.	13.00	40.00

CRIME PATROL
EC (1948-1950)

7 Captain Crime. Previous title: International Crime Patrol.	125.00	400.00
8-14	105.00	340.00
15 1st: Crypt Keeper. (12-1/50)	700.00	2500.00
16 Title changes to The Crypt Of Terror with #17.	400.00	1500.00

CRIME REPORTER
ST. JOHN (1948)

1 "Death Makes A Deadline!" (8/48)	50.00	150.00
2 Cover: Matt Baker. SOTI (10/48)	95.00	300.00
3 Cover: Matt Baker. "The Matinee Murders!" (12/48)	31.00	100.00

CRIME SMASHER
FAWCETT (1948)

1 "The Unlucky Rabbit's Foot!"	85.00	275.00

CRIME SMASHERS
RIBAGE (1950-1953)

1 SOTI	105.00	340.00
2 Cover: Kubert.	55.00	170.00
3-4	35.00	110.00
5 Art: Wallace Wood.	55.00	170.00
6-12	31.00	100.00
13-15	28.00	90.00

CRIME SUSPENSTORIES
EC (1950-1955)

1 "Murder May Boomerang."	180.00	575.00
1A Identical to #1, except #15 blacked out inside front cover.	280.00	900.00
2	105.00	340.00
3-6	80.00	250.00
7-8	70.00	230.00
9-12	55.00	170.00
13-15	45.00	140.00
16	55.00	170.00
17 Art: Williamson/Frazetta (6 pages).	55.00	180.00
18	35.00	110.00
19 SOTI	45.00	140.00
20 SOTI	55.00	170.00
21	35.00	110.00
22-23	45.00	140.00
24-27	35.00	110.00

CRIME SUSPENSTORIES
EC(COCHRAN) (1992-1994)

1 Reprints EC originals.	.75	2.00
2-9	.75	2.00
ANNUAL 1 Reprint: 1st 5 issues.	2.25	8.95

CRIMEFIGHTERS
MARVEL(ATLAS) (1948-1949)

1	25.00	80.00
2	16.00	50.00
3	13.00	40.00
4-9	10.00	30.00
10 Also see Crime Fighters (2 words).	10.00	30.00

CRIMES BY WOMEN
FOX (1948-1951)

1	140.00	460.00
2	85.00	280.00
3 SOTI	85.00	280.00
4-5	70.00	230.00
6	85.00	280.00
7-9	70.00	230.00
10 SOTI	85.00	280.00
11 "Bow And Arrow Killer!" (2/50)	70.00	230.00
12-15	70.00	230.00
54 Reprint (1954).	35.00	110.00

CRIMES INCORPORATED
FOX (1950-1951)

NO# 132 page giant.	25.00	80.00
1 (#12 inside).	16.00	50.00
2 Title changes to Crime Incorporated.	13.00	40.00
3	13.00	40.00

CRIMINALS ON THE RUN
NOVELTY (1948-1949)

1 (V4#1 on cover). Previous title: Young King Cole.	25.00	80.00
2 (V4#2 on cover).	17.00	55.00
3 (V4#3 on cover).	17.00	55.00
4 (V4#4 on cover).	17.00	55.00
5 (V4#5 on cover).	17.00	55.00
6 (V4#6 on cover).	17.00	55.00
7 Cover: L. B. Cole. (V4#7 on cover).	25.00	80.00
8 (V4#8 on cover).	17.00	55.00
9 (V4#9 on cover).	17.00	55.00
10 Title changes to Crime Fighting Detective with #11.	14.00	44.00

CRISIS ON INFINITE EARTHS
DC (1985-1986)

1 1st: Pariah. 1st: Blue Beetle II.	2.50	9.00
2 1st: Anti-Monitor.	2.00	7.00
3	1.75	6.00
4 1st: Lady Quark. 1st & origin: Dr. Light II.	1.75	6.00
5	1.75	6.00
6 1st: Captain Atom.	1.75	6.00
7 Death: Supergirl. Double size.	2.50	9.00
8 Death: Flash.	2.75	10.00
9-12	1.75	6.00

CRITTERS
FANTAGRAPHICS (1986-1990)

1	1.00	3.00
2-12	.75	2.00
13-22	.50	1.50
23 Alan Moore.	1.50	5.00
24-49	.50	1.50
50 Double size.	1.50	5.00

CROSS
DARK HORSE (1995-CURRENT)

0	.75	2.50

CROSSFIRE
ECLIPSE (1984-1988)

1-26	.30	1.00

CROSSFIRE AND RAINBOW
ECLIPSE (1986)

1-3	.30	1.00
4 Cover: Dave Stevens.	.75	2.00

CROSSOVER CLASSICS: THE MARVEL/DC COLLECTION
MARVEL/DC COMICS (1995)

TPB Reprints company crossovers.	7.00	22.95

CROW, THE
CALIBER (1989-1990)

1	26.00	85.00
1 (2ND) 2nd printing.	1.50	5.00
1 (3RD) 3rd printing.	1.00	3.00
2	14.00	45.00
2 (2ND) 2nd printing.	1.00	3.00
2 (3RD) 3rd printing.	1.00	3.00
3 Limited print run.	16.00	50.00
4	11.00	35.00

CROW, THE
KITCHEN SINK (1992)

1-2	2.25	8.00
3	4.00	12.00
TPB The Crow Collected. Reprints all Crow stories with some new material.	5.00	15.95

CROWN COMICS
MCCOMBS (1944-1949)

1	55.00	170.00
2-3 Art: Matt Baker.	25.00	80.00
4-6 Cover/Art: Matt Baker.	35.00	110.00
7 Cover: Baker. Art: Feldstein, Kamen.	35.00	110.00

8 Art: Matt Baker. 26.00 85.00
9 17.00 55.00
10 Begin: Voodah. 20.00 65.00
11-19 20.00 65.00

CRUSADER FROM MARS
ZIFF-DAVIS (1952)
1 70.00 230.00
2 55.00 170.00

CRUSADER RABBIT
DELL FOUR COLOR SERIES (1956-1957)
735 (10/56) 55.00 180.00
805 (5/57) 50.00 160.00

CRUSADERS
GUILD (1982) MAGAZINE SIZE
1 1st: Southern Knights. Title changes to Southern Knights with #2. 1.75 6.00

CRY FOR DAWN
CFD (1989-1994)
1 Art: Joseph Linsner (all issues). 50.00 150.00
1 (2ND) 2nd printing. 19.00 60.00
1 (3RD) 3rd printing. With Dawn Poster. 10.00 30.00
2 20.00 60.00
3 15.00 45.00
4 10.00 30.00
5 13.00 40.00
6-7 2.75 10.00
8 2.25 8.00
9 1.50 5.00
4A Signed & numbered. 20.00 65.00
5 (2ND) 2nd printing (new cover). 7.00 20.00
5A Signed & numbered. Rare. 26.00 85.00
6A-9A Signed & numbered. 16.00 50.00

CRY FOR DAWN: SUBTLE VIOLENTS
SEE SUBTLE VIOLENTS

CRYIN' LION COMICS
WILLIAM H. WISE (1944-1945)
1 25.00 80.00
2-3 13.00 40.00

CRYING FREEMAN (PART 1)
VIZ (1989)
1 1st: Crying Freeman. 1.25 4.50
2-8 1.00 3.50

CRYING FREEMAN (PART 2)
VIZ (1990)
1-9 1.25 4.00

CRYING FREEMAN (PART 3)
VIZ (1991)
1-10 1.50 5.00

CRYING FREEMAN (PART 4)
VIZ (1992)
1-3 1.50 5.00
4-8 .75 2.75

CRYING FREEMAN (PART 5)
VIZ (1992)
1-11 .75 2.75

CRYPT OF SHADOWS
MARVEL (1973-1975)
1 Reprint: Adventure Into Terror #7. 1.50 5.00
2-6 1.00 3.00
7-12 .75 2.00
13-21 .50 1.50

CRYPT OF TERROR
EC (1950)
17 Previous title: Crime Patrol. 500.00 1700.00
18 300.00 1100.00
19 "Ghost Ship!" Title changes to Tales From The Crypt #20. 310.00 1000.00

CRYPT OF TERROR, THE
EC(COCHRAN) (1992-1994)
1 Reprints EC originals. .75 2.00
2-10 .75 2.00

CRYPT OF TERROR
EAST COAST (1973)
1 Reprint. 1.25 4.00

CURLY KAYOE
DELL FOUR COLOR SERIES (1958)
871 (1/58) 8.00 25.00

CURLY KAYOE COMICS
UFS (1946-1947)
1 16.00 50.00
2 11.00 35.00
3-8 7.00 20.00

CURSE OF RUNE
MALIBU (1995-CURRENT)
1 Two different covers exist. .75 2.50
2-3 .75 2.50

CUSTER'S LAST FIGHT
AVON (1950)
NO# "Massacre At Little Big Horn" 25.00 80.00

CYBERFORCE
IMAGE (1992-1993)
0 Origin: Cyberforce. .75 2.50
1 1st: Ripclaw. 1st: Ballistic. 1st: Heatwave. 1st: Cyberforce. 1st: Stryker. 1st: Cyblade. 1st: Impact. 1st: Velocity. 1st: Timmie. 1st: Cyberdata. With Image #0 coupon. 2.25 8.00
1 (GOLD) 6.00 17.00
1A Without coupon. .75 2.00
2 1.00 3.00
2 (SILVER) 5.00 15.00
3 .75 2.00
3 (GOLD) 5.00 15.00
4 .75 2.00
TPB Reprints mini-series plus new material. 4.00 12.95

CYBERFORCE
IMAGE/TOP COW (1993-CURRENT)
1 1.00 3.00
2-7 .50 1.95
8 Image X book. .75 2.50
9-10 .50 1.95
10 GOLD-10 SILVER Limited edition (500) from 1995 Oz Con. 8.00 25.00
10A Alternate cover (painted backgrounds). 1.75 6.00
11-12 .50 1.95
13-15 .75 2.25
ANNUAL 1 .75 2.50
ASHCAN 1 (San Diego) 2.25 8.00
ASHCAN 1A Signed & numbered. 2.75 10.00
SB 1-SB 2 Sourcebook. .75 2.50
TPB "Assault With A Deadly Woman" Reprints issues #4-7. 2.50 9.95

CYBERFORCE ORIGINS SPECIAL
IMAGE (1994-CURRENT)
1 O: Cyblade. .75 2.50
2 O: Stryker. .75 2.50

CYBERFORCE/CODENAME STRYKEFORCE: OPPOSING FORCES
IMAGE (1995)
1 .75 2.50

CYBERFROG
HALL OF HEROES (1994)
1 1st: Cyberfrog. 2.75 10.00
2 2.75 10.00

CYBERRAD
CONTINUITY (1991-1992)
1 Art: Neal Adams. .75 2.50
2-7 .75 2.50
TRADE PB 2.75 10.00

CYBERRAD
CONTINUITY (1993-1994)
1 Deathwatch 2000, pt.7. .75 2.50
2 Deathwatch 2000, pt.14. .75 2.50

CYBERSPACE 3000
MARVEL (1993-1994)
1 .75 2.95
2-12 .50 1.75

CYBLADE/SHI SPECIAL
IMAGE/CRUSADE (1995)
1 The Battel For Independents. .75 2.95

CYBORG
CANNON (1989)
1 Movie tie-in (distributed through video promotion). With photos inside. .30 1.00

CYBRID
MAXIMUM PRESS (1995-CURRENT)
1 .75 2.95

CYCLONE COMICS
BILBARA (1940)
1 (6/40) 145.00 480.00
2 (7/40) 110.00 360.00
3 (8/40) 85.00 270.00
4 (9/40) 85.00 270.00
5 (11/40) 85.00 270.00

CYCLOPS: RETRIBUTION
MARVEL (1994)
TPB Reprints Marvel Comics Presents story. 1.50 5.95

DAFFY
DELL/GOLD KEY/WHITMAN (1953-1983)
1 (#457) From the 4-Color Series. (3/53) 17.00 55.00
2 (#536) From the 4-Color Series. (2/54) 8.00 25.00
3 (#615) From the 4-Color Series. (2/55) 8.00 25.00
4-11 5.00 15.00
12-19 2.25 8.00
20-40 1.50 5.00
41-60 1.00 3.00
61-100 .50 1.50
101-145 .30 1.00

DAGAR, DESERT HAWK
FOX (1948-1949)
14 Previous title: All Great. 85.00 270.00
15 55.00 180.00
16-17 50.00 150.00
18-20 40.00 120.00
21 SOTI. "Flood of Death." 65.00 210.00
22-23 40.00 120.00

DAGWOOD COMICS
HARVEY (1950-1965)
1 16.00 50.00
2 10.00 30.00
3-6 8.00 25.00
7-12 7.00 20.00
13-24 5.00 15.00
25-50 4.00 12.00
51-80 2.25 8.00
81-100 2.00 7.00
101-130 1.75 6.00
131-140 1.50 5.00

DAISY AND HER PUPS
HARVEY (1951-1952)
1 (#21 on cover). 2.75 10.00
2 (#22 on cover). 2.25 8.00
3 (#23 on cover). 2.25 8.00
4 (#24 on cover). 2.25 8.00
5 (#25 on cover). 2.25 8.00
6 (#26 inside). 2.25 8.00
7 (#27 inside). 2.25 8.00
8-18 2.00 7.50

DAISY COMICS
EASTERN (1936)
NO# Joe Palooka, Buck Rogers and others. 75.00 240.00

DAISY DUCK'S DIARY
DELL FOUR COLOR SERIES (1954-1961)
600 (11/54) 11.00 35.00
659 (11/55) 7.00 20.00
743 (11/56) 7.00 20.00
858 (11/57) 8.00 25.00
948 (11/58) 7.00 20.00
1055 Art: Carl Barks. (11/59) 23.00 75.00
1150 Art: Carl Barks. (12/60) 23.00 75.00
1247 (11/61) 7.00 20.00

DAISY HANDBOOK
DAISY (1946-1955)
1 Red Ryder & more. (1946) 65.00 200.00
2 Art: Basil Wolverton. (1948) 65.00 200.00
3 (No#) Red Ryder Gun Book. 50.00 150.00

DAKOTA LIL
FAWCETT (1949)
NO# Movie photo cover (George Montgomery, Marie Windsor, Rod Cameron). From the Fawcett Movie Comic series. 50.00 160.00

DAKTARI
DELL (1967-1969)
1 TV photo covers on all issues. 6.00 18.00
2-4 2.75 10.00

DALE EVANS COMICS
DC (1948-1952)
1 Photo covers on issues #1, 2, 4-14. 125.00 400.00
2 70.00 230.00
3 35.00 110.00
4-6 55.00 170.00
7-8 35.00 110.00
9-11 31.00 100.00
12-14 28.00 90.00
15-18 25.00 80.00
19-24 20.00 65.00

DALE EVANS, QUEEN OF THE WEST
DELL (1953-1959)
1 (#479) From the 4-Color Series. Photo cover. (7/53) 40.00 125.00

CYBERFORCE MINI-SERIES #1

CYBERFORCE REG. SERIES #3

DALE EVANS COMICS #2

DAMAGE #15

DANGER UNLIMITED #1

DAREDEVIL #9

DAREDEVIL #38

DAREDEVIL #254

2 (#528) From the 4-Color Series. Photo cover. (1/54) 20.00 65.00
3 Photo covers on all issues. 19.00 60.00
4 16.00 50.00
5-12 13.00 40.00
13-22 11.00 35.00

DALGODA
FANTAGRAPHICS (1984-1986)
1-20 .30 1.00

DALTON BOYS, THE
AVON (1951)
1 19.00 60.00

DAMAGE
DC (1994-CURRENT)
0 .50 1.95
1-4 .50 1.75
5-12 .50 1.95
13-15 .75 2.25

DAMAGE CONTROL
MARVEL (1989)
1-4 .30 1.00

DAMAGE CONTROL
MARVEL (1989-1990)
1-4 .30 1.00

DAMAGE CONTROL
MARVEL (1991)
1-4 .30 1.00

DAN'L BOONE
ME (1955-1957)
1 16.00 50.00
2-8 8.00 25.00

DANCES WITH DEMONS
MARVEL (1993)
1 .75 2.95
2-6 .50 1.95

DANDY COMICS
EC (1947-1948)
1 50.00 160.00
2 40.00 120.00
3-7 29.00 95.00

DANGER
COMIC MEDIA (1953-1954)
1 Cover/Art: Don Heck. 16.00 50.00
2-3 8.00 25.00
4 Drug abuse story. 13.00 40.00
5 Art: Don Heck. 10.00 30.00
6-14 8.00 25.00

DANGER AND ADVENTURE
CHARLTON (1955-1956)
22 Previous title:This Magazine Is Haunted. App: Ibis. 16.00 50.00
23 App: Nyoka. 16.00 50.00
24-27 10.00 30.00

DANGER IS OUR BUSINESS
IW (1964)
9 Reprints #1 of the Toby series. 13.00 40.00

DANGER IS OUR BUSINESS
TOBY (1953-1955)
1 Art: Frank Frazetta, Al Williamson. 65.00 200.00
2 10.00 30.00
3 8.00 25.00
4-10 7.00 20.00

DANGER IS THEIR BUSINESS (A-1 SERIES)
ME (1952)
11 (A-1 #50). 16.00 50.00

DANGER MAN
DELL FOUR COLOR SERIES (1961)
1231 TV photo cover. (9/61) 19.00 60.00

DANGER TRAIL
DC (1950-1951)
1 Art: Alex Toth in all issues. "Hunters Of The Whispering Gallery!" and others. 230.00 750.00
2 "Hangman's House!" and others. 190.00 600.00
3 "Thunder Over Thailand!" and others. 250.00 800.00
4 "Reign Of The Scarlet Umbrella!" and others. 155.00 500.00
5 "Rendezvous In Rio!" and others. (3-4/51) 155.00 500.00

DANGER UNLIMITED
DARK HORSE (1994)
1-4 .75 2.00
TPB Reprints issues #1-4 with additional material. 5.00 14.95

DANIEL BOONE
DELL FOUR COLOR SERIES (1961)
1163 (3/61) 13.00 40.00

DANIEL BOONE
GOLD KEY (1965-1969)
1 TV photo covers on all issues. 16.00 50.00
2 13.00 40.00
3-6 10.00 30.00
7-12 7.00 20.00
13-15 5.00 15.00

DANNY BLAZE
CHARLTON (1955)
1 10.00 30.00
2 Title changes to Nature Boy with #3. 7.00 20.00

DANNY THOMAS SHOW, THE
DELL FOUR COLOR SERIES (1961)
1180 TV photo cover. (4/61) 35.00 110.00
1249 TV photo cover. (11/61) 28.00 90.00

DARBY O'GILL AND THE LITTLE PEOPLE
DELL FOUR COLOR SERIES (1959)
1024 Disney movie photo cover. (8/59) 22.00 70.00

DARBY O'GILL AND THE LITTLE PEOPLE
GOLD KEY (1970)
10251-001 Disney movie photo cover. 5.00 15.00

DAREDEVIL
MARVEL (1964-CURRENT)
1 1st & Origin: Daredevil in "The Origin Of Daredevil!" 400.00 1350.00
2 App: Electro. "The Evil Menace Of Electro!" by Lee/Orlando. 140.00 450.00
3 1st & Origin: The Owl. "The Owl, Ominous Overlord Of Crime!" by Lee/Orlando. 80.00 250.00
4 1st: Purple Man. "Killgrave, The Unbelievable Purple Man!" by Lee/Orlando. 65.00 200.00
5 1st: Matador. "The Mysterious Masked Matador!" by Lee/Wood. 55.00 180.00
6 "Trapped By The Fellowship Of Fear!" by Lee/Wood. 40.00 125.00
7 1st: red costume. "Daredevil Battles Sub-Mariner!" 65.00 200.00
8 1st: Stiltman. "The Stiltman Cometh!" by Lee/Wood. 35.00 110.00
9 "That He May See!" by Lee/Wood. 31.00 100.00
10 "While The City Sleeps!" by Lee/Wood. 31.00 100.00
11 "A Time To Unmask!" by Lee/Powell. 31.00 100.00
12 1st: Plunderer, App: Ka-Zar. "Sightless, In A Savage Land!" by Lee/Romita. 31.00 100.00
13 "The Secret Of Ka-Zar's Origin!" by Lee/Romita. 20.00 65.00
14 App: Ka-Zar, Plunderer. "If This Be Justice!" by Lee/Romita. 20.00 65.00
15 "And Men Shall Call Him...Ox!" by Lee/Romita. 20.00 65.00
16 1st: Masked Marauder, App: Spider-Man. "Enter...Spider-Man!" by Lee/Romita. 26.00 85.00
17 App: Spider-Man. "None Are So Blind...!" by Lee/Romita. 25.00 80.00
18 1st & Origin: Gladiator. "There Shall Come A Gladiator!" by Lee/Romita. 14.00 45.00
19 App: Gladiator, Masked Marauder. "Alone..Against The Underworld!" by Lee/Romita. 14.00 45.00
20 App: The Owl. "The Verdict Is: Death!" by Lee/Colan. 13.00 40.00
21 App: The Owl. "The Trap Is Sprung!" by Lee/Colan. 13.00 40.00
22 "The Tri-Man Lives!" by Lee/Colan. 13.00 40.00
23 "DD Goes Wild!" by Lee/Colan. 13.00 40.00
24 App: Ka-Zar. "The Mystery Of The Midnight Stalker!" by Lee/Colan. 13.00 40.00
25 1st: Leap-Frog. "Enter: The Leap-Frog!" by Lee/Colan. 10.00 30.00
26 "Stilt-Man Strikes Again!" 8.00 25.00
27 "Matt Murdock Must Die!" App: Spider-Man. 11.00 36.00
28 "Thou Shalt Not Covet Thy Neighbor's Planet!" 8.00 25.00
29 "Unmasked!" 8.00 25.00
30 App: Thor. "...If There Should Be A Thunder God!" 8.00 25.00
31 "Blind Man's Bluff!" 8.00 25.00
32 "To Fight The Impossible Fight!" 8.00 25.00
33 "Behold The Beetle!" 8.00 25.00
34 "To Squash A Beetle!" 8.00 25.00
35 "Daredevil Dies First!" 8.00 25.00
36 "The Name Of The Game Is...Mayhem!" 8.00 25.00
37 "Don't Look Now, But It's...Dr. Doom!" 7.00 20.00
38 "The Living Prison!" App: Fantastic Four. 7.00 20.00
39 "Deadlier Than Ever...The Unholy Three!" 7.00 20.00
40 "The Fallen Hero!" 7.00 20.00
41 "The Death Of Mike Murdock!" 7.00 20.00
42 1st: Jester. "Nobody Laughs At...The Jester!" 7.00 20.00
43 Origin retold: Daredevil. "In Combat With Captain America!" 7.00 20.00
44 "I, Murderer!" 7.00 20.00
45 "The Dismal Dreggs Of Defeat!" 7.00 20.00
46 "The Final Jest!" 7.00 20.00
47 "Brother, Take My Hand!" 7.00 20.00
48 "Farewell To Foggy!" 7.00 20.00
49 4.00 12.00
50 Art: Barry Smith. "If In Battle I Fail..!" 5.00 15.00
51 Art: Barry Smith. 5.00 15.00
52 Art: Barry Smith. "The Night Of The Panther!" 5.00 15.00
53 Origin retold. "As It Was In The Beginning!" 6.00 18.00
54 1st 15 cent cover price. 2.75 10.00
55-76 2.75 10.00
77 4.00 12.00
78-99 2.75 10.00
100 Origin retold. 7.00 20.00
101-104 1.75 6.00
105 Art: Jim Starlin. Origin: Moondragon. 4.00 12.00
106-113 1.25 4.50
114 1.75 6.00
115-130 1.25 4.00
131 1st & Origin: new Bullseye. 7.00 22.00
132 Bullseye. 1.50 5.00
133-137 1.00 3.00
138 Ghost Rider. 1.75 6.00
139-145 1.00 3.00
146 1.75 6.00
147-157 1.00 3.00
158 Begin: Frank Miller art. 16.00 50.00
159 8.00 25.00
160-161 7.00 20.00
162 Art: Steve Ditko (no Miller). 4.00 12.00
163 4.00 12.00
164 Origin retold. 4.00 12.00
165-167 4.00 12.00
168 1st: Elektra by Frank Miller. (1/80) 13.00 40.00
169 Elektra. 4.00 12.00
170 4.00 12.00
171-173 2.00 7.00
174 Elektra. 2.00 7.00
175 Elektra. 2.25 8.00
176-180 Elektra. 1.75 6.00
181 Death: Elektra. Double size. 4.00 12.00
182-184 Punisher. 1.75 6.00
185-189 1.00 3.50
190 Return: Elektra. 1.50 5.00
191-195 .75 2.00
196 Wolverine. 4.00 11.00
197-199 .75 2.00
200 1.00 3.50
201-218 .75 2.00
219-220 1.00 3.00
221-226 .75 2.00
227 1.75 6.00
228-233 1.00 3.50
234-237 .75 2.00
238 Sabretooth. 1.50 5.00
239-240 .75 2.00
241 Art: Todd McFarlane. .75 2.00
242-247 .75 2.00
248-249 Wolverine. 2.25 8.50
250-251 .75 2.00
252 1.50 5.00
253 .75 2.00
254 1st & Origin: Typhoid Mary. 5.00 15.00
255-256 Typhoid Mary. 2.25 8.00
257 Crossover with Punisher #10. 1.75 6.00
258 .75 2.00
259-260 Typhoid Mary. 1.00 3.00
261-271 .75 2.00
272 1.00 3.00
273-291 .75 2.00
292-293 Punisher. .75 2.00
294 .75 2.00
295 Ghost Rider. .75 2.00
296 .75 2.00
297 Typhoid Mary. 1.25 4.00
298 1.00 3.50
299 1.00 3.00
300 Double size. 1.25 4.50
301-318 .50 1.50
319 Fall From Grace prologue. 2.75 10.00
320 Fall From Grace pt.1 2.25 8.00
321 Fall From Grace (pt.2). Glow-in-the-dark cover. 1.25 4.00
321A Regular cover. .75 2.00

322 Fall From Grace pt.3 .... 1.00 3.00
323 Fall From Grace pt.4 .... 1.00 3.00
324 Fall From Grace pt.5 .... .75 2.50
325 Fall From Grace final chapter. ...... .75 2.75
326-327 .... .75 2.00
328-343 .... .50 1.50
344 .... .50 1.95

DAREDEVIL ANNUAL
MARVEL (1967-CURRENT)

1 King-Size Special. New stories. (9/67) 9.00 28.00
2 King-Size Special. (2/71) 2.25 8.00
3 Special. (1/72) 1.75 6.00
4 1st: Mind-Master. (1976) 1.50 5.00
5 (#4 on cover) Atlantis Attacks. (1989) 1.50 5.00
6 (1990) 1.00 3.50
7 (1991) .... .75 2.00
8 (1992) .... .75 2.25
9 Polybagged with card. (1993) ...... .75 2.95
10 (1994) .... .75 2.95

DAREDEVIL COMICS
LEV GLEASON (1941-1956)

1 "Daredevil Battles Hitler!" 1300.00 5000.00
2 .... 500.00 1900.00
3 .... 310.00 1000.00
4 .... 260.00 850.00
5 .... 220.00 700.00
6 .... 200.00 650.00
7-11 .... 160.00 525.00
12 Origin: The Claw. 250.00 825.00
13 Begin: Little Wise Guys. 220.00 700.00
14 .... 120.00 390.00
15 .... 145.00 480.00
16-17 .... 110.00 360.00
18 New origin: Daredevil. 230.00 750.00
19-20 .... 95.00 300.00
21 Begin: The Claw. 145.00 480.00
22-30 .... 65.00 210.00
31 Death: The Claw. 145.00 480.00
32-37 .... 50.00 150.00
38 Origin retold: Daredevil. 65.00 210.00
39-48 .... 40.00 120.00
49-68 .... 28.00 90.00
69 End: Daredevil. 28.00 90.00
70-71 .... 16.00 50.00
72-78 .... 14.00 45.00
79 Return: Daredevil. 19.00 60.00
80 Daredevil. 16.00 50.00
81-90 .... 11.00 35.00
91-100 .... 10.00 30.00
101-134 .... 8.00 25.00

DAREDEVIL: MAN WITHOUT FEAR
MARVEL (1993-1994)

1 .... 1.50 5.00
2 .... 1.25 4.00
3-5 .... 1.00 3.00
TPB Reprints issues #1-5. .... 5.00 15.95

DARING ADVENTURES
I.W./SUPER (1963-1964)

9 Reprint. 7.00 20.00
10-18 .... 7.00 20.00

DARING ADVENTURES
ST. JOHN (1953)

1 3-D comic (with glasses). Cover & art: Joe Kubert.
.... 55.00 175.00

DARING ADVENTURES
ST. JOHN (1954)

6 Cover: Matt Baker. From Approved Comics series.
.... 13.00 40.00

DARING ADVENTURES
SUPER (1963-1964)

10-11 .... 2.75 10.00
12 Reprint: Phantom Lady. 19.00 60.00
13-14 .... 2.75 10.00
15 Reprint: Hooded Menace #1. ...... 10.00 30.00
16 Reprint: Dynamic #12. .... 2.75 10.00
17 Reprint: Green Lama #3 by Raboy. 7.00 20.00
18 .... 8.00 25.00

DARING COMICS
MARVEL(TIMELY) (1944-1945)

9 Begin: Human Torch & Sub-Mariner. 180.00 575.00
10-12 .... 155.00 500.00

DARING LOVE
GILMORE (1953)

1 .... 8.00 25.00

DARING MYSTERY COMICS
MARVEL(TIMELY) (1940-1942)

1 .... 3100.00 12000.00
2 .... 1100.00 4300.00
3 .... 700.00 2700.00
4 .... 500.00 1800.00
5 1st & Begin: The Falcon. (6/40) 500.00 1800.00
6 Cover/Art: Simon & Kirby. (9/40) 600.00 2200.00
7 .... 600.00 2000.00
8 .... 400.00 1500.00

DARK, THE
AUGUST HOUSE (1995-CURRENT)

1 .... .75 2.50
1A Foil cover, signed & numbered. ...... .75 2.50
2-5 .... .75 2.50

DARK, THE
CONTINUM (1992)

1 .... 1.25 4.00
2-4 .... .75 2.50

DARK, THE
CONTINUM (1993-1994)

1 Red foil cover. 1.00 3.50
2 .... 1.00 3.00
3 .... .75 2.50
4 Foil cover. .... .75 2.50
5-7 .... .75 2.50

DARK CONVENTION BOOK, THE
CONTINUM (1992-1993)

1 Released at 1992 San Diego Comic Convention.
.... 8.00 25.00
2 Released at 1993 ComicFest. 5.00 15.00

DARK CRYSTAL, THE
MARVEL (1983)

1 Movie Adaptation. .... .30 1.00
2 .... .30 1.00

DARK DOMINION
DEFIANT (1993-1994)

1 .... 1.00 3.00
2 .... .75 2.75
3 .... .75 2.50
4 .... .75 2.95
5-11 .... .75 2.50

DARK GUARD
MARVEL (1993)

1 .... .75 2.95
2-7 .... .50 1.75

DARK HOLD
MARVEL (1992-1994)

1 .... .75 2.00
2-16 .... .50 1.50

DARK HORSE COMICS
DARK HORSE (1992-1994)

1 .... 1.00 3.50
2-7 .... .75 2.50
8 1st & Begin: X. 5.00 15.00
9 .... 2.50 9.00
10 End: X. 1.50 5.00
11-25 .... .75 2.50

DARK HORSE DOWNUNDER
DARK HORSE (1994)

1-3 .... .75 2.50

DARK HORSE PRESENTS
DARK HORSE (1986-CURRENT)

1 1st: Concrete. 6.00 18.00
1 (2ND) 2nd printing. 1.00 3.00
2 Concrete. 2.75 10.00
3 Concrete. 2.00 7.00
4 Concrete. 1.75 6.50
5-6 Concrete. 1.50 5.50
7 .... 1.00 3.75
8 Concrete. 1.50 5.00
9 .... 1.00 3.75
10 1st: Masque (later called Mask). (9/87)
.... 5.00 15.00
11 Masque. 2.75 10.00
12 Concrete; Masque. 2.75 10.00
13 Masque. 2.75 10.00
14 Concrete; Masque. 2.75 10.00
15 Masque. 2.75 10.00
16 Concrete; Masque. 2.75 10.00
17 .... 1.00 3.75
18 Concrete; Masque. 2.75 10.00
19 Masque. 2.75 10.00
20 Masque. Double size. 2.75 10.00
21 Masque. (8/88) 2.75 10.00
22 1st: Duckman. 1.50 5.00
23 .... 1.00 3.25
24 1st & Origin: Aliens. 8.00 25.00
25-27 .... .75 2.50
28 .... 1.00 3.25
29-31 .... .75 2.50
32 .... 1.25 4.00
33 .... .75 2.50
34 Aliens. 2.50 9.00
35 Predator. 2.50 9.00
36 1st: Aliens vs. Predator. 2.50 9.00
36A Painted cover. 2.75 10.00
37-39 .... .75 2.50
40 Double size. 1.00 3.00
41 .... .75 2.50
42-43 Aliens. 1.00 3.75
44-45 .... .75 2.50
46 Predator. 1.00 3.00
47 .... .75 2.50
48-50 .... .75 2.25
51 Begin: Sin City by Frank Miller. ... 1.00 3.00
52-53 .... 1.00 3.00
54 1st & Begin: Next Men by John Byrne. 2.25 8.00
55 .... 1.75 6.00
56 Double size Annual (3.95). 1.50 5.00
57 Double size. 1.50 5.00
58-61 .... .75 2.25
62 End: Sin City. .... .75 2.25
63-66 .... .75 2.25
67 Double size (3.95). .... .75 2.25
68-84 .... .75 2.25
85-91 .... .75 2.50
92-93 .... 1.75 6.00
94 .... .75 2.50
95 .... 1.75 6.00
96-99 .... .75 2.50

DARK HORSE PRESENTS: ALIENS
DARK HORSE (1992)

1 Reprints Aliens stories originally published in DHP #24, 42, 43, 56, and 5th Anniversary Special. 1.25 4.95
PLATINUM Limited. 2.75 10.00

DARK HORSE PRESENTS: FIFTH ANNIVERSARY SPECIAL
DARK HORSE (1991)

NO# 1st Sin City 2.75 10.00

DARK MANSION OF FORBIDDEN LOVE
DC (1971)

1 .... 5.00 16.00
2 .... 4.00 11.00
3-4 .... 2.25 8.75

DARK MYSTERIES
MERIT (1951-1955)

1 Cover/Art: Wallace Wood. 110.00 360.00
2 Cover/Art: Wood/Harrison. 75.00 240.00
3-6 .... 40.00 120.00
7-9 .... 29.00 95.00
10 .... 40.00 120.00
11-13 .... 23.00 75.00
14 .... 29.00 95.00
15-18 .... 22.00 70.00
19 .... 40.00 120.00
20 .... 31.00 100.00
21-22 .... 19.00 60.00
23 1st Code Approved issue. 20.00 65.00
24 .... 16.00 50.00
25 .... 19.00 60.00

DARK SHADOWS
AJAX (1957-1958)

1 .... 16.00 50.00
2-3 .... 14.00 46.00

DARK SHADOWS
GOLD KEY (1969-1976)

1 Begin: TV photo cover. With poster. 60.00 190.00
1A Without poster. 20.00 65.00
2 .... 31.00 100.00
3 With pull-out poster. 35.00 110.00
3A Without poster. 20.00 65.00
4 "The Man Who Could Not Die!" ... 22.00 70.00
5-6 .... 22.00 70.00
7 End: photo covers. 22.00 70.00
8-12 .... 15.00 48.00
13-24 .... 10.00 33.00
25-35 .... 9.00 27.00
DIGEST Special. Photo cover. 19.00 60.00

DARK SHADOWS
INNOVATION (1992)

1 TV tie-in. 1.00 3.00
2-4 .... .75 2.50

DARKER IMAGE
IMAGE (1993)

1 1st: Deathblow. 1st: The Maxx. 1st: Bloodwulf.
.... 1.25 5.00
1A Black & white promo. 4.00 12.00
1B Gold version. 6.00 18.00
ASHCAN 1 .... 1.00 3.00

DARK HORSE COMICS #9

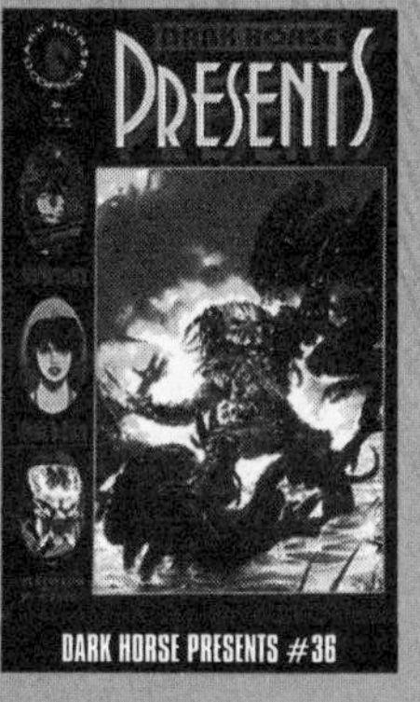

DARK HORSE PRESENTS #36

DARKER IMAGE #1

DARKHAWK #43

DARKSTARS #5

A DATE WITH JUDY #2

DAWN #1

DAZZLER #8

FAMOUS • FIRSTS

DAREDEVIL COMICS #1

Until this comic, superheroes had it easy. But then came the debut of The Claw, comics' first super-powered villain. Featured in his own series in the book, Claw primarily fought The Ghost and was finally killed in issue #31.

DARKHAWK
MARVEL (1991-1995)
1 1st & Origin: Darkhawk. 1.00 3.00
2-14 .... .40 1.25
15-49 .... .50 1.25
50 .... .40 1.25
ANNUAL 1 (1992) .... .75 2.00
ANNUAL 2 1st: Dreamkiller. Polybagged with card. (1993)
.... .75 2.00
ANNUAL 3 (1994) .... .75 2.00

DARKMAN
MARVEL (1990)
1 Movie Adaptation. .... .30 1.00
2-3 .... .30 1.00

DARKSTARS
DC (1992-CURRENT)
0 .... .50 1.95
1 1st: Darkstars. 1.00 3.00
2-6 .... .75 2.00
7-21 .... .50 1.75
22-30 .... .50 1.95
31-34 .... .75 2.25

DARLING LOVE
ARCHIE (1949-1952)
1 .... 15.00 48.00
2 .... 10.00 30.00
3-11 .... 8.00 24.00

DARLING ROMANCE
MLJ (1949-1951)
1 .... 20.00 65.00
2 .... 10.00 33.00
3-7 .... 9.00 27.00

DATE WITH DANGER
STANDARD (1952-1953)
5-6 .... 8.00 25.00

DATE WITH DEBBI
DC (1969-1972)
1 .... 5.00 16.00
2-3 .... 4.00 11.00
4-12 .... 1.75 6.50
13-18 .... 1.50 5.50

DATE WITH JUDY
DC (1947-1960)
1 .... 50.00 160.00
2 .... 25.00 80.00
3-6 .... 20.00 65.00
7-12 .... 17.00 55.00
13-24 .... 10.00 33.00
25-40 .... 9.00 27.00
41-45 .... 7.00 22.00
46 1st Code Approved issue. 5.00 16.00
47-60 .... 5.00 16.00
61-79 .... 4.00 13.00

DATE WITH MILLIE, A
MARVEL(ATLAS) (1959-1960)
1 .... 17.00 55.00
2-7 .... 9.00 28.00

DATE WITH MILLIE, A
MARVEL(ATLAS) (1956-1957)
1 .... 31.00 100.00
2 .... 14.00 46.00
3-5 .... 11.00 34.00
6-7 .... 7.00 23.00

DATE WITH PATSY, A
MARVEL(ATLAS) (1957)
1 .... 17.00 55.00

DAVID AND GOLIATH
DELL FOUR COLOR SERIES (1961)
1205 Movie photo cover. (7/61) ... 13.00 40.00

DAVID CASSIDY
CHARLTON (1972-1973)
1 .... 5.00 15.00
2-14 .... 2.75 10.00

DAVID LADD'S LIFE STORY
DELL (1962)
12-173-212 Movie photo cover. 13.00 40.00

DAVY CROCKETT
AVON (1951)
NO# "The Creek Rebellion" 19.00 60.00

DAVY CROCKETT
DELL (1955)
1 Dell Giant. Disney movie photo cover (Fess Parker).
.... 55.00 175.00

DAVY CROCKETT
DELL FOUR COLOR SERIES (1955)
631 "Indian Fighter" Disney movie photo cover (Fess Parker). (5/55) 28.00 90.00
639 "At The Alamo" Disney movie photo cover (Fess Parker). (7/55) 28.00 90.00
664 "The Great Keelboat Race" Disney movie photo cover (Fess Parker). (11/55) 25.00 80.00
671 "And The River Pirates" Disney movie photo cover (Fess Parker). (12/55) 25.00 80.00

DAVY CROCKETT
GOLD KEY (1963,1969)
1 TV photo cover (Fess Parker). 10.00 30.00
2 TV photo cover (Fess Parker). 7.00 20.00

DAWN
SIRIUS (1995-CURRENT)
1 .... 1.50 5.00
1A Black light cover. 7.00 20.00

DAZZLER
MARVEL (1981-1986)
1 1st Direct Sale comic available only through comic shops. App: X-Men. 1.00 3.00
2 App: X-Men. .... .75 2.25
3-20 .... .50 1.50
21 Double size. Photo cover. .... .50 1.50
22-37 .... .50 1.50
38 X-Men, Wolverine. .... .75 2.50
39-42 .... .50 1.75

DC 100 PAGE SUPER SPECTACULAR
DC (1971-1973)
4 Reprints: Weird Mystery Tales. Cover: Berni Wrightson.
.... .75 2.00
5 Reprints: Love Stories. .... .30 1.00
6 Reprints: World's Greatest Super-Heroes. Cover: Neal Adams.
.... 1.25 4.00
7 See Superman #245.
8 See Batman Comics #238.
9 See Our Army At War #242.
10 See Adventure Comics #416.
11 See Flash #214.
12 See Superboy #185.
13 See Superman #252.
14 Reprints: Detective #31, 32; Showcase #34.
.... 1.00 3.00
15 Reprints: Detective #65. .... 1.00 3.00
16 Reprints: All Star #37; Adventure #66. 1.00 3.00
17 Reprints: Detective #75. .... 1.00 3.00
18 Reprints: All Star #4. .... 1.00 3.00
19 Reprints: Adventure #40. .... 1.00 3.00
20 Reprints: Detective #66, 68. ...... 1.00 3.00
21 Reprints: Brave and the Bold #54. 1.00 3.00
22 Reprints: All-Flash Quarterly #13. ... 1.00 3.00

DC CHALLENGE
DC (1985-1986)
1-12 .... .20 .75

DC COMICS PRESENTS
DC (1978-1986)
1 Superman, Flash. 1.00 3.00
2 Flash. .... .50 1.25
3-25 .... .50 1.25
26 1st: New Teen Titans. 2.75 10.00
27-40 .... .50 1.25
41 Superman/Joker. 1.50 5.00
42-76 .... .50 1.25
77-78 Animal Man. 1.50 5.00
79-84 .... .50 1.25
85 Swamp Thing. 1.25 4.00
86-88 .... .50 1.50
89-93 .... .50 1.25
94 .... .50 1.50

95-96	.50	1.25
97	.50	1.75
ANNUAL 1 Superman. (1982)	.75	2.00
ANNUAL 2 Superwoman. (1983)	.50	1.25
ANNUAL 3 Captain Marvel. (1984)	.50	1.25
ANNUAL 4 Superwoman. (1985)	.50	1.25

DC SPECIAL
DC (1968-1977)

1	2.75	10.00
2-4	2.00	7.50
5 Sgt. Rock.	2.00	7.50
6-14	2.00	7.50
15	5.00	15.00
16-29	1.50	5.00

DC SPECIAL SERIES
DC (1977-1981)

1-2	1.00	3.00
3-12	.75	2.00
13-15	.50	1.50
16 Death: Jonah Hex.	1.50	5.00
17-20	.50	1.50
21 Art: Frank Miller.	5.00	15.00
22-26	.30	1.00
27 Batman vs. the Incredible Hulk.	2.25	8.00

DC SUPER-STARS
DC (1976-1978)

1 Double size.	1.50	5.00
2-7	.75	2.00
8 Reprint: Showcase #15.	.75	2.00
9	.30	1.00
10 Batman/Joker.	1.50	5.00
11-18	.75	2.00

DC UNIVERSE: TRINITY
DC (1993)

1-2 Foil cover.	.75	2.95

D-DAY
CHARLTON (1963-1968)

1-6	2.75	10.00

DEAD END CRIME STORIES
KIRBY (1949)

NO# Art: Bob Powell.	70.00	225.00

DEAD EYE WESTERN COMICS
HILLMAN (1948-1953)

1	16.00	50.00
2-3	13.00	40.00
4-12	8.00	25.00
V2#1-V2#2	7.00	20.00
V2#3-V2#4 Art: Krigstein.	7.00	20.00
V2#5-V2#12	7.00	20.00
V3#1 (4-5/53)	7.00	20.00

DEAD OF NIGHT
MARVEL (1973-1975)

1	1.00	3.00
2-10	.50	1.50
11 1st: Scarecrow.	.75	2.00

DEAD WHO WALK, THE
AVON (1952)

1	85.00	275.00

DEADBOLT
HALL OF HEROES (1993)

1 One shot.	2.00	7.50

DEADLINE
TOM ASTOR/DEADLINE (1980-CURRENT)

1 1st: Tankgirl.	5.00	15.00
2-15	2.25	8.00
16-23	1.75	6.00
24	1.50	5.00
25	1.75	6.00
26-71	1.50	5.00

DEADLY FOES OF SPIDER-MAN
MARVEL (1991)

1	1.25	4.00
2-4	1.00	3.00
TPB Reprints issues #1-4.	4.00	12.95

DEADMAN
DC (1985)

1	1.25	4.00
2-7	.75	2.00

DEADMAN
DC (1986)

1-4	.75	2.00

DEADMAN: EXORCISM
DC (1992)

1-2	1.25	4.95

DEADMAN: LOST SOULS
DC (1995)

TPB Reprints Exorcism & Love And Death mini-series.	6.00	19.95

DEADMAN: LOVE AFTER DEATH
DC (1990)

1-2	1.00	3.00

DEADPOOL
MARVEL (1993)

1	.75	2.00
2-4	.50	1.50

DEADPOOL
MARVEL (1994)

1-4	.50	1.50

DEADSHOT
DC (1988-1989)

1	.75	2.00
2-4	.50	1.50

DEADWORLD
ARROW (1986-1991)

1-28	.30	1.00

DEAR BEATRICE FAIRFAX
STANDARD (1950-1951)

5 Cover: Alex Schomburg in all issues.	10.00	30.00
6-9	10.00	30.00

DEAR LONELY HEART
ARTFUL (1951-1952)

1	19.00	60.00
2	10.00	30.00
3 Art: Matt Baker.	19.00	60.00
4-8	8.00	25.00

DEAR LONELY HEARTS
COMIC MEDIA (1953-1954)

1	8.00	25.00
2	5.00	15.00
3-8	2.75	10.00

DEARLY BELOVED
ZIFF-DAVIS (1952)

1 Photo cover.	16.00	50.00

DEATH 3
MARVEL (1993-1994)

1	.75	2.95
2-4	.50	1.75

DEATH DEALER
VEROTIK (1995-CURRENT)

1 Frank Frazetta cover	2.75	10.00

DEATH GALLERY
DC (1994)

1 One shot.	1.25	4.00

DEATH METAL
MARVEL (1993-1994)

1	.75	2.00
2-4	.30	1.00

DEATH OF CAPTAIN MARVEL
MARVEL (1994)

NO# Reprints Marvel Graphic Novel #1.	2.00	7.95

DEATH RATTLE
KITCHEN SINK (1985-1988)

1-7	.75	2.00
8 1st: "Xenozoic Tales"	2.25	8.00
9-18	.75	2.00

DEATH: THE HIGH COST OF LIVING
DC (1993)

1	2.25	8.00
1A Platinum edition.	6.00	20.00
2	2.75	10.00
3	1.50	5.00
3A Replacement book.	1.00	3.00
TPB Reprints issues #1-3.	4.00	12.95

DEATH VALLEY
CHARLTON (1955)

7-9	5.00	15.00

DEATH VALLEY
COMIC MEDIA (1953-1954)

1 "Inferno!"	13.00	40.00
2 "Fool's Gold!"	10.00	30.00
3-6	7.00	20.00

DEATH'S HEAD
MARVEL (1988-1989)

1	1.75	6.00
2-10	1.00	3.00
TPB	4.00	12.95

DEATH'S HEAD II
MARVEL (1992)

1 Mini-series.	1.25	4.00
1 (2ND) 2nd printing, Silver cover.	.50	1.50
2	1.00	3.00
2 (2ND) 2nd printing, Silver cover.	.50	1.50
3	1.25	4.00
4	1.00	3.00

DEATH'S HEAD II
MARVEL (1992-1993)

1	.75	2.00
2-18	.50	1.75

DEATH'S HEAD II AND DIE-CUT
MARVEL (1993)

1 Foil-embossed logo.	.75	2.95
2	.50	1.75

DEATHBLOW
IMAGE/WILDSTORM (1993-CURRENT)

1	1.00	3.00
2-5	.75	2.50
5A Cover variant.	4.00	12.00
6-10	.50	1.95
11-16	.75	2.50
16A Newsstand edition.	.50	1.95
17-18	.75	2.50
ASHCAN 1	2.25	8.00

DEATHLOK
MARVEL (1990)

1 1st & Origin: new Deathlok.	.75	2.00
2-4	.30	1.00

DEATHLOK
MARVEL (1991-1994)

1 Origin: Deathlok.	.50	1.50
1 (2ND) 2nd printing.	.30	1.00
2-34	.30	1.00
ANNUAL 1 (1992)	.75	2.00
ANNUAL 2 (1993)	.75	2.00

DEATHLOK SPECIAL
MARVEL (1991)

1 Reprints.	.30	1.00
2-4	.30	1.00

DEATHMARK
LIGHTNING (1994-CURRENT)

1	.75	2.75

DEATHMATE
IMAGE/VALIANT (1993-1994)

BLACK 1st: Gen 13. (9/93)	2.75	10.00
BLACK-A Gold edition.	8.00	25.00
BLUE (10/93)	1.25	4.00
BLUE-A Gold version.	2.75	10.00
EPILOGUE	.75	2.95
EPILOGUE-A Gold version.	2.75	10.00
PROLOGUE (9/93)	.75	2.95
RED	1.50	5.00
RED-A Gold version.	2.75	10.00
TOUR BOOK	2.00	7.00
YELLOW (10/93)	1.25	4.00
YELLOW-A Gold edition.	2.75	10.00

DEATHSTROKE: THE TERMINATOR
DC (1991-CURRENT)

0 (8/94)	.50	1.95
1 Origin: Deathstroke.	1.75	6.00
1 (2ND) 2nd printing.	.50	1.75
2-3	1.25	4.00
4-11	.75	2.00
12-37	.50	1.75
38-40	.50	1.95
41 Begin: Deathstroke The Hunted.	.50	1.95
42-44	.50	1.95
45 End: Deathstroke The Hunted.	.50	1.95
46-47	.50	1.95
48-49	.75	2.25
50 Double size.	1.00	3.50
51	.75	2.25
ANNUAL 1 (1992)	1.00	3.50
ANNUAL 2 Bloodlines, pt.18. (1993)	1.00	3.50
ANNUAL 3 Elseworlds story. (1994)	1.00	3.95
ANNUAL 4 (1995)	1.00	3.95
TPB Full Circle.	4.00	12.95

DEATHWRECK
MARVEL (1993-1994)

1-4	.30	1.00

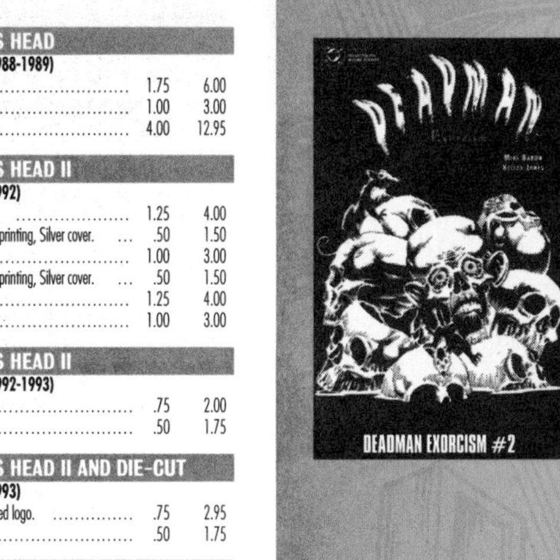

DEADMAN EXORCISM #2

DEADSHOT #1

DEATH GALLERY #1

DEATHLOK MINI-SERIES #1

DEFENDERS #147

DEMON #1

DENNIS THE MENACE #9

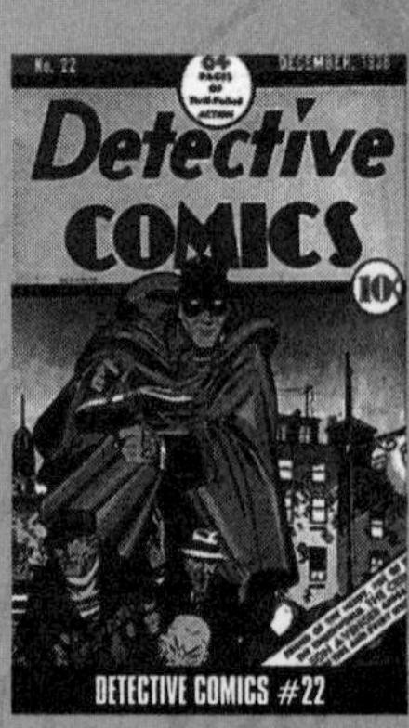

DETECTIVE COMICS #22

DEBBIE DEAN COMICS
CSP (1945)
1-2 ..... 16.00 50.00

DEEP, THE
MARVEL (1977)
1 Movie tie-in. ..... .75 2.00

DEFENDERS, THE
DELL (1962-1963)
1 (#12-176-211). TV tie-in. 5.00 15.00
2 (#12-176-304). TV tie-in. 5.00 15.00

DEFENDERS, THE
MARVEL (1972-1986)
1 Begin: Hulk, Sub-Mariner, Doctor Strange. 19.00 60.00
2 ..... 10.00 30.00
3 ..... 7.00 20.00
4 Joins: Valkyrie. 7.00 20.00
5 ..... 7.00 20.00
6-9 ..... 5.00 15.00
10 Hulk battles Thor. 7.00 20.00
11-14 ..... 2.50 9.00
15 Magneto. 7.00 20.00
16 Magneto. 4.00 12.00
17-20 ..... 2.00 7.00
21-23 ..... 1.75 6.00
24-25 Son of Satan. 1.75 6.00
26-29 Guardians Of The Galaxy. 2.75 10.00
30 ..... 1.50 5.00
31 Origin: Nighthawk. 1.50 5.00
32 Origin concludes. 1.50 5.00
33-60 ..... 1.50 5.00
61 ..... 1.75 6.50
62-75 ..... 1.25 4.00
76-95 ..... 1.00 3.00
96 Ghost Rider. 1.75 6.00
97-99 ..... .75 2.00
100 ..... 1.00 3.00
101-105 ..... .75 2.00
106 ..... 1.00 3.00
107-124 ..... .75 2.00
125 Begin: New Defenders. 1.00 3.00
126-149 ..... .75 2.00
150 ..... 1.00 3.00
151 ..... .75 2.00
152 ..... 1.00 3.00

DEFENDERS ANNUAL, THE
MARVEL (1976)
1 ..... 1.25 4.00

DEFENDERS OF DYNATRON CITY
MARVEL (1992)
1 TV tie-in. ..... .30 1.00
2-6 ..... .30 1.00

DELL GIANT COMICS
DELL (1959-1961)
21 Tom And Jerry Picnic Time. 31.00 100.00
22 Huey, Dewey And Louie Back To School. 23.00 75.00
23 Little Lulu And Tubby Halloween Fun. 26.00 85.00
24 Woody Woodpecker's Family Fun. 19.00 60.00
25 Tarzan's Jungle World. 25.00 80.00
26 Christmas Parade (Disney). Art: Barks (16 pages). 65.00 200.00
27 Man In Space (Disney). 31.00 100.00
28 Bugs Bunny's Winter Fun. 25.00 80.00
29 Little Lulu And Tubby In Hawaii. 22.00 70.00
30 Disneyland U.S.A. 31.00 100.00
31 Huckleberry Hound Summer Fun. 50.00 150.00
32 Bugs Bunny's Beach Party. 19.00 60.00
33 Daisy Duck And Uncle Scrooge Picnic Time. 25.00 80.00
34 Nancy And Sluggo Summer Camp. 19.00 60.00
35 Huey, Dewey And Louie Back To School. 19.00 60.00
36 Little Lulu And Witch Hazel Halloween Fun. 25.00 80.00
37 Tarzan King Of The Jungle. 28.00 90.00
38 Uncle Donald And His Nephews Family Fun. 19.00 60.00
39 Merry Christmas (Disney). 20.00 65.00
40 Woody Woodpecker's Christmas Parade. 19.00 60.00
41 Yogi Bear's Winter Sports. 50.00 150.00
42 Lulu And Tubby In Australia. 19.00 60.00
43 Mighty Mouse In Outer Space. 95.00 300.00
44 Around The World With Huckleberry And His Friends. 50.00 150.00
45 Nancy And Sluggo Summer Camp. 16.00 50.00
46 Bugs Bunny Beach Party. 16.00 50.00
47 Mickey And Donald In Vacationland. 25.00 80.00
48 The Flintstones (Bedrock Bedlam). 1st Flintstones in comics (8/61). 50.00 150.00
49 Huey, Dewey And Louie Back To School. 16.00 50.00
50 Little Lulu And Witch Hazel Trick 'N' Treat. 19.00 60.00
51 Tarzan King Of The Jungle. 16.00 50.00
52 Uncle Donald And His Nephews Dude Ranch. 16.00 50.00
53 Donald Duck Merry Christmas. 16.00 50.00
54 Woody Woodpecker's Christmas Party. 16.00 50.00
55 Daisy Duck And Uncle Scrooge Show Boat. 16.00 50.00

DELL JUNIOR TREASURY
DELL (1955-1957)
1 "Alice In Wonderland" 19.00 60.00
2 "Aladdin And The Wonderful Lamp" 16.00 50.00
3 "Gulliver's Travels" 10.00 30.00
4 "Adventures Of Mr. Frog And Miss Mousie" 13.00 40.00
5 "The Wizard Of Oz" 13.00 40.00
6 "Heidi" 10.00 30.00
7 "Santa And The Angel" 10.00 30.00
8 "Raggedy Ann And The Camel With The Wrinkled Knees" 10.00 30.00
9 Clementina The Flying Pig. 10.00 30.00
10 "The Adventures Of Tom Sawyer" 10.00 30.00

DELLA VISION
MARVEL(ATLAS) (1955)
1 ..... 25.00 80.00
2-3 ..... 16.00 50.00

DEMOLITION MAN
DC (1993-1994)
1 Movie adaptation. ..... .30 1.00
2-3 ..... .30 1.00

DEMON
DC (1972-1974)
1 Jack Kirby cover & art in all issues. 8.00 25.00
2-6 ..... 2.75 10.00
7-16 ..... 2.25 8.00

DEMON
DC (1987)
1 ..... .75 2.00
2 ..... .50 1.50
3-4 ..... .30 1.00

DEMON
DC (1990-1995)
0 (8/94) ..... .50 1.95
1 ..... 1.25 4.00
2 ..... 1.00 3.00
3-49 ..... .50 1.50
50 Double size. ..... .75 2.95
51-58 ..... .50 1.50
ANNUAL 1 (1992) 1.00 3.00
ANNUAL 2 Bloodlines, pt 20. (1993) 1.00 3.50

DENNIS THE MENACE
MARVEL (1981)
1-13 ..... .20 .50

DENNIS THE MENACE
STANDARD (1953-1979)
1 1st: Dennis The Menace. 50.00 150.00
2 ..... 23.00 75.00
3-8 ..... 19.00 60.00
9 1st Code Approved issue. 16.00 50.00
10-20 ..... 14.00 45.00
21-30 ..... 10.00 30.00
31-50 ..... 7.00 20.00
51-70 ..... 5.00 15.00
71-100 ..... 2.75 10.00
101-120 ..... 2.25 8.00
121-140 ..... 1.75 6.00
141-166 ..... 1.25 4.00

DENNIS THE MENACE AND HIS DOG RUFF
FAWCETT (1961)
1 ..... 8.00 25.00

DENNIS THE MENACE GIANTS
STANDARD (1955-1969)
NO# Giant Vacation Special. (Summer/55) 23.00 75.00
2-4 ..... 19.00 60.00
5-6 ..... 16.00 50.00
7 In Hollywood. 16.00 50.00
7 (2ND) In Hollywood. 2nd printing. (Summer/61) 10.00 30.00
8-10 ..... 16.00 50.00
11-12 ..... 13.00 40.00
13 Best Of Dennis The Menace. 13.00 40.00
14-18 ..... 13.00 40.00
19 Giant Christmas Issue. 13.00 40.00
20 ..... 13.00 40.00
21-30 ..... 10.00 30.00
31 All Year 'Round. 10.00 30.00
32 ..... 10.00 30.00
33 In California. 10.00 30.00
34-37 ..... 10.00 30.00
38 In Mexico. 10.00 30.00
38 (2ND) In Mexico. 2nd printing. (Summer/66) 1.50 5.00
39-40 ..... 10.00 30.00
41-45 ..... 7.00 20.00
46 Triple Feature. 7.00 20.00
47 ..... 7.00 20.00
48 Way Out Stories. 7.00 20.00
49-50 ..... 7.00 20.00
51 ..... 5.00 15.00
52 Sports Special. 5.00 15.00
53-60 ..... 5.00 15.00
61-67 ..... 2.75 10.00
68 In Hawaii. 2.75 10.00
69-70 ..... 2.75 10.00
71-75 ..... 1.75 6.00

DENNIS THE MENACE...AND AWAY WE GO!
HALL (1970)
NO# Giveaway with purchase of Caladryl (includes 2 Readi-Band bandages inside back cover). 2.75 10.00

DEPUTY, THE
DELL FOUR COLOR SERIES (1960-1961)
1077 TV photo cover (Henry Fonda). (2/60) 25.00 80.00
1130 TV photo cover (Henry Fonda). (9/60) 17.00 55.00
1225 TV photo cover (Henry Fonda). (9/61) 19.00 60.00

DEPUTY DAWG
DELL FOUR COLOR SERIES (1961-1962)
1238 TV tie-in. (10/61) 28.00 90.00
1299 TV tie-in. (3/62) 26.00 85.00

DEPUTY DAWG
GOLD KEY (1965)
10164-508 TV tie-in. 25.00 80.00

DEPUTY DAWG PRESENTS DINKY DUCK AND HASHIMOTO-SAN
GOLD KEY (1965)
10159-508 TV tie-in. 25.00 80.00

DESIGN FOR SURVIVAL
TWIN CIRCLE (1968)
NO# Anti-communism. 5.00 15.00

DESPERADO
LEV GLEASON (1948-1949)
1 ..... 16.00 50.00
2 ..... 11.00 35.00
3-5 ..... 8.00 25.00
6-8 ..... 7.00 20.00

DESTINATION MOON
FAWCETT (1950)
NO# Movie photo cover. From the Fawcett Movie Comic series. 155.00 500.00

DESTROYER DUCK
ECLIPSE (1982-1984)
1 1st: Groo The Wanderer. 1.50 5.00
2-7 ..... .75 2.00

DESTRUCTOR
ATLAS(SEABOARD) (1975)
1-4 ..... 1.00 3.00

DETECTIVE COMICS
DC (1937-CURRENT)
0 (8/94) ..... .75 2.00
1 ..... 16300.00 65000.00
2 ..... 2300.00 9000.00
3 ..... 1700.00 6500.00
4-6 ..... 900.00 3200.00
7-10 ..... 700.00 2600.00
11-16 ..... 600.00 2300.00
17 1st: Fu Manchu. 700.00 2600.00
18 Fu Manchu cover. 800.00 2800.00
19 ..... 600.00 2300.00
20 Begin: The Crimson Avenger. 1000.00 3900.00
21 ..... 500.00 1900.00
22 Crimson Avenger cover. 700.00 2600.00
23-26 ..... 500.00 1900.00
27 1st & Begin: Batman by Bob Kane (5/39) 35100.00 140000.00
28 2nd: Batman (not on cover). 4600.00 18000.00
29 3rd: Batman (2nd cover). 5600.00 22000.00
30 No Batman cover. 1300.00 5000.00

29 3rd: Batman (2nd cover).	5600.00	22000.00
30 No Batman cover.	1300.00	5000.00
31 Batman cover (9/39)	4100.00	16000.00
32 No Batman cover.	1300.00	5000.00
33 Origin: Batman.	6600.00	26000.00
34 No Batman cover.	1000.00	3900.00
35 Begin consecutive Batman covers. Classic hypo cover.	2600.00	10000.00
36-37	1000.00	3900.00
38 1st & Origin: Robin. (4/40)	6300.00	25000.00
39	1000.00	3900.00
40 1st & Origin: Clay Face.	1200.00	4500.00
41 1st Robin solo story.	700.00	2600.00
42-44	400.00	1500.00
45 1st Joker story in Detective Comics.	700.00	2600.00
46-48	400.00	1300.00
49 End: Clay Face.	400.00	1300.00
50	400.00	1300.00
51-55	310.00	1000.00
56 (10/41)	310.00	1000.00
57	310.00	1000.00
58 1st: Penguin.	700.00	2600.00
59 2nd: Penguin.	400.00	1300.00
60 Air Wave.	310.00	1000.00
61	310.00	1000.00
62 Cover/story: Joker.	400.00	1500.00
63	310.00	1000.00
64 1st & Origin: Boy Commandos by Simon & Kirby.	700.00	2600.00
65 1st Boy Commandos Simon & Kirby cover.	400.00	1300.00
66 1st & Origin: Two Face.	600.00	2000.00
67 1st Penguin cover.	400.00	1500.00
68 1st Two Face cover.	310.00	1000.00
69 Joker.	300.00	1100.00
70	250.00	825.00
71 Joker.	300.00	1100.00
72	240.00	775.00
73 Scarecrow.	240.00	775.00
74 Simon & Kirby.	240.00	775.00
75	240.00	775.00
76 Joker cover & story. Sandman in Boy Commandos story.	300.00	1100.00
77-79	240.00	775.00
80 Two Face.	280.00	900.00
81-82	210.00	675.00
83 Alfred.	220.00	700.00
84	210.00	675.00
85 Joker.	250.00	825.00
86-90	210.00	675.00
91 Joker.	240.00	775.00
92-97	200.00	650.00
97A Special Edition-U.S. Navy giveaway.	280.00	900.00
98	200.00	650.00
99 Penguin.	250.00	825.00
100 (6/45)	280.00	900.00
101	170.00	550.00
102 Joker.	240.00	775.00
103-108	170.00	550.00
109 Joker.	240.00	775.00
110-113	170.00	550.00
114 Joker.	220.00	700.00
115-117	155.00	500.00
118 The Joker in "The Royal Flush Crimes!"	220.00	700.00
119	155.00	500.00
120 Penguin.	280.00	900.00
121	155.00	500.00
122 1st Catwoman cover.	280.00	900.00
123	155.00	500.00
124 Joker.	200.00	650.00
125	155.00	500.00
126 Penguin.	240.00	775.00
127	155.00	500.00
128 Joker.	200.00	650.00
129-130	155.00	500.00
131-136	140.00	450.00
137 Joker.	155.00	500.00
138 Origin: Robotman.	280.00	900.00
139	140.00	450.00
140 1st Riddler in "The Riddler!" (10/48)	600.00	2300.00
141	140.00	450.00
142 2nd: Riddler.	240.00	775.00
143-148	140.00	450.00
149 Joker.	180.00	575.00
150-155	155.00	500.00
156 New Batmobile.	190.00	600.00
157-159	155.00	500.00
160 "The Globe-Trotter Of Crime" (6/50)	155.00	500.00
161-167	155.00	500.00
168 Origin: The Joker.	700.00	2600.00
169-170	155.00	500.00
171 Penguin.	220.00	700.00
172-179	155.00	500.00
180 Joker.	190.00	600.00
181-183	140.00	450.00
184 "The Human Firefly!"	140.00	450.00
185 "The Secret Of Batman's Utility Belt!"	140.00	450.00
186	140.00	450.00
187 Two Face.	155.00	500.00
188-189	140.00	450.00
190 Origin retold: Batman.	190.00	600.00
191-192	130.00	420.00
193 Joker.	155.00	500.00
194-202	130.00	420.00
203 Catwoman in "The Crimes Of The Catwoman!" (1/54)	155.00	500.00
204	130.00	420.00
205 Origin: Batcave.	180.00	575.00
206-210	130.00	420.00
211 Catwoman.	155.00	500.00
212-224	130.00	420.00
225 Lead story: "If I Were Batman!", 1st & Origin (pt.1): John Jones, Manhunter From Mars in backup story: "The Strange Experiment of Dr. Erdel!" (11/55)	1100.00	4000.00
226 Origin concludes.	270.00	875.00
227-229	110.00	360.00
230 1st: Mad Hatter.	115.00	375.00
231	70.00	225.00
232	70.00	220.00
233 1st & Origin: Batwoman. (7/56)	290.00	950.00
234	65.00	200.00
235 "Batman And His Costume!"	115.00	375.00
236	75.00	235.00
237	65.00	210.00
238	65.00	200.00
239	80.00	260.00
240	65.00	200.00
241-248	55.00	180.00
249 Batwoman.	55.00	180.00
250-253	55.00	180.00
254 Bat Hound.	55.00	180.00
255-260	55.00	180.00
261	40.00	130.00
262 Origin: Jackal.	40.00	130.00
263-264	40.00	130.00
265 Origin with new facts: Batman.	65.00	200.00
266	40.00	130.00
267 1st & Origin: Bat-Mite.	50.00	160.00
268-269	40.00	130.00
270-272	40.00	120.00
273	40.00	130.00
274-275	31.00	100.00
276 2nd: Bat-Mite.	35.00	110.00
277-280	31.00	100.00
281-292	23.00	75.00
293 Begin: Aquaman backup story.	25.00	80.00
294-297	23.00	75.00
298 1st S.A. Clay Face. 1st 12 cent cover price.	55.00	175.00
299-300	17.00	55.00
301	19.00	60.00
302-304	13.00	40.00
305-310	11.00	35.00
311	13.00	40.00
312-321	11.00	35.00
322 Batgirl.	11.00	35.00
323-325	11.00	35.00
326 End: Martian Manhunter.	11.00	35.00
327	16.00	50.00
328 Death: Alfred.	20.00	65.00
329-330	11.00	35.00
331	8.00	25.00
332 Joker.	10.00	30.00
333-340	8.00	25.00
341 Joker.	10.00	30.00
342-358	8.00	25.00
359 1st & Origin: New Batgirl.	14.00	45.00
360-364	8.00	25.00
365 Joker.	10.00	30.00
366-368	8.00	25.00
369 Art: Neal Adams.	11.00	35.00
370-371	8.00	25.00
372-386	5.00	15.00
387 Reprint: Detective #27 Batman story.	10.00	30.00
388 Joker. 1st 15 cent cover price.	7.00	20.00
389-390	5.00	15.00
391	2.75	10.00
392	4.00	12.00
393-394	2.75	10.00
395	7.00	20.00
396	2.75	10.00
397	7.00	20.00
398-399	2.75	10.00
400 Art: Neal Adams. 1st & Origin: Man-Bat.	10.00	30.00
401	2.75	10.00
402	7.00	20.00
403	2.75	10.00
404	7.00	20.00
405-406	2.75	10.00
407-408	7.00	20.00
409	4.00	11.00
410	7.00	20.00
411-420	2.75	10.00
421-436	2.50	9.00
437 1st: New Manhunter.	5.00	15.00
438 Begin: 100 pg. issues.	4.00	12.00
439-441	4.00	12.00
442-444	2.75	10.00
445 End: 100 pg. issues.	2.75	10.00
446-465	2.00	7.00
466-468	4.00	13.00
469-470	2.00	7.00
471-474	4.00	13.00
475-476 Art: Marshall Rogers. Joker.	7.00	22.00
477 Art: Neal Adams.	6.00	18.00
478-479	4.00	13.00
480	2.00	7.00
481	4.00	12.00
482	2.25	8.00
483	2.75	10.00
484-499	1.50	5.00
500	2.75	10.00
501-503	1.50	5.00
504 Joker.	2.25	8.00
505-512	1.50	5.00
513	1.75	6.00
514-523	1.50	5.00
524	1.75	6.00
525	1.50	5.00
526 500th issue anniversary.	5.00	14.00
527-531	1.00	3.50
532 Joker.	1.50	5.00
533-562	1.00	3.50
563-564	1.25	4.00
565-568	1.00	3.50
569-570 Joker.	2.00	7.00
571	1.00	3.50
572	1.50	5.00
573	1.00	3.50
574	1.50	5.00
575 Begin: Year 2.	2.75	10.00
576-577	2.25	8.00
578 End: Year 2.	2.25	8.00
579-597	1.00	3.00
598 Blind Justice, pt.1	1.75	6.00
599 pt.2	1.50	5.25
600 pt.3 50th Anniversary issue.	2.00	7.50
601-603	1.00	3.00
604-606	.75	2.25
607	.50	1.50
608	.75	2.25
609-621	.50	1.50
622	1.00	3.00
623	.75	2.25
624-626	.50	1.50
627	1.25	4.00
628-642	.50	1.50
643-654	.50	1.25
655	1.00	3.00
656 Bane.	2.25	8.00
657 Azrael & Robin.	2.25	8.00
658 Azrael.	2.00	7.50
659 Knightfall pt.2.	1.25	4.00
660 Knightfall pt.4. Bane.	1.00	3.00
661 Knightfall pt.6.	1.00	3.00
662 Knightfall pt.8.	1.00	3.00
663 Knightfall pt.10.	.75	2.50
664 Knightfall pt.12.	.75	2.50
665 Knightfall pt.16.	.75	2.50
666 Knightfall pt.18.	.75	2.50
667-669	.75	2.00
670-674	.50	1.50
675 Foil embossed cover.	.75	2.95
675A Regular edition.	.50	1.50
676 Double size.	1.25	4.00
677	1.00	3.00
678-679	.75	2.00
680-681	.50	1.50
682 Embossed cover.	.75	2.50
682A Regular cover.	.50	1.50
683-685	.50	1.50
686-689	.50	1.95

DETECTIVE COMICS ANNUAL

DC (1988-CURRENT)

1 (1988)	1.50	5.00
2 (1989)	1.50	5.50
3 (1990)	.75	2.50
4 Armageddon 2001. (1991)	.75	2.50
5 Darkness Within. (1992)	.75	2.50
6 Bloodlines, pt.14 (1993)	.75	2.50
7 Elseworlds story. (1994)	.75	2.95
8	1.00	3.95

DETECTIVE EYE

CENTAUR (1940)

1	310.00	1000.00
2	230.00	750.00

DETECTIVE COMICS #164

DETECTIVE COMICS #172

DETECTIVE COMICS #258

DETECTIVE COMICS #600

DETECTIVE COMICS #606

DICK COLE #6

DICK TRACY #42

DINOSAURS FOR HIRE #6

FAMOUS · FIRSTS

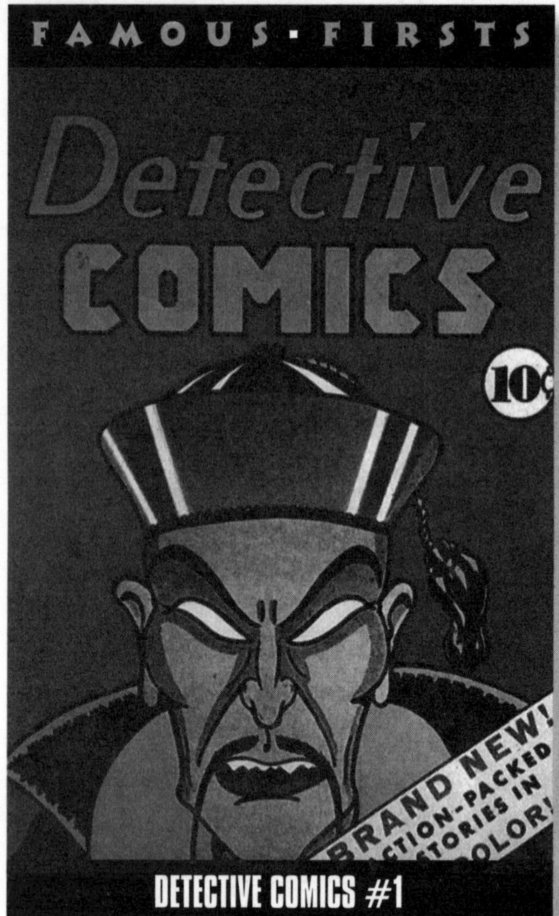

DETECTIVE COMICS #1

The very first comic with a specific theme proved so popular that National Allied Publishing took the comic's initials (DC) and became DC Comics. It featured many adventurers before Batman showed up.

DETECTIVE PICTURE STORIES
CENTAUR (1936-1937)

1	600.00	2000.00
2 Clock story.	250.00	800.00
3	220.00	700.00
4 Art: Will Eisner.	230.00	750.00
5 Clock story.	200.00	650.00

DETECTIVES, THE
DELL FOUR COLOR SERIES (1961)

1168 TV photo cover. (2/61)	19.00	60.00
1219 TV photo cover (Adam West).	19.00	60.00
1240 TV photo cover.	16.00	50.00

DETHGRIP
AXIS (1994)

1-3	.30	1.00

DEVIL CHIEF
DARK HORSE (1994)

NO# One-shot.	.75	2.50

DEVIL DINOSAUR
MARVEL (1978)

1 Cover/Art: Jack Kirby in all.	.75	2.00
2-9	.75	2.00

DEVIL DOG DUGAN
MARVEL(ATLAS) (1956)

1	14.00	44.00
2	9.00	27.00
3	5.00	16.00

DEVIL DOGS COMICS
STREET & SMITH (1942)

1	55.00	170.00

DIARY LOVES
QUALITY (1949-1953)

1	31.00	100.00
2	19.00	60.00
3	7.00	20.00
4 Art: Reed Crandall.	11.00	35.00
5-7	5.00	15.00
8-9 Art: Bill Ward.	10.00	30.00
10	5.00	15.00
11	2.75	10.00
12 Art: Bill Ward.	10.00	30.00
13-14	2.75	10.00
15-16 Art: Bill Ward.	10.00	30.00
17-20	2.75	10.00
21 Art: Bill Ward.	8.00	25.00
22-31	2.75	10.00

DIARY OF HORROR!
AVON (1952)

1 "Beware Of The Undead!" and more.	65.00	200.00

DIARY SECRETS
ST. JOHN (1949)

2 Cover: Matt Baker. From Blue Ribbon Comics 2nd series.	19.00	60.00

DIARY SECRETS
ST. JOHN (1952-1955)

10 Previous title: Teen Age Diary Secrets.	19.00	60.00
11-20	13.00	40.00
21-30	10.00	30.00
ANNUAL Art: Baker.	125.00	400.00

DICK COLE
CURTIS (1948-1950)

1	25.00	80.00
2	13.00	40.00
3-6	10.00	30.00
7-10	7.00	20.00

DICK POWELL (A-1 SERIES)
ME (1949)

22 (A-1 #22). Photo cover.	31.00	100.00

DICK QUICK ACE REPORTER
SEE: PICTURE NEWS

DICK TRACY
DELL FOUR COLOR SERIES (1944-1947)

34	110.00	350.00
56	95.00	300.00
96	70.00	225.00
133	55.00	175.00
163	45.00	135.00

DICK TRACY
DELL/HARVEY (1948-1961)

1	65.00	200.00
2-3	28.00	90.00
4-20	22.00	70.00
21-24	19.00	60.00
25 Begin: Harvey publication.	17.00	55.00
26-30	17.00	55.00
31-40	14.00	45.00
41-50	13.00	40.00
51-60	11.00	36.00
61-80	10.00	31.00
81-100	9.00	27.00
101-125	7.00	22.00
126-140	6.00	18.00
141-145 Double size.	7.00	22.00

DICK TRACY
SEE LARGE FEATURE COMICS (SERIES II) #3.

DICK TRACY AND DICK TRACY, JR.
CUPPLES & LEON (1933)

1933 (...And How They Captured "Stooge" Viller).	125.00	400.00

DICK TRACY AND SCOTTIE OF SCOTLAND YARD
SEE LARGE FEATURE COMICS #13.

DICK TRACY AND THE KIDNAPPED PRINCES
SEE LARGE FEATURE COMICS #15.

DICK TRACY BUSTER BROWN SHOES
GIVEAWAY (1944)

NO#	45.00	140.00

DICK TRACY FOILS THE MAD DOC HUMP
SEE LARGE FEATURE COMICS #11.

DICK TRACY GETS HIS MAN
SEE LARGE FEATURE COMICS #4.

DICK TRACY MEETS THE BLANK
SEE LARGE FEATURE COMICS #1

DICK TRACY POPPED WHEAT
GIVEAWAY (1947)

NO#	4.00	12.00

DICK TRACY THE RACKET BUSTER
SEE LARGE FEATURE COMICS #8.

DICK WINGATE OF THE U.S NAVY
TOBY (1953)

1	5.00	15.00

DICK'S ADVENTURES
DELL FOUR COLOR SERIES (1949)

245 (9/49)	11.00	35.00

DICKIE DARE
EASTERN (1941-1942)

1	40.00	130.00
2	28.00	90.00
3-4	22.00	70.00

DIE, MONSTER, DIE
DELL (1966)

12-175-603 Movie photo cover (Boris Karloff).	10.00	30.00

DIE-CUT
MARVEL (1993-1994)
1-5 .50 1.50

DIGITEK
MARVEL (1992-1993)
1-4 .50 1.50

DING DONG
ME (1946-1947)
1 (Summer/46) 16.00 50.00
2 (9/46) 8.00 25.00
3 (Winter/47) 5.00 15.00
4-5 5.00 15.00

DINKY COMICS
ST. JOHN (1949)
6 From Blue Ribbon Comics 2nd series. 5.00 15.00

DINOSAURS FOR HIRE
ETERNITY (1988-1989)
1-9 .75 2.00

DINOSAURS FOR HIRE
MALIBU (1993-1994)
1-14 .75 2.50

DINOSAURUS!
DELL FOUR COLOR SERIES (1960)
1120 Movie tie-in. (8/60) 16.00 50.00

DIRTY DOZEN, THE
DELL (1967)
12-180-710 Movie tie-in. 8.00 25.00

DIRTY PAIR
ECLIPSE (1988-1989)
1-4 1.50 5.00

DIRTY PAIR ANIME COMICS
VIZ (1994)
1-5 1.25 4.95

DIRTY PAIR BOOK III: A PLAGUE OF ANGELS
ECLIPSE (1990-1991)
1-5 1.25 4.00

DIRTY PAIR: FATAL BUT NOT SERIOUS
DARK HORSE (1995)
1-5 .75 2.95

DIRTY PAIR II
ECLIPSE (1989)
1-5 1.50 5.00

DIRTY PAIR: SIM HELL
DARK HORSE (1993)
1-4 1.00 3.25

DISNEYLAND BIRTHDAY PARTY
DELL (1958)
1 Dell Giant. Art: Carl Barks. 50.00 150.00

DISTANT SOIL, A
ARIA PRESS (1991-CURRENT)
1 1.50 5.00
1 (2ND) 2nd printing. .75 2.50
1 (3RD) 3rd printing. .75 2.50
1 (4TH) 4th printing. .75 2.50
2 1.00 3.50
2 (2ND) 2nd printing. .50 1.75
3 1.00 3.00
3 (2ND) 2nd printing. .50 1.75
4 1.00 3.00
4 (2ND) 2nd printing. .50 1.75
5-8 .75 2.00
9-10 .75 2.50

DISTANT SOIL, A
WARP GRAPHICS (1983-1985)
1 5.00 15.00
2-3 2.25 8.00
4-9 1.50 5.00

DIVER DAN
DELL (1962)
1 (#1254) From the 4-Color Series. TV photo cover. (2/62) 13.00 40.00
2 8.00 25.00

DIVISION 13
DARK HORSE (1994-1995)
1-4 .75 2.50

DIXIE DUGAN
COLUMBIA (1942-1949)
1 40.00 120.00
2 19.00 60.00
3 17.00 55.00
4-5 10.00 30.00
6-8 8.00 25.00
9-13 7.00 20.00

DIXIE DUGAN
PRIZE (1951-1954)
V3#1-V4#4 5.00 15.00

DIZZY DAMES
ACG (1952-1953)
1 11.00 35.00
2 7.00 20.00
3-6 5.00 15.00

DNAGENTS
ECLIPSE (1983-1985)
1-23 .50 1.50
24 Cover: Dave Stevens. .75 2.00

DO YOU BELIEVE IN NIGHTMARES?
ST. JOHN (1957-1958)
1 Art: Steve Ditko. 65.00 210.00
2 Art: Dick Ayers. 40.00 120.00

DOC SAVAGE
DC (1987)
1-4 .30 1.00

DOC SAVAGE
DC (1988-1990)
1-24 .30 1.00
ANNUAL 1 (1989) .30 1.00

DOC SAVAGE
GOLD KEY (1966)
1 (11/66) 13.00 40.00

DOC SAVAGE
MARVEL (1972-1974)
1 1.75 6.00
2-8 1.00 3.00

DOC SAVAGE
MARVEL (1975-1977) MAGAZINE
1 Movie photo cover (Ron Ely). 2.25 8.00
2-8 .75 2.00

DOC SAVAGE COMICS
STREET & SMITH (1940-1943)
1 500.00 1900.00
2 1st & Origin: Ajax. 250.00 825.00
3-4 145.00 480.00
5 1st & Origin: Astron. 130.00 420.00
6-7 110.00 360.00
8-12 95.00 300.00
13-20 85.00 270.00

DOC SAVAGE: CURSE OF THE FIRE GOD
DARK HORSE (1995-CURRENT)
1-3 .75 2.95

DOC SAVAGE GIANT SIZE
MARVEL (1975)
1 1.50 5.00

DOCTOR CHAOS
TRIUMPHANT (1993-1994)
0-10 .75 2.50

DOCTOR FATE
DC (1987)
1-4 1.00 3.00

DOCTOR FATE
DC (1989-1992)
1 .75 2.50
2-41 .50 1.75
ANNUAL 1 (1989) .75 2.50

DOCTOR SOLAR
GOLD KEY (1962-1982)
1 1st & Origin: Dr. Solar. 95.00 300.00
2 31.00 100.00
3-6 19.00 60.00
7-12 11.00 35.00
13-14 10.00 30.00
15 Origin retold: Dr. Solar. 10.00 30.00
16-24 10.00 30.00
25-26 7.00 20.00
27 (4/69) 7.00 20.00
28 (1981) 2.25 8.00
29-31 2.25 8.00

DOCTOR STRANGE
MARVEL (1968-1969)
169 Origin retold: Doctor Strange. "Now Unto Us Is Born...The Magician!" 35.00 110.00
170 "To Dream...Perchance To Die!" 16.00 50.00
171 "In The Shadow Of...Death!" 10.00 32.00
172 "I, Dormammu!" 10.00 32.00
173 "...When A World Awaits!" 10.00 32.00
174 "The Power And The Pendulum!" 10.00 32.00
175 "Unto Us...The Sons Of Satannish!" 10.00 32.00
176 "O Grave, Where Is Thy Victory?" 10.00 32.00
177 "Hail The Master!" 10.00 32.00
178 App: Black Knight. "...With One Beside Him!" 10.00 32.00
179 10.00 30.00
180 "Eternity, Eternity!" 10.00 30.00
181 "If A World Should Die Before I Wake..." 10.00 30.00
182 "...To Fight The Juggernaut!" 10.00 30.00
183 "Beware The Undying Ones!" 10.00 30.00

DOCTOR STRANGE
MARVEL (1974-1987)
1 10.00 30.00
2 5.00 16.00
3-10 2.25 8.00
11-26 1.50 5.00
27-29 1.00 3.50
30 1.00 3.00
31-81 .75 2.00
ANNUAL 1 (1976) .75 2.50

DOCTOR STRANGE CLASSICS
MARVEL (1984)
1-4 .30 1.00

DOCTOR STRANGE, SORCERER SUPREME
MARVEL (1988-CURRENT)
1 1.50 5.00
2 1.00 3.00
3-10 .75 2.25
11 1.50 5.00
12-49 .75 2.00
50 .75 2.95
51-59 .75 2.00
60 Midnight Sons. 1.25 4.00
61 Siege Of Darkness, pt.15. .75 2.50
62-74 .75 2.00
75 Double size. Foil stamped cover. 1.00 3.50
75A Regular cover. .75 2.50
76-81 .50 1.95
ANNUAL 2 (1992) 1.00 3.00
ANNUAL 3 (1993) .75 2.95
ANNUAL 4 (1994) .75 2.95

DOCTOR STRANGE: TRIUMPH AND TORMENT
MARVEL (1988)
GN 2.50 9.95
GN HC Hardcover. 5.00 14.95

DOCTOR STRANGE VS DRACULA
MARVEL (1994)
1 Reprint. .50 1.75

DOCTOR STRANGE/GHOST RIDER SPECIAL
MARVEL (1991)
1 1.00 3.25

DOCTOR STRANGE/SPIDER-MAN: WAY TO DUSTY DOOM
MARVEL (1994)
TPB 1.75 6.95

DOCTOR WHO
MARVEL (1984-1986)
1-23 .30 1.00

DOCTOR ZERO
MARVEL (1988-1989)
1-8 .30 1.00

DO-DO
NATIONWIDE (1950-1951)
1 5" x 7" format on all issues. 19.00 60.00
2-7 10.00 30.00

DODO AND THE FROG, THE
DC (1954-1957)
80 Previous title: Funny Stuff. 31.00 100.00
81-85 23.00 75.00
86-91 20.00 65.00
92 25.00 80.00

DIRTY PAIR: FATAL BUT NOT SERIOUS #1

DIVISION 13 #1

DOCTOR FATE #2

DOCTOR STRANGE #29

DOLL MAN #23

DONALD DUCK 4C #159

DONALD DUCK #250 (GLADSTONE)

DOOM 2099 #2

DOG OF FLANDERS, A
DELL FOUR COLOR SERIES (1960)
1088 Movie photo cover. (4/60) ... 10.00 30.00

DOGFACE DOOLEY
I.W.
1 Reprints A-1 series. ...3.00 ...12.00

DOGFACE DOOLEY (A-1 SERIES)
ME (1951-1953)
1 (A-1 #40). 8.00 25.00
2 (A-1 #43). 7.00 20.00
3 (A-1 #49). 7.00 20.00
4 (A-1 #53). 7.00 20.00
5 (A-1 #64). 7.00 20.00

DOGS OF WAR
DEFIANT (1994)
1-5 .75 2.50

DOLL MAN
QUALITY (1941-1953)
1 "Doll Man Battles The Phantom Duelist!" (Autumn/41) 400.00 1200.00
2 (Spring/42) 190.00 600.00
3 (Summer/42) 145.00 480.00
4 "The Dolls Of Death!" (Winter/42) 145.00 480.00
5 (Spring/43) 110.00 360.00
6 (Summer/43) 85.00 270.00
7 (Autumn/43) 85.00 270.00
8 1st: Torchy. (Spring/46) 100.00 330.00
9 (Summer/46) 75.00 240.00
10 "...Mauls The Murder Marionettes!" and more. (Autumn/46) 60.00 190.00
11 "The Doll Man Socks Crime Square In The Eye!" (Winter/46) 60.00 190.00
12 "Not Any Bigger, But Better!" (Spring/47) 60.00 190.00
13 "The Doll Man Blows Crime Sky High!" (Summer/47) 60.00 190.00
14 "The Doll Man Puts The Spotlight On Crime!" (Autumn/47) 60.00 190.00
15 "The Doll Man Faces Danger!" (Winter/47) 60.00 190.00
16 "The Doll Man Condenses For Action And Thrills!" 50.00 160.00
17 "...Deals Out Punishment For Crime!" 50.00 160.00
18 "...And The Redskins Scalp Crime!" 50.00 160.00
19 "...Is Fitted For A Cement Coffin!" 50.00 160.00
20 "...Destroys The Black Heart Of Nemo Black!" 50.00 160.00
21 "...Solves The Problem Of A Poison Pistol!" 50.00 160.00
22 "...Battles Tom Thumb, Miniature Master Of Menace!" 50.00 160.00
23 "...Meets The Minstrel, Musician Of Menace!" 50.00 160.00
24 "...Smashes The Perilous Elixir Of Youth!" 50.00 160.00
25 "...Short Circuits Thrawn, Lord Of Lightning!" 50.00 160.00
26-28 50.00 150.00
29-34 40.00 130.00
35 "The Prophet Of Doom!" 40.00 130.00
36 40.00 130.00
37 Origin: Dollgirl. 55.00 180.00
38-47 31.00 100.00

DOMINO CHANCE
CHANCE (1984-1985)
1 .75 2.00
2-6 .30 1.00
7 1st: Gizmo. .30 1.00
8 1st: full Gizmo story. .30 1.00
9-20 .30 1.00

DON FORTUNE
FORTUNE (1946-1947)
1 Art: C.C. Beck in all issues. 25.00 80.00
2-3 14.00 46.00
4-6 11.00 34.00

DON NEWCOMBE BASEBALL HERO
FAWCETT (1950)
NO# Photo cover. 85.00 270.00

DON WINSLOW OF THE NAVY
FAWCETT (1948-1955)
1 180.00 575.00
2 100.00 330.00
3 70.00 220.00
4-5 50.00 160.00
6 Patriotic flag cover. 50.00 160.00
7-12 35.00 110.00
13-18 25.00 80.00
19-24 19.00 60.00
25-30 17.00 55.00
31-40 14.00 44.00
41-50 12.00 38.00
51-63 10.00 33.00
64 Art: Matt Baker. 15.00 49.00
65 Photo cover. 15.00 49.00
66-69 Photo cover. 14.00 44.00
70-73 9.00 27.00

DON'T GIVE UP THE SHIP
DELL FOUR COLOR SERIES (1959)
1049 Movie photo cover (Jerry Lewis). (9/59) 16.00 50.00

DONALD AND MICKEY IN DISNEYLAND
DELL (1958)
1 Dell Giant. 23.00 75.00

DONALD AND MICKEY MERRY CHRISTMAS
DISNEY (1943-1949)
1943 Firestone giveaway. Reprints Walt Disney Comics & Stories #32, Barks art. 140.00 450.00
1944 Firestone giveaway. 125.00 400.00
1945 Firestone giveaway. 155.00 500.00
1946 Firestone giveaway. Santa's Stormy Visit. 125.00 400.00
1947-1948 Firestone giveaway. 95.00 300.00
1949 Firestone giveaway. 110.00 350.00

DONALD DUCK
ALSO SEE LARGE FEATURE COMICS #16.

DONALD DUCK
DELL (1952-1990)
26 "Trick Or Treat" by Carl Barks. 80.00 250.00
27 "...And The Flying Horse" 10.00 30.00
28 "...And Robert The Robot" 10.00 30.00
29-30 10.00 30.00
31-44 7.00 20.00
45 Art: Carl Barks (6 pgs). 16.00 50.00
46 "Secret Of Hondurica" by Carl Barks. 23.00 75.00
47-51 5.00 15.00
52 "Lost Peg-Leg Mine" by Carl Barks. 19.00 60.00
53 5.00 15.00
54 "Forbidden Valley" by Carl Barks. 19.00 60.00
55-59 5.00 15.00
60 "Donald Duck And The Titanic Ants" by Carl Barks. 16.00 50.00
61-67 4.00 12.00
68 Art: Carl Barks. 8.00 25.00
69-90 4.00 12.00
91-100 2.75 10.00
101-115 2.50 9.00
116-130 2.25 8.00
131-140 1.75 6.00
141-160 1.50 5.00
161-175 1.25 4.00
176-200 1.00 3.00
201-225 .75 2.50
226-245 .75 2.00

DONALD DUCK
DELL FOUR COLOR SERIES (1942-1961)
9 "Finds Pirate Gold!" Art: Carl Barks. 1700.00 6500.00
29 "The Mummy's Ring" Art: Carl Barks. 1300.00 4800.00
62 "Frozen Gold" Art: Carl Barks. 400.00 1200.00
108 "The Terror Of The River". 290.00 950.00
147 "Volcano Valley". 210.00 675.00
159 "The Ghost Of The Grotto" Art: Carl Barks. 190.00 600.00
178 "Christmas On Bear Mountain". 190.00 600.00
189 "The Old Castle's Secret" Art: Carl Barks. 170.00 550.00
199 "Sheriff Of Bullet Valley". 170.00 550.00
203 "The Golden Christmas Tree" Art: Carl Barks. 155.00 500.00
223 "Lost In The Andes." 155.00 500.00
238 "Voodoo Hoodoo" Art: Carl Barks. 140.00 450.00
256 "Luck Of The North" Art: Carl Barks. 95.00 300.00
263 "Land Of The Totem Poles". 95.00 300.00
275 "Ancient Persia". 95.00 300.00
282 "The Pixilated Parrot." 95.00 300.00
291 "The Magic Hourglass." 85.00 275.00
300 "Big-Top Bedlam." 95.00 300.00
308 "Dangerous Disguise." 80.00 250.00
318 "No Such Varmint". Art: Carl Barks. 80.00 250.00
328 "Old California." 80.00 250.00
339 "The Magic Fountain." Not by Barks. 19.00 60.00
348 "The Crocodile Collector." Cover: Carl Barks. 23.00 75.00
356 "Rags To Riches." Cover: Carl Barks. 23.00 75.00
367 "A Christmas For Shacktown." 70.00 225.00
379 "Southern Hospitality." Not by Barks. 14.00 45.00
394 "Malayalaya." Cover: Carl Barks. 20.00 65.00
408 "The Golden Helmet." 70.00 225.00
422 "The Gilded Man." 70.00 225.00
1051 "In Mathmagic Land". Disney movie tie-in. (8/59) 23.00 75.00
1109 "This Is Your Life...". Disney TV tie-in. (8/60) 50.00 150.00
1190 "And The Wheel". Disney movie tie-in. (11/61) 16.00 50.00
1198 "In Mathmagic Land". Disney movie tie-in. (2/61) 16.00 50.00

DONALD DUCK
GLADSTONE (1986-CURRENT)
246 2.25 8.00
247-249 1.00 3.00
250 Reprints "Donald Duck Finds Pirate Gold!" by Barks. 2.75 10.00
251-256 1.00 3.00
257 1.25 4.00
258-260 1.00 3.00
261-270 .75 2.00
271-277 .50 1.50
278-279 Double size. .75 2.50
280-285 .50 1.50

DONALD DUCK ALBUM
DELL FOUR COLOR SERIES (1959-1961)
995 (5/59) 8.00 25.00
1099 Cover: Carl Barks. (5/60) 8.00 25.00
1140 (10/60) 8.00 25.00
1182 (7/61) 8.00 25.00
1239 Cover: Carl Barks. (9/61) 8.00 25.00

DONALD DUCK AND THE PIRATES
DISNEY (1947)
W1 Disney Cheerios Premium. 7.00 20.00

DONALD DUCK BEACH PARTY
DELL (1954-1959)
1 Dell Giant. 31.00 100.00
2 20.00 65.00
3-6 19.00 60.00

DONALD DUCK BEACH PARTY
GOLD KEY (1965)
10158-509 8.00 25.00

DONALD DUCK COMIC PAINT BOOK
SEE LARGE FEATURE COMICS #20.

DONALD DUCK, COUNTER SPY
DISNEY (1947)
X1 Disney Cheerios Premium. 7.00 20.00

DONALD DUCK FUN BOOK
DELL (1953-1954)
1 Games and puzzles. 110.00 350.00
2 Giant edition. 95.00 300.00

DONALD DUCK IN DISNEYLAND
DELL (1955)
1 Dell Giant. 40.00 125.00

DONALD DUCK PILOTS A JET PLANE
DISNEY (1947)
Z1 Disney Cheerios Premium. 7.00 20.00

DONALD DUCK'S ATOM BOMB
DISNEY (1947)
Y1 Disney Cheerios Premium. Art: Carl Barks. 80.00 250.00

DONATELLO
MIRAGE (1986)
1 One-shot. 1.75 6.00

DONDI
DELL FOUR COLOR SERIES (1961)
1176 Movie photo cover. (1/61) 10.00 30.00
1276 (12/61) 10.00 30.00

DOOM 2099
MARVEL (1993-CURRENT)
1 Foil cover. 1.00 3.00
2-24 .50 1.50
25 Foil stamped, embossed cover. .75 2.95
25A Regular cover. .75 2.25
26-28 .50 1.50
29 Chromium cover. 1.00 3.50
29A Regular cover. .50 1.95
30-32 .50 1.95

DOOM PATROL
DC (1964-1973)
86 Previous title: My Greatest Adventures. 25.00 80.00
87 14.00 45.00
88 Origin: The Chief. 14.00 45.00
89-98 14.00 45.00

99 App: Beast. 14.00 45.00
100 Origin: Beast. 19.00 60.00
101 8.00 25.00
102 10.00 30.00
103-120 8.00 25.00
121 Death: The Doom Patrol. 22.00 70.00
122-123 Reprints. 1.00 3.00
124 1.00 3.00

DOOM PATROL
DC (1987-1994)
1 .75 2.00
2 .50 1.75
3 1st: Lodestone. .50 1.75
4 1st: Karma. .50 1.75
5-8 .50 1.50
9-16 .50 1.25
17 1.25 4.00
18 1.00 3.00
19 Origin: Grant Morrison scripts. 2.25 8.00
20-29 1.50 5.00
30-49 .75 2.00
50 1.00 3.00
51-52 .75 2.00
53-56 .50 1.50
57 .75 2.50
58-60 .50 1.50
61-62 .50 1.75
63 End: Morrison scripts. .50 1.75
64-65 .50 1.75
66-87 .50 1.95
ANNUAL 1 (1988) .50 1.50
ANNUAL 2 Children's Crusade. (1994) 1.00 3.95
TPB Crawling From The Wreckage. Reprints issues #19-25. 6.00 19.95

DOOM'S IV
IMAGE (1994)
1 1st: Doom's IV .75 2.50
2-4 .75 2.50
1/2 Wizard mail-away offer. 2.75 10.00
SOURCEBOOK .75 2.50

DOORWAY TO NIGHTMARE
DC (1978)
1-5 .30 1.00

DOPEY DUCK COMICS
MARVEL (1945-1946)
1 40.00 125.00
2 Title changes to Wacky Duck with #3. 25.00 80.00

DOROTHY LAMOUR
FOX (1950)
2 Previous title: Jungle Lil. Movie photo cover. 31.00 100.00
3 Movie photo cover. 31.00 100.00

DOTTY
ACE (1948-1949)
35 8.00 25.00
36-38 5.00 15.00
39-40 2.75 10.00

DOTTY DRIPPLE AND TAFFY
DELL FOUR COLOR SERIES (1955-1958)
646 (9/55) 7.00 20.00
691 (4/56) 7.00 20.00
718 (8/56) 5.00 15.00
746 (11/56) 5.00 15.00
801 (5/57) 7.00 20.00
903 (5/58) 7.00 20.00

DOUBLE ACTION COMICS
DC (1940)
2 Same cover as Adventure #37. 3100.00 12000.00

DOUBLE COMICS
ELLIOT (1940-1944)
1 (NO#) 128 pages (1940). 400.00 1200.00
2 (NO#) 128 pages (1941). 310.00 1000.00
3 (NO#) 128 pages (1942). 230.00 750.00
4 (NO#) 128 pages (1943). 230.00 750.00
5 (NO#) 128 pages (1944). 230.00 750.00

DOUBLE DARE ADVENTURES
HARVEY (1966-1967)
1 Art: Simon & Kirby. Origin: Bee Man. (12/66) 11.00 34.00
2 (3/67) 9.00 28.00

DOUBLE DRAGON
MARVEL (1991)
1-6 .20 .50

DOUBLE EDGE: ALPHA
MARVEL (1995)
1 Chromium cover. 1.75 5.50

DOUBLE IMPACT
HIGH IMPACT (1995-CURRENT)
1 1st: China & Jazz. Chromium cover. 2.25 8.50
1A Limited prismatic/rainbow cover. 7.00 20.00
2 1.25 4.00
2A Alternate (nude) cover in black bag. 7.00 20.00
2B Alternate (nude) cover in silver bag. 10.00 30.00
3 .75 2.95

DOUBLE LIFE OF PRIVATE STRONG
ARCHIE (1959)
1 1st & Origin: The Fly. Origin: The Shield. Cover & art: Simon & Kirby. 130.00 430.00
2 Cover & art: Simon & Kirby. 95.00 300.00

DOUBLE TROUBLE WITH GOOBER
DELL FOUR COLOR SERIES (1952-1954)
417 (8/52) 7.00 20.00
471 (5/53) 5.00 15.00
516 (11/53) 5.00 15.00
556 (4/54) 5.00 15.00

DOUBLE UP COMICS
ELLIOT (1941)
1 Pocket size. 125.00 400.00

DOWN WITH CRIME
FAWCETT (1951-1952)
1 "The Houdini Of Crime!" (11/51) 29.00 95.00
2-4 14.00 44.00
5-7 12.00 38.00

D.P.7
MARVEL (1986-1989)
1-32 .30 1.00
ANNUAL 1 (1987) .30 1.00

DR. BOBBS
DELL FOUR COLOR SERIES (1949)
212 (1/49) 10.00 30.00

DR. FU MANCHU
I.W. (1964)
1 16.00 50.00

DR. KILDARE
DELL (1962-1965)
1 (#1337) From the 4-Color Series. TV photo cover. 13.00 40.00
2 TV photo covers on all issues. 10.00 30.00
3-9 10.00 30.00

DR. WHO AND THE DALEKS
DELL (1966)
12-190-612 Movie photo cover. 25.00 80.00

DRACULA
DELL (1962-1973)
1 (#12-231-212) Movie tie-in. 2.75 10.00
2 Origin: New Dracula. 1.75 6.00
3-4 1.50 5.00
6 Reprint. (7/72) 1.00 3.00
7-8 Reprint. 1.00 3.00

DRACULA (BRAM STOKER'S...)
TOPPS (1992-1993)
1 With trading cards. Movie tie-in. .75 2.95
1A Red foil cover. 8.00 25.00
2-4 .75 2.95
TPB Reprints issues #1-4, foil enhanced cover. 5.00 13.95

DRACULA LIVES
MARVEL (1973-1975) MAGAZINE
1 2.75 10.00
2-13 1.50 5.00
ANNUAL (1975) 1.50 5.00

DRACULA: VLAD THE IMPALER
TOPPS (1993)
1-3 .75 2.95

DRACULA VS. ZORRO
TOPPS (1993)
1-3 .75 2.95

DRAG 'N WHEELS
CHARLTON (1968-1973)
30-59 2.75 10.00

DRAG STRIP HOTRODDERS
CHARLTON (1963-1967)
1 8.00 25.00
2 5.00 15.00
3 4.00 12.00
4-6 2.75 10.00
7-16 2.50 9.00

DRAGON: BLOOD AND GUTS
IMAGE/HIGH BROW (1995)
1-3 .75 2.50

DRAGON FORCE
AIRCEL (1988-1989)
1-13 .75 2.00

DRAGON'S CLAWS
MARVEL(UK) (1988-1989)
1 .75 2.00
2-4 .50 1.75
5 1st: full Death's Head II. 2.25 8.00
6-10 .50 1.75

DRAGONLANCE
DC (1988-1991)
1-34 .50 1.50

DRAGONSLAYER
MARVEL (1981)
1 Movie Adaptation. .30 1.00
2 .30 1.00

DRAGOON WELLS MASSACRE
DELL FOUR COLOR SERIES (1957)
815 Movie photo cover. (7/57) 19.00 60.00

DRAMA
SIRIUS (1994)
1A Limited, signed & numbered. 10.00 30.00
1 One shot. App: Dawn. 2.75 10.00

DREADSTAR
MALIBU (1994-CURRENT)
1 1st: Kalla (female Dreadstar). .75 2.50
2-6 .75 2.50

DREADSTAR
MARVEL(EPIC)/FIRST (1982-1991)
1 Origin: Dreadstar. 1.25 4.50
2-26 .50 1.50
27 Begin First publication. .50 1.50
28-64 .50 1.50
ANNUAL 1 (1983) 1.00 3.00

DREADSTAR AND COMPANY
MARVEL (1985)
1-6 .30 1.00

DREADWOLF
LIGHTNING (1994)
1 1.00 3.50

DREAM BOOK OF LOVE (A-1 SERIES)
ME (1954)
1 (A-1 #106). Art: Bob Powell. 17.00 55.00
2 (A-1 #114). 17.00 55.00
3 (A-1 #123). Movie photo cover. 17.00 55.00

DREAM BOOK OF ROMANCE (A-1 SERIES)
ME (1954)
5 (A-1 #92). 11.00 34.00
6 (A-1 #101). Movie photo cover (Marlon Brando). 25.00 80.00
7 (A-1 #109). Art: Bob Powell. 13.00 40.00
8 (A-1 #110). Movie photo cover. 14.00 46.00
9 (A-1 #124). 11.00 34.00

DREAM CORRIDOR
SEE HARLAN ELLISON'S DREAM CORRIDOR

DREAM OF LOVE
IW (1958)
8-9 2.75 10.00

DROIDS
MARVEL(STAR) (1986-1987)
1 TV cartoon tie-in. .75 2.00
2-8 .30 1.00

DRUM BEAT
DELL FOUR COLOR SERIES (1955)
610 Movie photo cover (Alan Ladd). (1/55) 25.00 80.00

DUCK ALBUM
DELL FOUR COLOR SERIES (1951-1957)
353 Cover: Carl Barks. (10/51) 13.00 40.00
450 (2/53) 11.00 35.00
492 (8/53) 7.00 22.00
531 (1/54) 7.00 22.00
560 (5/54) 7.00 20.00
586 (9/54) 7.00 20.00
611 (1/55) 7.00 20.00

DRAMA #1

DREADSTAR #14 (MARVEL)

DREADWOLF #1

DROIDS #1

DUNE #1

DURANGO KID #1

THE EAGLE #3

EERIE #9 (AVON)

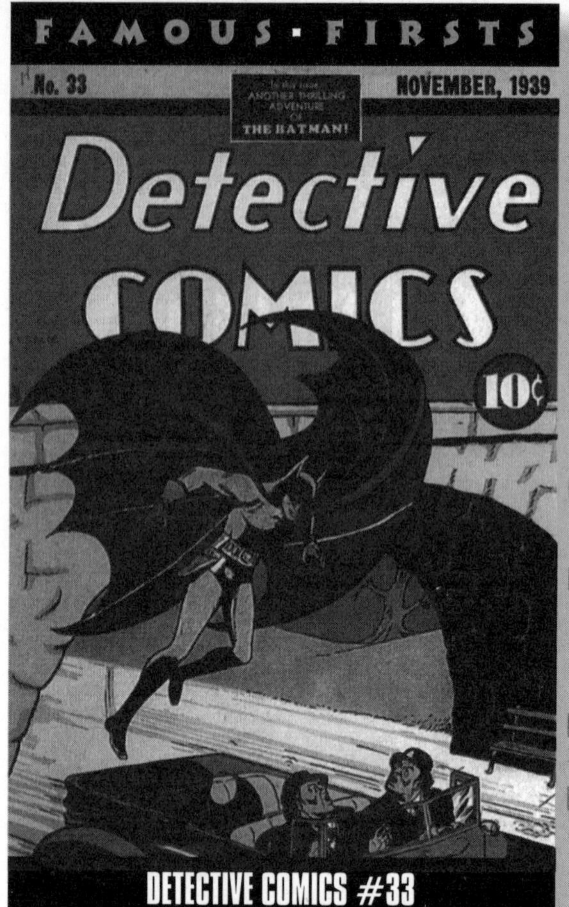

DETECTIVE COMICS #33

It took six issues for DC to reveal how Bruce Wayne became Batman. The two-page summation shows Thomas and Martha Wayne being shot by a robber, Bruce's vow of vengeance, and that symbolic bat flying through the window.

649 (9/55) 7.00 20.00
686 (3/56) 7.00 20.00
726 (9/56) 7.00 20.00
782 (3/57) 8.00 25.00
840 (9/57) 7.00 20.00

DUDLEY
PRIZE (1949-1950)
1 .... 19.00 60.00
2-3 .... 10.00 30.00

DUMBO
DELL FOUR COLOR SERIES (1949-1956)
234 "Sky Voyage" (7/49) 20.00 65.00
668 (12/55) 13.00 40.00
668A Cover variant-Mouse on trunk. (1/56)
.... 11.00 35.00

DUMBO
GOLD KEY (1963)
10090-310 Disney movie tie-in. 5.00 15.00

DUMBO AND THE CIRCUS MYSTERY
DISNEY (1947)
Y3 Disney Cheerios Premium. 5.00 15.00

DUMBO COMIC PAINT BOOK
SEE LARGE FEATURE COMICS #19.

DUNC AND LOO
SEE: AROUND THE BLOCK WITH DUNC AND LOO.

DUNE
MARVEL (1985)
1 Movie Adaptation. .... .75 2.00
2-3 .... .75 2.00

DURANGO KID
ME (1949-1955)
1 Begin: Frank Frazetta art. Photo cover (Charles Starrett).
.... 100.00 330.00
2 Photo cover (Charles Starrett). 70.00 220.00
3-5 Photo cover (Charles Starrett). 55.00 170.00
6-10 .... 29.00 95.00
11-15 .... 23.00 75.00
16 End: Frank Frazetta art. 23.00 75.00
17 Origin: Durango Kid. 26.00 85.00
18-30 .... 17.00 55.00
31 Return: Red Scorpion. 14.00 44.00
32-41 .... 17.00 55.00

DYNAMIC ADVENTURES
IW (1964)
9 Reprint. 2.25 8.00

DYNAMIC CLASSICS
DC (1978)
1 Art: Neal Adams. 1.00 3.00

DYNAMIC COMICS
CHESLER (1941-1948)
1 Origin: Major Victory. 210.00 675.00
2 .... 115.00 370.00
3 .... 85.00 280.00
4-7 .... 55.00 170.00
8 .... 70.00 230.00
9 .... 65.00 200.00
10 .... 60.00 190.00
11-16 .... 55.00 170.00
17 SOTI 70.00 230.00
18-20 .... 35.00 110.00
21-25 .... 31.00 100.00

DYNAMITE
COMIC MEDIA (1953-1954)
1 .... 23.00 75.00
2 .... 16.00 50.00
3-8 .... 13.00 40.00
9 Title changes to Johnny Dynamite with issue #10.
.... 13.00 40.00

DYNAMO
TOWER (1966-1967)
1 Art: Wallace Wood. 10.00 30.00
2-4 .... 7.00 20.00

DYNAMO JOE
FIRST (1986-1988)
1-15 .... .30 1.00
SPECIAL 1 (1987) .... .30 1.00

EAGLE
APPLE (1986-1989)
1 .... .75 2.00
2-26 .... .50 1.50

EAGLE, THE
FOX (1941-1942)
1 .... 230.00 750.00
2 Origin: Spider Queen. 155.00 500.00
3-4 .... 115.00 370.00

EAGLE
RHP (1945)
1 .... 31.00 100.00
2 .... 22.00 70.00

EARTH 4
CONTINUITY (1993-1994)
1 (No. 0 on inside) Deathwatch 2000, pt.6. .75 2.50
2 Deathwatch 2000, pt.11. .... .75 2.50
3 Deathwatch 2000, pt.18. Tyvek cover. .75 2.50
V2#1-V2#2 .... .75 2.50
V2#3 (Vol.2 absent from issue number). .75 2.50

EARTH MAN ON VENUS, AN
AVON (1951)
NO# Art: Wallace Wood. 155.00 500.00

EASTER WITH MOTHER GOOSE
DELL FOUR COLOR SERIES (1946-1949)
103 .... 45.00 140.00
140 .... 31.00 100.00
185 (3/48) 28.00 90.00
220 (3/49) 28.00 90.00

ECLIPSO
DC (1992-1994)
1 .... .50 1.50
2-18 .... .50 1.25
ANNUAL 1 Bloodlines, pt.19. 1st: Prism. (1993)
.... .75 2.50

ECLIPSO: THE DARKNESS WITHIN
DC (1992)
1A With gem attached. 1.25 4.00
1B Newsstand (without gem). .... .50 1.50
2 .... .75 2.50

ECTOKID
MARVEL (1993-1994)
1-10 .... .50 1.50

ECTOKID UNLEASHED
MARVEL (1994)
1 .... .75 2.95

EDDIE STANKY
FAWCETT (1951)
NO# Photo cover. 65.00 200.00

EDGAR BERGEN PRESENTS CHARLIE MCCARTHY
WHITMAN (1938)
764 Big Little Book tie-in. Large size. 190.00 600.00

EERIE
AVON (1951-1954)
1 .... 75.00 240.00
2 Cover/Art: Wallace Wood. 95.00 300.00
3-5 Cover: Wallace Wood. 75.00 240.00
6 .... 31.00 100.00
7 Art: Joe Kubert. 55.00 180.00
8 .... 31.00 100.00
9 Art: Joe Kubert. 40.00 120.00
10-11 .... 29.00 95.00
12 Dracula. 40.00 120.00
13-14 .... 29.00 95.00
15-17 .... 25.00 80.00

EERIE
I.W. (1964)
1-2 .... 5.00 15.00

EERIE
WARREN (1966-1983) MAGAZINE
1 Black & white, 24 pages. 80.00 250.00
2 Cover: Frank Frazetta. 17.00 55.00
3 Cover: Frank Frazetta. 10.00 31.00
4 8.00 25.00
5 Cover: Frazetta. 8.00 25.00
6 8.00 25.00
7-8 Cover: Frazetta. 8.00 25.00
9-10 8.00 25.00
11-30 6.00 18.00
31-50 4.00 12.00
51-59 2.75 10.00
60 Summer Giant. 4.00 12.00
61-75 2.25 8.75
76-90 2.00 7.50
91-100 1.75 6.25
101-120 1.50 5.00
121-139 1.00 3.75

EERIE ADVENTURES
ZIFF-DAVIS (1951)
1 40.00 125.00

EERIE COMICS
AVON (1947)
1 1st horror comic? "The Eyes Of The Tiger!" by Jerry Robinson. 250.00 800.00

EGYPT
DC (1995-CURRENT)
1-2 .75 2.50

EH!
CHARLTON (1953-1954)
1 40.00 125.00
2 Cover/Art: Dick Ayers. 25.00 80.00
3-5 22.00 70.00
6 Art: Dick Ayers. 22.00 70.00
7 22.00 70.00

EIGHTBALL
FANTAGRAPHICS (1989-CURRENT)
1 Begin: Like A Velvet Glove. 2.75 10.00
1 (2ND) 2nd printing. .75 2.95
1 (3RD) 3rd printing. .75 2.95
1 (4TH) 4th printing. .75 2.95
1 (5TH) 5th printing. .75 2.95
1 (6TH) 6th printing. .75 2.95
2 1.50 5.00
2 (2ND) 2nd printing. .75 2.75
2 (3RD) 3rd printing. .75 2.75
2 (4TH) 4th printing. .75 2.75
3 1.50 5.00
3 (2ND) 2nd printing. .75 2.95
3 (3RD) 3rd printing. .75 2.75
3 (4TH) 4th printing. .75 2.75
4 1.50 5.00
4 (2ND) 2nd printing. .75 2.75
4 (3RD) 3rd printing. .75 2.75
4 (4TH) 4th printing. .75 2.75
5 1.50 5.00
5 (2ND) 2nd printing. .75 2.75
6 1.00 3.00
6 (2ND) 2nd printing. .75 2.75
7 .75 2.75
7 (2ND) 2nd printing. .75 2.75
8 .75 2.95
8 (2ND) 2nd printing. .75 2.95
9 .75 2.75
10 End: Like A Velvet Glove. .75 2.75
11 Begin: Ghost World. .75 2.95
12 .75 2.75
13 Printing error. .75 2.95
13 (2ND) 2nd printing. .75 2.95
14-15 .75 2.95

EIGHTY PAGE GIANT
DC (1964-1971)
1 Superman Annual. (8/64) 95.00 300.00
2 Jimmy Olsen. 55.00 175.00
3 Lois Lane. 50.00 150.00
4 The Flash. 50.00 150.00
5 Batman (25th anniversary). 50.00 150.00
6 Superman. 31.00 100.00
7 Sgt. Rock's Prize Battle Tales. 40.00 125.00
8 Secret Origins. 80.00 250.00
9 The Flash. 40.00 120.00
10 Superboy. 31.00 100.00
11 Superman. 31.00 100.00
12 Batman. 31.00 100.00
13 Jimmy Olsen. 31.00 100.00
14 Lois Lane. 31.00 100.00
15 World's Finest (Superman & Batman). 31.00 100.00

EIGHTY SEVENTH PRECINCT
DELL (1962)
1 (#1309) From the 4-Color Series. TV photo cover. (4/62) 23.00 75.00
2 TV photo cover. 13.00 40.00

EL CID
DELL FOUR COLOR SERIES (1962)
1259 Movie photo cover. 16.00 50.00

EL DORADO
DELL (1967)
12-240-710 Movie photo cover (John Wayne). 28.00 90.00

ELEKTRA ASSASSIN
MARVEL (1986-1987)
1 1.50 5.00
2 1.25 4.00
3-8 1.00 3.00

ELEKTRA LIVES AGAIN
MARVEL (1991)
GN Hardcover Graphic Novel. 8.00 24.95

ELEKTRA: ROOT OF EVIL
MARVEL (1995)
1 Mini-series. Foil stamped cover. 1.25 4.00
2 Foil stamped cover. 1.00 3.50
3-4 1.00 3.50

ELEKTRA SAGA
MARVEL (1984)
1 1.75 6.00
2-4 1.50 5.50

ELEMENTALS
COMICO (1984-1988)
1 1st: Destroyers. 2.00 7.00
2 1.75 6.00
3 1.00 3.50
4-10 .75 2.50
11-29 .75 2.00

ELEMENTALS
COMICO (1989-CURRENT)
1-28 .75 2.50
29 Poster edition. 1.25 4.95
29A Regular edition. .75 2.50
30 Prism foil enhanced cover. 1.25 4.95
30A Regular edition. .75 2.50
31-34 .75 2.50
SPECIAL 1-SPECIAL 2 .75 2.00

ELEMENTALS: OBLIVION WAR
COMICO (1992)
1-2 .75 2.95

ELEMENTALS: SEX SPECIAL
COMICO (1992-1993)
1 .75 2.95
1A Gold edition. 1.25 4.95
2 .75 2.95
2A 2nd printing. .75 2.95
3-7 .75 2.95

ELEMENTALS: STRIKE FORCE LEGACY
COMICO (1992)
1 1.00 3.95

ELEVEN OR ONE: AN ANGRY CHRIST COMIC
SIRIUS (1995)
1 One shot. 1.25 4.00

ELFLORD
AIRCEL (1986-1989)
1 1.00 3.00
2-20 .75 2.00

ELFQUEST
MARVEL(EPIC) (1985-1988)
1-32 .50 1.50

ELFQUEST
WARP GRAPHICS (1978-1985) MAGAZINE
1 1st print, $1 cover price. 13.00 40.00
1 (2ND) 2nd printing. 4.00 11.00
1 (3RD) 3rd printing. 1.75 6.00
2 1st print, $1 cover price. "Raid At Sorrow's End." 7.00 20.00
2 (2ND) 2nd printing. 1.50 5.00
2 (3RD) 3rd printing. 1.00 3.00
3 1st print, $1 cover price. "The Challenge." 7.00 20.00
3 (2ND) 2nd printing. 1.50 5.00
3 (3RD) 3rd printing. 1.00 3.00
4 1st print, $1 cover price. "Wolfsong." 7.00 20.00
4 (2ND) 2nd printing. 1.50 5.00
4 (3RD) 3rd printing. 1.00 3.00
5 1st print, $1 cover price. "Voice Of The Sun." 7.00 20.00
5 (2ND) 2nd printing. 1.50 5.00
5 (3RD) 3rd printing. 1.00 3.00
6 1st print, $1.25 cover price. "The Quest Begins." 7.00 20.00
6 (2ND) 2nd printing. 1.25 4.00
6 (3RD) 3rd printing. .75 2.00
7 1st print, $1.25 cover price. "The Dreamberry Tales." 4.00 13.00
7 (2ND) 2nd printing. 1.25 4.00
8 1st print, $1.25 cover price. "Hands Of The Symbol Maker." 4.00 13.00
8 (2ND) 2nd printing. 1.25 4.00
9 1st print, $1.25 cover price. "The Lodestone." 4.00 13.00
9 (2ND) 2nd printing. 1.25 4.00
10 1st print, $1.50 cover price. "The Forbidden Grove." 2.50 9.00
11 "Lair Of The Bird Spirits." 2.50 9.00
12 "What Is The Way?" 2.50 9.00
13 "The Secret Of The Wolfriders." 2.50 9.00
14 "The Fall." 2.50 9.00
15 "The Quest Usurped." 2.50 9.00
16 1st: A Distant Soil. 7.00 20.00
17-21 2.25 8.00

ELFQUEST: BLOOD OF TEN CHIEFS
WARP GRAPHICS (1993-CURRENT)
1-18 .75 2.50

ELFQUEST GATHERUM, THE
FANTAGRAPHICS (1981)
NO# Oversize b&w trade paperback with color covers dedicated to fans of Elfquest. $6.95 cover price. Richard & Wendy Pini drawn on the front cover by Wendy Pini. 5.00 15.00

ELFQUEST: HIDDEN YEARS
WARP GRAPHICS (1992-CURRENT)
1-14 .75 2.50
15 Double size. .75 2.50
16-21 .75 2.50
22 .75 2.50

ELFQUEST: JINK
WARP GRAPHICS (1994-CURRENT)
1-4 .75 2.25
5 .75 2.50
6 .75 3.00

ELFQUEST: KINGS OF THE BROKEN WHEEL
WARP GRAPHICS (1993)
1 1.00 4.00
2-6 .75 2.00

ELFQUEST: NEW BLOOD
WARP GRAPHICS (1992-CURRENT)
1-29 .75 2.50

ELFQUEST: REBELS
WARP GRAPHICS (1994-CURRENT)
1-4 .75 2.25
5-7 .75 2.50

ELFQUEST: SHARDS
WARP GRAPHICS (1994-CURRENT)
1-7 .75 2.50
8-9 .75 2.50

ELFQUEST: SIEGE AT BLUE MOUNTAIN
WARP GRAPHICS (1987-1988)
1 2.75 10.00
2 1.75 6.00
3-4 1.25 4.50
5-8 1.25 4.00

ELFQUEST: WAVE DANCERS
WARP GRAPHICS (1993-1994)
1 .75 2.50
2-6 .75 2.25

ELIMINATOR
MALIBU (1995)
0 (4/95) .75 2.95
1 .75 2.50
1A Black cover edition. 1.00 3.95
2-3 .75 2.50

ELLERY QUEEN
DELL FOUR COLOR SERIES (1961-1962)
1165 (2/61) 19.00 60.00
1243 (10/61) 16.00 50.00
1289 (2/62) 14.00 45.00

ELEMENTALS SEX SPECIAL #4

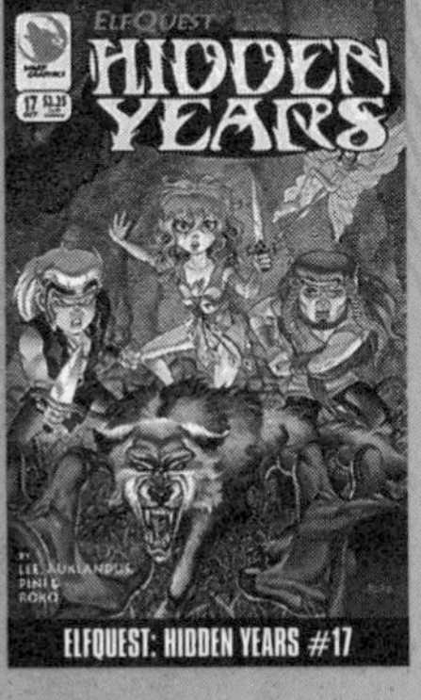

ELFQUEST: HIDDEN YEARS #17

ELFQUEST: NEW BLOOD #27

ELIMINATOR #1

ETERNAL WARRIOR #2

ETERNAL WARRIOR #7

EVIL ERNIE: REVENGE #4

EXCALIBER #42

ELLERY QUEEN
SUPERIOR (1949)
1 .... 55.00 175.00
2-4 .... 31.00 100.00

ELLERY QUEEN
ZIFF-DAVIS (1952)
1 .... 50.00 150.00
2 .... 40.00 120.00

ELMER FUDD
DELL FOUR COLOR SERIES (1953-1962)
470 (5/53) 7.00 20.00
558 (5/54) 5.00 15.00
628 (5/55) 5.00 15.00
689 (3/56) 5.00 15.00
725 (9/56) 5.00 15.00
783 (3/57) 5.00 15.00
841 (9/57) 5.00 15.00
888 (3/58) 5.00 15.00
938 (9/58) 5.00 15.00
977 (3/59) 5.00 15.00
1032 (9/59) 7.00 20.00
1081 (2/60) 5.00 15.00
1131 (9/60) 7.00 20.00
1171 (3/61) 7.00 20.00
1222 (8/61) 7.00 20.00
1293 (2/62) 8.00 25.00

ELSIE COMICS
D.S. (1957)
1-2 Bordon Milk giveaway. 10.00 30.00

ELSIE THE COW COMICS
D.S. (1949-1950)
1 .... 31.00 100.00
2-3 .... 23.00 75.00

ELVEN
MALIBU (1994-1995)
0 Double size. .... .75 2.95
1-4 .... .75 2.50

E-MAN
ALPHA PRODUCTIONS (1993-CURRENT)
1 Bagged with poster. 1.00 3.25
1A Regular edition. No poster. .... .75 2.75
2-4 .... 1.00 3.25
2A-3A Regular edition. No poster. .... .75 2.75
4A Regular edition. No poster. .... .75 2.75

E-MAN
CHARLTON (1973-1975)
1 1st & Origin: E-Man. 7.00 20.00
2 Art: Steve Ditko. 5.00 15.00
3 .... 2.50 9.00
4 Art: Steve Ditko. 5.00 15.00
5 .... 5.00 15.00
6-7 Art: John Byrne. 2.75 10.00
8 .... 4.00 12.00
9-10 Art: John Byrne. 2.75 10.00

E-MAN: FUTURE TENSE
ALPHA PRODUCTIONS (1995-CURRENT)
1 .... .75 2.75

E-MAN RETURNS
ALPHA (1993)
1 .... .50 1.50

EMIL AND THE DETECTIVES
GOLD KEY (1965)
10120-502 Disney movie photo cover. 7.00 20.00

ENDLESS GALLERY, THE
DC COMICS (1995)
1 .... 1.00 3.50

ENEMY
DARK HORSE (1994)
1-5 .... .75 2.50

ENIGMA
DC/VERTIGO (1993)
1 .... 1.50 4.00
2 .... 1.00 3.00
3-8 .... .75 2.50

ENSIGN PULVER
DELL (1964)
12-257-410 Movie tie-in. 7.00 20.00

EPIC ILLUSTRATED
MARVEL (1980-1986) MAGAZINE
1 Cover: Frank Frazetta. 1.50 5.00
2-25 .... 1.00 3.00
26 The Galactus Story, chapter 1. .... 1.00 3.00
27-31 .... 1.00 3.00
32 "The Ages Of Cerebus" portfolio. 1.00 3.00
33-34 .... 1.00 3.00

ERNIE COMICS
ACE (1948-1949)
22 Previous title: Andy Comics. 8.00 25.00
23 .... 7.00 20.00
24 .... 5.00 15.00
25 Title changes to All Love Romances with #26.
.... 5.00 15.00

ESCAPADE IN FLORENCE
GOLD KEY (1963)
10043-301 Disney TV movie photo cover (Annette Funicello).
.... 13.00 40.00

ESCAPE FROM DEVIL'S ISLAND
AVON (1952)
1 Cover: Kinstler. 40.00 125.00

ESPIONAGE
DELL (1964)
1-2 .... 4.00 12.00

ETERNAL WARRIOR
VALIANT (1992-CURRENT)
1 Origin: Eternal Warrior. Origin: Armstrong. 1.25 5.00
1A Gold logo variant. 2.25 8.00
1B Gold logo, Gold foil. 2.25 8.00
2-3 .... .75 2.50
4 1st: Bloodshot (cameo). 1.00 3.00
5 1st: full Bloodshot. .... .75 2.50
6 Master Darque. .... .75 2.50
7 .... .75 2.50
8 Combined with Archer & Armstrong #8. .... .75 2.50
9 .... .75 2.50
10-15 .... .75 2.25
16-17 Bloodshot. .... .75 2.25
18 Doctor Mirage. .... .75 2.25
19-25 .... .75 2.25
26 Combined with Archer & Armstrong #26. .75 2.25
27-32 .... .75 2.25
33 .... .50 1.95
34 .... .75 2.25
35-44 .... .75 2.50
YEARBOOK 1-YEARBOOK 2 .... 1.00 3.95

ETERNALS, THE
MARVEL (1976-1978)
1 Cover/Art: Jack Kirby in all issues. 1st & Origin: Eternals.
.... 1.25 4.00
2-19 .... .75 2.00
ANNUAL 1 (1977) 1.00 3.00

ETERNALS, THE
MARVEL (1985-1986)
1-12 .... .50 1.50

ETERNITY SMITH
HEROIC (1987-1988)
1 .... .75 2.50
2-9 .... .50 1.50

ETERNITY SMITH
RENEGADE (1986-1987)
1 1st: Eternity Smith. 1.50 5.00
2 .... 1.00 3.00
3-5 .... .75 2.00

EVE OF THE STORM
RIVAL (1995-CURRENT)
1 .... 1.50 5.00
2-3 .... 1.00 3.50

EVERYTHING HAPPENS TO HARVEY
DC (1953-1954)
1 .... 50.00 160.00
2 .... 29.00 95.00
3 .... 25.00 80.00
4-7 .... 20.00 65.00

EVERYTHING'S DUCKY
DELL FOUR COLOR SERIES (1961)
1251 Movie tie-in. (11/61) 13.00 40.00

EVIL ERNIE
CHAOS! (1995)
0 New Year's Evil. 1.50 5.00

EVIL ERNIE
ETERNITY (1991-1992)
1 1st: Evil Ernie. 1st: Lady Death. 35.00 110.00
2 1st: Lady Death cover. 25.00 80.00
3-4 Lady Death. 16.00 55.00
5 .... 16.00 50.00

EVIL ERNIE: REVENGE
CHAOS! (1994-1995)
1 App: Lady Death. 2.00 7.50
1A White, glow-in-the-dark limited edition. 13.00 40.00
2 .... 1.25 4.50
3-4 .... 1.00 3.00

EVIL ERNIE: THE RESURRECTION
CHAOS! (1993)
1 (GOLD) Limited. 16.00 50.00
1 .... 4.00 12.00
2 Holo-lithographic enhanced cover. 4.00 12.00
3 .... 4.00 12.00
4 .... 2.75 10.00
TPB Reprints issues #1-4. .... 5.00 14.95

EVIL ERNIE VS THE SUPERHEROES
CHAOS! (1995)
1 .... .75 2.95

EVIL ERNIE: YOUTH GONE WILD
CHAOS (1994)
TPB Reprints original 5-issue series from Eternity.
.... 2.50 9.95

EVIL KNIEVEL
MARVEL & IDEAL (1974)
NO# Giveaway. 1.50 5.00

EXCALIBUR
MARVEL (1988-CURRENT)
1 1st: Widget. 1st: Crazy Gang. 1.50 5.00
2-19 .... 1.00 3.00
20-49 .... .75 2.00
50 .... .75 2.75
51-57 .... .50 1.75
58 .... 1.00 3.00
59-70 .... .50 1.75
71 Hologram cover. 2.00 7.50
72-74 .... .50 1.75
75 Holo-grafic foil cover. Double size. 1.00 3.50
75A Newsstand edition. .... .75 2.25
76-80 .... .50 1.75
81 .... .50 1.95
82 Prismatic foil-stamped cover. Double size.
.... 1.00 3.50
82A Regular cover. .... .75 2.50
83 Deluxe edition. .... .50 1.95
83A Regular edition. .... .50 1.50
84 Deluxe edition. .... .50 1.95
84A Regular edition. .... .50 1.50
85 Deluxe edition. .... .50 1.95
85A Regular edition. .... .50 1.50
86 Deluxe edition (with card). .... .50 1.95
86A Regular edition (no card). .... .50 1.50
87-89 .... .50 1.95
ANNUAL 1 Polybagged with card. .... .75 2.95
ANNUAL 2 .... .75 2.95

EXCALIBUR: MOJO MAYHEM
MARVEL (1989)
NO# 1.00 3.00

EXCALIBUR SPECIAL
MARVEL (1987)
1 .... .75 2.50
2 .... .75 2.00

EXCALIBUR: THE SWORD IS DRAWN
MARVEL (1988)
NO# 1st Excalibur comic. (4/88) 2.75 10.00
NO# (2ND) 2nd printing. (10/88) .... .75 2.00
NO# (3RD) 3rd printing. (12/89) .... .75 2.00
NO#A New story. (4/92) 1.00 3.00

EXCALIBUR: XX CROSSING
MARVEL (1992)
1 .... .75 2.50

EXCITING COMICS
STANDARD (1940-1949)
1 1st & Origin: The Mask. 240.00 775.00
2 .... 110.00 360.00
3-6 .... 95.00 300.00
7-8 .... 75.00 240.00
9 1st & Origin: The Black Terror. 310.00 1000.00
10-14 .... 110.00 360.00
15 Begin: The Liberator. 95.00 300.00
16-20 .... 65.00 210.00
21-27 .... 50.00 150.00
28 Begin: Schomburg covers. 60.00 190.00
29-36 .... 50.00 150.00
37-50 .... 40.00 120.00
51 1st & Begin: Miss Masque. 75.00 240.00
52-55 .... 55.00 180.00
56-58 .... 65.00 210.00
59 Art: Frank Frazetta. 70.00 220.00
60-66 .... 50.00 150.00

67-69 31.00 100.00

EXCITING ROMANCES
FAWCETT (1949-1953)
1 19.00 60.00
2-5 11.00 35.00
6-12 8.00 25.00

EXILE EARTH
RIVER CITY (1994)
1 .50 1.50

EXILES
MALIBU (1993)
1 1st: Exiles. Bagged w/ Ultraverse card. 1.00 3.00
1 (GOLD) 1.50 5.00
1A Unbagged. .50 1.95
1B Hologram. 1.50 5.00
1C Ultra-limited foil cover. 1.50 5.00
2 .50 1.50
3 w/ Rune 0 coupon. .50 1.50
4 .50 1.50

EX-MUTANTS
ETERNITY/AMAZING (1986-1988)
1-8 .75 2.00
SPECIAL .75 2.00
WINTER .75 2.25

EX-MUTANTS
MALIBU (1992-1994)
1 .50 1.95
1A Prism cover. 2.25 8.00
2-10 .50 1.95
11-18 .75 2.25

EX-MUTANTS: SHATTERED EARTH
ETERNITY (1988-1989)
1-3 .75 2.00
4-5 1.00 3.00
6-14 .75 2.00

EXOTIC ROMANCES
QUALITY (1955-1956)
22 Previous title: True War Romances. 10.00 30.00
23-26 7.00 22.00
27-28 Art: Matt Baker. 10.00 30.00
29 7.00 20.00
30-31 Art: Matt Baker. 8.00 25.00

EXPLORER JOE
ZIFF-DAVIS (1951-1952)
1 13.00 40.00
2 10.00 30.00

EXPOSED
DS (1948-1949)
1 22.00 70.00
2 25.00 80.00
3-5 13.00 40.00
6-7 SOTI 50.00 150.00
8-9 10.00 30.00

EXTRA!
EC (1955)
1 23.00 75.00
2-5 16.00 50.00

EXTREME
IMAGE (1993)
0 Send away coupon book from Extreme Tourbook '93. 2.75 10.00
0A Limited edition. 7.00 20.00
1 .75 2.95

EXTREME JUSTICE
DC (1994-CURRENT)
0-4 .50 1.50
5-8 .50 1.75

EXTREME SACRIFICE
IMAGE (1995)
EPILOGUE-PRELUDE Polybagged with card. .75 2.50

EXTREME STUDIOS TOUR BOOK '93
EXTREME (1992)
1 With coupon. 2.75 10.00
1A Without coupon. .75 2.00
1B Signed by all 12 artists. 5.00 15.00
1C Gold. 2.75 10.00

EXTREMIST, THE
DC (1993)
1 .75 2.50
1 PLATINUM 2.75 10.00
2 .75 2.25
3-4 .50 1.95

FACE, THE
COLUMBIA (1941-1942)
1 85.00 275.00
2 Title changes to Tony Trent with #3. 55.00 175.00

FACE, THE
DC (1994)
1 Vertigo one-shot. 1.25 4.95

FACTOR X
MARVEL (1995)
1 Deluxe edition. 1.50 5.00
2 Deluxe edition. 1.00 3.50
3-4 1.00 3.00

FAIRY TALE PARADE
DELL (1942-1946)
1 Cover & art: Walt Kelly on all issues. 155.00 500.00
2 80.00 250.00
3-5 55.00 175.00
6-9 40.00 125.00

FAIRY TALE PARADE
DELL FOUR COLOR SERIES (1944-1946)
50 Art: Walt Kelly. 65.00 200.00
69 Art: Walt Kelly. 50.00 150.00
87 40.00 130.00
104 Art: Walt Kelly. 45.00 140.00
114 31.00 100.00
121 23.00 75.00

FALCON
MARVEL (1983-1984)
1-4 .30 1.00

FALL OF THE ROMAN EMPIRE, THE
GOLD KEY (1964)
10118-407 Movie photo cover. 7.00 20.00

FALLEN ANGELS
MARVEL (1987)
1-8 .75 2.00

FALLING IN LOVE
DC (1955-1973)
1 55.00 170.00
2 26.00 85.00
3-6 20.00 65.00
7-12 17.00 55.00
13-30 10.00 33.00
31-46 9.00 27.00
47 1st 12 cent cover price. 7.00 22.00
48-70 5.00 16.00
71-100 4.00 11.00
101-120 2.25 8.75
121-143 1.75 6.50

FAMILY AFFAIR
GOLD KEY (1970)
1 TV photo covers on all issues. 10.00 30.00
2 7.00 20.00
3-4 5.00 15.00

FAMILY FUNNIES
HARVEY (1950-1951)
1 8.00 25.00
2 6.00 18.00
3-8 4.00 12.00

FAMILY MAN
DC (1995)
1-3 1.25 4.95

FAMOUS CRIMES
FOX (1948-1951)
1 Reprint: Phantom Lady #16. 55.00 170.00
2 55.00 170.00
3 SOTI 55.00 180.00
4-6 28.00 90.00
7 SOTI "Tarzan The Wyoming Killer!" 50.00 150.00
8-12 25.00 80.00
13-20 17.00 55.00

FAMOUS FIRST EDITIONS
DC (1974-1978)
F-4 Limited Collectors' Gold Mint Series. Whiz Comics #1 reprint in large, oversize format. 5.00 15.00
F-5 Limited Collectors' Silver Mint Series. Batman Comics #1 reprint in large, oversize format. 7.00 20.00
F-6 Limited Collectors' Series. Wonder Woman #1 reprint in large, oversize format. 5.00 15.00
F-7 Limited Collectors' Series. All Star Comics #3 reprint in large, oversize format. 5.00 15.00
F-8 Limited Collectors' Series. Flash Comics #1 reprint in large, oversize format. 5.00 15.00
C-26 Limited Collectors' Gold Mint Series. Action #1 reprint in large, oversize format. 5.00 15.00
C-28 Limited Collectors' Silver Mint Series. Detective #27 reprint in large, oversize format. 7.00 20.00
C-30 Limited Collectors' Bronze Mint Series. Sensation Comics #1 reprint in large, oversize format. 2.75 10.00
C-61 Limited Collectors' Series. Superman #1 reprint in large, oversize format. 7.00 20.00

FAMOUS FUNNIES
EASTERN (1933-1955)
NO#A "A Carnival Of Comics" Giveaway used to test demand for interest in comics. 2300.00 9000.00
NO#B "Series 1" 1st 10 cent comic book in the modern format sold to the public. (2/34) 4600.00 18000.00
1 1st monthly comic book magazine in the modern format. 1st comic book sold through newsstand distribution. 3300.00 13000.00
2 800.00 3000.00
3 Begin: Buck Rogers. 900.00 3300.00
4 290.00 950.00
5 220.00 700.00
6-10 160.00 525.00
11-16 110.00 360.00
17 (12/35) 110.00 360.00
18 110.00 360.00
19-30 75.00 240.00
31-40 55.00 175.00
41-50 40.00 130.00
51-60 29.00 95.00
61-70 26.00 85.00
71-80 25.00 80.00
81-90 20.00 65.00
91-100 17.00 55.00
101-110 14.00 44.00
111-130 12.00 38.00
131-150 9.00 27.00
151-200 7.00 22.00
201-208 5.00 16.00
209 Begin: Buck Rogers feature. Begin: Frank Frazetta covers. (12/53) 70.00 220.00
210-215 70.00 220.00
216 End: Buck Rogers feature. End: Frank Frazetta covers. (3/55) 70.00 220.00
217-218 5.00 16.00

FAMOUS GANG BOOK OF COMICS
EASTERN (1942)
NO# Porky Pig, Bugs Bunny. 155.00 500.00

FAMOUS GANGSTERS
AVON (1951-1952)
1-3 40.00 125.00

FAMOUS INDIAN TRIBES
DELL (1962)
12-624-209 "The Sioux" 2.75 10.00

FAMOUS MONSTERS OF FILMLAND
WARREN (1961-1980)
1 1st: Warren horror magazine. 250.00 825.00
2 100.00 330.00
3 115.00 380.00
4 150.00 490.00
4A With cover sticker-ultra rare. 200.00 650.00
5 115.00 380.00
6 70.00 220.00
7 Roland. 50.00 160.00
7A Tomorrows Monster. 50.00 160.00
7B Zacherly Channel 9. 70.00 220.00
8-9 60.00 190.00
10 50.00 160.00
11-12 60.00 190.00
13 100 pages. 70.00 220.00
14 40.00 130.00
15 50.00 160.00
16-18 45.00 140.00
19-20 31.00 100.00
21 Bride of Frankenstein. 70.00 220.00
22 Dracula, 5th anniversary issue. 70.00 220.00
23 Son of Kong. 35.00 110.00
24 35.00 110.00
25 King Kong. 40.00 130.00
26-30 25.00 80.00
31-34 15.00 49.00
35-37 10.00 33.00
38 20.00 65.00
39-45 7.00 22.00
46 9.00 27.00
47-49 7.00 22.00
50 Gorgo cover. 7.00 22.00
51 5.00 16.00
52 Barnabas (Dark Shadows) Collins cover. 5.00 16.00
53-55 5.00 16.00
56 Frankenstein. 17.00 55.00
57-69 4.00 13.00
70-79 Do not exist, see Monster World.
80-81 4.00 11.00
82 Dark Shadows. 14.00 44.00
83-99 4.00 11.00
100 9.00 27.00

EXTREME JUSTICE #0

FACTOR X #1

FALLEN ANGELS #2

FAMOUS FUNNIES #209

FANTASTIC COMICS #4

FANTASTIC FEARS #1

FANTASTIC FOUR #1

FANTASTIC FOUR #39

FAMOUS • FIRSTS

FANTASTIC FOUR #5

It took The FF five issues to "Meet Doctor Doom," their perennial arch foe. When Doom attacks, Reed Richards recognizes the voice of his former college rival Victor Von Doom, whose face was scarred in an unauthorized lab experiment.

101-107 .... 2.25 8.75
108 King Kong. 7.00 22.00
109-113 .... 2.25 8.75
114 Japanese Monsters. 20.00 65.00
115-117 .... 2.25 8.75
118 20 Million Miles to Earth. 5.00 16.00
119-162 .... 1.75 6.50
163 .... 7.00 22.00
164-189 .... 1.50 5.50
190-191 .... 4.00 11.00

FAMOUS MONSTERS OF FILMLAND YEARBOOK
WARREN (1962-1982) MAGAZINE
1962 .... 35.00 110.00
1963 .... 26.00 85.00
1964 .... 17.00 55.00
1965 .... 16.00 50.00
1966 .... 11.00 34.00
1967 .... 9.00 28.00
1968-1970 .... 5.00 14.00
1971 .... 9.00 28.00
1972 .... 14.00 46.00
1973-1981 .... 8.00 25.00
1982 .... 6.00 17.00

FAMOUS MONSTERS SPEAK
WARREN (1963)
RECORD 16.00 50.00

FAMOUS STARS
ZIFF-DAVIS (1950-1952)
1 Movie photo cover (James Stewart & Shelly Winters in Winchester '73). 40.00 130.00
2 Photo cover (Betty Hutton). 25.00 80.00
3 Movie photo cover (Farley Granger & Ann Blyth in Our Very Own). 25.00 80.00
4 Movie photo cover (Robert Mitchum & Jane Russell in His Kind Of Woman). 25.00 80.00
5 Photo cover (Elizabeth Taylor). 25.00 80.00
6 Movie photo cover (Jeff Chandler & Evelyn Keyes in The Iron Man). 25.00 80.00

FAMOUS STORIES
DELL (1942)
1-2 .... 40.00 120.00

FANG
SIRIUS (1995)
1 .... 1.25 4.50
2-3 .... .75 2.95

FANGORIA (MAGAZINE)
STARLOG (1980-CURRENT)
1 .... 10.00 30.00
2-10 .... 7.00 20.00
11-20 .... 2.75 10.00
21-100 .... 1.50 5.00

FANTAGOR (UNDERGROUND)
R.CORBEN (1970-1972)
1 .... 10.00 30.00
2 Publisher: Rip Off Press. 7.00 20.00
3-4 Publisher: Last Gasp. 4.00 12.00

FANTASTIC
YOUTHFUL (1952)
8 Previous title: Captain Science. 50.00 150.00
9 Title changes to Beware with #10. .... 31.00 100.00

FANTASTIC ADVENTURES
SUPER (1963-1964)
9-18 .... 2.75 10.00

FANTASTIC COMICS
AJAX (1954-1955)
10-11 .... 19.00 60.00

FANTASTIC COMICS
FOX (1939-1941)
1 Origin: Samson. 500.00 1900.00
2 .... 280.00 900.00
3 Rare. Classic cover. 1100.00 4000.00
4-6 .... 155.00 500.00
7 Cover: Joe Simon. (6/40) 140.00 450.00
8-10 .... 140.00 450.00
11-23 .... 110.00 350.00

FANTASTIC FABLES
SILVER WOLF (1987)
1 Art: Tim Vigil. 1.00 3.00
2 Art: Tim Vigil. 1.50 5.00

FANTASTIC FEARS
AJAX/FARRELL (1953-1954)
1 Has #7 on cover (5/53) 31.00 100.00
2 Has #8 on cover (7/53) 23.00 75.00
3-4 .... 16.00 50.00
5 Art: Steve Ditko (his 3rd published work (1/54), see Black Magic V4#4 and Captain 3-D #1). 155.00 500.00
6 .... 65.00 200.00
7 .... 19.00 60.00
8-9 .... 16.00 50.00

FANTASTIC FIRSTS
MARVEL (1994)
HC 7.00 20.00

FANTASTIC FORCE
MARVEL (1994-CURRENT)
1 Foil-stamped cover. .... .75 2.50
2-11 .... .50 1.75

FANTASTIC FOUR
MARVEL (1961-CURRENT)
ASHCAN 1-ASHCAN 2 .... .20 .75
1 1st & Origin: The Fantastic Four. 1st: Mole Man. 3500.00 14000.00
1A Golden Record set (1966). 33-1/3 album still-sealed with reprint comic (identical to FF 1 but without cover price and ads). 65.00 200.00
1B Golden Record reprint comic removed from album set (identical to FF 1 but without cover price and ads). 35.00 110.00
2 1st: Skrulls. "The Skrulls From Outer Space!" by Lee/Kirby. 700.00 2700.00
3 1st: FF in costumes. 500.00 1800.00
4 1st: Silver-Age Sub-Mariner. "The Coming Of The Sub-Mariner!" by Lee/Kirby. 600.00 2200.00
5 1st & Origin: Dr. Doom. "Meet Dr. Doom!" by Lee/Kirby. 600.00 2300.00
6 App: Sub-Mariner, Dr. Doom. "The Diabolical Duo Join Forces!" by Lee/Kirby. 300.00 1200.00
7 1st: Kurrgo. "The Master Of Planet X!" by Lee/Kirby. 160.00 525.00
8 1st: Puppet Master, Alicia Masters. "Prisoners Of The Puppet-Master!" by Lee/Kirby. 180.00 575.00
9 App: Sub-Mariner. "The End Of The Fantastic Four!" by Lee/Kirby. 160.00 525.00
10 App: Dr. Doom. "The Return Of Doctor Doom!" by Lee/Kirby. 160.00 525.00
11 Origin retold: Fantastic Four, 1st: Impossible Man. "A Visit With The Fantastic Four!" & "The Impossible Man!" by Lee/Kirby. 140.00 450.00
12 1st: Thing vs. Hulk in "The Fantastic Four Meet The Hulk!" by Lee/Kirby. 250.00 850.00
13 1st: Watcher, 1st: Red Ghost. "The Red Ghost!" by Lee/Kirby. 95.00 300.00
14 "The Sub-Mariner Strikes!" 80.00 250.00
15 1st: Mad Thinker. "The Mad Thinker And His Awesome Android!" 80.00 250.00
16 "The Return Of Doctor Doom!" (7/63) 80.00 250.00
17 "In The Clutches Of Doctor Doom!" 80.00 250.00
18 "The All-Powerful Super-Skrull!" (9/63) 80.00 250.00
19 1st: Rama-Tut. "Prisoners Of The Pharoah!" by Lee/Kirby. 80.00 250.00
20 1st: Molecule Man. "The Mysterious Molecule Man!" by Lee/Kirby. 80.00 250.00
21 "The Hate-Monger!" 50.00 150.00
22 .... 40.00 125.00
23 "The Master Plan Of Doctor Doom!" 40.00 125.00
24 "The Infant Terrible!" 40.00 125.00
25 "The Incredible Hulk Versus The Thing!" 100.00 350.00
26 Conclusion of the classic The Thing Vs. The Hulk battle in "The Avengers Take Over!" (5/64) 85.00 290.00
27 "The Search For The Sub-Mariner!" 40.00 125.00
28 App: X-Men. 55.00 175.00
29 App: The Watcher. "It Started On Yancy Street!" (8/64) 31.00 100.00
30 .... 31.00 100.00
31 "The Mad Menace Of The Macabre Mole Man!" 23.00 75.00
32 "Death Of A Hero!" 23.00 75.00

No.	Description	Good	NM
33	"On The Side Of...Sub-Mariner!"	23.00	75.00
34	"A House Divided!"	23.00	75.00
35	"Calamity On The Campus!"	23.00	75.00
36	1st: Frightful Four. "The Frightful Four!"	31.00	100.00
37	"Behold! A Distant Star!"	23.00	75.00
38	"Defeated By The Frightful Four!"	23.00	75.00
39	"A Blind Man Shall Lead Them!"	23.00	75.00
40	"The Battle Of The Baxter Building!"	23.00	75.00
41	"The Brutal Betrayal Of Ben Grimm!"	19.00	60.00
42	"To Save You, Why Must I Kill You?"	19.00	60.00
43	"Lo, There Shall Be An Ending!"	19.00	60.00
44	1st: Gorgon. "The Gentleman's Name Is Gorgon!" (11/65)	19.00	60.00
45	1st: The Inhumans. "Among Us Hide...The Inhumans!"	19.00	60.00
46	"Those Who Would Destroy Us!"	19.00	60.00
47	"Beware, The Hidden Land!"	19.00	60.00
48	1st: Galactus & Silver Surfer in "The Coming Of Galactus!" and "Also Introducing The Sensational Silver Surfer!" (3/66)	250.00	800.00
49	2nd: Silver Surfer. "If This Be Doomsday!"	65.00	200.00
50	3rd: Silver Surfer. "The Saga Of The Silver Surfer!" (5/66)	65.00	200.00
51	"This Man...This Monster!"	11.00	35.00
52	1st: Black Panther.	25.00	80.00
53	Origin: Black Panther. "The Way It Began!"	20.00	65.00
54	"Whosoever Finds The Evil Eye..!"	11.00	35.00
55	"The Peerless Power Of The Silver Surfer!"	14.00	45.00
56	App: Silver Surfer. "Klaw, The Murderous Master Of Sound!"	11.00	35.00
57	App: Silver Surfer. "Enter...Doctor Doom!"	14.00	45.00
58	App: Silver Surfer. "The Dismal Dregs Of Defeat!"	11.00	35.00
59	App: Silver Surfer. "Doomsday!"	11.00	35.00
60	App: Silver Surfer. "The Peril And The Power!"	13.00	40.00
61	"Where Stalks The Sandman?"	11.00	35.00
62	"...And One Shall Save Him!"	13.00	40.00
63	"Blastaar, The Living Bomb-Burst!"	11.00	35.00
64	"The Sentry Sinister!"	13.00	40.00
65	"I Accuse!"	13.00	40.00
66	Origin: Him (no appearance). "What Lurks Behind The Beehive?"	14.00	45.00
67	1st & Origin (pt.2): Him (Warlock).	22.00	70.00
68	"His Mission: Destroy The Fantastic Four!"	11.00	35.00
69	"By Ben Betrayed!"	10.00	30.00
70	"When Fall The Mighty!"	10.00	30.00
71		10.00	30.00
72	"Where Soars The Silver Surfer!"	11.00	35.00
73		10.00	30.00
74	App: Silver Surfer. "When Calls Galactus!"	11.00	35.00
75	App: Silver Surfer. "Worlds Within Worlds!"	11.00	35.00
76	App: Silver Surfer. "...Stranded In Sub-Atomica!"	10.00	30.00
77	App: Silver Surfer. "...Shall Earth Endure?"	10.00	30.00
78	"The Thing No More!"	8.00	25.00
79	"This Monster Forever!"	8.00	25.00
80	"Where Treads The Living Totem!"	8.00	25.00
81	"Enter...The Exquisite Elemental!"	8.00	25.00
82		8.00	25.00
83	"Shall Man Survive?"	8.00	25.00
84	"The Name Is Doom!"	7.00	20.00
85	App: Dr. Doom. "Within This Tortured Land!"	7.00	20.00
86	App: Dr. Doom. "Victims!"	7.00	20.00
87	App: Dr. Doom. "The Power And The Pride!"	7.00	20.00
88	"A House There Was!"	7.00	20.00
89	"The Madness Of The Mole Man!" 1st 15 cent cover price.	6.00	18.00
90	"The Skrull Takes A Slave!"	6.00	18.00
91	"The Thing Enslaved!"	6.00	18.00
92	"Ben Grimm Killer Vs. Torgo!"	6.00	18.00
93	"Arena Of Death!"	6.00	18.00
94	"The Return Of The Frightful Four!"	8.00	25.00
95	"If The F.F. Fails, It Means...World War III!"	7.00	20.00
96	"The Mad Thinker And His Androids Of Death!"	7.00	20.00
97	"The Monster From The Lost Lagoon!"	7.00	20.00
98	"Doomsday On The Moon!"	7.00	20.00
99	"The Torch Goes Wild!"	7.00	20.00
100	"The Long Journey Home!" (7/70)	22.00	70.00
101-102	End: Kirby Art	7.00	20.00
103-107		2.75	10.00
108	Kirby Art	7.00	20.00
109-111		2.75	10.00
112	Hulk vs. The Thing.	13.00	40.00
113-114		2.50	9.00
115		2.75	10.00
116	Double size.	2.50	9.00
117-120		2.50	9.00
121-123	Silver Surfer.	4.00	12.00
124		2.00	7.00
125-149		1.50	5.00
150		1.75	6.00
151-154		1.00	3.00
155-157	Silver Surfer.	1.50	5.00
158		1.50	5.00
159-163		1.00	3.00
164		1.50	5.00
165		1.00	3.00
166-167	Hulk vs. The Thing.	1.00	3.00
168		1.50	5.00
169-171		1.00	3.00
172-175		1.50	5.00
176-199		1.00	3.00
200	Double size.	1.25	4.00
201-208		.75	2.50
209	Begin: John Byrne art.	1.50	5.00
210-211		1.50	5.00
212-216		1.00	3.50
217	App: Dazzler.	1.00	3.50
218		1.50	5.00
219-220		1.00	3.50
221	End: John Byrne art.	1.00	3.50
222-231		1.00	3.00
232	Begin: John Byrne art.	1.25	4.50
233-236		1.00	3.50
237-238		1.00	3.00
239		1.25	4.00
240-241		1.00	3.00
242-243		1.00	3.50
244		1.50	5.00
245-249		1.00	3.00
250	App: Spider-Man. Double size.	1.00	3.00
251-261		1.00	3.00
262	Origin: Galactus.	1.00	3.00
263-272		.75	2.50
273	1st: Nathaniel Richards.	1.25	4.00
274-285		.75	2.50
286	2nd: X-Factor. Story continues in X-Factor 1.	.75	2.50
287-292		.75	2.50
293	End: Byrne art.	.75	2.50
294-295		.75	2.00
296		1.00	3.00
297-299		.75	2.00
300		1.00	3.00
301-305		.75	2.00
306	Begin: New Fantastic Four team.	.75	2.00
307-318		.75	2.00
319	Double size.	.75	2.00
320-336		.75	2.00
337		1.25	4.50
338-346		.50	1.50
347	Wolverine, Spider-Man, Hulk, Ghost Rider.	1.75	6.00
347 (2ND)	2nd printing (Gold version).	.75	2.75
348	Wolverine, Spider-Man, Hulk, Ghost Rider.	1.50	5.00
348 (2ND)	2nd printing (Gold version).	.75	2.50
349	Wolverine, Spider-Man, Hulk, Ghost Rider.	1.50	5.00
350	Double size.	.75	2.50
351-357		.50	1.75
358		.75	2.25
359-365		.50	1.50
366-369		.50	1.25
370		.75	2.00
371	White embossed cover.	1.50	5.50
371 (2ND)	2nd printing (Red embossed cover).	.75	2.50
372-374		.50	1.25
375	Double size.	.75	2.95
376	Polybagged with Dirt magazine. Double size.	.75	2.95
376A	Without Dirt magazine.	.50	1.25
377-380		.50	1.25
381	Death: Reed Richards & Dr. Doom.	2.00	7.50
382		1.25	4.50
383-386		.75	2.00
387	Die-cut foil cover.	1.25	4.00
387A	Regular edition.	.50	1.25
388-393		.50	1.50
394	Neon ink cover, bagged with insert & print.	.75	2.95
394A	Regular cover.	.50	1.50
395-397		.50	1.50
398	Prismatic foil stamped cover.	.75	2.50
398A	Regular cover.	.50	1.50
399	Prismatic foil stamped cover.	.75	2.50
399A	Regular cover.	.50	1.50
400	Double size prismatic foil stamped cover.	1.00	3.95
401-403		.50	1.50

FANTASTIC FOUR ANNUAL

MARVEL (1963-CURRENT)

No.	Description	Good	NM
1	Origin retold: Fantastic Four. (1963)	140.00	475.00
2	Origin: Dr. Doom. "The Final Victory Of Doctor Doom!" (1964)	95.00	300.00
3	Marriage: Reed & Sue Richards. "The Wedding Of Sue And Reed!" (1965)	32.00	125.00
4	King Size Special. (1966)	15.00	60.00
5	King-Size Special. 1st: solo Silver Surfer story. (1967)	35.00	110.00
6	King-Size Special. (1968)	14.00	45.00
7	King-Size Special. (1969)	7.00	20.00
8	King-Size Special. (1970)	2.75	10.00
9	King-Size Special. (1971)	2.75	10.00
10	King-Size Special. (1973)	2.75	10.00
11	(1976)	2.25	8.00
12	(1977)	2.00	7.00
13	(1978)	2.00	7.00
14	(1979)	2.00	7.00
15	(1980)	2.00	7.00
16	(1981)	2.00	7.00
17	(1983)	2.00	7.00
18	(1984)	2.00	7.00
19	(1985)	2.00	7.00
20	(1987)	2.00	7.00
21	Evolutionary Wars. (1988)	1.25	4.00
22	Atlantis Attacks. (1989)	1.25	4.50
23	Future Present. (1990)	1.50	5.00
24	(1991)	.75	2.25
25	(1992)	.75	2.25
26	Polybagged with card. (1993)	.75	2.95
27	(1994)	.75	2.95

FANTASTIC FOUR: ATLANTIS RISING

MARVEL (1995)

No.	Description	Good	NM
1-2		1.00	3.95

FANTASTIC FOUR BOOK AND RECORD SET

POWER RECORDS (1974)

No.	Description	Good	NM
PR-13	Reprints issue #126 (origin retold).	2.75	10.00

FANTASTIC FOUR MARVEL MILESTONE

MARVEL (1994)

No.	Description	Good	NM
1	Reprints issue #1, metallic ink cover.	.75	2.95

FANTASTIC FOUR ROAST

MARVEL (1982)

No.	Description	Good	NM
1	One-shot.	.75	2.00

FANTASTIC FOUR SPECIAL EDITION

MARVEL (1984)

No.	Description	Good	NM
1	Cover & art: John Byrne.	.75	2.50

FANTASTIC FOUR UNLIMITED

MARVEL (1993-CURRENT)

No.	Description	Good	NM
1-11		1.00	3.95

FANTASTIC FOUR VS. X-MEN

MARVEL (1987)

No.	Description	Good	NM
1		1.25	4.00
2-4		1.00	3.00

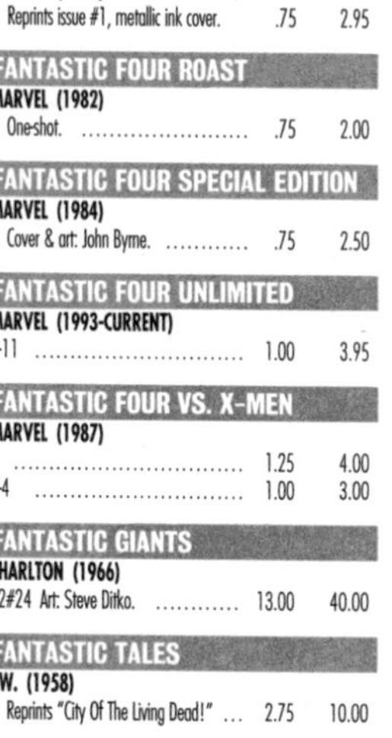

FANTASTIC GIANTS

CHARLTON (1966)

No.	Description	Good	NM
V2#24	Art: Steve Ditko.	13.00	40.00

FANTASTIC TALES

I.W. (1958)

No.	Description	Good	NM
1	Reprints "City Of The Living Dead!"	2.75	10.00

FANTASTIC VOYAGE

GOLD KEY (1967-1969)

No.	Description	Good	NM
1	(8/69)	7.00	20.00
2	(12/69)	5.00	15.00
10178-702	Movie photo cover. (2/67)	10.00	30.00

FANTASTIC VOYAGES OF SINBAD, THE

GOLD KEY (1965-1967)

No.	Description	Good	NM
1		7.00	20.00
2	"The Spell Of The Golden Scimitar."	7.00	20.00

FANTASTIC WORLDS

STANDARD (1952-1953)

No.	Description	Good	NM
5	"Triumph Over Terror!" (9/52)	40.00	130.00
6	"The Cosmic Terror" (11/52)	35.00	110.00
7	"The Asteroid God!" (1/53)	25.00	80.00

FANTASY ILLUSTRATED

NEW MEDIA (1982) MAGAZINE

No.	Description	Good	NM
1-2		.75	2.95

FANTASY MASTERPIECES

MARVEL (1966-1967)

No.	Description	Good	NM
1	Photo of Stan Lee on inside front cover. (2/66)	10.00	30.00

FANTASTIC FOUR #100

FANTASTIC FOUR ANNUAL #2

FANTASY MASTERPIECES #9

FANTASY MASTERPIECES #11

a
b
c
d
e
f
g
h
i
j
k
l
m
n
o
p
q
r
s
t
u
v
w
x
y
z

FATE #0

FAWCETT'S FUNNY ANIMALS #12

FEATURE FUNNIES #16

FELIX THE CAT #22

2 Reprint: Strange Tales #89. .... 2.75 10.00
3 Double size giant. 4.00 12.00
4-8 .... 4.00 12.00
9 Origin Human Torch (reprint from Marvel Mystery #1). 4.00 13.00
10 Reprints All Winners #19. .... 2.75 10.00
11 Reprint origin Toro from Human Torch #1. Becomes Marvel Super Heroes #12. .... 2.75 10.00

FANTASY MASTERPIECES

MARVEL (1979-1981)
1 Reprint: Silver Surfer #1. .... 1.50 5.00
2 Reprint: Silver Surfer #2. .... 1.25 4.00
3 Reprint: Silver Surfer #3. .... 1.25 4.00
4 Reprint: Silver Surfer #4. .... 1.25 4.00
5 Reprint: Silver Surfer #5. .... 1.25 4.00
6 Reprint: Silver Surfer #6. .... 1.25 4.00
7 Reprint: Silver Surfer #7. .... 1.25 4.00
8 Reprint: Silver Surfer #8. .... 1.25 4.00
9 Reprint: Silver Surfer #9. .... 1.25 4.00
10 Reprint: Silver Surfer #10. .... 1.25 4.00
11 Reprint: Silver Surfer #11. .... 1.25 4.00
12 Reprint: Silver Surfer #12. .... 1.25 4.00
13 Reprint: Silver Surfer #13. .... 1.25 4.00
14 Reprint: Silver Surfer #14. .... 1.25 4.00

FANTASY QUARTERLY

IPS (1978)
1 1st: Elfquest in "Fire And Flight" by Richard and Wendy Pini. Black & white fanzine with color covers printed on newsprint. Low distribution. 16.00 50.00

FANTOMAN

CENTAUR (1940)
2 Previous title: Amazing Adventure Funnies. 250.00 800.00
3-4 .... 220.00 700.00

FARMER'S DAUGHTER, THE

STANHALL (1954)
1 .... 16.00 50.00
2-4 .... 10.00 30.00

FAST FICTION

FAMOUS AUTHORS (1949-1950)
1 The Scarlet Pimpernel. 50.00 150.00
2 Captain Blood. 31.00 100.00
3 She. 50.00 150.00
4 The 39 Steps. 31.00 100.00
5 Beau Geste. 31.00 100.00

FASTEST GUN ALIVE, THE

DELL FOUR COLOR SERIES (1956)
741 Movie photo cover (Glenn Ford). (9/56) 19.00 60.00

FAT AND SLAT

EC (1947-1948)
1 1st & Origin: Voltage. 70.00 220.00
2-4 .... 35.00 110.00

FATE

DC (1994-CURRENT)
0 Begin: new Dr. Fate. .... .50 1.95
1 .... 1.00 3.00
2-11 .... .75 2.25

FATMAN THE HUMAN FLYING SAUCER

LIGHTNING (1967)
1 1st & Origin: Fatman by C.C. Beck. 16.00 50.00
2 Art: C.C. Beck. 13.00 42.00
3 Art: C.C. Beck. 15.00 48.00

FAUST

NORTHSTAR/REBEL (1989-1994)
1 Art: Tim Vigil in all. 13.00 40.00
1A Premier Tour Edition. 16.00 50.00
1 (2ND) 2nd printing. 2.50 9.00
1 (3RD) 3rd printing. .... .75 2.50
2 .... 10.00 30.00
2 (2ND) 2nd printing. .... .75 2.50
2 (3RD) 3rd printing. .... .75 2.50
3 .... 5.00 15.00
3 (2ND) 2nd printing. .... .75 2.50
4 .... 2.25 8.00
5-6 .... 1.50 6.00
7 Begin Rebel publication. 1.25 5.00
8-9 .... .75 3.50
10 .... .75 3.50

FAVORITE COMICS

GIVEAWAY (1934)
1 .... 95.00 300.00
2-3 .... 65.00 200.00

FAWCETT MINIATURES

FAWCETT (1946)
NO#-1 Captain Marvel And The Horn Of Plenty. 3-3/4" x 5". 22.00 70.00
NO#-2 Captain Marvel Jr. in The Case Of The Poison Press. 22.00 70.00
NO#-3 Captain Marvel And The Raiders From Space. 22.00 70.00
NO#-4 Delecta Of The Planets. Art: C.C. Beck. 40.00 120.00

FAWCETT MOVIE COMICS

FAWCETT (1949-1952)
7 "Gunmen of Abilene"-Rocky Lane photo cover. Art: Bob Powell. (1950) See: Dakota Lil, Copper Canyon, Destination Moon, Montana, Pioneer Marshal, Powder River Rustlers, and Singing Guns for NO# issues. 50.00 160.00
8 "King Of The Bullwhip"-Lash LaRue photo cover. Art: Bob Powell. (1950) 80.00 250.00
9 "The Old Frontier"-Monte Hale photo cover. Art: Bob Powell. (2/51, mis-dated 2/50). 40.00 125.00
10 "The Missourians"-Monte Hale photo cover. (4/51) 31.00 100.00
11 "The Thundering Trail"-Lash LaRue photo cover. (6/51) 65.00 200.00
12 "Rustlers On Horseback"-Rocky Lane photo cover. (8/51) 50.00 160.00
13 "Warpath"-Edmond O'Brien photo cover. (10/51) 28.00 90.00
14 "The Last Outpost"-Ronald Reagan & Rhonda Fleming photo cover. (12/51) 55.00 175.00
15 "The Man From Planet X"-photo cover. (2/52) 400.00 1200.00
16 "Ten Tall Men"-Burt Lancaster photo cover. (4/52) 19.00 60.00
17 "Rose of Cimarron"-Jack Buetel & Mala Powers photo cover. (6/52) 23.00 75.00
18 "The Brigand"-Anthony Dexter photo cover. (8/52) 23.00 .... 75.00
19 "Carbine Williams"-James Stewart photo cover. (10/52) 31.00 100.00
20 "Ivanhoe"-Robert Taylor, Joan Fontaine & Elizabeth Taylor photo cover. (12/52) 40.00 125.00

FAWCETT'S FUNNY ANIMALS

FAWCETT (1942-1956)
1 1st: Hoppy The Marvel Bunny. 80.00 250.00
2 .... 31.00 100.00
3-6 .... 23.00 75.00
7-12 .... 16.00 50.00
13-24 .... 11.00 35.00
25-50 .... 8.00 25.00
51-75 .... 5.00 15.00
76-91 .... 4.00 12.00

FBI STORY, THE

DELL FOUR COLOR SERIES (1959)
1069 Movie photo cover (James Stewart). (11/59) 22.00 70.00

FEAR

MARVEL (1970-1976)
1 .... 2.75 10.00
2-8 .... 1.50 5.00
9 Title changes to Adventure Into Fear with #10. .... 1.50 5.00

FEARLESS FAGAN

DELL FOUR COLOR SERIES (1952)
441 (12/52) 8.00 25.00

FEATURE BOOKS

DAVID MCKAY (1937-1948)
NO# (1A) Popeye And The "Jeep" (later reprinted in #3). 900.00 3300.00
NO# (1B) Dick Tracy The Detective (later reprinted in #4). 900.00 3300.00
1 Zane Grey's King Of The Royal Mounted. 135.00 440.00
2 Popeye. 150.00 490.00
3 Popeye And The "Jeep" 150.00 490.00
4 Dick Tracy The Detective. 270.00 875.00
5 Popeye And His Poppa. 100.00 330.00
6 Dick Tracy The Detective. 200.00 650.00
7 Little Orphan Annie (#1). 170.00 550.00
8 Secret Agent X-9. .... 70.00 220.00
9 Dick Tracy And The Famon Boys. ... 200.00 650.00
10 Popeye And Susan. (2/38) 100.00 330.00
11 Annie Rooney. 50.00 160.00
12 Blondie. 100.00 330.00
13 Inspector Wade. 100.00 330.00
14 Popeye in "Wild Oats" 135.00 440.00
15 Barney Baxter In The Air. 50.00 160.00
16 Red Eagle. 29.00 95.00
17 Gang Busters (1st time in comics). 100.00 330.00
18-19 Mandrake The Magician. 60.00 190.00
20 The Phantom. 135.00 440.00
21 The Lone Ranger. 135.00 440.00
22 The Phantom. 85.00 270.00
23 Mandrake The Magician in Teiba Castle. 60.00 190.00
24 The Lone Ranger. 135.00 440.00
25 Flash Gordon On The Planet Mongo. 115.00 380.00
26 Prince Valiant. 170.00 550.00
27 Blondie. 25.00 80.00
28 Blondie And Dagwood. 25.00 80.00
29 Blondie At Home Sweet Home. ... 25.00 80.00
30 The Katzenjammer Kids. 25.00 80.00
31 Blondie Keeps The Home-Fires Burning. 25.00 80.00
32 The Katzenjammer Kids. 25.00 80.00
33 The Romance Of Flying. 25.00 80.00
34 Blondie Home Is Our Castle. 25.00 80.00
35 The Katzenjammer Kids "Boys Will Be Boys." 25.00 80.00
36 Blondie On The Home Front. 25.00 80.00
37 The Katzenjammer Kids "Clever Boys These Kids!" 25.00 80.00
38 Blondie "The Model Homemaker." 25.00 80.00
39 The Phantom. 70.00 220.00
40 Blondie in "Home-Made Laughs!" 25.00 80.00
41 The Katzenjammer Kids. 25.00 80.00
42 Blondie in "Home-Spun Yarns!" ... 25.00 80.00
43 Blondie "Home-Cooked Scraps!!" 25.00 80.00
44 Katzenjammer Kids in "Monkey Business." 25.00 80.00
45 Blondie in "Home Of The Free-And The Brave!" 25.00 80.00
46 Mandrake The Magician in the Fire World. 50.00 160.00
47 Blondie in "Eaten Out Of House And Home!" 25.00 80.00
48 The Maltese Falcon. 135.00 440.00
49 Perry Mason "The Case Of The Lucky Legs." 25.00 80.00
50 The Case Of The Shoplifter's Shoe (A Perry Mason Mystery). 25.00 80.00
51 Rip Kirby "The Mystery Of The Mangler." 25.00 80.00
52 Mandrake The Magician in The Land Of X. 25.00 80.00
53 The Phantom in Safari Suspense. ... 25.00 80.00
54 Rip Kirby "The Case Of The Master Menace" 25.00 80.00
55 Mandrake The Magician in "The 5-Numbers Treasure Hunt!" 25.00 80.00
56 The Phantom Destroys The Sky Band. 25.00 80.00
57 The Phantom in The Blue Gang. ... 25.00 80.00

FEATURE COMICS

QUALITY (1939-1950)
21 Previous title: "Feature Funnies." ... 65.00 210.00
22 .... 50.00 165.00
23 1st: Charlie Chan. (8-39) 60.00 190.00
24-26 .... 50.00 165.00
27 1st & Origin: Doll Man by Lou Fine. (12/39) 800.00 3000.00
28 .... 310.00 1000.00
29-30 .... 180.00 575.00
31 .... 155.00 500.00
32 .... 145.00 480.00
33-36 .... 140.00 450.00
37 End: Lou Fine art on Doll Man. ... 110.00 350.00
38-43 .... 65.00 200.00
44 Begin: Reed Crandall art on Doll Man. 95.00 300.00
45-50 .... 55.00 180.00
51-60 .... 50.00 150.00
61-70 .... 40.00 120.00
71-80 .... 29.00 95.00
81-90 .... 28.00 90.00
91-99 .... 25.00 80.00
100 .... 29.00 95.00
101-120 .... 23.00 75.00
121-130 .... 22.00 70.00
131-138 .... 19.00 60.00
139 End: Doll Man. 19.00 60.00
140 Begin: Stuntman Stetson. 7.00 20.00
141-144 .... 7.00 20.00

FEATURE FILMS

DC (1950)
1 "Captain China"-John Payne photo cover. 85.00 280.00
2 "Riding High"-Bing Crosby photo cover. 85.00 280.00
3 "The Eagle And The Hawk"-John Payne & Rhonda Fleming photo cover. 85.00 280.00
4 "Fancy Pants"-Bob Hope & Lucille Ball photo cover. 85.00 280.00

FEATURE FUNNIES

CHESLER (1937-1939)
1 Joe Palooka, Mickey Finn, Lala Palooza, The Bumble Family, Jane Arden, etc. 500.00 1800.00
2 .... 250.00 825.00
3 Begin: The Clock. 220.00 700.00
4 .... 220.00 700.00
5-7 .... 190.00 600.00

8-10 .... 145.00 480.00
11-15 .... 130.00 420.00
16-19 .... 110.00 360.00
20 Title changes to Feature Comics with #21. .... 110.00 360.00

FEATURE PRESENTATION, A
FOX (1950)
5 The Black Tarantula. 50.00 150.00
6 Moby Dick. 31.00 100.00

FEATURE STORIES MAGAZINE
FOX (1950)
3 Jungle Thrills. 25.00 80.00
4 .... 23.00 75.00

FELIX THE CAT
DELL FOUR COLOR SERIES (1942-1947)
15 .... 130.00 425.00
46 "And The Haunted Castle" 95.00 300.00
77 .... 85.00 275.00
119 .... 60.00 190.00
135 .... 45.00 140.00
162 .... 35.00 110.00

FELIX THE CAT
DELL/TOBY/HARVEY (1948-1961)
1 .... 31.00 100.00
2 .... 16.00 50.00
3-6 .... 11.00 35.00
7-19 .... 8.00 25.00
20 Begin: Toby publication. 10.00 30.00
21-31 .... 7.00 20.00
3D(#1) With glasses. 55.00 175.00
32-61 .... 7.00 20.00
62 Begin: Harvey publication. 5.00 15.00
63-80 .... 2.75 10.00
81-90 .... 2.25 8.00
91-100 .... 1.75 6.00
101-118 .... 1.50 5.00
1952-1953 100 page Annual. 65.00 200.00
1954 100 page Annual. 50.00 150.00

FELIX'S NEPHEWS INKY AND DINKY
HARVEY (1957-1958)
1 .... 14.00 45.00
2-7 .... 7.00 20.00

FEMFORCE
AMERICOMICS (1985-CURRENT)
1 .... 1.50 5.00
2 .... 1.00 3.00
3-33 .... .75 2.50
34-62 .... .75 2.75
63-68 .... .75 2.95
69 Polybagged with pog. .... .75 2.95
69A Regular edition (no pog). .... .75 2.95
70-71 .... .75 2.95
72 Polybagged with compact comic (Sentinels Of Justice #1). 1.00 3.95
72A Regular edition. .... .75 2.95
73 Polybagged with compact comic #2. .... 1.00 3.95
73A Regular edition. .... .75 2.95
74 Polybagged with Heike print. 1.25 4.95
74A Regular edition. .... .75 2.95
75 Polybagged with Gorby mini-poster. 1.25 4.95
75A Regular edition. .... .75 2.95
76 Polybagged with compact comic. 1.00 3.95
76A Regular edition. .... .75 2.95
77 .... .75 2.95
78 Polybagged with Compact Comic. 1.25 4.95
78A Regular edition. .... .75 2.95
79 Polybagged with supplements. 1.50 5.90
79A Regular edition. .... .75 2.95
80 Polybagged with supplements. 1.50 5.90
80A Regular edition. .... .75 2.95
81 Polybagged with supplements. 1.50 5.90
81A Regular edition. .... .75 2.95
82 Polybagged with supplements. 1.50 5.90
82A Regular edition. .... .75 2.95
83 Polybagged with Ms. Victory print. 1.00 3.95
83A Regular edition. .... .75 2.95
84 Polybagged with Femforce Index #4B. 1.50 5.90
84A Regular edition. .... .75 2.95
85 Polybagged with card. 1.25 4.95
85A Regular edition. .... .75 2.95
86 Polybagged with Femforce Index #5. .... 1.50 5.90
86A Regular edition. .... .75 2.95

FEMFORCE: FRIGHTBOOK
AMERICOMICS (1995)
1 .... .75 2.95

FEMFORCE: UNTOLD ORIGIN
AMERICOMICS
1 O: Femforce. 1.25 4.95

FEMFORCE UP-CLOSE
AMERICOMICS (1992-CURRENT)
1-3 .... .75 2.75
4 .... .75 2.95
5 Bagged with sticker. 1.00 3.95
5A Regular edition. .... .75 2.95
6 Bagged with sticker. 1.00 3.95
6A Regular edition. .... .75 2.95
7 Bagged with sticker. 1.00 3.95
7A Regular edition. .... .75 2.95
8 Baged with sticker. 1.00 3.95
8A Regular edition. .... .75 2.95
9 .... .75 2.95
10 Bagged with compact comic. 1.00 3.95
10A Regular edition. .... .75 2.95
11 .... .75 2.95

FERRET, THE
MALIBU (1993-CURRENT)
1 Die-cut. .... .75 2.50
2 With poster. .... .75 2.50
2A w/o poster. .... .50 1.95
3 With poster. .... .75 2.50
3A w/o poster. .... .50 1.95
4 With poster. .... .75 2.50
4A w/o poster. .... .50 1.95
5-11 .... .75 2.25

FEUD
MARVEL (1993)
1-4 .... .50 1.50

FEVER FEW
KITCHEN SINK (1972)
1 .... 7.00 20.00

FIBBER MCGEE & MOLLY (A-1 SERIES)
ME (1949)
25 (A-1 #25). Radio tie-in. 11.00 35.00

FIGHT AGAINST CRIME
STORY (1951-1954)
1 "Scorpion Of Crime." 31.00 100.00
2 .... 16.00 50.00
3 .... 13.00 40.00
4 .... 16.00 50.00
5 .... 13.00 40.00
6-8 .... 10.00 30.00
9 Drug story. 31.00 100.00
10-12 .... 26.00 85.00
13 .... 22.00 70.00
14 "Death Trap" 22.00 70.00
15 .... 22.00 70.00
16 .... 26.00 85.00
17 E. C. swipe. 31.00 100.00
18-19 .... 25.00 80.00
20 Gruesome cover. 50.00 150.00
21 Title changes to Fight Against The Guilty with #22. .... 23.00 75.00

FIGHT AGAINST THE GUILTY
STORY (1954-1955)
22 Previous title: Fight Against Crime. (12/54) 17.00 55.00
23 (3/55) 16.00 50.00

FIGHT COMICS
FICTION HOUSE (1940-1954)
1 Art: Will Eisner. Origin: Spy Fighter. 400.00 1300.00
2 .... 155.00 500.00
3 Begin: Rip Regan. 120.00 390.00
4 Cover: Lou Fine. 140.00 450.00
5 .... 120.00 390.00
6-10 .... 80.00 260.00
11-14 .... 70.00 220.00
15 1st: Super American. 120.00 390.00
16 Begin: Captain Fight. 120.00 390.00
17-18 .... 60.00 190.00
19 End: Captain Fight. 60.00 190.00
20 .... 60.00 190.00
21-30 .... 40.00 130.00
31 .... 35.00 110.00
32 Begin: Tiger Girl. 35.00 110.00
33-40 .... 35.00 110.00
41-50 .... 31.00 100.00
51 Origin: Tiger Girl. 50.00 150.00
52-60 .... 28.00 90.00
61-86 .... 23.00 75.00

FIGHT THE ENEMY
TOWER (1966-1967)
1 .... 8.00 25.00
2-3 .... 7.00 20.00

FIGHTIN' ARMY
CHARLTON (1956-1984)
16 Previous title: Soldier And Marine Comics. 8.00 25.00
17-19 .... 2.75 10.00
20 Art: Steve Ditko. 7.00 20.00
21-30 .... 2.75 10.00
31-40 .... 2.25 8.00
41-50 .... 2.00 7.00
51-60 .... 1.75 6.00
61-75 .... 1.50 5.00
76-100 .... 1.25 4.00
101-120 .... 1.00 3.00
121-130 .... .75 2.00
131-150 .... .30 1.00
151-172 .... .20 .50

FIGHTIN' MARINES
ST. JOHN (1954)
11 Cover & art: Matt Baker. From Approved Comics series. 10.00 30.00

FIGHTIN' MARINES
ST. JOHN/CHARLTON (1951-1984)
1 (#15) Cover&art: Matt Baker. (8/51) 40.00 125.00
2 1st: Canteen Kate by Baker. 35.00 110.00
3-6 .... 28.00 90.00
7-9 .... 23.00 75.00
10 .... 7.00 20.00
11-13 .... 2.75 10.00
14 Begin: Charlton publishing. Canteen Kate. 7.00 20.00
15-16 .... 7.00 20.00
17 Canteen Kate. 10.00 30.00
18-24 .... 2.75 10.00
25 Double size. (3/58) 8.00 25.00
26 100 page Giant. (8/58) 13.00 40.00
27-30 .... 2.75 10.00
31-50 .... 2.25 8.00
51-60 .... 2.00 7.00
61-81 .... 1.75 6.00
82 100 page Giant. 5.00 15.00
83-100 .... 1.25 4.00
101-132 .... .75 2.50
133-140 .... .75 2.00
141-160 .... .30 1.00
161-176 .... .20 .50

FIGHTIN' NAVY
CHARLTON (1956-1984)
74 Previous title: Don Winslow. 7.00 20.00
75-80 .... 2.75 10.00
81-90 .... 2.25 8.00
91-110 .... 2.00 7.00
111-124 .... 1.50 5.00
125 (1966) 1.50 5.00
126 (1983) .... .30 1.00
127-133 .... .30 1.00

FIGHTIN' TEXAN, THE
ST. JOHN (1952)
16 Previous title: The Texan. 7.00 20.00
17 .... 2.75 10.00

FIGHTING AMERICAN
DC (1994)
1-5 .... .30 1.00

FIGHTING AMERICAN
HARVEY (1966)
1 Reprint: 1954 #1. .... 7.00 20.00

FIGHTING AMERICAN
PRIZE (1954-1955)
1 Origin: Fighting American & Speedboy. 290.00 950.00
2 Art: Simon & Kirby in all issues. 145.00 480.00
3-4 .... 130.00 420.00
5-7 .... 110.00 360.00

FIGHTING DANIEL BOONE
AVON (1953)
NO# Art: Kinstler. 25.00 80.00

FIGHTING DAVY CROCKETT
AVON (1955)
9 Previous title: Kit Karson. 10.00 30.00

FIGHTING FRONTS!
HARVEY (1952-1953)
1 .... 10.00 30.00
2 Art: Bob Powell. 11.00 35.00
3 Art: Bob Powell. 7.00 20.00
4-5 .... 4.00 12.00

FIGHTING INDIANS OF THE WILD WEST
AVON (1952)
1 .... 16.00 50.00
2 .... 10.00 30.00

FEM FORCE UP-CLOSE #6

THE FERRET #3

FEUD #4

FIGHTING AMERICAN #6

a b c d e f g h i j k l m n o p q r s t u v w x y z

FIREARM #8

FIRESTAR #2

FIRESTORM THE NUCLEAR MAN #50

FLASH #105 (1ST SERIES)

FLASH COMICS #1

This book features not only the origin of Jay Garrick, the first Flash, but it also introduces Johnny Thunder and the Golden Age Hawkman, who alternate cover appearances with The Flash. All three later join the Justice Society of America.

FIGHTING LEATHERNECKS
TOBY (1952)

1	16.00	50.00
2	10.00	30.00
3-6	8.00	25.00

FIGHTING MAN
AJAX (1952-1953)

1	10.00	30.00
2	5.00	15.00
3-8	2.75	10.00

FIGHTING MAN ANNUAL
AJAX (1952)

1 100 page giant.	50.00	150.00

FIGHTING PRINCE OF DONEGAL, THE
GOLD KEY (1967)

10193-701 Disney movie tie-in.	5.00	15.00

FIGHTING UNDERSEA COMMANDOS
AVON (1952-1953)

1	13.00	40.00
2	8.00	25.00
3-5	7.00	20.00

FIGHTING YANK
NEDOR (1942-1949)

1	240.00	775.00
2	110.00	360.00
3	75.00	240.00
4	55.00	180.00
5	50.00	150.00
6-12	40.00	120.00
13-18	31.00	100.00
19-24	29.00	95.00
25 Begin: Jerry Robinson art.	40.00	120.00
26-29	29.00	95.00

FILM FUNNIES
MARVEL(ATLAS) (1949-1950)

1 Begin: Krazy Krow.	31.00	100.00
2	28.00	90.00

FILM STARS ROMANCES
STAR (1950)

1 Photo insert cover (Dan Dailey, Gregory Peck & Rudolph Valentino).	40.00	125.00
2 Movie photo cover (Robert Taylor & Elizabeth Taylor in Conspirator).	40.00	125.00
3 Movie photo cover (Robert Cummings & Lizabeth Scott in Paid In Full).	40.00	125.00

FIRE AND BLAST
NFPA (1952)

NO# Fire prevention giveaway.	23.00	75.00

FIREARM
MALIBU (1993-CURRENT)

0 Video tape and comic package.	2.75	10.00
1	.75	2.50
1A Silver foil cover.	2.75	10.00
2 With Rune #0 coupon.	.75	2.50
3-10	.50	1.95
11	1.00	3.50
12-17	.50	1.95
18	.75	2.50

FIREHAIR
I.W. (1962)

8 Reprint.	7.00	20.00

FIREHAIR COMICS
FICTION HOUSE (1948-1952)

1	55.00	180.00
2 Title changes to Pioneer West Romances with #3.	28.00	90.00
7 Previous title: Pioneer West Romances.	16.00	50.00

8-11	13.00	43.00

FIRESTAR
MARVEL (1986)

1 App: New Mutants & X-Men.	1.00	3.00
2 Art: Art Adams. App: Wolverine.	.50	1.50
3-4	.50	1.50

FIRESTORM
DC (1978)

1 1st & Origin: Firestorm.	1.00	3.00
2-5	.50	1.50

FIRESTORM THE NUCLEAR MAN
DC (1987-1990)

65 Previous title: Fury Of Firestorm.	.30	1.00
66-99	.30	1.00
100 Double size	.75	2.00
ANNUAL 5 1st: New Firestorm. (1987)	.50	1.75

FIRST AMERICANS, THE
DELL FOUR COLOR SERIES (1957)

843 (9/57)	11.00	35.00

FIRST CHRISTMAS
FICTION HOUSE (1953)

NO# Cover: Kelly Freas. Oversized 3 Dimension comic (with glasses).	80.00	250.00

FIRST ISSUE SPECIAL
DC (1975-1976)

1 1st: Atlas. Cover & art: Kirby.	.50	1.50
2 Green Team.	.50	1.50
3 Metamorpho.	.50	1.50
4 Lady Cop.	.50	1.50
5 Manhunter by Kirby.	.50	1.50
6 Dingbats.	.50	1.50
7 The Creeper.	.50	1.50
8 1st & origin: Warlord. Cover & art: Mike Grell.	2.75	10.00
9 Dr. Fate.	.50	1.50
10 The Outsiders.	.50	1.50
11 Code Name: Assassin.	.50	1.50
12 New Starman.	.50	1.50
13 Return Of The New Gods.	.50	1.50

FIRST MEN IN THE MOON
GOLD KEY (1965)

10132-503 Movie photo cover.	8.00	25.00

FISH POLICE
FISHWRAP/COMICO/APPLE (1985-1990)

1	1.75	6.00
1 (2ND) 2nd printing.	.50	1.50
2	1.00	3.00
2 (2ND) 2nd printing.	.50	1.50
3-5	.75	2.00
6 Begin: Comico publication.	.75	2.00
7-17	.50	1.50
18 Begin: Apple publication.	.50	1.50
19-26	.50	1.50

FISH POLICE
MARVEL (1992)

1 Reprint.	.30	1.00
2-6	.30	1.00

FLAME, THE
AJAX (1955)

1 Has #5 on cover.	55.00	180.00
2-3	50.00	150.00

FLAME, THE
FOX (1940-1942)

1 Art: Lou Fine.	600.00	2000.00
2	280.00	925.00
3 Art: Bob Powell.	190.00	600.00
4-8	160.00	525.00

FLAMING CARROT
AV/RENEGADE/DARK HORSE (1984-1993)

1	17.00	55.00
2	10.00	30.00
3	7.00	22.00
4-5	6.00	18.00
6 Begin: Renegade publishing.	5.00	15.00
7	2.75	10.00
8-9	2.25	8.00
10-14	1.50	5.00
15	1.25	4.00
15A Variant without cover price.	2.50	9.00
16-17	1.25	4.00
18 Begin: Dark Horse publication.	1.25	4.00
19-23	1.25	4.00
24 Anniversary issue (2.50 cover).	1.25	4.00
25 With trading cards.	1.00	3.00
26	1.00	3.00
27-28	.75	2.25

29-31 .75 2.50

FLAMING CARROT COMICS
KILLIAN BARRACKS (1981)
1 Magazine size (8.5 x 11). 28.00 90.00

FLARE
HEROIC (1988-1989)
1-3 .30 1.00

FLARE
HEROIC (1990-1994)
1-16 .30 1.00
ANNUAL 1 .30 1.00

FLARE ADVENTURES
HEROIC (1992-1993)
1 .30 1.00
2 Issues #2-12 flip format with Champions Classics. .30 1.00
3-12 .30 1.00

FLARE FIRST EDITION
HEROIC (1991-1993)
1 Reprints. .30 1.00
2-11 .30 1.00

FLASH
DC (1959-1985)
105 Origin retold: Flash. "Master Of Mirrors!" 1200.00 4300.00
106 Origin: Grodd. "The Pied Piper Of Peril!" 300.00 1050.00
107 "Amazing Race Against Time!" 140.00 475.00
108 "The Speed Of Doom!" 140.00 475.00
109 "Return Of The Mirror-Master!" (11/59) 115.00 425.00
110 1st & Origin: Kid Flash. "Challenge Of The Weather Wizard!" 320.00 1050.00
111 "Invasion Of The Cloud Creatures!" 80.00 260.00
112 1st & Origin: Elongated Man. "Mystery Of The Elongated Man!" 95.00 325.00
113 1st & Origin: Trickster. 70.00 240.00
114 65.00 200.00
115-116 55.00 170.00
117 1st & Origin: Captain Boomerang. 65.00 200.00
118-119 45.00 140.00
120 Team up: Flash & Kid Flash. 45.00 140.00
121 35.00 115.00
122 1st & Origin: The Top. 35.00 115.00
123 1st: Golden Age Flash in S.A. 1st: Earth II. 230.00 750.00
124 31.00 100.00
125 1st 12 cent cover price. 25.00 80.00
126-128 25.00 80.00
129 2nd Golden-Age Flash. Re-intro: JSA (Cameo). Lead story: "Double Danger On Earth!" (6/62) 70.00 220.00
130 25.00 80.00
131 Green Lantern. 25.00 80.00
132-136 25.00 80.00
137 App: Golden Age Flash. 1st full JSA story (since re-intro into Silver Age). 110.00 360.00
138 23.00 75.00
139 1st & Origin: Professor Zoom. 31.00 100.00
140 22.00 70.00
141-150 16.00 50.00
151 App: Golden Age Flash. 22.00 70.00
152-159 14.00 45.00
160 80 page Giant #G-21. 17.00 60.00
161-167 11.00 35.00
168 App: Green Lantern. 13.00 40.00
169 80 page Giant #G-34. 17.00 60.00
170 App: Golden Age Flash. 11.00 35.00
171-172 8.00 26.00
173 App: Golden Age Flash. 8.00 26.00
174 9.00 28.00
175 2nd:Superman/Flash race. "Race To The End Of The Universe!" (12/67) 35.00 115.00
176 Giant size. 7.00 22.00
177 7.00 22.00
178 80 page Giant #G-46. 14.00 50.00
179 7.00 22.00
180-186 4.00 13.00
187 80 page Giant #G-58. 12.00 40.00
188-195 4.00 13.00
196 80 page Giant #G-70. 12.00 40.00
197-200 4.00 11.00
201-204 2.00 7.50
205 Giant #G-82. 5.00 20.00
206-210 2.00 7.00
211 Reprint: Flash #104. 2.00 7.00
212 2.00 7.00
213 Reprint: Flash #137. 2.00 7.00
214 DC 100 Page Super Spectacular #11. 2.75 10.00
215 Reprint: Showcase #4. 4.00 13.00
216 2.00 7.00
217-219 Art: Neal Adams. 6.00 18.00
220 2.25 8.00
221-225 2.00 7.00
226 Art: Neal Adams. 2.75 10.00
227-228 1.75 6.00
229 100 page Giant. 5.00 15.00
230-231 1.00 3.00
232 100 page Giant. 5.00 15.00
233 5.00 15.00
234-242 1.00 3.00
243 Death: The Top. 1.00 3.00
244-266 1.00 3.00
267 How Flash got his costume. 1.00 3.00
268-288 1.00 3.00
289 1st George Perez art for DC. 2.00 7.00
290 1.00 3.00
291-299 .75 2.50
300 25th Anniversary. .75 2.50
301-302 .75 2.50
303 Return: the Top. .75 2.50
304 .75 2.50
305-306 1.00 3.00
307-349 .75 2.50
350 Double size. 1.50 5.00
ANNUAL 1 (1963) 95.00 300.00

FLASH
DC (1987-CURRENT)
0 (8/94) 1.00 3.00
1 2.75 10.00
2 1.75 6.00
3 1.50 5.00
4 1.25 4.00
5-6 1.00 3.50
7-13 1.00 3.00
14-18 .75 2.50
19-49 .75 2.00
50 Duble size. 1.50 5.50
51-71 .50 1.50
72 .75 2.00
73 1.25 4.00
74-75 1.00 3.00
76-78 .50 1.50
79 .75 2.50
80 Foil enhanced cover. .75 2.50
80A Newsstand edition. .50 1.50
81-87 .50 1.50
88-90 1.00 3.00
91 1.75 6.00
92 1st: Impulse. 4.00 12.00
93 1.75 6.00
94 Zero Hour, pt 3. 1.50 5.00
95 1.25 4.00
96-99 .75 2.00
100 Double size. Holographic foil enhanced cover. 1.25 4.50
100A Alternate cover (no enhancement). .75 2.50
101 .75 2.00
102-105 .50 1.75
SPECIAL 1 50th Anniversary. (1990) 1.00 3.00

FLASH ANNUAL
DC (1987-CURRENT)
1 (1987) 1.25 4.00
2 (1988) .75 2.50
3 History of all Flashes. (1989) .75 2.50
4 (1991) 1.00 3.50
5 (1992) 1.25 4.50
6 Bloodlines. (1993) .75 2.50
7 Elseworlds story. (1994) .75 2.95
8 (1995) 1.00 3.50

FLASH COMICS
DC (1940-1949)
1 1st & origin: The Flash. 1st & Origin: Hawkman. (1/40) 16300.00 65000.00
2 1200.00 4600.00
3 900.00 3500.00
4-5 700.00 2600.00
6 2nd: Flash cover. 1000.00 3700.00
7-10 500.00 1900.00
11-15 400.00 1300.00
16-23 310.00 1000.00
24 Hawkgirl. 400.00 1300.00
25-28 240.00 775.00
29 1st & Origin: Ghost Patrol. 240.00 775.00
30-36 240.00 775.00
37-38 200.00 650.00
39 "Play Of The Year" by Gardner Fox. Hawkman cover. (3/43) 200.00 650.00
40-48 200.00 650.00
49-60 170.00 550.00
61 150.00 490.00
62 Begin: Joe Kubert art on Hawkman. 200.00 650.00
63-66 150.00 490.00
67-72 160.00 525.00
73-79 180.00 575.00
80 Begin: The Atom. 160.00 525.00
81-85 200.00 650.00
86 Debut: The Black Canary. 400.00 1300.00
87-90 220.00 725.00
91 230.00 750.00
92 1st solo story: Black Canary. 400.00 1500.00
93-97 240.00 775.00
98 Atom gets new costume. 310.00 1000.00
99 310.00 1000.00
100-103 Scarce. 500.00 1900.00
104 Origin retold: Flash. Scarce. 1100.00 4000.00

FLASH COMICS (WHEATIES GIVEAWAY)
DC (1946)
NO# 700.00 2500.00

FLASH COMICS ASHCAN
FAWCETT (JAN., 1940)
1 12 pages, b&w ashcan used during copyright process. 1st & Origin: Captain Thunder (name changed to Captain Marvel-see Whiz Comics 2). 8 copies known to exist. 5100.00 20000.00

FLASH GORDON
DC (1988)
1-9 .20 .75

FLASH GORDON
DELL FOUR COLOR SERIES (1942-1953)
10 Cover & art: Alex Raymond. 130.00 425.00
84 95.00 300.00
173 "Adventure In Opto" (11/47) 31.00 100.00
190 (6/48) 31.00 100.00
204 (12/48) 25.00 80.00
247 "Adventure On Artico" (9/49) 23.00 75.00
424 "Test Flight In Space" (9/52) 17.00 55.00
512 (11/53) 10.00 30.00

FLASH GORDON
GOLD KEY (1965)
1 One shot. 7.00 20.00

FLASH GORDON
HARVEY (1950-1951)
1 Art: Alex Raymond 31.00 100.00
2-4 23.00 75.00
5 Black & White. Sent to subscribers only. 65.00 200.00

FLASH GORDON
KING/CHARLTON/GOLD KEY (1966-1982)
1 7.00 20.00
2-10 4.00 12.00
11 5.00 15.00
12 Begin: Charlton publication. 5.00 15.00
13 Art: Jeff Jones (15 pages). 7.00 20.00
14-18 2.75 10.00
19 Begin: Gold Key publication. 2.25 8.00
20-21 2.25 8.00
22-25 1.75 6.00
26-28 1.25 4.00
29-37 1.00 3.00

FLASH TV SPECIAL
DC (1991)
1 TV photo cover. 1.00 3.95

FLINTSTONES, THE
CHARLTON (1970-1977)
1 13.00 40.00
2 7.00 20.00
3-7 5.00 15.00
8 Double size. Summer Vacation. 8.00 25.00
9-12 2.75 10.00
13-24 2.25 8.00
25-50 1.75 6.00

FLINTSTONES
DELL/GOLD KEY (1961-1970)
2 See Dell Giant #48 for #1. 23.00 75.00
3-4 19.00 60.00
5-6 16.00 50.00
7 Begin Gold Key publication. 14.00 45.00
8-10 13.00 40.00
11 1st: Pebbles. (6/63) 19.00 60.00
12-15 11.00 35.00
16 1st: Bamm-Bamm. (1/64) 16.00 50.00
17-23 10.00 30.00
24 1st: Gruesomes. 11.00 35.00
25-33 10.00 30.00
34 1st: Great Gazoo. 13.00 40.00
35-40 8.00 25.00
41-48 7.00 20.00
49-55 5.00 15.00
56-60 4.00 12.00

FLINTSTONES, THE
HARVEY (1992-1994)
1-13 .50 1.25

FLASH #110 (1ST SERIES)

FLASH #75 (2ND SERIES)

FLASH COMICS #10

FLASH GORDON #2 (HARVEY)

THE FLY #4

FORBIDDEN PLANET #1

FORCE WORKS #4

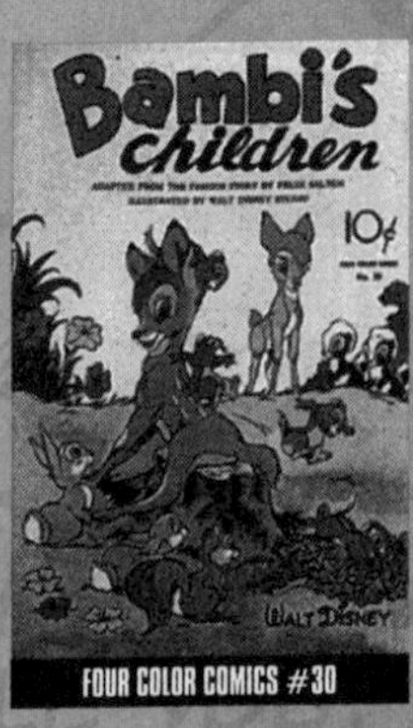

FOUR COLOR COMICS #30

FLINTSTONES, THE
MARVEL (1977-1979)
1-9 .... .75 2.00

FLINTSTONES AT N.Y. WORLD'S FAIR, THE
J.W. BOOKS
NO# No date, circa 1964. .... 13.00 40.00
NO#2 1965 on cover. 2.75 10.00

FLINTSTONES BIGGER AND BOULDER
GOLD KEY (1962)
1 (30013-211) 80 page giant. 23.00 75.00
2 (1966), reprints #1. .... 10.00 30.00

FLINTSTONES WITH PEBBLES AND BAMM-BAMM, THE
GOLD KEY (1965)
30028-511 100 page Gold Key Giant. 16.00 50.00

FLIP
HARVEY (1954)
1 .... 23.00 75.00
2 Art: Bob Powell. 19.00 60.00

FLIPPER
GOLD KEY (1966-1967)
1 Photo cover, TV tie-in. 13.00 40.00
2-3 Photo cover. 7.00 20.00

FLIPPITY & FLOP
DC (1951-1960)
1 .... 60.00 190.00
2 .... 40.00 125.00
3-6 .... 29.00 95.00
7-12 .... 25.00 80.00
13-20 .... 20.00 65.00
21 1st Code Approved issue. 17.00 55.00
22-30 .... 16.00 50.00
31-36 .... 12.00 39.00
37-47 .... 10.00 33.00

FLOATERS
DARK HORSE (1993)
1-6 .... .75 2.50

FLOOD RELIEF
MALIBU (1994)
1 Red Cross benefit issue. 1.50 5.00

FLY, THE
ARCHIE (1983-1984)
1 Art: Steve Ditko. .... .50 1.50
2-9 .... .50 1.50

FLY, THE
IMPACT (1991-1992)
1-17 .... .30 1.00
ANNUAL 1 .... .75 2.50

FLY BOY
ZIFF-DAVIS (1952-1953)
1 .... 19.00 60.00
2 .... 13.00 40.00
3-4 .... 10.00 30.00

FLYBOY
ST. JOHN (1954)
5 From Approved Comics series. 10.00 30.00

FLYING A'S RANGE RIDER
DELL (1953-1959)
2 See Range Rider #404 for 1st issue. 13.00 40.00
3-6 .... 11.00 35.00
7-12 .... 8.00 25.00
13-18 .... 7.00 20.00
19-20 .... 5.00 15.00
21 .... 5.00 15.00
22-24 .... 5.00 15.00

FLYING ACES
KEY (1955)
1 .... 8.00 25.00
2-5 .... 5.00 15.00

FLYING NUN, THE
GOLD KEY (1968)
1 Photo cover. TV tie-in. 11.00 35.00
2 Photo-cover. 7.00 20.00
3-4 .... 4.00 12.00

FLYING SAUCERS
AVON (1950)
1 Art: Wallace Wood. 100.00 325.00
1A 1951 reprint (slight cover variant). 95.00 300.00

FLYING SAUCERS
DELL (1967)
1 .... 5.00 15.00
2-4 .... 2.50 9.00

FLYMAN
MIGHTY (1965-1966)
32-33 .... 10.00 30.00
34-39 .... 8.00 25.00

FOLLOW THE SUN
DELL (1962)
1 (01-280-207) 8.00 25.00
2 (12-280-211) 8.00 25.00

FOODANG
AUGUST HOUSE (1995-CURRENT)
1 Color reprint of Continum issue, foil enhanced cover.
.... .75 2.50
1A Signed & numbered, foil cover. .... .75 2.50
2-4 .... .75 2.50

FOODANG
CONTINUM (1994)
1 Foil enhanced cover. .... .50 1.95

FOODINI
CONTINENTAL (1950)
1 .... 17.00 55.00
2 .... 10.00 30.00
3-4 .... 7.00 20.00

FOOFUR
MARVEL(STAR) (1987-1988)
1 TV Cartoon. .... .20 .50
2-6 .... .20 .50

FOOLKILLER
MARVEL (1990-1991)
1 1st & Origin: Foolkiller III. .... .75 2.00
2 Origin: Foolkiller I & II. .... .30 1.00
3 1st: Foolkiller in costume. .... .30 1.00
4-10 .... .30 1.00

FOOTBALL THRILLS
ZIFF-DAVIS (1952)
1 .... 55.00 180.00
2 .... 40.00 120.00

FOR A NIGHT OF LOVE
AVON (1951)
NO# 50.00 150.00

FORBIDDEN LOVE
QUALITY (1950)
1 Art: Reed Crandall. Photo cover. 100.00 325.00
2-3 Photo cover. 50.00 150.00
4 Photo cover. Art: Bill Ward. 55.00 175.00

FORBIDDEN PLANET
INNOVATION (1992)
1 Movie Adaptation. .... .75 2.50
2-4 .... .75 2.50

FORBIDDEN TALES OF DARK MANSION
DC (1972-1974)
5 Previous title: Dark Mansion Of Forbidden Love.
.... 1.50 5.00
6-15 .... 1.50 5.00

FORBIDDEN WORLDS
ACG (1951-1967)
1 Williamson/Frazetta art, 10 pgs. 280.00 900.00
2 .... 145.00 480.00
3 Art: Williamson/Wood. 130.00 420.00
4 .... 75.00 240.00
5 Art: Williamson. 95.00 300.00
6 Art: Williamson. 75.00 240.00
7-12 .... 50.00 150.00
13-18 .... 31.00 100.00
19-24 .... 28.00 90.00
25-33 .... 23.00 75.00
34 Marilyn Monroe inside FC photo & ad. (10/54)
.... 28.00 90.00
35 (8/55) 19.00 60.00
36-48 .... 16.00 50.00
49-54 .... 15.00 48.00
55-60 .... 13.00 42.00
61-64 .... 11.00 36.00
65 "There's A New Moon Tonight" 13.00 42.00
66-72 .... 11.00 36.00
73 1st: Herbie. 75.00 240.00
74-85 .... 11.00 36.00
86 .... 13.00 42.00
87-90 .... 11.00 36.00
91-93 .... 8.00 24.00
94 Herbie. 19.00 60.00
95-100 .... 8.00 24.00
101-109 .... 6.00 18.00
110 Herbie. 11.00 36.00
111-113 .... 6.00 18.00
114 1st Herbie cover and story. 11.00 36.00
115 .... 6.00 18.00
116 Herbie. 11.00 36.00
117-124 .... 6.00 18.00
125 1st & Origin: Magicman. 8.00 24.00
126-139 .... 6.00 18.00
140 Mark Midnight by Steve Ditko. 8.00 24.00
141-145 .... 4.00 12.00

FORCE WORKS
MARVEL (1994-CURRENT)
1 Double size, pop-up cover. 1.25 4.50
1A Regular cover. .... .50 1.75
1B Ashcan edition. .... .20 .75
2 .... .50 1.25
3-4 .... .50 1.50
5 Polybagged with neon ink cover, insert & print.
.... .75 2.95
5A Regular cover. .... .50 1.50
6-11 .... .50 1.50
12 .... .75 2.50
13-15 .... .50 1.50

FOREIGN INTRIGUES
CHARLTON (1956)
13 Previous title: Johnny Dynamite. 7.00 20.00
14 .... 7.00 20.00
15 Title changes to Battlefield Action with issue #16.
.... 7.00 20.00

FOREST FIRE
AFA (1950)
NO# 1st: Smokey the Bear. Giveaway. 31.00 100.00

FOREVER, DARLING
DELL FOUR COLOR SERIES (1956)
681 Movie photo cover (Lucy & Desi). (2/56)
.... 26.00 85.00

FOREVER PEOPLE
DC (1971-1972)
1 1st: Forever People & Darkseid. Cover & art: Kirby in all issues. 12.00 38.00
2 .... 8.00 26.00
3-6 .... 7.00 22.00
7-8 .... 4.00 12.00
9-10 Deadman. 4.00 12.00
11 .... 4.00 12.00

FOREVER PEOPLE
DC (1988)
1-6 .... .30 1.00

FORTY BIG PAGES OF MICKEY MOUSE
WHITMAN (1936)
945 40 pages, cardboard covers. 400.00 1200.00

FOUR COLOR COMICS
DELL (1941-1962)
1 Little Joe. 110.00 350.00
2 Harold Teen. 65.00 200.00
3 Alley Oop. 115.00 375.00
4 Smilin' Jack. 110.00 350.00
5 Raggedy Ann And Andy. 115.00 375.00
6 Smitty. 50.00 150.00
7 Smokey Stover. 65.00 200.00
8 Tillie The Toiler. 50.00 150.00
9 Donald Duck Finds Pirate Gold. Barks art.
.... 1700.00 6500.00
10 Flash Gordon By Alex Raymond. 130.00 425.00
11 Wash Tubbs. 70.00 225.00
12 Bambi (#1). 115.00 375.00
13 Mr. District Attorney (#1). 65.00 200.00
14 Smilin' Jack. 80.00 250.00
15 Felix The Cat (#1). 130.00 425.00
16 Porky Pig and the Secret Of The Haunted House (#1).
.... 125.00 400.00
17 Popeye. 110.00 350.00
18 Little Orphan Annie's Junior Commandos.
.... 95.00 300.00
19 Thumper meets the Seven Dwarfs. 115.00 375.00
20 Barney Baxter. 50.00 150.00
21 Oswald The Rabbit (#1). 80.00 250.00
22 Tillie The Toiler. 31.00 100.00
23 Raggedy Ann And Andy. Walt Kelly art. 95.00 300.00
24 Gang Busters. 70.00 225.00
25 Andy Panda (#1). 95.00 300.00
26 Popeye. 100.00 325.00
27 Mickey Mouse and the Seven-Colored Terror.
.... 170.00 550.00
28 Wash Tubbs. 50.00 150.00
29 Donald Duck and the Mummy's Ring. Barks art.
.... 1300.00 4800.00

30 Bambi's Children. 110.00 350.00
31 Moon Mullins. 40.00 125.00
32 Smitty. 31.00 100.00
33 Bugs Bunny "Public Nuisance No.1". 125.00 400.00
34 Dick Tracy. 110.00 350.00
35 Smokey Stover. 25.00 80.00
36 Smilin' Jack. 50.00 150.00
37 Bringing Up Father. 50.00 150.00
38 Roy Rogers Comics (#1). 190.00 600.00
39 Oswald The Rabbit. 55.00 175.00
40 Barney Google And Snuffy Smith. 50.00 150.00
41 Mother Goose and Nursery Rhyme Comics.
55.00 175.00
42 Tiny Tim. 40.00 125.00
43 Popeye. 70.00 225.00
44 Terry And The Pirates. 95.00 300.00
45 Raggedy Ann. 70.00 225.00
46 Felix The Cat and the Haunted Castle. 95.00 300.00
47 Gene Autry in The Ghost Mine. 110.00 350.00
48 Porky Pig (Porky of The Mounties & Porky and the Pirate). July, 1944; Barks art. 200.00 650.00
49 Snow White And The Seven Dwarfs. 110.00 350.00
50 Fairy Tale Parade. Walt Kelly art. 65.00 200.00
51 Bugs Bunny finds the Lost Treasure. 65.00 200.00
52 Little Orphan Annie. 65.00 200.00
53 Wash Tubbs. 40.00 125.00
54 Andy Panda. 65.00 200.00
55 Tille The Toiler. 28.00 90.00
56 Dick Tracy. 95.00 300.00
57 Gene Autry "Raiders of the Range". 95.00 300.00
58 Smilin' Jack. 50.00 150.00
59 Mother Goose And Nursery Rhyme Comics.
50.00 150.00
60 Tiny Folks Funnies. 31.00 100.00
61 Santa Clause Funnies. Walt Kelly art. 55.00 180.00
62 Donald Duck in Frozen Gold. Barks art.
400.00 1200.00
63 Roy Rogers Comics. 125.00 400.00
64 Smokey Stover. 19.00 60.00
65 Smitty. 25.00 80.00
66 Gene Autry. "Trail of Terror". 95.00 300.00
67 Oswald The Rabbit. 40.00 125.00
68 Mother Goose And Nursery Rhyme Comics.
50.00 150.00
69 Fairy Tale Parade. Walt Kelly art. 50.00 150.00
70 Popeye And Wimpy. 65.00 200.00
71 Three Caballeros. Walt Kelly art. 190.00 600.00
72 Raggedy Ann. 55.00 180.00
73 The Gumps (#1). 25.00 80.00
74 Marge's Little Lulu (#1). 200.00 650.00
75 Gene Autry and The Wildcat. 80.00 250.00
76 Little Orphan Annie. 55.00 180.00
77 Felix The Cat. 85.00 275.00
78 Porky Pig and the Bandit Twins. 55.00 175.00
79 Mickey Mouse in the Riddle Of The Red Hat.
190.00 600.00
80 Smilin' Jack. 35.00 110.00
81 Moon Mullins. 22.00 70.00
82 The Lone Ranger. 1st: Lone Ranger Four Color comic.
85.00 275.00
83 Gene Autry. "Outlaw Trail". 80.00 250.00
84 Flash Gordon. 95.00 300.00
85 Andy Panda. "The Mad Dog Mystery". 40.00 125.00
86 Roy Rogers Comics. 95.00 300.00
87 Fairy Tale Parade. 40.00 130.00
88 Bugs Bunny's Great Adventure. 50.00 150.00
89 Tillie The Toiler. 25.00 80.00
90 Christmas With Mother Goose. 50.00 150.00
91 Santa Claus Funnies. Walt Kelly art. 50.00 150.00
92 The Wonderful Adventures Of Pinocchio. Walt Kelly art.
85.00 275.00
93 Gene Autry in The Bandit Of Black Rock.
65.00 200.00
94 Winnie Winkle. 25.00 80.00
95 Roy Rogers Comics. 95.00 300.00
96 Dick Tracy. 70.00 225.00
97 Marge's Little Lulu. 70.00 225.00
98 The Lone Ranger. 65.00 200.00
99 Smitty. 23.00 75.00
100 Gene Autry Comics. 70.00 225.00
101 Terry And The Pirates. Last issue to carry the "Four Color Comic" emblem. 65.00 200.00
102 Oswald The Rabbit. 31.00 100.00
103 Easter With Mother Goose. 45.00 140.00
104 Fairy Tale Parade. Walt Kelly art. 45.00 140.00
105 Albert The Alligator And Pogo Possum (#1). Walt Kelly art.
190.00 600.00
106 Tillie The Toiler. 19.00 60.00
107 Little Orphan Annie. 50.00 150.00
108 Donald Duck in "The Terror of the River"
290.00 950.00
109 Roy Rogers Comics. 80.00 250.00
110 Marge's Little Lulu. 50.00 150.00
111 Captain Easy. 25.00 80.00
112 Porky Pig's Adventure In Gopher Gulch.
31.00 100.00
113 Popeye. 28.00 90.00
114 Fairy Tale Parade. 31.00 100.00
115 Marge's Little Lulu. 45.00 135.00
116 Mickey Mouse and the House of Many Mysteries.
55.00 175.00
117 Roy Rogers Comics. 55.00 175.00
118 The Lone Ranger. 60.00 190.00
119 Felix The Cat. 60.00 190.00
120 Marge's Little Lulu. 40.00 125.00
121 Fairy Tale Parade. 23.00 75.00
122 Henry (#1). 23.00 75.00
123 Bugs Bunny's Dangerous Venture. 25.00 80.00
124 Roy Rogers Comics. 55.00 175.00
125 The Lone Ranger. 55.00 175.00
126 Christmas With Mother Goose. Walt Kelly art.
31.00 100.00
127 Popeye. 31.00 100.00
128 Santa Claus Funnies. Walt Kelly art. 31.00 100.00
129 Uncle Remus and his tales of Brer Rabbit (#1).
50.00 150.00
130 Andy Panda. 19.00 60.00
131 Marge's Little Lulu. 40.00 120.00
132 Tille The Toiler. 19.00 60.00
133 Dick Tracy. 55.00 175.00
134 Tarzan and the Devil Ogre. 125.00 400.00
135 Felix The Cat. 45.00 140.00
136 The Lone Ranger. 50.00 150.00
137 Roy Rogers Comics. 55.00 175.00
138 Smitty. 19.00 60.00
139 Marge's Little Lulu. 35.00 110.00
140 Easter With Mother Goose. 31.00 100.00
141 Mickey Mouse and the Submarine Pirates.
55.00 175.00
142 Bugs Bunny and the Haunted Mountains.
25.00 80.00
143 Oswald The Rabbit and the Prehistoric Egg.
16.00 50.00
144 Roy Rogers Comics. 55.00 175.00
145 Popeye. 28.00 90.00
146 Marge's Little Lulu. 31.00 100.00
147 Donald Duck in Volcano Valley. 210.00 675.00
148 Albert The Alligator And Pogo Possum. Walt Kelly art.
145.00 475.00
149 Smilin' Jack. 25.00 80.00
150 Tillie The Toiler. 17.00 55.00
151 The Lone Ranger. 40.00 130.00
152 Little Orphan Annie. 28.00 90.00
153 Roy Rogers Comics. 50.00 150.00
154 Andy Panda. 19.00 60.00
155 Henry. 13.00 40.00
156 Porky Pig and the Phantom. 22.00 70.00
157 Mickey Mouse and the Beanstalk. Movie tie-in.
55.00 175.00
158 Marge's Little Lulu. 28.00 90.00
159 Donald Duck in the Ghost Of The Grotto. Barks art.
190.00 600.00
160 Roy Rogers Comics. 50.00 150.00
161 Tarzan and the Fires Of Tohr. 100.00 330.00
162 Felix The Cat. 35.00 110.00
163 Dick Tracy. 45.00 135.00
164 Bugs Bunny finds the Frozen Kingdom. 22.00 70.00
165 Marge's Little Lulu. 25.00 80.00
166 Roy Rogers Comics. 50.00 150.00
167 The Lone Ranger. 31.00 100.00
168 Popeye. 28.00 90.00
169 Woody Woodpecker Man Hunter of the North" (#1).
35.00 110.00
170 Mickey Mouse on Spook's Island. 45.00 140.00
171 Charlie McCarthy (#1). 40.00 125.00
172 Christmas With Mother Goose. 31.00 100.00
173 Flash Gordon. 31.00 100.00
174 Winnie Winkle. 14.00 45.00
175 Santa Claus Funnies. 28.00 90.00
176 Tillie The Toiler. 16.00 50.00
177 Roy Rogers Comics. 50.00 150.00
178 Donald Duck "Christmas On Bear Mountain".
190.00 600.00
179 Uncle Wiggily (#1). 40.00 120.00
180 Ozark Ike (#1). 16.00 50.00
181 Mickey Mouse in Jungle Magic. 45.00 140.00
182 Porky Pig in Ever-Never Land. 22.00 70.00
183 Oswald The Rabbit. 16.00 50.00
184 Tillie The Toiler. 16.00 50.00
185 Easter With Maher Goose. 28.00 90.00
186 Bambi. 25.00 80.00
187 Bugs Bunny and the Dreadful Dragon. 22.00 70.00
188 Woody Woodpecker. 22.00 70.00
189 Donald Duck in The Old Castle's Secret. Barks art.
170.00 550.00
190 Flash Gordon. 31.00 100.00
191 Porky Pig To The Rescue. 22.00 70.00
192 The Brownies (#1). 31.00 100.00
193 Tom And Jerry in Double Trouble (#1).
40.00 125.00
194 Mickey Mouse in the World Under The Sea.
45.00 140.00
195 Tillie The Toiler. 13.00 40.00
196 Charlie McCarthy in The Haunted Hide-Out. Photo (insert) cover. 31.00 100.00
197 Zane Grey's Spirit Of The Border (#1). 22.00 70.00
198 Andy Panda. 19.00 60.00
199 Donald Duck in Sheriff Of Bullet Valley.
170.00 550.00
200 Bugs Bunny, Super Sleuth. 19.00 60.00
201 Christmas With Mother Goose. 28.00 90.00
202 Woody Woodpecker. 16.00 50.00
203 Donald Duck in "The Golden Christmas Tree". Barks art.
155.00 500.00
204 Flash Gordon. 25.00 80.00
205 Santa Claus Funnies. 28.00 90.00
206 Little Orphan Annie. 16.00 50.00
207 King Of The Royal Mounted. 31.00 100.00
208 Brer Rabbit Does It Again! 23.00 75.00
209 Harold Teen. 8.00 25.00
210 Tippie And Cap Stubbs. 8.00 25.00
211 Little Beaver (#1). 16.00 50.00
212 Dr. Bobbs. 10.00 30.00
213 Tillie The Toiler. 11.00 35.00
214 Mickey Mouse and his Sky Adventure.
31.00 100.00
215 Sparkle Plenty. 23.00 75.00
216 Andy Panda and the Police Pup. 13.00 40.00
217 Bugs Bunny in Court Jester. 23.00 75.00
218 3 Little Pigs and the Wonderful Magic Lamp.
23.00 75.00
219 Swee' Pea. 20.00 65.00
220 Easter With Mother Goose. 28.00 90.00
221 Uncle Wiggily. 22.00 70.00
222 Zane Grey's West Of The Pecos. 16.00 50.00
223 Donald Duck "Lost In The Andes". 155.00 500.00
224 Little Iodine (#1). 23.00 75.00
225 Oswald The Rabbit. 11.00 35.00
226 Porky Pig and Spoofy, the Spook. 16.00 50.00
227 Seven Dwarfs. 25.00 80.00
228 The Mark Of Zorro. 55.00 175.00
229 Smokey Stover. 8.00 25.00
230 Zane Grey's Sunset Pass. 16.00 50.00
231 Mickey Mouse and the Rajah's Treasure.
31.00 100.00
232 Woody Woodpecker. 16.00 50.00
233 Bugs Bunny, Sleepwalking Sleuth. 23.00 75.00
234 Dumbo in Sky Voyage. 20.00 65.00
235 Tiny Tim. 13.00 40.00
236 Zane Grey's Heritage Of The Desert. 16.00 50.00
237 Tillie The Toiler. 10.00 30.00
238 Donald Duck in "Voodoo Hoodoo". Barks art.
140.00 450.00
239 Adventure Bound. 10.00 30.00
240 Andy Panda. 13.00 40.00
241 Porky Pig, Mighty Hunter. 16.00 50.00
242 Tippie And Cap Stubbs. 10.00 30.00
243 Thumper Follows His Nose. 19.00 60.00
244 The Brownies. 25.00 80.00
245 Dick's Adventures. 11.00 35.00
246 Zane Grey's Thunder Mountain. 11.00 35.00
247 Flash Gordon. 23.00 75.00
248 Mickey Mouse and the Black Sorcerer.
31.00 100.00
249 Woody Woodpecker in the Globe Trotter.
16.00 50.00
250 Bugs Bunny in Diamond Daze. 23.00 75.00
251 Hubert At Camp Moonbeam. 11.00 35.00
252 Pinocchio. 23.00 75.00
253 Christmas With Mother Goose. Walt Kelly art.
28.00 90.00
254 Santa Claus Funnies. Walt Kelly art. 28.00 90.00
255 Zane Grey's The Ranger. 11.00 35.00
256 Donald Duck in "Luck Of The North". Barks art.
95.00 300.00
257 Little Iodine. 16.00 50.00
258 Andy Panda and the Balloon Race. 13.00 40.00
259 Santa and the Angel. 11.00 35.00
260 Porky Pig, Hero Of The Wild West. 16.00 50.00
261 Mickey Mouse and The Missing Key. 31.00 100.00
262 Raggedy Ann And Andy. 14.00 45.00
263 Donald Duck in "Land Of The Totem Poles".
95.00 300.00
264 Woody Woodpecker In The Magic Lantern.
14.00 45.00
265 Zane Grey's King Of The Royal Mounted.
20.00 65.00
266 Bugs Bunny On The Isle Of Hercules. 19.00 60.00
267 Little Beaver. 8.00 25.00
268 Mickey Mouse's Surprise Visitor. 31.00 100.00
269 Johnny Mack Brown in Law for the Badlands (#1). Photo cover. 45.00 140.00
270 Zane Grey's Drift Fence. 11.00 35.00
271 Porky Pig in Phantom Of The Plains. 16.00 50.00
272 Cinderella. 20.00 65.00
273 Oswald The Rabbit. 10.00 30.00
274 Bugs Bunny, Hare-Brained Reporter. 19.00 60.00
275 Donald Duck in "Ancient Persia". 95.00 300.00
276 Uncle Wiggily. 16.00 50.00
277 Porky Pig in Desert Adventure. 16.00 50.00
278 Bill Elliott Comics (#1). Photo cover. 31.00 100.00
279 Mickey Mouse and Pluto Battle The Giant Ants.
25.00 80.00

FOUR COLOR COMICS #40

FOUR COLOR COMICS #123

FOUR COLOR COMICS #192

FOUR COLOR COMICS #253

FOUR COLOR COMICS #383

FOUR COLOR COMICS #401

FOUR COLOR COMICS #435

FOUR COLOR COMICS #445

FAMOUS · FIRSTS

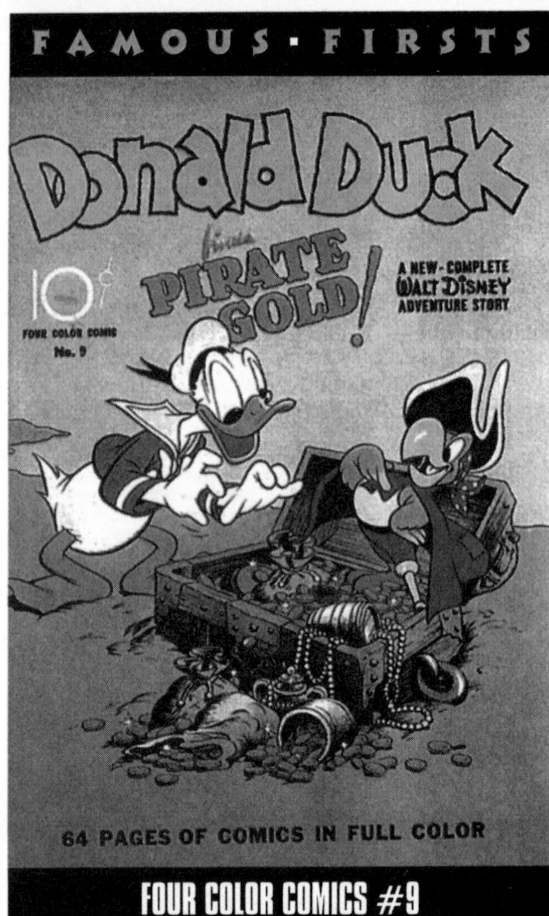

FOUR COLOR COMICS #9

This issue presents the first comics work in the Four Color series by the most popular "Duck" artist, Carl Barks. Working in Disney's animation department, Barks was picked to turn storyboards for an animation feature into a comic.

280 Andy Panda in the Isle Of Mechanical Men. 13.00 40.00
281 Bugs Bunny in The Great Circus Mystery. 19.00 60.00
282 Donald Duck and The Pixilated Parrot. 95.00 300.00
283 Zane Grey's King Of The Royal Mounted. 22.00 70.00
284 Porky Pig in "The Kingdom Of Nowhere". 16.00 50.00
285 Bozo The Clown and His Minikin Circus (#1). 31.00 100.00
286 Mickey Mouse and the Uninvited Guest. 25.00 80.00
287 Gene Autry's Champion in The Ghost Of Black Mountain (#1). Color photo front and back covers. (8/50) 25.00 80.00
288 Woody Woodpecker in Klondike Gold. 14.00 45.00
289 Bugs Bunny in "Indian Trouble". 19.00 60.00
290 The Chief. 11.00 35.00
291 Donald Duck in "The Magic Hourglass". 85.00 275.00
292 The Cisco Kid Comics (#1). 50.00 150.00
293 The Brownies. 22.00 70.00
294 Little Beaver. 8.00 25.00
295 Porky Pig in "President Porky". ... 16.00 50.00
296 Mickey Mouse in Private Eye For Hire. 25.00 80.00
297 Andy Panda in The Haunted Inn. 13.00 40.00
298 Bugs Bunny, Sheik For A Day. ... 19.00 60.00
299 Buck Jones and the Iron Horse Trail (#1). 28.00 90.00
300 Donald Duck in "Big-Top Bedlam". 95.00 300.00
301 Zane Grey's The Mysterious Rider. 11.00 35.00
302 Santa Claus Funnies. 8.00 25.00
303 Porky Pig in The Land Of The Monstrous Flies. 11.00 35.00
304 Mickey Mouse in "Tom-Tom Island". 19.00 60.00
305 Woody Woodpecker. 8.00 25.00
306 Raggedy Ann + Andy. 13.00 40.00
307 Bugs Bunny in Lumberjack Jackrabbit. 16.00 50.00
308 Donald Duck in "Dangerous Disguise". 80.00 250.00
309 Betty Betz' Dollface And Her Gang. 13.00 40.00
310 Zane Grey's King Of The Royal Mounted. 14.00 45.00
311 Porky Pig in "Midget Horses Of Hidden Valley". 11.00 35.00
312 Tonto (#1). 25.00 80.00
313 Mickey Mouse in "The Mystery Of The Double-Cross Ranch" (#1). 19.00 60.00
314 Zane Grey's Ambush. 11.00 35.00
315 Oswald The Rabbit. 8.00 25.00
316 Rex Allen (#1). Photo cover. ... 40.00 130.00
317 Bugs Bunny in "Hair Today, Gone Tomorrow." 16.00 50.00
318 Donald Duck in "No Such Varmint". Barks art. 80.00 250.00
319 Gene Autry's Champion in The Trail To Danger. 11.00 35.00
320 Uncle Wiggily (#1). 14.00 45.00
321 Little Scouts (#1). 5.00 15.00
322 Porky Pig in "Roaring Rockets." ... 11.00 35.00
323 Susie Q. Smith. 10.00 30.00
324 I Met A Handsome Cowboy. 17.00 55.00
325 Mickey Mouse in the Haunted Castle. 19.00 60.00
326 Andy Panda. 8.00 25.00
327 Bugs Bunny and The Rajah's Elephant. 16.00 50.00
328 Donald Duck in Old California. ... 80.00 250.00
329 Roy Roger's Trigger. (#1) 25.00 80.00
330 Porky Pig Meets The Bristled Bruiser. 11.00 35.00
331 Alice In Wonderland. 23.00 75.00
332 Little Beaver. 8.00 25.00
333 Zane Grey's Wilderness Trek. ... 11.00 35.00
334 Mickey Mouse and Yukon Gold. ... 19.00 60.00
335 Francis The Talking Mule (#1). Movie tie-in. 23.00 75.00
336 Woody Woodpecker. 8.00 25.00
337 The Brownies. 8.00 25.00
338 Bugs Bunny and the Rocking Horse Thieves. 16.00 50.00
339 Donald Duck and the Magic Fountain (not by Barks). 19.00 60.00
340 Zane Grey's King Of The Royal Mounted. 14.00 45.00
341 Unbirthday Party with Alice In Wonderland. 19.00 60.00
342 Porky Pig in The Lucky Peppermint Mine. 8.00 25.00
343 Mickey Mouse in the Ruby Eye Of Homar-Guy-Am. 16.00 50.00
344 Sergeant Preston from Challenge Of The Yukon (#1). 25.00 80.00
345 Andy Panda ...in Scotland Yard. ... 8.00 25.00
346 Zane Grey's Hide-out. 11.00 35.00
347 Bugs Bunny the Frigid Hare. 16.00 50.00
348 Donald Duck The Crocodile Collector. Cover: Carl Barks. 23.00 75.00
349 Uncle Wiggily. 14.00 45.00
350 Woody Woodpecker. 8.00 25.00
351 Porky Pig and the Grand Canyon Giant. 8.00 25.00
352 Mickey Mouse "The Mystery Of Painted Valley". 16.00 50.00
353 Duck Album. Cover: Carl Barks. ... 13.00 40.00
354 Raggedy Ann + Andy. 13.00 40.00
355 Bugs Bunny "Hot-Rod Hare". ... 16.00 50.00
356 Donald Duck in "Rags To Riches". Cover: Carl Barks. 23.00 75.00
357 Zane Grey's Comeback! 10.00 30.00
358 Andy Panda. 8.00 25.00
359 Frosty The Snowman. 14.00 45.00
360 Porky Pig in "Tree Of Fortune". ... 8.00 25.00
361 Santa Claus Funnies. 7.00 20.00
362 Mickey Mouse and the Smuggled Diamonds. 16.00 50.00
363 Zane Grey's King Of The Royal Mounted. 11.00 35.00
364 Woody Woodpecker. 8.00 25.00
365 The Brownies. 8.00 25.00
366 Bugs Bunny "Uncle Buckskin Comes To Town". 16.00 50.00
367 Donald Duck in "A Christmas For Shacktown". 70.00 225.00
368 Beany And Cecil featuring Cecil the Seasick Sea Serpent (#1). 50.00 150.00
369 The Lone Ranger's Famous Horse Hi-Yo Silver (#1). 22.00 70.00
370 Porky Pig in "Trouble In The Big Trees". 8.00 25.00
371 Mickey Mouse "The Inca Idol Case". 16.00 50.00
372 Zane Grey's Riders Of The Purple Sage. 8.00 25.00
373 Sergeant Preston Of The Yukon. 14.00 45.00
374 Woody Woodpecker. 8.00 25.00
375 John Carter Of Mars. 50.00 155.00
376 Bugs Bunny, "The Magic Sneeze". 16.00 50.00
377 Susie Q. Smith. 8.00 25.00
378 Tom Corbett, Space Cadet (#1). 40.00 130.00
379 Donald Duck in Southern Hospitality (not by Barks). 14.00 45.00
380 Raggedy Ann + Andy. 10.00 30.00
381 Marge's Tubby "Captain Yo-Yo" (#1). 25.00 80.00
382 Snow White And The Seven Dwarfs. Reprints part of Four Color #49; Movie tie-in. (3/52) 19.00 60.00
383 Andy Panda. 5.00 15.00
384 Zane Grey's King Of The Royal Mounted. 11.00 35.00
385 Porky Pig in The Isle Of Missing Ships. 8.00 25.00
386 Uncle Scrooge in "Only A Poor Old Man" (#1). 230.00 750.00
387 Mickey Mouse in High Tibet. ... 16.00 50.00
388 Oswald The Rabbit. 7.00 20.00
389 Andy Hardy Comics (#1). 10.00 30.00
390 Woody Woodpecker. 8.00 25.00
391 Uncle Wiggily. 10.00 30.00
392 The Lone Ranger's Famous Horse Hi-Yo Silver. 10.00 30.00
393 Bugs Bunny. 16.00 50.00
394 Donald Duck in Malayalaya. Cover: Carl Barks. 20.00 65.00
395 Zane Grey's Forlorn River. 8.00 25.00
396 Tales Of The Texas Rangers. TV photo cover. 26.00 85.00
397 Sergeant Preston Of The Yukon. 14.00 45.00
398 The Brownies. 8.00 25.00
399 Porky Pig in The Lost Gold Mine. ... 8.00 25.00
400 Tom Corbett, Space Cadet. 23.00 75.00
401 Mickey Mouse and Goofy's Mechanical Wizard. 11.00 35.00
402 Mary Jane And Sniffles Comics. ... 20.00 65.00
403 Li'l Bad Wolf. 10.00 30.00
404 The Range Rider Comics. TV photo cover. 26.00 85.00
405 Woody Woodpecker. 8.00 25.00
406 Tweety And Sylvester (#1). 16.00 50.00
407 Bugs Bunny in "The Foreign-Legion Hare." 11.00 35.00
408 Donald Duck and the Golden Helmet. 70.00 225.00
409 Andy Panda. 5.00 15.00
410 Porky Pig in The Water Wizard. ... 8.00 25.00

411 Mickey Mouse and the Old Sea Dog. 11.00 35.00
412 Zane Grey's Nevada. 8.00 25.00
413 Robin Hood. Movie photo cover. 25.00 80.00
414 Beany And Cecil in "Horse-Fly Hubbub". 40.00 125.00
415 Rootie Kazootie (#1). TV tie-in. 23.00 75.00
416 Woody Woodpecker. 8.00 25.00
417 Double Trouble With Goober. 7.00 20.00
418 Rusty Riley, A Boy, A Horse, And A Dog. 10.00 30.00
419 Sergeant Preston Of The Yukon. 14.00 45.00
420 Bugs Bunny in "The Mysterious Buckaroo." 11.00 35.00
421 Tom Corbett, Space Cadet. 19.00 60.00
422 Donald Duck and The Gilded Man. 70.00 225.00
423 Rhubarb, Owner Of the Brooklyn Ball Club. 10.00 30.00
424 Flash Gordon featuring "Test Flight In Space". 17.00 55.00
425 The Return Of Zorro. 40.00 120.00
426 Porky Pig in "The Scalawag Leprechaun." 8.00 25.00
427 Mickey Mouse and the Wonderful Whizzix. 11.00 35.00
428 Uncle Wiggily. 10.00 30.00
429 Pluto in "Why Dogs Leave Home." 11.00 35.00
430 Marge's Tubby, The Shadow Of A Man-Eater. 17.00 55.00
431 Woody Woodpecker. 8.00 25.00
432 Bugs Bunny and the Rabbit Olympics. 11.00 35.00
433 Zane Grey's Wildfire. 8.00 25.00
434 Rin Tin Tin in Dark Danger (#1). Photo cover. 45.00 140.00
435 Frosty The Snowman. 8.00 25.00
436 The Brownies. 7.00 20.00
437 John Carter Of Mars. 35.00 110.00
438 Annie Oakley (#1). TV tie-in. 31.00 100.00
439 Little Hiawatha. 11.00 35.00
440 Black Beauty. 10.00 30.00
441 Fearless Fagan. 8.00 25.00
442 Peter Pan. 16.00 50.00
443 Ben Bowie and his Mountain Men (#1). 16.00 50.00
444 Marge's Tubby. 17.00 55.00
445 Charlie McCarthy. 11.00 35.00
446 Captain Hook and Peter Pan. 17.00 55.00
447 Andy Hardy Comics. 5.00 15.00
448 Beany And Cecil. 35.00 110.00
449 Zane Grey's Tappan's Burro. 8.00 25.00
450 Duck Album. 11.00 35.00
451 Rusty Riley. 8.00 25.00
452 Raggedy Ann + Andy. 10.00 30.00
453 Susie Q. Smith. 8.00 25.00
454 Krazy Kat Comics. 10.00 30.00
455 Johnny Mack Brown Comics. Photo cover. 14.00 45.00
456 Uncle Scrooge Back To The Klondike (#2). 130.00 425.00
457 Daffy (#1). 17.00 55.00
458 Oswald The Rabbit. 5.00 15.00
459 Rootie Kazootie. TV tie-in. 16.00 50.00
460 Buck Jones. 8.00 25.00
461 Marge's Tubby. 16.00 50.00
462 The Little Scouts. 5.00 15.00
463 Petunia. 8.00 25.00
464 Bozo featuring "Bozo The Capitol Clown". 20.00 65.00
465 Francis The Famous Talking Mule. 11.00 35.00
466 Rhubarb, The Millionaire Cat. 7.00 20.00
467 Zane Grey's Desert Gold. 8.00 25.00
468 Goofy. 19.00 60.00
469 Bettle Bailey (#1). 19.00 60.00
470 Elmer Fudd. 7.00 20.00
471 Double Trouble With Goober. 5.00 15.00
472 Wild Bill Elliott. Photo cover. 16.00 50.00
473 Li'l Bad Wolf. 8.00 25.00
474 Mary Jane And Sniffles. 17.00 55.00
475 The Two Mouseketeers. 14.00 45.00
476 Rin Tin Tin. TV photo cover. 20.00 65.00
477 Beany And Cecil. 35.00 110.00
478 Charlie McCarthy. 10.00 30.00
479 Dale Evans, Queen Of The West (#1). 40.00 125.00
480 Andy Hardy. 5.00 15.00
481 Annie Oakley And Tagg. 17.00 55.00
482 The Brownies. 7.00 20.00
483 Little Beaver. 7.00 20.00
484 Zane Grey's River Feud. 8.00 25.00
485 The Little People. 14.00 45.00
486 Rusty Riley. 8.00 25.00
487 Mowgli Jungle Book. 11.00 35.00
488 John Carter of Mars. 25.00 80.00
489 Tweety And Sylvester. 7.00 22.00
490 Jungle Jim. 13.00 40.00
491 Silvertip. Art: Raymond Kinstler. 20.00 65.00
492 Duck Album. 7.00 22.00
493 Johnny Mack Brown. Photo cover. 11.00 35.00
494 The Little King. 17.00 55.00
495 Uncle Scrooge (#3). 95.00 300.00
496 The Green Hornet. 55.00 175.00
497 The Sword Of Zorro. 29.00 95.00
498 Bugs Bunny's Album. 8.00 25.00
499 Spike And Tyke (#1). 7.00 20.00
500 Buck Jones. 7.00 20.00
501 Francis The Famous Talking Mule. 11.00 35.00
502 Rootie Kazootie. TV tie-in. 16.00 50.00
503 Uncle Wiggily. 11.00 35.00
504 Krazy Kat. 10.00 30.00
505 The Sword And The Rose. Disney movie photo cover. 11.00 35.00
506 The Little Scouts. 4.00 12.00
507 Oswald The Rabbit. 5.00 15.00
508 Bozo. 20.00 65.00
509 Pluto. 11.00 35.00
510 Son Of Black Beauty. 8.00 25.00
511 Zane Grey's Outlaw Trail. 8.00 25.00
512 Flash Gordon. 10.00 30.00
513 Ben Bowie and his Mountain Men. 10.00 30.00
514 Frosty The Snowman. 8.00 25.00
515 Andy Hardy. 5.00 15.00
516 Double Trouble With Goober. 5.00 15.00
517 Chip 'N' Dale (#1). 10.00 30.00
518 Rivets. 5.00 15.00
519 Steve Canyon. 16.00 50.00
520 Wild Bill Elliott. Photo cover. 13.00 40.00
521 Beetle Bailey. 10.00 30.00
522 The Brownies. 7.00 20.00
523 Rin Tin Tin. 20.00 65.00
524 Tweety And Sylvester. 8.00 25.00
525 Santa Claus Funnies. 5.00 15.00
526 Napoleon. 5.00 15.00
527 Charlie McCarthy. 8.00 25.00
528 Dale Evans, Queen Of The West. Photo cover. 20.00 65.00
529 Little Beaver. 7.00 20.00
530 Beany And Cecil. 35.00 110.00
531 Duck Album. 7.00 22.00
532 Zane Grey's The Rustlers. 8.00 25.00
533 Raggedy Ann + Andy. 10.00 30.00
534 Western Marshal. 13.00 40.00
535 I Love Lucy Comics (#1). TV photo cover. 95.00 300.00
536 Daffy. 8.00 25.00
537 Stormy And Pluto. 8.00 25.00
538 The Mask Of Zorro. 31.00 100.00
539 Ben And Me. 5.00 15.00
540 Knights Of The Round Table. Photo cover. 16.00 50.00
541 Johnny Mack Brown. Photo cover. 13.00 40.00
542 Super Circus featuring Mary Hartline. 13.00 40.00
543 Uncle Wiggily. 10.00 30.00
544 Rob Roy. Disney movie photo cover. 22.00 70.00
545 The Wonderful Adventures Of Pinocchio. 13.00 40.00
546 Buck Jones. 8.00 25.00
547 Francis The Famous Talking Mule. 11.00 35.00
548 Krazy Kat. 7.00 20.00
549 Oswald The Rabbit. 7.00 20.00
550 The Little Scouts. 5.00 15.00
551 Bozo. 20.00 65.00
552 Beetle Bailey. 10.00 30.00
553 Susie Q. Smith. 7.00 20.00
554 Rusty Riley. 7.00 20.00
555 Zane Grey's Range War. 8.00 25.00
556 Double Trouble With Goober. 5.00 15.00
557 Ben Bowie and his Mountain Men. 8.00 25.00
558 Elmer Fudd. 5.00 15.00
559 I Love Lucy Comics (#2). TV photo cover. 55.00 180.00
560 Duck Album. 7.00 20.00
561 Mr. Magoo and Gerald McBoing Boing. 22.00 70.00
562 Goofy. 10.00 30.00
563 Rhubarb, The Millionaire Cat. 5.00 15.00
564 Li'l Bad Wolf. 5.00 15.00
565 Jungle Jim. 7.00 20.00
566 Son Of Black Beauty. 7.00 20.00
567 Prince Valiant. Movie photo cover. 20.00 65.00
568 Gypsy Colt. 11.00 35.00
569 Priscilla's Pop. 10.00 30.00
570 Beany And Cecil. 35.00 110.00
571 Charlie McCarthy. 7.00 20.00
572 Silvertip. 10.00 30.00
573 The Little People. 7.00 20.00
574 The Hand Of Zorro. 31.00 100.00
575 Annie Oakley And Tagg. 17.00 55.00
576 Angel (#1). 7.00 20.00
577 Spike And Tyke. 2.75 10.00
578 Steve Canyon. 10.00 30.00
579 Francis The Famous Talking Mule. 10.00 30.00
580 Luke Short in Six Gun Ranch. 7.00 20.00
581 Chip 'N' Dale. 5.00 15.00
582 Mowgli Jungle Book. 7.00 20.00
583 Zane Grey's The Lost Wagon Train. 8.00 25.00
584 Johnny Mack Brown. "Killer's Trail". 11.00 35.00
585 Bugs Bunny's Album. 7.00 20.00
586 Duck Album. 7.00 20.00
587 The Little Scouts. 2.75 10.00
588 King Richard And The Crusaders. Movie photo cover. 23.00 75.00
589 Buck Jones. 5.00 15.00
590 Hansel And Gretel. 11.00 35.00
591 Western Marshal. 10.00 30.00
592 Super Circus. 10.00 30.00
593 Oswald The Rabbit. 5.00 15.00
594 Bozo. 20.00 65.00
595 Pluto. 7.00 20.00
596 Turok, Son Of Stone (#1). 190.00 600.00
597 The Little King. 13.00 40.00
598 Captain Davy Jones. 7.00 20.00
599 Ben Bowie and his Mountain Men. 7.00 20.00
600 Daisy Duck's Diary. 11.00 35.00
601 Frosty The Snowman. 7.00 20.00
602 Mr. Magoo And Gerald McBoing Boing. 20.00 65.00
603 The Two Mouseketeers. 7.00 20.00
604 Zane Grey's Shadow On The Trail. 8.00 25.00
605 The Brownies. 5.00 15.00
606 Sir Lancelot. 17.00 55.00
607 Santa Claus Funnies. 5.00 15.00
608 Silvertip. "Valley Of Vanishing Men". 11.00 35.00
609 The Littlest Outlaw. 10.00 30.00
610 Drum Beat. Movie photo cover (Alan Ladd). 25.00 80.00
611 Duck Album. 7.00 20.00
612 Little Beaver. 5.00 15.00
613 Western Marshal. 10.00 30.00
614 20,000 Leagues Under The Sea. Disney movie tie-in. 13.00 40.00
615 Daffy. 8.00 25.00
616 Zane Grey's To The Last Man. 8.00 25.00
617 The Quest Of Zorro. 31.00 100.00
618 Johnny Mack Brown. 11.00 35.00
619 Krazy Kat. 7.00 20.00
620 Mowgli Jungle Book. 7.00 20.00
621 Francis The Famous Talking Mule. 10.00 30.00
622 Beetle Bailey. 7.00 22.00
623 Oswald The Rabbit. 5.00 15.00
624 Treasure Island. 7.00 20.00
625 Beaver Valley. 7.00 20.00
626 Ben Bowie And His Mountain Men. 7.00 20.00
627 Goofy. 10.00 30.00
628 Elmer Fudd. 5.00 15.00
629 Lady And The Tramp. Disney movie tie-in. 13.00 40.00
630 Priscilla's Pop. 5.00 15.00
631 Davy Crockett, Indian Fighter. Disney movie photo cover (Fess Parker). 28.00 90.00
632 Zane Grey's Fighting Caravans. 8.00 25.00
633 The Little People. 7.00 20.00
634 Lady And The Tramp Album. 7.00 20.00
635 Beany And Cecil. 35.00 110.00
636 Chip 'N' Dale. 5.00 15.00
637 Silvertip. 10.00 30.00
638 Spike And Tyke. 5.00 15.00
639 Davy Crockett At The Alamo. Disney movie photo cover (Fess Parker). 28.00 90.00
640 Western Marshal. 8.00 25.00
641 Steve Canyon. 10.00 30.00
642 The Two Mouseketeers. 7.00 20.00
643 Wild Bill Elliott. "Mystery Of Furnace Valley". 11.00 35.00
644 Sir Walter Raleigh. Movie photo cover. 16.00 50.00
645 Johnny Mack Brown. 8.00 25.00
646 Dotty Dripple And Taffy. 7.00 20.00
647 Bugs Bunny's Album. 7.00 20.00
648 Jace Pearson Of The Texas Rangers. 11.00 35.00
649 Duck Album. 7.00 20.00
650 Prince Valiant. 10.00 30.00
651 King Colt. 8.00 25.00
652 Buck Jones. 5.00 15.00
653 Smokey The Bear. 14.00 45.00
654 Pluto. 7.00 20.00
655 Francis The Famous Talking Mule. 8.00 25.00
656 Turok, Son Of Stone (#2). 95.00 300.00
657 Ben Bowie and his Mountain Men. 7.00 20.00
658 Goofy. 10.00 30.00
659 Daisy Duck's Diary. 7.00 20.00
660 Little Beaver. 5.00 15.00
661 Frosty The Snowman. 7.00 20.00
662 Zoo Parade. 11.00 35.00
663 Winky Dink. 16.00 50.00
664 Davy Crockett in The Great Keelboat Race. Disney movie photo cover. 25.00 80.00
665 The African Lion. 11.00 35.00
666 Santa Claus Funnies. 5.00 15.00
667 Silvertip And The Stollen Stallion. 10.00 30.00
668 Dumbo. 13.00 40.00
669 Robin Hood. Disney movie photo cover. 10.00 30.00
670 Mouse Musketeers. 7.00 20.00
671 Davy Crockett And The River Pirates. Disney movie photo cover. 25.00 80.00

FOUR COLOR COMICS #509

FOUR COLOR COMICS #547

FOUR COLOR COMICS #586

FOUR COLOR COMICS #699

672 Quentin Durward. Movie photo cover. 14.00 45.00
673 Buffalo Bill, Jr. (#1). 16.00 50.00
674 The Little Rascals. 16.00 50.00
675 Steve Donovan, Western Marshal. 16.00 50.00
676 Will-Yum! 7.00 20.00
677 Little King. 13.00 40.00
678 The Last Hunt. Movie photo cover. 14.00 45.00
679 Gunsmoke (#1). TV photo cover. 40.00 125.00
680 Out Our Way With The Worry Wart. 7.00 20.00
681 Forever, Darling. Movie photo cover (Lucille Ball and Desi Arnaz). 26.00 85.00
682 When Knighthood Was In Flower. 11.00 35.00
683 Hi And Lois. 7.00 20.00
684 Helen Of Troy. Movie photo cover. 28.00 90.00
685 Johnny Mack Brown. 10.00 30.00
686 Duck Album. 7.00 20.00
687 The Indian Fighter. 11.00 35.00
688 Alexander The Great. Movie photo cover. 16.00 50.00
689 Elmer Fudd. 5.00 15.00
690 The Conqueror. Movie photo cover (John Wayne). 40.00 125.00
691 Dotty Dripple And Taffy. 7.00 20.00
692 The Little People. 7.00 20.00
693 Song Of The South. Disney movie tie-in. 8.00 25.00
694 Super Circus. 10.00 30.00
695 Little Beaver. 5.00 15.00
696 Krazy Kat. 8.00 25.00
697 Oswald The Rabbit. 5.00 15.00
698 Francis The Famous Talking Mule. 10.00 30.00
699 Prince Valiant. "The Secret of the Flames". 11.00 35.00
700 Water Birds And The Olympic Elk. Disney movie tie-in. 11.00 35.00
701 Jiminy Cricket. 13.00 40.00
702 The Goofy Success Story. 11.00 35.00
703 Scamp. 11.00 35.00
704 Priscilla's Pop. 7.00 20.00
705 Brave Eagle. 11.00 35.00
706 Bongo And Lumpjaw. 7.00 20.00
707 Corky And White Shadow. 10.00 30.00
708 Smokey The Bear. 8.00 25.00
709 The Searchers. Movie photo cover (John Wayne). 160.00 525.00
710 Francis The Famous Talking Mule. 10.00 30.00
711 Mouse Musketeers. 5.00 15.00
712 The Great Locomotive Chase. Disney movie photo cover. 11.00 35.00
713 The Animal World. Movie tie-in. 11.00 35.00
714 Spin And Marty. Disney TV tie-in. 23.00 75.00
715 Timmy. 5.00 15.00
716 Man In Space. Disney TV tie-in. 10.00 30.00
717 Moby Dick. Movie photo cover 19.00 60.00
718 Dotty Dripple And Taffy. 5.00 15.00
719 Prince Valiant. "The Peril of the Round Table". 11.00 35.00
720 Gunsmoke. "The Hunter". TV photo cover. 16.00 50.00
721 Captain Kangaroo. TV photo cover. 40.00 120.00
722 Johnny Mack Brown. 8.00 25.00
723 Santiago. Movie photo cover (Alan Ladd). 28.00 90.00
724 Bugs Bunny's Album. 5.00 15.00
725 Elmer Fudd. 5.00 15.00
726 Duck Album. 7.00 20.00
727 The Nature Of Things. 10.00 30.00
728 Mouse Musketeers. 5.00 15.00
729 Bob, Son Of Battle. 7.00 20.00
730 Smokey Stover. 5.00 15.00
731 Silvertip and The Fighting Four. 10.00 30.00
732 The Challenge Of Zorro. 28.00 90.00
733 Buck Jones. 5.00 15.00
734 Cheyenne (#1). TV photo cover (Clint Walker). 31.00 100.00
735 Crusader Rabbit (#1). TV tie-in. 55.00 180.00
736 Pluto. 8.00 25.00
737 Steve Canyon. 11.00 35.00
738 Westward Ho, The Wagons. Disney movie photo cover (Fess Parker). 16.00 50.00
739 Luke Short's Bounty Guns. 8.00 25.00
740 Chilly Willy. 8.00 25.00
741 The Fastest Gun Alive. Movie photo cover (Glen Ford). 19.00 60.00
742 Buffalo Bill, Jr. TV photo cover. 10.00 30.00
743 Daisy Duck's Diary. 7.00 20.00
744 Little Beaver. 5.00 15.00
745 Francis The Famous Talking Mule. 10.00 30.00
746 Dotty Dripple And Taffy. 5.00 15.00
747 Goofy. 10.00 30.00
748 Frosty The Snowman. 7.00 20.00
749 Secrets Of Life. 11.00 35.00
750 The Great Cat Family. 11.00 35.00
751 Our Miss Brooks. 16.00 50.00
752 Mandrake The Magician. 19.00 60.00
753 The Little People. 7.00 20.00
754 Smokey The Bear. 7.00 20.00
755 The Littlest Snowman. 7.00 20.00
756 Santa Claus Funnies. 5.00 15.00
757 The True Story Of Jesse James. Movie photo cover. 22.00 70.00
758 Bear Country. 11.00 35.00
759 Circus Boy. TV photo cover of Monkee's Mickey Dolenz. 25.00 80.00
760 The Hardy Boys. Disney TV photo cover. 28.00 90.00
761 Howdy Doody. 22.00 70.00
762 The Sharkfighters. Movie photo cover. 28.00 90.00
763 Grandma Duck's Farm Friends. 13.00 40.00
764 Mouse Musketeers. 5.00 15.00
765 Will-Yum! 7.00 20.00
766 Buffalo Bill, Jr. TV photo cover. 8.00 25.00
767 Spin And Marty. Disney TV photo cover. 16.00 50.00
768 Steve Donovan, Western Marshal. TV photo cover. 13.00 40.00
769 Gunsmoke. "The Marshal's Gamble". TV photo cover. 16.00 50.00
770 Brave Eagle. TV Photo cover 8.00 25.00
771 Brand Of Empire. 7.00 20.00
772 Cheyenne. TV photo cover (Clint Walker). 16.00 50.00
773 The Brave One. Movie photo cover. 11.00 35.00
774 Hi And Lois. 7.00 20.00
775 Sir Lancelot And Brian. "The Knight of the Red Plume". TV photo cover. 22.00 70.00
776 Johnny Mack Brown. Photo cover. 8.00 25.00
777 Scamp. 8.00 25.00
778 The Little Rascals. TV tie-in. 8.00 25.00
779 Lee Hunter, Indian Fighter. 11.00 35.00
780 Captain Kangaroo. TV photo cover. 31.00 100.00
781 Fury. TV photo cover. 22.00 70.00
782 Duck Album. 8.00 25.00
783 Elmer Fudd. 5.00 15.00
784 Around The World In 80 Days. Movie photo cover. 16.00 50.00
785 Circus Boy. TV photo cover (Mickey Dolenz). 25.00 80.00
786 Cinderella. 8.00 25.00
787 Little Hiawatha. 8.00 25.00
788 Prince Valiant. "Trial By Arms". 11.00 35.00
789 Silvertip. "Valley Thieves". 10.00 30.00
790 The Wings of Eagles. Movie photo cover (John Wayne). 40.00 125.00
791 The 77th Bengal Lancers. TV photo cover. 16.00 50.00
792 Oswald the Rabbit. 5.00 15.00
793 Morty Meekle. 7.00 20.00
794 The Count of Monte Cristo. Movie tie-in. 22.00 70.00
795 Jiminy Cricket. 10.00 30.00
796 Madeleine and Genevieve. 8.00 25.00
797 Gunsmoke. TV photo cover. 16.00 50.00
798 Buffalo Bill, Jr. TV photo cover. 8.00 25.00
799 Priscilla's Pop. 7.00 20.00
800 The Buccaneers. TV photo cover. 16.00 50.00
801 Dotty Dripple and Taffy. 7.00 20.00
802 Goofy. 11.00 35.00
803 Cheyenne. TV photo cover (Clint Walker). 16.00 50.00
804 Steve Canyon. 11.00 35.00
805 Crusader Rabbit. 50.00 160.00
806 Scamp. 8.00 25.00
807 Savage Range. 8.00 25.00
808 Spin and Marty. TV photo cover. 16.00 50.00
809 The Little People. 7.00 20.00
810 Francis The Famous Talking Mule. 8.00 25.00
811 Howdy Doody. TV tie-in. 19.00 60.00
812 The Big Land. Movie photo cover (Alan Ladd). 23.00 75.00
813 Circus Boy. TV photo cover (The Monkees' Mickey Dolenz). 25.00 80.00
814 Covered Wagons, Ho! 10.00 30.00
815 Dragoon Wells Massacre. Movie photo cover. 19.00 60.00
816 Brave Eagle. TV photo cover. 8.00 25.00
817 Little Beaver. 5.00 15.00
818 Smokey the Bear (6/57). 7.00 20.00
819 Mickey Mouse in Magicland. 10.00 30.00
820 The Oklahoman. Movie photo cover. 20.00 65.00
821 Wringle Wrangle. Movie photo cover (Fess Parker). 16.00 50.00
822 Paul Revere's Ride with Johnny Tremain. Disney TV tie-in. 23.00 75.00
823 Timmy. 5.00 15.00
824 The Pride and the Passion. Movie photo cover (Frank Sinatra & Cary Grant). 20.00 65.00
825 The Little Rascals. TV tie-in. 8.00 25.00
826 Spin and Marty and Annette. Disney TV photo cover. 40.00 125.00
827 Smokey Stover. 5.00 15.00
828 Buffalo Bill, Jr. TV photo cover. 8.00 25.00
829 Tales of the Pony Express. 8.00 25.00
830 The Hardy Boys. TV photo cover. 19.00 60.00
831 No Sleep 'Til Dawn. Movie photo cover. 16.00 50.00
832 Lolly and Pepper. 8.00 25.00
833 Scamp. 8.00 25.00
834 Johnny Mack Brown. Photo cover. 8.00 25.00
835 Silvertip. "The Fake Rider". 10.00 30.00
836 Man in Flight. Disney TV tie-in. 11.00 35.00
837 All-American Athlete Cotton Woods. 13.00 40.00
838 Bugs Bunny's Life Story Album. 8.00 25.00
839 The Vigilantes. Movie tie-in. 16.00 50.00
840 Duck Album. 7.00 20.00
841 Elmer Fudd. 5.00 15.00
842 The Nature of Things. 11.00 35.00
843 The First Americans. 11.00 35.00
844 Gunsmoke. TV photo cover. 14.00 45.00
845 The Land Unknown. Movie tie-in. 35.00 115.00
846 Gun Glory. Movie photo cover. 31.00 100.00
847 Perri. 7.00 20.00
848 Marauder's Moon. 7.00 20.00
849 Prince Valiant. "Quest for the Grail". 11.00 35.00
850 Buck Jones. 5.00 15.00
851 The Story of Mankind. Movie photo cover (Hedy Lamarr & Vincent Price). 16.00 50.00
852 Chilly Willy. 5.00 15.00
853 Pluto. 7.00 20.00
854 The Hunchback of Notre Dame. Movie photo cover. 31.00 100.00
855 Broken Arrow. TV photo cover. 11.00 35.00
856 Buffalo Bill, Jr. TV photo cover. 8.00 25.00
857 The Goofy Adventure Story. 8.00 25.00
858 Daisy Duck's Diary. 8.00 25.00
859 Topper and Neil. TV tie-in. 7.00 20.00
860 Wyatt Earp (#1). TV photo cover. 28.00 90.00
861 Frosty the Snowman. 8.00 25.00
862 The Truth About Mother Goose. 13.00 40.00
863 Francis the Famous Talking Mule. 8.00 25.00
864 The Littlest Snowman. 7.00 20.00
865 Andy Burnett. TV photo cover. 19.00 60.00
866 Mars and Beyond. Movie tie-in. 13.00 40.00
867 Santa Claus Funnies. 7.00 20.00
868 The Little People. 7.00 20.00
869 Old Yeller. Disney movie photo cover. 17.00 55.00
870 Little Beaver. 5.00 15.00
871 Curly Kayoe. 8.00 25.00
872 Captain Kangaroo. TV photo cover. 31.00 100.00
873 Grandma Duck's Farm Friends. 8.00 25.00
874 Old Ironsides. Movie tie-in. 16.00 50.00
875 Trumpets West. 7.00 20.00
876 Tales of Wells Fargo. TV photo cover. 23.00 75.00
877 Frontier Doctor. TV photo cover (Rex Allen). 28.00 90.00
878 Peanuts (#1). 40.00 125.00
879 Brave Eagle. TV photo cover. 8.00 25.00
880 Steve Donovan, Western Marshal. TV photo cover. 10.00 30.00
881 The Captain and the Kids. 7.00 20.00
882 Zorro. Disney TV photo cover. 40.00 125.00
883 The Little Rascals. TV tie-in. 8.00 25.00
884 Hawkeye and the Last of the Mohicans. TV photo cover. 16.00 50.00
885 Fury. TV photo cover. 16.00 50.00
886 Bongo and Lumpjaw. 7.00 20.00
887 The Hardy Boys. TV photo cover. 19.00 60.00
888 Elmer Fudd. 5.00 15.00
889 Clint and Mac. TV photo cover. 23.00 75.00
890 Wyatt Earp. TV photo cover. 17.00 55.00
891 The Light in the Forest. Disney movie photo cover (Fess Parker). 16.00 50.00
892 Maverick (#1). TV photo cover (James Garner). 40.00 125.00
893 Jim Bowie. TV photo cover. 13.00 40.00
894 Oswald the Rabbit. 5.00 15.00
895 Wagon Train (#1). TV photo cover. 23.00 75.00
896 The Adventures of Tinker Bell. 10.00 30.00
897 Jiminy Cricket. 5.00 15.00
898 Silvertip. 10.00 30.00
899 Goofy. 7.00 20.00
900 Prince Valiant. "The Island of Thunder". 11.00 35.00
901 Little Hiawatha. 8.00 25.00
902 Will-Yum! 7.00 20.00
903 Dotty Dripple and Taffy. 7.00 20.00
904 Lee Hunter, Indian Fighter. 8.00 25.00
905 Annette. TV photo cover. 50.00 150.00
906 Francis the Famous Talking Mule. 8.00 25.00
907 Sugarfoot. TV photo cover. 31.00 100.00
908 The Little People and the Giant. 7.00 20.00
909 Smitty. 7.00 20.00
910 The Vikings. Movie photo cover (Kirk Douglas). 23.00 75.00
911 The Gray Ghost. Movie photo cover. 19.00 60.00
912 Leave it to Beaver. TV photo cover. 55.00 175.00
913 The Left-Handed Gun. Movie photo cover (Paul Newman). 25.00 80.00
914 No Time for Sergeants. Movie photo cover (Andy Griffith). 22.00 70.00
915 Casey Jones. TV photo cover. 14.00 45.00
916 Red Ryder Ranch Comics. 7.00 20.00
917 The Life of Riley. TV photo cover (William Bendix). 31.00 100.00

918 Beep Beep, the Roadrunner (#1). 22.00 70.00
919 Boots and Saddles. TV photo cover. 17.00 55.00
920 Zorro. "Ghost of the Mission". Disney TV photo cover. 31.00 100.00
921 Wyatt Earp. TV photo cover. 17.00 55.00
922 Johnny Mack Brown. Photo cover. 7.00 20.00
923 Timmy. 5.00 15.00
924 Colt .45 (#1). TV photo cover. 20.00 65.00
925 Last of the Fast Guns. Movie photo cover. 16.00 50.00
926 Peter Pan. 8.00 25.00
927 Top Gun. 7.00 20.00
928 Sea Hunt (#1). TV photo cover (Lloyd Bridges). 25.00 80.00
929 Brave Eagle. TV photo cover. 7.00 20.00
930 Maverick. TV photo cover (James Garner). 26.00 85.00
931 Have Gun, Will Travel (#1). TV photo cover (Richard Boone). 25.00 80.00
932 Smokey the Bear (His Life Story). 5.00 15.00
933 Zorro. "Garcia's Secret". Disney TV photo cover. 31.00 100.00
934 Restless Gun. TV photo cover. 23.00 75.00
935 King of the Royal Mounted. 8.00 25.00
936 The Little Rascals. TV tie-in. 8.00 25.00
937 Ruff and Reddy (#1). TV tie-in. 28.00 90.00
938 Elmer Fudd. 5.00 15.00
939 Steve Canyon. 8.00 25.00
940 Lolly and Pepper. 8.00 25.00
941 Pluto. 7.00 20.00
942 Pony Express. TV tie-in. 10.00 30.00
943 White Wilderness. Movie tie-in. 11.00 35.00
944 The 7th Voyage of Sindbad. Movie tie-in. 31.00 100.00
945 Maverick. TV photo cover (James Garner). 23.00 75.00
946 The Big Country. Movie photo cover. 16.00 50.00
947 Broken Arrow. TV photo cover. 11.00 35.00
948 Daisy Duck's Diary. 7.00 20.00
949 High Adventure (Lowell Thomas'). TV photo cover. 11.00 35.00
950 Frosty the Snowman. 7.00 20.00
951 The Lennon Sisters Life Story. TV photo cover. 40.00 125.00
952 Goofy. 7.00 20.00
953 Francis the Famous Talking Mule. 8.00 25.00
954 Man in Space. Disney movie tie-in. 13.00 40.00
955 Hi and Lois. 5.00 15.00
956 Ricky Nelson. TV photo cover. 35.00 110.00
957 Buffalo Bee. TV tie-in. 19.00 60.00
958 Santa Claus Funnies. 7.00 20.00
959 Christmas Stories. 7.00 20.00
960 Zorro. "The Eagle's Brood". Disney TV photo cover. 31.00 100.00
961 Jace Pearson's Tales of the Texas Rangers. TV photo cover. 11.00 35.00
962 Maverick. TV photo cover (James Garner). 23.00 75.00
963 Johnny Mack Brown. Photo cover. 7.00 20.00
964 The Hardy Boys. TV photo cover. 19.00 60.00
965 Grandma Duck's Farm Friends. 7.00 20.00
966 Tonka. Movie photo cover (Sal Mineo). 16.00 50.00
967 Chilly Willy. 5.00 15.00
968 Tales of Wells Fargo. TV photo cover (Dale Robertson). 20.00 65.00
969 Peanuts. 23.00 75.00
970 Lawman (#1). TV photo cover. 22.00 70.00
971 Wagon Train. TV photo cover. 13.00 40.00
972 Tom Thumb. Movie tie-in. 28.00 90.00
973 Sleeping Beauty and the Prince. 16.00 50.00
974 The Little Rascals. TV tie-in. 8.00 25.00
975 Fury. TV photo cover. 14.00 45.00
976 Zorro. Disney TV photo cover. 31.00 100.00
977 Elmer Fudd. 5.00 15.00
978 Lolly and Pepper. 7.00 20.00
979 Oswald the Rabbit. 5.00 15.00
980 Maverick. TV photo cover (James Garner & Jack Kelly). 19.00 60.00
981 Ruff and Reddy. TV tie-in. 13.00 40.00
982 The New Adventures of Tinker Bell. 11.00 35.00
983 Have Gun, Will Travel. TV photo cover. 16.00 50.00
984 Sleeping Beauty's Fairy Godmothers. 13.00 40.00
985 The Shaggy Dog. Movie photo cover (Annette Funicello movie photo backcover). 13.00 40.00
986 Restless Gun. TV photo cover. 16.00 50.00
987 Goofy. 7.00 20.00
988 Little Hiawatha. 7.00 20.00
989 Jiminy Cricket. 7.00 20.00
990 Huckleberry Hound. TV tie-in. 23.00 75.00
991 Francis the Famous Talking Mule. 8.00 25.00
992 Sugarfoot. TV photo cover. 28.00 90.00
993 Jim Bowie. TV photo cover. 14.00 45.00
994 Sea Hunt. TV photo cover (Lloyd Bridges). 16.00 50.00
995 Donald Duck Album. 8.00 25.00
996 Zane Grey's Nevada. 8.00 25.00
997 Walt Disney Presents (The 9 Lives of Elfego Baca). TV photo cover. 13.00 40.00
998 Ricky Nelson. TV photo cover. 31.00 100.00
999 Leave it to Beaver. TV photo cover. 50.00 150.00
1000 The Gray Ghost. Movie photo cover. 16.00 50.00
1001 Lowell Thomas' High Adventure. TV photo cover. 11.00 35.00
1002 Buffalo Bee. TV tie-in. 13.00 40.00
1003 Zorro. Disney TV photo cover. 25.00 80.00
1004 Colt .45. TV photo cover. 16.00 50.00
1005 Maverick. TV photo cover. 19.00 60.00
1006 Hercules. Movie tie-in. 25.00 80.00
1007 John Paul Jones. Movie photo cover. 13.00 40.00
1008 Beep Beep, the Road Runner. 16.00 50.00
1009 The Rifleman (#1). TV photo cover. 40.00 125.00
1010 Grandma Duck's Farm Friends. Barks art. 20.00 65.00
1011 Buckskin. TV photo cover. 22.00 70.00
1012 Last Train from Gun Hill. Movie photo cover. 19.00 60.00
1013 Bat Masterson (#1). TV photo cover. 20.00 65.00
1014 The Lennon Sisters. TV photo cover. 35.00 110.00
1015 Peanuts. 23.00 75.00
1016 Smokey the Bear Nature Stories. 5.00 15.00
1017 Chilly Willy. 5.00 15.00
1018 Rio Bravo. Movie photo cover (John Wayne, Dean Martin and Ricky Nelson). 55.00 175.00
1019 Wagon Train. TV photo cover. 11.00 35.00
1020 Jungle Jim. 5.00 15.00
1021 Jace Pearson's Tales of the Texas Rangers. TV photo cover. 11.00 35.00
1022 Timmy. 5.00 15.00
1023 Tales of Wells Fargo. TV photo cover. 19.00 60.00
1024 Darby O'Gill and the Little People. Disney movie photo cover. 22.00 70.00
1025 Vacation in Disneyland. Barks art. 23.00 75.00
1026 Spin and Marty. TV photo cover. 16.00 50.00
1027 The Texan. TV photo cover. 14.00 45.00
1028 Rawhide. TV photo cover (Clint Eastwood). 65.00 200.00
1029 Boots and Saddles. TV photo cover. 11.00 35.00
1030 The Little Rascals. TV tie-in. 8.00 25.00
1031 Fury. TV photo cover. 14.00 45.00
1032 Elmer Fudd. 7.00 20.00
1033 Steve Canyon. Photo cover. 10.00 30.00
1034 Nancy and Sluggo. 7.00 20.00
1035 Lawman. TV photo cover. 11.00 35.00
1036 The Big Circus. Movie tie-in. 11.00 35.00
1037 Zorro. Disney TV photo cover (Annette Funicello). 31.00 100.00
1038 Ruff And Reddy. TV tie-in. 13.00 40.00
1039 Pluto. 7.00 20.00
1040 Quick Draw McGraw (#1). 25.00 80.00
1041 Sea Hunt. TV photo cover. 19.00 60.00
1042 The Three Chipmunks. 7.00 20.00
1043 The Three Stooges. Movie photo cover. 40.00 125.00
1044 Have Gun, Will Travel. TV photo cover. 14.00 45.00
1045 Restless Gun . TV photo cover. 16.00 50.00
1046 Beep Beep, The Road Runner. 13.00 40.00
1047 Gyro Gearloose. Cover & art: Carl Barks. 31.00 100.00
1048 The Horse Soldiers. Movie photo cover (John Wayne). 50.00 150.00
1049 Don't Give Up The Ship. Movie photo cover (Jerry Lewis). 16.00 50.00
1050 Huckleberry Hound. TV tie-in. 13.00 40.00
1051 Donald In Mathmagic Land. 23.00 75.00
1052 Ben-Hur. Movie tie-in. 19.00 60.00
1053 Goofy. 7.00 20.00
1054 Huckleberry Hound Winter Fun. 14.00 45.00
1055 Daisy Duck's Diary. Art: Carl Barks. 23.00 75.00
1056 Yellowstone Kelly. Movie photo cover (Clint Walker). 14.00 45.00
1057 Mickey Mouse Album. 8.00 25.00
1058 Colt .45. TV photo cover. 16.00 50.00
1059 Sugarfoot. TV photo cover. 20.00 65.00
1060 Journey to the Center of the Earth. Movie photo cover. 31.00 100.00
1061 Buffalo Bee. 10.00 30.00
1062 Christmas Stories. 7.00 20.00
1063 Santa Claus Funnies. 7.00 20.00
1064 Bug's Bunny Merry Christmas. 10.00 30.00
1065 Frosty The Snowman. 8.00 25.00
1066 77 Sunset Strip. TV photo cover. 31.00 100.00
1067 Yogi Bear. 31.00 100.00
1068 Francis the Famous Talking Mule. 7.00 20.00
1069 The FBI Story. Movie photo cover (James Stewart). 22.00 70.00
1070 Solomon and Sheba. Movie photo cover. 19.00 60.00
1071 The Real McCoys. TV photo cover. 28.00 90.00
1072 Blythe (Marge's). 10.00 30.00
1073 Grandma Duck's Farm Friends. Barks art. 31.00 100.00
1074 Chilly Willy. 5.00 15.00
1075 Tales of Wells Fargo. TV photo cover. 19.00 60.00
1076 The Rebel. TV photo cover. 22.00 70.00
1077 The Deputy. TV photo cover (Henry Fonda). 25.00 80.00
1078 The Three Stooges. Photo cover. 25.00 80.00
1079 The Little Rascals. TV tie-in. 7.00 20.00
1080 Fury. TV photo cover. 13.00 40.00
1081 Elmer Fudd. 5.00 15.00
1082 Spin and Marty. TV photo cover. 14.00 45.00
1083 Men into Space. TV photo cover. 14.00 45.00
1084 Speedy Gonzales. 8.00 25.00
1085 The Time Machine. Movie tie-in. 25.00 80.00
1086 Lolly and Pepper. 7.00 20.00
1087 Peter Gunn. TV photo cover. 23.00 75.00
1088 A Dog of Flanders. Movie photo cover. 10.00 30.00
1089 Restless Gun. TV photo cover. 16.00 50.00
1090 Francis the Famous Talking Mule. 7.00 20.00
1091 Jacky's Diary. 10.00 30.00
1092 Toby Tyler. Movie photo cover. 19.00 60.00
1093 MacKenzie's Raiders. Movie photo cover. 13.00 40.00
1094 Goofy. 5.00 15.00
1095 Gyro Gearloose. Art: Carl Barks. 19.00 60.00
1096 The Texan. TV photo cover. 14.00 45.00
1097 Rawhide. TV photo cover (Clint Eastwood). 45.00 140.00
1098 Sugarfoot. TV photo cover. 17.00 55.00
1099 Donald Duck Album. Cover: Carl Barks. 8.00 25.00
1100 Annette's Life Story. TV photo cover. 50.00 150.00
1101 Kidnapped (Robert Louis Stevenson's). Movie photo cover. 10.00 30.00
1102 Wanted: Dead or Alive. TV photo cover (Steve McQueen). 16.00 50.00
1103 Leave it to Beaver. TV photo cover. 50.00 150.00
1104 Yogi Bear Goes to College. TV tie-in. 19.00 60.00
1105 Oh! Susanna Gale Storm. TV photo cover. 16.00 50.00
1106 77 Sunset Strip. TV photo cover. 22.00 70.00
1107 Buckskin. TV photo cover. 16.00 50.00
1108 The Troubleshooters. TV photo cover. 16.00 50.00
1109 This is Your Life, Donald Duck. TV tie-in. 50.00 150.00
1110 Bonanza. TV photo cover. 65.00 200.00
1111 Shotgun Slade. TV tie-in. 13.00 40.00
1112 Pixie and Dixie and Mr. Jinks. TV tie-in. 7.00 20.00
1113 Tales of Wells Fargo. TV photo cover. 19.00 60.00
1114 Huckleberry Finn. Movie photo cover. 13.00 40.00
1115 Ricky Nelson. TV photo cover. 31.00 100.00
1116 Boots and Saddles. TV photo cover. 11.00 35.00
1117 The Boy and the Pirates. Movie photo cover. 13.00 40.00
1118 The Sword and the Dragon. Movie photo cover. 22.00 70.00
1119 Smokey the Bear Nature Stories. 7.00 20.00
1120 Dinosaurus. Movie tie-in. 16.00 50.00
1121 Hercules Unchained. Movie tie-in. 22.00 70.00
1122 Chilly Willy. 7.00 20.00
1123 Tombstone Territory. TV photo cover. 19.00 60.00
1124 Whirlybirds. TV photo cover. 16.00 50.00
1125 Laramie. TV photo cover. 19.00 60.00
1126 Sundance. TV photo cover. 19.00 60.00
1127 The Three Stooges. Photo cover. 23.00 75.00
1128 Rocky and His Friends. TV tie-in. 65.00 200.00
1129 Pollyanna. Disney movie photo cover. 22.00 70.00
1130 The Deputy. TV photo cover (Henry Fonda). 17.00 55.00
1131 Elmer Fudd. 7.00 20.00
1132 Space Mouse. 11.00 35.00
1133 Fury. TV photo cover. 13.00 40.00
1134 Real McCoys. TV photo cover. 26.00 85.00
1135 Mouse Musketeers. 7.00 20.00
1136 Jungle Cat. Movie photo cover. 13.00 40.00
1137 The Little Rascals. TV tie-in. 8.00 25.00
1138 The Rebel. TV photo cover. 19.00 60.00
1139 Spartacus. Movie photo cover (Kirk Douglas). 26.00 85.00
1140 Donald Duck Album. 8.00 25.00
1141 Huckleberry Hound for President. TV tie-in. 13.00 40.00
1142 Johnny Ringo. TV photo cover. 16.00 50.00
1143 Pluto. 8.00 25.00
1144 The Story of Ruth. Movie photo cover. 25.00 80.00
1145 The Lost World. Movie photo cover. 25.00 80.00
1146 Restless Gun. TV photo cover. 17.00 55.00
1147 Sugarfoot. TV photo cover. 16.00 50.00

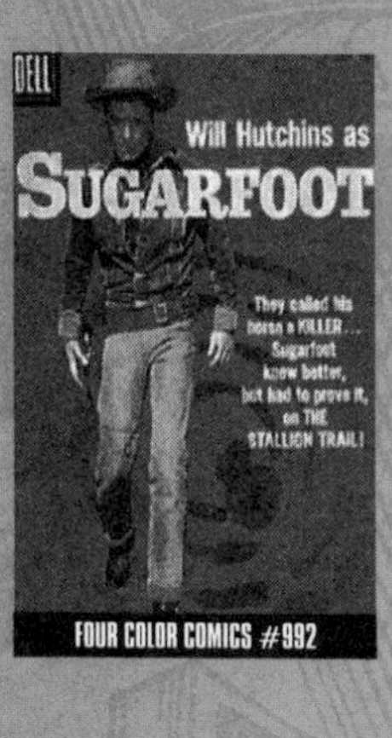

FOUR COLOR COMICS #992

FOUR COLOR COMICS #1023

FOUR COLOR COMICS #1102

FOUR COLOR COMICS #1128

FOUR COLOR COMICS (1ST SERIES) #2

FOUR COLOR COMICS (1ST SERIES) #10

FOUR COLOR COMICS (1ST SERIES) #18

FOUR FAVORITES #2

FAMOUS • FIRSTS

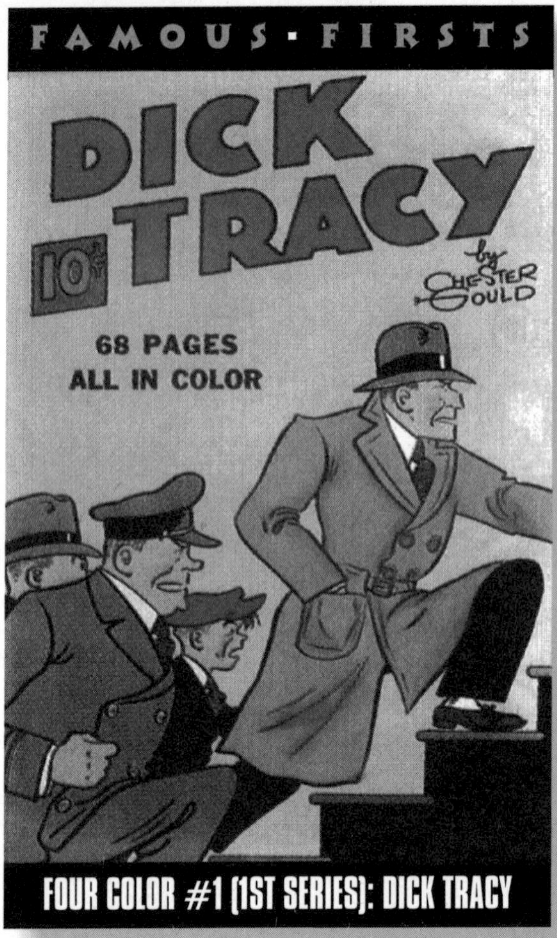

FOUR COLOR #1 (1ST SERIES): DICK TRACY

The book that launched the popular *Four Color* series, this series reproduced recolored comic strip sequences. Later issues included Terry and the Pirates, Little Orphan Annie and Mickey Mouse.

1148 I Aim at the Stars. (The Wernher Von Braun Story), Movie photo cover. 19.00 60.00
1149 Goofy. 7.00 20.00
1150 Daisy Duck's Diary. Art: Carl Barks. 23.00 75.00
1151 Mickey Mouse Album. 7.00 20.00
1152 Rocky and His Friends. TV tie-in. 55.00 175.00
1153 Frosty the Snowman. 8.00 25.00
1154 Santa Claus Funnies. 8.00 25.00
1155 North to Alaska. Movie photo cover (John Wayne). 40.00 125.00
1156 Swiss Family Robinson. Disney movie photo cover. 23.00 75.00
1157 Master of the World. Movie tie-in. 16.00 50.00
1158 Three Worlds of Gulliver. Movie photo cover. 19.00 60.00
1159 77 Sunset Strip. TV photo cover. 19.00 60.00
1160 Rawhide. TV photo cover (Clint Eastwood). 50.00 150.00
1161 Grandma Duck's Farm Friends. Art: Carl Barks. 23.00 75.00
1162 Yogi Bear Joins the Marines. TV tie-in. 19.00 60.00
1163 Daniel Boone. 13.00 40.00
1164 Wanted: Dead or Alive. TV photo cover (Steve McQueen). 16.00 50.00
1165 Ellery Queen. 19.00 60.00
1166 Rocky and His Friends. TV tie-in. 50.00 150.00
1167 Tales of Wells Fargo. TV photo cover. 16.00 50.00
1168 The Detectives. TV photo cover. 19.00 60.00
1169 New Adventures of Sherlock Holmes. 31.00 100.00
1170 The Three Stooges. Photo cover. 23.00 75.00
1171 Elmer Fudd. 7.00 20.00
1172 Fury. TV photo cover. 11.00 35.00
1173 The Twilight Zone. TV tie-in. 55.00 175.00
1174 The Little Rascals. TV tie-in. 8.00 25.00
1175 Mouse Musketeers. 7.00 20.00
1176 Dondi. Movie photo cover. 10.00 30.00
1177 Chilly Willy. 5.00 15.00
1178 Ten Who Dared. Movie tie-in. 8.00 25.00
1179 The Swamp Fox. Disney TV photo cover (Leslie Nielson). 19.00 60.00
1180 The Danny Thomas Show. TV photo cover. 35.00 110.00
1181 Texas John Slaughter. TV photo cover. 10.00 30.00
1182 Donald Duck Album. 8.00 25.00
1183 101 Dalmatians. Disney movie tie-in. 19.00 60.00
1184 Gyro Gearloose. Art: Carl Barks. 23.00 75.00
1185 Sweetie Pie. 10.00 30.00
1186 Yak Yak. Art: Jack Davis. 11.00 35.00
1187 The Three Stooges. Photo cover. 23.00 75.00
1188 Atlantis, the Lost Continent. Movie photo cover. 26.00 85.00
1189 Greyfriars Bobby. Movie photo cover. 14.00 45.00
1190 Donald and the Wheel. Movie tie-in. Cover: Carl Barks. 16.00 50.00
1191 Leave it to Beaver. TV photo cover. 50.00 150.00
1192 Ricky Nelson. TV photo cover. 31.00 100.00
1193 The Real McCoys. TV photo cover. 23.00 75.00
1194 Pepe. Movie photo cover. 8.00 25.00
1195 National Velvet. TV photo cover. 25.00 80.00
1196 Pixie and Dixie and Mr. Jinks. TV tie-in. 7.00 20.00
1197 The Aquanauts. TV photo cover. 19.00 60.00
1198 Donald In Mathmagicland. Movie tie-in. 16.00 50.00
1199 The Absent-Minded Professor. Movie photo cover. 16.00 50.00
1200 Hennessey. TV photo cover. 13.00 40.00
1201 Goofy. 7.00 20.00
1202 Rawhide. TV photo cover (Clint Eastwood). 50.00 150.00
1203 Pinocchio. 10.00 30.00
1204 Scamp. 7.00 20.00
1205 David and Goliath. Movie photo cover. 13.00 40.00
1206 Lolly and Pepper. 7.00 20.00
1207 The Rebel. TV photo cover. 19.00 60.00
1208 Rocky and His Friends. TV tie-in. 50.00 150.00
1209 Sugarfoot. TV photo cover. 16.00 50.00
1210 The Parent Trap. Disney TV photo cover. 16.00 50.00
1211 77 Sunset Strip. TV photo cover. 17.00 55.00
1212 Chilly Willy. 7.00 20.00
1213 Mysterious Island. Movie photo cover. 19.00 60.00
1214 Smokey the Bear. 7.00 20.00
1215 Tales of Wells Fargo. TV photo cover. 19.00 60.00
1216 Whirleybirds. TV photo cover. 16.00 50.00
1218 Fury. TV photo cover. 13.00 40.00
1219 The Detectives. TV photo cover (Adam West). 19.00 60.00
1220 Gunslinger. TV photo cover. 17.00 55.00
1221 Bonanza. TV photo cover. 50.00 160.00
1222 Elmer Fudd. 7.00 20.00
1223 Laramie. TV photo cover. 13.00 40.00
1224 The Little Rascals. TV tie-in. 8.00 25.00
1225 The Deputy. TV photo cover (Henry Fonda). 19.00 60.00
1226 Nikki, Wild Dog of the North. Movie photo cover. 10.00 30.00
1227 Morgan the Pirate. Movie photo cover. 19.00 60.00
1229 Thief of Baghdad. Movie photo cover. 26.00 85.00
1230 Voyage to the Bottom of the Sea. Movie photo (insert) cover. 22.00 70.00
1231 Danger Man. TV photo cover. 19.00 60.00
1232 On the Double. Movie tie-in. 13.00 40.00
1233 Tammy Tell Me True. Movie tie-in. 19.00 60.00
1234 The Phantom Planet. Movie tie-in. 13.00 40.00
1235 Mister Magoo. 19.00 60.00
1236 King of Kings. Movie photo cover. 16.00 50.00
1237 The Untouchables. TV photo cover. 28.00 90.00
1238 Deputy Dawg. TV tie-in. 28.00 90.00
1239 Donald Duck Album. Cover: Carl Barks. 8.00 25.00
1240 The Detectives. TV photo cover. 16.00 50.00
1241 Sweetie Pie. 10.00 30.00
1242 King Leonardo and His Short Subjects. TV tie-in. 26.00 85.00
1243 Ellery Queen. 16.00 50.00
1244 Space Mouse. 10.00 30.00
1245 New Adventures of Sherlock Holmes. 28.00 90.00
1246 Mickey Mouse Album. 7.00 20.00
1247 Daisy Duck's Diary. 7.00 20.00
1248 Pluto. 7.00 20.00
1249 The Danny Thomas Show. TV photo cover. 28.00 90.00
1250 The Four Horsemen of the Apocalypse. Movie photo cover. 16.00 50.00
1251 Everything's Ducky. Movie tie-in. 13.00 40.00
1252 The Andy Griffith Show. TV photo cover. 80.00 250.00
1253 Space Man (#1). 19.00 60.00
1254 Diver Dan. TV photo cover. 13.00 40.00
1255 The Wonders of Aladdin. Movie tie-in. 19.00 60.00
1256 Kona (#1). 13.00 40.00
1257 Car 54, Where Are You? (#1). TV photo cover. 19.00 60.00
1258 The Frogmen (#1). 16.00 50.00
1259 El Cid. Movie photo cover. 16.00 50.00
1260 The Horsemasters. Movie photo cover (Annette Funicello). 23.00 75.00
1261 Rawhide. TV photo cover (Clint Eastwood). 50.00 150.00
1262 The Rebel. TV photo cover. 19.00 60.00
1263 77 Sunset Strip. TV photo cover. 16.00 50.00
1264 Pixie and Dixie and Mr. Jinks. Hanna-Barbera TV tie-in. 8.00 25.00
1265 The Real McCoys. TV photo cover. 22.00 70.00
1266 Spike and Tyke. 7.00 20.00
1267 Gyro Gearloose. Cover & art: Carl Barks (4 pages). 19.00 60.00
1268 Oswald The Rabbit. 7.00 20.00
1269 Rawhide. TV photo cover (Clint Eastwood). 50.00 150.00
1270 Bullwinkle And Rocky. TV tie-in. 50.00 150.00
1271 Yogi Bear Birthday Party. Hanna-Barbera TV tie-in. 19.00 60.00
1272 Frosty The Snowman. 8.00 25.00
1273 Hans Brinker. Movie photo cover. 13.00 40.00
1274 Santa Claus Funnies. 8.00 25.00
1275 Rocky and His Friends. TV tie-in. 45.00 140.00
1276 Dondi. 10.00 30.00
1278 King Leonardo and His Short Subjects. TV tie-in. 25.00 80.00
1279 Grandma Duck's Farm Friends. 10.00 30.00
1280 Hennessey. TV photo cover. 13.00 40.00
1281 Chilly Willy. 7.00 20.00
1282 Babes in Toyland. Movie photo cover (Annette Funicello). 25.00 80.00

1283 Bonanza. TV photo cover. 45.00 135.00
1284 Laramie. TV photo cover. 13.00 40.00
1285 Leave It to Beaver. TV photo cover. 50.00 150.00
1286 The Untouchables. TV photo cover. 28.00 90.00
1287 Man From Wells Fargo. TV photo cover.
.... 19.00 60.00
1288 The Twilight Zone. TV tie-in. ... 31.00 100.00
1289 Ellery Queen. 14.00 45.00
1290 Mouse Musketeers. 7.00 20.00
1291 77 Sunset Strip. TV photo cover. 16.00 50.00
1293 Elmer Fudd. 8.00 25.00
1294 Ripcord. TV tie-in. 13.00 40.00
1295 Mister Ed, the Talking Horse. TV photo cover.
.... 31.00 100.00
1296 Fury. TV photo cover. 13.00 40.00
1297 The Little Rascals. TV tie-in. ... 8.00 25.00
1298 The Hathaways. TV photo cover. 13.00 40.00
1299 Deputy Dawg. TV tie-in. 26.00 85.00
1300 The Comancheros. Movie photo cover (John Wayne).
.... 40.00 120.00
1301 Adventures in Paradise. TV tie-in. 13.00 40.00
1302 Johnny Jason, Teen Reporter. ... 10.00 30.00
1303 Lad: A Dog. Movie photo cover. 10.00 30.00
1304 Nellie the Nurse. 13.00 40.00
1305 Mister Magoo. 19.00 60.00
1306 Target: The Corrupters. TV tie-in. 13.00 40.00
1307 Margie. TV tie-in. 10.00 30.00
1308 Tales of the Wizard of Oz. TV tie-in. 19.00 60.00
1309 87th Precinct. TV photo cover. 23.00 75.00
1310 Huck and Yogi Winter Sports. TV tie-in.
.... 19.00 60.00
1311 Rocky and His Friends. TV tie-in. 50.00 150.00
1312 National Velvet. TV photo cover. 19.00 60.00
1313 Moon Pilot. Disney movie photo cover.
.... 19.00 60.00
1328 The Underwater City. Movie photo cover.
.... 19.00 60.00
1330 Brain Boy (#1). 16.00 50.00
1332 Bachelor Father. TV tie-in. 16.00 50.00
1333 Short Ribs. 14.00 45.00
1335 Aggie Mack. 10.00 30.00
1336 On Stage. 10.00 30.00
1341 The Andy Griffith Show. TV photo cover.
.... 65.00 200.00
1348 Yak Yak. Art: Jack Davis. 10.00 30.00
1349 Yogi Bear Visits the U.N. TV photo cover.
.... 26.00 85.00
1350 Comanche. Movie photo cover (reprint of "Tonka" with Sal Mineo). 13.00 40.00
1354 Calvin & the Colonel (#1). TV tie-in. 13.00 40.00

FOUR COLOR COMICS (SERIES 1)

DELL (1939-1942)

NO#(1) Dick Tracy. 68 pages. 1300.00 5000.00
NO#(2) Don Winslow Of The Navy #1. 310.00 1000.00
NO#(3) Myra North (Special Nurse). 190.00 600.00
4 Donald Duck. 1940. 64 pages. ... 1700.00 6500.00
5 Smilin' Jack #1. 68 pages. 140.00 450.00
6 Dick Tracy. 68 pages. 310.00 1000.00
7 Gang Busters. 66 pages. 85.00 275.00
8 Dick Tracy. 68 pages. 180.00 575.00
9 Terry And The Pirates. 145.00 475.00
10 Smilin' Jack. 68 pages. 130.00 425.00
11 Smitty #1. 68 pages. 95.00 300.00
12 Little Orphan Annie. 68 pages. ... 125.00 400.00
13 Walt Disney's Reluctant Dragon. Movie tie-in. 1941.
.... 300.00 1100.00
14 Moon Mullins #1. 68 pages. 85.00 275.00
15 Tillie The Toiler #1. 68 pages. ... 85.00 275.00
16 Mickey Mouse Outwits The Phantom Blot (#1) by Floyd Gottfredson. The first Mickey Mouse comic in the Four Color series. 68 pages. (1941) 1800.00 7000.00
17 Walt Disney's Dumbo The Flying Elephant. Movie tie-in.
.... 400.00 1500.00
18 Jiggs And Maggie "Bringing Up Father" #1. 68 pages.
.... 95.00 300.00
19 Barney Google And Snuffy Smith #1. First comic with "Four Color Comic" on the cover. 68 pages. 95.00 300.00
20 Tiny Tim. 68 pages. 70.00 225.00
21 Dick Tracy. 68 pages. 155.00 500.00
22 Don Winslow Of The Navy. 68 pages. 65.00 200.00
23 Gang Busters. 65.00 200.00
24 Captain Easy. 68 pages. 85.00 275.00
25 Popeye. 68 pages. 155.00 500.00

FOUR FAVORITES

ACE (1941-1947)

1 Begin: Raven, Lash Lightning. 200.00 650.00
2 .... 100.00 330.00
3 .... 70.00 220.00
4-5 .... 60.00 190.00
6-8 .... 50.00 160.00
9 Art: Harvey Kurtzman. 70.00 220.00
10 Cover & Art: Harvey Kurtzman. ... 85.00 270.00
11 Art: Harvey Kurtzman. 70.00 220.00
12 Art: L.B. Cole. 50.00 160.00
13-18 .... 29.00 95.00
19-24 .... 20.00 65.00
25-26 .... 17.00 55.00
27-29 .... 14.00 44.00
30-32 .... 10.00 33.00

FOUR HORSEMEN OF THE APOCALYPSE, THE

DELL FOUR COLOR SERIES (1961)

1250 Movie photo cover. (11/61) ... 16.00 50.00

FOUR MOST

NOVELTY (1941-1950)

V1#1 Begin: Dick Cole, Target, Cadet, Edison Bell.
.... 155.00 500.00
V1#2 .... 65.00 200.00
V1#3 .... 50.00 150.00
V1#4 .... 40.00 125.00
V2#1-V2#4 .... 16.00 50.00
V3#1-V3#4 .... 11.00 35.00
V4#1-V4#4 .... 10.00 30.00
V5#1-V8#5 .... 8.00 25.00
37-41 .... 8.00 25.00

FOUR STAR BATTLE TALES

DC (1973)

1-5 .... .75 2.00

FOUR STAR SPECTACULAR

DC (1976)

1-6 .... .75 2.00

FOX AND THE CROW

DC (1951-1968)

1 .... 210.00 675.00
2 .... 105.00 340.00
3-6 .... 70.00 230.00
7-12 .... 55.00 170.00
13-18 .... 45.00 140.00
19-22 .... 35.00 110.00
23 1st Code Approved issue. 26.00 85.00
24-29 .... 23.00 75.00
30-40 .... 20.00 65.00
41-46 .... 17.00 55.00
47-55 .... 14.00 46.00
56-65 .... 13.00 40.00
66-75 .... 11.00 34.00
76-85 .... 9.00 29.00
86-94 .... 7.00 23.00
95 1st & Origin: Stanley And His Monster. 9.00 29.00
96-100 .... 6.00 17.00
101-108 .... 4.00 11.00

FOXHOLE

CHARLTON (1954-1956)

1 Cover: Jack Kirby. 40.00 120.00
2 Cover & Art: Jack Kirby. 29.00 95.00
3-5 Cover: Kirby. 15.00 48.00
6 Cover & Art: Kirby. 28.00 90.00
7 .... 4.00 12.00

FOXY FAGAN COMICS

DEARFIELD (1946-1948)

1 .... 19.00 60.00
2-7 .... 8.00 25.00

FRACTURED FAIRY TALES

GOLD KEY (1962)

10022-210 TV cartoon tie-in. 31.00 100.00

FRANCIS THE FAMOUS TALKING MULE

DELL FOUR COLOR SERIES (1951-1960)

335 Movie tie-in. 52 pages. (6/51) 23.00 75.00
465 (4/53) 11.00 35.00
501 (10/53) 11.00 35.00
547 (4/54) 11.00 35.00
579 (8/54) 10.00 30.00
621 (4/55) 10.00 30.00
655 (10/55) 8.00 25.00
698 (4/56) 10.00 30.00
710 (7/56) 10.00 30.00
745 (11/56) 10.00 30.00
810 (6/57) 8.00 25.00
863 (11/57) 8.00 25.00
906 (5/58) 8.00 25.00
953 (11/58) 8.00 25.00
991 (5/59) 8.00 25.00
1068 (11/59) 7.00 20.00
1090 (4/60) 7.00 20.00

FRANK BUCK

FOX (1950)

1 (70) Photo cover. 22.00 70.00
2 (71) 20.00 65.00
3 .... 19.00 60.00

FRANKENSTEIN

DELL (1963-1967)

1 (12-283-305) Movie tie-in. 5.00 15.00
2 (1966) 2.75 10.00
3-4 .... 2.75 10.00

FRANKENSTEIN COMICS

PRIZE (1945-1954)

1 Begin & Origin: Frankenstein by Dick Briefer.
.... 160.00 525.00
2 .... 85.00 270.00
3-6 .... 60.00 190.00
7-12 .... 45.00 140.00
13-16 .... 40.00 120.00
17 End: Comedy series. 40.00 120.00
18 Begin: Horror series. 55.00 180.00
19-20 .... 40.00 120.00
21-24 .... 31.00 100.00
25-33 .... 29.00 95.00

FRANKENSTEIN, JR

GOLD KEY (1967)

1 .... 5.00 15.00

FRANKENSTEIN MONSTER, THE

SEE: MONSTER OF FRANKENSTEIN

FRANKENSTEIN-DRACULA WAR, THE

TOPPS (1995)

1-3 .... .75 2.50

FRANKIE AND LANA

MARVEL (1949)

12 Previous title: Frankie Comics. 7.00 20.00
13-14 .... 7.00 20.00
15 Title changes to Frankie Fuddle Comics with #16.
.... 7.00 20.00

FRANKIE COMICS

MARVEL (1946-1948)

4 Previous title: Movie Tunes. 10.00 30.00
5-10 .... 10.00 30.00
11 Title changes to Frankie And Lana with #12.
.... 10.00 30.00

FRANKIE FUDDLE COMICS

MARVEL (1949)

16 Previous title: Frankie And Lana. ... 7.00 20.00
17 .... 7.00 20.00

FREAK FORCE

IMAGE/HIGH BROW (1993-1995)

1 1st: Freak Force. .... .75 2.00
2-7 .... .75 2.00
8 1st: Kill Cat. .... .75 2.50
9 .... .75 2.00
10-18 .... .75 2.50

FREEDOM AGENT

GOLD KEY (1963)

1 .... 2.25 8.00

FREEDOM FIGHTERS

DC (1976-1978)

1 .... .75 2.00
2-15 .... .30 1.00

FREEDOM TRAIN

STREET & SMITH (1948)

NO# Giveaway. 10.00 30.00

FREEJACK

NOW (1992)

1 Movie tie-in. .... .75 2.50

FREEX

MALIBU (1993-CURRENT)

1 1st: the Freex. Bagged with Ultraverse card.
.... 1.00 3.00
1A Unbagged edition. .... .50 1.95
1B Hologram edition. 2.25 8.00
1C Ultra limited foil edition. 1.50 5.00
1D Gold hologram edition. 2.25 8.00
2 .... .75 2.00
3 .... .50 1.95
4 With Rune #0 coupon. .... .75 2.50
5-14 .... .50 1.95
15 .... 1.00 3.50
16 .... .50 1.95
17-18 .... .75 2.50
GIANT 1 .... .75 2.50

FRIENDLY GHOST CASPER, THE

HARVEY (1958-1989)

1 .... 40.00 125.00
2 .... 19.00 60.00
3-10 .... 13.00 40.00
11-15 .... 10.00 30.00
16-24 .... 7.00 20.00
25-30 .... 5.00 15.00

FOUR MOST #8

FRANKENSTEIN #23 [PRIZE]

FREAK FORCE #6

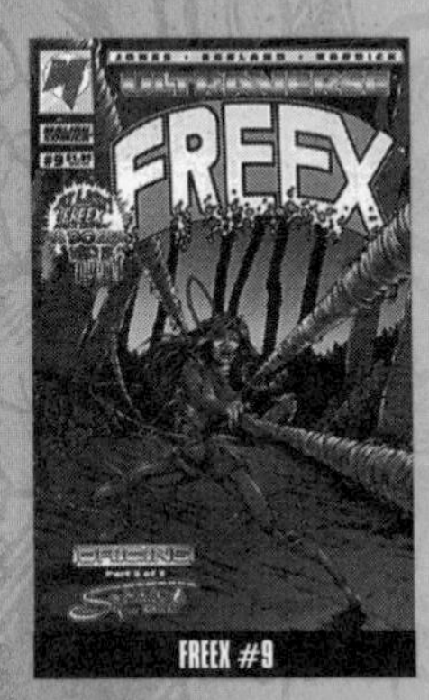

FREEX #9

FUNLAND COMICS #1

THE FUNNIES #10

FUNNIES ON PARADE #1

FURY #1 (MARVEL)

31-40 ... 2.75 10.00
41-50 ... 2.25 8.00
51-60 ... 1.75 6.00
61-75 ... 1.50 5.00
76-100 ... 1.25 4.00
101-150 ... 1.00 3.00
151-200 ... .75 2.00
201-230 ... .50 1.50
231-250 ... .30 1.00

FRISKY ANIMALS
STAR (1951-1954)
44 Previous title: Frisky Fables. ... 14.00 45.00
45-58 ... 14.00 45.00

FRISKY ANIMALS ON PARADE
AJAX (1957-1958)
1 ... 16.00 50.00
2 ... 7.00 20.00
3 ... 10.00 30.00

FRISKY FABLES
NOVELTY PRESS (1945-1950)
1 Cover&art: Al Fago in all issues 1-38. 16.00 50.00
2 ... 10.00 30.00
3 ... 8.00 25.00
4 (V2#1) ... 5.00 15.00
5-12 ... 5.00 15.00
13 (V2#10) ... 4.00 12.00
14-15 ... 4.00 12.00
16 (V3#1) ... 4.00 12.00
17-27 ... 4.00 12.00
28 (V4#1) ... 2.75 10.00
29-37 ... 2.75 10.00
38 (V5#4) ... 2.75 10.00
39 Begin L.B. Cole covers. ... 11.00 35.00
40-42 ... 11.00 35.00
43 Title changes to Frisky Animals with #44. ... 11.00 35.00

FRITZI RITZ
UFS/ST. JOHN/DELL (1948-1958)
2 ... 8.00 25.00
3-7 ... 7.00 20.00
8-26 ... 2.75 10.00
27-29 ... 5.00 15.00
30-36 ... 4.00 12.00
37-59 ... 2.75 10.00

FROGMEN, THE
DELL (1962-1965)
1 (#1258) From the 4-Color Series. (2/62) ... 16.00 50.00
2-3 ... 10.00 30.00
4 ... 7.00 20.00
5 Art: Alex Toth. ... 8.00 25.00
6-8 ... 4.00 12.00
9-11 ... 2.75 10.00

FROM BEYOND THE UNKNOWN
DC (1969-1973)
1 ... 2.75 10.00
2 ... 1.50 5.00
3-10 ... 1.25 4.00
11-25 ... 1.00 3.00

FROM HELL
MAD LOVE/KITCHEN SINK (1993-CURRENT)
1 ... 2.75 11.00
1 (2ND) 2nd printing. ... 1.25 5.00
1 (3RD) 3rd printing. ... 1.25 5.00
1 (4TH) 4th printing. ... 1.25 5.00
2 ... 1.75 6.00
2 (2ND) 2nd printing. ... 1.25 5.00
2 (3RD) 3rd printing. ... 1.25 5.00
3 ... 1.75 6.00
3 (2ND) 2nd printing. ... 1.25 5.00
4-8 ... 1.25 5.00

FROM HELL
MAD LOVE/TUNDRA (1991-1993)
1 ... 2.75 11.00
1 (2ND) 2nd printing. ... 1.50 5.00
2 ... 1.50 6.00

FROM HERE TO INSANITY
CHARLTON (1955-1956)
8 Previous title: Eh! ... 16.00 50.00
9 ... 13.00 40.00
10 Cover&art: Steve Ditko (3 pgs.). ... 31.00 100.00
11-12 Art: Jack Kirby. ... 50.00 150.00
13 (V3#1 inside). Magazine size (ala Mad Magazine). Art: Steve Ditko (3 pgs.), Basil Wolverton (5 pgs.). ... 80.00 250.00

FROM THE DARKNESS
ADVENTURE
1-4 ... .50 1.50

FRONT PAGE COMIC BOOK
HARVEY (1945)
1 Art: Joe Kubert. ... 65.00 200.00

FRONTIER DOCTOR
DELL FOUR COLOR SERIES (1958)
877 TV photo cover. (2/90) ... 28.00 90.00

FRONTIER FIGHTERS
DC (1955-1956)
1 Featuring Davy Crockett in "Challenge Of Black Warrior!", Kit Carson and Buffalo Bill Cody. (9-10/55) 125.00 400.00
2 Davy Crockett in "The Rifle Named Betsey!", Kit Carson, and Buffalo Bill. (11-12/55) ... 75.00 240.00
3 Davy Crockett, Kit Carson, and Buffalo Bill. (1-2/56) ... 65.00 200.00
4 Davy Crockett, Kit Carson, and Buffalo Bill. (3-4/56) ... 65.00 200.00
5 Davy Crockett. (5-6/56) ... 65.00 200.00
6 "Renegade Fur Traders!" (7-8/56) ... 65.00 200.00
7 Davy Crockett in "The Frontier Barrel-Maker!" (9-10/56) ... 65.00 200.00
8 Davy Crockett as "King Of Lost Valley!" (11-12/56) ... 65.00 200.00

FRONTIER ROMANCES
AVON (1949-1950)
1 SOTI ... 65.00 200.00
2 ... 40.00 125.00

FRONTIER WESTERN
MARVEL(ATLAS) (1956-1957)
1 ... 25.00 80.00
2-3 ... 17.00 55.00
4 ... 10.00 33.00
5 ... 14.00 44.00
6-10 ... 9.00 27.00

FRONTLINE COMBAT
EC (1951-1954)
1 ... 145.00 480.00
2 ... 75.00 240.00
3 ... 55.00 180.00
4 "Airburst" by Harvey Kurtzman. ... 50.00 150.00
5 ... 40.00 120.00
6-10 ... 31.00 100.00
11-15 ... 29.00 95.00

FROSTY THE SNOWMAN
DELL FOUR COLOR SERIES (1951-1961)
359 (11/51) ... 14.00 45.00
435 (11/52) ... 8.00 25.00
514 (11/53) ... 8.00 25.00
601 (11/54) ... 7.00 20.00
661 (11/55) ... 7.00 20.00
748 (11/56) ... 7.00 20.00
861 (11/57) ... 8.00 25.00
950 (12/58) ... 7.00 20.00
1065 (12/59) ... 8.00 25.00
1153 (12/60) ... 8.00 25.00
1272 (12/61) ... 8.00 25.00

FRUITMAN SPECIAL
HARVEY (1969)
1 ... 10.00 30.00

F-TROOP
DELL (1966-1967)
1 TV tie-in. Photo covers on all issues. 13.00 40.00
2 ... 7.00 20.00
3-7 ... 5.00 15.00

FUGITIVES FROM JUSTICE
ST. JOHN (1952)
1 ... 19.00 60.00
2-3 ... 16.00 50.00
4 ... 10.00 30.00
5 ... 8.00 25.00

FUGITOID
MIRAGE (1985)
1 One-shot; Story ties into TMNT #5. ... 1.75 6.00

FUN PARADE COMICS
FP (1955)
45 Canadian. Millie The Model story. ... 7.00 20.00

FUNLAND
ZIFF-DAVIS (1949)
NO# ... 23.00 75.00

FUNLAND COMICS
CROYDEN (1945)
1 ... 23.00 75.00

FUNNIES, THE
DELL (1936-1942)
1 ... 400.00 1300.00
2 1st: Scribbly by Sheldon Mayer. ... 170.00 550.00
3 ... 125.00 410.00
4-5 ... 115.00 380.00
6-10 ... 95.00 300.00
11-20 ... 70.00 220.00
21-29 ... 50.00 160.00
30 1st & Origin: John Carter of Mars. 170.00 550.00
31-34 ... 85.00 270.00
35 Begin: Mr. District Attorney. ... 85.00 280.00
36-40 ... 60.00 190.00
41-44 ... 50.00 160.00
45 1st & Origin: Phantasmo. (7/40) 100.00 330.00
46-50 ... 70.00 220.00
51-55 ... 60.00 190.00
56 End: John Carter of Mars. ... 60.00 190.00
57 1st & Origin: Captain Midnight. Begin series: Captain Midnight. ... 270.00 875.00
58 1st full Captain Midnight cover. ... 170.00 550.00
59-60 ... 85.00 270.00
61 Begin: Andy Panda. ... 95.00 300.00
62-63 ... 85.00 270.00
64 1st & Origin: Woody Woodpecker. End: Captain Midnight. Becomes New Funnies #65. ... 200.00 650.00

FUNNIES ANNUAL, THE
AVON (1959)
1 Reprints newspaper strips. ... 80.00 250.00

FUNNIES ON PARADE
EASTERN (1933)
NO# Printed for Procter & Gamble as a premium, 32 pgs. with slick cover. Generally considered the first true comic book. ... 2600.00 10000.00

FUNNY 3-D
HARVEY (1953)
1 With glasses. ... 19.00 60.00

FUNNY FILMS
ACG (1949-1954)
1 ... 20.00 65.00
2 ... 10.00 33.00
3-10 ... 9.00 27.00
11-29 ... 5.00 16.00

FUNNY FOLKS
DC (1946-1950)
1 1st & Begin: Nutsy Squirrel. ... 100.00 320.00
2 ... 40.00 120.00
3-6 ... 28.00 90.00
7-12 ... 19.00 60.00
13-15 ... 16.00 50.00
16 Begin: Hollywood Funny Folks on cover. 16.00 50.00
17-18 ... 16.00 50.00
19-25 ... 12.00 39.00
26 Title changes to Hollywood Funny Folks. ... 12.00 39.00

FUNNY FROLICS
MARVEL(TIMELY) (1945-1946)
1 ... 40.00 120.00
2 ... 19.00 60.00
3-4 ... 13.00 43.00
5 Art: Harvey Kurtzman. ... 19.00 60.00

FUNNY FUNNIES
NEDOR (1943)
1 ... 23.00 75.00

FUNNY PAGES
CENTAUR(COMICS MAGAZINE) (1936-1940)
2 Previous title: The Comics Magazine. 400.00 1500.00
3-5 ... 310.00 1000.00
6 (11/36) 1st: The Clock (2 pg. story). First original masked hero in comics. Two page serialized story ends in issue 9. Second serialized story begins in issue 10, continues in issue 11, and is left unfinished. ... 400.00 1500.00
7-10 ... 155.00 500.00
11 End: The Clock. ... 155.00 500.00
12 (V2#1) (9/37) ... 125.00 400.00
13 (V2#2) ... 125.00 400.00
14 (V2#3) ... 125.00 400.00
15 (V2#4) ... 125.00 400.00
16 (V2#5) ... 125.00 400.00
17 (V2#6) ... 125.00 400.00
18 (V2#7) ... 125.00 400.00
19 (V2#8) ... 125.00 400.00
20 (V2#9) ... 125.00 400.00
21 (V2#10) 1st: Arrow by Gustavson. 600.00 2000.00
22 (V2#11) ... 250.00 800.00
23 (V2#12) ... 250.00 800.00
24 (V3#1) ... 200.00 650.00
25 (V3#2) ... 200.00 650.00
26 (V3#3) ... 200.00 650.00
27 (V3#4) ... 200.00 650.00
28 (V3#5) ... 200.00 650.00
29 (V3#6) ... 200.00 650.00
30 (V3#7) 1st: Arrow cover. ... 250.00 800.00

31 (V3#8) 200.00 650.00
32 (V3#9) 200.00 650.00
33 (V3#10) 230.00 750.00
34 (V4#1) App: The Owl. Classic cover. 310.00 1000.00
35 (V3#5) 200.00 650.00
36-39 200.00 650.00
40-42 190.00 600.00

FUNNY PICTURE STORIES
CENTAUR(COMICS MAGAZINE) (1936-1939)
1 1st complete Clock story (see Funny Pages 6). Begin: The Clock. 600.00 2000.00
2 Clock story. 310.00 1000.00
3-6 190.00 600.00
7-9 155.00 500.00
10 (V2#1) 155.00 500.00
11 (V2#2) 1st published work: Jack Cole. 230.00 750.00
12 (V2#3) 155.00 500.00
13 (V2#4) 140.00 450.00
14 (V2#5) 140.00 450.00
15 (V2#6) 140.00 450.00
16 (V2#7) 140.00 450.00
17 (V2#8) 140.00 450.00
18 (V2#9) 140.00 450.00
19 (V2#10) 110.00 350.00
20 (V2#11) 110.00 350.00
21 (V3#1) 110.00 350.00
22 (V3#2) 110.00 350.00
23 (V3#3). Becomes Comic Pages #24 (V3#4). 110.00 350.00

FUNNY STUFF
DC (1944-1954)
1 (Summer/44) 250.00 800.00
2 (Fall/44) 125.00 410.00
3 (Winter/44) 85.00 270.00
4 (Spring/45) 85.00 270.00
5 (Summer/45) 85.00 270.00
6 (Fall/45) 85.00 270.00
7 (Winter/45) 65.00 200.00
8 (4/46) 65.00 200.00
9 (5/46) 65.00 200.00
10 (6/46) 65.00 200.00
11 (7/46) 65.00 200.00
12 (8/46) 65.00 200.00
13-17 40.00 130.00
18 1st: Dodo & The Frog. 65.00 200.00
19-20 40.00 130.00
21 31.00 100.00
22 Superman app. (cameo). 85.00 270.00
23-24 31.00 100.00
25-36 20.00 65.00
37-50 17.00 55.00
51-60 13.00 41.00
61-79 9.00 27.00

FUNNY TUNES
AVON (1953-1954)
1 11.00 35.00
2-3 8.00 25.00

FUNNY TUNES
SEE ANIMATED FUNNY COMIC-TUNES.

FUNNY WORLD
MARBAK (1947-1948)
1 All issues reprint strips. 7.00 20.00
2-3 5.00 15.00

FUNNYMAN
ME (1948)
1 Art: Jerry Siegel & Joe Schuster in all issues. (1/48) 60.00 190.00
2 (3/48) 50.00 150.00
3 (4/48) 40.00 120.00
4 (5/48) 40.00 120.00
5 (7/48) 40.00 120.00
6 (8/48) 40.00 120.00

FUNTASTIC WORLD OF HANNA BARBERA, THE
MARVEL (1977)
1-3 .75 2.50

FURTHER ADVENTURES OF INDIANA JONES, THE
MARVEL (1983-1986)
1-34 .20 .50

FURY
DELL FOUR COLOR SERIES (1957-1962)
781 TV photo cover. (3/57) 22.00 70.00
885 TV photo cover. (3/58) 16.00 50.00
975 TV photo cover. (3/59) 14.00 45.00
1031 TV photo cover. (9/59) 14.00 45.00
1080 TV photo cover. (2/60) 13.00 40.00
1133 TV photo cover. (8/60) 13.00 40.00
1172 TV photo cover. (3/61) 11.00 35.00
1218 TV photo cover. (8/61) 13.00 40.00
1296 TV photo cover. (2/62) 13.00 40.00

FURY
GOLD KEY (1962)
10020-211 Photo cover. 7.00 20.00

FURY
MARVEL (1994)
1 .75 2.95

FURY OF FIRESTORM
DC (1982-1987)
1 .75 2.00
2-61 .50 1.25
61A Superman test logo. 12.00 50.00
62-63 .50 1.25
64 Title changes to Firestorm The Nuclear Man with #65. .50 1.25
ANNUAL 1 (1983) .50 1.25
ANNUAL 2 (1984) .50 1.25
ANNUAL 3 (1985) .50 1.25
ANNUAL 4 (1986) .50 1.25

FURY OF HELLINA
LIGHTNING (1995-CURRENT)
1 .75 3.50
1A Signed & numbered limited edition. 2.50 9.95

FURY OF S.H.I.E.L.D.
MARVEL (1995)
1 .75 2.50
2-3 .50 1.95
4 Includes de-coder card. .75 2.50

FUTURE COMICS
MCKAY (1940)
1 Begin: Lone Ranger. (6/40) 400.00 1200.00
2 (7/40) 220.00 700.00
3 (8/40) 190.00 600.00
4 (9/40) 190.00 600.00

FUTURE WORLD COMICS
DOUGHERTY (1946)
1 31.00 100.00
2 23.00 75.00

FUTURIANS, THE
AARDWOLF PUBLICATIONS (1995)
0 One shot. .75 2.95

G-8 AND HIS BATTLE ACES
GOLD KEY (1966)
1 (10184-610). Pulp character. 5.00 15.00

GABBY HAYES ADVENTURE COMICS
TOBY (1953)
1 Photo cover. "Ambush At Terror Canyon!" 23.00 75.00

GABBY HAYES WESTERN
FAWCETT/CHARLTON (1948-1957)
1 Photo covers on all. 80.00 250.00
2 40.00 125.00
3 25.00 80.00
4-6 22.00 70.00
7-12 20.00 65.00
13-18 19.00 60.00
19-24 16.00 50.00
25-30 13.00 40.00
31-40 11.00 35.00
41-42 10.00 30.00
43 "Vittles For Villains" 10.00 30.00
44-49 10.00 30.00
50 (1/53) 10.00 30.00
51 Begin: Charlton publication. 5.00 15.00
52-59 5.00 15.00

GAGS
UNITED FEATURES (1937)
1 13.00 40.00

GALACTIC GUARDIANS
MARVEL (1994)
1-4 .30 1.00

GALLANT MEN
GOLD KEY (1963)
10085-310 TV photo cover. 2.75 10.00

GAMBIT
MARVEL (1993-1994)
1 Gold embossed cover. 1.75 6.00
1A Gold edition. 8.00 25.00
2-4 1.25 4.00

GAMBIT AND THE X-TERNALS
MARVEL (1995)
1 1.25 4.50
2-4 1.00 3.00

GAMES OF FUN
EASTERN (1934)
NO# 8-1/2 x 5-1/2" with spine at the top. Contains newspaper strip reprints. Color covers, B&W interior. 10.00 30.00

GANG BUSTERS
DC (1947-1959)
1 140.00 460.00
2 70.00 230.00
3-6 55.00 170.00
7-12 45.00 140.00
13 35.00 110.00
14 Photo cover. Art: Frank Frazetta (8 pages). 65.00 200.00
15-16 35.00 110.00
17 Art: Frank Frazetta (8 pages). 65.00 200.00
18 35.00 110.00
19-25 26.00 85.00
26 Art: Jack Kirby. 29.00 95.00
27-30 22.00 70.00
31-36 20.00 65.00
37-44 17.00 55.00
45 1st Code Approved issue. 16.00 50.00
46-50 14.00 46.00
51-60 13.00 40.00
61-67 11.00 34.00

GANG BUSTERS
DELL FOUR COLOR SERIES (1943)
24 70.00 225.00

GANG BUSTERS
SEE LARGE FEATURE COMICS #10, 17.

GANGSTERS AND GUN MOLLS
AVON (1951-1952)
1 "Big Jim" Colosimo, Evelyn Ellis, Pete Parakis. 65.00 200.00
2 Bonnie Parker, The Kissing Bandit, The Wild Genna Brothers. 50.00 150.00
3 Juanita Perez, Crime's Homicide Squad, Insurance For Death, Marie Swain "Rod-Baby." 40.00 125.00
4 Mara Hite, Elkins Boys, Alice Cort. 31.00 100.00

GANGSTERS CAN'T WIN
DS (1948-1949)
1 31.00 100.00
2 16.00 50.00
3-6 13.00 40.00
7-9 10.00 30.00

GARGOYLE
MARVEL (1985)
1-4 .30 1.00

GARRISON'S GORILLAS
DELL (1968-1969)
1 TV tie-in. Photo covers on all issues. 7.00 20.00
2-5 5.00 15.00

GASOLINE ALLEY
STAR (1950-1951)
1 31.00 100.00
2-3 23.00 75.00

GASP!
ACG (1967)
1 "Those Terrible Teen-Agers!" 9.00 27.00
2 "Vengeful Spirit!" 4.00 13.00
3 "Sorry, You've Got The Wrong Ghosts!" 4.00 11.00
4 "You've Got To Relax!" 4.00 11.00

GAY COMICS
MARVEL(TIMELY) (1944-1949)
1 1st: Millie The Model. (5/44) 100.00 320.00
18 Art: Basil Wolverton. (Fall/44) 50.00 160.00
19-29 Art: Basil Wolverton. 40.00 130.00
30-31 14.00 45.00
32 10.00 32.00
33 12.00 39.00
34 16.00 50.00
35 10.00 32.00
36-37 12.00 39.00
38-40 10.00 32.00

GAY PURR-EE
GOLD KEY (1963)
30017-301 Movie tie-in. 8.00 25.00

FURY OF SHIELD #3

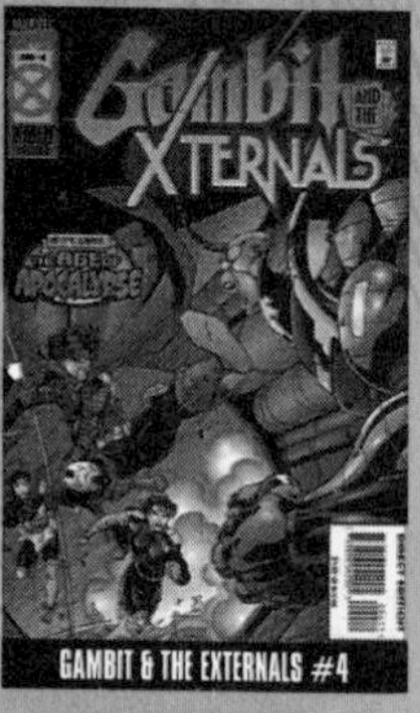
GAMBIT & THE EXTERNALS #4

GEN13 (MINI-SERIES) #1

GEN13 #1G

GENERATION X #2

GEOMANCER #6

GHOST #2

GHOST IN THE SHELL #2

GAY COMICS #1

This 1944 title had a very different meaning than it does today, offering teenage humor strips. It debuted Millie the Model, who proved so popular she was given her own book that lasted until 1973.

GEM COMICS
SPOTLIGHT (1945)

1 (4/45)	40.00	120.00

GEN13
IMAGE (1994)

0 (7/94)	2.00	7.00
1 See Deathmate Black for 1st appearance.	13.00	40.00
1 (2ND) 2nd printing.	2.25	8.00
2	10.00	35.00
3	7.00	22.00
4	4.00	12.00
5	2.25	8.00
5A Variant cover.	5.00	16.00
1/2 Wizard mail-away offer.	13.00	40.00
TPB Reprints entire mini-series.	4.00	12.95
TPB HC Hardcover version, signed & numbered.	12.00	39.95

GEN13
IMAGE (1995-CURRENT)

1A Charge! cover by J. Scott Campbell & Alex Garner.	2.50	9.00
1B Thumbs up cover by J. Scott Campbell & Alex Garner.	2.50	9.00
1C X-Babies parody cover by Art Adams.	7.00	20.00
1D Heavy Metal parody cover by Simon Bisley.	7.00	20.00
1E McFarlane Spider-Man parody cover by John Cleary.	7.00	20.00
1F Mass merchandising cover by Michael Golden.	7.00	20.00
1G Victoria's Secret catalog parody cover by Michael Lopez.	7.00	20.00
1H Janet Jackson parody cover by Jason Pearson.	7.00	20.00
1I Brady Bunch parody cover by J. Scott Campbell & Chuck Gibson.	7.00	20.00
1J Paper doll cover by J. Scott Campbell & Tom McWeeney.	7.00	20.00
1K Sandman parody cover by Joe Dunn.	7.00	20.00
1L Pulp Fiction parody cover by Anthony M. Cox.	7.00	20.00
1M Do-it-yourself cover by J. Scott Campbell.	7.00	20.00
2 Includes 2 cards.	1.00	4.00
2A Newsstand version.	.50	2.00
3-4	.75	3.00
SET 1 Collector's pack (all 13 covers with slipcase) plus a Jim Lee signed chromium cover edition.	85.00	275.00
SET 2 Collector's pack plus a J. Scott Campbell signed chromium cover edition.	65.00	200.00
SET 3 Collector's pack plus a Brandon Choi signed chromium cover edition.	50.00	175.00
SET 4 Collector's pack plus an Alex Garner signed chromium cover edition.	40.00	150.00

GENE AUTRY
DELL FOUR COLOR SERIES (1944-1946)

47 "The Ghost Mine"	110.00	350.00
57 "Raiders Of The Range"	95.00	300.00
66 "Trail Of Terror"	95.00	300.00
75 "And The Wildcat"	80.00	250.00
83 "Outlaw Trail"	80.00	250.00
93 "The Bandit Of Black Rock"	65.00	200.00
100 Photo cover.	70.00	225.00

GENE AUTRY COMICS
DELL (1946-1959)

1	100.00	330.00
2 Begin: Photo covers.	50.00	160.00
3-6	35.00	110.00
7-12	26.00	85.00
13-18	23.00	75.00
19-24	20.00	65.00
25-30	17.00	55.00
31-40	15.00	49.00
41-50	12.00	38.00
51-56	10.00	33.00
57-65	9.00	27.00
66-80	8.00	24.00
81-99	6.00	19.00
100	7.00	22.00
101-110	6.00	19.00
111 End: Photo covers.	6.00	19.00
112-121	5.00	15.00
NO# (1950) Quaker Oats giveaway (2.5 x 6.75", 5 different issues).	20.00	65.00

GENE AUTRY COMICS
FAWCETT/DELL (1942-1944)

1 "The Mark Of Cloven Hoof"	600.00	2200.00
2	270.00	875.00
3 "The Secret Of The Aztec Treasure"	170.00	550.00
4 "The Outlaw Of Smokey Valley"	170.00	550.00
5 "The Mystery Of Paint Rock Canyon"	170.00	550.00
6 "Outlaw Round-Up"	170.00	550.00
7 "Border Bullets"	135.00	440.00
8 "Blazing Guns"	135.00	440.00
9 "Range Robbers"	135.00	440.00
10 "Fightin' Buckaroo" & "Danger's Trail"	135.00	440.00
11 Begin: Dell publication. (1943)	115.00	380.00
12 "Down Mexico Way" (1944)	100.00	330.00

GENE AUTRY'S CHAMPION
DELL (1950-1955)

1 (#287) From the 4-Color Series. "The Ghost Of Black Mountain" (8/50)	25.00	80.00
2 (#319) From the 4-Color Series. "The Trail To Danger" (3/51)	11.00	35.00
3 (8/51)	7.00	22.00
4-10	4.00	13.00
11-19	4.00	11.00

GENE DOGS
MARVEL (1993-1994)

1 Bagged w/ trading cards.	.75	2.00
2-8	.50	1.50

GENERATION NEXT
MARVEL (1995)

1	1.50	5.50
2	1.25	4.00
3	1.00	3.50
4	1.00	3.00

GENERATION X
MARVEL (1994-CURRENT)

PREVIEW Intro to new team.	.20	.75
1 Chrome cover.	1.75	6.00
2 Deluxe edition.	1.25	4.00
2A Regular edition.	.50	1.50
3 Deluxe edition.	1.00	3.00
3A Regular edition.	.50	1.50
4 Deluxe edition.	1.00	3.00
4A Regular edition.	.50	1.50
5-7	.50	1.95

GENERIC COMIC BOOK
MARVEL (1984)

1	.30	1.00

GENESIS
MALIBU (1993)

0 Chromium cover.	1.00	3.50
0A Gold foil cover.	2.75	10.00

GENTLE BEN
DELL (1968-1969)

1 TV photo covers on all issues.	7.00	20.00
2-5	2.75	10.00

GEOMANCER
VALIANT (1994-1995)

1	1.00	3.00
2-8	.75	2.25

GEORGE PAL'S PUPPETOONS
FAWCETT (1945-1949)

1 Captain Marvel cover.	85.00	270.00
2	35.00	110.00
3-6	20.00	65.00
7-12	17.00	55.00
13-19	14.00	44.00

GEORGIE COMICS
MARVEL/TIMELY (1945-1952)

1 (Spring/45)	35.00	110.00
2 (Summer/45)	17.00	55.00
3 (Fall/45)	14.00	44.00
4 (1/46)	14.00	44.00
5 (4/46)	14.00	44.00
6 (Summer/46)	14.00	44.00
7 (9/46)	10.00	33.00
8 (11/46)	10.00	33.00

9 (1/47) 10.00 33.00
10 (4/47) 10.00 33.00
11 (6/47) 10.00 33.00
12 (9/47) 10.00 33.00
13-18 9.00 27.00
19-24 7.00 22.00
25 Cover: Peter Driben. 14.00 44.00
26-30 5.00 16.00
31-39 4.00 11.00

GERALD MCBOING-BOING AND MR. MAGOO
DELL (1952-1953)
1 10.00 30.00
2 7.00 20.00
3-5 5.00 15.00

GERONIMO INDIAN FIGHTER
AVON (1950-1952)
1 20.00 65.00
2-3 13.00 40.00
4 11.00 35.00

GET LOST
MIKEROSS (1954)
1 28.00 90.00
2 19.00 60.00
3 16.00 50.00

GET SMART
DELL (1966-1967)
1 TV photo covers on all issues. 20.00 65.00
2 14.00 45.00
3 13.00 40.00
4 11.00 35.00
5-8 10.00 30.00

GETALONG GANG, THE
MARVEL(STAR) (1985-1986)
1 TV cartoon tie-in. .20 .50
2-6 .20 .50

G-FORCE
MARVEL (1994)
1-4 .20 .50

GHOST
DARK HORSE (1994)
TPB Reprints all Ghost appearances to date. 2.25 8.95

GHOST
DARK HORSE (1995-CURRENT)
1 2.00 7.00
2 1.50 5.00
3-4 1.00 3.50

GHOST BREAKERS
STREET & SMITH (1948)
1 Cover/Art: Bob Powell. 60.00 190.00
2 Cover/Art: Bob Powell. 50.00 160.00

GHOST COMICS
FICTION HOUSE (1951-1954)
1 110.00 360.00
2 55.00 180.00
3-5 50.00 150.00
6 "The Sleepers In The Crypt" 50.00 150.00
7-11 40.00 120.00

GHOST IN THE SHELL, THE
DARK HORSE (1995)
1 1.75 6.00
2 2.25 8.00
3 1.50 5.00
4 1.25 4.00
5-6 1.00 3.95

GHOST MANOR
CHARLTON (1968-1971)
1 2.25 8.00
2 1.50 5.00
3-6 1.25 4.00
7-12 1.00 3.00
13-18 .75 2.00
19 Title changes to Ghostly Haunts .75 2.00

GHOST MANOR
CHARLTON (1971-1984)
1 2.25 8.00
2 1.25 4.00
3-10 1.00 3.00
11-30 .75 2.00
31-54 .50 1.50
55-77 .30 1.00

GHOST MOTHER COMICS (UNDERGROUND)
PIRATE PRESS (1969)
1 Digest size. 13.00 40.00

GHOST RIDER
MARVEL (1967)
1 1st & Origin: The Ghost Rider (western). 11.00 35.00
2-5 4.00 12.00
6 Art: Dick Ayers. 4.00 12.00
7 4.00 12.00

GHOST RIDER
MARVEL (1973-1983)
1 17.00 55.00
2 6.00 18.00
3-5 4.00 12.00
6-9 2.25 8.00
10 Reprint: Marvel Spotlight #5. 2.75 10.00
11-19 2.25 8.00
20 Story continues in Daredevil #138. 2.25 8.00
21-30 1.75 6.00
31-49 1.50 5.00
50 Double size. 1.50 5.00
51-67 1.00 3.00
68 Origin retold. 1.00 3.00
69-76 1.00 3.00
77 Origin retold. 1.00 3.00
78-79 1.00 3.00
80 1.50 5.00
81 Death: Ghost Rider. 2.00 7.00

GHOST RIDER
MARVEL (1990-CURRENT)
1 1st & Origin: new Ghost Rider. 2.25 7.00
1 (2ND) 2nd printing. 1.00 3.00
2 1.00 4.00
3-5 1.00 3.00
5 (2ND) 2nd printing (Gold). .75 2.00
6 Punisher. 1.00 3.00
7-14 1.00 3.00
15 Glow-in-the-dark cover. 1.00 3.00
15 (2ND) 2nd printing. .75 2.00
16-27 .75 2.00
28 Double size. .75 2.50
29-30 .50 1.50
31 Double size. .50 1.50
32-49 .50 1.50
50 Anniversary issue, foil cover. 1.00 3.00
50A Regular edition. .75 2.00
51-60 .50 1.50
61 Double size. .75 2.50
62-65 .50 1.95
ANNUAL 1 (1993) .75 2.95
ANNUAL 2 (1994) .75 2.95

GHOST RIDER (A-1 SERIES)
ME (1950-1954)
1 (A-1 #27). Art: Dick Ayers (all issues). Origin: Ghost Rider. 100.00 330.00
2 (A-1 #29). Cover: Frazetta. 85.00 270.00
3 (A-1 #31). Cover: Frazetta. 85.00 270.00
4 (A-1 #34). "The Greedy Ghosts Of Boot Hill" Cover: Frazetta. 85.00 270.00
5 (A-1 #37). Cover: Frazetta. 85.00 270.00
6 (A-1 #44). 40.00 130.00
7 (A-1 #51). 40.00 130.00
8 (A-1 #57). 35.00 110.00
9 (A-1 #69). 35.00 110.00
10 (A-1 #71). "Ghost Rider vs Frankenstein!" 40.00 130.00
11 (A-1 #75). 26.00 85.00
12 (A-1 #80). 26.00 85.00
13 (A-1 #84). 26.00 85.00
14 (A-1 #112). 26.00 85.00

GHOST RIDER 2099
MARVEL (1994-CURRENT)
1 Prismatic foil cover. .75 2.25
1A Regular edition. .50 1.50
2-16 .50 1.50
17 .50 1.95

GHOST RIDER: FEAR
MARVEL (1992)
1 Bookshelf format. App: Captain America. 1.50 5.95

GHOST RIDER/BLAZE: SPIRITS OF VENGEANCE
MARVEL (1992-1994)
1 Polybagged. .75 2.00
2-11 .50 1.50
12 Glow-in-the-dark cover. .75 2.95
13 .75 2.25
14-22 .50 1.50

GHOST SPECIAL
DARK HORSE (1994)
1 One-shot. 2.25 8.00

GHOST STORIES
DELL (1962-1973)
1 (12295-211). 10.00 30.00
2 5.00 15.00
3-6 4.00 12.00
7-12 2.75 10.00
13-20 2.25 8.00
21-30 1.75 6.00
31-37 1.50 5.00

GHOSTDANCING
DC (1995)
1 Mini-series. .75 2.50
2 .50 1.95
3-6 .75 2.50

GHOSTLY HAUNTS
CHARLTON (1971-1978)
20 Previous title: Ghost Manor. 1.25 4.00
21-40 1.25 4.00
41-50 1.00 3.00
51-58 .75 2.00

GHOSTLY TALES
CHARLTON (1966-1984)
55 Previous title: "Blue Beetle." 2.75 10.00
56-60 2.25 8.00
61-80 1.75 6.00
81-100 1.50 5.00
101-130 1.25 4.00
131-150 1.00 3.00
151-169 .75 2.00

GHOSTLY WEIRD STORIES
STAR (1953-1954)
120 Previous title: Blue Bolt Weird. 40.00 120.00
121-124 28.00 90.00

GHOSTS
DC (1971-1982)
1 5.00 14.00
2 2.50 9.50
3-6 2.00 7.00
7-12 1.75 6.00
13-20 1.50 5.00
21-40 1.00 3.50
41-80 .75 2.25
81-100 .50 1.75
101-112 .30 1.00

G.I. COMBAT
QUALITY/DC (1952-1987)
1 110.00 350.00
2 50.00 150.00
3-6 35.00 110.00
7-12 28.00 90.00
13-24 22.00 70.00
25-43 16.00 50.00
44 Begin: DC publication. (1/57) 85.00 300.00
45-48 45.00 160.00
49-60 31.00 110.00
61-66 23.00 80.00
67 1st: Tank Killer. 31.00 100.00
68 Prototype issue. 35.00 110.00
69-72 19.00 62.00
73-84 17.00 56.00
85-86 14.00 46.00
87 1st: Haunted Tank. 45.00 140.00
88-90 14.00 46.00
91 1st 12 cent cover price. 11.00 36.00
92-96 11.00 36.00
97-107 8.00 26.00
108 App: Sgt. Rock. 11.00 36.00
109-113 7.00 22.00
114 Origin: Haunted Tank. 28.00 90.00
115-120 5.00 16.00
121-136 4.00 11.00
137 1st 15 cent cover price. 2.25 8.00
138 1st: The Losers. 4.00 12.00
139-145 1.75 6.00
146-148 Double size. 1.50 5.00
149-200 1.25 4.00
201-281 1.00 3.00
282-288 .75 2.00

G.I. JOE
CUSTOM (1967)
NO# (America's Moveable Fighting Man). Toy tie-in. 5.00 15.00

G.I. JOE
MARVEL (1982-1994)
1 1.00 3.00
2-59 .50 1.50

GHOST RIDER #7 (2ND SERIES)

G.I. COMBAT #26

G.I. JOE #41 (MARVEL)

G.I. JOE #50 (MARVEL)

GIANT SIZE AVENGERS #1

GIANT SIZE X-MEN #1

GIVE ME LIBERTY #2

GLORY #2

60 Art: Todd McFarlane. .50 1.50
61-155 .30 1.00

G.I. JOE
ZIFF-DAVIS (1950-1957)
1 (#10) 16.00 50.00
2 (#11) 11.00 35.00
3 (#12)-4 (#13) 10.00 30.00
5 (#14) (1951) 10.00 30.00
6-10 8.00 25.00
11-17 7.00 20.00
18 100 page Giant. 25.00 80.00
19-30 6.00 18.00
31-51 5.00 15.00

G.I. JOE AND THE TRANSFORMERS
MARVEL (1987)
1-4 .30 1.00
TPB 1.25 4.95

G.I. JOE: EUROPEAN MISSIONS
MARVEL (1988-1989)
1-16 .30 1.00

G.I. JOE ORDER OF BATTLE
MARVEL (1986-1987)
1-4 .30 1.00

G.I. JOE SPECIAL MISSIONS
MARVEL (1986-1989)
1-28 .30 1.00

G.I. JOE YEARBOOK
MARVEL (1984-1988)
1-5 .50 1.00

G.I. SWEETHEARTS
QUALITY (1953-1955)
32 Previous title: Diary Loves. 7.00 20.00
33-45 5.00 15.00

G.I. WAR BRIDES
SUPERIOR (1954-1955)
1 7.00 20.00
2 5.00 15.00
3-8 2.75 10.00

G.I. WAR TALES
DC (1973)
1-4 .50 1.50

GIANT COMICS EDITIONS
ST. JOHNS (1948-1950)
1 Mighty Mouse. 90.00 290.00
2 Abbie an' Slats. 17.00 55.00
3 Terry-Toons. 50.00 160.00
4 Various rebound crime comics including Red Seal 16. 100.00 330.00
5 Police Case Book. 75.00 240.00
5A Terry-Toons Album. 50.00 160.00
6 Western Picture Stories. 70.00 220.00
7 Rebound teenage romance comics. 25.00 80.00
8 The Adventures Of Mighty Mouse. 50.00 160.00
9 Romance And Confession Stories. 70.00 220.00
10 Terry-Toons Album. 40.00 130.00
11 Cover: Matt Baker. Western Picture Stories. 70.00 220.00
12 Classic Matt Baker cover. Diary Secrets. 135.00 440.00
13 Romances. 50.00 160.00
14 Mighty Mouse Album. 50.00 160.00
15 Cover: Matt Baker. Romances. 50.00 160.00
16 Abbott & Costello, Casper, and Little Audrey. 50.00 160.00
17 (NO#) Mighty Mouse Album. 40.00 130.00

GIANT-SIZE AVENGERS
MARVEL (1974-1975)
1 1st: Nuklo. 1st: Miss America. 1st: Bova, All Winners Squad. (8/74) 2.50 9.00
2 (11/74) 1.75 6.50
3 (2/75) 1.50 5.00
4 (6/75) 1.75 6.00
5 (12/75) 1.00 3.00

GIANT-SIZE CAPTAIN AMERICA
MARVEL (1975)
1 Reprint: Tales Of Suspense #59-63. 1.50 5.00

GIANT-SIZE CAPTAIN MARVEL
MARVEL (1975)
1 1.50 5.00

GIANT-SIZE CHILLERS
MARVEL (1974)
1 "The Curse Of Dracula!" Title changes to Giant-Size Dracula. 1.25 4.25

GIANT-SIZE CHILLERS
MARVEL (1975)
1-3 .75 2.75

GIANT-SIZE CONAN THE BARBARIAN
MARVEL (1974-1975)
1 Reprint: Conan #3. 2.25 8.00
2 Reprint: Conan #5. 1.50 5.50
3 Reprint: Conan #6. 1.50 5.50
4 Reprint: Conan #7. 1.50 5.50
5 Reprint: Conan #14, 15. 1.50 5.50

GIANT-SIZE CREATURES FEATURING WEREWOLF
MARVEL (1974)
1 1st & origin: Tigra, The Were-Woman. Title changes to: Giant-Size Werewolf By Night with #2. 1.50 5.00

GIANT-SIZE DAREDEVIL
MARVEL (1975)
1 Reprint: Annual #1. 2.75 10.00

GIANT-SIZE DEFENDERS
MARVEL (1974-1975)
1 2.75 10.00
2 1.75 6.00
3-5 1.50 5.00

GIANT-SIZE DOCTOR STRANGE
MARVEL (1975)
1 "This Dream...This Doom!" 1.50 5.00

GIANT-SIZE DRACULA
MARVEL (1974-1975)
2 "Vengeance Of The Elder Gods!" (1974) Previous title: "Giant-Size Chillers." 1.00 3.00
3 "Slow Death On The Killing Ground!" 1.00 3.00
4 "The Demon Of Devil's Lake!" 1.00 3.00
5 "The Fine Art Of Dying!" John Byrne's 1st work for Marvel. 2.00 7.00

GIANT-SIZE FANTASTIC FOUR
MARVEL (1974-1975)
2 Previous title: Giant-Size Super-Stars. 2.00 7.00
3 2.00 7.00
4 1st Madrox. 2.50 9.00
5-6 1.75 6.00

GIANT-SIZE INCREDIBLE HULK
MARVEL (1975)
1 2.75 10.00

GIANT-SIZE INVADERS
MARVEL (1975)
1 "Hordes Of Hitler!" 2.00 7.50

GIANT-SIZE IRON MAN
MARVEL (1975)
1 Reprints Tales Of Suspense #49, 57, 58. 1.75 6.00

GIANT-SIZE KID COLT
MARVEL (1975)
1-3 1.50 5.00

GIANT-SIZE MARVEL TRIPLE ACTION
MARVEL (1975)
1-2 .75 2.50

GIANT-SIZE MASTER OF KUNG FU
MARVEL (1974-1975)
1 1.75 6.50
2 1.50 5.00
3-4 1.25 4.00

GIANT-SIZE POWER MAN
MARVEL (1975)
1 1.00 3.00

GIANT-SIZE SPIDER-MAN
MARVEL (1974-1975)
1 Art: Kirby/Ditko. 5.00 16.00
2-3 2.25 8.00
4 3rd App: Punisher. 13.00 40.00
5-6 1.75 6.00

GIANT-SIZE SUPER-HEROES FEATURING SPIDER-MAN
MARVEL (1974)
1 Morbius, Man-Wolf. 11.00 35.00

GIANT-SIZE SUPER-STARS
MARVEL (1974)
1 Featuring The Fantastic Four. App: Black Panther, Hulk vs. Thing. Title changes to Giant-Size Fantastic Four with #2. 6.00 18.00

GIANT-SIZE SUPER-VILLAIN TEAM-UP
MARVEL (1975)
1 2.00 7.00
2 1.50 5.50

GIANT-SIZE THOR
MARVEL (1975)
1 5.00 15.00

GIANT-SIZE WEREWOLF BY NIGHT
MARVEL (1974-1975)
2 Previous title: Giant-Size Creatures Featuring Werewolf. 1.25 4.00
3-5 1.25 4.00

GIANT-SIZE X-MEN
MARVEL (1975)
1 1st & origin: The New X-Men (Nightcrawler, Storm, Colossus, Thunderbird, Wolverine). 2nd full app: Wolverine. 100.00 350.00
2 Reprints X-Men #57-59. 10.00 30.00

GIDGET
DELL (1966)
1 TV photo cover (Sally Field). 10.00 30.00
2 TV photo cover (Sally Field). 8.00 25.00

GIFT COMICS
FAWCETT (1942-1949)
1 Captain Marvel, Bulletman, others. 324 pages. 400.00 1500.00
2 324 pages. 400.00 1200.00
3 324 pages. 240.00 775.00
4 148 pages. 190.00 625.00

GIGGLE COMICS
CRESTON/ACG (1943-1955)
1 40.00 120.00
2 19.00 60.00
3-6 13.00 40.00
7-12 10.00 30.00
13-30 8.00 25.00
31-50 7.00 20.00
51-63 5.00 15.00
64 Begin: ACG publication. 5.00 15.00
65-70 5.00 15.00
71-99 4.00 12.00

GILGAMESH II
DC (1989)
1 Cover/Art: Jim Starlin. .75 2.00
2-4 .75 2.00

GINGER
ARCHIE (1951-1954)
1 22.00 70.00
2 11.00 36.00
3-6 10.00 30.00
7-10 Katy Keene. 15.00 48.00

GIRL COMICS
MARVEL(ATLAS) (1949-1952)
1 Photo cover. 23.00 75.00
2 13.00 40.00
3 Art: Bill Everett. Elizabeth Taylor photo cover. 19.00 60.00
4-6 11.00 35.00
7-11 8.00 25.00
12 Title changes to Girl Confessions with #13. 8.00 25.00

GIRL CONFESSIONS
MARVEL(ATLAS) (1952-1954)
13 Previous title: Girl Comics. 8.00 25.00
14-20 7.00 20.00
21-30 6.00 18.00
31-35 5.00 15.00

GIRL FROM U.N.C.L.E.
GOLD KEY (1967)
1 TV photo covers on all issues. 13.00 40.00
2-5 8.00 25.00

GIRLS LOVE STORIES
DC (1949-1973)
1 Photo cover. 85.00 270.00
2 40.00 130.00
3-10 29.00 95.00
11-20 25.00 80.00
21-33 17.00 55.00
34 1st Code Approved issue. 15.00 49.00
35-40 14.00 44.00
41-50 10.00 33.00
51-70 9.00 27.00
71-83 7.00 22.00
84 1st 12 cent cover price. 6.00 19.00
85-100 6.00 19.00

101-109 .... 5.00 16.00
110-120 .... 4.00 13.00
121-140 .... 4.00 11.00
141-150 .... 2.25 8.75
151-160 .... 1.75 6.50
161-170 .... 1.25 4.25
171-180 .... 1.00 3.25

GIRLS' ROMANCES
DC (1950-1971)
1 .... 85.00 270.00
2 .... 40.00 130.00
3-6 .... 35.00 110.00
7-12 .... 26.00 85.00
13-18 .... 23.00 75.00
19-24 .... 17.00 55.00
25-31 .... 12.00 38.00
32 1st Code Approved issue. 10.00 33.00
33-40 .... 10.00 33.00
41-50 .... 9.00 27.00
51-70 .... 7.00 22.00
71-80 .... 5.00 16.00
81 1st 12 cent cover price. 4.00 11.00
82-100 .... 4.00 11.00
101-108 .... 2.50 9.75
109 Cover & App: The Beatles. 14.00 44.00
110-120 .... 2.25 8.75
121-133 .... 2.00 7.50
134 Cover: Neal Adams. 2.50 9.75
135-140 .... 1.75 6.50
141-150 .... 1.25 4.25
151-160 .... 1.00 3.25

GIVE ME LIBERTY
DARK HORSE (1990-1991)
1-4 .... 1.25 4.95
TPB Reprints issues #1-4. .... 6.00 19.95

GIZMO
CHANCE (1985)
1 One shot. 1.50 5.00

GIZMO
MIRAGE (1986-1987)
1 .... 1.00 3.00
2-6 .... .75 2.00

GLADSTONE COMIC ALBUM
GLADSTONE (1987-1990)
1-15 .... 1.50 5.00
16-28 .... 1.25 4.00

GLAMOROUS ROMANCES
ACE (1949-1956)
41 Previous title: Dotty. 8.00 25.00
42-60 .... 5.00 15.00
61-69 .... 4.00 12.00
70 Photo cover. 4.00 12.00
71-80 .... 2.75 10.00
81 1st Code Approved issue. 2.25 8.00
82-90 .... 2.25 8.00

GLORY
IMAGE/EXTREME (1995-CURRENT)
1 .... 1.00 4.50
1A Variant cover. 1.50 6.00
2-5 .... .75 2.50
TPB Reprints isssues #1-4. .... 2.50 9.95

GNOME MOBILE, THE
GOLD KEY (1967)
10207-710 Disney movie tie-in. 7.00 20.00

GOBBLEDY GOOK
MIRAGE (1984)
1 1st: TMNT (24 pages). 75.00 225.00
2 Early TMNT (24 pages). 60.00 200.00

GOBBLEDY GOOK
MIRAGE (1986)
1 8 page TMNT story. 2.75 10.00

GOD'S HEROES IN AMERICA
CATECHETICAL GUILD (1956)
307 .... 2.25 8.00

GODDESS
DC (1995)
1 .... 1.00 3.50
2-4 .... .75 2.95

GODWHEEL
MALIBU (1995)
0 .... .75 2.50
1-3 .... .75 2.50
TPB Reprints issues #0-3. .... 2.50 9.95

GODZILLA
DARK HORSE (1988)
1 .... 1.75 6.50
2-6 .... 1.00 3.25
SPECIAL Color. 1.00 3.50
TPB Reprints issues 1-6. .... 6.00 17.95

GODZILLA
DARK HORSE (1995-CURRENT)
0 Reprints stories from Dark Horse Comics. .75 2.50
1-2 .... .75 2.50

GODZILLA
MARVEL (1977-1979)
1 .... 2.00 7.00
2 .... 1.50 5.00
3-10 .... 1.25 4.00
11-24 .... .75 2.75

GODZILLA VS BARKLEY
DARK HORSE (1993)
1 .... .75 2.95

GODZILLA VS HERO ZERO
DARK HORSE (1995)
1 .... .75 2.50

GOING STEADY
ST. JOHN (1954-1955)
10 Previous title: Teen Age Temptations. 19.00 60.00
11 .... 13.00 40.00
12-13 .... 10.00 30.00
14 .... 13.00 40.00

GOING STEADY WITH BETTY
AVON (1949)
1 Title changes to Betty And Her Steady with #2.
.... 31.00 100.00

GOLD DIGGER
ANTARCTIC (1992-1993)
1 Mini series. 2.25 8.00
2-3 .... 1.75 6.00
4 .... 1.50 5.00
TPB Reprints issues #1-4 .... 2.50 9.95

GOLD DIGGER
ANTARCTIC (1993-CURRENT)
1 .... 2.75 10.00
2-3 .... 2.25 8.00
4 .... 1.75 6.00
5 Misnumbered as #0. .... 1.75 6.00
6-8 .... 1.25 4.00
9-10 .... 1.00 3.50
11-22 .... .75 2.75
TPB Reprints issues #1-4. .... 2.50 9.95

GOLDEN AGE
DC (1993-1994)
1-4 .... 1.25 4.95
TPB Reprints issues #1-4. .... 6.00 19.95

GOLDEN AGE GREATS
AC (1994-CURRENT)
1 Reprints. 2.50 9.95
2-4 .... 2.50 9.95
5 .... 4.00 11.95

GOLDEN ARROW
FAWCETT (1942-1947)
1 .... 50.00 160.00
2 .... 35.00 110.00
3 .... 25.00 80.00
4-6 .... 20.00 65.00

GOLDEN COMICS DIGEST
GOLD KEY (1969-1976)
1 Bugs Bunny, Tom & Jerry, Woody Woodpecker.
.... 2.75 10.00
2 Hanna-Barbera TV Fun Favorites. 2.75 10.00
3 Tom & Jerry, Woody Woodpecker. 1.75 6.00
4 Tarzan. 2.75 10.00
5 Tom & Jerry, Woody Woodpecker, Bugs Bunny.
.... 1.75 6.00
6 Bugs Bunny. 1.75 6.00
7 Hanna-Barbera TV Fun Favorites. 2.25 8.00
8 Tom & Jerry, Woody Woodpecker, Bugs Bunny.
.... 1.75 6.00
9 Tarzan. 2.75 10.00
10 Bugs Bunny. 1.50 5.00
11 Hanna-Barbera TV Fun Favorites. 1.50 5.00
12 Tom & Jerry, Bugs Bunny. 1.50 5.00
13 Tom & Jerry. 1.50 5.00
14 Bugs Bunny Fun Packed Funnies. 1.50 5.00
15 Tom & Jerry, Bugs Bunny, Woody Woodpecker.
.... 1.50 5.00
16 Woody Woodpecker. 1.50 5.00
17 Bugs Bunny. 1.50 5.00
18 Tom & Jerry. 1.50 5.00
19 Little Lulu. 1.50 5.00
20 Woody Woodpecker. 1.50 5.00
21 Bugs Bunny Showtime. 1.25 4.00
22 Tom & Jerry Winter Wingding. 1.25 4.00
23 Little Lulu and Tubby Fun Fling. 1.25 4.00
24 Woody Woodpecker Fun Festival. 1.25 4.00
25 Tom & Jerry. 1.25 4.00
26 Bugs Bunny Halloween Hulla-Boo-Loo. 1.25 4.00
27 Little Lulu and Tubby in Hawaii. 1.25 4.00
28 Tom & Jerry. 1.25 4.00
29 Little Lulu and Tubby. 1.25 4.00
30 Bugs Bunny Vacation Funnies. 1.25 4.00
31 Turok Son Of Stone. 1.00 3.00
32 Woody Woodpecker Summer Fun. 1.00 3.00
33 Little Lulu and Tubby Halloween Fun. 1.00 3.00
34 Bugs Bunny Winter Funnies. 1.00 3.00
35 Tom & Jerry Snowtime Funtime. 1.00 3.00
36 Little Lulu and Her Friends. 1.00 3.00
37 Woody Woodpecker County Fair. 1.00 3.00
38 The Pink Panther. 1.00 3.00
39 Bugs Bunny Summer Fun. 1.00 3.00
40 Little Lulu. 1.00 3.00
41 Tom & Jerry Winter Carnival. .... .75 2.00
42 Bugs Bunny. .... .75 2.00
43 Little Lulu in Paris. .... .75 2.00
44 Woody Woodpecker Family Fun Festival. .75 2.00
45 The Pink Panther. .... .75 2.00
46 Little Lulu and Tubby. .... .75 2.00
47 Bugs Bunny. .... .75 2.00
48 The Lone Ranger. 1.50 5.00

GOLDEN LAD
SPARK (1945-1946)
1 1st & Origin: Golden Lad. 80.00 250.00
2 .... 40.00 125.00
3 .... 31.00 100.00
4 (4/46) 31.00 100.00
5 App: Flame. 40.00 125.00

GOLDEN WEST RODEO TREASURE
DELL (1957)
1 100 page Dell Giant. 25.00 80.00

GOMER PYLE
GOLD KEY (1966-1967)
1 TV photo covers on all. 13.00 40.00
2-3 .... 10.00 30.00

GOOD GUYS
DEFIANT (1993-1994)
1 .... 1.00 3.50
2-10 .... .75 2.50

GOODBYE, MR. CHIPS
GOLD KEY (1970)
10246-006 Movie photo cover. 7.00 20.00

GOOFY
DELL FOUR COLOR SERIES (1953-1962)
468 (5/53) 19.00 60.00
562 (5/54) 10.00 30.00
627 (5/55) 10.00 30.00
658 (11/55) 10.00 30.00
702 "Success Story" (5/56) 11.00 35.00
747 (11/56) 10.00 30.00
802 (6/57) 11.00 35.00
857 "Adventure Story" (11/57) 8.00 25.00
899 (5/58) 7.00 20.00
952 (11/58) 7.00 20.00
987 (5/59) 7.00 20.00
1053 (11/59) 7.00 20.00
1094 (5/60) 5.00 15.00
1149 (11/60) 7.00 20.00
1201 (8/62) 7.00 20.00

GOOFY COMICS
STANDARD (1943-1953)
1 .... 40.00 130.00
2 .... 20.00 65.00
3-12 .... 14.00 44.00
13-24 .... 10.00 33.00
25-40 .... 7.00 22.00
41-48 .... 5.00 16.00

GOOFY LOST IN THE DESERT
DISNEY (1947)
X2 Disney Cheerios Premium. 2.75 10.00

GORGO
CHARLTON (1961-1965)
1 Movie tie-in. Art: Steve Ditko. 50.00 160.00
2-3 Cover/Art: Steve Ditko. 35.00 110.00
4 Cover: Steve Ditko. 20.00 65.00
5-10 .... 17.00 55.00
11 Art: Steve Ditko. 20.00 65.00
12 .... 9.00 27.00
13-16 Art: Steve Ditko. 14.00 44.00

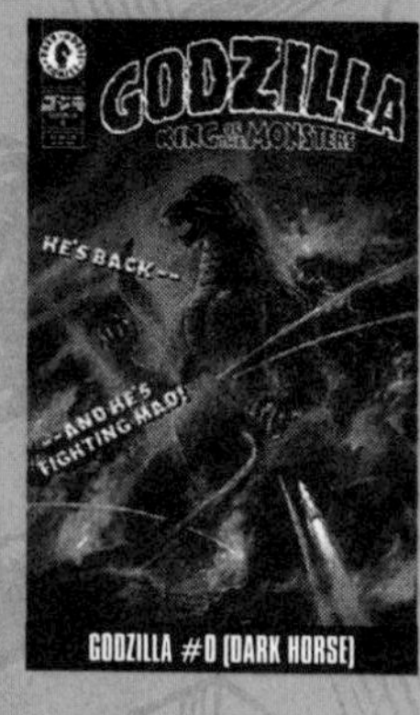

GODZILLA #0 (DARK HORSE)

GOLDEN ARROW #1

GOLDEN LAD #1

GRAVESTONE #1

a b c d e f g h i j k l m n o p q r s t u v w x y z

GREAT COMICS #1

GREEN ARROW #0 (2ND SERIES)

GREEN ARROW: THE WONDER YEAR #1

GREEN HORNET #2 (3RD SERIES)

GREEN LANTERN COMICS #1

DC's Golden Age Green Lantern, Alan Scott, scored his own title after a run in *All-American Comics.* Appearing for only 38 issues, the character is still around, having been de-aged and changed into the hero known as Sentinel.

17-23 .... 7.00 22.00

GORGO'S REVENGE
CHARLTON (1962)
NO# Title changes to The Return Of Gorgo with #2. .... 10.00 30.00

GOTHAM BY GASLIGHT
DC (1989)
NO# One-shot. 1.00 3.95

GOVERNOR AND J.J., THE
GOLD KEY (1970)
1 TV photo covers on all issues. 8.00 25.00
2 .... 5.00 15.00
3 .... 2.75 10.00

GRAFIK MUZIK
CALIBER (1990)
1 .... 1.00 3.50
2-4 .... .75 2.50

GRAND PRIX
CHARLTON (1967-1970)
16 Previous title: Hot Rod Racers. 7.00 20.00
17-20 .... 6.00 18.00
21-31 .... 5.00 15.00

GRANDMA DUCK'S FARM FRIENDS
DELL FOUR COLOR SERIES (1957-1962)
763 (1/57) 13.00 40.00
873 (1/58) 8.00 25.00
965 (1/59) 7.00 20.00
1010 Art: Carl Barks. (7/59) 20.00 75.00
1073 Art: Carl Barks. (1/60) 20.00 75.00
1161 Art: Carl Barks. (2/61) 20.00 75.00
1279 (1/62) 10.00 30.00

GRAPHIC FANTASY
AJAX (1981)
1-2 .... .30 1.00

GRAVESTONE
MALIBU (1993-CURRENT)
1 .... .75 2.25
2 Direct market edition (with poster). .... .75 2.25
2A Newsstand edition (without poster). .... .50 1.95
3-9 .... .75 2.25

GRAY GHOST, THE
DELL FOUR COLOR SERIES (1958-1959)
911 Movie photo cover. (6/58) 19.00 60.00
1000 Movie photo cover. (6/59) 16.00 50.00

GREAT ACTION COMICS
I.W. (1958)
1 .... 2.25 8.00
8 Reprint: Phantom Lady 15. .... 23.00 75.00
9 Reprint: Phantom Lady 23. .... 23.00 75.00

GREAT CAT FAMILY, THE
DELL FOUR COLOR SERIES (1956)
750 Disney movie tie-in. (11/56) 11.00 35.00

GREAT COMICS
GREAT (1941-1942)
1 1st & Origin: The Great Zarro. (11/41) 220.00 700.00
2 (12/41) 110.00 360.00
3 Hitler cover. Movie tie-in: The Lost City. (1/42) 220.00 700.00

GREAT COMICS
NOVACK (1945)
1 Cover: L.B. Cole. 50.00 150.00

GREAT EXPLOITS
DECKER (1957)
1 .... 10.00 30.00

GREAT LOCOMOTIVE CHASE, THE
DELL FOUR COLOR SERIES (1956)
712 Disney movie photo cover. (7/56) 11.00 35.00

GREAT LOVER ROMANCES
TOBY (1951-1955)
1 Photo cover. 16.00 50.00
2 Photo cover. 8.00 25.00
3 Photo cover. 5.00 15.00
4-5 Title variance: Young Lover Romances. Photo cover. 5.00 15.00
6-9 .... 5.00 15.00
10 Photo cover (Rita Hayworth). 8.00 25.00
11 Photo cover (same shot as #2). 5.00 15.00
12-14 .... 5.00 15.00
15 Photo cover (Elizabeth Taylor). 5.00 15.00
16-22 .... 5.00 15.00

GREAT RACE, THE
DELL (1966)
12-299-603 Movie photo cover. 8.00 25.00

GREAT WESTERN (A-1 SERIES)
ME (1954)
8 (A-1 #93). 23.00 75.00
9 (A-1 #105). 16.00 50.00
10 (A-1 #113). 16.00 50.00
11 (A-1 #127). 16.00 50.00

GREEN ARROW
DC (1983)
1 .... 1.25 4.00
2 .... .75 2.25

GREEN ARROW
DC (1988-CURRENT)
0 (8/94) .... .50 1.95
1 .... 1.75 6.00
2 .... 1.00 3.00
3-54 .... .75 2.00
55-74 .... .50 1.50
75 .... .75 2.50
76-86 .... .50 1.50
87-90 .... .50 1.95

GREEN ARROW ANNUAL
DC (1988-CURRENT)
1 (1988) 1.25 4.00
2 (1989) 1.00 3.25
3 (1990) 1.00 3.00
4 (1991) 1.00 3.00
5 (1992) 1.00 3.00
6 (1993) 1.00 3.50

GREEN ARROW: THE LONG BOW HUNTERS
DC (1987)
1 1st: Shado. 2.25 8.00
1 (2ND) 2nd printing. .... .75 2.00
2 .... 1.75 6.00
2 (2ND) 2nd printing. .... .75 2.00
3 .... 1.75 6.00
TPB Reprints issues #1-3. .... 4.00 12.95

GREEN ARROW: THE WONDER YEAR
DC (1993)
1-4 .... .30 1.00

GREEN GIANT COMICS
PELICAN (1940)
1 Green Giant, Master Mystic, Mundoo, Black Arrow, Dr. Nerod; Origin: Colossus. 1800.00 7000.00

GREEN HORNET, THE
DELL FOUR COLOR SERIES (1953)
496 (9/53) 55.00 175.00

GREEN HORNET, THE
GOLD KEY (1966-1967)
1 TV Photo covers on all issues. "Ring Of Terror!" 40.00 125.00
2-3 .... 28.00 90.00

GREEN HORNET, THE
NOW (1989-1991)
1 .... 2.25 8.00
2 .... 1.50 5.00
3-6 .... 1.25 4.00
7 .... 1.00 3.00
8-14 .... .75 2.00

GREEN HORNET, THE
NOW (1991-CURRENT)
1-37 .... .50 1.50

38-46 .75 2.50
ANNUAL 1 (1992) .50 1.50
ANNUAL 2 (1993) .50 1.50

GREEN HORNET: ANNIVERSARY SPECIAL
NOW (1992)
1-3 .75 2.00

GREEN HORNET COMICS
HARVEY (1940-1949)
1 1st: Green Hornet. 500.00 1800.00
2 250.00 825.00
3 200.00 650.00
4-5 145.00 480.00
6 (8/41) 145.00 480.00
7 (6/42) 130.00 420.00
8-12 110.00 360.00
13-18 95.00 300.00
19-24 85.00 270.00
25-30 75.00 240.00
31 Begin: The Man In Black. 85.00 270.00
32-38 65.00 210.00
39 Stuntman by Simon & Kirby. 75.00 240.00
40-45 55.00 180.00
46 "Case Of The Marijuana Racket!" 55.00 180.00
47 55.00 180.00

GREEN HORNET: DARK TOMORROW
NOW (1993)
1-3 .75 2.50

GREEN HORNET: SOLITARY SENTINEL
NOW (1992-1993)
1-3 .75 2.50

GREEN JET COMICS, THE
METROPOLITAN (1950)
1 Giveaway (5.25 x 8.5, bound at top). Contains Green Lama by Mac Raboy. 35.00 110.00

GREEN LAMA
SPARK (1944-1946)
1 Cover/Art: Mac Raboy on all issues. 220.00 700.00
2 130.00 420.00
3-8 110.00 360.00

GREEN LANTERN
DC (1960-1986)
1 Origin retold: Green Lantern (see Showcase #22). "Menace Of The Giant Puppet!" 700.00 2600.00
2 1st: Pieface. "Secret Of The Golden Thunderbolts!" 180.00 575.00
3 "Amazing Theft Of The Power Lamp!" 100.00 330.00
4 "The Diabolical Missile From Qward!" 80.00 260.00
5 1st & Origin: Hector Hammond. "The Power Ring That Vanished!" 80.00 260.00
6 "World Of Living Phantoms!" 70.00 225.00
7 1st & Origin: Sinestro. 55.00 180.00
8-9 50.00 165.00
10 1st 12 cent cover price. 50.00 165.00
11-12 50.00 165.00
13 Flash. 65.00 200.00
14 1st & Origin: Sonar. 40.00 125.00
15 40.00 125.00
16 1st & Origin: Star Sapphire. 50.00 150.00
17 "The Spy-Eye That Doomed Green Lantern!" 35.00 115.00
18-19 35.00 115.00
20 App: Flash. 40.00 130.00
21 1st & Origin: Dr. Polaris. 31.00 100.00
22-23 31.00 100.00
24 1st & Origin: Shark. "The Shark That Hunted Human Prey!" and "The Strange World Named Green Lantern!" 31.00 100.00
25 "War Of The Weapon Wizards!" 31.00 100.00
26-30 31.00 100.00
31 23.00 75.00
32 "The Power Battery Peril!" 23.00 75.00
33-39 23.00 75.00
40 First mention of Crisis. Origin: Guardians. (10/65) 100.00 325.00
41-42 17.00 55.00
43 App: Flash. 17.00 55.00
44 17.00 55.00
45 App: Golden Age Green Lantern. 23.00 75.00
46-48 19.00 60.00
49 "The Spectacular Robberies Of TV's Master Villain!" 19.00 60.00
50 "Thraxon The Powerful Vs. Green Lantern The Powerless!" (1/67) 19.00 60.00
51 11.00 35.00
52 App: GA Green Lantern. 16.00 50.00
53-58 11.00 35.00
59 1st: Guy Gardner. (3/68) 60.00 180.00
60 8.00 25.00
61 App: GA Green Lantern. 13.00 40.00
62-69 8.00 25.00
70 1st 15 cent cover price. 6.00 18.00
71-75 5.00 15.00
76 Begin: Neal Adams art. 35.00 120.00
77 16.00 50.00
78 Art: Neal Adams. 13.00 40.00
79-80 Art: Neal Adams. 11.00 35.00
81 Art: Neal Adams. (12/70) 10.00 30.00
82-84 Art: Neal Adams. 10.00 30.00
85 Art: Neal Adams. Drug/hypo cover. Drug story. (8-9/71) 13.00 40.00
86 Art: Neal Adams. GA reprint. 13.00 40.00
87 Art: Neal Adams. 1st: John Stewart. 10.00 30.00
88 Art: Neal Adams. Spiro Agnew anti-establishment cover. (4-5/71) 2.00 7.00
89 Art: Neal Adams. Golden Age Green Lantern reprint from #38, "The Impossible Mr. Paradox!". 7.00 20.00
90 Art: Mike Grell. 1.50 5.00
91-92 1.50 5.00
93-95 1.25 4.00
96-99 1.00 3.00
100 1st: Airwave II. Double size. 1.50 5.00
101 1.50 5.00
102 1.25 4.00
103 1.00 3.00
104-107 1.50 5.00
108-110 Backup story: GA Green Lantern. 1.50 5.00
111 Origin retold. 1.25 4.00
112 Origin retold: GA Green Lantern. 2.25 8.00
113-115 1.00 3.00
116 1st: Guy Gardner as Green Lantern. 8.00 25.00
117-118 1.00 3.00
119-122 .75 2.00
123 1.75 6.00
124-140 .75 2.00
141 1st: Omega Men. 1.50 5.00
142-143 1.00 3.50
144 1.00 3.00
145-149 .75 2.00
150 Double size Anniversary issue. 1.00 3.00
151-181 .75 2.00
182 John Stewart becomes Green Lantern. .75 2.00
183-187 .75 2.00
188 1.25 4.00
189-193 .75 2.00
194 Battle: Guy Gardner/Hal Jordan. .75 2.00
195 Guy Gardner becomes Green Lantern. 4.00 12.00
196-197 .75 2.00
198 1.00 3.00
199 .75 2.00
200 Double size. Becomes Green Lantern Corps. #201. .75 2.00

GREEN LANTERN
DC (1990-CURRENT)
0 (8/94) 1.25 4.00
1 1.00 3.00
2-12 .75 2.00
13 Double size. .75 2.00
14-18 .75 2.00
19 50th Anniversary issue. .75 2.00
20-24 .50 1.50
25 Battle: Guy Gardner/Hal Jordan. .75 2.00
26 .25 1.00
27-45 .25 1.00
46 Reign of the Supermen, pt.19. 2.50 9.00
47 Green Arrow. 1.75 6.00
48 1st: Kyle Rayner. 2.00 7.00
49 1.25 4.50
50 Glow-in-the-dark cover. 1.50 5.50
51 1.00 3.50
52 .75 2.00
53-54 .50 1.50
55 .75 2.00
56-62 .50 1.50
63-66 .50 1.75
ANNUAL 1 Darkness Within. (1992) .75 2.50
ANNUAL 2 Bloodlines, pt.7. (1993) .75 2.50
ANNUAL 3 Elseworlds story. (1994) .75 2.95
TPB The Road Back. Reprints issues #1-8. (1992) 2.25 8.95

GREEN LANTERN COMICS
DC (1941-1949)
1 Origin retold (from All-American #16). 6300.00 25000.00
2 "Secret Of The Golden Thunderbolts" 1200.00 4600.00
3 700.00 2700.00
4 700.00 2500.00
5 500.00 1800.00
6 500.00 1600.00
7-8 400.00 1500.00
9 "The School For Vandals!" (Late Fall, '43) 400.00 1200.00
10 1st & Origin: Vandal Savage. 400.00 1300.00
11 300.00 1100.00
12 1st & Origin: Gambler. "Doiby Dickles Enters High Sassiety!" (Summer, '44) 300.00 1100.00
13-15 280.00 925.00
16-20 270.00 875.00
21-26 250.00 800.00
27 1st & Origin: Sky Pirate. 250.00 800.00
28 "The Tricks Of The Sportsmaster!" 250.00 800.00
29-30 250.00 800.00
31-34 230.00 750.00
35-38 270.00 875.00

GREEN LANTERN CORPS
DC (1986-1988)
201 1st: new Corps. Previous title: Green Lantern. .50 1.50
202-223 .50 1.50
224 Double size. 1.00 3.50
ANNUAL 1 See Tales Of The Green Lantern Corps.
ANNUAL 2 (1986) .75 2.75
ANNUAL 3 (1987) .75 2.50

GREEN LANTERN CORPS QUARTERLY
DC (1992-1994)
1-5 .75 2.50
6-8 .75 2.95

GREEN LANTERN EMERALD DAWN
DC (1989-1990)
1 Origin: Hal Jordan. 1.75 6.00
2 1.25 4.00
3-6 .75 2.00
TPB Reprints issues #1-6. 1.25 4.95

GREEN LANTERN: EMERALD DAWN II
DC (1991)
1 .75 2.00
2-6 .50 1.25

GREEN LANTERN: GANTHET'S TALE
DC (1992)
NO# 1.50 5.95

GREEN LANTERN: MOSIAC
DC (1992-1993)
1-2 .75 2.00
3-18 .50 1.25

GREEN LANTERN/GREEN ARROW
DC (1983-1984)
1 Series reprints original Green Lanterns #'s 76-89. 1.00 3.00
2-7 1.00 3.00

GREEN MASK
FOX (1940-1944)
1 Origin The Green Mask. 300.00 1100.00
2 180.00 575.00
3 Art: Bob Powell. 125.00 400.00
4 95.00 310.00
5 70.00 230.00
6 65.00 200.00
7-9 55.00 170.00
10-11 45.00 140.00

GREEN MASK
FOX (1945-1946)
1 (Volume 2) 31.00 100.00
2 28.00 90.00
3 25.00 80.00
4-6 22.00 70.00

GREEN PLANET, THE
CHARLTON (1962)
NO# 13.00 40.00

GRENDEL
COMICO (1983-1984)
1 19.00 60.00
2-3 13.00 40.00

GRENDEL
COMICO (1986-1991)
1 1.50 5.00
2 1.25 4.00
3 1.00 3.50
4 Cover: Dave Stevens. 1.00 3.50
5-6 1.00 3.50
7-10 1.00 3.00
11-15 .75 2.00
16 Mage. 1.25 4.00
17-19 Mage. .75 2.25
20-32 .75 2.25
33 Double size. .75 2.25
34-40 .75 2.25

GRENDEL CLASSICS
DARK HORSE (1995-CURRENT)
1 Reprints. 1.00 3.95

GREEN LANTERN #4

GREEN LANTERN #19

GREEN LANTERN COMICS #8

GRIFTER ONE-SHOT

GROO THE WANDERER #116

GUARDIANS OF THE GALAXY #46

GUY GARDNER, WARRIOR #20

HAMMER OF GOD: BUTCH #2

GRENDEL: DEVIL BY THE DEED
DARK HORSE (1993)
- 1 Reprints 1st Grendel Graphic Novel (new cover & pin-ups). 1.00 3.95

GRENDEL TALES
DARK HORSE (1993-1994)
- 1-6 .75 2.95
- TPB Reprints issues #1-6. 6.00 17.95

GRENDEL TALES: DEVIL IN OUR MIDST
DARK HORSE (1994)
- 1-5 .75 2.95

GRENDEL TALES: DEVIL'S CHOICES
DARK HORSE (1995)
- 1-4 .75 2.95

GRENDEL TALES: DEVILS AND DEATHS
DARK HORSE (1994)
- 1-2 .75 2.95

GRENDEL TALES: HOMECOMING
DARK HORSE (1994-1995)
- 1-3 .75 2.95

GRENDEL TALES: THE DEVIL'S HAMMER
DARK HORSE (1994)
- 1 .75 2.50
- 2-3 .75 2.95

GRENDEL: WAR CHILD
DARK HORSE (1992-1993)
- 1 1.50 5.00
- 2-9 1.00 3.00
- 10 Double size (3.50). 1.25 4.00
- HC Limited signed edition. Reprints #1-10. 30.00 99.95
- TPB Reprints issues #1-10 plus new material. 6.00 18.95

GRENDEL/BATMAN
DC (1993)
- 2 Part 2 of Batman/Grendel. 1.25 4.95

GREY LEGACY
FRAGILE ELITE (1993)
- 1 .75 2.50

GREYFRIARS BOBBY
DELL FOUR COLOR SERIES (1961)
- 1189 Movie photo cover. (11/61) 14.00 45.00

GRIFTER
IMAGE (1995)
- 1 One shot. 1.75 7.00

GRIFTER
IMAGE (1995-CURRENT)
- 1 With cards. 1.50 5.00
- 1A Newsstand edition (no cards). .50 2.00
- 2-3 .75 3.00

GRIM GHOST, THE
ATLAS(SEABOARD) (1975)
- 1 Origin: Grim Ghost. .75 2.00
- 2-3 .30 1.00

GRIM WIT
LAST GASP (1972)
- 1 2.75 10.00
- 2 1.75 6.00

GRIMJACK
FIRST (1984-1991)
- 1 .50 1.50
- 2-25 .50 1.25
- 26 Teenage Mutant Ninja Turtles (2nd time in full color). 1.75 6.00
- 27-74 .50 1.25
- 75 (5.95) 1.50 5.95
- 76-81 .50 1.25

GRIMM'S GHOST STORIES
GOLD KEY (1972-1982)
- 1 1.50 5.00
- 2 1.00 3.00
- 3-4 .75 2.00
- 5 Art: Williamson. .75 2.00
- 6-7 .75 2.00
- 8 Art: Williamson. .75 2.00
- 9-12 .75 2.00
- 13-16 .50 1.50
- 17 Art: Reed Crandall. .50 1.50
- 18-24 .50 1.50
- 25-40 .50 1.25
- 41-60 .30 1.00

GRIN AND BEAR IT
SEE LARGE FEATURE COMICS #28.

G.R.I.P., THE
ECLIPSE (1994)
- 1-2 .50 1.50

GRIPS
SILVERWOLF (1986)
- 1 Cover/Art: Tim Vigil in all issues. 8.00 25.00
- 2 5.00 15.00
- 3-4 4.00 12.00

GRIT GRADY COMICS
HOLYOKE (1944-1945)
- 1 From the Holyoke One-Shot series. 19.00 60.00

GROO
IMAGE (1995-CURRENT)
- 1-8 .50 1.95

GROO CHRONICLES, THE
MARVEL(EPIC) (1989-1990)
- 1 1.75 6.00
- 2-6 1.00 3.00

GROO SPECIAL
ECLIPSE (1984)
- 1 Cover/Art: Sergio Aragones. 10.00 30.00

GROO THE WANDERER
MARVEL (1985-1994)
- 1 2.00 7.00
- 2 1.50 5.00
- 3-12 1.25 4.00
- 13-28 1.00 3.00
- 29 1.25 4.00
- 30-41 .75 2.00
- 42-49 .50 1.25
- 50 Double size. .50 1.25
- 51-86 .50 1.25
- 87-99 .75 2.25
- 100 (2.95) .75 2.95
- 101-120 .75 2.95

GROO, THE WANDERER
PACIFIC (1982-1984)
- 1 Cover&art: Sergio Aragones in all issues. 8.00 25.00
- 2 5.00 15.00
- 3-7 2.75 10.00
- 8 4.00 12.00

GROOVY
MARVEL (1968)
- 1 Monkees, Ringo Starr, Sonny & Cher, Mamas and Papas photos inside. 9.00 27.00
- 2-3 7.00 22.00

GUADALCANAL DIARY
DAVID MCKAY (1945)
- NO# From the American Library series. 40.00 125.00

GUARDIANS OF METROPOLIS
DC (1994)
- 1-4 .50 1.50

GUARDIANS OF THE GALAXY
MARVEL (1990-1995)
- 1 1.50 5.00
- 2 .75 2.00
- 3 .50 1.50
- 4-8 .75 2.00
- 9 1st full App: Rancor. .75 2.00
- 10-12 .75 2.00
- 13 1st: Spirit Of Vengeance. .75 2.00
- 14 Spirit Of Vengeance continued. .75 2.00
- 15 .75 2.00
- 16 Double size. .75 2.00
- 17-20 .75 2.00
- 21 App: Rancor. .50 1.50
- 22-23 .50 1.50
- 24 Silver Surfer. .50 1.50
- 25 Prism cover. (2.50) .75 2.50
- 26-38 .50 1.25
- 39 Embossed foil cover. Dr. Doom vs. Rancor. (2.95) .75 2.95
- 40-49 .50 1.25
- 50 Foil embossed cover. Double size. .75 2.95
- 50A Regular cover. .50 1.25
- 51-61 .50 1.25
- 62 Double size. .75 2.50
- TPB Reprints issues #1-6. 4.00 12.95

GUARDIANS OF THE GALAXY ANNUAL
MARVEL (1991-CURRENT)
- 1 (1991) .75 2.50
- 2 1st: Galactic Guardians. (1992) .75 2.50
- 3 Bagged with trading card. (1993) .75 2.95
- 4 (1994) .75 2.95

GULLIVER'S TRAVELS
DELL (1965-1966)
- 1 5.00 15.00
- 2 2.75 10.00
- 3 2.25 8.00

GUMPS, THE
DELL (1947)
- 1 19.00 60.00
- 2 16.00 50.00
- 3 13.00 40.00
- 4-5 10.00 30.00

GUMPS, THE
DELL FOUR COLOR SERIES (1945)
- 73 25.00 80.00

GUN GLORY
DELL FOUR COLOR SERIES (1957)
- 846 Movie photo cover. (10/57) 31.00 100.00

GUN RUNNER
MARVEL (1993)
- 1 Bagged w/ cards. .75 2.75
- 2-6 .50 1.75

GUN THAT WON THE WEST
WINCHESTER (1956)
- NO# "The Story Of Winchester." 8.00 25.00

GUNFIGHTER
EC (1948-1950)
- 5 App: Moon Girl. 100.00 330.00
- 6 App: Moon Girl. 70.00 220.00
- 7-13 50.00 160.00
- 14 Title changes to Haunt Of Fear with #15. 50.00 160.00

GUNFIGHTERS IN HELL
REBEL (1993)
- 1-2 .30 1.00

GUNFIRE
DC (1994-1995)
- 0-10 .30 1.00

GUNHAWK
MARVEL (1950-1951)
- 12 19.00 60.00
- 13-18 14.00 45.00

GUNHAWKS
MARVEL (1972-1973)
- 1 1.25 4.00
- 2 1.00 3.00
- 3-7 .75 2.00

GUNS AGAINST GANGSTERS
CURTIS (1948-1949)
- 1 31.00 100.00
- 2 19.00 60.00
- 3-6 13.00 40.00
- V2#1 10.00 30.00
- V2#2 13.00 40.00

GUNSLINGER
DELL FOUR COLOR SERIES (1961)
- 1220 TV photo cover. (8/61) 17.00 55.00

GUNSLINGER
MARVEL (1973)
- 2 Previous title: Tex Dawson. .75 2.00
- 3 .75 2.00

GUNSMITH CATS
DARK HORSE (1995-CURRENT)
- 1-6 .75 2.95

GUNSMOKE
DELL (1956-1961)
- 1 (#679) From the 4-Color Series. TV photo cover. (2/56) 40.00 125.00
- 2 (#720) From the 4-Color Series. "The Hunter", TV photo cover. (8/56) 16.00 50.00
- 3 (#769) From the 4-Color Series. "The Marshal's Gamble", TV photo cover (James Arness). (2/57) 16.00 50.00
- 4 (#797) From the 4-Color Series. TV photo cover (James Arness). (5/57) 16.00 50.00
- 5 (#844) From the 4-Color Series. TV photo cover (James Arness). (8/57) 14.00 45.00

6-12 13.00 40.00
13-20 10.00 30.00
21-27 8.00 25.00

GUNSMOKE
GOLD KEY (1969-1970)
1 8.00 25.00
2-3 5.00 15.00
4-6 2.75 10.00

GUNSMOKE
YOUTHFUL (1949-1952)
1 Begin: Masked Marvel by Graham Ingels. 50.00 150.00
2-3 31.00 100.00
4-6 19.00 60.00
7-10 11.00 35.00
11-14 8.00 25.00
15-16 10.00 30.00

GUNSMOKE FILM STORY
GOLD KEY (1962)
30008-211 100 page Giant. 19.00 60.00

GUNSMOKE WESTERN
ATLAS (1955-1963)
32 19.00 60.00
33-36 13.00 40.00
37-40 11.00 35.00
41-45 10.00 30.00
46-50 8.00 25.00
51-60 7.00 20.00
61-70 5.00 15.00
71 4.00 12.00
72 Origin: Kid Colt. 4.00 12.00
73-77 4.00 12.00

GUY GARDNER
DC (1992-CURRENT)
0 (8/94) .50 1.50
1-16 .50 1.50
17 Title changes to Guy Gardner, Warrior. .50 1.50
18 .50 1.50
19 Twilight aftermath. 1.75 6.00
20 vs. Hal Jordan. 1.50 5.00
21 vs. Hal Jordan. 1.25 4.50
22-24 .50 1.50
25 Double size. .75 2.50
26-28 .50 1.50
29 Double "barn door" type cover. .75 2.95
29A Regular cover. .50 1.50
30 .50 1.50
31-34 .50 1.75
ANNUAL 1 (1995) 1.00 3.50

GUY GARDNER REBORN
DC (1992)
1 App: Lobo. 1.25 4.95
2-3 1.25 4.95

GYPSY COLT
DELL FOUR COLOR SERIES (1954)
568 (6/54) 11.00 35.00

GYRO GEARLOOSE
DELL (1962)
01-329-207 7.00 20.00

GYRO GEARLOOSE
DELL FOUR COLOR SERIES (1959-1961)
1047 Cover & art: Carl Barks. (11/59) 31.00 100.00
1095 Art: Carl Barks. (4/60) 19.00 60.00
1184 Art: Carl Barks. (12/61) 23.00 75.00
1267 Cover & art: Carl Barks. (11/60) 19.00 60.00

HA HA COMICS
CRESTON/ACG (1943-1955)
1 40.00 130.00
2 20.00 65.00
3-6 14.00 44.00
7-12 10.00 33.00
13-24 9.00 28.00
25-36 8.00 24.00
37-50 6.00 19.00
51-70 5.00 16.00
71-80 4.00 13.00
81 Begin: ACG publication. 4.00 11.00
82-90 4.00 11.00
91-94 2.25 8.75
95 3-D effect cover. 14.00 44.00
96-99 2.25 8.75

HACKER FILES, THE
DC (1992-1993)
1-12 .30 1.00

HALL OF HEROES
HALL OF HEROES (1993)
1 1st: Deadbolt. 5.00 15.00
2-3 .75 2.50

HALLELUJAH TRAIL, THE
DELL (1966)
12-307-602 Movie photo (inserts) cover. 10.00 30.00

HAMMER OF GOD: BUTCH
DARK HORSE (1994)
1 .75 2.95
2-3 .75 2.50

HAND OF FATE
ACE (1951-1955)
8 Previous title: Men Against Crime. 45.00 140.00
9 26.00 85.00
10 23.00 75.00
11-18 20.00 65.00
19 22.00 70.00
20-23 17.00 55.00
24 25.00 80.00
25-26 17.00 55.00

HANGMAN COMICS
MLJ (1942-1943)
2 Previous title: Special Comics. 310.00 1000.00
3 200.00 650.00
4 155.00 500.00
5-6 180.00 575.00
7-8 170.00 550.00

HANK
PENTAGON (1946)
NO# Coulton Waugh newspaper strip reprints. 10.00 30.00

HANNA-BARBERA BANDWAGON
GOLD KEY (1962-1963)
1 Giant size. App: Augie Doggie. 19.00 60.00
2 Giant size. 16.00 50.00
3-4 8.00 25.00

HANNA-BARBERA SUPER TV HEROES
GOLD KEY (1968-1969)
1 31.00 100.00
2 23.00 75.00
3 Space Ghost. 23.00 75.00
4-5 16.00 50.00
6-7 Space Ghost. 23.00 75.00

HANS BRINKER
DELL FOUR COLOR SERIES (1962)
1273 Movie photo cover. (2/62) 13.00 40.00

HANS CHRISTIAN ANDERSEN
ZIFF-DAVIS (1953)
NO# Movie photo cover (with Danny Kaye). 40.00 125.00

HANSEL AND GRETEL
DELL FOUR COLOR SERIES (1954)
590 (10/54) 11.00 35.00

HAP HAZARD COMICS
ACE (1944-1949)
1 19.00 60.00
2 10.00 30.00
3-4 8.00 25.00
5-6 7.00 20.00
7-12 5.00 15.00
13 2.75 10.00
14 Cover: Al Feldstein. 10.00 30.00
15-24 2.75 10.00

HAPPIEST MILLIONAIRE, THE
GOLD KEY (1968)
10221-804 Disney movie tie-in. 5.00 15.00

HAPPY BIRTHDAY, MARTHA WASHINGTON
DARK HORSE (1995)
NO# One shot. .75 2.95

HAPPY COMICS
NEDOR/STANDARD (1943-1950)
1 40.00 130.00
2 20.00 65.00
3-6 15.00 49.00
7-12 10.00 33.00
13-20 9.00 27.00
21-31 7.00 22.00
32 Art: Frank Frazetta (7 pages). 20.00 65.00
33 Art: Frank Frazetta (12 pages). 35.00 110.00
34-40 7.00 22.00

HAPPY DAYS
GOLD KEY (1979-1980)
1 TV photo covers on all issues. 2.25 8.00
2 1.50 5.00
3-6 1.00 3.00

HAPPY HOULIHANS
EC (1947)
1 Origin: Moon Girl. 85.00 270.00
2 Title changes to Saddle Justice with #3. 40.00 130.00

HARBINGER
VALIANT (1992-1995)
0 With Trade Paperback. 1.75 6.00
0A Sendaway; pink logo. 6.00 18.00
1 1st: Harbinger. 6.00 18.00
1A Coupon cut out. .75 2.00
2 2.75 10.00
2A Coupon cut out. .75 2.00
3 1.75 6.00
3A Coupon cut out. .75 2.00
4 1.75 6.00
4A Coupon cut out. .75 2.00
5 1.75 6.00
5A Coupon cut out. .75 2.00
6 Death: Torque. 1.25 4.00
6A Coupon cut out. .30 1.00
7 1.00 3.00
8-9 Unity. 1.00 3.00
10 1st: H.A.R.D. Corps. 1.00 3.00
11 Elfquest crossover. .75 2.00
12-13 .75 2.00
14 1st: Stronghold. .75 2.00
15-18 .75 2.00
19 1st: Stunner. .75 2.00
20-24 .75 2.00
25 (3.50 cp) .75 2.00
26-40 .75 2.00
41 .75 2.50
TPB Bagged with #0 and trading card. 5.00 15.00

HARBINGER FILES: HARADA
VALIANT (1994)
1-2 .75 2.50

HARD BOILED
DARK HORSE (1990-1991)
1 Art: Frank Miller in all issues. 1.75 6.50
2-3 1.75 6.00
HC Signed and numbered. Reprints issues #1-3 with extra pages. 30.00 99.95
TPB Reprints issues #1-3. 5.00 14.95

H.A.R.D. CORPS
VALIANT (1992-1995)
1 1.00 3.00
1A Gold logo variant. 2.75 10.00
2-5 .75 2.50
5A With Comic Defense logo. .75 2.50
6-9 .75 2.25
10 Turok. .75 2.25
11-30 .75 2.25

HARD ROCK COMICS
REVOLUTIONARY (1993-CURRENT)
1-27 .75 2.50

HARDCASE
MALIBU (1993-CURRENT)
0 8 page San Diego Comic Con special. 1.00 3.50
1 1st: Hardcase. 1.25 4.00
1B Hologram edition. 2.25 8.00
1C Ultra limited/foil edition. 1.25 4.00
1D Gold hologram edition. 2.25 8.00
2 Polybagged with trading card. 1.00 3.00
3-22 .75 2.00
23-25 .75 2.50

HARDWARE
DC (1993-CURRENT)
1 Direct Market. 1.00 3.00
1A Newsstand. .50 1.75
1B Platinum edition. 1.50 5.00
2-15 .50 1.50
16 Collector's "barn-door" cover version. 1.00 3.95
16A Regular edition. .50 1.95
17 .50 1.50
18-24 .50 1.75
25 Double size. .75 2.95
26-28 .50 1.75
29 .30 1.00
30-31 .75 2.50

HARDY BOYS, THE
DELL FOUR COLOR SERIES (1956-1959)
760 TV photo cover. (12/56) 28.00 90.00
830 "The Secret Of The Old Mill" TV photo cover. (8/57) 19.00 60.00

HARBINGER #23

H.A.R.D. CORPS #8

HARDCASE #5

HARDWARE #1

a b c d e f g h i j k l m n o p q r s t u v w x y z

HAUNT OF FEAR #8

HAUNTED THRILLS #2

HAUNTED THRILLS #10

HAVOK & WOLVERINE: MELTDOWN #2

FAMOUS • FIRSTS

HEROIC COMICS #1

You gotta love a comic that stars the Purple Zombie! It also features Hydroman by Bill Everett, who earlier created the Sub-Mariner. But starting with #16, it cover-featured everyday heroes, especially soldiers in combat.

887 TV photo cover. (1/58) 19.00 60.00
964 TV photo cover. (1/59) 19.00 60.00

HARDY BOYS, THE
GOLD KEY (1970-1971)
1 TV tie-in. 4.00 12.00
2-4 .... 2.00 7.00

HARLAN ELLISON'S DREAM CORRIDOR
DARK HORSE (1995-CURRENT)
1 .... 1.25 4.50
2-3 .... 1.00 3.50
4-5 .... .75 2.95
SPECIAL 1 .... 1.50 5.50

HARLEM GLOBETROTTERS
GOLD KEY (1972-1975)
1 TV cartoon tie-in. 1.50 5.00
2-12 .... .75 2.50

HAROLD TEEN
CUPPLES & LEON (1931)
1931 .... 31.00 100.00

HAROLD TEEN
DELL FOUR COLOR SERIES (1942-1949)
2 .... 65.00 200.00
209 .... 8.00 25.00

HARSH REALM
HARRIS (1994)
1-5 .... .75 2.95

HARVEY
MARVEL (1970-1972)
1 .... 2.75 10.00
2 .... 1.75 6.00
3-6 .... 1.25 4.00

HARVEY 3-D HITS
HARVEY (1954)
1 Featuring Sad Sack. With glasses. ... 40.00 125.00

HARVEY COMICS HITS
HARVEY (1951-1953)
51 The Phantom. 31.00 100.00
52 Steve Canyon's Air Power. 16.00 50.00
53 Mandrake. 23.00 75.00
54 Tim Tyler's Tales Of Jungle Terror. 13.00 40.00
55 Love Stories Of Mary Worth. 7.00 20.00
56 The Phantom. 23.00 75.00
57 Rip Kirby Exposes The Kidnap Racket by Alex Raymond. 23.00 75.00
58 Girls In White. 7.00 20.00
59 Tales Of The Invisible (featuring Scarlet O'Neil). 13.00 40.00
60 Paramount Animated Comics (#1). Baby Huey, Casper. 70.00 225.00
61 Casper The Friendly Ghost (previously Casper The Friendly Ghost #5, becomes Casper The Friendly Ghost #7). 65.00 200.00
62 Paramount Animated Comics (#2). 16.00 50.00

HARVEY COMICS LIBRARY
SEE TEENAGE DOPE SLAVES #1 & BLACKMAIL TERROR #2

HARVEY HITS
HARVEY (1957-1967)
1 The Phantom. 35.00 110.00
2 Rags Rabbit. 2.75 10.00
3 Richie Rich. 125.00 400.00
4 Little Dot's Uncles. 20.00 65.00
5 Stevie, Mazie's Boy Friend. 2.75 10.00
6 The Phantom. 23.00 75.00
7 Wendy The Good Little Witch. 23.00 75.00
8 Sad Sack's Army Life. 8.00 25.00
9 Richie Rich's Golden Deeds. 70.00 225.00
10 Little Lotta's Lunch-Box. 16.00 50.00
11 Little Audrey's Summer Fun. 10.00 30.00
12 The Phantom. Cover: Jack Kirby. ... 16.00 50.00
13 Little Dot's Uncles. 13.00 40.00
14 Herman and Katnip. 2.75 10.00
15 The Phantom. 17.00 55.00
16 Wendy The Good Little Witch. 13.00 40.00
17 Sad Sack's Army Life. 7.00 20.00
18 Buzzy And The Crow. 4.00 12.00
19 Little Audrey. 7.00 20.00
20 Casper And Spooky. 9.00 28.00
21 Wendy The Good Little Witch. 7.00 22.00
22 Sad Sack's Army Life. 2.75 10.00
23 Wendy The Good Little Witch. 7.00 20.00
24 Little Dot's Uncles. 10.00 30.00
25 Herman And Catnip. 2.25 8.00
26 The Phantom. 14.00 45.00
27 Wendy The Good Little Witch. 7.00 20.00
28 Sad Sack's Army Life. 2.25 8.00
29 Harvey-Toon. 6.00 18.00
30 Wendy The Good Little Witch. 7.00 20.00
31 Herman And Katnip. 1.50 5.00
32 Sad Sack's Army Life. 1.50 5.00
33 Wendy The Good Little Witch. 7.00 20.00
34 Harvey-Toon. 2.75 10.00
35 Friday Funnies. 1.50 5.00
36 The Phantom. 11.00 35.00
37 Casper And Nightmare. 5.00 15.00
38 Harvey-Toon. 2.75 10.00
39 Sad Sack's Army Life. 1.50 5.00
40 Funday Funnies. 1.00 3.00
41 Herman And Katnip. 1.00 3.00
42 Harvey-Toon. 1.50 5.00
43 Sad Sack's Army Life. 1.50 5.00
44 The Phantom. 11.00 35.00
45 Casper And Nightmare. 4.00 12.00
46 Harvey-Toon. 1.50 5.00
47 Sad Sack's Army Life. 1.50 5.00
48 The Phantom. 10.00 30.00
49 Stumbo The Giant. 13.00 40.00
50 Harvey-Toon. 1.50 5.00
51 Sad Sack's Army Life. 1.50 5.00
52 Casper And Nightmare. 4.00 12.00
53 Harvey-Toon. 1.50 5.00
54 Stumbo The Giant. 7.00 22.00
55 Sad Sack's Army Life. 1.50 5.00
56 Casper And Nightmare. 4.00 12.00
57 Stumbo The Giant. 7.00 22.00
58 Sad Sack's Army Life. 1.50 5.00
59 Casper And Nightmare. 4.00 12.00
60 Stumbo The Giant. 7.00 22.00
61 Sad Sack's Army Life. 1.50 5.00
62 Casper And Nightmare. 4.00 12.00
63 Stumbo The Giant. 7.00 22.00
64 Sad Sack's Army Life. 1.50 5.00
65 Casper And Nightmare. 2.75 10.00
66 Stumbo The Giant. 7.00 22.00
67 Sad Sack's Army Life. 1.50 5.00
68 Casper And Nightmare. 2.75 10.00
69 Stumbo The Giant. 7.00 22.00
70 Sad Sack's Army Life. 1.50 5.00
71 Casper And Nightmare. 2.25 8.00
72 Stumbo The Giant. 7.00 22.00
73 Little Sad Sack. 1.50 5.00
74 Sad Sack's Muttsy. 1.50 5.00
75 Casper And Nightmare. 2.25 8.00
76 Little Sad Sack. 1.50 5.00
77 Sad Sack's Muttsy. 1.50 5.00
78 Stumbo The Giant. 7.00 22.00
79 Little Sad Sack. 1.50 5.00
80 Sad Sack's Muttsy. 1.50 5.00
81 Little Sad Sack. 1.50 5.00
82 Sad Sack's Muttsy. 1.50 5.00
83 Little Sad Sack. 1.50 5.00
84 Sad Sack's Muttsy. 1.50 5.00
85 Gabby Gob. 1.50 5.00
86 G.I. Juniors. 1.50 5.00
87 Sad Sack's Muttsy. 1.50 5.00
88 Stumbo The Giant. 7.00 22.00
89 Sad Sack's Muttsy. 1.50 5.00
90 Gabby Gob. 1.50 5.00
91 G.I. Juniors. 1.50 5.00
92 Sad Sack's Muttsy. 1.50 5.00
93 Sadie Sack. 1.50 5.00
94 Gabby Gob. 1.50 5.00
95 G.I. Juniors. 1.50 5.00
96 Sad Sack's Muttsy. 1.50 5.00
97 Gabby Gob. 1.50 5.00
98 G.I. Juniors. 1.50 5.00
99 Sad Sack's Muttsy. 1.50 5.00
100 Gabby Gob. 1.50 5.00
101 G.I. Juniors. 1.50 5.00
102 Sad Sack's Muttsy. 1.50 5.00
103 Gabby Gob. 1.50 5.00
104 G.I. Juniors. 1.50 5.00
105 Sad Sack's Muttsy. 1.50 5.00
106 Gabby Gob. 1.50 5.00
107 G.I. Juniors. 1.50 5.00

108 Sad Sack's Muttsy.	1.50	5.00
109 Gabby Gob.	1.50	5.00
110 G.I. Juniors.	1.50	5.00
111 Sad Sack's Muttsy.	1.50	5.00
112 G.I. Juniors.	1.50	5.00
113 Sad Sack's Muttsy.	1.50	5.00
114 G.I. Juniors.	1.50	5.00
115 Sad Sack's Muttsy.	1.50	5.00
116 G.I. Juniors.	1.50	5.00
117 Sad Sack's Muttsy.	1.50	5.00
118 G.I. Juniors.	1.50	5.00
119 Sad Sack's Muttsy.	1.50	5.00
120 G.I. Juniors.	1.50	5.00
121 Sad Sack's Muttsy.	1.50	5.00
122 G.I. Juniors.	1.50	5.00

HATARI!
DELL (1963)

12-340-301 Movie tie-in (John Wayne).	13.00	40.00

HATE
FANTAGRAPHICS (1990-CURRENT)

1 1st: Buddy Bradley.	7.00	20.00
1 (2ND) 2nd printing.	.75	2.50
1 (3RD) 3rd printing.	.75	2.50
1 (4TH) 4th printing.	.75	2.50
2	5.00	15.00
2 (2ND) 2nd printing.	.75	2.50
2 (3RD) 3rd printing.	.75	2.50
2 (4TH) 4th printing.	.75	2.50
3	2.75	10.00
3 (2ND) 2nd printing.	.75	2.50
3 (3RD) 3rd printing.	.75	2.50
4	2.75	10.00
4 (2ND) 2nd printing.	.75	2.50
4 (3RD) 3rd printing.	.75	2.50
5	2.75	10.00
5 (2ND) 2nd printing.	.75	2.50
5 (3RD) 3rd printing.	.75	2.50
6	2.00	7.00
6 (2ND) 2nd printing.	.75	2.50
6 (3RD) 3rd printing.	.75	2.50
7	1.75	6.00
8	1.50	5.00
8 (2ND) 2nd printing.	.75	2.50
8 (3RD) 3rd printing.	.75	2.50
9	1.50	5.00
9 (2ND) 2nd printing.	.75	2.50
10	1.50	5.00
10 (2ND) 2nd printing.	.75	2.50
11	1.25	4.00
11 (2ND) 2nd printing.	.75	2.50
12	1.25	4.00
13-14	.75	2.50
15	1.00	3.25
16-19	.75	2.95

HATHAWAYS, THE
DELL FOUR COLOR SERIES (1962)

1298 TV photo cover. (2/62)	13.00	40.00

HAUNT OF FEAR
EC (1950-1954)

1 (#15)	600.00	2100.00
2 (#16)	220.00	700.00
3 (#17) Origin: Crypt of Terror, Haunt of Fear, & Vault of Horror. SOTI	240.00	775.00
4	160.00	525.00
5	145.00	480.00
6	130.00	420.00
7	110.00	360.00
8	95.00	300.00
9	85.00	270.00
10	75.00	240.00
11	65.00	210.00
12	60.00	190.00
13	55.00	180.00
14 Origin: Old Witch.	95.00	300.00
15-18	55.00	180.00
19 SOTI	85.00	270.00
20	50.00	150.00
21-22	40.00	120.00
23 SOTI	50.00	150.00
24-28	40.00	120.00

HAUNT OF FEAR
EC(COCHRAN) (1992-1994)

1 Reprints EC original: The Haunt Of Fear #15 (1950).	.75	2.00
2 Reprint: The Haunt Of Fear #16 (1950).	.50	1.50
3 Reprint: The Haunt Of Fear #17 (1950).	.50	1.50
4 Reprint: The Haunt Of Fear #4.	.75	2.00
5 Reprint: The Haunt Of Fear #5.	.75	2.00
6 Reprint: The Haunt Of Fear #6.	.75	2.00
7 Reprint: The Haunt Of Fear #7.	.75	2.00
8 Reprint: The Haunt Of Fear #8.	.75	2.00
9	.75	2.00
ANNUAL 1 Reprint: 1st 5 issues.	2.25	8.95

HAUNT OF FEAR
EAST COAST (1974)

12 Reprint.	1.50	5.00
23 Reprint.	1.25	4.00

HAUNT OF FEAR, THE
GLADSTONE (1991)

1 Reprints EC originals: Haunt Of Fear #17 & Weird Science-Fantasy #28.	1.00	3.00
2	1.00	3.00

HAUNT OF HORROR, THE
MARVEL (1974-1975) MAGAZINE

1	2.75	10.00
2-5	1.50	5.00

HAUNTED THRILLS
AJAX (1952-1954)

1	35.00	110.00
2	25.00	80.00
3-5	20.00	65.00
6-12	17.00	55.00
13-18	14.00	44.00

HAVE GUN WILL TRAVEL
DELL (1958-1962)

1 (#931) From the 4-Color Series. TV photo cover. (8/58)	25.00	80.00
2 (#983) From the 4-Color Series. TV photo cover. (4/59)	16.00	50.00
3 (#1044) From the 4-Color Series. TV photo cover. (10/59)	14.00	45.00
4 Photo covers on all issues.	11.00	35.00
5-10	10.00	30.00
11-14	8.00	25.00

HAVOK AND WOLVERINE: MELTDOWN
MARVEL (1988-1989)

1	1.50	5.00
2-4	1.25	4.00

HAWK, THE
SEE THE HAWK (FROM APPROVED COMICS SERIES #1)

HAWK, THE
ST. JOHN (1953)

1 3-D comic (with glasses). Cover: Matt Baker.	50.00	150.00

HAWK, THE
ST. JOHN (1954)

1 From Approved Comics series. (Issue #5 in Ziff-Davis series).	10.00	30.00
7 From Approved Comics series. (Issue #6 in Ziff-Davis series).	10.00	30.00

HAWK, THE
ZIFF-DAVIS (1951-1955)

1	25.00	80.00
2	13.00	40.00
3-8	10.00	30.00
9-10 Cover/Art: Matt Baker.	16.00	50.00
11	10.00	30.00
12 Cover/Art: Matt Baker.	16.00	50.00

HAWK AND DOVE
DC (1988-1989)

1 Cover/Art: Rob Liefeld (all issues).	.75	2.00
2-5	.30	1.00

HAWK AND DOVE
DC (1989-1991)

1-28	.30	1.00

HAWK AND THE DOVE
DC (1968-1969)

1 Cover/Art: Steve Ditko.	13.00	40.00
2 Cover/Art: Steve Ditko.	11.00	35.00
3 Begin: Gil Kane cover & art.	8.00	25.00
4-6	8.00	25.00

HAWKEYE
MARVEL (1983)

1 Origin: Hawkeye.	.75	2.50
2-4	.75	2.00

HAWKEYE
MARVEL (1994)

1-4	.50	1.75

HAWKEYE AND THE LAST OF THE MOHICANS
DELL FOUR COLOR SERIES (1958)

884 TV photo cover. (3/58)	16.00	50.00

HAWKMAN
DC (1964-1968)

1 "Master Of The Sky-Weapons!"	130.00	450.00
2	50.00	160.00
3	26.00	90.00
4 1st & Origin: Zantanna.	35.00	110.00
5	25.00	80.00
6	23.00	80.00
7-10	19.00	60.00
11-15	13.00	40.00
16-27	8.00	25.00

HAWKMAN
DC (1986-1987)

1-SPECIAL 1	.30	1.00

HAWKMAN
DC (1993-CURRENT)

0 (8/94)	.50	1.95
1 Foil enhanced cover.	1.25	4.00
2-11	.50	1.75
12-20	.50	1.95
21-24	.75	2.25
ANNUAL 1 Bloodlines pt17. (1993)	1.00	3.50

HAWKWORLD
DC (1989)

1 New costume for Hawkman.	1.75	6.00
2-3	1.25	4.00

HAWKWORLD
DC (1990-1993)

1	1.00	3.00
2	.50	1.50
3-32	.30	1.00
ANNUAL 1 Flash. (1990)	.75	2.95
ANNUAL 2 Armageddon 2001. (1991)	.75	2.95
ANNUAL 2A 2nd printing (silver).	.75	2.95
ANNUAL 3 Eclipso. (1992)	.30	1.00

HEAD COMIX (UNDERGROUND)
VIKING PRESS/BALLANTINE (1968)

1 (HC) Hardcover. $4.95 cover price. Published by Viking Press.	250.00	800.00
1 (SC) Softcover. $2.50 cover price. Published by Viking Press.	31.00	100.00

HEADLINE COMICS
PRIZE (1943-1956)

1 "Begin The Jr. Rangers!" (Feb/43)	70.00	220.00
2 "The Jr. Rangers, Uncle Sam's Battling Nephews, Nip The Nippons!" (3/43)	35.00	110.00
3 "Jr. Rangers Crash Through Second Front!" (4/43)	25.00	80.00
4 "The Jr. Rangers Discover Hitler's Secret Weapon!" (Summer/43)	20.00	65.00
5 "Jr. Rangers Invade Italy!" (Fall/43)	20.00	65.00
6 (Winter/43)	20.00	65.00
7 (Spring/44)	20.00	65.00
8 Hitler on cover. (Summer/44)	35.00	110.00
9 (Fall/44)	17.00	55.00
10 (Mid-Winter/44)	17.00	55.00
11 (Winter/44)	17.00	55.00
12 "Heroes Of Yesterday!" (Spring/45)	17.00	55.00
13-15	14.00	44.00
16 Origin: Atomic Man.	35.00	110.00
17-18	12.00	38.00
19 Art: Simon & Kirby.	35.00	110.00
20-21	12.00	38.00
22	10.00	33.00
23-24 Art: Simon & Kirby.	26.00	85.00
25-35 Cover/Art: Simon & Kirby.	26.00	85.00
36 Art: Simon & Kirby.	23.00	75.00
37	10.00	33.00
38-44	5.00	16.00
45 Art: Jack Kirby.	9.00	27.00
46-50	5.00	16.00
51-55	4.00	11.00
56 Art: Simon & Kirby.	12.00	38.00
57-60	4.00	11.00
61-70	2.25	8.75
71-77	1.75	6.50

HEAP, THE
SKYWALD (1971)

1	1.25	4.00

HEART THROBS
QUALITY/DC (1949-1972)

1 Cover: Bill Ward.	65.00	200.00
2 Cover/Art: Bill Ward.	31.00	100.00
3	10.00	30.00
4 Photo cover. Art: Bill Ward.	16.00	50.00
5 Photo cover.	10.00	30.00
6 Art: Bill Ward.	16.00	50.00
7	10.00	30.00
8 Art: Bill Ward.	16.00	50.00

HAWK & DOVE #28

HAWKEYE #1 (2ND SERIES)

HAWKMAN #0 (3RD SERIES)

HELLBLAZER #23

HELLSHOCK #2

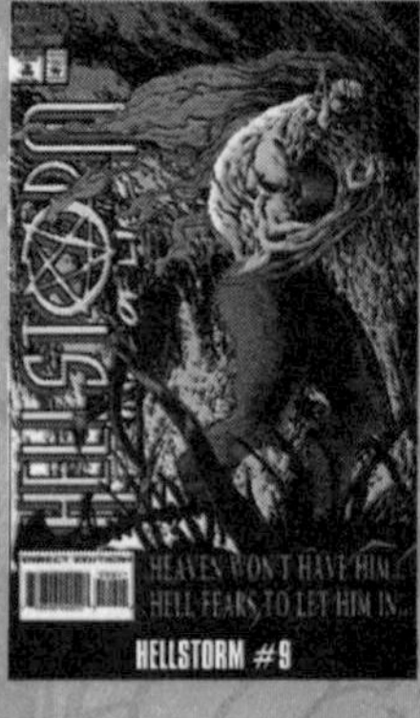

HELLSTORM
HEAVEN WON'T HAVE HIM!
HELL FEARS TO LET HIM IN...

HELLSTORM #9

HERCULES: PRINCE OF POWER #1 (1ST SERIES)

HEROES AGAINST HUNGER

9 Movie photo cover (Jane Russell & Robert Mitchum) ... 19.00 60.00
10 Art: Bill Ward. ... 16.00 50.00
11-14 ... 7.00 20.00
15 Art: Bill Ward. ... 13.00 40.00
16-20 ... 7.00 20.00
21 Cover: Bill Ward. ... 10.00 30.00
22-30 ... 7.00 20.00
31-33 ... 6.00 18.00
34 1st Code Approved issue. ... 5.00 15.00
35-46 ... 4.00 12.00
47 Begin: DC publication. ... 31.00 100.00
48-50 ... 19.00 60.00
51-60 ... 13.00 40.00
61-70 ... 10.00 30.00
71-74 ... 7.00 20.00
75 1st 12 cent cover price. ... 5.00 15.00
76-80 ... 5.00 15.00
81-100 ... 4.00 12.00
101 App: The Beatles. ... 7.00 20.00
102-110 ... 2.75 10.00
111-125 ... 2.25 8.00
126-140 ... 1.75 6.00
141-146 ... 1.25 4.00

HEARTS OF DARKNESS
MARVEL (1992)
1 Ghost Rider, Punisher, Wolverine. ... 1.25 4.95

HEAVY METAL
METAL MAMMOTH (1974-CURRENT) MAGAZINE
1 ... 20.00 65.00
2 ... 11.00 35.00
3 ... 5.00 15.00
4-5 ... 2.75 10.00
6-10 ... 2.25 8.00
11-100 ... 1.50 5.00

HECKLE AND JECKLE
DELL (1966-1967)
1 ... 5.00 15.00
2-3 ... 2.75 10.00

HECKLE AND JECKLE
GOLD KEY (1962-1963)
1 ... 8.00 25.00
2-4 ... 5.00 15.00

HECKLE AND JECKLE
ST. JOHN (1949)
1 From Blue Ribbon Comics 2nd series. 25.00 80.00
3 (2nd issue) From Blue Ribbon Comics 2nd series. ... 25.00 80.00

HECKLE AND JECKLE COMICS
ST. JOHN/PINES (1952-1959)
3 ... 25.00 80.00
4-6 ... 14.00 44.00
7-20 ... 9.00 27.00
21-24 ... 5.00 16.00
25 Begin: Pines publication. ... 5.00 16.00
26-34 ... 5.00 16.00

HECKLER, THE
DC (1992-1993)
1-7 ... .20 .50

HECTOR COMICS
KEY (1953-1954)
1 ... 5.00 15.00
2-3 ... 2.75 10.00

HECTOR HEATHCOTE
GOLD KEY (1964)
10111-403 TV tie-in. ... 7.00 20.00

HECTOR THE INSPECTOR
SEE TOP FLIGHT COMICS

HEDY DEVINE COMICS
MARVEL(ATLAS) (1947-1952)
22 1st: Hedy Devine. ... 16.00 50.00
23-30 ... 13.00 40.00
31-50 ... 10.00 30.00

HEDY WOLFE
MARVEL(ATLAS) (1957)
1 Patsy Walker's Rival! ... 11.00 35.00

HEE HAW
CHARLTON (1970-1971)
1 TV tie-in. ... 5.00 15.00
2 ... 2.75 10.00
3-7 ... 2.25 8.00

HEIGH-YO SILVER! THE LONE RANGER
SEE LARGE FEATURE COMICS #3

HELEN OF TROY
DELL FOUR COLOR SERIES (1956)
684 Movie photo cover. (3/56) ... 28.00 90.00

HELL RIDER
SKYWALD (1971) MAGAZINE
1-2 ... 2.75 10.00

HELL'S ANGEL
MARVEL (1992)
1-7 ... .30 1.00

HELLBLAZER
DC (1988-CURRENT)
1 ... 7.00 22.00
2-5 ... 4.00 11.00
6-12 ... 1.75 6.50
13-18 ... 1.50 5.50
19 Sandman appearance. ... 2.75 10.00
20-23 ... 1.50 5.00
24 With Shocker movie poster. ... 1.50 5.00
25-26 ... 1.25 4.00
27 ... 2.75 10.00
28-49 ... 1.25 4.00
50 ... 1.25 4.50
51-55 ... .75 3.00
56-59 ... .75 3.00
60 1st Genesis ... 2.25 8.00
61 Genesis ... 1.50 5.00
62 ... .75 3.00
63 Begin: Vertigo. ... 1.00 3.00
64-65 ... .75 ... 3.00
66-88 ... .50 1.95
89-93 ... .75 2.25
ANNUAL 1 (1989) ... 1.50 5.00
SPECIAL 1 ... 1.00 3.95

HELLBOY
DARK HORSE (1994)
1 ... 1.75 6.00
2-4 ... 1.50 5.00

HELLHOUNDS: PANZER CORPS
DARK HORSE (1994)
1-6 ... .50 1.50

HELLINA
LIGHTNING (1994)
1 ... 1.50 ... 5.00
1A Limited edition, numbered, silver metallic ink. ... 4.00 15.00
1B Signed & numbered. ... 4.00 15.00
TPB Reprints. ... 2.25 8.95

HELLINA: KISS OF DEATH
LIGHTNING (1995)
1 ... 1.00 4.00
1A Variant cover (nude), certified & numbered. ... 2.50 9.95

HELLINA: TAKING BACK THE NIGHT
LIGHTNING (1995)
1 ... 1.00 4.00
1A Variant cover (nude), certified & numbered. ... 2.50 9.95

HELLO PAL
HARVEY (1943)
1 Photo cover (Mickey Rooney). Begin: Rocketman and Rocketgirl. ... 115.00 380.00
2 Photo cover (Charlie McCarthy). ... 75.00 240.00
3 Photo cover (Bob Hope). ... 75.00 240.00

HELLRAISER
MARVEL (1989-1993)
1 "Clive Barker's..." ... 1.75 6.00
2 ... 1.50 5.00
3-20 ... 1.25 4.00

HELLRAISER: BOOK OF THE DAMNED
MARVEL (1991)
1-4 ... 1.25 4.95

HELLRAISER: DARK HOLIDAY SPECIAL
MARVEL (1992)
1 ... 1.25 4.95

HELLRAISER: SUMMER SPECIAL
MARVEL (1992)
1 ... 1.50 5.95

HELLSHOCK
IMAGE (1994)
1 1st: Hellshock. ... .75 3.00
2-4 ... .50 2.00
4A Variant cover. ... 1.75 7.00

HELLSTORM
MARVEL (1993-CURRENT)
1 Parchment cover. ... .75 2.95
2-19 ... .75 2.00

HELP KEEP OUR LAND BEAUTIFUL
SCSA (1961)
NO# Soil Conservation Society of America giveaway, 16 pgs. ... 2.75 10.00

HE-MAN
TOBY (1954)
1 ... 13.00 40.00
2 ... 8.00 25.00

HE-MAN
ZIFF-DAVIS (1952)
1 Art: Bob Powell. ... 16.00 50.00

HENNESSEY
DELL FOUR COLOR SERIES (1961-1962)
1200 TV photo cover. (7/61) ... 13.00 40.00
1280 TV photo cover. (1/62) ... 13.00 40.00

HENRY
DELL (1948-1961)
1 ... 14.00 45.00
2 ... 7.00 20.00
3-10 ... 4.00 12.00
11-20 ... 2.75 10.00
21-40 ... 2.25 8.00
41-65 ... 1.50 5.00

HENRY
DELL FOUR COLOR SERIES (1946-1947)
122 (10/46) ... 23.00 75.00
155 (7/47) ... 13.00 40.00

HENRY ALDRICH COMICS
DELL (1950-1954)
1 ... 16.00 50.00
2 ... 8.00 25.00
3-6 ... 7.00 20.00
7-12 ... 5.00 15.00
13-22 ... 2.75 10.00

HEPCATS
DOUBLE DAIMOND (1989-CURRENT)
1 ... 11.00 35.00
1A Special edition (with new material). ... 7.00 20.00
2 ... 8.00 25.00
2A Special edition (with new material). ... 2.00 7.00
3 ... 5.00 15.00
4-9 ... 2.75 10.00
10-12 ... .75 2.50
TPB The Collegiate Hepcats. ... 2.50 9.95
TPB Snowblind Part One ... 4.00 ... 14.00

HERBIE
ACG (1964-1967)
1 ... 50.00 160.00
2 ... 23.00 75.00
3-4 ... 17.00 55.00
5 Beatles spoof. ... 22.00 70.00
6-7 ... 15.00 49.00
8 1st & Origin: The Fat Fury. ... 20.00 65.00
9-12 ... 15.00 49.00
13-18 ... 12.00 38.00
19-23 ... 10.00 33.00

HERBIE
DARK HORSE (1992-1993)
1-2 ... .75 2.50
3 Cover/Art: Bob Burden. ... .75 2.50
4-6 ... .75 2.50

HERCULES
CHARLTON (1967-1968)
1 ... 2.75 10.00
2 ... 1.50 5.00
3-6 ... 1.00 3.00
7 ... .75 2.00
8 Magazine size. ... 2.75 10.00
9-13 ... .75 2.00

HERCULES
DELL FOUR COLOR SERIES (1959-1960)
1006 Movie tie-in. (7/59) ... 25.00 80.00
1121 "Unchained". Movie tie-in. (8/60) 22.00 70.00

HERCULES, PRINCE OF POWER
MARVEL (1982)
1-4 ... .30 1.00

HERCULES, PRINCE OF POWER
MARVEL (1984)
1-4 .30 1.00

HERCULES UNBOUND
DC (1975-1977)
1-12 .30 1.00

HERE'S HOWIE
DC (1952-1954)
1 40.00 130.00
2 20.00 65.00
3-6 17.00 55.00
7-12 14.00 44.00
13-18 10.00 33.00

HERMES VS. THE EYEBALL KID
DARK HORSE (1994-1995)
1-3 .75 2.95

HERO FOR HIRE
MARVEL (1972-1973)
1 1st & Origin: Luke Cage. 16.00 50.00
2 5.00 16.00
3 1st: Mace. 5.00 16.00
4-5 5.00 16.00
6-7 2.75 10.00
8-9 Dr. Doom. 2.75 10.00
10-12 2.50 9.00
13 2.00 7.00
14 Origin retold: Luke Cage. 2.00 7.00
15 2.00 7.00
16 Origin: Stiletto. Title changes to Power Man with #17. 2.00 7.00

HEROES AGAINST HUNGER
DC (1986)
1 App: Batman & Superman. Famine relief. 1.25 4.50

HEROES FOR HOPE STARRING THE X-MEN
MARVEL (1985)
1 Famine relief. 1.75 6.00

HEROES, INC. PRESENTS
GANG (1969, 1976)
NO# Cover: Wallace Wood. Art: Steve Ditko & Wallace Wood. 16.00 50.00
2 Cover & art: Wallace Wood. 10.00 30.00

HEROIC COMICS
FF (1940-1955)
1 1st & Origin: Hydroman by Bill Everett; 1st & Origin: Purple Zombie. 190.00 600.00
2 95.00 300.00
3-6 65.00 200.00
7 1st & Origin: Man O' Metal. 70.00 225.00
8-11 40.00 125.00
12 1st & Origin: Music Master by Bill Everett. 50.00 150.00
13 Art: Reed Crandall, Lou Fine. 50.00 150.00
14 1st & Origin: Rainbow Boy. 50.00 150.00
15 1st: Downbeat. 40.00 125.00
16-20 31.00 100.00
21-24 25.00 80.00
25-30 20.00 65.00
31-36 16.00 50.00
37-42 11.00 35.00
43-48 8.00 25.00
49-60 7.00 20.00
61-64 5.00 15.00
65 Art: Frank Frazetta. 13.00 40.00
66 Art: Frazetta. 7.00 20.00
67 Art: Frazetta. 8.00 25.00
68 5.00 15.00
69 Art: Frazetta. 13.00 40.00
70-71 Art: Frazetta. 8.00 25.00
72 Art: Frazetta. 13.00 40.00
73 Art: Frazetta. 8.00 25.00
74 5.00 15.00
75 Art: Frazetta. 7.00 20.00
76-80 5.00 15.00
81-83 Art: Frazetta. 5.00 15.00
84-85 2.75 10.00
86-87 Art: Frazetta. 8.00 25.00
88-97 2.75 10.00

HEROIC SUPER-SPECTACULAR
HEROIC (1992)
1 Only 1500 copies printed (mis-printed cover-Southern Knights #35), actual cover on back. 2.75 10.00

HEX
DC (1985-1987)
1-10 .30 1.00
11-12 Future Batman. .30 1.00
13-18 .30 1.00

HEY THERE, IT'S YOGI BEAR
GOLD KEY (1964)
10122-409 Movie tie-in. 13.00 40.00

HI AND LOIS
CHARLTON (1969-1971)
1 2.25 8.00
2-6 1.25 4.00
7-11 .75 2.00

HI AND LOIS
DELL FOUR COLOR SERIES (1956-1958)
683 (3/56) 7.00 20.00
774 (3/57) 7.00 20.00
955 (11/58) 5.00 15.00

HIGH CHAPPARAL
GOLD KEY (1968)
10226-808 TV photo cover. 10.00 30.00

HI-JINX COMICS
ACG (1947-1948)
1 16.00 50.00
2 8.00 25.00
3-7 7.00 20.00

HILLBILLY COMICS
CHARLTON (1955-1956)
1 11.00 35.00
2-5 7.00 20.00

HILLY ROSE'S SPACE ADVENTURE
ASTRO (1995-CURRENT)
1-2 .75 2.95

HI-SCHOOL ROMANCE
HARVEY (1949-1958)
1 Photo cover. 16.00 50.00
2 8.00 25.00
3-6 7.00 20.00
7-12 5.00 15.00
13-18 4.00 12.00
19-24 2.75 10.00
25-36 2.25 8.00
37-48 1.75 6.00
49-60 1.25 4.00
61-75 1.00 3.00

HI-SPOT COMICS
HAWLEY (1940)
2 David Innes Of Pellucidar by Edgar Rice Burroughs. See Red Ryder Comics for previous and subsequent issues. 220.00 700.00

HISTORY OF THE DC UNIVERSE
DC (1986)
1 Art: George Perez. 1.75 6.00
2 1.75 6.00
HARDCOVER Limited edition (regular edition HC is $30.00). 19.00 60.00

HIT COMICS
QUALITY (1940-1950)
1 (7/40) 700.00 2500.00
2 (8/40) 400.00 1200.00
3 (9/40) 310.00 1000.00
4 (10/40) 230.00 750.00
5 Classic cover. (11/40) 800.00 3000.00
6 (12/40) 190.00 625.00
7 (1/41) 170.00 550.00
8 (2/41) 170.00 550.00
9 (3/41) 170.00 550.00
10 (4/41) 170.00 550.00
11 (5/41) 170.00 550.00
12 (6/41) 170.00 550.00
13-18 160.00 525.00
19-24 145.00 480.00
25 1st & Origin: Kid Eternity. 230.00 750.00
26 155.00 500.00
27-29 105.00 340.00
30-31 85.00 280.00
32 App: Plasticman. 95.00 310.00
33-36 65.00 210.00
37-40 50.00 160.00
41-44 40.00 130.00
45-48 35.00 110.00
49-59 31.00 100.00
60 End: Kid Eternity. 31.00 100.00
61-65 Cover/Art: Reed Crandall. 26.00 85.00

HITCHHIKER'S GUIDE TO THE GALAXY
DC (1993)
1-3 1.00 3.00

HI-YO SILVER, LONE RANGER'S FAMOUS HORSE
DELL (1952-1960)
1 (#369) From the 4-Color Series. (1/52) 22.00 70.00
2 (#392) From the 4-Color Series. (4/52) 10.00 30.00
3-6 5.00 15.00
7-12 4.00 12.00
13-18 2.75 10.00
19-24 2.25 8.00
25-30 1.75 6.00
31-36 1.50 5.00

HI-YO SILVER THE LONE RANGER TO THE RESCUE
SEE LARGE FEATURE COMICS #7

-

HOGAN'S HEROES
DELL (1966-1967)
1 TV photo cover and tie-in all issues. 10.00 30.00
2 7.00 20.00
3 6.00 18.00
4-8 5.00 15.00

HOKUM & HEX
MARVEL (1993-1994)
1 Razorline title. .75 2.50
2-9 .50 1.75

HOLIDAY COMICS
FAWCETT (1942)
1 Giant 196 pgs. Captain Marvel, Spy Smasher, Nyoka, Golden Arrow, Ibis, and Lance O'Casey. 310.00 1000.00

HOLIDAY COMICS
STAR (1951-1952)
1 Merry Christmas issue. 35.00 110.00
2 Animals On Parade. 35.00 110.00
3-4 Animals On Parade. 23.00 75.00
5 Merry Christmas issue. 20.00 65.00
6 Animals On Parade. 20.00 65.00
7 Animals On Parade. 17.00 55.00
8 Merry Christmas issue. 17.00 55.00

HOLLYWOOD COMICS
NEW AGE (1944)
1 16.00 50.00

HOLLYWOOD CONFESSIONS
ST. JOHN (1949)
1 Cover&art: Joe Kubert. 31.00 100.00
2 Cover&art: Joe Kubert. Scarcer. 55.00 175.00

HOLLYWOOD DIARY
QUALITY (1949-1950)
1 19.00 60.00
2 Photo cover. 16.00 50.00
3 Photo cover. 13.00 40.00
4-5 Photo cover. 10.00 30.00

HOLLYWOOD FILM STORIES
PRIZE (1950)
1 Movie tie-in and photo cover (June Allyson). 28.00 90.00
2 Movie tie-in and photo cover (Lizabeth Scott). 19.00 60.00
3 Movie tie-in and photo cover (Barbara Stanwyck). 16.00 50.00
4 Movie tie-in and photo cover (Betty Hutton). 13.00 40.00

HOLLYWOOD FUNNY FOLKS
DC (1950-1954)
27 Previous title: "Funny Folks." 25.00 80.00
28-30 20.00 65.00
31-40 17.00 55.00
41-50 14.00 44.00
51-60 12.00 38.00

HOLLYWOOD PICTORIAL ROMANCES
ST. JOHN (1950)
3 Art: Matt Baker. Photo cover. 35.00 110.00

HOLLYWOOD SECRETS
QUALITY (1949-1950)
1 40.00 130.00
2 35.00 110.00
3-4 Photo cover. 12.00 38.00
5 Lex Barker (Tarzan) photo cover. 17.00 55.00
6 Photo cover. 10.00 33.00

HOLYOKE ONE-SHOT
SEE INDIVIDUAL TITLES.
- Grit Grady, Rusty Dugan, Miss Victory, Mr. Miracle, U.S. Border Patrol, Captain Fearless, Z-2, Blue Streak, Citizen Smith, Captain Stone.

HEX #11

HEROES FOR HOPE #1

HITCHHIKER'S GUIDE TO THE GALAXY #3

HOLLYWOOD FILM STORIES #4

HOPALONG CASSIDY #11

HORRIFIC #7

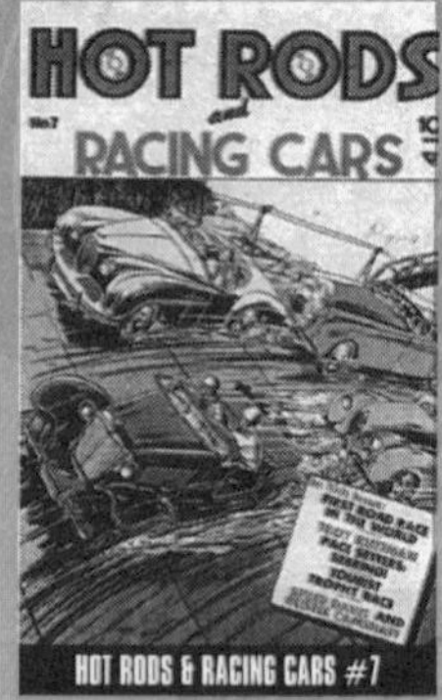

HOT RODS & RACING CARS #7

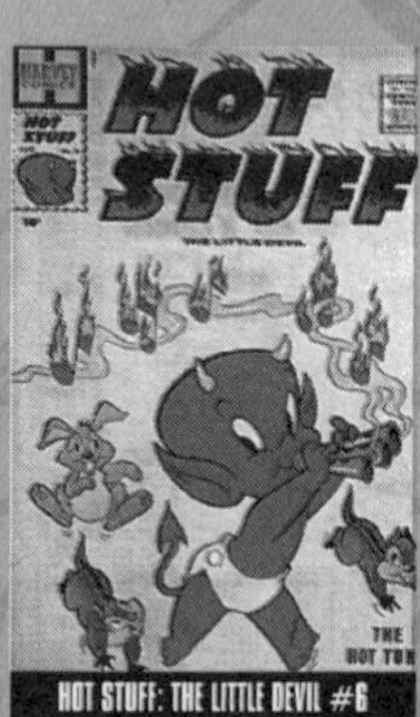

HOT STUFF: THE LITTLE DEVIL #6

HOUSE OF SECRETS #92

This issue holds the first appearance of Swamp Thing, who gained his own title in 1972, and later brought a whole new level of emotional and psychological horror to comics in the '80s with *Saga of the Swamp Thing*.

HOMAGE SWIMSUIT SPECIAL

IMAGE

1 .... 1.00 3.00

HOME RUN (A-1 SERIES)

ME (1953)

3 (A-1 #89). Photo cover (Stan Musial). 65.00 200.00

HOMER HOOPER

MARVEL(ATLAS) (1953)

1 (7/53) 17.00 55.00
2 (8/53) 10.00 33.00
3 (9/53) 9.00 27.00
4 (12/53) 9.00 27.00

HOMER, THE HAPPY GHOST

MARVEL(ATLAS) (1955-1958)

1 Dan DeCarlo cover & art in all issues. 35.00 110.00
2 .... 20.00 65.00
3-6 .... 14.00 44.00
7-10 .... 12.00 38.00
11-22 .... 10.00 33.00

HONEY WEST

GOLD KEY (1966)

1 (#10186-609). TV photo cover. ... 16.00 50.00

HOODED HORSEMAN, THE

ACG (1952-1953)

21 Previous title: "Blazing West." ... 16.00 50.00
22 .... 10.00 30.00
23-27 .... 8.00 25.00

HOODED HORSEMAN, THE

ACG (1954-1956)

18 Previous title: "Out Of The Night." 13.00 40.00
19 .... 8.00 25.00
20-27 .... 7.00 20.00

HOODED MENACE, THE

AVON (1951)

NO # 65.00 200.00

HOORAY COMICS

TENDON (1946)

1 Featuring 'Rusty Red' The Battling Bantam.
.... 11.00 35.00

HOOT GIBSON WESTERN

FOX (1950)

3 Art: Wallace Wood. "Rip Roaring Six Gun Cowboy" (9/50)
.... 40.00 130.00
5 Photo cover. "Rip-Roaring Movie Star" (5/50)
.... 35.00 110.00
6 Photo cover. "Smashing Six-Gun Tornado Of The West"
(7/50) 35.00 110.00

HOOT GIBSON'S WESTERN ROUNDUP

FOX (1950)

1 132 pages. 80.00 250.00

HOPALONG CASSIDY

FAWCETT/DC (1943-1959)

1 "Vultures Of The V-Bar-8" (2/43) 700.00 2400.00
2 (Summer '46) 135.00 440.00
3 "Blazing Trails" (Fall/46) 100.00 330.00
4 (Winter/46) 85.00 270.00
5 "Death In The Saddle!" Photo cover. (3/47)
.... 70.00 220.00
6 (4/47) 60.00 190.00
7 (5/47) 50.00 160.00
8 "The Phantom Stagecoach!" Photo cover. (6/47)
.... 45.00 140.00
9 "The Lost Stockade!" (7/47) ... 40.00 130.00
10 (8/47) 40.00 130.00
11 "The Desperate Jeeters!" Photo cover. (9/47)
.... 40.00 120.00
12 "The Mysterious Message!" (10/47) 40.00 120.00
13 "The Human Target!" Photo cover. (11/47)
.... 40.00 120.00
14 "Land Of The Lawless!" Photo cover. (12/47)
.... 40.00 120.00
15 "Death Holds The Reins!" Photo cover. (1/48)
.... 40.00 120.00
16 "Webfoot's Revenge!" Photo cover. (2/48)
.... 29.00 95.00
17 "The Hangman's Noose!" Photo cover. (3/48)
.... 29.00 95.00
18 "The Ghost Of Dude Ranch!" Photo cover. (4/48)
.... 29.00 95.00
19 Photo cover. (5/48) 29.00 95.00
20 "The Notorious Nellie Blaine!" (6/48) 29.00 95.00
21-29 .... 26.00 85.00
30-34 Painted cover. 10.00 33.00
35-36 Photo cover. 19.00 60.00
37-41 Painted cover. 12.00 38.00
42 Photo cover. 15.00 49.00
43-50 .... 15.00 49.00
51-60 .... 12.00 38.00
61-70 .... 10.00 33.00
71-85 .... 9.00 27.00
86 Begin: DC publication. 35.00 110.00
87 .... 29.00 95.00
88-90 .... 25.00 80.00
91-98 .... 22.00 70.00
99 1st Code Approved issue. 20.00 65.00
100-107 .... 17.00 55.00
108 End: photo covers. 17.00 55.00
109-112 .... 14.00 44.00
113-120 .... 9.00 27.00
121-130 .... 7.00 22.00
131-135 .... 5.00 16.00
BOND BREAD Giveaway. (1951) ... 40.00 130.00

HOPPY THE MARVEL BUNNY

FAWCETT (1945-1947)

1 (12/45) 50.00 160.00
2 (1/46) 25.00 80.00
3 (2/46) 22.00 70.00
4 (3/46) 22.00 70.00
5 (4/46) 22.00 70.00
6 (5/46) 22.00 70.00
7-12 .... 19.00 60.00
13-15 .... 15.00 49.00

HORACE & DOTTY DRIPPLE

HARVEY (1952-1955)

25-43 .... 1.25 4.00

HORIZONTAL LIEUTENANT, THE

DELL (1962)

01-348-210 Movie tie-in. 7.00 20.00

HORRIFIC

COMIC MEDIA (1952-1954)

1 .... 35.00 110.00
2 .... 17.00 55.00
3 .... 22.00 70.00
4-6 .... 17.00 55.00
7-9 .... 14.00 46.00
10-13 .... 13.00 40.00

HORROR FROM THE TOMB

PREMIER (1954)

1 Title changes to Mysterious Stories with #2.
.... 35.00 110.00

HORRORS, THE

STAR (1953-1954)

11 Horrors of War. 28.00 90.00
12 Horrors Of War. 28.00 90.00
13 Horrors of Mystery. 28.00 90.00
14-15 Horrors Of The Underworld. ... 28.00 90.00

HORSE SOLDIERS, THE

DELL FOUR COLOR SERIES (1959)

1048 Movie tie-in (John Wayne). (9/59)
.... 50.00 150.00

HORSE WITHOUT A HEAD, THE

GOLD KEY (1964)

10109-401 Disney TV movie tie-in. ... 5.00 15.00

HORSEMASTERS, THE

DELL FOUR COLOR SERIES (1961)

1260 Movie photo cover (Annette Funicello). (11/61)
.... 23.00 75.00

HOT DOG (A-1 SERIES)

ME (1954-1955)

1 (A-1 #107). 7.00 20.00
2 .... 2.75 10.00
3 (A-1 #115). 5.00 15.00
4 (A-1 #136). 5.00 15.00

HOT ROD AND SPEEDWAY COMICS

HILLMAN (1952-1953)

1	35.00	110.00
2	26.00	85.00
3-6	17.00	55.00

HOT ROD COMICS

FAWCETT (1952-1953)

1 Cover/Art: Bob Powell on all issues.	55.00	180.00
2	40.00	120.00
3	28.00	90.00
4-5	22.00	70.00
6-7	19.00	60.00

HOT ROD KING

ZIFF-DAVIS (1952)

1 "The Masked Driver!"	50.00	150.00

HOT ROD RACERS

CHARLTON (1964-1967)

1	14.00	44.00
2	10.00	33.00
3-4	9.00	27.00
5-6	7.00	22.00
7	6.00	19.00
8-11	5.00	16.00
12-15	4.00	13.00

HOT RODS AND RACING CARS

CHARLTON (1951-1973)

1	40.00	130.00
2	26.00	85.00
3	25.00	80.00
4-6	20.00	65.00
7-12	17.00	55.00
13-18	15.00	49.00
19-24	14.00	44.00
25-34	12.00	38.00
35 Double size (64 pages).	17.00	55.00
36-40	10.00	33.00
41-50	9.00	27.00
51-60	7.00	22.00
61-70	6.00	19.00
71-90	5.00	15.00
91-100	4.00	11.00
101-110	2.25	8.75
111-120	1.75	6.50

HOT STUFF SIZZLERS

HARVEY (1960-1974)

1	16.00	50.00
2	8.00	25.00
3-6	4.00	12.00
7-20	2.75	10.00
21-40	1.50	5.00
41-50	1.00	3.00
51-59	.75	2.00

HOT STUFF THE LITTLE DEVIL

HARVEY (1957-1991)

1	50.00	150.00
2 1st: Stumbo The Giant.	31.00	100.00
3-6	22.00	70.00
7-12	14.00	45.00
13-20	10.00	30.00
21-30	7.00	20.00
31-40	5.00	15.00
41-50	2.75	10.00
51-60	2.25	8.00
61-70	1.75	6.00
71-80	1.50	5.00
81-90	1.25	4.00
91-100	1.00	3.00
101-105	.75	2.00
106-112 Giant size.	1.25	4.00
113-140	.50	1.50
141-177	.30	1.00

HOT WHEELS

DC (1970-1971)

1	13.00	40.00
2	7.00	20.00
3	10.00	30.00
4 Cover: Neal Adams.	7.00	20.00
5	7.00	20.00
6 Cover/Art: Neal Adams.	10.00	30.00

HOUSE II

MARVEL (1987)

1 Movie adaptation.	.75	2.00

HOUSE OF HAMMER

TOP SELLER/QUALITY (1976-1984) MAGAZINE

1 Dracula movie (1958) adaptation, others.	4.00	12.00
2-9	2.25	8.00
10 Werewolf issue.	2.25	8.00
11-12	2.25	8.00
13 Plague Of The Zombies adaptation, others.	2.50	9.00
14 1,000,000 Years B.C. adaptation, others.	2.50	9.00
15	2.00	7.00
16 Star Wars issue.	5.00	15.00
17-18	2.25	8.00

HOUSE OF MYSTERY

DC (1951-1983)

1 "Wanda Was A Werewolf!" (12-1/51)	300.00	1100.00
2 "I Was A Dead Man!" (2-3/52)	130.00	425.00
3 "The Dummy Of Death!" (4-5/52)	110.00	350.00
4 "The Man With The Evil Eye!" (6-7/52)	85.00	275.00
5 "I Was A Witch!" (8/52)	80.00	250.00
6 "The Monster In Clay!" (9/52)	65.00	200.00
7 "The Nine Lives Of Roger Denham!" (10/52)	65.00	200.00
8 "Tattoos Of Doom!" (11/52)	65.00	200.00
9 "Secret Of The Little Black Bag!" (12/52)	55.00	175.00
10 "Wishes Of Doom!" (1/53)	55.00	175.00
11 "The Grim Game Of 'Ghost'!" (2/53)	55.00	175.00
12 "Secret Of The Matador's Sword!" (3/53)	55.00	175.00
13 "The Theater Of 1,000 Thrills!" (4/53)	55.00	175.00
14 "The Deadly Dolls!" (5/53)	55.00	175.00
15 "The Man Who Could Change People!" (6/53)	50.00	150.00
16 "The Man Who Killed His Shadow!" (7/53)	50.00	150.00
17 "Station G-H-O-S-T!" (8/53)	50.00	150.00
18 "The Devil Bird!" (9/53)	50.00	150.00
19 "The Strange Faces Of Death!" (10/53)	50.00	150.00
20 "Mr. Mortem!" (11/53)	50.00	150.00
21-26	40.00	125.00
27-32	31.00	100.00
33-35	26.00	85.00
36 1st Code Approved issue.	31.00	100.00
37-50	22.00	70.00
51-60	17.00	55.00
61	20.00	65.00
62	16.00	50.00
63	20.00	65.00
64	16.00	50.00
65-66	20.00	65.00
67	16.00	50.00
68-69	13.00	40.00
70	17.00	55.00
71	11.00	35.00
72	17.00	55.00
73-75	11.00	35.00
76	17.00	55.00
77-83	11.00	35.00
84-85	17.00	55.00
86-99	11.00	35.00
100	13.00	40.00
101-116	10.00	30.00
117 1st 12 cent cover price.	8.00	25.00
118-119	8.00	25.00
120	10.00	32.00
121-142	7.00	20.00
143 Begin: J'onn J'onzz.	65.00	200.00
144	31.00	100.00
145-155	19.00	60.00
156 1st & Origin: Robby Reed.	28.00	90.00
157-159	19.00	60.00
160 Robby Reed as Plastic Man.	28.00	90.00
161-168	14.00	45.00
169 1st & Origin: Gem Girl.	14.00	45.00
170-173	14.00	45.00
174 Begin: Mystery format.	2.75	10.00
175-177	2.75	10.00
178 Art: Neal Adams.	7.00	20.00
179 Art: Berni Wrightson (his 1st pro work-3 pages). 1st 15 cent cover price.	19.00	60.00
180 Art: Wrightson (5 pages).	2.75	10.00
181 Art: Wrightson (10 pages).	2.75	10.00
182	2.25	8.00
183 Art: Wrightson (3 pages).	2.75	10.00
184	1.75	6.00
185	2.50	9.00
186 Art: Neal Adams, Berni Wrightson.	5.00	15.00
187	1.25	4.00
188 Art: Wrightson.	4.00	11.00
189-190	1.25	4.00
191 Art: Wrightson.	4.00	11.00
192-193	1.25	4.00
194	1.00	3.00
195 Double size.	10.00	30.00
196-198	1.00	3.00
199	1.50	5.00
200-203	1.00	3.00
204 Cover/Art: Wrightson.	5.00	15.00
205-206	1.00	3.00
207	1.25	4.00
208-223	1.00	3.00
224 Art: Adams, Wrightson. Begin: 100 page issues.	5.00	16.00
225-228	1.50	5.00
229 End: 100 page issues.	1.50	5.00
230-235	1.25	4.00
236 Art: Steve Ditko.	1.25	4.00
237-321	1.25	4.00

HOUSE OF SECRETS

DC (1956-1978)

1 "The Hand Of Doom!" (11/56)	250.00	800.00
2 "The Mask Of Fear!" (2/57)	95.00	300.00
3 Cover/Art: Jack Kirby. "The Three Prophecies!" (4/57)	80.00	275.00
4 Art: Kirby. "Master Of The Unknown!" (6/57)	60.00	200.00
5 "The Man Who Hated His Hair!" (8/57)	31.00	100.00
6 "Experiment 1000!" (10/57)	31.00	100.00
7 "The Island Of The Enchantress!" (12/57)	28.00	90.00
8 Art: Kirby. "The Electrified Man!" (2/58)	50.00	150.00
9 "The Jigsaw Creatures!" (4/58)	28.00	90.00
10 "I Was A Prisoner Of The Sea!" (6/58)	28.00	90.00
11 "The Man Who Couldn't Stop Growing!" (8/58)	28.00	90.00
12 Cover/Art: Kirby. "The Hole In The Sky!" (9/58)	50.00	150.00
13 "The Face In The Mist!" (10/58)	22.00	70.00
14 "The Man Who Stole Air!" (11/58)	22.00	70.00
15 "The Creature In The Camera!" (12/58)	22.00	70.00
16 "We Matched Wits With A Gorilla Genius!" (1/59)	22.00	70.00
17 "Lady In The Moon!" (2/59)	22.00	70.00
18 (3/59)	22.00	70.00
19 (4/59)	17.00	55.00
20 "The Incredible Fireball Creatures!" (5/59)	17.00	55.00
21 (6/59)	17.00	55.00
22 (7/59)	17.00	55.00
23 1st & Begin: Mark Merlin.	50.00	160.00
24	17.00	55.00
25-27	14.00	45.00
28 (1/60)	14.00	45.00
29-30	14.00	45.00
31-50	11.00	35.00
51 1st 12 cent cover price.	10.00	30.00
52-57	10.00	30.00
58 Origin: Mark Merlin.	10.00	30.00
59-60	10.00	30.00
61 1st & Begin: Eclipso.	50.00	155.00
62	20.00	65.00
63-65	17.00	55.00
66 1st: Eclipso cover.	35.00	105.00
67 Art: Alex Toth.	16.00	50.00
68-72	14.00	45.00
73 Mark Merlin becomes Prince Ra-Man.	14.00	45.00
74-79	14.00	45.00
80 End: Eclipso, Prince Ra-Man.	14.00	45.00
81 Begin: Mystery format.	2.75	10.00
82-89	2.75	10.00
90 Art: Neal Adams. (3/71)	2.75	10.00
91	2.75	10.00
92 1st & Origin: Swamp Thing by Len Wein and Berni Wrightson. (7/71)	115.00	400.00
93	1.25	4.00
94 Wrightson inks, Toth art. (10-11/71)	1.25	4.00
95-154	1.25	4.00

HOUSE OF TERROR

ST. JOHN (1953)

1 First 3-D comic devoted to the horror genre (with glasses). Includes art by Joe Kubert and Matt Baker.	65.00	200.00

HOW AVIATION CADETS ARE TRAINED AT NAVY PRE-FLIGHT SCHOOLS

SEE AVIATION CADETS

HOW THE WEST WAS WON

GOLD KEY (1963)

10074-307 Movie tie-in.	7.00	20.00

HOWARD THE DUCK

MARVEL (1976-1986)

1 App: Spider-Man.	4.00	11.00
2-11	.75	2.00
12 Cameo: Kiss. (3/77)	1.25	4.00
13 1st full app: Kiss. (6/77)	1.25	4.00
14-33	.50	1.50

HOUSE OF MYSTERY #7

HOUSE OF MYSTERY #19

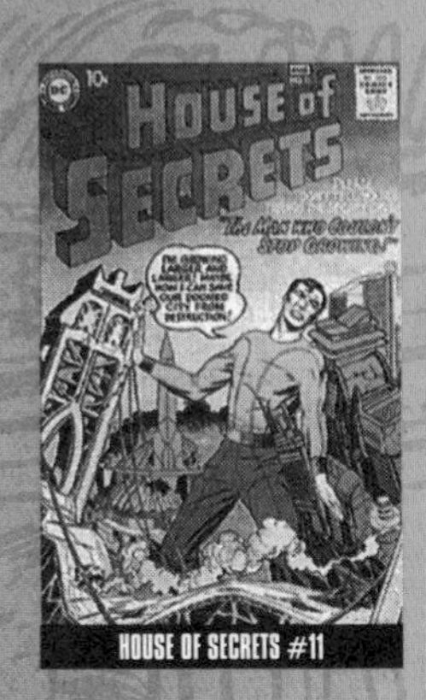

HOUSE OF SECRETS #11

HULK 2099 #2

THE HUNTRESS #1

HYPERKIND UNLEASHED #1

ICEMAN #1

ICON #14

ANNUAL 1 .50 1.50

HOWARD THE DUCK
MARVEL (1979-1981) MAGAZINE
1-9 .75 2.00

HOWARD THE DUCK: THE MOVIE
MARVEL (1987)
1 Movie adaptation. .30 1.00
2-3 .30 1.00

HOWDY DOODY
DELL (1950-1956)
1 1st TV tie-in comic book. Photo cover. 115.00 380.00
2 Photo covers through #5. 50.00 160.00
3-5 26.00 85.00
6 SOTI. 35.00 110.00
7-12 20.00 65.00
13-25 14.00 44.00
26-38 10.00 33.00

HOWDY DOODY
DELL FOUR COLOR SERIES (1957)
761 TV tie-in. (1/57) 22.00 70.00
811 (7/57) 19.00 60.00

H.R. PUFNSTUF
GOLD KEY (1970-1972)
1-8 2.75 10.00

HUBERT
DELL FOUR COLOR SERIES (1949)
251 "At Camp Moonbeam" (10/49) 11.00 35.00

HUCK AND YOGI WINTER SPORTS
DELL FOUR COLOR SERIES (1962)
1310 TV tie-in. (4/62) 19.00 60.00

HUCKLEBERRY FINN
DELL FOUR COLOR SERIES (1960)
1114 Movie photo cover. (7/60) 13.00 40.00

HUCKLEBERRY HOUND
DELL (1960-1970)
3-9 10.00 30.00
10-17 7.00 22.00
18-19 14.00 45.00
20-30 5.00 15.00
31-43 2.75 10.00

HUCKLEBERRY HOUND
DELL FOUR COLOR SERIES (1959-1960)
990 TV tie-in. (5/59) 23.00 75.00
1050 TV tie-in. (10/59) 13.00 40.00
1054 TV tie-in. (12/59) 14.00 45.00
1141 "For President" TV tie-in. (10/60) 16.00 50.00

HULK
SEE INCREDIBLE HULK

HULK 2099
MARVEL (1994-1995)
1 Foil stamped cover. .75 2.50
2-6 .50 1.50
7-10 .50 1.95

HUMAN FLY
I.W. (1963)
1 Reprint. 2.75 10.00
10 2.75 10.00

HUMAN FLY, THE
MARVEL (1977-1979)
1 Origin: Human Fly. App: Spider-Man. .75 2.00
2 App: Ghost Rider. 1.75 6.00
3-8 .50 1.50
9 App: Daredevil. .50 1.50
10-12 .50 1.50
13-19 .50 1.25

HUMAN TARGET
DC (1991)
1 TV tie-in. .75 2.00

HUMAN TORCH, THE
MARVEL (1974-1975)
1 Reprint: Strange Tales #101. 1.50 6.00
2 Reprint: Strange Tales #102. 1.25 5.00
3 Reprint: Strange Tales #103. 1.25 5.00
4 Reprint: Strange Tales #104. 1.25 5.00
5 Reprint: Strange Tales #105. 1.25 5.00
6 Reprint: Strange Tales #106. 1.25 5.00
7 Reprint: Strange Tales #107. 1.25 5.00
8 Reprint: Strange Tales #108. 1.25 5.00

HUMAN TORCH
MARVEL (TIMELY/ATLAS) (1940-1954)
2 (#1) (Fall/40) 3300.00 13000.00
3 (#2) (Winter/40) 900.00 3200.00
4 (#3) (Spring/41) 700.00 2600.00
5 (#4) (Summer/41) 500.00 1900.00
5 Battle: Human Torch, Sub-Mariner. (Fall/41) 500.00 1900.00
6-7 310.00 1000.00
8 Battle: Human Torch, Sub-Mariner. 400.00 1500.00
9 310.00 1000.00
10 Battle: Human Torch, Sub-Mariner. 400.00 1300.00
11-12 250.00 825.00
13-15 240.00 775.00
16-17 220.00 700.00
18-20 200.00 650.00
21-25 180.00 575.00
26 "Her Diary Of Terror!" (Spring, '47). 180.00 575.00
27-30 180.00 575.00
31-32 145.00 480.00
33 App: Captain America. 170.00 550.00
34 145.00 480.00
35 App: Captain America. (1949) 170.00 550.00
36 (1954). 140.00 450.00
37-38 120.00 390.00

HUMBUG
HUMBUG (1957-1958)
1 28.00 90.00
2 13.00 40.00
3-6 10.00 30.00
7-9 8.00 25.00
10-11 Magazine size. 11.00 35.00

HUMPHREY COMICS
HARVEY (1948-1952)
1 Art: Bob Powell #'s 1-6. 16.00 50.00
2-6 10.00 30.00
7-8 7.00 20.00
9 Origin: Humphrey. 10.00 30.00
10 7.00 20.00
11-12 5.00 15.00
13-22 2.75 10.00

HUNCHBACK OF NOTRE DAME, THE
DELL FOUR COLOR SERIES (1957)
854 Movie photo cover. (7/57) 31.00 100.00

HUNTED
FOX (1950)
1 (#13) SOTI 40.00 125.00
2 31.00 100.00

HUNTER'S HEART
DC/PARADOX (1995)
1-3 1.25 4.95

HUNTRESS
DC (1989-1990)
1 .50 1.50
2-19 .30 1.00

HUNTRESS, THE
DC (1994)
1-4 .20 .50

HURRICANE COMICS
CAMBRIDGE HOUSE (1945)
1 19.00 60.00

HYBRIDS
CONTINUITY (1993)
1-4 .30 1.00

HYDE-25
HARRIS (1995-CURRENT)
0 Includes reprint of Vampirella #1 (Warren). .75 2.95

HYPER MYSTERY COMICS
HYPER (1940)
1 Begin: Hyper, the Phenomenal. (5/40) 280.00 900.00
2 (6/40) 220.00 700.00

HYPERKIND
MARVEL (1993-1994)
1 Prismatic foil cover. .75 2.50
2-9 .50 1.75

HYPERKIND UNLEASHED
MARVEL (1994)
1 .75 2.95

I AIM AT THE STARS
DELL FOUR COLOR SERIES (1960)
1148 Movie photo cover. (10/60) 19.00 60.00

I DREAM OF JEANNIE
DELL (1965-1966)
1 TV photo cover. 20.00 65.00
2 TV photo cover. 17.00 55.00

I LOVE LUCY COMICS
DELL (1954-1962)
1 (#535) From the 4-Color Series (2/54). TV photo cover. 95.00 300.00
2 (#559) From the 4-Color Series (5/54). TV photo cover. 55.00 180.00
3-6 31.00 100.00
7-12 25.00 80.00
13-18 22.00 70.00
19-24 19.00 60.00
25-30 16.00 50.00
31-35 13.00 40.00

I LOVE LUCY FEATURING 3 DIMENSION
DESILU (1953)
1 Magazine size (with glasses). 100.00 330.00

I LOVE YOU
CHARLTON (1955-1980)
7 Previous title: In Love. 16.00 50.00
8-19 5.00 15.00
20-29 2.25 8.00
30-59 1.50 5.00
60 Elvis Presley cover & story. 19.00 60.00
61-100 .75 2.00
101-130 .30 1.00

I LOVE YOU
FAWCETT (1950)
1 Photo cover. 19.00 60.00

I, LUSIPHUR
MULEHIDE (1991-1992)
1 All issues magazine size. 8.00 25.00
2-3 7.00 20.00
4-9 5.00 15.00
10 Title changes to Poison Elves with #11. 5.00 15.00

I MET A HANDSOME COWBOY
DELL FOUR COLOR SERIES (1951)
324 (3/51) 17.00 55.00

I SPY
GOLD KEY (1966-1968)
1 TV photo cover on all issues. 31.00 100.00
2 23.00 75.00
3-6 19.00 60.00

I'M A COP (A-1 SERIES)
ME (1954)
1 (A-1 #111). Cover/Art: Bob Powell. 14.00 45.00
2 (A-1 #126). Cover/Art: Bob Powell. 13.00 40.00
3 (A-1 #128). Cover/Art: Bob Powell. 10.00 30.00

I'M DICKENS...HE'S FENSTER
DELL (1963)
1 TV photo cover. 7.00 20.00
2 TV photo cover. 5.00 15.00

IBIS, THE INVINCIBLE
FAWCETT (1943-1948)
1 Origin: Ibis. Cover: Mac Raboy. 310.00 1000.00
2 160.00 525.00
3 125.00 400.00
4-6 105.00 340.00

ICEMAN
MARVEL (1984-1985)
1-4 .30 1.00

ICICLE
HEROIC (1992-1993)
1-5 .30 1.00

ICON
DC (1993-CURRENT)
1 .75 2.95
1A Newsstand version, unbagged. .50 1.50
2-14 .50 1.50
15-24 .50 1.75
25 Double size. .75 2.95
26 .50 1.75
27-29 .75 2.50

IDEAL, A CLASSICAL COMIC
MARVEL(TIMELY) (1948-1949)
1 Antony and Cleopatra. 65.00 200.00
2 The Corpses of Dr. Sacotti. 50.00 150.00
3 Joan of Arc. 40.00 120.00
4 Richard the Lion-Hearted. 50.00 150.00
5 "Love And Romance", photo cover, becomes Love Romances #6. 40.00 120.00

IDEAL COMICS
MARVEL(TIMELY) (1944-1946)
1 Begin: Super Rabbit. 40.00 120.00
2 23.00 75.00
3-4 19.00 60.00

IDOL
MARVEL (1992)
1-3 .30 1.00

IF THE DEVIL WOULD TALK
CATHECHETICAL GUILD (1950)
NO# 95.00 300.00
NO# (2ND) 2nd printing (1958). 65.00 200.00

IMAGE
IMAGE (1993)
0 1st: Troll. Send-away issue. 1.75 6.00

IMAGES OF SHADOWHAWK
IMAGE (1993-1994)
1-3 .50 1.95

IMMORTALIS
MARVEL (1993)
1 Foil-stamped cover. .75 2.95
2-4 .50 1.75

IMPACT
EC (1955)
1 35.00 110.00
2 20.00 65.00
3-5 17.00 55.00

IMPULSE
DC (1995-CURRENT)
1 1.00 3.50
2 .75 2.00
3-6 .50 1.75

IN LOVE
MAINLINE/CHARLTON (1954-1955)
1 Art: Simon & Kirby. 31.00 100.00
2 Art: Simon & Kirby. 23.00 75.00
3-4 Art: Simon & Kirby. 16.00 50.00
5 Cover: Simon & Kirby. 11.00 35.00
6 Title changes to I Love You with #7. 5.00 15.00

IN SEARCH OF THE CASTAWAYS
GOLD KEY (1963)
10048-303 Disney movie photo cover. 13.00 40.00

IN THE DAYS OF THE MOB
HAMPSHIRE (1971) MAGAZINE
1 2.75 10.00

INCOMPLETE DEATH'S HEAD
MARVEL (1993-1994)
1 .75 2.95
2-10 .50 1.75

INCREDIBLE HULK, THE
MARVEL (1962-1963)
1 1st & origin: The Hulk (grey) in "The Coming Of The Hulk!" by Jack Kirby. (5/62) 2100.00 8000.00
2 1st: Green Hulk in "The Terror Of The Toad Men!" by Kirby & Ditko. (7/62) 500.00 1800.00
3 Origin retold. 1st: Ringmaster. (9/62) 400.00 1200.00
4 "The Monster And The Machine!" & "Mongu!! Gladiator From Space!" by Jack Kirby. 310.00 1000.00
5 "Beauty And The Beast!" by Kirby. 310.00 1000.00
6 "The Metal Master!" by Steve Ditko. (3/63) 400.00 1400.00

INCREDIBLE HULK, THE
MARVEL (1968-CURRENT)
102 Origin retold. Previous title: Tales To Astonish. 50.00 150.00
103 "The Space Parasite!" 20.00 65.00
104 "Ring Around The Rhino!" 19.00 60.00
105 1st: Missing Link. "This Monster Unleashed!" 16.00 50.00
106 "Above The Earth...A Titan Rages!" 13.00 40.00
107 "Ten Rings Hath...The Mandarin!" 13.00 40.00
108 "Monster Triumphant!" 13.00 40.00
109 "The Monster And The Man-Beast!" 10.00 30.00
110 "Umbu, The Unliving!" 10.00 30.00
111 "Shanghaied In Space!" 8.00 25.00
112 "The Brute Battles On!" 8.00 25.00
113 "Where Fall The Shifting Sands!" 8.00 25.00
114 "At Last I Will Have My Revenge!" 8.00 25.00
115 "Lo, The Leader Lives!" 8.00 25.00
116 "The Eve Of...Annihilation!" 8.00 25.00
117 "World's End?" 8.00 25.00
118 1st 15 cent cover price. 5.00 15.00
119 "At The Mercy Of...Maximus The Mad!" 5.00 15.00
120 "On The Side Of...The Evil Inhumans!" 5.00 15.00
121 5.00 15.00
122 Hulk battles The Thing. 8.00 25.00
123-126 5.00 15.00
127-140 2.50 9.00
141 1st: Doc Samson. 2.50 9.00
142 2.25 8.00
143-144 1.75 6.00
145 Origin retold. Double size. 2.50 9.00
146-149 1.75 6.00
150 App: Havok & Polaris. 2.50 9.00
151-161 1.75 6.00
162 1st: Wendigo. 2.25 8.00
163-171 1.75 6.00
172 Origin retold: Juggernaut. App: X-Men. 2.00 7.00
173-175 1.75 6.00
176 App: Warlock (cameo). 7.00 20.00
177 Warlock. 7.00 20.00
178 Warlock reborn. 7.00 20.00
179 1.50 5.00
180 1st: cameo app. Wolverine. 28.00 90.00
181 1st: full appearance Wolverine. (11/74) 115.00 380.00
182 App: Wolverine (cameo). See Giant-size X-Men #1 for 2nd full appearance. 19.00 60.00
183-189 1.25 4.00
190 1.50 5.00
191-199 1.25 4.00
200 Anniversary issue. App: Silver Surfer. 8.00 25.00
201-233 1.00 3.00
234 1st: Quasar. 1.00 3.00
235-249 1.00 3.00
250 Double size. 2.25 8.00
251-271 .75 2.50
272-273 1.25 4.00
274-299 .75 2.50
300 1.00 3.00
301-311 .75 2.50
312 Origin retold. .75 2.50
313 .75 2.50
314 Begin: John Byrne cover/art. 1.50 5.00
315-317 1.00 3.00
318 1.25 4.00
319 Bruce Banner marries Betty Talbot. 2.25 8.00
320-323 .75 2.75
324 App: Grey Hulk. 2.75 10.00
325 .75 2.50
326 Battle: Grey Hulk vs. Green Hulk. .75 2.50
327-329 .75 2.50
330 Begin: Todd McFarlane art. 5.00 16.00
331 4.00 12.00
332-334 2.25 8.00
335 1.00 3.00
336-339 1.50 5.00
340 App: Wolverine. 8.00 25.00
341-344 1.50 5.00
345 1.75 6.00
346 End: McFarlane art. 1.50 5.00
347-349 .75 2.00
350 Double size. Hulk battles The Thing. 1.50 5.00
351-366 .75 2.00
367 Begin: Dale Keown art. 2.50 9.00
368 Cover/Art: Sam Kieth. 1.50 5.00
369-371 Cover/Art: Dale Keown. 1.25 4.00
372 Art: Dale Keown. 2.75 10.00
373-376 Art: Dale Keown. 1.25 4.00
377 1st: new Hulk. Art: Dale Keown. 4.00 12.00
377 (2ND) 2nd printing. 1.25 4.00
377 (3RD) 3rd printing. .50 1.50
378 .50 1.50
379 Art: Dale Keown. 1.25 4.00
380 1.00 3.00
381-388 1.25 4.00
389-392 1.00 3.00
393 30th Anniversary issue. 1.50 5.00
394-397 .75 2.00
398 End: Dale Keown art. .75 2.00
399 .75 2.00
400 Foil cover (2.50 cp). 1.00 3.00
400 (2ND) 2nd printing. .75 2.00
401-417 .50 1.50
418 Marriage: Rick & Marlo. Collector's edition (wedding invite cover). .75 2.50
418A Regular edition. .50 1.50
419 .75 2.00
420-424 .50 1.50
425 Hologram cover. 1.00 3.50
425A Regular cover. .75 2.25
426 Deluxe edition. .50 1.95
426A Regular edition. .50 1.50
427-433 .50 1.95
ASHCAN .20 .75

INCREDIBLE HULK AND WOLVERINE, THE
MARVEL (1986)
1 Reprints Incredible Hulk #'s 180-182. 2.75 10.00
1 (2ND) 2nd printing. 1.25 4.00

INCREDIBLE HULK ANNUAL
MARVEL (1968-CURRENT)
1 King-Size Special. "A Refuge Divided!" (1968) 17.00 55.00
2 King-Size Special. (1969) 9.00 28.00
3 King-Size Special. (1971) 2.25 8.00
4 Special. (1972) 2.00 7.00
5 (1976) 1.50 5.00
6 (1977) 1.50 5.00
7 Art: John Byrne/Bob Layton. (1978) 1.75 6.50
8 (1979) 2.25 8.00
9 (1980) 1.25 4.00
10 (1981) 1.25 4.00
11 (1982) 1.25 4.00
12 (1983) 1.25 4.00
13 (1984) 1.25 4.00
14 (1985) 1.25 4.00
15 (1986) 1.25 4.00
16 Lifeform, pt.3 (1990) 1.25 4.00
17 (1991) .75 2.00
18 (1992) .75 2.25
19 (1993) .75 2.95
20 (1994) .75 2.95

INCREDIBLE HULK: FUTURE IMPERFECT
MARVEL (1992-1993)
1-2 1.50 5.95
TPB Reprints issues #1-2. 4.00 12.95

INCREDIBLE HULK KING-SIZE SPECIAL
SEE INCREDIBLE HULK ANNUAL

INCREDIBLE MR. LIMPET, THE
DELL (1964)
12-370-408 Movie photo cover (Don Knotts). 11.00 35.00

INCREDIBLE SCIENCE FICTION
EC (1955-1956)
30 Previous title: Weird Science-Fantasy. 75.00 240.00
31-32 75.00 240.00
33 Cover & art: Wallace Wood. Reprint: Weird Fantasy #18. 75.00 240.00

INCREDIBLE SCIENCE FICTION
EC(COCHRAN) (1994)
1 All issues reprint originals. .75 2.00
2-10 .75 2.00

INDEPENDENT PUBLISHERS GROUP SPOTLIGHT
HEROIC (1993)
0 San Diego Con giveaway. 2.75 10.00

INDIAN BRAVES
ACE (1951)
1 11.00 35.00
2-4 7.00 20.00

INDIAN CHIEF
DELL (1951-1959)
3 Previous title: The Chief. 7.00 20.00
4-11 4.00 12.00
12 1st: White Eagle. 7.00 20.00
13-33 2.75 10.00

INDIAN FIGHTER, THE
DELL FOUR COLOR SERIES (1956)
687 Movie photo cover (Kirk Douglas). (3/56) 11.00 35.00

INDIAN FIGHTER
YOUTHFUL (1950-1952)
1 13.00 40.00
2 10.00 30.00
3-11 7.00 20.00

INDIAN WARRIORS
STAR (1951-1953)
3-D(#1) With glasses. 50.00 150.00
7 Previous title: White Rider. 16.00 50.00
8 Title changes to Western Crime Cases with #9. 13.00 40.00

INDIANA JONES AND THE FATE OF ATLANTIS
DARK HORSE (1991)
1-4 .30 1.00

INDIANA JONES AND THE IRON PHOENIX
DARK HORSE (1994-1995)
1-4 .30 1.00

INCREDIBLE HULK, THE #377

INCREDIBLE HULK: FUTURE IMPERFECT #1

INDIANA JONES & THE FATE OF ATLANTIS #1

INDIANA JONES & THE IRON PHOENIX #4

a b c d e f g h i j k l m n o p q r s t u v w x y z

a b c d e f g h i j k l m n o p q r s t u v w x y z

INSTANT PIANO #3

THE INVISIBLES #2

IRON MAN #169

IRON MAN #282

INCREDIBLE HULK,THE #1

Bruce Banner is hit by a gamma bomb and turned into a gray monster. He lasted six issues, but later was turned green and joined the Sub-Mariner in *Tales to Astonish*, which became *The Incredible Hulk* with issue #102.

INDIANA JONES AND THE LAST CRUSADE
MARVEL (1989)
1 Movie tie-in. .30 1.00
2-4 .30 1.00

INDIANA JONES AND THE SHRINE OF THE SEA DEVIL
DARK HORSE (1994)
1 One shot (reprinted from Dark Horse Comics #3-6. .75 2.50

INDIANA JONES AND THE SPEAR OF DESTINY
DARK HORSE (1995)
1-4 .75 2.50

INDIANA JONES AND THE TEMPLE OF DOOM
MARVEL (1984)
1 Movie tie-in. .30 1.00
2-3 .30 1.00

INDIANA JONES: THE ARMS OF GOLD
DARK HORSE (1994)
1-4 .30 1.00

INDIANA JONES: THE GOLDEN FLEECE
DARK HORSE (1994)
1-2 .30 1.00

INDIANA JONES: THUNDER IN THE ORIENT
DARK HORSE (1993-1994)
1-6 .30 1.00

INDIANAPOLIS 500, THE
(1957)
NO# Digest size. 25.00 80.00

INDIANS
FICTION HOUSE (1950-1953)
1 Begin: Long Bow. 40.00 120.00
2 19.00 60.00
3-6 15.00 48.00
7-12 11.00 36.00
13-17 10.00 30.00

INFERIOR FIVE
DC (1967-1972)
1 See Showcase #62 for 1st app. 13.00 40.00
2 7.00 22.00
3-12 4.00 12.00

INFINITY CRUSADE
MARVEL (1993)
1 Gold foil cover. 1.00 3.00
2-6 .75 2.00

INFINITY GAUNTLET
MARVEL (1991)
1 Thanos. 1.50 5.00
2 Return: Adam Warlock. 1.00 3.00
3-6 .75 2.00
TPB Reprints entire Gauntlet series. 8.00 24.95

INFINITY, INC.
DC (1984-1988)
1 1.00 3.00
2-13 .75 2.00
14 Begin: Todd McFarlane art. 1.50 5.00
15-17 .75 2.00
18 Begin: Crisis crossover. .75 2.00
19-23 .75 2.00
24 End: Crisis crossover. .75 2.00
25-36 .75 2.00
37 End: McFarlane art. .75 2.00
38-49 .50 1.50
50 Double size. .75 2.00
51-53 .50 1.50
ANNUAL 1 (1985) 1.25 4.00
ANNUAL 2 (1988) .75 2.00

INFINITY WAR
MARVEL (1992)
1 Thanos, Magus. 1.25 4.00
2 Origin: Magus. 1.00 3.00
3-6 1.00 3.00

INFORMER
FTP (1954)
1 16.00 50.00
2 10.00 30.00
3-5 7.00 20.00

INHUMANOIDS
MARVEL(STAR) (1987)
1 TV tie-in. .20 .50
2-4 .20 .50

INHUMANS
MARVEL (1975-1977)
1 1.50 5.00
2 1.25 4.00
3 1st: Shatterstar. 1.00 3.00
4 1.00 3.00
5 Death: Shatterstar. 1.00 3.00
6-12 1.00 3.00
SPECIAL 1 Inhumans vs. Maximus. .75 2.00

INKY AND DINKY
SEE FELIX'S NEPHEWS INKY AND DINKY

INSECT FEAR (UNDERGROUND)
PRINT MINT (1970)
1 25.00 80.00
2 13.00 40.00
3 7.00 20.00

INSIDE CRIME
FOX (1950)
1 #3 inside (7/50). 31.00 100.00
2 SOTI (9/50) 31.00 100.00
3 No# shown. 25.00 80.00

INSTANT PIANO
DARK HORSE (1994-CURRENT)
1 1.75 6.00
2-4 1.00 3.95

INTERNATIONAL COMICS
EC (1947)
1 135.00 440.00
2 100.00 330.00
3-4 85.00 270.00
5 Title changes to International Crime Patrol with #6. 85.00 270.00

INTERNATIONAL CRIME PATROL
EC (1948)
6 App: Moon Girl. Previous title: International Comics. Title changes to Crime Patrol with #7. 155.00 500.00

INTERPLANETARY LIZARDS OF THE TEXAS PLAINS
LEADBELLY (1991-1992)
1-8 .30 1.00

INTERVIEW WITH THE VAMPIRE
INNOVATION (1992-1994)
1 1.75 6.00
2-4 1.00 3.00
5-12 .75 2.00

INTIMATE
CHARLTON (1957-1958)
1 2.75 10.00
2 2.25 8.00
3 Title changes to Tee-Age Love with V2#4. 1.75 6.00

INTIMATE CONFESSIONS
REALISTIC (1951-1953)
1 Cover/Art: Kinstler. 95.00 300.00
2 16.00 50.00
3 Cover/Art: Kinstler. 22.00 70.00
4-8 19.00 60.00

INVADERS
GOLD KEY (1967-1968)
1 TV tie-in. Photo cover on all issues. 10.00 30.00
2-4 7.00 20.00

INVADERS, THE
MARVEL (1975-1979)

1 ... 4.00 12.00
2-5 ... 2.00 7.00
6-9 ... 1.50 5.50
10 Reprint: Captain America #22. ... 1.50 5.50
11-19 ... 1.50 5.50
20 Reprint: Motion Picture Funnies #1. 2.00 7.50
21 Reprint: Marvel Mystery #10. ... 1.25 4.00
22-23 ... 1.25 4.00
24 Reprint: Marvel Mystery #17. ... 1.25 4.00
25-40 ... 1.25 4.00
41 Double size. ... 1.25 4.00
ANNUAL 1 Cover/Art: Alex Schomburg. (1977)
... 2.75 10.00

INVADERS
MARVEL (1993)

1-4 ... .30 1.00

INVASION
DC (1988-1989)

1 1st: L.E.G.I.O.N. ... 1.25 4.00
2-3 ... 1.00 3.00
SPECIAL 1 Daily Planet (tabloid size). ... .75 2.50

INVISIBLE BOY
ST. JOHN (1954)

2 Cover: Saunders. From Approved Comics series.
... 23.00 75.00

INVISIBLE SCARLET O'NEILL
HARVEY (1950-1951)

1 ... 16.00 50.00
2-3 ... 8.00 25.00

INVISIBLES, THE
DC (1994-CURRENT)

1 ... 1.00 3.50
2-12 ... .75 2.50

IRON FIST
MARVEL (1975-1977)

1 Iron Fist battles Iron Man. John Byrne art in all.
... 16.00 50.00
2-5 ... 6.00 18.00
6-7 ... 2.75 10.00
8 Origin retold. ... 2.75 10.00
9-13 ... 2.75 10.00
14 1st: Sabretooth. ... 50.00 160.00
15 App: New X-Men. ... 13.00 40.00
15A 35 cent cover variant with UPC code. 23.00 75.00

IRON MAN
MARVEL (1968-CURRENT)

1 Origin retold. Lead story: "Alone Against A.I.M." See Tales To Astonish #39 for 1st appearance. ... 110.00 350.00
2 ... 31.00 100.00
3 ... 25.00 80.00
4 ... 22.00 70.00
5-6 ... 19.00 60.00
7-15 ... 11.00 35.00
16 1st 15 cent issue cover price. ... 8.00 25.00
17-20 ... 8.00 25.00
21-24 ... 7.00 20.00
25-40 ... 5.00 15.00
41-42 ... 4.00 12.00
43 Double size. ... 4.00 12.00
44 1st 20 cent issue cover price. ... 4.00 12.00
45-46 ... 4.00 12.00
47 Origin retold. ... 8.00 25.00
48 ... 4.00 12.00
49-53 ... 2.75 10.00
54 Iron Man battles Sub-Mariner. ... 5.00 15.00
55 1st: Thanos. (2/73) ... 12.00 40.00
56 Art: Jim Starlin. ... 3.00 10.00
57-60 ... 2.75 10.00
61-79 ... 1.75 6.00
80-99 ... 1.50 5.00
100 Anniversary issue. ... 5.00 15.00
101-117 ... 1.50 5.00
118 Art: John Byrne. ... 1.75 6.00
119 ... 1.50 5.00
120 Sub-Mariner. ... 1.50 5.00
121 Sub-Mariner. ... 1.25 4.00
122-127 ... 1.25 4.00
128 ... 1.50 5.00
129-149 ... 1.00 3.00
150 Double size. ... 1.75 6.00
151-168 ... 1.00 3.00
169 Tony Stark resigns Iron Man armor. 4.00 12.00
170 James Rhodes dons Iron Man armor as Iron Man II.
... 4.00 12.00
171-190 ... 1.00 3.00
191 Return: Tony Stark as Iron Man. ... 1.50 5.00
192 ... 1.25 4.00
193-199 ... 1.00 3.00
200 New armor (red & silver). Double size. 1.75 6.00
201-213 ... 1.00 3.00
214 App: New Spider-Woman. ... 1.00 3.00
215-224 ... 1.00 3.00
225 Armor Wars. Double size. ... 1.25 4.00
226-232 ... 1.00 3.00
233 ... .75 2.00
234 Spider-Man. ... .75 2.00
235-241 ... .75 2.00
242 ... 1.00 3.00
243 ... .75 2.00
244 Origin retold: Iron Man. ... 1.50 5.00
245-249 ... .75 2.00
250 Dr. Doom. Double size. ... 1.00 3.00
251-257 ... .75 2.00
258-274 ... .50 1.50
275 Double size. ... .50 1.50
276-280 ... .50 1.50
281 1st: War Machine armor. ... 2.00 7.00
282 ... 1.25 4.00
283-287 ... .50 1.50
288 ... .75 2.50
289 ... .50 1.50
290 ... .75 2.95
291-299 ... .50 1.50
300 Embossed foil cover. ... 1.25 4.50
300A Regular cover. ... .75 2.50
301-309 ... .50 1.50
310 Neon ink cover (with insert & acetate print).
... .75 2.95
310A Regular cover. ... .50 1.50
311 ... .50 1.50
312 Double size. ... .75 2.25
313-316 ... .50 1.50
317 Flip book (with War Machine, U.S. Agent, & Hawkeye).
... .75 2.50
318-319 ... .50 1.50

IRON MAN 2020
MARVEL (1994)

NO# Prestige format. ... 1.50 5.95

IRON MAN AND SUB-MARINER
MARVEL (1968)

1 One shot pre-dates Iron Man #1. (4/68)
... 40.00 125.00

IRON MAN ANNUAL
MARVEL (1970-CURRENT)

1 King-Size Special. Reprints Tales Of Suspense #71, 79, 80, 82. (8/70) ... 7.00 22.00
2 King-Size Special. Reprints Tales Of Suspense #81, 82, 91. (11/71) ... 2.25 8.00
3 (6/76) ... 1.75 6.00
4 (8/77) ... 1.75 6.00
5 (12/82) ... 1.50 5.00
6 (11/83) ... 1.50 5.00
7 (10/84) ... 1.50 5.00
8 (10/86) ... 1.50 5.00
9 (1987) ... 1.50 5.00
10 (1989) ... 1.25 4.50
11 (1990) ... 1.25 4.00
12 (1991) ... .75 2.25
13 (1992) ... .75 2.25
14 Polybagged with card. (1993) ... .75 2.95
15 (1994) ... .75 2.95

IRON MAN: CRASH
MARVEL (1988)

GN Computer-generated book. ... 4.00 12.95

IRON MAN: IRON MANUAL
MARVEL (1993)

1 ... .50 1.75

IRON MAN SPECIAL
MARVEL (1970-1971)

1 Reprint: Tales Of Suspense #'s 71, 79, 80, 82.
... 7.00 20.00
2 Reprint: Tales Of Suspense #'s 81, 82, 91.
... 2.25 8.00

IRONJAW
ATLAS(SEABOARD) (1975)

1 ... .50 1.50
2-4 ... .30 1.00

IRONWOOD
EROS/FANTAGRAPHICS (1991-CURRENT)

1 ... 2.75 10.00
1 (2ND) 2nd printing. ... .75 2.75
2 ... 1.50 5.00
2 (2ND) 2nd printing. ... .75 2.75
3 ... 1.50 5.00
3 (2ND) 2nd printing. ... .75 2.75
3 (3RD) 3rd printing. ... .75 2.75
4 ... 1.25 4.00
4 (2ND) 2nd printing. ... .75 2.75
5 ... 1.25 4.00
5 (2ND) 2nd printing. ... .75 2.75
6 ... 1.25 4.00
6 (2ND) 2nd printing. ... .75 2.75
7 ... 1.25 4.00
7 (2ND) 2nd printing. ... .75 2.75
8 ... 1.25 4.00
8 (2ND) 2nd printing. ... .75 2.75
9 ... .75 2.75
9 (2ND) 2nd printing. ... .75 2.75
10 ... .75 2.50

IS THIS TOMORROW?
CATECHETICAL GUILD (1947)

1-BLANK CR ... 28.00 90.00
1-NO PRICE ... 16.00 50.00
1(10 CENT) ... 23.00 75.00

ISIS
DC (1976-1978)

1 TV tie-in. ... .75 2.00
2-6 ... .30 1.00
7 Origin: Isis. ... .30 1.00
8 ... .30 1.00

ISLAND OF DR. MOREAU, THE
MARVEL (1977)

1 Movie tie-in. ... 1.00 3.00

IT REALLY HAPPENED
WISE (1945-1947)

1 Ben Franklin; Jan Christiaan Smuts; Kit Carson; Lieutenant Lakin, R.N. ... 25.00 80.00
2 Manuel Quezon; Joseph Mazzini; Bernardo O'Higgins; Sevier of Tennessee. ... 17.00 55.00
3 Col. Carlson; Andrews of Asia; Gen. Jomini; Lt. Childers.
... 12.00 38.00
4 Dr. David Livingstone; Rear Admiral Wilkes; Maj. Alexander Pokryshkin; Sir Martin Frobisher; Chaplain Albert J. Hoffman.
... 10.00 33.00
5 Lou Gehrig; Lewis Carroll; Amelia Earhart; Israel Putnam.
... 25.00 80.00
6 John J. McGraw; Joan of Arc; John Adams; John Quincy Adams; Ernie Pyle. ... 10.00 33.00
7 Teddy Roosevelt; Sir Walter Raleigh; Jefferson Davis; John J. Audubon. ... 10.00 33.00
8 Mayor LaGuardia; Roy Rogers; Sister Kenny; Manuel Camacho.
... 25.00 80.00
9 William O'Dwyer; Frank Buck; George Eastman; Captain Kidd.
... 10.00 33.00
10 LeRoy Grumman; Nathaniel Greene; Sir Richard Burton; Honus Wagner. ... 20.00 65.00
11 Bob Crosby; Robert Burns; Lincoln Ellsworth; Glenn Cunningham. ... 14.00 44.00

IT'S ABOUT TIME
GOLD KEY (1967)

10195-701 TV photo cover. ... 7.00 20.00

IT'S GAMETIME
DC (1955-1956)

1 ... 140.00 460.00
2-4 ... 115.00 370.00

ITCHY & SCRATCHY COMICS
BONGO (1993-CURRENT)

1 TV cartoon tie-in. ... 1.00 3.50
2-3 ... .50 1.95

ITCHY AND SCRATCHY COMICS: HOLIDAY HIJINKS SPECIAL
BONGO (1994)

1 TV cartoon tie-in. ... .75 2.25

IVANHOE
DELL (1963)

12-373-309 Movie tie-in. ... 5.00 15.00

IWO JIMA
FOX (1950)

12 Photo cover. ... 40.00 120.00

JAB
ADHESIVE (1992-1993)

1 1st: Too Much Coffee Man. ... 1.50 8.00
2-3 ... .75 2.50

JACE PEARSON OF THE TEXAS RANGERS
DELL (1952-1959)

2 TV photo cover on all issues. ... 10.00 30.00
3-6 ... 8.00 25.00
7 "The Cover-Up" ... 7.00 20.00
8-12 ... 7.00 20.00
13-20 ... 5.00 15.00

IT REALLY HAPPENED #7

ITCHY & SCRATCHY #2

JAB #2

JACKIE GLEASON & THE HONEYMOONERS #12

JACKPOT COMICS #5

JESSE JAMES #4

JINGLE JANGLE #6

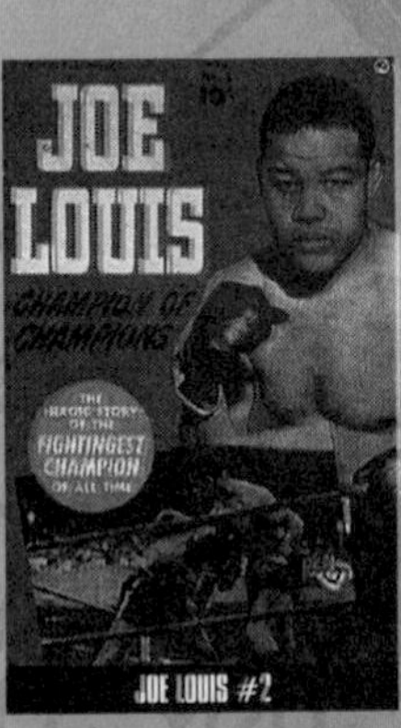

JOE LOUIS #2

JACE PEARSON'S TALES OF THE TEXAS RANGERS
DELL FOUR COLOR SERIES (1952-1959)
396 TV tie-in. Photo cover. (5/52) 26.00 85.00
648 TV photo cover. (9/55) 11.00 35.00
961 TV photo cover. (1/59) 11.00 35.00
1021 TV photo cover. (8/59) 11.00 35.00

JACK ARMSTRONG
PARENTS' INSTITUTE (1947-1949)
1 "Arctic Mystery!" (11/47) 35.00 110.00
2 "Den Of The Golden Dragon!" (12/47) 17.00 55.00
3 "Lost Valley Of Ice!" (1/48) 14.00 46.00
4 "Land Of The Leopard Men!" (2/48) 14.00 46.00
5 "Racketeers Of The Ring!" (3/48) 14.00 46.00
6 14.00 46.00
7-8 13.00 40.00
9 "Mystery Of The Midgets!" (10/48) 13.00 40.00
10 "Secret Cargo!" (3/49) 13.00 40.00
11 13.00 40.00
12 "Madman's Island!" (7/49) 13.00 40.00
13 13.00 40.00

JACK OF HEARTS
MARVEL (1984)
1-4 .30 1.00

JACK O FROST
SEE UNEARTHLY SPECTACULARS

JACK THE GIANT-KILLER
DELL (1963)
12-374-301 Movie tie-in. 16.00 50.00

JACKIE GLEASON
ST. JOHN (1948)
1 TV tie-in. 160.00 525.00
2 140.00 450.00

JACKIE GLEASON
ST. JOHN (1955)
1 TV tie-in and photo cover. 125.00 400.00
2 105.00 340.00
3-5 85.00 280.00

JACKIE GLEASON AND THE HONEYMOONERS
DC (1956-1958)
1 TV tie-in. 210.00 675.00
2 155.00 500.00
3-6 125.00 400.00
7-12 115.00 370.00

JACKIE JOYNER-KERSEE IN HIGH HURDLES
DC (1992)
NO# Kellogg's giveaway. .75 2.00

JACKIE ROBINSON, BASEBALL HERO
FAWCETT (1950-1952)
1 (NO#) Photo cover on all issues. 190.00 600.00
2 110.00 360.00
3 100.00 330.00
4-6 85.00 270.00

JACK-IN-THE-BOX COMICS
CPC (1946-1947)
1 "Stitches" (2/46) 16.00 50.00
11 Previous title: Yellowjacket Comics. 16.00 50.00
12 7.00 20.00
13 Art: Basil Wolverton (3 pages). 23.00 75.00
14-15 7.00 20.00
16 Title changes to Cowboy Western Comics with #17. 7.00 20.00

JACKPOT COMICS
MLJ (1941-1943)
1 Begin: The Black Hood, Mr. Justice, Steel Sterling. 400.00 1500.00
2 230.00 750.00
3 190.00 625.00
4 Begin: Archie. 1st: Mrs. Grundy. 400.00 1500.00
5 1st: Mr. Weatherbee. 1st: Reggie (cameo). 310.00 1000.00
6 230.00 750.00
7 190.00 625.00
8-9 160.00 525.00

JACKY'S DIARY
DELL FOUR COLOR SERIES (1960)
1091 (4/60) 10.00 30.00

JAGUAR, THE
IMPACT (1991-1992)
1-14 .30 1.00
ANNUAL 1 With trading card. .75 2.50

JAGUAR GOD
VEROTIK (1995-CURRENT)
1 Frank Frazetta cover 2.00 6.00

JAM: URBAN ADVENTURE, THE
DARK HORSE (1995)
8 .75 2.95

JAMBOREE COMICS
ROUND (1946)
1 26.00 85.00
2 17.00 55.00

JAMES BOND 007: THE QUASIMODO GAMBIT
DARK HORSE (1995)
1-3 1.00 3.95

JAMES BOND: FOR YOUR EYES ONLY
MARVEL (1981)
1 Movie adaptation. .30 1.00
2 .30 1.00

JANN OF THE JUNGLE
MARVEL(ATLAS) (1955-1957)
8 Previous title: Jungle Tales. 35.00 110.00
9-10 17.00 55.00
11-15 14.00 44.00
16 Art: Al Williamson (5 pages). 25.00 80.00
17 Art: Al Williamson. 25.00 80.00

JASON AND THE ARGONAUTS
DELL (1963)
12-376-310 Movie photo cover. 22.00 70.00

JASON GOES TO HELL
TOPPS (1993-1994)
1-2 .75 2.95

JEANIE COMICS
MARVEL(ATLAS) (1947-1949)
13 20.00 65.00
14-15 14.00 44.00
16 20.00 65.00
17-19 14.00 44.00
20-27 10.00 33.00

JEEP COMICS
LEFFINGWELL (1944-1948)
1 Begin: Captain Power. 25.00 80.00
2 19.00 60.00
3 Dinosaur cover. 23.00 75.00

JEFF JORDAN, U.S. AGENT
DS (1947)
1 10.00 30.00

JEMM, SON OF SATURN
DC (1984-1985)
1-12 .20 .50

JESSE JAMES
AVON (1950-1956)
1 Reprint: Cowpuncher #1. 23.00 75.00
2 Art: Joe Kubert. 22.00 70.00
3 Reprint: Cowpuncher #2. 19.00 60.00
4 7.00 20.00
5-6 Art: Joe Kubert. 19.00 60.00
7 Art: Joe Kubert. 14.00 45.00
8 Art: Raymond Everett Kinstler. 13.00 40.00
9 7.00 20.00
15-16 Art: Raymond Everett Kinstler. 10.00 30.00
17-19 5.00 15.00
20 Art: Williamson/Frazetta. 19.00 60.00
21-29 5.00 15.00

JESSE JAMES
REALISTIC (1953)
NO# Reprint. 10.00 32.00

JET ACES
FICTION HOUSE (1952)
1 19.00 60.00
2-4 10.00 30.00

JET DREAM
GOLD KEY (1968)
1 4.00 12.00

JET FIGHTERS
STANDARD (1952-1953)
5 16.00 50.00
6 Circus Pilot. 8.00 25.00
7 Iron Curtains For Ivan. 16.00 50.00

JET POWER
I.W. (1963)
1-2 Reprint. 2.75 10.00

JET POWERS (A-1 SERIES)
ME (1950-1951)
1 (A-1 #30). Begin: Powell art. 40.00 125.00
2 (A-1 #32). 31.00 100.00
3 (A-1 #35). Art: Williamson/Evans. 40.00 125.00
4 (A-1 #38). "The Rain Of Sleep!" classic drug story. 65.00 200.00

JET PUP 3D
DIMENSIONS (1953)
1 A 3D Features book. With glasses. 70.00 225.00

JETSONS, THE
CHARLTON (1970-1973)
1 Hanna-Barbera TV tie-in. 19.00 60.00
2 9.00 27.00
3-6 7.00 22.00
7-12 4.00 13.00
13-20 4.00 11.00

JETSONS, THE
GOLD KEY (1963-1970)
1 Hanna-Barbera TV tie-in. 70.00 230.00
2 35.00 110.00
3-6 26.00 85.00
7-12 22.00 70.00
13-24 17.00 55.00
25-36 13.00 40.00

JETTA OF THE 21ST CENTURY
STANDARD (1952-1953)
5 26.00 85.00
6-7 17.00 55.00

JIGSAW
HARVEY (1966)
1 1st & Origin: Jigsaw by Reed Crandall. 6.00 18.00
2 4.00 12.00

JIM
FANTAGRAPHICS (1987-1990)
1 All issues are magazine size. 7.00 20.00
2 5.00 15.00
3-4 2.75 10.00

JIM
FANTAGRAPHICS (1994-CURRENT)
1 1.25 4.00
1 (2ND) 2nd printing. .75 2.95
2 1.00 3.50
2 (2ND) 2nd printing. .75 2.95
3-5 .75 2.95

JIM BOWIE
CHARLTON (1955-1957)
15 Previous title: Danger. 7.00 20.00
16 5.00 15.00
17-18 2.75 10.00

JIM BOWIE
DELL FOUR COLOR SERIES (1958-1959)
893 TV photo cover. (4/58) 13.00 40.00
993 TV photo cover. (5/59) 14.00 45.00

JIM HARDY COMIC BOOK
SPOTLIGHT (1944)
NO# 128 Pg. Giant. 65.00 200.00

JIM HARDY COMICS
ST. JOHN (1947-1948)
2 From the Treasury Of Comics series. (7/47) 16.00 50.00
5 From the Treasury Of Comics series. (1/48) 13.00 40.00

JIM RAY'S AVIATION SKETCHBOOK
VITAL (1946)
1 31.00 100.00
2 23.00 75.00

JIMBO
BONGO (1995-CURRENT)
1 TV cartoon tie-in. .75 2.95

JIMINY CRICKET
DELL FOUR COLOR SERIES (1956-1959)
701 Disney. (5/56) 13.00 40.00
795 (5/57) 10.00 30.00
897 (4/58) 5.00 15.00
989 (5/59) 7.00 20.00

JIMMY DURANTE (A-1 SERIES)
ME (1948)
18 (A-1 #18), photo cover. 55.00 180.00
20 (A-1 #20), photo cover. 55.00 180.00

JIMMY WAKELY
DC (1949-1952)
1 Photo cover. Art: Alex Toth in most issues. 115.00 380.00
2 Photo cover. 95.00 300.00

3-4 Art: Frank Frazetta. Photo cover. 85.00 270.00
5 Photo cover. 70.00 220.00
6-7 Art: Frank Frazetta. Photo cover. 85.00 270.00
8-15 60.00 190.00
16-18 50.00 160.00

JINGLE JANGLE COMICS
EASTERN (1942-1949)
1 50.00 160.00
2 25.00 80.00
3-6 20.00 65.00
7-12 17.00 55.00
13-18 14.00 44.00
19-24 12.00 38.00
25-36 9.00 27.00
37-42 6.00 19.00

JOAN OF ARC (A-1 SERIES)
ME (1949)
21 (A-1 #21), Ingrid Bergman movie photo cover. Also see "Ideal-A Classical Comic." 55.00 175.00

JOE LOUIS CHAMPION OF CHAMPIONS
FAWCETT (1950)
1 Photo cover. Life story. 125.00 400.00
2 Photo cover. 85.00 280.00

JOE PALOOKA
COLUMBIA (1942-1944)
1 125.00 410.00
2 75.00 240.00
3-4 60.00 190.00

JOE PALOOKA
HARVEY (1945-1961)
1 85.00 270.00
2 40.00 130.00
3 35.00 110.00
4 28.00 90.00
5 Art: Simon & Kirby. Boy Explorers. 55.00 175.00
6-7 25.00 80.00
8-12 20.00 65.00
13-14 17.00 55.00
15 1st & Origin: Humphrey. 1st: Atoma by Bob Powell. (12/47) 35.00 110.00
16-18 15.00 49.00
19-24 14.00 44.00
25-26 12.00 38.00
27 App: Little Max. 12.00 38.00
28-30 12.00 38.00
31-34 10.00 33.00
35 App: Little Max. 10.00 33.00
36 10.00 33.00
37-40 9.00 27.00
41 Front cover features a photo of Bing Crosby reading a Joe Palooka comic. 10.00 33.00
42-48 7.00 22.00
49-60 5.00 16.00
61-72 4.00 13.00
73-85 4.00 11.00
86-99 2.25 8.75
100 Anniversary issue. 5.00 16.00
101-115 2.25 8.75
116 Giant size. 10.00 33.00
117-118 Giant size. 7.00 22.00

JOE PALOOKA VISITS THE LOST CITY
MTA (1945)
1 One Shot, 160 pgs. 250.00 800.00

JOE R. LANSDALE'S BY BIZARRE HANDS.
DARK HORSE (1994)
1-3 .75 2.50

JOE YANK
STANDARD (1952-1954)
5 8.00 25.00
6 11.00 35.00
7-8 7.00 20.00
9 6.00 18.00
10-16 5.00 15.00

JOHN BYRNE'S NEXT MEN
DARK HORSE (1992-CURRENT)
0 Reprint: Dark Horse Presents #54-57. 1.75 6.50
1 2.00 7.00
1 (2ND) 2nd printing. .75 2.50
2 1st: Sathanas. 1.50 5.00
3 1.25 4.00
4-18 .75 2.50
19 Faith #1. 1.00 3.00
20 Faith #2. 1.00 3.00
21 Faith #3. 1.00 3.00
22 Faith #4. 1.00 3.00
23 Power #1. .75 2.50
24 Power #2. .75 2.50
25 Power #3. .75 2.50
26 Power #4. .75 2.50
27 Lies #1. .75 2.50
28 Lies #2. .75 2.50
29 Lies #3. .75 2.50
30 Lies #4. .75 2.50

JOHN CARTER OF MARS
DELL FOUR COLOR SERIES (1952-1953)
375 (2/52) 50.00 155.00
437 (11/52) 35.00 110.00
488 (8/53) 25.00 80.00

JOHN CARTER OF MARS
GOLD KEY (1964)
1 (10104-404) 7.00 20.00
2 (10104-407) 5.00 15.00
3 (10104-410) 4.00 12.00

JOHN CARTER, WARLORD OF MARS
MARVEL (1977-1979)
1 Origin: John Carter. .30 1.00
2-17 .30 1.00
18 Art: Frank Miller. .50 1.50
19-28 .30 1.00
ANNUAL 1-ANNUAL 2 (1978) .30 1.00
ANNUAL 3 (1979) .30 1.00

JOHN F. KENNEDY, CHAMPION OF FREEDOM
WORDEN & CHILDS (1964)
NO# Photo cover of JFK. 16.00 50.00

JOHN F. KENNEDY LIFE STORY
DELL (1964)
12-378-410 Photo cover. 13.00 40.00

JOHN PAUL JONES
DELL FOUR COLOR SERIES (1959)
1007 Movie photo cover. (9/59) 13.00 40.00

JOHN STEED, EMMA PEEL
GOLD KEY (1968)
1 TV photo cover (The Avengers). 65.00 200.00

JOHN STEELE SECRET AGENT
GOLD KEY (1964)
1 16.00 50.00

JOHN WAYNE ADVENTURE COMICS
TOBY (1949-1955)
1 Photo cover. 250.00 800.00
2 Photo cover. 125.00 400.00
3 Flying Tigers movie tie-in & photo cover "The Flying Sheriff." 125.00 400.00
4 105.00 340.00
5-6 95.00 310.00
7 85.00 280.00
8 105.00 340.00
9-11 70.00 230.00
12 65.00 200.00
13 No photo cover. 35.00 110.00
14 Sands of Iowa Jima movie photo cover. 65.00 200.00
15-16 No photo cover. 35.00 110.00
17 Photo cover. 65.00 200.00
18 No photo cover. 55.00 170.00
19-24 35.00 110.00
25 Hondo movie tie-in & photo cover. 65.00 200.00
26-27 Photo cover. 65.00 200.00
28 Movie photo cover "She Wore A Yellow Ribbon." Lead story: "Dead Man's Boots!" 65.00 200.00
29-31 Photo cover. 65.00 200.00

JOHNNY DANGER
TOBY (1950)
1 Movie photo cover. 40.00 120.00

JOHNNY DANGER PRIVATE DETECTIVE
TOBY (1954)
1 Photo cover. 16.00 50.00

JOHNNY DYNAMITE
CHARLTON (1955-1956)
10 Previous title: Dynamite. 7.00 20.00
11 7.00 20.00
12 Title changes to Foreign Intrigues with issue #13. 7.00 20.00

JOHNNY DYNAMITE
DARK HORSE (1994)
1-4 .75 2.95

JOHNNY HAZARD
STANDARD (1948-1949)
1 40.00 125.00
5 19.00 60.00
6-8 16.00 50.00
35 8.00 25.00

JOHNNY JASON, TEEN REPORTER
DELL (1962)
1 (#1302) From the 4-Color Series. (2/62) 10.00 30.00
2 (01380-208) 5.00 15.00

JOHNNY MACK BROWN
DELL (1950-1952)
2 TV tie-in & photo covers on all issues. 20.00 65.00
3 17.00 55.00
4 14.00 44.00
5 12.00 38.00
6-10 10.00 33.00

JOHNNY MACK BROWN COMICS
DELL FOUR COLOR SERIES (1950-1959)
269 "Law For The Badlands". Photo cover. (3/50) 45.00 140.00
455 Photo cover. (3/53) 14.00 45.00
493 Photo cover. (9/53) 11.00 35.00
541 Photo cover. (3/54) 13.00 40.00
584 "Killer's Trail". Photo cover. (9/54) 11.00 35.00
618 Photo cover. (2/55) 11.00 35.00
645 Photo cover. (9/55) 8.00 25.00
685 Photo cover. (3/56) 10.00 30.00
722 Photo cover. (9/56) 8.00 25.00
776 Photo cover. (3/57) 8.00 25.00
834 Photo cover. (9/57) 8.00 25.00
922 Photo cover. (6/58) 7.00 20.00
963 Photo cover. (2/59) 7.00 20.00

JOHNNY RINGO
DELL FOUR COLOR SERIES (1960)
1142 TV photo cover. (11/60) 16.00 50.00

JOHNNY THUNDER
DC (1973)
1 Reprints from All American Western in all. .75 2.00
2-3 .75 2.00

JO-JO COMICS
FOX (1946-1947)
1 (No# on cover). 17.00 55.00
2 9.00 27.00
3-5 7.00 22.00
6 Title changes to Jo-Jo Congo King with #7. 7.00 22.00

JO-JO CONGO KING
FOX (1947-1949)
7 1st: Jo-Jo Congo King (7/47). Previous title: Jo-Jo Comics. 105.00 340.00
7A (9/47) 85.00 280.00
8-11 70.00 230.00
12 (3/48) 70.00 230.00
14 (4/48) 65.00 200.00
15-18 65.00 200.00
19-24 55.00 170.00
25-29 45.00 140.00

JOKER
DC (1975-1976)
1 "The Joker's Double Jeopardy!" 7.00 20.00
2 2.50 9.00
3 The Creeper. 2.50 9.00
4 Green Arrow. 2.50 9.00
5 2.50 9.00
6 Sherlock Holmes. 2.50 9.00
7 Lex Luthor. 2.50 9.00
8 Scarecrow. 2.50 9.00
9 Catwoman. 2.50 9.00

JOKER COMICS
TIMELY (1942-1950)
1 1st: Powerhouse Pepper by Wolverton. 310.00 1000.00
2 1st: Tessie The Typist. Art: Wolverton. 155.00 500.00
3 Art: Wolverton in all issues. 80.00 250.00
4-5 80.00 250.00
6-12 55.00 180.00
13-18 50.00 160.00
19-24 50.00 150.00
25-27 40.00 120.00
28 Begin: Millie The Model. 40.00 120.00
29-30 40.00 120.00
31 End: Powerhouse Pepper. 40.00 120.00
32 Begin: Hedy. 12.00 37.00
33-42 12.00 37.00

JOLLY JINGLES
MLJ (1943-1945)
10 Previous title: Jackpot Comics. 1st & Origin: Super Duck. 75.00 240.00
11 40.00 120.00
12 28.00 90.00
13-16 22.00 70.00

JOE YANK #5

JOHN BYRNE'S NEXT MEN #7

JOHN WAYNE ADVENTURE COMICS #6

JO-JO CONGO KING #18

JONAH HEX: TWO GUN MOJO #2

JOURNEY INTO MYSTERY #65

JOURNEY INTO MYSTERY #89

JOURNEY INTO MYSTERY #109

FAMOUS · FIRSTS

JUMBO COMICS No. 1 SEPT.
64 PAGES Bigger & Better Funnies 10¢
BIG PAGES–BIG PICTURES–BIG TYPE–EASY TO READ

JUMBO COMICS #1

This anthology offered plenty, including industry-giant Jack Kirby's first comics artwork. But readers tended to linger over Sheena, Queen of the Jungle, who soon became the sole cover feature.

JON JUAN
TOBY (1950)

1 By Siegel/Schomburg. SOTI	31.00	100.00

JONAH HEX
DC (1977-1985)

1 See All Star Western #10 for 1st appearance.	11.00	38.00
2	5.00	18.00
3-6	4.00	12.00
7-8 Hex's face explained.	5.00	15.00
9-12	4.00	12.00
13-18	2.25	8.00
19-24	1.25	4.00
25-30	1.00	3.50
31 Origin retold.	1.00	3.50
32 Origin retold pt2.	1.00	3.50
33-40	1.00	3.50
41-60	1.00	3.00
61-91	.75	2.00
92 Story continues in Hex #1.	.75	2.00

JONAH HEX AND OTHER WESTERN TALES
DC (1979-1980)

1 100 page digests.	.30	1.00
2-3	.30	1.00

JONAH HEX: RIDERS OF THE WORM AND SUCH
DC (1995)

1 Mini-series.	.75	2.95
2-5	.75	2.95

JONAH HEX: TWO-GUN MOJO
DC (1993)

1	1.75	6.00
1A Platinum edition (no cover price).	5.00	15.00
2-5	1.25	4.00
TPB Reprints issues #1-5.	4.00	12.95

JONNI THUNDER
DC (1985)

1-4	.30	1.00

JONNY DEMON
DARK HORSE (1994)

1-3	.75	2.50

JONNY QUEST
GOLD KEY (1964)

10139-412 TV tie-in.	85.00	275.00

JONNY QUEST CLASSICS
COMICO (1987)

1-4	.30	1.00

JOSIE
ARCHIE (1963-1982)

1	35.00	110.00
2	14.00	44.00
3-6	9.00	27.00
7-12	6.00	17.00
13-24	4.00	13.00
25-40	4.00	11.00
41-50	2.25	8.75
51-60	1.75	6.50
61-70	1.50	5.50
71-80	1.00	3.75
81-90	.75	2.00
91-106	.30	1.00

JOURNEY
AV/FANTAGRAPHICS (1983-1986)

1	1.25	4.00
2	.75	2.00
3-28	.30	1.00

JOURNEY INTO FEAR
SUPERIOR (1951-1954)

1	70.00	230.00
2	35.00	110.00
3	31.00	100.00
4	28.00	90.00
5-6	26.00	85.00
7-12	22.00	70.00
13-14	17.00	55.00
15 SOTI	26.00	85.00
16-18	17.00	55.00
19-21	16.00	50.00

JOURNEY INTO MYSTERY
MARVEL (1972-1975)

1	2.75	10.00
2	1.25	4.00
3-5	1.00	3.50
6 Begin: reprints.	1.00	3.00
7-12	1.00	3.00
13-19	.75	2.50

JOURNEY INTO MYSTERY
MARVEL(ATLAS) (1952-1966)

1	400.00	1500.00
2	160.00	525.00
3-4	130.00	425.00
5	115.00	375.00
6	95.00	315.00
7-12	80.00	265.00
13-14	70.00	225.00
15 "Till Death Do Us Part!"	70.00	225.00
16-18	70.00	225.00
19-22	55.00	180.00
23 1st Code Approved issue.	50.00	150.00
24-32	50.00	150.00
33 Art: Al Williamson.	70.00	225.00
34-36	45.00	140.00
37	35.00	110.00
38	55.00	175.00
39-50	35.00	105.00
51 Art: Jack Kirby/Wallace Wood.	35.00	105.00
52-57	35.00	105.00
58 Fantastic Four #1 cover prototype (5/60). Same design as FF#1 by Ditko, 1 1/2 years earlier.	35.00	105.00
59-61	35.00	105.00
62 The Hulk prototype. "The Coming Of The Hulk pt 1." Cover and 13 page story by Kirby/Ditko. (11/60)	55.00	180.00
63-65	31.00	100.00
66 The Hulk prototype (3/61). "Return Of The Hulk!" Cover and 13 page story by Kirby.	55.00	180.00
67-69	31.00	100.00
70 The Sandman prototype (7/61). "The Sandman Cometh!" Cover and 13 page story.	31.00	100.00
71-72	31.00	100.00
73 Spider-Man prototype "The Spider Strikes!" Cover and 7 page story by Kirby. (10/61)	65.00	215.00
74-77	31.00	100.00
78 Dr. Strange prototype "The Sorcerer!" Cover and 6 page story by Kirby. (3/62)	50.00	160.00
79 Mr. Hyde prototype (4/62). "The Midnight Monster!" Cover and 7 page story by Kirby.	22.00	70.00
80-82	22.00	70.00
83 1st & origin: Thor. (8/62)	900.00	3300.00
83A Golden Record set (1966). 33-1/3 record album still-sealed with reprint comic (identical to J.I.M. 83 but without cover price and ads).	50.00	150.00
83B Golden Record reprint, removed from record set (identical to J.I.M. 83 but without cover price and ads).	23.00	75.00
84 2nd Thor.	240.00	775.00
85 1st: Loki. 3rd Thor.	140.00	475.00
86 1st full app. Odin. 4th Thor.	90.00	285.00
87 5th Thor.	70.00	225.00
88 6th Thor.	70.00	225.00
89 Origin retold: Thor.	70.00	225.00
90-92 Art: Joe Sinnott.	40.00	120.00
93 1st: Radioactive Man. Art: Jack Kirby.	40.00	120.00
94-96 Art: Joe Sinnott.	31.00	100.00
97 Art: Jack Kirby.	40.00	130.00
98	28.00	90.00
99 1st Sutur, Mr. Hyde.	25.00	80.00
100	25.00	80.00
101-102	19.00	60.00
103 1st Enchantress.	19.00	60.00
104-106	19.00	60.00
107 1st Grey Gargoyle.	19.00	60.00
108	19.00	60.00
109 App: Magneto (10/64)	29.00	100.00
110	19.00	60.00
111	16.00	50.00
112 Thor battles The Hulk.	45.00	140.00
113	16.00	50.00
114 1st & origin: Absorbing Man.	16.00	50.00
115 In depth Origin: Loki.	23.00	75.00
116-117	16.00	50.00
118 1st: Destoyer.	16.00	50.00
119-124	16.00	50.00

125 Title changes to Thor #126. 16.00 50.00

JOURNEY INTO MYSTERY ANNUAL
MARVEL (1965)
1 1st: Hercules. 40.00 125.00

JOURNEY INTO UNKNOWN WORLDS
MARVEL(ATLAS) (1950-1957)
1 (#36) "The End Of The Earth!" 310.00 1000.00
2 (#37) Cover & art: Bill Everett. "When Worlds Collide!" 190.00 625.00
3 (#38) 155.00 500.00
4-6 115.00 370.00
7 "Planet Of Terror" by Basil Wolverton. 155.00 500.00
8-10 80.00 250.00
11-13 70.00 230.00
14 "One Of Our Graveyards Is Missing" by Basil Wolverton. 115.00 370.00
15 "They Crawl By Night" by Basil Wolverton. 115.00 370.00
16-17 55.00 180.00
18-19 Art: Matt Fox. 55.00 180.00
20-30 50.00 150.00
31-33 40.00 120.00
34 1st Code approved issue. 23.00 75.00
35-40 23.00 75.00
41-48 19.00 60.00
49 "Invasion Of The Metal Men!" 19.00 60.00
50 19.00 60.00
51-59 17.00 55.00

JOURNEY TO THE CENTER OF THE EARTH
DELL FOUR COLOR SERIES (1959)
1060 Movie photo cover (Pat Boone, James Mason). (11/59) 31.00 100.00

JUDE, THE FORGOTTEN SAINT
CATECHETICAL GUILD (1953)
NO# 5.00 15.00

JUDGE COLT
GOLD KEY (1969-1970)
1 2.00 7.00
2 1.75 6.00
3-4 1.50 5.00

JUDGE DREDD
DC (1994-CURRENT)
1 1.00 3.00
2-10 .50 2.00
11-15 .75 2.25

JUDGE DREDD
EAGLE/QUALITY (1983-1986)
1 Begin: Cover&Art by Brian Bolland. 5.00 15.00
2 2.75 10.00
3-9 2.25 8.00
10 End: Cover/Art by Brian Bolland. 2.25 8.00
11-14 1.25 4.50
15 Cover&art: Brian Bolland. 1.25 4.50
16-20 1.25 4.50
21-35 1.00 3.00

JUDGE DREDD
QUALITY/FLEETWAY (1986-1991)
1 1.50 5.00
2-49 1.00 3.00
50 .75 2.50
51-59 .75 2.25
60 Title changes to Judge Dredd Classics with #61. .75 2.25

JUDGE DREDD: AMERICA
QUALITY/FLEETWAY
BOOK 1-BOOK 2 .75 2.95

JUDGE DREDD AND THE ANGEL GANG
TITAN (1995)
TPB 8.00 23.50

JUDGE DREDD CLASSICS
QUALITY/FLEETWAY (1991-1993)
61 Previously title: Judge Dredd. .50 2.00
62-77 .50 2.00

JUDGE DREDD CRIME FILES
EAGLE/QUALITY (1985-1986)
1-6 .75 2.00

JUDGE DREDD: FUTURE CRIME
SQ PRODUCTIONS (1995)
GN Reprints. 2.00 7.95

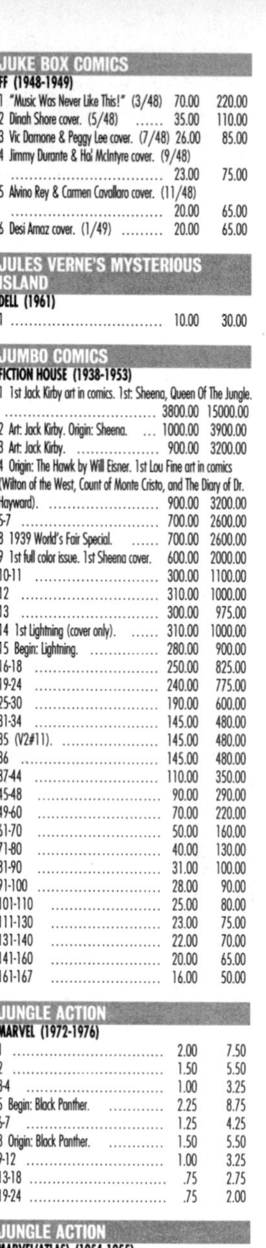

JUDGE DREDD: LEGENDS OF THE LAW
DC (1994-CURRENT)
1-6 .50 1.95
7-10 .75 2.25

JUDGE DREDD MEGA COLLECTION
SQ PRODUCTIONS (1995)
GN Hardcover. Reprints. 5.00 14.95

JUDGE DREDD: RAPTAUR
QUALITY/FLEETWAY
BOOK 1-BOOK 2 .75 2.95

JUDGE DREDD: THE EARLY CASES
EAGLE (1986)
1-6 .75 2.25

JUDGE DREDD: THE JUDGE CHILD QUEST
EAGLE (1984)
1-5 .75 2.50

JUDGE DREDD: THE OFFICIAL MOVIE ADAPTATION
DC (1995)
NO# Softcover movie tie-in. 1.50 5.95

JUDGE DREDD'S HARDCASE PAPERS
FLEETWAY/QUALITY (1987)
1 Reprints. 1.50 5.95
2-4 1.50 5.95

JUDGE PARKER
ARGO (1956)
1 Newspaper reprints. 7.00 20.00

JUDGEMENT DAY
LIGHTNING (1993-1994)
1 Gold prism cover. 1.50 5.00
2 Polybagged with card. 1.00 3.50
2A Signed & numbered. 2.50 9.95
3-10 .75 2.95

JUDO JOE
JAY-JAY (1953)
1 10.00 30.00
2-3 7.00 20.00

JUDOMASTER
CHARLTON (1966-1967)
89-98 5.00 15.00

JUDY CANOVA
FOX FEATURES (1950)
1 (#23, 5/50) Cover & art: Wallace Wood. 31.00 100.00
2 (#24, 7/50) Cover & art: Wallace Wood. 31.00 100.00
3 Cover & art: Wallace Wood. (9/50) 31.00 100.00

JUGHEAD
ARCHIE (1965-1987)
122 Previous title: Archie's Pal, Jughead. 4.00 11.00
123 2.25 8.00
124-150 2.25 8.75
151-175 1.50 5.50
176-200 1.00 3.25
201-250 .75 2.00
251-300 .50 1.50
301-352 .30 1.00

JUGHEAD AS CAPTAIN HERO
ARCHIE (1966-1967)
1 10.00 33.00
2 7.00 22.00
3-5 5.00 16.00
6-7 4.00 11.00

JUGHEAD'S FANTASY
ARCHIE (1960)
1 40.00 130.00
2 22.00 70.00
3 17.00 55.00

JUGHEAD'S FOLLY
ARCHIE (1957)
1 (One Shot). Jughead as Elvis Presley. 95.00 300.00

JUGHEAD'S JOKES
ARCHIE (1967-1982)
1 15.00 49.00
2 7.00 22.00
3-6 4.00 11.00
7-24 1.50 5.50
25-40 1.00 3.25
41-60 .75 2.00
61-78 .30 1.00

JUKE BOX COMICS
FF (1948-1949)
1 "Music Was Never Like This!" (3/48) 70.00 220.00
2 Dinah Shore cover. (5/48) 35.00 110.00
3 Vic Damone & Peggy Lee cover. (7/48) 26.00 85.00
4 Jimmy Durante & Hal McIntyre cover. (9/48) 23.00 75.00
5 Alvino Rey & Carmen Cavallaro cover. (11/48) 20.00 65.00
6 Desi Arnaz cover. (1/49) 20.00 65.00

JULES VERNE'S MYSTERIOUS ISLAND
DELL (1961)
1 10.00 30.00

JUMBO COMICS
FICTION HOUSE (1938-1953)
1 1st Jack Kirby art in comics. 1st: Sheena, Queen Of The Jungle. 3800.00 15000.00
2 Art: Jack Kirby. Origin: Sheena. 1000.00 3900.00
3 Art: Jack Kirby. 900.00 3200.00
4 Origin: The Hawk by Will Eisner. 1st Lou Fine art in comics (Wilton of the West, Count of Monte Cristo, and The Diary of Dr. Hayward). 900.00 3200.00
5-7 700.00 2600.00
8 1939 World's Fair Special. 700.00 2600.00
9 1st full color issue. 1st Sheena cover. 600.00 2000.00
10-11 300.00 1100.00
12 310.00 1000.00
13 300.00 975.00
14 1st Lightning (cover only). 310.00 1000.00
15 Begin: Lightning. 280.00 900.00
16-18 250.00 825.00
19-24 240.00 775.00
25-30 190.00 600.00
31-34 145.00 480.00
35 (V2#11). 145.00 480.00
36 145.00 480.00
37-44 110.00 350.00
45-48 90.00 290.00
49-60 70.00 220.00
61-70 50.00 160.00
71-80 40.00 130.00
81-90 31.00 100.00
91-100 28.00 90.00
101-110 25.00 80.00
111-130 23.00 75.00
131-140 22.00 70.00
141-160 20.00 65.00
161-167 16.00 50.00

JUNGLE ACTION
MARVEL (1972-1976)
1 2.00 7.50
2 1.50 5.50
3-4 1.00 3.25
5 Begin: Black Panther. 2.25 8.75
6-7 1.25 4.25
8 Origin: Black Panther. 1.50 5.50
9-12 1.00 3.25
13-18 .75 2.75
19-24 .75 2.00

JUNGLE ACTION
MARVEL(ATLAS) (1954-1955)
1 Begin: Leopard Girl. 45.00 140.00
2 45.00 140.00
3 35.00 110.00
4 1st Code approved issue. 28.00 90.00
5-6 25.00 80.00

JUNGLE ADVENTURES
SUPER (1963)
10 Reprints in all issues. 5.00 15.00
12-18 5.00 15.00

JUNGLE BOOK, THE
GOLD KEY (1968)
30033-803 Disney movie tie-in. 7.00 20.00
6022-801 Disney movie tie-in. 7.00 20.00

JUNGLE CAT
DELL FOUR COLOR SERIES (1960)
1136 Movie photo cover. (9/60) 13.00 40.00

JUNGLE COMICS
FICTION HOUSE (1940-1954)
1 1st & Origin: Kaanga, Tabu, Wizard of the Jungle, White Panther and Wambi. 500.00 1900.00
2 Begin: Fantomah; Red Panther. 280.00 900.00
3 240.00 775.00
4 220.00 700.00
5 200.00 650.00
6 180.00 575.00
7 155.00 500.00
8-9 145.00 480.00
10-12 140.00 450.00

JOURNEY INTO UNKNOWN WORLDS #26

JUDGE DREDD #1 (1ST SERIES)

JUDGE DREDD: LEGENDS OF THE LAW #9

JUDGEMENT DAY #4

a b c d e f g h i j k l m n o p q r s t u v w x y z

JUNGLE COMICS #71

JUNGLE COMICS #78

JUSTICE LEAGUE OF AMERICA #22

JUSTICE LEAGUE OF AMERICA #29

13-14	120.00	390.00
15-18	100.00	320.00
19-24	80.00	260.00
25 Vol. 2 #1 appears on the cover instead of #25.	75.00	240.00
26-30	70.00	220.00
31-40	60.00	190.00
41-50	55.00	180.00
51-60	50.00	160.00
61-70	50.00	150.00
71-80	45.00	140.00
81-90	40.00	130.00
91-97	35.00	110.00
98 SOTI.	60.00	190.00
99-110	35.00	110.00
111-120	31.00	100.00
121-130	29.00	95.00
131-163	25.00	80.00

JUNGLE DRUMS
CPI (1952)

20 Canadian.	8.00	25.00

JUNGLE GIRL
FAWCETT (1942)

1 Movie photo cover. Title changes to Nyoka with #2.	170.00	550.00

JUNGLE JIM
CHARLTON (1969-1970)

22 Art: Steve Ditko.	8.00	25.00
23-26	8.00	25.00
27-28 Art:Steve Ditko.	8.00	25.00

JUNGLE JIM
DELL (1953-1959)

3-6	5.00	16.00
7-12	4.00	12.00
13-19	2.75	10.00

JUNGLE JIM
DELL FOUR COLOR SERIES (1953-1959)

490 (8/53)	13.00	40.00
565 (6/54)	7.00	20.00
1020 (8/59)	5.00	15.00

JUNGLE JIM
KING (1967)

5 Reprint.	1.50	5.00

JUNGLE JIM
STANDARD (1949-1951)

11	10.00	30.00
12-15	8.00	24.00
16-20	5.00	16.00

JUNGLE JO
FOX (1950-1951)

1	45.00	140.00
2	31.00	100.00
3-6	28.00	90.00

JUNGLE LIL
FOX (1950)

1	50.00	150.00

JUNGLE TALES
MARVEL(ATLAS) (1954-1955)

1 Begin: Jann Of The Jungle.	35.00	110.00
2	25.00	80.00
3-6	20.00	65.00
7 Title changes to Jann Of The Jungle with #8.	20.00	65.00

JUNGLE TALES OF TARZAN
CHARLTON (1964-1965)

1	7.00	20.00
2-5	4.00	12.00

JUNGLE THRILLS
STAR (1952-1953)

3-D(#1) With glasses.	65.00	200.00
16 Cover: L.B. Cole. Reprint: Phantom Lady and Rulah. Becomes Terrors of the Jungle #17.	50.00	150.00

JUNGLE TWINS, THE
GOLD KEY (1972-1975)

1	1.50	5.00
2-6	.75	2.00
7-18	.30	1.00

JUNIE PROM COMICS
DEARFIELD (1947-1949)

1	16.00	50.00
2-6	8.00	25.00

JUNIOR COMICS
FOX (1947-1948)

9 Cover & art: Al Feldstein.	95.00	300.00
10-16 Cover & art: Al Feldstein.	80.00	250.00

JUNIOR HOPP COMICS
STANMOR (1952)

1	10.00	30.00
2-3	7.00	20.00

JUNIOR MISS
MARVEL(TIMELY) (1947-1950)

24	16.00	50.00
25	10.00	30.00
26-30	8.00	24.00
31-39	6.00	18.00

JURASSIC PARK
TOPPS (1993)

1	1.25	4.50
1A Newsstand edition.	1.00	3.00
2	1.00	3.25
2A Newsstand edition.	.75	2.50
3	.75	2.95
3A Newsstand edition.	.75	2.50
4	.75	2.95
4A Newsstand edition.	.75	2.50
ANNUAL 1	1.00	3.95

JURASSIC PARK ADVENTURES
TOPPS (1994-CURRENT)

1-10	.50	1.95

JURASSIC PARK: RAPTOR
TOPPS (1993)

1-2	.75	2.95

JURASSIC PARK: RAPTORS ATTACK!
TOPPS (1994)

1-4	.75	2.50

JURASSIC PARK: RAPTORS HIJACK
TOPPS (1994)

1-2	.75	2.50

JUST MARRIED
CHARLTON (1958-1976)

1	7.00	20.00
2	2.75	10.00
3-12	2.25	8.00
13-24	1.75	6.00
25-40	1.25	4.00
41-60	1.00	3.00
61-80	.75	2.50
81-100	.75	2.00
101-114	.30	1.00

JUSTICE
MARVEL (1986-1989)

1-32	.30	1.00

JUSTICE
MARVEL(ATLAS) (1948-1955)

4	17.00	55.00
5-9	14.00	44.00
10 Begin: photo covers.	17.00	55.00
11-14	17.00	55.00
15 End: photo covers.	17.00	55.00
16-30	10.00	33.00
31-40	9.00	27.00
41-52	7.00	22.00

JUSTICE: FOUR BALANCE
MARVEL (1994)

1-2	.50	1.75

JUSTICE, INC.
DC (1975)

1	.30	1.00
2-4 Art: Jack Kirby.	.30	1.00

JUSTICE LEAGUE (INTERNATIONAL #7-25; AMERICA #26-UP)
DC (1987-CURRENT)

0 (8/94)	.50	1.50
1 1st: Maxwell Lord.	2.00	7.00
2	1.25	4.00
3	1.00	3.00
3A Limited test edition (Superman logo instead of DC logo).	18.00	60.00
4-6	1.00	3.00
7 Begin: Justice League International.	1.25	4.00
8-23	.75	2.00
24	1.25	4.00
25	.75	2.00
26 Begin: Justice League America.	.75	2.00
27-30	.75	2.00
31-35	1.00	3.00
36-61	.75	2.00
62-68	.50	1.50
69 Doomsday battle.	1.75	6.00
70 Begin: Funeral For A Friend.	1.25	4.00
70A Newsstand edition (without outer cover).	.75	2.00
71	1.00	3.00
71A Newsstand edition (without outer cover).	.50	1.50
72-91	.50	1.50
92 Zero Hour.	.75	2.00
93-99	.50	1.50
100 Double size, holographic foil cover.	1.00	3.95
100A Regular cover.	.75	2.95
101-104	.50	1.75
ANNUAL 1 (1987)	1.25	4.00
ANNUAL 2 (1988)	1.25	4.00
ANNUAL 3 (1989)	1.00	3.00
ANNUAL 4 (1990)	.75	2.00
ANNUAL 5 Armageddon 2001. (1991)	.75	2.00
ANNUAL 5A 2nd printing (silver).	.75	2.00
ANNUAL 6 (1992)	.75	2.00
ANNUAL 7 Bloodlines, pt.15 (1993)	.75	2.00
ANNUAL 8 Elseworlds story. (1994)	.75	2.00
ANNUAL 9 Year One. (1995)	.75	2.00

JUSTICE LEAGUE ARCHIVES
DC COMICS (1993)

1 Hardcover. Reprints: Brave & Bold #28-30, JLA (1st) #1-6.	12.00	39.95
2 Hardcover. Reprints: JLA (1st) #7-14.	12.00	39.95
3 Hardcover. Reprints: JLA (1st) #15-22.	15.00	49.95

JUSTICE LEAGUE EUROPE
DC (1989-1994)

1	1.00	3.00
2-19	.75	2.00
20-49	.50	1.25
50 Double size, anniversary issue. Team changes name to Justice League International.	.75	2.50
51-68	.50	1.25
ANNUAL 1 (1990)	.75	2.00
ANNUAL 2 (1991)	.75	2.00
ANNUAL 3 (1992)	.75	2.00
ANNUAL 4 (1993)	.75	2.00
ANNUAL 5 Elseworlds story. (1994)	.75	2.95

JUSTICE LEAGUE OF AMERICA
DC (1960-1987)

1 1st & origin: Despero in "World Of No Return!" (11/60)	700.00	2700.00
2 "Secret Of The Sinister Sorcerers!" (1/61)	190.00	625.00
3 1st & origin: Kanjar Ro. "Slave Ship Of Space!" (3/61)	140.00	450.00
4 Green Arrow joins JLA. "Doom Of The Star Diamond!" (5/61)	95.00	315.00
5 1st & origin: Dr. Destiny. "When Gravity Went Wild!" (7/61)	70.00	230.00
6 1st & origin: Professor Amos Fortune. "The Wheel Of Misfortune!" (9/61)	60.00	190.00
7 "The Cosmic Fun-House!" (11/61)	60.00	190.00
8 1st 12-cent cover price. "For Sale...The Justice League!" (1/62)	60.00	190.00
9 Origin: JLA. "The Origin Of The Justice League!" (2/62)	105.00	340.00
10 "The Fantastic Fingers Of Felix Faust!" (3/62)	60.00	190.00
11-13	45.00	140.00
14 The Atom joins JLA. (9/62)	45.00	140.00
15 "Challenge Of The Untouchable Aliens!" (11/62)	45.00	140.00
16-18	35.00	110.00
19-20	31.00	100.00
21 "Crisis On Earth-One!" (8/63) featuring the first full re-introduction of The Justice Society from the Golden Age. 1st Silver-Age Hourman, Dr. Fate.	65.00	215.00
22 "Crisis On Earth-Two!", part 2 of JSA story.	55.00	180.00
23-28	19.00	60.00
29 App: JSA in "Crisis On Earth-Three!" 1st Silver-Age Starman.	19.00	60.00
30 App: JSA.	19.00	60.00
31	19.00	60.00
32 1st & origin: Brain Storm.	13.00	40.00
33-34	13.00	40.00
35-36	10.00	30.00
37 App: JSA in "The Earth Without A Justice League!"	19.00	60.00
38 App: JSA.	19.00	60.00
39 80 Pg. Giant G-16.	23.00	75.00
40-41	10.00	30.00
42-45	8.00	25.00
46 1st Silver-Age Sandman. App: Batman, Wildcat, Solomon Grundy, JSA.	28.00	90.00
47 App: JSA.	8.00	25.00
48 80 Pg. Giant G-29.	11.00	35.00
49-54	5.00	16.00
55 Debut: Earth II Robin.	16.00	50.00
56 "Justice League Vs. Justice Society!"	7.00	20.00

57	5.00	16.00
58 80 Pg. Giant G-41.	10.00	30.00
59-60	5.00	16.00
61-63	2.75	10.00
64 App: JSA. 1st & Origin: Red Tornado in "Stormy Return Of Red Tornado!"	5.00	15.00
65-66	2.75	10.00
67 80 Pg. Giant G-53.	8.00	25.00
68-70	2.75	10.00
71	2.50	9.00
72	2.00	7.00
73 1st 15-cent issue.	2.00	7.00
74-75	2.00	7.00
76 80 Pg. Giant G-65.	5.00	15.00
77	2.00	7.00
78-84	1.50	5.00
85	5.00	15.00
86	1.50	5.00
87	2.75	10.00
88-92	1.50	5.00
93 80 Pg. Giant G-89.	5.00	15.00
94 Reprint: Adventure Comics #40, 61. Double size.	10.00	30.00
95 Double size.	2.75	10.00
96 Reprint: Adventure Comics #48. Double size.	1.50	5.00
97 Double size. Origin retold: JLA.	1.50	5.00
98 Double size.	1.50	5.00
99 Double size. Golden-Age reprints.	1.50	5.00
100	2.25	8.00
101-102 JSA.	1.50	5.00
103-106	1.50	5.00
107	2.75	10.00
108-109	1.50	5.00
110 Begin: 100 page issues.	1.75	6.00
111	1.75	6.00
112 Reprint: Adventure Comics #61 (1st Starman).	1.75	6.00
113-114	1.75	6.00
115	1.00	3.00
116 End: 100 page issues.	1.00	3.00
117-128	1.00	3.00
129-136	.75	2.00
137 Superman battles Shazam.	.75	2.00
138-192	.75	2.00
193 1st All-Star Squadron.	.75	2.00
194-199	.75	2.00
200 Anniversary issue.	1.25	4.00
201-232	.50	1.50
233 Begin: new JLA.	.50	1.50
234-243	.50	1.50
244-245 Crisis.	.50	1.50
246-249	.50	1.50
250	1.00	3.00
251-257	.50	1.50
258 Death: Vibe.	.50	1.50
259	.50	1.50
260 Death: Steel.	.50	1.50
261	1.25	4.00

JUSTICE LEAGUE OF AMERICA ANNUAL

DC (1983-1985)

1 (1983)	1.50	5.00
2 Debut: new JLA. (1984)	1.25	4.00
3 Crisis. (1985)	1.25	4.00

JUSTICE LEAGUE QUARTERLY

DC (1990-1993)

1-17	.75	2.50

JUSTICE LEAGUE TASK FORCE

DC (1993-CURRENT)

0 (8/94)	.75	2.00
1 w/ membership card.	.75	2.50
2-4	.50	1.75
5	.75	2.50
6-28	.50	1.75

JUSTICE MACHINE

COMICO (1987-1989)

1-29	.30	1.00
ANNUAL 1 (1987)	.30	1.00

JUSTICE MACHINE

NOBLE (1981-1984)

1 Cover: John Byrne. Issues #1-3 are magazine size.	2.50	9.00
2	1.75	6.00
3	1.25	4.00
4-5 Flip book: Cobalt Blue.	1.00	3.00
ANNUAL 1 1st: Elementals (1984).	1.75	6.00

JUSTICE SOCIETY OF AMERICA

DC (1991)

1	.50	1.50
2-8	.30	1.00

JUSTICE SOCIETY OF AMERICA

DC (1992-1993)

1-10	.30	1.00

JUSTICE TRAPS THE GUILTY

PRIZE (1947-1958)

1 Cover & art: Simon & Kirby on issue #s 1-21.	65.00	210.00
2	31.00	100.00
3-6	28.00	90.00
7-12	23.00	75.00
13 SOTI.	16.00	50.00
14-20	15.00	48.00
21-29	10.00	30.00
30 Cover & art: Simon & Kirby.	15.00	48.00
31-40	6.00	18.00
41-50	5.00	14.00
51-57	4.00	12.00
58 SOTI.	28.00	90.00
59-75	4.00	12.00
76 Art: Joe Orlando.	4.00	12.00
77-92	4.00	12.00

KA'A'NGA COMICS

FICTION HOUSE (1949-1954)

1	75.00	240.00
2	40.00	120.00
3	28.00	90.00
4-6	22.00	70.00
7-12	19.00	60.00
13-20	15.00	48.00
IW 1-IW 8	4.00	12.00

KAANGA JUNGLE KING

I.W. (1964)

1 Reprints original series.	7.00	20.00

KABUKI: CIRCLE OF BLOOD

CALIBER (1995-CURRENT)

1 Origin: Kabuki.	1.75	6.00
2-4	.75	2.95

KABUKI COMPILATION

CALIBER (1995)

1 Reprints Fear The Reaper & Dance Of Death.	2.00	7.95

KABUKI: DANCE OF DEATH

LONDON NIGHT STUDIOS (1995-CURRENT)

1, 1A	1.50	5.00

KABUKI: FEAR THE REAPER

CALIBER (1994)

1 1st: Kabuki. One shot.	1.75	6.00

KAMANDI: AT EARTH'S END

DC (1993)

1-6	.30	1.00

KAMANDI, THE LAST BOY ON EARTH

DC (1972-1978)

1 1st & origin: Kamandi.	8.00	25.00
2	5.00	16.00
3-6	2.75	10.00
7-12	2.50	9.00
13-24	1.75	6.00
25 1st 25-cent cover price.	1.00	3.00
26-28	1.00	3.00
29 Superman.	1.00	3.00
30	1.00	3.00
31 Debut: Pyra.	1.00	3.00
32 Jack Kirby biography (4 pages).	1.25	4.00
33-58	1.00	3.00
59	1.50	5.00

KAMUI

ECLIPSE (1987-1990)

1	2.75	10.00
2	1.75	6.00
3-6	1.50	5.00
7-12	1.25	4.00
13-37	1.00	3.00

KARATE KID

DC (1976-1978)

1-15	.30	1.00

KASCO KOMICS

KASCO (1945-1949)

1 Art: Bill Woggon (1945 giveaway).	19.00	60.00
2 Art: Bill Woggon (1949 giveaway).	10.00	30.00

KATY KEENE

ARCHIE (1949-1961)

1 Art: Bill Woggon (all issues).	140.00	460.00
1 (3-D) With glasses.	65.00	200.00
2	70.00	230.00
3-6	60.00	190.00
7-12	50.00	150.00
13-18	40.00	130.00
19-24	35.00	110.00
25-30	25.00	80.00
31-44	22.00	70.00
45-62	19.00	60.00
ANNUAL 1	80.00	260.00
ANNUAL 2-ANNUAL 6	65.00	210.00

KATY KEENE FASHION BOOK

ARCHIE (1955-1959)

1	60.00	190.00
2	40.00	130.00
3-6	29.00	95.00
7-12	20.00	65.00
13-18	16.00	50.00
19-23	12.00	39.00

KATY KEENE PINUP PARADE

ARCHIE (1955-1961)

1	60.00	190.00
2	40.00	130.00
3 (1957)	31.00	100.00
4-6	29.00	95.00
7	23.00	75.00
8 Parody of MAD magazine.	29.00	95.00
9-15	20.00	65.00

KATY KEENE SPECIAL

ARCHIE (1983-1990)

1-33	.30	1.00

KATY KEENE SPECTACULAR

ARCHIE (1956)

1	50.00	160.00

KATZENJAMMER KIDS, THE

MCKAY/STANDARD (1947-1954)

1	19.00	60.00
2	10.00	30.00
3-4	7.00	20.00
5-12	5.00	15.00
13-20	2.75	10.00
21-27	1.75	6.00

KA-ZAR

MARVEL (1970-1971)

1 Cover & art: Jack Kirby (all issues). App: X-Men, Avengers, Daredevil.	4.00	12.00
2 Origin: Ka-Zar.	2.50	9.00
3	2.25	8.00

KA-ZAR

MARVEL (1974-1977)

1-20	.75	2.00

KA-ZAR THE SAVAGE

MARVEL (1981-1984)

1-34	.30	1.00

KEEN DETECTIVE FUNNIES

CENTAUR (1938-1940)

8 Reprint: Funny Picture Stories 1.	310.00	1000.00
9 Art: Will Eisner (Tex Martin story).	170.00	550.00
10-11	140.00	450.00
18-22	125.00	400.00
23 Debut: Air Man.	190.00	600.00
24 Air Man.	190.00	600.00
V2#1 Begin: The Eye Sees.	155.00	500.00
V2#2	125.00	400.00
V2#3	125.00	400.00
V2#4-V2#6	125.00	400.00
V2#7 1st & origin: The Masked Marvel.	250.00	800.00
V2#10-V3#1	125.00	400.00
V2#12 Origin: The Eye Sees.	170.00	550.00

KEEN KOMICS

CENTAUR (1939)

1 (Oversized)	400.00	1500.00
2 Art: Carlos Burgos on Cut Carson.	125.00	400.00
3	125.00	400.00

KEN MAYNARD WESTERN

FAWCETT (1950-1952)

1 Photo covers on all.	100.00	330.00
2	70.00	220.00
3	60.00	190.00
4	50.00	160.00
5	40.00	130.00
6-8	35.00	110.00

KEN SHANNON

QUALITY (1951-1953)

1 Art: Reed Crandall in all issues.	31.00	100.00
2	19.00	60.00
3-5	16.00	50.00
6 "The Weird Vampire Mob!" by Reed Crandall (cover & art).	25.00	80.00

KA'A'NGA COMICS #16

KAMANDI: THE LAST BOY ON EARTH #1

KATY KEENE #2

KA-ZAR #1 (1ST SERIES)

KID COLT OUTLAW #40

KID ETERNITY #1 [QUALITY]

KING CONAN #16

KING OF KINGS #1236

FAMOUS • FIRSTS

LEADING COMICS #1

DC used its second-rate heroes to create a second-team *Justice Society of America*. Called The Seven Soldiers of Victory, it featured The Vigilante, Green Arrow, The Star Spangled Kid, The Shining Knight and The Crimson Avenger.

7-10	13.00	40.00

KENT BLAKE OF THE SECRET SERVICE
MARVEL(ATLAS) (1951-1953)

1	16.00	50.00
2	10.00	30.00
3-6	8.00	25.00
7-14	7.00	20.00

KERRY DRAKE DETECTIVE CASES
ME/HARVEY (1944-1952)

NO# From the A-1 series.	31.00	100.00
2	19.00	60.00
3-5	16.00	50.00
6-10	10.00	30.00
11-20	7.00	20.00
21-25	5.00	15.00
26-33	2.75	10.00

KEWPIES
WILL EISNER PUB. (1949)

1 Art: Will Eisner.	65.00	200.00

KEY COMICS
CM (1944-1946)

1 Begin: The Key.	40.00	120.00
2	19.00	60.00
3-5	16.00	50.00

KID COLT OUTLAW
MARVEL (1948-1979)

NO# "He Lived By His Guns" 1950 giveaway by Wisco 99, Carnation, Klarer, and other companies. Miniature size.	80.00	250.00
1 App: Two-Gun Kid.	145.00	480.00
2	65.00	210.00
3-6	60.00	190.00
7-10	45.00	140.00
11 Origin: Kid Colt.	60.00	190.00
12	45.00	140.00
13-24	40.00	120.00
25-30	28.00	90.00
31-35	22.00	70.00
36-40	19.00	60.00
41-50	15.00	48.00
51-60	11.00	35.00
61-75	10.00	30.00
76-90	8.00	25.00
91-100	7.00	20.00
101 1st 12-cent cover price.	5.00	15.00
102-110	5.00	15.00
111-120	4.00	12.00
121-130	2.75	10.00
131-139	2.25	8.00
140 Begin: reprints of earlier issues.	2.25	8.00
141-150	2.25	8.00
151-160	1.75	6.00
161-180	1.50	5.00
181-200	1.25	4.00
201-210	1.00	3.00
211-229	.75	2.00

KID COWBOY
ST. JOHN (1954)

4 From Approved Comics series.	7.00	20.00

KID COWBOY
ZIFF-DAVIS (1950-1954)

1	8.00	25.00
2	5.00	15.00
3-6	2.75	10.00
7-12	1.75	6.00
13-14	1.25	4.00

KID ETERNITY
DC (1991)

1 Origin: Kid Eternity by Grant Morrison.	1.50	5.00
2 Origin continued.	1.50	5.00
3 Origin concludes.	1.50	5.00

KID ETERNITY
DC(VERTIGO) (1993-1994)

1-16	.50	1.95

KID ETERNITY
QUALITY (1946-1949)

1 See also: HIT COMICS.	120.00	390.00
2	75.00	240.00
3	65.00	210.00
4-6	55.00	180.00
7-12	50.00	150.00
13-18	40.00	120.00

KID KOMICS
MARVEL(TIMELY) (1943-1946)

1 Art: Basil Wolverton (7 pgs.). App: Sub-Mariner.	500.00	1800.00
2 Begin: The Young Allies.	310.00	1000.00
3	230.00	750.00
4 App: Sub-Mariner.	190.00	625.00
5-6	155.00	500.00
7-10	115.00	370.00

KID MOVIE KOMICS
MARVEL(TIMELY) (1946)

11 Last issue of Kid Komics with minor title change. Funny animal stories.	50.00	150.00

KID SLADE GUNFIGHTER
MARVEL(ATLAS) (1957)

5 Previous title: Matt Slade, Gunfighter.	10.00	30.00
6	8.00	25.00
7-8	7.00	20.00

KIDNAPPED
DELL FOUR COLOR SERIES (1960)

1101 Movie photo cover. (5/60)	10.00	30.00

KIDNAPPED
GOLD KEY (1963)

10080-306 Disney movie photo cover. Reprints Four Color #1101.	5.00	15.00

KILL RAZOR SPECIAL
IMAGE/TOP COW (1995)

1 One shot.	1.00	3.00

KILL YOUR BOYFRIEND
DC (1995)

1 One-shot.	1.25	4.95

KILLER INSTINCT
IMAGE (1993)

1 Tour Book, unsigned.	1.75	6.00
1A Signed by artists/writers.	14.00	45.00

KILLERS
ME (1947-1948)

1 Killers Three. SOTI.	110.00	360.00
2 "Dying, Dying, Dead!" about smoking dope.	130.00	420.00

KILLFRENZY
MARVEL (1994)

1 1st: Killfrenzy.	.50	1.95
2	.50	1.95

KILLPOWER: THE EARLY YEARS
MARVEL (1993)

1 Foil-embossed cover.	.75	2.95
2-9	.50	1.75

KILROYS, THE
ACG (1947-1955)

1	23.00	75.00
2	10.00	30.00
3-6	8.00	25.00
7-12	7.00	20.00
13-20	5.00	15.00
21-30	2.75	10.00
31-40	2.25	8.00
41-47	1.75	6.00
48-49 3-D effect.	2.75	10.00
50-54	1.75	6.00

KINDRED
IMAGE/WILDSTORM (1994)

1 1st: Kindred. 1st: Bloodmoon.	2.50	9.50
2	1.75	6.50
3	1.50	5.50
3A Variant cover.	4.00	12.50
4	.75	2.50
TPB Reprints issues #1-4.	2.50	9.95

KING COMICS
DAVID MCKAY (1936-1952)

1 1st: Flash Gordon in comics. Art: Alex Raymond (through issue #115).	1300.00	4800.00

2 ..... 600.00 2200.00
3 ..... 400.00 1500.00
4 ..... 400.00 1300.00
5 ..... 300.00 1100.00
6 ..... 200.00 650.00
7 ..... 170.00 550.00
8 ..... 150.00 490.00
9-12 ..... 135.00 440.00
13-15 ..... 115.00 380.00
16-20 ..... 100.00 330.00
21-30 ..... 85.00 270.00
31-40 ..... 75.00 240.00
41-49 ..... 70.00 220.00
50 Begin: Lone Ranger. 75.00 240.00
51-53 ..... 70.00 220.00
54-60 ..... 60.00 190.00
61 Begin: The Phantom. 65.00 200.00
62-65 ..... 55.00 170.00
66-70 ..... 40.00 130.00
71-80 ..... 35.00 110.00
81-90 ..... 26.00 85.00
91-99 ..... 23.00 75.00
100 ..... 26.00 85.00
101-110 ..... 22.00 70.00
111-120 ..... 17.00 55.00
121-130 ..... 14.00 44.00
131-140 ..... 10.00 33.00
141-150 ..... 9.00 27.00
151-154 ..... 7.00 22.00
155 End: Flash Gordon. 7.00 22.00
156-159 ..... 5.00 16.00

KING CONAN
MARVEL (1980-1983)
1 ..... .75 2.00
2-18 ..... .30 1.00
19 Title changes to Conan The King with #20. .30 1.00

KING KONG
GOLD KEY (1968)
30036-809 Movie tie-in. 7.00 20.00

KING LEONARDO AND HIS SHORT SUBJECTS
DELL FOUR COLOR SERIES (1961-1962)
1242 TV tie-in. (10/61) 26.00 85.00
1278 TV tie-in. (1/62) 25.00 80.00

KING LEONARDO AND HIS SHORT SUBJECTS
GOLD KEY (1962-1963)
1 TV cartoon tie-in. 20.00 65.00
2 ..... 10.00 33.00
3-4 ..... 7.00 22.00

KING OF DIAMONDS
DELL (1962)
01-391-209 TV photo cover. 7.00 20.00

KING OF KINGS
DELL FOUR COLOR SERIES (1961)
1236 Movie photo cover. 16.00 50.00

KING OF THE BAD MEN OF DEADWOOD
AVON (1950)
NO# 19.00 60.00

KING OF THE ROYAL MOUNTED
DELL (1952-1958)
8 ..... 10.00 30.00
9-12 ..... 7.00 20.00
13-18 ..... 5.00 16.00
19-28 ..... 4.00 12.00

KING OF THE ROYAL MOUNTED
DELL FOUR COLOR SERIES (1948-1958)
207 (12/48) 31.00 100.00
265 (2/50) 20.00 65.00
283 (7/50) 22.00 70.00
310 (1/51) 14.00 45.00
340 (7/51) 14.00 45.00
363 (12/51) 11.00 35.00
384 (3/52) 11.00 35.00
935 (9/58) 8.00 25.00

KING OF THE ROYAL MOUNTED
SEE LARGE FEATURE COMICS #9.

KING RICHARD AND THE CRUSADERS
DELL FOUR COLOR SERIES (1954)
588 Movie photo cover. (10/54) 23.00 75.00

KING SOLOMON'S MINES
AVON (1951)
NO# 50.00 150.00

KISS
SEE MARVEL COMICS SUPER SPECIAL

KISS CLASSIC
MARVEL (1995)
TPB Reprints: Marvel Comics Super Special #1,5.
..... 2.75 10.00

KIT CARSON
AVON (1950-1955)
1 (No#). "Indian Scout" 16.00 50.00
2 ..... 10.00 30.00
3 "Fights The Comanche Raiders" 8.00 25.00
4 ..... 7.00 20.00
5 "And The Trail Of Doom" 7.00 20.00
6-8 ..... 7.00 20.00

KIT CARSON & THE BLACKFEET WARRIORS!
REALISTIC (1953)
NO# 10.00 30.00

KITTY PRYDE AND WOLVERINE
MARVEL (1984-1985)
1 ..... 1.75 6.00
2 ..... 1.50 5.00
3-6 ..... 1.00 3.00

KNIGHTHAWK
ACCLAIM/WINDJAMMER (1995)
1 Mini-series. ..... .75 2.50
2-6 ..... .75 2.50

KNIGHTHAWK THE PROTECTOR
CONTINUITY (1993)
1-3 ..... .75 2.50

KNIGHTMARE
IMAGE (1995-CURRENT)
1-6 ..... .75 2.50

KNIGHTS OF PENDRAGON
MARVEL UK (1990-1991)
1-18 ..... .75 2.00

KNIGHTS OF THE ROUND TABLE
DELL (1964)
12-397-401 ..... 7.00 20.00

KNIGHTS OF THE ROUND TABLE
DELL FOUR COLOR SERIES (1954)
540 Photo cover. (3/54) 16.00 50.00

KNOCK KNOCK WHO'S THERE
WHITMAN (1936)
801 Featuring Enoch Knox. 16.00 50.00

KNOCKOUT ADVENTURES
FICTION HOUSE (1953)
1 Reprint: Fight Comics 53. ..... 19.00 60.00

KNOWING'S NOT ENOUGH
UNITED STATES STEEL (1956)
NO# Giveaway. Sparling cover (full color race car).
..... 16.00 50.00

KO KOMICS
GERONA (1945)
1 ..... 50.00 150.00

KOBALT
DC (1994-1995)
1-13 ..... .50 1.75
14-15 ..... .75 2.50
16 ..... 1.00 3.95

KOBRA
DC (1976-1977)
1 1st Kobra. ..... .50 1.50
2-7 ..... .30 1.00

KOKEY KOALA
TOBY (1952)
1 ..... 11.00 35.00

KOKO AND KOLA
ME (1946-1950)
1 ..... 10.00 30.00
2 ..... 7.00 20.00
3-5 ..... 5.00 15.00

KOKO AND KOLA (A-1 SERIES)
ME (1950)
6 (A-1 #28). 5.00 15.00

KOMIC KARTOONS
MARVEL(TIMELY) (1945)
1-2 ..... 19.00 60.00

KOMIK PAGES
HARRY A. CHESLER (1945)
10(#1) 23.00 75.00

KONA
DELL (1962-1967)
1 (#1256) From the 4-Color Series. (2/62)
..... 13.00 40.00
2-6 ..... 8.00 25.00
7-12 ..... 7.00 20.00
13-21 ..... 5.00 15.00

KONG THE UNTAMED
DC (1975-1976)
1 1st Kong. ..... .50 1.50
2-5 ..... .30 1.00

KONGA
CHARLTON (1960-1965)
1 Movie tie-in. 50.00 160.00
2 ..... 25.00 80.00
3-6 ..... 20.00 65.00
7-12 ..... 17.00 55.00
13-23 ..... 14.00 44.00

KONGA'S REVENGE
CHARLTON (1963-1964)
2 Previous title: Return Of Konga. 10.00 33.00
3 ..... 9.00 27.00

KORAK, SON OF TARZAN
GOLD KEY/DC (1964-1975)
1 ..... 10.00 30.00
2 ..... 7.00 20.00
3-6 ..... 5.00 15.00
7-12 ..... 4.00 12.00
13-20 ..... 2.75 10.00
21-30 ..... 2.25 8.00
31-40 ..... 1.75 6.00
41-45 ..... 1.50 5.00
46 Begin: DC publication. 1.25 4.00
47-50 ..... 1.00 3.00
51-58 ..... .75 2.00
59 Title changes to Tarzan Family with #60. .75 2.00

KRAZY KAT COMICS
DELL (1951-1952)
1 ..... 11.00 35.00
2 ..... 7.00 20.00
3-5 ..... 5.00 15.00

KRAZY KAT COMICS
DELL FOUR COLOR SERIES (1953-1956)
454 (2/53) 10.00 30.00
504 (10/53) 10.00 30.00
548 (4/54) 7.00 20.00
619 (4/55) 7.00 20.00
696 (4/56) 8.00 25.00

KRAZY KOMICS
MARVEL(TIMELY) (1942-1947)
1 ..... 65.00 210.00
2 ..... 40.00 120.00
3-6 ..... 28.00 90.00
7-11 ..... 23.00 75.00
12 Artists draw themselves into story. 40.00 125.00
13-15 ..... 19.00 60.00
16-20 ..... 16.00 50.00
21-26 ..... 12.00 37.00

KRAZY KOMICS
MARVEL(TIMELY) (1948)
1 Art: Basil Wolverton (10 pages). 80.00 260.00
2 Art: Basil Wolverton (10 pages). 55.00 180.00

KRAZY KROW COMICS
MARVEL(TIMELY) (1945)
1 (Summer/45) 31.00 100.00
2 (Fall/45) 19.00 60.00
3 (Winter/45) 19.00 60.00

KRAZY LIFE HILARIOUS COMICS
FOX (1945)
1 Title changes to Nutty Life with #2. ..... 23.00 75.00

KREE/SKRULL WAR
MARVEL (1983)
1 ...Starring the Avengers. Reprint: The Avengers #93-94.
..... 1.00 3.00
2 Reprint: The Avengers #95-97. ..... 1.00 3.00

KRULL
MARVEL (1983)
1 Movie tie-in. ..... .30 1.00

KNIGHTMARE #3

KOBALT #8

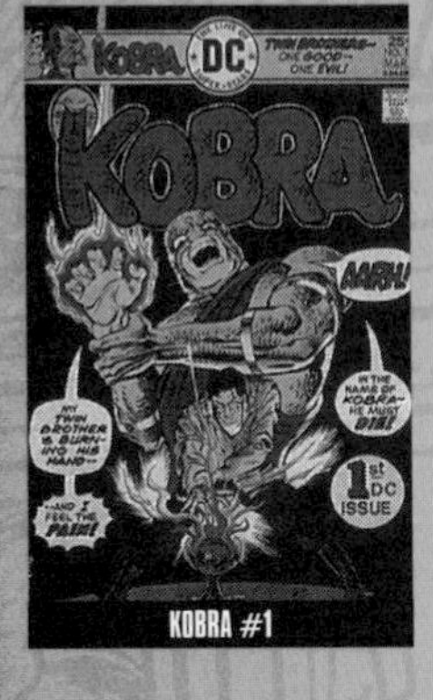

KOBRA #1

KRAZY KOMICS #3 (1ST SERIES)

KRUSTY COMICS #3

LADY DEATH: BETWEEN HEAVEN & HELL #4

LADY JUSTICE #2

LADY RAWHIDE #1

2 .30 1.00

KRUSTY COMICS
BONGO COMICS (1995)
1 TV cartoon tie-in. .75 2.25
2-3 .75 2.25

KRYPTON CHRONICLES
DC (1981)
1 Pre-Crisis history. .50 1.50
2-3 .50 1.25

KULL AND THE BARBARIANS
MARVEL (1975) MAGAZINE
1-3 .75 2.00

KULL THE CONQUEROR
MARVEL (1971-1978)
1 1.50 5.00
2-10 1.00 3.50
11-29 1.00 3.00

KULL THE CONQUEROR
MARVEL (1982-1983)
1-2 .30 1.00

KULL THE CONQUEROR
MARVEL (1983-1985)
1-10 .30 1.00

LA PACIFICA
DC (1994-1995)
1-3 1.25 4.95

LABOR IS A PARTNER
CATECHETICAL GUILD (1949)
NO# 23.00 75.00

LAD: A DOG
DELL (1962)
1 (#1303) From the 4-Color Series. Movie photo cover. 10.00 30.00
2 4.00 12.00

LADY AND THE TRAMP
DELL (1955)
1 100 page giant. 25.00 80.00

LADY AND THE TRAMP
DELL FOUR COLOR SERIES (1955)
629 Disney. (5/55) 13.00 40.00
634 "Album". Disney. (6/55) 7.00 20.00

LADY AND THE TRAMP
GOLD KEY (1963)
10042-301 Disney movie tie-in. 7.00 20.00

LADY ARCANE
HEROIC (1992-1993)
1-4 .30 1.00

LADY DEATH
CHAOS! (1994)
1/2 Wizard mail-away offer. 8.00 25.00
1/2 (GOLD) 13.00 45.00
1/2 VELVET 16.00 55.00
1 Art: Stephen Hughes. Chromium cover. 22.00 70.00
1A Gold foil edition (signed by creative team). 31.00 100.00
2 14.00 45.00
3 8.00 25.00
ASHCAN 1 Limited to 5000. 2.75 10.00
ASHCAN 2 Halloween edition. 1.75 6.00
TPB The Reckoning. Reprints issues #1-3. 1.75 6.95

LADY DEATH: BETWEEN HEAVEN AND HELL
CHAOS! (1995)
1 2.25 8.00
1A Limited edition, signed & numbered. 13.00 40.00
1B Black velvet edition. 16.00 50.00
1C Limited commemorative edition. 8.00 25.00
2 1.25 4.50
3-4 .75 2.75

LADY DEATH IN LINGERIE
CHAOS COMICS! (1995)
1 1.00 3.50
1A Leather edition 10.00 35.00

LADY DEATH SWIMSUIT SPECIAL
CHAOS! COMICS (1994)
1 4.00 12.00
1A Red velvet edition. 14.00 45.00

LADY FOR A NIGHT
REPUBLIC (1942)
NO# Movie giveaway (4 pages). From the Cinema Comics Herald series. 16.00 50.00

LADY JUSTICE
TEKNO (1995-CURRENT)
1 1.00 3.50
2-4 .50 1.95

LADY LUCK
QUALITY (1949-1950)
86 Previous title: Smash Comics. 100.00 330.00
87 95.00 300.00
88-90 85.00 270.00

LADY RAWHIDE
TOPPS (1995)
1 .75 4.00
SPECIAL Reprints Zorro #2 & 3. 1.25 6.00

LAFF-A-LYMPICS
MARVEL (1978-1979)
1 Hanna-Barbera cartoon TV tie-in. .30 1.00
2-13 .30 1.00

LAFFY-DAFFY COMICS
RURAL HOME (1945)
1 10.00 30.00

LANA
MARVEL (1948-1949)
1 31.00 100.00
2 16.00 50.00
3-6 11.00 35.00
7 Title changes to Little Lana with #8. 11.00 35.00

LANCE O'CASEY
FAWCETT (1946-1948)
1 50.00 160.00
2 25.00 80.00
3-4 20.00 65.00

LANCELOT AND GUINEVERE
DELL (1963)
12-416-310 Movie tie-in. 13.00 40.00

LANCER
GOLD KEY (1969)
1 TV photo cover on all issues. 5.00 15.00
2-3 2.75 10.00

LAND OF THE GIANTS
GOLD KEY (1968-1969)
1 TV photo cover on all issues. 10.00 30.00
2 7.00 20.00
3 5.00 15.00
4-5 2.75 10.00

LAND OF THE LOST COMICS
EC (1946-1948)
1 Radio show tie-in. 60.00 190.00
2 40.00 130.00
3 35.00 110.00
4-9 25.00 80.00

LAND UNKNOWN, THE
DELL FOUR COLOR SERIES (1957)
845 Movie tie-in. (8/57) 35.00 115.00

LARAMIE
DELL (1962)
01-418-207 TV photo cover. (7/62) 10.00 30.00

LARAMIE
DELL FOUR COLOR SERIES (1960-1962)
1125 TV photo cover. (8/60) 19.00 60.00
1223 TV photo cover. (8/61) 13.00 40.00
1284 TV photo cover. (1/62) 13.00 40.00

LAREDO
GOLD KEY (1966)
10179-606 TV tie-in photo cover. 2.75 10.00

LARGE FEATURE COMICS
DELL (1939-1942)
1 Dick Tracy Meets The Blank. 300.00 1100.00
2 Terry And The Pirates (#1, 1939). 130.00 430.00
3 Heigh-Yo Silver! The Lone Ranger. Exists in same format as Whitman #710. Rare. Dated 1939. 140.00 460.00
4 Dick Tracy Gets His Man. (1939) 180.00 575.00
5 Tarzan Of The Apes. Art: Hal Foster. 250.00 800.00
6 Terry And The Pirates. 105.00 340.00
7 Hi-Yo Silver. The Lone Ranger To The Rescue. 180.00 575.00
8 Dick Tracy, The Racket Buster. 145.00 480.00
9 Zane Grey's King Of The Royal Mounted. 80.00 250.00
10 Gang Busters. 125.00 400.00
11 Dick Tracy Foils The Mad Doc Hump. 180.00 575.00
12 Smilin' Jack. 105.00 340.00
13 Dick Tracy And Scottie Of Scotland Yard. 155.00 500.00
14 Smilin' Jack Helps G-Men Solve A Case! 85.00 280.00
15 Dick Tracy And The Kidnapped Princes. (1941) 155.00 500.00
16 Donald Duck. 600.00 2000.00
17 Gang Busters. (1941) 65.00 200.00
18 Phantasmo, The Master Of The World. 55.00 170.00
19 Dumbo Comic Paint Book. 400.00 1300.00
20 Donald Duck Comic Paint Book. 600.00 2300.00
21 Private Buck. 35.00 110.00
22 Nuts And Jolts. 26.00 85.00
23 The Nebbs. 35.00 110.00
24 Popeye in "Thimble Theatre" 105.00 340.00
25 Smilin' Jack And The Secret Of The Everglades. 105.00 340.00
26 Smitty. 55.00 170.00
27 Terry And The Pirates by Caniff. 105.00 340.00
28 Grin And Bear It. 26.00 85.00
29 Moon Mullins. 45.00 140.00
30 Tillie The Toiler. 35.00 110.00

LARGE FEATURE COMICS
DELL (1942-1943)
NO# 1001 Hours Of Fun. 20.00 65.00
1 Peter Rabbit by Harrison Cady. 105.00 340.00
2 Winnie Winkle. 35.00 110.00
3 Dick Tracy. (1942) 140.00 460.00
4 Tiny Tim. 55.00 170.00
5 Toots And Casper. 26.00 85.00
6 Terry And The Pirates. 85.00 280.00
7 Pluto Saves The Ship. 1st Carl Barks story. 210.00 675.00
8 Bugs Bunny. 1st Bugs Bunny comic book. 210.00 675.00
9 Bringing Up Father. 35.00 110.00
10 Popeye. 85.00 280.00
11 Barney Google And Snuffy Smith. 45.00 140.00
12 Private Buck. 20.00 65.00

LARRY DOBY BASEBALL HERO
FAWCETT (1950)
NO# Photo cover. 140.00 450.00

LARS OF MARS
ZIFF-DAVIS (1951)
10 Origin. Painted cover. (4-5/51) 95.00 300.00
11 Painted cover. 75.00 240.00

LASH LARUE WESTERN
FAWCETT/CHARLTON (1949-1961)
1 Photo covers on issues #1-47. 125.00 400.00
2 55.00 175.00
3 40.00 125.00
4-6 31.00 100.00
7-12 28.00 90.00
13-25 25.00 80.00
26-28 22.00 70.00
29 "Marked For Murder!" 22.00 70.00
30-40 22.00 70.00
41-46 19.00 60.00
47 Begin: Charlton publication. End: Photo covers. 19.00 60.00
48-60 13.00 40.00
61-70 10.00 30.00
71-84 7.00 20.00

LASSIE
DELL/GOLD KEY (1950-1969)
1 TV tie-in photo cover. 25.00 80.00
2 Begin: painted covers. 12.00 38.00
3-6 10.00 33.00
7-12 9.00 27.00
13-20 7.00 22.00
21-30 6.00 17.00
31-40 5.00 15.00
41-50 4.00 11.00
51-58 2.25 8.75
59 Begin: Gold Key publication. 2.25 8.75
60 2.25 8.75
61-70 1.75 6.50

LAST AMERICAN, THE
MARVEL(EPIC) (1990-1991)
1-4 .75 2.00

LAST DAYS OF THE JUSTICE SOCIETY
DC (1986)
1 .75 2.50

LAST HUNT, THE
DELL FOUR COLOR SERIES (1956)
678 Movie photo cover. (2/56) 14.00 45.00

LAST OF THE COMANCHES
AVON (1953)
NO# Cover & Art: Raymond Kinstler. 19.00 60.00

LAST OF THE FAST GUNS
DELL FOUR COLOR SERIES (1958)
925 Movie photo cover. (8/58) 16.00 50.00

LAST OF THE VIKING HEROES
GENESIS WEST (1987-1991)
1 .30 1.00
2 .30 1.00
3 .30 1.00
4-12 .30 1.00
SS#1 Summer Special. Cover: Frank Frazetta. (1988) .75 2.50
SS#2 Summer Special. (1990) .75 2.50
SS#3 Summer Special. (1991) .75 2.50

LAST ONE, THE
DC (1993)
1-6 .30 1.00

LAST STARFIGHTER, THE
MARVEL (1984)
1 Movie tie-in. .30 1.00
2-3 .30 1.00

LAST TEMPTATION OF ALICE COOPER, THE
MARVEL (1994)
1-2 1.50 5.00
3 1.75 6.00
TPB Reprints: Issues #1-3. 5.00 15.00

LAST TRAIN FROM GUN HILL
DELL FOUR COLOR SERIES (1959)
1012 Movie photo cover. (7/59) 19.00 60.00

LATEST COMICS
SPOTLIGHT (1945)
1 25.00 80.00
2 13.00 40.00

LAUGH COMICS
ARCHIE (1946-1987)
20 Previous title: Black Hood. Begin: Archie. 110.00 360.00
21 55.00 180.00
22-25 50.00 150.00
26-30 31.00 100.00
31-40 23.00 75.00
41-50 16.00 50.00
51-60 13.00 42.00
61-70 10.00 30.00
71-80 8.00 24.00
81-90 6.00 19.00
91-99 5.00 14.00
100 8.00 24.00
101-110 4.00 12.00
111-128 2.50 9.50
129 1st 12 cent issue. 2.50 9.50
130 2.50 9.50
131-160 2.00 7.00
161-180 1.75 6.00
181-200 1.25 4.75
201-222 1.00 3.50
223 1st: That Wilken Boy story. 1.00 3.50
224-240 1.00 3.50
241-300 .75 2.25
301-350 .50 1.75
351-400 .30 1.00

LAUGH COMIX
MLJ (1944)
46 Previous title: Top-Notch Comics. 28.00 90.00
47 22.00 70.00
48 Title changes to Suzie Comics with #49. 22.00 70.00

LAUREL AND HARDY
DELL (1962-1963)
1 (12-423-210) TV tie-in. 10.00 30.00
2-4 7.00 20.00

LAUREL AND HARDY
GOLD KEY (1967)
1 7.00 20.00
2 5.00 15.00

LAUREL AND HARDY
ST. JOHN (1949)
1 105.00 340.00
2-3 65.00 200.00
26-28 Reprint. 26.00 85.00

LAW AGAINST CRIME
SEE LAW-CRIME.

LAW BREAKERS
CHARLTON (1951-1952)
1 35.00 110.00
2 17.00 55.00
3 12.00 38.00
4 "The White Death!" Drug abuse story. 20.00 65.00
5-6 10.00 33.00
7 "The Deadly Dopesters!" Drug abuse story. 20.00 65.00
8 10.00 33.00
9 Title changes to Law Breakers Suspense Stories with #10. 10.00 33.00

LAW BREAKERS SUSPENSE STORIES
CHARLTON (1953)
10 Previous title: "Law Breakers." 11.00 36.00
11 Severed tongues cover. 75.00 240.00
12-14 11.00 36.00
15 Acid-in-face cover. Becomes Strange Suspense Stories #16. 40.00 120.00

LAW OF DREDD
FLEETWAY/QUALITY (1989-1992)
1 1.00 3.00
2 .75 2.50
3-33 .50 1.95

LAWBREAKERS ALWAYS LOSE
MARVEL (1948-1949)
1 35.00 110.00
2 17.00 55.00
3-6 14.00 46.00
7 SOTI 35.00 110.00
8 11.00 34.00
9-10 Photo cover. 14.00 46.00

LAW-CRIME
ESSENKAY (1948)
1 "Ramond Hamilton Dies In Chair" 85.00 270.00
2 "Strangled Beauty Puzzles Police" 55.00 180.00
3 "Lipstick Slayer Sought" SOTI 95.00 300.00

LAWDOG
MARVEL (1993-1994)
1-13 .50 1.50

LAWDOG VS. GRIMROD
MARVEL (1993)
1 .50 1.50

LAWMAN
DELL (1959-1962)
1 (#970) From the 4-Color Series. TV photo cover. (2/59) 22.00 70.00
2 (#1035) From the 4-Color Series. TV photo cover. (11/59) 11.00 35.00
3 10.00 30.00
4 8.00 25.00
5-7 7.00 20.00
8-11 5.00 15.00

LAWRENCE (OF ARABIA)
DELL (1963)
12-426-308 Movie tie-in. 10.00 30.00

LEADING COMICS
DC (1941-1955)
1 Begin: Crimson Avenger, Green Arrow, Vigilante. Lead story: "Blueprint For Crime!" 700.00 2400.00
2 310.00 1000.00
3 220.00 700.00
4 190.00 600.00
5 145.00 480.00
6 140.00 450.00
7 130.00 420.00
8-9 120.00 390.00
10-11 110.00 360.00
12 "The Million Dollar Challenge!" 110.00 360.00
13 110.00 360.00
14 End: Super Hero issues. 110.00 360.00
15 Begin: Funny animal issues. 55.00 180.00
16 40.00 120.00
17-22 29.00 95.00
23 1st: Peter Porkchops. 50.00 150.00
24-30 22.00 70.00
31-33 19.00 60.00
34 Title changes to Leading Screen Comics. 15.00 48.00
35-40 13.00 42.00
41-50 11.00 36.00
51-60 10.00 30.00
61-77 8.00 24.00

LEAGUE OF CHAMPIONS
HEROIC (1990-1994)
1-13 .30 1.00

LEAVE IT TO BEAVER
DELL (1962)
01-428-207 TV photo cover. 35.00 110.00

LEAVE IT TO BEAVER
DELL FOUR COLOR SERIES (1958-1962)
912 TV photo cover. (6/58) 55.00 175.00
999 TV photo cover. (6/59) 50.00 150.00
1103 TV photo cover. (6/60) 50.00 150.00
1191 TV photo cover. (6/61) 50.00 150.00
1285 TV photo cover. (2/62) 50.00 150.00

LEAVE IT TO BINKY
DC (1948-1970)
1 50.00 160.00
2 25.00 80.00
3 20.00 65.00
4 17.00 55.00
5 App: Superman (cameo). 25.00 80.00
6-12 14.00 44.00
13-24 12.00 38.00
25-45 10.00 33.00
46 1st Code Approved issue. 9.00 27.00
47-59 7.00 22.00
60 (10/59) 7.00 22.00
61 (6-7/68) 5.00 16.00
62-63 4.00 11.00
64-71 2.25 8.75

LEE HUNTER, INDIAN FIGHTER
DELL FOUR COLOR SERIES (1957-1958)
779 (3/57) 11.00 35.00
904 (5/58) 8.00 25.00

LEFT-HANDED GUN, THE
DELL FOUR COLOR SERIES (1958)
913 Movie photo cover (Paul Newman). (7/58) 25.00 80.00

LEGACY
MAJESTIC (1993-1994)
0 .75 2.50
1 Enhanced cover. .75 2.50
2-7 .75 2.50

LEGACY OF SUPERMAN
DC (1993)
1 .75 2.50

LEGEND OF LOBO, THE
GOLD KEY (1963)
10059-303 Disney movie photo cover. 5.00 15.00

LEGEND OF MOTHER SARAH, THE
DARK HORSE (1995-CURRENT)
1-5 .75 2.50
6-7 .75 2.95

LEGEND OF SUPREME
IMAGE (1994-CURRENT)
1-4 .75 2.50

LEGEND OF YOUNG DICK TURPIN, THE
GOLD KEY (1966)
10176-605 TV photo (insert) cover. 2.75 10.00

LEGENDS
DC (1986-1987)
1 1st: New Captain Marvel. .75 2.50
2 .50 1.50
3 1st: New Suicide Squad. .50 1.50
4-5 .50 1.50
6 1st: New Justice League. 1.25 4.00
TPB Reprints issues #1-6. 2.50 9.95

LEGENDS OF DANIEL BOONE, THE
DC (1955-1956)
1 (10-11/55) 100.00 325.00
2 "Daniel Boone's Rookie Rangers!" 70.00 230.00
3 "The Shawnee Raiders!" 65.00 200.00
4 "Paleface Medicine Man!" 55.00 170.00
5 "The Last Stand!" 55.00 170.00
6 "The Outlaw Fort!" 55.00 170.00
7 "Daniel Boone's Young Buckskin Pal!" 55.00 170.00
8 "The Four-Legged Frontiersmen!" (10/56) 55.00 170.00

LEGENDS OF ELFINWILD, THE
WEHNER (1987)
1 .20 .50

LEGENDS OF NASCAR
VORTEX (1990-1993)
1 Bill Elliott. .75 2.00
2 Richard Petty. .75 2.00
3 Ken Schrader. .75 2.00
4 Bobby Allison. .75 2.00
5-16 .75 2.00

LEGENDS OF THE DARK KNIGHT
SEE BATMAN: LEGENDS OF THE DARK KNIGHT.

LASH LARUE WESTERN #29

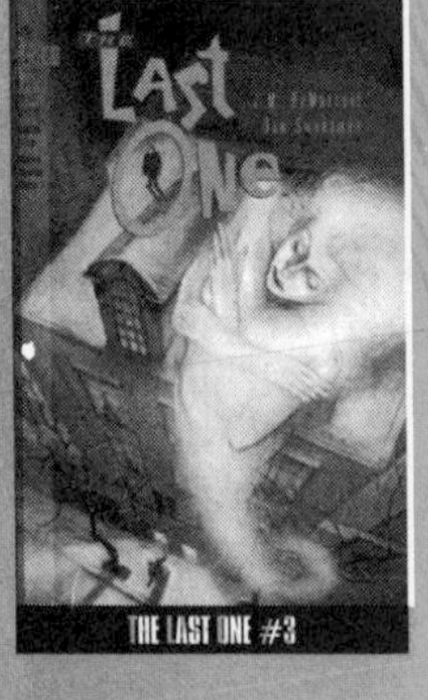

THE LAST ONE #3

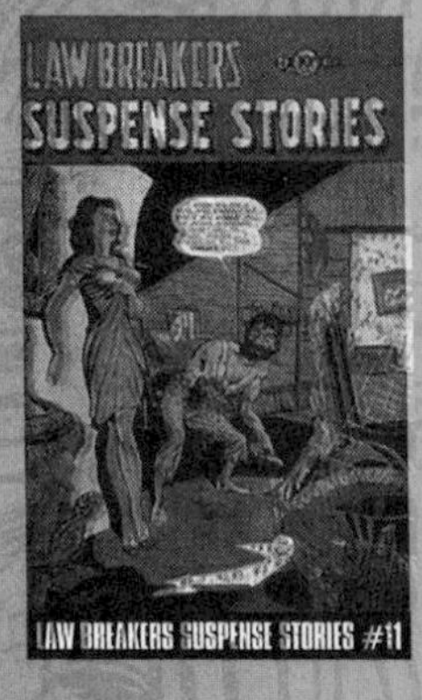

LAW BREAKERS SUSPENSE STORIES #11

LEADING COMICS #2

L.E.G.I.O.N. '94 #62

LEGION OF SUPER-HEROES #53 (4TH SERIES)

LIBERTY COMICS #11

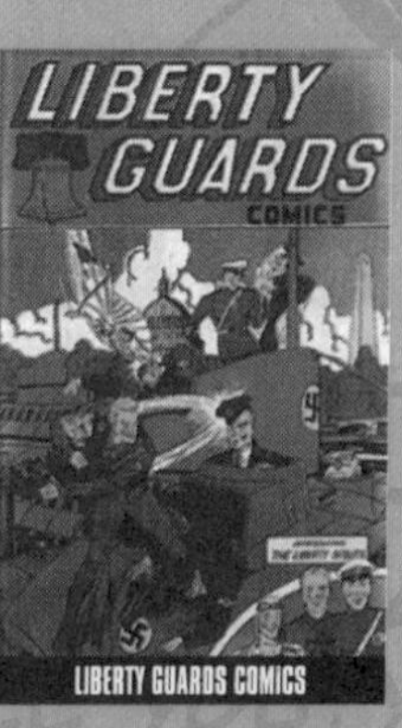
LIBERTY GUARDS COMICS

FAMOUS · FIRSTS

LITTLE DOT #1

Little Dot loved to collect dots, but more important for comics history, she had this friend called Richie Rich. He makes his first appearance here as the world's richest boy, and soon has more comic titles than dollar bills.

LEGENDS OF THE WORLD'S FINEST
DC (1994)
1-3 .... 1.25 4.95

L.E.G.I.O.N.
DC (1989-1994)
1 Begin: LEGION '89. .... 1.50 5.00
2-10 .... 1.25 4.00
11 Begin: LEGION'90. .... .75 2.00
12-22 .... .75 2.00
23 Begin: LEGION'91. .... .75 2.25
24-34 .... .75 2.25
35 Begin: LEGION'92. .... .50 1.50
36-46 .... .50 1.50
47 Begin: LEGION'93. .... .50 1.50
48-61 .... .50 1.75
62 Begin: LEGION'94. .... .50 1.75
63-69 .... .50 1.75
70 .... 1.25 4.00
ANNUAL 1 (1990) 1.25 4.50
ANNUAL 2 (1991) .... .75 2.95
ANNUAL 3 (1992) .... .75 2.95
ANNUAL 4 Bloodlines, pt.23 (1993) ... 1.00 3.50
ANNUAL 5 Elseworlds story. (1994) ... 1.00 3.50

LEGION OF MONSTERS, THE
MARVEL (1975) MAGAZINE
1 1st & Origin: Legion of Monsters. Cover: Neal Adams. 5.00 15.00

LEGION OF SUBSTITUTE HEROES
DC (1985)
1 .... .30 1.00

LEGION OF SUPER-HEROES
DC (1973)
1 .... 1.75 6.00
2-4 .... 1.00 3.00

LEGION OF SUPER-HEROES
DC (1980-1984)
259 Previous title: Superboy. 1.25 4.00
260-270 .... .75 2.00
271-284 .... .50 1.25
285-286 Art: Keith Giffen (backup story). .50 1.25
287 Begin: Keith Giffen art on Legion. ... .50 1.25
288-299 .... .50 1.25
300 Double size anniversary issue. ... 1.00 3.00
301-312 .... .50 1.25
313 Title changes to Tales Of The Legion Of Super-Heroes with #314. .... .50 1.25
ANNUAL 1 (1982) .... .75 2.50
ANNUAL 2 (1983) .... .75 2.25
ANNUAL 3 (1984) .... .75 2.25

LEGION OF SUPER-HEROES
DC (1984-1989)
1 .... 1.00 3.00
2-3 .... .50 1.50
4 Death: Karate Kid. .... .50 1.50
5 Death: Nemesis Kid. .... .50 1.50
6-15 .... .50 1.50
16 Crisis crossover. .... .75 2.00
17 Origin retold: Legion. .... .75 2.00
18 Crisis crossover. .... .75 2.00
19-36 .... .50 1.50
37 Begin: Superboy's Death story. ... 2.00 7.00
38 Death: Superboy. 2.75 10.00
39-44 .... .50 1.50
45 Double size 30th anniversary issue. 1.00 3.00
46-49 .... .50 1.50
50 Double size. Death: Time Trapper. ... .50 1.50
51-61 .... .50 1.50
62 Death: Magnetic Kid. .... .50 1.50
63 .... .50 1.50
ANNUAL 1 "Who Shot Laurel Kent?" (1985) 1.00 3.00
ANNUAL 2 (1986) .... .75 2.75
ANNUAL 3 (1987) .... .75 2.75
ANNUAL 4 (1988) .... .75 2.75

LEGION OF SUPER-HEROES
DC (1989-CURRENT)
0 .... .50 1.95
1-5 .... .75 2.50
6-7 .... .75 2.25
8 Origin retold: Legion. .... .75 2.25
9-25 .... .75 2.25
26-30 .... .75 2.00
31-37 .... .50 1.75
38 Death appearance. 1.75 6.00
39-49 .... .50 1.75
50 Double size. Vs. B.I.O.N. 1.00 3.50
51-53 .... .50 1.75
54 Die cut, foil-stamped cover. .... .75 2.95
55-58 .... .50 1.75
59-68 .... .50 1.95
69-73 .... .75 2.25
ANNUAL 1 (1990) 1.00 3.50
ANNUAL 2 (1991) 1.00 3.50
ANNUAL 3 (1992) 1.00 3.50
ANNUAL 4 Bloodlines, pt.12 (1993) ... 1.00 3.50
ANNUAL 5 Elseworlds story. (1994) ... 1.00 3.50
ANNUAL 6 (1995) 1.00 3.95

LEGION OF THE NIGHT, THE
MARVEL (1991)
1 1st: Legion Of The Night. 1.50 5.00
2 Fin Fang Foom. 1.50 5.00

LEGIONNAIRES
DC (1992-CURRENT)
0 (8/94) .... .75 2.25
1 Polybagged with trading card. ...... .50 1.25
2-9 .... .50 1.25
10-17 .... .50 1.50
18 Zero Hour, pt 4. .... .75 2.50
19-25 .... .50 1.50
26 .... .50 1.75
27-30 .... .75 2.25
ANNUAL 1 Elseworlds story. (1994) ... .75 2.95
ANNUAL 2 Year One. (1995) 1.00 3.95

LEGIONNAIRES 3
DC (1986)
1-4 .... .50 1.50

LENNON SISTERS, THE
DELL FOUR COLOR SERIES (1958-1959)
951 "Life Story". TV photo cover. (11/58) 40.00 125.00
1014 TV photo cover. (7/59) 35.00 110.00

LEONARDO
MIRAGE (1986)
1 From: Teenage Mutant Ninja Turtles. 2.50 9.00

LET'S PRETEND
D.S. (1950)
1 Radio tie-in. 22.00 70.00
2-3 .... 16.00 50.00

LETHAL FOES OF SPIDER-MAN
MARVEL (1993)
1-4 .... .50 1.75

LETHAL STRYKE
LONDON NIGHT STUDIOS (1995-CURRENT)
1 1st: Lethal Stryke. 1.00 4.00

LETHARGIC COMICS
ALPHA
1 .... .75 2.50
1A Signed re-release with original drawing. 1.50 5.00
2-9 .... .75 2.50

LI'L ABNER
HARVEY/TOBY (1947-1955)
61 .... 50.00 150.00
62 .... 23.00 75.00
63-65 .... 19.00 60.00
66-70 .... 16.00 50.00
71-80 .... 13.00 40.00
81-90 .... 10.00 30.00
91-97 .... 8.00 25.00

LI'L ABNER & THE CREATURES FROM DROP-OUTER SPACE
GIVEAWAY
NO# 16.00 50.00

LI'L ABNER JOINS THE NAVY
TOBY (1950)
NO# Dated 3-29-50 inside back cover. 16.00 50.00

LI'L BAD WOLF
ELL FOUR COLOR SERIES (1952-1954)
03 (6/52) 10.00 30.00
73 (6/53) 8.00 25.00
64 (6/54) 5.00 15.00

LI'L GENIUS
HARLTON (1954-1965)
.... 11.00 35.00
.... 7.00 20.00
-12 .... 5.00 15.00
13-15 .... 4.00 12.00
16-17 Double size. 7.00 20.00
18 100 page giant. 13.00 40.00
19-24 .... 2.75 10.00
25-53 .... 1.75 6.00

LIBERTY COMICS
GREEN (1945-1946)
10 Reprints Hangman #8. .... 25.00 80.00
11 .... 17.00 55.00
12 App: Black Hood. 23.00 75.00
14-15 .... 9.00 27.00

LIBERTY GUARDS COMICS
CENTAUR(CMO) (1942)
NO# Cover: Gustavson. Same cover as Liberty Scouts #2, contents are from Man Of War Comics #1. Title changed from Liberty Scouts due to complaint from Boy Scouts of America.
.... 95.00 300.00

LIBERTY SCOUTS
CENTAUR (1941)
2 Origin: Fire-Man by Gustavson. ... 250.00 800.00
3 1st & Origin: The Sentinal by Gustavson.
.... 250.00 800.00

LIFE OF CAPTAIN MARVEL
MARVEL (1985)
1 Reprints of Thanos storyline by Jim Starlin. .75 2.00
2-5 .... .75 2.00

LIFE OF GROO, THE
GRAPHITTI DESIGNS (1995)
GN 4.00 12.95

LIFE OF POPE JOHN PAUL II
MARVEL (1983)
1 .... .50 1.50

LIFE OF RILEY, THE
DELL FOUR COLOR SERIES (1958)
917 TV photo cover (William Bendix). (7/58)
.... 31.00 100.00

LIFE STORIES OF AMERICAN PRESIDENTS
DELL (1957)
1 Dell Giant. 11.00 35.00

LIFE STORY
FAWCETT (1949-1953)
1 Photo covers on all issues. 14.00 45.00
2 .... 7.00 20.00
3-6 .... 5.00 15.00
7-47 .... 2.75 10.00

LIFE WITH ARCHIE
ARCHIE (1958-1991)
1 .... 65.00 210.00
2 .... 31.00 100.00
3-6 .... 22.00 70.00
7-12 .... 19.00 60.00
13-18 .... 15.00 48.00
19-24 .... 11.00 36.00
25-30 .... 8.00 24.00
31-36 .... 6.00 18.00
37-44 .... 4.00 12.00
45 1st: Man From R.I.V.E.R.D.A.L.E. story. 4.00 12.00
46 Origin: Pureheart. 4.00 12.00
47 .... 4.00 12.00
48 Origin: Evilheart (Reggie). 1st: Superteen (Betty).
.... 4.00 12.00
49-59 .... 2.50 9.50
60 1st: The Archies (band). 2.50 9.50
61-75 .... 2.00 7.00
76-90 .... 1.75 6.00
91-100 .... 1.25 4.75
101-125 .... 1.00 3.50
126-150 .... .75 2.25
151-171 .... .30 1.00
172 Special Bicentennial issue. (8/76) .30 1.00
173-200 .... .30 1.00
201-286 .... .20 .50

LIFE WITH MILLIE
MARVEL(ATLAS) (1960-1962)
8 Previous title: A Date With Millie. ... 10.00 33.00
9 .... 9.00 27.00
10 .... 7.00 22.00
11-15 .... 5.00 16.00
16-20 .... 4.00 13.00

LIFE WITH SNARKY PARKER
FOX (1950)
1 TV photo cover & tie-in. 55.00 175.00

LIGHT AND DARKNESS WAR
MARVEL(EPIC) (1988-1989)
1-6 .... .30 1.00

LIGHT IN THE FOREST, THE
DELL FOUR COLOR SERIES (1958)
891 Movie photo cover (Fess Parker). (3/58)
.... 16.00 50.00

LIGHTNING COMICS
ACE (1940-1942)
4 Previous title: Sure-Fire Comics. ... 140.00 460.00
5 .... 105.00 340.00
6 Begin: Dr. Nemesis. 85.00 280.00
7 (V2#1) 70.00 230.00
8 (V2#2) 70.00 230.00
9 (V2#3) 70.00 230.00
10 (V2#4) 70.00 230.00
11 (V2#5) 70.00 230.00
12 (V2#6) 70.00 230.00
13 (V3#1) 70.00 230.00

LIMITED COLLECTORS' EDITION
DC (1973-1978) OVERSIZE COMICS
C-20 Rudolph The Red-Nosed Reindeer. 2.25 8.00
C-21 Shazam. 1.50 5.00
C-22 Tarzan. Cover&art:Joe Kubert. ... 1.50 5.00
C-23 House Of Mystery. 1.75 6.00
C-24 Rudolph The Red-Nosed Reindeer. 1.25 4.00
C-25 Batman. Cover & art: Neal Adams. TV show tie-in.
.... 2.75 10.00
C-27 Shazam. TV tie-in. 1.50 5.00
C-29 Tarzan. 1.25 4.00
C-30 Super-Heroes Battle Super-Gorillas. 1.50 5.00
C-31 Superman. 1.75 6.00
C-32 Ghosts. 1.25 4.00
C-33 Rudolph The Red-Nosed Reindeer. 1.00 3.00
C-34 Christmas With The Super-Heroes. 2.25 8.00
C-35 Shazam. TV tie-in. 1.25 4.00
C-36 The Bible. 1.75 6.00
C-37 Batman. All-villain issue. ... 2.75 10.00
C-38 Superman. 1.50 5.00
C-39 Secret Origins Of The Super-Villains. 1.25 4.00
C-40 Dick Tracy. 1.50 5.00
C-41 Super Friends. 1.50 5.00
C-42 Rudolph The Red-Nosed Reindeer. 1.25 4.00
C-43 Christmas With The Super-Heroes. 1.75 6.00
C-44 Batman. 2.25 8.00
C-45 More Secret Origins Of The Super-Villains.
.... 1.50 5.00
C-46 Justice League Of America. ... 1.75 6.00
C-47 Superman Salutes The Bicentennial. 1.50 5.00
C-48 Superman Vs. The Flash. Reprints Superman 199 and Flash 175. 2.25 8.00
C-49 Superboy And The Legion Of Super-Heroes.
.... 1.25 4.00
C-50 Rudolph The Red-Nosed Reindeer. 1.00 3.00
C-51 Batman. Cover & art: Neal Adams. 2.75 10.00
C-52 The Best Of DC. Cover & art: Neal Adams.
.... 2.00 7.00
C-57 Welcome Back, Kotter. TV tie-in. 1.50 5.00
C-58 Super-Heroes Battle Super-Gorillas. 1.25 4.00
C-59 Batman's Strangest Cases. 2.75 10.00

LINDA CARTER STUDENT NURSE
MARVEL(ATLAS) (1961-1963)
1 .... 10.00 33.00
2 .... 7.00 22.00
3 .... 5.00 16.00
4-9 .... 4.00 11.00

LINDA LARK
DELL (1961-1963)
1 .... 2.75 10.00
2 .... 1.50 5.00
3-8 .... 1.00 3.00

LINUS, THE LIONHEARTED
GOLD KEY (1965)
10155-509 TV tie-in. 16.00 50.00

LION, THE
GOLD KEY (1963)
10035-301 Movie photo cover. 7.00 20.00

LION KING, THE
MARVEL (1994)
1 Movie adaptation. .... .75 2.50

LION OF SPARTA
DELL (1963)
12-439-301 Movie photo (insert) cover. 5.00 15.00

LIPPY THE LION AND HARDY HAR HAR
GOLD KEY (1963)
10049-303 TV cartoon (Hanna-Barbera) tie-in.
.... 19.00 60.00

LISA COMICS
BONGO (1995-CURRENT)
1 TV cartoon tie-in. .... .75 2.25

LITTLE AL OF THE F.B.I.
ZIFF-DAVIS (1950-1951)
10-11 Painted cover by Norman Saunders. 19.00 60.00

LITTLE AL OF THE SECRET SERVICE
ZIFF-DAVIS (1951)
1 (#10 on cover) Painted cover by Norman Saunders.
.... 16.00 50.00
2-3 Painted cover by Norman Saunders. 13.00 40.00

LITTLE ANGEL
STANDARD (1954-1959)
5 .... 8.00 25.00
6 .... 6.00 18.00
7 .... 5.00 15.00
8-15 .... 2.75 10.00

LITTLE ANNIE ROONEY
ST. JOHN (1948)
1 .... 16.00 50.00
2 .... 8.00 25.00
3 .... 7.00 20.00

LITTLE ARCHIE
ARCHIE (1956-1983)
1 .... 95.00 300.00
2 .... 50.00 150.00
3 .... 40.00 120.00
4-6 .... 31.00 100.00
7-12 .... 28.00 90.00
13-18 .... 19.00 60.00
19-24 .... 13.00 42.00
25-30 .... 10.00 30.00
31-40 .... 6.00 18.00
41-50 .... 4.00 12.00
51-60 .... 2.50 9.50
61-84 .... 2.00 7.00
85-100 .... 1.00 3.50
101-120 .... .75 2.25
121-150 .... .30 1.00
151-181 .... .20 .50

LITTLE ARCHIE MYSTERY
ARCHIE (1963)
1 .... 23.00 75.00
2 .... 11.00 36.00

LITTLE AUDREY
ST. JOHN/HARVEY (1948-1957)
1 1st: Little Audrey. 50.00 150.00
2 .... 23.00 75.00
3-6 .... 19.00 60.00
7-8 .... 16.00 50.00
9-10 .... 13.00 40.00
11-12 .... 10.00 30.00
13-18 .... 7.00 20.00
19-24 .... 5.00 15.00
25 Begin: Harvey publication. 13.00 40.00
26-28 App: Casper. 7.00 20.00
29-31 .... 5.00 15.00
32-35 App: Casper. 7.00 20.00
36-40 .... 4.00 12.00
41-53 .... 2.75 10.00

LITTLE AUDREY AND MELVIN
HARVEY (1962-1973)
1 .... 11.00 35.00
2 .... 7.00 20.00
3 .... 5.00 15.00
4-6 .... 4.00 12.00
7-12 .... 2.75 10.00
13-18 .... 2.25 8.00
19-24 .... 1.75 6.00
25-30 .... 1.50 5.00
31-36 .... 1.25 4.00
37-48 .... 1.00 3.00
49-50 .... .75 2.00
51-53 Double size. 1.00 3.00
54-61 .... .75 2.00

LITTLE AUDREY CLUBHOUSE
HARVEY (1961)
1 64 page giant. 10.00 30.00

LIFE WITH ARCHIE #2

LIFE WITH MILLIE #8

LION KING, THE #1

LISA COMICS #1

a b c d e f g h i j k l m n o p q r s t u v w x y z

LITTLE AUDREY #7

LITTLE DOT #13

LITTLE IODINE 4C #224

LITTLE LULU 4C #131

LITTLE AUDREY YEARBOOK
ST. JOHN (1950)
1 260 page giant. 125.00 400.00

LITTLE BEAVER
DELL (1951-1953)
3-8 5.00 15.00

LITTLE BEAVER
DELL FOUR COLOR SERIES (1949-1958)
211 (1/49) 16.00 50.00
267 (2/50) 8.00 25.00
294 (9/50) 8.00 25.00
332 (5/51) 8.00 25.00
483 (7/53) 7.00 20.00
529 (1/54) 7.00 20.00
612 (1/55) 5.00 15.00
660 (11/55) 5.00 15.00
695 (4/56) 5.00 15.00
744 (11/56) 5.00 15.00
817 (8/57) 5.00 15.00
870 (1/58) 5.00 15.00

LITTLE BIT
JUBILEE (1949)
1-2 5.00 15.00

LITTLE DOT
HARVEY (1953-1976)
1 1st: Richie Rich. 1st: Little Lotta. 110.00 350.00
2 1st: Freckles. 1st: Pee Wee. 55.00 175.00
3 31.00 100.00
4-5 23.00 75.00
6 1st: Richie Rich cover. 31.00 100.00
7-12 19.00 60.00
13-24 14.00 45.00
25-30 10.00 30.00
31-36 7.00 20.00
37-42 5.00 15.00
43-48 4.00 12.00
49-60 2.25 8.00
61-70 1.75 6.00
71-80 1.50 5.00
81-90 1.00 3.00
91-110 .75 2.00
111-130 .50 1.50
131-150 .30 1.00
151-164 .20 .50

LITTLE DOT DOTLAND
HARVEY (1962-1973)
1 10.00 30.00
2 5.00 15.00
3-6 2.75 10.00
7-12 2.25 8.00
13-18 1.75 6.00
19-24 1.50 5.00
25-40 1.25 4.00
41-50 1.00 3.00
51-61 .75 2.00

LITTLE EVA
ST. JOHN (1952-1956)
1 16.00 50.00
2 8.00 25.00
3-6 7.00 20.00
7-12 5.00 15.00
13-18 2.75 10.00
19-24 2.25 8.00
25-31 1.75 6.00

LITTLE EVA 3-D COMICS
ST. JOHN (1953)
1 With glasses (1/2 price if glasses are missing). 23.00 75.00
2 With glasses. 16.00 50.00

LITTLE GIANT COMICS
CENTAUR (1938-1939)
1 125.00 400.00
2-4 95.00 300.00

LITTLE GIANT DETECTIVE FUNNIES
CENTAUR (1938-1939)
1 Oblong, 128 pages. 125.00 400.00
2-3 No copies known to exist. 95.00 300.00
4 95.00 300.00

LITTLE GIANT MOVIE FUNNIES
CENTAUR (1938)
1 125.00 400.00
2 95.00 300.00

LITTLE HIAWATHA
DELL FOUR COLOR SERIES (1952-1959)
439 (12/52) 11.00 35.00
787 (4/57) 8.00 25.00
901 (5/58) 8.00 25.00
988 (5/59) 7.00 20.00

LITTLE IODINE
DELL (1950-1962)
1 16.00 50.00
2 8.00 25.00
3-6 7.00 20.00
7-12 5.00 15.00
13-18 4.00 12.00
19-24 2.75 10.00
25-30 2.25 8.00
31-36 1.75 6.00
37-42 1.50 5.00
43-48 1.25 4.00
49-56 1.00 3.00

LITTLE IODINE
DELL FOUR COLOR SERIES (1949)
224 (4/49) 23.00 75.00
257 (12/49) 16.00 50.00

LITTLE JOE
DELL FOUR COLOR SERIES (1942)
1 110.00 350.00

LITTLE KING, THE
DELL FOUR COLOR SERIES (1953-1956)
494 (9/53) 17.00 55.00
597 (10/54) 13.00 40.00
677 (2/56) 13.00 40.00

LITTLE KIP COMICS
WP (1965)
NO# (3/4" x 1") .20 .50

LITTLE LANA
MARVEL (1949-1950)
8 Previous title: Lana. 10.00 30.00
9 10.00 30.00

LITTLE LOTTA
HARVEY (1955-1976)
1 50.00 150.00
2 23.00 75.00
3 19.00 60.00
4-6 16.00 50.00
7-12 13.00 40.00
13-18 10.00 30.00
19-24 8.00 25.00
25-30 7.00 20.00
31-36 5.00 15.00
37-42 2.75 10.00
43-50 2.25 8.00
51-60 1.75 6.00
61-70 1.50 5.00
71-80 1.25 4.00
81-90 1.00 3.00
91-100 .75 2.00
101-110 .30 1.00
111-121 .20 .50

LITTLE LOTTA FOODLAND
HARVEY (1963-1972)
1 16.00 50.00
2 8.00 25.00
3 7.00 20.00
4-6 4.00 12.00
7-12 2.25 8.00
13-18 1.00 3.00
19-24 .75 2.00
25-29 .30 1.00

LITTLE LULU
DELL (1948-1984)
1 85.00 270.00
2 40.00 130.00
3 35.00 110.00
4-6 28.00 90.00
7-12 22.00 70.00
13-18 19.00 60.00
19-24 16.00 50.00
25-30 14.00 45.00
31-36 11.00 36.00
37-48 9.00 27.00
49-60 7.00 22.00
61-80 6.00 18.00
81-100 5.00 16.00
101-130 2.75 10.00
131-164 2.50 9.00
165-166 Giant size. 7.00 22.00
167-180 2.00 7.00
181-190 1.25 4.50
191-210 .75 2.50
211-220 .50 1.75
221-268 .20 .75

LITTLE LULU
DELL FOUR COLOR SERIES (1945-1947)
74 200.00 650.00
97 70.00 225.00
110 50.00 150.00
115 45.00 135.00
120 40.00 125.00
131 40.00 120.00
139 35.00 110.00
146 31.00 100.00
158 28.00 90.00
165 25.00 80.00

LITTLE LULU & TUBBY HALLOWEEN FUN
DELL (1957-1958)
2 100 page Giant. (10/58) 20.00 65.00
6 100 page Giant. (10/57) 20.00 65.00

LITTLE LULU AND TUBBY AT SUMMER CAMP
DELL (1957-1958)
2 100 page giant. (10/58) 28.00 90.00
5 100 page giant. (10/57) 28.00 90.00

LITTLE LULU AND TUBBY IN ALASKA
DELL (1959)
1 100 page Giant. 16.00 50.00

LITTLE LULU ON VACATION
DELL (1954)
1 100 page Giant. 55.00 170.00

LITTLE LULU TRICK 'N' TREAT
GOLD KEY (1962)
1 9.00 27.00

LITTLE LULU TUBBY ANNUAL
DELL (1953-1954)
1 Giant size. (3/53) 65.00 200.00
2 Giant size. (3/54) 55.00 175.00

LITTLE MAX COMICS
HARVEY (1949-1961)
1 16.00 50.00
2 10.00 30.00
3-6 8.00 25.00
7-9 7.00 20.00
10-12 6.00 18.00
13-20 4.00 12.00
21-30 2.50 9.00
31-40 2.00 7.00
41-50 1.75 6.00
51-60 1.50 5.00
61-69 1.00 3.00
70-73 .75 2.00

LITTLE MERMAID, THE
DISNEY (1992)
1 Movie adaptation. .75 2.00
2-4 .75 2.00

LITTLE MISS MUFFET
STANDARD (1948-1949)
11 10.00 30.00
12-13 7.00 20.00

LITTLE NEMO IN SLUMBERLAND
CUPPLES & LEON (1909)
1909 10" x 14", Cardboard covers, features color interior by Winsor McCay. 600.00 2000.00

LITTLE NEMO IN SLUMBERLAND
MCKAY (1945)
1945 28 pages, softcover, B&W reprints from 1905 and 1911. 10.00 30.00

LITTLE ORPHAN ANNIE
CUPPLES & LEON (1926-1934)
1926 First book in the series. 100 pages, hardcover. Contains strip reprints from 1926. 65.00 200.00
1927 In The Circus. Hardcover, 100 pages. Daily strip reprints from 1927. 50.00 150.00
1928 And The Haunted House. 100 pages, hardbound. Contains B&W daily strip reprints from 1928. 40.00 125.00
1929 Bucking The World. 100 pages, hardcover. Daily strip reprints from 1929. 40.00 125.00
1930 Never Say Die. 100 pages, hardcover. Daily strip reprints from 1930. 31.00 100.00
1931 Shipwrecked. 100 pages, hardcover. Daily strip reprints from 1931. 31.00 100.00
1932 A Willing Helper. 100 pages. Hardcover. Daily strip reprints from 1932. 31.00 100.00
1933 In Cosmic City. 100 pages, hardcover. Daily strip reprints from 1933. 31.00 100.00
1934 Uncle Dan. 100 pages, hardcover. Daily strip reprints from 1934. 31.00 100.00

LITTLE ORPHAN ANNIE
DELL (1948)

1	20.00	65.00
2-3	11.00	36.00

LITTLE ORPHAN ANNIE
DELL FOUR COLOR SERIES (1942-1948)

18 "Junior Commandos"	95.00	300.00
52	65.00	200.00
76	55.00	180.00
107	50.00	150.00
152	28.00	90.00
206	16.00	50.00

LITTLE ORPHAN ANNIE JUNIOR COMMANDOS GIVEAWAY
K.K. (1944)

NO# Same cover art from 4-Color series #18.	40.00	125.00

LITTLE ORPHAN ANNIE POPPED WHEAT GIVEAWAY
GIVEAWAY (1947)

NO#	2.75	10.00

LITTLE PEOPLE, THE
DELL FOUR COLOR SERIES (1953-1958)

485 (8/53)	14.00	45.00
573 (7/54)	7.00	20.00
633 (6/55)	7.00	20.00
692 (4/56)	7.00	20.00
753 (11/56)	7.00	20.00
809 (6/57)	7.00	20.00
868 (12/57)	7.00	20.00
908 "And The Giant" (5/58)	7.00	20.00

LITTLE RASCALS, THE
DELL FOUR COLOR SERIES (1956-1962)

674 TV tie-in. (1/56)	16.00	50.00
778 (3/57)	8.00	25.00
825 (8/57)	8.00	25.00
883 (3/58)	8.00	25.00
936 (9/58)	8.00	25.00
974 (3/59)	8.00	25.00
1030 (9/59)	8.00	25.00
1079 (2/60)	7.00	20.00
1137 (8/60)	8.00	25.00
1174 (2/61)	8.00	25.00
1224 (9/61)	8.00	25.00
1297 (2/62)	8.00	25.00

LITTLE SCOUTS, THE
DELL FOUR COLOR SERIES (1951-1954)

321 (3/51)	5.00	15.00
462 (4/53)	5.00	15.00
506 (10/53)	4.00	12.00
550 (4/54)	5.00	15.00
587 (10/54)	2.75	10.00

LITTLE STOOGES, THE
GOLD KEY (1972-1974)

1	2.75	10.00
2	1.75	6.00
3	1.25	4.00
4-7	1.00	3.00

LITTLEST OUTLAW, THE
DELL FOUR COLOR SERIES (1954)

609 (11/54)	10.00	30.00

LITTLEST SNOWMAN, THE
DELL FOUR COLOR SERIES (1956-1957)

755 (12/56)	7.00	20.00
864 (12/57)	7.00	20.00

LIVING BIBLE COMIC BOOK SERIES
LIVING BIBLE (1945-1946)

1 The Life Of Paul.	26.00	85.00
2 Joseph And His Brethren.	20.00	65.00
3 Chaplains At War.	26.00	85.00

LOBO
DC (1990-1991)

1	1.50	5.00
1 (2ND) 2nd printing.	.75	2.50
2-4	1.25	4.00

LOBO
DC (1993-CURRENT)

0 (8/94)	1.00	3.50
1 Foil embossed "zipper" cover.	1.75	6.00
2	1.25	4.00
3	1.00	3.50
4-15	.50	1.75
16-20	.75	2.25
ANNUAL 1 Bloodlines, pt.1. (1993)	1.00	3.50
ANNUAL 2 Elseworlds story. (1994)	1.00	3.50

LOBO
DELL (1965-1966)

1-2	1.75	6.00

LOBO: A CONTRACT ON GAWD
DC (1994)

1-4	.50	1.75

LOBO: BLAZING CHAIN OF LOVE
DC (1992)

1	.50	1.50

LOBO: BOUNTY HUNTING FOR FUN AND PROFIT
DC (1995)

1	1.25	4.95

LOBO: CONVENTION SPECIAL
DC (1993)

1	.50	1.75

LOBO: IN THE CHAIR
DC (1994)

1	.50	1.95

LOBO: INFANTICIDE
DC (1992)

1-4	.50	1.50

LOBO PARAMILITARY CHRISTMAS SPECIAL
DC (1991)

1	.75	2.39

LOBO: PORTRAIT OF A VICTIM
DC (1993)

1 One shot.	.50	1.75

LOBO: PORTRAITS OF A BASTICH
DC (1995)

1 One shot.	1.00	3.50

LOBO: UNAMERICAN GLADIATORS
DC (1993)

1-4	.50	1.75

LOBO'S BACK
DC (1992)

1	1.00	3.00
2	.75	2.00
3-4	.50	1.50

LOBO'S BIG BABE SPRING BREAK SPECIAL
DC (1995)

1	.50	1.95

LOBOCOP
DC (1994)

1	.50	1.95

LOGAN'S RUN
MARVEL (1977)

1-5	.50	1.25
6 1st: Thanos solo story.	2.25	6.00
7	.50	1.25

LOLLY AND PEPPER
DELL (1962)

01-459-207	4.00	12.00

LOLLY AND PEPPER
DELL FOUR COLOR SERIES (1957-1961)

832 (9/57)	8.00	25.00
940 (10/58)	8.00	25.00
978 (4/59)	7.00	20.00
1086 (4/60)	7.00	20.00
1206 (8/61)	7.00	20.00

LONE EAGLE
AJAX (1954)

1	13.00	40.00
2	8.00	25.00
3-4	7.00	20.00

LONE RANGER
DELL (1948-1962)

1	95.00	310.00
2	50.00	150.00
3	40.00	130.00
4-6	35.00	110.00
7-12	28.00	90.00
13-18	22.00	70.00
19-30	16.00	50.00
31-36	14.00	45.00
37-42	11.00	36.00
43-48	9.00	27.00
49-60	7.00	22.00
61-80	6.00	18.00
81-99	5.00	16.00
100 Anniversary issue.	6.00	18.00
101-111	4.00	13.00
112 Begin: Clayton Moore photo covers.	31.00	100.00
113-117	19.00	60.00
118 Special anniversary issue.	31.00	100.00
119-125	16.00	50.00
126-136	13.00	40.00
137-145	10.00	30.00

LONE RANGER, THE
DELL FOUR COLOR SERIES (1945-1947)

82	85.00	275.00
98	65.00	200.00
118	60.00	190.00
125	55.00	175.00
136	50.00	150.00
151	40.00	130.00
167	31.00	100.00

LONE RANGER
GOLD KEY (1964-1977)

1	4.00	13.00
2	2.50	9.00
3	2.00	7.00
4-6	1.50	5.25
7-12	1.25	4.50
13-18	1.00	3.00
19-28	.50	1.75

LONE RANGER
WRATHER (1969)

NO# Giveaway.	5.00	15.00

LONE RANGER AND TONTO, THE
TOPPS (1994)

1-4	.75	2.50
TPB Reprints issues #1-4.	2.50	9.95

LONE RANGER CHEERIOS GIVEAWAY
GIVEAWAY (1954)

1 16 color pages. Measures 2-1/2" by 7". Newsprint covers.	16.00	50.00

LONE RANGER COMICS
LONE RANGER, INC. (1938)

NO#	500.00	1800.00

LONE RANGER GOLDEN WEST
DELL/GOLD KEY (1955, 1966)

3 100 page giant.	55.00	175.00
30029-610 Reprints earlier issue.	16.00	50.00

LONE RANGER MOVIE STORY
DELL (1956)

NO# Clayton Moore photo cover.	110.00	350.00

LONE RANGER'S WESTERN TREASURY, THE
DELL (1953-1954)

1 100 page giant.	65.00	200.00
2 100 page giant.	40.00	125.00

LONE RIDER
SUPERIOR (1951-1955)

1	19.00	60.00
2	10.00	30.00
3	8.00	25.00
4-10	7.00	20.00
11-26	5.00	15.00

LONE WOLF AND CUB
FIRST (1987-1991)

1-2	2.00	7.00
3-10	1.25	4.00
11-41	1.00	3.00
42-47	1.00	3.50

LONG BOW
FICTION HOUSE (1951-1953)

1	17.00	55.00
2	9.00	27.00
3	7.00	22.00
4-9	5.00	16.00

LONG HOT SUMMER, THE
DC (1995)

1 Holographic foil-stamped cover.	.75	2.95
2-3	.75	2.50

LITTLE MAX COMICS #1

THE LITTLE MERMAID #1

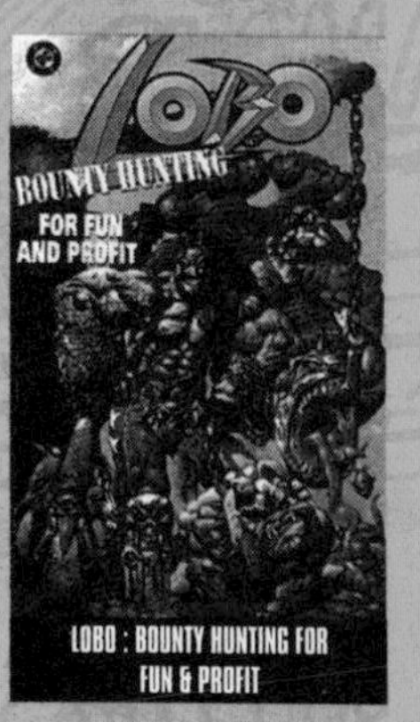

LOBO : BOUNTY HUNTING FOR FUN & PROFIT

LOBO: BIG BABE SPRING BREAK SPECIAL

LOOSE CANNON #1

LORD PUMPKIN #0

LORNA THE JUNGLE GIRL #25

LOST UNIVERSE #2

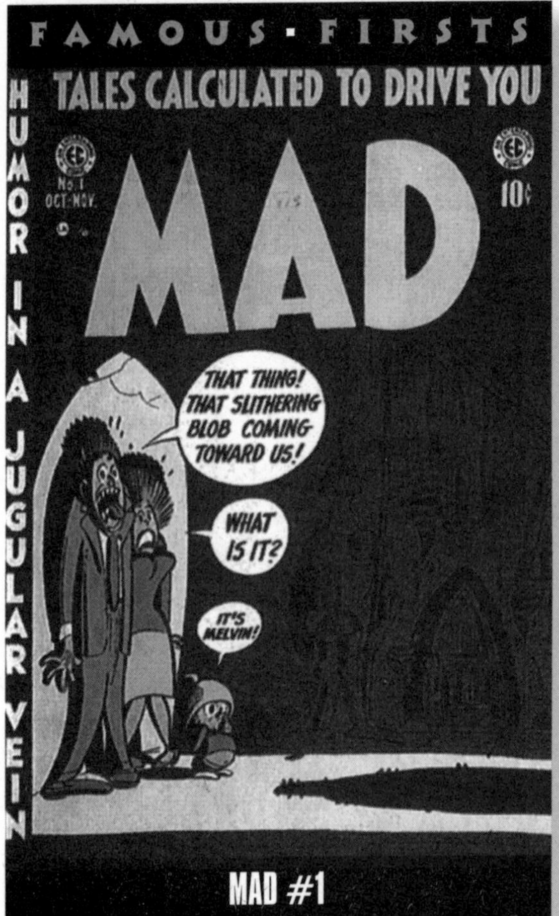

MAD #1

Created by Harvey Kurtzman to parody comic strips and comic books, *Mad* proved influential with a generation of wide-eyed kids. With #24, it became a magazine in order to avoid restrictions by the Comics Code.

LONG JOHN SILVER AND THE PIRATES
CHARLTON (1956-1957)
30-32 .... 5.00 15.00

LONGSHOT
MARVEL (1985-1986)
1 1st: Longshot. Art Adams cover & art on all issues. 2.75 10.00
2-3 .... 2.00 7.00
4 App: Spider-Man. 2.00 7.00
5 .... 2.00 7.00
6 Double size. 2.00 7.00

LOONEY TUNES
DC (1994-CURRENT)
1-14 .... .30 1.00

LOONEY TUNES
GOLD KEY (1975-1984)
1 .... .50 1.50
2-47 .... .20 .75

LOONEY TUNES (AND MERRIE MELODIES)
DELL (1941-1962)
1 Begin: Porky Pig, Bugs Bunny. 68 pages. 900.00 3200.00
2 .... 250.00 800.00
3 .... 210.00 675.00
4 .... 180.00 575.00
5 .... 155.00 500.00
6 .... 140.00 460.00
7-9 .... 125.00 400.00
10-12 .... 105.00 340.00
13-18 .... 85.00 280.00
19-24 .... 80.00 250.00
25-30 .... 70.00 230.00
31-36 .... 65.00 200.00
37-42 .... 55.00 170.00
43-48 .... 45.00 140.00
49-60 .... 35.00 110.00
61-70 .... 28.00 90.00
71-80 .... 20.00 65.00
81-90 .... 14.00 46.00
91-100 .... 11.00 34.00
101-110 .... 7.00 23.00
111-120 .... 6.00 17.00
121-130 .... 4.00 13.00
131-150 .... 4.00 11.00
151-180 .... 2.50 9.00
181-200 .... 1.75 6.75
201-220 .... 1.25 4.50
221-246 .... .75 2.25

LOOSE CANNON
DC (1995)
1 Mini-series. .... .50 1.75
2-4 .... .50 1.75

LORD JIM
GOLD KEY (1965)
10156-509 Movie photo cover. 5.00 15.00

LORD PUMPKIN
MALIBU (1994)
0 (8/94) .... .75 2.50
0A Newstand edition. Variant cover. (12/94) .... .75 2.50

LORNA THE JUNGLE GIRL
MARVEL(ATLAS) (1953-1957)
1 Origin: Lorna The Jungle Girl. 35.00 110.00
2 .... 17.00 55.00
3 .... 14.00 44.00
4-6 .... 10.00 33.00
7-12 .... 7.00 22.00
13-20 .... 5.00 16.00
21-26 .... 4.00 11.00

LOST IN SPACE
GOLD KEY (1973-1982)
37 Previous title: Space Family Robinson. 1.25 4.75
38-40 .... 1.00 3.50
41-50 .... .75 2.25
51-59 .... .30 1.00

LOST IN SPACE
INNOVATION (1991-1993)
1 .... 1.00 3.50
2-5 .... .75 2.75
6-12 .... .75 2.50
ANNUAL 1 .... 1.00 3.50
ANNUAL 2 .... .75 2.75

LOST IN SPACE: ARRIVAL
INNOVATION (1994)
1 Polybagged with card, gold foil-stamped cover. 1.25 4.95
1A Polybagged with card, silver foil-stamped cover. .... .75 2.95
2-3 .... .75 2.50

LOST IN SPACE: PROJECT ROBINSON
INNOVATION (1993)
1-2 .... .75 2.50

LOST UNIVERSE
TEKNO (1994-CURRENT)
0 (7/95) .... .75 2.25
1 (Gene Roddenberry's...) .... .75 2.50
2-7 .... .50 1.95

LOST WORLD, THE
DELL FOUR COLOR SERIES (1960)
1145 Movie photo cover. 25.00 80.00

LOST WORLDS
STANDARD (1952)
5 Alice In Terrorland by Toth. 40.00 130.00
6 Outlaws Of Space. 29.00 95.00

LOVE ADVENTURES
MARVEL(ATLAS) (1949-1952)
1 Photo cover. 19.00 60.00
2 Movie photo cover. 16.00 50.00
3 .... 10.00 30.00
4 .... 7.00 20.00
5-9 .... 5.00 15.00

LOVE AND ROCKETS
FANTAGRAPHICS (1982-CURRENT)
1 Color cover. (Fall/82) 16.00 50.00
1 (2ND) 2nd printing. 1.00 3.95
1 (3RD) 3rd printing. 1.00 3.95
1A Black & white cover (800 printed). 19.00 60.00
2 .... 8.00 25.00
2 (2ND) 2nd printing. 1.00 3.95
3 .... 5.00 15.00
3 (2ND) 2nd printing. 1.00 3.95
4 .... 5.00 15.00
4 (2ND) 2nd printing. 1.00 3.95
5 .... 5.00 15.00
5 (2ND) 2nd printing. .... .75 2.50
6 .... 1.75 6.00
6 (2ND) 2nd printing. .... .75 2.50
7 .... 1.75 6.00
7 (2ND) 2nd printing. .... .75 2.50
8 .... 1.75 6.00
8 (2ND) 2nd printing. .... .75 2.50
9 .... 1.75 6.00
9 (2ND) 2nd printing. .... .75 2.50
10 .... 1.75 6.00
10 (2ND) 2nd printing. .... .75 2.50
11 .... 1.25 4.95
11 (2ND) 2nd printing. .... .75 2.50
12 .... 1.25 4.00
12 (2ND) 2nd printing. .... .75 2.50
13 .... 1.25 4.00
13 (2ND) 2nd printing. .... .75 2.50
14 .... 1.00 3.00
14 (2ND) 2nd printing. .... .75 2.50
15 .... 1.00 3.00
15 (2ND) 2nd printing. .... .75 2.50
16 .... 1.00 3.00
16 (2ND) 2nd printing. .... .75 2.50
17-20 .... 1.00 3.00
21-28 .... .75 2.25
29-34 .... .75 2.50
35-39 .... .75 2.75
40 .... 1.00 3.50
41-46 .... .75 2.95

LOVE AT FIRST SIGHT
ACE (1949-1956)
1 .... 13.00 40.00
2 .... 7.00 20.00
3-6 .... 5.00 15.00

7-12 2.75 10.00
13-20 2.25 8.00
21-42 1.75 6.00

LOVE BUG, THE
GOLD KEY (1969)
10237-906 Disney movie photo cover. 7.00 20.00

LOVE CLASSICS
MARVEL (1949-1950)
1 14.00 44.00
2 Virginia Mayo movie (White Heat) cover. 10.00 33.00

LOVE CONFESSIONS
QUALITY (1949-1956)
1 31.00 100.00
2 16.00 50.00
3 13.00 40.00
4-6 10.00 30.00
7-12 7.00 20.00
13-20 5.00 15.00
21-30 4.00 12.00
31-54 2.75 10.00

LOVE DRAMAS
MARVEL (1949-1950)
1 20.00 65.00
2 Title changes to True Secrets with #3. 14.00 44.00

LOVE PROBLEMS & ADVICE ILLUSTRATED
HARVEY (1949-1957)
1 14.00 45.00
2 7.00 20.00
3-10 5.00 15.00
11-31 2.75 10.00
32-37 2.25 8.00
38 Cover: Simon & Kirby. 7.00 20.00
39-43 2.25 8.00
44 Title changes to Romance Stories Of True Love with #45. 2.25 8.00

LOVE ROMANCES
MARVEL(TIMELY/ATLAS) (1949-1963)
6 Previous title: Ideal, A Classical Comic. 14.00 44.00
7 10.00 33.00
8-12 7.00 22.00
13-24 5.00 16.00
25-106 4.00 11.00

LOVE SCANDALS
QUALITY (1950)
1 23.00 75.00
2 Photo cover. 10.00 30.00
3 7.00 20.00
4 Art: Bill Ward. 16.00 50.00
5 8.00 25.00

LOVELORN
ACG (1949-1954)
1 16.00 50.00
2 8.00 25.00
3-6 7.00 20.00
7-12 4.00 12.00
13-24 2.75 10.00
25-40 2.00 7.00
41-48 1.50 5.00
49-50 3-D effect story. 22.00 70.00
51 3-D effect story. Becomes Confessions of the Lovelorn #52. 22.00 70.00

LOVERS LANE
LEV GLEASON (1949-1954)
1 10.00 30.00
2 7.00 20.00
3-10 5.00 15.00
11-20 2.75 10.00
21-30 2.00 7.00
31-41 1.50 5.00

LOWELL THOMAS' HIGH ADVENTURE
DELL FOUR COLOR SERIES (1958-1959)
949 TV photo cover. (11/58) 11.00 35.00
1001 TV photo cover. (8/59) 11.00 35.00

LT. ROBIN CRUSOE, U.S.N.
GOLD KEY (1966)
10191-610 Disney movie photo cover. 5.00 15.00

LUCKY COMICS
CONSOLIDATED (1944-1946)
1 19.00 60.00
2 10.00 30.00
3-5 7.00 20.00

LUCKY FIGHTS IT THROUGH
EDUCATIONAL (1949)
NO# 16 page giveaway, VD education. 250.00 800.00

LUCKY STAR
NATION-WIDE (1950-1953)
1 8.00 25.00
2 5.00 15.00
3-14 2.75 10.00

LUCY SHOW, THE
GOLD KEY (1963-1964)
1 TV photo covers on all issues. 20.00 65.00
2 14.00 44.00
3-5 10.00 33.00

LUKE CAGE, HERO FOR HIRE
SEE HERO FOR HIRE

LUKE CAGE, POWER MAN
SEE POWER MAN

LUKE SHORT'S...
DELL FOUR COLOR SERIES (1954-1958)
580 "Six Gun Ranch" (8/54) 7.00 20.00
651 "King Colt" (9/55) 8.00 25.00
739 "Bounty Guns" (10/56) 8.00 25.00
771 "Brand Of Empire" (3/57) 7.00 20.00
807 "Savage Range" (6/57) 8.00 25.00
848 "Marauders' Moon" (10/57) 7.00 20.00
875 "Trumpets West" (2/58) 7.00 20.00
927 "Top Gun" (8/58) 7.00 20.00

LYNCH MOB
CHAOS! (1994-1995)
1 1st: Mother Mayhem. 1.00 3.50
1A Refractor foil cover. 4.00 12.50
2-3 .75 2.50
3A Premium edition. 2.25 8.00
4 .75 2.50

MACHINE, THE
DARK HORSE (1994-1995)
1-4 .75 2.50

MACHINE MAN
MARVEL (1978-1981)
1 .75 2.00
2-17 .50 1.50
18 App: Alpha Flight. .50 1.50
19 1st: Jack-O-Lantern (who later becomes Hobgoblin II). 5.00 15.00

MACHINE MAN
MARVEL (1984-1985)
1 .75 2.00
2 1st: Iron Man 2020 (cameo). .75 2.00
3 1st: Iron Man 2020 (full). .75 2.50
4 .75 2.00

MACHINE MAN 2020
MARVEL (1994-1995)
1 Reprints. .75 2.00
2-4 .75 2.00

MACK BOLAN: THE EXECUTIONER
INNOVATION (1993-1994)
1 1st: Mack Bolan. Black over-cover with red foil enhancement. 1.00 3.95
1A Tyvek cover with metallic ink logo. 1.00 3.50
1B Cardstock cover with gold & red foil logo. .75 2.95
2-8 .75 2.50

MACKENZIE'S RAIDERS
DELL FOUR COLOR SERIES (1960)
1093 Movie photo cover. (6/60) 13.00 40.00

MACROSS
COMICO (1984)
1 2.25 8.00

MAD
EC (1952-CURRENT)
1 1300.00 4800.00
2 280.00 900.00
3 190.00 600.00
4 160.00 525.00
5 Low distribution. 250.00 825.00
6-12 130.00 420.00
13-15 110.00 360.00
16-23 95.00 300.00
24 Begin: Magazine size issues. 220.00 700.00
25 110.00 360.00
26-29 75.00 240.00
30 1st: Alfred E. Neuman. 95.00 300.00
31 55.00 180.00
32 50.00 150.00
33-36 40.00 120.00
37-40 25.00 80.00
41-50 19.00 60.00
51-60 15.00 48.00
61-70 11.00 36.00
71-80 10.00 30.00
81-90 8.00 24.00
91-100 7.00 21.00
101-104 6.00 18.00
105 Batman TV show spoof. 7.00 20.00
106-120 5.00 15.00
121-150 4.00 12.00
151-180 2.75 10.00
181-200 2.25 8.00
201-250 1.75 6.00
251-300 1.25 4.00
301-320 1.00 3.00
321-340 .75 2.00

MAD ABOUT MILLIE
MARVEL (1969-1970)
1 10.00 30.00
2 6.00 18.00
3-17 4.00 12.00
ANNUAL 1 (1971) 6.00 18.00

MAD DOG
MARVEL (1993-1994)
1 TV tie-in (Bob). .50 1.25
2-6 .50 1.25

MAD FOLLIES
EC (1963-1969)
1 (NO#) (1963) 55.00 180.00
2 (1964) 40.00 120.00
3 (1965) 28.00 90.00
4 (1966) 31.00 100.00
5 (1967) 23.00 75.00
6 (1968) 19.00 60.00
7 (1969) 17.00 55.00

MAD FOR KEEPS
EC (1958)
HC Hardcover. Reprint: early Mads. Cover is taken from Mad #30. 230.00 750.00

MAD HATTER
OW (1946)
1 Costumed hero. 65.00 200.00
2 50.00 150.00

MAD MONSTER PARTY?
DELL (1968)
12-460-801 Movie photo cover (Claymation). 10.00 30.00

MAD SPECIAL
EC (1970-CURRENT)
NO# Star Trek Spectacular. 1.25 4.00
1 (Fall/70) 19.00 60.00
2 (Spring/71) 11.00 35.00
3 10.00 30.00
4-10 8.00 25.00
11-20 7.00 20.00
21-30 5.00 15.00
31-40 2.75 10.00
41-50 2.25 8.00
51-70 1.75 6.00
71-75 1.50 5.00
76 Collector's Series #1. 1.50 5.00
77-78 1.50 5.00
79 Collector's Series #2. 1.50 5.00
80-81 1.50 5.00
82 Collector's Series #3. 1.50 5.00
83-84 1.50 5.00
85 Collector's Series #4. 1.50 5.00
86-87 1.50 5.00
88 Collector's Series #5. 1.50 5.00
89 Polybagged with trading cards. 1.25 4.00
90 1.00 3.00
91 Collector's Series #6. 1.00 3.00
92-93 1.00 3.00
94 Collector's Series #7. 1.00 3.00
95-96 1.00 3.00
97 Collector's Series #8. Includes Spy Vs. Spy Combat Card game. 1.00 3.00
98-99 1.00 3.00
100 Collector's Series #9. 1.00 3.00
101-102 1.00 3.00
103 Collector's Special #10. 1.00 3.00

MADBALLS
MARVEL(STAR) (1986-1988)
1-10 .30 1.00

MADELEINE AND GENEVIEVE
DELL FOUR COLOR SERIES (1957)
796 (5/57) 8.00 25.00

LUCKY STAR #2

MAD #36

MAD #39

MAD #50

MADMAN COMICS #1

MAGNUS, ROBOT FIGHTER #0 (VALIANT)

MAGNUS, ROBOT FIGHTER #21 (VALIANT)

MAGNUS, ROBOT FIGHTER/NEXUS #1

MADHOUSE
AJAX/FARRELL (1954)

1 .... 35.00 110.00
2 .... 17.00 55.00
3-4 .... 14.00 44.00

MADMAN
TUNDRA (1992)

1 .... 2.25 8.00
2 .... 1.75 6.00
2A 2nd printing. 1.00 3.95
3 .... 1.50 5.50
TPB Oddity Odyssey. Reprints issues #1-3. 7.00 20.00

MADMAN ADVENTURES
TUNDRA (1992-1993)

1 .... 1.75 6.00
2 .... 1.25 4.50
3 .... 1.00 3.50

MADMAN ADVENTURES COLLECTION
KITCHEN SINK (1995)

TPB Reprints: Madman Adventures #1-3. 5.00 14.95

MADMAN COMICS
LEGEND/DARK HORSE (1994-CURRENT)

1 .... 1.75 6.00
2-7 .... 1.00 3.50
8 .... .75 2.95

MAGE
COMICO (1984-1986)

1 .... 4.00 11.00
2 .... 2.25 8.00
3-5 .... 1.50 5.00
6 Begin: Grendel (1st time in color). ... 7.00 20.00
7 .... 2.00 7.00
8-12 .... 1.25 4.00
13 Death: Grendel. 1.25 4.00
14 .... 1.25 4.00
15 Double size with pullout poster. ... 1.50 5.50

MAGIC AGENT
ACG (1962)

1 .... 7.00 20.00
2-3 .... 4.00 12.00

MAGIC COMICS
MCKAY (1939-1949)

1 Begin: Blondie, Popeye, Mandrake. 270.00 875.00
2 .... 135.00 440.00
3 .... 100.00 330.00
4 .... 85.00 270.00
5 .... 70.00 220.00
6 .... 50.00 160.00
7-12 .... 40.00 130.00
13-16 .... 35.00 110.00
17 Begin: The Lone Ranger. 40.00 130.00
18-20 .... 35.00 110.00
21-30 .... 26.00 85.00
31-40 .... 20.00 65.00
41-50 .... 14.00 44.00
51-70 .... 10.00 33.00
71-80 .... 7.00 22.00
81-100 .... 5.00 16.00
101-123 .... 4.00 11.00

MAGIC SWORD, THE
DELL (1962)

01-496-209 Movie photo cover. 10.00 30.00

MAGIC: THE GATHERING...ANTIQUITIES WAR
ACCLAIM/ARMADA (1995)

1-2 Mini-series. .... .75 2.50

MAGIC: THE GATHERING...FALLEN EMPIRES
ACCLAIM/ARMADA (1995)

1 Mini-series. Polybagged with card pack. .75 2.75
2 .... .75 2.50

MAGIC: THE GATHERING...ICE AGE
ACCLAIM/ARMADA (1995)

1 Mini-series. .... .75 2.50
2-3 .... .75 2.50
4 Polybagged with tokens. .... .75 2.50

MAGIC: THE GATHERING...NIGHTMARE
ACCLAIM/ARMADA (1995)

1 One shot. .... .75 2.50

MAGIC: THE GATHERING...THE SHADOW MAGE
ACCLAIM/ARMADA (1995)

1 Mini-series. .... .75 2.50
2-3 .... .75 2.50
4 Polybagged with tokens. .... .75 2.50

MAGIC: THE GATHERING...WAYFARER
ACCLAIM/ARMADA (1995)

1-2 Mini-series. .... .75 2.50

MAGIK
MARVEL (1983-1984)

1-4 .... .30 1.00

MAGILLA GORILLA
CHARLTON (1970-1971)

1 TV cartoon tie-in. 7.00 22.00
2-5 .... 4.00 13.00

MAGILLA GORILLA
GOLD KEY (1964-1968)

1 TV cartoon tie-in. 14.00 44.00
2-10 .... 7.00 22.00

MAGNETO
MARVEL (1993)

0 Giveaway. (12/93) 1.50 6.00
0A Gold edition. 2.25 8.00
0B Platinum edition. 2.75 10.00

MAGNUS, ROBOT FIGHTER
GOLD KEY (1963-1977)

1 1st & Origin: Magnus. 1st: Aliens. ... 80.00 250.00
2 .... 40.00 125.00
3-4 .... 31.00 100.00
5-6 .... 25.00 80.00
7-12 .... 19.00 60.00
13-24 .... 11.00 35.00
25-27 .... 10.00 30.00
28 End: Aliens backup story. 10.00 30.00
29 Begin: Reprints. 2.75 10.00
30-46 .... 2.75 10.00

MAGNUS, ROBOT FIGHTER
VALIANT (1991-CURRENT)

0 Send away version with card. 7.00 20.00
0A Available in stores, without card. ... 1.25 4.00
1 .... 2.50 9.00
1A Coupon cut out. .... .75 2.00
2 .... 1.75 6.00
2A Coupon cut out. .... .75 2.00
3 .... 1.25 4.00
3A Coupon cut out. .... .50 1.50
4 .... 1.25 4.00
4A Coupon cut out. .... .50 1.50
5 .... 1.25 4.00
5A Coupon cut out. .... .30 1.00
6 .... 1.00 3.00
6A Coupon cut out. .... .30 1.00
7 1st: X-O Armor. 1.00 3.00
7A Coupon cut out. .... .30 1.00
8 .... 1.00 3.00
8A Coupon cut out. .... .30 1.00
9-11 .... .75 2.00
12 1st: new Turok. Giant size. 4.00 12.00
13-20 .... .75 2.00
21 .... 1.00 3.00
21A Gold edition. 1.75 6.00
22-23 .... .75 2.00
24 1st: Rai & The Future Force. ...... .75 2.00
25 Silver foil cover. .... .75 2.00
26-28 .... .75 2.00
29 Eternal Warrior. .... .75 2.00
30-55 .... .75 2.00
56-60 .... .75 2.50
YEARBOOK 1 (1994) 1.00 3.95

MAGNUS ROBOT FIGHTER 4000 A.D.
VALIANT (1990-1991)

1 (7.95) Trade paperback. 2.25 8.00
2 .... 2.25 8.00

MAGNUS ROBOT FIGHTER/NEXUS
VALIANT/DARK HORSE (1993)

1 .... 1.00 3.00
2 .... .75 2.95

MAI THE PSYCHIC GIRL
ECLIPSE (1987-1989)

1-28 .... .50 1.50

MAJOR HOOPLE COMICS
NEDOR (1943)

1 .... 50.00 150.00

MAJOR INAPAK, THE SPACE ACE
ME (1951)

1 Cover/Art: Bob Powell. (Thousands of copies surfaced in the 1970's). .... .75 2.00

MAJOR VICTORY COMICS
CHESLER (1944-1945)

1 Origin: Major Victory. 95.00 300.00
2 .... 60.00 190.00
3 .... 35.00 110.00

MALIBU COMICS: COLLECTOR'S GUIDE TO THE ULTRAVERSE
MALIBU (1994)

1 Index of all Ultraverse titles. .... .30 .99

MAMMOTH COMICS
K.K. (1938)

1 80 pages, oversize, contains strip reprints. 190.00 600.00

MAN COMICS
MARVEL(ATLAS) (1949-1953)

1 .... 20.00 65.00
2 .... 10.00 33.00
3-6 .... 7.00 22.00
7-12 .... 5.00 16.00
13-20 .... 4.00 11.00
21-28 .... 2.25 8.75

MAN FROM ATLANTIS
MARVEL (1978)

1-7 .... .30 1.00

MAN FROM U.N.C.L.E.
GOLD KEY (1965-1969)

1 TV photo covers on all issues. 25.00 80.00
2 .... 17.00 55.00
3-8 .... 10.00 33.00
9-15 .... 9.00 27.00
16-22 .... 7.00 22.00

MAN FROM WELLS FARGO
DELL (1962)

01-495-207 TV tie-in, photo cover. ... 10.00 30.00

MAN FROM WELLS FARGO
DELL FOUR COLOR SERIES (1962)

1287 TV photo cover. 19.00 60.00

MAN IN BLACK
HARVEY (1957-1958)

1 Cover/Art: Bob Powell (all issues). ... 20.00 65.00
2-4 .... 14.00 44.00

MAN IN FLIGHT
DELL FOUR COLOR SERIES (1957)

836 Disney movie tie-in. (9/57) ... 11.00 35.00

MAN IN SPACE
DELL FOUR COLOR SERIES (1956-1959)

716 Disney movie tie-in. (8/56) ... 10.00 30.00
954 Disney movie tie-in. (2/59) ... 13.00 40.00

MAN O' MARS
FICTION HOUSE (1953)

1 Space Rangers. 75.00 240.00

MAN OF STEEL, THE
DC (1986)

1 Cover/art: John Byrne on all issues. 1st & origin: post-Crisis Superman. Full figure cover. 1.50 5.00
1A Chest shot cover. 1.25 4.00
2 1st: new Lois Lane. .... .75 2.00
3 App: Batman. .... .50 1.75
4 Debut: new Lex Luthor. .... .75 2.00
5 1st: new Bizarro. .... .75 2.00
6 .... .50 1.75
TPB Reprints issues #1-6. .... 4.00 12.95
TPB-C Send away limited edition. 14.00 45.00

MAN OF WAR
MALIBU (1993-CURRENT)

1 Direct edition (with poster). .... .75 2.50
1A Newsstand edition. .... .50 1.95
2 With poster. .... .75 2.50
2A Newsstand edition. .... .50 1.95
3 With poster. .... .75 2.50
3A Newsstand edition. .... .50 1.95
4 With poster. .... .75 2.50
4A Newsstand edition. .... .50 1.95
5 With poster. .... .75 2.25
5A Newsstand edition. .... .50 1.95
6-12 .... .75 2.25

MAN OF WAR COMICS
CENTAUR (1941-1942)

1 Cover & art: Paul Gustavson. 310.00 1000.00
2 Cover & art: Paul Gustavson. 250.00 800.00

MANBAT
DC (1976)

1 .... 1.75 6.00

2 1.50 5.00
SPECIAL 1 1.00 3.75

MANDRAKE THE MAGICIAN
DELL FOUR COLOR SERIES (1956)
752 (11/56) 19.00 60.00

MANDRAKE THE MAGICIAN
KING (1966-1967)
1 7.00 20.00
2 4.00 12.00
3-7 2.25 8.00
8 Art: Jeff Jones (4 pages). 7.00 20.00
9 2.25 8.00
10 Art: Alex Raymond (14 pages). 8.00 25.00

MANGAZINE
ANTARCTIC (1985-1986)
1-10 .30 1.00

MANHUNT!
ME (1947-1953)
1 1st & Begin: Space Ace. 55.00 170.00
2 35.00 110.00
3-6 28.00 90.00
7 End: Space Ace. 25.00 80.00
8 1st & Begin: Trail Colt. 20.00 65.00
9 20.00 65.00
10 Art: Graham Ingels. 20.00 65.00
11 Art: Frank Frazetta (7 pages). 35.00 110.00
12 20.00 65.00

MANHUNT (A-1 SERIES)
ME (1952)
13 (A-1 #63). Reprint: Trail Colt #1 by Frazetta. 31.00 100.00
14 (A-1 #77). 19.00 60.00

MANHUNTER
DC (1984)
1 App: Batman. .75 2.50

MANHUNTER
DC (1988-1990)
1-24 .30 1.00

MANHUNTER
DC (1994-CURRENT)
0 (8/94) .50 1.95
1-6 .50 1.95
7-10 .75 2.25

MAN-THING
MARVEL (1974-1975)
1 Begin: Man-Thing. 2nd: Howard The Duck (part 2 of story from FEAR #19). 5.00 15.00
2 2.25 8.00
3 1st: Foolkiller. 1.75 6.00
4 Origin: Foolkiller. 1.00 3.00
5 Begin: Mike Ploog art. 1.00 3.00
6-10 1.00 3.00
11 End: Mike Ploog art. 1.00 3.00
12-22 1.00 3.00

MAN-THING
MARVEL (1979-1981)
1 1.25 4.00
2-11 .75 2.00

MAN-THING GIANT SIZE
MARVEL (1974-1975)
1 1.75 6.00
2-3 1.00 3.00
4-5 Howard The Duck. 1.50 5.00

MANTRA
MALIBU (1983-CURRENT)
1 Polybagged with Ultraverse card. 1.25 4.50
1A Unbagged edition, without card. .50 1.95
1B Hologram edition. 2.75 10.00
1C Ultra limited foil edition. 1.50 5.00
1D Gold hologram edition. 2.75 10.00
2 1.00 3.00
3-4 .75 2.50
5-9 .50 1.95
10 Archimage Quest pt.1, with Ultraverse Premiere #2. 1.00 3.50
11-17 .50 1.95
18-24 .75 2.50
ASHCAN 1 1.50 5.00
GIANT SIZE .75 2.50

MANTRA: SPEAR OF DESTINY
MALIBU (1995)
1-2 .75 2.50

MANY GHOSTS OF DR. GRAVES, THE
CHARLTON (1967-1982)
1 2.75 10.00
2 1.50 5.00
3-12 1.25 4.00
13-30 1.00 3.00
31-50 .75 2.00
51-72 .30 1.00

MANY LOVES OF DOBIE GILLIS
DC (1960-1964)
1 65.00 200.00
2 29.00 95.00
3-6 26.00 85.00
7-12 22.00 70.00
13-18 19.00 60.00
19-26 15.00 48.00

MARCH OF COMICS
K.K. (1946-1982)
1 (No#) How Santa Got His Red Suit. 60.00 190.00
2 (No#) Goldilocks. 60.00 190.00
3 (No#) Our Gang. 85.00 270.00
4 (No#) Donald Duck. 1700.00 6500.00
5 Andy Panda. 35.00 110.00
6 Popular Fairy Tales. 40.00 130.00
7 Oswald The Lucky Rabbit. 40.00 130.00
8 Mickey Mouse. 150.00 490.00
9 Gloomey Bunny. 19.00 60.00
10 Santa Claus. 15.00 49.00
11 Santa Claus. 14.00 44.00
12 Santa's Toys. 14.00 44.00
13 Santa's Surprise. 14.00 44.00
14 Santa's Kitchen. 14.00 44.00
15 Hip-It-Ty Hop. 14.00 44.00
16 Woody Woodpecker. 23.00 75.00
17 Roy Rogers. 60.00 190.00
18 Popular Fairy Tales. 22.00 70.00
19 Uncle Wiggily. 19.00 60.00
20 Donald Duck. 900.00 3300.00
21 Tom And Jerry. 22.00 70.00
22 Andy Panda. 19.00 60.00
23 Raggedy Ann + Andy. 28.00 90.00
24 Felix The Cat. 50.00 150.00
25 Gene Autry. 60.00 190.00
26 Our Gang. 50.00 150.00
27 Mickey Mouse. 110.00 350.00
28 Gene Autry. 60.00 190.00
29 Easter. 9.00 27.00
30-31 Santa Claus. 7.00 22.00
32 Does not exist.
33 A Christmas Carol. 7.00 22.00
34 Woody Woodpecker. 19.00 60.00
35 Roy Rogers. 60.00 190.00
36 Felix The Cat. 40.00 120.00
37 Popeye. 29.00 95.00
38 Oswald The Lucky Rabbit. 14.00 44.00
39 Gene Autry. 60.00 190.00
40 Andy And Woody. 14.00 44.00
41 Donald Duck. 600.00 2200.00
42 Porky Pig. 14.00 44.00
43 Henry. 12.00 38.00
44 Bugs Bunny. 19.00 60.00
45 Mickey Mouse. 95.00 300.00
46 Tom And Jerry. 19.00 60.00
47 Roy Rogers. 55.00 170.00
48-50 Santa Claus. 6.00 19.00
51 Felix The Cat. 29.00 95.00
52 Popeye. 25.00 80.00
53 Oswald The Lucky Rabbit. 14.00 44.00
54 Gene Autry. 50.00 150.00
55 Andy and Woody. 14.00 44.00
56 Donald Duck. 70.00 230.00
57 Porky Pig. 14.00 44.00
58 Henry. 9.00 27.00
59 Bugs Bunny. 15.00 49.00
60 Mickey Mouse. 60.00 190.00
61 Tom And Jerry. 14.00 44.00
62 Roy Rogers. 50.00 150.00
63-64 Santa Claus. 6.00 19.00
65 Jingle Bells. 6.00 19.00
66 Popeye. 22.00 70.00
67 Oswald The Lucky Rabbit. 12.00 38.00
68 Roy Rogers. 45.00 140.00
69 Donald Duck. 60.00 190.00
70 Tom And Jerry. 12.00 38.00
71 Porky Pig. 12.00 38.00
72 Krazy Kat. 15.00 49.00
73 Roy Rogers. 40.00 120.00
74 Mickey Mouse. 50.00 150.00
75 Bugs Bunny. 14.00 44.00
76 Andy And Woody. 12.00 38.00
77 Roy Rogers. 35.00 110.00
78 Gene Autry. 35.00 110.00
79 Andy Panda. 7.00 22.00
80 Popeye. 20.00 65.00
81 Oswald The Lucky Rabbit. 7.00 22.00
82 Tarzan. Photo cover (Lex Barker). 29.00 95.00
83 Bugs Bunny. 10.00 33.00
84 Henry. 5.00 16.00
85 Woody Woodpecker. 5.00 16.00
86 Roy Rogers. 29.00 95.00
87 Krazy Kat. 14.00 44.00
88 Tom And Jerry. 9.00 27.00
89 Porky Pig. 5.00 16.00
90 Gene Autry. 29.00 95.00
91 Roy Rogers And Santa. 29.00 95.00
92 Christmas With Santa. 5.00 16.00
93 Woody Woodpecker. 5.00 16.00
94 Indian Chief. 15.00 49.00
95 Oswald The Lucky Rabbit. 5.00 16.00
96 Popeye. 17.00 55.00
97 Bugs Bunny. 9.00 27.00
98 Tarzan. Photo cover (Lex Barker). 35.00 110.00
99 Porky Pig. 5.00 16.00
100 Roy Rogers. 25.00 80.00
101 Henry. 5.00 16.00
102 Tom Corbett. 40.00 130.00
103 Tom And Jerry. 5.00 16.00
104 Gene Autry. 25.00 80.00
105 Roy Rogers. 25.00 80.00
106 Santa's Helpers. 5.00 16.00
107 Does not exist.
108 Fun With Santa. 5.00 16.00
109 Woody Woodpecker. 5.00 16.00
110 Indian Chief. 9.00 27.00
111 Oswald The Lucky Rabbit. 5.00 16.00
112 Henry. 5.00 16.00
113 Porky Pig. 5.00 16.00
114 Tarzan. 35.00 110.00
115 Bugs Bunny. 7.00 22.00
116 Roy Rogers. 25.00 80.00
117 Popeye. 17.00 55.00
118 Flash Gordon. 23.00 75.00
119 Tom And Jerry. 5.00 16.00
120 Gene Autry. 25.00 80.00
121 Roy Rogers. 25.00 80.00
122 Santa's Surprise. 4.00 11.00
123 Santa's Christmas Book. 4.00 11.00
124 Woody Woodpecker. 5.00 16.00
125 Tarzan. Photo cover (Lex Barker). 29.00 95.00
126 Oswald The Lucky Rabbit. 5.00 16.00
127 Indian Chief. 7.00 22.00
128 Tom And Jerry. 5.00 16.00
129 Henry. 4.00 11.00
130 Porky Pig. 5.00 16.00
131 Roy Rogers. 25.00 80.00
132 Bugs Bunny. 5.00 16.00
133 Flash Gordon. 22.00 70.00
134 Popeye. 12.00 38.00
135 Gene Autry. 22.00 70.00
136 Roy Rogers. 22.00 70.00
137 Gifts From Santa. 4.00 11.00
138 Fun At Christmas. 4.00 11.00
139 Woody Woodpecker. 5.00 16.00
140 Indian Chief. 7.00 22.00
141 Oswald The Lucky Rabbit. 5.00 16.00
142 Flash Gordon. 22.00 70.00
143 Porky Pig. 5.00 16.00
144 Tarzan. 28.00 90.00
145 Tom And Jerry. 5.00 16.00
146 Roy Rogers. Photo cover. 25.00 80.00
147 Henry. 4.00 11.00
148 Popeye. 12.00 38.00
149 Bugs Bunny. 5.00 16.00
150 Gene Autry. 22.00 70.00
151 Roy Rogers. 22.00 70.00
152 The Night Before Christmas. 4.00 11.00
153 Merry Christmas. 4.00 11.00
154 Tom And Jerry. 5.00 16.00
155 Tarzan. Photo cover. 28.00 90.00
156 Oswald The Lucky Rabbit. 5.00 16.00
157 Popeye. 10.00 33.00
158 Woody Woodpecker. 5.00 16.00
159 Indian Chief. 7.00 22.00
160 Bugs Bunny. 5.00 16.00
161 Roy Rogers. 19.00 60.00
162 Henry. 4.00 11.00
163 Rin Tin Tin. 10.00 33.00
164 Porky Pig. 5.00 16.00
165 The Lone Ranger. 14.00 44.00
166 Santa And His Reindeer. 4.00 11.00
167 Roy Rogers And Santa. 19.00 60.00
168 Santa Claus' Workshop. 4.00 11.00
169 Popeye. 10.00 33.00
170 Indian Chief. 7.00 22.00
171 Oswald The Lucky Rabbit. 4.00 11.00
172 Tarzan. 22.00 70.00
173 Tom And Jerry. 4.00 11.00
174 The Lone Ranger. 14.00 44.00
175 Porky Pig. 4.00 11.00
176 Roy Rogers. 17.00 55.00
177 Woody Woodpecker. 4.00 11.00
178 Henry. 4.00 11.00
179 Bugs Bunny. 4.00 11.00
180 Rin Tin Tin. 9.00 27.00

MAN OF STEEL #3

MANHUNTER #9 (2ND SERIES)

MAN-THING #1

MANTRA #8

MARCH OF COMICS #5

MARCH OF COMICS #8

MARCH OF COMICS #69

MARCH OF COMICS #75

FAMOUS • FIRSTS

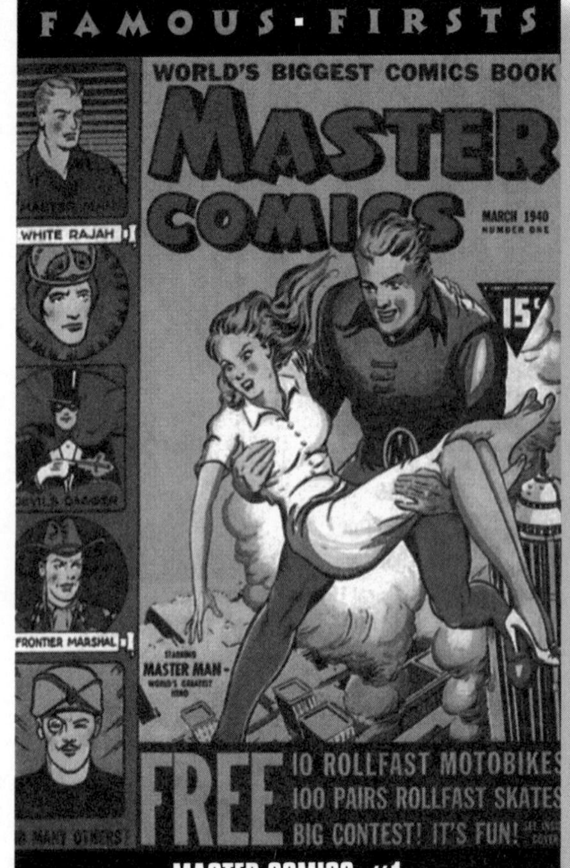

MASTER COMICS #1

This rare comic features the first appearance of Masterman and several other little known heroes. It's also one of the first oversized comics, measuring 10 inches by 13 inches. Issue #22 began Captain Marvel Jr.'s long run.

181	Happy Holiday.	2.25	8.75
182	Happi Tim.	4.00	11.00
183	Welcome Santa.	2.25	8.75
184	Woody Woodpecker.	4.00	11.00
185	Tarzan. Photo cover.	22.00	70.00
186	Oswald The Lucky Rabbit.	4.00	11.00
187	Indian Chief.	7.00	22.00
188	Bugs Bunny.	4.00	11.00
189	Henry.	4.00	11.00
190	Tom And Jerry.	4.00	11.00
191	Roy Rogers.	17.00	55.00
192	Porky Pig.	4.00	11.00
193	The Lone Ranger.	14.00	44.00
194	Popeye.	9.00	27.00
195	Rin Tin Tin.	9.00	27.00
196	Does not exist.		
197	Santa Is Coming.	2.25	8.75
198	Santa's Helper.	2.25	8.75
199	Huckleberry Hound.	10.00	33.00
200	Fury.	9.00	27.00
201	Bugs Bunny.	4.00	11.00
202	Space Explorer.	19.00	60.00
203	Woody Woodpecker.	4.00	11.00
204	Tarzan.	17.00	55.00
205	Mighty Mouse.	10.00	33.00
206	Roy Rogers. Photo cover.	17.00	55.00
207	Tom And Jerry.	4.00	11.00
208	The Lone Ranger. Photo cover (Clayton Moore).	22.00	70.00
209	Porky Pig.	4.00	11.00
210	Lassie.	9.00	27.00
211	Does not exist.		
212	Christmas Eve.	2.25	8.75
213	Here Comes Santa.	2.25	8.75
214	Huckleberry Hound.	9.00	27.00
215	Hi Yo Silver.	9.00	27.00
216	Rocky And His Friends.	26.00	85.00
217	Lassie.	7.00	22.00
218	Porky Pig.	4.00	11.00
219	Journey To The Sun.	9.00	27.00
220	Bugs Bunny.	4.00	11.00
221	Roy And Dale. Photo cover.	15.00	49.00
222	Woody Woodpecker.	4.00	11.00
223	Tarzan.	17.00	55.00
224	Tom And Jerry.	4.00	11.00
225	The Lone Ranger.	10.00	33.00
226	Christmas Treasury.	2.25	8.75
227	Does not exist.		
228	Letters To Santa.	2.25	8.75
229	The Flintstones.	22.00	70.00
230	Lassie.	7.00	22.00
231	Bugs Bunny.	4.00	11.00
232	The Three Stooges.	22.00	70.00
233	Bullwinkle.	28.00	90.00
234	Smokey The Bear.	5.00	16.00
235	Huckleberry Hound.	9.00	27.00
236	Roy And Dale.	12.00	38.00
237	Mighty Mouse.	7.00	22.00
238	The Lone Ranger.	10.00	33.00
239	Woody Woodpecker.	4.00	11.00
240	Tarzan.	14.00	44.00
241	Santa Claus Around The World.	2.25	8.75
242	Santa's Toyland.	2.25	8.75
243	The Flintstones.	20.00	65.00
244	Mister Ed. TV Photo cover.	14.00	44.00
245	Bugs Bunny.	4.00	11.00
246	Popeye.	7.00	22.00
247	Mighty Mouse.	7.00	22.00
248	The Three Stooges.	22.00	70.00
249	Woody Woodpecker.	4.00	11.00
250	Roy And Dale.	12.00	38.00
251	Little Lulu And Witch Hazel.	26.00	85.00
252	Tarzan.	14.00	44.00
253	Yogi Bear.	10.00	33.00
254	Lassie.	7.00	22.00
255	Santa's Christmas List.	2.25	8.75
256	Christmas Party.	2.25	8.75
257	Mighty Mouse.	7.00	22.00
258	The Sword In The Stone. Disney movie tie-in.	20.00	65.00
259	Bugs Bunny.	4.00	11.00
260	Mister Ed.	10.00	33.00
261	Woody Woodpecker.	4.00	11.00
262	Tarzan.	14.00	44.00
263	Donald Duck.	19.00	60.00
264	Popeye.	7.00	22.00
265	Yogi Bear.	7.00	22.00
266	Lassie.	5.00	16.00
267	Little Lulu.	20.00	65.00
268	The Three Stooges.	20.00	65.00
269	A Jolly Christmas.	2.25	8.75
270	Santa's Little Helpers.	2.25	8.75
271	The Flintstones.	20.00	65.00
272	Tarzan.	14.00	44.00
273	Bugs Bunny.	4.00	11.00
274	Popeye.	7.00	22.00
275	Little Lulu.	17.00	55.00
276	The Jetsons.	40.00	120.00
277	Daffy Duck.	4.00	11.00
278	Lassie.	5.00	16.00
279	Yogi Bear.	7.00	22.00
280	The Three Stooges.	20.00	65.00
281	Tom And Jerry.	2.25	8.75
282	Mister Ed.	10.00	33.00
283	Santa's Visit.	2.25	8.75
284	Christmas Parade.	2.25	8.75
285	Astro Boy.	80.00	260.00
286	Tarzan.	12.00	38.00
287	Bugs Bunny.	4.00	11.00
288	Daffy Duck.	4.00	11.00
289	The Flintstones.	19.00	60.00
290	Mister Ed. TV photo cover.	9.00	27.00
291	Yogi Bear.	7.00	22.00
292	The Three Stooges. Photo cover.	20.00	65.00
293	Little Lulu.	14.00	44.00
294	Popeye.	7.00	22.00
295	Tom And Jerry.	2.25	8.75
296	Lassie. TV photo cover.	5.00	16.00
297	Christmas Bells.	2.25	8.75
298	Santa's Sleigh.	2.25	8.75
299	The Flintstones.	19.00	60.00
300	Tarzan.	12.00	38.00
301	Bugs Bunny.	4.00	11.00
302	Laurel And Hardy. Photo cover.	12.00	38.00
303	Daffy Duck.	1.50	5.50
304	The Three Stooges. Photo cover.	19.00	60.00
305	Tom And Jerry.	1.50	5.50
306	Daniel Boone. TV photo cover (Fess Parker).	12.00	38.00
307	Little Lulu.	12.00	38.00
308	Lassie. TV photo cover.	5.00	16.00
309	Yogi Bear.	5.00	16.00
310	The Lone Ranger. TV photo cover (Clayton Moore).	22.00	70.00
311	Santa's Show.	2.25	8.75
312	Christmas Album.	2.25	8.75
313	Daffy Duck.	1.50	5.50
314	Laurel And Hardy.	10.00	33.00
315	Bugs Bunny.	4.00	11.00
316	The Three Stooges.	15.00	49.00
317	The Flintstones.	15.00	49.00
318	Tarzan.	10.00	33.00
319	Yogi Bear.	5.00	16.00
320	Space Family Robinson (Lost In Space).	31.00	100.00
321	Tom And Jerry.	1.50	5.50
322	The Lone Ranger.	9.00	27.00
323	Little Lulu.	7.00	22.00
324	Lassie. TV photo cover.	5.00	16.00
325	Fun With Santa.	2.25	8.75
326	Christmas Story.	2.25	8.75
327	The Flintstones.	15.00	49.00
328	Space Family Robinson (Lost In Space).	31.00	100.00
329	Bugs Bunny.	4.00	11.00
330	The Jetsons.	26.00	85.00
331	Daffy Duck.	1.50	5.50
332	Tarzan.	9.00	27.00
333	Tom And Jerry.	1.50	5.50
334	Lassie.	4.00	11.00
335	Little Lulu.	7.00	22.00
336	The Three Stooges.	15.00	49.00
337	Yogi Bear.	5.00	16.00
338	The Lone Ranger.	9.00	27.00
339	Did not exist.		
340	Here Comes Santa.	2.25	8.75
341	The Flintstones.	15.00	49.00
342	Tarzan.	9.00	27.00
343	Bugs Bunny.	2.25	8.75
344	Yogi Bear.	5.00	16.00
345	Tom And Jerry.	1.50	5.50
346	Lassie.	4.00	11.00
347	Daffy Duck.	1.50	5.50
348	The Jetsons.	22.00	70.00
349	Little Lulu.	7.00	22.00
350	The Lone Ranger.	9.00	27.00
351	Beep-Beep, The Road Runner.	4.00	11.00

352 Space Family Robinson (Lost In Space).	31.00	100.00
353 Beep-Beep, The Road Runner.	4.00	11.00
354 Tarzan.	7.00	22.00
355 Little Lulu.	7.00	22.00
356 Scooby Doo, Where Are You?	5.00	16.00
357 Daffy Duck And Porky Pig.	1.50	5.50
358 Lassie.	4.00	11.00
359 Baby Snoots.	4.00	11.00
360 H.R. Pufnstuf. TV photo cover.	5.00	16.00
361 Tom And Jerry.	1.50	5.50
362 Smokey The Bear.	1.50	5.50
363 Bugs Bunny And Yosemite Sam.	2.25	8.75
364 The Banana Splits. TV photo cover.	5.00	16.00
365 Tom And Jerry.	1.50	5.50
366 Tarzan.	7.00	22.00
367 Bugs Bunny And Porky Pig.	2.25	8.75
368 Scooby Doo.	5.00	16.00
369 Little Lulu.	5.00	16.00
370 Lassie. TV photo cover.	4.00	11.00
371 Baby Snoots.	2.25	8.75
372 Smokey The Bear.	1.50	5.50
373 The Three Stooges.	14.00	44.00
374 Wacky Witch.	1.50	5.50
375 Beep-Beep, The Road Runner and Daffy Duck.	1.50	5.50
376 The Pink Panther.	4.00	11.00
377 Baby Snoots.	2.25	8.75
378 Turok, Son Of Stone.	40.00	120.00
379 Heckle And Jeckle.	1.50	5.50
380 Bugs Bunny And Yosemite Sam.	1.50	5.50
381 Lassie.	4.00	11.00
382 Scooby Doo.	5.00	16.00
383 Smokey The Bear.	1.50	5.50
384 The Pink Panther.	1.50	5.50
385 Little Lulu.	4.00	11.00
386 Wacky Witch.	1.50	5.50
387 Beep-Beep, The Road Runner and Daffy Duck.	1.50	5.50
388 Tom And Jerry.	1.50	5.50
389 Little Lulu.	4.00	11.00
390 The Pink Panther.	1.50	5.50
391 Scooby Doo.	4.00	11.00
392 Bugs Bunny And Yosemite Sam.	1.50	5.50
393 Heckle And Jeckle.	1.50	5.50
394 Lassie.	1.50	5.50
395 Woodsy The Owl.	1.50	5.50
396 Baby Snoots.	1.50	5.50
397 Beep-Beep The Road Runner and Daffy Duck.	1.50	5.50
398 Wacky Witch.	1.50	5.50
399 Turok, Son Of Stone.	28.00	90.00
400 Tom And Jerry.	1.50	5.50
401 Baby Snoots.	1.50	5.50
402 Daffy Duck.	1.50	5.50
403 Bugs Bunny.	1.50	5.50
404 Space Family Robinson (Lost In Space).	23.00	75.00
405 Cracky.	1.00	3.25
406 Little Lulu.	4.00	11.00
407 Smokey The Bear.	1.50	5.50
408 Turok, Son Of Stone.	20.00	65.00
409 The Pink Panther.	1.00	3.25
410 Wacky Witch.	1.00	3.25
411 Lassie.	1.50	5.50
412 New Terrytoons.	1.00	3.25
413 Daffy Duck.	1.00	3.25
414 Space Family Robinson (Lost In Space).	20.00	65.00
415 Bugs Bunny.	1.00	3.25
416 Beep-Beep, The Road Runner.	1.00	3.25
417 Little Lulu.	4.00	11.00
418 The Pink Panther.	1.00	3.25
419 Baby Snoots.	1.00	3.25
420 Woody Woodpecker.	1.00	3.25
421 Tweety And Sylvester.	1.00	3.25
422 Wacky Witch.	1.00	3.25
423 Little Monsters.	1.00	3.25
424 Cracky.	1.00	3.25
425 Daffy Duck.	1.00	3.25
426 Underdog.	5.00	16.00
427 Little Lulu.	1.50	5.50
428 Bugs Bunny.	1.00	3.25
429 The Pink Panther.	1.00	3.25
430 Beep-Beep, The Road Runner.	1.00	3.25
431 Baby Snoots.	1.00	3.25
432 Lassie.	1.50	5.50
433 Tweety And Sylvester.	1.00	3.25
434 Wacky Witch.	1.00	3.25
435 New Terrytoons.	1.00	3.25
436 Cracky.	1.00	3.25
437 Daffy Duck.	1.00	3.25
438 Underdog.	4.00	11.00
439 Little Lulu.	1.50	5.50
440 Bugs Bunny.	1.00	3.25
441 The Pink Panther.	1.00	3.25
442 The Road Runner.	1.00	3.25
443 Baby Snoots.	1.00	3.25
444 Tom And Jerry.	1.00	3.25
445 Tweety And Sylvester.	1.00	3.25
446 Wacky Witch.	1.00	3.25
447 Mighty Mouse.	1.50	5.50
448 Cracky.	1.00	3.25
449 The Pink Panther.	1.00	3.25
450 Baby Snoots.	1.00	3.25
451 Tom And Jerry.	1.00	3.25
452 Bugs Bunny.	1.00	3.25
453 Popeye.	1.00	3.25
454 Woody Woodpecker.	1.00	3.25
455 The Road Runner.	1.00	3.25
456 Little Lulu.	1.50	5.50
457 Tweety And Sylvester.	1.00	3.25
458 Wacky Witch.	1.00	3.25
459 Mighty Mouse.	1.50	5.50
460 Daffy Duck.	1.00	3.25
461 The Pink Panther.	1.00	3.25
462 Baby Snoots.	1.00	3.25
463 Tom And Jerry.	1.00	3.25
464 Bugs Bunny.	1.00	3.25
465 Popeye.	1.00	3.25
466 Woody Woodpecker.	1.00	3.25
467 Underdog.	4.00	11.00
468 Little Lulu.	1.00	3.25
469 Tweety And Sylvester.	1.00	3.25
470 Wacky Witch.	1.00	3.25
471 Mighty Mouse.	1.50	5.50
472 Heckle And Jeckle.	1.00	3.25
473 The Pink Panther.	1.00	3.25
474 Baby Snoots.	1.00	3.25
475 Little Lulu.	1.00	3.25
476 Bugs Bunny.	1.00	3.25
477 Popeye.	1.00	3.25
478 Woody Woodpecker.	1.00	3.25
479 Underdog.	2.25	8.75
480 Tom And Jerry.	1.00	3.25
481 Tweety And Sylvester.	1.00	3.25
482 Wacky Witch.	1.00	3.25
483 Mighty Mouse.	1.50	5.50
484 Heckle And Jeckle.	1.00	3.25
485 Baby Snoots.	1.00	3.25
486 The Pink Panther.	1.00	3.25
487 Bugs Bunny.	1.00	3.25
488 Little Lulu.	1.00	3.25

MARCH OF CRIME

FOX (1948-1951)

NO# (1948) 132 pages.	190.00	600.00
NO# (1949) 132 pages.	160.00	525.00
1 (#7 on cover).	55.00	180.00
2 Art: Wallace Wood.	55.00	180.00
3	28.00	90.00

MARCO POLO

CHARLTON (1962)

NO# Movie tie-in.	25.00	80.00

MARGE'S LITTLE LULU

SEE LITTLE LULU

-

MARGE'S TUBBY AND HIS CLUBHOUSE PALS

DELL (1956)

1 100 Page Giant.	28.00	90.00

MARGIE

DELL (1962)

1 (#1307) From the 4-Color Series. TV tie-in. (3/62)	10.00	30.00
2 TV tie-in, photo cover.	7.00	20.00

MARGIE COMICS

MARVEL (1946-1949)

35 Previous title: Comedy Comics.	13.00	40.00
36	8.00	25.00
37-40	7.00	20.00
41-48	5.00	15.00
49 Title changes to Reno Browne with #50.	5.00	15.00

MARINE WAR HEROES

CHARLTON (1964-1967)

1	2.75	10.00
2	2.00	7.00
3-18	1.50	5.00

MARINES AT WAR

MARVEL(ATLAS) (1957)

5 Previous title: Tales Of The Marines.	4.00	12.00
6-7	4.00	12.00

MARINES ATTACK

CHARLTON (1964-1966)

1	2.75	10.00
2-9	1.75	6.00

MARINES IN ACTION

MARVEL(ATLAS) (1955-1957)

1	11.00	36.00
2	8.00	24.00
3-14	5.00	14.00

MARINES IN BATTLE

MARVEL(ATLAS) (1954-1958)

1	20.00	65.00
2	10.00	33.00
3-10	7.00	22.00
11-25	5.00	16.00

MARK, THE

DARK HORSE (1993)

1-4	.75	2.50

MARK, THE

DARK HORSE (1995-CURRENT)

1-2	.75	2.50

MARK 5

IMAGE (1995-CURRENT)

1-5	.75	2.50

MARK STEEL

AMERICAN IRON & STEEL (1967)

1967 Giveaway. Art: Neal Adams.	2.75	10.00

MARK TRAIL

PINES (1958)

1	7.00	20.00
2-5	2.75	10.00
SPECIAL 1 "Adventure Book Of Nature."	13.00	40.00

MARKSMAN, THE

HEROIC (1988)

1-5	.30	1.00
ANNUAL 1 (1988)	.30	1.00

MARMADUKE MOUSE

QUALITY (1946-1956)

1	17.00	55.00
2	9.00	27.00
3-20	6.00	19.00
21-40	4.00	11.00
41-65	1.75	6.50

MARRIED WITH CHILDREN

NOW (1990-1991)

1 TV tie-in.	1.25	4.00
1 (2ND)	.75	2.00
2	1.00	3.00
2 (2ND)	.50	1.75
3	.50	1.75

MARRIED WITH CHILDREN

NOW (1992)

1-8	.75	2.00
SPECIAL 1 (1992)	.75	2.00

MARS AND BEYOND

DELL FOUR COLOR SERIES (1957)

866 Movie tie-in. (12/57)	13.00	40.00

MARS ATTACKS

TOPPS (1994)

1-5	.75	2.95
TPB Reprints issues #1-6 plus new story.	4.00	12.95

M.A.R.S. PATROL TOTAL WAR

GOLD KEY (1966-1969)

3 Previous title: Total War.	7.00	20.00
4-10	2.75	10.00

MARSHALL LAW

MARVEL(EPIC) (1987-1989)

1-6	1.00	3.00

MARTHA WASHINGTON GOES TO WAR

DARK HORSE (1994)

1	1.25	4.50
2	1.25	4.00
3-5	1.00	3.50

MARTIN KANE

FOX (1950)

1 (#4) SOTI	40.00	120.00
2	28.00	90.00

MARVEL ACTION HOUR: FANTASTIC FOUR

MARVEL (1994-1995)

1 Polybagged with insert and acetate print.	.75	2.95
1A Regular edition.	.50	1.50
2-8	.50	1.50

MARCH OF CRIME #3

MARINES IN BATTLE #3

THE MARK #4 (MINI-SERIES)

MARRIED WITH CHILDREN #2

MARVEL COMICS PRESENTS #72

MARVEL DOUBLE FEATURE #11

MARVEL MASTERPIECES #1

MARVEL MYSTERY COMICS #57

MARVEL ACTION HOUR: IRON MAN
MARVEL (1994-1995)
1 Polybagged with insert and acetate print. .75 2.95
1A Regular edition. .50 1.50
2-8 .50 1.50

MARVEL ADVENTURE
MARVEL (1975-1976)
1 Reprints Daredevil books. .30 1.00
2-6 .30 1.00

MARVEL AGE
MARVEL (1982-1992)
1-200 .20 .50

MARVEL AND DC PRESENT
MARVEL/DC (1982)
1 The Uncanny X-Men and The New Teen Titans. 6.00 18.00

MARVEL BOY
MARVEL (1950-1951)
1 Origin: Marvel Boy. 140.00 450.00
2 Title changes to Astonishing with #3. 110.00 350.00

MARVEL CHILLERS
MARVEL (1975-1976)
1 1st: Modred The Mystic. 1.50 5.00
2 Modred. 1.25 4.00
3 Origin: Tigra. .75 2.00
4-7 .50 1.50

MARVEL CLASSICS COMICS
MARVEL (1976-1978)
1 1.25 4.00
2-27 1.00 3.00
28 1st: Mike Grell art. 2.00 7.00
29-36 .75 2.00

MARVEL COLLECTORS' ITEM CLASSICS
MARVEL (1965-1969)
1 Reprints Fantastic Four #2, Amazing Spider-man #3, Tales To Astonish #36 and Journey Into Mystery #97. Square-bound Giant-Size issue. 16.00 50.00
2 10.00 30.00
3-6 8.00 25.00
7-12 5.00 15.00
13-21 2.75 10.00
22 Reprint: Tales To Astonish #27 (1st Ant-Man). Becomes Marvel's Greatest Comics. 4.00 12.00

MARVEL COMICS
MARVEL(TIMELY) (1939)
1 1st Marvel comic book. 1st: Human Torch, The Angel, Ka-Zar. Origin: Sub-Mariner by Bill Everett. 21300.00 85000.00

MARVEL COMICS PRESENTS
MARVEL (1988-CURRENT)
1 2.75 10.00
2 1.50 5.00
3-4 1.25 4.00
5-10 1.00 3.00
11-18 .75 2.00
19 1st: Damage Control. .75 2.00
20-24 .75 2.00
25 1st & Origin: Nth Man. .75 2.00
26-37 .75 2.00
38 1.25 4.00
39-47 .75 2.00
48-50 1.50 5.00
51-53 Wolverine by Liefeld. 1.25 4.00
54-62 2.00 7.00
63-71 .75 2.00
72 Begin: Origin Wolverine (Weapon X). 2.25 8.00
73-83 1.50 5.00
84 End: Origin Wolverine. 1.50 5.00
85 Begin: Wolverine by Sam Kieth. 2.25 8.00
86-88 1.50 5.00
89 2.25 8.00
90-91 .75 2.00
92 1.25 4.00
93-99 .75 2.00
100 Anniversary issue. Ghost Rider/Wolverine. 1.00 3.00
101-175 .50 1.50

MARVEL COMICS SUPER SPECIAL, A
MARVEL (1977-1986) MAGAZINE
1 Kiss. 40 pages comics plus photos and features. 19.00 60.00
2 Conan. Movie tie-in. .75 2.00
3 Close Encounters of the Third Kind. Movie tie-in. .75 2.00
4 The Beatles Story. Wrap-around cover, comics, photos and features. 4.00 12.00
5 Kiss. 13.00 40.00
6 Jaws II. Movie tie-in. .75 2.00
7 Sgt. Pepper. Movie tie-in. 2.75 10.00
8 Battlestar Galactica. TV & movie tie-in. .75 2.00
9 Conan. .75 2.00
10 Star-Lord. .75 2.00
11 Warriors Of The Shadow Realm. Begin: Weirdworld epic. (6/79) 1.00 3.00
12 Warriors Of The Shadow Realm. 1.00 3.00
13 Warriors Of The Shadow Realm. End: Weirdworld epic. .75 2.00
14 Meteor. Movie tie-in. .75 2.00
15 Star Trek. Movie adaptation. 1.00 3.00
16 The Empire Strikes Back. Movie adaptation. 1.25 4.00
17 Xanadu. Movie adaptation. .75 2.00
18 Raiders Of The Lost Ark. Movie adaptation. .75 2.00
19 For Your Eyes Only. Movie adaptation. .75 2.00
20 Dragonslayer. Movie adaptation. .75 2.00
21 Conan. .75 2.00
22 Bladerunner. Movie adaptation. .75 2.00
23 Annie. Movie adaptation. .75 2.00
24 The Dark Crystal. Movie adaptation. .75 2.00
25 Rock And Rule. Movie adaptation. .75 2.00
26 Octopussy. Movie adaptation. .75 2.00
27 Return Of The Jedi. Movie adaptation. 1.25 4.00
28 Krull. Movie adaptation. .75 2.00
29 Greystoke, The Legend Of Tarzan. Movie adaptation. .75 2.00
30 Indiana Jones And The Temple Of Doom. Movie adaptation. .75 2.00
31 The Last Star Fighter. Movie adaptation. .75 2.00
32 The Muppets Take Manhattan. Movie adaptation. .75 2.00
33 Buckaroo Banzai. Movie adaptation. .75 2.00
34 Sheena. Movie adaptation. .75 2.00
35 Conan The Destroyer. Movie adaptation. .75 2.00
36 Dune. Movie adaptation. .75 2.00
37 2010. Movie adaptation. .75 2.00
38 Red Sonja. Movie adaptation. .75 2.00
39 Santa Claus. Movie adaptation. .75 2.00
40 Labyrinth. Movie adaptation. .75 2.00
41 Howard The Duck. Movie adaptation. .75 2.00

MARVEL DOUBLE FEATURE
MARVEL (1973-1977)
1 1.00 3.00
2-21 .75 2.00

MARVEL FAMILY
FAWCETT (1945-1954)
1 Origin retold: Capt. Marvel, Capt. Marvel Jr., Mary Marvel. 280.00 900.00
2 155.00 500.00
3 125.00 400.00
4 110.00 350.00
5 95.00 300.00
6-12 80.00 250.00
13-24 65.00 200.00
25-40 50.00 150.00
41-60 31.00 100.00
61-70 28.00 90.00
71-89 25.00 80.00

MARVEL FANFARE
MARVEL (1982-1991)
1 Spider-Man/Angel. 1st: Paul Smith art. 1.75 6.00
2 Spider-Man/Ka-Zar. 2.00 7.00
3-4 X-Men. 1.50 5.00
5-32 .75 2.50
33 X-Men, Wolverine. .75 2.50
34-50 .75 2.50
51 Silver Surfer. Double size. .75 2.50
52-60 .75 2.50

MARVEL: FANTASTIC FOUR
MARVEL (1995-CURRENT)
1 .30 1.00

MARVEL FEATURE
MARVEL (1971-1973)
1 1st & Origin: The Defenders. Double size. 23.00 75.00
2 2nd: Defenders. Double size. 13.00 40.00
3 Defenders. 13.00 40.00
4 Begin: Antman (1st app. since 1965). 5.00 15.00
5-7 2.50 9.00
8 Reprint: Tales To Astonish #44. 2.50 9.00
9 2.50 9.00
10 End: Antman. 2.50 9.00
11 1st: Thing solo story (Thing battles Hulk). 2.50 9.00
12 Thing, Iron Man vs. Thanos. 2.50 9.00

MARVEL FEATURE
MARVEL (1975-1976)
1 Begin: Red Sonja (pre-Red Sonja #1). 1.25 4.00
2-7 .75 2.00

MARVEL FUMETTI BOOK
MARVEL (1984)
1 All photos. .30 1.00

MARVEL GRAPHIC NOVEL
MARVEL (1982-1989)
1 Death Of Captain Marvel by Jim Starlin. (All prices are for 1st printings). 8.00 25.00
2 Elric: The Dreaming City. 2.75 10.00
3 Dreadstar by Jim Starlin. 2.75 10.00
4 1st & Origin: The New Mutants. 7.00 20.00
4 (2-3RD) 2nd & 3rd printings. 1.50 5.95
5 X-Men in God Loves, Man Kills. 5.00 14.00
5 (2-5TH) 2nd thru 5th printings. 2.50 9.95
6 The Star Slammers. 2.25 8.00
7 Killraven. 2.00 7.00
8 Super Boxers. 2.25 8.00
9 The Futurians. 4.00 11.00
10 Heartburst. 2.25 8.00
11 Void Indigo. 2.75 10.00
12 The Dazzler. 2.75 10.00
13 Starstruck. 2.00 7.00
14 Swords Of The Swashbucklers. 2.00 7.00
15 The Raven Banner. 1.75 6.00
16 The Aladdin Effect. 1.75 6.00
17 Revenge Of The Living Monolith. 2.25 8.00
18 She-Hulk. 2.50 9.00
19 Conan in The Witch Queen Of Acheron. 1.75 6.00
20 Greenberg The Vampire. 1.75 6.00
21 Marada The She Wolf. 1.75 6.00
22 The Amazing Spider-Man in Hooky by Berni Wrightson. 4.00 11.00
23 Dr. Strange. 1.75 6.00
24 Daredevil in Love And War. 2.50 9.00
25 Alien Legion. 1.75 6.00
26 Dracula. 1.75 6.00
27 Avengers in Emperor Doom. 1.75 6.00
28 Conan The Reaver. 1.75 6.00
29 The Big Change (Hulk battles The Thing). 1.75 6.00
30 A Sailor's Story. 1.75 6.00
31 Wolfpack. 1.75 6.00
32 The Death Of Groo. 5.00 16.00
33 Thor. 1.75 6.00
34 Cloak & Dagger in Predator & Prey. 1.75 6.00
35 The Shadow in Hitler's Astrologer. 2.75 10.00
36 Willow (movie adaptation). 2.00 7.00
37 Hercules. 2.00 7.00
38 Silver Surfer in Judgement Day. 4.00 12.00

MARVEL MASTERPIECES
MARVEL (1993)
1 Pin-ups by Joe Jusko. .75 2.95
2-4 .75 2.95

MARVEL MASTERPIECES II
MARVEL (1994-CURRENT)
1-2 .75 2.95

MARVEL MASTERWORKS
MARVEL (1988-1992)
1 Deluxe hardcover reprint of Spider-Man #'s 1-10. 11.00 34.95
2 Deluxe hardcover reprint of Fantastic Four #'s 1-10. 11.00 34.95
3 Deluxe hardcover reprint of X-Men #'s 1-10. 11.00 34.95
4 Deluxe hardcover reprint of Avengers #'s 1-10. 11.00 34.95
5 Deluxe hardcover reprint of Spider-Man #'s 11-20. 11.00 34.95
6 Deluxe hardcover reprint of Fantastic Four #'s 11-20. 11.00 34.95
7 Deluxe hardcover reprint of X-Men #'s 11-21. 11.00 34.95
8 Deluxe hardcover reprint of Incredible Hulk #'s 1-6. 11.00 34.95
9 Deluxe hardcover reprint of Avengers #'s 11-20. 11.00 34.95
10 Deluxe hardcover reprint of Spider-Man #'s 21-30 and Annual #1. 11.00 34.95
11 Deluxe hardcover reprint of X-Men #'s 94-100 and Giant-Sized #1. 11.00 34.95
12 Deluxe hardcover reprint of X-Men #'s 101-110. 11.00 34.95
13 Deluxe hardcover reprint of Fantastic Four #'s 21-30 and Annual #1. 11.00 34.95
14 Deluxe hardcover reprint of Tales Of Suspense (Captain America) #'s 59-81. 11.00 34.95
15 Deluxe hardcover reprint of Silver Surfer #'s 1-5. 11.00 34.95
16-19 11.00 34.95
20 Deluxe hardcover reprint of Tales Of Suspense (Iron Man) #'s 39-50. 11.00 34.95
21-22 11.00 34.95

MARVEL MOVIE PREMIERE
MARVEL (1975)
1 Movie tie-in "The Land That Time Forgot!" 1.50 5.00

MARVEL MYSTERY COMICS

MARVEL(TIMELY) (1939-1949)

2 Begin: Human Torch, Sub-Mariner, Ka-Zar. (12/39) Previous title: Marvel Comics. 3300.00 13000.00
3 1300.00 5000.00
4 1st: Electro; The Ferret. 1200.00 4500.00
5 Scarce. 2400.00 9500.00
6-7 700.00 2600.00
8 1st: Sub-Mariner/Human Torch battle. 900.00 3200.00
9 Battle: Sub-Mariner/Human Torch. Scarce. 2600.00 10000.00
10 Battle: Sub-Mariner/Human Torch. 700.00 2600.00
11 600.00 2000.00
12 Cover: Jack Kirby. 500.00 1900.00
13 1st & Begin: The Vision by Simon & Kirby. (11/40) 600.00 2300.00
14-16 400.00 1300.00
17 Human Torch/ Sub-Mariner. 400.00 1500.00
18 400.00 1300.00
19 Origin: Toro. 300.00 1100.00
20 Origin: The Angel. 300.00 1100.00
21 1st & Begin: The Patriot. (7/41) 300.00 1100.00
22-24 310.00 1000.00
25-26 280.00 900.00
27 End: Ka-Zar. 300.00 975.00
28-30 250.00 825.00
31 End: Sub-Mariner. 240.00 775.00
32-33 220.00 700.00
33A Black & White-Rare (3 known copies), cover of Marvel Mystery #33, contents combination of Capt. America #18 and Marvel Mystery #33, squarebound. 1900.00 7500.00
34-40 220.00 700.00
41-48 200.00 650.00
49 Origin: Miss America. (11/43) 240.00 775.00
50 200.00 650.00
51-52 180.00 575.00
53 "Master Plan for Destruction!" (3/44) 180.00 575.00
54-60 180.00 575.00
61-74 155.00 500.00
75 Begin: Young Allies. (8/46) 155.00 500.00
76-79 155.00 500.00
80 1st: Captain America in Marvel Mystery. (1/47) 240.00 775.00
81 Captain America. 200.00 650.00
82 1st & Origin: Namora. "The Coming Of Namora!" 280.00 900.00
83 End: Young Allies. 155.00 500.00
84 Begin: Sub-Mariner; Blonde Phantom. 220.00 700.00
85 155.00 500.00
86-88 Captain America. 200.00 650.00
89 1st: solo Captain America. 240.00 775.00
90-91 Captain America. 200.00 650.00
92 Origin retold: Human Torch in "The Birth Of The Torch". 1st: The Witness in "The Choice!" Captain America. (6/49) Becomes Marvel Tales #93. 310.00 1000.00

MARVEL PREMIERE

MARVEL (1972-1981)

1 Origin: Warlock (Him). 14.00 45.00
2 Warlock. 8.00 25.00
3 Begin: Dr. Strange. 10.00 30.00
4 4.00 12.00
5-7 2.50 9.00
8 4.00 12.00
9 2.50 9.00
10 Death: Ancient One. 4.00 12.00
11-13 1.50 5.00
14 End: Dr. Strange. (3/74) 1.50 5.00
15 1st & origin: Iron Fist. (5/74) 17.00 55.00
16 Origin (part 2): Iron Fist. 8.00 25.00
17-24 4.00 13.00
25 Art: John Byrne. End: Iron Fist. 7.00 20.00
26-27 1.75 6.00
28 Legion Of Monsters. 2.75 10.00
29-46 1.25 4.00
47 1st & Origin: new Antman. 1.25 4.00
48-49 1.25 4.00
50 Alice Cooper. 2.75 10.00
51-53 Black Panther. 1.00 3.00
54-56 1.00 3.00
57 1st app. Dr. Who in the U.S. 1.00 3.00
58-61 Dr. Who. 1.00 3.00

MARVEL PRESENTS

MARVEL (1975-1977)

1 1st & origin: Bloodstone. 2.00 7.00
2 Origin (part 2): Bloodstone. 1.50 5.00
3 Begin: Guardians of the Galaxy. 5.00 16.00
4-7 4.00 12.00
8 Reprint: Silver Surfer #2 (plus new pages). 4.00 12.00
9-12 4.00 12.00

MARVEL PREVIEW

MARVEL (1975-1980) MAGAZINE

1 Man-Gods From Beyond The Stars. .75 2.00
2 Punisher cover and story, "Death Sentence". Origin: The Punisher. 40.00 125.00
3 Blade The Vampire-Slayer. .75 2.00
4 Origin: Star-Lord. .75 2.00
5-6 Sherlock Holmes. .75 2.00
7 Satana. .75 2.00
8 Legion Of Monsters. 2.75 10.00
9 Origin: Man-God. .75 2.00
10 The Mighty Thor. .75 2.00
11 Star-Lord. .75 2.00
12 Haunt Of Horror. .75 2.00
13 The UFO Connection. .75 2.00
14-15 Star-Lord. .75 2.00
16 Detectives. .75 2.00
17 Black Mark. .75 2.00
18 Star-Lord. .75 2.00
19 Kull. .75 2.00
20 Bizarre Adventures. .75 2.00
21 Moon Knight (pre-Moon Knight #1). 1.50 5.00
22 King Arthur. .75 2.00
23 Bizarre Adventures. .75 2.00
24 .75 2.00

MARVEL SAGA

MARVEL (1985-1987)

1-25 .30 1.00

MARVEL SPECTACULAR

MARVEL (1973-1975)

1 Thor reprints. .30 1.00
2-19 .30 1.00

MARVEL SPOTLIGHT

MARVEL (1971-1977)

1 Origin: Red Wolf. 11.00 35.00
2 1st & Origin: Werewolf By Night. 13.00 40.00
3 7.00 20.00
4 End: Werewolf By Night. 7.00 20.00
5 1st & Origin: Ghost Rider (motorcycle). 20.00 70.00
6-8 7.00 20.00
9-10 4.00 12.00
11 End: Ghost Rider. 5.00 15.00
12 Origin: Son Of Satan. 7.00 20.00
13-27 1.75 6.00
28-29 Moon Knight. 4.00 11.00
30-31 1.50 5.00
32 2.25 8.00
33 1.50 5.00

MARVEL SPOTLIGHT

MARVEL (1979-1981)

1-11 .30 1.00

MARVEL SUPER ACTION

MARVEL (1976) MAGAZINE SIZE

1 Punisher cover and story, "Accounts Settled, Accounts Due". (1/76) 19.00 60.00

MARVEL SUPER ACTION

MARVEL (1977-1981)

1 Reprint: Captain America #100. .50 1.50
2-3 .50 1.50
4 Reprint: Marvel Boy #1. .50 1.50
5-37 .50 1.50

MARVEL SUPER HERO CONTEST OF CHAMPIONS

SEE CONTEST OF CHAMPIONS

MARVEL SUPER HEROES

MARVEL (1966) ONE SHOT

1 Reprints Daredevil #1. Giant-size, 64 pages. 21.00 68.00

MARVEL SUPER HEROES MEGAZINE

MARVEL (1994-CURRENT)

1 Reprints. .75 2.95
2-6 .75 2.95

MARVEL SUPER-HEROES

MARVEL (1967-1982)

12 1st & origin: Captain Marvel of The Kree (12/67). Previous title: Fantasy Masterpieces. 31.00 100.00
13 2nd: Captain Marvel. 17.00 55.00
14 Never-reprinted Spider-Man story. (5/68) 26.00 85.00
15-16 5.00 14.00
17 Origin: Black Knight. 5.00 14.00
18 1st & origin: Guardians Of The Galaxy. 16.00 50.00
19 Ka-Zar. 5.00 14.00
20 1st: solo Doctor Doom. (5/69) 8.00 25.00
21-30 2.00 7.00
31 End: Double size 64 page issues. 2.00 7.00
32-105 .75 2.00

MARVEL SUPER-HEROES

MARVEL (1990-CURRENT)

1 1.00 3.50
2-8 .75 2.95
9-12 .75 2.50
13-15 .75 2.75

MARVEL SUPER-HEROES SECRET WARS

SEE SECRET WARS

MARVEL TALES

MARVEL (1949-1957)

93 Previous title: Marvel Mystery Comics. 190.00 625.00
94 130.00 430.00
95-96 115.00 370.00
97 App: Sun Girl. 125.00 400.00
98-101 95.00 310.00
102 "The End Of The World!" by Basil Wolverton. 125.00 400.00
103 95.00 310.00
104 "Gateway To Horror!" by Basil Wolverton. 115.00 370.00
105 80.00 250.00
106-107 55.00 180.00
108-112 50.00 160.00
113-120 50.00 150.00
121-131 40.00 120.00
132 1st Code Approved issue. 31.00 100.00
133-140 26.00 85.00
141-146 23.00 75.00
147 Art: Steve Ditko. 26.00 85.00
148-159 23.00 75.00

MARVEL TALES

MARVEL (1964-1995)

1 Reprints: Amazing Fantasy 15, Amazing Spider-Man 1 (Part 2 story), Incredible Hulk 1, Tales To Astonish 35, Tales To Astonish 49, Sgt. Fury 1, Tales Of Suspense 39, Tales Of Suspense 48 and Journey Into Mystery 83. 70.00 230.00
2 Reprint: X-Men #1, Avengers #1. 22.00 70.00
3 Reprint: Strange Tales #101. 13.00 40.00
4-5 7.00 20.00
6-8 4.00 12.00
9 Reprint: Amazing Spider-Man #14. 5.00 14.00
10 4.00 12.00
11-31 2.00 7.00
32 End: 68 page double size issues. 2.00 7.00
33 1.50 5.00
34-105 1.25 4.00
106 Reprint: Amazing Spider-Man #129. 1.25 4.00
107-136 .75 2.00
137 Reprint: Amazing Fantasy #15. 2.00 7.00
138 Reprint: Amazing Spider-Man #1. 1.75 6.00
139-152 1.00 3.00
153-199 .75 2.00
200 Double size. .75 2.00
201-208 .75 2.00
209 Reprint: Amazing Spider-Man #129. 2.00 7.00
210-214 1.25 4.50
215-221 .75 2.00
222-285 .30 1.00
286 Metallic ink cover. .75 2.00
286A Regular edition. .30 1.00
287-291 .30 1.00

MARVEL TEAM-UP

MARVEL (1972-1985)

1 Begin: Spider-Man team-ups. 22.00 70.00
2 8.00 25.00
3 Morbius. 14.00 45.00
4 X-Men. 14.00 45.00
5-10 4.00 12.00
11-14 2.50 9.00
15 Ghost Rider. 1st: Orb. 2.50 9.00
16-20 2.25 8.00
21-22 1.75 6.00
23 X-Men. 1.75 6.00
24 1st: Moondog. 1.75 6.00
25-29 1.75 6.00
30-45 1.50 5.00
46 Deathlok. 1.50 5.00
47 1.50 5.00
48 Iron Man. 1st: Wraith. 1.50 5.00
49-52 1.50 5.00
53 X-Men, Hulk. 1st John Byrne art on X-Men (also see X-Men 108). (1/77) 4.00 13.00
54 Art: John Byrne. 1.50 5.00
55 Warlock. Art: John Byrne. 1.50 5.00
56-57 1.25 4.00
58 Ghost Rider. 1.25 4.00
59 Begin: John Byrne art. 1.50 5.00
60-61 1.50 5.00
62-64 1.25 4.00
65 1st & Origin: Captain Britain. 1.25 4.00
66-68 1.25 4.00
69 Havok. 1.25 4.00
70 End: John Byrne art. 1.25 4.00
71-74 1.00 3.00

MARVEL MYSTERY COMICS #64

MARVEL SPOTLIGHT #5

MARVEL SUPER-HEROES #20 (2ND SERIES)

MARVEL TEAM-UP #13

MARVEL TEAM-UP #55

MARVEL TEAM-UP #150

MARVEL TWO-IN-ONE #13

THE MASK RETURNS #4

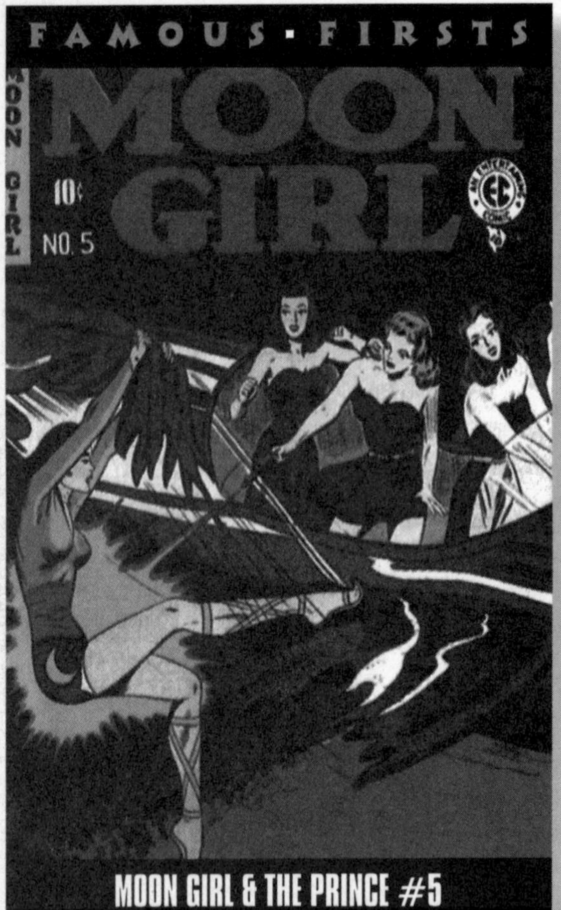

MOON GIRL & THE PRINCE #5

Moon Girl was a minor superheroine without much future, so Entertaining Comics' publisher William Gaines tried something different for a back-up story. As a result, "Zombie Terror" became EC's first horror tale.

75 Art: John Byrne. 1.00 3.00
76-78 1.00 3.00
79 Art: John Byrne. 1.00 3.00
80-85 1.00 3.00
86 Guardians Of The Galaxy. 1.00 3.00
87-90 1.00 3.00
91 Ghost Rider. 1.00 3.00
92-99 1.00 3.00
100 1st: Karma. Origin: Storm. 5.00 15.00
101-116 1.00 3.00
117 Wolverine cover and story. 5.00 14.00
118 Professor X. .75 2.50
119-140 .75 2.50
141 Daredevil. Alien costume appears (same date as Amazing Spider-Man 252). .75 2.50
142-149 .75 2.50
150 X-Men. Double size. 1.50 5.50

MARVEL TEAM-UP ANNUAL

MARVEL (1976-1984)

1 App: new X-Men by John Byrne. 5.00 15.00
2 1.25 4.00
3-4 1.00 3.00
5 .75 2.00
6 New Mutants. 1.00 3.00
7 .75 2.00

MARVEL TREASURY EDITION

MARVEL (1974-1981)

1 Spider-Man. 1.75 6.50
2 Fantastic Four. Reprints first Silver Surfer saga. 1.50 5.00
3 The Mighty Thor. 1.25 4.00
4 Conan The Barbarian by Barry Smith. 1.25 4.00
5 The Hulk. Reprints Hulk #3. 1.25 4.00
6 Doctor Strange. 1.25 4.00
7 The Mighty Avengers. 1.50 5.00
8 Giant Super-Hero Holiday Grab Bag. 1.50 5.50
9 Giant Super-Hero Team-Up. 1.25 4.00
10 The Mighty Thor. 1.25 4.00
11 Fantastic Four. 1.25 4.00
12 Howard The Duck. 1.25 4.00
13 Giant Super-Hero Holiday Grab-Bag. 1.25 4.00
14 Spider-Man. 1.25 4.00
15 Conan The Barbarian by Barry Smith and Neal Adams. 1.25 4.50
16 Giant Super-Hero Team-Up (The Defenders). 1.00 3.50
17 The Hulk. 1.00 3.50
18 Marvel Team-Up (The Astonishing Spider-Man). 1.50 5.00
19 Conan The Barbarian. 1.25 4.50
20 The Rampaging Hulk. 1.00 3.00
21 Fantastic Four. 1.00 3.00
22 Spider-Man. 1.00 3.00
23 Conan The Barbarian. 1.00 3.00
24 The Rampaging Hulk. 1.00 3.00
25 Spider-Man Vs. The Hulk At The Winter Olympics. 1.00 3.00
26 The Hulk. App: Wolverine. 1.75 6.00
27 Spider-Man. 1.00 3.50
28 Spider-Man/Superman. 2.00 7.00
SPECIAL 1 Super-Hero Holiday Grab-Bag. (1974) 1.25 4.00
SPECIAL 2 Captain America's Bicentennial Battles. (1976) 1.25 4.00

MARVEL TRIPLE ACTION

MARVEL (1972-1979)

1 Double size. .75 2.00
2-47 .30 1.00

MARVEL TWO-IN-ONE

MARVEL (1974-1983)

1 Begin: Thing team-ups. 8.00 25.00
2-4 2.50 9.00
5 Guardians Of The Galaxy. 5.00 15.00
6 Dr. Strange. Origin: Valkyrie. 5.00 16.00
7 1.75 6.00
8 Ghost Rider (early app). 2.50 9.00
9 2.50 9.00
10 1.50 5.00
11-12 1.00 3.00
13 1.00 3.00
14 Son Of Satan. 1.00 3.00
15 Morbius. 1.75 5.00
16-26 1.00 3.00
27 Deathlok. 1.00 3.00
28-29 1.00 3.00
30 2nd: Spider-Woman. 1.00 3.00
31-50 1.00 3.00
51 The Beast. 1.50 5.00
52-53 1.00 3.00
54 Death: Deathlok by John Byrne. 1.75 6.00
55 1.00 3.00
56-68 .75 2.00
69 Guardians Of The Galaxy. .75 2.00
70-79 .75 2.00
80 Ghost Rider. 1.25 4.00
81-99 .75 2.00
100 Double size. .75 2.00

MARVEL TWO-IN-ONE ANNUAL

MARVEL (1976-1982)

1 1.25 4.00
2 Death: Thanos by Jim Starlin. 5.00 15.00
3-4 1.00 3.00
5-7 .75 2.50

MARVEL'S GREATEST COMICS

MARVEL (1969-1981)

23 Previous title: Marvel Collectors' Item Classics. Begin: Fantastic Four reprints. 1.00 3.00
24-29 1.00 3.00
30 End: Double size issues. 1.00 3.00
31-34 .75 2.00
35 Reprint: Fantastic Four #48. 1.50 5.00
36 Reprint: Fantastic Four #49. 1.25 4.00
37 Reprint: Fantastic Four #50. 1.25 4.00
38-96 .30 1.00

MARVELS

MARVEL (1993-1994)

0 Companion to series. (6/94) 1.25 4.50
1 2.75 10.00
2 2.50 9.00
3 2.00 7.00
4 Spider-Man focus. 1.75 6.00
HC Hardcover, reprints #1-4 with unpublished art. 11.00 34.95

MARVELS OF SCIENCE

CHARLTON (1946)

1 1st Charlton comic. 35.00 110.00
2-4 17.00 55.00

MARY JANE AND SNIFFLES COMICS

DELL FOUR COLOR SERIES (1952-1953)

402 (6/52) 20.00 65.00
474 (6/53) 17.00 55.00

MARY MARVEL COMICS

FAWCETT (1945-1948)

1 220.00 700.00
2 "The Magic Yarn" (6/46). 110.00 360.00
3 95.00 300.00
4 75.00 240.00
5-7 55.00 180.00
8 App: Bulletman. 55.00 180.00
9-10 55.00 180.00
11-15 50.00 150.00
16-20 40.00 120.00
21-28 29.00 95.00

MARY POPPINS

GOLD KEY (1965)

10136-501 Disney movie photo cover. 8.00 25.00

MARY SHELLY'S FRANKENSTEIN

TOPPS (1994-1995)

1 Polybagged with card. .75 2.95
1A Regular edition (w/o card). Alternate cover. .75 2.50
2 Polybagged with card. .75 2.95
2A Regular edition (w/o card). Alternate cover. .75 2.50
3 Polybagged with card. .75 2.95
3A Regular edition (w/o card). Alternate cover. .75 2.50
4 Polybagged with card. .75 2.95
4A Regular edition (w/o card). Alternate cover. .75 2.50
TPB Reprints issues #1-4. 2.50 9.95

MASK, THE
DARK HORSE (1991)
0 Reprints Mask stories from Mayhem. (12/91) 1.50 5.50
1 (8/91) 2.75 10.00
2-3 2.25 8.00
4 (10/91) 1.75 6.00

MASK, THE
DARK HORSE (1995)
1 "The Mask Strikes Back" .75 2.50
2-6 .75 2.50

MASK COMICS
RHP (1945)
1 Cover: L. B. Cole. 250.00 825.00
2 Cover: L. B. Cole. 130.00 420.00
3 Cover: L. B. Cole. 75.00 240.00

MASK LIMITED-EDITION COLLECTION, THE
DARK HORSE (1995)
NO# Two volume set. Collects The Mask (mini-series) and The Mask Returns. Signed and numbered. 30.00 99.95

MASK OF DR. FU MANCHU, THE
AVON (1951)
1 Cover & art: Wallace Wood. 130.00 425.00

MASK RETURNS, THE
DARK HORSE (1992-1993)
1 1.00 3.50
2 .75 2.75
3-4 .75 2.50
TPB Reprints mini-series. 5.00 14.95

MASK: THE HUNT FOR GREEN OCTOBER
DARK HORSE (1995)
1-4 .75 2.50

MASK: THE MOVIE
DARK HORSE (1994)
1 Movie adaptation. .75 2.50
2 .75 2.50

MASKED BANDIT!, THE
AVON (1952)
NO# Art: Kinstler. 19.00 60.00

MASKED MARVEL
CENTAUR(ULTEM) (1940)
1 310.00 1000.00
2 250.00 800.00
3 200.00 650.00

MASKED PILOT
R.S. CALENDER (1939)
NO# 16.00 50.00

MASKED RAIDER, THE
CHARLTON (1955-1961)
1 14.00 44.00
2 7.00 22.00
3-6 4.00 11.00
7-30 1.75 6.50

MASKED RANGER
PREMIER (1954-1955)
1 50.00 150.00
2 22.00 70.00
3 20.00 65.00
4-9 19.00 60.00

MASQUE OF RED DEATH, THE
DELL (1964)
12-490-410 Movie photo cover (Vincent Price). 7.00 20.00

MASTER COMICS
FAWCETT (1940-1953)
1 1st & Origin: Masterman. Issues #1-6 are oversized. 2400.00 9500.00
2 700.00 2400.00
3 400.00 1200.00
4-5 290.00 950.00
6 End: Masterman. 290.00 950.00
7 Begin: Bulletman. 400.00 1400.00
8 290.00 950.00
9-10 220.00 700.00
11 1st & Origin: Minute-Man. 400.00 1500.00
12 220.00 700.00
13 1st & Origin: Bulletgirl. 400.00 1200.00
14-16 190.00 600.00
17-20 160.00 525.00
21 Captain Marvel, Bulletman battle Captain Nazi. 700.00 2400.00
22 Begin: Captain Marvel Jr. 700.00 2400.00
23 400.00 1200.00
24-30 145.00 480.00
31-40 110.00 360.00
41-45 95.00 300.00
46-47 75.00 240.00
48 1st: Bulletboy. 85.00 270.00
49 65.00 210.00
50 1st: Radar. 1st: Nyoka. 75.00 240.00
51-54 55.00 180.00
55-60 50.00 150.00
61-65 40.00 120.00
66-70 31.00 100.00
71-75 28.00 90.00
76-80 23.00 75.00
81-90 20.00 65.00
91-94 19.00 60.00
95 Begin: Tom Mix. 19.00 60.00
96-133 19.00 60.00

MASTER OF KUNG FU
MARVEL (1974-1983)
17 Previous title: Special Marvel Edition. 7.00 20.00
18 5.00 15.00
19 Man-Thing. 2.75 10.00
20-24 2.75 10.00
25-36 2.00 7.00
37-60 1.25 5.00
61-99 1.00 4.00
100 Double size. 1.00 4.00
101-117 1.00 3.00
118 Double size. 1.00 4.00
119-124 .75 2.00
125 Double size. 1.00 3.00
ANNUAL 1 Iron Fist. (4/76) 7.00 20.00

MASTER OF KUNG FU: BLEEDING BLACK
MARVEL (1991)
1 1.00 3.00

MASTER OF THE WORLD
DELL FOUR COLOR SERIES (1961)
1157 Movie tie-in. (7/61) 16.00 50.00

MATT SLADE GUNFIGHTER
MARVEL(ATLAS) (1956)
1 20.00 65.00
2 14.00 44.00
3 10.00 33.00
4 Title changes to Kid Slade Gunfighter with #5. 10.00 33.00

MAUS
PANTHEON/FANTAGRAPHICS (1986-1991)
TPB A Survivor's Tale. 2.25 8.95
VOL 1 My Father Bleeds History. 6.00 18.00
VOL 2 And Here My Troubles Began. 6.00 18.00

MAVERICK
DELL (1958-1962)
1 (#892) From the 4-Color Series. TV photo cover. (4/58) 40.00 125.00
2 (#930) From the 4-Color Series. TV photo cover. (7/58) 26.00 85.00
3 (#945) From the 4-Color Series. TV photo cover. (10/58) 23.00 75.00
4 (#962) From the 4-Color Series. TV photo cover. (1/59) 23.00 75.00
5 (#980) From the 4-Color Series. TV photo cover. (4/59) 19.00 60.00
6 (#1005) From the 4-Color Series. TV photo cover. (7/59) 19.00 60.00
7-14 14.00 45.00
15-19 11.00 35.00

MAVERICKS, THE
DAGGER (1993-1994)
1-6 .75 2.00

MAVERICKS: THE NEW WAVE
DAGGER (1994)
1-3 .75 2.50

MAXIMORTAL, THE
TUNDRA (1992-1993)
1-4 1.00 3.95
5-6 .75 2.95

MAXIMUM OVERLOAD
DARK HORSE (1993)
1-5 1.00 3.95

MAXX, THE
IMAGE (1993-CURRENT)
1/2 Wizard giveaway. 2.75 10.00
1/2A Gold edition in binder. 7.00 20.00
1 1.50 5.00
1A Glow in the dark cover. 8.00 25.00
2-3 1.50 5.00
4-10 1.00 3.00
11-12 .75 2.25
13-15 .75 2.25
16-18 .50 1.95

MAYA
DELL (1966)
12-495-612 Movie photo cover. 5.00 15.00

MAYA
GOLD KEY (1968)
1 (10218-803). TV photo cover. 2.75 10.00

MAYHEM
DARK HORSE (1989)
1 App: Masque (Mask) in all issues. 5.00 15.00
2-4 2.75 10.00

MAZIE
NATION-WIDE/HARVEY (1950-1958)
1 19.00 60.00
2-7 8.00 25.00
8-12 2.25 8.00
13 Begin Harvey publication. 1.50 5.00
14-28 1.50 5.00

MCHALE'S NAVY
DELL (1963)
1 TV tie-in, photo covers on all issues. 8.00 25.00
2-3 7.00 20.00

MCHALE'S NAVY
DELL (1964)
12-500-412 Movie photo cover (Ernest Borgnine). 8.00 25.00

MCKEEVER AND THE COLONEL
DELL (1963)
1 TV tie-in, photo cover. 10.00 30.00
2-3 7.00 20.00

MCLINTOCK!
GOLD KEY (1964)
10110-403 Movie photo cover (John Wayne). 31.00 100.00

MD
EC (1955-1956)
1 20.00 65.00
2 16.00 50.00
3-5 11.00 34.00

MECHA
DARK HORSE (1995)
SPECIAL .75 2.95

MEDAL OF HONOR COMICS
STAFFORD (1947)
1 16.00 50.00

MEET ANGEL
DC (1969)
7 Previous title: Angel & The Ape. 2.75 10.00

MEET CORLISS ARCHER
FOX (1948)
1 85.00 270.00
2 65.00 210.00
3 40.00 120.00

MEET MERTON
TOBY (1953-1954)
1 9.00 27.00
2 5.00 16.00
3-4 4.00 11.00

MEET THE NEW POST-GAZETTE SUNDAY FUNNIES
PITTSBURGH POST GAZETTE
NO# 16 page newspaper insert. 115.00 380.00

MEGALITH
CONTINUITY (1989-1991)
1-14 .75 2.50

MEGALITH
CONTINUITY (1993-1994)
0 Silver edition. Giveaway. 1.50 5.00
0A Red edition. Giveaway. 1.50 5.00
1 Deathwatch 2000, pt.5. Polybagged with card. .75 2.50
2 Deathwatch 2000, pt.10. .75 2.50
3 Deathwatch 2000, pt.16. Tyvek cover. .75 2.50
4-7 Rise Of Magic. .75 2.50
8-12 .75 2.50

MASTER COMICS #22

THE MAXIMORTAL #4

THE MAXX #6

MAYHEM #1

MELTING POT #1

METAL MEN (MINI-SERIES) #2

METAMORPHO #1

METROPOLIS S.C.U. #3

MEGATON
MEGATON (1983-1987)
1 Begin: Vanguard. 2.00 7.00
2 .... 1.50 5.00
3 1st: Savage Dragon. 5.00 15.00
4 Savage Dragon. 2.75 10.00
5-7 .... 1.00 3.00
8 Youngblood preview. 5.00 15.00
EXPLOSION 1st: Youngblood by Liefeld. (1987)
.... 7.00 20.00

MEGATON MAN
KITCHEN SINK (1984-1986)
1-10 .... .75 2.00

MEL ALLEN SPORTS COMICS
STANDARD (1949-1950)
5 .... 28.00 90.00
6 Lou Gehrig. 23.00 75.00

MELTDOWN
SEE HAVOK AND WOLVERINE: MELTDOWN

MELTING POT
KITCHEN SINK (1993-1994)
1 .... 1.00 3.50
2-3 .... .75 2.95
4 .... 1.00 3.50

MELVIN MONSTER
DELL (1965-1969)
1 Art: John Stanley (all issues). 23.00 75.00
2-10 .... 13.00 40.00

MELVIN THE MONSTER
MARVEL(ATLAS) (1956-1957)
1 .... 25.00 80.00
2-6 .... 16.00 50.00

MEN IN ACTION
AJAX (1957-1958)
1 .... 10.00 33.00
2 .... 5.00 16.00
3-9 .... 4.00 11.00

MEN IN ACTION
MARVEL(ATLAS) (1952)
1 .... 19.00 60.00
2 .... 10.00 33.00
3-6 .... 7.00 22.00
7 Art: Krigstein. 10.00 33.00
8 .... 7.00 22.00
9 Title changes to Battle Brady with issue #10.
.... 7.00 22.00

MEN INTO SPACE
DELL FOUR COLOR SERIES (1960)
1083 Disney TV photo cover. (3/60) 14.00 45.00

MEN OF WAR
DC (1977-1980)
1 Enemy Ace. .... .75 2.00
2-8 .... .30 1.00
9 Unknown Soldier. .... .30 1.00
10-26 .... .30 1.00

MEN'S ADVENTURES
MARVEL(ATLAS) (1950-1954)
4 Previous title: True Adventures. 29.00 95.00
5 .... 19.00 60.00
6-8 .... 15.00 48.00
9 Begin: All war stories. 11.00 36.00
10-19 .... 8.00 24.00
20 End: War stories. 8.00 24.00
21 Begin: Horror stories. 13.00 42.00
22-25 .... 11.00 36.00
26 End: Horror stories. 11.00 36.00
27-28 App: Captain America, Human Torch, Sub-Mariner.
.... 155.00 500.00

MENACE
MARVEL(ATLAS) (1953-1954)
1 Art: Bill Everett. 85.00 270.00
2 .... 55.00 180.00
3-4 .... 50.00 150.00
5 1st & origin: Zombie by Bill Everett. 65.00 210.00
6-7 .... 40.00 120.00
8-11 .... 29.00 95.00

MEPHISTO VS...
MARVEL (1987)
1 Fantastic Four. 1.00 3.00
2 X-Factor. .... .75 2.00
3 X-Men. .... .75 2.00
4 Avengers. .... .75 2.00

MERCY
DC (1993)
1 Vertigo one-shot. 1.50 5.95

MERRILL'S MARAUDERS
DELL (1963)
12-510-301 Movie photo cover. 5.00 15.00

MERRY CHRISTMAS FROM SEARS TOYLAND, A
SEARS & ROEBUCK GIVEAWAY (1939)
NO# Oversize 16 page giveaway dated 1939. Features Color and B&W strip reprints on each page. Strips include Terry, Little Orphan Annie, Dick Tracy, Mutt & Jeff, and others.
.... 50.00 150.00

METAL HURLANT
LES HUMANOIDES (1974)
1 .... 31.00 100.00

METAL MEN
DC (1963-1978)
1 "The Rain Of The Missile Men!" See Showcase #37 for 1st app. 115.00 400.00
2 .... 45.00 140.00
3-6 .... 25.00 80.00
7 .... 16.00 50.00
8 "The Playground Of Terror!" 16.00 50.00
9 "The Robot Juggernaut!" 16.00 50.00
10-12 .... 16.00 50.00
13-20 .... 11.00 36.00
21 .... 8.00 25.00
22-26 .... 7.00 20.00
27 Origin retold: Metal Men. 14.00 45.00
28-30 .... 7.00 20.00
31-40 .... 5.00 15.00
41 (1970) 5.00 15.00
42 (1973) 2.00 7.00
43-44 .... 2.00 7.00
45 (1976) 1.25 4.00
46-56 .... 1.25 4.00

METAL MEN
DC (1993-1994)
1 Foil cover. 1.00 3.75
2-4 .... .50 1.25

METAMORPHO
DC (1965-1968)
1 .... 26.00 85.00
2-3 .... 14.00 44.00
4 .... 8.00 25.00
5-6 .... 8.00 25.00
7-9 .... 6.00 20.00
10 1st & Origin: Element Girl. 9.00 27.00
11-17 .... 5.00 15.00

METAMORPHO
DC (1993)
1-4 .... .50 1.50

METAPHYSIQUE
MALIBU (1995)
1 Mini-series. .... .75 2.95
2-3 .... .75 2.95
ASHCAN .... .30 1.00

METEOR COMICS
BAIRD (1945)
1 Captain Wizard. 50.00 150.00

METEOR MAN
MARVEL (1993-1994)
1 Movie tie-in. .... .50 1.25
2-6 .... .50 1.25

METROPOLIS S.C.U.
DC (1994)
1-4 .... .50 1.50

MEZZ GALACTIC TOUR
DARK HORSE (1994)
1 Nexus spin-off. .... .75 2.50

MIAMI MICE
RIP OFF (1986-1987)
1-10 .... .30 1.00

MICHAEL JORDAN TRIBUTE
REVOLUTIONARY (1993)
1 .... .75 2.95

MICHAELANGELO
MIRAGE (1986)
1 From Teenage Mutant Ninja Turtles. One shot.
.... 4.00 12.00
1(2ND) 1.50 5.00

MICKEY AND DONALD
GLADSTONE (1988-1990)
1 .... 1.00 3.00
2-18 .... .50 1.25

MICKEY FINN
EASTERN (1942-1949)
1 .... 35.00 110.00
2 .... 17.00 55.00
3 .... 14.00 44.00
4-6 .... 9.00 27.00
7-15 .... 7.00 22.00

MICKEY MOUSE
DELL FOUR COLOR SERIES (1943-1957)
27 "And The Seven-Colored Terror" ... 170.00 550.00
79 "The Riddle Of The Red Hat" Story & art: Carl Barks.
.... 190.00 600.00
116 "The House Of Many Mysteries" 55.00 175.00
141 "And The Submarine Pirates" ... 55.00 175.00
157 "And The Beanstalk" Disney movie tie-in.
.... 55.00 175.00
170 "On Spook's Island" 45.00 140.00
181 "Jungle Magic" 45.00 140.00
194 "The World Under The Sea" 45.00 140.00
214 "And His Sky Adventure" 31.00 100.00
231 "And The Rajah's Treasure" 31.00 100.00
248 "And The Black Sorcerer" 31.00 100.00
261 "And The Missing Key" 31.00 100.00
268 "Surprise Visitor" 31.00 100.00
279 "...And Pluto Battle The Giant Ants" 25.00 80.00
286 "And The Uninvited Guest" 25.00 80.00
296 "Private Eye For Hire" 25.00 80.00
304 "Tom-Tom Island" 19.00 60.00
313 "The Mystery Of The Double-Cross Ranch"
.... 19.00 60.00
325 "The Haunted Castle" 19.00 60.00
334 "And Yukon Gold" 19.00 60.00
343 "The Ruby Eye Of Homar-Guy-Am" 16.00 50.00
352 "The Mystery Of Painted Valley" 16.00 50.00
362 "And The Smuggled Diamonds" ... 16.00 50.00
371 "The Inca Idol Case" 16.00 50.00
387 "High Tibet" 16.00 50.00
401 "And Goofy's Mechanical Wizard" 11.00 35.00
411 "And The Old Sea Dog" 11.00 35.00
427 "And The Wonderful Whizzix" ... 11.00 35.00
819 "In Magicland" (7/57) 10.00 30.00

MICKEY MOUSE
DELL/GOLD KEY/GLADSTONE (1952-1990)
28-30 .... 7.00 20.00
31-50 .... 5.00 15.00
51-75 .... 4.00 12.00
76-84 .... 2.75 10.00
85 Begin: Gold Key publication. 2.75 10.00
86-100 .... 2.75 10.00
101-130 .... 2.25 8.00
131-150 .... 1.50 5.00
151-218 .... .75 2.00
219 1st Gladstone publication. 1.25 4.00
220-230 .... .75 2.50
231-256 .... .30 1.00

MICKEY MOUSE ADVENTURES
DISNEY (1990-1991)
1-18 .... .50 1.50

MICKEY MOUSE ALBUM
DELL FOUR COLOR SERIES (1959-1961)
1057 (11/59) 8.00 25.00
1151 (11/60) 7.00 20.00
1246 (11/61) 7.00 20.00

MICKEY MOUSE ALMANAC
DELL (1957)
1 100 page Giant. 95.00 300.00

MICKEY MOUSE AND THE HAUNTED HOUSE
DISNEY (1947)
W4 Disney Cheerios Premium. 7.00 20.00

MICKEY MOUSE AT THE RODEO
DISNEY (1947)
X4 Disney Cheerios Premium. 7.00 20.00

MICKEY MOUSE BIRTHDAY PARTY
DELL (1953)
1 100 page Giant. 95.00 300.00

MICKEY MOUSE BOOK
BIBO & LANG (1930)
NO# 1st: Disney book. 1st & origin: Mickey Mouse, Minnie Mouse. Cover: UB Iwerks. 1300.00 5000.00

MICKEY MOUSE CLUB PARADE
DELL (1955)
1 Dell Giant. Reprint: 4-Color #16. ... 95.00 300.00

MICKEY MOUSE IN FANTASYLAND
DELL (1957)
- 1 100 page Giant. 31.00 100.00

MICKEY MOUSE IN FRONTIERLAND
DELL (1956)
- 1 100 page Giant. 31.00 100.00

MICKEY MOUSE MAGAZINE
DISNEY (1933-1935)
- V1#1 (11/33) 190.00 600.00
- V1#2-V1#12 95.00 300.00
- V2#1-V2#12 50.00 150.00

MICKEY MOUSE MAGAZINE
WESTERN (1935-1940)
- V1#1 Large size, 25 cents, Summer, 1935. Introduces Disney characters to the comics field (in a magazine format), ultimately becomes Walt Disney's Comics & Stories, one of the longest-running comics series. 2200.00 8500.00
- V1#2 300.00 1100.00
- V1#3 200.00 650.00
- V1#4 170.00 550.00
- V1#5 1st Donald Duck cover. 200.00 650.00
- V1#6-V1#12 135.00 440.00
- V2#1-V2#2 100.00 330.00
- V2#3 Special 100 page Christmas issue. 500.00 1600.00
- V2#4-V2#12 100.00 330.00
- V2#10 1st full color issue. 135.00 440.00
- V3#1-V3#2 100.00 330.00
- V3#3 1st Snow White. 200.00 650.00
- V3#4-V3#5 Snow White. 170.00 550.00
- V3#6 100.00 330.00
- V3#7 Seven Dwarfs on cover. 100.00 330.00
- V3#8-V3#12 100.00 330.00
- V4#1 Movie tie-in. Contains the complete story to "Brave Little Tailor", cover features a scene from the movie. 100.00 330.00
- V4#2 100.00 330.00
- V4#3 Ferdinand The Bull. 100.00 330.00
- V4#4-V4#5 85.00 270.00
- V4#6 The Ugly Duckling. (3/39) 100.00 330.00
- V4#7 (4/39) 100.00 330.00
- V4#8 100.00 330.00
- V4#9-V4#12 85.00 270.00
- V5#1 85.00 270.00
- V5#2 1st Pinocchio (cameo). 135.00 440.00
- V5#3 Pinocchio. 170.00 550.00
- V5#4-V5#5 Donald Duck. 100.00 330.00
- V5#6-V5#7 100.00 330.00
- V5#8 End: Magazine size issues. 100.00 330.00
- V5#9 Begin: Comic size issues. 115.00 380.00
- V5#10-V5#11 100.00 330.00
- V5#12 Transition issue. Becomes Walt Disney's Comics And Stories #1. 700.00 2700.00

MICKEY MOUSE MEETS THE WIZARD
DISNEY (1947)
- Y4 Disney Cheerios Premium. 7.00 20.00

MICKEY MOUSE STORYBOOK
DAVID MCKAY (1931-1934)
- 1 Sunday strip reprints in all issues. 400.00 1300.00
- 2 310.00 1000.00
- 3 84 pages of full color. 310.00 1000.00
- 4 310.00 1000.00

MICKEY MOUSE SUMMER FUN
DELL (1958-1959)
- 1 Giant size. 28.00 90.00
- 2 Giant size. 28.00 90.00

MICKEY MOUSE'S SECRET ROOM
DISNEY (1947)
- Z4 Disney Cheerios Premium. 7.00 20.00

MICRA
COMICS INTERVIEW (1986-1987)
- 1 1.00 3.00
- 2-4 .75 2.00
- 5-7 .50 1.75

MICRONAUTS
MARVEL (1979-1984)
- 1 .75 2.00
- 2-59 .30 1.00
- ANNUAL 1-ANNUAL 2 Cover/Art: Steve Ditko. 1.00 3.00

MICRONAUTS
MARVEL (1984-1986)
- 1-20 .20 .50

MIDGET COMICS
ST. JOHN (1950)
- 1 Matt Baker cover. 19.00 60.00
- 2 Tex West, Cowboy Marshall. 11.00 36.00

MIDNIGHT
AJAX/FARRELL (1957-1958)
- 1 13.00 40.00
- 2-6 7.00 20.00

MIDNIGHT MEN
MARVEL (1993-1994)
- 1 Metallic ink embossed cover. .75 2.50
- 2-10 .50 1.95

MIDNIGHT MYSTERY
ACG (1961)
- 1 14.00 44.00
- 2 7.00 22.00
- 3-7 5.00 16.00

MIDNIGHT SONS
MARVEL (1994)
- ASHCAN .20 .75

MIDNIGHT SONS UNLIMITED
MARVEL (1993)
- 1-9 1.00 3.95

MIDNIGHT TALES
CHARLTON (1972-1976)
- 1 1.00 3.00
- 2-18 .30 1.00

MIGHTY COMICS
RADIO (1966-1967)
- 40 Previous title: Flyman. 4.00 12.00
- 41 The Shield. 4.00 12.00
- 42 Black Hood. 4.00 12.00
- 43-44 4.00 12.00
- 45 Shield and Hangman. 4.00 12.00
- 46-50 4.00 12.00

MIGHTY CRUSADERS
MIGHTY (1965-1966)
- 1 Origin: The Shield. 10.00 33.00
- 2 Origin: The Comet. 7.00 22.00
- 3 Origin: Fly-Man. 5.00 16.00
- 4 1st: Silver Age Hangman. 7.00 22.00
- 5 Debut: Ultra-Men. 5.00 16.00
- 6 5.00 16.00
- 7 Origin: Fly-Girl. 7.00 22.00

MIGHTY CRUSADERS
RED CIRCLE (1983-1985)
- 1-13 .30 1.00

MIGHTY HEROES, THE
DELL (1967)
- 1 13.00 40.00
- 2-4 10.00 30.00

MIGHTY MAGNOR
MALIBU (1993)
- 1 Art: Sergio Aragones in all issues. Direct market version. 1.00 3.95
- 1A Newsstand edition. .50 1.95
- 2-6 .50 1.95

MIGHTY MARVEL WESTERN, THE
MARVEL (1968-1976)
- 1 Begin: Kid Colt, Rawhide Kid reprints. 1.75 6.50
- 2-12 1.00 3.25
- 13-46 .30 1.00

MIGHTY MIDGET COMICS
FAWCETT (1942-1943)
- 11-A Captain Marvel. 4"x5". Interior art is duotone. 14.00 44.00
- 11-B Bulletman #11 on cover (same cover as Bulletman #3). 4"x5". Interior art is duotone. 14.00 44.00
- 11-C Captain Marvel Jr. 4"x5". 14.00 44.00
- 11-D Balbo The Magician Boy. 4"x5". 14.00 44.00
- 11-E Ibis The Invincible. 4"x5". 14.00 44.00
- 11-F Spy Smasher. 4"x5". 14.00 44.00

MIGHTY MORPHIN' POWER RANGERS
HAMILTON (1994-1995)
- 1 TV tie-in. .50 1.95
- 2-6 .50 1.95
- TPB Reprints issues #1-6. 2.50 9.95

MIGHTY MORPHIN' POWER RANGERS SAGA
HAMILTON (1995)
- 1-2 Mini-series. .50 1.95

MIGHTY MORPHIN' POWER RANGERS
HAMILTON (1995-CURRENT)
- 1 TV tie-in. .50 1.95
- 2-3 .50 1.95

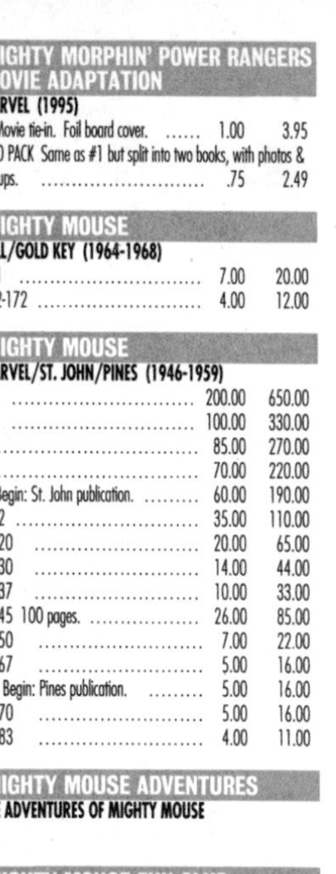

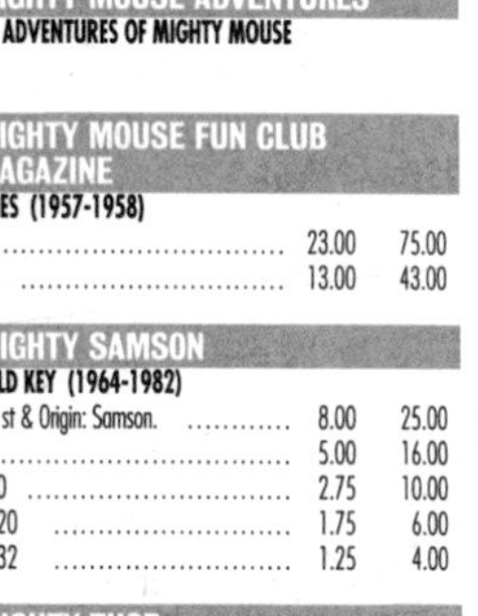

MIGHTY MORPHIN' POWER RANGERS MOVIE ADAPTATION
MARVEL (1995)
- 1 Movie tie-in. Foil board cover. 1.00 3.95
- TWO PACK Same as #1 but split into two books, with photos & pin-ups. .75 2.49

MIGHTY MOUSE
DELL/GOLD KEY (1964-1968)
- 161 7.00 20.00
- 162-172 4.00 12.00

MIGHTY MOUSE
MARVEL/ST. JOHN/PINES (1946-1959)
- 1 200.00 650.00
- 2 100.00 330.00
- 3 85.00 270.00
- 4 70.00 220.00
- 5 Begin: St. John publication. 60.00 190.00
- 6-12 35.00 110.00
- 13-20 20.00 65.00
- 21-30 14.00 44.00
- 31-37 10.00 33.00
- 38-45 100 pages. 26.00 85.00
- 46-50 7.00 22.00
- 51-67 5.00 16.00
- 68 Begin: Pines publication. 5.00 16.00
- 69-70 5.00 16.00
- 71-83 4.00 11.00

MIGHTY MOUSE ADVENTURES
SEE ADVENTURES OF MIGHTY MOUSE

-

MIGHTY MOUSE FUN CLUB MAGAZINE
PINES (1957-1958)
- 1 23.00 75.00
- 2-6 13.00 43.00

MIGHTY SAMSON
GOLD KEY (1964-1982)
- 1 1st & Origin: Samson. 8.00 25.00
- 2 5.00 16.00
- 3-10 2.75 10.00
- 11-20 1.75 6.00
- 21-32 1.25 4.00

MIGHTY THOR
SEE THOR

-

MIKE BARNETT, MAN AGAINST CRIME
FAWCETT (1951-1952)
- 1 23.00 75.00
- 2 13.00 40.00
- 3-4 10.00 30.00
- 5 "Market For Morphine!" 13.00 40.00
- 6 10.00 30.00

MIKE DANGER
TEKNO (1995-CURRENT)
- 1-3 .50 1.95

MIKE SHAYNE PRIVATE EYE
DELL (1962)
- 1 2.75 10.00
- 2-3 1.75 6.00

MILITARY COMICS
QUALITY (1941-1945)
- 1 1st & Origin: Blackhawk. 1300.00 5000.00
- 2 500.00 1900.00
- 3 1st & Origin: Chop Chop. 400.00 1300.00
- 4 310.00 1000.00
- 5-7 290.00 950.00
- 8-11 220.00 700.00
- 12 Begin: Blackhawk by Reed Crandall. 240.00 775.00
- 13-16 160.00 525.00
- 17-21 140.00 450.00
- 22 End: Reed Crandall Blackhawk. 140.00 450.00
- 23-35 120.00 390.00
- 36-42 110.00 360.00
- 43 Title changes to Modern Comics with #44. 110.00 360.00

MILK AND CHEESE
SLAVE LABOR (1991-CURRENT)
- 1 5.00 15.00
- 1 (2-6TH) 2nd thru 6th printings. .75 2.50
- 2 2.25 8.00
- 2 (2-3RD) 2nd & 3rd printings. .75 2.50
- 3 2.00 7.00
- 3 (2-3RD) 2nd & 3rd printings. .75 2.50
- 4 1.50 5.00
- 4 (2ND) 2nd printing. .75 2.50
- 5 .75 2.50

MIDNIGHT SONS UNLIMITED #7

MIDNIGHT TALES #1

MIGHTY MORPHIN' POWER RANGERS THE MOVIE

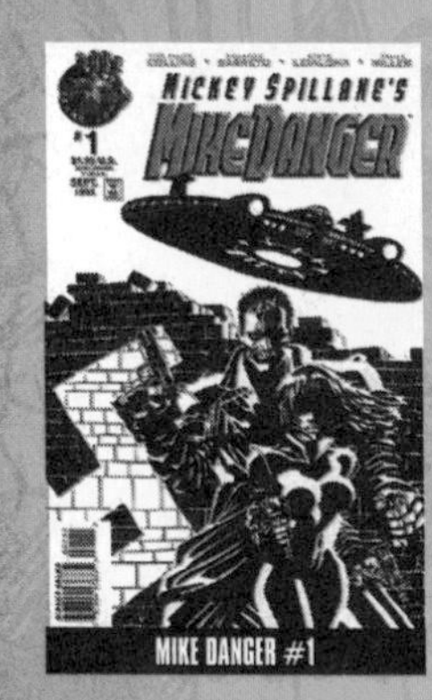

MIKE DANGER #1

MILLENNIUM #3

MILLIE THE MODEL #9

MIRACLEMAN #20

MOBFIRE #1

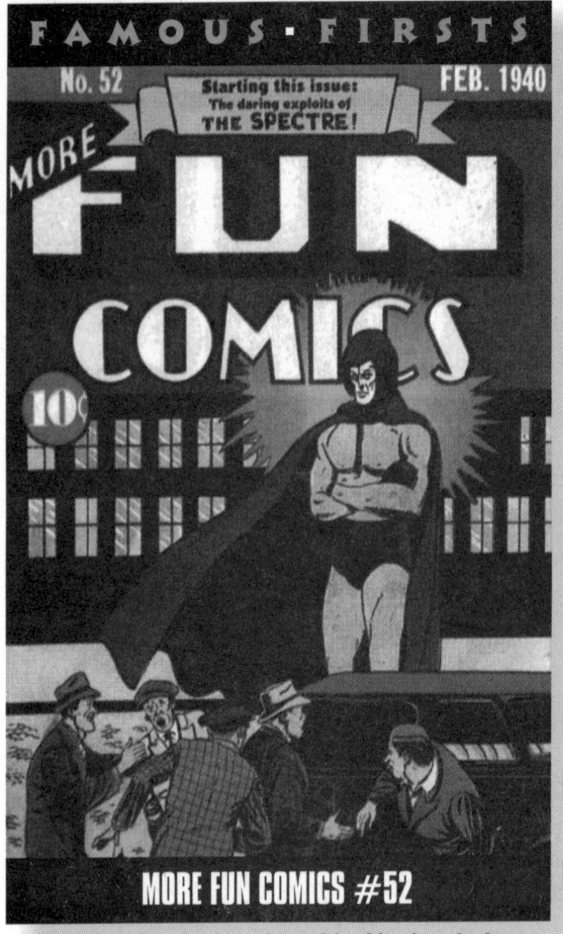

FAMOUS • FIRSTS
No. 52
FEB. 1940
Starting this issue: The daring exploits of THE SPECTRE!
MORE FUN
COMICS
10¢

MORE FUN COMICS #52

You've gotta love an avenging spirit of justice who hangs out in a comic called *More Fun*. When Detective Jim Corrigan is killed and dumped in the river, he becomes The Spectre, who lives on in DC's comics today.

5 (2ND) 2nd printing. .75 2.50
6 .75 2.50

MILLENNIUM
DC (1988)
1-8 .50 1.75

MILLIE, THE LOVABLE MONSTER
DELL (1962-1973)
1 (#12-523-211) 8.00 25.00
2-3 7.00 20.00
4-6 2.75 10.00

MILLIE THE MODEL
MARVEL(TIMELY/ATLAS) (1945-1973)
1 Origin: Millie. 110.00 350.00
2 70.00 220.00
3-10 40.00 130.00
11-15 26.00 85.00
16-20 20.00 65.00
21-30 14.00 44.00
31-50 10.00 33.00
51-75 7.00 22.00
76-100 5.00 16.00
101-120 4.00 11.00
121-160 2.25 8.75
161-207 1.50 5.50
ANNUAL 1 (1962) 25.00 80.00
ANNUAL 2 (1963) 20.00 65.00
ANNUAL 3 (1964) 14.00 44.00
ANNUAL 4 (1965) 14.00 44.00
ANNUAL 5 (1966) 14.00 44.00
ANNUAL 6 (1967) 14.00 44.00
ANNUAL 7 (1968) 14.00 44.00
ANNUAL 8 (1969) 14.00 44.00
ANNUAL 9 (1970) 14.00 44.00
ANNUAL 10 (1971) 14.00 44.00

MILT GROSS FUNNIES
GROSS (1947)
1-2 10.00 30.00

MILTON THE MONSTER AND FEARLESS FLY
GOLD KEY (1966)
1 (10175-605). 11.00 35.00

MINUTEMAN
FAWCETT (1941-1942)
1 280.00 900.00
2-3 145.00 480.00

MIRACLE COMICS
HILLMAN (1940-1941)
1 280.00 900.00
2 140.00 460.00
3-4 105.00 340.00

MIRACLE OF THE WHITE STALLIONS, THE
GOLD KEY (1963)
10065-306 Disney movie tie-in. 5.00 15.00

MIRACLEMAN
ECLIPSE (1985-1988)
1 Begin: Alan Moore. .75 2.00
2-15 .75 2.00
16 End: Alan Moore. .50 1.75
17 Begin: Neil Gaiman. .50 1.75
18-22 .50 1.75
23 End: Neil Gaiman. .50 1.75
24-28 .50 1.75
SPECIAL 3-D comic. 1.00 3.00

MIRACLEMAN: THE APOCRYPHA
ECLIPSE (1991-1992)
1-3 .75 2.50

MIRACLEMAN TRIUMPHANT
ECLIPSE (1994-CURRENT)
1 .75 2.95

MISADVENTURES OF MERLIN JONES, THE
GOLD KEY (1964)
10115-405 Disney movie photo cover (Annette Funicello). 7.00 20.00

MISS AMERICA COMICS
MARVEL(TIMELY) (1944)
1 Starring Patsy Walker. 190.00 600.00

MISS BEVERLY HILLS OF HOLLYWOOD
DC (1949-1950)
1 "Beverly Meets Alan Ladd!" (3-4/49) 95.00 300.00
2 "Bev Goes To Eve Arden's Party!" ... 65.00 200.00
3 "Dorothy Lamour in Road To Stardom" 55.00 175.00
4 "Beverly Meets Betty Hutton in Red, White, And Blue" 55.00 175.00
5 "Bev Meets Bob (The Great Lover) Hope!" 55.00 175.00
6 (1-2/50) 55.00 175.00
7-8 50.00 150.00
9 "Meet Wendell Corey, Hollywood's Newest Screen Sensation!" (7-8/50) Partial photo cover. 50.00 150.00

MISS FURY
MARVEL(TIMELY) (1942-1946)
1 "Introducing the unique, exciting and glamorous Miss Fury" by Tarpe Mills. 400.00 1500.00
2 270.00 875.00
3 190.00 625.00
4 155.00 500.00
5-8 130.00 430.00

MISS LIBERTY COMIC BOOK
BURTEN (1945)
1 Title changes to Liberty Comics #10. 65.00 200.00

MISS MELODY LANE OF BROADWAY
DC (1950)
1 Photo inserts on all covers. 16.00 50.00
2-3 50.00 165.00

MISS PEACH
DELL (1963)
1 14.00 45.00

MISS VICTORY
HOLYOKE (1944-1945)
3 From the Holyoke One-Shot series. Origin retold: Cat Man. 50.00 150.00

MISSION: IMPOSSIBLE
DELL (1967-1969)
1 TV photo covers on all issues. 13.00 40.00
2-5 10.00 30.00

MISTER ED, THE TALKING HORSE
DELL FOUR COLOR SERIES (1962)
1295 TV photo cover. (2/62) 31.00 100.00

MISTER ED, THE TALKING HORSE
GOLD KEY (1962-1964)
1 TV tie-in, photo covers on all issues. 17.00 55.00
2-6 10.00 33.00

MISTER MAGOO
DELL (1961-1964)
1 (#1235) From the 4-Color Series. (3/61) 19.00 60.00
2 (#1305) From the 4-Color Series. (3/62) 19.00 60.00
3-5 13.00 40.00
6 16.00 50.00

MISTER MIRACLE
DC (1971-1978)
1 1st: Mister Miracle. Jack Kirby cover/art in all issues. 10.00 30.00
2 6.00 18.00
3 2.75 10.00
4-8 25 cent double size issue. 2.75 10.00
9 Origin: Mister Miracle. 2.50 9.00
10 2.50 9.00
11-17 1.75 6.00
18 (1974). 1.75 6.00
19 (1977) 1.25 4.00
20-25 1.25 4.00

MISTER MIRACLE
DC (1989-1991)
1 .30 1.50
2-8 .50 1.50
9 1st: Maxi-Man. .50 1.50

10-12 .50 1.50
13-14 Lobo. .50 1.50
15-21 .50 1.50
22 1st: new Mister Miracle. .50 1.50
23-28 .50 1.50

MISTER MIRACLE SPECIAL
DC (1987)
1 .75 2.00

MISTER MYSTERY
MEDIA (1951-1954)
1 75.00 240.00
2 60.00 190.00
3 50.00 160.00
4-6 50.00 150.00
7 "The Brain Bats Of Venus!" by Basil Wolverton. 145.00 480.00
8-10 40.00 120.00
11 "Robot Woman!" by Basil Wolverton. 75.00 240.00
12 "Shangri-La!" 110.00 360.00
13-17 40.00 120.00
18 "Robot Woman!" by Basil Wolverton. 65.00 210.00
19 40.00 120.00

MISTER UNIVERSE
MEDIA (1951-1952)
1 25.00 80.00
2-3 17.00 55.00
4-5 14.00 44.00

MISTER X
VORTEX (1984-1988)
1 1.75 6.00
2 1.00 3.00
3-14 .75 2.00

MISTER X
VORTEX (1989-1990)
1-12 .75 2.00

MITZI COMICS
MARVEL(TIMELY) (1948)
1 Title changes to Mitzi's Boy Friend Comics with #2. 31.00 100.00

MITZI'S BOY FRIEND COMICS
MARVEL(TIMELY) (1948-1949)
2 Previous title: Mitzi Comics. 13.00 42.00
3-6 11.00 36.00
7 Title changes to Mitzi's Romances with #8. 13.00 42.00

MITZI'S ROMANCES
MARVEL(TIMELY) (1949)
8 Previous title: Mitzi's Boy Friend Comics. 11.00 36.00
9-10 11.00 36.00

MOBFIRE
DC (1994-1995)
1-6 .75 2.50

MOBY DICK
DELL FOUR COLOR SERIES (1956)
717 Movie photo cover. (8/56) 19.00 60.00

MOBY DUCK
GOLD KEY (1967-1980)
1 (Walt Disney's). 1.75 6.00
2-5 1.50 5.00
6-10 1.00 3.00
11-30 .75 2.00
31-47 .30 1.00

MOD SQUAD
DELL (1969-1971)
1 TV tie-in. Photo cover. 8.00 25.00
2 5.00 15.00
3-8 2.75 10.00

MODEL BY DAY
RIP OFF PRESS (1990)
1 1.50 5.00
2 1.00 3.00

MODEL FUN
HARLE (1954-1955)
2-5 With Bobby Benson. 7.00 20.00

MODELING WITH MILLIE
MARVEL(ATLAS) (1963-1967)
21 Previous title: Life With Millie. 12.00 38.00
22-30 7.00 22.00
31-54 4.00 13.00

MODERN COMICS
QUALITY (1945-1950)
44 Previous title: Military Comics. 95.00 310.00
45-52 65.00 210.00
53 Begin: Torchy by Bill Ward. (9/46) 75.00 240.00
54-60 50.00 160.00
61-70 50.00 150.00
71-77 40.00 130.00
78 1st: Madame Butterfly. "Blackhawk Against Madame Butterfly!" 40.00 130.00
79-80 40.00 130.00
81-102 40.00 120.00

MODERN LOVE
EC (1949-1950)
1 105.00 340.00
2 85.00 280.00
3 70.00 230.00
4-6 105.00 340.00
7-8 70.00 230.00

MODNIKS
GOLD KEY (1967-1968)
1 (10206-708) 2.75 10.00
2 1.75 6.00

MOE & SHMOE COMICS
O.S. (1948)
1 13.00 40.00
2 10.00 30.00

MOLLY O'DAY
AVON (1945)
1 1st Avon comic. 80.00 250.00

MONKEES, THE
DELL (1967-1969)
1 TV photo cover. 26.00 85.00
2 TV photo cover. 14.00 44.00
3-4 TV photo cover. 10.00 33.00
5 5.00 16.00
6-7 TV photo cover. 10.00 33.00
8-9 5.00 16.00
10 TV photo cover. 10.00 33.00
11-17 4.00 11.00

MONOLITH
COMICO (1991-1992)
1-4 .75 2.50

MONROES, THE
DELL (1967)
1 TV photo cover. 2.75 10.00

MONSTER
FICTION HOUSE (1953)
1 55.00 180.00
2 "The Dark Abysmal." 40.00 120.00

MONSTER CRIME COMICS
HILLMAN (1952)
1 140.00 450.00

MONSTER HUNTERS
CHARLTON (1975-1979)
1 2.25 8.00
2 Art: Steve Ditko. 5.00 15.00
3-5 1.25 4.00
6 Art: Steve Ditko. 2.25 8.00
7 1.25 4.00
8 Art: Steve Ditko. 2.25 8.00
9 1.00 3.00
10 Art: Steve Ditko. 2.25 8.00
11-12 .75 2.00
13 Art: Steve Ditko. 1.75 6.00
14 Art: Steve Ditko (entire issue). 5.00 15.00
15 Art: Steve Ditko. 1.75 6.00
16-17 .75 2.00
18 Art: Steve Ditko. 1.75 6.00

MONSTER MENACE
MARVEL (1993-1994)
1-4 .50 1.25

MONSTER OF FRANKENSTEIN
MARVEL (1973-1975)
1 6.00 18.00
2-5 2.50 9.00
6 Begin title variant: The Frankenstein Monster. 2.50 9.00
7 2.50 9.00
8 Dracula. 2.75 10.00
9 Death: Dracula. 2.75 10.00
10-12 2.00 7.00
13-18 1.25 4.00

MONSTER WORLD
WARREN (1964-1967) MAGAZINE
1 5.00 16.00
2 The Munsters TV photo cover. 4.00 11.00
3 Low distribution. 14.00 44.00
4-8 1.50 5.50
9 Addams Family TV photo cover. 4.00 11.00
10 1.50 5.50

MONSTERS OF THE MOVIES
MARVEL (1974-1975) MAGAZINE
1 2.75 10.00
2-7 1.50 5.00

MONSTERS ON THE PROWL
MARVEL (1971-1974)
9 Previous title: Chamber Of Darkness. Reprints (including cover): Tales To Astonish #12. 1.50 5.50
10 Reprints (including cover variation): Journey Into Mystery #71. 1.00 3.25
11-15 1.00 3.25
16 1.50 5.50
17 Reprints Tales Of Suspense #14. 1.00 3.25
18 Reprints Tales Of Suspense #22. 1.00 3.25
19-20 1.00 3.25
21-22 .75 2.00
23 Reprints (including cover): Strange Tales #87. .75 2.00
24 .75 2.00
25 Reprints (including cover): Tales Of Suspense #20. .75 2.00
26 Reprints (including cover): Strange Tales #95. .75 2.00
27 Reprint (including cover): Amazing Adventures #6 (1961). .75 2.00
28 Reprints (including cover): Amazing Adventures #5 (1961). .75 2.00
29 Reprints (including cover): Tales To Astonish #34. .75 2.00
30 Reprints Tales Of Suspense #9. .75 2.00

MONSTERS UNLEASHED
MARVEL (1973-1975) MAGAZINE
1 1.75 6.50
2-11 1.00 3.25
ANNUAL 1 .75 2.00

MONTANA
FAWCETT (1950)
NO# Movie photo cover (Errol Flynn & Alexis Smith). From the Fawcett Movie Comic series. 35.00 110.00

MONTE HALE WESTERN
FAWCETT (1948-1956)
29 Previous title: Mary Marvel. 80.00 250.00
30 40.00 125.00
31-40 25.00 80.00
41-44 19.00 60.00
45-50 16.00 50.00
51-60 13.00 40.00
61-82 10.00 30.00
83 Begin Charlton publication. 10.00 30.00
84-88 7.00 22.00

MONTY HALL OF THE U.S. MARINES
TOBY (1951-1953)
1 11.00 35.00
2 7.00 20.00
3-11 5.00 15.00

MOON, A GIRL, ROMANCE
EC (1949-1950)
9 App: Moon Girl. 140.00 460.00
10-11 110.00 350.00
12 135.00 440.00

MOON GIRL
EC (1947-1949)
1 Origin: Moon Girl. 180.00 575.00
2 100.00 330.00
3-4 75.00 240.00
5 EC's 1st horror story: "Zombie Terror!" 200.00 650.00
6-8 100.00 330.00

MOON KNIGHT
MARVEL (1980-1984)
1 2.00 7.00
2-14 1.00 3.00
15 1st Direct Sale issue. 1.25 4.00
16-34 .75 2.00
35 X-Men. 1.25 4.00
36-38 .75 2.00

MOON KNIGHT
MARVEL (1985)
1 .50 1.50
2-6 .50 1.50

MOON KNIGHT
MARVEL (1989-1994)
1 1.50 5.00
2 1.00 3.00
3-7 .75 2.00

MONSTER OF FRANKENSTEIN #1

MONSTERS OF THE MOVIES #2

MONTY HALL OF THE U.S. MARINES #1

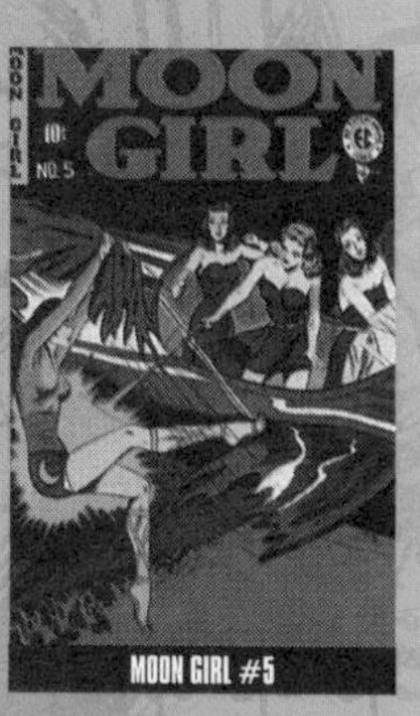

MOON GIRL #5

a b c d e f g h i j k l m n o p q r s t u v w x y z

MOON KNIGHT #2 (2ND SERIES)

MOON KNIGHT #1 (3RD SERIES)

MORBIUS REVISITED #2

MORE FUN COMICS #53

8-9 Punisher. .75 2.00
10-18 .75 2.00
19-21 Spider-Man, Punisher. .75 2.00
22-24 .75 2.00
25 Ghost Rider. .75 2.00
26-34 .75 2.00
35-49 .50 1.50
50 Die cut cover (2.95). 1.00 3.50
51-54 .50 1.50
55 Begin: Stephen Platt art. 4.00 12.00
56 2.25 8.00
57 1.75 6.00
58 1.00 3.00
59 Death: Bloodline. 1.00 3.00
60 End: Stephan Platt art. Death: Moon Knight. 1.75 6.00
SPECIAL 1 (1992) .75 2.50

MOON KNIGHT: DIVIDED WE FALL
MARVEL (1992)
1 1.25 4.95

MOON KNIGHT SPECIAL EDITION
MARVEL (1983-1984)
1 Reprints from Hulk magazine. .75 2.00
2-3 .75 2.00

MOON MULLINS
ACG (1948-1949)
1 31.00 100.00
2-8 10.00 30.00

MOON MULLINS
DELL FOUR COLOR SERIES (1943-1945)
31 40.00 125.00
81 22.00 70.00

MOON MULLINS
SEE LARGE FEATURE COMICS #29.

MOON PILOT
DELL FOUR COLOR SERIES (1962)
1313 Movie photo cover. (3/62) 19.00 60.00

MOONSHADOW
DC (1994-1995)
1-12 .75 2.25

MOONSHADOW
MARVEL (1983-1984)
1 Origin: Moonshadow. 2.75 10.00
2 1.50 5.00
3-6 1.25 4.00
7-12 1.00 3.00
TPB 4.00 10.95

MOON-SPINNERS, THE
GOLD KEY (1964)
10124-410 Disney movie photo cover. 5.00 15.00

MOPSY
ST. JOHN (1948-1953)
1 26.00 85.00
2 14.00 44.00
3-12 10.00 33.00
13-19 7.00 22.00

MORBIUS REVISITED
MARVEL (1993)
1-5 .50 1.50

MORBIUS: THE LIVING VAMPIRE
MARVEL (1992-1995)
1 1.25 4.00
2-5 1.00 3.00
6-11 .75 2.00
12 Midnight Massacre, pt.4. .75 2.00
13-24 .75 2.00
25 .75 2.50
26-32 .50 1.95

MORE FUN COMICS
DC (1936-1947)
7 Previous title: New Fun Comics. Oversized, paper cover. (1/36) 1300.00 5000.00
8 "Spike" (2/36) 1300.00 5000.00
9 1st comic-sized issue (3-4/36). 1800.00 7000.00
10 "No Swimming" (5/36) 800.00 3000.00
11 (7/36) 700.00 2600.00
12 (8/36) 600.00 2200.00
13 (9/36) 600.00 2200.00
14 1st: Dr. Occult in costume (Superman prototype) (10/36). 3100.00 12000.00
15 Dr. Occult (11/36). 1200.00 4500.00
16 "X-Mas Number." End: Dr. Occult (12/36). 1200.00 4500.00
17 900.00 3200.00
18-20 500.00 1900.00
21-25 400.00 1300.00
26-28 310.00 1000.00
29 End: Humor covers. 310.00 1000.00
30-40 240.00 775.00
41-50 210.00 675.00
51 Cameo: The Spectre (one panel on last page). 900.00 3200.00
52 1st & Origin: The Spectre. (2/40) 11300.00 45000.00
53 Origin (part 2): The Spectre. 5100.00 20000.00
54 1700.00 6500.00
55 1st: Dr. Fate. (5/40) 2400.00 9500.00
56 1st Dr. Fate cover. 900.00 3200.00
57 700.00 2600.00
58 900.00 3200.00
59-60 600.00 2300.00
61 Dr. Fate cover. 600.00 2000.00
62-64 500.00 1800.00
65 600.00 2000.00
66 500.00 1800.00
67 Origin: Dr. Fate. 1300.00 5000.00
68 Doctor Fate. (6/41) 400.00 1500.00
69-70 400.00 1500.00
71 1st & Origin: Johnny Quick. 1200.00 4500.00
72 300.00 1100.00
73 1st & Origin: Aquaman. 1st: Green Arrow & Speedy. 2300.00 9000.00
74 2nd: Aquaman. 400.00 1500.00
75-80 310.00 1000.00
81-88 280.00 900.00
89 Origin: Green Arrow & Speedy team in "Birth Of The Battling Bowmen!" 280.00 900.00
90 280.00 900.00
91 The Green Arrow in "Silks, Spice, And Everything Nice" 220.00 700.00
92 220.00 700.00
93 Green Arrow and Speddy (misspelled on cover) in "The Case Of The Corny Crook." 220.00 700.00
94-97 220.00 700.00
98 End: Dr. Fate. 220.00 700.00
99 220.00 700.00
100 Anniversary issue. 240.00 775.00
101 1st & Origin: Superboy. End: Spectre. (1-2/45) 1800.00 7000.00
102 2nd: Superboy. 400.00 1500.00
103 280.00 900.00
104 1st Superboy cover. 240.00 775.00
105 200.00 650.00
106 180.00 575.00
107 End: Superboy, Johnny Quick. 180.00 575.00
108 Begin: Genius Jones. 50.00 150.00
109-124 40.00 130.00
125 Superman cover. 155.00 500.00
126 40.00 130.00
127 60.00 190.00

MORE SEYMOUR
ARCHIE (1963)
1 4.00 11.00

MORE TRASH FROM MAD
EC (1958-1969)
NO# Includes an 8 page color insert "Katchandhammer Kids!" 55.00 180.00
2 40.00 120.00
3-4 35.00 110.00
5-6 26.00 85.00
7 17.00 55.00
8 13.00 43.00
9-12 12.00 37.00

MORGAN THE PIRATE
DELL FOUR COLOR SERIES (1961)
1227 Movie photo cover. 19.00 60.00

MORSE FUNNIES (UNDERGROUND)
ALBERT MORSE (1974)
1 1st printing, 1 drawing per one-sided page. Cover: Robert Crumb. 400.00 1500.00
1A 2nd printing. Art on each page. Cover: Robert Crumb. 400.00 1500.00

MORTAL KOMBAT
MALIBU (1994)
0 .75 2.95
1 Video game tie-in. .75 2.95
1A Gold foil cover. 2.75 10.00
2-6 .75 2.95

MORTAL KOMBAT: BARAKA
MALIBU (1995)
1 One shot. .75 2.95

MORTAL KOMBAT: BATTLEWAVE
MALIBU (1995)
1-6 .75 2.95

MORTAL KOMBAT: GORO, PRINCE OF PAIN
MALIBU (1994)
1-3 .75 2.95

MORTAL KOMBAT: KUNG LAO
MALIBU (1995)
1 .75 2.95

MORTAL KOMBAT: RAYDEN/KANO
MALIBU (1995)
1 Foil-stamped cover. 1.25 4.95
1A Regular cover. .75 2.95
2-3 .75 2.95

MORTAL KOMBAT: TOURNAMENT EDITION BATTLE FINALE
MALIBU (1994)
1 Double size. 1.00 3.95

MORTAL KOMBAT: TOURNAMENT EDITION BATTLE FINALE
MALIBU (1994)
1 Double size. 1.00 3.95

MORTAL KOMBAT: U.S. SPECIAL FORCES
MALIBU (1995)
1 1.00 3.50
2 .75 2.95

MORTY MEEKLE
DELL FOUR COLOR SERIES (1957)
793 (4/57) 7.00 20.00

MOSES AND THE TEN COMMANDMENTS
DELL (1957)
1 100 page Giant. 25.00 80.00

MOTHER GOOSE AND NURSERY RHYME COMICS
DELL FOUR COLOR SERIES (1944-1945)
41 Art: Walt Kelly (all issues). 55.00 175.00
59 (12/44) 50.00 150.00
68 (4/45) 50.00 150.00

MOTION PICTURE COMICS
FAWCETT (1950-1953)
101 Monte Hale in "The Vanishing Westerner." 60.00 190.00
102 Rocky Lane in "Code Of The Silver Sage." 50.00 160.00
103 Rocky Lane in "Covered Wagon Raid." 50.00 160.00
104 Rocky Lane in "Vigilante Hideout." Art: Powell. 50.00 160.00
105 Audie Murphy in "The Red Badge Of Courage." Art: Powell. 70.00 220.00
106 George Montgomery in "The Texas Rangers." 50.00 160.00
107 Rocky Lane in "Frisco Tornado." 50.00 160.00
108 John Derek in "Mask Of The Avenger." 35.00 110.00
109 Rocky Lane in "Rough Riders Of Durango." 50.00 160.00
110 "When Worlds Collide." 170.00 550.00
111 Lash LaRue in "The Vanishing Outpost." 50.00 160.00
112 Jon Hall in "Brave Warrior." 26.00 85.00
113 George Murphy in "Walk East On Beacon." 26.00 85.00
114 George Montgomery in "Cripple Creek." 26.00 85.00

MOTION PICTURE FUNNIES WEEKLY
FIRST FUNNIES (1939)
1 1st & Origin: Sub-Mariner (pre-dates Marvel Comics #1). 2300.00 9000.00
2-4 Only covers exist for issues 2-4, the comics were never printed. A small number of covers were found in the estate of the publisher. 190.00 600.00

MOTORHEAD
DARK HORSE (1995-CURRENT)
1-3 .75 2.50

MOTORMOUTH
MARVEL UK (1992-1993)
1 1st & Origin: Motormouth. 1.00 3.00
2 1st: Killpower. .75 2.00
3-12 .50 1.75

MOTORMOUTH & KILLPOWER
MARVEL (1992)
1 Foil stamped cover. .75 2.50
2-6 .50 1.75

MOUSE MUSKETEERS
DELL (1957-1960)
8-21 .... 2.25 8.00

MOUSE MUSKETEERS
DELL FOUR COLOR SERIES (1956-1962)
670 (1/56) 7.00 20.00
711 (8/56) 5.00 15.00
728 (9/56) 5.00 15.00
764 (1/15) 5.00 15.00
1135 (9/60) 7.00 20.00
1175 (3/61) 7.00 20.00
1290 (2/62) 7.00 20.00

MOUSE ON THE MOON, THE
DELL (1963)
12-530-312 Movie photo cover. 11.00 35.00

MOVIE COMICS
DC (1939)
1 "Gunga Din","Son Of Frankenstein","The Great Man Votes","Fisherman's Wharf" & "Scouts To The Rescue" part 1; Wheelan "Minute Movies" begin. Photo cover. 600.00 2300.00
2 "Stagecoach","The Saint Strikes Back","King Of The Turf","Scouts To The Rescue" part 2,"Arizona Legion". Movie photo cover. 500.00 1700.00
3 "East Side Of Heaven","Mystery In The White Room","Four Feathers","Mexicali Rose" with Gene Autry, "Spirit Of Culver","Many Secrets","The Mikado". Movie photo cover. 310.00 1000.00
4 "Captain Fury", Gene Autry in "Blue Montana Skies","Streets Of New York" with Jackie Cooper, "Oregon Trail" part 1 with Johnny Mack Brown, "Big Town Czar" with Barton MacLane, & "Star Reporter" with Warren Hull. Movie photo cover. 280.00 900.00
5 "Man In The Iron Mask","Five Came Back","Wolf Call","The Girl & The Gambler","The House Of Fear","The Family Next Door","Oregon Trail" part 2. Movie photo cover. 250.00 800.00
6 "The Phantom Creeps","Chumps at Oxford" & "The Oregon Trail" part 3. Movie photo cover. 250.00 800.00

MOVIE COMICS
FICTION HOUSE (1946-1947)
1 Begin: Big Town, Johnny Danger. ... 85.00 270.00
2 "White Tie & Tails" with William Bendix. 55.00 180.00
3 "Andy Hardy" starring Mickey Rooney. 55.00 180.00
4 Mitzi In Hollywood by Matt Baker. ... 75.00 240.00

MOVIE LOVE
FAMOUS FUNNIES (1950-1953)
1 "Mrs. Mike" & "The Big Wheel", photo cover. 17.00 55.00
2 Photo cover (Myrna Loy). 10.00 33.00
3 Photo cover. 9.00 27.00
4 Photo cover (Paulette Goddard). ... 9.00 27.00
5-7 Photo cover. 9.00 27.00
8 Art: Williamson/Frazetta. Photo cover. 50.00 160.00
9 Photo cover. 9.00 27.00
10 Art: Frank Frazetta. Photo cover ... 50.00 160.00
11 Photo cover. 7.00 22.00
12 Photo cover (Dean Martin & Jerry Lewis). 7.00 22.00
13 Photo cover (Ronald Reagan). ... 17.00 55.00
14-22 Photo cover. 7.00 22.00

MOVIE THRILLERS
ME (1949)
1 Movie photo cover "Rope Of Sand" (Burt Lancaster). 60.00 190.00

MOVIE TOWN ANIMAL ANTICS
DC (1950-1954)
24 Previous title: Animal Antics. 17.00 55.00
25-40 .... 14.00 44.00
41-51 .... 12.00 38.00

MOVIE TUNES
MARVEL (1946)
3 Previous title: Animated Movie-Tunes Comics. Title changes to Frankie Comics with #4. .... 19.00 60.00

MOWGLI JUNGLE BOOK
DELL FOUR COLOR SERIES (1953-1955)
487 (8/53) 11.00 35.00
582 (8/54) 7.00 20.00
620 (4/55) 7.00 20.00

MR. AND MRS. J. EVIL SCIENTIST
GOLD KEY (1963-1966)
1 (10093-311) Flintstones TV tie in. (11/63) 13.00 40.00
2-4 .... 7.00 20.00

MR. ANTHONY'S LOVE CLINIC
HILLMAN (1949-1950)
1 Photo cover. 14.00 44.00
2 .... 9.00 27.00
3-5 .... 7.00 22.00

MR. BUG GOES TO TOWN
PARAMOUNT (1941)
NO# Movie giveaway (4 pages). From the Cinema Comics Herald series. 23.00 75.00

MR. BUGG GOES TO TOWN
K.K. (1941)
NO# 48 page cartoon movie tie-in. ... 125.00 400.00

MR. DISTRICT ATTORNEY
DC (1948-1959)
1 Radio/TV tie-in. 155.00 500.00
2 .... 70.00 220.00
3-6 .... 50.00 160.00
7-12 .... 40.00 120.00
13-18 .... 29.00 95.00
19-24 .... 25.00 80.00
25-30 .... 20.00 65.00
31-43 .... 17.00 55.00
44 1st Code Approved issue. 14.00 44.00
45-67 .... 12.00 38.00

MR. DISTRICT ATTORNEY
DELL FOUR COLOR SERIES (1942)
13 .... 65.00 200.00

MR. FIXITT
APPLE (1992)
1 .... .75 2.00

MR. FIXITT
HEROIC (1993)
1 .... .75 2.00

MR. HERO, THE NEWMATIC MAN
TEKNO-COMIX (1994-CURRENT)
1 (Neil Gaiman's...) 1.25 4.50
2-10 .... .50 1.95

MR. MAGOO
DELL FOUR COLOR SERIES (1954)
561 "And Gerald McBoing Boing". (5/54) 22.00 70.00
602 "And Gerald McBoing Boing". (11/54) 20.00 65.00

MR. MIRACLE COMICS
HOLYOKE (1944-1945)
4 From the Holyoke One-Shot series. ... 16.00 50.00

MR. MONSTER
DARK HORSE (1988)
1 .... 1.50 5.00
2-6 .... 1.00 3.00

MR. MONSTER
ECLIPSE (1985-1987)
1 .... 2.75 10.00
2 .... 1.75 6.00
3-10 .... 1.00 3.00

MR. MONSTER VS THE NAZIS FROM MARS
ATOMEKA (1988)
1 .... 1.25 4.95

MR. T AND THE T-FORCE
NOW (1993-1994)
1 Polybagged with gold foil-stamped card. .50 1.95
1A Newsstand edition, polybagged with card. .50 1.95
1B Signed Gold edition. 10.00 30.00
2 Polybagged with gold foil-stamped card. .50 1.95
2A Newsstand edition. polybagged with card. .50 1.95
3 Polybagged with gold foil-stamped card. .50 1.95
3A Newsstand edition, polybagged with card. .50 1.95
4-14 .... .50 1.95

MS. MARVEL
MARVEL (1977-1979)
1 1st: Ms. Marvel. 1.50 5.00
2 Origin: Ms. Marvel. 1.25 4.00
3-8 .... 1.00 3.00
9 1st: Deathbird. 1.50 5.00
10-12 .... 1.00 3.00
13-15 .... .75 2.00
16 Cameo: Mystique. 4.00 12.00
17 .... 1.50 5.00
18 1st: Mystique (full app.). 5.00 14.00
19 .... .75 2.00
20 New costume. .... .75 2.00
21-23 .... .75 2.00

MS. MYSTIC
CONTINUITY (1988-1991)
1 Reprints Pacific series #1. .... 1.25 4.00
2 Reprints Pacific series #2. .... 1.00 3.25
3 .... .75 2.75
4-9 .... .75 2.50

MS. MYSTIC
CONTINUITY (1993)
1 Deathwatch 2000, pt.8. .... .75 2.50
2 Deathwatch 2000, pt.12. .... .75 2.50
3 Deathwatch 2000, pt.18. .... .75 2.50

MS. MYSTIC
CONTIUNUITY (1993-1994)
1-4 .... .75 2.50

MS. MYSTIC
PACIFIC (1982-1984)
1 Origin: Ms. Mystic. Cover/Art: Neal Adams. 1.75 6.00
2 Cover/Art: Neal Adams. 1.25 4.00

MS. TREE
ECLIPSE/AV/RENEGADE (1983-1989)
1-49 .... .75 2.00
50 With flexidisc. 1.25 4.00

MUGGSY MOUSE (A-1 SERIES)
ME (1951-1954)
1 (A-1 #33). 10.00 30.00
2 (A-1 #36). 10.00 30.00
3 (A-1 #39). 7.00 20.00
4 (A-1 #95). 7.00 20.00
5 (A-1 #99). 7.00 20.00

MULLKON EMPIRE
TEKNO (1995-CURRENT)
1-4 .... .50 1.95

MUMMY, THE
DELL (1962)
12-537-211 Movie tie-in. 8.00 25.00

MUMMY, THE
INNOVATION (1990-1991)
1 "Ramses the Damned" .... .50 1.50
2-12 .... .50 1.50

MUNSTERS
GOLD KEY (1965-1968)
1 TV photo covers on all issues. 45.00 140.00
2 .... 22.00 70.00
3-6 .... 17.00 55.00
7-12 .... 15.00 49.00
13-16 .... 14.00 44.00

MURCIELAGA SHE-BAT
HEROIC (1993)
1-3 .... .50 1.50

MURDER INCORPORATED
FOX (1948-1951)
1 "For Adults Only" on cover. 60.00 190.00
2 "For Adults Only" on cover. 40.00 130.00
3-7 .... 23.00 75.00
8 SOTI 26.00 85.00
9-15 .... 20.00 65.00
16 (#5 inside). 17.00 55.00
17 (#2 inside). 14.00 44.00
18 (#3 inside). 14.00 44.00

MURDEROUS GANGSTERS
AVON (1951-1952)
1 Pretty Boy Floyd, Legs Diamond. ... 50.00 160.00
2 Baby Face Nelson. 35.00 110.00
3 Nick Marek, Tony & Bud Fenner, Jed Hawkins. 25.00 80.00
4 "Murder By Needle!" drug story. ... 35.00 110.00

MUSIC MAN, THE
DELL (1963)
12-538-301 Movie tie-in. 5.00 15.00

MUTINY ON THE BOUNTY
GOLD KEY (1963)
10040-302 Movie photo cover (Marlon Brando). 8.00 25.00

MUTT AND JEFF
BALL (1910-1916)
1910 Oblong, hardcover, 68 pages. 125.00 400.00
1911-1916 .... 125.00 400.00

MUTT AND JEFF
DC/DELL/HARVEY (1939-1965)
1 (Summer/39) 270.00 875.00
2 (Summer/40) 135.00 440.00
3 (Summer/41) 100.00 330.00
4 (Winter/41) 70.00 220.00
5 (Summer/42) 70.00 220.00

MORE FUN COMICS #85

MORTAL KOMBAT #3

MR. HERO #1

MS. MARVEL #9

MY GREATEST ADVENTURE #20

MY GREATEST ADVENTURE #85

MY NAME IS HOLOCAUST #5

MYSTERIOUS ISLAND #1213

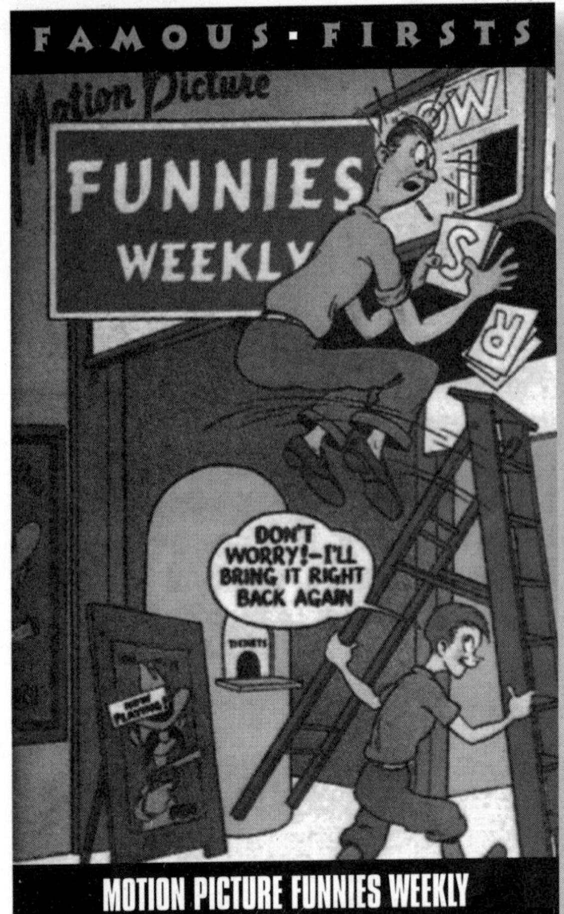

MOTION PICTURE FUNNIES WEEKLY

This comic, created as a giveaway at movie theaters, features the first appearance of Bill Everett's Sub-Mariner. The character later was sold to Marvel, which expanded the story and printed it in *Marvel Comics* #1.

6 (Fall/42)	50.00	160.00
7 (Winter/42)	50.00	160.00
8 (2-3/43)	50.00	160.00
9 (4-5/43)	40.00	130.00
10 (6-7/43)	40.00	130.00
11 (Fall/43)	40.00	130.00
12 (Winter/43)	40.00	130.00
13 (Spring/44)	35.00	110.00
14 (Summer/44)	35.00	110.00
15 (Fall/45)	35.00	110.00
16-18	35.00	110.00
19-30	20.00	65.00
31-40	15.00	49.00
41-50	12.00	38.00
51-75	9.00	27.00
76-100	7.00	22.00
101-103	5.00	16.00
104 Begin: Dell publication.	5.00	16.00
105-110	5.00	16.00
111-115	4.00	11.00
116 Begin: Harvey publication.	4.00	11.00
117-148	4.00	11.00

MUTT AND JEFF JOKES

HARVEY (1960-1961)

1-3	5.00	15.00

MUTT AND JEFF NEW JOKES

HARVEY (1963-1965)

1-4	2.75	10.00

MY CONFESSION

FOX (1949-1950)

7 Previous title: Western True Crime.	31.00	100.00
8-10	31.00	100.00

MY DATE COMICS

HILLMAN (1947-1948)

1 Cover & art: Simon & Kirby.	50.00	150.00
2	40.00	120.00
3	31.00	100.00
4	29.00	95.00

MY FAVORITE MARTIAN

GOLD KEY (1964-1966)

1 TV photo covers on all issues.	25.00	80.00
2	12.00	38.00
3-9	10.00	33.00

MY FRIEND IRMA

MARVEL(ATLAS) (1950-1955)

3 Radio/TV tie-in.	17.00	55.00
4 Art: Harvey Kurtzman (10 pages).	22.00	70.00
5	17.00	55.00
6-8	14.00	44.00
9-12	10.00	33.00
13-20	7.00	22.00
21-30	5.00	16.00
31-40	4.00	11.00
41-48	2.25	8.75

MY GIRL PEARL

MARVEL(ATLAS) (1955-1961)

1	14.00	44.00
2	7.00	22.00
3-6	4.00	11.00
7-11	1.50	5.50

MY GREATEST ADVENTURE

DC (1955-1964)

1	250.00	800.00
2	115.00	375.00
3-5	80.00	260.00
6 Begin: Science Fiction format.	80.00	260.00
7-12	55.00	175.00
13-15	40.00	125.00
16-18 Art: Jack Kirby.	50.00	150.00
19	31.00	100.00
20-21 Art: Jack Kirby.	50.00	150.00
22-24	31.00	100.00
25-27	23.00	75.00
28 Art: Jack Kirby.	50.00	150.00
29-40	23.00	75.00
41-61	16.00	50.00
62 1st 12 cent cover price.	11.00	35.00
63-79	7.00	20.00
80 1st & Origin: Doom Patrol. 1st & Origin: Elasti-girl, Robotman, Negative Man. (6/63)	100.00	325.00
81-84	31.00	100.00
85 Title changes to Doom Patrol with #86.	31.00	100.00

MY GREATEST THRILLS IN BASEBALL

GIVEAWAY (1960)

NO# Mickey Mantle.	110.00	350.00

MY LIFE

FOX (1948-1949)

4 Previous title: Meet Corliss Archer. SOTI.	40.00	130.00
5	17.00	55.00
6	20.00	65.00
7	14.00	44.00
8-9	9.00	27.00
10 Art: Wallace Wood.	20.00	65.00

MY LITTLE MARGIE

CHARLTON (1954-1964)

1	50.00	160.00
2	25.00	80.00
3-12	14.00	44.00
13-19	10.00	33.00
20 100 page giant.	17.00	55.00
21-30	9.00	27.00
31-40	7.00	22.00
41-54	5.00	16.00

MY LOVE MEMOIRS

FOX (1949-1950)

9 Previous title: Women Outlaws.	16.00	50.00
10-12	16.00	50.00

MY NAME IS CHAOS

DC (1992)

1-4	1.25	4.95

MY NAME IS HOLOCAUST

DC (1995)

1 Mini-series.	.75	2.50
2-5	.75	2.50

MY OWN ROMANCE

MARVEL(ATLAS) (1949-1960)

4 Previous title: My Romance.	16.00	50.00
5-12	10.00	30.00
13-42	7.00	20.00
43 1st Code-Approved issue.	5.00	15.00
44-60	5.00	15.00
61-76	2.75	10.00

MY PAL DIZZY

METROPOLITAN (1950)

1 Giveaway (5.25 x 8.5, bound at top).	2.75	10.00

MY PAST THRILLING CONFESSIONS

FOX (1949-1950)

7 Previous title: Western Thrillers.	14.00	44.00
8-10	10.00	33.00
11 Art: Wallace Wood.	23.00	75.00

MY ROMANCE

MARVEL (1948-1949)

1	23.00	75.00
2	13.00	40.00
3 Title changes to My Own Romance with #4.	13.00	40.00

MYS-TECH WARS

MARVEL (1993)

1-3	.50	1.75

MYSTERIES OF SCOTLAND YARD (A-1 SERIES)

ME (1954)

1 (A-1 #121).	22.00	70.00

MYSTERIES OF UNEXPLORED WORLDS

CHARLTON (1956-1965)

1	55.00	180.00
2	22.00	70.00
3-4 Art: Steve Ditko.	28.00	90.00
5-6 Cover/Art: Steve Ditko.	40.00	120.00
7 64 pages. Art: Steve Ditko.	40.00	120.00
8-9 Art: Steve Ditko.	28.00	90.00
10-11 Cover/Art: Steve Ditko.	40.00	120.00
12 Art: Steve Ditko.	28.00	90.00
13-18	8.00	24.00
19 Art: Steve Ditko.	28.00	90.00

20 .... 8.00 24.00
21-24 Art: Steve Ditko. 28.00 90.00
25 .... 6.00 18.00
26 Art: Steve Ditko. 28.00 90.00
27-30 .... 6.00 18.00
31-45 .... 4.00 12.00
46 1st & Origin: Son Of Vulcan. 8.00 24.00
47-48 Son Of Vulcan. 6.00 18.00

MYSTERIES WEIRD AND STRANGE
SUPERIOR/DYNAMIC (1953-1955)
1 .... 35.00 110.00
2 .... 17.00 55.00
3-11 .... 14.00 44.00

MYSTERIOUS ADVENTURES
STORY (1951-1955)
1 .... 60.00 190.00
2 .... 35.00 110.00
3-6 .... 26.00 85.00
7-10 .... 23.00 75.00
11 SOTI 29.00 95.00
12-20 .... 23.00 75.00
21-25 .... 20.00 65.00

MYSTERIOUS ISLAND
DELL FOUR COLOR SERIES (1962)
1213 Movie photo cover. (1/62) ... 19.00 60.00

MYSTERIOUS ISLE
DELL (1963)
1 .... 2.75 10.00

MYSTERIOUS STORIES
PREMIER (1955)
2 Previous title: Horror From The Tomb. 40.00 120.00
3 .... 23.00 75.00
4-7 .... 19.00 60.00

MYSTERIOUS SUSPENSE
CHARLTON (1968)
1 "Return Of The Question!" by Steve Ditko (cover & art).
.... 14.00 44.00

MYSTERY COMICS
WISE (1944)
1 Lead story: "Brad Spencer-Wonderman."
.... 130.00 420.00
2-3 .... 75.00 240.00
4 .... 65.00 210.00

MYSTERY IN SPACE
DC (1951-1981)
1 Art: Frank Frazetta (8 pgs.) 500.00 1800.00
2 .... 220.00 700.00
3-6 .... 170.00 550.00
7-12 .... 125.00 400.00
13-18 .... 70.00 225.00
19 "The Mad Planet" by Virgil Finlay. (4-5/54)
.... 75.00 275.00
20-24 .... 70.00 220.00
25 .... 65.00 200.00
26-30 .... 55.00 175.00
31-52 .... 50.00 150.00
53 Begin: Adam Strange. 300.00 1100.00
54 .... 110.00 350.00
55 .... 70.00 225.00
56-60 .... 40.00 130.00
61-71 .... 31.00 100.00
72 1st 12 cent cover price. 23.00 75.00
73-74 .... 20.00 65.00
75 Justice League crossover. 65.00 200.00
76-80 .... 20.00 65.00
81-86 .... 14.00 45.00
87 Begin: Hawkman. 55.00 180.00
88-89 Hawkman. 40.00 120.00
90 Adam Strange/Hawkman team-up. (3/64)
.... 40.00 120.00
91 .... 7.00 20.00
92 Begin: Space Ranger. 8.00 25.00
93-102 .... 8.00 25.00
103 End: Space Ranger. 8.00 25.00
104-109 .... 2.75 10.00
110 (9/66) 2.75 10.00
111 (8/80) 1.00 3.00
112-117 .... 1.00 3.00

MYSTERY MEN COMICS
FOX (1939-1942)
1 1st: Blue Beetle. 1300.00 5000.00
2 .... 280.00 900.00
3 .... 240.00 775.00
4-6 .... 200.00 650.00
7-12 .... 120.00 390.00
13-24 .... 100.00 320.00
25-31 .... 80.00 260.00

MYSTERY TALES
MARVEL(ATLAS) (1952-1957)
1 .... 115.00 370.00
2 .... 55.00 180.00
3-6 .... 50.00 150.00
7 "The Ghost Hunter!" 40.00 120.00
8-12 .... 40.00 120.00
13-24 .... 31.00 100.00
25-36 .... 26.00 85.00
37-46 .... 23.00 75.00
47 Art: Steve Ditko, Bob Powell. 28.00 90.00
48-54 .... 23.00 75.00

MYSTERY TALES
SUPER (1964)
16 Reprints in all issues. 2.25 8.00
17-18 .... 2.25 8.00

MYSTIC
MARVEL(ATLAS) (1951-1957)
1 .... 95.00 310.00
2 .... 65.00 200.00
3 .... 50.00 150.00
4 "The Den Of The Devil-Bird!" by Basil Wolverton.
.... 95.00 310.00
5 .... 40.00 120.00
6 "The Eye Of Doom!" by Basil Wolverton.
.... 95.00 310.00
7-12 .... 31.00 100.00
13-20 .... 26.00 85.00
21-36 .... 23.00 75.00
37 1st Code Approved issue. 19.00 60.00
38-56 .... 16.00 50.00
57 "Trapped In The Ant-Hill!" 28.00 90.00
58-61 .... 16.00 50.00

MYSTIC COMICS
MARVEL(TIMELY) (1940-1942)
1 1st & Origin: Blue Blaze. 2300.00 9000.00
2 .... 700.00 2600.00
3 Origin: Hercules. (6/40) 600.00 2000.00
4 Origin: Thin Man & Black Widow. ... 600.00 2000.00
5 Origin: Black Marvel. 500.00 1900.00
6 Origin: The Challenger & The Destroyer.
.... 500.00 1900.00
7 1st & Origin: The Witness. (12/41) 500.00 1800.00
8-10 .... 400.00 1300.00

MYSTIC COMICS
MARVEL(TIMELY) (1944-1945)
1 Begin: Human Torch, The Angel, The Destroyer.
.... 310.00 1000.00
2 End: Human Torch. 190.00 625.00
3 End: The Angel. 170.00 550.00
4 The Young Allies. (3/45) 155.00 500.00

MYSTICAL TALES
MARVEL(ATLAS) (1956-1957)
1 Art: Bill Everett. 50.00 150.00
2 .... 25.00 80.00
3-8 .... 20.00 65.00

NAKED PREY, THE
DELL (1966)
12-545-612 Movie photo cover. 7.00 20.00

NAM
MARVEL (1986-1993)
1 .... 1.25 4.00
2-12 .... .75 2.50
13-51 .... .75 2.00
52 Punisher. 1.00 3.00
52 (2ND) 2nd printing (blue). .... .50 1.75
53 Punisher. .... .75 2.00
54-74 .... .50 1.75
75 Double size. .... .50 1.75
76-84 .... .50 1.75

NAMOR, THE SUB-MARINER
MARVEL (1990-CURRENT)
1 Cover/Art: John Byrne issues 1-25. ... 1.00 3.00
2-6 .... .75 2.00
7-15 .... .50 1.50
16 Punisher. .... .50 1.50
17-22 .... .50 1.50
23 Wolverine. Return of Iron Fist. ...... .75 2.00
24 Wolverine, Iron Fist. .... .75 2.00
25 Origin: Iron Fist. .... .75 2.50
26 1st Jae Lee art on Namor. 1.75 6.00
27 .... 1.25 4.00
28-29 .... 1.00 3.00
30-31 .... .75 2.00
32-49 .... .30 1.00
50 Silver/transparent cover. Double size. .75 2.95
50A Regular edition. .... .30 1.00
51-62 .... .30 1.00
ANNUAL 1 (1991) .... .75 2.00
ANNUAL 2 (1992) .... .75 2.25
ANNUAL 3 Polybagged with card. (1993) .75 2.95
ANNUAL 4 (1994) .... .75 2.95

NAMORA
MARVEL (TIMELY) (1948)
1 App: Sub-Mariner. 310.00 1000.00
2 App: Blonde Phantom & Sub-Mariner. 240.00 775.00
3 App: Sub-Mariner. 240.00 775.00

NANCY AND SLUGGO
DELL FOUR COLOR SERIES (1959)
1034 "Summer Camp" (9/59) 7.00 20.00

NANCY AND SLUGGO
ST. JOHN/DELL/GOLD KEY (1955-1963)
121 Previous title: Sparkler Comics. ... 7.00 20.00
122-145 .... 4.00 12.00
146 Begin: Dell publication. Begin: Peanuts by Schultz. (9/57)
.... 8.00 25.00
147-187 .... 2.75 10.00
188 Begin: Gold Key publication. 1.75 6.00
189-192 .... 1.75 6.00

NANCY AND SLUGGO
UNITED FEATURES (1949-1954)
16 .... 10.00 30.00
17-23 .... 5.00 15.00

NANCY AND SLUGGO TRAVEL TIME
DELL (1958)
1 100 page Giant. 23.00 75.00

NANNY AND THE PROFESSOR
DELL (1970)
1 (01-546-008) TV photo cover. 10.00 30.00
2 TV photo cover. 7.00 20.00

NAPOLEON
DELL FOUR COLOR SERIES (1954)
526 (1/54) 5.00 15.00

NAPOLEON AND UNCLE ELBY
EASTERN (1942)
1 .... 31.00 100.00

NATIONAL COMICS
QUALITY (1940-1949)
1 1st & Begin: Uncle Sam. 700.00 2400.00
2 .... 400.00 1200.00
3 .... 250.00 825.00
4 .... 190.00 600.00
5 1st & Begin: Quicksilver. 220.00 700.00
6-8 .... 190.00 600.00
9-12 .... 145.00 480.00
13-16 Art: Lou Fine. 160.00 525.00
17 .... 130.00 420.00
18 .... 145.00 480.00
19-24 .... 110.00 360.00
25-30 .... 95.00 300.00
31-40 .... 65.00 210.00
41-50 .... 40.00 130.00
51-60 .... 25.00 80.00
61-70 .... 20.00 65.00
71-75 .... 16.00 50.00

NATIONAL VELVET
DELL (1962)
01-556-207 Photo cover. 5.00 15.00
12-556-210 Photo cover. 2.75 10.00

NATIONAL VELVET
DELL FOUR COLOR SERIES (1961-1962)
1195 TV photo cover. (4/61) 25.00 80.00
1312 TV photo cover. (2/62) 19.00 60.00

NATIONAL VELVET
GOLD KEY (1962-1963)
1 Photo cover. 5.00 15.00
2 .... 5.00 15.00

NATURE BOY
CHARLTON (1956-1957)
3 Origin: Nature Boy. Previous title: Danny Blaze.
.... 40.00 130.00
4-5 .... 29.00 95.00

NATURE OF THINGS, THE
DELL FOUR COLOR SERIES (1956-1957)
727 Disney movie tie-in. (9/56) ... 10.00 30.00
842 (9/57) 11.00 35.00

NAUGHTY BITS
FANTAGRAPHICS (1990-CURRENT)
1 1st: Bitchy Bitch. 2.75 10.00
1 (2ND) 2nd printing. .... .75 2.50
2 .... 1.50 5.00
2 (2ND) 2nd printing. .... .75 2.50
3 .... 1.25 4.00

NAM #82

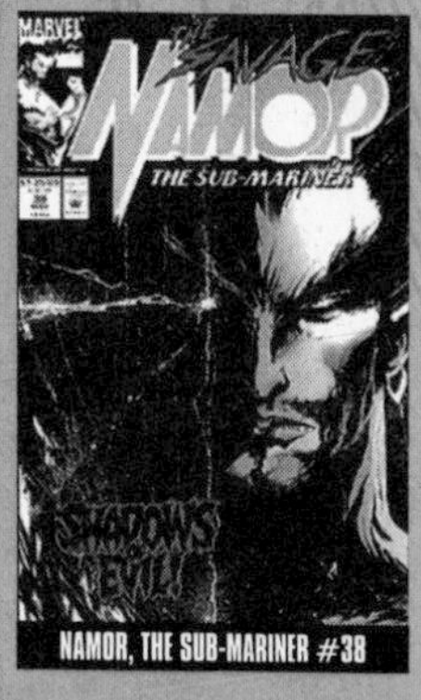

NAMOR, THE SUB-MARINER #38

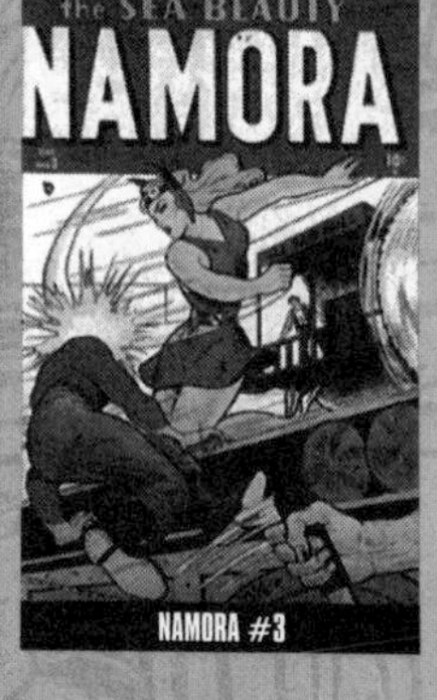

NAMORA #3

NATIONAL COMICS #4

NATURE BOY #4

NAVY HEROES #1

NEGATIVE BURN #24

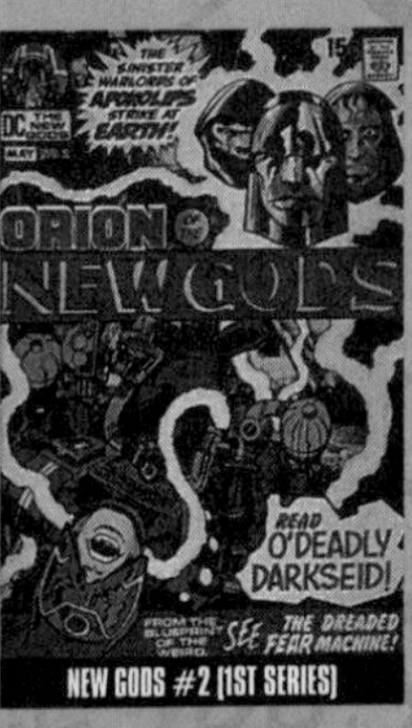

NEW GODS #2 (1ST SERIES)

3 (2ND) 2nd printing.	.75	2.50
4	1.25	4.00
4 (2ND) 2nd printing.	.75	2.50
5	1.00	3.00
5 (2ND) 2nd printing.	.75	2.50
6	1.00	3.00
6 (2ND) 2nd printing.	.75	2.50
7	.75	2.50
7 (2ND) 2nd printing.	.75	2.50
8	1.00	3.00
8 (2ND) 2nd printing.	.75	2.50
9-14	.75	2.50
15-16	.75	2.75

NAVY ACTION
MARVEL(ATLAS) (1954-1957)

1 Art: Bob Powell.	16.00	50.00
2	8.00	25.00
3-10	5.00	16.00
11	2.75	10.00
12-14 Sailor Sweeney.	2.75	10.00
15-18	2.75	10.00

NAVY COMBAT
MARVEL(ATLAS) (1955-1958)

1 Art: Don Heck.	16.00	50.00
2	8.00	25.00
3-11	6.00	18.00
12 Art: Reed Crandall.	10.00	30.00
13-16	5.00	15.00
17 Art: Al Williamson.	8.00	25.00
18-20	2.75	10.00

NAVY HEROES
ALMANAC (1945)

1	16.00	50.00

NAVY HISTORY AND TRADITION
STOKES WALESBY (1958-1961)

1772-1778-1940-1945 Department Of The Navy giveaway.	8.00	25.00

NAVY TALES
MARVEL(ATLAS) (1957)

1	13.00	40.00
2-4	10.00	30.00

NAZA: STONE AGE WARRIOR
DELL (1963-1966)

1 (#12-555-401)	5.00	15.00
2-9	2.75	10.00

NEBBS, THE
SEE LARGE FEATURE COMICS #23.

NECROMANTRA/LORD PUMPKIN
MALIBU (1995)

1 Mini-series, flip book.	.75	2.95
2-4	.75	2.95
4A Alternate cover by Kyle Hotz.	.75	2.95

NECROSCOPE
MALIBU (1992)

1-2	.75	2.00

NEGATIVE BURN
CALIBER (1993-CURRENT)

1	1.50	5.00
2	1.00	3.00
3 Bone preview.	5.00	15.00
4-12	.75	2.95
13 Strangers In Paradise.	1.50	5.00
14-24	.75	2.95
25	1.00	3.95
TPB "Best Of Year One", reprints. (1995)	2.50	9.95

NEGRO HEROES
PMI (1947-1948)

1	140.00	450.00
2 Jackie Robinson.	155.00	500.00

NEGRO ROMANCES
FAWCETT/CHARLTON (1950-1955)

1 Photo cover.	230.00	750.00
2 Photo cover.	190.00	625.00
3 Photo cover. (10/50)	190.00	625.00
4 Reprint: issue #2. (5/55)	155.00	500.00

NELLIE THE NURSE
DELL FOUR COLOR SERIES (1962)

1304 (3/62)	13.00	40.00

NELLIE THE NURSE
MARVEL(ATLAS) (1945-1952)

1	50.00	160.00
2	26.00	85.00
3	20.00	65.00
4	17.00	55.00
5 App: Georgie.	20.00	65.00
6-10	14.00	44.00
11-20	10.00	33.00
21-36	7.00	22.00

NESTROBBER
BLUE SKY BLUE (1992)

1	.30	1.00

NEW ADVENTURE COMICS
DC (1937-1938)

12 Previous title: New Comics.	1000.00	3700.00
13-14	800.00	3000.00
15	600.00	2200.00
16	500.00	1800.00
17	400.00	1500.00
18-24	400.00	1200.00
25-30	300.00	1100.00
31 Title changes to Adventure Comics with issue #32.	300.00	1100.00

NEW ADVENTURES OF CHARLIE CHAN, THE
DC (1958-1959)

1 "Charlie Chan's Invisible Club!" (6/58)	125.00	400.00
2 "Menace Of The Giant Statues" (8/58)	80.00	250.00
3 "The Two Lives Of Charlie Chan!" (10/58)	65.00	200.00
4 "Case Of The Vanishing Man!" (12/58)	65.00	200.00
5 "Challenge Of The Crimson Clown!" (2/59)	65.00	200.00
6 "Trail Across The Sky!" (4/59)	65.00	200.00

NEW ADVENTURES OF SHERLOCK HOLMES
DELL FOUR COLOR SERIES (1961)

1169 (3/61)	31.00	100.00
1245 (11/61)	28.00	90.00

NEW ADVENTURES OF SPEED RACER
NOW (1993-1994)

1-11	.50	1.95

NEW ADVENTURES OF SUPERBOY, THE
DC (1980-1984)

1-54	.30	1.00

NEW BOOK OF COMICS
DC (1937-1938)

1 Reprints New Fun #1-4, More Fun #9.	3300.00	13000.00
2 Reprints Dr. Occult by Siegel & Shuster.	1700.00	6500.00

NEW COMICS
DC (1935-1936)

1	3300.00	13000.00
2 1st: Federal Men by Siegel & Shuster.	1700.00	6500.00
3-6	1000.00	3900.00
7-10	700.00	2600.00
11 Title changes to New Adventures Comics with #12.	700.00	2600.00

NEW FUN COMICS
DC (1935)

1 1st DC comic. 1st comic to contain original stories. (2/35)	8300.00	33000.00
2	3300.00	13000.00
3	1900.00	7500.00
4-5	1800.00	7000.00
6 1st: Dr. Occult by Siegel & Shuster (pre-Superman character). (10/35) Becomes More Fun Comics #7.	3300.00	13000.00

NEW FUNNIES
DELL (1942-1962)

65 Previous title: The Funnies. Begin: Andy Panda, Oswald.	95.00	300.00
66-70	55.00	175.00
71-75	40.00	120.00
76 Andy Panda by Carl Barks.	95.00	300.00
77-78	31.00	100.00
79-80	28.00	90.00
81-90	22.00	70.00
91-100	13.00	40.00
101-110	10.00	30.00
111-120	7.00	20.00
121-150	4.00	12.00
151-200	1.75	6.00
201-220	1.00	3.00
221-250	.75	2.00
251-288	.30	1.00

NEW GODS, THE
DC (1971-1978)

1 1st: Orion.	11.00	35.00
2 2nd: full Darkseid app.	6.00	18.00
3	5.00	15.00
4 Begin: Double size (.25).	5.00	15.00
5-6	5.00	15.00
7 Origin: Orion.	2.75	10.00
8	2.75	10.00
9 End: Double size (.25).	2.75	10.00
10	2.25	8.00
11 (10-11/72)	2.25	8.00
12 (7/77)	1.25	4.00
13-19	1.25	4.00

NEW GODS
DC (1984)

1-6	.75	2.00

NEW GODS, THE
DC (1989-1991)

1-28	.30	1.00

NEW MUTANTS
MARVEL (1983-1991)

1 Origin: Karma.	2.75	10.00
2	1.75	6.00
3-9	1.25	4.50
10 1st: Magma.	1.25	4.50
11-15	1.25	4.00
16 1st: Thunderbird II.	1.50	5.00
17	1.25	4.00
18 Debut: new Warlock.	2.75	10.00
19-20	1.25	4.00
21 Origin: Warlock. Double size.	2.75	10.00
22-24	1.00	3.00
25 1st (cameo): D. Haller (Legion).	4.00	12.00
26	6.00	18.00
27 1st: Haller as Legion.	5.00	16.00
28 Origin: Legion.	4.00	12.00
29 1st: Guido (Strong Guy).	1.00	3.00
30-43	1.00	3.00
44 App: Legion.	2.75	10.00
45	1.00	3.00
46 Mutant Massacre.	1.00	3.00
47-49	1.00	3.00
50 Return: Professor X. Double size.	1.25	4.00
51-58	1.00	3.00
59 Fall Of The Mutants.	1.00	3.00
60-61 Fall Of The Mutants.	.75	2.00
62-72	.75	2.00
73	.75	2.50
74 1st: X-Terminators.	.75	2.00
75 Magneto.	1.25	4.00
76-84	.75	2.00
85 Cover: Rob Liefeld.	1.25	4.00
86 Begin: Rob Liefeld art. 1st: Cable (cameo).	2.75	10.00
87 1st: Cable. 1st: Stryfe.	10.00	30.00
87 (2ND) 2nd printing.	.30	1.00
88	4.00	12.00
89-91	2.25	8.00
92 No Liefeld art.	1.25	4.00
93	2.25	8.00
94 Cable battles Wolverine.	2.25	8.00
95	2.25	8.00
95 (2ND) 2nd printing.	1.00	3.00
96-97	2.25	8.00
98 1st: Deadpool. 1st: Gideon. 1st: Vanessa (as Domino).	2.50	9.00
99 1st: Feral. 1st: Shatterstar.	2.25	8.00
100 1st: X-Force.	2.75	10.00
100 (2ND) 2nd printing, Gold.	1.25	4.00
100 (3RD) 3rd printing, Silver.	.50	1.50

NEW MUTANTS ANNUAL
MARVEL (1984-1993)

1 1st: Lila Cheney. (1984)	1.75	6.50
2 1st: Psylocke. 1st: Meggan. (1986)	1.25	4.00
3 (1987)	1.25	4.00
4 Evolutionary War. (1988)	1.50	5.00
5 Atlantis Attacks. 1st: Rob Liefeld art on New Mutants. (1989)	2.75	10.00
6 Days Of Future Past. (1990)	1.50	5.00
7 2nd: X-Force. (1991)	1.25	4.00

NEW PEOPLE, THE
DELL (1970)

1	2.75	10.00
2	1.75	6.00

NEW SHADOWHAWK, THE
IMAGE (1995-CURRENT)

1	.75	2.50

NEW TALENT SHOWCASE
DC (1984-1985)

1-19	.30	1.00

NEW TEEN TITANS
DC (1980-1984)
1 1st & Origin: Cyborg, Starfire. 1st: Grant Wilson. 5.00 15.00
2 1st: Deathstroke, Wintergreen, Trigon. 5.00 15.00
3 Origin: Raven, Starfire. 1st & Origin: Psimon. 1.50 5.00
4 Origin: Trigon. 1.50 5.00
5 .... 1.50 5.00
6 .... 1.00 3.00
7 Origin: Cyborg. 1.00 3.00
8-9 .... 1.00 3.00
10 2nd: Deathstroke. Origin: Changeling. 2.25 8.00
11-28 .... .75 2.00
29-33 .... .50 1.25
34 Deathstroke. 1.50 5.00
35-36 .... .50 1.25
37 Batman. .... .50 1.25
38 .... .50 1.25
39 Last: Dick Grayson Robin. 1.50 5.00
40 Title changes to Tales Of The Teen Titans with #41. .... .50 1.25
ANNUAL 1 (1982) 1.00 3.75
ANNUAL 2 (1983) 1.00 3.50

NEW TEEN TITANS
DC (1984-1988)
1 Begin: George Perez cover & art. ... 1.50 5.00
2-9 .... 1.00 3.00
10-12 .... .75 2.00
13-14 Crisis. .... .75 2.00
15-19 .... .75 2.00
20 Return: original Teen Titans. .... .75 2.00
21-48 .... .75 2.00
49 Title changes to New Titans with #50. .75 2.00
ANNUAL 1 1st: The Vanguard. .... .75 2.50
ANNUAL 2 Origin: Baron Blood. .... .75 2.50
ANNUAL 3-ANNUAL 4 .... .75 2.50

NEW TEEN TITANS DRUG AWARENESS GIVEAWAY
DC (1983)
1 1st: Protector. From the Keebler Co. ... .75 2.00
2 From American Soft Drinks. .... .50 1.50
3 From IBM Corporation. .... .50 1.50

NEW TERRYTOONS
DELL (1960-1962)
1 1st Deputy Dog. 8.00 25.00
2-8 .... 5.00 15.00

NEW TERRYTOONS
GOLD KEY (1962-1979)
1 (30010-210) 80 page giant. 16.00 50.00
2 (300010-301) 80 page giant. ... 13.00 40.00
3-12 .... 5.00 15.00
13-24 .... 2.75 10.00
25-35 .... 1.75 6.00
36-54 .... .75 2.00

NEW TICK, THE
NEW ENGLAND COMICS
1 One shot. 1.00 3.25

NEW TITANS, THE
DC (1988-CURRENT)
0 (8/94) .... .50 1.95
50 Cover & art: George Perez. Previous title: New Teen Titans (2nd series). 1.00 3.00
51-58 .... .75 2.00
59 End: George Perez art. .... .75 2.00
60 A Lonely Place Of Dying, pt.2. ...... 1.50 5.00
61 A Lonely Place Of Dying, pt.4. ...... 1.50 5.00
62-65 Deathstroke. .... .75 2.00
66-70 .... .75 2.00
71 Titans Hunt. 1.50 5.00
72-75 Titans Hunt. 1.25 4.00
76 .... 1.00 3.00
77-85 .... .75 2.00
86-91 .... .50 1.50
92 .... .50 1.50
93-99 .... .50 1.50
100 .... 1.00 3.50
101-111 .... .50 1.75
112-121 .... .50 1.95
122-124 .... .75 2.25
125 Double size. 1.00 3.50
ANNUAL 5 (1989) 1.00 3.75
ANNUAL 6 (1990) 1.00 3.75
ANNUAL 7 Armageddon 2001. (1991) 1.25 4.00
ANNUAL 8 Eclipso. (1992) 1.00 3.75
ANNUAL 9 Bloodlines, pt.5. (1993) ... 1.00 3.50
ANNUAL 10 Elseworlds story. (1994) 1.00 3.50
ANNUAL 11 (1995) 1.00 3.95

NEW TWO-FISTED TALES VOL.II
DARK HORSE (1994)
1 .... 1.25 4.95

NEW WARRIORS, THE
MARVEL (1990-CURRENT)
1 .... 2.00 7.00
1 (2ND) 2nd printing. .... .75 2.00
2 .... 1.25 4.00
3-6 .... 1.00 3.00
7 App: Punisher (cameo). 1.00 3.00
8-9 App: Punisher. 1.00 3.00
10 .... 1.00 3.00
11 App: Wolverine. 1.00 3.00
12-18 .... 1.00 3.00
19-24 .... .75 2.00
25 Die-cut cover. Double size. .... .75 2.00
26-39 .... .50 1.25
40 Gold foil cover. .... .75 2.00
40A Regular cover. .... .50 1.25
41-49 .... .50 1.25
50 Glow-in-the-dark cover. .... .75 2.95
50A Regular cover. .... .50 1.50
51-59 .... .50 1.50
60 Double size. .... .75 2.50
61-62 .... .75 2.00
ANNUAL 1 (1991) 1.50 5.50
ANNUAL 2 (1992) .... .75 2.25
ANNUAL 3 1st: Void. Polybagged with card. (1993) .... .75 2.95
ANNUAL 4 (1994) .... .75 2.95
TPB Reprints: Thor #411-412, New Warriors #1-4. .... 4.00 12.95

NEW WORLD
METROPOLITAN (1950)
1 Giveaway (5.25 x 8.5, bound at top). 13.00 40.00

NEW YORK HERALD COMIC SECTION PAINT BOOK, THE
NEW YORK HERALD (1914)
1 Strip reprints, black & white interior. 40.00 125.00

NEW YORK WORLD'S FAIR
DC (1939-1940)
1939 1st: Sandman (publication arrived on newsstands a few weeks before Adventure #40. Also see Adventure #40). "96 pages in full color!" Cardboard covers. Features the classic "Blond Superman" on the front cover. 5100.00 20000.00
1940 1940 issue. "96 pages in full color!" Superman, Batman and Robin, The Sandman, Slam Bradley. 2600.00 10000.00

NEWMEN
IMAGE (1994-CURRENT)
1 1st: NewMen. 1.00 3.00
2-4 .... .75 2.25
5-16 .... .75 2.50

NEXT MAN
COMICO (1985)
1 .... 1.00 3.00
2-5 .... .50 1.50

NEXT MEN
SEE JOHN BYRNE'S NEXT MEN

NEXT NEXUS
FIRST (1989)
1-4 .... 1.00 3.00

NEXUS
CAPITAL (1981-1982) MAGAZINE
1 1st: Nexus. 7.00 20.00
2 .... 2.75 10.00
3 With flexi disc. 2.25 8.00

NEXUS
FIRST (1983-1991)
1 .... 1.75 6.00
2-5 .... 1.25 4.00
6 Trialogue Trilogy. 1.25 4.50
7-8 Trialogue Trilogy. .... .75 2.50
9-54 .... .75 2.50
55-80 .... .75 2.25

NEXUS: ALIEN JUSTICE
DARK HORSE (1992-1993)
1-3 .... 1.00 3.95

NEXUS LEGENDS
FIRST (1989-1991)
1 Reprints. .... .75 2.25
2-23 .... .75 2.00

NEXUS: OUT OF THE VORTEX
DARK HORSE (1995)
1-3 .... .75 2.50

NEXUS: THE LIBERATOR
DARK HORSE (1992)
1-4 .... .75 2.50

NEXUS: THE ORIGIN
DARK HORSE (1992)
1 .... 1.00 3.95

NEXUS: THE WAGES OF SIN
DARK HORSE (1995)
1-4 .... .75 2.95

NICK FURY, AGENT OF S.H.I.E.L.D.
MARVEL (1968-1971)
1 Art: Jim Steranko (#s 1-3, 5). Cover: Jim Steranko (#s1-7) 11.00 35.00
2 .... 8.00 25.00
3 .... 7.00 20.00
4 Origin retold: Nick Fury. 6.00 18.00
5 .... 6.00 18.00
6-7 .... 4.00 12.00
8-10 .... 1.50 5.00
11 .... 1.25 4.50
12 Cover & art: Barry Smith. 1.25 4.50
13 1st: Super-Patriot. 1.00 3.00
14 1st 15 cent cover price. 1.00 3.00
15 1st & Death: Bullseye I. 7.00 20.00
16-18 Double size (.25 cp). 1.00 3.00

NICK FURY AGENT OF SHIELD
MARVEL (1983-1984)
1-2 .... .75 2.50

NICK FURY, AGENT OF S.H.I.E.L.D.
MARVEL (1989-1993)
1 .... 1.00 3.00
2 .... .75 2.00
3-9 .... .50 1.50
10 Captain America. .... .50 1.50
11-12 .... .50 1.50
13 Return: Yellow Claw. .... .50 1.50
14-26 .... .50 1.50
27-29 Wolverine. .... .50 1.50
30-31 Deathlok. .... .50 1.50
32-47 .... .50 1.50

NICK FURY VS. SHIELD
MARVEL (1988)
1 .... 1.75 6.00
2 .... 1.50 5.00
3 .... 1.25 4.00
4-5 .... 1.00 3.00
6 SHIELD disbanded. 1.00 3.00

NICKEL COMICS
DELL (1938)
1 Pocket size (5 1/2 x 7 1/2"). ... 115.00 380.00

NICKEL COMICS
FAWCETT (1940)
1 1st & Origin: Bulletman. 400.00 1500.00
2 Bulletman. 230.00 750.00
3 Bulletman. 155.00 500.00
4-7 Bulletman. 115.00 370.00
8 World's Fair issue (no Bulletman). ... 95.00 310.00

NIGHT BEFORE CHRISTMASK, THE
DARK HORSE (1994)
HC 2.50 9.95

NIGHT FORCE, THE
DC (1982-1983)
1-14 .... .20 .50

NIGHT GLIDER
TOPPS (1993)
1 Polybagged with card. .... .75 2.95

NIGHT MAN, THE
MALIBU (1993-CURRENT)
1 1st: Night Man, Deathmask. With #0 coupon. 1.00 3.00
1A Silver foil cover. 1.75 6.00
2 .... .75 2.25
3-15 .... .50 1.95
16 .... 1.00 3.50
17-23 .... .75 2.50
ANNUAL 1 .... 1.00 3.95

NIGHT NURSE
MARVEL (1972-1973)
1 .... 2.25 8.00
2-4 .... 1.75 6.00

NIGHT OF MYSTERY
AVON (1953)
NO# 55.00 175.00

NIGHT OF THE GRIZZLY
DELL (1966)
12-558-612 Movie photo cover. 8.00 25.00

NEW MUTANTS ANNUAL #2

THE NEW SHADOWHAWK #2

THE NEW WARRIORS #10

NEXUS #69

a
b
c
d
e
f
g
h
i
j
k
l
m
n
o
p
q
r
s
t
u
v
w
x
y
z

NIGHTSTALKERS #5

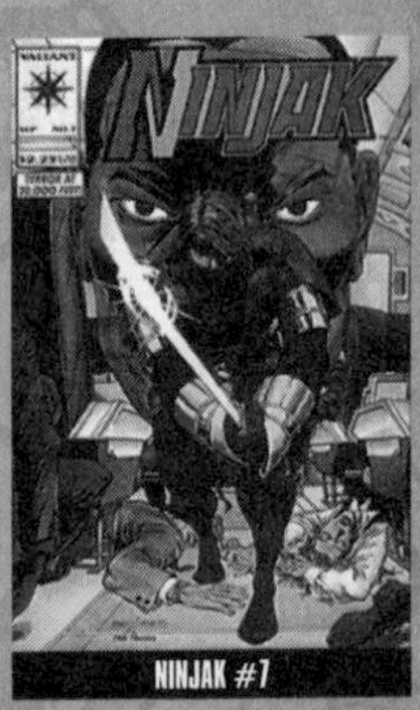

NINJAK #7

NOCTURNE #1

NONE BUT THE BRAVE #12-565-506

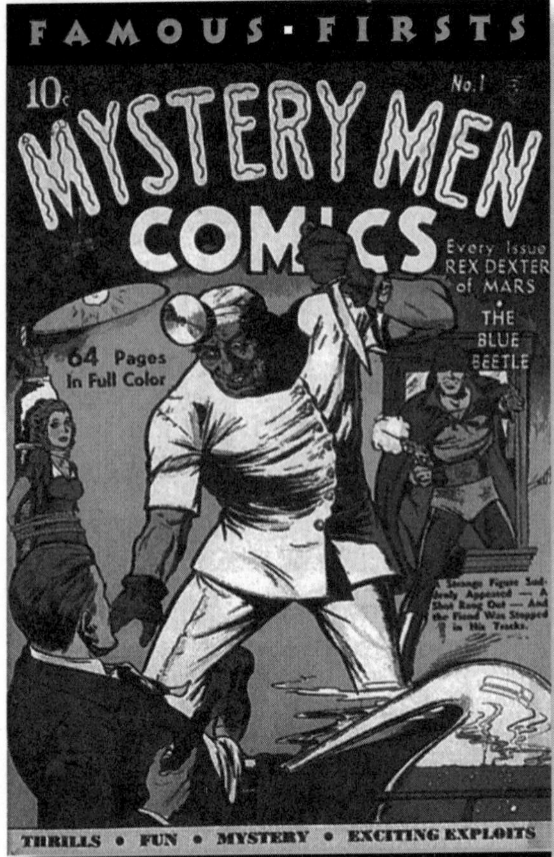

MYSTERY MEN COMICS #1

The Blue Beetle, who enjoyed long careers at Charlton and DC, makes his debut here and becomes the primary cover feature with issue #6. That guy coming in the window is the Green Mask, who didn't fare as well.

NIGHT RIDER
MARVEL (1974-1975)
1 Reprints Marvel's western Ghost Rider series. .75 2.00
2-6 .30 1.00

NIGHT THRASHER
MARVEL (1993-1995)
1 Embossed holo-graphix foil cover. .75 2.95
2-9 .50 1.75
10-21 .50 1.95

NIGHT THRASHER: FOUR CONTROL
MARVEL (1992-1993)
1-4 .75 2.00

NIGHT VISION
REBEL (1992)
1-3 1.00 3.00

NIGHTBREED
MARVEL (1990-1993)
1 1.00 3.50
2 1.00 3.00
3-6 .75 2.50
7-23 .75 2.25
24 .75 2.50
TPB Reprints #1-4. 2.50 9.95

NIGHTCAT
MARVEL (1992)
1 .75 2.00

NIGHTCRAWLER
MARVEL (1985-1986)
1 1.25 4.00
2 .75 2.00
3 Alternate X-Men. .75 2.00
4 .75 2.00

NIGHTCRY
CRY FOR DAWN (1993)
1 Horror anthology. 1.25 4.95

NIGHTMARE
SKYWALD (1970-1975) MAGAZINE
1 4.00 12.00
2-23 1.50 5.00
ANNUAL (1972) 1.50 5.00
SPECIAL (Winter/73) 1.50 5.00

NIGHTMARE
ST. JOHN (1953-1954)
10 Cover: Joe Kubert. Previous title: Weird Horrors. 65.00 210.00
11 45.00 140.00
12 Cover: Joe Kubert. 40.00 120.00
13 Title changes to Amazing Ghost Stories with #14. 29.00 95.00

NIGHTMARE
ZIFF-DAVIS (1952)
1 65.00 210.00
2 55.00 180.00
3 45.00 140.00

NIGHTMARE AND CASPER
HARVEY (1963-1964)
1 10.00 30.00
2-5 4.00 12.00

NIGHTMARK
ALPHA (1994)
1 Blood & Honor. .75 2.50
SPECIAL 1 .75 2.50

NIGHTSTALKERS
MARVEL (1992-1994)
1 .75 2.00
2-18 .50 1.50

NIGHTVENGER
AXIS (1994)
1-2 .50 1.95

NIGHTWATCH
MARVEL (1994)
1 Spider-Man. Prismatic foil cover. .75 2.50
1A Newsstand edition. .50 1.25
2-7 .50 1.50

NIGHTWING
DC (1995-CURRENT)
1-2 .75 2.25

NIGHTWING: ALFRED'S RETURN
DC (1995)
1 1.00 3.50

NIKKI, WILD DOG OF THE NORTH
DELL FOUR COLOR SERIES (1961)
1226 Movie photo cover. (9/61) 10.00 30.00

NIKKI, WILD DOG OF THE NORTH
GOLD KEY (1964)
10141-412 Disney movie tie-in. 5.00 15.00

NINA'S NEW AND IMPROVED ALL-TIME GREATEST COLLECTOR'S ITEM CLASSICS
DARK HORSE (1994)
1 .75 2.50

NINJAK
VALIANT (1994-CURRENT)
00 (4/95) .75 2.50
1 Chromium cover. 1.25 4.00
1A Gold edition. 2.00 7.00
2 1.00 3.00
3-13 .75 2.00
14-28 .75 2.50
YEARBOOK 1 1.00 3.95

NINTENDO COMICS SYSTEM
VALIANT (1990-1991)
1-2 .75 2.00

NO ESCAPE
MARVEL (1994)
1 Movie adaptation. .50 1.50
2-3 .50 1.50

NO SLEEP 'TIL DAWN
DELL FOUR COLOR SERIES (1957)
831 Movie photo cover. (9/57) 16.00 50.00

NO TIME FOR SERGEANTS
DELL (1965)
1 TV photo covers on all issues. 10.00 30.00
2-3 7.00 20.00

NO TIME FOR SERGEANTS
DELL FOUR COLOR SERIES (1958)
914 Movie photo cover (Andy Griffith). (7/58) 22.00 70.00

NOCTURNALS, THE
MALIBU (1995)
1 .75 2.95
1A Newsstand edition (different cover). .75 2.95
2-6 .75 2.95

NOCTURNE
MARVEL (1995-CURRENT)
1-4 .50 1.50

NOMAD
MARVEL (1990-1991)
1-2 1.00 3.00
3 .75 2.00
4 .50 1.75

NOMAD
MARVEL (1992-1994)
1-25 .50 1.50

NOMAN
TOWER (1966-1967)
1 14.00 44.00
2 9.00 27.00

NONE BUT THE BRAVE
DELL (1965)
12-565-506 Movie tie-in (Frank Sinatra). 13.00 40.00

NOODNIK COMICS
COMIC MEDIA (1953-1954)
1 (3-D) With glasses. 50.00 160.00
2-5 9.00 27.00

NORMALMAN
AV/RENEGADE (1984-1985)
1 2.75 10.00
2-5 1.50 5.00
6-12 1.00 3.00
ANNUAL 1 (1986) 1.50 5.00

NORMALMAN/MEGATON MAN SPECIAL
IMAGE (1994)
NO# 1st: Gareb Shamus. .75 2.50

NORTH TO ALASKA
DELL FOUR COLOR SERIES (1960)
1155 Movie photo cover (John Wayne). (12/60) 40.00 125.00

NORTHSTAR
MARVEL (1994)
1-4 .50 1.50

NORTHSTAR PRESENTS: JAMES O'BARR
NORTHSTAR (1994)
NO# .75 2.50
NO# (GOLD) 1.25 4.95

NORTHSTAR PRESENTS: JAMES O'BARR
NORTHSTAR (1994)
1 .75 2.50
1 (GOLD) Limited. 1.25 4.95

NORTHWEST MOUNTIES
ST. JOHN (1948-1949)
1 40.00 130.00
2 35.00 110.00
3-12 26.00 85.00

NORTHWEST MOUNTIES
ST. JOHN (1954)
12 Cover: Matt Baker. From Approved Comics series. 13.00 40.00

NOT BRAND ECHH
MARVEL (1967-1969)
1 8.00 25.00
2 5.00 16.00
3 4.00 12.00
4 X-Men spoof. 5.00 16.00
5-8 4.00 12.00
9-13 Double size giant. 5.00 15.00

NOVA
MARVEL (1976-1979)
1 1st & Origin: Nova. 5.00 15.00
2 2.25 8.00
3 1.75 6.00
4-5 1.50 5.00
6 1st: Sphinx. 1.50 5.00
7-10 1.50 5.00
11 1.25 4.00
12 Spider-Man. 1.25 4.00
13-25 1.25 4.00

NOVA
MARVEL (1994-1995)
1 Gold cover. .75 2.50
1A Regular cover. .50 1.50
2-18 .50 1.50

NTH MAN
MARVEL (1989-1990)
1-7 .30 1.00
8 1st Dale Keown art for Marvel. 1.50 5.00
9-16 .30 1.00

NUCLEUS
HERO (1979)
1 App: Cerebus. 10.00 30.00

NUKLA
DELL (1965-1966)
1 1st & Origin: Nukla. 8.00 25.00
2 5.00 15.00
3 2.75 10.00
4 Art: Steve Ditko. (9/66) 8.00 25.00

NURSERY RHYMES
ZIFF-DAVIS (1951)
1 (#10 on cover) 20.00 66.00
2 14.00 44.00

NUTS!
PREMIERE (1954)
1 31.00 100.00
2-5 25.00 80.00

NUTS AND JOLTS
SEE LARGE FEATURE COMICS #22.

-

NUTSY SQUIRREL
DC (1954-1957)
61 Previous title: Hollywood Funny Folks. 20.00 66.00
62-64 17.00 55.00
65-72 14.00 44.00

NUTTY COMICS
FAWCETT (1946)
1 23.00 75.00

NUTTY COMICS
HARVEY (1945-1947)
NO# 10.00 30.00
2 8.00 25.00
3-4 7.00 20.00
5-8 5.00 15.00

NUTTY LIFE
FOX (1946)
2 Previous title: Krazy Life Hilarious Comics. 13.00 40.00

NYOKA THE JUNGLE GIRL
CHARLTON (1955-1957)
14 Previous title: Zoo Funnies. 11.00 35.00
15-22 11.00 35.00

NYOKA THE JUNGLE GIRL
FAWCETT (1945-1953)
2 Previous title: Jungle Girl. 100.00 330.00
3 50.00 160.00
4-5 40.00 130.00
6-12 35.00 110.00
13-24 26.00 85.00
25 Movie photo cover. 20.00 65.00
26-29 20.00 65.00
30 Begin: Movie photo covers. 20.00 65.00
31-36 15.00 49.00
37-50 12.00 38.00
51-60 9.00 27.00
61-69 7.00 22.00
70 End: Movie photo covers. 7.00 22.00
71-77 7.00 22.00

OAKY DOAKS
EASTERN (1942)
1 31.00 100.00

OBNOXIO THE CLOWN
MARVEL (1983)
1 ...Vs. The X-Men. .30 1.00

OCCULT FILES OF DR. SPEKTOR, THE
GOLD KEY (1973-1982)
1 2.75 10.00
2-6 1.50 5.00
7-13 .75 2.00
14 App: Dr. Solar. 1.75 6.00
15-25 .75 2.00

ODELL'S ADVENTURES IN 3-D
SEE ADVENTURES IN 3-D.

-

OFFICER OUTBODY
MARVEL (1993)
1-5 .50 1.95

OFFICIAL HANDBOOK OF THE MARVEL UNIVERSE, THE
MARVEL (1983-1984)
1 1.50 5.00
2 1.00 3.00
3-15 .75 2.50

OFFICIAL HANDBOOK OF THE MARVEL UNIVERSE
MARVEL (1985-1988)
1 1.00 3.50
2-20 .50 1.50

OFFICIAL HANDBOOK OF THE MARVEL UNIVERSE, THE
MARVEL (1989-1990)
1-8 .50 1.50

OFFICIAL HAWKMAN INDEX, THE
ICG (1986)
1-2 .30 1.00

OFFICIAL INDEX TO THE AVENGERS
MARVEL (1994-1995)
1 Indexes #1-60. .50 1.95
2 Indexes #61-122. .50 1.95
3 Indexes #123-180. .50 1.95
4 Indexes #181-240. .50 1.95
5 Indexes #241-299. .50 1.95
6 Indexes #300-360. .50 1.95

OFFICIAL INDEX TO THE X-MEN
MARVEL
1 Indexes Uncanny #1-15 . .50 1.95
2 .50 1.95
3 Indexes Uncanny #123-180. .50 1.95

OFFICIAL JUSTICE LEAGUE OF AMERICA INDEX, THE
ECLIPSE (1986-1987)
1-8 .30 1.00

OFFICIAL LEGION OF SUPER-HEROES INDEX, THE
ECLIPSE (1986-1987)
1-5 .30 1.00

OFFICIAL MARVEL INDEX TO MARVEL TEAM-UP
MARVEL (1986)
1-6 .30 1.00

OFFICIAL MARVEL INDEX TO THE AMAZING SPIDER-MAN
MARVEL (1985)
1-9 .75 2.00

OFFICIAL MARVEL INDEX TO THE AVENGERS, THE
MARVEL (1987-1988)
1-7 .30 1.00

OFFICIAL MARVEL INDEX TO THE FANTASTIC FOUR
MARVEL (1985-1986)
1-5 .30 1.00

OFFICIAL MARVEL INDEX TO THE X-MEN, THE
MARVEL (1987-1988)
1-8 .30 1.00

OFFICIAL ROY ROGERS RIDERS CLUB COMICS
DELL (1952)
NO# Scarce comic given away to members of the Riders Club. 65.00 200.00

OFFICIAL TEEN TITANS INDEX, THE
ECLIPSE (1985-1986)
1-5 .30 1.00

O.G. WHIZ
GOLD KEY (1971-1979)
1 13.00 40.00
2 12.00 38.00
3 7.00 20.00

OH MY GODDESS!
DARK HORSE (1994-1995)
1-3 1.00 3.00
4-6 .75 2.50

OH MY GODDESS! PART 2
DARK HORSE (1995)
1-5 .75 2.50

OH! SUSANNA
DELL FOUR COLOR SERIES (1960)
1105 TV photo cover (Gale Storm). (6/60) 16.00 50.00

OK COMICS
ACE (1940)
1 100.00 330.00
2 Origin: Mister Mist. 100.00 330.00

OKAY COMICS
UNITED FEATURES (1940)
1 The Captain And The Kids. 64 pages. 50.00 150.00

OKLAHOMAN, THE
DELL FOUR COLOR SERIES (1957)
820 Movie photo cover. (6/57) 20.00 65.00

OKTANE
DARK HORSE (1995)
1-4 .75 2.50

THE OFFICIAL HAWKMAN INDEX #2

OFFICIAL INDEX TO THE X-MEN #1

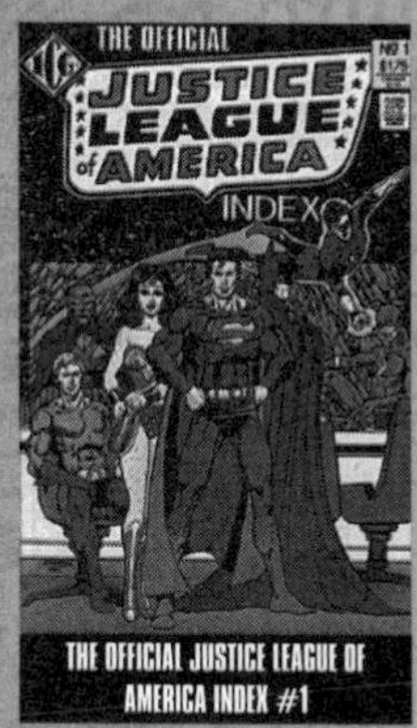

THE OFFICIAL JUSTICE LEAGUE OF AMERICA INDEX #1

OH MY GODDESS #4

THE OMEGA MEN #1

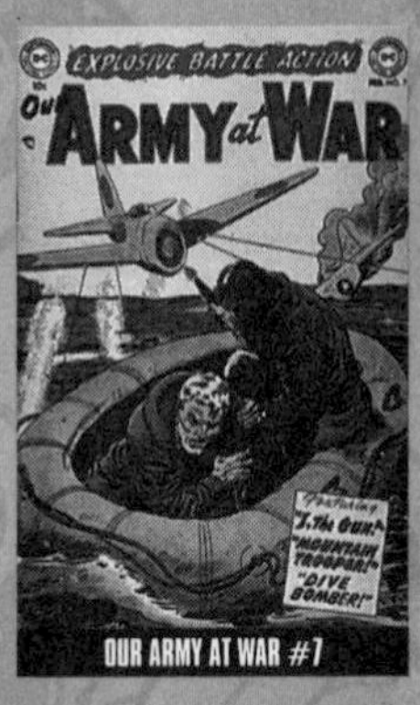
OUR ARMY AT WAR #7

OUR ARMY AT WAR #153

OUR GANG COMICS #4

OLD IRONSIDES
DELL FOUR COLOR SERIES (1958)
874 Movie tie-in. (1/58) 16.00 50.00

OLD YELLER
DELL FOUR COLOR SERIES (1958)
869 Disney movie photo cover. (1/58) 17.00 55.00

OLD YELLER
GOLD KEY (1966)
10168-601 Disney movie photo cover. 7.00 20.00

OMAC
DC (1974-1975)
1 Origin: Omac by Jack Kirby. 1.75 6.00
2 Jack Kirby art in all issues. 1.25 4.00
3-8 .... 1.00 3.00

OMAC: ONE MAN ARMY CORPS
DC (1991)
1 Cover/Art: John Byrne in all issues. ... 1.25 4.00
2-4 .... 1.25 4.00

OMAHA THE CAT DANCER
KITCHEN SINK (1986-CURRENT)
0 Reprints: Bizarre Sex #9. (11/93) 1.25 4.00
1 .... 2.50 9.00
2 .... 1.50 5.00
3-6 .... 1.00 3.25
7-11 .... .75 2.75
12-17 .... .75 2.50
18-21 .... .75 2.95

OMAHA THE CAT DANCER
STEEL DRAGON (1984)
1 .... 1.75 6.00
2 .... 1.50 5.00

OMEGA
NORTH STAR (1988)
1 Reprints Rebel Studios version. 8.00 25.00
2 .... .75 2.00

OMEGA
REBEL (1987)
1 Art: Tim Vigil. 22.00 70.00

OMEGA MEN, THE
DC (1982-1986)
1 .... .75 2.00
2 .... .50 1.50
3 1st: Lobo (cameo). 2.75 10.00
4 .... .50 1.50
5 2nd app: Lobo. 1.50 5.00
6-8 .... .50 1.25
9 3rd: Lobo. 1.00 3.00
10 1st full Lobo story. 2.00 7.00
11-18 .... .50 1.25
19 Lobo (cameo). 1.50 5.00
20 Origin: Lobo. 1.50 5.00
21-30 .... .50 1.25
31 Crisis. .... .50 1.25
32-36 .... .50 1.25
37 Lobo. 2.00 7.00
38 .... .50 1.75
ANNUAL 1 (1984) .... .50 1.75
ANNUAL 2 (1985) .... .50 1.50

OMEGA THE UNKNOWN
MARVEL (1976-1977)
1 1st: Omega. 1.50 5.00
2 .... .75 2.50
3-7 .... .75 2.00
8 1st: new Foolkiller (Greg Salinger). ... 1.50 5.00
9 1st: full app. new Foolkiller. 2.00 7.00
10 .... .75 2.00

OMEN
NORTHSTAR (1989)
1 Cover/Art: Tim Vigil in all issues. ... 5.00 15.00
1 (2ND) 2nd printing. 1.00 3.00
2 .... 2.75 10.00
3 .... 1.75 6.00

OMNI COMIX
PENTHOUSE (1995-CURRENT)
1 Included with Omni magazine. 1.00 3.50
2 .... 1.00 3.95

ON STAGE
DELL FOUR COLOR SERIES (1962)
1336 (4/62) 10.00 30.00

ON THE DOUBLE
DELL FOUR COLOR SERIES (1961)
1232 Movie tie-in. 13.00 40.00

ON THE SPOT
FAWCETT (1948)
NO# Photo insert cover of Pretty Boy Floyd.
.... 50.00 160.00

ONE HUNDRED AND ONE DALMATIANS
DELL FOUR COLOR SERIES (1961)
1183 Disney movie tie-in. (2/61) ... 19.00 60.00

ONE HUNDRED AND ONE DALMATIANS
GOLD KEY (1970)
10247-002 Disney movie tie-in. 7.00 20.00

ONE MILLION YEARS AGO
ST. JOHN (1953)
1 1st & Origin: Tor. Title changes to 3-D Comi cs with #2.
.... 25.00 80.00

OPERATION BIKINI
DELL (1963)
12-597-310 Movie photo cover. 7.00 20.00

OPERATION CROSSBOW
DELL (1965)
12-590-512 Movie tie-in. 7.00 20.00

OPERATION KNIGHTSTRIKE
IMAGE (1995-CURRENT)
1-3 .... .75 2.50

OPERATION PERIL
ACG (1950-1953)
1 .... 35.00 110.00
2 .... 17.00 55.00
3-6 .... 14.00 44.00
7-16 .... 10.00 33.00

OPERATION SURVIVAL
GIS (1957)
NO# Civil Defense giveaway. Li'l Abner on cover only.
.... 7.00 20.00

OPTIC NERVE
ADRIAN TOMINE (1990)
1 Photocopy mini-comics. 5.00 15.00
2-5 .... 5.00 15.00
6 .... 1.50 5.00
7 .... .75 2.00

OPTIC NERVE
DRAWN & QUARTERLY (1995-CURRENT)
1 .... 1.25 4.00

ORIGINAL GHOST RIDER, THE
MARVEL (1992-1993)
1 Reprint: Marvel Spotlight #5. .... .50 1.75
2 Reprint: Marvel Spotlight #6. .... .50 1.75
3-21 .... .50 1.75

ORIGINAL GHOST RIDER RIDES AGAIN, THE
MARVEL (1991-1992)
1 Reprints: Ghost Rider #68-69. All issues are reprints.
.... .75 2.25
2 .... .50 1.75
3-7 .... .50 1.50

OSCAR COMICS
MARVEL (1947-1949)
1 (#24) 16.00 50.00
2 (#25) Art: Basil Wolverton (minor). 13.00 40.00
3-9 .... 10.00 30.00
10 title changes to Awful Oscar with #11. 10.00 30.00

OSWALD THE RABBIT
DELL FOUR COLOR SERIES (1943-1961)
21 .... 80.00 250.00
39 .... 55.00 175.00
67 (4/45) 40.00 125.00
102 (4/46) 31.00 100.00
143 "And The Prehistoric Egg" (4/47) 16.00 50.00
183 (3/48) 16.00 50.00
225 (4/49) 11.00 35.00
273 (4/50) 10.00 30.00
315 (2/51) 8.00 25.00
388 (4/52) 7.00 20.00
458 "Full Moon Ahead" (4/53) 5.00 15.00
507 (10/53) 5.00 15.00
549 (4/54) 7.00 20.00
593 (10/54) 5.00 15.00
623 (4/55) 5.00 15.00
697 (4/56) 5.00 15.00
792 (4/57) 5.00 15.00
894 (4/58) 5.00 15.00
979 (4/59) 5.00 15.00
1268 (11/61) 7.00 20.00

OTHERS, THE
IMAGE (1995-CURRENT)
0 Reprints (3/95) .... .30 1.00
1-4 .... .75 2.50

OUR ARMY AT WAR
DC (1952-1977)
1 .... 280.00 900.00
2 .... 125.00 400.00
3 .... 95.00 300.00
4 Art: Al Krigstein. 80.00 250.00
5-6 .... 80.00 250.00
7-12 .... 55.00 175.00
13 Art: Al Krigstein. 65.00 200.00
14-24 .... 40.00 125.00
25-31 .... 31.00 100.00
32 1st Code Approved issue. 31.00 100.00
33-36 .... 26.00 85.00
37-50 .... 23.00 75.00
51-60 .... 22.00 70.00
61-72 .... 19.00 60.00
73-80 .... 16.00 50.00
81 1st: Sgt. Rock. "The Rock Of Easy Co.!"
.... 400.00 1300.00
82 App: Sgt. Rock (cameo). 100.00 325.00
83 Art: Joe Kubert. Sgt. Rock. 130.00 425.00
84 .... 50.00 160.00
85 1st & Origin: Ice Cream Soldier. ... 55.00 170.00
86-90 .... 50.00 155.00
91 1st: all Sgt. Rock issue. 115.00 380.00
92-94 .... 31.00 100.00
95 1st: Bulldozer. 31.00 100.00
96 .... 31.00 100.00
97-108 .... 23.00 75.00
109-127 .... 14.00 45.00
128 Origin: Sgt. Rock. 45.00 135.00
129-139 .... 10.00 30.00
140 All Sgt. Rock. 8.00 25.00
141-150 .... 7.00 20.00
151 1st: Enemy Ace. 50.00 150.00
152 .... 5.00 15.00
153 2nd: Enemy Ace. 20.00 65.00
154 .... 5.00 15.00
155 Enemy Ace. 10.00 30.00
156-157 .... 5.00 15.00
158 1st & Origin: Iron Major. 8.00 25.00
159-163 .... 5.00 15.00
164 80 page Giant #G-19. .... 11.00 35.00
165-176 .... 5.00 15.00
177 80 page Giant #G-32. .... 10.00 30.00
178-181 .... 4.00 12.00
182-183 .... 7.00 20.00
184-185 .... 4.00 12.00
186 .... 7.00 20.00
187-189 .... 4.00 11.00
190 80 page Giant #G-44. .... 7.00 20.00
191-199 .... 2.75 10.00
200 .... 4.00 12.00
201 .... 2.00 7.00
202 .... .75 2.00
203 80 page Giant #G-56. .... 5.00 15.00
204-205 No Sgt. Rock. .... .75 2.00
206-215 .... .75 2.00
216 80 page Giant #G-68. .... 2.75 10.00
217-228 .... 1.50 5.00
229 80 page Giant #G-80. .... 2.75 10.00
230-239 .... 1.50 5.00
240 Art: Neal Adams. 2.25 8.00
241 .... 1.75 6.00
242 DC 100 Page Super Spectacular #9. 1.75 6.00
243-260 .... 1.50 5.00
261-279 .... 1.25 4.50
280 200th Anniversary issue. 1.25 4.50
281-300 .... 1.25 4.50
301 Title changes to Sgt. Rock with #302. 1.25 4.50

OUR FIGHTING FORCES
DC (1954-1978)
1 .... 160.00 525.00
2 .... 80.00 250.00
3 .... 70.00 220.00
4 1st Code Approved issue. 55.00 180.00
5-6 .... 50.00 155.00
7-9 .... 40.00 130.00
10 Art: Wallace Wood. 45.00 140.00
11-12 .... 35.00 105.00
13-18 .... 29.00 95.00
19-24 .... 25.00 80.00
25-30 .... 20.00 65.00
31-40 .... 17.00 55.00
41 Unknown Soldier prototype. 26.00 85.00
42-44 .... 17.00 55.00
45 1st: Gunner & Sarge. 55.00 180.00
46 .... 35.00 105.00
47-50 .... 19.00 60.00
51-56 .... 10.00 30.00
57-62 .... 8.00 25.00
63-64 .... 7.00 20.00

65 1st 12 cent cover price. 5.00 15.00
66-75 2.75 10.00
76-80 2.25 8.00
81-90 2.00 7.00
91-93 1.25 4.00
94 End: Gunner & Sarge. 1.25 4.00
95-122 1.25 4.00
123 Begin: The Losers. 1.25 4.00
124-128 1.25 4.00
129-181 1.00 3.00

OUR FLAG COMICS
ACE (1941-1942)
1 Begin: Captain Victory. 300.00 1100.00
2 1st & Origin: The Flag. 200.00 650.00
3-5 150.00 490.00

OUR GANG COMICS
DELL (1942-1949)
1 140.00 450.00
2 65.00 200.00
3-5 40.00 125.00
6 50.00 150.00
7 31.00 100.00
8 Begin: Benny Burro by Carl Barks. 65.00 200.00
9-10 50.00 150.00
11-12 31.00 100.00
13-18 25.00 80.00
19-35 19.00 60.00
36 End: Carl Barks art. 19.00 60.00
37-40 16.00 50.00
41-50 13.00 40.00
51-59 10.00 30.00

OUR LADY OF FATIMA
CATECHETICAL GUILD (1955)
395 Giveaway. 8.00 25.00

OUR LOVE STORY
MARVEL (1969-1976)
1 2.75 10.00
2 1.00 3.00
3-4 .75 2.00
5 Art: Jim Steranko. 2.75 10.00
6-13 .50 1.50
14-38 .30 1.00

OUR MISS BROOKS
DELL FOUR COLOR SERIES (1956)
751 TV photo cover. (11/56) 16.00 50.00

OUT OF THE NIGHT
ACG (1952-1954)
1 Art: Al Williamson. 85.00 270.00
2 Art: Al Williamson. 60.00 190.00
3 35.00 110.00
4 Art: Al Williamson. 60.00 190.00
5-12 26.00 85.00
13-16 20.00 65.00
17 Title changes to The Hooded Horseman with #18. 20.00 65.00

OUT OF THE SHADOWS
STANDARD (1952-1954)
5 55.00 180.00
6 40.00 120.00
7-9 29.00 95.00
10-14 22.00 70.00

OUT OF THE VORTEX
DARK HORSE (1993-1994)
1 1.25 4.00
2-11 .75 2.00
12 .75 2.50

OUT OF THIS WORLD
AVON (1950)
1 One-shot, 130 pg. pulp magazine with 32 page color comic insert. "Lunar Station" & "Man Eating Lizards" by Kubert, "Crom The Barbarian" by Giunta. 50.00 150.00

OUT OF THIS WORLD
CHARLTON (1956-1959)
1 40.00 120.00
2 19.00 60.00
3-6 Art: Steve Ditko. 40.00 120.00
7 Cover/Art: Steve Ditko. 55.00 180.00
8-12 Art: Steve Ditko. 40.00 120.00
13-15 11.00 36.00
16 Art: Steve Ditko. 40.00 120.00

OUT OUR WAY WITH WORRY WART
DELL FOUR COLOR SERIES (1956)
680 (2/56) 7.00 20.00

OUTER LIMITS, THE
DELL (1964-1969)
1 TV tie-in. 13.00 40.00
2 7.00 20.00
3-6 5.00 15.00
7-12 2.75 10.00
13-18 1.75 6.00

OUTER SPACE
CHARLTON (1958-1968)
17 Previous title: This Magazine Is Haunted (2nd series). 19.00 60.00
18-20 Art: Steve Ditko. 22.00 70.00
21-24 15.00 48.00
25 (12/59) 15.00 48.00

OUTER SPACE
CHARLTON (1968)
V2#1 Art: Steve Ditko. 10.00 30.00

OUTLANDERS
DARK HORSE (1988-1992)
1-33 .75 2.00

OUTLAW FIGHTERS
MARVEL(ATLAS) (1954-1955)
1 16.00 50.00
2-5 10.00 30.00

OUTLAW KID, THE
MARVEL (1970-1975)
1 1.50 5.00
2 1.25 4.00
3-6 .75 2.00
7-12 .50 1.50
13-30 .30 1.00

OUTLAW KID, THE
MARVEL(ATLAS) (1954-1957)
1 Origin: The Outlaw Kid. 40.00 120.00
2 19.00 60.00
3-6 13.00 40.00
7-12 10.00 30.00
13-19 7.00 20.00

OUTLAWS
DS (1948-1949)
1 40.00 125.00
2 31.00 100.00
3 19.00 60.00
4-8 13.00 40.00
9 Art: Frank Frazetta (7 pages). 70.00 220.00

OUTLAWS
STAR (1952-1954)
10 Cover: L. B. Cole (all issues). Previous title: Western Crime Cases. 10.00 30.00
11-14 7.00 20.00

OUTLAWS OF THE WEST
CHARLTON (1957-1980)
11 Previous title: Cody Of The Pony Express (2nd series). 10.00 30.00
12 7.00 20.00
13-17 5.00 15.00
18 Art: Steve Ditko. 23.00 75.00
19-30 2.75 10.00
31-60 1.75 6.00
61-88 1.00 3.00

OUTLAWS OF THE WILD WEST
AVON (1952)
1 128 page Giant. 31.00 100.00

OUTSIDERS, THE
DC (1985-1988)
1-28 .50 1.50
ANNUAL 1 (1986) .75 2.00
SPECIAL 1 .50 1.50

OUTSIDERS, THE
DC (1993-CURRENT)
0 .50 1.95
1-ALPHA 1st Technocrat, Faust. .50 1.75
1-OMEGA Death: Looker. .50 1.75
2-9 .50 1.75
10-18 .50 1.95
19-23 .75 2.25

OXYDOL-DREFT GIVEAWAY
OXYDOL-DREFT (1950)
1 Li'l Abner in "The Mystery Of The Cave!" 19.00 60.00
2 Daisy Mae in "Ham Sangwidges", also "Cousin Weakeyes". 19.00 60.00
3 Shmoo in "Washable Jones Travels". 19.00 60.00
4 John Wayne The Cowboy Trouble Shooter. 31.00 100.00
5 Archie In "Mask Me No Questions". 19.00 60.00
6 Paul Terry's Terry-Toon Comics starring Mighty Mouse. 19.00 60.00

OZ
CALIBER PRESS (1994-CURRENT)
1-2 1.50 5.00
3-7 .75 2.95

OZARK IKE
DELL FOUR COLOR SERIES (1948)
180 (2/48) 16.00 50.00

OZARK IKE
STANDARD (1948-1952)
11-25 7.00 20.00

PACIFIC PRESENTS
PACIFIC (1982-1984)
1 The Rocketeer by Dave Stevens. 1.75 6.00
2 "The Rocketeer, Chapter 4" by Dave Stevens. "The Missing Man Meets The Payne Family" by Steve Ditko. 1.25 4.00
3-4 .75 2.00

PACT, THE
IMAGE (1994)
1-3 .50 1.95

PAGEANT OF COMICS
ST. JOHN (1947)
1 Mopsy. 10.00 30.00
2 Jane Arden. 7.00 20.00

PALOOKA-VILLE
DRAWN & QUARTERLY (1991-CURRENT)
1 1.50 5.00
1 (2ND) 2nd printing. .75 2.95
2 1.25 4.00
2 (2ND) 2nd printing. .75 2.95
3-7 .75 2.95

PANCHO VILLA
AVON (1950)
NO# 25.00 80.00

PANIC
EC (1954-1956)
1 35.00 110.00
2 17.00 55.00
3-4 14.00 44.00
5-8 10.00 33.00
9 1st Code Approved issue. 9.00 27.00
10-11 7.00 22.00
12 Low distribution. 35.00 110.00

PARADOX
DARK VISIONS (1994)
1-2 .75 2.95

PARAMOUNT ANIMATED COMICS
HARVEY (1953-1956)
1 Begin: Baby Huey. 25.00 80.00
2 13.00 40.00
3-6 10.00 30.00
7 Begin: Baby Huey covers. 16.00 50.00
8-22 8.00 25.00

PARENT TRAP, THE
DELL FOUR COLOR SERIES (1961)
1210 Disney movie photo cover. (8/61) 16.00 50.00

PAROLE BREAKERS
AVON (1951-1952)
1 50.00 165.00
2 35.00 110.00
3 27.00 88.00

PARTRIDGE FAMILY, THE
CHARLTON (1971-1973)
1 TV tie-in. 6.00 18.00
2-4 4.00 12.00
5 Summer special. 8.00 24.00
6-21 2.50 9.50

PAT BOONE
DC (1959-1960)
1 TV tie-in & photo covers on all issues. "Pat Tells His Story!" 70.00 220.00
2 "Pat Meets Shirley!" (12/59) 50.00 160.00
3 "The Golden Years" (2/60) 40.00 130.00
4 (4/60) 40.00 130.00
5 "Fashions Ala Francaise" (6/60) 40.00 130.00

PAT THE BRAT
ARCHIE (1955-1959)
1 13.00 42.00
2-3 10.00 30.00
4 (#5-14 do not exist) 10.00 30.00
15-32 5.00 15.00
33 Title changes to The Adventures Of Pipsqueak with #34. 5.00 15.00

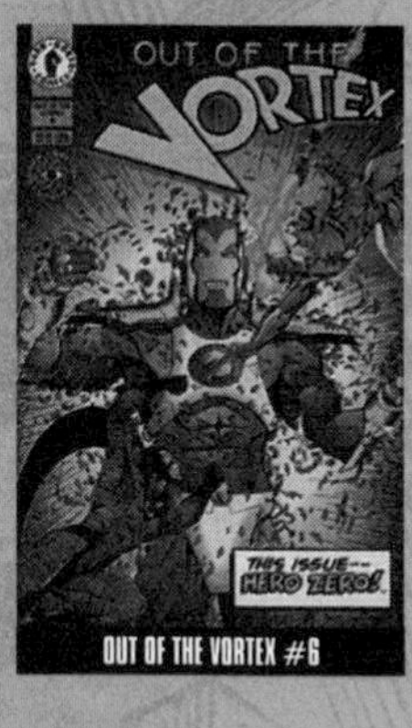

OUT OF THE VORTEX #6

THE OUTSIDERS #3 (2ND SERIES)

THE PACT #1

PARAMOUNT ANIMATED COMICS #4

PATCHES #5

PATSY WALKER #4

PENTHOUSE COMIX #7

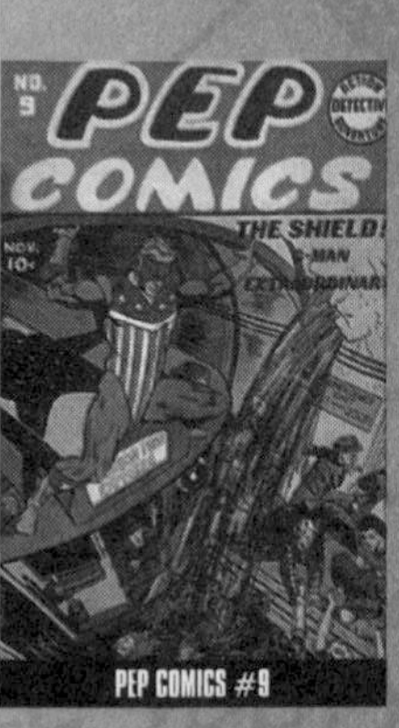

PEP COMICS #9

FAMOUS · FIRSTS

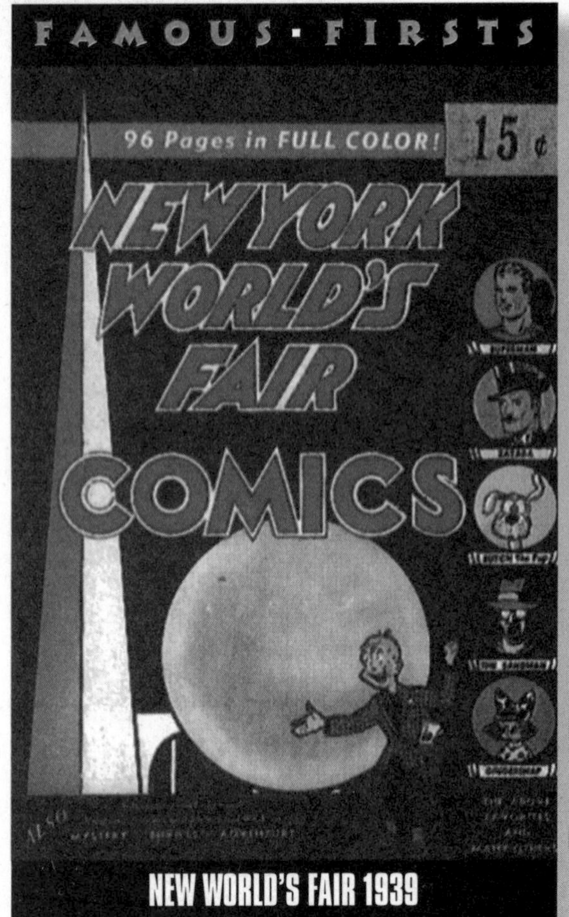

96 Pages in FULL COLOR!
15¢
NEW YORK WORLD'S FAIR
COMICS

NEW WORLD'S FAIR 1939

This comic offers two firsts: It's the first event-oriented book, tying into the World's Fair (a different edition appeared in 1940). It also debuted the Golden Age Sandman, appearing just before *Adventure Comics* #40.

PATCHES
RURAL HOME (1945-1947)

1 Cover: L.B. Cole. 28.00 90.00
2-4 .... 16.00 50.00
5 Danny Kaye cover & story. 16.00 50.00
6 .... 16.00 50.00
7 Hopalong Cassidy cover & story. 16.00 50.00
8 Smiley Burnette cover & story. 16.00 50.00
9-10 .... 16.00 50.00
11 Red Skelton cover & story. 16.00 50.00

PATSY AND HEDY
MARVEL(ATLAS) (1952-1967)

1 .... 17.00 55.00
2 .... 10.00 33.00
3-6 .... 9.00 27.00
7-12 .... 7.00 22.00
13-30 .... 5.00 16.00
31-60 .... 4.00 11.00
61-80 .... 1.75 6.50
81-100 .... 1.25 4.25
101-110 .... .75 2.00
ANNUAL 1 .... 10.00 33.00

PATSY AND HER PALS
MARVEL(ATLAS) (1953-1957)

1 .... 25.00 80.00
2 .... 10.00 33.00
3-12 .... 7.00 22.00
13-29 .... 4.00 11.00

PATSY WALKER
MARVEL(ATLAS) (1945-1965)

1 .... 70.00 220.00
2 .... 35.00 110.00
3-6 .... 26.00 85.00
7-12 .... 20.00 65.00
13-18 .... 17.00 55.00
19-30 .... 14.00 44.00
31-50 .... 10.00 33.00
51-60 .... 7.00 22.00
61-80 .... 4.00 13.00
81-100 .... 2.25 8.75
101-124 .... 1.50 5.50

PATSY WALKER FASHION PARADE
MARVEL (1966)

1 Giant-size annual. 13.00 40.00

PATTY POWERS
MARVEL(ATLAS) (1956)

4 .... 13.00 40.00
5-7 .... 10.00 30.00

PAUL REVERE'S RIDE
DELL FOUR COLOR SERIES (1957)

822 "With Johnny Tremain" (8/57) 23.00 75.00

PAUL TERRY'S COMICS
ST. JOHN (1951-1955)

85A Same as Terry-Toons #85 (but with title change). 10.00 30.00
86A Same as Terry-Toons #86 (but with title change). 10.00 30.00
87 Previous title: Terry-Toons. 7.00 20.00
88-104 .... 7.00 20.00
105-106 100 page giant. 11.00 35.00
107-124 .... 7.00 20.00
125 Title changes to Adventures Of Mighty Mouse with #126. .... 7.00 20.00

PAWNEE BILL
STORY (1951)

1-3 .... 10.00 30.00

PEACEMAKER, THE
CHARLTON (1967)

1-5 .... 2.75 10.00

PEANUTS
DELL (1958-1962)

1 (#878) From the 4-Color Series. (2/58) 40.00 125.00
2 (#969) From the 4-Color Series. (2/59) 23.00 75.00
3 (#1015) From the 4-Color Series. (8/59) 23.00 75.00
4 .... 14.00 44.00
5-8 .... 10.00 33.00
9-13 .... 7.00 22.00

PEANUTS
GOLD KEY (1963-1964)

1 .... 10.00 33.00
2-4 .... 7.00 22.00

PEBBLES & BAMM BAMM
CHARLTON (1972-1976)

1 .... 10.00 30.00
2 .... 5.00 15.00
3-12 .... 2.25 8.00
13-20 .... 1.50 5.00
21-36 .... 1.00 3.00

PEBBLES FLINTSTONE
GOLD KEY (1963)

10088-309 .... 19.00 60.00

PEEP SHOW
DRAWN & QUARTERLY (1992-CURRENT)

1-7 .... .75 2.50

PENALTY!
ACE (1955-1956)

47 Previous title: Crime Must Pay The Penalty. 2.75 10.00
48 .... 2.75 10.00

PENDRAGON II
MARVEL (1992-1993)

1-12 .... .50 1.75
13-14 Death's Head II. .... .50 1.75
15 .... .50 1.75

PENNY
AVON (1947-1949)

1 .... 10.00 30.00
2-6 .... 5.00 15.00

PENTHOUSE COMIX
PENTHOUSE (1994-CURRENT)

1 1st: Hericane. 7.00 22.00
1 (2ND) 2nd printing (includes new material). 1.75 6.00
2 .... 5.00 15.00
3 .... 2.75 10.00
4-6 .... 1.75 6.00
6A Newsstand edition (magazine size). 1.75 6.00
7 .... 1.75 6.00
7A Newsstand edition (magazine size). 1.75 6.00

PENTHOUSE MEN'S ADVENTURE
PENTHOUSE (1995-CURRENT)

1 .... 1.25 4.95
1A Newsstand edition (magazine size). 1.25 4.95
2 .... 1.25 4.95
2A Newsstand edition (magazine size). 1.25 4.95
3-4 (Magazine size) 1.25 4.95

PEP COMICS
MLJ (1940-1987)

1 1st: The Shield, The Rocket. 1st & Origin: The Comet by Jack Cole. 1100.00 4300.00
2 Origin: The Rocket. 400.00 1200.00
3 .... 250.00 825.00
4-5 .... 220.00 700.00
6-10 .... 160.00 525.00
11 1st: Dusty (Shield's sidekick). 220.00 700.00
12 1st & Origin: Fireball. 220.00 700.00
13-15 .... 145.00 480.00
16 Origin: Madame Satan. 210.00 675.00
17 1st & Origin: Hangman. Death: The Comet. 500.00 1800.00
18-21 .... 110.00 360.00
22 1st: Archie, Betty, Jughead. (12/41) 1300.00 5000.00
23 .... 290.00 950.00
24-25 .... 220.00 700.00
26 1st: Veronica. (4/42) 290.00 950.00
27-29 .... 200.00 650.00
30 1st: Mrs. Grundy. 220.00 700.00
31 1st: Mr. Lodge. 220.00 700.00
32-35 .... 160.00 525.00
36 1st cover featuring Archie. 220.00 700.00
37-40 .... 130.00 420.00
41 Begin: Archie covers. 145.00 480.00
42-46 .... 100.00 330.00

47 End: Hangman. ... 100.00 330.00
48 Begin: Black Hood. ... 85.00 270.00
49-50 ... 75.00 240.00
51-59 ... 65.00 200.00
60 Begin: Katy Keene. ... 65.00 200.00
61 ... 45.00 140.00
62 1st: Lil Jinx. ... 45.00 140.00
63-65 ... 45.00 140.00
66-70 ... 40.00 120.00
71-80 ... 28.00 90.00
81-90 ... 22.00 70.00
91-100 ... 16.00 50.00
101-120 ... 11.00 36.00
121-140 ... 8.00 24.00
141-149 ... 6.00 18.00
150-151 ... 8.00 24.00
152 1st 12 cent cover. ... 8.00 24.00
153 ... 8.00 24.00
154 End: Katy Keene. ... 8.00 24.00
155-160 ... 8.00 24.00
161-167 ... 4.00 12.00
168 App: Jaguar. ... 6.00 18.00
169-180 ... 2.50 9.50
181-200 ... 2.00 7.00
201-220 ... 1.25 4.75
221-240 ... .75 2.25
241-275 ... .30 1.00
276-410 ... .20 .50
411 ... .20 .75

PEPE
DELL FOUR COLOR SERIES (1961)
1194 Movie photo cover. (4/61) ... 8.00 25.00

PERFECT CRIME, THE
CROSS (1949-1953)
1 Art: Bob Powell. ... 35.00 110.00
2 Art: Bob Powell. ... 20.00 65.00
3-4 Art: Bob Powell. ... 17.00 55.00
5-11 ... 17.00 55.00
12-15 ... 14.00 44.00
16-17 ... 10.00 30.00
18 "Super-Cargo" drug abuse story. ... 26.00 85.00
19-25 ... 10.00 30.00
26 Drug abuse story. ... 26.00 85.00
27-29 ... 10.00 30.00
30 Gruesome cover. ... 25.00 80.00
31-33 ... 10.00 30.00

PERFECT LOVE
ZIFF-DAVIS (1951-1953)
1 (#10) ... 16.00 50.00
2 ... 10.00 30.00
3-10 ... 7.00 20.00

PERG
LIGHTNING (1993-CURRENT)
1 Glow-in-the-dark cover. ... 1.25 4.00
2 ... 1.00 3.00
3 ... .75 2.95
4 1st: Hellina. ... .75 2.95
4A Platinum version. ... 1.75 6.00
5-7 ... 1.25 4.00
8 Hellina ... 1.25 4.00

PERRI
DELL FOUR COLOR SERIES (1957)
847 (10/57) ... 7.00 20.00

PERSONAL LOVE
FAMOUS FUNNIES (1950-1955)
1 Photo cover on all issues. ... 16.00 50.00
2 ... 8.00 25.00
3-10 ... 7.00 20.00
11-23 ... 4.00 12.00
24-25 Art: Frank Frazetta. ... 65.00 200.00
26 ... 2.75 10.00
27-28 Art: Frank Frazetta. ... 65.00 200.00
29-31 ... 2.75 10.00
32 Art: Frank Frazetta. ... 70.00 225.00
33 ... 2.75 10.00

PERSONAL LOVE
PRIZE (1957-1959)
1 ... 8.00 25.00
2-6 ... 4.00 12.00
V2#1-V2#6 ... 2.75 10.00
V3#1 Art: Wallace Wood. ... 5.00 15.00
V3#2 ... 2.25 8.00

PERSONALITY CLASSICS
PERSONALITY (1991)
1 John Wayne. ... .50 1.50
2-4 ... .50 1.50

PETER CANNON, THUNDERBOLT
DC (1992-1993)
1-12 ... .30 1.00

PETER COTTONTAIL
KEY (1954)
1 ... 8.00 25.00
2 ... 5.00 15.00
3-D(#1) With glasses. ... 31.00 100.00

PETER GUNN
DELL FOUR COLOR SERIES (1960)
1087 TV photo cover. (4/60) ... 23.00 75.00

PETER PAN
DELL FOUR COLOR SERIES (1952-1958)
442 Disney movie tie-in. (12/52) ... 16.00 50.00
926 Disney movie tie-in. (8/58) ... 8.00 25.00

PETER PAN
GOLD KEY (1963)
10086-309 Disney movie tie-in. ... 7.00 20.00

PETER PAN TREASURE CHEST
DELL (1953)
1 Dell Giant, Disney. ... 190.00 600.00

PETER PANDA
DC (1953-1958)
1 ... 60.00 190.00
2 ... 29.00 95.00
3-5 ... 20.00 65.00
6-10 ... 17.00 55.00
11-31 ... 14.00 44.00

PETER PARKER
SEE SPECTACULAR SPIDER-MAN

PETER PORKCHOPS
DC (1949-1960)
1 See Leading Comics #23 for 1st app. ... 90.00 290.00
2 ... 40.00 130.00
3-6 ... 31.00 100.00
7-12 ... 26.00 85.00
13-18 ... 22.00 70.00
19-30 ... 16.00 50.00
31-40 ... 12.00 39.00
41-50 ... 10.00 33.00
51-62 ... 6.00 19.00

PETER PORKER, THE SPECTACULAR SPIDER-HAM
MARVEL(STAR) (1985-1987)
1-17 ... .30 1.00

PETER POTAMUS
GOLD KEY (1965)
1 TV tie-in. ... 13.00 40.00

PETER RABBIT
FAGO (1958)
1 ... 7.00 20.00

PETER RABBIT
SEE LARGE FEATURE COMICS (SERIES II) #1.

PETER RABBIT COMICS
AVON (1947-1956)
1 ... 55.00 175.00
2 ... 40.00 125.00
3-6 ... 31.00 100.00
7-12 ... 7.00 20.00
13-34 ... 2.75 10.00

PETTICOAT JUNCTION
DELL (1964-1965)
1 TV photo cover on all issues. ... 13.00 40.00
2-5 ... 8.00 25.00

PETUNIA
DELL FOUR COLOR SERIES (1953)
463 (4/53) ... 8.00 25.00

PHANTASMO
SEE LARGE FEATURE COMICS #18.

PHANTOM, THE
DC (1988)
1-4 ... .30 1.00

PHANTOM, THE
DC (1989-1990)
1-13 ... .30 1.00

PHANTOM
GOLD KEY/KING/CHARLTON (1962-1977)
1 ... 16.00 50.00
2 ... 9.00 27.00
3-12 ... 6.00 18.00
13-17 ... 4.00 13.00
18 Begin: King publication. ... 2.50 9.00
19-29 ... 2.50 9.00
30 Begin: Charlton publication. ... 2.00 7.00
31-35 ... 2.00 7.00
36 Art: Steve Ditko. ... 4.00 13.00
37-38 ... 2.00 7.00
39 Art: Steve Ditko. ... 4.00 13.00
40-50 ... 1.25 4.50
51-60 ... .75 2.50
61-74 ... .50 1.75

PHANTOM FORCE
IMAGE/GENESIS WEST (1993-CURRENT)
1 ... .75 2.50
2 ... .50 1.95
3 Begin Genesis West publication. ... .75 2.50
4-10 ... .75 2.50

PHANTOM LADY
AJAX (1954-1955)
1 (Vol1#5). Art: Matt Baker. ... 120.00 390.00
2-4 ... 100.00 330.00

PHANTOM LADY
FOX (1947-1949)
13 1st & Begin: Phantom Lady by Matt Baker.
... 400.00 1500.00
14 ... 310.00 1000.00
15 ... 280.00 900.00
16 ... 240.00 775.00
17 SOTI ... 500.00 1900.00
18-23 ... 240.00 775.00

PHANTOM PLANET, THE
DELL FOUR COLOR SERIES (1961)
1234 Movie tie-in. ... 13.00 40.00

PHANTOM STRANGER
DC (1952-1953)
1 "Who Is The Phantom Stranger?" (8-9/52)
... 310.00 1000.00
2 "The Killer Shadow" (10-11/52) ... 220.00 700.00
3 ... 190.00 600.00
4 (2-3/53) ... 190.00 600.00
5 (4-5/53) ... 190.00 600.00
6 "The Doorway In The Sky!" (6-7/53) 190.00 600.00

PHANTOM STRANGER, THE
DC (1969-1976)
1 1st: Silver-Age Phantom Stranger. ... 19.00 60.00
2 ... 8.00 25.00
3 ... 6.00 18.00
4 Art: Neal Adams. ... 8.00 25.00
5-6 ... 5.00 15.00
7 ... 2.75 10.00
8-12 ... 2.50 9.00
13-14 ... 1.75 6.00
15 Begin: 25 cent double size issues. ... 1.75 6.00
16-18 ... 1.75 6.00
19 End: 25 cent double size issues. ... 1.50 5.00
20-22 ... 1.50 5.00
23 Begin: Spawn Of Frankenstein by Mike Kaluta.
... 2.25 8.00
24 ... 1.75 6.00
25-29 ... 1.50 5.00
30 End: Spawn Of Frankenstein. ... 1.50 5.00
31-38 ... 1.25 4.00
39-41 Deadman. ... 1.50 5.00

PHANTOM STRANGER
DC (1987-1988)
1-4 ... .30 1.00

PHANTOM WITCH DOCTOR, THE
AVON (1952)
1 ... 55.00 175.00

PHANTOM ZONE, THE
DC (1982)
1-4 ... .30 1.00

PHIL RIZZUTO BASEBALL HERO
FAWCETT (1951)
NO# Photo cover. ... 125.00 400.00

PHOENIX
ATLAS(SEABOARD) (1975)
1 Origin: Phoenix. ... .75 2.00
2-4 ... .30 1.00

PHOENIX: THE UNTOLD STORY
MARVEL (1984)
1 Reprint: X-Men #137. ... 2.75 10.00

PEP COMICS #19

PHANTOM LADY #18

THE PHANTOM STRANGER #2 (MINI-SERIES)

PHIL RIZZUTO BASEBALL HERO

a b c d e f g h i j k l m n o p q r s t u v w x y z

PICTORAL ROMANCES #5

PICTURE NEWS #4

PICTURE STORIES FROM AMERICAN HISTORY #4

PITT #3

PICNIC PARTY
DELL (1955-1957)

6 Dell Giant. Disney. Previous title: Vacation Parade.	31.00	100.00
7	20.00	65.00
8	23.00	75.00

PICTORIAL ROMANCES
ST. JOHN (1950-1954)

4	23.00	75.00
5	19.00	60.00
6-17	13.00	40.00
18-20 100 pages.	25.00	80.00
21-24	13.00	40.00

PICTURE NEWS
LAFAYETTE (1946-1947)

1	31.00	100.00
2	19.00	60.00
3-9	16.00	50.00
10 "Dick Quick Ace Reporter" on cover.	16.00	50.00

PICTURE PARADE
GILBERTON (1953)

1	19.00	60.00
2-3	11.00	36.00
4 Title changes to Picture Progress with #5.	11.00	36.00

PICTURE PROGRESS
GILBERTON (1954-1955)

5 Previous title: Picture Parade.	4.00	12.00
6-9	4.00	12.00
V2#1 The Story Of Flight.	4.00	12.00
V2#2-V2#3	4.00	12.00
V2#4 The Star Spangled Banner.	4.00	12.00
V2#5 1954 News In Review.	4.00	12.00
V2#6-V2#7	4.00	12.00
V2#8 The Time Of The Cave Man.	4.00	12.00
V2#9	4.00	12.00
V3#1 The Man Who Discovered America.	4.00	12.00
V3#2	4.00	12.00

PICTURE STORIES FROM AMERICAN HISTORY
DC (1945-1947)

1	31.00	100.00
2-4	16.00	50.00

PICTURE STORIES FROM SCIENCE
EC (1947)

1	25.00	80.00
2	17.00	55.00

PICTURE STORIES FROM THE BIBLE (OLD TESTAMENT)
DC (1942-1943)

1	23.00	75.00
2-4	16.00	50.00
1943 232 pages.	31.00	100.00
1945 Hardcover, 232 pages.	31.00	100.00

PICTURE STORIES FROM THE BIBLE (NEW TESTAMENT)
DC (1944-1946)

1-3	16.00	50.00

PICTURE STORIES FROM WORLD HISTORY
EC (1947)

1	25.00	80.00
2	20.00	65.00

PINHEAD & FOODINI
FAWCETT (1951-1952)

1	45.00	140.00
2	22.00	70.00
3-4	15.00	48.00

PINK PANTHER, THE
GOLD KEY (1971-1984)

1 TV tie-in.	7.00	20.00
2	2.75	10.00
3-12	1.75	6.00
13-40	1.25	4.00
41-60	.75	2.00
61-87	.30	1.00

PINOCCHIO
DELL FOUR COLOR SERIES (1946-1962)

92 "The Wonderful Adventures Of..."	85.00	275.00
252 (Disney).	23.00	75.00
545 "The Wonderful Adventures Of..."	13.00	40.00
1203 (3/62)	10.00	30.00

PIN-UP PETE
MINOAN (1952)

1	23.00	75.00

PIONEER MARSHALL
FAWCETT (1950)

NO# Movie photo cover (Monte Hale). From the Fawcett Movie Comic series.	50.00	150.00

PIONEER PICTURE STORIES
STREET & SMITH (1941-1943)

1	35.00	110.00
2	17.00	55.00
3-9	10.00	33.00

PIONEER WEST ROMANCES
FICTION HOUSE (1950-1951)

3 Previous title: Firehair.	23.00	75.00
4-5	17.00	55.00
6 Title changes back to Firehair with #7.	17.00	55.00

PIRACY
EC (1954-1955)

1 Art: Williamson.	40.00	130.00
2	35.00	110.00
3-7	25.00	80.00

PIRANA
SEE THRILL-O-RAMA

PIRATES COMICS
HILLMAN (1950)

1	19.00	60.00
2	13.00	40.00
3-4	10.00	30.00

PITT
IMAGE/TOP COW (1993-CURRENT)

1 1st: Pitt.	2.25	8.00
2	1.50	5.00
3	2.25	8.00
4-8	.75	2.50
9-10	.50	1.95
ASHCAN 1	2.75	10.00

PIXIE AND DIXIE AND MR. JINKS
DELL FOUR COLOR SERIES (1960-1961)

1112 TV tie-in. (7/60)	7.00	20.00
1196 TV tie-in. (6/61)	7.00	20.00
1264 TV tie-in. (11/61)	8.00	25.00

PIXIE PUZZLE ROCKET TO ADVENTURE LAND
AVON (1952)

1	16.00	50.00

PLAN 9 FROM OUTER SPACE
MALIBU

GN	1.25	4.95

PLANET COMICS
BLACKTHORNE (1988)

1-3	.75	2.00

PLANET COMICS
FICTION HOUSE (1940-1954)

1 Cover: Eisner/Fine. 1st science-fiction anthology series in comics.	1700.00	6500.00
2	500.00	1800.00
3	400.00	1400.00
4-5	400.00	1200.00
6-7	310.00	1000.00
8-12	280.00	900.00
13-14	220.00	700.00
15 Begin: Mars, God Of War.	400.00	1200.00
16-18	200.00	650.00
19-24	190.00	600.00
25-30	160.00	525.00
31-40	140.00	450.00
41-50	110.00	360.00
51-53	75.00	240.00
54 "The Lost World" (5/48).	75.00	240.00
55-60	75.00	240.00
61-73	50.00	150.00

PLANET COMICS
I. W. (1958)

1 Reprints Planet Comics #70.	8.00	25.00
8 Reprints Planet Comics #72.	8.00	25.00
9 Reprints Planet Comics #73.	8.00	25.00

PLANET OF THE APES
ADVENTURE (1990-1992)

1	1.25	4.00
1A Limited edition.	1.75	6.00
2-24	.75	2.00

PLANET OF THE APES
MARVEL (1974-1977) MAGAZINE

1	1.75	6.00
2	1.00	3.00
3-6	.75	2.00
7-29	.50	1.50

PLANET OF THE APES: BLOOD OF THE APES
ADVENTURE (1991-1992)

1-4	.75	2.00

PLANET OF THE APES: FORBIDDEN ZONE
ADVENTURE (1992-1993)

1-4	.75	2.00

PLANET OF THE APES: SINS OF THE FATHERS
ADVENTURE (1993)

1	.75	2.00

PLANET OF VAMPIRES
ATLAS(SEABOARD) (1975)

1	.75	2.00
2-3	.30	1.00

PLASM
DEFIANT (1993)

0 Diamond Preview giveaway.	2.75	10.00
BINDER Card binder for "Warriors Of Plasm" card set.	14.00	45.00
BINDER (2) 2nd printing.	6.00	18.00

PLASMER
MARVEL (1993-1994)

1	.75	2.50
2-7	.50	1.95

PLASTIC MAN
DC (1988-1989)

1-4	.30	1.00

PLASTIC MAN
QUALITY (1943-1956)

1 (NO#) "Game Of Death!"	900.00	3500.00
2 (NO#) "The Gay Nineties Nightmare!" (2/44)	290.00	950.00
3 (Spring/46)	220.00	700.00
4	190.00	600.00
5	145.00	480.00
6-12	115.00	380.00
13-18	100.00	330.00
19-30	75.00	240.00
31-40	55.00	180.00
41-64	50.00	150.00

PLASTICMAN
DC (1966-1977)

1 1st: Silver-Age Plasticman.	17.00	55.00
2	8.00	25.00
3-6	7.00	20.00
7 Origin: Plasticman.	8.00	25.00
8 1st 15 cent cover price.	5.00	14.00
9	5.00	14.00
10 (1968)	5.00	14.00
11 (1976)	1.50	5.00
12-20	1.50	5.00

PLAYFUL LITTLE AUDREY
HARVEY (1957-1976)

1	23.00	75.00
2	10.00	30.00
3-6	7.00	20.00
7-12	5.00	16.00
13-30	2.75	10.00
31-60	2.00	7.00
61-80	1.50	5.00
81-99	1.00	3.00
100 Giant size.	1.50	5.00
101 Giant Size.	1.50	5.00
102-103 Giant size.	1.50	5.00
104-121	.75	2.00

PLOP!
DC (1973-1976)

1 All issues contain art by Sergio Aragones except #23.	1.50	5.00
2-22	1.50	5.00
23	.75	2.00
24	1.50	5.00

PLUTO
DELL FOUR COLOR SERIES (1952-1961)

429 "Why Dogs Leave Home" (10/52)	11.00	35.00
509 (10/53)	11.00	35.00
595 (10/54)	7.00	20.00
654 (10/55)	7.00	20.00
736 (10/56)	8.00	25.00
853 (10/57)	7.00	20.00
941 (10/58)	7.00	20.00
1039 (10/59)	7.00	20.00
1143 (11/60)	8.00	25.00

1248 (10/61) 7.00 20.00

PLUTO JOINS THE F.B.I.
DISNEY (1947)
W3 Disney Cheerios Premium. 5.00 15.00

PLUTO SAVES THE SHIP
SEE LARGE FEATURE COMICS (SERIES II) #7.

PLUTO TURNS SLEUTH HOUND
DISNEY (1947)
Z2 Disney Cheerios Premium. 5.00 15.00

POCKET COMICS
HARVEY (1941-1942)
1 1st & Origin: The Black Cat. 1st Harvey comic.
.... 190.00 600.00
2 Includes Black Cat (2nd app.), Spirit of '76, Red Blazer, and The Zebra. (9/41) 95.00 300.00
3-4 .... 75.00 240.00

POGO PARADE
DELL (1953)
1 100 page giant edition. Walt Kelly Pogo reprints from Animal Comics. 80.00 250.00

POGO POSSUM
DELL (1949-1954)
1 Cover & art: Walt Kelly (all issues). 135.00 440.00
2 .... 60.00 190.00
3-6 .... 40.00 130.00
7-12 .... 29.00 95.00
13-16 .... 25.00 80.00

POISON ELVES
MULEHOUSE GRAPHICS (1993-1995)
11 Previous title: I, Lusipher. 2.25 8.00
12 .... 2.25 8.00
13 .... 7.00 20.00
14 .... 2.25 8.00
15 .... 4.00 12.00
15 (2ND) 2nd printing. (1994) 1.50 5.00
16-17 .... 2.25 8.00
17 (2ND) 2nd printing. (1994) 1.50 5.00
18-20 .... 1.50 5.00

POISON ELVES
SIRIUS (1995-CURRENT)
1 .... 1.50 5.00
2-4 .... .75 2.50

POLICE AGAINST CRIME
PREMIERE (1954-1955)
1 Art: Jay Disbrow. 19.00 60.00
2 .... 11.00 35.00
3-5 .... 8.00 25.00
6-9 .... 5.00 15.00

POLICE COMICS
QUALITY (1941-1953)
1 1st & Origin: Plastic Man by Jack Cole. 1st: Phantom Lady.
.... 1600.00 6000.00
2 .... 400.00 1400.00
3 .... 310.00 1000.00
4 .... 290.00 950.00
5 Begin: Plastic Man covers. 290.00 950.00
6-7 .... 280.00 900.00
8 1st & Origin: Manhunter. 400.00 1200.00
9-10 .... 280.00 900.00
11 1st: Spirit (in comics). 400.00 1200.00
12 Ebony. 250.00 825.00
13 Woozy Winks. 250.00 825.00
14-18 .... 200.00 650.00
19 .... 190.00 600.00
20 App: The Raven. 200.00 650.00
21-22 .... 190.00 600.00
23 End: Phantom Lady. 190.00 600.00
24-30 .... 145.00 480.00
31-36 .... 130.00 420.00
37-42 .... 100.00 330.00
43-50 .... 75.00 240.00
51-60 .... 60.00 190.00
61-70 .... 50.00 150.00
71-100 .... 40.00 120.00
101 End: Manhunter. 28.00 90.00
102 .... 28.00 90.00
103 End: Plastic Man covers. 28.00 90.00
104-127 .... 28.00 90.00

POLICE LINEUP
AVON (1951-1952)
1 .... 31.00 100.00
2 "The Religious Murder Cult!" 40.00 125.00
3-4 Art: Raymond Everett Kinstler. ... 19.00 60.00

POLICE TRAP
MAINLINE/CHARLTON (1954-1955)
1 Cover: Simon & Kirby. 29.00 95.00
2-4 Cover: Simon & Kirby. 19.00 60.00
5-6 Cover & art: Simon & Kirby. 28.00 90.00

POLICE TRAP
SUPER (1963-1964)
11 Reprints (all issues). 1.50 5.00
16-18 .... 1.50 5.00

POLLYANNA
DELL FOUR COLOR SERIES (1960)
1129 Movie photo cover. (8/60) ... 22.00 70.00

POPEYE
DELL FOUR COLOR SERIES (1942-1947)
17 "And Wimpy" 110.00 350.00
26 .... 100.00 325.00
43 .... 70.00 225.00
70 "And Wimpy" 65.00 200.00
113 .... 28.00 90.00
127 (12/46) 31.00 100.00
145 .... 28.00 90.00
168 (10/47) 28.00 90.00

POPEYE
DELL/GOLD KEY/KING/CHARLTON (1948-1984)
1 .... 50.00 150.00
2 .... 25.00 80.00
3-6 .... 22.00 70.00
7-12 .... 19.00 60.00
13-24 .... 16.00 50.00
25-40 .... 13.00 40.00
41-45 .... 8.00 25.00
46 Origin: Wallace Maximillion Smith the 97th (better known as Swee'Pea). 11.00 35.00
47-65 .... 8.00 25.00
66 Begin: Gold Key publication. Giant size. 11.00 35.00
67 Giant size. 11.00 35.00
68-70 .... 7.00 20.00
71-80 .... 5.00 15.00
81 Begin: King publication. 2.75 10.00
82-90 .... 2.75 10.00
91-93 .... 1.75 6.00
94 Begin: Charlton publication. 1.75 6.00
95-110 .... 1.75 6.00
111-130 .... 1.25 4.00
131-138 .... .75 2.00
139 Resume Gold Key publication. ...... .75 2.00
140-150 .... .75 2.00
151-171 .... .30 1.00

POPEYE
SEE LARGE FEATURE COMICS (SERIES I) #24, (SERIES II) #10

POPEYE CARTOON BOOK
SAALFIELD (1934)
2095 "A Sly Fisherman." 8-1/2"x13". Full color strip reprints. 40 page version. 155.00 500.00
2095-A 12 page version. 95.00 300.00

POPULAR COMICS
DELL (1936-1948)
1 Newspaper strip reprints. 1st: Dick Tracy (in comics).
.... 500.00 1600.00
2 .... 230.00 750.00
3 .... 200.00 650.00
4 .... 170.00 550.00
5 Begin: Tom Mix. 170.00 550.00
6-12 .... 135.00 440.00
13-24 .... 100.00 330.00
25-40 .... 75.00 240.00
41-45 .... 55.00 170.00
46 1st & Origin: Martan, the Marvel Man. 70.00 220.00
47-50 .... 55.00 170.00
51 Origin: The Voice. 55.00 170.00
52-59 .... 55.00 170.00
60 1st & Origin: Professor Supermind and Son.
.... 70.00 220.00
61-70 .... 40.00 130.00
71 .... 35.00 110.00
72 Begin: The Owl. 35.00 110.00
73-75 .... 35.00 110.00
76-78 Captain Midnight. 50.00 160.00
79-84 .... 35.00 110.00
85 End: The Owl. 35.00 110.00
86-100 .... 23.00 75.00
101-110 .... 20.00 65.00
111-130 .... 17.00 55.00
131-145 .... 14.00 44.00

POPULAR TEEN-AGERS
STAR (1950-1954)
5 Previous title: School Day Romances. 22.00 70.00
6-8 .... 22.00 70.00

9 "Romances" 11.00 35.00
10-13 "Love" 11.00 35.00
14 "Love" Art: Wallace Wood. 22.00 70.00
15-23 "Love" 10.00 30.00

PORKY PIG
DELL (1952-1962)
25 .... 7.00 20.00
26 .... 2.75 10.00
27-40 .... 2.00 7.00
41-50 .... 1.50 5.00
51-81 .... 1.00 3.00

PORKY PIG
DELL FOUR COLOR SERIES (1942-1952)
16 "And The Secret Of The Haunted House"
.... 125.00 400.00
48 "Porky Of The Mounties" & "Porky And The Pirate"
.... 200.00 650.00
78 "And The Bandit Twins" 55.00 175.00
112 "Adventure In Gopher Gulch" ... 31.00 100.00
156 "And The Phantom" 22.00 70.00
182 "Ever-Never Land" 22.00 70.00
191 "To The Rescue" 22.00 70.00
226 "And Spoofy, The Spook" 16.00 50.00
241 "Mighty Hunter" 16.00 50.00
260 "Hero Of The Wild West" 16.00 50.00
271 "Phantom Of The Plains" 16.00 50.00
277 "Desert Adventure" 16.00 50.00
284 "The Kingdom Of Nowhere" 16.00 50.00
295 "President Porky" 16.00 50.00
303 "The Land Of The Monstrous Flies" 11.00 35.00
311 "Midget Horses Of Hidden Valley" 11.00 35.00
322 "Roaring Rockets" 11.00 35.00
330 "Meets The Bristled Bruiser" 11.00 35.00
342 "The Lucky Peppermint Mine" ... 8.00 25.00
351 "And The Grand Canyon Giant" ... 8.00 25.00
360 "Tree Of Fortune" 8.00 25.00
370 "Trouble In The Big Trees" 8.00 25.00
385 "The Isle Of Missing Ships" 8.00 25.00
399 "The Lost Gold Mine" 8.00 25.00
410 "The Water Wizard" 8.00 25.00
426 "The Scalawag Leprechaun" 8.00 25.00

PORKY PIG
GOLD KEY (1965-1984)
1 .... 1.50 5.00
2-5 .... 1.00 3.00
6-10 .... .75 2.00
11-50 .... .30 1.00
51-109 .... .20 .50

PORKY'S BOOK OF TRICKS
GIVEAWAY (1942)
NO# "A Christmas Book Of Surprises" 70.00 220.00

POWDER RIVER RUSTLERS
FAWCETT (1950)
NO# Movie photo cover (Rocky Lane). From the Fawcett Movie Comic series. 55.00 170.00

POWER & GLORY
MALIBU (1994-CURRENT)
1 .... 1.00 3.00
1A Alternate cover. 1.00 3.00
1B With bonus book, blue foil, gold stamp. 1.50 5.00
1C With limited edition serigraph. 1.50 5.00
1D Gold version. 2.25 8.00
1E Silver version. 2.25 8.00
1F Playbbagged, newsstand version. ... 1.00 3.00
2-4 .... .75 2.50
TPB Reprints issues #1-4. .... 4.00 12.95

POWER COMICS
HOLYOKE (1944-1945)
1 Cover: L.B. Cole. 130.00 420.00
2 .... 110.00 360.00
3-4 Cover: L.B. Cole. 110.00 360.00

POWER MAN
MARVEL (1974-1978)
17 Previous title: Hero For Hire. 4.00 11.00
18-20 .... 2.25 8.00
21-27 .... 1.50 5.00
28-47 .... 1.25 4.50
48-49 Art: John Byrne. 1.00 3.50
50 Begin: Power Man & Iron Fist. ...... .50 1.25
51-56 .... .50 1.25
57 App: new X-Men. 1.50 5.00
58-65 .... .50 1.25
66 2nd: Sabretooth. 14.00 45.00
67-77 .... .50 1.25
78 3rd: Sabretooth. 7.00 22.00
79-83 .... .50 1.25
84 4th: Sabretooth. 7.00 22.00
85-124 .... .50 1.25
125 Death: Iron Fist. Double size. ...... .50 1.75
ANNUAL 1 (1976) 1.25 4.00

PIXIE & DIXIE & MR. JINX #1112

PLANET COMICS #42

PLASMER #2

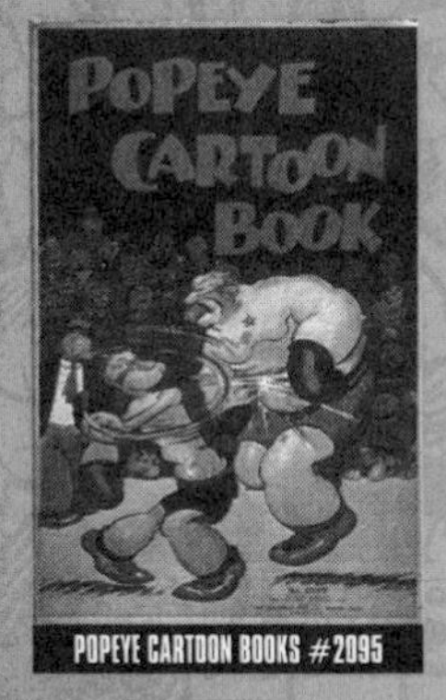

POPEYE CARTOON BOOKS #2095

PREDATOR #1

PREDATOR: BIG GAME #1

PRIME #12

PRIMORTALS #2

FAMOUS • FIRSTS

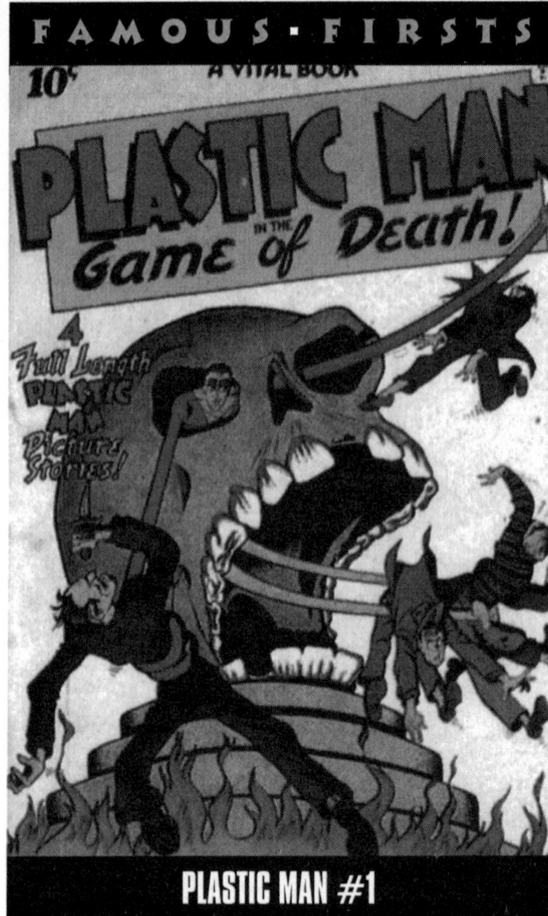

PLASTIC MAN #1

Jack Cole's brilliant stretchable hero, a former criminal named Eel O'Brien, combines dramatic super-doing with plenty of slapstick comedy. Plastic Man graduated into his own comic two years after debuting in *Police Comics* #1.

GIANT-SIZE (1975) .50 1.25

POWER OF PRIME, THE
MALIBU (1995-CURRENT)
1-2 .75 2.50

POWER OF SHAZAM, THE
DC (1994)
1 .75 2.50
2-3 .75 2.00
4-8 .50 1.75
GN Captain Marvel. 6.00 19.95
TPB 2.50 9.95

POWER OF THE MARK
DARK HORSE (1993)
1-4 .75 2.50

POWER PACK
MARVEL (1984-1991)
1 1st & Origin: Power Pack. .75 2.00
2-18 .30 1.00
19 Wolverine. 1.50 5.00
20-26 .30 1.00
27 Sabretooth, Wolverine. 1.50 5.00
28-45 .30 1.00
46 Punisher. .30 1.00
47-62 .30 1.00

POWER PACK: HOLIDAY SPECIAL
MARVEL (1992)
1 .75 2.95

POWERHOUSE PEPPER COMICS
MARVEL (1943-1948)
1 Art: Basil Wolverton in all issues. 220.00 700.00
2 110.00 360.00
3-4 95.00 300.00
5 130.00 420.00

POWERMOWERMAN AND POWER MOWER SAFETY (UNDERGROUND)
FRANK BURGMEIER (1966)
NO# 50.00 150.00

PREACHER
DC (1995-CURRENT)
1 1st: Preacher. 1.75 6.50
2 1.25 4.50
3 1.00 3.00
4-7 .75 2.50

PREDATOR
DARK HORSE (1989-1990)
1 2.75 10.00
1 (2ND) 2nd printing. 1.25 4.00
2 1.75 6.00
3-4 1.25 4.00

PREDATOR 2
DARK HORSE (1991)
1 Movie adaptation. .75 2.50
2 .75 2.50

PREDATOR: BAD BLOOD
DARK HORSE (1993)
1-4 .75 2.50

PREDATOR: BIG GAME
DARK HORSE (1991)
1 1.25 4.00
2-4 .75 2.50
TPB Reprints issues #1-4. 5.00 13.95

PREDATOR: BLOODY SANDS OF TIME
DARK HORSE (1992)
1-2 .75 2.50

PREDATOR: COLD WAR
DARK HORSE (1991)
1-4 1.00 3.00

PREDATOR: INVADERS FROM THE FOURTH DIMENSION
DARK HORSE (1994)
NO# One-shot. 1.00 3.95

PREDATOR: JUNGLE TALES
MARVEL (1995)
1 One-shot. .75 2.95

PREDATOR: RACE WAR
DARK HORSE (1993)
0-4 .75 2.50

PREDATOR VS. MAGNUS ROBOT FIGHTER
DARK HORSE/VALIANT (1992-1993)
1 1.25 4.00
1A Platinum. 1.75 6.00
1B Gold. 1.50 5.00
2 1.00 3.00

PREZ
DC (1973-1974)
1 1.00 3.00
2-4 .75 2.00

PRIDE AND THE PASSION, THE
DELL FOUR COLOR SERIES (1957)
824 Movie photo cover (Frank Sinatra). (8/57) 20.00 65.00

PRIDE OF THE YANKEES, THE
ME (1949)
NO# Photo cover. The story of Lou Gehrig. 145.00 480.00

PRIMAL FORCE
DC (1994-CURRENT)
0 (8/94) .50 1.95
1-7 .50 1.95
8-12 .75 2.25

PRIME
MALIBU (1993-CURRENT)
1/2 Send away (Wizard) with hologram cover and certificate of authenticity. 2.75 10.00
1 1st: Prime, Prototype. Ultraverse #0 card. 2.25 8.00
1A Hologram edition. 4.00 12.00
1B Ultra-limited foil edition. 4.00 12.00
1D Gold hologram edition. 4.00 12.00
2 Polybagged with card. 2.25 8.00
3 Origin: Prime. 1.50 5.00
4 Cover has Prime on top. Polybagged. 1.75 6.00
4A Cover has Prototype on top. Polybagged. 1.75 6.00
4B Prime on top (unbagged). 1.25 4.00
4C Prototype on top (unbagged). 1.25 4.00
5 With coupon. .75 2.25
6-11 .75 2.25
12 1.00 3.00
13 Double size. .75 2.95
13A Variant cover. 2.25 8.00
14-19 .50 1.95
20-26 .75 2.50
ANNUAL 1 1.00 3.95
ASHCAN 1 .20 .75
ASHCAN NO# 2.25 8.00
TPB Prime Time. Reprints issues #1-4. (1994) 2.50 9.95

PRIMER
COMICO (1982-1984)
1 2.00 7.00
2 1st: Grendel. 20.00 65.00
3-4 1.25 4.00
5 1st Sam Kieth art in comics. 7.00 20.00
6 1st: Evangelyne. 5.00 15.00

PRIMORTALS, THE
TEKNO-COMIX (1994-CURRENT)
1 (Leonard Nimoy's...) 1.50 5.00
2 1.00 3.50
3-7 .75 2.25
8-10 .50 1.95

PRINCE AND THE PAUPER, THE
DELL (1962)
01-654-207 Disney movie tie-in. 7.00 20.00

PRINCE NAMOR, THE SUB-MARINER
MARVEL (1984)
1-4 .30 1.00

PRINCE VALIANT
DELL FOUR COLOR SERIES (1954-1958)
567 Movie photo cover. (6/54) 20.00 65.00
650 (9/55) 10.00 30.00
699 "The Secret Of The Flames" (4/56) 11.00 35.00
719 "The Peril Of The Round Table" (8/56) 11.00 35.00
788 "Trial By Arms" (4/57) 11.00 35.00
849 "Quest For The Grail" (12/57) 11.00 35.00
900 "The Island Of Thunder" (5/58) 11.00 35.00

PRINCE VANDAL
TRIUMPHANT (1993-1995)
0-10 .75 2.50

PRISCILLA'S POP
DELL FOUR COLOR SERIES (1954-1957)
569 (7/54) 10.00 30.00
630 (5/55) 5.00 15.00
704 (5/56) 7.00 20.00
799 (5/57) 7.00 20.00

PRISON BREAK!
AVON (1951-1952)
1 50.00 150.00
2 31.00 100.00
3 25.00 80.00
4-5 23.00 75.00

PRISON RIOT!
AVON (1952)
1 "Mutiny At Bradburn!" 31.00 100.00

PRISON TO PRAISE
LOGOS (1974)
NO# .30 1.00

PRISONER, THE
DC (1988-1989)
1 Book A. TV tie-in. 1.00 3.50
2 Book B. 1.00 3.50
3 Book C. 1.00 3.50
4 Book D. 1.00 3.50

PRIVATE BUCK
SEE LARGE FEATURE COMICS (SERIES I) #21, (SERIES II) #12

PRIVATE EYE
SEE MIKE SHAYNE

PRIZE COMICS
PRIZE (1940-1948)
1 400.00 1200.00
2 190.00 625.00
3-6 155.00 500.00
7 1st: Green Lama. 310.00 1000.00
8-9 155.00 500.00
10-12 130.00 430.00
13 1st & Origin: Yank and Doodle. 155.00 500.00
14-20 115.00 370.00
21-24 95.00 310.00
25-30 85.00 280.00
31-40 55.00 180.00
41-50 40.00 120.00
51-60 28.00 90.00
61-62 23.00 75.00
63 Cover/Art: Simon & Kirby. 28.00 90.00
64-67 23.00 75.00
68 Title changes to Prize Comics Western with #69. 23.00 75.00

PRIZE COMICS WESTERN
PRIZE (1948-1956)
69 Previous title: Prize Comics. 25.00 80.00
70-75 17.00 55.00
76 Movie photo cover (Canadian Pacific with Randolph Scott). 25.00 80.00
77 Movie photo cover (Streets Of Laredo with William Holden). 25.00 80.00
78 Movie photo cover (Roughshod with Robert Sterling). 25.00 80.00
79 Movie photo cover (Stage To Chino with George O'Brien). 25.00 80.00
80-82 Photo cover. 20.00 65.00
83-84 20.00 65.00
85 1st: American Eagle. 35.00 110.00
86-90 20.00 65.00
91-99 17.00 55.00
100 Anniversary issue. (7-8/53) 17.00 55.00
101-110 14.00 44.00
111-119 10.00 33.00

PRIZE MYSTERY
KEY (1955)
1 10.00 30.00

2-3 7.00 20.00

PROJECT A-KO
MALIBU (1994)
1 1.25 4.00
2-4 .75 2.95

PROJECT A-KO 2
CPM (1995)
1-3 .75 2.95

PROJECT A-KO 0
ANTARCTIC PRESS (1994)
0 Digest size. 1.50 5.00

PROJECT X: THUMP'N GUTS
KITCHEN SINK (1993)
1 1.25 4.95

PROPELLERMAN
DARK HORSE (1993-1994)
1-7 .75 2.95

PROPHET
IMAGE (1993-1995)
1 With coupon for Prophet #0. 1.00 3.00
1A Gold edition. 2.25 8.00
2 1st: Judas. .75 2.50
3 .75 2.50
4 .50 1.95
4A Platt cover. 4.00 12.00
5 Begin: Stephan Platt art. 1.50 5.00
6 1.25 4.00
7 .50 1.95
8-10 .75 2.50

PROPHET
IMAGE (1995-CURRENT)
1, 1A .75 2.50
ANNUAL 1 (1995) .75 2.50
SOURCEBOOK .75 2.95

PROTECTORS, THE
MALIBU (1992-1994)
1 Direct market edition, with poster. .75 2.50
1A Newsstand version, without poster. .50 1.95
2-4 .75 2.50
5 Hole through book. .75 2.50
6-11 .75 2.50
12-20 .75 2.25

PROTOTYPE
MALIBU (1993-CURRENT)
0 (6/94) .75 2.50
1 1st: Veil. Polybagged with card. 1.00 3.50
1A Unbagged without card. .50 1.95
1B Hologram edition. 2.25 8.00
1C Ultra-limited foil edition. 2.25 8.00
1D Gold hologram edition. 2.25 8.00
2-3 .75 2.00
4-12 .50 1.95
13 With Ultraverse Premiere #6. 1.00 3.50
14-17 .50 1.95
18 .75 2.50
GS 1 Giant size. .75 2.50

PROTOTYPE: TURF WAR
MALIBU (1995)
1-3 .75 2.50

PRUDENCE & CAUTION
DEFIANT (1994)
1 1.00 3.25
2-4 .75 2.50

PSI-LORDS: REIGN OF THE STARWATCHERS
VALIANT (1994-1995)
1 Chromium cover. 1.00 3.50
2-3 .75 2.25
4 Begin title variant: Psi-Lords. .75 2.25
5-10 .75 2.25

PSYBA-RATS, THE
DC (1995)
1 .75 2.50
2-3 .50 1.50

PSYCHO
SKYWALD (1971-1975) MAGAZINE
1 4.00 12.00
2-24 1.50 5.00
ANNUAL (1972) 1.50 5.00

PSYCHOANALYSIS
EC (1955)
1 25.00 80.00
2-4 17.00 55.00

PSYCHONAUTS
MARVEL (1993-1994)
1-4 1.25 4.95

PT 109
GOLD KEY (1964)
10123-409 Movie tie-in (photo insert). (Based on the true story of John F. Kennedy). 11.00 35.00

PUBLIC ENEMIES
DS (1948-1949)
1 19.00 60.00
2 SOTI 25.00 80.00
3-6 13.00 40.00
7-9 10.00 30.00

PUNCH AND JUDY COMICS
HILLMAN (1944-1951)
1 (1944) 23.00 75.00
2 (Fall/48) 11.00 35.00
3-12 8.00 25.00
V2#1 7.00 20.00
V2#2 Art: Jack Kirby. 22.00 70.00
V2#3-V2#9 5.00 16.00
V2#10-V2#12 Art: Jack Kirby. 22.00 70.00
V3#1-V3#2 Art: Jack Kirby. 22.00 70.00
V3#3-V3#9 5.00 16.00

PUNCH COMICS
CHESLER (1941-1948)
1 145.00 480.00
2 (#s 3-8 do not exist) 75.00 240.00
9 Begin: Rocketman. 75.00 240.00
10 40.00 120.00
11-12 31.00 100.00
13-19 29.00 95.00
20 Unusual cover (semi-nudity). 75.00 240.00
21-26 25.00 80.00

PUNISHER
MARVEL (1986)
1 Mini-series. 7.00 20.00
2 2.75 10.00
3-5 2.25 8.00

PUNISHER
MARVEL (1987-1995)
1 2.75 10.00
2 1.50 5.00
3-7 1.25 4.00
8-9 1.75 6.00
10 Crossover with Daredevil #257. 2.25 8.00
11-17 1.25 4.00
18-23 1.00 3.00
24-49 .75 2.00
50 1.00 3.00
51-56 .75 2.00
57 Double cover version. .75 2.00
57A Newsstand version (photo cover only). .75 2.00
58 .75 2.00
59 .75 2.50
60-66 .50 1.50
67-74 .50 1.25
75 Embossed cover, double size. .75 2.50
76-84 .50 1.25
85 Prequel to Suicide Run. .50 1.25
86 Suicide Run, foil cover. .50 1.25
87-99 .50 1.25
100 Prismatic cover. 1.00 3.95
100A Regular cover. .75 2.95
101-104 .50 1.25

PUNISHER
MARVEL (1989-1990) MAGAZINE
1 All issues are reprints. 1.00 3.00
2-16 .75 2.00

PUNISHER 2099
MARVEL (1993-CURRENT)
1-24 .50 1.50
25 Enhanced cover. .75 2.95
25A Regular cover. .50 1.50
26-27 .50 1.50
28-33 .50 1.95

PUNISHER: A MAN NAMED FRANK
MARVEL (1994)
1 Prestige format. 1.75 6.95

PUNISHER ANNUAL
MARVEL (1988-CURRENT)
1 Evolutionary War. (1988) 1.75 6.00
2 Atlantis Attacks. (1989) 1.00 3.00
3 Lifeform, pt.1 (1990) 1.00 3.00
4 (1991) .75 2.00
5 (1992) .75 2.00
6 1st: Phalanx. Polybagged with card. (1993) .75 2.95

PROPHET #2 (1ST SERIES)

PROTOTYPE #5

PUNISHER (MINI-SERIES) #1

PUNISHER 2099 #2

PUNISHER ARMORY #3

PUNISHER WAR JOURNAL #44

PUNISHER: WAR ZONE #24

PUNISHER/BATMAN: DEADLY KNIGHTS

7 (1994) .... .75 2.95

PUNISHER ARMORY
MARVEL (1990-1992)
1 Punisher's weapons arsenal. 2.50 9.00
2 .... 2.00 7.00
3-10 .... .75 2.00

PUNISHER: BACK-TO-SCHOOL SPECIAL
MARVEL (1992-CURRENT)
1 (1992) .... .75 2.95
2 (1993) .... .75 2.95
3 (1994) .... .75 2.95

PUNISHER: BLOODLINES
MARVEL (1991)
NO# Prestige format. 1.50 5.95

PUNISHER CLASSIC
MARVEL (1989)
1 .... 1.50 5.00

PUNISHER: CRUISE HARD
MARVEL (1994)
NO# .... .75 2.95

PUNISHER: DIE HARD IN THE BIG EASY
MARVEL (1992)
1 .... 1.25 4.95

PUNISHER: G-FORCE
MARVEL (1992)
NO# 1.25 4.95

PUNISHER: HOLIDAY SPECIAL
MARVEL (1992-CURRENT)
1 (1992) Foil-stamped cover. .... .75 2.95
2 (1993) .... .75 2.95
3 (1994) .... .75 2.95

PUNISHER MEETS ARCHIE
MARVEL/ARCHIE (1994)
1 .... 1.00 3.95

PUNISHER MOVIE COMIC
MARVEL (1989-1990)
1 Movie adaptation. .... .50 1.50
2-3 .... .50 1.50
TPB 1.50 5.95

PUNISHER: NO ESCAPE
MARVEL (1990)
1 App: Captain America, Paladin. 1.50 5.00

PUNISHER: P.O.V.
MARVEL (1991)
1-4 .... 1.25 4.95

PUNISHER: RETURN TO BIG NOTHING
MARVEL (1989)
HC 6.00 16.95
SC 4.00 12.95

PUNISHER: ROUGH CUT
MARVEL
1 One shot. .... .75 2.50

PUNISHER: SPINNING DOOMSDAY'S WEB
MARVEL (1992)
GN App: Black Widow. 2.50 9.95

PUNISHER: SUMMER SPECIAL
MARVEL (1991-1994)
1 (1991) 1.00 3.00
2 (1992) 1.00 3.00
3 (1993) .... .75 2.50
4 (1994) .... .75 2.95

PUNISHER: THE GHOST OF INNOCENTS
MARVEL (1993)
1-2 .... 1.50 5.95

PUNISHER: THE ORIGIN OF MICROCHIP
MARVEL (1993)
1-2 .... .50 1.50

PUNISHER: THE PRIZE
MARVEL (1990)
1 .... 1.25 4.95

PUNISHER WAR JOURNAL
MARVEL (1988-1995)
1 Begin: Jim Lee cover & art. 1.25 4.00
2 Daredevil. 1.00 3.00
3 Daredevil. .... .75 2.00
4 1st: Sniper. .... .75 2.00
5 Sniper. .... .75 2.00
6 Wolverine. 1.00 3.00
7 Wolverine. .... .75 2.00
8-11 .... .75 2.00
12 End: Jim Lee cover & art. .... .75 2.00
13-16 .... .75 2.00
17-19 Art: Jim Lee. .... .75 2.00
20-28 .... .75 2.00
29-30 Ghost Rider. .... .75 2.00
31-42 .... .75 2.00
43-60 .... .50 1.50
61 Suicide Run (pt.1). 1.00 3.00
62 .... 1.00 3.00
63 .... .50 1.50
64 Suicide Run (pt.10). Die-cut cover. .... .75 2.95
64A Regular cover. .... .50 1.50
65-74 .... .50 1.50
75 Double size. .... .75 2.00
76-80 .... .50 1.50

PUNISHER: WAR ZONE
MARVEL (1992-1995)
1 .... 1.00 3.00
2-5 .... .75 2.00
6-22 .... .50 1.50
23 Suicide Run (pt.2). Embossed cover. .... .50 1.50
24 .... .50 1.50
25 Suicide Run (pt.8). .... .50 1.50
26-41 .... .50 1.50
ANNUAL 1 Polybagged with card. (1993) .... .75 2.95
ANNUAL 2 (1994) .... .75 2.95

PUNISHER: YEAR ONE
MARVEL (1994-1995)
1-4 .... .75 2.50

PUNISHER/BATMAN: DEADLY KNIGHTS
MARVEL/DC (1994)
NO# 1.25 4.95

PUNISHER/WOLVERINE: AFRICAN SAGA
MARVEL (1989)
1 Prestige format. Reprints: Punisher War Journal #6-7.
.... 1.50 5.95

PUNX
ACCLAIM (1995)
1 .... .75 2.50

PUPPET COMICS
DOUGHERTY (1946)
1-2 .... 10.00 30.00

PURPLE CLAW, THE
TOBY (1953)
1 .... 50.00 165.00
2 .... 35.00 110.00
3 .... 27.00 88.00

PUSSYCAT
MARVEL (1968)
1 .... 31.00 100.00

QUACK!
STAR REACH (1976-1977)
1 Cover/Art: Frank Brunner. 1.50 5.00
2 .... .75 2.00
3 The Beavers by Dave Sim. 1.25 4.00
4-6 .... .50 1.50

QUADRANT
QUADRANT (1983-1986) MAGAZINE
1 Art: Peter Hsu in all issues. 2.25 8.00
2 .... 1.00 3.00
3-7 .... .50 1.50

QUASAR
MARVEL (1989-1994)
1 Origin: Quasar. .... .75 2.00
2-5 .... .30 1.00
6 App: Venom. 1.00 3.00
7 App: Spider-Man. .... .30 1.00
8-13 .... .30 1.00
14 Cover: Todd McFarlane. .... .30 1.00
15 .... .30 1.00
16 Double size. .... .30 1.00
17-24 .... .30 1.00
25 Double size. .... .30 1.00
26-49 .... .30 1.00
50 Holo-grafix foil enhanced-cover. Double size.
.... .75 2.00
51-60 .... .30 1.00

QUEEN OF THE DAMNED
INNOVATION (1991-1992)
1-9 .... .75 2.50

QUENTIN DURWARD
DELL FOUR COLOR SERIES (1956)
672 Movie photo cover. (1/56) 14.00 45.00

QUESTION, THE
DC (1987-1990)
1-36 .... .30 1.00

QUESTION QUARTERLY, THE
DC (1990-1992)
1-5 .... .30 1.00

QUESTPROBE
MARVEL (1984-1985)
1-4 .... .20 .50

QUICK DRAW MCGRAW
CHARLTON (1970-1972)
1 TV cartoon tie-in. 7.00 22.00
2-8 .... 5.00 16.00

QUICK DRAW MCGRAW
DELL/GOLD KEY (1959-1969)
1 (#1040) From the 4-Color Series. TV tie-in. (12/59)
.... 25.00 80.00
2 .... 14.00 45.00
3-6 .... 10.00 30.00
7-11 .... 7.00 20.00
12 Begin: Gold Key publication. 80 pages. 19.00 60.00
13 80 pages. 19.00 60.00
14-15 .... 5.00 15.00

QUICK-TRIGGER WESTERN
MARVEL(ATLAS) (1956-1957)
12 Art: Matt Baker. Previous title: Cowboy Action.
.... 12.00 38.00
13-15 .... 9.00 27.00
16 Art: Jack Kirby. 9.00 27.00
17 .... 9.00 27.00
18 Art: Matt Baker. 9.00 27.00
19 .... 9.00 27.00

Q-UNIT
HARRIS (1993)
1 Polybagged. .... .75 2.95

RACE FOR THE MOON
HARVEY (1958)
1 .... 16.00 50.00
2-3 Cover & art: Jack Kirby/Al Williamson. 26.00 85.00

RACK & PAIN
DARK HORSE (1994)
1-4 .... .75 2.50

RACKET SQUAD
CAPITOL (1952-1958)
1 .... 31.00 100.00
2 .... 16.00 50.00
3-4 .... 13.00 40.00
5 App: Dr. Neff. 16.00 50.00
6 App: Dr. Neff. 13.00 40.00
7-10 .... 10.00 30.00
11 Cover/Art: Steve Ditko. 50.00 150.00
12 Cover (classic)/Art: Steve Ditko. 70.00 225.00
13 .... 16.00 50.00
14 .... 11.00 35.00
15-20 .... 10.00 30.00
21-28 .... 7.00 20.00
29 Double size. 13.00 40.00

RADICAL DREAMER
BLACKBALL (1994)
0-2 .... .75 2.00
3-4 .... .75 2.50

RADICAL DREAMER
MARK'S GIANT ECONOMY SIZE (1995-CURRENT)
1-3 .... .75 2.95

RADIOACTIVE MAN
BONGO (1993-1995)
1 TV cartoon (Simpson's) tie-in. 1.25 4.00
2 (#88) .... .75 2.25
3 (#216) .... .50 1.95
4 (#412) .... .75 2.25
5 (#679) .... .75 2.25
6 (#1000) .... .75 2.25

RAGGEDY ANN + ANDY
DELL (1946-1949)
1 .... 40.00 130.00
2 .... 28.00 90.00
3-6 .... 19.00 60.00

7-12 16.00 50.00
13-20 11.00 36.00
21-30 7.00 22.00
31-39 4.00 13.00

RAGGEDY ANN AND ANDY
DELL (1955)
1 Dell Giant. 23.00 75.00

RAGGEDY ANN AND ANDY
DELL (1964-1966)
1 2.50 9.00
2 1.50 5.25
3-4 1.00 3.50

RAGGEDY ANN AND ANDY
DELL FOUR COLOR SERIES (1942-1954)
5 115.00 375.00
23 (6/43) 95.00 300.00
45 70.00 225.00
72 55.00 180.00
262 (1/50) 14.00 45.00
306 (12/50) 13.00 40.00
354 (10/51) 13.00 40.00
380 (3/52) 10.00 30.00
452 (2/53) 10.00 30.00
533 (2/54) 10.00 30.00

RAGGEDY ANN AND ANDY
GOLD KEY (1971-1973)
1 1.50 5.00
2-6 1.00 3.00

RAGMAN
DC (1976-1977)
1 1st & Origin: Ragman. 1.50 5.00
2 Origin (pt.2): Ragman. 1st: Opal. 1.00 3.50
3-5 1.00 3.00

RAGMAN
DC (1991-1992)
1 1st: new Ragman. .75 2.00
2-8 .50 1.50

RAGMAN: CRY OF THE DEAD
DC (1993-1994)
1-6 .50 1.75

RAI
VALIANT (1992-1995)
0 Origin: Rising Spirit. (9/92) 2.00 7.00
1 Flip book with Magnus Robot Fighter #5. 2.50 9.00
2 Flip book with Magnus Robot Fighter #6. 2.00 7.00
3-4 4.00 12.00
5 1.00 3.00
6-8 .75 2.00
9 1st: Future Force. Begin title variant: Rai And The Future Force. .75 2.00
9A Gold edition. 1.50 5.00
10-33 .75 2.00
TPB Polybagged with #0. 4.00 11.95

RAIDERS OF THE LOST ARK
MARVEL (1981)
1 Movie adaptation. .75 2.00
2-3 .30 1.00

RALPH KINER HOME RUN KING
FAWCETT (1950)
NO# Photo cover. 110.00 350.00

RAMAR OF THE JUNGLE
TOBY (1954-1956)
1 TV tie-in starring Jon Hall. 25.00 80.00
2 (9/55) 17.00 55.00
3-5 14.00 44.00

RAMPAGING HULK
MARVEL (1977-1978) MAGAZINE
1 1.50 5.00
2 App: original X-Men. 2.75 10.00
3-8 .75 2.00
9 Hulk battles Thor. 1.50 5.00

RANGE BUSTERS
CHARLTON (1955)
8 10.00 30.00
9-10 7.00 20.00

RANGE BUSTERS
FOX (1950-1951)
1 19.00 60.00
2-8 13.00 40.00

RANGE RIDER COMICS, THE
DELL FOUR COLOR SERIES (1952)
404 TV photo cover. (6/52) 26.00 85.00

RANGE ROMANCES
QUALITY (1949-1950)
1 Cover/Art: Gustavson. 31.00 100.00
2 Cover/Art: Reed Crandall. 40.00 125.00
3-5 23.00 75.00

RANGERS COMICS
FICTION HOUSE (1941-1953)
1 300.00 975.00
2 145.00 480.00
3-5 120.00 390.00
6-7 100.00 320.00
8-10 80.00 260.00
11-20 60.00 190.00
21 1st & Origin: Firehair. 80.00 260.00
22-27 40.00 130.00
28 1st & Origin: Tiger Man. 45.00 140.00
29-30 40.00 130.00
31-40 31.00 100.00
41-50 23.00 75.00
51-60 20.00 65.00
61-69 16.00 50.00

RANGO
DELL (1967)
1 TV photo cover (Tim Conway). 6.00 18.00

RANMA 1/2 (PART 1)
VIZ (1992)
1 16.00 50.00
2-3 5.00 15.00
4-5 1.50 5.00
6 2.75 10.00
7 1.50 5.00
TPB VOL 1 Reprints issues #1-7. (1993) 6.00 16.95

RANMA 1/2 (PART 2)
VIZ (1993)
1 2.75 10.00
2-8 1.50 5.00
9 2.00 7.50
10-11 1.00 3.50
TPB VOL 2 Reprints issues #1-6. (1994) 5.00 15.95
TPB VOL 3 Reprints issues #6-11. (1994) 5.00 15.95

RANMA 1/2 (PART 3)
VIZ (1993-1994)
1-13 .75 2.75

RANMA 1/2 (PART 4)
VIZ (1995-CURRENT)
1-8 .75 2.75

RAPHAEL
MIRAGE (1985)
1 Teenage Mutant Ninja Turtle tie-in. 2.25 8.00

RARE BIT FIENDS
KING HELL (1994-CURRENT)
1 1.25 4.00
2-13 .75 2.95

RASCALS IN PARADISE
DARK HORSE (1994)
1 Deluxe, oversized format. 1.00 3.95
2-3 1.00 3.95

RAT PATROL, THE
DELL (1967-1969)
1 TV tie-in and photo cover. 11.00 35.00
2 8.00 25.00
3-6 7.00 20.00

RAVAGE 2099
MARVEL (1992-1995)
1 1st: Ravage 2099. .50 1.25
2-24 .50 1.25
25 Double size, foil stamped cover. .75 2.95
25A Regular cover. .75 2.00
26-33 .50 1.25

RAVEN, THE
DELL (1963)
12-680-309 Movie photo cover (Vincent Price). 10.00 30.00

RAVEN
RENAISSANCE (1993)
1-7 .75 2.50

RAVER
MALIBU (1993-1994)
1 .50 1.95
1A Prism enhanced cover. .75 2.95
2-5 .50 1.95

RAW (UNDERGROUND)
RAW (1980)
1 31.00 100.00
2-3 23.00 75.00
4-7 16.00 50.00

RAW MEDIA MAG
REBEL (1991)
1 1.50 5.00
2 1.00 3.00

RAWHIDE
DELL (1962)
01-684-208 Clint Eastwood photo cover. 31.00 100.00

RAWHIDE
DELL FOUR COLOR SERIES (1959-1962)
1028 TV photo cover (Clint Eastwood) on all issues. (9/59) 65.00 200.00
1097 (5/60) 45.00 140.00
1160 (2/61) 50.00 150.00
1202 (6/61) 50.00 150.00
1261 (11/61) 50.00 150.00
1269 (2/62) 50.00 150.00

RAWHIDE
GOLD KEY (1963-1964)
1 (10071-307) Clint Eastwood photo cover. 23.00 75.00
2 19.00 60.00

RAWHIDE KID
MARVEL (1985)
1-4 .30 1.00

RAWHIDE KID
MARVEL(ATLAS) (1955-1979)
1 145.00 480.00
2 75.00 240.00
3-6 40.00 130.00
7-12 29.00 95.00
13-22 19.00 60.00
23 Origin: Rawhide Kid by Jack Kirby. 40.00 120.00
24-30 15.00 48.00
31-40 11.00 36.00
41-50 10.00 30.00
51-70 8.00 24.00
71-80 6.00 19.00
81-90 5.00 14.00
91-99 2.50 9.50
100 Origin retold: Rawhide Kid (with new facts). 6.00 18.00
101-110 2.00 7.00
111-120 1.25 4.75
121-130 1.00 3.50
131-140 .75 2.25
141-151 .30 1.00
SPECIAL 1 (1971) 4.00 12.00

RAY, THE
DC (1992)
1 1st: new Ray. 4.00 12.00
2 2.25 8.00
3 1.50 5.00
4 2.50 9.00
5 1.25 4.00
6 2.00 7.00

RAY, THE
DC (1994-CURRENT)
0 (8/94) .75 2.25
1 Foil embossed cover. 1.00 3.50
1A Regular edition. .50 1.75
2-17 .75 2.25
ANNUAL 1 (1995) 1.00 3.95
TPB In A Blaze Of Power. Reprints mini-series. 2.50 9.95

RAY BRADBURY COMICS
TOPPS (1993-1994)
1-4 .75 2.95

RAZOR
LONDON NIGHT (1993-CURRENT)
0 (2ND) 2nd printing. (8/92) 1.00 3.00
0 1st: Razor. (4/92) 10.00 30.00
0B First "Razor" story redrawn. (4/95) 1.00 3.00
1 13.00 40.00
2 Art: James O'Barr. 6.00 18.00
2A Limited edition. 9.00 28.00
3 5.00 15.00
3A Limited edition. 7.00 20.00
4 2.75 10.00
4A Limited edition. 5.00 15.00
5 Cover: Joseph Michael Linsner. 5.00 15.00
6 O: Razor. 2.75 10.00
7-8 2.25 8.00
9 1.75 6.00

QUASAR #48

RADIOACTIVE MAN #3

RAI #1

THE RAY (MINI-SERIES) #4

RAZOR: BURN #2

REAL LIFE COMICS #48

REBELS 94 #0

RED SONJA #1

FAMOUS • FIRSTS

REAL FACT COMICS #6

This comic rambled through time to present bios of famous adventurers. This issue's importance comes from its introduction of Tommy Tomorrow, Virgil Finlay's fictional hero who continued adventuring into the Silver Age.

10 1st: Stryke. 5.00 15.00
11-12 .... 1.50 5.00
13 Begin title variant: Razor Uncut. ... 1.00 3.00
14-15 .... 1.00 3.00
ANNUAL 1 1st: Shi. 13.00 40.00
ANNUAL 2 .... 1.75 6.00

RAZOR AND SHI SPECIAL
LONDON NIGHT (1994)
1 Reprints Razor Annual #1 (plus new material).
.... 2.75 10.00
1A Platinum version. 8.00 25.00

RAZOR: BURN
LONDON NIGHT (1994-1995)
1 .... 1.50 5.50
2 .... 1.25 4.50
2A Platinum cover. 5.00 15.00
3 .... 1.25 4.00
4-5 .... 1.00 3.00

RAZOR: SWIMSUIT SPECIAL
LONDON NIGHT (1995)
1 .... 1.00 3.00
1A Platinum edition. 6.00 18.00

RAZOR: THE SUFFERING
LONDON NIGHT (1994)
1 .... 1.75 6.00
1A Director's Cut version (contains new material).
.... 1.75 6.00
2 .... 1.75 6.00
2A Director's Cut version (new material). 1.75 6.00

RAZOR VS DARK ANGEL
LONDON NIGHT STUDIOS/BONEYARD PRESS
NO# Reprints Final Nail #1, with 36 pages of new art and new ending. 1.50 5.95

RAZOR/DARK ANGEL: THE FINAL NAIL
LONDON NIGHT/BONEYARD (1994)
1 .... 1.00 3.50
2 .... .75 2.95

RAZORLINE: THE FIRST CUT
MARVEL (1993)
1 Preview of Clive Barker's Universe. ... .20 .75

REAL ADVENTURE COMICS
GILMORE (1955)
1 Title changes to Action Adventure Comics with #2.
.... 5.00 15.00

REAL CLUE CRIME STORIES
HILLMAN (1947-1953)
V2#4 Cover & art: Simon & Kirby. Previous title: Clue Comics.
.... 60.00 190.00
V2#5-V2#7 Cover/Art: Simon & Kirby. 40.00 130.00
V2#8-V2#12 .... 10.00 33.00
V3#1-V3#8 .... 7.00 22.00
V3#9 SOTI 14.00 44.00
V3#10-V3#12 .... 7.00 22.00
V4#1-V4#12 .... 7.00 22.00
V5#1-V6#12 .... 5.00 16.00
V7#1-V8#3 .... 4.00 11.00

REAL FACT COMICS
DC (1946-1949)
1 Art: Simon & Kirby. "The True Story Of America's Airborne Forest Rangers!" 110.00 360.00
2 Art: Simon & Kirby. "P. T. Barnum" (5-6/46)
.... 55.00 180.00
3 "The Story Of H. G. Wells, Mr. Future!" (7-8/46)
.... 40.00 120.00
4 Art: Virgil Finlay. "The Exciting Story Of Jimmy Stewart" (9-10/46) 55.00 180.00
5 "The True Story Of Batman And Robin" (11-12/46)
.... 290.00 950.00
6 1st & Origin: Tommy Tomorrow in "The First Man To Reach Mars!" by Virgil Finlay (1-2/47) ... 220.00 700.00
7 "Hollywood's Immortal Douglas Fairbanks"
.... 40.00 120.00
8 2nd: Tommy Tomorrow in "Operation Luna!" by Virgil Finlay (5-6/47) 110.00 360.00
9 Art: Simon & Kirby. "Daredevil Drivers Of The Indianapolis Speedway" (7-8/47) 50.00 150.00
10 "How Your Favorite Movie Serials Are Made featuring Columbia Pictures' The Vigilante!" (9-10/47)
.... 55.00 180.00
11 "Behind The Scenes With The F.B.I." (11-12/47)
.... 29.00 95.00
12 "The Marshall Who Fought Outlaws With His Fists!" (1-2/48) 29.00 95.00
13 Tommy Tomorrow in "The Thrilling Log Of A Pioneer Space Expedition!" (3-4/48) 110.00 360.00
14 "Will Rogers Diary Of Death!" ... 25.00 80.00
15 "The Last War On Earth!" (7-8/48) 25.00 80.00
16 "How The Four Reno Brothers Terrorized The West!"
.... 75.00 240.00
17 "I Guard An Armored Car!" (11-12/48)
.... 25.00 80.00
18 "The Mystery Man Of Tombstone" (1-2/49)
.... 25.00 80.00
19 "I Am A Camera Cop" 25.00 80.00
20 "How The Arson Squad Traps Firebugs!"
.... 25.00 80.00
21 "A Day In The Life Of A Paratrooper!" (7-8/49)
.... 25.00 80.00

REAL FUNNIES
NEDOR (1943)
1 .... 31.00 100.00
2-3 .... 19.00 60.00

REAL GHOSTBUSTERS, THE
NOW (1988-1992)
1-28 .... .30 1.00

REAL HEROES COMICS
PMI (1941-1946)
1 Franklin D. Roosevelt. 40.00 130.00
2 J. Edgar Hoover. 23.00 75.00
3-5 .... 14.00 44.00
6 Lou Gehrig. 26.00 85.00
7-16 .... 10.00 33.00

REAL LIFE COMICS
NEDOR (1941-1952)
1 .... 60.00 190.00
2 .... 20.00 65.00
3 Classic Hitler cover. 35.00 110.00
4-6 .... 17.00 55.00
7-12 .... 14.00 44.00
13-23 .... 12.00 38.00
24 Babe Ruth. 17.00 55.00
25-26 .... 10.00 33.00
27 Cover: Alex Schomburg. 17.00 55.00
28-40 .... 9.00 27.00
41-49 .... 7.00 22.00
50 Art: Frank Frazetta (5 pages). ... 35.00 110.00
51 .... 7.00 22.00
52 Art: Frank Frazetta. 35.00 110.00
53-59 .... 7.00 22.00

REAL MCCOYS, THE
DELL FOUR COLOR SERIES (1960-1961)
1071 TV photo covers on all issues. (1/60)
.... 28.00 90.00
1134 (9/60) 26.00 85.00
1193 (5/61) 23.00 75.00
1265 (11/61) 22.00 70.00

REAL SCREEN COMICS
DC (1945-1959)
1 Begin: The Fox & Crow. 200.00 650.00
2 .... 85.00 270.00
3-5 .... 60.00 190.00
6-12 .... 35.00 110.00
13-24 .... 26.00 85.00
25-40 .... 20.00 65.00
41-50 .... 15.00 49.00
51-60 .... 12.00 38.00
61-100 .... 9.00 27.00
101-110 .... 7.00 22.00
111-128 .... 5.00 16.00

REAL SPORTS COMICS
HILLMAN (1948)
1 Art: Bob Powell (12 pages). Title changes to All Sports Comics with #2. .... 55.00 175.00

REAL WEST ROMANCES
PRIZE (1949-1950)
1 "Wild Hosses And Ornery Women" Art: Simon & Kirby. Photo covers on all issues. 28.00 90.00
2 "Heartbroken Bronco Buster" 17.00 55.00
3 "In Love With His Ranch-Boss!" Art: Simon & Kirby. 17.00 55.00
4 "Lovin' Or Feudin'!" Art: Simon & Kirby. 26.00 85.00
5 "Gun-Totin' Bride!" Art: Simon & Kirby. 20.00 65.00
6 Art: Simon & Kirby. 17.00 55.00
V2#1 Art: Simon & Kirby. 13.00 40.00

REAL WESTERN HERO
FAWCETT (1948-1949)
70 Tom Mix, Hopalong Cassidy, Monte Hale. Previous title: Wow Comics. 50.00 160.00
71-74 .... 35.00 110.00
75 Title changes to Western Hero with #76. .... 35.00 110.00

REALISTIC ROMANCES
REALISTIC (1951-1954)
1 .... 23.00 75.00
2 .... 10.00 30.00
3-8 .... 8.00 25.00
15-17 .... 7.00 20.00

REALM, THE
ARROW (1986-1989)
1 .... 1.25 4.00
2 .... .75 2.00
3 .... .50 1.50
4 1st: Deadworld. 2.75 10.00
5-19 .... .50 1.50

RE-ANIMATOR
ADVENTURE (1991-1992)
1 Movie adaptation. .... .75 2.00
2-3 .... .75 2.00

REAP THE WILD WIND
PARAMOUNT (1942)
NO# Movie giveaway (4 pages). From the Cinema Comics Herald series. 31.00 100.00

REBEL, THE
DELL FOUR COLOR SERIES (1960-1961)
1076 TV photo covers on all issues. (2/60) 22.00 70.00
1138 (10/60) 19.00 60.00
1207 (8/61) 19.00 60.00
1262 (11/61) 19.00 60.00

R.E.B.E.L.S.
DC (1994-CURRENT)
0 (8/94) .... .50 1.95
1 Begin '94 season. .... .50 1.95
2-4 .... .50 1.95
5 Begin: '95 season. .... .50 1.95
6-7 .... .50 1.95
8-11 .... .75 2.25

RECORD BOOK OF FAMOUS POLICE CASES
ST. JOHN (1949)
NO# Cover: Matt Baker. Art: Joe Kubert. 55.00 175.00

RED ARROW
PL (1951)
1 .... 8.00 25.00
2-3 .... 5.00 15.00

RED CIRCLE COMICS
RURAL HOME (1945)
1 Begin: The Prankster. 35.00 110.00
2 .... 17.00 55.00
3-4 .... 10.00 33.00

RED CIRCLE SORCERY
SEE SORCERY

RED DRAGON COMICS
STREET & SMITH (1943-1944)
5 Previous title: Trail Blazers. 100.00 330.00
6 .... 85.00 270.00
7-9 .... 70.00 220.00

RED DRAGON COMICS
STREET & SMITH (1947-1949)
1 Begin: Red Dragon. 115.00 380.00
2 Cover: Ed Cartier. 100.00 330.00
3 1st: Dr. Neff, Ghost Breaker. 85.00 270.00
4 Cover: Ed Cartier. 115.00 380.00
5-7 .... 70.00 220.00

RED FOX
HARRIER/VALKYRIE (1986-1988)
1 .... 1.50 5.00
2 .... 1.25 4.00
3 .... .75 2.50
4-20 .... .75 2.00

RED FOX (A-1 SERIES)
ME (1954)
15 (A-1 #108). 19.00 60.00

RED HAWK (A-1 SERIES)
ME (1953)
11 (A-1 #90). Cover/Art: Bob Powell. 16.00 50.00

RED ICEBERG
IMPACT (1960)
NO# Anti-communism. 50.00 150.00

RED MASK
I.W. (1958)
1-3 .... 2.25 8.00

RED MASK
ME (1954-1957)
42 Previous title: Tim Holt. 23.00 75.00
43 .... 16.00 50.00
44-46 .... 13.00 40.00
47-54 .... 10.00 30.00

RED MOUNTAIN FEATURING QUANTRELL'S RAIDERS
AVON (1952)
NO# Movie tie-in. 31.00 100.00

RED RAVEN COMICS
MARVEL(TIMELY) (1940)
1 1st & Origin: Red Raven. 1st signed work by Jack Kirby. 2100.00 8000.00

RED RYDER COMICS
HAWLEY/DELL (1940-1957)
NO# (1950) Wells Lamont Company giveaway. 45.00 140.00
1 (9/40) 250.00 825.00
2 Does not exist. See Hi-Spot Comics #2.
3 (8/41) 135.00 440.00
4-5 .... 100.00 330.00
6 Begin: Dell publication. 85.00 270.00
7-10 .... 60.00 190.00
11-20 .... 50.00 160.00
21-30 .... 35.00 110.00
31-39 .... 26.00 85.00
40 Begin: photo back covers. 26.00 85.00
41-50 .... 20.00 65.00
51-56 .... 17.00 55.00
57 End: photo back covers. 17.00 55.00
58-60 .... 17.00 55.00
61-70 .... 14.00 44.00
71-90 .... 10.00 33.00
91-98 .... 7.00 22.00
99 Begin: Jim Bannon photo covers. 7.00 22.00
100-105 .... 7.00 22.00
106 End: Jim Bannon photo covers. 7.00 22.00
107-110 .... 7.00 22.00
111-130 .... 5.00 16.00
131-151 .... 4.00 11.00

RED RYDER RANCH COMICS
DELL FOUR COLOR SERIES (1958)
916 (7/58) 7.00 20.00

RED SEAL COMICS
CHESLER (1945-1947)
14 .... 70.00 220.00
15 .... 50.00 160.00
16 SOTI 85.00 270.00
17-21 App: Lady Satan. 40.00 130.00
22 Rocketman. 50.00 160.00

RED SONJA
MARVEL (1977-1979)
1 Also see Marvel Feature. 1.00 3.00
2-6 .... .75 2.00
7-15 .... .30 1.00

RED SONJA
MARVEL (1983)
1 .... .75 2.50
2 .... .75 2.00

RED SONJA
MARVEL (1983-1986)
1-2 .... .75 2.00
3-6 .... .50 1.25
7-13 .... .30 1.00

RED SONJA: THE MOVIE
MARVEL (1985)
1 Movie adaptation. .... .30 1.00
2 .... .30 1.00

RED WARRIOR
MARVEL(ATLAS) (1951)
1 .... 17.00 55.00
2 .... 10.00 33.00
3-6 .... 7.00 22.00

RED WOLF
MARVEL (1972-1973)
1 .... 1.75 6.00
2-9 .... 1.00 3.00

REDDY GOOSE
WESTERN (1958-1962)
1 (NO#) Giveaway (International Shoe Company). 11.00 35.00
2-16 .... 5.00 15.00

REDDY KILOWATT
EDUCATIONAL (1946-1960)
1 "Reddy Made Magic" (1946) 16.00 50.00
1A "Reddy Made Magic" (1958) 10.00 30.00
2 "Wizard Of Light" (1956) 8.00 25.00
2A "Wizard Of Light" (1958) 8.00 25.00
3 "The Space Kite" (1956) 8.00 25.00
3A "The Space Kite" (1960) 8.00 25.00

REDSKIN
YOUTHFUL (1950-1952)
1 .... 13.00 40.00
2 .... 7.00 20.00
3-12 .... 4.00 12.00

REFORM SCHOOL GIRL!
REALISTIC (1951)
NO# Photo cover. SOTI 200.00 650.00

REG'LAR FELLERS
CUPPLES & LEON (1928)
1928 Softcover, 36 pages. 31.00 100.00

REGGIE
ARCHIE (1963-1980)
15 Previous title: Archie's Rival Reggie. 14.00 44.00
16-18 .... 10.00 33.00
19 Title changes to Reggie And Me. 9.00 27.00
20-30 .... 5.00 16.00
31-49 .... 4.00 11.00
50 Begin: Giant size issues. 4.00 11.00
51-67 .... 1.50 5.50
68 End: Giant size issues. 1.50 5.50
69-70 .... 1.50 5.50
71-90 .... .75 2.00
91-126 .... .30 1.00

REGGIE'S WISE-GUY JOKES
ARCHIE (1968-1981)
1 .... 4.00 13.00
2 .... 1.75 6.50
3-6 .... 1.25 4.25
7-12 .... 1.00 3.25
13-24 .... .75 2.00
25-55 .... .30 1.00

REGULATORS
IMAGE/SHADOWLINE (1995-CURRENT)
1-2 .... .75 2.50

REMEMBER PEARL HARBOR
STREET & SMITH (1942)
NO# 65.00 200.00

REN & STIMPY
MARVEL (1992-CURRENT)
1A Polybagged with Ren scratch & sniff air fowler. 2.75 10.00
1B Polybagged with Stimpy scratch & sniff air fowler. 2.75 10.00
1 (2ND) 2nd printing. .... .75 2.00
2 .... 1.25 5.00
3-5 .... 1.50 5.00
6 Spider-Man. 1.50 5.00
7 .... 1.00 3.00
8-10 .... .75 2.50
11-17 .... .75 2.00
18-24 .... .75 2.00
25 Die-cut cover. .... .75 2.95
25A Regular edition. .... .75 2.00
26-33 .... .75 2.00
TPB VOL 1 Pick Of The Litter. Reprints issues #1-4, with new material. 4.00 12.95
TPB VOL 2 Tastes Like Chicken. Reprints issues #5-8. .... 4.00 12.95
TPB VOL 3 Reprints issues #9-12. .... 4.00 12.95

RED WARRIOR #2

REDSKIN #6

REGULATORS #2

REN & STIMPY #5

REPTILICUS #1

THE RETURN OF GORGO #2

REX ALLEN #4

RICHIE RICH #14

TPB VOL 4 Your Pals. Reprints issues #13-16. 4.00 12.95
TPB VOL 5 Seeck Little Monkeys. Reprints issues #17-20. 4.00 12.95

REN AND STIMPY: EENTERACTEEVE SPECIAL
MARVEL (1995)
1 Error: pages printed out of order. .75 2.95
1A Corrected version. .75 2.95

REN AND STIMPY: FOUR SWERKS SPECIAL
MARVEL (1994)
NO# .75 2.95

REN AND STIMPY HOLIDAY SPECIAL
MARVEL (1994)
1 Reprints plus new material. .75 2.95

REN AND STIMPY: MASTERS OF TIME AND SPACE
MARVEL (1994)
NO# .75 2.95

REN AND STIMPY: POWDERED TOAST MAN
MARVEL (1993)
1 Double size issue. .75 2.95

REN AND STIMPY: POWDERED TOAST MAN'S CEREAL SERIAL SPECIAL
MARVEL (1995)
1 .75 2.95

REN AND STIMPY: SUMMER JOBS SPECIAL
MARVEL (1994)
NO# .50 1.95

REN AND STIMPY: VIRTUAL STUPIDITY
MARVEL (1995)
1 .75 2.95

RENO BROWNE
MARVEL (1950)
50 Previous title: Margie Comics. Movie photo cover on all issues. 31.00 100.00
51-52 23.00 75.00

REPTILICUS
CHARLTON (1961)
1 Movie tie-in. 20.00 65.00
2 Title changes to Reptisaurus with #3. 14.00 46.00

REPTISAURUS
CHARLTON (1962-1963)
3 Previous title: Reptilicus. 7.00 23.00
4-8 6.00 17.00
SPECIAL 1 7.00 23.00

REQUIEM FOR DRACULA
MARVEL (1993)
NO# Reprint: Tomb Of Dracula #69, 70. .75 2.00

RESTAURANT AT THE END OF THE UNIVERSE, THE
DC (1995)
1 Adaptation of 2nd book in the "Hitchhiker's Guide" series. 1.50 5.95
2-3 1.50 5.95

RESTLESS GUN
DELL FOUR COLOR SERIES (1958-1960)
934 TV photo cover. (9/58) 23.00 75.00
986 TV photo cover. (4/59) 16.00 50.00
1045 TV photo cover. (11/59) 16.00 50.00
1089 TV photo cover. (4/60) 16.00 50.00
1146 TV photo cover. (11/60) 17.00 55.00

RETURN OF GORGO, THE
CHARLTON (1963-1964)
2 Movie tie-in. Cover & art: Steve Ditko. Previous title: Gorgo's Revenge. 19.00 60.00
3 Cover/Art: Steve Ditko. 16.00 50.00

RETURN OF KONGA, THE
CHARLTON (1962)
NO# 14.00 46.00

RETURN TO JURASSIC PARK
TOPPS (1995-CURRENT)
1-1A .75 2.50
3-4 .75 2.95

REVENGERS
CONTINUITY (1985-1989)
1 Starring Megalith. .75 2.00
2-6 .75 2.00

REX ALLEN COMICS
DELL (1951-1959)
1 (#316) From the 4-Color Series. (2/51) Photo covers on all issues. 40.00 130.00
2 13.00 40.00
3-6 8.00 25.00
7-12 7.00 20.00
13-18 5.00 15.00
19-31 2.75 10.00

REX DEXTER OF MARS
FOX (1940)
1 400.00 1400.00

REX HART
MARVEL(TIMELY) (1949-1950)
6 Previous title: Blaze Carson. Photo covers on all issues. 28.00 90.00
7 "Mystery At The Bar-Z Ranch!" 17.00 55.00
8 "The Hombre Who Killed His Friend!" 17.00 55.00

REX THE WONDER DOG
SEE ADVENTURES OF REX THE WONDER DOG

RHUBARB
DELL FOUR COLOR SERIES (1952-1954)
423 "Owner Of The Brooklyn Ball Club" (9/52) 10.00 30.00
466 "The Millionaire Cat" (4/53) 7.00 20.00
563 "The Millionaire Cat" (6/54) 5.00 15.00

RIBTICKLER
FOX (1945-1947)
1 13.00 40.00
2 7.00 20.00
3 2.75 10.00
4-9 1.75 6.00

RICHARD DRAGON, KUNG-FU FIGHTER
DC (1975-1977)
1-18 .30 1.00

RICHIE RICH
HARVEY (1960-1991)
1 125.00 400.00
2 65.00 200.00
3-6 31.00 100.00
7-12 19.00 60.00
13-18 13.00 40.00
19-24 7.00 20.00
25-40 5.00 15.00
41-80 2.75 10.00
81-100 1.75 6.00
101-111 1.00 3.00
112 Begin: Double size issues. 1.25 4.00
113-115 1.25 4.00
116 End: Double size issues. 1.25 4.00
117-150 .30 1.00
151-254 .20 .50

RICHIE RICH DOLLARS AND CENTS
HARVEY (1963-1982)
1 16.00 50.00
2 7.00 20.00
3-12 2.25 8.00
13-24 1.25 4.00
25-50 .75 2.00
51-109 .20 .50

RICHIE RICH MILLIONS
HARVEY (1961-1982)
1 19.00 60.00
2 7.00 20.00
3-12 2.75 10.00
13-24 1.50 5.00
25-50 1.00 3.00
51-70 .30 1.00
71-113 .20 .50

RICHIE RICH PROFITS
HARVEY (1974-1982)
1 1.00 3.00
2-6 .75 2.00
7-12 .30 1.00
13-47 .20 .50

RICHIE RICH SUCCESS STORIES
HARVEY (1964-1982)
1 16.00 50.00
2 7.00 20.00
3-6 2.75 10.00
7-12 1.50 5.00
13-24 1.00 3.00
25-50 .75 2.00
51-105 .20 .50

RICKY
STANDARD (1953)
5 2.25 8.00

RICKY NELSON
DELL FOUR COLOR SERIES (1958-1961)
956 TV photo cover. (12/58) 35.00 110.00
998 TV photo cover. (7/59) 31.00 100.00
1115 TV photo cover. (7/60) 31.00 100.00
1192 TV photo cover. (3/61) 31.00 100.00

RIFLEMAN, THE
DELL/GOLD KEY (1959-1964)
1 (#1009) From the 4-Color Series. TV photo cover (Chuck Connors). (7/59) 40.00 125.00
2 TV photo covers on all issues. 20.00 65.00
3-6 17.00 55.00
7-12 14.00 44.00
13 Begin: Gold Key publication. 10.00 33.00
14-20 10.00 33.00

RIMA, THE JUNGLE GIRL
DC (1974-1975)
1-7 .30 1.00

RIN TIN TIN
DELL/GOLD KEY (1952-1963)
1 (#434) From the 4-Color Series. "Dark Danger." TV photo covers on all issues. (11/52) 45.00 140.00
2 (#476) From the 4-Color Series. (6/53) 20.00 65.00
3 (#523) From the 4-Color Series. (12/53) 20.00 65.00
4 13.00 40.00
5-8 11.00 35.00
9-12 8.00 25.00
13-18 7.00 20.00
19-38 5.00 15.00

RING OF BRIGHT WATER
DELL (1969)
01-701-910 Movie tie-in. 5.00 15.00

RINGO KID, THE
MARVEL (1970-1976)
1 1.00 3.00
2-30 .30 1.00

RINGO KID WESTERN
MARVEL(ATLAS) (1954-1957)
1 35.00 110.00
2 17.00 55.00
3-6 10.00 33.00
7-12 9.00 27.00
13-21 7.00 22.00

RIO BRAVO
DELL FOUR COLOR SERIES (1959)
1018 Movie photo cover (John Wayne, Dean Martin). (6/59) 55.00 175.00

RIO CONCHOS
GOLD KEY (1965)
10143-503 Movie tie-in (photo insert). 13.00 40.00

RIOT
MARVEL(ATLAS) (1954-1956)
1 19.00 60.00
2-6 16.00 50.00

RIOT GEAR
TRIUMPHANT (1993-1994)
0 .75 2.50
1 1st: Riot Gear. With coupon. .75 2.50
2-11 .75 2.50

RIP HUNTER, TIME MASTER
DC (1961-1965)
1 See Showcase #20 for 1st app. "The 1,000-Year-Old Curse!" 125.00 400.00
2 55.00 175.00
3-5 26.00 85.00
6 Art: Alex Toth. 1st 12 cent cover price. 20.00 65.00
7 Art: Alex Toth. 20.00 65.00
8-12 17.00 55.00
13-18 16.00 50.00
19-24 14.00 45.00
25-29 13.00 40.00

RIP IN TIME
FANTAGOR (1986-1987)
1-5 .30 1.00

RIPCLAW
IMAGE/TOP COW (1995)
1/2 Wizard mail-away offer. 2.75 10.00
1/2 (GOLD) 7.00 20.00
1/2A Chicago Con version (3500). ... 8.00 25.00
1/2B San Diego Con version (3500). 8.00 25.00
1/2C Dragon Con version (3500). ... 8.00 25.00
1 .... 1.00 4.00
2-4 .... .75 2.50

RIPCORD
DELL FOUR COLOR SERIES (1962)
1294 TV tie-in. (2/62) 13.00 40.00

RIPFIRE
MALIBU (1995-CURRENT)
0 .... .75 2.50

RIPLEY'S BELIEVE IT OR NOT!
GOLD KEY (1967-1980)
4 Previous title: Ripley's Believe It Or Not True War Stories."
.... 2.75 10.00
5 .... 1.50 5.00
6-12 .... 1.00 3.00
13-50 .... .75 2.00
51-94 .... .30 1.00

RIPLEY'S BELIEVE IT OR NOT!
HARVEY (1953-1954)
1 Art: Bob Powell. 16.00 50.00
2-4 .... 10.00 30.00

RIPLEY'S BELIEVE IT OR NOT TRUE GHOST STORIES
GOLD KEY (1965-1966)
1 .... 7.00 20.00
2 Title changes to Ripley's Believe It Or Not True War Stories.
.... 2.75 10.00

RIPLEY'S BELIEVE IT OR NOT TRUE WAR STORIES
GOLD KEY (1966)
3 .... 5.00 15.00

RIVETS
DELL FOUR COLOR SERIES (1953)
518 (12/53) 5.00 15.00

ROB ROY
DELL FOUR COLOR SERIES (1954)
544 Disney movie photo cover. (3/54) 22.00 70.00

ROBIN
DC (1991)
1 Origin: Robin. 1.50 5.00
1 (2ND) 2nd printing. .... .75 2.25
1 (3RD) 3rd printing. .... .50 1.50
2 .... 1.00 3.25
2 (2ND) 2nd printing. .... .30 1.00
3 .... 1.00 3.00
4 .... .75 2.50
5 .... .50 1.75

ROBIN
DC (1993-CURRENT)
0 (8/94) .... .75 2.50
1 Embossed foil cover. 1.25 4.00
1A Newsstand version. .... .50 1.75
2-7 .... .50 1.50
8 1st: Bruce back in Batman costume. 1.25 4.00
9 .... .75 2.50
10 .... .75 2.00
11-13 .... .50 1.50
14 Embossed cover. .... .75 2.50
14A Regular cover. .... .50 1.50
15-16 .... .50 1.50
17-20 .... .50 1.95
ANNUAL 1 (1992) .... .75 2.50
ANNUAL 2 Bloodlines, pt.10. (1993) ... .75 2.50
ANNUAL 3 Elseworlds story. (1994) ... .75 2.95
ANNUAL 4 (1995) .... .75 2.95

ROBIN 3000
DC (1993)
1-2 .... 1.25 4.95

ROBIN: A HERO REBORN
DC (1991)
TPB Reprint: Batman Comics #455-457, Robin #1-5.
.... 1.25 4.95

ROBIN HOOD
DELL (1963)
1 One shot. 2.75 10.00

ROBIN HOOD
DELL FOUR COLOR SERIES (1952-1955)
413 Disney movie photo cover. (8/52) 25.00 80.00
669 Disney movie photo cover. (12/55) 10.00 30.00

ROBIN HOOD
DISNEY (FLOUR GIVEAWAY) (1952)
NO# Measures 5" x 7-1/4" 5.00 15.00

ROBIN HOOD
GOLD KEY (1965)
10163-506 Disney movie tie-in. 5.00 15.00

ROBIN HOOD
ME (1955-1957)
1 (#52 on cover) TV tie-in and photo cover. 25.00 80.00
2 (#53 on cover) 20.00 65.00
3-4 .... 20.00 65.00
5 Title changes to Adventures Of Robin Hood with #6.
.... 20.00 65.00

ROBIN HOOD TALES
QUALITY/DC (1956-1957)
1 .... 40.00 120.00
2 .... 22.00 70.00
3-5 .... 19.00 60.00
6 .... 15.00 48.00
7 Begin: DC publication. 50.00 150.00
8-14 .... 31.00 100.00

ROBIN II: JOKER'S WILD
DC (1991)
SET Deluxe: comes with every version of all four issues (14 in all), slipcase; Limited to 25,000. ...... 10.00 30.00
SET Collects all versions of #1, with hologram card.
.... 2.75 10.00
1A Batman cover, with hologram. ...... .50 1.50
1B Joker close-up cover, with hologram. .50 1.50
1C Joker in straightjacket cover, with hologram.
.... .50 1.50
1D Joker with video screens cover, with hologram.
.... .50 1.50
1 Death: Mr. Freeze. Newsstand version, without hologram.
.... .30 1.00
2 SET Collects all versions of #2, with hologram card.
.... 2.25 8.00
2A Dartboard cover, with hologram. ... .50 1.50
2B Room of Paintings cover, with hologram. .50 1.50
2C Museum cover, with hologram. ...... .50 1.50
2 Newsstand version, without hologram. .30 1.00
3 Newsstand version, without hologram. .30 1.00
3 SET Collects all versions of #3, with hologram card.
.... 1.75 6.00
3A Robin swinging cover, with hologram. .50 1.50
3B Robin on rooftop cover, with hologram. .50 1.50
4 SET Collects both versions of #4, with hologram card.
.... 1.25 4.00
4A Robin vs. Joker cover, with hologram. .50 1.50
4 Newsstand version, without hologram. .30 1.00

ROBIN III: CRY OF THE HUNTRESS
DC (1992-1993)
1 .... .75 2.50
1A Newsstand version. .... .50 1.25
2 .... .75 2.50
2A Newsstand version. .... .50 1.25
3 .... .75 2.50
3A Newsstand version. .... .50 1.25
4 .... .75 2.50
4A Newsstand version. .... .50 1.25
5 .... .75 2.50
5A Newsstand version. .... .50 1.25
6 .... .75 2.50
6A Newsstand version. .... .50 1.25

ROBIN: TRAGEDY AND TRIUMPH
DC (1993)
TPB Reprint: Detective Comics #618-621, Robin II #1-4.
.... 2.50 9.95

ROBOCOP
MARVEL (1987) MAGAZINE
1 Movie adaptation. 1.00 3.00

ROBOCOP
MARVEL (1990-1992)
1 Movie tie-in. 1.25 4.00
2-7 .... .75 2.00
8-22 .... .50 1.50

ROBOCOP 2
MARVEL (1990)
1 Movie adaptation. .... .75 2.00
2-3 .... .75 2.00

ROBOCOP 2
MARVEL (1990) MAGAZINE
1 Movie adaptation. 1.00 3.00

ROBOCOP 3
DARK HORSE (1992)
1-3 .... .75 2.50

ROBOCOP: PRIME SUSPECT
DARK HORSE (1992-1993)
1-4 .... .75 2.50

ROBOCOP: ROULETTE
DARK HORSE (1993)
1-4 .... .75 2.50

ROBOCOP VERSUS THE TERMINATOR
DARK HORSE (1992)
1 .... .75 2.50
1A Platinum edition. 2.75 10.00
2-4 .... .75 2.50

ROBOTECH DEFENDERS
DC (1985)
1-2 .... .30 1.00

ROBOTECH: FIREWALKERS
ETERNITY
1 .... .75 2.50

ROBOTECH: GENESIS
ETERNITY
1 Origin: Zor. .... .75 2.95
1A Expanded (2500). 1.50 5.95
2-3 .... .75 2.95
4-6 .... .75 2.50

ROBOTECH GRAPHIC NOVEL
COMICO (1986)
1 .... 1.50 5.00

ROBOTECH II: CYBER-PIRATES
ETERNITY
1 .... .75 2.00

ROBOTECH II: HANDBOOK
ETERNITY
SC Soft cover. 5.00 14.95

ROBOTECH II: MALCONTENT UPRISINGS
ETERNITY
1-12 .... .75 2.00

ROBOTECH II: RETURN TO MACROSS
ETERNITY
1-13 .... .75 2.50

ROBOTECH II: THE SENTINELS
ETERNITY
1 .... 1.25 4.00
2-3 .... 1.00 3.50
4-16 .... .75 2.00

ROBOTECH II: THE SENTINELS BOOK II
ETERNITY
1-21 .... .75 2.50
SWIMSUIT Spectacular. .... .75 2.95

ROBOTECH II: THE SENTINELS BOOK III
ETERNITY (1993-1994)
1-8 .... .75 2.50

ROBOTECH: INVID WAR
ETERNITY
1-16 .... .75 2.50

ROBOTECH INVID WAR: AFTERMATH
ETERNITY
1-6 .... .75 2.50

ROBOTECH MASTERS
COMICO (1985-1988)
1 .... 1.00 3.00
2-23 .... .75 2.00

ROBOTECH SPECIAL
COMICO (1988)
1 .... .50 1.50

ROBOTECH: THE LEGEND OF ZOR
ETERNITY
1 With trading cards. .... .50 1.95
1A Limited edition. 1.50 5.95

ROBOTECH: THE MACROSS SAGA
COMICO (1985-1989)
1 .... 7.00 20.00
2 .... 1.75 6.00
3-5 .... 1.25 4.00

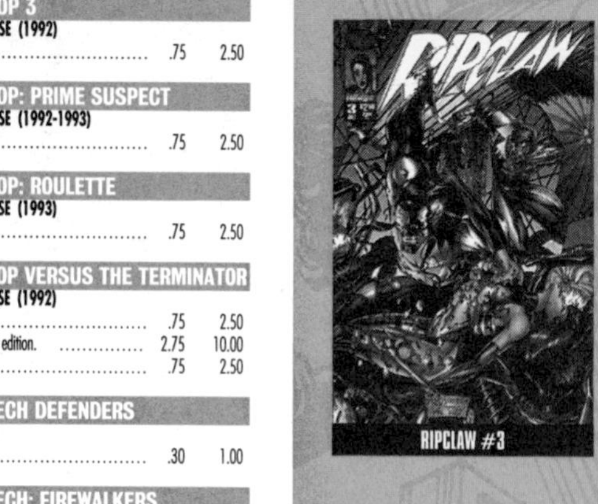
RIPCLAW #3

ROBIN ANNUAL #3

ROBIN 3000#1

ROBOCOP: ROULETTE #1

ROGUE #2

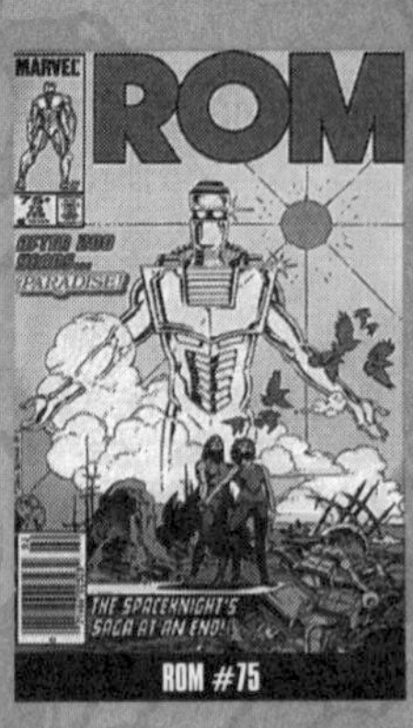

ROM #75

ROY ROGERS COMICS #6

RUDOLPH, THE RED NOSED REINDEER #57

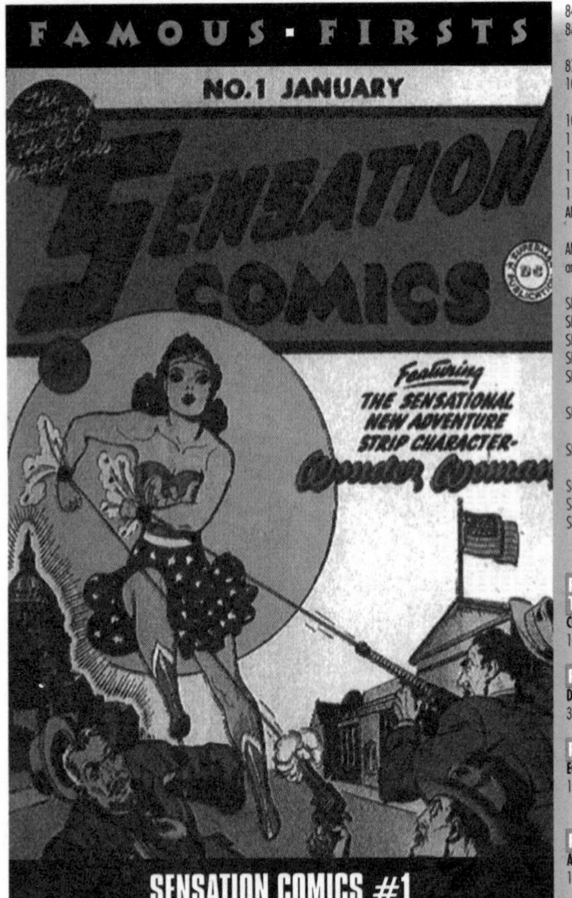

SENSATION COMICS #1

Continued from *All-Star Comics* #8, this comic finishes revealing the origin of Wonder Woman who comes to man's world and takes on Diana Prince's identity. Plus, Wildcat and Mr. Terrific make their debut.

6-7 .... 1.00 3.00
8-36 .... .75 2.00

ROBOTECH: THE NEW GENERATION
COMICO (1985-1988)
1-25 .... .75 2.00

ROBOTIX
MARVEL (1986)
1 One shot. .... .30 1.00

ROBOTMEN OF THE LOST PLANET
AVON (1952)
1 .... 135.00 440.00

ROCK 'N' ROLL COMICS
REVOLUTIONARY (1989-CURRENT)
1 Guns N Roses. 2.25 8.00
1 (2-7TH) 2nd through 7th printings. ... .75 2.50
2 Metallica. 1.50 5.00
2 (2-6TH) 2nd through 6th printings. ... .75 2.50
3-7 .... .75 2.50
8 Skid Row (never published).
9-69 .... .75 2.50
70-72 .... .75 2.25
SPECIAL Women In Rock. .... .75 2.50

ROCKET COMICS
HILLMAN (1940)
1 .... 280.00 920.00
2 .... 180.00 575.00
3 .... 140.00 460.00

ROCKET KELLY
FOX (1944-1946)
NO# Dated 1944. .... 35.00 110.00
1 (Fall, 1945) 28.00 90.00
2 .... 25.00 80.00
3-5 .... 20.00 65.00

ROCKET SHIP X
FOX (1951)
1 "Out Of This World" (9/51) 55.00 180.00

ROCKET TO THE MOON
AVON (1951)
NO# 135.00 440.00

ROCKET'S BLAST COMICCOLLECTOR (FANZINE)
SFCA (1961-1982)
1 All issues 1-40 are very low circulation, title pages state from 250 to 700 copies printed. 50.00 150.00
2-10 .... 11.00 35.00
11-28 .... 7.00 20.00
29 Title changes to RB-CC. 6.00 18.00
30 (1964) 5.00 15.00
31 Roy Thomas sells his "All Star" collection.
.... 8.00 25.00
32-46 .... 5.00 15.00
47 Cover: Wally Wood (1967). 5.00 15.00
48-49 .... 5.00 15.00
50 Anniversary special issue. 7.00 20.00
51-53 .... 2.75 10.00
54 Cover: Wally Wood. 5.00 15.00
55 .... 2.75 10.00
56 Cover: Wally Wood. 5.00 15.00
57 .... 2.75 10.00
58 (1968). 2.75 10.00
59-70 .... 2.75 10.00
71 .... 1.50 5.00
72 Color Werewolf cover by Juanillo. ... 2.75 10.00
73 .... 1.50 5.00
74 1st pre-publication ad for Overstreet's Comic Book Price Guide (1970). 7.00 20.00
75-80 .... 1.50 5.00
81 Cover: Richard Corben. 2.75 10.00
82 .... 1.50 5.00
83 Cover: Richard Corben. 2.75 10.00
84-85 .... 1.50 5.00
86 Full color horror cover by Berni Wrightson.
.... 7.00 20.00
87-99 .... 1.50 5.00
100 Anniversary issue with checklist of all RB-CC to date.
.... 7.00 20.00
101-113 .... 1.50 5.00
114 Cover: Berni Wrightson. 2.75 10.00
115-116 .... 1.50 5.00
117 Cover: Berni Wrightson. 2.75 10.00
118-155 .... 1.50 5.00
ANNUAL 1 Includes material from early issues.
.... 16.00 50.00
ANNUAL 2 Massive "Fandom" issue. 154 pg. square bound annual with lots of articles and art from earlier issues.
.... 16.00 50.00
SPECIAL 1 Timely Comics checklist. ... 10.00 30.00
SPECIAL 1A 2nd printing. 5.00 15.00
SPECIAL 1B 3rd printing. Color cover. ... 2.75 10.00
SPECIAL 2 Human Torch cover (1963). 5.00 15.00
SPECIAL 3 Story Of "All-American Comics." (1964).
.... 2.75 10.00
SPECIAL 4 Commie Fighters of the 50s (Fall, 1964).
.... 2.75 10.00
SPECIAL 5 Stars Of "Star-Spangled Comics" (Winter, 1964).
.... 2.75 10.00
SPECIAL 6 Stars of Quality Comics Group. 2.75 10.00
SPECIAL 7 EC/Sci Fi Comics. 2.75 10.00
SPECIAL 8 Full color cover of Captain Marvel (1970).
.... 2.75 10.00

ROCKETEER ADVENTURE MAGAZINE, THE
COMICO (1988-1989)
1-2 Cover/Art: Dave Stevens. 2.75 10.00

ROCKETEER ADVENTURE MAGAZINE
DARK HORSE (1995)
3 .... 1.00 3.00

ROCKETEER SPECIAL EDITION, THE
ECLIPSE (1984)
1 "The Rocketeer, Chapter 5" by Dave Stevens. (11/84)
.... 8.00 25.00

ROCKETMAN
AJAX (1952)
1 .... 65.00 200.00

ROCKETS AND RANGE RIDERS
RICHFIELD (1957)
NO# Giveaway. 16.00 50.00

ROCKY AND HIS FIENDISH FRIENDS
GOLD KEY (1962-1963)
1 80 page giant. 55.00 180.00
2-3 80 page giant. 40.00 120.00
4-5 .... 23.00 75.00

ROCKY AND HIS FRIENDS
DELL FOUR COLOR SERIES (1960-1962)
1128 TV tie-in. (8/60) 65.00 200.00
1152 TV tie-in. (11/60) 55.00 175.00
1166 TV tie-in. (2/61) 50.00 150.00
1208 TV tie-in. (8/61) 50.00 150.00
1275 TV tie-in. (12/61) 50.00 150.00
1311 TV tie-in. (3/62) 50.00 150.00

ROCKY HORROR PICTURE SHOW
CALIBER (1990)
1 Movie adaptation. 1.50 5.00
2-3 .... 1.00 3.00

ROCKY LANE WESTERN
FAWCETT/CHARLTON (1949-1959)
1 Photo covers #s 1-60. .... 115.00 380.00
2 .... 50.00 160.00
3-6 .... 35.00 110.00
7-12 .... 23.00 75.00
13-24 .... 17.00 55.00
25-40 .... 12.00 38.00
41-55 .... 9.00 27.00
56 Begin: Charlton publication. (2/54) 7.00 22.00
57-87 .... 5.00 16.00

ROD CAMERON WESTERN
FAWCETT (1950-1953)
1 Photo covers on all issues. 85.00 270.00
2 .... 35.00 110.00
3 .... 23.00 75.00
4-6 .... 17.00 55.00
7-20 .... 14.00 44.00

ROGER RABBIT
DISNEY (1990-1991)
1 Movie tie-in. 1.00 3.00
2 .... .75 2.00

3-18 .50 1.50

ROGUE
MARVEL (1994-1995)
1 Foil-stamped cover. 1.25 4.50
2-3 1.00 3.00
4 Foil-stamped cover. 1.00 3.00

ROLY POLY COMICS
GREEN (1945-1946)
NO# (1945) 31.00 100.00
10 (1/46) 16.00 50.00
11-14 16.00 50.00
15 App: Blue Circle. 23.00 75.00

ROM
MARVEL (1979-1986)
1 1st & Origin: Rom. Toy tie-in. .75 2.00
2-16 .30 1.00
17-18 X-Men. .75 2.00
19-75 .20 .50
ANNUAL 1-ANNUAL 4 .30 1.00

ROMANCE STORIES OF TRUE LOVE
HARVEY (1957-1958)
45 Previous title: Love Problems & Advice Illustrated. 2.75 10.00
46-51 2.75 10.00
52 Art: Matt Baker. 7.00 20.00

ROMANCE TRAIL
DC (1949-1950)
1 Photo covers on all issues. 70.00 230.00
2-6 35.00 115.00

ROMANCES OF THE WEST
MARVEL (1949-1950)
1 "The Cowpoke Who Lassoed My Heart!" Movie photo cover (Calamity Jane And Sam Bass with Yvonne De Carlo and Howard Duff). 29.00 95.00
2 Photo cover. 20.00 65.00

ROMANTIC HEARTS
MERIT (1953-1955)
1 7.00 20.00
2 2.75 10.00
3-12 1.75 6.00

ROMANTIC HEARTS
STORY (1951-1952)
1 10.00 30.00
2 5.00 15.00
3-10 2.75 10.00

ROMANTIC LOVE
AVON (1949-1954)
1 23.00 75.00
2-5 13.00 40.00
6 Marijuana use in "Thrill Crazy" story. 23.00 75.00
7-23 10.00 30.00

ROMANTIC PICTURE NOVELETTES
ME (1946)
1 A complete Mary Worth adventure. 10.00 30.00

ROMANTIC SECRETS
CHARLTON (1955-1964)
5 2.75 10.00
6-10 1.50 5.00
11-20 .75 2.00
21-51 .30 1.00
52 Title changes to Time For Love V2#53. .30 1.00

ROMANTIC SECRETS
FAWCETT (1949-1953)
1 Photo cover. 13.00 40.00
2 7.00 20.00
3-6 5.00 15.00
7-12 2.75 10.00
13-39 1.50 5.00

ROMANTIC STORY
FAWCETT/CHARLTON (1949-1973)
1 13.00 40.00
2 7.00 20.00
3-10 2.75 10.00
11-22 1.50 5.00
23 Begin: Charlton publication. 1.50 5.00
24-40 1.50 5.00
41-80 .75 2.00
81-130 .20 .75

ROMANTIC WESTERN
FAWCETT (1949-1950)
1 Photo covers on all issues. 23.00 75.00
2 Art: Al Williamson. 26.00 85.00
3 16.00 50.00

RONALD MCDONALD
CHARLTON (1970-1971)
1 2.75 10.00
2 2.00 7.00
3-4 1.50 5.00

RONIN
DC (1983-1984)
1 Cover/Art: Frank Miller in all issues. 1.75 6.00
2-5 1.00 3.00
6 1.50 5.00
TPB Reprint: Issues #1-6. 4.00 12.95

ROOK
HARRIS (1995)
0 .75 2.95

ROOK, THE (MAGAZINE)
WARREN (1979-1982)
1 5.00 15.00
2-5 2.75 10.00
6-14 1.50 5.00

ROOM 222
DELL (1970)
1 TV tie-in. 7.00 20.00
2-4 2.75 10.00

ROOTIE KAZOOTIE
DELL (1952-1954)
1 (#415) From the 4-Color Series. TV tie-in. (8/52) 23.00 75.00
2 (#459) From the 4-Color Series. TV tie-in. (4/53) 16.00 50.00
3 (#502) From the 4-Color Series. TV tie-in. (10/53) 16.00 50.00
4-6 11.00 35.00

ROSE
HEROIC (1992-1993)
1-5 .30 1.00

ROSE & GUNN
BISHOP PRESS (1995-CURRENT)
1 1.50 5.00
2-3 .75 2.95

ROUNDUP
DS (1948-1949)
1 Western Crime Stories. 16.00 50.00
2 Western Crime Stories. 10.00 30.00
3-5 Thrill-Packed Western Stories. 10.00 30.00

ROWLF
RIP OFF (1971)
1 1.50 5.00

ROY CAMPANELLA BASEBALL HERO
FAWCETT (1950)
NO# Photo cover. 110.00 350.00

ROY ROGERS AND TRIGGER
GOLD KEY (1967)
1 Photo cover. 5.00 15.00

ROY ROGERS COMICS
DELL (1948-1961)
1 Photo covers on all issues. 140.00 460.00
2 70.00 230.00
3-6 55.00 170.00
7-12 45.00 140.00
13-24 31.00 100.00
25-30 26.00 85.00
31-40 20.00 65.00
41-50 17.00 55.00
51-60 14.00 46.00
61-80 11.00 34.00
81-145 7.00 23.00

ROY ROGERS COMICS
DELL FOUR COLOR SERIES (1944-1947)
38 First western photo cover comic. (3/44) 190.00 600.00
63 Photo cover. 125.00 400.00
86 Photo cover. (10/45) 95.00 300.00
95 Photo cover. (2/46) 95.00 300.00
109 Photo cover. 80.00 250.00
117 Photo cover. (9/46) 55.00 175.00
124 Photo cover. (11/46) 55.00 175.00
137 Photo cover. (2/47) 55.00 175.00
144 Photo cover. (4/47) 55.00 175.00
153 Photo cover. Lead story: "The Mad Marksman" (7/47) 50.00 150.00
160 Photo cover. (8/47) 50.00 150.00
166 Photo cover. (10/47) 50.00 150.00
177 Photo cover. (12/47) 50.00 150.00

ROY ROGERS' TRIGGER
DELL (1951-1955)
1 (#329) From the 4-Color Series. No photo cover. (5/51) 25.00 80.00
2 Photo cover. (9-11/51) 10.00 30.00
3-6 7.00 20.00
7-17 2.75 10.00

RUDOLPH, THE RED NOSED REINDEER
DC (1950-1962)
1950 19.00 60.00
1951 14.00 45.00
1952-1955 10.00 30.00
1956-1962 7.00 20.00

RUFF AND REDDY
DELL (1958-1962)
1 (#937) From the 4-Color Series. TV tie-in. 1st: Hanna Barbera comic. (9/58) 28.00 90.00
2 (#981) From the 4-Color Series. TV tie-in. (4/59) 13.00 40.00
3 (#1038) From the 4-Color Series. TV tie-in. (10/59) 13.00 40.00
4-12 7.00 20.00

RUGGED ACTION
MARVEL(ATLAS) (1954-1955)
1 10.00 30.00
2-4 6.00 18.00

RUINS
MARVEL (1995)
1-2 Acetate outer cover. 1.25 4.95

RULAH JUNGLE GODDESS
FOX (1948-1949)
17 Previous title: "Zoot Comics." 120.00 390.00
18 "Land Of Giants!" (9/48) 100.00 330.00
19-20 95.00 300.00
21 SOTI 100.00 330.00
22 SOTI 95.00 300.00
23-27 75.00 240.00

RUN, BUDDY, RUN
GOLD KEY (1967)
10204-706 TV photo cover. 2.75 10.00

RUNAWAY, THE
DELL (1964)
12-707-412 Movie tie-in. 8.00 25.00

RUNE
MALIBU (1994-CURRENT)
0 Send away issue (coupon redemption). (11/93) 4.00 12.00
1 1.00 3.00
1A Ultra limited foil edition. 1.75 6.00
2 .50 1.95
3 1.00 3.50
4-9 .50 1.95
GIANT SIZE #1 .75 2.50
TPB Reprints issues #1-5. (1995) 4.00 12.95

RUNE/SILVER SURFER
MALIBU/MARVEL (1995)
1 Deluxe format. Flip cover. 1.50 5.95
1A Regular edition. Different cover. .75 2.95

RUNE/WRATH
MALIBU (1994)
ASHCAN Bound in Diamond Previews. .50 1.25
ASHCAN A Gold foil limited (5000). 2.75 10.00

RUST
NOW (1987-1989)
1-15 .30 1.00
V2#1-V2#7 .20 .50

RUSTY COMICS
MARVEL (1947-1949)
12 Previous title: Kid Movie Comics. 19.00 60.00
13 10.00 30.00
14 Powerhouse Pepper. 19.00 60.00
15-22 8.00 24.00

RUSTY DUGAN COMICS
HOLYOKE (1944-1945)
2 From the Holyoke One-Shot series. 16.00 50.00

RUSTY RILEY
DELL FOUR COLOR SERIES (1952-1954)
418 "...A Boy, A Horse, And A Dog" (8/52) 10.00 30.00
451 (2/53) 8.00 25.00
486 (8/53) 8.00 25.00
554 (4/54) 7.00 20.00

RUGGED ACTION #1

RUINS #1

RUNE #2

RUNE #5

SACHS & VIOLENS #3

THE SAINT #1

SAMSON #1

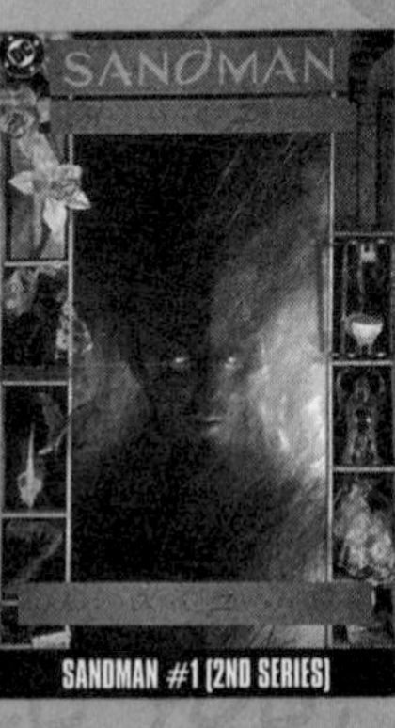

SANDMAN #1 (2ND SERIES)

SAARI
PL (1951)
1 "The Jungle Goddess" 50.00 150.00

SABRETOOTH
MARVEL (1993)
1 Die-cut cover. 1.75 6.00
2-4 .... 1.25 4.00

SABRETOOTH CLASSICS
MARVEL (1994-CURRENT)
1 Reprints. .... .50 1.50
2-15 .... .50 1.50

SABRINA THE TEENAGE WITCH
ARCHIE (1971-1983)
1 .... 10.00 32.00
2 .... 5.00 15.00
3 .... 2.25 8.00
4-5 .... 1.75 6.00
6-10 .... 1.50 5.00
11-20 .... 1.00 3.00
21-50 .... .75 2.00
51-77 .... .30 1.00

SABU "ELEPHANT BOY"
FOX (1950)
1 (#30). Movie tie-in, photo cover. ... 26.00 85.00
2 Photo cover. 17.00 55.00

SACHS & VIOLENS
MARVEL (1993)
1 Embossed cover. .... .75 2.75
1A Platinum edition. 2.25 8.00
2-4 .... .75 2.25

SAD SACK AND THE SARGE
HARVEY (1957-1982)
1 .... 16.00 50.00
2 .... 8.00 25.00
3-12 .... 4.00 12.00
13-25 .... 1.75 6.00
26-50 .... 1.00 3.00
51-75 .... .50 1.50
76-155 .... .20 .50

SAD SACK COMICS
HARVEY (1949-1982)
1 .... 50.00 150.00
2 .... 23.00 75.00
3-6 .... 16.00 50.00
7-12 .... 11.00 35.00
13-24 .... 6.00 18.00
25-50 .... 2.25 8.00
51-93 .... 1.50 5.00
94-100 .... .75 2.00
101-150 .... .30 1.00
151-287 .... .20 .50

SAD SACK LAUGH SPECIAL
HARVEY (1958-1977)
1 .... 10.00 30.00
2 .... 5.00 15.00
3-6 .... 2.75 10.00
7-12 .... 1.75 6.00
13-25 .... 1.00 3.00
26-93 .... .50 1.50

SAD SACK'S ARMY LIFE
HARVEY (1963-1971)
1 .... 8.00 25.00
2-5 .... 5.00 15.00
6-10 .... 4.00 12.00
11-15 .... 2.75 10.00
16-20 .... 2.25 8.00
21-34 .... 1.50 5.00
35-40 .... 1.00 3.00
41-61 .... .75 2.00

SADDLE JUSTICE
EC (1948-1949)
3 Previous title: Happy Houlihans. ... 85.00 280.00
4 .... 85.00 280.00
5-7 .... 80.00 250.00
8 Title changes to Saddle Romances with #9.
.... 80.00 250.00

SADDLE ROMANCES
EC (1949-1950)
9 Previous title: "Saddle Justice." ... 85.00 280.00
10 Art: Wally Wood (his 1st at EC). ... 95.00 310.00
11 .... 85.00 280.00

SADE SPECIAL
BISHOP PRESS (1995-CURRENT)
1 App: Razor. 1.50 5.50

SAFETY-BELT MAN
SIRIUS (1994-CURRENT)
1 .... 1.50 5.00
2-4 .... 1.00 3.00

SAGA OF CRYSTAR, CRYSTAL WARRIOR, THE
MARVEL (1983-1985)
1-11 .... .30 1.00

SAGA OF RA'S AL GHUL, THE
DC (1988)
1-4 .... .30 1.00

SAGA OF SWAMP THING, THE
DC (1982-1986)
1 Origin retold: Swamp Thing. 1.00 3.00
2-19 .... .75 2.00
20 Begin: Alan Moore scripts. 5.00 15.00
21 New Origin: Swamp Thing. 4.00 13.00
22-25 .... 4.00 12.00
26-29 .... 2.50 9.00
30-33 .... 1.75 6.00
34-36 .... 1.00 3.50
37 1st: John Constantine. 5.00 15.00
38-40 .... 1.50 5.00
41-44 .... .75 2.75
45 Title changes to Swamp Thing with #46. .75 2.75
ANNUAL 1 Movie tie-in. (1982) ...... .75 2.75
ANNUAL 2 Resurrection: Abby by Alan Moore. (1985)
.... 1.50 5.00
ANNUAL 3 (1987) .... .75 2.50
TPB Reprints issues #21-27. .... 4.00 12.95

SAGA OF THE ORIGINAL HUMAN TORCH, THE
MARVEL (1990)
1-4 .... .30 1.00

SAGA OF THE SUB-MARINER, THE
MARVEL (1988-1989)
1-12 .... .30 1.00

SAINT, THE
AVON (1947-1952)
1 .... 100.00 330.00
2 .... 50.00 160.00
3-5 .... 40.00 130.00
6 App: Miss Fury. 60.00 190.00
7-8 .... 35.00 110.00
9-12 .... 25.00 80.00

SAINT SINNER
MARVEL (1993-CURRENT)
1 Razorline title. Prismatic foil cover. ... .75 2.50
2-7 .... .50 1.75
8 .... .50 1.95

SAM HILL PRIVATE EYE
CLOSE-UP (1950-1951)
1 .... 16.00 50.00
2 .... 7.00 20.00
3-7 .... 5.00 15.00

SAMSON
AJAX (1955)
12 App: Wonder Boy. 35.00 110.00
13 App: Rocketman, Wonder Boy. ... 35.00 110.00
14 .... 25.00 80.00

SAMSON
FOX (1940-1941)
1 Art: Bob Powell. 280.00 900.00
2 .... 140.00 450.00
3-6 .... 100.00 320.00

SAMSON AND DELILAH
FOX (1950)
11 "A Spectacular Feature (Formerly My Confession)"
.... 25.00 80.00

SAMURAI
AIRCEL (1985-1987)
1 .... 1.50 5.00
2-6 .... 1.00 3.00
7-16 .... .75 2.00

SAMUREE
ACCLAIM/WINDJAMMER (1995)
1 .... 1.00 3.50
2 .... .75 2.50

SAMUREE
CONTINUITY (1987-1992)
1-9 .... .30 1.00

SAMUREE
CONTINUITY (1993-1994)
1 Rise Of Magic tie-in. .... .75 2.50
2-3 Rise Of Magic. .... .75 2.50
4-9 .... .75 2.50

SANCTUARY (PART 1)
VIZ (1992)
1-9 .... 1.25 4.95

SANCTUARY (PART 2)
VIZ (1993-1994)
1-9 .... 1.25 4.95

SANCTUARY (PART 3)
VIZ (1994-1995)
1-8 .... 1.00 3.25

SANDMAN, THE
DC (1974-1976)
1 Art: Jack Kirby (all issues). 2.50 9.00
2-6 .... 1.50 5.00

SANDMAN
DC (1989-CURRENT)
1 1st: new Sandman. 20.00 66.00
2 .... 11.00 35.00
3-5 .... 9.00 28.00
6-7 .... 7.00 20.00
8 1st: Death. 16.00 50.00
8A Limited edition (inside front cover editorial by Karen Berger).
.... 50.00 160.00
9-14 .... 5.00 14.00
15-18 .... 2.75 10.00
18A Error (1st 3 panels on first page are blue).
.... 25.00 80.00
19 .... 2.50 9.00
19A Error (switched pages). 13.00 40.00
20-21 .... 2.50 9.00
22 1st: Daniel. 8.00 25.00
23-25 .... 2.50 9.00
26-30 .... 1.75 6.00
31-35 .... 1.50 5.00
36-39 .... 1.25 4.00
40-45 .... 1.00 3.00
46 Begin: Vertigo series. 1.25 4.00
47-49 .... 1.00 3.00
50 Double size anniversary issue. 1.00 3.50
50A Platinum edition (black cover with stars).
.... 16.00 50.00
51-56 .... 1.00 3.00
57 Kindly Ones, pt.1. .... 1.25 4.00
58 Kindly Ones, pt.2. .... 1.00 3.00
59-68 .... .75 2.50
69 .... 1.00 3.75
70 .... 1.00 3.25
71 .... .75 2.50

SANDMAN: A GALLERY OF DREAMS
DC (1994)
1 .... .75 2.95

SANDMAN MIDNIGHT THEATRE
DC (1995)
1 One shot. 1.75 6.95

SANDMAN MYSTERY THEATRE
DC (1993-CURRENT)
1 .... 1.00 3.00
2-30 .... .75 2.25
ANNUAL 1 (1994) 1.00 3.95

SANDMAN SPECIAL
DC (1991)
1 .... 1.00 3.50

SANDS OF THE SOUTH PACIFIC
TOBY (1953)
1 .... 19.00 60.00

SANTA AND THE ANGEL
DELL FOUR COLOR SERIES (1949)
259 A 2 in 1 book; "Santa At The Zoo" on back cover.
(12/49) 11.00 35.00

SANTA CLAUS CONQUERS THE MARTIANS
DELL (1966)
1A Sealed with Golden Record. 50.00 160.00
12-725-603 Movie photo cover. 20.00 65.00

SANTA CLAUS FUNNIES
DELL (1942-1943)
1 (No # on cover) Art: Walt Kelly. ... 65.00 200.00
2 Art: Walt Kelly. 31.00 100.00

SANTA CLAUS FUNNIES
DELL (1952)
1 Dell Giant. 25.00 80.00

SANTA CLAUS FUNNIES
DELL FOUR COLOR SERIES (1944-1961)
61 Art: Walt Kelly. 55.00 180.00
91 Art: Walt Kelly. 50.00 150.00
128 Art: Walt Kelly. 31.00 100.00
175 Art: Walt Kelly. (12/47) 28.00 90.00
205 Art: Walt Kelly. (12/48) 28.00 90.00
254 Art: Walt Kelly. (11/49) 26.00 85.00
302 8.00 25.00
361 7.00 20.00
525 (12/53) 5.00 15.00
607 (12/54) 5.00 15.00
666 (12/55) 5.00 15.00
756 (12/56) 5.00 15.00
867 (12/57) 7.00 20.00
958 (12/58) 7.00 20.00
1063 (12/59) 5.00 15.00
1154 (12/60) 8.00 25.00
1274 (12/61) 8.00 25.00

SANTA CLAUS FUNNIES
W. T. GRANT (1940)
1 Giveaway. 10.00 30.00

SANTA CLAUS PARADE
ZIFF-DAVIS (1951-1955)
1 (No # on cover, dated 1951) 25.00 80.00
2 19.00 60.00
3 (1/55) 19.00 60.00

SANTIAGO
DELL FOUR COLOR SERIES (1956)
723 Movie photo cover (Alan Ladd). (9/56) 28.00 90.00

SATANIKA
VEROTIK (1995-CURRENT)
1 2.50 8.00

SATAN'S SIX
TOPPS (1993)
1 All issues polybagged with cards. .75 2.95
2-4 .75 2.95

SAVAGE DRAGON
IMAGE (1992-1993)
1 Four different posters available. 1.50 5.00
2 1.00 3.50
3 With Image #0 coupon. 1.00 3.50
3A Without Image #0 coupon. .75 2.00

SAVAGE DRAGON
IMAGE/HIGH BROW (1993-CURRENT)
1 1st: Ricochet. 1st: Barbaric. 1.00 3.00
2 .75 2.95
3-12 .50 1.95
13 Image X book. .75 2.50
13A Erik Larsen version. .50 1.95
14-21 .75 2.50

SAVAGE DRAGON VS THE SAVAGE MEGATON MAN
IMAGE (1993)
1 One shot. .50 1.95
1A Gold foil cover. 2.75 10.00

SAVAGE SHE-HULK, THE
MARVEL (1980-1982)
1 1st & Origin: She-Hulk. 1.75 6.00
2-10 1.00 3.00
11-12 Morbius. 1.00 3.00
13-25 .75 2.00

SAVAGE SWORD OF CONAN
MARVEL (1974-1995) (MAGAZINE)
1 Cover: Boris Vallejo. 25.00 80.00
2 Cover: Neal Adams. 11.00 35.00
3 Art: Barry Smith, Neal Adams. 7.00 20.00
4 Cover: Boris Vallejo. 5.00 15.00
5 Cover: Boris Vallejo. 2.75 10.00
6 2.75 10.00
7 Cover: Boris Vallejo. 2.25 8.00
8 2.25 8.00
9-10 Cover: Boris Vallejo. 2.25 8.00
11 2.00 7.00
12 Cover: Boris Vallejo. 2.00 7.00
13-18 2.00 7.00
19-30 1.75 6.00
31-39 1.50 5.00
40 1.75 6.00
41-90 1.50 5.00
91-99 1.25 4.00
100 (5/84) 1.50 5.00
101-130 1.25 4.00
131-149 1.00 3.50
150 1.50 5.00
151-175 1.00 3.50
176-185 1.00 3.00
186-193 .75 2.75
194-199 .75 2.25
200 (8/92) .75 2.25
201-235 .75 2.25
ANNUAL 1 (Special #1 in indicia). (Summer/75) 2.25 8.00

SAVAGE TALES
MARVEL (1971-1975) MAGAZINE
1 Starring Conan The Barbarian by Roy Thomas & Barry Smith. 1st & Origin: Manthing. 40.00 125.00
2 Art: Barry Smith, Berni Wrightson. 14.00 45.00
3 Art: Barry Smith, Al Williamson. 10.00 30.00
4 Cover: Neal Adams. Art: Neal Adams, Joe Maneely, Barry Smith. 7.00 20.00
5 End: Conan. 7.00 20.00
6 Begin: Ka-Zar. 1.75 6.00
7 1.50 5.00
8-11 1.25 4.00
12 Annual #1 on cover (featuring Ka-Zar). 1.25 4.00

SAVAGE TALES
MARVEL (1985-1987) MAGAZINE
1 1st: The Nam. .75 2.00
2-9 .30 1.00

SCAMP
DELL (1958-1961)
5-10 4.00 12.00
11-16 2.75 10.00

SCAMP
DELL FOUR COLOR SERIES (1956-1961)
703 (5/56) 11.00 35.00
777 (3/57) 8.00 25.00
806 (6/57) 8.00 25.00
833 (9/57) 8.00 25.00
1204 (7/61) 7.00 20.00

SCAMP
GOLD KEY (1969-1979)
1 2.75 10.00
2-10 1.50 5.00
11-20 .75 2.50
21-45 .50 1.50

SCARAB
DC (1993-1994)
1 Vertigo title. .50 1.95
2-8 .50 1.95

SCARECROW OF ROMNEY MARSH, THE
GOLD KEY (1964-1965)
1 (10112-404). Disney TV tie-in. 5.00 15.00
2-3 5.00 15.00

SCARLET WITCH
MARVEL (1994)
1-4 .50 1.75

SCAVENGERS
TRIUMPHANT (1993-1994)
1 1.25 4.00
2-13 .75 2.50

SCHISM
DEFIANT (1994)
1-4 1.00 3.25

SCHOOL DAY ROMANCES
STAR (1949-1950)
1 23.00 75.00
2 16.00 50.00
3 Photo insert on cover. 17.00 55.00
4 Photo inserts on cover (including Ronald Reagan). Title changes to Popular Teen-Agers with #5. 23.00 75.00

SCIENCE COMICS
EXPORT (1951)
1 11.00 36.00

SCIENCE COMICS
FOX (1940)
1 1st & Origin: Dynamo. 700.00 2500.00
2 310.00 1000.00
3 280.00 900.00
4 Art: Jack Kirby. 310.00 1000.00
5-6 240.00 775.00
7-8 200.00 650.00

SCIENCE COMICS
HUMOR (1946)
1 10.00 30.00
2-5 7.00 20.00

SCOOP COMICS
HOLYOKE (1941-1944)
1 Debut: Rocketman. 155.00 500.00
2 75.00 240.00
3 55.00 180.00
8 40.00 120.00

SCORPION
ATLAS(SEABOARD) (1975)
1 Cover: Howard Chaykin. .75 2.00
2 Art: Berni Wrightson. .30 1.00
3 .30 1.00

SCORPION CORPS
DAGGER (1993-1994)
1 .75 2.75
2-9 .75 2.50

SCOTLAND YARD
CHARLTON (1955-1956)
1 16.00 50.00
2-4 10.00 30.00

SCOUT
ECLIPSE (1985-1987)
1-24 .50 1.75

SCREAM
SKYWALD (1973-1975) MAGAZINE
1 2.75 10.00
2 1.25 4.00
3 1.25 4.00
4-11 1.25 4.00

SCREAM COMICS
ACE (1944-1948)
1 17.00 55.00
2 12.00 38.00
3-10 7.00 22.00
11-18 5.00 16.00
19 Title changes to Andy Comics with #20. 5.00 16.00

SCRIBBLY
DC (1948-1952)
1 Cover/Art: Sheldon Mayer in all issues. 280.00 900.00
2 180.00 575.00
3-6 140.00 460.00
7-12 105.00 340.00
13-15 70.00 230.00

SCUD, THE DISPOSABLE ASSASSIN
FIREMAN PRESS (1993-CURRENT)
1 2.00 7.00
2-3 1.50 5.00
4-5 1.25 4.00
6-7 .75 2.95

SEA DEVILS
DC (1961-1967)
1 "The Sea Devils Battle The Octopus Man!" (See Showcase 27 for 1st app.) 110.00 350.00
2 55.00 175.00
3 1st 12 cent issue. 40.00 120.00
4-6 25.00 80.00
7-12 17.00 55.00
13-18 13.00 40.00
19-24 10.00 30.00
25-35 8.00 25.00

SEA HOUND, THE
AVON (1945-1949)
1(NO#) (Captain Silver's Log Of...) 13.00 40.00
2 (9-10/45) 7.00 20.00
3 (7/49) 5.00 15.00
4 5.00 15.00

SEA HUNT
DELL (1958-1962)
1 (#928) From the 4-Color Series. TV photo cover (Lloyd Bridges). (8/58) 25.00 80.00
2 (#994) From the 4-Color Series. TV photo cover (Lloyd Bridges). (5/59) 16.00 50.00
3 (#1041) From the 4-Color Series. TV photo cover (Lloyd Bridges). (10/59) 19.00 60.00
4-13 13.00 40.00

SEARCHERS, THE
DELL FOUR COLOR SERIES (1956)
709 Movie photo cover (John Wayne). (6/56) 160.00 525.00

SEBASTIAN O
DC (1993)
1 Vertigo title. .50 1.95
2-3 .50 1.95

SANDMAN #8 (2ND SERIES)

SATAN'S SIX #1

SAVAGE DRAGON #15

SCARLET WITCH #4

SECOND LIFE OF DR. MIRAGE #10

SECRET WEAPONS #1

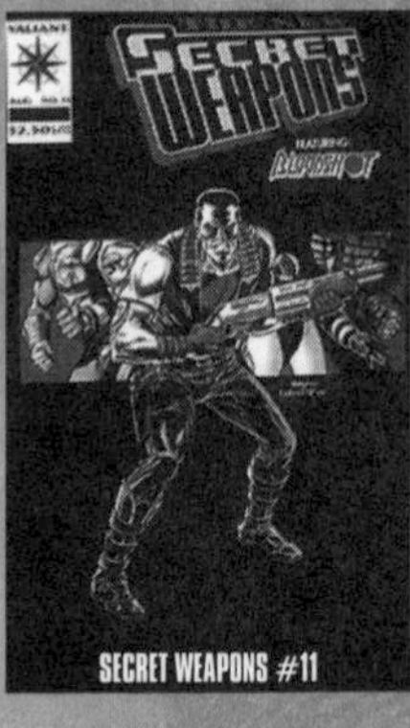

SECRET WEAPONS #11

SENSATION COMICS #53

FAMOUS · FIRSTS

SHOWCASE #22

Once DC's reboot of The Flash in *Showcase* #4 proved popular, the company revived another Golden Age hero. The result was a science-fiction oriented Green Lantern, a charter member of the Justice League of America.

SECOND LIFE OF DR. MIRAGE, THE
VALIANT (1993-1995)
1 .75 2.50
1 (GOLD) 1.75 6.00
2-19 .75 2.00

SECRET AGENT
GOLD KEY (1966-1968)
1 TV photo cover. 19.00 60.00
2 TV photo cover. 13.00 40.00

SECRET CITY SAGA
TOPPS (1993)
0 .75 2.95
1 Art: Steve Ditko (all issues). .75 2.95
2-4 .75 2.95

SECRET DEFENDERS
MARVEL (1993-1995)
1 Dr. Strange, Wolverine, Nomad. Foil-stamped cover. .75 2.75
2-11 .50 1.75
12 Prism-foil cover. .75 2.50
13-14 .50 1.75
15-24 .50 1.95
25 Double size. .75 2.50

SECRET DIARY OF EERIE ADVENTURES
AVON (1953)
NO# Giant 100 page book. 220.00 700.00

SECRET HEARTS
DC (1949-1971)
1 "Make-Believe Sweetheart" Photo cover. (9-10/49) 70.00 220.00
2 35.00 110.00
3-6 26.00 85.00
7-12 20.00 65.00
13-24 14.00 44.00
25-50 9.00 27.00
51-75 5.00 16.00
76 1st 12 cent cover price. 2.25 8.75
77-100 2.25 8.75
101-120 1.25 4.25
121-140 .75 2.00
141-153 .30 1.00

SECRET MISSIONS
ST. JOHN (1950)
1 28.00 90.00

SECRET MYSTERIES
RIBAGE (1954-1955)
16 20.00 65.00
17-19 12.00 38.00

SECRET ORIGINS
DC (1961)
1 Giant size one-shot. Reprint: World's Finest 71, Showcase 17, Green Lantern 1, Detective 225, Showcase 4, Showcase 6, Wonder Woman 105. 85.00 280.00

SECRET ORIGINS
DC (1973-1974)
1 2.75 10.00
2 1.75 6.00
3-4 1.50 5.00
5-7 1.25 4.50

SECRET ORIGINS
DC (1986-1990)
1 Origin retold: Superman. 1.25 4.00
2-5 .75 2.00
6 Golden-Age Batman. 1.25 4.00
7-12 .75 2.00
13 Origin: Nightwing. 1.00 3.00
14-38 .75 2.00
39 Animal Man. 1.00 3.00
40-50 .75 2.00
ANNUAL 1-3 .75 2.00
SPECIAL 1 .75 2.00

SECRET SIX
DC (1968-1969)
1 1st & Origin: Secret Six. 13.00 40.00
2-3 7.00 20.00
4-7 5.00 15.00

SECRET SOCIETY OF SUPER-VILLAINS
DC (1976-1978)
1 .75 2.50
2-15 .50 1.50

SECRET SQUIRREL
GOLD KEY (1966)
1 TV tie-in. 23.00 75.00

SECRET SQUIRREL KITE FUN BOOK
SCE (1966)
1966 11.00 35.00

SECRET STORY ROMANCES
MARVEL(ATLAS) (1953-1956)
1 13.00 40.00
2 7.00 20.00
3-11 5.00 15.00
12-20 2.75 10.00
21 Title changes to True Tales Of Love with #22. 2.75 10.00

SECRET WARS
MARVEL (1984-1985)
1 1st: Beyonder. 1.50 5.00
2-6 1.00 3.00
7 1st: new Spider-Woman. 1.00 3.00
8 1st & Origin: Spider-Man's alien costume. 6.00 18.00
9-11 .75 2.50
12 Double size. 1.00 3.00
TPB Reprints issues #1-12. 6.00 19.95

SECRET WARS II
MARVEL (1985-1986)
1 .75 2.00
2-8 .50 1.75
9 Death: Beyonder. .75 2.00

SECRET WEAPONS
VALIANT (1993-1995)
1 .50 1.50
2-23 .50 1.50

SECRETS BEHIND THE COMICS
FAMOUS ENTERPRISES (1947)
NO# By Stan Lee. Includes Captain America & Bucky, Blonde Phantom, Powerhouse Pepper, Millie The Model, et al. Lee's instructional guide to drawing comics, with illustrations by many of the great Timely Comics artists. 155.00 500.00

SECRETS OF HAUNTED HOUSE
DC (1975-1982)
1 1.25 4.00
2 1.00 3.00
3-12 .75 2.00
13-46 .30 1.00

SECRETS OF LIFE
DELL FOUR COLOR SERIES (1956)
749 Disney movie photo cover. (11/56) 11.00 35.00

SECRETS OF SINISTER HOUSE
DC (1972-1974)
5 Previous title: Sinister House Of Secret Love. .75 2.00
6-9 .75 2.00
10 Art: Neal Adams. 1.75 6.00
11-18 .50 1.50

SECRETS OF THE LEGION OF SUPER-HEROES
DC (1981)
1-3 .30 1.00

SECRETS OF THE VALIANT UNIVERSE
VALIANT (1994)
1 Included with Wizard's Valiant Special. 1.00 3.00
2-3 .75 2.25

SECRETS OF YOUNG BRIDES
CHARLTON (1957-1964)
5 8.00 25.00
6-10 5.00 15.00
11-25 2.75 10.00
26-44 1.75 6.00

SECRETS OF YOUNG BRIDES
CHARLTON (1975-1976)
1-9 .75 2.00

SECTAURS
MARVEL (1985-1986)
1-10 .30 1.00

SEDUCTION OF THE INNOCENT!
ECLIPSE (1985-1986)
1 .75 2.00
1 (3-D) Cover: Dave Stevens. 1.00 3.00
2-6 .75 2.00

SEDUCTION OF THE INNOCENT
NY: RINEHART & CO.
1953-01 The infamous critical dissertation of American comic books by Fredric Wertham, M.D. With dust jacket and bibliography page intact. 1st edition. 280.00 900.00
1953-02 Without bibliography page. 110.00 350.00

SEEKER
SKY (1994)
1-3 .75 2.50

SENSATION COMICS
DC (1942-1952)
1 "Featuring The Sensational New Adventure Strip Character—Wonder Woman!" Origin: Wonder Woman (continued from ALL STAR #8). 1st & Origin: Wildcat. 1st & Origin: Mr. Terrific. 3100.00 12000.00
2 700.00 2600.00
3-6 300.00 975.00
7-8 240.00 775.00
9-10 200.00 650.00
11-12 155.00 500.00
13-18 140.00 450.00
19-24 120.00 390.00
25-30 110.00 350.00
31-33 90.00 290.00
34 Begin: Sargon The Sorcerer. 100.00 320.00
35-40 80.00 260.00
41-50 70.00 220.00
51-60 60.00 190.00
61-67 50.00 160.00
68 1st & Origin: The Huntress. (8/47) 70.00 220.00
69-80 50.00 160.00
81 SOTI 60.00 190.00
82-85 40.00 130.00
86 App: The Atom. 60.00 190.00
87-90 40.00 130.00
91-93 31.00 100.00
94 "S.O.S. Wonder Woman!" 60.00 190.00
95-99 31.00 100.00
100-106 80.00 260.00
107 1st Mystery format issue. 80.00 260.00
108 80.00 260.00
109 Title changes to Sensation Mystery #110. 80.00 260.00

SENSATION MYSTERY
DC (1952-1953)
110 Previous title: "Sensation Comics." (7-8/52) 70.00 220.00
111 "The Spectre In The Flame" (9-10/52) 70.00 220.00
112 "Death Has Five Guesses!" 70.00 220.00
113 (1-2/53) 70.00 220.00
114 "The Haunted Diamond" 70.00 220.00
115 "The Phantom Castle!" 70.00 220.00
116 Johnny Peril in "The Toy Assassins!" (7-8/53) 70.00 220.00

SENSATIONAL POLICE CASES
AVON (1952-1954)
1(NO#) Giant 100 page book. (1952) 65.00 200.00
2-4 10.00 30.00

SENSATIONAL SHE-HULK, THE
MARVEL (1989-1994)
1 Begin: John Byrne art & scripts. .75 2.50
2-7 .50 1.50
8 End: John Byrne. .50 1.50
9-30 .50 1.50
31 Resume: John Byrne art & scripts. .50 1.50
32-49 .50 1.50
50 End: John Byrne art. Embossed green foil cover, double size. .75 2.95
51-60 .50 1.50

SENSATIONAL SHE-HULK: CEREMONY
MARVEL (1989)
1-2 1.25 4.00

SENSATIONAL SPIDER-MAN
MARVEL (1989)
1 80 page one shot. 1.50 5.95

SERGEANT BILKO
DC (1957-1960)
1 TV tie-in. 125.00 400.00
2 65.00 200.00
3-6 55.00 170.00
7-18 45.00 140.00

SERGEANT PRESTON OF THE YUKON
DELL (1951-1959)
1 (#344) From the 4-Color Series. "Challenge Of The Yukon". (8/51) 25.00 80.00
2 (#373) From the 4-Color Series. (2/52) 14.00 45.00
3 (#397) From the 4-Color Series. (5/52) 14.00 45.00
4 (#419) From the 4-Color Series. (8/52) 14.00 45.00
5-10 5.00 15.00
11-18 2.75 10.00
19 Begin: photo covers. 7.00 20.00
20-29 7.00 20.00

SEVEN DWARFS
DELL FOUR COLOR SERIES (1949)
227 Disney. (5/49) 25.00 80.00

SEVEN DWARFS AND THE ENCHANTED MOUNTAIN, THE
DISNEY (1947)
Z3 Disney Cheerios Premium. 5.00 15.00

SEVEN SEAS COMICS
LEADER (1946-1947)
1 Art: Matt Baker (in all issues). 105.00 340.00
2 85.00 280.00
3-6 70.00 230.00

SEVENTH VOYAGE OF SINBAD, THE
DELL FOUR COLOR SERIES (1958)
944 Movie photo cover. (9/58) 31.00 100.00

SEVENTY SEVEN SUNSET STRIP
DELL (1962)
01-742-209 TV photo cover. 16.00 50.00

SEVENTY SEVEN SUNSET STRIP
DELL FOUR COLOR SERIES (1960-1962)
1066 TV photo covers on all issues. (1/60) 31.00 100.00
1106 (6/60) 22.00 70.00
1159 (1/61) 19.00 60.00
1211 (8/61) 17.00 55.00
1263 (11/61) 16.00 50.00
1291 (2/62) 16.00 50.00

SEVENTY SEVEN SUNSET STRIP
GOLD KEY (1962-1963)
1 TV photo cover. 16.00 50.00
2 TV photo cover. 13.00 40.00

SEVENTY SEVENTH BENGAL LANCERS, THE
DELL FOUR COLOR SERIES (1957)
791 TV photo cover. (4/57) 16.00 50.00

SEX WARRIOR
DARK HORSE (1994)
1 1st: Dakini, the Sex Warrior. .75 2.50
2 .75 2.50

SEYMOUR MY SON
ARCHIE (1963)
1 7.00 22.00

SGT. BILKO'S PRIVATE DOBERMAN
DC (1958-1960)
1 TV tie-in. 70.00 230.00
2 35.00 110.00
3-4 26.00 85.00
5 Photo cover. 28.00 90.00
6-8 26.00 85.00
9 Photo cover. 28.00 90.00
10-11 26.00 85.00

SGT. FURY AND HIS HOWLING COMMANDOS
MARVEL (1963-1981)
1 1st & Origin: Sgt. Fury and the Howling Commandos in "Meet The Howling Commandos." 220.00 750.00
2 "Seven Doomed Men!" 70.00 250.00
3 App: Reed Richards. "Midnight On Massacre Mountain!" 35.00 125.00
4 "Lord Ha-Ha's Last Laugh!" 35.00 115.00
5 "At The Mercy Of Baron Strucker!" 35.00 115.00
6 "The Fangs Of The Fox!" 35.00 115.00
7 "The Court-Martial Of Sgt. Fury!" 28.00 90.00
8 "The Death Ray Of Dr. Zemo!" 28.00 90.00
9 "Mission: Capture Hitler!" 28.00 90.00
10 1st: Captain Savage. "On To Okinawa!" 28.00 90.00
11 "The Crackdown Of Capt. Flint!" 28.00 90.00
12 28.00 90.00
13 App: Captain America. (12/64) 70.00 235.00
14 1st: Blitz Squad. 16.00 50.00
15-20 16.00 50.00
21-24 11.00 35.00
25 App: Red Skull. 11.00 35.00
26-30 11.00 35.00
31-33 7.00 20.00
34 Origin retold: Howling Commandos. 7.00 20.00
35-50 7.00 20.00
51-60 5.00 16.00
61-75 4.00 12.00
76-99 2.75 10.00
100 App: Stan Lee. Anniversary issue. 2.75 10.00
101-125 2.25 8.00
126-150 1.75 6.00
151-167 1.50 5.00

SGT. FURY ANNUAL
MARVEL (1965-1971)
1 31.00 100.00
2 (1966) 9.00 28.00
3 (1967) 5.00 16.00
4-7 2.75 10.00

SGT. ROCK
DC (1977-1988)
302 Previous title: Our Army At War. 2.75 10.00
303-325 1.75 6.00
326-360 1.25 4.00
361-399 1.00 3.00
400 1.25 4.00
401-422 1.00 3.00
ANNUAL 2 (1982) 1.25 4.00
ANNUAL 3 (1983) 1.00 3.00
ANNUAL 4 (1984) 1.00 3.00

SGT. ROCK SPECIAL
DC (1988-1992)
1 1.00 3.00
1A (1992 one-shot) 1.25 4.00
2-20 .75 2.50

SGT. ROCK'S PRIZE BATTLE TALES
DC (1964)
1 35.00 110.00

SHADE THE CHANGING MAN
DC (1977-1978)
1 1st & Origin: Shade. Cover/Art/Stories: Steve Ditko (in all issues). 2.00 6.00
2 1.25 4.00
3-8 1.00 3.00

SHADE THE CHANGING MAN
DC (1990-CURRENT)
1 1.25 4.00
2 1.00 3.00
3-20 .75 2.00
21-31 .50 1.75
32 Begin: Vertigo series. .50 1.75
33-35 .50 1.75
36-49 .50 1.95
50 .75 2.95
51-58 .50 1.95
59-63 .75 2.25

SHADO: SONG OF THE DRAGON
DC (1992)
1-4 1.25 4.95

SHADOW, THE
ARCHIE (1964-1965)
1 (Not the pulp character). 10.00 32.00
2 6.00 18.00
3-8 5.00 15.00

SHADOW, THE
DC (1973-1975)
1 Art: Mike Kaluta. 8.00 25.00
2 6.00 18.00
3 Art: Kaluta/Wrightson. 7.00 20.00
4 Art: Mike Kaluta. 6.00 18.00
5 Art: Mike Kaluta. 2.50 9.00
6 Art: Mike Kaluta. 6.00 18.00
7-12 2.50 9.00

SHADOW, THE
DC (1986)
1 1.50 5.00
2-4 1.00 3.00

SHADOW, THE
DC (1987-1989)
1 1.25 4.00

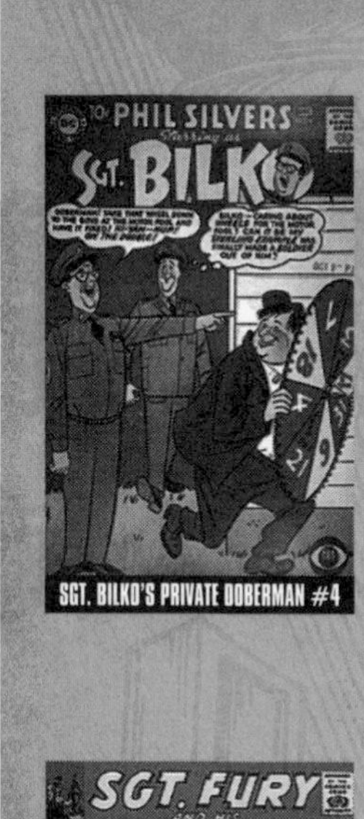

SGT. BILKO'S PRIVATE DOBERMAN #4

SGT. FURY #13

SHADE, THE CHANGING MAN #58

THE SHADOW #1 (2ND SERIES)

SHADOW OF THE BAT #0

SHADOWHAWK III #1

SHADOWMAN #16

SHAMAN'S TEARS #1

2-19 .75 2.00
ANNUAL 1 (1987) 1.00 3.00
ANNUAL 2 (1988) 1.00 3.00

SHADOW AND DOC SAVAGE, THE
DARK HORSE (1995-CURRENT)
1 .75 2.95

SHADOW AND THE MYSTERIOUS 3
DARK HORSE (1994)
NO# One-shot. .75 2.95

SHADOW CABINET
DC (1994)
0 Shadow War crossover. 1st DC #0. .75 2.50
1-13 .50 1.75
14-16 .75 2.50

SHADOW COMICS
STREET & SMITH (1940-1949)
V1#1 Shadow, Doc Savage, Nick Carter, Bill Barnes. 800.00 2800.00
V1#2 280.00 900.00
V1#3 (5/40) 220.00 725.00
V1#4 210.00 675.00
V1#5 End: Doc Savage. 190.00 625.00
V1#6 155.00 500.00
V1#7 1st & Origin: The Hooded Wasp. 180.00 575.00
V1#8-V1#9 140.00 460.00
V1#10-V1#12 125.00 400.00
V2#1-V2#2 105.00 340.00
V2#3 1st & Origin: Supersnipe. 140.00 460.00
V2#4-V2#6 85.00 280.00
V2#7 (10/42) 85.00 280.00
V2#8-V2#9 85.00 280.00
V2#10-V2#12 80.00 250.00
V3#1-V3#12 70.00 230.00
V4#1 65.00 200.00
V4#2 "The Brain Of Nippon". 65.00 200.00
V4#3-V4#12 65.00 200.00
V5#1-V5#12 65.00 200.00
V6#1-V6#11 65.00 200.00
V6#12 Begin: Bob Powell cover & art. 65.00 200.00
V7#1-V7#6 70.00 230.00
V7#7 (10/47) 70.00 230.00
V7#8-V7#12 70.00 230.00
V8#1-V8#12 70.00 230.00
V9#1-V9#3 70.00 230.00
V9#4 (7/49) 70.00 230.00
V9#5 70.00 230.00

SHADOW EMPIRES: FAITH CONQUERS
DARK HORSE (1994)
1-4 .75 2.95

SHADOW: HELL'S HEAT WAVE
DARK HORSE (1995)
1-3 .75 2.95

SHADOW: IN THE COILS OF LEVIATHAN
DARK HORSE (1993)
1 1.25 4.00
2-4 1.00 3.00
TPB Reprints issues #1-4. 5.00 13.95

SHADOW OF THE BAT
DC (1992-CURRENT)
0 1.00 3.00
1 1st: Jeremiah Arkham. Begin: The Last Arkham. Deluxe polybagged edition. 1.50 5.00
1A Regular edition. 1.00 3.00
2-3 .75 2.50
4 End: The Last Arkham. .75 2.50
5-6 .75 2.50
7-15 .75 2.00
16 Knightfall tie-in. 1.00 3.00
17-18 Knightfall tie-in. .75 2.50
19-28 .75 2.00
29 1.00 3.25
30 .75 2.50
31-34 .50 1.95
35 Embossed cover. .75 2.95
35A Regular edition. .50 1.95
36-42 .50 1.95
ANNUAL 1 (1993) 1.00 3.50
ANNUAL 2 Elseworlds story. (1994) .75 2.50

SHADOW OF THE BATMAN
DC (1985-1986)
1 Reprints: Detective Comics in all issues. 2.50 9.00
2-3 1.75 6.00
4 Joker. 2.25 8.00
5 1.75 6.00

SHADOW RIDERS
MARVEL UK (1993)
1 Cable. .75 2.50
2 .75 2.50
3-4 .50 1.75

SHADOW STRIKES, THE
DC (1989-1992)
1 1.00 3.00
2-28 .75 2.50
ANNUAL 1 1.25 4.00

SHADOW, THE (MOVIE ADAPTATION)
DARK HORSE (1994)
1-2 .75 2.50

SHADOWHAWK
IMAGE (1992-1993)
1 With Image #0 coupon. Silver foil cover. 1.50 5.00
1A Without coupon. .75 2.00
1B Newsstand version. .75 2.00
2 App: Spawn. 1.25 4.00
3 Glow-in-the-dark cover. 1.00 3.00
4 Savage Dragon. .75 2.50
ASHCAN 1.50 5.00

SHADOWHAWK GALLERY
IMAGE (1994)
1 .50 1.95

SHADOWHAWK II
IMAGE (1993)
1 Die-cut cover ($3.50 cp). 1.00 3.00
2 Identity revealed: Shadowhawk. 1.00 3.00
3 Fold-up cover. 1.00 3.00
ASHCAN Silver version. 1.50 5.00

SHADOWHAWK III
IMAGE/SHADOWLINE INK (1993-1995)
0 (9/94) .75 2.50
1 New secrets revealed. 1.00 3.00
1A Gold edition. 1.50 5.00
2-4 .75 2.00
5 Numbered as #12. .75 2.00
6 (#13) .75 2.00
7 (#14) .75 2.50
8 (#15) .75 2.50
9 (#16) .75 2.50
10 (#17) .75 2.50
11 (#18) .75 2.50
ASHCAN 1.50 5.00
SPECIAL 1 Flip book. 1.00 3.50

SHADOWHAWK/VAMPIRELLA: CREATURES OF THE NIGHT
IMAGE/HARRIS (1995)
2 First issue listed as Vampirella/Shadowhawk. 1.25 4.95

SHADOWMAN
ACCLAIM/VALIANT (1992-CURRENT)
0 Origin: Shadowman. Chromium cover. (2/94) 1.00 3.00
0A Regular cover. .75 2.00
1 1st: Shadowman. 2.75 10.00
2-3 1.75 6.00
4-5 1.00 3.00
6-7 .75 2.00
8 1st: Master Darque. 1.50 5.00
9-15 .75 2.00
16 1st: Dr. Mirage. 1.00 3.00
17-40 .75 2.00
41-42 .75 2.50
TPB Reprints issues #1-3,6. Includes Darque Passages comic. 2.50 9.95
YEARBOOK 1 1.00 3.95

SHADOWMASTERS
MARVEL (1989-1990)
1-4 .30 1.00

SHADOWS FALL
DC COMICS (1994-1995)
1-6 .75 2.95

SHAGGY DOG, THE
DELL FOUR COLOR SERIES (1959)
985 Movie photo cover (Annette Funicello photo back cover). (5/59) 13.00 40.00

SHAGGY DOG/THE ABSENT-MINDED PROFESSOR
GOLD KEY (1967)
30032-708 Disney movie tie-ins (combo comic reprints 4-Color books #985 & 1199). 8.00 25.00

SHAMAN'S TEARS
IMAGE/AXIS (1993-CURRENT)
1 1st & begin origin: Joshua Brand. 1.00 3.50
2 .75 2.50
3-9 .50 1.95
10-11 .75 2.50

SHANNA, THE SHE-DEVIL
MARVEL (1972-1973)
1 1st: Shanna. 1.50 5.00
2 1.00 3.00
3-5 .75 2.00

SHARKFIGHTERS, THE
DELL FOUR COLOR SERIES (1957)
762 Movie photo cover. (1/57) 28.00 90.00

SHARP COMICS
H. C. BLACKERBY (1945-1946)
1 65.00 200.00
2 50.00 150.00

SHAZAM!
DC (1973-1978)
1 1st: revival of original Captain Marvel since the Golden-Age. 1.25 4.00
2 Intro: Mr. Mind. .75 2.00
3-7 .75 2.00
8 100 page issue. 1.00 3.00
9 .75 2.00
10 End: C.C. Beck art. .75 2.00
11 .75 2.00
12 Begin: 100 page issues. 1.00 3.00
13-16 1.00 3.00
17 End: 100 page issues. 1.00 3.00
18-24 .75 2.00
25 1st: Isis. .75 2.00
26-35 .75 2.00

SHAZAM: THE NEW BEGINNING
DC (1987)
1 1st & Origin: new Captain Marvel. .50 1.50
2-4 .50 1.25

SHEENA, QUEEN OF THE JUNGLE
FICTION HOUSE (1942-1953)
1 400.00 1200.00
2 190.00 625.00
3 (Spring/43) 130.00 430.00
4 (Fall/48) 55.00 180.00
5 55.00 180.00
6 (Spring/50) 40.00 120.00
7 40.00 120.00
8-12 31.00 100.00
13-18 26.00 85.00

SHE-HULK
SEE SAVAGE OR SENSATIONAL SHE-HULK

SHERIFF BOB'S CHUCK WAGON
AVON (1950)
1 16.00 50.00

SHERIFF OF TOMBSTONE
CHARLTON (1958-1961)
1 11.00 35.00
2 7.00 20.00
3-6 5.00 15.00
7-17 2.75 10.00

SHERLOCK HOLMES
DC (1975)
1 .75 2.00

SHERRY THE SHOWGIRL
MARVEL(ATLAS) (1956-1957)
1 13.00 40.00
2 7.00 20.00
3-7 2.75 10.00

SHI
CRUSADE (1994-CURRENT)
1 10.00 30.00
1A Fan appreciation issue, new cover and art. 1.00 3.00
1B Fan appreciation, no logo. 2.00 7.50
1C Comic-Con version, gold Crusade logo. 8.00 25.00
2 6.00 18.00
2A San Diego Con commemmerative version (3000, b & w). 10.00 30.00
2B Ashcan version. 5.00 15.00
3 3.00 10.00
4 2.00 6.00
5 1.25 4.00
5A Variant cover. 7.00 20.00
6 .75 2.50
6A Chicago Comic Con commemmorative version (cover to Tomo

#1, interior Shi #6). 5.00 15.00

SHI: SENRYAKU
CRUSADE (1995-CURRENT)
1 .... .75 2.95

SHIELD
MARVEL (1973)
1 .... 1.50 5.00
2-5 .... .75 2.00

SHIELD WIZARD COMICS
MLJ (1940-1944)
1 Origin: The Shield. 500.00 1800.00
2 .... 270.00 875.00
3-4 .... 190.00 625.00
5-6 .... 155.00 500.00
7-8 .... 130.00 430.00
9-13 .... 115.00 370.00

SHOCK DETECTIVE CASES
STAR (1952)
20 Previous title: "Crime Fighting Detective."
.... 16.00 50.00
21 Title changes to Spook with #22. 16.00 50.00

SHOCK ILLUSTRATED
EC (1955-1956)
1 .... 11.00 35.00
2 .... 13.00 40.00
3 Rare (only 100 copies printed). ... 250.00 800.00

SHOCK SUSPENSTORIES
EC (1952-1955)
1 .... 150.00 490.00
2 .... 85.00 270.00
3 .... 70.00 220.00
4 SOTI 75.00 240.00
5 .... 60.00 190.00
6-7 .... 70.00 220.00
8-11 .... 50.00 160.00
12 "The Monkey" drug story. 60.00 190.00
13 Art: Frank Frazetta. 70.00 220.00
14-15 .... 40.00 130.00
16-18 .... 35.00 110.00

SHOCK SUSPENSTORIES
EC(COCHRAN) (1992-1994)
1 Reprints EC original. 1.00 3.00
2-3 .... .50 1.50
4-10 .... .75 2.00
ANNUAL 1 Reprint: 1st 5 issues. 2.25 8.95

SHOCK SUSPENSTORIES
EAST COAST (1974)
12 .... 1.50 5.00

SHOCKING MYSTERY CASES
STAR (1952-1954)
50 Previous title: "Thrilling Crime Cases." 50.00 160.00
51 .... 25.00 80.00
52-60 .... 17.00 55.00

SHOGUN WARRIORS
MARVEL (1979-1980)
1 Toy tie-in. .... .75 2.00
2-20 .... .30 1.00

SHORT RIBS
DELL FOUR COLOR SERIES (1962)
1333 (4/62) 14.00 45.00

SHOTGUN MARY
ANTARCTIC (1995-1996)
1 Mini-series. .... .75 2.95

SHOTGUN SLADE
DELL FOUR COLOR SERIES (1960)
1111 TV tie-in. (7/60) 13.00 40.00

SHOWCASE
DC (1956-1978)
1 Fire Fighters. "Fourth Alarm!" 600.00 2000.00
2 Kings Of The Wild. "Rider Of The Winds!" (5-6/56)
.... 180.00 575.00
3 The Frogmen! (8/56) 190.00 600.00
4 "Presenting The Flash!" 1st & origin: Silver-Age Flash. (10/56) 5100.00 20000.00
5 Manhunters in "The Human Eel!" (12/56)
.... 220.00 700.00
6 1st & Origin: Challengers Of The Unknown by Jack Kirby (2/57) 800.00 3000.00
7 Challengers Of The Unknown (4/57) 400.00 1500.00
8 The Flash in "The Secret Of The Empty Box!" (6/57)
.... 1600.00 6000.00
9 Superman's Girl Friend Lois Lane. "Mrs. Superman!"
.... 800.00 3000.00
10 Superman's Girl Friend Lois Lane. "The Forbidden Box From Krypton!" (10/57) 500.00 1600.00
11 Challengers Of The Unknown. "The Day The Earth Blew Up!"
.... 300.00 1150.00
12 Challengers Of The Unknown. "Menace Of The Ancient Vials!" by Jack Kirby. (2/58) 300.00 1100.00
13 The Flash in "Around The World In 80 Minutes!" by Infantino. Origin: Mr. Element. (4/58) 800.00 2800.00
14 The Flash in "Giants Of The Time-World!" by Infantino. Origin: Dr. Alchemy. (6/58) 800.00 2800.00
15 The Space Ranger. 1st: Space Ranger. (8/58)
.... 400.00 1300.00
16 The Space Ranger. (10/58) 200.00 660.00
17 Adventures On Other Worlds. 1st: Adam Strange. "The Planet And The Pendulum!" (12/58) 500.00 1700.00
18 Adventures On Other Worlds. App: Adam Strange in "The Dozen Dooms Of Adam Strange!" ... 250.00 800.00
19 Adam Strange in "Adventures On Other Worlds" (4/59)
.... 250.00 800.00
20 Rip Hunter...Time Master. 1st & Origin: Rip Hunter. "Prisoners Of 100 Million B.C.!" 190.00 600.00
21 Rip Hunter...Time Master. (8/59) 95.00 300.00
22 Green Lantern. 1st & Origin: Green Lantern (Silver-Age). "Menace Of The Runaway Missile!" by Gil Kane. (10/59)
.... 1100.00 4200.00
23 Green Lantern. "The Invisible Destroyer!"
.... 400.00 1200.00
24 Green Lantern in "The Creature That Couldn't Die!" (2/60)
.... 400.00 1200.00
25 Rip Hunter...Time Master in "Captives Of The Medieval Sorcerer" (4/60) 65.00 200.00
26 Rip Hunter...Time Master in "The Aliens From 2000 B.C.!" (6/60) 65.00 200.00
27 1st: Sea Devils. "The Golden Monster!" (8/60)
.... 190.00 600.00
28 The Sea Devils in "The Undersea Prison!" (10/60)
.... 85.00 275.00
29 The Sea Devils in "The Last Dive Of The Sea Devils!" (12/60) 85.00 275.00
30 Aquaman And Aqualad in "The Creatures From Atlantis!" (2/61) 155.00 500.00
31 Aquaman And Aqualad in "The Sea Beasts From One Billion, B.C.!" 85.00 280.00
32 Aquaman And Aqualad in "The Creature King Of The Sea!" (6/61) 85.00 280.00
33 Aquaman And Aqualad in "Prisoners Of The Aqua-Planet!" 80.00 .... 260.00
34 1st & Origin: The Atom in "Battle Of The Tiny Titans!" (10/61) 400.00 1200.00
35 The Atom in "Dooms From Beyond!" 170.00 560.00
36 The Atom in "Prisoner In a Test Tube!"
.... 140.00 460.00
37 1st: Metal Men in "The Flaming Doom!"
.... 170.00 550.00
38 The Metal Men in "The Nightmare Menace!"
.... 100.00 325.00
39 The Metal Men in "The Deathless Doom!"
.... 70.00 230.00
40 The Metal Men in "The Day The Metal Men Melted!" (10/62) 70.00 230.00
41-42 Tommy Tomorrow. 31.00 100.00
43 Dr. No (James Bond). Movie tie-in (photo cover inside FC; 4/63). 100.00 330.00
44 Tommy Tomorrow. "Wanted For Treason: Tommy Tomorrow!" 19.00 60.00
45 Sgt. Rock. 50.00 150.00
46-47 Tommy Tomorrow. 17.00 55.00
48-49 Cave Carson. 11.00 35.00
50-51 I Spy. 13.00 40.00
52 Cave Carson. "Prisoners Of The Lost World!"
.... 13.00 40.00
53-54 G.I. Joe. 13.00 40.00
55 Dr. Fate & Hourman. 1st: Golden-Age Green Lantern in Silver-Age. 1st: Solomon Grundy (Silver-Age).
.... 80.00 250.00
56 Dr. Fate & Hourman. 20.00 65.00
57-58 Enemy Ace. 22.00 70.00
59 Teen Titans. "The Return Of The Teen Titans!" (12/65)
.... 20.00 65.00
60 The Spectre. 1st: Spectre (Silver-Age). 60.00 190.00
61 The Spectre. "Beyond The Sinister Barrier!"
.... 28.00 90.00
62 1st & Origin: Inferior Five. 16.00 50.00
63 Inferior Five. 7.00 20.00
64 The Spectre. "The Ghost Of Ace Chance!"
.... 23.00 75.00
65 Inferior Five. 7.00 20.00
66-67 B'wana Beast. 2.75 10.00
68-69 Maniaks. 2.75 10.00
70 Binky. 2.75 10.00
71 Maniaks. 2.75 10.00
72 Top Gun. 2.75 10.00
73 1st & Origin: The Creeper by Steve Ditko.
.... 20.00 65.00
74 1st & Origin: Anthro. 14.00 45.00
75 1st & Origin: Hawk & The Dove. ... 19.00 60.00
76 1st: Bat Lash. 10.00 30.00
77 1st: Angel & Ape. 10.00 30.00
78 1st: Jonny Double. 4.00 12.00
79 1st: Dolphin. 6.00 18.00
80 Phantom Stranger. 2.75 10.00
81 Windy & Willy. 2.00 7.00
82 1st: Nightmaster. "Some Forbidden Fate!"
.... 13.00 40.00
83 Nightmaster. "Sing A Song Of Sorcery!"
.... 13.00 40.00
84 Nightmaster. "Come Darkness, Come Death!"
.... 13.00 40.00
85-87 Firehair. 2.75 10.00
88-90 Jason's Quest. 1.50 5.00
91 Manhunter 2070. .... 1.50 5.00
92 Origin: Manhunter 2070. .... 1.50 5.00
93 Manhunter 2070. .... 1.50 5.00
94 1st & Origin: new Doom Patrol & Robotman.
.... 2.25 8.00
95 The Doom Patrol. Origin: Celsius. ... 2.25 8.00
96 The Doom Patrol. 2.25 8.00
97 Origin: Power Girl. 1.25 4.00
98 Origin continued: Power Girl. 1.25 4.00
99 Power Girl. 1.25 4.00
100 Anniversary edition. Features most Showcase characters.
.... 1.75 6.00
101 Hawkman. "Mystery In Space" App: Adam Strange, Hawkgirl. 1.25 4.00
102 Hawkman. :Strange Adventures" App: Adam Strange.
.... 1.25 4.00
103 Hawkman. "Adventures On Other Worlds" App: Adam Strange. 1.25 4.00
104 O.S.S. Spies At War. 1.25 4.00

SHOWCASE '93
DC (1993)
1-4 .... .50 1.95
5-6 .... .75 2.75
7 Knightfall tie-in (pt.13). 1.25 4.00
8 Knightfall tie-in (pt.14). 1.00 3.75
9-11 .... .75 2.25
12 .... .50 1.95

SHOWCASE '94
DC (1994)
1-7 .... .50 1.95
8 .... 1.00 3.00
9 .... .75 2.50
10 Azrael story. 1.00 3.00
11 .... .75 2.50
12 .... .50 1.95

SHOWCASE '95
DC (1994-CURRENT)
1-4 .... .75 2.50
5-8 .... .75 2.95

SHOWGIRLS
MARVEL(ATLAS) (1957)
1 .... 13.00 40.00
2 .... 8.00 25.00

SHROUD, THE
MARVEL (1994)
1-4 .... .50 1.75

SIDESHOW
AVON (1949)
1 .... 31.00 100.00

SILLY SYMPHONIES
DELL (1952-1959)
1 100 page giant. 65.00 200.00
2-3 100 page giant. 50.00 150.00
4-6 100 page giant. 40.00 120.00
7 100 page giant. 50.00 150.00
8-9 100 page giant. 31.00 100.00

SILVER SABLE
MARVEL (1992-1995)
1 Silver embossed cover. .... .75 2.00
2-3 .... .50 1.25
4-5 Dr. Doom. .... .50 1.25
6-17 .... .50 1.25
18-19 Venom. .... .50 1.25
20-24 .... .50 1.25
25 .... .75 2.00
26-35 .... .50 1.50

SILVER STAR
PACIFIC (1983-1984)
1-6 .... .30 1.00

SILVER STREAK COMICS
LEV GLEASON (1939-1946)
1 Begin: The Claw by Cole (12/39) 2300.00 9000.00
2 Cover/Art: Simon & Kirby. 700.00 2500.00
3 1st & Origin: The Silver Streak (3/40) 600.00 2000.00
4 .... 310.00 1000.00
5 .... 280.00 900.00
6 1st & Origin: Daredevil (9/40) ... 2300.00 9000.00

SHI #1

SHOCK SUSPENSTORIES #9

SHOWCASE #4

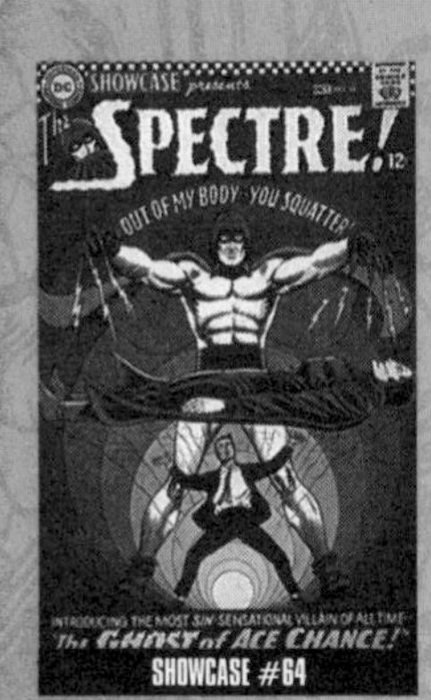

SHOWCASE #64

SILVER SURFER #3 (1ST SERIES)

SILVER SURFER #63 (2ND SERIES)

SIMPSONS COMICS #1

SIMPSONS COMICS #5

SILVER STREAK COMICS #6

The industry's first Daredevil (not to be confused with Marvel's Daredevil) was tortured as a child, leaving him mute and with a boomerang-shaped scar on his chest. He grows up to fight criminals with his wits and boomerang.

7 Daredevil battles The Claw. 1100.00 4000.00
8 Daredevil battles The Claw. 600.00 2000.00
9 Daredevil battles The Claw. 400.00 1500.00
10 1st & Origin: Captain Battle. Daredevil battles The Claw. 310.00 1000.00
11 Daredevil battles The Claw. 220.00 700.00
12-16 ...... 155.00 500.00
17 End: Daredevil. 155.00 500.00
18 1st & Begin: The Saint. 125.00 400.00
19-20 ...... 110.00 350.00
21 (5/42) 110.00 350.00
22 Begin: Reprints. (1946) 40.00 125.00
23-24 ...... 40.00 125.00
25 (NO#) (11/46) 70.00 225.00

SILVER SURFER
MARVEL (1968-1970)
1 Squarebound. Origin: The Silver Surfer. "The Origin Of The Silver Surfer!" (8/68). 125.00 400.00
2 "When Lands The Surfer!" 40.00 125.00
3 1st: Mephisto. "The Power And The Prize!" 40.00 125.00
4 Low distribution. 115.00 380.00
5 "And Who Shall Mourn For Him?" ... 23.00 75.00
6 "Worlds Without End!" 23.00 75.00
7 "The Heir Of Frankenstein!" End: Double-size squarebound issues. 23.00 75.00
8 "Introducing: The Ghost!" 16.00 50.00
9 "...To Steal The Surfer's Soul!" ... 16.00 50.00
10 "A World He Never Made!" 16.00 50.00
11 "O, Bitter Victory!" 12.00 38.00
12 "Gather, Ye Witches!" 12.00 38.00
13 "The Dawn Of The Doomsday Man!" 12.00 38.00
14 Spider-Man crossover. 19.00 60.00
15 Silver Surfer battles Human Torch. 12.00 38.00
16 vs. Mephisto. 12.00 38.00
17 "The Surfer Must Kill!" 12.00 38.00
18 Cover & art: Jack Kirby. "...The Unbeatable Inhumans!" 12.00 38.00

SILVER SURFER
MARVEL (1982) ONE-SHOT
1 Art: John Byrne. 2.50 9.00

SILVER SURFER
MARVEL (1987-CURRENT)
1 Origin retold: The Silver Surfer. 2.75 10.00
2 ...... 1.75 6.00
3-5 ...... 1.50 5.00
6-10 ...... 1.25 4.00
11-13 ...... 1.00 3.00
14 ...... 1.25 4.00
15 Begin: Ron Lim cover & art. 2.25 8.00
16-20 ...... 1.25 4.00
21-30 ...... 1.00 3.00
31 ...... 1.50 5.00
32 No Ron Lim cover & art. 1.00 3.00
33 ...... 1.00 3.00
34 Return: Thanos (cameo). 3.00 9.00
35 1st: Thanos (full story). 2.25 8.00
36 History of Thanos. 2.00 7.00
37 1st: Drax. 2.00 7.00
38 Silver Surfer battles Thanos. 2.00 7.00
39 Art: Jim Starlin. 1.75 6.00
40 ...... 1.75 6.00
41-45 ...... 1.50 5.00
46 Return: Adam Warlock. 1.75 6.00
47 ...... 1.75 6.00
48-49 ...... 1.50 5.00
50 Embossed silver foil cover. 2.75 10.00
50 (2ND) 2nd printing. 1.00 3.00
50 (3RD) 3rd printing. ...... .50 1.50
51-59 ...... 1.00 3.00
60-64 ...... .75 2.00
65-67 ...... .50 1.50
68-74 ...... .50 1.50
75 Foil embossed cover. Double size. ... .75 2.50
76 ...... .50 1.50
77-81 ...... .50 1.25
82 Double size. ...... .50 1.75
83-84 ...... .50 1.25
85 Polybagged with Dirt Magazine. ... .75 2.95
85A Without Dirt Magazine. ...... .50 1.25
86-91 ...... .50 1.25
92-99 ...... .50 1.50
100 Double size, hologram cover. 1.00 3.95
100A Regular cover. ...... .75 2.25
101-107 ...... .50 1.50

SILVER SURFER
MARVEL (1988-1989)
1 Art: Moebius. 1.00 3.00
2 Art: Moebius. ...... .75 2.00

SILVER SURFER ANNUAL
MARVEL (1988-CURRENT)
1 ...... 2.00 7.00
2 ...... 1.25 4.00
3 ...... 1.25 4.00
4-5 ...... .75 2.25
6-7 ...... .75 2.95

SILVER SURFER: RESURRECTION
MARVEL (1993)
1-4 ...... .75 2.50

SILVER SURFER VS. DRACULA
MARVEL (1994)
1 Reprint: Tomb Of Dracula #50. ...... .50 1.75

SILVERTIP
DELL FOUR COLOR SERIES (1953-1958)
491 (8/53) 20.00 65.00
572 (7/54) 10.00 30.00
608 "Valley Of Vanishing Men" (12/54) 11.00 35.00
637 (7/55) 10.00 30.00
667 "And The Stolen Stallion" (12/55) 10.00 30.00
731 "And The Fighting Four" (10/56) 10.00 30.00
789 "Valley Thieves" (4/57) 10.00 30.00
835 "The Fake Rider" (9/57) 10.00 30.00
898 (5/58) 10.00 30.00

SIMPSONS COMICS
BONGO (1993-CURRENT)
1 ...... 1.00 3.00
2-3 ...... .50 1.95
4-10 ...... .75 2.25

SIMPSONS COMICS AND STORIES
WELSH (1993)
1 Polybagged. 1.00 3.00
1A Newsstand edition. ...... .50 1.50

SIN CITY
DARK HORSE (1992)
HC 8.00 25.00
SC 5.00 15.00

SIN CITY, A DAME TO KILL FOR
DARK HORSE (1993-1994)
1 By Frank Miller. 2.00 7.00
1 (2ND) 2nd printing. ...... .75 2.95
2 ...... 1.25 4.50
2 (2ND) 2nd printing. ...... .75 2.95
3 ...... 1.25 4.00
3 (2ND) 2nd printing. ...... .75 2.95
4-6 ...... 1.00 3.50
TPB Reprints issues #1-6 (with 10 new pages). 5.00 15.00

SIN CITY: THE BABE WORE RED AND OTHER STORIES
DARK HORSE (1994)
NO# One-shot. 1.00 3.50

SIN CITY: THE BIG FAT KILL
DARK HORSE (1994-1995)
1 ...... 1.50 5.00
2 ...... 1.25 4.00
3-5 ...... 1.00 3.50

SINGING GUNS
FAWCETT (1950)
NO# Movie photo cover (Vaughn Monroe). 50.00 150.00

SINGLE SERIES
UNITED FEATURES (1938-1942)
1 The Captain And The Kids. (1938) 135.00 440.00
1A Captain And The Kids #1. Second edition, reprinted Dec. 29, 1939. ...... 70.00 220.00
2 Broncho Bill. 70.00 220.00
3 Ella Cinders. 70.00 220.00
4 Li'l Abner (#1). 100.00 330.00
5 Fritzi Ritz. 50.00 160.00
5A Fritzi Ritz (reprint, 1939). 35.00 110.00
6 Jim Hardy (#1). 60.00 190.00
7 Frankie Doodle. (1939) 50.00 160.00

8 Peter Pat. 40.00 130.00
9 Strange As It Seems. 40.00 130.00
10 Little Mary Mixup. 40.00 130.00
11 Mr. And Mrs. Beans. 40.00 130.00
11A Mr. And Mrs. Beans (reprint giveaway from New York World's Fair, 1939). 40.00 130.00
12 Joe Jinks. 40.00 130.00
13 Looy Dot Dope & Colonel Wowser. 40.00 130.00
14 Billy Make Believe. 35.00 110.00
15 How It Began. (1939) 40.00 130.00
16 Illustrated Gags. (1940) 25.00 80.00
17 Danny Dingle. 35.00 110.00
18 Li'l Abner (#2). 85.00 270.00
19 Broncho Bill (#2). 50.00 160.00
20 Tarzan. 200.00 650.00
21 Ella Cinders (#2). 50.00 160.00
22 Iron Vic. 40.00 130.00
23 Tailspin Tommy. 50.00 160.00
24 Alice In Wonderland/Through The Looking Glass. 70.00 220.00
25 Abbie An' Slats. 50.00 160.00
26 Little Mary Mixup (#2). 40.00 130.00
27 Jim Hardy. (1942) 40.00 130.00
28 Ella Cinders And Abbie An' Slats. 40.00 130.00

SINISTER HOUSE OF SECRET LOVE, THE
DC (1971-1972)
1 1.25 4.00
2-3 1.00 3.00
4 Title changes to Secrets Of Sinister House with #5. 1.00 3.00

SIR LANCELOT
DELL FOUR COLOR SERIES (1954-1957)
606 (12/54) 17.00 55.00
775 "...And Brian". "The Knight Of The Red Plume". (3/57) Movie photo cover. 22.00 70.00

SIR WALTER RALEIGH
DELL FOUR COLOR SERIES (1955)
644 Movie photo cover. (8/55) 16.00 50.00

SISTERHOOD OF STEEL
MARVEL (1984-1986)
1-8 .30 1.00

SIX BLACK HORSES
DELL (1963)
12-750-301 Movie photo cover. 7.00 20.00

SIX FROM SIRIUS
MARVEL(EPIC) (1984)
1-4 .30 1.00

SIX GUN HEROES
FAWCETT/CHARLTON (1950-1965)
1 Photo covers on #s 1-24. 70.00 220.00
2 35.00 110.00
3-6 25.00 80.00
7-12 20.00 65.00
13-23 14.00 44.00
24 Begin: Charlton publication. 14.00 44.00
25 14.00 44.00
26-30 12.00 38.00
31-50 9.00 27.00
51-83 4.00 11.00

SIX GUN WESTERN
MARVEL(ATLAS) (1957)
1 20.00 65.00
2-3 17.00 55.00
4 10.00 33.00

SIX MILLION DOLLAR MAN
CHARLTON (1976-1977) MAGAZINE
1 TV tie-in. .75 2.00
2-7 .75 2.00

SIX MILLION DOLLAR MAN, THE
CHARLTON (1976-1978)
1 TV photo cover. .75 2.00
2-9 .30 1.00

SKELETON HAND
ACG (1952-1953)
1 50.00 160.00
2 29.00 95.00
3-6 25.00 80.00

SKI PARTY
DELL (1965)
12-743-511 Movie photo cover. 8.00 25.00

SKIN GRAFT
DC (1993)
1-4 .75 2.50

SKIPPY'S OWN BOOK OF COMICS
GIVEAWAY (1934)
NO# 4th comic book in the modern format. 1st full color comic book devoted to a single character. 1100.00 4000.00

SKRULL KILL KREW
MARVEL (1995-CURRENT)
1 .75 2.95

SKULL KILLER
FREE PRESS (1975)
1 2.75 10.00

SKULL THE SLAYER
MARVEL (1975-1976)
1 1st & Origin: Skull. .75 2.00
2-8 .30 1.00

SKY BLAZERS
HAWLEY (1940)
1 Radio tie-in. 70.00 220.00
2 40.00 130.00

SKY PILOT
ZIFF-DAVIS (1950-1951)
10 Cover: Norman Saunders. 10.00 30.00
11 Cover: Norman Saunders. 7.00 20.00

SKY ROCKET COMICS
CHESLER (1944)
NO# 23.00 75.00

SKY SHERIFF
DS (1948)
1 Starring Breeze Lawson. 13.00 40.00

SKYMAN
COLUMBIA (1941-1948)
1 Origin: Skyman, The Face. 135.00 440.00
2 App: Yankee Doodle. (1941) 60.00 190.00
3 (1948) 40.00 130.00
4 35.00 110.00

SLAM BANG COMICS
FAWCETT (1940)
1 400.00 1200.00
2 95.00 310.00
3 155.00 500.00
4-6 95.00 310.00
7 Title changes to "Western Desperado Comics" with #8. 95.00 310.00

SLAPSTICK
MARVEL (1992-1993)
1-4 .30 1.00

SLAPSTICK COMICS
CMD (1946)
NO# 25.00 80.00

SLASH-D DOUBLECROSS
ST. JOHN (1950)
NO# Pocket Comics. 25.00 80.00

SLAVE GIRL
ETERNITY (1989)
1 .75 2.25

SLAVE GIRL COMICS
AVON (1949)
1 100.00 330.00
2 70.00 220.00

SLEEPING BEAUTY
DELL FOUR COLOR SERIES (1959)
973 "And The Prince" (5/59) 16.00 50.00
984 "...Fairy Godmothers" (4/59) 13.00 40.00

SLEEPING BEAUTY
GOLD KEY (1970)
30042-009 Disney movie tie-in. With poster. 5.00 15.00

SLEEPWALKER
MARVEL (1991-1994)
1 1st: Sleepwalker. 1.75 6.00
2 1.25 4.50
3 1.00 3.75
4-6 1.00 3.50
7-8 1.00 3.25
9 .75 2.50
10 .75 2.25
11-13 .75 2.00
14 .50 1.50
15-18 .50 1.25
19 Die-cut cover. .75 2.00
20-24 .50 1.25
25 Holo-grafix foil cover. .75 2.95

26-33 .50 1.25
SPECIAL 1 (1992) .75 2.00

SLICK CHICK COMICS
LEADER (1947)
1 16.00 50.00
2-3 8.00 25.00

SLUDGE
MALIBU (1993-CURRENT)
1 1st: Sludge. With coupon for Rune #0. .75 2.50
1A Silver foil cover. 1.75 6.00
2 .50 1.95
3 1st: Lord Pumpkin & Pistol. 1.00 3.00
4-11 .50 1.95
12 Flip book with Ultraverse Premiere #8. 1.00 3.50
13 .50 1.95

SLUDGE: RED X-MAS
MALIBU (1994)
1 Holiday one-shot. .75 2.50

SLUGGER
LEV GLEASON (1956)
1 Little Wise Guys spin-off. 5.00 15.00

SMALL KILLING, A
DARK HORSE (1993)
GN 80 page graphic novel. 4.00 11.95

SMASH COMICS
QUALITY (1939-1949)
1 400.00 1200.00
2 155.00 500.00
3 105.00 340.00
4-5 80.00 250.00
6-13 55.00 180.00
14 1st: The Ray by Lou Fine. (9/40) 400.00 1500.00
15 230.00 750.00
16 190.00 625.00
17 170.00 550.00
18 1st & Origin: Midnight by Jack Cole. 230.00 750.00
19-20 155.00 500.00
21 115.00 370.00
22 End: The Ray by Lou Fine. 115.00 370.00
23-24 95.00 310.00
25 1st & Origin: Wildfire. 115.00 370.00
26-30 85.00 280.00
31-32 65.00 210.00
33 Origin: The Marksman. 80.00 250.00
34-39 55.00 180.00
40 End: The Ray. 55.00 180.00
41 40.00 120.00
42 Begin: Lady Luck. 31.00 100.00
43-50 26.00 85.00
51-60 23.00 75.00
61-84 19.00 60.00
85 Title changes to Lady Luck with #86. 19.00 60.00

SMASH HIT SPORTS COMICS
ESSANKAY (1949)
1 26.00 85.00

SMILEY BURNETTE WESTERN
FAWCETT (1950)
1 Photo covers all issues. 50.00 160.00
2-4 35.00 110.00

SMILIN' JACK
DELL (1948-1949)
1 14.00 45.00
2 7.00 22.00
3-8 4.00 13.00

SMILIN' JACK
DELL FOUR COLOR SERIES (1942-1947)
4 110.00 350.00
14 80.00 250.00
36-58 50.00 150.00
80 35.00 110.00
149 25.00 80.00

SMILIN' JACK
SEE LARGE FEATURE COMICS #12, 14, 25.

SMILIN' JACK POPPED WHEAT
GIVEAWAY (1947)
NO# 16 pages 1.50 5.00

SMITTY
CUPPLES & LEON (1928-1933)
1928 25.00 80.00
1929-1933 20.00 65.00

SMITTY
DELL (1948-1949)
1 14.00 45.00

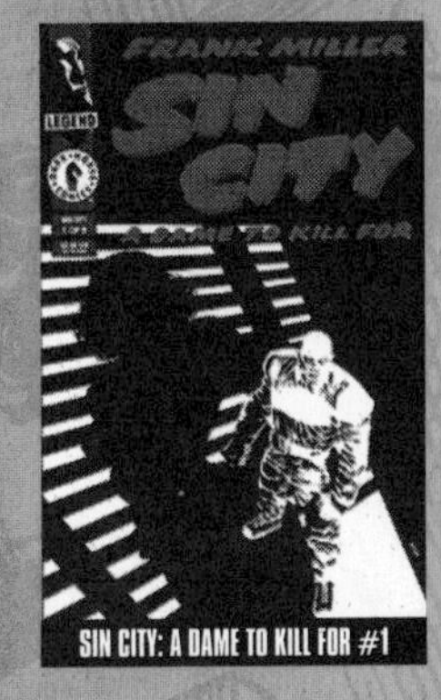

SIN CITY: A DAME TO KILL FOR #1

SLUDGE #6

SMASH COMICS #21

SMASH HIT SPORTS COMICS #1

SOLAR #3

SOLAR #15

SOLITAIRE #7

SON OF SINBAD #1

2 ..... 6.00 18.00
3-7 ..... 2.50 9.00

SMITTY
DELL FOUR COLOR SERIES (1942-1958)
6 ..... 50.00 150.00
32 ..... 31.00 100.00
65 (3/45) 25.00 80.00
99 (3/46) 23.00 75.00
138 ..... 19.00 60.00
909 ..... 7.00 20.00

SMITTY
SEE LARGE FEATURE COMICS #26.

SMOKEY STOVER
DELL FOUR COLOR SERIES (1942-1957)
7 ..... 65.00 200.00
35 ..... 25.00 80.00
64 (2/45) 19.00 60.00
229 (5/49) 8.00 25.00
730 (10/56) 5.00 15.00
827 (8/57) 5.00 15.00

SMOKEY THE BEAR
DELL FOUR COLOR SERIES (1955-1961)
653 (10/55) 14.00 45.00
708 (6/56) 8.00 25.00
754 (11/56) 7.00 20.00
818 (6/57) 7.00 20.00
932 "His Life Story" (8/58) 5.00 15.00
1016 "Nature Stories" (8/59) 5.00 15.00
1119 "Nature Stories". (8/60) 7.00 20.00
1214 (8/61) 7.00 20.00

SMOKY
DELL (1967)
12-746-702 Movie tie-in. 5.00 15.00

SNAGGLEPUSS
GOLD KEY (1962-1963)
1 TV tie-in. 13.00 40.00
2-4 ..... 7.00 20.00

SNAP COMICS
CHESLER (1945)
9 ..... 16.00 50.00

SNAPPY COMICS
PRIZE (1945)
1 ..... 19.00 60.00

SNIFFY THE PUP
STANDARD (1949-1952)
5 ..... 7.00 20.00
6-17 ..... 2.25 8.00

SNOOPER AND BLABBER DETECTIVES
GOLD KEY (1962-1963)
1 TV cartoon tie-in. 10.00 30.00
2-3 ..... 7.00 20.00

SNOW WHITE AND THE SEVEN DWARFS
DELL FOUR COLOR SERIES (1944-1952)
49 Disney movie tie-in. 110.00 350.00
382 Disney movie tie-in. 19.00 60.00

SNOW WHITE AND THE SEVEN DWARFS GIVEAWAY
DISNEY (1952-1958)
1952 Presented by Bendix Washing Machines. 8.00 25.00
1955 "The Milky Way" presented by American Dairy Association. 10.00 30.00
1958 "Mystery Of The Missing Magic" 8.00 25.00

SNOW WHITE AND THE SEVEN DWARFS
GOLD KEY (1963)
10091-310 Disney movie tie-in. 7.00 20.00

SOLAR
ACCLAIM/VALIANT (1991-CURRENT)
1 Origin: Solar. Second Death, pt.1. ..... 2.00 7.00
2 Origin continued. Second Death, pt.2. 1.50 5.00
3 Origin continued. Second Death, pt.3. 2.00 7.00
4 Origin concludes. Second Death, pt.4. 1.00 3.00
5-9 ..... 1.00 3.00
10 1st: Eternal Warrior. Black embossed cover. 4.00 12.00
10 (2ND) 2nd printing. ..... .75 2.00
11 1st: full Eternal Warrior. 2.00 7.00
12-13 ..... .75 2.00
14 1st: Bender. 1.25 4.00
15 Climax to battle with Bender. ..... .75 2.00
16-23 ..... .75 2.00
24-45 ..... .75 2.25
46-49 ..... .75 2.50
50 Giant size. ..... .75 2.95
51-52 ..... .75 2.50
TPB Reprints issues #1-4, does not include Alpha & Omega chapters. 2.50 9.95

SOLARMAN
MARVEL (1989)
1 ..... .30 1.00

SOLDIER AND MARINE COMICS
CHARLTON (1954-1956)
11 Art: Bob Powell. 5.00 16.00
12 Photo cover. 4.00 11.00
13-15 ..... 4.00 11.00
V2#9 ..... 2.25 8.75

SOLDIER COMICS
FAWCETT (1952-1953)
1 ..... 15.00 48.00
2 ..... 8.00 24.00
3-6 ..... 5.00 14.00
7-11 ..... 2.50 9.50

SOLDIERS OF FORTUNE
ACG (1951-1953)
1 ..... 25.00 80.00
2 ..... 14.00 44.00
3-9 ..... 10.00 33.00
10-13 ..... 4.00 11.00

SOLITAIRE
MALIBU (1993-1994)
1 Polybagged with cards. ..... .75 2.50
1A Newsstand edition. ..... .50 1.95
1B Silver foil cover. 2.25 8.00
2-12 ..... .50 1.95

SOLO
MARVEL (1994-1995)
1 Spider-Man. ..... .50 1.75
2-4 ..... .50 1.75

SOLO AVENGERS
MARVEL (1987-1989)
1-19 ..... .30 1.00
20 Title changes to Avengers Spotlight with #21. ..... .30 1.00

SOLOMON AND SHEBA
DELL FOUR COLOR SERIES (1959)
1070 Movie photo cover. (12/59) ... 19.00 60.00

SOLUTION, THE
MALIBU (1993-CURRENT)
0 Send away issue (free with Rune #0). (11/93) 2.75 10.00
1 ..... .50 1.95
1A Silver foil cover. 1.50 5.00
2 With coupon for Rune #0. ..... .75 2.50
3-15 ..... .50 1.95
16 Flip book with Ultraverse Premiere #10. 1.00 3.50
17 ..... .75 2.50

SON OF BLACK BEAUTY
DELL FOUR COLOR SERIES (1953-1954)
510 (11/53) 8.00 25.00
566 (6/54) 7.00 20.00

SON OF CELLULOID
ECLIPSE (1991)
1 ..... .30 1.00

SON OF FLUBBER
GOLD KEY (1963)
10057-304 Disney movie tie-in. 7.00 20.00

SON OF SATAN
MARVEL (1975-1977)
1 ..... 4.00 12.00
2 Origin: The Possessor. 2.00 7.00
3-8 ..... 1.50 5.00

SON OF SINBAD
ST. JOHN (1950)
1 "The Curse Of The Caliph's Dancer" by Joe Kubert. 50.00 160.00

SONG OF THE SOUTH
DELL FOUR COLOR SERIES (1956)
693 Disney movie tie-in. (4/56) 8.00 25.00

SONS OF KATIE ELDER, THE
DELL (1965)
12-748-511 Movie photo cover (John Wayne, Dean Martin). 23.00 75.00

SORCERY
RED CIRCLE (1974-1975)
6 Previous title: Chilling Adventures In Sorcery. .75 2.00
7-11 ..... .75 2.00

SORORITY SECRETS
TOBY (1954)
1 ..... 7.00 20.00

SOUL
FLASHPOINT (1994)
1 ..... .75 2.00

SOUL SEARCHERS AND COMPANY
CLAYPOOL (1993-1994)
1-4 ..... .75 2.50
5-7 ..... .75 2.95
8-12 ..... .75 2.50

SOUTHERN KNIGHTS
GUILD/CI/HEROIC (1983-1992)
2 Previous title: Crusaders. 1.50 5.00
3 ..... 1.00 3.00
4-36 ..... .50 1.50

SOVEREIGN 7
DC COMICS (1995-CURRENT)
1 ..... 1.00 3.00
2-3 ..... .50 1.95

SPACE: 1999
CHARLTON (1975-1976)
1 TV tie-in. 1.25 4.00
2 ..... 1.00 3.00
3 Begin: John Byrne art. 1.50 5.00
4-6 ..... 1.50 5.00

SPACE: 1999
CHARLTON (1975-1976) MAGAZINE
1 ..... 1.25 4.00
2-8 ..... .75 2.00

SPACE ACE (A-1 SERIES)
ME (1952)
5 (A-1 #61). 65.00 200.00

SPACE ACTION
ACE (1952)
1 ..... 105.00 340.00
2-3 ..... 80.00 250.00

SPACE ADVENTURES
CAPITOL/CHARLTON (1952-1964)
1 ..... 65.00 210.00
2 ..... 31.00 100.00
3-6 ..... 25.00 80.00
7-9 ..... 22.00 70.00
10-11 Cover/Art: Steve Ditko. 65.00 210.00
12 Cover: Steve Ditko. 65.00 210.00
13-14 Blue Beetle. 28.00 90.00
15 Rocky Jones (TV tie-in, photo insert). 23.00 75.00
16-18 Rocky Jones. 23.00 75.00
19 ..... 23.00 75.00
20 First Trip To The Moon (reprint: Destination Moon). 23.00 75.00
21-22 ..... 19.00 60.00
23 Space Trip To The Moon. 19.00 60.00
24-27 Art: Steve Ditko. 28.00 90.00
28-30 ..... 15.00 48.00
31-32 Art: Steve Ditko. 28.00 90.00
33 1st & Origin: Captain Atom by Steve Ditko. One of the first Super-Hero characters created by Ditko. 110.00 360.00
34-40 Art: Steve Ditko. 50.00 150.00
41-59 ..... 8.00 24.00

SPACE ADVENTURES
CHARLTON (1967-1979)
1 (#60) 1st & Origin: Paul Mann. ... 8.00 24.00
2 Art: Steve Ditko. 5.00 15.00
3-4 ..... 2.75 10.00
5-6 Art: Steve Ditko. 5.00 15.00
7 ..... 2.75 10.00
8 Art: Steve Ditko. 5.00 15.00
9 Reprint: Space Adventures #33. (1978) .75 2.25
10 (1979) ..... .50 1.75
11-13 ..... .50 1.75

SPACE BUSTERS
ZIFF-DAVIS (1952)
1 ..... 100.00 330.00
2-3 ..... 85.00 275.00

SPACE COMICS
AVON (1954)
4-5 ..... 10.00 30.00

SPACE DETECTIVE
AVON (1951-1952)
1 Art: Wood. "Opium Smugglers Of Venus!" 190.00 625.00
2 "Batwomen Of Mercury!" 110.00 360.00
3-4 65.00 210.00

SPACE DETECTIVE
I.W.
1 Reprints in all issues. 5.00 15.00
8-9 5.00 15.00

SPACE FAMILY ROBINSON
GOLD KEY (1962-1969)
1 (#10031-212) 70.00 220.00
2 35.00 110.00
3-6 17.00 55.00
7-12 12.00 38.00
13-24 9.00 27.00
25-36 5.00 16.00

SPACE FUNNIES
ARCHIVAL (1989)
1 1.50 5.95

SPACE GHOST
GOLD KEY (1967)
10199-703 TV tie-in. 95.00 300.00

SPACE GIANTS, THE
BONEYARD (1993)
1 .75 2.00

SPACE GIANTS, THE
FBN (1979)
NO# One-shot. First American comic book dealing with Japanese animation. 1.75 6.00

SPACE KAT-ETS, THE
POWER (1953)
1 With glasses. 40.00 125.00

SPACE MAN
DELL (1962-1972)
1 (#1253) From the 4-Color Series. (1/62) 19.00 60.00
2 8.00 25.00
3-6 6.00 17.00
7 4.00 11.00
8 (1964) 4.00 11.00
9 (1972) 4.00 11.00
10 4.00 11.00

SPACE MOUSE
AVON (1953-1954)
1 12.00 38.00
2 7.00 22.00
3-5 5.00 16.00

SPACE MOUSE
DELL FOUR COLOR SERIES (1960-1961)
1132 (8/60) 11.00 35.00
1244 (10/61) 10.00 30.00

SPACE MOUSE
GOLD KEY (1962-1963)
1 7.00 20.00
2-5 5.00 15.00

SPACE PATROL
ZIFF-DAVIS (1952)
1 TV tie-in. Cover: Saunders. 135.00 440.00
2 Cover: Saunders. 100.00 330.00

SPACE SQUADRON
MARVEL(ATLAS) (1951-1952)
1 105.00 340.00
2 85.00 280.00
3-4 70.00 230.00
5 Title changes to Space Worlds with #6. 70.00 230.00

SPACE THRILLERS!
AVON (1954)
NO# 190.00 600.00

SPACE WAR
CHARLTON (1959-1979)
1 25.00 80.00
2 17.00 55.00
3 14.00 44.00
4-6 Cover/Art: Steve Ditko. 35.00 110.00
7 9.00 27.00
8 Cover/Art: Steve Ditko. 35.00 110.00
9 7.00 22.00
10 Cover/Art: Steve Ditko. 35.00 110.00
11-15 5.00 16.00
16-20 4.00 11.00
21-27 1.75 6.50
28-30 Cover/Art: Steve Ditko. 14.00 44.00
31 Cover/Art: Steve Ditko. 17.00 55.00
32 1.00 3.25
33-34 Cover/Art: Steve Ditko. 14.00 44.00

SPACE WESTERN COMICS
CHARLTON (1952-1953)
40 Previous title: Cowboy Western Comics. 85.00 270.00
41-42 70.00 220.00
43-44 60.00 190.00
45 Title changes to Cowboy Western Comics with #46. 60.00 190.00

SPACE WORLDS
MARVEL(ATLAS) (1952)
6 Previous title: "Space Squadron." 65.00 200.00

SPACED (UNDERGROUND)
ANTHONY SMITH (1982-1988)
1 5.00 15.00
2 2.75 10.00
3-4 1.50 5.00
5-6 1.00 3.00
7-13 .30 1.00

SPACEHAWK
DARK HORSE (1989-1990)
1 Cover & art: Basil Wolverton. Reprints. .75 2.00
2-5 .75 2.00

SPACEMAN (SPEED CARTER)
MARVEL(ATLAS) (1953-1954)
1 105.00 340.00
2 70.00 230.00
3-6 65.00 200.00

SPACEMEN
WARREN (1963-1965) MAGAZINE
1 8.00 25.00
2-4 7.00 20.00
5-8 5.00 15.00
YEARBOOK (1965) 8.00 25.00

SPANDEX TIGHTS: ADVENTURES OF THE AEROBIC DUO
LOST CAUSE PRODUCTIONS (1994-CURRENT)
1 .50 1.95
2-5 .75 2.25

SPANDEX TIGHTS VS. MIGHTY AWFUL SOUR RANGERS
LOST CAUSE PRODUCTIONS (1995-CURRENT)
1 .75 2.50

SPARK MAN
FRANCES M. MCQUEENY (1945)
1 Origin: Spark Man. 35.00 110.00

SPARKIE
ZIFF-DAVIS (1951-1952)
1 (...Radio Pixie), radio tie-in. 26.00 85.00
2 Title changes to Big Jon And Sparkie with issue #3. 20.00 65.00

SPARKLE COMICS
UNITED FEATURES (1948-1954)
1 16.00 50.00
2 8.00 25.00
3-6 7.00 20.00
7-12 5.00 15.00
13-33 2.75 10.00

SPARKLE PLENTY
DELL FOUR COLOR SERIES (1949)
215 Dick Tracy tie-in. (2/49) 23.00 75.00

SPARKLER COMICS
UNITED FEATURE (1940)
1 50.00 160.00
2 35.00 110.00

SPARKLER COMICS
UNITED FEATURES (1941-1955)
1 1st & Origin: Sparkman. 280.00 925.00
2 135.00 440.00
3-6 100.00 330.00
7-12 70.00 220.00
13-18 50.00 160.00
19-24 40.00 130.00
25-30 35.00 110.00
31-40 25.00 80.00
41-50 20.00 65.00
51-70 17.00 55.00
71-80 14.00 44.00
81-90 10.00 33.00
91-100 9.00 27.00
101-120 5.00 16.00

SPARKLING LOVE
AVON (1950)
1 23.00 75.00

SPARKLING STARS
HOLYOKE (1944-1948)
1 19.00 60.00
2 10.00 30.00
3 7.00 20.00
4-33 2.75 10.00

SPARKPLUG
HEROIC (1993)
1-2 .30 1.00

SPARKY WATTS
COLUMBIA (1942-1949)
1 40.00 130.00
2 20.00 65.00
3 16.00 50.00
4 14.00 45.00
5-10 11.00 36.00

SPARTACUS
DELL FOUR COLOR SERIES (1960)
1139 Movie photo cover (Kirk Douglas). (11/60) 26.00 85.00

SPARTAN: WARRIOR SPIRIT
IMAGE (1995)
1 .75 2.50

SPAWN
IMAGE (1992-CURRENT)
1 1st: Spawn. Cover/Art: Todd McFarlane in most issues. 5.00 16.00
2 1st: Violator. 4.00 12.00
3 4.00 12.00
4 With Image #0 coupon. 5.00 16.00
4A Without coupon. 1.00 3.00
5 2.75 10.00
6 2.25 8.00
7 Begin: The Quest. 1.75 6.00
8 1.75 6.00
9 1st: Angela. 2.25 8.00
10 App: Cerebus. 1.50 5.00
11-13 1.25 4.00
14 Return: Violator. 1.00 3.00
15 1.00 3.00
16-17 1.00 3.50
18 1.50 5.00
19 (Note: #19 & 20 shipped after #25) 1.50 5.00
20 1.50 5.00
21-23 .75 2.25
24-30 1.00 3.00
31 .75 2.25
32 .75 2.25
33-36 .75 2.25
TPB Reprints issues #1-5. 2.50 9.95

SPAWN: BLOOD FEUD
IMAGE (1995)
1-2 .75 2.25

SPAWN-BATMAN: RED SCARE
IMAGE/DC (1994)
NO# Crossover with Batman/Spawn:War Devil. 1.25 5.00

SPECIAL COMICS
MLJ (1941-1942)
1 Origin retold: The Hangman, origin: The Boy Buddies, Death: The Comet. 400.00 1500.00

SPECIAL EDITION COMICS
FAWCETT (1940)
1 One-shot. 1st comic devoted entirely to Captain Marvel: "Captain Marvel and the Haunted House!", "Capt. Marvel and Gamblers Of Death", "Capt. Marvel and Sivana The Weather Wizard." 1900.00 7500.00

SPECIAL EDITION X-MEN
MARVEL (1983)
1 Reprints Giant-Size X-Men #1. 5.00 15.00

SPECIAL MARVEL EDITION
MARVEL (1971-1974)
1 Featuring The Mighty Thor. 1.25 4.00
2-4 1.00 3.50
5 Starring Sgt. Fury. .75 2.25
6-14 .75 2.25
15 1st & Begin: Shang-Chi, Master of Kung Fu. 8.00 25.00
16 1st: Midnight. Title changes to Master Of Kung Fu with #17. 6.00 18.00

SOVEREIGN SEVEN #1

SPACE ADVENTURES #2

SPAWN #8

SPAWN #21

a b c d e f g h i j k l m n o p q r s t u v w x y z

SPECTACULAR SPIDER-MAN #17

SPECTACULAR SPIDER-MAN #120

SPECTRE #8 (1ST SERIES)

SPIDER-MAN #1 PLATINUM

STAR SPANGLED COMICS #7

After six covers featuring the Star-Spangled Kid and Stripesy, this issue introduces Joe Simon and Jack Kirby's Newsboy Legion and The Guardian. Revived during Kirby's 1970s stint at DC, they still appear in the Superman family.

SPECIES
DARK HORSE (1995)

1 Movie adaptation. 1.25 4.00
2 .... 1.00 3.00

SPECTACULAR ADVENTURES
ST. JOHN (1950)

2 Previous title: Adventures In Romance. 8.00 25.00

SPECTACULAR SPIDER-MAN
MARVEL (1968) MAGAZINE

1 Origin retold & updated: Spider-Man. Black & white story. 16.00 50.00
2 Cover & Story: Green Goblin. Full color. 22.00 70.00

SPECTACULAR SPIDER-MAN (PETER PARKER)
MARVEL (1976-CURRENT)

1 Origin retold. 14.00 45.00
2 .... 5.00 16.00
3-5 .... 2.75 10.00
6-8 Morbius. 4.00 12.00
9-21 .... 2.00 7.00
22 Moon Knight. 2.50 9.00
23 Moon Knight. 2.00 7.00
24-25 .... 2.00 7.00
26 .... 1.75 6.00
27 App: Daredevil by Frank Miller. ... 6.00 17.00
28 App: Daredevil by Frank Miller. ... 5.00 14.00
29-37 .... 1.50 5.00
38 Morbius. 1.50 5.00
39-55 .... 1.50 5.00
56 1st: Spider-Man/Jack-O-Lantern battle. 5.00 15.00
57-59 .... 1.50 5.00
60 Origin retold: Spider-Man. Double size. 1.50 5.50
61-63 .... 1.25 4.00
64 1st: Cloak & Dagger. 4.00 11.00
65-68 .... 1.00 3.00
69-70 Cloak & Dagger. 2.25 8.00
71-74 .... 1.00 3.00
75 Double size. 1.50 5.00
76-80 .... 1.00 3.00
81-82 Punisher. 2.50 9.00
83 Origin retold: Punisher. 1.75 6.00
84 .... 1.00 3.00
85 Hobgoblin gains powers of the original Green Goblin. 7.00 20.00
86-89 .... 1.00 3.00
90 Crossover with Amazing Spider-Man #252. .... 2.00 7.00
91-99 .... 1.00 3.00
100 Kingpin. Double size. 1.50 5.00
101-115 .... .75 2.75
116 Sabretooth. 1.75 6.00
117-118 .... .75 2.75
119 Sabretooth. 1.75 6.00
120-129 .... .75 2.50
130 Hobgoblin. .... .75 2.50
131 Kraven's Last Hunt, pt.3. .... 2.50 9.00
132 Kraven's Last Hunt, pt.6. .... 2.50 9.00
133 "I Am Spider!" 2.00 7.00
134-139 .... 1.00 3.00
140 Punisher (cameo). 1.25 4.00
141-143 App: Punisher. 1.25 4.00
144-146 .... 1.00 3.00
147 1st: new Hobgoblin (Macendale). 6.00 18.00
148 .... 1.00 3.00
149 .... 2.75 10.00
150-157 .... 1.00 3.00
158 1st: Cosmic Spider-Man. 4.00 13.00
159 Cosmic Spider-Man. 2.25 8.00
160 .... 1.75 6.50
161 Hobgoblin. .... .75 2.50
162-163 Hobgoblin. 1.25 4.00
164-183 .... .50 1.75
184-188 .... .50 1.50
189 Hologram cover ($2.95 cp). 2.50 9.00
189 (2ND) 2nd printing. 1.00 3.25
190-196 .... .50 1.50
197-199 .... .75 2.00
200 Holo-grafix foil cover. 1.25 4.00
201-202 .... .50 1.50
203 Maximum Carnage. .... .75 2.00
204-212 .... .50 1.50
213 Metallic ink cover. .... .75 2.95
213A Regular edition. .... .50 1.50
214-216 .... .50 1.50
217 Foil stamped cover. 1.50 5.00
217A Regular edition. .... .75 2.50
218-219 .... .50 1.50
220 Double size. 1.00 3.00
221 Death: Doctor Octopus. 1.00 3.00
222 .... .75 2.00
223 Enhanced cover. 1.00 3.50
223A Regular cover. .... .75 2.50
224 .... .75 2.00
225 Double size, 3-D holodisk cover. ... 1.25 4.50
225A Regular cover. .... .75 2.95
226 .... 1.00 3.00
227 .... .50 1.50

SPECTACULAR SPIDER-MAN ANNUAL
MARVEL (1979-CURRENT)

1 (1979) 1.50 5.00
2 1st & Origin: Rapier. (1980) 1.25 4.50
3 (1981) 1.25 4.50
4 (1984) 1.25 4.50
5 1st: ACE. (1985) 1.25 4.25
6 (1986) 1.25 4.25
7 (1987) 1.25 4.25
8 Evolutionary War. (1988) 1.25 4.00
9 Atlantis Attacks. (1989) 1.25 4.00
10 Art: Todd McFarlane. (1990) 1.00 3.50
11 (1991) .... .75 2.00
12 (1992) .... .75 2.25
13 Polybagged with card. (1993) ... .75 2.95
14 (1994) .... .75 2.95

SPECTACULAR SPIDER-MAN SUPER-SIZE SPECIAL
MARVEL (1995)

1 Flip book. 1.00 3.95

SPECTRE
DC (1967-1969)

1 .... 25.00 80.00
2-5 Cover/Art: Neal Adams. 16.00 50.00
6-8 .... 8.00 25.00
9 Art: Berni Wrightson. 9.00 28.00
10 .... 7.00 20.00

SPECTRE, THE
DC (1987-1989)

1 .... 1.00 3.00
2 .... .75 2.75
3-9 .... .75 2.00
10-11 Batman, Millenium. .... .50 1.75
12-31 .... .50 1.75
ANNUAL 1 .... .75 2.50

SPECTRE, THE
DC (1992-CURRENT)

0 (8/94) 1.00 3.00
1 Glow-in-the-dark cover. 2.50 8.50
2-3 .... 1.50 5.50
4 .... 1.25 4.00
5-7 .... 1.00 3.00
8 Glow-in-the-dark cover. 1.25 4.00
9-12 .... 1.00 3.00
13 Glow-in-the-dark cover. .... .75 2.50
14-20 .... .50 1.75
21 .... 1.00 3.00
22-29 .... .50 1.95
30-33 .... .75 2.25

SPEED COMICS
BROOKWOOD (1939-1947)

1 1st & Origin: Shock Gibson. 280.00 900.00
2 .... 140.00 460.00
3 .... 85.00 280.00
4-5 .... 70.00 230.00
6-11 .... 55.00 180.00
12 Begin: The Wasp. 70.00 230.00
13 Begin: Captain Freedom. 85.00 280.00
14 Begin: 100 page pocket size. 70.00 230.00
15 .... 70.00 230.00
16 End: 100 page pocket size. Nazi "demons" cover. 70.00 230.00
17 Begin: Black Cat. 105.00 340.00
18-20 .... 55.00 180.00
21-24 .... 55.00 170.00
25-30 .... 45.00 140.00
31-44 .... 35.00 110.00

SPEED MERCHANTS
HOLLYWOOD PRESS (1947)
1 1st comic devoted to auto racing. Rare. 80.00 250.00

SPEED SMITH, THE HOT ROD KING
ZIFF-DAVIS (1952)
1 Cover: Norman Saunders. 55.00 175.00

SPEEDBALL
MARVEL (1988-1989)
1 Art: Steve Ditko (all issues). .30 1.00
2-11 .30 1.00

SPEEDY GONZALES
DELL FOUR COLOR SERIES (1960)
1084 (3/60) 8.00 25.00

SPELLBOUND
MARVEL(ATLAS) (1952-1957)
1 "Step Into My Coffin!" 85.00 280.00
2 45.00 140.00
3-6 35.00 110.00
7-12 28.00 90.00
13-20 25.00 80.00
21-23 20.00 65.00
24 1st Code approved issue. 20.00 65.00
25-28 20.00 65.00
29 Art: Steve Ditko. 25.00 80.00
30-34 17.00 55.00

SPIDER-MAN
MARVEL (1990-CURRENT)
1 Begin: Todd McFarlane cover & art. 2.25 8.00
1A Black cover, bagged 8.00 25.00
1B Green cover. 1.75 6.00
1C Green cover, w/UPC. 4.00 12.00
1D Green cover, bagged. 5.00 15.00
1E Green cover w/UPC, bagged 2.25 8.00
1F Platinum cover. Limited edition (10,000) sent only to specialty shops, contains 10 extra pages of new artwork. 65.00 200.00
1G 2nd print, Gold cover 1.75 6.00
1H 2nd print, Gold cover w/UPC 6.00 18.00
2 1.75 6.50
3 1.75 6.00
4-5 1.50 5.00
6-7 Ghost Rider, Hobgoblin. 1.75 6.00
8 Begin: Wolverine story. 1.50 5.00
9-11 1.25 4.00
12 End: Wolverine story. 1.25 4.00
13 Return: Spider-Man's black costume. 1.50 5.00
14 1.50 5.00
15 1.25 4.00
16 X-Force, crossover with X-Force 3. 1.50 5.00
17 1.00 3.00
18-25 .75 2.00
26 Origin retold: Spider-Man. (3.50) 1.25 4.00
27-45 .75 2.00
46 Hobgoblin. Metallic ink cover. .75 2.95
46A Regular edition. .50 1.50
47-49 .50 1.95
50 Holo-grafix cover. Double size. 1.00 3.95
50A Regular edition. .75 2.50
51 Flip book with 2 foil stamped covers. 1.25 4.00
51A Regular edition. .75 2.75
52-53 .50 1.95
54 Double size. .75 2.75
55-56 .50 1.95
57 Double size. .75 2.95
57A Regular edition. .75 2.50
58-62 .50 1.95

SPIDER-MAN 2099
MARVEL (1992-CURRENT)
1 Origin: Miguel O'Hara (Spider-Man 2099). 1.50 5.00
2 Origin continued. 1.25 4.00
3 .75 2.50
4 .75 2.00
5-22 .50 1.50
23 .75 2.95
24 .50 1.50
25 Double size anniversary issue with foil stamped cover. .75 2.95
25A Regular edition. .75 2.25
26-31 .50 1.50
32-35 .50 1.95
ANNUAL 1 (1994) .75 2.95

SPIDER-MAN ADVENTURES
MARVEL (1994-CURRENT)
1A Regular cover edition. .50 1.50
1 Foil-stamped embossed cover. .75 2.95
2-9 .50 1.50

SPIDER-MAN AND DAREDEVIL
MARVEL (1984)
1 One shot. Reprint: Spectacular Spider-Man #26-28. 1.00 3.00

SPIDER-MAN AND HIS AMAZING FRIENDS
MARVEL (1981)
1 TV tie-in. One shot; "The Triumph of the Green Goblin!" 1.75 6.00

SPIDER-MAN CLASSICS
MARVEL (1993-CURRENT)
1 Reprints in all issues. .50 1.25
2-14 .50 1.25
15 Metallic ink cover. .75 2.95
15A Regular edition. .50 1.25
16 .50 1.25

SPIDER-MAN: FRIENDS AND ENEMIES
MARVEL (1994-1995)
1-4 .50 1.95

SPIDER-MAN: FUNERAL FOR AN OCTOPUS
MARVEL (1995)
1 .75 2.50
2 .75 2.00
3 .50 1.50

SPIDER-MAN: MAXIMUM CLONAGE ALPHA
MARVEL (1995)
1 Maximum Clonage, p1. 1.25 4.95

SPIDER-MAN: MAXIMUM CLONAGE OMEGA
MARVEL (1995)
1 Concludes Maximum Clonage series. 1.25 4.95

SPIDER-MAN MEGAZINE
MARVEL (1994)
1-6 Reprints. .75 2.95

SPIDER-MAN: MUTANT AGENDA
MARVEL (1994)
0 Keepsake edition for crossover with comic strip. .50 1.25
1-3 .50 1.75

SPIDER-MAN: POWER OF TERROR
MARVEL (1994-1995)
1-4 .50 1.95

SPIDER-MAN SAGA
MARVEL (1991-1992)
1-4 .75 2.95

SPIDER-MAN SPECIAL EDITION: TRIAL OF VENOM
MARVEL (1992)
1 5.00 15.00

SPIDER-MAN: SUPER SIZE SPECIAL
MARVEL (1995)
1 1.00 3.95

SPIDER-MAN: THE ARACHNIS PROJECT
MARVEL (1994)
1-6 .50 1.75

SPIDER-MAN: THE CLONE JOURNALS
MARVEL (1995)
NO# One-shot. .50 1.95

SPIDER-MAN: THE JACKAL FILES
MARVEL (1995)
NO# One-shot. .50 1.95

SPIDER-MAN: THE LOST YEARS
MARVEL (1995-CURRENT)
1-2 .75 2.95

SPIDER-MAN UNLIMITED
MARVEL (1993-CURRENT)
1 Maximum Carnage, pt.1. 1.50 5.00
2 Maximum Carnage, pt.14. 1.25 4.50
3-10 1.00 3.95

SPIDER-MAN VS DR. DOOM
MARVEL (1995)
1 Reprints Amazing Spider-Man issues #349-350. 1.75 6.95

SPIDER-MAN VS. DRACULA
MARVEL (1994)
1 Reprint: Giant-size Spider-Man #1. .50 1.75

SPIDER-MAN VS. WOLVERINE
MARVEL (1987)
1 Death: Ned Leeds. 7.00 20.00
1 (2ND) 2nd printing. (1990) 1.25 4.95

SPIDER-MAN: WEB OF DOOM
MARVEL (1994)
1-3 .50 1.75

SPIDER-MAN/X-FACTOR: SHADOWGAMES
MARVEL (1994)
1-3 .50 1.95

SPIDER-WOMAN
MARVEL (1978-1983)
1 Origin: Spider-Woman. 1.75 6.50
2-12 .75 2.50
13-36 .75 2.00
37 X-Men. 1.25 4.00
38 X-Men. 1.25 4.50
39-49 .75 2.00
50 Death: Spider-Woman. Double size. 1.25 4.00

SPIDER-WOMAN
MARVEL (1993-1994)
1-4 .50 1.75

SPIDEY SUPER STORIES
MARVEL (1974-1982)
1 Origin (simplified): Spider-Man. 1.00 3.00
2-38 .75 2.00
39 Thanos. .75 2.50
40-44 .50 1.50
45 Silver Surfer. .75 2.50
46-57 .30 1.00

SPIKE AND TYKE
DELL (1955-1961)
4-24 2.25 8.00

SPIKE AND TYKE
DELL FOUR COLOR SERIES (1953-1961)
499 (9/53) 7.00 20.00
577 (8/54) 2.75 10.00
638 (8/55) 5.00 15.00
1266 (11/61) 7.00 20.00

SPIN AND MARTY
DELL (1958-1959)
5 TV photo cover (all issues). 10.00 30.00
6-9 10.00 30.00

SPIN AND MARTY
DELL FOUR COLOR SERIES (1956-1960)
714 Disney TV photo covers on all issues (Mickey Mouse Club series). (6/56) 23.00 75.00
767 (2/57) 16.00 50.00
808 (6/57) 16.00 50.00
826 "And Annette". 40.00 125.00
1026 (9/59) 16.00 50.00
1082 (3/60) 14.00 45.00

SPIRAL ZONE
DC (1988)
1-4 .30 1.00

SPIRIT, THE
FICTION HOUSE (1952-1954)
1 Not by Eisner. 50.00 160.00
2 Begin: Will Eisner art. 70.00 220.00
3-4 50.00 160.00
5 60.00 190.00

SPIRIT, THE
HARVEY (1966-1967)
1-2 Eisner reprint with 9 new pages of art. 11.00 35.00

SPIRIT, THE
KITCHEN SINK (1973)
1 Cover/Art: Will Eisner. 5.00 15.00
2 Cover/Art: Will Eisner. 2.75 10.00

SPIRIT, THE
KITCHEN SINK (1983-1992)
1-87 .75 2.00

SPIRIT, THE
QUALITY (1944-1950)
1 "Wanted Dead Or Alive!" 135.00 440.00
2 "Crime Doesn't Pay!" 85.00 270.00
3 "Murder Runs Wild!" 60.00 190.00
4 "...Flirts With Death!" 50.00 160.00
5 50.00 160.00
6-11 35.00 110.00
12 Begin: Covers by Will Eisner. 70.00 220.00
13-17 70.00 220.00
18-21 75.00 240.00
22 Classic Eisner cover. 100.00 330.00

SPIDER-MAN 2099 #25

SPIDER-MAN UNLIMITED #1

SPIDER-WOMAN #1

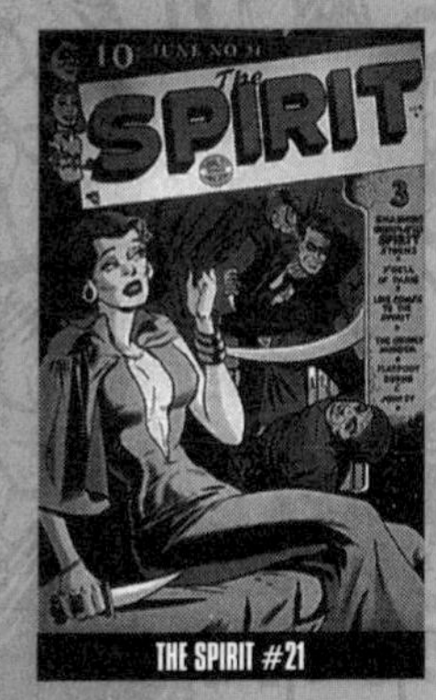

THE SPIRIT #21

a b c d e f g h i j k l m n o p q r s t u v w x y z

SPYKE #4

STAMP COMICS #1

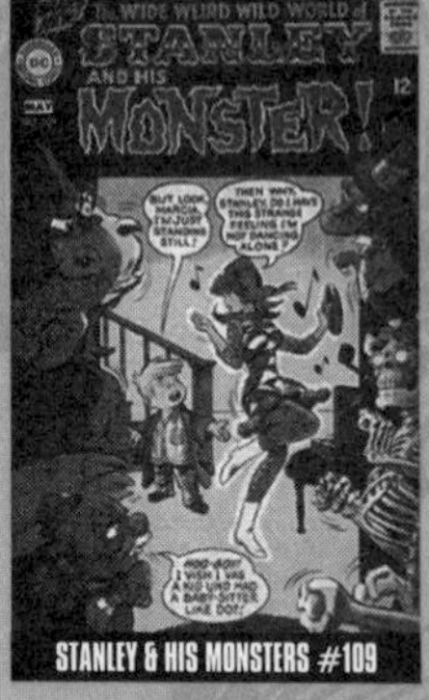

STANLEY & HIS MONSTERS #109

STAR SPANGLED COMICS #1

SPIRIT, THE
SUPER
11 Reprints Quality Spirit #19 by Eisner. 2.75 10.00
12 Reprints Quality Spirit #17 by Fine. 2.75 10.00

SPIRIT, THE
WARREN (1974-1983) MAGAZINE
1-41 .50 1.50

SPIRIT WEEKLY COMIC BOOK
EISNER (1940-1952)
1 1st & origin: The Spirit. Cover & art: Will Eisner in all issues. (6/2/40) 125.00 400.00
2 (6/9/40) 55.00 175.00
3 (6/16/40) 31.00 100.00
4 (6/23/40) 23.00 75.00
5 (6/30/40) 23.00 75.00
6 (7/7/40) 23.00 75.00
7 (7/14/40) 23.00 75.00
8 (7/21/40) 23.00 75.00
9 (7/28/40) 20.00 65.00
10 (8/4/40) 19.00 60.00
11-582 7.00 20.00

SPIRITMAN
EISNER (1944)
1 35.00 110.00
2 25.00 80.00

SPIRITS OF VENGEANCE
SEE GHOST RIDER/BLAZE: SPIRITS OF VENGEANCE

SPITFIRE AND THE TROUBLESHOOTERS
MARVEL (1986-1987)
1-8 .30 1.00
9 Title changes to Codename: Spitfire with #10. .30 1.00

SPITFIRE COMICS
ELLIOT (1944)
132 31.00 100.00
133 28.00 90.00

SPITFIRE COMICS
HARVEY (1941)
1 100 pages, small digest size. Origin: The Fly-Man. 95.00 300.00
2 65.00 200.00

SPLATTER
NORTHSTAR (1991)
1-6 .30 1.00

SPLITTING IMAGE
IMAGE (1993)
1-2 .50 1.95

SPOOF
MARVEL (1970-1973)
1 1.25 4.00
2-5 .75 2.50

SPOOK
STAR (1953-1954)
22 "...Detective Cases" 26.00 85.00
23 Begin: "... Tales Of Suspense And Mystery" 17.00 55.00
24 SOTI 22.00 70.00
25-27 17.00 55.00
28-29 App: Rulah. 20.00 65.00
30 17.00 55.00

SPOOK COMICS
BAILY (1946)
1 40.00 120.00

SPOOKY THE TUFF LITTLE GHOST
HARVEY (1955-1980)
1 40.00 125.00
2 22.00 70.00
3-10 13.00 40.00
11-20 7.00 20.00
21-40 2.75 10.00
41-60 1.75 6.00
61-90 1.25 4.00
91-110 1.00 3.00
111-130 .75 2.00
131-161 .30 1.00

SPORT COMICS
STREET & SMITH (1940-1941)
1 1st comic book devoted to sports. Lou Gehrig life story. 105.00 340.00
2 Gene Tunney life story. 35.00 110.00
3 Rookies to Stars story (Rizzuto, Priddy, Novikoff, Stringer, Reiser). 70.00 230.00
4 Football cover and stories. Becomes True Sport Picture Stories #5. 70.00 230.00

SPORT STARS
MARVEL (1949)
1 Knute Rockne life story. Becomes Sports Action #2. 31.00 100.00

SPORT STARS
PMI (1946-1947)
1 Photo insert covers on all issues. Story Of Johnny Weismuller, "How Tarzan Got That Way." 35.00 110.00
2 Jack Dempsey, The Manassa Mauler. 26.00 85.00
3 Di Mag(gio) Is Back! 31.00 100.00
4 Pepper Martin, Diamond Terror. 17.00 55.00
5-6 26.00 85.00

SPORTS ACTION
MARVEL(ATLAS) (1950-1952)
2 George Gipp life story. Previous title: "Sport Stars." 35.00 110.00
3 Art: Bill Everett. 29.00 95.00
4-11 17.00 55.00
12 Art: Bill Everett. 29.00 95.00
13 Art: Krigstein. 29.00 95.00
14 17.00 55.00

SPY CASES
MARVEL(ATLAS) (1950-1953)
1 (#26) 23.00 75.00
2 (#27)-3 (#28) 13.00 40.00
4-6 10.00 30.00
7-12 7.00 20.00
13-19 5.00 15.00

SPY FIGHTERS
MARVEL(ATLAS) (1951-1953)
1 19.00 60.00
2 13.00 40.00
3-15 8.00 25.00

SPY HUNTERS
ACG (1949-1953)
3 19.00 60.00
4-6 13.00 40.00
7-12 10.00 30.00
13-24 7.00 20.00

SPY SMASHER
FAWCETT (1941-1943)
1 Begin: Spy Smasher. 600.00 2200.00
2 Cover: Mac Raboy. 310.00 1000.00
3-4 230.00 750.00
5 Cover: Mac Raboy. 190.00 625.00
6 Cover & art: Mac Raboy. 190.00 625.00
7 Art: Mac Raboy. 190.00 625.00
8-9 155.00 500.00
10 "Did Spy Smasher Kill Hitler?" 180.00 575.00
11 155.00 500.00

SPYKE
MARVEL (1993)
1 Metallic ink cover. .75 2.50
2-4 .50 1.95

SPYMAN
HARVEY (1966-1967)
1 1st published work: Jim Starlin. 11.00 36.00
2-3 8.00 24.00

SQUAD, THE
MALIBU (1994)
-B—C .75 2.25
0-A .75 2.25

SQUADRON SUPREME
MARVEL (1985-1986)
1 1.00 3.50
2 .75 2.50
3-12 .50 1.75

STALKER
DC (1975-1976)
1 1st & origin: Stalker by Steve Ditko. 1.25 4.00
2-4 Cover & art: Steve Ditko/Wallace Wood. 1.00 3.00

STAMP COMICS
YOUTHFUL (1951-1952)
1 23.00 75.00
2 13.00 40.00
3-7 10.00 30.00

STANLEY & HIS MONSTER
DC (1993)
1-4 .50 1.50

STANLEY AND HIS MONSTER!
DC (1968)
109 Previous title: "Fox And The Crow." 5.00 14.00
110-112 5.00 14.00

STAR
IMAGE (1995)
1-2 .75 2.50

STAR BLAZERS
ARGO PRESS (1995-CURRENT)
0-1 .75 2.95

STAR BLAZERS
COMICO (1987)
1-4 .50 1.75

STAR BLAZERS
COMICO (1989)
1-2 .75 2.00
3-5 .75 2.50

STAR BRAND
MARVEL (1986-1989)
1-19 .30 1.00

STAR COMICS
CENTAUR(CHESLER) (1937-1939)
1 Issues 1-6 are oversized. 310.00 1000.00
2 155.00 500.00
3-5 125.00 400.00
6 (9/37) 125.00 400.00
7 (10-11/37) 125.00 400.00
8 (12/37) 125.00 400.00
9 (1/38) 125.00 400.00
10 (3/38) 190.00 600.00
11 140.00 450.00
12-15 95.00 300.00
16 Begin: The Phantom Rider. 110.00 350.00
17 (V2#1) 95.00 300.00
18 (V2#2) 95.00 300.00
19 (V2#3) 95.00 300.00
20 (V2#4) 95.00 300.00
21 (V2#5) 95.00 300.00
22 (V2#6) 95.00 300.00
23 (V2#7) 95.00 300.00

S.T.A.R. CORPS
DC (1993-1994)
1-6 .50 1.50

STAR HUNTERS
DC (1977-1978)
1-7 .75 2.00

STAR PRESENTATIONS
FOX (1950)
3 Dr. Jekyll And Mr. Hyde (5/50). Art: Wood & Harrison. 95.00 300.00

STAR RANGER
CENTAUR(CHESLER) (1937-1938)
1 (2/37) 280.00 900.00
2 155.00 500.00
3-6 125.00 400.00
7-9 110.00 350.00
10 (3/38) 110.00 350.00
11 110.00 350.00
12 Title changes to Cowboy Comics with #13. 110.00 350.00

STAR RANGER FUNNIES
CENTAUR (1938-1939)
15 Art: Will Eisner. Previous title: Cowboy Comics. 230.00 750.00
16 (V2#1) 155.00 500.00
17 (V2#2) 125.00 400.00
18 (V2#3) 125.00 400.00
19 (V2#4) 125.00 400.00
20 (V2#5) 125.00 400.00

STAR SLAMMERS
MALIBU (1994)
1 Gold stamp. .75 2.50
2-5 .75 2.50

STAR SPANGLED COMICS
DC (1941-1952)
1 700.00 2600.00
2 310.00 1000.00
3-4 240.00 775.00
5-6 155.00 500.00
7 1st & origin & begin: The Newsboy Legion by Joe Simon and Jack Kirby. 1st & Origin: the Guardian. 1300.00 5000.00
8 Origin: TNT. 400.00 1300.00
9-10 300.00 1100.00
11-12 310.00 1000.00
13-18 280.00 900.00

19 240.00 775.00
20 Begin: Liberty Belle. 240.00 775.00
21-24 240.00 775.00
25-28 220.00 700.00
29 End: Simon & Kirby art. 220.00 700.00
30-35 120.00 390.00
36-40 100.00 320.00
41-50 80.00 260.00
51-64 70.00 220.00
65 Begin: Robin stories. 300.00 1100.00
66 240.00 775.00
67-68 155.00 500.00
69 1st & Origin: Tomahawk. 240.00 775.00
70-75 145.00 480.00
76-80 140.00 450.00
81-85 110.00 350.00
86-87 Batman (cameo). 200.00 650.00
88 Begin: Batman series. 200.00 650.00
89-90 155.00 500.00
91-93 145.00 480.00
94 End: Batman series. 145.00 480.00
95 End: Robin covers. 140.00 450.00
96 Batman (cameo). 110.00 350.00
97 80.00 260.00
98 Batman (cameo). 100.00 320.00
99 80.00 260.00
100 90.00 290.00
101-109 60.00 190.00
110-111 Batman (cameo). 80.00 260.00
112 Batman & Robin story. 120.00 390.00
113 Art: Frank Frazetta (10 pages). 110.00 350.00
114 Origin retold: Robin. 140.00 450.00
115 App: Batman. 120.00 390.00
116 70.00 220.00
117 App: Batman. 120.00 390.00
118-119 60.00 190.00
120 Batman (cameo). 80.00 260.00
121 End: Tomahawk covers. 60.00 190.00
122 1st & origin: Ghost Breaker. (11/51) 80.00 260.00
123-126 60.00 190.00
127 Batman (cameo). 70.00 220.00
128-129 60.00 190.00
130 Batman (cameo). Becomes Star Spangled War Stories. 70.00 220.00

STAR SPANGLED WAR STORIES

DC (1952-1977)

1 (#131) Previous title: Star Spangled Comics. 170.00 550.00
2 (#132) 115.00 375.00
3 (11/52) 95.00 300.00
3 (#133) (10/52) 100.00 325.00
4-6 85.00 275.00
7-12 65.00 200.00
13-18 50.00 150.00
19-24 40.00 125.00
25-30 31.00 100.00
31 1st Code Approved issue. 25.00 80.00
32-36 22.00 70.00
37-44 19.00 60.00
45 23.00 75.00
46-48 19.00 60.00
49-60 16.00 52.00
61-66 15.00 48.00
67 Easy Co. (no Sgt. Rock). 15.00 48.00
68-83 15.00 48.00
84 Origin: M. Marie. 26.00 85.00
85-89 M. Marie. 20.00 65.00
90 1st: Dinosaur story. 75.00 235.00
91 10.00 33.00
92 Dinosaur cover & story. 35.00 115.00
93 10.00 33.00
94-95 Dinosaur cover & story. 29.00 95.00
96 Begin: Dinosaur stories. 29.00 95.00
97-99 29.00 95.00
100 35.00 110.00
101-125 20.00 64.00
126 No Dinosaur story. 8.00 25.00
127-133 14.00 45.00
134 Art: Neal Adams. 25.00 80.00
135-136 16.00 50.00
137 End: Dinosaur stories. 16.00 50.00
138 Begin: Enemy Ace by Joe Kubert. 20.00 65.00
139 Origin: Enemy Ace. 14.00 45.00
140-145 8.00 25.00
146 1st 15 cent cover price. 7.00 20.00
147-149 5.00 16.00
150 End: Enemy Ace by Kubert. 5.00 16.00
151 1st: Unknown Soldier. 13.00 40.00
152-153 4.00 12.00
154 Origin: Unknown Soldier. 8.00 25.00
155 2.75 10.00
156 2.25 8.50
157 App: Sgt. Rock. 1.50 5.00
158-161 1.50 5.00
162-175 1.25 4.00
176-203 1.00 3.50
204 Title changes to Unknown Soldier with #205. 1.00 3.50

STAR TREK

DC (1984-1988)

1 3.00 10.00
2-4 1.75 6.00
5 1.50 5.00
6-20 1.25 4.00
21-33 1.00 3.00
34-49 .75 2.00
50 1.00 3.00
51-56 .75 2.00
ANNUAL 1 (1985) 1.00 3.50
ANNUAL 2 (1986) 1.00 3.00
ANNUAL 3 (1988) 1.00 3.00

STAR TREK

DC (1989-CURRENT)

1 2.50 8.00
2 1.25 4.00
3-5 1.00 3.00
6-12 .75 2.50
13-25 .75 2.50
26-49 .75 2.00
50 Double size anniversary issue. 1.00 3.50
51-70 .75 2.00
71-74 .75 2.50
75 Double size. 1.00 3.95
ANNUAL 1 (1990) 1.00 3.50
ANNUAL 2 (1991) 1.00 3.50
ANNUAL 3 (1992) 1.00 3.50
ANNUAL 4 (1993) 1.00 3.50
ANNUAL 5 (1994) 1.00 3.95
SPECIAL 1 1.00 3.50
SPECIAL 2 (1995) 1.00 3.95

STAR TREK

GOLD KEY (1967-1979)

1 Begin: TV photo covers. 125.00 420.00
2 70.00 225.00
3-6 50.00 160.00
7-8 40.00 125.00
9 End: photo covers. 40.00 125.00
10-12 20.00 65.00
13-24 17.00 55.00
25-36 14.00 45.00
37-61 8.00 25.00

STAR TREK

MARVEL (1980-1982)

1 Movie adaptation. 1.75 6.50
2 1.25 4.00
3-18 .75 2.50

STAR TREK BOOK AND RECORD SET

POWER RECORDS (1975)

PR-25 Passage To Moauv. 2.75 10.00
PR-26 The Crier In Emptiness. 2.75 10.00
PR-46 Robot Masters. 2.75 10.00

STAR TREK: DEEP SPACE NINE

MALIBU (1993-CURRENT)

0 (12/94) .75 2.95
1 TV tie-in. Direct market version, regular cover. 1.00 3.00
1 (GOLD) 1.50 5.00
1A Newsstand version. Photo cover. .50 1.95
1B Dual Foil collector's limited edition, enhanced gold & silver foil logo. 1.75 6.00
2-24 .75 2.50
25 Double size. 1.00 3.50
26 .75 2.50
ANNUAL 1 1.00 3.95
SPECIAL 1 1.00 3.50

STAR TREK: DEEP SPACE NINE HEARTS AND MINDS

MALIBU (1994)

1 .75 2.50
1A Hologram version. 2.25 8.00
2-4 .75 2.50

STAR TREK: DEEP SPACE NINE THE MAQUIS

MALIBU (1995)

1 .75 2.50
1A Photo cover edition. .75 2.50
2-3 .75 2.50

STAR TREK: DEEP SPACE NINE...CELEBRITY SERIES

MALIBU (1995-CURRENT)

1 .75 2.95
1A Signed by Mark "Sarek" Lenard. 6.00 19.95

STAR TREK: DEEP SPACE NINE...LIGHTSTORM

MALIBU (1994)

1 1.00 3.50
1A Silver-foil edition. 2.25 8.00

STAR TREK: GENERATIONS

DC (1994)

1A Prestige format. 1.50 5.95
1B 3.95 cover price edition. 1.00 3.95

STAR TREK MOVIE SPECIAL

DC (1984-1987)

III The Search For Spock. .50 1.50
IV The Voyage Home. .50 1.50
V The Final Frontier. .75 2.00
VI The Undiscovered Country. .75 2.95
VI(A) The Undiscovered Country. Prestige format. 1.50 5.95

STAR TREK: THE MODALA IMPERATIVE

DC (1991)

1-4 .75 2.00
TPB 6.00 19.95

STAR TREK: THE NEXT GENERATION

DC (1988)

1 4.00 12.00
2 2.50 9.00
3-6 1.25 4.00

STAR TREK: THE NEXT GENERATION

DC (1989-CURRENT)

1 4.00 12.00
2 2.00 7.50
3 1.75 6.50
4-6 1.50 5.00
7-12 1.25 4.00
13-30 1.00 3.00
31-49 .75 2.50
50 Double size. .75 2.50
51-74 .75 2.50
75 Double size. 1.25 4.00
ANNUAL 1 1.25 4.00
ANNUAL 2-ANNUAL 4 1.25 4.00
ANNUAL 5 1.25 4.00
SPECIAL 1 (1993) 1.00 3.50
SPECIAL 2 1.25 4.00

STAR TREK: THE NEXT GENERATION—DEEP SPACE NINE

DC/MALIBU (1994)

1 Each publisher released two issues. .75 2.50
1A Gold foil edition from Malibu. 2.75 10.00
2 .75 2.50

STAR TREK: THE NEXT GENERATION—SHADOWHEART

DC (1994-1995)

1-4 .50 1.95

STAR TREK: THE NEXT GENERATION—THE MODALA IMPERATIVE

DC (1991)

1-4 .50 1.75

STAR TREK: THE NEXT GENERATION—THE SERIES FINALE

DC (1994)

1 Prestige format. 1.00 3.95

STAR TREK: VOYAGER—THE PREMIERE EPISODE

MALIBU (1995)

1 TV adaptation. .75 2.50
2 .75 2.50

STAR WARS

MARVEL (1977-1986)

1 11.00 35.00
1 (UPC) Rare test version with 35-cent cover price and UPC code in box at lower left corner. Estimated 1500 copies printed and distributed to test response to higher cover price. 115.00 375.00
2 5.00 15.00
3 4.00 12.00
4-6 2.00 8.00
7-10 1.50 5.50
11-15 1.25 4.50
16-24 1.00 3.50
25-38 1.00 3.00
39-44 Empire Strikes Back adapt. 2.25 8.00
45-91 .75 2.00
92 Double size. .75 2.00
93-99 .75 2.00
100 Double size. .75 2.00

STAR SPANGLED WAR STORIES #53

STAR TREK ANNUAL #4 (2ND SERIES)

STAR TREK NEXT GENERATION SERIES FINALE

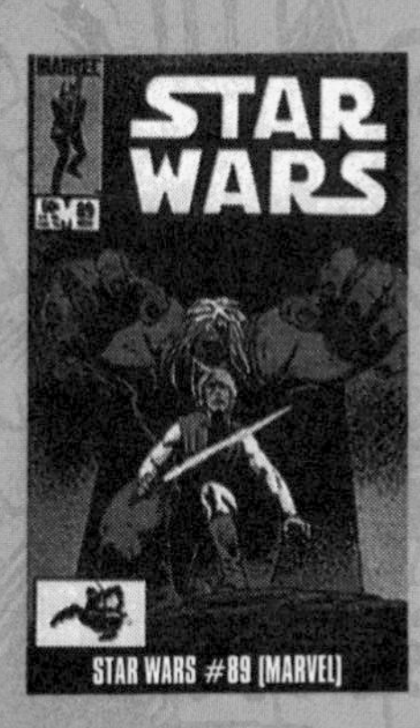

STAR WARS #89 (MARVEL)

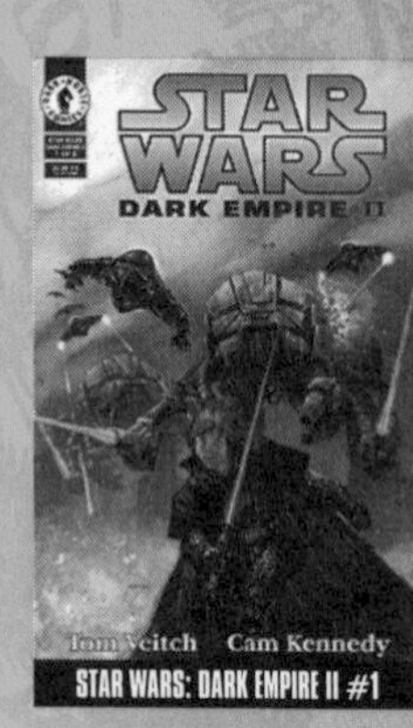

STAR WARS: DARK EMPIRE II #1

STAR TREK: JABBA THE HUTT ONE-SHOT

STARMAN #11 (2ND SERIES)

STEEL #18

FAMOUS • FIRSTS
AMAZING SCIENCE-FICTION TALES!
52 BIG PAGES
STRANGE ADVENTURES
SCOOP! A thrilling preview of Hollywood's smash interplanetary epic
"DESTINATION MOON"

STRANGE ADVENTURES #1

DC launched its first science fiction anthology series with this issue from 1950. It features a photo cover from the classic film Destination Moon. The series later introduced such unique characters as Animal Man and Deadman.

101-106 .75 2.00
107 8.00 25.00
ANNUAL 1 (1979) 1.00 3.00
ANNUAL 2 (1982) .75 2.50
ANNUAL 3 (1983) .75 2.50

STAR WARS: DARK EMPIRE
DARK HORSE (1991-1992)
1 10.00 30.00
1 GOLD 11.00 35.00
1 PLATINUM 11.00 35.00
1 (2ND) 1.50 5.00
2 10.00 30.00
2 GOLD 11.00 35.00
2 PLATINUM 11.00 35.00
2 (2ND) 1.00 3.00
3 5.00 15.00
3 GOLD 7.00 20.00
3 PLATINUM 7.00 20.00
3 (2ND) .75 2.00
4 4.00 12.00
4 GOLD 5.00 15.00
4 PLATINUM 5.00 15.00
5 4.00 12.00
5 GOLD 5.00 15.00
5 PLATINUM 5.00 15.00
6 2.75 10.00
6 GOLD 5.00 15.00
6 PLATINUM 5.00 15.00
TPB Reprints issues #1-6. 6.00 16.95

STAR WARS: DARK EMPIRE II
DARK HORSE (1994-1995)
1 2.00 7.00
2 1.25 4.50
3 1.25 4.00
4-6 1.00 3.25

STAR WARS: DROIDS
DARK HORSE (1994-1995)
1 Solo series for C3PO & R2-D2. 1.00 3.50
2-6 .75 2.50
SPECIAL Reprints Dark Horse Comics stories. (1/95) .75 2.50
TPB Reprints issues #1-6 plus Dark Horse Comics and Star Wars Galaxy magazine stories. 6.00 17.95

STAR WARS: DROIDS
DARK HORSE (1995-CURRENT)
1-5 .75 2.50

STAR WARS: EMPIRE'S END
DARK HORSE (1995)
1-2 .75 2.95

STAR WARS: HEIR TO THE EMPIRE
DARK HORSE (1995-1996)
1-2 .75 2.95

STAR WARS IN 3-D
BLACKTHORN (1987-1988)
1 1.50 5.00
2-3 1.00 3.00

STAR WARS: JABBA THE HUTT
DARK HORSE (1995)
NO# The Gaar Suppoon Hit. One shot. .75 2.50

STAR WARS: JABBA THE HUTT—THE DYNASTY TRAP
DARK HORSE (1995)
NO# One shot. .75 2.50

STAR WARS: JABBA THE HUTT—THE HUNGER OF PRINCESS NAMPI
DARK HORSE (1995)
NO# One shot. .75 2.50

STAR WARS: RETURN OF THE JEDI
MARVEL (1983-1984)
1-4 .50 1.50

STAR WARS: RIVER OF CHAOS
DARK HORSE (1995)
1-4 1.00 3.00

STAR WARS: TALES OF THE JEDI
DARK HORSE (1993-1994)
1 1.75 6.00
2-3 1.50 5.00
4-5 1.00 3.00
TPB Reprints issues #1-5. 5.00 14.95

STAR WARS: TALES OF THE JEDI - FREEDON NADD UPRISING
DARK HORSE (1994)
1-2 .75 2.50

STAR WARS: TALES OF THE JEDI- DARK LORDS OF THE SITH
DARK HORSE (1994-1995)
1 Polybagged with card. 1.00 3.00
2-6 .75 2.50

STAR WARS: TALES OF THE JEDI— THE SITH WAR
DARK HORSE (1995-1996)
1-4 .75 2.50

STAR WARS UK
MARVEL(UK) (1993)
1 .75 2.95

STAR WARS: X-WING - ROGUE SQUADRON
DARK HORSE (1995-CURRENT)
1-4 .75 2.95

STARBLAST
MARVEL (1994)
1-4 .50 1.50

STARCHILD
TALIESIN (1992-CURRENT)
0 (4/93) 1.50 5.00
1 12.00 35.00
1 (2ND) 2nd printing. (2/94) .75 2.50
2 5.00 15.00
2 (2ND) 2nd printing. (2/94) .75 2.50
3 2.25 8.00
4 1.00 3.00
5-12 .75 2.50

STARFIRE
DC (1976-1977)
1-8 .50 1.50

STARLET O'HARA IN HOLLYWOOD
STANDARD (1948-1949)
1 25.00 80.00
2 17.00 55.00
3-4 14.00 44.00

STAR-LORD SPECIAL EDITION
MARVEL (1982)
1 One shot. Art: John Byrne/Terry Austin. 1.75 6.00

STARMAN
DC (1988-1992)
1 Origin: Starman. .30 1.00
2-27 .30 1.00
28 Tie-in with Superman #50. .75 2.00
29-45 .30 1.00

STARMAN
DC (1994-CURRENT)
0-1 1.50 4.50
2-3 1.00 3.50
4-5 1.00 3.50
6-7 1.00 3.00
8-11 .75 2.25

STARR FLAGG, UNDERCOVER GIRL (A-1 SERIES)
ME (1952-1954)
5 (A-1 #62). 70.00 220.00
6 (A-1 #98). 60.00 190.00
7 (A-1 #118). 60.00 190.00

STARS AND STRIPES COMICS
CENTAUR (1941)
2 400.00 1500.00
3 Origin: Dr. Synthe. 280.00 900.00
4 1st & Origin: The Stars And Stripes. 250.00 800.00
5 (11/41) 190.00 600.00
6 (12/41) #5 on cover. 190.00 600.00

STARSLAYER
PACIFIC (1981-1985)
1 1st & Origin: Starslayer. 1.50 5.00
2 1st & Origin: Rocketeer by Dave Stevens. 5.00 15.00
3 The Rocketeer, pt.2. 2.75 10.00
4 1.00 3.00
5 2nd: Groo The Wanderer. 1.50 5.00
6-9 .75 2.00
10 1st: Grimjack. .75 2.00
11-34 .30 1.00

STARTLING COMICS
NEDOR (1940-1948)
1 Origin: Capt. Future, Mystico. 270.00 875.00
2 135.00 440.00
3 100.00 330.00
4 85.00 270.00
5-6 70.00 220.00
7-9 60.00 190.00
10 1st & Origin: The Fighting Yank. 300.00 975.00
11-15 60.00 190.00
16 Origin: The Four Comrades. 70.00 220.00
17 50.00 160.00
18 Begin: Pyroman. 110.00 350.00
19 60.00 190.00
20 Begin: The Oracle. 50.00 160.00
21-30 40.00 130.00
31-43 35.00 110.00
44 Begin: Lance Lewis, Space Detective. 70.00 220.00
45 55.00 170.00
46-48 50.00 150.00
49 Classic Alex Schomburg cover. 310.00 1000.00
50-53 40.00 130.00

STARTLING TERROR TALES
STAR (1952-1953)
10 70.00 220.00
11 50.00 160.00
12-14 25.00 80.00

STARTLING TERROR TALES
STAR (1953-1954)
4-11 17.00 55.00

STARWATCHERS
VALIANT (1994)
1 Wraparound Chromium cover. 1.00 3.50
2-4 .75 2.25

S.T.A.T.
MAJESTIC (1993)
1 .75 2.25
2-6 .75 2.50

STATIC
DC/MILESTONE (1993-CURRENT)
1 Origin: Static. 1.00 3.50
1A Newsstand version. .50 1.50
1B Platinum version. 1.50 5.00
2-13 .50 1.50
14 .75 2.50
15-24 .50 1.75
25 Double size. 1.00 3.95
26 .75 2.50
27 .30 .99

STEEL
DC (1993-CURRENT)
0 .50 1.50
1-15 .50 1.50
16-19 .50 1.95
ANNUAL 1 Elseworlds story. (1994) .75 2.95
ANNUAL 2 (1995) 1.00 3.95

STEEL, THE INDESTRUCTIBLE MAN
DC (1978)
1-5 .30 1.00

STEVE CANYON
DELL FOUR COLOR SERIES (1953-1959)
519 (12/53) 16.00 50.00
578 (8/54) 10.00 30.00
641 (10/55) 10.00 30.00
737 (10/56) 11.00 35.00
804 (5/57) 11.00 35.00
939 (9/58) 8.00 25.00
1033 Photo cover. (9/59) 10.00 30.00

STEVE CANYON COMICS
HARVEY (1948)
1 Origin: Steve Canyon. 28.00 90.00
2 16.00 50.00
3-6 14.00 45.00

STEVE DONOVAN, WESTERN MARSHAL
DELL FOUR COLOR SERIES (1956-1958)
675 TV photo cover. (2/56) 16.00 50.00
768 TV photo cover. (2/57) 13.00 40.00
880 TV photo cover. (2/58) 10.00 30.00

STEVE ROPER
FAMOUS FUNNIES (1948)
1 11.00 36.00
2 6.00 18.00
3-5 2.75 10.00

STEVE ZODIAC AND THE FIREBALL XL-5
GOLD KEY (1964)
10108-401 TV tie-in. 13.00 40.00

STORIES BY FAMOUS AUTHORS ILLUSTRATED
SEABOARD (1950-1951)
1 The Scarlet Pimpernel. Reprints Fast Fiction #1. 50.00 150.00
2 Captain Blood. Reprints Fast Fiction #2. 50.00 150.00
3 She. Reprints Fast Fiction #3. 55.00 175.00
4 The 39 Steps. Reprints Fast Fiction #4. 40.00 125.00
5 Beau Geste. Reprints Fast Fiction #5. 40.00 125.00
6 Macbeth. 40.00 125.00
7 The Window. 31.00 100.00
8 Hamlet. 31.00 100.00
9 Nicholas Nickleby. 31.00 100.00
10 Romeo And Juliet by Shakespeare. 31.00 100.00
11 Ben Hur (1/51). 31.00 100.00
12 La Svengali. 31.00 100.00
13 Scaramouche (3/51). 31.00 100.00

STORMWATCH
IMAGE (1993-CURRENT)
0 Polybagged with card. (6/93) .75 2.50
1 1st: Stormwatch. .50 1.95
2 1st: Strafe. .50 1.95
3 1st: Backlash. 1.50 5.00
4-8 .50 1.95
9 1st: Defile. .75 2.50
10 .50 1.95
10A Variant cover. 2.50 9.50
11-16 .50 1.95
17-21 .75 2.50
22 (Includes 2 cards). .75 2.50
22A Newsstand edition (no cards). .50 1.95
23-24 .75 2.50
25 Images Of Tomorrow (shipped after #9). .75 2.50
26 .75 2.50
ASHCAN 1 1.50 5.00
SOURCEBOOK .75 2.50
YEARBOOK 1 1.00 3.50

STORMY AND PLUTO
DELL FOUR COLOR SERIES (1954)
537 (2/54) 8.00 25.00

STORY OF HARRY S. TRUMAN, THE
DEMOCRATIC NATIONAL COMMITTEE (1948)
NO# Giveaway. 16.00 50.00

STORY OF MANKIND, THE
DELL FOUR COLOR SERIES (1958)
851 Movie photo cover (Vincent Price & Hedy Lamarr). (1/58) 16.00 50.00

STORY OF RUTH, THE
DELL FOUR COLOR SERIES (1960)
1144 Movie photo cover. (9/60) 25.00 80.00

STRAIGHT ARROW
ME (1950-1956)
1 55.00 175.00
2 28.00 90.00
3 Cover: Frank Frazetta. 40.00 125.00
4-6 22.00 70.00
7-12 16.00 50.00
13-21 13.00 40.00
22 Cover: Frank Frazetta. 25.00 80.00
23-30 10.00 30.00
31-40 8.00 25.00
41-55 7.00 20.00

STRAIGHT ARROW'S FURY (A-1 SERIES)
ME (1954)
1 (A-1 #119). 16.00 50.00

STRANGE
AJAX (1957-1958)
1 25.00 80.00
2 15.00 48.00
3-6 11.00 36.00

STRANGE ADVENTURES
DC (1950-1973)
1 Movie photo cover (Destination Moon). 500.00 1600.00
2 250.00 800.00
3-6 155.00 500.00
7-8 125.00 400.00
9 Origin: Captain Comet (6/51). 260.00 850.00
10-12 125.00 400.00
13-18 95.00 300.00
19-20 80.00 250.00
21 "The Monster That Fished For Men!" 80.00 250.00
22-24 80.00 250.00
25-36 65.00 200.00
37-38 55.00 175.00
39 SOTI 80.00 250.00
40-48 55.00 175.00
49 End: Captain Comet. 55.00 175.00
50-53 35.00 110.00
54 1st Code Approved issue. 31.00 100.00
55-75 22.00 70.00
76-99 16.00 50.00
100 23.00 75.00
101-116 10.00 30.00
117 1st & Origin: Atomic Knights. 110.00 350.00
118-119 10.00 30.00
120 2nd: Atomic Knights. 50.00 150.00
121-122 10.00 30.00
123 3rd: Atomic Knights. 25.00 80.00
124-125 8.00 25.00
126 4th: Atomic Knights. 25.00 80.00
127-128 8.00 25.00
129 Atomic Knights. 13.00 40.00
130-131 8.00 25.00
132 Atomic Knights. 13.00 40.00
133-134 8.00 25.00
135 1st 12 cent cover price. Atomic Knights. 13.00 40.00
136-137 7.00 20.00
138 Atomic Knights. 13.00 40.00
139-140 7.00 20.00
141 Atomic Knights. 13.00 40.00
142-143 7.00 20.00
144 Atomic Knights. 13.00 40.00
145-146 7.00 20.00
147 Atomic Knights. 13.00 40.00
148-149 7.00 20.00
150 Atomic Knights. 10.00 33.00
151-152 7.00 20.00
153 Atomic Knights. 9.00 27.00
154-155 7.00 20.00
156 Atomic Knights. 9.00 27.00
157-159 7.00 20.00
160 Atomic Knights. 9.00 27.00
161-179 4.00 11.00
180 1st & Origin: Animal Man. 50.00 160.00
181-183 2.25 8.00
184 2nd: Animal Man. 30.00 100.00
185-187 2.25 8.00
188-189 Art: Steve Ditko. 2.25 8.00
190 3rd: Animal Man (1st time in costume). (7/66) 35.00 110.00
191-194 1.25 4.00
195 1st full-length Animal Man story. 20.00 60.00
196-200 1.25 4.00
201 2nd full-length Animal Man story. 20.00 60.00
202-204 1.25 4.00
205 1st & Origin: Deadman. 16.00 50.00
206 Begin: Neal Adams art. 11.00 35.00
207-210 8.00 25.00
211-215 5.00 16.00
216 End: Deadman. End: Adams art. 5.00 16.00
217-218 Art: Murphy Anderson. Atomic Knights backup story. 1.25 4.00
219 Art: Murphy Anderson. Atomic Knights backup story. 1st 15 cent cover price. 1.25 4.00
220-221 Art: Murphy Anderson. Atomic Knights backup story. 1.25 4.00
222 Art: Murphy Anderson. Atomic Knights backup story. 2.75 10.00
223-226 Art: Murphy Anderson. Atomic Knights backup story. 1.25 4.00
227 1.25 4.00
228 Art: Neal Adams. 1.25 4.00
229-234 1.25 4.00
235 Art: Neal Adams. 1.25 4.00
236-244 1.25 4.00

STRANGE AS IT SEEMS
EASTERN (1937)
2 Previous title: The John Hix Scrapbook. 40.00 125.00

STRANGE ATTRACTORS
RETROGRAFIX (1993)
1-2 .75 2.00

STRANGE COMBAT TALES
MARVEL (1993)
1-3 .75 2.50

STRANGE CONFESSIONS
ZIFF-DAVIS (1952)
1 Photo covers on all issues. 65.00 210.00

STORMWATCH #5

STRANGE ADVENTURES #9

STRANGE ADVENTURES #19

STRANGE ADVENTURES #24

a
b
c
d
e
f
g
h
i
j
k
l
m
n
o
p
q
r
s
t
u
v
w
x
y
z

STRANGE TALES #106 (1ST SERIES)

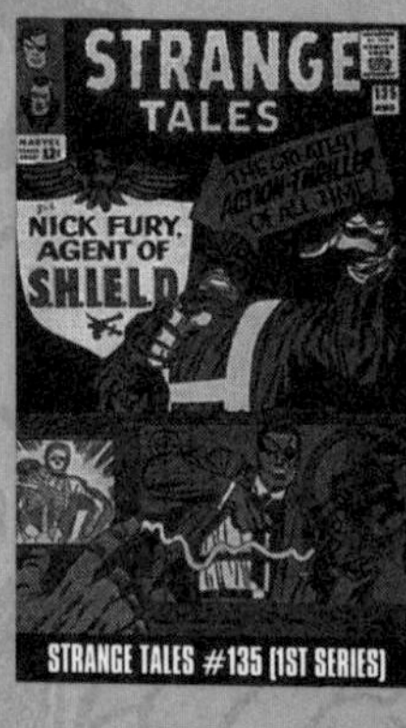

STRANGE TALES #135 (1ST SERIES)

STRANGE TALES #161 (1ST SERIES)

STRANGE TALES #180 (1ST SERIES)

2-4 ... 50.00 160.00

STRANGE FANTASY
AJAX (1952-1954)

1 (#2) (8/52) ... 55.00 180.00
2 (10/52) ... 45.00 140.00
3 ... 40.00 120.00
4 Rocket Man. ... 29.00 95.00
5-6 ... 22.00 70.00
7 Madam Satan. ... 31.00 100.00
8 ... 22.00 70.00
9 ... 29.00 95.00
10 ... 28.00 90.00
11-14 ... 22.00 70.00

STRANGE MYSTERIES
I.W./SUPER (1963-1964)

9-18 Reprints in all issues. ... 2.75 10.00

STRANGE MYSTERIES
SUPERIOR (1951-1955)

1 ... 75.00 240.00
2 ... 40.00 120.00
3-6 ... 25.00 80.00
7-9 ... 22.00 70.00
10 SOTI. ... 28.00 90.00
11-12 ... 22.00 70.00
13-18 ... 19.00 60.00
19-21 ... 15.00 48.00

STRANGE PLANETS
IW (1958)

1 Reprint. ... 13.00 40.00
9 Reprint. ... 16.00 50.00

STRANGE PLANETS
SUPER (1963-1964)

10 Reprints in all issues. ... 8.00 25.00
11 ... 8.00 25.00
12 ... 8.00 25.00
13 ... 8.00 25.00
14 ... 8.00 25.00
15 ... 8.00 25.00
16 ... 8.00 25.00
17-18 ... 8.00 25.00

STRANGE SPORTS STORIES
DC (1973-1974)

1 ... 2.75 10.00
2-6 ... 1.50 5.00

STRANGE STORIES FROM ANOTHER WORLD
FAWCETT (1952-1953)

2 Cover: Norman Saunders (on all issues). Previous title: "Unknown World." ... 75.00 240.00
3-5 ... 55.00 180.00

STRANGE STORIES OF SUSPENSE
MARVEL(ATLAS) (1955-1957)

5 Previous title: Rugged Action. ... 55.00 180.00
6-8 ... 31.00 100.00
9-12 ... 25.00 80.00
13-16 ... 22.00 70.00

STRANGE SUSPENSE STORIES
CHARLTON (1967-1969)

1 ... 7.00 22.00
2 ... 4.00 13.00
3-9 ... 2.25 8.75

STRANGE SUSPENSE STORIES
FAWCETT/CHARLTON (1952-1976)

1 ... 110.00 360.00
2 ... 75.00 240.00
3-4 ... 55.00 180.00
5 #s 6-15 and 23-26 do not exist. ... 55.00 180.00
16 Begin: Charlton publication. ... 40.00 120.00
17 ... 28.00 90.00
18 Cover & art: Steve Ditko. ... 55.00 180.00
19 Cover & art: Steve Ditko. ... 65.00 210.00
20 Cover & art: Steve Ditko. ... 55.00 180.00
21 ... 28.00 90.00
22 Cover: Steve Ditko. ... 40.00 120.00
27 1st Code Approved issue. ... 16.00 50.00
28-30 ... 13.00 42.00
31-33 Cover & art: Steve Ditko. ... 28.00 90.00
34 Cover & art: Steve Ditko. ... 55.00 180.00
35 Cover & art: Steve Ditko. ... 28.00 90.00
36 Art: Steve Ditko. Double size. ... 40.00 120.00
37 Cover & art: Steve Ditko. ... 28.00 90.00
38 ... 11.00 36.00
39 Art: Steve Ditko. ... 22.00 70.00
40 Cover & art: Steve Ditko. ... 22.00 70.00
41 Art: Steve Ditko. ... 22.00 70.00
42-44 ... 11.00 36.00
45 Cover & art: Steve Ditko. ... 22.00 70.00
46 ... 11.00 36.00
47-48 Cover & art: Steve Ditko. ... 22.00 70.00
49 ... 11.00 36.00
50-51 Cover & art: Steve Ditko. ... 22.00 70.00
52-53 Art: Steve Ditko. ... 15.00 48.00
54-60 ... 10.00 30.00
61-70 ... 6.00 18.00
71-74 ... 4.00 12.00
75 Reprint: Space Adventures #33 by Ditko. ... 28.00 90.00
76-77 ... 11.00 36.00

STRANGE TALES
MARVEL (1987-1988)

1-19 ... .50 1.25

STRANGE TALES
MARVEL(ATLAS) (1951-1976)

1 ... 400.00 1500.00
2 ... 160.00 525.00
3-4 ... 130.00 425.00
5 "The Room Without A Door!" ... 130.00 425.00
6 ... 130.00 425.00
7-12 ... 85.00 280.00
13-24 ... 65.00 215.00
25-34 ... 50.00 160.00
35 1st Code Approved issue. ... 45.00 140.00
36-50 ... 35.00 115.00
51-66 ... 31.00 100.00
67 Quicksilver prototype (2/59). "I Was The Invisible Man!" Seven page story by Kirby/Sinnott. 1st Kirby/Ditko/Lee issue. ... 35.00 110.00
68 ... 35.00 110.00
69 Professor X prototype (6/59). "The World That Was Lost!" Story by Kirby/Sinnott. ... 35.00 110.00
70 Giant Man prototype (8/59). "A Giant Walks The Earth!" by Kirby (5 pages). ... 35.00 110.00
71-72 ... 35.00 110.00
73 Ant Man prototype (2/60). "Grottu, King Of The Insects!" Cover and six page story by Kirby/Ditko. ... 35.00 110.00
74 ... 35.00 110.00
75 Iron Man prototype (6/60). "I Made The Hulk Live!" Five page story by Don Heck. ... 35.00 110.00
76 Human Torch prototype (8/60). "I Am Dragoom! The Flaming Invader!" Cover and seven page story by Kirby. ... 35.00 110.00
77 ... 35.00 110.00
78 Ant Man prototype (11/60). "The Worm Man!" Five page story by Ditko. ... 35.00 110.00
79 Dr. Strange prototype (12/60). "I Was In The Clutches Of The Living Shadow!" Seven page story by Kirby. ... 55.00 175.00
80 ... 31.00 100.00
81-82 ... 26.00 85.00
83 ... 35.00 110.00
84 Magneto prototype (5/61). "Magneto!" Cover and 13 page story by Kirby. ... 50.00 165.00
85-88 ... 26.00 85.00
89 1st: Fin Fang Foom. Art: Jack Kirby. ... 70.00 225.00
90-91 ... 26.00 85.00
92 Ancient One prototype. (1/62) "Somewhere Sits The Lama!" Five page story by Don Heck. ... 26.00 85.00
93 1st 12 cent cover price. ... 23.00 75.00
94 The Thing prototype (3/62). "Pildorr, The Plunderer From Outer Space!" Cover and seven page story by Kirby/Sinnott. ... 35.00 115.00
95-96 ... 22.00 70.00
97 Aunt May & Uncle Ben prototype (6/62). "Goodbye To Linda Brown!" Five page story by Ditko. ... 100.00 350.00
98-100 ... 22.00 70.00
101 Begin: Human Torch series. ... 220.00 725.00
102 ... 70.00 230.00
103 ... 50.00 165.00
104 "The Human Torch Meets Paste-Pot Pete!" ... 55.00 180.00
105 ... 50.00 160.00
106 App: Fantastic Four. ... 40.00 120.00
107 ... 50.00 150.00
108-109 ... 40.00 120.00
110 Lead story: "The Human Torch vs The Wizard and Paste-Pot Pete!", 1st & origin: Dr. Strange in "Dr. Strange, Master Of Black Magic!" by Steve Ditko. ... 280.00 950.00
111 2nd: Dr. Strange. ... 65.00 215.00
112-113 ... 31.00 100.00
114 3rd & begin: Dr. Strange series. ... 65.00 210.00
115 Eight page story "The Origin Of Dr. Strange!" by Lee/Ditko; Origin: The Sandman. "The Sandman Strikes". (12/63) ... 95.00 310.00
116 "The Human Torch Battles The Thing!" ... 25.00 80.00
117 ... 20.00 65.00
118 ... 28.00 90.00
119 App: Spider-Man. ... 23.00 75.00
120 ... 26.00 85.00
121-122 ... 14.00 45.00
123 1st: Beetle. ... 14.00 45.00
124 ... 14.00 45.00
125 ... 11.00 35.00
126 ... 13.00 40.00
127-129 ... 11.00 35.00
130 "The Human Torch and The Thing meet The Beatles!" (3/65) ... 13.00 40.00
131-133 ... 8.00 25.00
134 End: Human Torch. ... 8.00 25.00
135 Begin: Nick Fury. ... 22.00 70.00
136 ... 8.00 25.00
137 ... 11.00 35.00
138-145 ... 8.00 25.00
146 End: Dr. Strange by Ditko. ... 8.00 25.00
147 ... 8.00 25.00
148 Origin: Ancient One. ... 16.00 50.00
149-150 ... 7.00 22.00
151 1st Jim Steranko art for Marvel. ... 14.00 45.00
152-156 ... 7.00 20.00
157 ... 8.00 25.00
158 ... 7.00 20.00
159 Art: Jim Starlin. Captain America cover. Origin retold: Nick Fury. ... 7.00 20.00
160-166 ... 7.00 20.00
167 ... 10.00 30.00
168 App: X-Men. (5/68) ... 7.00 20.00
169 1st & Origin: Brother Voodoo. (9/73) ... 1.00 3.50
170-177 ... 1.00 3.50
178 Begin: Warlock. Origin retold: Warlock & Him. ... 7.00 20.00
179-181 App: Warlock. ... 2.75 10.00
182-188 ... 1.00 3.50

STRANGE TALES ANNUAL
MARVEL(ATLAS) (1962-1963)

1 1st Marvel annual. ... 95.00 300.00
2 New Spider-Man story. (7/63) ... 110.00 355.00

STRANGE TALES MARVEL MILESTONE
MARVEL (1995)

1 Metallic ink cover. Reprints #110. ... .75 2.95

STRANGE TALES OF THE UNUSUAL
MARVEL(ATLAS) (1955-1957)

1 Art: Bob Powell. ... 65.00 210.00
2 ... 31.00 100.00
3-4 ... 29.00 95.00
5 Art: Steve Ditko. ... 40.00 120.00
6 ... 29.00 95.00
7 Art: Jack Kirby. ... 29.00 95.00
8-11 ... 22.00 70.00

STRANGE TERRORS
ST. JOHN (1952-1953)

1 ... 65.00 210.00
2-5 ... 40.00 120.00
6-7 100 page issue. ... 75.00 240.00

STRANGE WORLD OF YOUR DREAMS
PRIZE (1952-1953)

1 Art: Simon & Kirby. ... 100.00 330.00
2-3 Art: Simon & Kirby. ... 75.00 240.00
4 ... 55.00 180.00

STRANGE WORLDS
AVON (1950-1955)

1 ... 125.00 400.00
2 SOTI ... 105.00 340.00
3 Art: Frank Frazetta. ... 210.00 675.00
4 ... 105.00 340.00
5 ... 85.00 280.00
6 ... 70.00 230.00
7 ... 55.00 170.00
8 ... 45.00 140.00
9 #s 10-17 do not exist. ... 45.00 140.00
18-19 ... 35.00 110.00
20 Begin: war stories. 1st Code Approved issue. ... 11.00 34.00
21-22 ... 7.00 23.00

STRANGE WORLDS
MARVEL(ATLAS) (1958-1959)

1 Art: Steve Ditko & Jack Kirby. ... 115.00 370.00
2 Cover & art: Steve Ditko. ... 65.00 200.00
3 Art: Jack Kirby. ... 55.00 180.00
4 ... 55.00 170.00
5 Art: Steve Ditko. ... 55.00 170.00

STRANGERS, THE
MALIBU (1993-CURRENT)

1 1st: Atom Bob. ... 1.00 3.00
1B Hologram edition. ... 2.25 8.00
1C Ultra limited foil edition. ... 1.25 4.00
1D Gold hologram edition. ... 2.25 8.00
2 Bagged with Ultraverse card. ... 1.00 3.00
3-6 ... .75 2.00
7-12 ... .50 1.95
13 ... 1.00 3.50
14-20 ... .50 1.95
21-26 ... .75 2.50
ANNUAL 1 ... 1.00 3.95

ASHCAN 1 Signed. 1.50 5.00
ASHCAN 1A Unsigned. .... .75 2.00
TPB Jumpstart. Reprints issues #1-4. .... 2.50 9.95

STRANGERS IN PARADISE
ABSTRACT (1994-CURRENT)
1 .... 1.50 5.50
1 (2ND) 2nd printing. .... .75 2.75
2-5 .... .75 2.75

STRANGERS IN PARADISE
ANTARCTIC (1993-1994)
1 1st: Katchoo. 10.00 30.00
1 (2ND) 2nd printing. 2.75 10.00
1 (3RD) 3rd printing. 1.50 5.00
2 .... 7.00 20.00
3 .... 2.75 10.00
TPB Reprints issues #1-3 (plus extra story). 1.75 6.95

STRAWBERRY SHORTCAKE
MARVEL(STAR) (1985-1986)
1-7 .... .30 1.00

STRAY BULLETS
EL CAPITAN (1995-CURRENT)
1 .... 2.00 6.50
1 (2ND) 2nd printing. .... .75 2.75
1 (3RD) 3rd printing. .... .75 2.75
2 .... .75 2.95
2 (2ND) 2nd printing. 1.00 3.50
3 .... .75 2.95
3 (2ND) 2nd printing. .... .75 2.95
4 .... .75 2.95
5 .... 1.00 3.50

STRAY TOASTERS
MARVEL (1988-1989)
1-4 .... .50 1.50

STREET COMIX PRESENTS
STREET ENTERPRISES (1973)
1 Rip Kirby. 1.50 5.00
2 Flash Gordon. 1.50 5.00

STREETS
DC (1993)
1-3 .... 1.00 3.00

STRICTLY PRIVATE
EASTERN (1942)
1 No date but early 40's. Ads for Heroic Comics #8 on back cover. Digest size with G.I. cartoons on every page.
.... 40.00 125.00
2 .... 23.00 75.00

STRONGMAN (A-1 SERIES)
ME (1955)
1 (A-1 #130). Cover & art: Bob Powell. 50.00 160.00
2 (A-1 #132). Art: Bob Powell. 35.00 110.00
3 (A-1 #134). Art: Bob Powell. 35.00 110.00
4 (A-1 #139). Art: Bob Powell. 35.00 110.00

STRYFE'S STRIKE FILE
MARVEL (1993)
1 .... .75 2.00
1 (2ND) 2nd printing. Gold logo. ...... .50 1.75

STRYKE
LONDON NIGHT STUDIOS (1995)
0 Full color special. (2/95) 1.50 5.00
1/2 Bagged w/ Tarot card. 1.00 3.00

STRYKE: NATURAL BORN KILLER
LONDON NIGHT STUDIOS (1995-CURRENT)
1 .... 1.00 3.00

STUNTMAN COMICS
HARVEY (1946)
1 Origin Stuntman by Jack Kirby and Joe Simon.
.... 180.00 575.00
2 Cover & art: Kirby & Simon. 125.00 400.00
3 Digest-size, b&w, mailed to subscribers only.
.... 105.00 340.00

STUPID
IMAGE (1993)
1 Spawn parody. .... .50 1.95

STUPID HEROES
MIRAGE (1993)
1-3 .... .75 2.75

STYGMATA
EXPRESS/ENTITY (1994-CURRENT)
0 Foil enhanced cover. .... .75 2.95
1-3 .... .75 2.95

SUB-MARINER
MARVEL (1968-1974)
1 Origin: Sub-Mariner. 28.00 90.00
2 .... 8.00 25.00
3-10 .... 7.00 20.00
11-13 .... 5.00 15.00
14 .... 10.00 30.00
15 .... 4.00 12.00
16 1st 15 cent cover price. 4.00 12.00
17-18 .... 4.00 12.00
19 1st: Sting Ray. 5.00 15.00
20 Dr. Doom. 4.00 12.00
21-22 .... 4.00 12.00
23-24 .... 2.00 7.00
25 Origin: Atlantis. 2.25 8.00
26 .... 2.00 7.00
27-28 .... 2.75 10.00
29-33 .... 2.00 7.00
34 App: Hulk, Silver Surfer. 2.75 10.00
35 Avengers battle. 2.75 10.00
36-39 .... 2.00 7.00
40 Spider-Man. 2.75 10.00
41-49 .... 1.50 5.00
50 1st: Namorita. 1.75 6.00
51-72 .... 1.50 5.00
SPECIAL 1 (1971) 1.75 6.00
SPECIAL 2 (1972) 1.50 5.00

SUB-MARINER
MARVEL (1988-1989)
1-12 .... .50 1.75

SUB-MARINER COMICS
MARVEL (TIMELY/ATLAS) (1941-1955)
1 Begin: Sub-Mariner, The Angel. 2600.00 10000.00
2 .... 900.00 3200.00
3 .... 600.00 2300.00
4 .... 500.00 1800.00
5-6 .... 400.00 1300.00
7-8 .... 310.00 1000.00
9-10 .... 280.00 900.00
11-12 .... 240.00 775.00
13-18 .... 200.00 650.00
19-20 .... 155.00 500.00
21 End: Angel. 155.00 500.00
22 .... 140.00 450.00
23 App: Human Torch, Namora. 155.00 500.00
24 .... 140.00 450.00
25 Begin: The Blonde Phantom. 180.00 575.00
26-28 .... 140.00 450.00
29 App: Human Torch. 155.00 500.00
30 .... 140.00 450.00
31 App: Captain America. 200.00 650.00
32 Origin: Sub-Mariner. (7/49) 310.00 1000.00
33 (4/54) 155.00 500.00
34-35 App: Human Torch. 140.00 450.00
36-38 .... 140.00 450.00
39 1st Code Approved issue. 140.00 450.00
40-42 .... 140.00 450.00

SUBTLE VIOLENTS
CRY FOR DAWN (1991)
1 1st: Rhyder. 10.00 30.00

SUBURBAN JERSEY NINJA SHE-DEVILS
MARVEL (1992)
1 .... .50 1.50

SUGAR & SPIKE
DC (1956-1971)
1 (4-5/56) Cover & art: Sheldon Mayer (all issues).
.... 280.00 900.00
2 .... 125.00 400.00
3 .... 110.00 350.00
4-6 .... 100.00 325.00
7-12 .... 80.00 250.00
13-18 .... 65.00 200.00
19-30 .... 50.00 150.00
31-40 .... 31.00 100.00
41-50 .... 25.00 80.00
51-60 .... 19.00 60.00
61-75 .... 16.00 50.00
76-90 .... 13.00 40.00
91-98 .... 10.00 30.00

SUGAR BOWL COMICS
FAMOUS FUNNIES (1948)
1 .... 25.00 80.00
2 .... 14.00 44.00
3-4 .... 10.00 33.00

SUGARFOOT
DELL FOUR COLOR SERIES (1958-1961)
907 TV photo covers on all issues. (5/58)
.... 31.00 100.00
992 (5/59) 28.00 90.00
1059 (11/59) 20.00 65.00
1098 (5/60) 17.00 55.00
1147 (11/60) 16.00 50.00
1209 (9/61) 16.00 50.00

SUICIDE SQUAD
DC (1987-1992)
1 .... 1.00 3.00
2-9 .... .50 1.50
10 .... .75 2.50
11-12 .... .50 1.50
13 .... 1.00 3.00
14-26 .... .50 1.50
27-30 .... .75 2.50
31-39 .... .50 1.50
40 .... .50 1.75
41-43 .... .50 1.50
44-49 .... .50 1.25
50 .... .75 2.00
51-66 .... .50 1.25
ANNUAL 1 .... .75 2.25

SUMMER FUN
SEE MICKEY MOUSE SUMMER FUN

SUMMER LOVE
CHARLTON (1965-1968)
46-47 App: The Beatles. 19.00 60.00
48 .... 1.50 5.00

SUMMER MAGIC
GOLD KEY (1963)
10076-309 Disney movie photo cover. 5.00 15.00

SUN FUN KOMIKS
SUN (1939)
1 .... 70.00 225.00

SUN GIRL
MARVEL (1948)
1 .... 220.00 700.00
2 Begin: Blonde Phantom. 190.00 600.00
3 .... 190.00 600.00

SUNDANCE
DELL FOUR COLOR SERIES (1960)
1126 TV photo cover. (8/60) 19.00 60.00

SUNNY, AMERICA'S SWEETHEART
FOX (1947-1948)
11 .... 85.00 270.00
12-14 .... 70.00 220.00

SUNSET CARSON
CHARLTON (1951)
1 Movie photo cover. 115.00 380.00
2 .... 85.00 270.00
3-4 .... 60.00 190.00

SUPER BOOK OF COMICS
WESTERN (1943)
NO# Dick Tracy. 85.00 275.00
1 Dick Tracy And The Smuggling Ring. 80.00 250.00
2-10 .... 16.00 50.00

SUPER BOOK OF COMICS
WESTERN (1944-1948)
NO# Bugs Bunny. (1948) 10.00 30.00
1 Dick Tracy. (All issues were giveaways with various sponsors).
.... 10.00 30.00
2 Bugs Bunny. 10.00 30.00
3 Terry And The Pirates. 10.00 30.00
4 Andy Panda. 10.00 30.00
5 Smokey Stover. 10.00 30.00
6 Porky Pig. 10.00 30.00
7 Smilin' Jack. 10.00 30.00
8 Oswald The Rabbit. 10.00 30.00
9 Alley Oop. 10.00 30.00
10 Elmer Fudd. 10.00 30.00
11 Little Orphan Annie. 10.00 30.00
12 Woody Woodpecker. 10.00 30.00
13 Dick Tracy. 10.00 30.00
14 Bugs Bunny. 10.00 30.00
15 Andy Panda. 10.00 30.00
16 Terry And The Pirates. 10.00 30.00
17 Smokey Stover. 10.00 30.00
18 Porky Pig. 10.00 30.00
19 Smilin' Jack. 10.00 30.00
20 Oswald The Rabbit. 10.00 30.00
21 Gasoline Alley. 10.00 30.00
22 Elmer Fudd. 10.00 30.00
23 Little Orphan Annie. 10.00 30.00
24 Woody Woodpecker. 10.00 30.00
25 Dick Tracy. 10.00 30.00
26 Bugs Bunny. 10.00 30.00
27 Andy Panda. 10.00 30.00
28 Terry And The Pirates. 10.00 30.00
29 Smokey Stover. 10.00 30.00

STRANGE WORLDS #2

SUB-MARINER #1 [1ST SERIES]

SUB-MARINER #8 [1ST SERIES]

SUB-MARINER #48 [1ST SERIES]

a
b
c
d
e
f
g
h
i
j
k
l
m
n
o
p
q
r
s
t
u
v
w
x
y
z

SUPER CIRCUS #1

SUPER POWERS #3

SUPERBOY #7 (1ST SERIES)

SUPERBOY ANNUAL #1 (1ST SERIES)

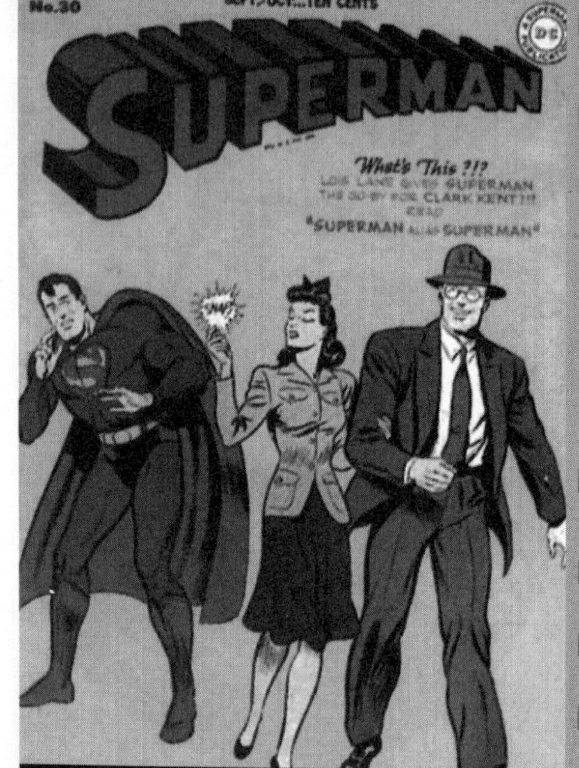

SUPERMAN #30

This issue features the first appearance and origin of Mr. Mxyztplk, the impish practical joker who would harass Superman for years to come, and still does today. And just for the record, it's pronounced "miks yeez pit'l ik."

30 Porky Pig. 10.00 30.00

SUPER CAT
AJAX (1957-1958)
1 8.00 24.00
2-4 5.00 14.00

SUPER CIRCUS
CROSS (1951)
1 Photo inserts on cover (cast members including Mary Hartline). TV tie-in. 16.00 50.00
2 Photo inserts on cover. 10.00 30.00
3-5 7.00 20.00

SUPER CIRCUS
DELL FOUR COLOR SERIES (1954-1956)
542 "Featuring Mary Hartline." (3/54) 13.00 40.00
592 (10/54) 10.00 30.00
694 (4/56) 10.00 30.00

SUPER COMICS
DELL (1938-1949)
1 400.00 1200.00
2 190.00 600.00
3 125.00 400.00
4-6 95.00 300.00
7-12 70.00 225.00
13-18 50.00 150.00
19-24 40.00 125.00
25-29 31.00 100.00
30 Movie tie-in (The Sea Hawk). 65.00 200.00
31-40 25.00 80.00
41-50 22.00 70.00
51-60 19.00 60.00
61-70 16.00 50.00
71-80 13.00 40.00
81-90 10.00 30.00
91-100 7.00 20.00
101-121 4.00 12.00

SUPER DUCK COMICS
MLJ (1944-1960)
1 Origin: Super Duck. 85.00 280.00
2-6 35.00 110.00
7-12 20.00 65.00
13-20 14.00 46.00
21-30 9.00 28.00
31-50 6.00 17.00
51-94 4.00 11.00

SUPER FRIENDS
DC (1976-1981)
1 .75 2.00
2-47 .50 1.50

SUPER FUNNIES
SUPERIOR (1953-1954)
1 (3-D) Presents Dopey Duck. With glasses. 55.00 180.00
2 Title changes to Super Western Funnies with #3. 11.00 35.00

SUPER GREEN BERET
LIGHTNING (1967)
1 Origin: Tod Holton: Super Green Beret. 7.00 20.00
2 7.00 20.00

SUPER HEROES
DELL (1967)
1 1st & origin: Fab 4. 8.00 25.00
2-4 5.00 15.00

SUPER HEROES BATTLE SUPER GORILLAS
DC (1976)
1 Reprints. Double size. 1.50 5.00

SUPER HEROES FEATURING SPIDER-MAN
MARVEL (1974)
1 Giant-Size. Versus Man-Wolf. 16.00 50.00

SUPER MAGIC COMICS
STREET & SMITH (1941)
1 Title changes to Super Magician Comics with #2. 150.00 490.00

SUPER MAGICIAN COMICS
STREET & SMITH (1941-1947)
V1#2 Previous title: Super Magic Comics. 50.00 160.00
V1#3 35.00 110.00
V1#4 29.00 95.00
V1#5-V1#7 26.00 85.00
V1#8 App: Abbott & Costello. 35.00 110.00
V1#9-V1#12 26.00 85.00
V2#1 App: The Shadow. 45.00 140.00
V2#2-V3#4 17.00 55.00
V3#5 Origin: Mr. Twilight. 17.00 55.00
V3#6-V3#7 17.00 55.00
V3#8 Mis-numbered V4#8 (12/44) 17.00 55.00
V3#9-V3#12 17.00 55.00
V4#1-V4#7 14.00 44.00
V4#8 (12/45) 14.00 44.00
V4#9-V5#6 14.00 44.00
V5#7-V5#8 Featuring Red Dragon. 40.00 130.00

SUPER MARIO BROTHERS
VALIANT (1991)
1 1st Valiant comic. .75 2.00
2-5 .75 2.00

SUPER POWERS
DC (1984)
1-5 .30 1.00

SUPER POWERS
DC (1985)
1-6 .30 1.00

SUPER POWERS
DC (1986)
1-4 .30 1.00

SUPER RABBIT
MARVEL(TIMELY) (1944-1948)
1 115.00 370.00
2 80.00 250.00
3-5 55.00 180.00
6 Origin: Super Rabbit. (Spring/46) 65.00 210.00
7-8 40.00 120.00
9-10 31.00 100.00
11-14 23.00 75.00

SUPER SOLDIERS
MARVEL (1993)
1 .75 2.50
2-8 .50 1.75

SUPER SPY
CENTAUR (1940)
1 280.00 900.00
2 170.00 550.00

SUPER WESTERN COMICS
YOUTHFUL (1950-1951)
1 Presents Buffalo Bill (& others). 13.00 40.00
2-4 8.00 25.00

SUPER WESTERN FUNNIES
SUPERIOR (1954)
3 Featuring the Phantom Ranger. Previous title: Super Funnies. 7.00 20.00
4 Featuring the Phantom Ranger. 7.00 20.00

SUPERBOY
DC (1949-1979)
1 See More Fun Comics #101 for 1st appearance. (3-4/49) 1100.00 4000.00
2 "Smallville Celebrates Superboy Day" 400.00 1400.00
3-4 250.00 825.00
5 "Superboy Meets Supergirl!" (11-12/49) 190.00 625.00
6 190.00 625.00
7 "The Boy Of Steel Vs. Humpty Dumpty!" 160.00 525.00
8 160.00 525.00
9 "Another Adventure Of Humpty Dumpty, The Hobby Robber!" 130.00 425.00
10-12 130.00 425.00
13 "The Boy Of Steel In A Super-Boy Scout Adventure!" 115.00 375.00
14 "The Boy From Mars!" 115.00 375.00
15 "The Golden Superboy Coins!" 115.00 375.00

16 "The Strange Costumes Of Superboy!" (9-10/51) 100.00 325.00
17 "Superboy's Double!" 100.00 325.00
18 "The Men Who Doubted Superboy!" 100.00 325.00
19 "The Death Of Young Clark Kent!" (4-5/52) 80.00 260.00
20 "The Ghost That Haunted Smallville!" 80.00 260.00
21 "Lana Lang, Magician!" 80.00 260.00
22 "Meet The New Clark Kent!" 80.00 260.00
23 "The Super-Superboy!" 80.00 260.00
24 "The Super-Fat Boy Of Steel!" 80.00 260.00
25 "The Cinderella Of Smallville!" (4-5/53) 65.00 210.00
26 "The Super-Tot Of Smallville!" 65.00 210.00
27 "Clark Kent, Runaway!" 65.00 210.00
28 "The Man Who Defeated Superboy!" (10-11/53) 65.00 210.00
29 "The Puppet Superboy!" 65.00 210.00
30 "The Giant Who Came To Smallville!" 65.00 210.00
31 "The Amazing Elephant Boy From Smallville!" 50.00 160.00
32 "His Majesty, King Superboy!" 50.00 160.00
33 "The Crazy Costumes Of The Boy Of Steel!" 50.00 160.00
34 "The Hep-Cats Of Smallville!" (6/54) 50.00 160.00
35 "The Boy Oracle Of Smallville!" 50.00 160.00
36 "Superboy's Sister!" 50.00 160.00
37 "Thaddeus Lang, Genius!" 50.00 160.00
38 "The Boy Of Steel Meets Bongo, Public Chimp No. 1!" (1/55) 50.00 160.00
39 1st Code Approved issue. 40.00 130.00
40-48 35.00 105.00
49 1st: Metallo. (6/56) 35.00 110.00
50-60 28.00 90.00
61-67 25.00 80.00
68 1st & origin: Bizarro. (10-11/58) 130.00 425.00
69-75 16.00 50.00
76 17.00 55.00
77 16.00 50.00
78 Origin retold: Mr. Mxyzptlk. 25.00 80.00
79 16.00 50.00
80 Superboy meets Supergirl. (4/60) 23.00 75.00
81 13.00 40.00
82 1st: Bizarro Krypto. 13.00 40.00
83-85 13.00 40.00
86 App: Legion. (1/61) 26.00 85.00
87-88 13.00 40.00
89 1st: Mon-el. 65.00 200.00
90-92 10.00 33.00
93 App: Legion. 1st 12 cent cover price. 10.00 33.00
94-97 7.00 22.00
98 1st & origin: Ultra Boy. 13.00 40.00
99 7.00 22.00
100 Origin retold: Superboy (10/62). 40.00 125.00
101-117 5.00 15.00
118 6.00 18.00
119-120 5.00 15.00
121-123 2.75 10.00
124 1st: Insect Queen. 2.75 10.00
125-128 2.25 8.00
129 80 page Giant #G-22. 7.00 20.00
130-137 1.50 5.00
138 80 page Giant #G-35. 1.50 5.00
139-144 1.50 5.00
145-146 1.25 4.00
147 80 page Giant #G-47. 7.00 20.00
148-155 1.50 5.00
156 80 page Giant #G-59. 5.00 15.00
157-164 1.25 4.00
165 80 page Giant #G-71. 5.00 15.00
166-168 1.25 4.00
169-173 1.00 3.00
174 80 page Giant #G-83. 5.00 15.00
175-176 1.00 3.00
177-184 .75 2.50
185 DC 100 Page Super Spectacular #12. .75 2.50
186-196 .75 2.50
197 Begin: Legion series. 1.75 6.00
198-199 .75 2.50
200 1.50 5.00
201 .75 2.50
202 100 page issue. .75 2.50
203 1.00 3.50
204 .75 2.50
205 100 page issue. .75 2.50
206-210 .75 2.50
211-230 .75 2.00
231 Title changes to Superboy And The Legion Of Super-Heroes. .75 2.00
232-237 .75 2.00
238-239 .50 1.25
240 .75 2.00
241-257 .50 1.25
258 Title changes to Legion Of Super Heroes with #259. .50 1.25

SUPERBOY

DC (1990-1991)

1 TV tie-in. .50 1.50
2-12 .30 1.00
13 Title changes to Adventures Of Superboy. .30 1.00
14-21 .30 1.00

SUPERBOY

DC (1994-CURRENT)

0 .50 1.50
1 .75 2.00
2-15 .50 1.50
16-19 .50 1.95
ANNUAL 1 Elseworlds story. (1994) .75 2.95
SPECIAL 1 .50 1.25

SUPERBOY ANNUAL

DC (1964)

1 28.00 90.00

SUPERCAR

GOLD KEY (1962-1963)

1 TV tie-in. 40.00 120.00
2-4 31.00 100.00

SUPERGIRL

DC (1972-1974)

1 .75 2.50
2-10 .75 2.00

SUPERGIRL

DC (1982-1984)

1 "Daring New Adventures Of..." until issue #14. .30 1.00
2-23 .30 1.00

SUPERGIRL

DC (1994)

1 .75 2.00
2-4 .50 1.50

SUPERGIRL MOVIE SPECIAL

DC (1985)

1 Movie tie-in. .75 2.00

SUPERGIRL/TEAM LUTHOR SPECIAL

DC (1993)

1 .75 2.50

SUPERIOR STORIES

NESBIT (1955)

1 "The Invisible Man." 16.00 50.00
2 "The Pirate Of The Gulf." 16.00 50.00
3 "The Wreck Of The Grosvenor." 16.00 50.00
4 "The Texas Ranger." Photo insert cover. 16.00 50.00

SUPERMAN

DC (1939-1986)

1 "The Complete Story Of The Daring Exploits Of The One And Only Superman!" Reprints first four ACTION stories, plus 6 new pages. 23800.00 95000.00
2 "64 Pages In Full Color!" (Fall/39) 2600.00 10000.00
3 1400.00 5500.00
4 App: Lex Luthor. 1100.00 4100.00
5 App: Luthor. 900.00 3200.00
6-7 700.00 2600.00
8-9 600.00 2000.00
10 1st: bald Luthor. 600.00 2300.00
11-13 400.00 1500.00
14 Patriotic cover. 600.00 2000.00
15 400.00 1300.00
16 Lois Lane cover. 400.00 1300.00
17-18 300.00 1100.00
19-23 300.00 975.00
24 Patriotic flag cover. 310.00 1000.00
25-29 250.00 825.00
30 1st & origin: Mr. Mxyztplk. 300.00 1100.00
31-33 200.00 650.00
33A Special Edition-U.S. Navy giveaway. 200.00 650.00
34 200.00 650.00
34A Special Edition-U.S. Navy giveaway. 200.00 650.00
35-40 200.00 650.00
41-49 155.00 500.00
50 "The Task That Stumped Superman!" (1-2/48). 155.00 500.00
51-52 140.00 450.00
53 10th Anniversary Issue. Origin retold: Superman. "The Origin Of Superman!" Same date as Batman Comics #47 (7-8/49). 400.00 1500.00
54-60 130.00 420.00
61 Origin retold: Superman. 280.00 900.00
62-72 120.00 390.00
72A Giveaway; cover variant (price blacked out). 155.00 500.00
73-74 120.00 390.00
74A Same cover and contents as #75 but misnumbered. (3-4/52) 155.00 500.00
75 120.00 390.00
76 App: Batman. "The Mightiest Team On Earth!" where they learn each other's identity. 300.00 1100.00
77 "The Man Who Went To Krypton!" 110.00 350.00
78-80 110.00 350.00
81-95 100.00 320.00
96 1st Code Approved issue. 90.00 290.00
97-99 80.00 260.00
100 Anniversary issue. (9-10/55) 400.00 1500.00
101-110 55.00 180.00
111-120 50.00 150.00
121-122 40.00 125.00
123 Supergirl tryout. 50.00 150.00
124-126 40.00 125.00
127 1st & origin: Titano. 50.00 150.00
128 40.00 125.00
129 1st: Lori Lamaris. "The Ghost Of Lois Lane!" 50.00 150.00
130 40.00 125.00
131 29.00 95.00
132 App: Batman & Robin. 31.00 100.00
133-139 29.00 95.00
140 1st: Bizarro Supergirl, Bizarro Jr. 35.00 105.00
141 22.00 70.00
142 App: Batman. 22.00 70.00
143 "Bizarro Meets Frankenstein!" 22.00 70.00
144-145 22.00 70.00
146 Superman's life story. 31.00 100.00
147 1st: Legion of Super-Villians. 26.00 85.00
148 17.00 55.00
149 App: Legion. 23.00 75.00
150-156 14.00 45.00
157 1st: Gold Kryptonite. 16.00 50.00
158 16.00 50.00
159-162 14.00 45.00
163-166 11.00 35.00
167 New Origin: Brainiac. 16.00 50.00
168-180 11.00 35.00
181-182 8.00 25.00
183 80 page Giant #G-18. 11.00 35.00
184-186 8.00 25.00
187 80 page Giant #G-23. 11.00 35.00
188-192 8.00 25.00
193 80 page Giant #G-31. 11.00 35.00
194-196 8.00 25.00
197 80 page Giant #G-36. 11.00 35.00
198 8.00 25.00
199 1st: Superman/Flash race. 40.00 130.00
200 "Super-Brother Against Super-Brother!" (10/67) 7.00 20.00
201 5.00 15.00
202 "Tales Of The Bizarro World" all Bizarro issue. 80 page Giant #G-42. (1/67) 8.00 25.00
203-206 5.00 15.00
207 80 page Giant #G-48. 8.00 25.00
208-211 5.00 15.00
212 80 page Giant #G-54. 8.00 25.00
213-216 5.00 15.00
217 80 page Giant #G-60. 8.00 25.00
218-221 5.00 15.00
222 80 page Giant #G-66. 8.00 25.00
223-226 5.00 15.00
227 80 page Giant #G-72. 8.00 25.00
228-231 5.00 15.00
232 80 page Giant #G-78. 8.00 25.00
233-238 5.00 15.00
239 80 page Giant #G-84. 8.00 25.00
240 2.75 10.00
241-244 Double size. 2.25 8.00
245 DC 100 page Spectacular #7. 2.50 9.00
246-248 1.75 6.00
249 1st & Origin: Terra Man by Neal Adams. 2.75 10.00
250-251 1.00 3.00
252 DC 100 Page Super Spectacular #13. 2.25 8.00
253 1.50 5.00
254 Art: Neal Adams. 2.25 8.00
255-263 1.00 3.00
264 1st: Steve Lombard. 1.00 3.00
265-271 1.00 3.00
272 100 page issue. 1.50 5.00
273-277 .75 2.50
278 100 page issue. 1.50 5.00
279-283 .50 1.75
284 100 page issue. 1.50 5.00
285-291 .50 1.50
292 Origin retold: Lex Luthor. .75 2.00
293-299 .50 1.75
300 Origin retold: Superman. 1.75 6.00
301-399 .50 1.50
400 Double size anniversary issue. 1.25 4.00
401-410 .50 1.50
411 Tribute to Julius Schwartz. .50 1.50
412-413 .50 1.50
414-415 Crisis. .50 1.50
416-422 .50 1.50
423 Title changes to Adventures Of Superman with #424. 2.25 8.00

SUPERBOY #17 (3RD SERIES)

FROM THE PAGES OF SUPERMAN!
SUPERGIRL
REIGN OF TOMORROW!

SUPERGIRL (MINI-SERIES) #1

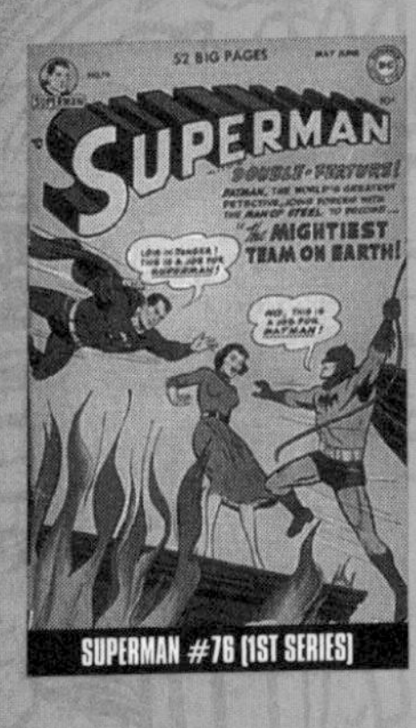

SUPERMAN #76 (1ST SERIES)

SUPERMAN #205 (1ST SERIES)

a
b
c
d
e
f
g
h
i
j
k
l
m
n
o
p
q
r
s
t
u
v
w
x
y
z

SUPERMAN #1 (2ND SERIES)

SUPERMAN #75 (2ND SERIES)

SUPERMAN'S GIRLFRIEND LOIS LANE #37

SUPERMAN'S GIRLFRIEND LOIS LANE #70

SUPERMAN
DC (1987-CURRENT)
0 (8/94) 1.00 3.50
1 Begin: John Byrne cover & art. 1st & Origin: New Metallo. 1.75 6.00
2 .... 1.00 3.00
3 .... .75 2.50
4-6 .... .75 2.00
7 1st & Origin: Rampage. .... .75 2.50
8 .... .75 2.00
9 Joker. 1.25 4.00
10 .... .75 2.00
11 1st: new Mr. Mxyzptlk. .... .75 2.00
12 .... 1.00 3.00
13 1st: Toyman. .... .75 2.00
14-20 .... .75 2.00
21 1st: Matrix. .... .75 2.00
22 End: John Byrne cover & art. .... .75 2.00
23 .... .75 2.00
24-40 .... .50 1.75
41 .... .50 1.75
42-49 .... .50 1.75
50 Clark Kent proposes to Lois Lane. ... 1.50 5.00
50 (2ND) 2nd printing. .... .50 1.50
51 .... .75 2.00
52 .... .50 1.50
53 Lois learns Clark's secret I.D. .... .75 2.00
53 (2ND) 2nd printing. .... .30 1.00
54-56 .... .50 1.50
57 .... .50 1.50
58-59 .... .50 1.50
60 1st: Agent Liberty. .... .75 2.75
61-65 .... .50 1.50
66 Panic In The Sky. 2.75 10.00
67 .... .50 1.50
68-72 .... .50 1.25
73 Cameo: Doomsday. 1.75 6.00
74 Doomsday, pt.2. .... 2.50 9.00
75 Death Of Superman (bagged). ... 8.00 25.00
75 (2ND) 2nd printing. 1.25 4.00
75 (3RD) 3rd printing. .... .75 2.50
75 (4TH) 4th printing. .... .75 2.50
75A Limited platinum edition. 23.00 75.00
75B Newsstand version. 2.75 10.00
76 Funeral For A Friend. 1.00 3.00
77 Funeral For A Friend. .... .75 2.00
78 Reign Of The Supermen, pt.3. Collectors edition. .... .75 2.00
78A Newsstand edition. .... .50 1.50
79 Memorial service for Clark Kent. ... 1.00 3.00
80 .... .75 2.00
81 .... .75 2.50
82 True Superman revealed. Chromium cover. 1.50 5.00
82A Newsstand edition. 1.00 3.50
83-99 .... .50 1.50
100 Double size, holographic foil-enhanced cover. 1.25 4.50
100A Alternate (non-enhanced) cover. ... .75 2.95
101-104 .... .50 1.95
TRADE PB "The Death of Superman" reprints all Doomsday issues. 1.25 4.95

SUPERMAN (MINIATURE)
DC (1955)
1 "The Superman Time Capsule!", Kellogg's Sugar Smacks giveaway. 95.00 300.00
1A "Duel In Space", Kellogg's Sugar Smacks giveaway. 95.00 300.00
1B "The Supershow Of Metropolis", Kellogg's Sugar Smacks giveaway. 95.00 300.00

SUPERMAN AND THE GREAT CLEVELAND FIRE
DC (1948)
NO# Rare four-page giveaway in full color. 190.00 600.00

SUPERMAN ANNUAL
DC (1960-1986)
1 1st: DC annual in the Silver Age. "An All-Star Collection Of The Greatest Super-Stories Ever Published!" (10/60) 130.00 425.00
2 Super-Villian issue. Includes Titano, Brainiac, Metallo, Bizarro, etc. (Winter/60) 65.00 200.00
3 "The Strange Lives Of Superman!" plus "Secrets Of Superman's Fortress Of Solitude!" (Summer/61) 50.00 150.00
4 "Featuring Superman's Most Famous Adventures in Time, Space, and on Alien Worlds!" (Winter/61) 40.00 125.00
5 All Krypton issue. 26.00 85.00
6 .... 23.00 75.00
7 .... 17.00 55.00
8 Origins issue (1963) 14.00 45.00
9 (1983) 1.50 5.00
10 .... 1.50 5.00
11 (1985) 1.50 5.00
12 (1986) 1.00 3.00

SUPERMAN ANNUAL
DC (1987-CURRENT)
1 .... .75 2.75
2 .... 1.25 4.75
3 Armageddon 2001. .... 1.75 6.00
3 (2ND) 2nd printing. .... .75 2.00
4-5 .... .75 2.50
6 Elseworlds story. (1994) .... .75 2.95
7 (1995) 1.00 3.95

SUPERMAN ARCHIVES
DC (1992)
1 Hardcover reprints Golden Age #s 1-4. 12.00 39.95
2 Hardcover reprints Golden Age #s 5-8. 12.00 39.95
3 Hardcover reprints Golden Age #s 9-12. 12.00 39.95
4 Hardcover reprints Golden Age #s 13-16. 15.00 49.95

SUPERMAN FAMILY, THE
DC (1974-1982)
164 Previous title: Superman's Pal Jimmy Olsen. .... .75 2.00
165-176 .... 1.50 5.00
177-181 .... .75 2.00
182 .... 1.00 3.00
183-222 .... .50 1.50

SUPERMAN FOR EARTH
DC (1994)
1 Ecology one shot. 1.25 4.95

SUPERMAN: FROM THE 1930S TO THE 1970S
DC (1971)
NO# Hardcover book, with dustjacket. First edition. 16.00 50.00

SUPERMAN GALLERY
DC (1993)
1 Superman by various artists. .... .75 2.95

SUPERMAN IV MOVIE SPECIAL
DC (1987)
1 Movie tie-in. .... .75 2.00

SUPERMAN: KAL
DC (1995)
1 Prestige format. Elseworlds story. ... 1.50 5.95

SUPERMAN: LEGACY OF SUPERMAN
DC (1993)
1 One shot. Cover: Art Adams. .... .75 2.50

SUPERMAN MOVIE SPECIAL
DC (1983)
1 Movie tie-in, different versions exist. ... .75 2.00

SUPERMAN POST CEREAL MINIATURE
DC (1979)
NO# 1.50 5.00

SUPERMAN RECORD
DC/GOLDEN RECORDS (1966)
NO# Complete set includes record, comic (The Origin Of Superman!), metal pin, iron-on decal, & membership card to the "Supermen Of America" club, in a blue record box. 80.00 250.00

SUPERMAN SPECIAL
DC (1983-1985)
1 Cover & art: Gil Kane. 2.25 8.50
2-3 .... 1.00 3.00

SUPERMAN SPECIAL
DC (1992)
1 .... 1.00 3.50

SUPERMAN: SPEEDING BULLETS
DC (1993)
1 Prestige format. 1.25 4.95

SUPERMAN: THE EARTH STEALERS
DC (1988)
1 .... 1.00 3.95

SUPERMAN: THE MAN OF STEEL
DC (1991-CURRENT)
0 (8/94) 1.00 3.00
1 (1995) .... .75 2.95
2-16 .... .50 1.25
17 1st: Doomsday (cameo). 1.75 6.00
18 1st: full Doomsday. 1.75 6.00
19 Doomsday. 1.75 6.00
20-21 Funeral For A Friend. 1.00 3.00
22 Reign Of The Supermen, pt.2. Collector's edition. .... .50 1.95
22A Newsstand edition. .... .50 1.50
23 .... .75 2.50
24 .... .75 2.00
25 .... 1.00 3.00
26 .... .75 2.00
27-29 .... .50 1.50
30 Collector's edition (with vinyl clings). 1.00 3.00
30A Regular edition. .... .50 1.75
31-44 .... .50 1.50
45-48 .... .50 1.95
ANNUAL 1 (1992) .... .75 2.50
ANNUAL 2 Bloodlines, pt.2. (1993) ... .75 2.50
ANNUAL 3 Elsworlds story. (1994) ... .75 2.95

SUPERMAN: THE MAN OF TOMORROW
DC (1995-CURRENT)
1 .... .50 1.95

SUPERMAN: THE SECRET YEARS
DC (1985)
1-4 .... .50 1.25

SUPERMAN THREE-DIMENSION ADVENTURES
DC (1953)
NO# Origin retold: Superman. With glasses. 220.00 700.00

SUPERMAN: UNDER A YELLOW SUN
DC (1994)
NO# Softcover. 1.50 5.95

SUPERMAN VS. ALIENS
DC/DARK HORSE (1995)
1 .... 1.75 6.00
2-3 .... 1.25 4.95

SUPERMAN VS. THE AMAZING SPIDER-MAN
DC/MARVEL (1976)
1 Treasury edition, 100 pages. 5.00 15.00

SUPERMAN WORKBOOK
DC (1945)
NO# 400.00 1200.00

SUPERMAN'S GIRLFRIEND LOIS LANE
DC (1958-1974)
1 "The Witch Of Metropolis!" (3-4/58) 600.00 2400.00
2 "Superman's Forbidden Room!" (6/58) 190.00 600.00
3 "Lois Lane Adopts A Super Baby!" ... 95.00 300.00
4 "The Super-Courtship Of Lois Lane!" (10/58) 95.00 300.00
5 "The Fattest Girl In Metropolis!" ... 95.00 300.00
6 "Lois Lane, Convict!" (1/59) 95.00 300.00
7 "The Girl Who Stole Superman's Heart!" 65.00 200.00
8 "The Ugly Superman!" 65.00 200.00
9 "Superman's Mystery Song!" App: Pat Boone. 65.00 200.00
10 "Baby Lois Lane!" 65.00 200.00
11 "The Leopard Girl Of The Jungle!" 65.00 200.00
12 "Lana Lang, Girl Atlas!" (10/59) 65.00 200.00
13-18 .... 45.00 135.00
19-24 .... 31.00 100.00
25-29 .... 23.00 75.00
30 1st 12 cent cover price. 17.00 55.00
31-32 .... 13.00 40.00
33 App: Mon-el. 13.00 40.00
34-49 .... 13.00 40.00
50 App: Triplicate Girl, Phantom Girl, Shrinking Violet. 13.00 40.00
51-55 .... 8.00 25.00
56 App: Saturn Girl. 8.00 25.00
57-58 .... 8.00 25.00
59 Batman story. 8.00 25.00
60-67 .... 8.00 25.00
68 80 page Giant #G-26. .... 10.00 30.00
69 .... 7.00 20.00
70 1st: Silver Age app Catwoman. "The Catwoman's Black Magic!" 55.00 175.00
71 Catwoman story continued "Bad Luck For A Black Super-Cat!" 40.00 120.00
72-73 .... 4.00 12.00
74 1st: Bizarro Flash. 10.00 30.00
75-76 .... 4.00 12.00
77 80 page Giant #G-39. .... 8.00 25.00
78 .... 4.00 12.00
79-85 .... 2.25 8.00
86 80 page Giant #G-51. .... 5.00 15.00
87-94 .... 2.00 7.00
95 80 page Giant #G-63. .... 5.00 15.00
96-103 .... 1.75 6.00
104 80 page Giant #G-75. .... 4.00 12.00
105-112 .... 1.50 5.00
113 80 Pg. Giant #G-87. .... 4.00 12.00
114-137 .... 1.25 4.00

SUPERMAN'S GIRLFRIEND LOIS LANE ANNUAL
DC (1962-1963)
1 (1962) 31.00 100.00
2 (1963) 16.00 50.00

SUPERMAN'S PAL JIMMY OLSEN
DC (1954-1974)
1 "The Boy Of 100 Faces!" (9-10/54) 1000.00 3900.00
2 "The Flying Jimmy Olsen!" 280.00 900.00
3 "The Man Who Collected Excitement!" (1-2/55) 190.00 600.00
4 "King For A Day!" 1st Code Approved issue. (3-4/55) 130.00 425.00
5 "The Story Of Superman's Souvenirs!" 110.00 350.00
6 "The 100 Pieces Of Kryptonite!" (7-8/55) 110.00 350.00
7 "The King Of Marbles!" (9/55) 85.00 275.00
8 "Jimmy Olsen, Crooner!" (8/55) 70.00 225.00
9 "The Missile Of Steel!" 70.00 225.00
10 "Jungle Jimmy Olsen!" (2/56) 70.00 225.00
11 "T.N.T. Olsen, The Champ!" 70.00 225.00
12 "The Invisible Jimmy Olsen!" 70.00 225.00
13 "Jimmy Olsen's Super-Illusions!" 55.00 175.00
14 "The Boy Superman!" (8/56) 55.00 175.00
15-18 55.00 175.00
19-24 45.00 135.00
25-30 31.00 100.00
31-40 19.00 60.00
41-50 14.00 45.00
51-56 10.00 30.00
57 1st 12 cent cover price. 7.00 20.00
58-75 5.00 15.00
76-94 2.75 10.00
95 80 page Giant #G-25. 7.00 20.00
96-100 2.75 10.00
101-103 2.25 8.00
104 80 page Giant #G-38. 7.00 20.00
105-110 2.25 8.00
111-112 2.00 7.00
113 80 page Giant #G-50. 5.00 15.00
114-120 2.00 7.00
121 1.75 6.00
122 80 page Giant #G-62. 5.00 15.00
123-130 1.75 6.00
131 80 page Giant #G-74. 5.00 15.00
132-133 1.75 6.00
134 1st: Darkseid (cameo). 5.00 15.00
135-139 2.75 10.00
140 80 page Giant #G-86. 7.00 20.00
141 Jack Kirby self portrait. 2.25 8.00
142-148 2.25 8.00
149-162 1.75 6.00
163 Title changes to Superman Family with #164. 1.75 6.00

SUPERMAN/DOOMSDAY: HUNTER/PREY
DC (1994)
1 Return: Doomsday. 2.25 8.00
2-3 2.00 7.00

SUPERMAN-TIM
DC (1942-1950)
1 (9/42) 65.00 200.00
2 (10/42) 55.00 175.00
3 (11/42) 50.00 150.00
4 (12/42) 50.00 150.00
5 (1/43) 40.00 125.00
6 (2/43) 40.00 125.00
7 (3/43) 40.00 125.00
8 (4/43) 40.00 125.00
9 (5/43) 40.00 125.00
10 (6/43) 40.00 125.00
11 (7/43) 40.00 125.00
12 (8/43) 40.00 125.00
13 (9/43) 40.00 125.00
14 (10/43) 31.00 100.00
15 (11/43) 31.00 100.00
16 (12/43) 31.00 100.00
17 (1/44) 31.00 100.00
18 (2/44) 31.00 100.00
19 (3/44) 31.00 100.00
20 (4/44) 31.00 100.00
21 (5/44) 31.00 100.00
22 (6/44) 31.00 100.00
23 (7/44) 31.00 100.00
24 (8/44) 31.00 100.00
25 (9/44) 31.00 100.00
26 (10/44) 31.00 100.00
27 (11/44) 31.00 100.00
28 (12/44) 31.00 100.00
29 (1/45) 31.00 100.00
30 (2/45) 31.00 100.00
31 (3/45) 31.00 100.00
32 (4/45) 31.00 100.00
33 (5/45) 31.00 100.00
34 (6/45) 31.00 100.00
35 (7/45) 31.00 100.00
36 (8/45) 31.00 100.00
37 (9/45) 31.00 100.00
38 (10/45) 31.00 100.00
39 (11/45) 31.00 100.00
40 (12/45) 31.00 100.00
41 (1/46) 31.00 100.00
42 (2/46) 31.00 100.00
43 (3/46) 31.00 100.00
44 (4/46) 31.00 100.00
45 (5/46) 31.00 100.00
46 (6/46) 31.00 100.00
47 (7/46) 31.00 100.00
48 (8/46) 31.00 100.00
49 (9/46) 31.00 100.00
50 (10/46) 31.00 100.00
51 (11/46) 31.00 100.00
52 (12/46) 31.00 100.00
53 (1/47) 31.00 100.00
54 (2/47) 31.00 100.00
55 (3/47) 31.00 100.00
56 (4/47) 31.00 100.00
57 (5/47) 31.00 100.00
58 (6/47) 31.00 100.00
59 (7/47) 31.00 100.00
60 (8/47) 31.00 100.00
61 (9/47) 31.00 100.00
62 (10/47) 31.00 100.00
63 (11/47) 31.00 100.00
64 (12/47) 31.00 100.00
65 (1/48) 31.00 100.00
66 (2/48) 31.00 100.00
67 (3/48) 31.00 100.00
68 (4/48) 31.00 100.00
69 (5/48) 31.00 100.00
70 (6/48) 31.00 100.00
71 (7/48) 31.00 100.00
72 (8/48) 31.00 100.00
73 (9/48) 31.00 100.00
74 (10/48) 31.00 100.00
75 (11/48) 31.00 100.00
76 (12/48) 31.00 100.00
77 (1/49) 31.00 100.00
78 (2/49) 31.00 100.00
79 (3/49) 31.00 100.00
80 (4/49) 31.00 100.00
81 (5/49) 31.00 100.00
82 (6/49) 31.00 100.00
83 (7/49) 31.00 100.00
84 (8/49) 31.00 100.00
85 (9/49) 31.00 100.00
86 (10/49) 31.00 100.00
87 (11/49) 40.00 125.00
88 (12/49) 31.00 100.00
89 (1/50) 31.00 100.00
90 (2/50) 31.00 100.00
91 (3/50) 31.00 100.00
92 (4/50) 31.00 100.00
93 (5/50) 31.00 100.00

SUPERMOUSE
STANDARD/PINES (1948-1958)
1 35.00 110.00
2 17.00 55.00
3-6 14.00 44.00
7-12 9.00 27.00
13-18 7.00 22.00
19-30 5.00 16.00
31-45 4.00 11.00

SUPER-MYSTERY COMICS
ACE (1940-1949)
1 270.00 875.00
2 135.00 440.00
3 1st: Black Spider. 115.00 380.00
4 115.00 380.00
5 100.00 330.00
6-V2#1 85.00 270.00
V2#2-V2#6 75.00 240.00
V3#1 Begin: Vulcan & Black Ace. 70.00 220.00
V3#2 70.00 220.00
V3#3 Begin: The Sword. 85.00 270.00
V3#4-V3#6 70.00 220.00
V4#1 Art: L. B. Cole. 60.00 190.00
V4#2-V4#6 50.00 160.00
V5#1-V5#6 40.00 130.00
V6#1-V8#6 35.00 110.00

SUPERNATURAL THRILLERS
MARVEL (1972-1975)
1-15 .50 1.50

SUPERPATRIOT
IMAGE (1993)
1-4 .50 1.95

SUPERPATRIOT: LIBERTY & JUSTICE
IMAGE (1995-CURRENT)
1-2 .75 2.50

SUPERSNIPE COMICS
STREET & SMITH (1942-1949)
6 Previous title: Army And Navy Comics. 145.00 480.00
7-8 90.00 290.00
9 App: Doc Savage. 125.00 400.00
10-12 90.00 290.00
V2#1 65.00 210.00
V2#2 Mis-numbered V2#1 on cover (4/44) 65.00 210.00
V2#3 "Supersnipe and Huck Finn". 65.00 210.00
V2#4-V2#6 65.00 210.00
V2#7 "Wing Woowoo In Pistol Packin' Mom". 65.00 210.00
V2#8-V2#12 65.00 210.00
V3#1-V3#12 55.00 170.00
V4#1-V4#12 40.00 120.00
V5#1 35.00 110.00

SUPER-TEAM FAMILY
DC (1975-1978)
1 .75 2.00
2-15 .30 1.00

SUPER-VILLAIN TEAM-UP
MARVEL (1975-1980)
1-3 1.25 4.00
4 Dr. Doom vs. Namor. 1.25 4.00
5 1st: The Shroud. 1.25 4.00
6 1.25 4.00
7 Origin: Shroud. 1.25 4.00
8-17 1.25 4.00

SUPERWORLD COMICS
HUGO GERNSBACK (1940)
1 Cover: Frank R. Paul. 500.00 1800.00
2 290.00 950.00
3 220.00 700.00

SUPREME
IMAGE (1992-CURRENT)
1 1.00 3.00
1 GOLD Limited edition. 1.50 5.00
2-4 .75 2.00
5-11 .50 1.95
11A Alternate cover by Pedi. 1.50 5.00
12 Aftermath of Extreme Prejudice. 1.75 6.50
13-24 .75 2.50
25 Cover: Stephen Platt. Image of Tomorrow (shipped after #12). 1.75 6.00
26-30 .75 2.50
ANNUAL 1 .75 2.95
ASHCAN 1 2.75 10.00
ASHCAN 2 1.50 5.00

SUPREME: GLORY DAYS
IMAGE (1994)
1 .75 2.95
2 .75 2.50

SURE-FIRE COMICS
ACE (1940)
1 1st & Origin: "Flash" Lightning, Ace McCoy & Buck Steele. 210.00 675.00
2 125.00 400.00
3 105.00 340.00
4 Title changes to Lightning Comics with #5. 105.00 340.00

SUSIE Q. SMITH
DELL FOUR COLOR SERIES (1951-1954)
323 (3/51) 10.00 30.00
377 (2/52) 8.00 25.00
453 (2/53) 8.00 25.00
553 (4/54) 7.00 20.00

SUSPENSE
MARVEL(ATLAS) (1949-1953)
1 Movie photo cover (Peter Lorre, Sidney Greenstreet and Joan Lorring in "The Verdict"). 85.00 280.00
2 Movie photo cover (Dennis O'Keefe and Gale Storm in "Abandoned"). 55.00 170.00
3 45.00 140.00
4-11 35.00 110.00
12-18 26.00 85.00
19-29 20.00 65.00

SUSPENSE COMICS
CONTINENTAL (1943-1946)
1 Begin: Grey Mask. 180.00 575.00
2 125.00 400.00
3 Rare. Classic cover by Alex Schomburg. Art: L. B. Cole. 2600.00 10000.00
4-6 105.00 340.00

SUPERMAN'S GIRLFRIEND LOIS LANE #128

SUPERMAN'S PAL JIMMY OLSEN #110

SUPERMAN'S PAL JIMMY OLSEN #130

SUPERMAN/DOOMSDAY #2

a b c d e f g h i j k l m n o p q r s t u v w x y z

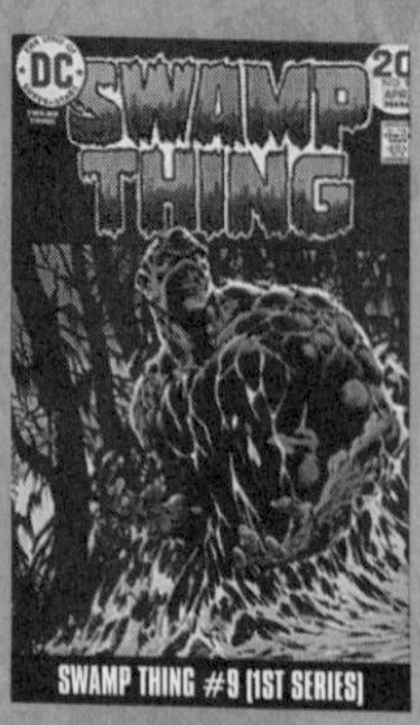

SWAMP THING #9 (1ST SERIES)

SWAMP THING #159 (2ND SERIES)

SWEETIE PIE #1

SWIFT ARROW #1

FAMOUS · FIRSTS

TALES OF SUSPENSE #39

The first appearance and origin of Iron Man sees Tony Stark trip a booby-trap mine in South Vietnam. With shrapnel threatening to stop his heart, he creates a life-saving chestplate and becomes Iron Man.

7 .... 85.00 280.00
8 Classic cover. 280.00 900.00
9-10 .... 85.00 280.00
11 Classic cover. 210.00 675.00
12 .... 85.00 280.00

SUSPENSE DETECTIVE
FAWCETT (1952-1953)
1 .... 55.00 180.00
2 .... 28.00 90.00
3-5 .... 20.00 65.00

SUZIE COMICS
MLJ (1945-1954)
49 Previous title: Laugh Comix. 35.00 110.00
50 .... 17.00 55.00
51-55 .... 14.00 46.00
56 Begin: Katy Keene. 14.00 46.00
57-60 .... 14.00 46.00
61-80 .... 11.00 34.00
81-100 .... 7.00 23.00

SWAMP FOX, THE
DELL FOUR COLOR SERIES (1961)
1179 TV photo cover (Leslie Nielsen). (2/61)
.... 19.00 60.00

SWAMP THING
DC (1972-1976)
1 Cover & Art: Wrightson #s 1-10. ... 22.00 75.00
2 .... 10.00 30.00
3-6 .... 5.00 16.00
7 App: Batman. 8.00 25.00
8-10 .... 4.00 13.00
11-24 .... 1.25 4.00

SWAMP THING
DC (1986-CURRENT)
46 Previous title: Saga Of Swamp Thing. 1.25 4.00
47-49 .... .75 2.50
50 Double size. 1.00 3.50
51 .... 1.25 4.00
52 Arkham Asylum. 1.25 4.00
53 Batman. 1.50 5.00
54-64 .... .75 2.50
65-66 .... .75 2.00
67 .... 1.00 3.50
68-78 .... .75 2.00
79 .... 1.00 3.00
80 .... .75 2.00
81 .... 1.00 3.00
82-83 .... .75 2.00
84 App: Sandman. 2.75 10.00
85-137 .... .75 2.00
138-149 .... .75 2.00
150 Double size. .... .75 2.95
151-153 .... .75 2.00
154-158 .... .75 2.25
ANNUAL 4 Batman. 1.00 3.50
ANNUAL 5-ANNUAL 6 .... 1.00 3.25
ANNUAL 7 Children's Crusade. 1.00 3.95

SWEE' PEA
DELL FOUR COLOR SERIES (1949)
219 Popeye tie-in. (3/49) 20.00 65.00

SWEET LOVE
HARVEY (1949-1950)
1 Photo covers on all issues. 8.00 25.00
2 .... 5.00 15.00
3-5 .... 2.75 10.00

SWEETHEART DIARY
FAWCETT/CHARLTON (1949-1962)
1 Photo cover. 19.00 60.00
2 Photo cover. 10.00 30.00
3-4 Art: Wallace Wood. Photo cover. 19.00 60.00
5-6 .... 16.00 50.00
7-12 .... 10.00 30.00
13-18 .... 7.00 20.00
19-31 .... 5.00 15.00
32 Begin: Charlton publication. 7.00 20.00
33-40 .... 4.00 12.00
41-50 .... 2.25 8.00
51-65 .... 1.50 5.00

SWEETHEARTS
CHARLTON (1954-1973)
23-30 .... 2.75 10.00
31-39 .... 2.25 8.00
40 Photo cover (Tommy Sands). 8.00 25.00
41 .... 2.25 8.00
42 Photo cover (Ricky Nelson). 8.00 25.00
43-45 .... 2.25 8.00
46 Photo cover (Jimmy Rodgers). 8.00 25.00
47-60 .... 1.75 6.00
61-80 .... 1.25 4.00
81-100 .... .75 2.50
101-137 .... .50 1.50

SWEETHEARTS
FAWCETT (1948-1954)
68 Previous title: Captain Midnight. Photo cover (Robert Mitchum). (10/48) 23.00 75.00
69-70 .... 13.00 40.00
71-80 .... 8.00 25.00
81-90 .... 5.00 15.00
91-100 .... 2.75 10.00
101-118 .... 2.25 8.00
119 Movie photo cover (Don't Bother To Knock, Richard Widmark & Marilyn Monroe). 65.00 200.00
120-122 .... 2.25 8.00

SWEETIE PIE
DELL FOUR COLOR SERIES (1961)
1185 (4/61) 10.00 30.00
1241 (10/61) 10.00 30.00

SWIFT ARROW
AJAX/FARRELL (1954)
1 .... 13.00 40.00
2 .... 8.00 25.00
3-5 .... 7.00 20.00

SWIFT ARROW
AJAX/FARRELL (1957)
1 .... 7.00 20.00
2-3 .... 4.00 12.00

SWING WITH SCOOTER
DC (1966-1972)
1 .... 10.00 30.00
2 .... 6.00 18.00
3-6 .... 4.00 12.00
7-12 .... 2.50 9.50
13-24 .... 1.75 6.00
25-36 .... 1.25 4.75

SWISS FAMILY ROBINSON
DELL FOUR COLOR SERIES (1960)
1156 Disney movie photo cover. (12/60)
.... 23.00 75.00

SWISS FAMILY ROBINSON
GOLD KEY (1969)
10236-904 Disney movie photo cover. 7.00 20.00

SWORD AND THE DRAGON, THE
DELL FOUR COLOR SERIES (1960)
1118 Movie photo cover. (6/60) ... 22.00 70.00

SWORD AND THE ROSE, THE
DELL FOUR COLOR SERIES (1953)
505 Disney TV tie-in. (10/53) 11.00 35.00

SWORD IN THE STONE, THE
GOLD KEY (1964)
30019-402 Disney movie tie-in. 13.00 40.00

SWORD OF SORCERY
DC (1973)
1 .... 1.25 4.00
2-5 .... .75 2.00

SWORD OF THE ATOM
DC (1983)
1-4 .... .30 1.00

SWORDS OF THE SWASHBUCKLERS
MARVEL (1985-1987)
1-12 .... .30 1.00

SYMBOLS OF JUSTICE
HIGH IMPACT STUDIOS (1995-CURRENT)
1 1:Symbols of Justice. .... .75 2.95
2 .... .75 2.95

SYPHONS
NOW (1994)
1 .75 2.50

TABOO
SPIDERBABY/TUNDRA (1988-CURRENT) GRAPHIC NOVEL FORMAT
1-5 5.00 15.00
6 Neil Gaiman story, includes Sweeney Todd ashcan insert. (9.95c) 5.00 15.00
7-8 5.00 15.00

TAFFY COMICS
RURAL HOME (1945-1948)
1 Cover: L.B. Cole. 23.00 75.00
2 Cover: L.B. Cole. 13.00 40.00
3-4 10.00 30.00
5 Van Johnson cover. 10.00 30.00
6 Perry Como cover. 10.00 30.00
7 Dane Clark cover. 7.00 20.00
8 Glenn Ford cover. 7.00 20.00
9 Lon McCallister photo cover. 7.00 20.00
10 John Hodiak cover. 7.00 20.00
11 Mickey Rooney cover. 7.00 20.00
12 7.00 20.00

TAILGUNNER JO
DC (1988-1989)
1-6 .30 1.00

TAILSPIN TOMMY
CUPPLES & LEON (1932)
NO# 100 page hardcover. 65.00 200.00

TAINTED
DC (1994)
1 1.25 4.95

TALE OF ONE BAD RAT, THE
DARK HORSE (1994-1995)
1-4 .75 2.95

TALES CALCULATED TO DRIVE YOU BATS
ARCHIE (1961-1962)
1 14.00 44.00
2 9.00 27.00
3-7 7.00 22.00

TALES FROM THE CRYPT
EC (1950-1955)
20 Lead story: "The Thing From The Sea!" (10-11/50). Previous title: The Crypt Of Terror. 270.00 875.00
21 210.00 675.00
22 155.00 500.00
23-24 130.00 430.00
25-30 110.00 350.00
31 115.00 370.00
32 95.00 310.00
33 "Lower Berth!" by Jack Davis. 155.00 500.00
34-42 95.00 310.00
43 Cover: Jack Davis "Four-Way Split" 95.00 310.00
44-46 95.00 310.00

TALES FROM THE CRYPT
EC(COCHRAN) (1992-1994)
1 Reprint EC original: The Crypt Of Terror #17. 1.00 3.00
2 Reprint: The Crypt Of Terror #18. .50 1.50
3 Reprint: The Crypt Of Terror #19. .50 1.50
4 Reprint: Tales From The Crypt #20. .75 2.00
5 Reprint: Tales From The Crypt #21. .75 2.00
6 Reprint: Tales From The Crypt #22. .75 2.00
ANNUAL 1 Reprint: 1st 5 issues. 2.25 8.95

TALES FROM THE CRYPT
GLADSTONE (1990-1991)
1 Reprints EC originals: Tales From The Crypt #33 & Crime Suspenstories #17. 1.50 5.00
2 Reprints: Tales From The Crypt #35 & Crime Suspenstories #18. 1.00 3.00
3 Reprints: Tales From The Crypt #39 & Crime Suspenstories #1. 1.00 3.00
4 Reprints: Tales From The Crypt #18 & Crime Suspenstories #16. 1.25 4.00
5 Reprints: Tales From The Crypt #45 & Crime Suspenstories #5. 1.00 3.00
6 Reprints: Tales From The Crypt #42 & Crime Suspenstories #27. 1.00 3.00

TALES FROM THE GREAT BOOK
FAMOUS FUNNIES (1955-1956)
1 The Story Of Sampson; Daniel. 9.00 27.00
2 Joshua Marches On Jericho. 7.00 22.00
3 Joash The Boy King. 7.00 22.00
4 Young David; The Little Captive Maid; Moses And Miriam. 7.00 22.00

TALES FROM THE TOMB
DELL (1962)
1 (02-810-210) 11.00 35.00

TALES FROM THE TOMB
EERIE (1969-1975) MAGAZINE
V5#3 1.50 5.00

TALES OF ASGARD
MARVEL (1968)
1 One shot. 8.00 25.00

TALES OF EVIL
ATLAS/SEABOARD (1975)
1-3 .75 2.00

TALES OF GHOST CASTLE
DC (1975)
1-3 .30 1.00

TALES OF HORROR
TOBY (1952-1954)
1 55.00 180.00
2 28.00 90.00
3-6 22.00 70.00
7-13 19.00 60.00

TALES OF SUSPENSE
MARVEL(ATLAS) (1959-1968)
1 310.00 1000.00
2 125.00 400.00
3 115.00 375.00
4 110.00 350.00
5-6 80.00 250.00
7 Lava Man prototype. (1/60) "I Fought The Molten Man-Thing!" Cover and five page story by Kirby/Ditko. 80.00 250.00
8 70.00 225.00
9 Iron Man prototype. (5/60) "The Return Of The Living Robot!" Five page story by Don Heck. 95.00 300.00
10-12 65.00 210.00
13-15 50.00 150.00
16 Iron Man prototype. (4/61) "The Thing Called Metallo!" Cover and 13 page story by Kirby. 70.00 230.00
17-25 50.00 150.00
26 1st 12 cent cover price. 31.00 100.00
27 25.00 80.00
28 Stone Men prototype. (4/62) "Back From The Dead!" Cover and five page story by Kirby. 40.00 125.00
29-30 25.00 80.00
31 Dr. Doom prototype. (7/62) "The Monster In The Iron Mask!" Cover and seven page story by Kirby. 40.00 125.00
32 Dr. Strange prototype. (8/62) "Sazzik, The Sorcerer!" Six page story by Kirby. 50.00 150.00
33-34 25.00 80.00
35 The Watcher prototype. (11/62) "The Challenge Of Zarkorr!" Cover and seven page story by Kirby. 40.00 125.00
36-38 25.00 80.00
39 Debut & Origin: Iron Man in "Iron Man Is Born!" (3/63) 800.00 2800.00
40 Iron Man's new armor. 300.00 1100.00
41 180.00 575.00
42-45 75.00 240.00
46-47 50.00 150.00
48 New Iron Man armor by Steve Ditko. 55.00 175.00
49 1st X-Men, Avengers crossover. 40.00 140.00
50 1st: Mandarin. 20.00 65.00
51 1st: Scarecrow. 23.00 75.00
52 1st: Black Widow. (4/64) 31.00 100.00
53 Origin: The Watcher. 20.00 65.00
54-56 16.00 50.00
57 1st & Origin: Hawkeye. 31.00 100.00
58 Captain America battles Iron Man. 65.00 200.00
59 Begin: Captain America, Iron Man double feature. 65.00 200.00
60 2nd: Hawkeye. 26.00 85.00
61 14.00 45.00
62 Origin: Mandarin. 14.00 45.00
63 1st Silver Age origin Captain America. (3/65) 50.00 155.00
64 1st: Silver Age Red Skull. 20.00 65.00
65-66 23.00 75.00
67-78 10.00 30.00
79 11.00 35.00
80-81 7.00 20.00
82-98 10.00 30.00
99 Title changes to Captain America with #100. 10.00 30.00

TALES OF SUSPENSE MARVEL MILESTONE
MARVEL (1994)
1 Reprint (with metallic ink cover). .75 2.95

TALES OF SUSPENSE MARVEL SELECT EDITION
MARVEL (1994)
1 Prestige format. All new story. 1.75 6.95

TALES OF TERROR
DELL (1963)
12-793-302 Movie tie-in. 10.00 30.00

TALES OF TERROR
TOBY (1952)
1 28.00 90.00

TALES OF TERROR ANNUAL
EC (1951-1953)
NO#(1951) 900.00 3300.00
2(1952) 400.00 1400.00
3(1953) "128 spine-tingling pages featuring 16 of EC's best yarns from 1952." 310.00 1000.00

TALES OF THE BEANWORLD
ECLIPSE (1985-1991)
1 5.00 15.00
2 2.25 8.00
3-10 1.50 5.00
11-19 1.00 3.00

TALES OF THE FRITO KID
FRITO (1955)
NO# "The Haunted Mesa", 16 page giveaway (4 1/4" x 5"). 7.00 20.00

TALES OF THE GREEN BERET
DELL (1967-1969)
1 5.00 15.00
2-5 2.75 10.00

TALES OF THE GREEN HORNET
NOW (1990-1993)
1-2 .50 1.75
V2#1-V2#4 .50 1.95
V3#1 Polybagged with card (hologram). .75 2.75
V3#2-V3#3 .75 2.50

TALES OF THE GREEN LANTERN CORPS
DC (1981)
1-3 .50 1.25
ANNUAL 1 .30 1.00

TALES OF THE LEGION OF SUPER-HEROES
DC (1984-1987)
314 Previous title: Legion Of Super-Heroes. .75 2.00
315-320 .75 2.00
321-354 .30 1.00

TALES OF THE MARINES
MARVEL(ATLAS) (1957)
4 Previous title: Devil-Dog Dugan. 8.00 25.00

TALES OF THE MARVELS: BLOCKBUSTER
MARVEL (1995)
1 1.50 5.95

TALES OF THE MYSTERIOUS TRAVELER
CHARLTON (1956-1959)
1 70.00 230.00
2 Art: Steve Ditko. 65.00 200.00
3 Cover & art: Steve Ditko. 70.00 230.00
4-6 Cover & art: Steve Ditko. 85.00 280.00
7-9 Art: Steve Ditko. 70.00 230.00
10-11 Cover & art: Steve Ditko. 80.00 250.00
12-13 26.00 85.00

TALES OF THE NEW TEEN TITANS
DC (1982)
1-4 .75 2.25

TALES OF THE PONY EXPRESS
DELL FOUR COLOR SERIES (1957-1958)
829 TV tie-in. (8/57) 8.00 25.00
942 (10/58) 10.00 30.00

TALES OF THE TEEN TITANS
DC (1984-1988)
41 Previous title: New Teen Titans (1980-1984 series). .75 2.00
42-43 .75 2.00
44 1.00 3.00
45-59 .75 2.00
60-91 .30 1.00
ANNUAL 3 1.00 3.00
ANNUAL 4-ANNUAL 5 .50 1.25

TALES OF SUSPENSE #42

TALES OF SUSPENSE #49

TALES OF SUSPENSE #59

TALES OF THE NEW TEEN TITANS #2

a b c d e f g h i j k l m n o p q r s t u v w x y z

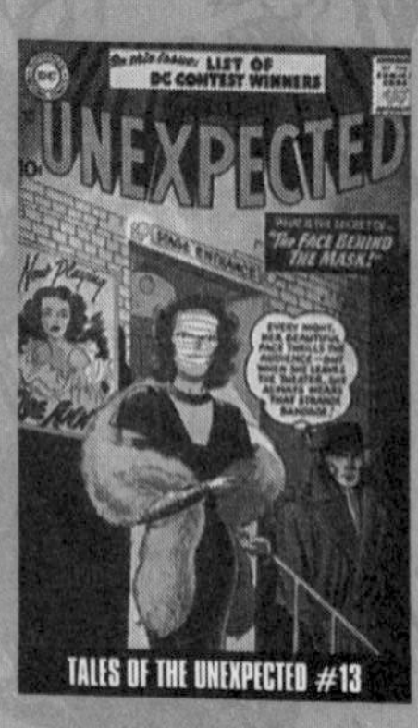

TALES OF THE UNEXPECTED #13

TALES TO ASTONISH #96

TALES TO ASTONISH #101

TANK GIRL MOVIE ADAPTATION

TALES OF THE TEENAGE MUTANT NINJA TURTLES
MIRAGE (1987-1989)

1 .... 2.25 8.00
2-3 .... 1.25 4.00
4-7 .... 1.00 3.00

TALES OF THE TEXAS RANGERS
SEE JACE PEARSON'S TALES OF THE TEXAS RANGERS.

TALES OF THE UNEXPECTED
DC (1956-1968)

1 "The Cartoon That Came To Life!" (2-3/56) 250.00 800.00
2 "The Gorilla Who Saved The World!" (4-5/56) 110.00 350.00
3 "The Master Of 100 Wigs!" (7/56) 95.00 300.00
4 "The House Where Dreams Come True!" (8/56) 80.00 250.00
5 "The Second Life Of Geoffrey Hawkes!" 65.00 200.00
6 "The Girl In The Bottle!" (10/56) 65.00 200.00
7 "The Face In The Clock!" 55.00 175.00
8 "The 3-D Camera That Could Rob!" 55.00 175.00
9 "The Man Who Ate Fire!" (1/57) 55.00 175.00
10 "Slave To The Wizard's Lamp!" ... 55.00 175.00
11 "The Man Who Hated Green!" ... 55.00 175.00
12 "The Indestructible Man!" 55.00 175.00
13 "The Face Behind The Mask!" ... 40.00 125.00
14 "The Green Gorilla!" 40.00 125.00
15 "City Of Three Dooms" (7/57) ... 40.00 125.00
16 .... 40.00 125.00
17 "The Impossible Voyage!" 40.00 125.00
18 .... 40.00 125.00
19 "The Menace Of The Fireball!" ... 31.00 100.00
20-24 .... 31.00 100.00
25-30 .... 25.00 80.00
31-39 .... 22.00 70.00
40 "Battle Of The Colossal Creatures!" plus Begin: Space Ranger (8/59) 190.00 600.00
41-42 .... 70.00 225.00
43 1st Space Ranger cover. 130.00 425.00
44-48 .... 55.00 180.00
49 .... 40.00 130.00
50-51 .... 35.00 110.00
52-53 .... 28.00 90.00
54 Dinosaur cover & story. 28.00 90.00
55-60 .... 28.00 90.00
61-67 .... 23.00 75.00
68 1st 12 cent cover price. 14.00 44.00
69-81 .... 14.00 44.00
82 End: Space Ranger. 14.00 44.00
83-90 .... 7.00 20.00
91-100 .... 5.00 15.00
101-103 .... 2.75 10.00
104 Title changes to Unexpected with #105. .... 2.75 10.00

TALES OF THE WIZARD OF OZ
DELL FOUR COLOR SERIES (1962)

1308 TV tie-in. (3/62) 19.00 60.00

TALES OF THE ZOMBIE
MARVEL (1973-1975) MAGAZINE

1 .... 4.00 13.00
2 Cover: Boris Vallejo. 2.25 8.75
3-10 .... 1.50 5.50
ANNUAL 1.50 5.50

TALES OF WELLS FARGO
DELL FOUR COLOR SERIES (1958-1961)

876 TV photo covers on all issues. (2/58) 23.00 75.00
968 (2/59) 20.00 65.00
1023 (8/59) 19.00 60.00
1075 (2/60) 19.00 60.00
1113 (7/60) 19.00 60.00
1167 (3/61) 16.00 50.00
1215 (10/61) 19.00 60.00

TALES TO ASTONISH
MARVEL (1979-1981)

1-14 .... .30 1.00

TALES TO ASTONISH
MARVEL(ATLAS) (1959-1968)

1 .... 310.00 1000.00
2 Cover: Steve Ditko. 130.00 425.00
3-4 .... 95.00 300.00
5 Stone Men prototype. (9/59) "I Was Trapped By The Things On Easter Island!" Cover and five page story by Kirby. 110.00 350.00
6 "I Saw The Invasion Of The Stone Men!" (11/59) 80.00 250.00
7 Toad Men prototype. (1/60) "We Meet In The Swamp!" Five page story by Kirby/Ditko. 80.00 250.00
8-9 .... 65.00 200.00
10 "I Was Trapped By Titano! The Monster That Time Forgot!" (7/60) 80.00 250.00
11-12 .... 65.00 200.00
13-14 .... 50.00 150.00
15 Electro prototype. (1/61) "The Blip!" Cover and seven page story by Kirby. 65.00 200.00
16 Stone Men prototype. (2/61) "Thorr, The Unbelievable!" Cover and seven page story by Kirby. ... 65.00 200.00
17-24 .... 50.00 150.00
25-26 .... 31.00 100.00
27 1st: Ant-Man in "The Man In The Anthill!" (1/62) 700.00 2500.00
28 1st 12 cent cover price. 28.00 90.00
29-34 .... 28.00 90.00
35 1st: Ant-Man in costume. "The Return Of The Ant-Man!" (9/62) 400.00 1200.00
36 .... 125.00 400.00
37-40 .... 65.00 200.00
41-43 .... 40.00 130.00
44 1st & origin: The Wasp. (6/63) 65.00 200.00
45 .... 31.00 100.00
46 "...When Cyclops Walks The Earth!" 31.00 100.00
47-48 .... 31.00 100.00
49 Ant-Man becomes Giant Man. 50.00 150.00
50-51 .... 20.00 65.00
52 1st & origin: Black Knight. (2/64) 20.00 65.00
53-56 .... 20.00 65.00
57 App: Spider-Man. 26.00 85.00
58 .... 20.00 65.00
59 Giant Man battles Hulk. 31.00 100.00
60 Giant Man/Hulk double feature origin. 40.00 125.00
61-64 .... 14.00 45.00
65 "The New Giant-Man!" 16.00 50.00
66-68 .... 13.00 40.00
69 End: Giant Man. 13.00 40.00
70 Begin: Hulk/Sub-Mariner double features. 19.00 60.00
71-80 .... 8.00 26.00
81 1st: Boomerang. 8.00 26.00
82 Sub-Mariner battles Iron Man. 13.00 40.00
83-91 .... 8.00 26.00
92 .... 10.00 30.00
93 Hulk battles Silver Surfer (1st full story outside of Fantastic Four). 10.00 30.00
94-99 .... 8.00 26.00
100 Hulk battles Sub-Mariner. 10.00 30.00
101 Title changes to Incredible Hulk with #102. .... 16.00 50.00

TALLY-HO COMICS
BAILY (1944)

NO# 60.00 190.00

TALOS OF THE WILDERNESS SEA
DC (1987)

1 .... .75 2.50

TALULLAH
METROPOLITAN (1950)

1 Giveaway (4.25 x 8.5, bound at top). 2.75 10.00

TAMMY TELL ME TRUE
DELL FOUR COLOR SERIES (1961)

1233 Movie tie-in. 19.00 60.00

TANK GIRL
DC (1995)

1 Movie tie-in. 1.50 5.95

TANK GIRL
DARK HORSE (1991)

1 Reprints Deadline magazine series from U.K. 1.50 5.00
2 .... 1.00 3.50
3-4 .... 1.00 3.00
TPB Vol. 1. Reprints #1-4. .... 5.00 14.95

TANK GIRL
DARK HORSE (1993)

1 .... 1.00 3.50
2-4 .... .75 2.50
TPB Vol. 2. Reprints 2nd series 1-4. ... 6.00 17.95

TANK GIRL: THE ODYSSEY
DC (1995)

1-4 .... .75 2.25

TARGET COMICS
NOVELTY (1940-1949)

V1#1 .... 600.00 2100.00
V1#2 .... 310.00 1000.00
V1#3 .... 290.00 950.00
V1#4 .... 250.00 825.00
V1#5 1st & begin: Spacehawk in "Spacehawk And The Creeping Death From Neptune" by Basil Wolverton. 600.00 2200.00
V1#6 1st & begin: Chameleon by Bill Everett. 290.00 950.00
V1#7 Classic Spacehawk cover by Wolverton. 700.00 2400.00
V1#8-V1#9 .... 250.00 825.00
V1#10 1st: The Target. 310.00 1000.00
V1#11 Origin: The Target. 290.00 950.00
V1#12 .... 250.00 825.00
V2#1-V2#12 .... 130.00 420.00
V3#1-V3#9 .... 110.00 360.00
V3#10 End: Spacehawk by Wolverton. 110.00 360.00
V3#11-V3#12 .... 28.00 90.00
V4#1-V4#12 .... 19.00 60.00
V5#1-V5#8 .... 15.00 48.00
V6#1-V6#12 .... 11.00 36.00
V7#1-V9#12 .... 8.00 24.00
V10#1-V10#2 .... 8.00 24.00
V10#3 Title changes to Target Western Romances with #106. .... 8.00 24.00

TARGET: THE CORRUPTERS
DELL (1962)

1 (#1306) From the 4-Color Series. TV tie-in. (3/62) 13.00 40.00
2-3 .... 7.00 20.00

TARGET WESTERN ROMANCES
STAR (1949-1950)

106 Previous title: Target Comics. ... 25.00 80.00
107 .... 19.00 60.00

TARGITT
ATLAS(SEABOARD) (1975)

1-3 .... .75 2.00

TARZAN
DELL FOUR COLOR SERIES (1947)

134 "And The Devil Ogre" (2/47) ... 125.00 400.00
161 "And The Fires Of Tohr" (8/47) 100.00 330.00

TARZAN
DELL/GOLD KEY/DC (1948-1977)

1 "The White Savages Of Vari" 125.00 400.00
2 "The Captives Of Thunder Valley!" ... 65.00 200.00
3 "The Dwarfs Of Didona!" 40.00 130.00
4 "The Lone Hunter" 40.00 130.00
5 "The Men Of Greed" 40.00 130.00
6 "The Outlaws Of Pal-ul-don" 40.00 130.00
7 "The Valley Of The Monsters" 28.00 90.00
8 "The White Pygmies" 28.00 90.00
9 "The Men Of A-Lur" 28.00 90.00
10 "The Treasure Of The Bolgani" ... 28.00 90.00
11 "The Sable Lion" 28.00 90.00
12 "The Price Of Peace" 28.00 90.00
13 Begin: Lex Barker photo cover. ... 55.00 180.00
14-18 .... 35.00 110.00
19-24 .... 28.00 90.00
25-30 .... 16.00 50.00
31-40 .... 11.00 36.00
41-53 .... 9.00 27.00
54 End: Lex Barker photo covers. 9.00 27.00
55-79 .... 4.00 13.00
80 Begin: Gordon Scott photo covers. ... 7.00 22.00
81-100 .... 6.00 18.00
101-131 .... 2.50 9.00
132 Begin Gold Key publication. 1.50 5.25
133-150 .... 1.50 5.25
151-180 .... 1.00 3.50
181-206 .... .75 2.50
207 Begin DC publication. 2.00 7.00
208-212 .... 1.00 3.50
213-229 .... .75 2.50
230 100 page issue. 1.25 4.50
231-234 .... .75 2.50
235 100 page issue. 1.00 3.50
236-258 .... .75 2.50

TARZAN
MARVEL (1977-1979)

1 .... .75 2.00
2-29 .... .30 1.00
ANNUAL 1 (1977) .... .30 1.00
ANNUAL 2 (1978) .... .30 1.00
ANNUAL 3 (1979) .... .30 1.00

TARZAN FAMILY, THE
DC (1975-1976)

60 Previous title: Korak, Son Of Tarzan. .30 1.00
61-66 .... .30 1.00

TARZAN, KING OF THE JUNGLE
SEE DELL GIANT

TARZAN, LORD OF THE JUNGLE
GOLD KEY (1965)

1 .... 9.00 27.00

TARZAN OF THE APES
SEE LARGE FEATURE COMICS #5.

TARZAN: THE LOST ADVENTURE
DARK HORSE (1995)
1-4 .75 2.95

TARZAN VS PREDATOR AT THE EARTH'S CORE
DARK HORSE (1995)
1 .75 2.50

TARZAN VS. PREDATOR: AT THE EARTH'S CORE
DARK HORSE (1995)
1 .75 2.50

TARZAN VS PREDATOR AT THE EARTH'S CORE
DARK HORSE (1995)
2-4 .75 2.50

TARZAN'S JUNGLE ANNUAL
DELL (1952-1958)
1 20.00 65.00
2 14.00 45.00
3-7 10.00 31.00

TASMANIAN DEVIL AND HIS TASTY FRIENDS
GOLD KEY (1962)
1 TV tie-in. 25.00 80.00

TEAM 1: STORMWATCH
IMAGE (1995)
1 .75 2.50

TEAM 1: WILDCATS
IMAGE (1995)
1 .75 2.50

TEAM 7
IMAGE (1994-1995)
1 1.50 5.50
1A Variant cover. 2.75 10.00
2 1.00 3.50
3-4 .75 2.50

TEAM 7: OBJECTIVE HELL
IMAGE (1995)
1 .75 2.50
1A Newsstand version without cards. .50 1.95
2-3 .75 2.50

TEAM AMERICA
MARVEL (1982-1983)
1 Toy tie-in. .30 1.00
2-11 .30 1.00
12 Double size. .30 1.00

TEAM ANARCHY
DAGGER (1993-1994)
1 Foil cover. .75 2.75
2-12 .75 2.50

TEAM HELIX
MARVEL (1993)
1-4 .30 1.00

TEAM TITANS
DC (1992-1994)
1A Origin:Terra. .50 1.75
1B Origin: Mirage. .50 1.75
1C Origin: Nightrider. .50 1.75
1D Origin: Redwing. .50 1.75
1E Origin: Killowat. .50 1.75
2-21 .50 1.75
22-24 .50 1.95
ANNUAL 1 Bloodlines, pt 22. (1993) 1.00 3.50
ANNUAL 2 Elseworlds story. (1994) .75 2.95

TEAM YOUNGBLOOD
IMAGE (1993-CURRENT)
1-8 .50 1.95
9 1.50 5.00
10 .75 2.50
11 .50 1.95
12-20 .75 2.50

TEDDY ROOSEVELT AND HIS ROUGH RIDERS
AVON (1950)
1 "The Battle Of San Juan Hill" 28.00 90.00

TEEN BEAM
DC (1968)
2 Monkees photo cover. 7.00 20.00

TEEN BEAT
DC (1967)
1 Monkees photo cover. 10.00 30.00

TEEN COMICS
MARVEL (1947-1950)
21 Previous title: All Teen Comics. 14.00 44.00
22-30 10.00 33.00
31-35 7.00 22.00

TEEN LIFE
QUALITY (1945-1946)
3 Previous title: Young Life. 11.00 35.00
4 10.00 30.00
5 Jackie Robinson tells his own story. 16.00 50.00

TEEN TITANS
DC (1966-1978)
1 50.00 160.00
2 23.00 75.00
3-6 11.00 35.00
7-12 8.00 26.00
13-18 6.00 18.00
19 2.75 10.00
20 Begin: Neal Adams art. 7.00 22.00
21 7.00 22.00
22 Origin: Wonder Girl. End: Neal Adams art. 7.00 22.00
23 1st 15 cent cover price. 2.75 10.00
24-30 2.75 10.00
31-43 2.00 7.00
44-45 1.50 5.00
46 Joker's daughter joins. 2.75 10.00
47 1.50 5.00
48 1st: Bumblebee, Harlequin II. 2.75 10.00
49 1.50 5.00
50 1st: Teen Titans West. 2.75 10.00
51-52 1.50 5.00
53 Origin retold. 2.75 10.00

TEEN TITANS SPOTLIGHT
DC (1986-1988)
1-21 .30 1.00

TEENA
SEE A-1 COMICS #11, 12 & 15.

TEENAGE DIARY SECRETS
ST. JOHN (1949)
4 Cover & art: Matt Baker. From Blue Ribbon Comics 2nd series. 20.00 65.00
5 Cover: Matt Baker. From Blue Ribbon Comics 2nd series. 17.00 55.00

TEENAGE DIARY SECRETS
ST. JOHN (1949-1950)
6-8 10.00 30.00
9 Title changes to Diary Secrets with #10. 10.00 30.00

TEENAGE DOPE SLAVES
HARVEY (1952)
1 From Harvey Comics Library series. SOTI 135.00 440.00

TEEN-AGE HOTRODDERS
CHARLTON (1963-1967)
1 11.00 34.00
2-6 7.00 23.00
7-12 6.00 17.00
13-24 4.00 11.00

TEEN-AGE LOVE
CHARLTON (1958-1973)
4 (Volume 2). 7.00 20.00
5-6 5.00 15.00
7-12 2.75 10.00
13-30 2.25 8.00
31-60 1.50 5.00
61-80 1.00 3.00
81-96 .30 1.00

TEENAGE MUTANT NINJA TURTLES
ARCHIE (1990)
1 Movie adaptation. 1.50 5.00

TEENAGE MUTANT NINJA TURTLES
MIRAGE (1984-1993)
1 110.00 350.00
1 (2ND) 2nd printing. 16.00 50.00
1 (3RD) 3rd printing. 8.00 25.00
1 (4TH) 4th printing. 5.00 15.00
1 (5TH) 5th printing. 1.50 5.00
2 28.00 90.00
2 (2ND) 2nd printing. 2.75 10.00
2 (3RD) 3rd printing. 1.50 5.00
3 10.00 30.00
3 (2ND) 2nd printing. New back-up story. 1.25 4.00
4 6.00 18.00
4 (2ND) 2nd printing. 1.25 4.00
5 Begin: Fugitoid. 4.00 12.00
5 (2ND) 2nd printing. 1.25 4.00
6 2.75 10.00
6 (2ND) 2nd printing. 1.00 3.00
7 1st color issue. Art (4 pages): Richard Corben. 5.00 14.00
7 (2ND) 2nd printing. 1.00 3.00
8 App: Cerebus. 2.75 10.00
9-10 2.00 7.50
11-18 1.50 5.00
19-32 1.25 4.00
33 Full color issue. 1.00 3.00
34-35 1.00 3.00
36-61 .75 2.00
62 .75 2.25

TEENAGE MUTANT NINJA TURTLES ADVENTURES
ARCHIE (1988)
1 1.50 5.00
2-3 1.00 3.00

TEENAGE MUTANT NINJA TURTLES ADVENTURES
ARCHIE (1989-CURRENT)
1 1.50 5.00
2 1.25 4.00
3-5 1.00 3.00
6-15 .75 2.00
16-73 .50 1.50
SPECIAL 1 .75 2.50
SPECIAL 2-4 .75 2.50
SPECIAL 5-8 .50 1.95
SPECIAL 9 1st: Mole. .50 1.95
SPECIAL 10 .50 1.95
SPECIAL 11 The Fifth Turtle. .75 2.00

TEENAGE MUTANT NINJA TURTLES PRESENTS...THE MAY EAST SAGA
ARCHIE
1-3 .50 1.25

TEENAGE MUTANT NINJA TURTLES PRESENTS...MERDUDE & MICHAELANGELO
ARCHIE (1993)
1 One shot. .50 1.25

TEENAGE MUTANT NINJA TURTLES PRESENTS...APRIL O'NEIL
ARCHIE (1993)
1-2 .50 1.25

TEENAGE MUTANT NINJA TURTLES VOLUME 2
MIRAGE
1 Full color issues. .75 2.75
2-13 .75 2.75

TEENAGE MUTANT NINJA TURTLES/FLAMING CARROT: LAND OF GREEN FIRE
MIRAGE (1993-1994)
1-4 .75 2.75

TEEN-AGE ROMANCE
MARVEL (1960-1962)
77 Previous title: My Own Romance. 2.75 10.00
78-86 2.75 10.00

TEEN-AGE ROMANCES
ST. JOHN (1949-1955)
1 Cover & art: Matt Baker. 35.00 110.00
2-3 Cover & art: Matt Baker. 20.00 65.00
4-8 Art: Matt Baker. 14.00 44.00
9 Cover & art: Matt Baker. 20.00 65.00
10-12 Cover & art: Matt Baker. 17.00 55.00
13-19 All Baker art. 23.00 75.00
20 Cover & art: Matt Baker. 17.00 55.00
21-22 All Baker art. 23.00 75.00
23-25 Cover & art: Matt Baker. 17.00 55.00
26-27 Art: Matt Baker. 10.00 33.00
28-30 4.00 13.00
31-32 Cover: Baker. 4.00 13.00
33-34 Art: Matt Baker. 10.00 33.00
35 Cover & art: Matt Baker. 14.00 44.00
36-42 Art: Matt Baker. 10.00 33.00
43 Art: Matt Baker. 1st Code Approved issue. 10.00 33.00
44-45 Art: Matt Baker. 10.00 33.00

TEEN-AGE TEMPTATIONS
ST. JOHN (1952-1954)
1 Cover & art: Matt Baker. 40.00 130.00
2 Cover: Matt Baker. 14.00 44.00
3-7 Cover & art: Matt Baker. 20.00 65.00
8 Cover & art: Matt Baker. Marijuana story. 23.00 75.00
9 Cover & art: Matt Baker. 20.00 65.00

TEAM 7 #3

TEAM YOUNGBLOOD #9

TEAM TITANS #8

TEEN TITANS #3

TEKNOPHAGE #4

TERMINATOR #2 (DARK HORSE)

BLACK MAGIC · VOODOO · JUNGLE MYSTERY
TERRIFYING TALES
TYRANTS OF TERROR!

TERRIFYING TALES #11

THB #2

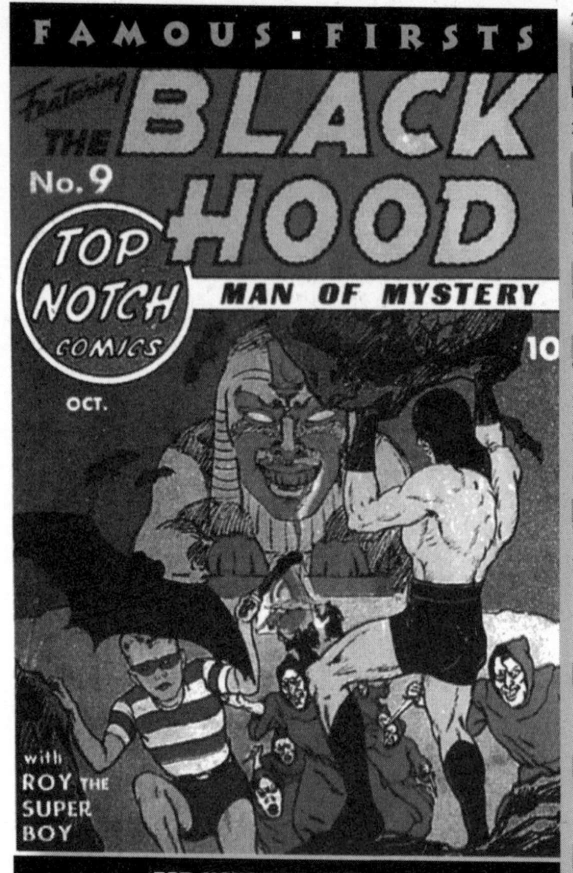

TOP NOTCH COMICS #9

The first eight issues featured a nifty guy with the catchy name "The Wizard." But this issue introduces The Black Hood, one of the first heroes in the Archie line. He returned in the 1960s and the 1980s.

TEENAGENTS
TOPPS (1993)
1 Polybagged with cards. .75 2.95
2-4 .75 2.95

TEGRA JUNGLE EMPRESS
FOX (1948)
1 Title changes to Zegra Jungle Empress with #2. SOTI 70.00 230.00

TEKNOPHAGE
TECHNO-COMIX (1995-CURRENT)
1-4 .50 1.95

TELEVISION PUPPET SHOW
AVON (1950)
1 16.00 50.00
2 13.00 40.00

TELL IT TO THE MARINES
TOBY (1952-1955)
1 19.00 60.00
2 10.00 30.00
3-6 7.00 20.00
7-12 4.00 12.00
13 Photo cover (John Wayne). 19.00 60.00
14-15 4.00 12.00

TEN WHO DARED
DELL FOUR COLOR SERIES (1960)
1178 Movie tie-in. (12/60) 8.00 25.00

TENSE SUSPENSE
FAGO (1958-1959)
1 9.00 28.00
2 7.00 23.00

TERMINAL POINT
DARK HORSE (1993)
1-2 .75 2.50

TERMINATOR, THE
DARK HORSE (1990)
1 1.25 4.00
2 1.00 3.00
3-4 1.00 3.00

TERMINATOR, THE
NOW (1988-1989)
1 2.00 7.00
2 1.00 3.00
3-17 .75 2.00

TERMINATOR 2: JUDGEMENT DAY
MARVEL (1991)
1 Movie adaptation. .30 1.00
2-3 .30 1.00

TERMINATOR: ALL MY FUTURES PAST, THE
NOW (1990)
1-2 .50 1.75

TERMINATOR: ENDGAME, THE
DARK HORSE (1992)
1-3 .75 2.50

TERMINATOR: HUNTERS AND KILLERS, THE
DARK HORSE (1992)
1-3 .75 2.50

TERMINATOR: SECONDARY OBJECTIVES, THE
DARK HORSE (1991)
1 1.00 3.00
2-4 .75 2.75

TERMINATOR: THE BURNING EARTH, THE
NOW (1990)
1 1.00 3.00
2-5 .75 2.00

TERMINATOR: THE ENEMY WITHIN, THE
DARK HORSE (1991-1992)
1 1.00 3.00
2-4 .75 2.50

TERRARISTS
MARVEL (1993)
1-4 .75 2.50

TERRIFIC COMICS
CONTINENTAL (1944)
1 Begin: Kid Terrific. 150.00 490.00
2 1st: Boomerang. 115.00 380.00
3 100.00 330.00
4 115.00 380.00
5 Classic Schomburg cover. 115.00 380.00
6 Cover & art: L.B. Cole. 115.00 380.00

TERRIFYING TALES
STAR (1953-1954)
11 "Tyrants Of Terror!" (Jo-Jo reprints). Previous title: Startling Terror Tales. 60.00 190.00
12 "The Image Of Horror!" 40.00 130.00
13 "The Death-Fire!" 70.00 220.00
14 "The Weird Idol!" 40.00 130.00
15 "The Grim Secret!" 40.00 130.00

TERROR ILLUSTRATED
EC (1955-1956)
1 Magazine size. 25.00 80.00
2 Magazine size. 15.00 49.00

TERROR INC.
MARVEL (1992-1993)
1 .75 2.50
2-13 .50 1.75

TERROR TALES
EERIE (1969-1976) MAGAZINE
V8#3-V9#3 1.50 5.00
V1#7 5.00 15.00

TERROR TALES
SEE BEWARE TERROR TALES

TERRORS OF THE JUNGLE
STAR (1952-1953)
17 Reprint: Rulah #21. Previous title: Jungle Thrills. (5/52) 60.00 190.00
18 Reprint: Jo Jo Congo King. (7/52) 35.00 110.00
19 Reprint: Jo Jo Congo King #16. (9/52) 26.00 85.00
20 Reprint: Jo Jo Congo King #17. (12/52) 26.00 85.00
21 (3/53) 35.00 110.00

TERRORS OF THE JUNGLE
STAR (1953-1954)
4 "Morass Of Death!" dinosaur cover. 45.00 137.50
5-10 35.00 110.00

TERRY AND THE PIRATES
DELL FOUR COLOR SERIES (1944-1946)
44 95.00 300.00
101 Last: 4-Color Series with "Four Color Comic" on cover. 65.00 200.00

TERRY AND THE PIRATES
HARVEY/CHARLTON (1947-1955)
3 Begin: Boy Explorers. 1st: Lady Dragon. 35.00 110.00
4 20.00 65.00
5-6 11.00 36.00
6A Puffed Wheat premium with ads on back cover and inside covers. 11.00 36.00
7-10 11.00 36.00
11 Art: Bob Powell. App: Man in Black. 14.00 45.00
12-18 9.00 27.00
19-25 6.00 18.00
26 (4/51) 4.00 13.00
27 Begin Charlton publication. (6/55) 4.00 13.00
28 4.00 13.00

TERRY AND THE PIRATES
SEE LARGE FEATURE COMICS (SERIES I) #2, 6, 27.
- Large Feature Comics (Series II) #6.

TERRY AND THE PIRATES POPPED WHEAT GIVEAWAY
GIVEAWAY (1938)
NO# 2.75 10.00

TERRY-TOONS
MARVEL(TIMELY)/ST. JOHN (1942-1951)
1 250.00 825.00
2 120.00 390.00
3 100.00 330.00
4-6 75.00 240.00
7-9 65.00 210.00
10-12 50.00 150.00
13-18 40.00 120.00
19-24 25.00 80.00
25-30 19.00 60.00
31-37 15.00 48.00
38 1st & begin: Mighty Mouse. (11/45) 250.00 825.00
39 110.00 360.00
40-41 75.00 240.00
42-45 55.00 180.00
46-49 40.00 120.00
50 1st: Heckle & Jeckle. (11/46) 75.00 240.00
51-52 40.00 120.00
53-59 19.00 60.00
60 Begin: St. John publication. 19.00 60.00
61-70 15.00 48.00
71-85 11.00 36.00
86 Title changes to Paul Terry's Comics starting with #87. 11.00 36.00

TERRY-TOONS
ST. JOHN (1952-1953)
1 26.00 85.00
2 14.00 44.00
3-6 10.00 33.00
7-9 9.00 27.00

TESSIE THE TYPIST COMICS
MARVEL(TIMELY) (1944-1949)
1 Art: Basil Wolverton. 125.00 400.00
2 Art: Basil Wolverton. 65.00 200.00
3 17.00 55.00
4-8 Art: Basil Wolverton. 40.00 130.00
9-13 Powerhouse Pepper by Basil Wolverton. 50.00 160.00
14-18 14.00 46.00
19-23 11.00 34.00

TEX DAWSON, GUN SLINGER
MARVEL (1973)
1 1.00 3.00

TEX FARRELL
DS (1948)
1 10.00 30.00

TEX GRANGER
PMI (1948-1950)
18 Previous title: Calling All Boys. 10.00 30.00
19-24 7.00 20.00

TEX MORGAN
MARVEL (1948-1950)
1 26.00 85.00
2 17.00 55.00
3-6 10.00 33.00
7-9 Photo cover. 23.00 75.00

TEX RITTER WESTERN
FAWCETT/CHARLTON (1950-1959)
1 Begin: Photo covers. 85.00 270.00
2 40.00 130.00
3-6 23.00 75.00
7-12 20.00 65.00
13-20 17.00 55.00
21 End: Photo covers. Begin Charlton publication. 14.00 44.00
22-30 7.00 22.00
31-46 4.00 13.00

TEX TAYLOR
MARVEL (1948-1950)
NO# "Draw Or Die Cowpoke!" or "An Exciting Adventure At The Gold Mine" 1950 giveaways of Wisco, Carnation, Klarer and other companies. 70.00 220.00
1 "Boot Hill Showdown For An Outlaw Buster!" 26.00 85.00
2 "When Two-Gun Terror Rides The Range!" 15.00 49.00
3 Thundering Hoofs And Blazing Guns!" 10.00 33.00
4 "Draw Or Die, Cowpoke!" Begin: photo covers. 20.00 65.00
5 "The Juggler Of Yellow Valley!" 20.00 65.00
6 "Mystery At Howling Gap!" 20.00 65.00
7 20.00 65.00
8 "The Mystery Of Devil-Tree Plateau!" 20.00 65.00
9 20.00 65.00

TEXAN, THE
DELL FOUR COLOR SERIES (1959-1960)
1027 TV photo cover. (9/59) 14.00 45.00
1096 TV photo cover. (5/60) 14.00 45.00

TEXAN, THE
ST. JOHN (1948-1951)
1 19.00 60.00
2-3 10.00 30.00
4-5 Cover & art: Matt Baker. 16.00 50.00
6 Cover: Matt Baker. 10.00 30.00
7-8 Cover & art: Matt Baker. 16.00 50.00
9 Cover: Matt Baker. 10.00 30.00
10 10.00 30.00
11 Cover & art: Matt Baker. 16.00 50.00
12 All Matt Baker issue. 23.00 75.00
13-15 Cover & art: Matt Baker. 16.00 50.00

TEXAS JOHN SLAUGHTER
DELL FOUR COLOR SERIES (1961):F3
1181 TV photo cover. (3/61) 10.00 30.00

THANOS QUEST
MARVEL (1990)
1 1.50 5.00
1 (2ND) 2nd printing. .75 2.00
2 1.50 5.00
2 (2ND) 2nd printing. .75 2.00

THAT DARN CAT
GOLD KEY (1966)
10171-602 Disney movie photo cover. 5.00 15.00

THB
HORSE PRESS (1984-1995)
1 3.00 10.00
1 (2ND) 2nd printing. 1.00 3.50
2 1.50 5.00
3 1.25 4.00
4-8 .75 2.95

T.H.E. CAT
DELL (1967)
1 TV photo cover (all issues). 8.00 25.00
2-4 5.00 16.00

THEY ALL KISSED THE BRIDE
COLUMBIA (1942)
NO# Movie giveaway (4 pages). From the Cinema Comics Herald series. 16.00 50.00

THIEF OF BAGHDAD
DELL FOUR COLOR SERIES (1961)
1229 Movie photo cover. 26.00 85.00

THIEVES AND KINGS
I BOX (1994-CURRENT)
1-6 .75 2.95

THIMBLE THEATRE STARRING POPEYE
SONNET (1931-1932)
1 By Segar. Cardboard covers with b/w strip reprints. 170.00 550.00
2 135.00 440.00

THING, THE
CHARLTON (1952-1954)
1 130.00 430.00
2 80.00 250.00
3 65.00 210.00
4-6 55.00 180.00
7 Classic horror cover. 115.00 370.00
8 55.00 180.00
9 SOTI 130.00 430.00
10 55.00 180.00
11 105.00 340.00
12-14 Cover & art: Steve Ditko. 130.00 430.00
15 Cover & art: Steve Ditko. "The Worm Turns." 130.00 430.00
16 65.00 210.00
17 Cover: Steve Ditko. 115.00 370.00

THING, THE
MARVEL (1983-1986)
1 .75 2.00
2-36 .50 1.25

THING FROM ANOTHER WORLD, THE
DARK HORSE (1991-1992)
1 Movie tie-in. 1.00 3.00
2 1.00 3.00

THING FROM ANOTHER WORLD: CLIMATE OF FEAR
DARK HORSE (1992)
1-4 .75 2.50

THING FROM ANOTHER WORLD: ETERNAL VOWS
DARK HORSE (1993-1994)
1-4 .75 2.50

THIRTY SECONDS OVER TOKYO
DAVID MCKAY (1944)
NO# Movie tie-in. From the American Library series. 55.00 175.00

THIS IS SUSPENSE
CHARLTON (1955)
23 Previous title: Strange Suspense Stories. Reprint: "Dr. Jekyll & Mr. Hyde" by Wallace Wood. 29.00 95.00
24-26 16.00 50.00

THIS IS WAR
STANDARD (1952-1953)
5-6 Art: Alex Toth. 13.00 40.00
7-8 7.00 20.00
9 Art: Alex Toth. 13.00 40.00

THIS MAGAZINE IS HAUNTED
CHARLTON (1957-1958)
12 Cover & art: Steve Ditko. Previous title: Zaza The Mystic. 60.00 187.50
13-14 Cover & art: Steve Ditko. 60.00 187.50
15 8.00 25.00
16 Art: Steve Ditko. Title changes to Outer Space with #17. 40.00 125.00

THIS MAGAZINE IS HAUNTED
FAWCETT (1951-1954)
1 80.00 250.00
2 55.00 180.00
3-5 40.00 120.00
6-8 31.00 100.00
9 23.00 75.00
10 Gruesome cover. 40.00 120.00
11-12 23.00 75.00
13 Gruesome cover. 40.00 120.00
14-15 19.00 60.00
16 Cover: Steve Ditko. 50.00 150.00
17 Cover & art: Steve Ditko. 65.00 210.00
18 Cover & art: Steve Ditko. 55.00 180.00
19 Cover: Steve Ditko. 50.00 150.00
20 19.00 60.00
21 Cover: Steve Ditko. 40.00 120.00

THOR
MARVEL (1966-CURRENT)
126 Previous title: Journey Into Mystery. 40.00 120.00
127-128 16.00 50.00
129 "The Verdict Of Zeus!" 16.00 50.00
130 "Thunder In The Underworld!" 16.00 50.00
131-133 16.00 50.00
134 1st: High Evolutionary. 19.00 60.00
135 Origin: High Evolutionary. 16.00 50.00
136-140 13.00 40.00
141-145 11.00 35.00
146 1st & Origin: The Inhumans. 14.00 45.00
147 Origin continued. 11.00 35.00
148-157 10.00 30.00
158 Origin retold: Thor. 22.00 70.00
159-161 10.00 30.00
162 Origin (pt.1): Galactus. 16.00 50.00
163-164 7.00 20.00
165 1st full appearance: Warlock. 13.00 40.00
166 2nd: Warlock. 13.00 40.00
167 6.00 18.00
168 Origin (pt.2): Galactus. 13.00 40.00
169 Origin (pt.3): Galactus. 13.00 40.00
170-178 6.00 18.00
179 End: Jack Kirby art. 6.00 18.00
180-181 Art: Neal Adams. 5.00 15.00
182-192 1.75 6.00
193 Silver Surfer. Double size. 11.00 35.00
194-200 1.75 6.00
201 1.50 5.00
202-224 1.25 4.00
225 1st: Firelord. 1.75 6.00
226 1.25 4.00
227-259 1.00 3.00
260 1.50 5.00
261-299 1.00 3.00
300 Double size. 1.75 6.00
301-305 1.00 3.00
306 1.75 6.00
307-336 1.00 3.00
337 1st: Beta Ray Bill. 2.25 8.00
338 Origin: Beta Ray Bill. 1.50 5.00
339 1.00 3.50

THIEF OF BAGHDAD #1229

THOR #132

THOR #144

THOR #166

THOR #460

THUNDERSTRIKE #11

THUNDERSTRIKE #23

TICK, THE #9

340-348 .... 1.00 3.00
349-372 .... .75 2.50
373 .... .75 2.25
374 X-Factor. 2.50 9.00
375-381 .... .75 2.00
382-383 .... 1.00 3.00
384 .... 1.50 5.00
385-386 .... .75 2.00
387-390 .... .50 1.75
391 .... 1.50 5.00
392-399 .... .50 1.75
400 .... 1.50 5.00
401-410 .... .50 1.50
411 1st: New Warriors (cameo). 2.00 7.00
412 1st: full New Warriors. 4.00 12.00
413-428 .... .50 1.50
429-430 .... 1.00 3.00
431 .... .50 1.50
432 1st: new Thor. Death: Loki. 1.00 3.00
433 Begin: new Thor. 1.75 6.50
434-435 .... 1.00 3.50
436-439 .... .50 1.50
440-443 .... 1.00 3.00
444-449 .... .50 1.25
450 Double size. .... .75 2.50
451-467 .... .50 1.25
468 .... .75 2.95
469-473 .... .50 1.25
474 .... .50 1.50
475 New costume. Multi-level cover. .... .75 2.95
475A Regular edition. .... .75 2.50
476-490 .... .50 1.50

THOR ANNUAL
MARVEL (1966-CURRENT)

2 King-Size Special. (9/66) 16.00 50.00
3 King-Size Special. (1/71) 5.00 15.00
4 King-Size Special. (12/71) 2.75 10.00
5-6 .... 2.50 9.00
7 .... 2.25 8.00
8-12 .... 2.00 7.00
13 .... 1.75 6.00
14 .... 1.50 5.50
15 .... 1.50 5.00
16-17 .... .75 2.25
18-19 .... .75 2.95

THOR CORPS
MARVEL (1993)

1-4 .... .50 1.75

THOSE MAGNIFICENT MEN IN THEIR FLYING MACHINES
GOLD KEY (1965)

10162-510 Movie photo cover. 5.00 15.00

THREE CABALLEROS
DELL FOUR COLOR SERIES (1945)

71 Art: Walt Kelly. Disney movie tie-in. 190.00 600.00

THREE CHIPMUNKS, THE
DELL FOUR COLOR SERIES (1959)

1042 (10/59) 7.00 20.00

THREE DIMENSION COMICS
ST. JOHN (1953)

1 Mighty Mouse. With 3-D glasses. ... 50.00 160.00
2-3 Mighty Mouse. With 3-D glasses. 40.00 130.00

THREE DIMENSIONAL E.C. CLASSICS
EC (1954)

1 With glasses. Becomes Three Dimensional Tales From The Crypt Of Terror #2. .... 190.00 600.00

THREE LITTLE PIGS
DELL FOUR COLOR SERIES (1949)

218 "And The Wonderful Magic Lamp" (3/49) 23.00 75.00

THREE MOUSEKETEERS, THE
DC (1956-1960)

1 .... 60.00 190.00
2 .... 35.00 110.00
3 .... 26.00 85.00
4-6 .... 20.00 65.00
7-12 .... 17.00 55.00
13-18 .... 14.00 44.00
19-26 .... 12.00 38.00

THREE MOUSEKETEERS, THE
DC (1970-1971)

1 .... 5.00 16.00
2 .... 4.00 11.00
3-7 .... 1.75 6.50

THREE MUSKETEERS, THE
MARVEL (1993)

1 Movie adaptation. .... .50 1.50
2 .... .50 1.50

THREE STOOGES
DELL/GOLD KEY (1959-1972)

1 (#1043) From the 4-Color Series. Photo cover. (10/59) 40.00 125.00
2 (#1078) From the 4-Color Series. Photo cover. (2/60) 25.00 80.00
3 (#1127) From the 4-Color Series. Photo cover. (8/60) 23.00 75.00
4 (#1170) From the 4-Color Series. Photo cover. (3/61) 23.00 75.00
5 (#1187) From the 4-Color Series. Photo cover. (5/61) 23.00 75.00
6-9 .... 17.00 55.00
10 Begin Gold Key publication. 14.00 46.00
11-14 .... 14.00 46.00
15 Movie tie-in. 14.00 46.00
16-18 .... 14.00 46.00
19-21 .... 13.00 40.00
22 Movie tie-in. 13.00 40.00
23-24 .... 13.00 40.00
25-30 .... 11.00 34.00
31-40 .... 7.00 23.00
41-55 .... 4.00 13.00

THREE STOOGES, THE
JUBILEE (1949)

1 Rare. 250.00 825.00
2 Rare. 190.00 600.00

THREE STOOGES
ST. JOHN (1953)

1 Splash page features caricatures of Joe Kubert and Norman Maurer at a drawing table introducing their new comic magazine. 145.00 480.00
2 (3-D) With glasses. 110.00 360.00
3 (3-D) With glasses. 95.00 300.00
4-7 .... 75.00 240.00

THREE STOOGES IN ORBIT, THE
GOLD KEY (1962)

30016-211 Movie photo cover. All photos with captions inside. 25.00 80.00

THREE STOOGES MEET HERCULES, THE
DELL (1962)

01-828-208 Movie photo cover. 22.00 70.00

THREE WORLDS OF GULLIVER
DELL FOUR COLOR SERIES (1961)

1158 Movie photo cover. (1/61) ... 19.00 60.00

THRILL COMICS
FAWCETT (JAN., 1940)

NO# (#1). 12 pages, b&w ashcan used to obtain copyright. See Whiz #2 and Flash Comics Ashcan. 1st & Origin: Captain Thunder (renamed Captain Marvel in Whiz 2). 3 copies are known to exist. 6300.00 25000.00

THRILLING COMICS
BETTER (1940-1951)

1 .... 250.00 800.00
2 .... 110.00 350.00
3 .... 85.00 275.00
4-6 .... 65.00 200.00
7 Alex Schomburg cover. 80.00 250.00
8-10 .... 50.00 150.00
11 Alex Schomburg cover. 80.00 250.00
12-17 .... 80.00 250.00
18 End: Alex Schomburg covers. 80.00 250.00
19 1st: American Crusader. 55.00 175.00
20-24 .... 31.00 100.00
25-30 .... 28.00 90.00
31-35 .... 25.00 80.00
36 Begin: Alex Schomburg covers. ... 50.00 150.00
37-52 .... 50.00 150.00
53 1st & Begin: Phantom Detective. ... 50.00 150.00
54-55 .... 50.00 150.00
56 1st & Begin: Princess Pantha. 50.00 150.00
57-64 .... 50.00 150.00
65 End: Phantom Detective. 50.00 150.00
66 .... 50.00 150.00
67-70 Art: Frank Frazetta. 65.00 200.00
71 Art: Frank Frazetta. End: Alex Schomburg covers. 65.00 200.00
72-73 Art: Frank Frazetta. 50.00 165.00
74 End: Princess Pantha. 26.00 85.00
75 .... 11.00 35.00
76-80 .... 10.00 30.00

THRILLING CRIME CASES
STAR (1950-1952)

41 Previous title: Four Most. 14.00 44.00
42-48 .... 10.00 33.00
49 Cover: L.B. Cole. Becomes Shocking Mystery Cases #50. .... 25.00 80.00

THRILLING TRUE STORY OF BASEBALL
FAWCETT (1952)

GIANTS Photo cover (with Willie Mays rookie photo-biography). 130.00 420.00
YANKEES Photo cover. 130.00 420.00

THRILLORAMA
HARVEY (1965-1966)

1 .... 4.00 12.00
2 Featuring Pirana. 2.75 10.00
3 .... 2.75 10.00

THRILLS OF TOMORROW
HARVEY (1954-1955)

17 Previous title: Tomb Of Terror. 19.00 60.00
18 .... 16.00 50.00
19 Begin: Stuntman by Simon & Kirby. 50.00 150.00
20 Cover & art: Simon & Kirby. 50.00 150.00

THUMPER
DELL FOUR COLOR SERIES (1943-1949)

19 "Meets The Seven Dwarfs" 115.00 375.00
243 "Follows His Nose" 19.00 60.00

THUN'DA (A-1 SERIES)
ME (1952-1953)

1 (A-1 #47). Origin: Thunda. Cover & art: Frank Frazetta. 190.00 600.00
2 (A-1 #56). 25.00 80.00
3 (A-1 #73). 22.00 70.00
4 (A-1 #78). 19.00 60.00
5 (A-1 #83). 19.00 60.00
6 (A-1 #86). 19.00 60.00

T.H.U.N.D.E.R. AGENTS
JC (1981) MAGAZINE SIZE

1 "JCP Features..." 1.00 3.00

T.H.U.N.D.E.R. AGENTS
JC (1983-1984)

1 New stories. 1.25 4.00
2 .... 1.00 3.00

T.H.U.N.D.E.R. AGENTS
TOWER (1965-1969)

1 1st & Origin: Dynamo, Noman, Menthor. Art: Wallace Wood. 29.00 95.00
2 .... 19.00 60.00
3-6 .... 13.00 42.00
7 Death: Menthor. 10.00 30.00
8 1st & Origin: Raven. 11.00 36.00
9-12 .... 10.00 30.00
13-16 .... 8.00 24.00
17 (12/67) 8.00 24.00
18 (9/68) 6.00 18.00
19 (11/68) 6.00 18.00
20 Double size special (all reprints). (11/69) 4.00 12.00

THUNDER BIRDS
20TH CENTURY FOX (1942)

NO# Movie giveaway (4 pages). From the Cinema Comics Herald series. 16.00 50.00

THUNDERBOLT
CHARLTON (1966-1967)

1 1st & Origin: Thunderbolt. 2.75 10.00
51 Previous title: Son Of Vulcan. 2.25 8.00
52-60 .... 1.50 5.00

THUNDERCATS
MARVEL(STAR) (1985-1988)

1 TV cartoon tie-in. .... .30 1.00
2-24 .... .30 1.00

THUNDERMACE
RAK (1986)

1 .... .75 2.00

THUNDERSTRIKE
MARVEL (1993-1995)

1 Foil cover. Double size. .... .75 2.95
2-7 .... .50 1.25
8-13 .... .50 1.50
13A Double Feature #1 (flip book with Code: Blue #1). .... .75 2.50
14 .... .50 1.50
14A Double Feature #2 (flip book with Code: Blue #2). .... .75 2.50
15 .... .50 1.50
15A Double Feature #3 (flip book with Code: Blue #3). .... .75 2.50
16 .... .50 1.50

16A Double Feature #4 (flip book with Code: Blue #4). .75 2.50
17-24 .50 1.50

TICK, THE
NEW ENGLAND PRESS (1988-1993)
SPECIAL 1 1st: Tick. Limited to 5000 numbered copies. 25.00 80.00
SPECIAL 2 Limited to 3000 numbered copies. 16.00 50.00
1 Reprints Special 1 with minor changes. 13.00 40.00
1 (2ND) 1.50 5.00
2 Reprints Special with minor changes. 8.00 25.00
2 2ND printing 1.25 4.00
2 3RD-5TH printings 1.00 3.00
3 5.00 15.00
4 1st: Paul The Samurai. 1st: Arthur. 4.00 12.00
4 2ND-5TH 1.00 3.00
5-6 2.25 8.00
7 1st: Chairface Chippendale. 2.25 8.00
8 2.25 8.00
8A No logo. 5.00 16.00
9-10 1.25 4.00
11-12 1.00 3.00
TPB 1 Omnibus I. Reprints #1-6. 5.00 13.95
TPB 2 Omnibus II. Reprints #7-10. 4.00 10.95

TICK: KARMA TORNADO!, THE
NEW ENGLAND PRESS (1994)
1 1.00 3.25
2-4 .75 2.75

TICK'S GIANT CIRCUS OF THE MIGHTY, THE
NEW ENGLAND PRESS (1992)
1 1.50 5.00
2 1.25 4.00

TIGER GIRL
GOLD KEY (1968)
10227-809 5.00 16.00

TIGER WALKS, A
GOLD KEY (1964)
10117-406 Disney movie photo cover. 5.00 15.00

TIGRESS
HEROIC (1992-1993)
1-6 .30 1.00

TILLIE THE TOILER
CUPPLES & LEON (1925-1933)
1 (1925) 25.00 80.00
2 25.00 80.00
3 By Russ Westover. Copyright 1932. 25.00 80.00
4-8 25.00 80.00

TILLIE THE TOILER
DELL FOUR COLOR SERIES (1942-1949)
8 50.00 150.00
22 31.00 100.00
55 28.00 90.00
89 25.00 80.00
106 19.00 60.00
132 (1/47) 19.00 60.00
150 17.00 55.00
176 (12/47) 16.00 50.00
184 16.00 50.00
195 13.00 40.00
213 11.00 35.00
237 10.00 30.00

TILLIE THE TOILER
SEE LARGE FEATURE COMICS #30.

TILLY AND TED IN TINKERTOYLAND
W. T. GRANT (1945)
NO# Giveaway. 7.00 20.00

TIM HOLT
ME (1948-1954)
1 (A-1 #14 on cover). Begin: photo covers. 115.00 380.00
2 (A-1 #17 on cover) 70.00 220.00
3 (A-1 #19 on cover) 60.00 190.00
4 Begin photo covers. 40.00 130.00
5-7 29.00 95.00
8-10 26.00 85.00
11 1st & Origin: The Ghost Rider by Dick Ayers. (11/49) 70.00 220.00
12-16 17.00 55.00
17 Ghost Rider cover by Frank Frazetta. "The Cowboy And The Clipper!" 55.00 170.00
18 End photo covers. 17.00 55.00
19 14.00 44.00
20 Origin & Begin: Red Mask. 20.00 65.00
21 Ghost Rider cover by Frazetta. 40.00 130.00
22 14.00 44.00
23 Cover: Frazetta. 35.00 110.00
24 14.00 44.00
25 1st: Black Phantom. 20.00 65.00
26-28 10.00 33.00
29 Photo cover. 10.00 33.00
30-32 10.00 33.00
33 End: Ghost Rider. 10.00 33.00
34 Horror format Ghost Rider. 17.00 55.00
35 Horror Ghost Rider story. 17.00 55.00
36-38 14.00 44.00
39-41 3-D effect. 20.00 65.00

TIM MCCOY
CHARLTON (1948-1949)
16 Retouched photo cover (Red River with John Wayne and Montgomery Clift). 70.00 220.00
17 Guest starring Rocky Lane. 50.00 160.00
18 Retouched movie photo cover (Two-Gun Justice). 50.00 160.00
19 Retouched photo cover. 50.00 160.00
20 "The Bring-Em-Back Kid!" 50.00 160.00
21 Guest starring Johnny Mack Brown. 50.00 160.00

TIM MCCOY, POLICE CAR 17
WHITMAN (1934)
674 Movie tie-in. Oversize, black & white interior. 70.00 220.00

TIM TYLER
BETTER (1942)
1 13.00 40.00

TIM TYLER COWBOY
STANDARD (1948-1950)
11 7.00 20.00
12-15 4.00 12.00

TIMBER WOLF
DC (1992-1993)
1-5 .30 1.00

TIMECOP
DARK HORSE (1994)
1 Movie adaptation. .75 2.50
2 .75 2.50

TIME FOR LOVE
CHARLTON (1966)
V2#53 Previous title: Romantic Secrets. 1.50 5.00

TIME FOR LOVE
CHARLTON (1967-1976)
1 1.50 5.00
2-47 1.00 3.00

TIME MACHINE, THE
DELL FOUR COLOR SERIES (1960)
1085 Movie photo cover. (3/60) 25.00 80.00

TIME MASTER
CONTINUITY (1994)
1-4 .75 2.50

TIME MASTERS
DC (1990)
1-8 .30 1.00

TIME TUNNEL, THE
GOLD KEY (1967)
1 TV photo cover. 8.00 25.00
2 TV photo cover. 7.00 20.00

TIMESPIRITS
MARVEL(EPIC) (1985-1986)
1-8 .30 1.00

TIMESTRYKE
MARVEL (1994)
1-2 .50 1.95

TIMEWALKER
VALIANT (1994-CURRENT)
1-15 .75 2.50
YEARBOOK 1 .75 2.95

TIMMY
DELL FOUR COLOR SERIES (1956-1959)
715 (8/56) 5.00 15.00
823 (8/57) 5.00 15.00
923 (8/58) 5.00 15.00
1022 (8/59) 5.00 15.00

TINY FOLKS FUNNIES
DELL FOUR COLOR SERIES (1944)
60 31.00 100.00

TINY TIM
DELL FOUR COLOR SERIES (1944-1949)
42 40.00 125.00
235 13.00 40.00

TINY TIM
SEE LARGE FEATURE COMICS (SERIES II) #4.

TINY TOT COMICS
EC (1946-1947)
1 55.00 175.00
2 35.00 110.00
3-6 28.00 90.00
7-10 23.00 75.00

TIP TOP COMICS
UNITED FEATURES (1936-1961)
1 1200.00 4400.00
2 300.00 1100.00
3 270.00 875.00
4 220.00 700.00
5 170.00 550.00
6-8 135.00 440.00
9-12 100.00 330.00
13-15 85.00 270.00
16-24 75.00 240.00
25-40 60.00 190.00
41-60 50.00 160.00
61-70 35.00 110.00
71-80 26.00 85.00
81-90 22.00 70.00
91-100 17.00 55.00
101-120 14.00 44.00
121-150 10.00 33.00
151-175 7.00 22.00
176-200 5.00 16.00
201-225 4.00 11.00

TIP TOPPER COMICS
UNITED FEATURES (1949-1954)
1 13.00 40.00
2 7.00 20.00
3-6 4.00 12.00
7-12 2.75 10.00
13-18 2.25 8.00
19-28 1.75 6.00

TIPPIE AND CAP STUBBS
DELL FOUR COLOR SERIES (1949)
210 (1/49) 8.00 25.00
242 (9/49) 10.00 30.00

T-MAN
QUALITY (1951-1956)
1 Art: Jack Cole. 40.00 125.00
2 23.00 75.00
3 19.00 60.00
4-5 Cover & art: Reed Crandall. 23.00 75.00
6-8 16.00 50.00
9-12 13.00 40.00
13-18 10.00 30.00
19-24 8.00 25.00
25 1st Code Approved issue. (5/55) 7.00 20.00
26-30 5.00 15.00
31-38 2.75 10.00

TNT COMICS
CPC (1946)
1 40.00 125.00

TOBY TYLER
DELL FOUR COLOR SERIES (1960)
1092 Disney movie photo cover. (3/60) 19.00 60.00

TOBY TYLER
GOLD KEY (1965)
10142-502 Disney movie photo cover. 7.00 20.00

TODAY'S BRIDES
AJAX/FARRELL (1955-1956)
1 8.00 25.00
2-4 5.00 15.00

TODAY'S ROMANCE
STANDARD (1952)
5 Photo covers on all issues. 8.00 25.00
6-8 5.00 15.00

TOKA
DELL (1964-1967)
1 5.00 15.00
2-6 2.25 8.00
7-10 1.50 5.00

TOM AND JERRY
DELL FOUR COLOR SERIES (1948)
193 "Double Trouble" (7/48) 40.00 125.00

TIM HOLT #17

TIM TYLER COWBOY #15

TIMECOP #1

TIMEWALKER #1

a b c d e f g h i j k l m n o p q r s t u v w x y z

TOM CORBETT SPACE CADET #3

TOM MIX COMICS #5

TOMAHAWK #11

TOMAHAWK #28

FAMOUS · FIRSTS

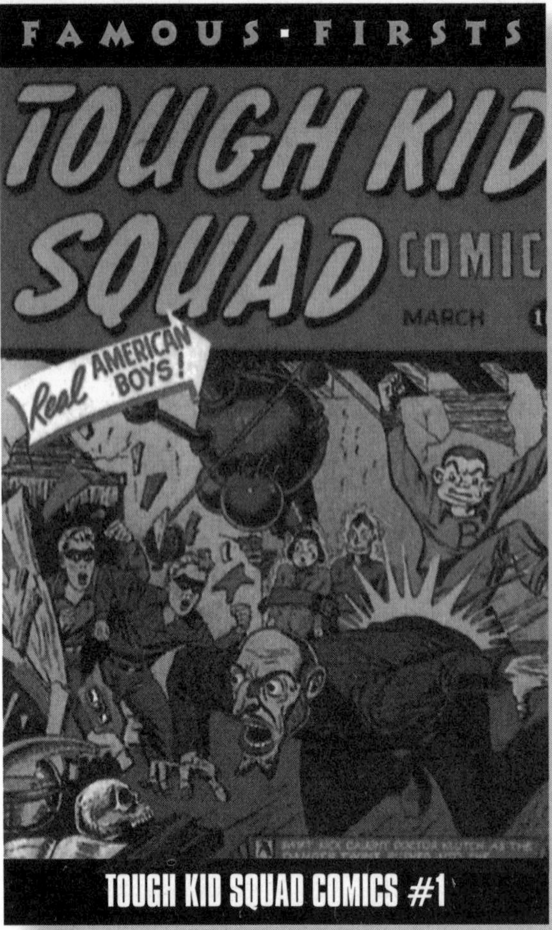

TOUGH KID SQUAD COMICS #1

Hoping for a hit equal to its *Young Allies* from a year earlier, Marvel launched *Tough Kid Squad*. The book features the Danger Twins and their gang, but failed to find an audience and only one issue was published.

TOM AND JERRY
DELL/GOLD KEY (1949-1982)

60 Previous title: Our Gang Comics.	13.00	40.00
61-65	10.00	30.00
66 Christmas cover.	10.00	30.00
67-76	7.00	20.00
77 Christmas cover.	7.00	20.00
78-90	7.00	20.00
91-100	4.00	12.00
101-120	2.75	10.00
121-140	2.25	8.00
141-175	1.75	6.00
176-212	1.25	4.00
213 Begin Gold Key publication.	5.00	15.00
214	5.00	15.00
215-250	1.00	3.00
251-275	.75	2.00
276-344	.30	1.00

TOM AND JERRY PICNIC TIME
DELL (1958)

1 100 page Dell Giant.	23.00	75.00

TOM AND JERRY WINTER CARNIVAL
DELL (1952-1953)

1 Droopy story by Carl Barks.	65.00	200.00
2 Droopy story by Carl Barks.	40.00	125.00

TOM AND JERRY'S BACK TO SCHOOL
DELL (1956)

1 100 page Dell Giant.	23.00	75.00

TOM AND JERRY'S SUMMER FUN
DELL (1954-1957)

1 100 page Dell Giant. Includes Droopy by Carl Barks.	40.00	125.00
2-4 100 page Dell Giant.	19.00	60.00

TOM AND JERRY'S TOY FAIR
DELL (1958)

1 100 page Dell Giant.	31.00	100.00

TOM AND JERRY'S WINTER FUN
DELL (1954-1958)

3 100 page Dell Giant.	25.00	80.00
4 100 page Dell Giant.	19.00	60.00
5 100 page Dell Giant.	19.00	60.00
6-7 100 page Dell Giant.	19.00	60.00

TOM CAT
CHARLTON (1956-1957)

4 Previous title: Bo.	11.00	35.00
5-7	8.00	25.00
8 Title changes to Atom The Cat with #9.	8.00	25.00

TOM CORBETT SPACE CADET
DELL (1952-1954)

1 (#378) From the 4-Color Series. (2/52)	40.00	130.00
2 (#400) From the 4-Color Series. TV tie-in. (5/52)	23.00	75.00
3 (#421) From the 4-Color Series. (8/52)	19.00	60.00
4-6	11.00	35.00
7-11	8.00	25.00

TOM CORBETT SPACE CADET
PRIZE (1955)

V2#1	45.00	140.00
V2#2-V2#3	35.00	110.00

TOM MIX COMICS
RALSTON-PURINA (1940-1942)

1 32 page giveaway, life story of Tom Mix.	300.00	1100.00
2	135.00	440.00
3-6	100.00	330.00
7-9	75.00	240.00
10 Begin title variant: Tom Mix Commandos Comics.	75.00	240.00
11-12	75.00	240.00

TOM MIX WESTERN
FAWCETT (1948-1953)

1 Photo cover.	135.00	440.00
2 Photo cover.	60.00	190.00
3 Retouched photo cover.	40.00	130.00
4 Photo cover.	40.00	130.00
5	40.00	130.00
6 Retouched photo cover.	40.00	130.00
7 Retouched photo cover.	29.00	95.00
8-12	29.00	95.00
13-18	25.00	80.00
19 Photo cover.	29.00	95.00
20-23	20.00	65.00
24 Begin: photo covers.	25.00	80.00
25-30	20.00	65.00
31-40	17.00	55.00
41-50	14.00	44.00
51-61	12.00	38.00

TOM TERRIFIC!
PINES (1957-1958)

1 TV cartoon tie-in.	65.00	210.00
2	45.00	140.00
3 Christmas issue.	35.00	110.00
4-6	29.00	95.00

TOM THUMB
DELL FOUR COLOR SERIES (1959)

972 Movie tie-in. (1/59)	28.00	90.00

TOM TOM THE JUNGLE BOY
ME (1946-1947)

1	11.00	35.00
2 Title changes to The Adventures Of Tom-Tom with #3.	8.00	25.00

TOMAHAWK
DC (1950-1972)

1 (9-10/50)	280.00	900.00
2 Art: Frank Frazetta (4 pages).	140.00	450.00
3 "Warpath!" (1-2/51)	110.00	360.00
4 "The Flying Frontiersman!"	100.00	330.00
5 "The Girl Who Was Chief!"	95.00	300.00
6 "King Of The Aztec Indians?"	95.00	300.00
7 "Voyage Of Fort Flotsam!" (9-10/51)	85.00	270.00
8 "The Mighty Magic Of Tomahawk!"	85.00	270.00
9 "The Traitor!" (1-2/52)	65.00	210.00
10 "Frontier Sabotage!"	65.00	210.00
11 "The Girl Who Hated Tomahawk!"	65.00	210.00
12 "The Man From Magic Mountain!"	65.00	210.00
13 "Dan Hunter's Betrayal!" (9-10/52)	50.00	160.00
14 "The Frontier Tinker!"	50.00	160.00
15 "The Wild-Men Of Wig-Wam Mountain!"	50.00	160.00
16 "The Riddle Of Fort Mystery!" (3-4/53)	50.00	160.00
17 "Castle In The Wilderness!"	50.00	160.00
18 "Bring In M'Sieur Pierre!"	50.00	160.00
19 "Red Man's Revenge!"	40.00	120.00
20 "Pioneer War Correspondent!"	40.00	120.00
21 "The Man With The Cane!" (1/54)	40.00	120.00
22 "Frontier Protection Racket!" (2/54)	40.00	120.00
23 "Tomahawk Runs The Gauntlet!" (3/54)	40.00	120.00
24 "The Adventure Of The Dancing Bear!"	40.00	120.00
25 "The Tenderfoot Frontiersman!"	28.00	90.00
26 "Fort Petticoat!"	28.00	90.00
27 "The Battle Without Weapons!"	28.00	90.00
28 "The Son Of Chief Deer-Trail!"	28.00	90.00
29 Art: Frank Frazetta (3 pages).	40.00	120.00
30	28.00	90.00
31 1st Code Approved issue.	25.00	80.00
32-40	22.00	70.00
41-50	19.00	60.00
51-56	16.00	50.00
57 Art: Frank Frazetta (3 pages).	22.00	70.00
58-60	15.00	48.00
61-77	13.00	42.00
78 1st 12 cent cover price.	11.00	36.00
79-80	10.00	30.00
81 1st: Miss Liberty.	10.00	30.00
82-90	8.00	24.00
91-95	6.00	18.00
96 1st & Origin: The Hood.	8.00	24.00
97-100	6.00	18.00
101-106	4.00	12.00
107 1st & Origin: Thunder-Man.	5.00	14.00
108-110	4.00	12.00
111-120	2.50	9.00
121-130	1.75	6.00
131-138	1.25	4.75
139 Reprint: Star Spangled Comics #113.	1.25	4.75
140	1.25	4.75

TOMB OF DARKNESS
MARVEL (1974-1976)
- 9 Previous title: "Beware." .75 2.00
- 10-23 .75 2.00

TOMB OF DRACULA
MARVEL (1972-1979)
- 1 1st: Dracula. 22.00 70.00
- 2 11.00 35.00
- 3-5 7.00 22.00
- 6-9 7.00 20.00
- 10 1st: Blade The Vampire Slayer. 7.00 20.00
- 11-20 5.00 15.00
- 21-49 2.25 8.00
- 50 App: Silver Surfer. 5.00 15.00
- 51-69 2.00 7.00
- 70 Death: Dracula. Double size. 2.00 7.00

TOMB OF DRACULA
MARVEL (1979-1980) MAGAZINE
- 1 2.25 8.00
- 2 Art: Steve Ditko. 1.50 5.00
- 3-6 1.25 4.00

TOMB OF DRACULA
MARVEL(EPIC) (1991-1992)
- 1-4 1.25 4.95

TOMB OF LIGEIA, THE
DELL (1965)
- 12-830-506 Movie tie-in. 8.00 25.00

TOMB OF TERROR
HARVEY (1952-1954)
- 1 40.00 130.00
- 2-3 19.00 60.00
- 4-6 16.00 50.00
- 7-12 15.00 48.00
- 13-15 All science-fiction issue. 29.00 95.00
- 16 All science-fiction issue. Title changes to Thrills Of Tomorrow with #17. 29.00 95.00

TOMBSTONE TERRITORY
DELL FOUR COLOR SERIES (1960)
- 1123 TV photo cover. (8/60) 19.00 60.00

TOMMY OF THE BIG TOP
KING/STANDARD (1948-1949)
- 10 7.00 20.00
- 11-12 5.00 15.00

TONKA
DELL FOUR COLOR SERIES (1959)
- 966 Movie photo cover (Sal Mineo). (1/59) 16.00 50.00

TONTO, THE LONE RANGER'S COMPANION
DELL (1951-1958)
- 1 (#312) From the 4-Color Series. (1/51) 25.00 80.00
- 2 10.00 30.00
- 3 8.00 25.00
- 4-6 7.00 20.00
- 7-12 5.00 15.00
- 13-18 2.75 10.00
- 19-33 1.75 6.00

TONY TRENT
COLUMBIA (1948)
- 3 Previous title: The Face. 13.00 40.00
- 4 10.00 30.00

TOO MUCH COFFEE MAN
ADHESIVE (1993-CURRENT)
- 1 2.25 8.00
- 1 (2ND) (3/94) .75 2.50
- 2 1.25 4.00
- 3 .75 2.50

TOODLES, THE
ZIFF-DAVIS (1951)
- 10 (7-8/51) 8.00 25.00

TOODLES TWINS, THE
ARGO (1956)
- 1 7.00 20.00

TOOL & DIE
FLASHPOINT (1994)
- 1 .75 2.00

TOONERVILLE TROLLEY
CUPPLES & LEON (1921)
- 1 Cardboard covers. 50.00 150.00

TOOTS AND CASPER
SEE LARGE FEATURE COMICS (SERIES II) #5.

TOP ADVENTURE COMICS
I.W. (1964)
- 1 Reprint. 2.75 10.00
- 2 Reprint. 2.25 8.00

TOP CAT
CHARLTON (1970-1973)
- 1 TV cartoon tie-in. 7.00 22.00
- 2 4.00 13.00
- 3-6 2.25 8.75
- 7-12 1.50 5.50
- 13-20 1.00 3.25

TOP CAT
DELL/GOLD KEY (1961-1970)
- 1 TV cartoon tie-in. 35.00 110.00
- 2 17.00 55.00
- 3 14.00 44.00
- 4-6 10.00 33.00
- 7-12 9.00 27.00
- 13-18 7.00 22.00
- 19-31 5.00 16.00

TOP COMICS
K.K./GOLD KEY (1967)
- 1-4 2.75 10.00

TOP DOG
MARVEL(STAR) (1985-1987)
- 1-14 .20 .50

TOP FLIGHT COMICS
ST. JOHN (1949)
- 1 Hector The Inspector. 10.00 30.00

TOP JUNGLE COMICS
I.W. (1964)
- 1 Reprint. 2.25 8.00

TOP LOVE STORIES
STAR (1951-1954)
- 3 L.B. Cole cover on all issues. 16.00 50.00
- 4-19 13.00 40.00

TOP NOTCH COMICS
MLJ (1939-1944)
- 1 1st & Origin: The Wizard. 700.00 2500.00
- 2 400.00 1200.00
- 3 310.00 1000.00
- 4 230.00 750.00
- 5 190.00 625.00
- 6 155.00 500.00
- 7-8 190.00 625.00
- 9 1st & Origin: The Black Hood. 600.00 2200.00
- 10 270.00 875.00
- 11-12 210.00 675.00
- 13-15 170.00 550.00
- 16-18 140.00 460.00
- 19-24 115.00 370.00
- 25-27 95.00 310.00
- 28 Begin title variant: Top-Notch Laugh Comics. 95.00 310.00
- 29-30 95.00 310.00
- 31-36 80.00 250.00
- 37-44 65.00 200.00
- 45 Title changes to Laugh Comix with #46. 65.00 200.00

TOP SECRET
HILLMAN (1952)
- 1 16.00 50.00

TOP SECRETS
STREET & SMITH (1947-1949)
- 1 Cover & art: Bob Powell. 40.00 130.00
- 2 Cover & art: Bob Powell. 28.00 90.00
- 3-6 Art: Bob Powell. 20.00 65.00
- 7 Cover & art: Bob Powell. 25.00 80.00
- 8-10 Art: Bob Powell. 17.00 55.00

TOP SPOT COMICS
TOP SPOT (1945)
- 1 25.00 80.00

TOPPER AND NEIL
DELL FOUR COLOR SERIES (1957)
- 859 TV tie-in. (11/57) 7.00 20.00

TOPS
LEV GLEASON (1949)
- 1 Jumbo size (.25 cp). 200.00 660.00
- 2 135.00 440.00

TOPS COMICS
CONSOLIDATED BOOK (1944)
- NO# 128 pages. Newspaper strip reprints. 50.00 160.00

TOPS IN ADVENTURE
ZIFF-DAVIS (1952)
- 1 132 pages. 65.00 200.00

TOPSY-TURVY COMICS
R.B. LEFFINGWELL (1945)
- 1 Starring Cookie. 16.00 50.00

TOR
DC (1975-1976)
- 1-6 .30 1.00

TOR
ST. JOHN (1954)
- 3 Previous title: 3-D Comics 16.00 50.00
- 4-5 16.00 50.00

TORCH OF LIBERTY SPECIAL
DARK HORSE (1994)
- 1 One shot. .75 2.50

TORCHY
QUALITY (1949-1950)
- 1 Cover: Bill Ward. 160.00 525.00
- 2 95.00 310.00
- 3 85.00 280.00
- 4 Art: Bill Ward (9 pages). 105.00 340.00
- 5-6 Cover & art: Bill Ward. 115.00 370.00
- 16 Super reprint. (1964) 7.00 23.00

TORMENTED, THE
STERLING (1954)
- 1-2 31.00 100.00

TOTAL WAR
GOLD KEY (1965)
- 1 8.00 25.00
- 2 Title changes to M.A.R.S. Patrol Total War with #3. 7.00 20.00

TOUGH KID SQUAD COMICS
MARVEL(TIMELY) (1942)
- 1 1st & Origin: Tough Kid Squad, The Human Top. 1300.00 5000.00

TOWER OF SHADOWS
MARVEL (1969-1971)
- 1 Art: Jim Steranko. 10.00 33.00
- 2 Art: Neal Adams. 5.00 16.00
- 3 Art: Barry Smith. 4.00 11.00
- 4 1.50 5.50
- 5 Art: Barry Smith. 4.00 11.00
- 6-7 1.50 5.50
- 8-9 Cover: Berni Wrightson. 2.25 8.75
- SPECIAL 1 Art: Neal Adams. 4.00 11.00

TOXIC CRUSADERS
MARVEL (1992)
- 1 TV cartoon tie-in. .30 1.00
- 2-8 .30 1.00

TOY TOWN COMICS
TOYTOWN (1945-1947)
- 1 L.B. Cole cover on all issues. 16.00 50.00
- 2-7 16.00 50.00

TOYBOY
CONTINUITY (1986-1989)
- 1 1st: Jason Kriter. .75 2.00
- 2-7 .75 2.00

TOYLAND COMICS
FICTION HOUSE (1947)
- 1 35.00 110.00
- 2 20.00 65.00
- 3-4 15.00 49.00

TRAIL BLAZERS
STREET & SMITH (1942)
- 1 True stories of American heroes. 35.00 110.00
- 2-4 25.00 80.00

TRAIL COLT (A-1 SERIES)
ME (1949)
- 1 (A-1 #24). Art: Frank Frazetta (7 pages). 50.00 150.00
- 2 (A-1 #26). Art: L.B. Cole (6 pages). 31.00 100.00

TRANSFORMERS, THE
MARVEL (1984-1991)
- 1-80 .30 1.00

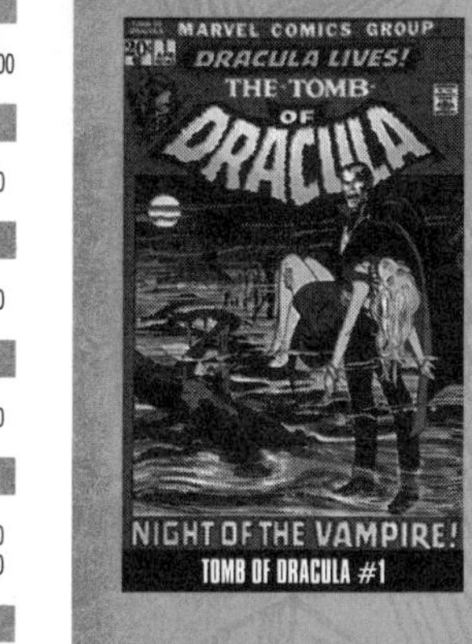

TOMB OF DRACULA #1

TOMB OF TERROR #10

TORCH OF LIBERTY SPECIAL

TRANSFORMERS #8

TRANSFORMERS: GENERATION 2 #1

TREASURE COMICS #5

TRENCHER #2

TRIBE #1 (IMAGE)

TRANSFORMERS: GENERATION 2
MARVEL (1993-1994)
1 Foil stamped cover. Double size. ... .30 1.00
1A Newsstand edition. ... .30 1.00
2-11 ... .30 1.00
12 Double size. ... .30 1.00

TRANSFORMERS: HEADMASTERS, THE
MARVEL (1987-1988)
1-4 ... .30 1.00

TRANSYLVANIA SPECIAL
CONTINUITY (1994)
1-2 ... .75 2.50

TRAPPED!
ACE (1954-1955)
1 ... 8.00 25.00
2-3 ... 5.00 16.00

TRAPPED!
HARVEY (1951)
1 (NO#) Giveaway. Anti-drug message. SOTI
... 2.75 10.00

TRAVELS OF JAIMIE MCPHEETERS, THE
GOLD KEY (1963)
1 ... 5.00 15.00

TREASURE COMICS
PRIZE (1943)
1 324 pages, 50 cent cover price. ... 400.00 1200.00

TREASURE COMICS
PRIZE (1945-1947)
1 ... 31.00 100.00
2 ... 16.00 50.00
3-6 ... 13.00 40.00
7 Art: Frank Frazetta (5 pages). ... 40.00 125.00
8 Art: Frank Frazetta. ... 40.00 125.00
9 ... 13.00 40.00
10 Cover & art: Simon & Kirby. ... 25.00 80.00
11-12 ... 13.00 40.00

TREASURE ISLAND
DELL (1962)
01-845-211 Movie tie-in. ... 10.00 30.00

TREASURE ISLAND
DELL FOUR COLOR SERIES (1955)
624 Disney movie photo cover. (4/55) 7.00 20.00

TREASURE ISLAND
GOLD KEY (1967)
10200-703 Disney movie photo cover. 7.00 20.00

TREASURY OF COMICS, A
ST. JOHN (1948-1949)
1 Over 500 pages. ... 190.00 600.00
2 ... 155.00 500.00

TREASURY OF DOGS, A
DELL (1956)
1 100 page Dell Giant. ... 23.00 75.00

TREASURY OF HORSES, A
DELL (1955)
1 100 page Dell Giant. ... 26.00 85.00

TRENCHER
IMAGE (1993)
1-4 ... .50 1.95

TRIBE
AXIS (1993-1994)
1 ... .75 2.50
2 1st: "Crush" Velvet. ... .75 2.50
3 ... .50 1.95

TRIBE
IMAGE (1993)
1 1st: Tribe. ... .75 2.00
1A Ivory edition. ... 1.50 5.00

TRIGGER TWINS
DC (1973)
1 ... 1.00 3.00

TRIPLE THREAT COMICS
GERONA (1945)
1 Beau Brummell, The Duke Of Darkness, King O'Leary.
... 14.00 45.00

TRIPLE-X
DARK HORSE (1994-1995)
1-7 ... 1.00 3.95

TRIUMPH
DC (1995)
1-4 ... .50 1.75

TROLL
IMAGE (1995)
1 ... .75 2.50

TROLL HALLOWEEN SPECIAL
IMAGE (1994)
1 Maxx. ... .75 2.95

TROLL II
IMAGE (1994)
1 ... 1.00 3.95

TROLL: ONCE A HERO
IMAGE (1994)
1 ... .75 2.50

TROLL STOCKING STUFFER
IMAGE (1994)
1 ... .75 2.95

TROLL THANKSGIVING SPECIAL
IMAGE (1994)
1 ... .75 2.95

TROLLORDS
TRU STUDIOS (1986-1989)
1-30 ... .30 1.00

TROUBLE WITH GIRLS, THE
COMICO/ETERNITY (1989-1990)
1-4 ... .30 1.00
5 Begin Eternity publication. ... .30 1.00
6-10 ... .30 1.00

TROUBLE WITH GIRLS, THE
MALIBU/ETERNITY (1987-1988)
1-6 ... .30 1.00
7 Begin Eternity publication. ... .30 1.00
8-14 ... .30 1.00
ANNUAL 1 (1988) ... .75 2.00

TROUBLE WITH GIRLS, THE
MARVEL (1994)
1 ... .75 2.50
2-4 ... .50 1.95

TROUBLESHOOTERS, THE
DELL FOUR COLOR SERIES (1960)
1108 TV photo cover. (6/60) ... 16.00 50.00

TRUE 3-D
HARVEY (1953-1954)
1 Art: Bob Powell. With glasses. ... 19.00 60.00
2 Art: Bob Powell. With glasses. ... 16.00 50.00

TRUE ADVENTURES
MARVEL (1950)
3 Previous title: True Western. Title changes to Men's Adventures with #4. ... 19.00 60.00

TRUE ANIMAL PICTURE STORIES
PMI (1947)
1-2 ... 10.00 30.00

TRUE AVIATION PICTURE STORIES
PMI (1942-1946)
1 ... 16.00 50.00
2 ... 10.00 30.00
3-6 ... 8.00 25.00
7-12 ... 7.00 20.00
13-15 ... 5.00 15.00

TRUE COMICS
TRUE (1941-1950)
1 ... 40.00 125.00
2 ... 23.00 75.00
3 Baseball Hall Of Fame. ... 28.00 90.00
4 ... 19.00 60.00
5 Joe Louis. ... 19.00 60.00
6 Baseball's World Series. ... 19.00 60.00
7-12 ... 13.00 40.00
13-16 ... 11.00 35.00
17 "The Beloved Bums-Brooklyn's Famous Dodgers"
... 14.00 45.00
18-24 ... 10.00 30.00
25-30 ... 8.00 25.00
31 "Red Grange-The Galloping Ghost" 10.00 30.00
32-40 ... 7.00 20.00
41-50 ... 5.00 15.00
51-54 ... 2.75 10.00
55 1st: Sad Sack. ... 10.00 30.00
56-60 ... 2.75 10.00
61-70 ... 2.00 7.50
71 Joe Di Maggio. ... 8.00 25.00
72 Jackie Robinson. ... 8.00 25.00
73 Walt Disney. ... 7.00 20.00
74-77 ... 2.00 7.50
78 Stan Musial. ... 7.00 20.00
79 ... 2.00 7.50
80-84 Distributed to subscribers only. 13.00 40.00

TRUE COMICS AND ADVENTURE STORIES
PMI (1965)
1 ... 1.50 5.00
2 ... 1.25 4.00

TRUE COMPLETE MYSTERY
MARVEL (1949)
5 Previous title: Complete Mystery. ... 23.00 75.00
6-8 Photo cover. ... 19.00 60.00

TRUE CONFIDENCES
FAWCETT (1949-1950)
1 Photo cover. ... 19.00 60.00
2-4 ... 10.00 30.00

TRUE CRIME CASES
ST. JOHN (1944)
NO# 100 page giant, 25 cent cover price. 70.00 220.00

TRUE CRIME COMICS
MAGAZINE VILLAGE (1947-1949)
2 Cover & art: Jack Cole. SOTI, "Dragging living people to death!" Classic drug story, "Murder, Morphine, And Me!"
... 250.00 800.00
3 Cover & art: Jack Cole. ... 180.00 575.00
4 Cover & art: Jack Cole. SOTI ... 140.00 460.00
5 Cover: Jack Cole. ... 85.00 280.00
6 Cover variant of issue #4. ... 35.00 110.00
V2#1 Partial photo cover. SOTI ... 125.00 400.00

TRUE GEIN
BONEYARD (1993)
1 ... .30 1.00

TRUE LIFE ROMANCE
FARRELL (1955-1956)
1 ... 10.00 30.00
2-3 ... 5.00 15.00

TRUE LIFE SECRETS
CHARLTON (1951-1956)
1 ... 13.00 40.00
2 ... 7.00 20.00
3-6 ... 5.00 15.00
7-12 ... 4.00 12.00
13-18 ... 2.75 10.00
19-29 ... 2.00 7.00

TRUE LIFE TALES
MARVEL (1949-1950)
1 (#8) Photo cover. ... 16.00 50.00
2 Photo cover. ... 16.00 50.00

TRUE LOVE CONFESSIONS
PREMIER (1954-1956)
1 ... 16.00 50.00
2 ... 8.00 25.00
3-11 ... 5.00 15.00

TRUE LOVE PICTORIAL
ST. JOHN (1952-1954)
1 Photo cover. ... 22.00 70.00
2 Cover: Matt Baker. ... 11.00 35.00
3-5 Cover & art: Matt Baker. ... 45.00 140.00
6-8 Cover & art: Matt Baker. ... 17.00 55.00
9 Cover: Matt Baker. ... 14.00 45.00
10-11 Cover & art: Matt Baker. ... 17.00 55.00

TRUE MOVIE AND TELEVISION
TOBY (1950-1951)
1 Photo cover (Elizabeth Taylor). ... 70.00 230.00
2 Photo cover. Art: Frazetta (illustration). 55.00 170.00
3 Photo cover (June Allyson). ... 45.00 140.00
4 Photo cover (Jane Powell). ... 35.00 110.00

TRUE SECRETS
MARVEL(ATLAS) (1950-1956)
3 Previous title: Love Dramas. ... 13.00 40.00
4 (2/51) ... 10.00 30.00
5 ... 7.00 20.00
6 Art: Bill Everett. ... 10.00 30.00
7-12 ... 7.00 20.00
13-21 ... 5.00 15.00
22 Art: Bill Everett. ... 7.00 20.00
23-28 ... 2.75 10.00
29 1st Code Approved issue. ... 2.25 8.00
30-40 ... 2.25 8.00

TRUE SPORT PICTURE STORIES
STREET & SMITH (1942-1949)
5 Joe Di Maggio cover & story. Previous title: Sport Comics. 40.00 120.00
6-12 20.00 65.00
V2#1-V2#6 17.00 55.00
V2#7 Stan Musial cover and story. 17.00 55.00
V2#8-V2#12 17.00 55.00
V3#1-V3#6 14.00 44.00
V3#7 Joe Di Maggio cover and story. 14.00 44.00
V3#8 Joe Louis cover and story. 14.00 44.00
V3#9-V4#9 14.00 44.00
V5#1 "The Satchel Paige story" 14.00 44.00
V5#2 14.00 44.00

TRUE STORIES OF ROMANCE
FAWCETT (1950-1951)
1 Photo cover. 13.00 40.00
2-3 Photo cover. 10.00 30.00

TRUE STORY OF JESSE JAMES, THE
DELL FOUR COLOR SERIES (1957)
757 Movie photo cover. (3/57) 22.00 70.00

TRUE SWEETHEART SECRETS
FAWCETT (1950-1953)
1 Photo covers on all issues. 16.00 50.00
2 Art: Wallace Wood. 23.00 75.00
3-6 13.00 40.00
7-11 10.00 30.00

TRUE TALES OF LOVE
MARVEL(ATLAS) (1956-1957)
22 Previous title: Secret Story Romances. 8.00 25.00
23-31 2.75 10.00

TRUE TO LIFE ROMANCES
STAR (1949-1954)
1 (#8) (11-12/49) 19.00 60.00
2 (#9) (1-2/50) 13.00 40.00
3 Movie photo cover ("The Doctor And The Girl" with Glenn Ford and Janet Leigh). 16.00 50.00
4 13.00 40.00
5 11.00 35.00
6-15 10.00 30.00
16-17 Art: Wallace Wood; Jay Disbrow. 19.00 60.00
18-23 8.00 25.00

TRUE WAR EXPERIENCES
HARVEY (1952)
1 8.00 25.00
2 5.00 15.00
3-4 2.75 10.00

TRUE WAR ROMANCES
QUALITY (1952-1955)
1 Photo cover. 13.00 40.00
2 7.00 20.00
3-6 5.00 15.00
7-20 2.75 10.00
21 1st Code Approved issue. Becomes Exotic Romances #22. 2.75 10.00

TRUE WESTERN
MARVEL (1949-1950)
1 "The True Unbelievable Story Behind Billy The Kid." Photo cover. 25.00 80.00
2 "Badmen Vs. Lawmen." Photo cover (Alan Ladd). Title changes to True Adventures with #3. 25.00 80.00

TRUMP
HMH (1957) MAGAZINE
1 16.00 50.00
2 11.00 35.00

TRUTH ABOUT MOTHER GOOSE, THE
DELL FOUR COLOR SERIES (1957)
862 (11/57) 13.00 40.00

TUBBY
DELL (1952-1961)
1 (#381) From the 4-Color Series. "Captain Yo-Yo" (3/52) 25.00 80.00
2 (#430) From the 4-Color Series. "The Shadow Of A Man-Eater" (10/52) 17.00 55.00
3 (#444) From the 4-Color Series. (1/53) 17.00 55.00
4 (#461) From the 4-Color Series. (4/53) 16.00 50.00
5 6.00 17.00
6-12 4.00 12.00
13-20 2.25 8.50
21-30 1.75 6.75
31-40 1.50 5.00
41-49 1.00 3.25

TUBBY AND THE LITTLE MEN FROM MARS
GOLD KEY (1964)
30020-410 64 page Giant-size. 10.00 30.00

TUFF GHOSTS
HARVEY (1962-1972)
1 Starring Spooky. 13.00 40.00
2-6 7.00 20.00
7-24 2.75 10.00
25-39 1.75 6.00
40-42 4.00 12.00
43 1.75 6.00

TUFFY
STANDARD (1949-1950)
5 7.00 20.00
6-9 4.00 12.00

TUROK, DINOSAUR HUNTER
VALIANT (1993-CURRENT)
0 .75 2.50
1 Special chromium foil cover. 1.00 3.00
1A Gold edition. 2.75 10.00
2-28 .75 2.50
29-30 1.00 3.00
31-34 .75 2.50
YEARBOOK 1 (1994) 1.00 3.95
YEARBOOK 2 .75 2.95

TUROK: SHAMAN'S TEARS
ACCLAIM/VALIANT (1995)
1-3 .75 2.50

TUROK SON OF STONE
DELL/GOLD KEY (1954-1982)
1 (#596) 1st & Origin: Turok. From the 4-Color Series. (12/54) 190.00 600.00
2 (#656) From the 4-Color Series. (10/55) 95.00 300.00
3 (3-5/56) 55.00 175.00
4-6 55.00 175.00
7-12 35.00 110.00
13-18 25.00 80.00
19-24 19.00 60.00
25-29 16.00 50.00
30 Begin Gold Key publication. 16.00 50.00
31-40 16.00 50.00
41-45 10.00 30.00
46-60 8.00 25.00
61-70 6.00 18.00
71-84 4.00 12.00
85-130 1.75 6.00

TUROK, SON OF STONE
GOLD KEY (1966)
30031-611 64 page giant-size issue (with either slick or paper covers). 19.00 60.00

TURTLE SOUP
MIRAGE (1987)
1 Teenage Mutant Ninja Turtles. 1.00 3.00

TV CASPER AND COMPANY
HARVEY (1963-1974)
1 Begin: 64 page giant-size, 25 cent cover price. 13.00 40.00
2-6 7.00 20.00
7-20 2.75 10.00
21-30 1.75 6.00
31 End: giant-size issues. 1.75 6.00
32-46 1.25 4.00

TV SCREEN CARTOONS
DC (1959-1961)
129 Previous title: Real Screen Comics. 17.00 55.00
130-138 14.00 46.00

TV STARS
MARVEL (1978-1979)
1-4 1.75 6.00

TV TEENS
CHARLTON (1954-1956)
1 (#14) 10.00 30.00
2 (#15) 7.00 20.00
3-13 5.00 15.00

TWEETY AND SYLVESTER
DELL (1952-1962)
1 (#406) From the 4-Color Series. (6/52) 16.00 50.00
2 (#489) From the 4-Color Series. (8/53) 7.00 22.00
3 (#524) From the 4-Color Series. (12/53) 8.00 25.00
4-37 2.25 8.00

TWEETY AND SYLVESTER
GOLD KEY (1963-1984)
1 2.25 8.00
2-30 1.25 4.00
31-60 .30 1.00
61-120 .20 .50

TWENTY THOUSAND LEAGUES UNDER THE SEA
DELL FOUR COLOR SERIES (1955)
614 Disney movie tie-in (2/55). 13.00 40.00

20,000 LEAGUES UNDER THE SEA
GOLD KEY (1963)
10095-312 Disney movie tie-in. 7.00 20.00

TWICE TOLD TALES
DELL (1964)
12-840-401 Movie photo cover (Vincent Price). 8.00 25.00

TWILIGHT ZONE, THE
DELL FOUR COLOR SERIES (1961-1962)
1173 TV tie-in. (3/61) 55.00 175.00
1288 TV tie-in. 31.00 100.00

TWILIGHT ZONE
GOLD KEY (1962-1982)
1 TV tie-in. 20.00 65.00
2 10.00 33.00
3-6 9.00 27.00
7-12 7.00 22.00
13-18 5.00 16.00
19-24 4.00 11.00
25-30 2.00 7.50
31-40 1.50 5.50
41-60 1.00 3.25
61-80 .75 2.00
81-92 .30 1.00

TWILIGHT ZONE
NOW (1991-1992)
1 .75 2.25
1A Prestige format. (4.95 cp) 1.50 5.50
1B Gold logo. (2.50 cp) 2.75 10.00
2-8 .50 1.95
9 3-D Special. (2.95 cp) .50 1.95
10-14 .50 1.95

TWILIGHT ZONE
NOW (1993)
1-4 .75 2.50

TWILIGHT ZONE (ONE SHOT)
NOW (1990)
1 Prestige format. (2.95 cp) 2.50 9.00
1A Newsstand edition (1.75 cp). 2.25 8.00

TWILIGHT ZONE 3-D WINTER SPECIAL
NOW
1 One shot. .75 2.95

TWILIGHT ZONE ANNIVERSARY SPECIAL
NOW (1992)
1 One shot. .75 2.50

TWILIGHT ZONE COMPUTER SPECIAL
NOW
1 Newsstand version of #2 (1993 series) with computer generated cover. .75 2.50

TWILIGHT ZONE SCIENCE FICTION SPECIAL
NOW
1 1.00 3.50

TWINKLE COMICS
SPOTLIGHT (1945)
1 25.00 80.00

TWISTED TALES
PACIFIC (1982-1984)
1-10 .30 1.00

TWO BIT THE WACKY WOODPECKER
TOBY (1952-1953)
1 16.00 50.00
2-3 8.00 25.00

TWO FACES COMMUNISM
CHRISTIAN ANTI-COMMUNISM CRUSADE (1961)
NO# Giveaway. 8.00 25.00

TWO-FISTED TALES
EC (1950-1955)
18 170.00 550.00

TRIUMPH #3

TROLL #1

TUBBY #8

TUROK DINOSAUR HUNTER #10

TWO-FISTED TALES ANNUAL 1952

TWO-GUN KID #55

TYRANT #2

ULTRAVERSE YEAR ZERO: DEATH OF THE SQUAD #4

FAMOUS · FIRSTS

UNCLE SCROOGE #1

"Only A Poor Old Man" launched Donald Duck's Uncle Scrooge into his own series of highly popular adventures. Originally in the Four Color series, Uncle Scrooge began its own numbering with #4, after *Four Color* #386, #456 and #495.

19 .... 125.00 410.00
20 .... 100.00 330.00
21 .... 85.00 270.00
22 .... 75.00 240.00
23 .... 70.00 220.00
24 .... 60.00 190.00
25 .... 50.00 160.00
26 .... 40.00 130.00
27-30 .... 35.00 110.00
31-32 .... 26.00 85.00
33 "Atom Bomb!" by Wallace Wood. 35.00 110.00
34-41 .... 23.00 75.00

TWO-FISTED TALES
EC(COCHRAN) (1992-1994)
1-3 .... .50 1.50
4-8 .... .75 2.00
9 Reprints. .... .75 2.00
ANNUAL 1 Reprint: 1st 5 issues. 2.25 8.95

TWO-FISTED TALES ANNUAL
EC (1952-1953)
1952 128 pages, 25 cent cover price. 170.00 550.00
1953 128 pages, 25 cent cover price. 135.00 440.00

TWO-GUN KID
MARVEL(ATLAS) (1948-1977)
1 "Hot Lead For Killer's Roost!" 170.00 550.00
2 .... 85.00 270.00
3 .... 70.00 220.00
4 .... 55.00 170.00
5 .... 50.00 160.00
6-12 .... 40.00 130.00
13-18 .... 35.00 110.00
19-24 .... 26.00 85.00
25-30 .... 20.00 65.00
31-40 .... 15.00 49.00
41-50 .... 12.00 38.00
51-59 .... 9.00 27.00
60 1st 12 cent cover price. 7.00 22.00
61-70 .... 5.00 16.00
71-80 .... 4.00 11.00
81-92 .... 2.25 8.75
93 Begin: reprints. 1st 15 cent cover price. 1.25 4.25
94-100 .... 1.00 3.25
101-110 .... .75 2.00
111-136 .... .30 1.00

TWO-GUN WESTERN
MARVEL(ATLAS) (1950-1952)
5 1st & Origin: Apache Kid. 26.00 85.00
6 .... 17.00 55.00
7-9 .... 14.00 44.00
10-14 .... 10.00 33.00

TWO-GUN WESTERN
MARVEL(ATLAS) (1956-1957)
4 Art: Steve Ditko 20.00 65.00
5 .... 17.00 55.00
6-8 .... 14.00 44.00
9-12 .... 10.00 33.00

TWO MOUSEKETEERS, THE
DELL FOUR COLOR SERIES (1953-1955)
475 (6/53) 14.00 45.00
603 (11/54) 7.00 20.00
642 (8/55) 7.00 20.00

TWO ON A GUILLOTINE
DELL (1965)
12-850-506 Movie tie-in. 7.00 20.00

TYRANT
SPIDERBABY GRAFIX (1994-CURRENT)
1-3 .... .75 2.95
3 (GOLD) 10.00 30.00
4-5 .... .75 2.95

UFO & OUTER SPACE
GOLD KEY (1978-1980)
14 Previous title: UFO Flying Saucers. ... .50 1.50
15-25 .... .50 1.50

UFO ENCOUNTERS
WESTERN (1978)
11192-11404 Giant size. 1.00 3.00

UFO FLYING SAUCERS
GOLD KEY (1968-1977)
2 (#1) 2.75 10.00
3 .... 1.50 5.00
4-6 .... 1.00 3.00
7-13 .... .75 2.00
30035-810 (10/68) 2.75 10.00

UFO MYSTERIES
WESTERN (1978)
11400-11404 Giant size. .... .75 2.00

ULTIMATE FACTOR X, THE
MARVEL (1995)
TPB Reprints issues #1-4 of Factor X. Gold etched cover. 2.25 8.95

ULTIMATE GAMBIT AND THE X-TERNALS, THE
MARVEL (1995)
TPB Reprints #1-4 of Gambit and the X-Ternals. Gold etched cover. 2.25 8.95

ULTIMATE GENERATION NEXT, THE
MARVEL (1995)
TPB Reprints issues #1-4 of Generation Next. 2.25 8.95

ULTRAFORCE
MALIBU (1994-1995)
0 Reprints both Wizard giveaways. ...... .75 2.50
0A With Wizard #35. .... .75 2.50
0B With Wizard #36. .... .75 2.50
1 Double size. .... .75 2.50
1 (GOLD) Hologram cover. 2.75 10.00
1A Newsstand version (variant cover). 1.50 5.00
2-5 .... .50 1.95
6-10 .... .75 2.50
ASHCAN .... .20 .75

ULTRAFORCE/AVENGERS
MALIBU/MARVEL (1995)
PRELUDE .... .75 2.50

ULTRAMAN
HARVEY (1993)
1 All issues also come in newsstand versions ($1.75). .... .75 2.50
2-3 .... .75 2.50

ULTRAVERSE YEAR ONE
MALIBU (1994)
0 Incentive/anthology book. 1.75 6.00
1 Double-size handbook. 1.25 4.95
2 .... .50 1.95

ULTRAVERSE YEAR ZERO: DEATH OF THE SQUAD
MALIBU (1995)
1-4 .... .75 2.95
SPECIAL 1 Double Feature. 1.00 3.95

ULTRAVERSE/MARVEL DREAM TEAM
MARVEL/MALIBU (1995)
1 .... 1.25 4.95

U.N. FORCE
GAUNTLET (1992-1993)
1-5 .... .30 1.00

UNCANNY TALES
MARVEL (1973-1975)
1-12 .... .75 2.50

UNCANNY TALES
MARVEL(ATLAS) (1952-1957)
1 .... 110.00 360.00
2 .... 55.00 180.00
3-6 .... 50.00 150.00
7-12 .... 40.00 120.00
13-18 .... 31.00 100.00
19-28 .... 28.00 90.00
29 1st Code Approved issue. 23.00 75.00
30-40 .... 19.00 60.00
41-56 .... 15.00 48.00

UNCANNY X-MEN
- SEE X-MEN

UNCANNY X-MEN AT THE STATE FAIR OF TEXAS, THE
MARVEL (1983)
NO# One-shot giveaway. 8.00 25.00

UNCANNY X-MEN IN DAYS OF FUTURE PAST, THE
MARVEL (1989)
NO# Squarebound (3.95 cp). 1.00 3.95

UNCENSORED MOUSE, THE
ETERNITY (1989)
1 Early Gottfredson strip reprints of Mickey Mouse. 1.50 5.00
2 Early Gottfredson strip reprints. 1.75 6.00

UNCLE CHARLIE'S FABLES
LEV GLEASON (1952)
1 10.00 30.00
2-5 7.00 20.00

UNCLE JOE'S FUNNIES
CENTAUR (1938)
1 Cover: Bill Everett. 115.00 375.00

UNCLE MILTY
TRUE CROSS (1950-1951)
1 TV tie-in, Milton Berle photo insert. 95.00 300.00
2 Photo insert (Milton Berle). 65.00 200.00
3-4 50.00 150.00

UNCLE SAM QUARTERLY
QUALITY (1941-1943)
1 Cover: Fine/Eisner. Origin: Uncle Sam. 500.00 1600.00
2 Cover & art: Lou Fine. 250.00 800.00
3 155.00 500.00
4-7 115.00 370.00
8 Title changes to Blackhawk Comics with #9. 115.00 370.00

UNCLE SCROOGE
DELL/GOLD KEY/GLADSTONE (1952-CURRENT)
1 (#386) From the 4-Color Series. "Only A Poor Old Man" (3/52) 230.00 750.00
2 (#456) From the 4-Color Series. "Back To The Klondike" (3/53) 130.00 425.00
3 (#495) From the 4-Color Series. (9/53) 95.00 300.00
4 50.00 150.00
5-7 31.00 100.00
8-10 25.00 80.00
11-18 19.00 60.00
19-30 14.00 45.00
31-39 11.00 35.00
40 Begin: Gold Key publication. 11.00 35.00
41-50 11.00 35.00
51-75 8.00 25.00
76-90 5.00 15.00
91-110 4.00 12.00
111-120 2.50 9.00
121-150 1.75 6.00
151-200 1.00 3.00
201-209 .75 2.00
210 Begin: Gladstone publication. .75 2.00
211-218 .75 2.00
219 "Son of the Sun" by Don Rosa. 2.25 8.00
220-287 .50 1.50

UNCLE SCROOGE ADVENTURES
GLADSTONE (1987-CURRENT)
1-30 .50 1.50

UNCLE SCROOGE AND DONALD DUCK
GOLD KEY (1965)
1 Reprints: "Only A Poor Old Man" from #1 (4-color #386). 11.00 35.00

UNCLE SCROOGE GOES TO DISNEYLAND
DELL (1957)
1 100 page Dell Giant. 50.00 150.00

UNCLE WIGGILY
DELL FOUR COLOR SERIES (1948-1954)
179 (1/48) 40.00 120.00
221 (3/49) 22.00 70.00
276 (5/50) 16.00 50.00
320 (3/51) 14.00 45.00
349 (9/51) 14.00 45.00
391 (4/52) 10.00 30.00
428 (10/52) 10.00 30.00
503 (10/53) 11.00 35.00
543 (3/54) 10.00 30.00

UNDERCOVER GIRL
SEE STARR FLAGG, UNDERCOVER GIRL

UNDERDOG
CHARLTON (1970-1972)
1 TV cartoon tie-in. 14.00 46.00
2 7.00 23.00
3-6 6.00 17.00
7-10 4.00 13.00

UNDERDOG
GOLD KEY (1975-1979)
1 TV cartoon tie-in. 11.00 34.00
2 6.00 17.00
3-6 4.00 11.00
7-12 1.75 6.75
13-23 1.25 4.50

UNDERDOG
SPOTLIGHT (1987)
1-3 .30 1.00

UNDERDOG SUMMER SPECIAL
HARVEY (1993)
1 64 pages. .75 2.25

UNDERSEA AGENT
TOWER (1966-1967)
1 14.00 44.00
2 9.00 27.00
3-6 7.00 22.00

UNDERSEA FIGHTING COMMANDOS
SEE FIGHTING UNDERSEA COMMANDOS

UNDERWATER
DRAWN & QUARTERLY (1994-CURRENT)
1-3 .75 2.95

UNDERWATER CITY, THE
DELL FOUR COLOR SERIES (1962)
1328 Movie photo cover. 19.00 60.00

UNDERWORLD
D.S. (1948-1949)
1 50.00 160.00
2 60.00 190.00
3 40.00 130.00
4 35.00 110.00
5 26.00 85.00
6-9 20.00 65.00

UNDERWORLD CRIME
FAWCETT (1952-1953)
1 35.00 110.00
2 25.00 80.00
3-6 20.00 65.00
7 17.00 55.00

UNDERWORLD STORY, THE
AVON (1950)
NO# Movie tie-in. 55.00 170.00

UNEARTHLY SPECTACULARS
HARVEY (1965-1967)
1 App: Tiger Boy and Company. 8.00 25.00
2-3 Starring Jack Q Frost. 7.00 20.00

UNEXPECTED, THE
DC (1968-1982)
105 Previous title: Tales Of The Unexpected. 5.00 16.00
106-113 4.00 11.00
114 1st 15 cent cover price. (8-9/69) 1.75 6.50
115-131 1.75 6.50
132-136 1.25 4.50
137-156 1.00 3.00
157-162 100 page issue. 1.75 6.00
163-188 .75 2.00
189 Begin 64 pages issues (1.00 cp). 1.00 3.00
190-194 1.00 3.00
195 End: $1.00 cover price issues. 1.00 3.00
196-223 .30 1.00

UNION
IMAGE/WILDSTORM (1993-1994)
0 Origin: Regent. .75 2.50
0A Variant cover. 2.50 9.00
1 1st: Union. .75 2.50
2-4 .50 1.95

UNION II
IMAGE/WILDSTORM (1995-CURRENT)
1-3 .75 2.50
4 Comes with 2 cards. .75 2.50
4A Newsstand edition (no cards). .50 1.95
5-6 .75 2.50

UNITED COMICS
UNITED FEATURES (1950-1953)
8 2.75 10.00
9-26 1.50 5.00

UNITED STATES FIGHTING AIR FORCE
SUPERIOR (1952-1956)
1 5.00 15.00
2 2.75 10.00
3-10 1.75 6.00
11-29 1.25 4.00

UNITED STATES MARINES, THE
TOBY (1943-1953)
NO# 8.00 25.00
2 5.00 15.00
3-4 2.75 10.00
5A From the A-1 series (#55). 2.75 10.00
6A From the A-1 series (#60). 2.75 10.00
7 2.75 10.00
7A From the A-1 series (#68). 2.75 10.00
8 2.75 10.00
8A From the A-1 series (#72). 2.75 10.00
9-11 2.75 10.00

UNITY
VALIANT (1992)
0 Unity pt.1. Giveaway. 1.00 3.00
0A Red bar version. 2.75 10.00
0B Gold bar version. 2.75 10.00
1 Epilogue: Unity. 1.00 3.00
1A Platinum cover. 2.75 10.00
1B Gold cover. 1.50 5.00
TPB 1 4.00 10.95
TPB 2-TPB 3 2.50 9.95
TPB 4 2.50 9.95

UNITY: THE LOST CHAPTERS
ACCLAIM/VALIANT (1994)
1 Double size. 1.00 3.95

UNIVERSAL PRESENTS DRACULA - THE MUMMY & OTHER STORIES
DELL (1963)
02-530-311 Giant size. 40.00 125.00

UNIVERSAL SOLDIER
NOW (1992)
1 Movie tie-in. Hologram cover. (Newsstand versions exist on all issues @ 1.95). .75 2.50
2-3 .75 2.50

UNKNOWN MAN, THE
AVON (1951)
NO# Movie tie-in. 50.00 160.00

UNKNOWN SOLDIER
DC (1977-1982)
205 Previous title: Star Spangled War Stories. .30 1.00
206-268 .30 1.00

UNKNOWN WORLD
FAWCETT (1952)
1 Cover: Norman Saunders. Becomes Strange Stories From Another World #2. 60.00 190.00

UNKNOWN WORLDS
ACG (1960-1967)
1 40.00 130.00
2 Dinosaurs. 22.00 70.00
3-8 15.00 49.00
9 Dinosaurs. 20.00 65.00
10-11 15.00 49.00
12 1st 12 cent cover price. 10.00 33.00
13-19 9.00 27.00
20-30 6.00 19.00
31-40 4.00 13.00
41-48 4.00 11.00
49-50 Art: Steve Ditko. 7.00 22.00
51-57 4.00 11.00

UNKNOWN WORLDS OF SCIENCE FICTION
MARVEL (1975-1976) MAGAZINE
1 1.50 5.00
2-6 1.25 4.00
SPECIAL 1 (1976) 1.25 4.00

UNLEASHED
TRIUMPHANT (1993)
0 .30 1.00

UNSANE
STAR (1954)
15 Cover: L.B. Cole. 31.00 100.00

UNSEEN
STANDARD (1952-1954)
5 45.00 140.00

UNION #0 VARIANT

UNION #4

UNITY #0

UNKNOWN WORLD #1

VALOR #17

VAMPIRELLA #69

VAMPIRELLA #73

VANGUARD #6

6-8 .... 31.00 100.00
9-12 .... 22.00 70.00
13-15 .... 17.00 55.00

UNTAMED
MARVEL (1993)
1 Embossed cover. .... .75 2.50
2-3 .... .50 1.95

UNTAMED LOVE
QUALITY (1950)
1 .... 40.00 130.00
2 Begin: photo covers. 20.00 65.00
3-5 .... 17.00 55.00

UNTOLD LEGEND OF THE BATMAN, THE
DC (1980)
1 Origin retold: Batman. Art: John Byrne. 1.75 6.00
2-3 .... 1.75 6.00

UNTOLD TALES OF SPIDER-MAN
MARVEL (1995-CURRENT)
1 .... .30 1.00

UNTOUCHABLES, THE
DELL (1962)
01-879-207 TV photo cover. 16.00 50.00
12-879-210 TV photo cover. 13.00 40.00

UNTOUCHABLES, THE
DELL FOUR COLOR SERIES (1961-1962)
1237 TV photo cover. (10/61) 28.00 90.00
1286 TV photo cover. (1/62) 28.00 90.00

UNUSUAL TALES
CHARLTON (1955-1965)
1 .... 40.00 120.00
2 .... 19.00 60.00
3-5 .... 15.00 48.00
6 Cover: Steve Ditko. 19.00 60.00
7-10 Cover & art: Steve Ditko. 40.00 120.00
11 Cover & art: Steve Ditko. 64 pages (double size).
.... 50.00 150.00
12 Art: Steve Ditko. 28.00 90.00
13 .... 11.00 36.00
14 Art: Steve Ditko. 28.00 90.00
15 Cover & art: Steve Ditko. 29.00 95.00
16-21 .... 8.00 24.00
22-23 Art: Steve Ditko. 19.00 60.00
24 .... 8.00 24.00
25-27 Art: Steve Ditko. 19.00 60.00
28 .... 8.00 24.00
29 Art: Steve Ditko. 19.00 60.00
30-49 .... 6.00 18.00

URTH 4
CONTINUITY (1990)
1-4 .... .75 2.00

U.S.AGENT
MARVEL (1993)
1-4 .... .30 1.00

U.S. BORDER PATROL COMICS
HOLYOKE (1944-1945)
5 From the Holyoke One-Shot series. ... 16.00 50.00

U.S. JONES
FOX (1941-1942)
1 .... 220.00 700.00
2 .... 160.00 525.00

U.S. PARATROOPS
AVON (1951-1952)
1 "Behind Enemy Lines!" 16.00 50.00
2 "Airborne Operation Killer!" 13.00 40.00
3 "Attack On Suchon Pass!" 10.00 30.00
4 "Airborne Assault On Gensan!" 10.00 30.00
5 "Destruction At Kumjom" 10.00 30.00
6 "Surprise Attack!" 10.00 30.00

U.S. TANK COMMANDOS
AVON (1952-1953)
1 .... 10.00 30.00
2 .... 5.00 15.00
3-4 .... 2.75 10.00

U.S.A. COMICS
MARVEL(TIMELY) (1941-1945)
1 Cover: Jack Kirby & Joe Simon. Rockman by Basil Wolverton. (8/41) 1600.00 6000.00
2 Begin: Captain Terror. Rockman by Basil Wolverton. (11/41)
.... 700.00 2500.00
3 (1/42) 500.00 1800.00
4 (7/42) 400.00 1500.00
5 Intro: Victory Boys. (Summer/42) 400.00 1200.00
6 Begin: Captain America. (12/42) 400.00 1500.00
7 (3/43) 300.00 1100.00
8 (5/43) 310.00 1000.00
9 (7/43) 250.00 800.00
10 (9/43) 190.00 625.00
11 (1/44) 190.00 625.00
12 (Spring/44) 190.00 625.00
13 (Summer/44) 155.00 500.00
14 (Fall/44) 155.00 500.00
15 (Spring/45) 155.00 500.00
16 (Summer/45) 155.00 500.00
17 (Fall/45) 155.00 500.00

U.S.A. IS READY!
DELL (1941)
1 One shot, 68 pages. 50.00 150.00

USAGI YOJIMBO
FANTAGRAPHICS (1987-CURRENT)
1 .... .75 2.00
2-35 .... .50 1.50
SPECIAL 1 (11/89) .... .75 2.00

USAGI YOJIMBO
MIRAGE (1993)
1-5 .... .75 2.75

USAGI YOJIMBO SUMMER SPECIAL
FANTAGRAPHICS (1986)
1 .... 1.00 3.00

UTTERLY STRANGE STORIES
UTTERLY STRANGE (1991)
1 One Shot. 6.00 18.00

V COMICS
FOX (1942)
1 .... 220.00 700.00
2 .... 160.00 525.00

VACATION COMICS (A-1 SERIES)
ME (1948)
1 (A-1 #16). 7.00 20.00

VACATION IN DISNEYLAND
DELL (1958)
1 100 page Dell Giant. 23.00 75.00

VACATION IN DISNEYLAND
DELL FOUR COLOR SERIES (1959)
1025 Art: Carl Barks. (8/59) 23.00 75.00

VACATION IN DISNEYLAND
GOLD KEY (1965)
30024-508 .... 4.00 12.00

VACATION PARADE
DELL (1950-1954)
1 Dell Giant. Art: Carl Barks. 190.00 600.00
2 Dell Giant. 31.00 100.00
3-5 Dell Giant. 19.00 60.00

VALERIA, THE SHE-BAT
ACCLAIM/WINDJAMMER (1995)
1 Reprints first Continuity series. .... .75 2.50
2 .... .75 2.50

VALERIA, THE SHE-BAT
CONTINUITY (1993-1994)
1 Art: Neal Adams. 1.00 3.00
1 (GOLD) 2.75 10.00
2-4 .... .75 2.50
5 Rise Of Magic. .... .75 2.50

VALLEY OF GWANGI, THE
DELL (1969)
01-880-912 Movie tie-in. 7.00 20.00

VALLEY OF THE DINOSAURS
CHARLTON (1975-1976)
1 TV cartoon tie-in. 1.50 5.50
2-6 .... 1.00 3.25
7-11 .... .75 2.00

VALOR
DC (1992-1994)
1-22 .... .50 1.25
23 .... 1.00 3.00

VALOR
EC (1955)
1 Cover & art: Wallace Wood. 40.00 130.00
2 Cover & art: Al Williamson. 35.00 110.00
3 .... 26.00 85.00
4 Cover: Wallace Wood. 35.00 110.00
5 Cover & art: Wallace Wood. 35.00 110.00

VAMPIRE COMPANION, THE
INNOVATION (1991)
1 .... 1.00 3.00
2-4 .... .75 2.50

VAMPIRE LESTAT, THE
INNOVATION (1990-1991)
1 .... 13.00 42.00
2 .... 7.00 21.00
3-5 .... 5.00 14.00
6-9 .... 4.00 11.00
10 .... 2.25 8.25
11-12 .... 2.00 7.00

VAMPIRE TALES
MARVEL (1973-1975) MAGAZINE
1 Begin: Morbius (1st solo Morbius series). 8.00 25.00
2 .... 4.00 12.00
3-4 .... 2.25 8.00
5 Origin: Morbius. 2.00 7.00
6-8 .... 1.50 5.00
9-11 .... 1.25 4.00
ANNUAL 1 (1975) 1.00 3.00

VAMPIRELLA
HARRIS (1992-1993)
0 (12/94) 1.50 5.00
1 .... 11.00 36.00
1 (2ND) 2nd printing. 4.00 12.00
2 .... 13.00 40.00
3 .... 5.00 15.00
4 .... 2.50 9.00
5 .... 1.75 6.00
TPB Black & white. 4.00 12.95

VAMPIRELLA
WARREN (1969-1988)
1 1st & Origin: Vampirella. Cover: Frazetta.
.... 95.00 300.00
2 Begin: Amazonia. 25.00 80.00
3 Scarcer. 65.00 200.00
4-6 .... 17.00 55.00
7 Cover: Frank Frazetta. 23.00 75.00
8 .... 23.00 75.00
9 Art: Barry Smith. 16.00 50.00
10 No Vampirella story. 6.00 18.00
11 1st & Origin: Pendragon. 11.00 35.00
12 .... 11.00 35.00
13-18 .... 8.00 24.00
19 (1973 Annual) 10.00 30.00
20-24 .... 8.00 24.00
25-26 .... 6.00 18.00
27 (1974 Annual) 8.00 25.00
28-30 .... 7.00 20.00
31 Cover: Frazetta. 7.00 20.00
32-36 .... 7.00 20.00
37 (1975 Annual) 8.00 25.00
38-40 .... 7.00 20.00
41-45 .... 5.00 15.00
46 Origin retold: Vampirella. 5.00 15.00
47-54 .... 5.00 15.00
55 Cover art from #36. .... 5.00 15.00
56-66 .... 5.00 15.00
67 Photo cover. 5.00 15.00
68 .... 5.00 15.00
69 Photo cover. 5.00 15.00
70 .... 5.00 15.00
71 Photo cover. 5.00 15.00
72-73 .... 5.00 15.00
74 Photo cover. 5.00 15.00
75 .... 5.00 15.00
76 Photo cover. 5.00 15.00
77-86 .... 5.00 15.00
87 Cover art from #52. .... 5.00 15.00
88-97 .... 5.00 15.00
98 Cover art from #53. .... 5.00 15.00
99 .... 5.00 15.00
100 92 page special. 7.00 20.00
101-110 .... 2.75 10.00
111 Giant Collector's Edition. 5.00 15.00
112 .... 2.75 10.00
113 Published by Harris. Scarce. 10.00 30.00
SPECIAL 1 (1977) 7.00 20.00

VAMPIRELLA ANNUAL
WARREN (1972)
1 New origin: Vampirella. 50.00 160.00

VAMPIRELLA CLASSIC
HARRIS (1995-CURRENT)
1-3 .... .75 2.95

VAMPIRELLA: MORNING IN AMERICA
DARK HORSE/HARRIS (1991-1992)
1-4 .... 1.25 4.50
TPB Limited edition. 11.00 35.00

VAMPIRELLA VS. THE CULT OF CHAOS
HARRIS (1993)
TPB Reprints Warren tales. ... 4.00 12.95

VAMPIRELLA/SHADOWHAWK: CREATURES OF THE NIGHT
HARRIS/IMAGE (1995)
1 Second issue listed as Shadowhawk/Vampirella. ... 1.25 4.95

VAMPS
DC (1994)
1 ... 1.25 4.00
2 ... .75 2.50
3-6 ... .75 2.25

VANGUARD
IMAGE (1993-1994)
1-6 ... .50 1.95

VANGUARD
MEGATON (1987)
1 Cover: Erik Larsen. ... 1.25 4.00

VANGUARD ILLUSTRATED
PACIFIC (1983-1984)
1-6 ... .50 1.50
7 1st: Mr. Monster. ... 1.75 6.00

VARIETY COMICS
FOX (1946-1950)
NO# Giant size (132 pages). (1946) 70.00 220.00
1 (1950) 128 pages. ... 60.00 190.00

VARIETY COMICS
RURAL HOME (1944-1946)
1 Origin: Captain Valiant. ... 29.00 95.00
2 ... 17.00 55.00
3 ... 12.00 38.00

VARSITY
PMI (1945)
1 ... 8.00 25.00

VAULT OF EVIL
MARVEL (1973-1975)
1 ... 1.75 6.00
2 ... 1.25 4.00
3-23 ... .75 2.50

VAULT OF HORROR, THE
EC (1950-1955)
12 Previous title: War Against Crime. 1000.00 3600.00
13 ... 220.00 700.00
14 ... 210.00 675.00
15 "Horror House!" ... 190.00 600.00
16 ... 145.00 480.00
17 ... 115.00 380.00
18 ... 100.00 320.00
19 ... 95.00 300.00
20-24 ... 75.00 240.00
25-30 ... 65.00 210.00
31-35 ... 55.00 180.00
36 "Pipe Dream" classic drug abuse story. 60.00 190.00
37 1st: Drusila (Vampirella prototype). 65.00 210.00
38-39 ... 55.00 180.00
40 Scarcer. ... 65.00 210.00

VAULT OF HORROR, THE
EC(COCHRAN) (1992-1994)
1 Reprints EC originals. ... .75 2.00
2-9 ... .75 2.00
ANNUAL 1 Reprint: 1st 5 issues. ... 2.25 8.95

VAULT OF HORROR
GLADSTONE (1990-1991)
1 Reprints EC originals: Vault Of Horror #34 & Haunt Of Fear #1. ... 1.00 3.00
2 Reprint: Vault Of Horror #27 & Haunt Of Fear #18. ... 1.00 3.00
3 Reprint: Haunt Of Fear #22 & Vault Of Horror #13 (1950). ... 1.00 3.00
4 Reprint: Vault Of Horror #23 & Haunt Of Fear #13 (1952). ... 1.00 3.00
5 Reprint: Vault Of Horror #19 & Weird Fantasy #8. ... 1.00 3.00
6 Reprint: Vault Of Horror #32 & Weird Fantasy #6. ... 1.00 3.00

VENGEANCE OF VAMPIRELLA
HARRIS (1994-CURRENT)
1 Red foil cover. ... 8.00 25.00
1A Gold edition. ... 14.00 45.00
1 (2ND) 2nd printing. ... 2.50 9.00
2 ... 5.00 15.00
3 ... 2.75 10.00
4 ... 2.25 8.00
5-7 ... 1.75 6.00
8 ... 2.00 7.00
9-10 ... 1.75 6.00
11-14 ... 1.00 3.50
15-16 ... .75 2.95

VENGEANCE SQUAD
CHARLTON (1975-1976)
1 ... 1.00 3.00
2-6 ... .75 2.00

VENOM: CARNAGE UNLEASHED
MARVEL (1995)
1-4 ... .75 2.95

VENOM: FUNERAL PYRE
MARVEL (1993)
1 Holo-grafix foil cover. ... .75 2.95
2-3 ... .75 2.95

VENOM: LETHAL PROTECTOR
MARVEL (1993)
1 Holografix cover ($2.95 cp). ... 1.50 5.00
1 (BLACK) Counterfeit. No value.
1 (GOLD) ... 8.00 25.00
2-6 ... 1.00 3.00
TPB Reprints issues #1-6. ... 5.00 15.95

VENOM: NIGHTS OF VENGEANCE
MARVEL (1994)
1 Foil stamped cover. ... .75 2.95
2-4 ... .75 2.95

VENOM: SEPARATION ANXIETY
MARVEL (1994-1995)
1-4 ... .75 2.95

VENOM: SINNER TAKES ALL
MARVEL (1995)
1 ... .75 2.95

VENOM SUPER SIZE SPECIAL
MARVEL (1995)
1 Flip book (Planet Of The Symbiotes, pt.3). 1.00 3.95

VENOM: THE ENEMY WITHIN
MARVEL (1994)
1-3 ... .75 2.95

VENOM: THE MACE
MARVEL (1994)
1 1st: Mace. ... .75 2.95
2-3 ... .75 2.95

VENOM: THE MADNESS
MARVEL (1993-1994)
1 Embossed cover. ... .75 2.95
2-3 ... .75 2.95

VENUS
MARVEL(ATLAS) (1948-1952)
1 1st & begin: Venus. ... 190.00 600.00
2 ... 95.00 300.00
3-6 ... 75.00 240.00
7-9 ... 65.00 210.00
10 Begin: Science Fiction stories. ... 110.00 360.00
11 Classic "The End Of The World!" cover & story. ... 110.00 360.00
12 ... 95.00 300.00
13 Begin: Venus by Bill Everett. ... 110.00 360.00
14-19 ... 110.00 360.00

VEROTIK
VEROTIK (1995-CURRENT)
1 ... 5.00 ... 15.00
2 ... 3.00 ... 10.00
3 ... 2.00 ... 6.00

VERTIGO JAM
DC (1993)
1 Sampler of Vertigo titles. ... 1.00 3.95

VERTIGO RAVE
DC (1994)
1 ... .30 1.00

VERTIGO VISIONS: DR. OCCULT
DC (1994)
1 ... 1.00 3.95

VERTIGO VISIONS: PHANTOM STRANGER
DC (1993)
1 ... 1.00 3.50

VERTIGO VISIONS: PREZ
DC (1995)
1 ... 1.00 3.95

VERTIGO VISIONS: THE GEEK
DC (1993)
1 Brother Power. ... 1.00 3.95

VERY BEST SURE FIRE COMICS
HOLYOKE (1945)
1 App: Captain Aero, Miss Victory. ... 70.00 230.00

VERY BEST SURE SHOT COMICS
HOLYOKE (1945)
1 Same cover art as Very Best Sure Fire Comics #1. Captain Aero, Miss Victory. ... 70.00 230.00

VIC FLINT
ARGO (1956)
1-2 ... 5.00 15.00

VIC FLINT
ST. JOHN (1948-1949)
1 ... 10.00 30.00
2-5 ... 7.00 20.00

VIC JORDAN
CIVIL SERVICE (1945)
1 Reprint: Newspaper strip. ... 13.00 40.00

VIC TORRY AND HIS FLYING SAUCER
FAWCETT (1951)
NO# Photo cover. One-shot. ... 85.00 270.00

VICKI
ATLAS SEABOARD (1975)
1 ... 1.00 3.00
2-4 ... .75 2.00

VICKY COMICS
ACE (1948-1949)
1 (NO#) (10/48) ... 2.75 10.00
2 (#4) (12/48) ... 2.75 10.00
3 (NO#) (2/49) ... 2.75 10.00
4 (4/49) ... 2.75 10.00
5 (6/49) ... 2.75 10.00

VICTORY
TOPPS (1994)
1 ... .75 2.50
1A Variant cover (Rob Liefeld). ... .75 2.50
2-5 ... .75 2.50

VICTORY COMICS
HILLMAN (1941)
1 Begin & Origin: Conqueror by Bill Everett. ... 400.00 1200.00
2 Cover & art: Bill Everett. ... 210.00 675.00
3-4 ... 140.00 460.00

VIDEO JACK
MARVEL (1987-1988)
1-6 ... .30 1.00

VIETNAM JOURNAL
APPLE (1987-1989)
1-11 ... .30 1.00

VIGILANTE
DC (1983-1988)
1-50 ... .30 1.00

VIGILANTES, THE
DELL FOUR COLOR SERIES (1957)
839 Movie tie-in. (9/57) ... 16.00 50.00

VIKINGS, THE
DELL FOUR COLOR SERIES (1958)
910 Movie photo cover (Kirk Douglas). (6/58) ... 23.00 75.00

VINTAGE MAGNUS
VALIANT (1992)
1-4 ... .75 2.00

VIOLATOR
IMAGE (1994)
1-3 ... .50 1.95

VIOLATOR VS. BADROCK
IMAGE (1995)
1-4 ... .75 2.50

VIPER
DC (1994)
1 TV tie-in. ... .50 1.95
2-3 ... .50 1.95

VIRGINIAN, THE
GOLD KEY (1963)
10060-306 TV photo cover. ... 9.00 28.00

VIRTUAL REALITY ZONE
GALAXINOVELS (1993)
1 Polybagged with poster & card. ... 1.00 3.95

VENOM: LETHAL PROTECTOR #1 GOLD

VENOM: LETHAL PROTECTOR #4

VERTIGO VISIONS: THE GEEK #1

VIOLATOR #1

VIRUS #2

VISION & SCARLET WITCH #1 (2ND SERIES)

VISITOR, THE #5

WANTED COMICS #12

WAR AGAINST CRIME! #11

This issue holds the honor of being the first by EC Publications to sport a horror cover, featuring the genre EC would exploit so successfully with its later titles *Vault of Horror* and *Tales From the Crypt*.

VIRUS
DARK HORSE (1993)
1-4 .... .75 2.50

VISION, THE
MARVEL (1994)
1-4 .... .50 1.75

VISION AND THE SCARLET WITCH, THE
MARVEL (1982-1983)
1-4 .... .30 1.00

VISION AND THE SCARLET WITCH, THE
MARVEL (1985-1986)
1-12 .... .30 1.00

VISIONS
VISION (1979-1983) FANZINE
1 1st & begin: Flaming Carrot. 31.00 100.00
2-3 .... 7.00 20.00
4 App: Flaming Carrot. 10.00 30.00
5 Cameo: Flaming Carrot. 5.00 15.00

VISITOR, THE
ACCLAIM/VALIANT (1994-1995)
1-13 .... .75 2.50

VOODA
AJAX (1955)
20 Cover & art: Matt Baker. Previous title: Voodoo.
.... 45.00 140.00
21-22 Art: Matt Baker. 35.00 110.00

VOODOO
AJAX (1952-1955)
1 Reprint: "South Sea Girl" by Matt Baker. 70.00 230.00
2 .... 55.00 170.00
3 .... 35.00 110.00
4-6 .... 28.00 90.00
7-12 .... 25.00 80.00
13-18 .... 22.00 70.00
19 Bondage cover. Becomes Vooda with #20.
.... 22.00 70.00
ANNUAL 1 100 pages, 25 cent cover price. (1952)
.... 105.00 340.00

VOODOO/ZEALOT: SKIN TRADE
IMAGE (1995)
1 .... 1.25 4.95

VORTEX
HALL OF HEROES (1993-1994)
1 1st work by Matt Martin. 7.00 20.00
2 .... 2.75 10.00
3-6 .... 1.00 3.00

VORTEX
VORTEX (1982-1988)
1 Art: Peter Hsu. 1.50 5.00
2 1st: Mister X. .... .75 2.00
3-11 .... .50 1.50
12 Art: Sam Kieth. .... .50 1.50
13-15 .... .50 1.50

VOYAGE TO THE BOTTOM OF THE SEA
DELL FOUR COLOR SERIES (1961)
1230 Movie photo (insert) cover. ... 22.00 70.00

VOYAGE TO THE BOTTOM OF THE SEA
GOLD KEY (1964-1970)
1 (10133-412) TV tie-in. 13.00 40.00
2 .... 10.00 30.00
3-6 .... 8.00 25.00
7-14 .... 7.00 20.00
15-16 Reprints. 2.75 10.00

VOYAGE TO THE DEEP
DELL (1962-1963)
1 .... 8.00 25.00
2-4 .... 5.00 15.00

WACKY DUCK COMICS
MARVEL (1946-1948)
3 (1946) Previous title: Dopey Duck Comics.
.... 20.00 65.00
4 .... 20.00 65.00
5 .... 10.00 33.00
6 (1947) 10.00 33.00
1 (8/48) 14.00 44.00
2 (10/48) 10.00 33.00

WACKY WITCH
GOLD KEY (1971-1975)
1 .... 2.75 10.00
2-10 .... 1.50 5.00
11-21 .... 1.00 3.00

WAGON TRAIN
DELL (1958-1962)
1 (#895) From the 4-Color Series. TV photo cover. (3/58)
.... 23.00 75.00
2 (#971) From the 4-Color Series. TV photo cover. (2/59)
.... 13.00 40.00
3 (#1019) From the 4-Color Series. TV photo cover. (8/59)
.... 11.00 35.00
4 TV photo covers on all issues. 8.00 25.00
5-6 .... 8.00 25.00
7-13 .... 7.00 20.00

WAGON TRAIN
GOLD KEY (1964)
1 TV photo covers on all issues. 8.00 25.00
2 .... 7.00 20.00
3-4 .... 4.00 12.00

WALLACE WOOD SKETCHBOOK
MATADOR (1970)
NO# Features sketches and art by Wallace Wood.
.... 31.00 100.00

WALT DISNEY COMIC DIGEST
GOLD KEY (1968-1976)
1-57 .... 1.00 3.00

WALT DISNEY PRESENTS
DELL (1959-1961)
1 (#997) From the 4-Color Series. "The Nine Lives Of Elfego Baca." TV photo covers on all issues. (6/59)
.... 11.00 35.00
2 .... 8.00 25.00
3-6 .... 6.00 18.00

WALT DISNEY SHOWCASE
GOLD KEY (1970-1980)
1 The Boatniks. Movie photo cover. ... 4.00 13.00
2 Moby Duck. 2.00 7.50
3 Bongo & Lumpjaw. 1.75 6.50
4 Pluto. 1.75 6.50
5 $1,000,000 Duck. Movie photo cover. 2.50 9.75
6 Bedknobs & Broomsticks. Movie tie-in. 2.50 9.75
7 Pluto. 1.75 6.50
8 Daisy And Donald. 1.75 6.50
9 101 Dalmatians. Movie tie-in. 2.00 7.50
10 Napoleon And Samantha. Movie photo cover.
.... 2.50 9.75
11 Moby Duck. 1.50 5.50
12 Dumbo. Movie tie-in. 1.75 6.50
13 Pluto. 1.50 5.50
14 The World's Greatest Athlete. Movie photo cover.
.... 2.50 9.75
15 The 3 Little Pigs. 1.75 6.50
16 Aristocats. Movie tie-in. 2.50 9.75
17 Mary Poppins. Movie photo cover. 2.50 9.75
18 Gyro Gearloose. 2.50 9.75
19 That Darn Cat. Movie photo cover. 2.50 9.75
20 Pluto. 1.75 6.50
21 Li'l Bad Wolf And The Three Little Pigs. 1.50 5.50
22 Alice In Wonderland Unbirthday Party. 2.00 7.50
23 Pluto. 1.75 6.50
24 Herbie Rides Again. Movie photo cover. 1.75 6.50
25 Old Yeller. Movie tie-in. 1.75 6.50
26 Lt. Robin Crusoe, USN. Movie photo cover.
.... 1.75 6.50
27 Island At The Top Of The World. Movie photo cover.
.... 2.00 7.50
28 Brer Rabbit, Bucky Bug. 1.75 6.50
29 Escape To Witch Mountain. Movie photo cover.
.... 2.00 7.50
30 Magica De Spell. 4.00 13.00
31 Bambi. Movie tie-in. 2.00 7.50
32 Spin And Marty. TV photo cover. ... 2.50 9.75
33 Pluto. 1.50 5.50
34 Paul Revere's Ride. TV tie-in. 1.50 5.50
35 Goofy. 1.50 5.50

36 Peter Pan. 1.50 5.50
37 Tinker Bell And Jiminy Cricket. 1.50 5.50
38 Mickey And The Sleuth (pt.1). 1.50 5.50
39 Mickey And The Sleuth (pt.2). 1.50 5.50
40 The Rescuers. Movie tie-in. 1.50 5.50
41 Herbie Goes To Monte Carlo. Movie photo cover. 1.75 6.50
42 Mickey And The Sleuth. 1.50 5.50
43 Pete's Dragon. Movie photo cover. 2.00 7.50
44 Return From Witch Mountain/In Search Of The Castaways. Movie(s) photo cover. 2.00 7.50
45 The Jungle Book. Movie tie-in. 2.00 7.50
46 The Cat From Outer Space/The Shaggy Dog. Movie(s) photo cover. 1.50 5.50
47 Mickey Mouse Surprise Party. 1.50 5.50
48 The Wonderful Adventures Of Pinocchio. 1.50 5.50
49 North Avenue Irregulars/Zorro. Movie(s) photo cover. 1.25 4.25
50 Bedknobs And Broomsticks/Mooncussers. Movie & TV photo cover. 1.25 4.25
51 101 Dalmations. Movie tie-in. 1.25 4.25
52 Unidentified Flying Oddball. Movie tie-in. 1.25 4.25
53 The Scarecrow. TV tie-in. 1.25 4.25
54 The Black Hole. Movie photo cover. 1.25 4.25

WALT DISNEY'S COMICS AND STORIES
DELL/GOLD KEY/GLADSTONE (1940-1986)

1 3300.00 13000.00
2 600.00 2200.00
3 300.00 975.00
4 230.00 750.00
4A Complimentary issue. 300.00 1100.00
5 170.00 550.00
6 135.00 440.00
7-12 115.00 380.00
13-24 85.00 270.00
25-30 70.00 220.00
31 Begin: Donald Duck by Carl Barks. 500.00 1900.00
32 300.00 975.00
33 200.00 650.00
34 170.00 550.00
35-36 135.00 440.00
37 Donald Duck not by Barks. 40.00 130.00
38-40 100.00 330.00
41-50 70.00 220.00
51-60 40.00 130.00
61-70 23.00 75.00
71-80 17.00 55.00
81-90 14.00 44.00
91-97 10.00 33.00
98 1st: Uncle Scrooge (in Walt Disney's Comics and Stories). 23.00 75.00
99-110 9.00 27.00
111-112 7.00 22.00
113 No Barks art. 2.25 8.75
114 7.00 22.00
115-116 No Barks art. 2.25 8.75
117 7.00 22.00
118-123 No Barks art. 2.25 8.75
124-130 7.00 22.00
131-150 5.00 16.00
151-200 4.00 11.00
201-250 2.25 8.75
251-263 1.75 6.50
264 Begin: Gold Key publication. 1.75 6.50
265-283 1.75 6.50
284-300 1.50 5.50
301-400 1.25 4.25
401-473 1.00 3.25
474 Begin: Whitman publication. .75 2.00
475-510 .75 2.00
511 Begin: Gladstone publication. .50 1.50
512-547 .50 1.50
548-595 .30 1.00

WALT DISNEY'S SLEEPING BEAUTY
DELL (1959)

1 100 page giant. 40.00 120.00

WAMBI, JUNGLE BOY
FICTION HOUSE (1942-1953)

1 85.00 270.00
2 40.00 130.00
3 (Spring/43) 35.00 110.00
4 (Fall/48) 20.00 65.00
5 17.00 55.00
6-8 14.00 44.00
9-18 10.00 33.00

WANDERERS
DC (1988-1989)

1-13 .30 1.00

WANDERING STAR
PEN AND INK (1993-CURRENT)

1 1st: Casandra Andrews. 10.00 30.00
1 2nd printing. 1.00 3.00
1 3rd printing. 1.00 3.00
2 2.75 10.00
3-7 1.00 3.00
8-9 .75 2.50

WANTED COMICS
TOYTOWN (1947-1953)

9 13.00 40.00
10-11 7.00 20.00
12 SOTI 13.00 40.00
13-17 7.00 20.00
18 "Satan's Cigarettes!" drug story. 22.00 70.00
19-24 7.00 20.00
25-38 5.00 15.00
39 "The Horror Weed!" drug story. 14.00 45.00
40-49 5.00 15.00
50 Begin: Horror stories. 16.00 50.00
51 16.00 50.00
52 End: Horror stories. 16.00 50.00
53 2.75 10.00

WANTED: DEAD OR ALIVE
DELL FOUR COLOR SERIES (1960-1961)

1102 TV photo cover (Steve McQueen). (5/60) 16.00 50.00
1164 TV photo cover (Steve McQueen). (5/61) 16.00 50.00

WANTED, THE WORLD'S MOST DANGEROUS VILLAINS
DC (1972-1973)

1 1.50 5.00
2 Reprint: Batman #25. 2.25 8.00
3-9 .75 2.00

WAR
CHARLTON (1975-1976)

1-48 .30 1.00

WAR, THE
MARVEL (1989-1990)

1-4 .75 2.00

WAR ACTION
MARVEL(ATLAS) (1952-1953)

1 23.00 75.00
2 13.00 40.00
3-14 8.00 25.00

WAR ADVENTURES
MARVEL(ATLAS) (1952-1953)

1 23.00 75.00
2 13.00 40.00
3-13 8.00 25.00

WAR AGAINST CRIME!
EC (1948-1950)

1 145.00 480.00
2 75.00 240.00
3 65.00 210.00
4-6 60.00 190.00
7-9 50.00 150.00
10 1st: Vault Keeper; Vault Of Horror. 400.00 1400.00
11 1st: Horror cover. 2nd: Vault Keeper. Becomes The Vault Of Horror. 250.00 825.00

WAR AND ATTACK
CHARLTON (1964-1967)

1 (1964) 2.75 10.00
54 (1966) 1.50 5.00
55-63 1.25 4.00

WAR BATTLES
HARVEY (1952-1953)

1 Art: Bob Powell. 10.00 30.00
2-3 Art: Bob Powell. 7.00 20.00
4-6 2.75 10.00
7 Art: Bob Powell. 5.00 15.00
8-9 2.75 10.00

WAR BIRDS
FICTION HOUSE (1952-1953)

1 20.00 65.00
2 15.00 49.00
3 12.00 38.00

WAR COMBAT
MARVEL(ATLAS) (1952)

1 19.00 60.00
2 10.00 30.00
3-5 7.00 20.00

WAR COMICS
DELL (1940-1941)

1 50.00 160.00
2 35.00 110.00
3 25.00 80.00
4 Title changes to War Stories with #5. 25.00 80.00

WAR COMICS
MARVEL(ATLAS) (1950-1957)

1 31.00 100.00
2 16.00 50.00
3-6 11.00 35.00
7-12 8.00 25.00
13-24 7.00 20.00
25-36 5.00 15.00
37-49 2.75 10.00

WAR DANCER
DEFIANT (1994)

1 1st: War Dancer. .75 2.50
2-3 .75 2.50
4 1.00 3.25
5-7 .75 2.50

WAR DOGS OF THE U.S. ARMY
AVON (1952)

1 16.00 50.00

WAR FURY
COMIC MEDIA (1952-1953)

1 Cover & art: Don Heck in all issues. 8.00 25.00
2-4 5.00 15.00

WAR GODS OF THE DEEP
DELL (1965)

12-900-509 Movie photo cover (Vincent Price). 7.00 20.00

WAR HEROES
ACE (1952-1953)

1 10.00 30.00
2 7.00 20.00
3-8 5.00 15.00

WAR HEROES
DELL (1942-1945)

1 31.00 100.00
2 16.00 50.00
3-5 13.00 40.00
6-11 10.00 30.00

WAR IS HELL
MARVEL (1973-1975)

1 .75 2.00
2-15 .30 1.00

WAR MACHINE
MARVEL (1994-CURRENT)

1 Foil embossed cover. .75 2.95
1A Newsstand version. .75 2.00
1B Ashcan edition. .20 .75
2-7 .50 1.50
8 Neon ink cover, polybagged with insert & acetate print. .75 2.95
8A Regular cover (no insert & print). .50 1.50
9-14 .50 1.50
15 Flip book with War Machine/U.S. Agent/Hawkeye mini series. .75 2.50
16-18 .50 1.50

WAR MAN
MARVEL (1993)

1 1st: Griffin. .75 2.50
2-3 .75 2.50

WAR OF THE GODS
DC (1991)

1-4 .30 1.00

WAR PARTY
LIGHTNING (1994)

1 1st: Deathmark. .75 2.95
2 .75 2.95

WAR REPORT
AJAX (1952-1953)

1 8.00 25.00
2-5 5.00 15.00

WAR STORIES
AJAX (1952-1953)

1 8.00 25.00
2-5 5.00 15.00

WAR STORIES
DELL (1942-1943)

5 Previous title: War Comics. 23.00 75.00
6-8 23.00 75.00

WAR VICTORY ADVENTURES
HARVEY (1942-1943)

1 (...COMICS) 5 cent cover price. 70.00 230.00
2 35.00 110.00
3 26.00 85.00

WAR DANCER #1

WAR FURY #3

WAR HEROES #7

WAR MACHINE #7

WARLOCK #9

WATCHMEN #2

WEAPON X #4

WEB OF SPIDER-MAN #100

WAR WAGON, THE
DELL (1967)
12-533-709 Movie photo cover (John Wayne). ... 22.00 70.00

WARBLADE: ENDANGERED SPECIES
IMAGE (1995)
1 ... .75 2.95
2-4 ... .75 2.50

WARCHILD
MAXIMUM PRESS (1994-1995)
0 (8/95) ... .75 2.50
1-4 ... .75 2.50

WARFRONT
HARVEY (1951-1967)
1 ... 10.00 30.00
2 ... 7.00 20.00
3-12 ... 5.00 15.00
13-24 ... 2.75 10.00
25-39 ... 1.75 6.00

WARHEADS
MARVEL (1992-1993)
1 ... .75 2.50
2-14 ... .50 1.75

WARLOCK
MARVEL (1972-1976)
1 ... 10.00 30.00
2-8 ... 2.75 10.00
9 Begin: Jim Starlin covers & art. 2nd: Thanos saga by Starlin continued from Strange Tales #181. ... 2.75 10.00
10 ... 7.00 20.00
11 ... 5.00 15.00
12-14 ... 2.25 8.00
15 ... 7.00 20.00

WARLOCK
MARVEL (1992)
1-6 ... .75 2.50

WARLOCK 5
AIRCEL (1986-1989)
1-22 ... .30 1.00

WARLOCK AND THE INFINITY WATCH
MARVEL (1992-1995)
1 ... 1.50 5.00
2 ... 1.00 3.00
3-6 ... .75 2.50
7-24 ... .50 1.50
25 Double size. ... .75 2.95
26-42 ... .50 1.50

WARLOCK CHRONICLES, THE
MARVEL (1993-1994)
1 Holo-grafic foil cover. ... .75 2.95
2-8 ... .75 2.00

WARLOCK SPECIAL EDITION
MARVEL (1982-1983)
1 Reprints: Thanos saga by Starlin. ... 2.00 7.00
2-6 ... 2.00 7.00

WARLORD
DC (1976-1989)
1 See First Issue Special #8 for origin & 1st app ... 5.00 15.00
2 ... 2.25 8.00
3 ... 1.75 6.00
4-10 ... 1.50 5.00
11-20 ... 1.25 4.00
21-41 ... 1.00 3.00
42-130 ... .75 2.00
131 1st DC work by Rob Liefeld. ... 1.00 3.00
132-133 ... .75 2.00
ANNUAL 1 (1982) ... .75 2.00
ANNUAL 2 (1983) ... .75 2.00
ANNUAL 3 (1984) ... .75 2.00
ANNUAL 4 (1985) ... .75 2.00
ANNUAL 5 (1986) ... .75 2.00

WARLORD
DC (1992)
1-6 ... .30 1.00

WARP
FIRST (1983-1985)
1-19 ... .30 1.00

WARPATH
KEY (1954-1955)
1 ... 10.00 30.00
2-3 ... 5.00 15.00

WARRIOR COMICS
H.C. BLACKERBY (1944)
1 Reprint: early DC stories. ... 50.00 150.00

WARRIOR NUN AREALA
ANTARCTIC PRESS (1994-1995)
1 1st: Warrior Nun Areala. ... 5.00 15.00
1 (2ND) 2nd printing. ... .75 2.95
1A Platinum version. ... 8.00 25.00
2 ... 2.25 8.00
3 ... 1.00 3.50
3A Polybagged with CD. ... 2.75 10.00

WARRIORS OF PLASM
DEFIANT (1993-1994)
0 Diamond Previews insert. ... 1.25 4.00
1 ... 1.00 3.00
2-3 ... .75 2.75
4 ... .75 2.95
5-14 ... .75 2.50

WARRIORS OF THE SHADOW REALM
SEE MARVEL COMICS SUPER SPECIAL #11-13.

WARSTRIKE
MALIBU (1994-1995)
1 ... .50 1.95
1A Silver foil cover. ... 2.75 10.00
2-7 ... .50 1.95

WARSTRIKE: PRELUDE TO GODWHEEL
MALIBU (1994)
1 One shot. ... .75 2.50

WARTIME ROMANCES
ST. JOHN (1951-1953)
1 Art: Matt Baker in all issues. ... 31.00 100.00
2-4 ... 16.00 50.00
5-12 ... 13.00 40.00
13-18 ... 10.00 30.00

WASH TUBBS
DELL FOUR COLOR SERIES (1942-1944)
11 ... 70.00 225.00
28 ... 50.00 150.00
53 ... 40.00 125.00

WASHABLE JONES AND THE SHMOO
TOBY (1953)
1 ... 35.00 110.00

WATCHMEN
DC (1986-1987)
1 ... 2.00 7.00
2 ... 1.25 4.00
3-12 ... 1.00 3.50
PORTFOLIO 1987. Signed and numbered. Edition limited to 2000. 12 color and duo-tone prints in a slipcase. ... 31.00 100.00
TPB Reprints issues #1-12. ... 6.00 16.95

WATER BIRDS AND THE OLYMPIC ELK
DELL FOUR COLOR SERIES (1956)
700 Disney movie tie-in. (4/56) ... 11.00 35.00

WEAPON X
MARVEL (1995)
TPB The Ultimate Weapon X. Reprints issues #1-4. ... 2.25 8.95
1 Deluxe edition. Previous title: Wolverine. 1.50 5.50
1 (2ND) 2nd printing. ... .50 1.95
2 ... 1.25 4.00
3-4 ... 1.00 3.00

WEAPON ZERO
IMAGE (1995)
T-1 #4. ... .75 2.50
T-2 #3. ... .75 2.50
T-3 #2. ... .75 2.50
T-4 #1 1st: Weapon Zero. ... .75 2.50

WEB, THE
DC(IMPACT) (1991-1992)
1-14 ... .30 1.00
ANNUAL 1 (1992) ... .75 2.50

WEB OF EVIL
QUALITY (1952-1954)
1 Begin: Jack Cole art. SOTI ... 80.00 250.00
2 ... 55.00 170.00
3 ... 40.00 130.00
4-11 ... 35.00 110.00
12-21 ... 26.00 85.00

WEB OF HORROR
MWM (1969-1970) MAGAZINE
1 Begin: Berni Wrightson. ... 13.00 40.00
2 ... 8.00 25.00
3 Cover & art: Berni Wrightson. ... 10.00 30.00

WEB OF MYSTERY
ACE (1951-1955)
1 ... 50.00 150.00
2 ... 25.00 80.00
3-6 ... 23.00 75.00
7-12 ... 20.00 65.00
13-27 ... 17.00 55.00
28-29 ... 14.00 44.00

WEB OF SPIDER-MAN
MARVEL (1985-CURRENT)
1 ...vs. Alien costume. ... 7.00 20.00
2 ... 3.00 10.00
3-8 ... 2.00 7.50
9-10 ... 2.00 7.00
11-15 ... 1.50 5.50
16-28 ... 1.50 5.00
29 Wolverine. ... 5.00 15.00
30 ... 4.00 13.00
31-32 ... 2.75 10.00
33-36 ... 1.25 4.50
37 ... 1.00 3.75
38 ... 1.75 6.00
39-47 ... 1.25 4.00
48 Origin: Hobgoblin II. ... 4.00 12.00
49 ... 1.25 4.00
50 Double size. ... 1.50 5.00
51-58 ... 1.00 3.00
59 Cosmic Spidey, Acts Of Vengeance. ... 2.25 8.00
60-61 Cosmic Spidey. ... 1.75 6.00
62-68 ... .75 2.50
69 ... 2.00 7.00
70 ... .75 2.50
71-85 ... .75 2.00
86 ... 1.00 3.00
87-89 ... .75 2.00
90 Hologram cover. ... 1.75 6.50
90 (2ND) 2nd printing. ... .75 2.95
91-99 ... .50 1.50
100 ... 1.00 3.50
101-103 ... .75 2.00
104-105 ... .50 1.50
106 Polybagged with Dirt magazine. ... 1.00 3.50
106A Without Dirt magazine. ... .50 1.50
107-112 ... .50 1.50
113 Metallic cover. ... 1.00 3.50
113A Regular edition. ... .50 1.50
114-116 ... .50 1.50
117 Foil stamped cover. Flip book. ... 1.75 6.00
117A Regular edition. ... .75 2.50
118 ... 1.00 3.00
119 ... .75 2.50
120 Double size. ... .75 2.50
121-122 ... .75 2.00
123-124 ... .50 1.50
125 Double size, with 3-D holodisk cover. ... 1.00 3.95
125A Regular edition. ... .75 2.95
126-128 ... .50 1.50

WEB OF SPIDER-MAN ANNUAL
MARVEL (1985-CURRENT)
1 ... 1.75 6.00
2 Art: Art Adams. ... 2.25 8.00
3 ... 1.25 4.00
4 ... 1.25 4.50
5-6 ... 1.25 4.00
7 ... .75 2.00
8 ... .75 2.25
9-10 ... .75 2.95

WEDDING BELLS
QUALITY (1954-1956)
1 ... 23.00 75.00
2 ... 13.00 40.00
3-8 ... 10.00 30.00
9-19 ... 8.00 25.00

WEEKENDER
RUCKER (1945-1946)
3-4 ... 31.00 100.00
5 (Vol.2,#1) ... 31.00 100.00

WEIRD, THE
DC (1988)
1-4 ... .30 1.00

WEIRD ADVENTURES
PL (1951)
1 ... 55.00 175.00
2 ... 40.00 125.00
3 ... 31.00 100.00

WEIRD ADVENTURES
ZIFF-DAVIS (1951)
10 .... 50.00 165.00

WEIRD CHILLS
KEY (1954)
1 Art: Wolverton. 65.00 200.00
2 Classic cover. 65.00 200.00
3 .... 31.00 100.00

WEIRD COMICS
FOX (1940-1942)
1 Cover: Lou Fine. 600.00 2100.00
2 Cover: Lou Fine. 280.00 925.00
3-4 .... 210.00 675.00
5 .... 190.00 625.00
6-8 .... 170.00 550.00
9-12 .... 145.00 470.00
13-20 .... 125.00 400.00

WEIRD FANTASY
EC (1950-1953)
1 (#13) 260.00 850.00
2 (#14) 140.00 460.00
3 (#15) 130.00 430.00
4 (#16) SOTI 140.00 460.00
5 (#17) 115.00 370.00
6-10 .... 85.00 280.00
11 .... 70.00 230.00
12 "Project...Survival!" by Wood. ... 70.00 230.00
13 .... 70.00 230.00
14 Art: Frazetta/Williamson. 95.00 310.00
15-19 .... 70.00 230.00
20 Art: Frazetta/Williamson. 95.00 310.00
21 Art: Frazetta/Williamson. 70.00 230.00
22 "The Silent Towns" 55.00 170.00

WEIRD FANTASY
EC(COCHRAN) (1992-1994)
1 Reprints EC original: Weird Fantasy #13 (1950). .... .75 2.00
2 Reprint: Weird Fantasy #14 (1950). .50 1.50
3 Reprint: Weird Fantasy #15 (1950). .50 1.50
4 Reprint: Weird Fantasy #16 (1950). .75 2.00
5 Reprint: Weird Fantasy #17 (1950). .75 2.00
6 Reprint: Weird Fantasy #6. .... .75 2.00
7 Reprint: Weird Fantasy #7. .... .75 2.00
8 Reprint: Weird Fantasy #8. .... .75 2.00
9 Reprint: Weird Fantasy #9. .... .75 2.00
ANNUAL 1 Reprint: 1st 5 issues. 2.25 8.95

WEIRD FANTASY
EASTERN (1974)
13 E.C. reprints. 1.75 6.00

WEIRD HORRORS
ST. JOHN (1952-1953)
1 .... 65.00 200.00
2 .... 35.00 110.00
3 .... 31.00 100.00
4-5 .... 28.00 90.00
6 Cover: William Ekgren. 65.00 200.00
7 Cover: William Ekgren. 80.00 250.00
8 Cover & art: Joe Kubert. 45.00 140.00
9 Cover & art: Joe Kubert. Title changes to Nightmare with #10. .... 45.00 140.00

WEIRD JUNGLE TALES
STAR (1953)
202 Cover: L.B. Cole. "The Wrath Of Kara!" 40.00 125.00

WEIRD MYSTERIES
GILLMORE (1952-1954)
1 .... 95.00 300.00
2 "Robot Woman" by Basil Wolverton. 140.00 450.00
3 .... 65.00 210.00
4 "The Man Who Never Smiled!" by Basil Wolverton. 130.00 420.00
5 "Swamp Monster!" by Basil Wolverton. 130.00 420.00
6 .... 65.00 210.00
7 SOTI 110.00 360.00
8 .... 65.00 210.00
9-10 .... 55.00 180.00
11-12 .... 50.00 150.00

WEIRD MYSTERY TALES
DC (1972-1975)
1 .... 1.50 5.00
2-24 .... 1.00 3.00

WEIRD SCIENCE
EC (1950-1953)
1 (#12) "Lost In The Microcosm" ... 290.00 950.00
2 (#13) 160.00 525.00
3 (#14) 145.00 480.00
4 (#15) 140.00 450.00
5 .... 110.00 360.00
6-10 .... 95.00 300.00
11-18 .... 75.00 240.00
19 Art: Frazetta/Williamson. SOTI ... 95.00 300.00
20-21 Art: Frazetta/Williamson. 95.00 300.00
22 Art: Frazetta/Williamson. Title changes to Weird Science-Fantasy with #23. .... 95.00 300.00

WEIRD SCIENCE
EC(COCHRAN) (1992-1994)
1 Reprints EC original: Weird Science #12 (1950). .... .75 2.00
2 Reprint: Weird Science #13 (1950). .50 1.50
3 Reprint: Weird Science #14 (1950). .50 1.50
4 Reprint: Weird Science #15 (1950). .75 2.00
5 Reprint: Weird Science #5. .... .75 2.00
6 Reprint: Weird Science #6. .... .75 2.00
7-10 .... .75 2.00
ANNUAL 1 Reprint: 1st 5 issues. 2.25 8.95

WEIRD SCIENCE
EASTERN (1974)
15 E.C. reprints. 1.50 5.00

WEIRD SCIENCE
GLADSTONE (1990-1991)
1 Reprints EC originals: Weird Science #22 & Weird Fantasy #1. .... 1.25 4.00
2 Reprints: Weird Science #16 & Weird Fantasy #17 (1950). 1.00 3.00
3 Reprints: Weird Science #9 & Weird Fantasy #14 (1950). 1.00 3.00
4 Reprints: Weird Science-Fantasy #27 & Weird Fantasy #11. .... 1.25 4.00

WEIRD SCIENCE-FANTASY
EC (1954-1955)
23 Cover & art: Wallace Wood. Previous title: Weird Science. 75.00 240.00
24 .... 75.00 240.00
25 Cover & art: Al Williamson. 75.00 240.00
26 Art: Wallace Wood. 65.00 210.00
27 Cover & art: Wallace Wood. 65.00 210.00
28 .... 75.00 240.00
29 Cover: Frank Frazetta. Title changes toIncredible Science Fiction with #30. .... 130.00 420.00

WEIRD SCIENCE-FANTASY
EC(COCHRAN) (1992-1994)
1 Reprints EC originals. .... .75 2.00
2-9 .... .75 2.00
ANNUAL 1 Reprint: 1st 5 issues. 2.25 8.95

WEIRD SCIENCE-FANTASY ANNUAL
EC (1952-1953)
1952 .... 400.00 1300.00
1953 .... 240.00 775.00

WEIRD SUSPENSE
ATLAS(SEABOARD) (1975)
1-3 .... .50 1.50

WEIRD TALES ILLUSTRATED
MILLENNIUM (1992)
1 .... 1.00 3.00
2 .... 1.50 5.00

WEIRD TALES OF THE FUTURE
SPM (1952-1953)
1 .... 110.00 360.00
2 Begin: Basil Wolverton cover & art. "Jumpin Jupiter" 190.00 600.00
3 .... 190.00 600.00
4 .... 145.00 480.00
5 End: Wolverton cover & art. 145.00 480.00
6 .... 75.00 240.00
7 "The Mind Movers" by Basil Wolverton. 110.00 360.00
8 .... 75.00 240.00

WEIRD TERROR
COMIC MEDIA (1952-1954)
1 .... 55.00 180.00
2-13 .... 40.00 120.00

WEIRD THRILLERS
ZIFF-DAVIS (1951-1952)
1 Photo cover. 75.00 240.00
2 .... 65.00 210.00
3 .... 55.00 180.00
4-5 .... 50.00 150.00

WEIRD WAR TALES
DC (1971-1983)
1 .... 1.25 4.00
2-3 .... 1.00 3.00
4-7 .... .75 2.50
8 Cover & art: Neal Adams. 1.25 4.00
9-20 .... .75 2.00
21-124 .... .30 1.00

WEIRD WESTERN TALES
DC (1972-1980)
12 Previous title: All Star Western (second series). .... .75 2.00
13-70 .... .75 2.00

WEIRD WONDER TALES
MARVEL (1973-1977)
1-22 .... .75 2.00

WEIRD WORLDS
DC (1972-1974)
1-10 .... .75 2.00

WELCOME BACK, KOTTER
DC (1976-1978)
1 TV tie-in. .... .75 2.00
2-10 .... .75 2.00

WENDY PARKER
MARVEL(ATLAS) (1953-1954)
1 .... 19.00 60.00
2 .... 10.00 30.00
3-8 .... 7.00 20.00

WENDY, THE GOOD LITTLE WITCH
HARVEY (1960-1976)
1 .... 14.00 45.00
2 .... 7.00 20.00
3-10 .... 5.00 15.00
11-15 .... 2.75 10.00
16-20 .... 2.25 8.00
21-25 .... 1.50 5.00
26-40 .... 1.00 3.00
41-50 .... .75 2.50
51-69 .... .75 2.00
70-74 .... .75 2.50
75-93 .... .30 1.00

WENDY WITCH WORLD
HARVEY (1961-1974)
1 .... 10.00 30.00
2-5 .... 5.00 15.00
6-10 .... 2.75 10.00
11-20 .... 1.50 5.00
21-30 .... .75 2.50
31-39 .... .75 2.00
40-53 .... .30 1.00

WEREWOLF
DELL (1966-1967)
1 .... 2.75 10.00
2-3 .... 1.75 6.00

WEREWOLF BY NIGHT
MARVEL (1972-1977)
1 .... 14.00 45.00
2 .... 7.00 20.00
3-6 .... 4.00 12.00
7-12 .... 2.75 10.00
13-20 .... 1.75 6.00
21-31 .... 1.50 5.00
32 1st & origin: Moon Knight. 19.00 60.00
33 2nd: Moon Knight. 8.00 25.00
34-36 .... 1.25 4.50
37 App: Moon Knight. 2.25 8.00
38-43 .... 1.00 3.50

WEST COAST AVENGERS
MARVEL (1984)
1 .... 1.50 5.00
2 .... 1.00 3.00
3-4 .... .75 2.00

WEST COAST AVENGERS
MARVEL (1985-1989)
1 .... 1.50 5.00
2 .... 1.00 3.00
3-45 .... .75 2.00
46 Title changes to Avengers West Coast with #47. .... .75 2.00

WEST COAST AVENGERS ANNUAL
MARVEL (1986-1988)
1-2 .... 1.00 3.00
3 Evolutionary War. (1988) 1.00 3.00

WESTERN ACTION THRILLERS
DELL (1937)
1 100 pages; Buffalo Bill, Laramie Joe, Two-Gun Thompson, & Wild West Bill. 170.00 550.00

WESTERN ADVENTURES COMICS
ACE (1948-1949)
1 (NO#) (10/48) 23.00 75.00
2 (NO#) (12/48) 13.00 40.00
3 (NO#) (2/49) SOTI 14.00 45.00
4-5 .... 10.00 30.00

WEIRD SCIENCE #10 (1ST SERIES)

WEIRD TERROR #7

WEREWOLF BY NIGHT #25

WEST COAST AVENGERS #27

a b c d e f g h i j k l m n o p q r s t u v w x y z

WESTERN COMICS #5

WESTERN COMICS #13

WESTERN ROUNDUP #1

WETWORKS #2

FAMOUS • FIRSTS

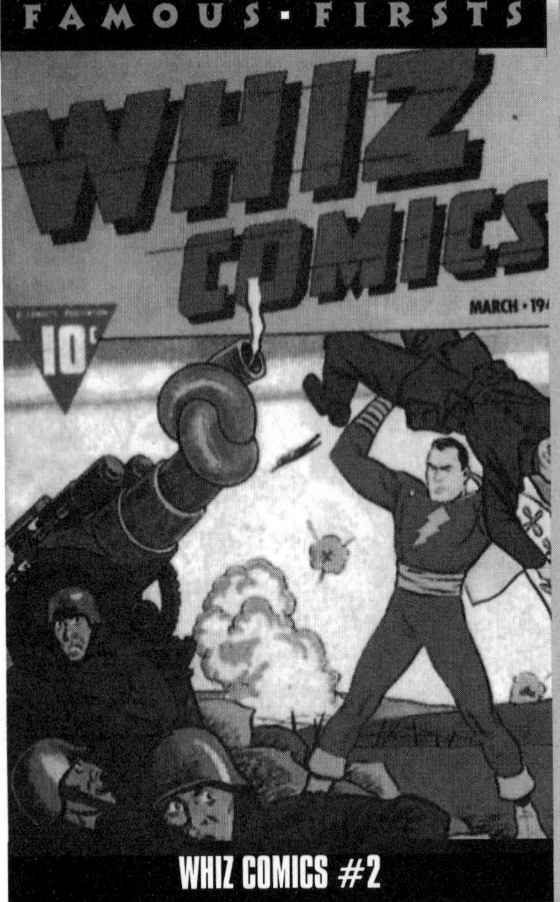

WHIZ COMICS #2

***Whiz* #2 marks the debut of Captain Marvel, Ibis the Invincible and Spy Smasher. Later, Captain Marvel became even more popular than Superman for awhile.**

6 Title changes to Western Love Trails with #7. 10.00 30.00

WESTERN BANDIT TRAILS
ST. JOHN (1949)
1 Cover: Matt Baker. 23.00 75.00
2 Cover: Matt Baker. 19.00 60.00
3 Cover & art: Matt Baker. 23.00 75.00

WESTERN BANDIT TRAILS
ST. JOHN (1954)
9 Cover: Matt Baker. From Approved Comics series. 13.00 40.00

WESTERN BANDITS
AVON (1952)
1 19.00 60.00

WESTERN COMICS
DC (1948-1961)
1 95.00 300.00
2 50.00 150.00
3-4 40.00 125.00
5 1st: Nighthawk. 40.00 125.00
6 40.00 125.00
7-12 31.00 100.00
13-18 23.00 75.00
19-30 19.00 60.00
31-40 16.00 50.00
41-49 13.00 40.00
50 1st Code Approved issue. 11.00 35.00
51-60 10.00 30.00
61-70 7.00 20.00
71-85 4.00 12.00

WESTERN CRIME BUSTERS
TROJAN (1950-1952)
1 31.00 100.00
2 16.00 50.00
3-5 13.00 40.00
6-7 Art: Wallace Wood. 50.00 150.00
8 13.00 40.00
9-10 Art: Wallace Wood. 50.00 150.00

WESTERN CRIME CASES
STAR (1951)
9 Cover: L.B. Cole. Previous title: Indian Warriors. Title changes to The Outlaws with #10. 10.00 30.00

WESTERN DESPERADO COMICS
FAWCETT (1940)
8 Previous title: Slam Bang Comics. 170.00 550.00

WESTERN FIGHTERS
HILLMAN (1948-1953)
1 50.00 150.00
2 16.00 50.00
3-10 10.00 30.00
11 Art: Al Williamson/Frank Frazetta. 40.00 125.00
12 10.00 30.00
V2#1 8.00 25.00
V2#10-V4#7 7.00 20.00
3-D(#1) Star publication. With glasses. 50.00 150.00

WESTERN FRONTIER
PLP (1951)
1 10.00 30.00
2-3 5.00 15.00

WESTERN GUNFIGHTERS
MARVEL (1970-1975)
1 Begin: Ghost Rider (western). 1.50 5.00
2-6 1.25 4.00
7-33 1.00 3.00

WESTERN GUNFIGHTERS
MARVEL(ATLAS) (1956-1957)
20 10.00 33.00
21 Art: Reed Crandall. 14.00 44.00
22 Art: Wallace Wood, Bob Powell. 20.00 65.00
23-27 10.00 33.00

WESTERN HEARTS
STANDARD (1949-1952)
1 Movie photo cover (Whip Wilson & Reno Browne). 23.00 75.00
2 Movie photo cover (Beverly Tyler & Jerome Courtland in Palomino). Art: Frazetta/Williamson. 25.00 80.00
3 Photo cover. 10.00 30.00
4 Photo cover. 8.00 25.00
5 Movie photo cover (Ray Milland & Hedy Lamar in Copper Canyon). 11.00 35.00
6 Movie photo cover (Fred MacMurray & Irene Dunne in Never A Dull Moment). 11.00 35.00
7 Photo cover. 8.00 25.00
8 Movie photo cover (Janis Carter & Randolph Scott in Santa Fe). 16.00 50.00
9 Movie photo cover (Whip Wilson & Reno Browne). 16.00 50.00
10 Photo cover. 8.00 25.00

WESTERN HERO
FAWCETT (1949-1952)
76 Tom Mix, Hoppy, Gabby. Previous title: Real Western Hero. 35.00 110.00
77-83 17.00 55.00
84 Begin: Photo covers. 25.00 80.00
85-90 20.00 65.00
91-100 17.00 55.00
101-112 14.00 44.00

WESTERN KID
MARVEL (1971-1972)
1-5 1.00 3.00

WESTERN KID
MARVEL(ATLAS) (1954-1957)
1 Origin: Western Kid. 20.00 65.00
2 10.00 33.00
3-17 7.00 22.00

WESTERN KILLERS
FOX (1948-1949)
59 (NO#) 26.00 85.00
60 31.00 100.00
61-64 26.00 85.00

WESTERN LIFE ROMANCES
MARVEL (1949-1950)
1 Movie photo cover (Reno Browne and Whip Wilson). 26.00 85.00
2 Movie photo cover (Gale Storm and Audie Murphy). 20.00 65.00

WESTERN LOVE
PRIZE (1949-1950)
1 Movie photo cover (Randolph Scott and Nancy Olson in Canadian Pacific). 40.00 130.00
2 Photo covers on all issues. 35.00 110.00
3-5 35.00 110.00

WESTERN LOVE TRAILS
ACE (1949-1950)
7 Previous title: Western Adventure Comics. 7.00 22.00
8-9 7.00 22.00

WESTERN MARSHAL
DELL FOUR COLOR SERIES (1954-1955)
534 (2/54) 13.00 40.00
591 (10/54) 10.00 30.00
613 (2/55) 10.00 30.00
640 (8/55) 8.00 25.00

WESTERN OUTLAWS
FOX (1948-1949)
17 35.00 110.00
18-20 22.00 70.00
21 25.00 80.00

WESTERN OUTLAWS
MARVEL(ATLAS) (1954-1957)
1 25.00 80.00
2 14.00 44.00
3 12.00 38.00
4 10.00 33.00
5-10 9.00 27.00
11-21 7.00 22.00

WESTERN OUTLAWS AND SHERIFFS
MARVEL(ATLAS) (1949-1952)
60 Previous title: Best Western. 31.00 100.00
61-73 25.00 80.00

WESTERN PICTURE STORIES
CENTAUR(CMC) (1937)

1 1st Western comic. Art: Will Eisner. 310.00 1000.00
2-3 Art: Will Eisner. 230.00 750.00
4 230.00 750.00

WESTERN ROUGH RIDERS
STANMOR (1954-1955)

1 13.00 40.00
2-4 8.00 25.00

WESTERN ROUNDUP
DELL (1952-1959)

1 Photo cover of Gene Autry, Roy Rogers, Johnny Mack Brown, Bill Elliott, and Rex Allen. Giant size. 65.00 200.00
2-10 Giant Size. 31.00 100.00
11-25 Giant Size. 23.00 75.00

WESTERN TALES
HARVEY (1955-1956)

31 Previous title: Witches Western Tales. 25.00 80.00
32-33 25.00 80.00

WESTERN TALES OF THE BLACK RIDER
MARVEL(ATLAS) (1955)

28 Previous title: Black Rider. 14.00 44.00
29-30 14.00 44.00
31 Title changes to Gunsmoke Western with #32. 14.00 44.00

WESTERN TEAM-UP
MARVEL (1973)

1 1.00 3.00

WESTERN THRILLERS
FOX (1948-1949)

1 40.00 130.00
2 20.00 65.00
3-5 17.00 55.00
6 Title changes to My Past Thrilling Confessions with #7. 17.00 55.00

WESTERN THRILLERS
MARVEL(ATLAS) (1954-1955)

1 17.00 55.00
2-3 10.00 33.00
4 Title changes to Cowboy Action with #5. 10.00 33.00

WESTERN TRAILS
MARVEL(ATLAS) (1957)

1 12.00 38.00
2 9.00 27.00

WESTERN TRUE CRIME
FOX (1948-1949)

1 (#15) 26.00 85.00
2 (#16) 20.00 65.00
3-5 17.00 55.00
6 Title changes to MY CONFESSION with #7. 17.00 55.00

WESTERN WINNERS
MARVEL (1949)

5 Previous title: All Western Winners. 40.00 130.00
6-7 35.00 110.00

WESTERNER COMICS, THE
TOYTOWN (1948-1951)

14 Wild Bill Pecos. 16.00 50.00
15-27 13.00 40.00
28-41 7.00 20.00

WESTWARD HO, THE WAGONS
DELL FOUR COLOR SERIES (1956)

738 Disney movie photo cover (Fess Parker). (10/56) 16.00 50.00

WETWORKS
IMAGE (1994-CURRENT)

1 1.75 6.00
2 1.25 4.50
2A Variant cover. 2.50 9.00
3-7 .75 2.50
8 Comes with 2 cards. .75 2.50
8A Newsstand edition (no cards). .50 1.95
9 .75 2.50
SOURCEBOOK .75 2.50

WHACK
ST. JOHN (1953-1954)

1 (3-D) With glasses. 40.00 120.00
2-3 19.00 60.00

WHAM COMICS
CENTAUR (1940)

1 310.00 1000.00
2 190.00 600.00

WHAM-O GIANT COMICS
WHAM-O (1967)

1 One shot. 7.00 20.00

WHAT IF...?
MARVEL (1977-1985)

1 Spider-Man Joined The Fantastic Four? 7.00 20.00
2 The Hulk Had The Brain Of Bruce Banner? 2.75 10.00
3 The Avengers Had Never Been? 2.00 7.00
4 The Invaders Had Stayed Together After World War Two? 2.00 7.00
5 Captain America Hadn't Vanished During World War Two? 2.00 7.00
6 The Fantastic Four Had Different Super-Powers? 2.00 7.00
7 Someone Else Besides Spider-Man Had Been Bitten By The Radioactive Spider? 1.75 6.00
8 The World Knew That Daredevil Is Blind? 1.75 6.00
9 The Avengers Had Fought Evil During The 1950's? 1.75 6.00
10 Jane Foster Had Found The Hammer Of Thor? 1.75 6.00
11 The Original Marvel Bullpen Had Become The Fantastic Four? 1.75 6.00
12 Rick Jones Had Become The Hulk? 1.75 6.00
13 Conan The Barbarian Walked The Earth Today? 1.75 6.00
14 Sgt. Fury Had Fought World War Two In Outer Space? 1.75 6.00
15 Nova Had Been Four Other People? 1.50 5.00
16 Shang-Chi, Master Of Kung Fu, Fought On The Side Of Fu Manchu? 1.50 5.00
17 Ghost Rider, Spider-Woman, Captain Marvel Were Villains? 2.00 7.00
18 Dr. Strange Were A Disciple Of Dormammu? 1.50 5.00
19 Spider-Man Had Never Become A Crimefighter? 1.50 5.00
20 The Avengers Fought The Kree-Skrull War Without Rick Jones? 1.50 5.00
21 Invisible Girl Of The Fantastic Four Married The Sub Mariner? 1.50 5.00
22 Dr. Doom Had Become A Hero? 1.50 5.00
23 The Hulk Had Become A Barbarian? 1.50 5.00
24 Spider-Man Had Rescued Gwen Stacy? 1.50 5.00
25 Thor And The Avengers Battled The Gods? 1.50 5.00
26 Captain America Had Been Elected President? 1.50 5.00
27 Phoenix Had Not Died? 2.25 8.00
28 Daredevil Became An Agent Of S.H.I.E.L.D.? 2.25 8.00
29 The Avengers Defeated Everybody? 1.25 4.00
30 Spider-Man's Clone Lived? 4.00 12.00
31 Wolverine Had Killed The Hulk? 4.00 13.00
32 The Avengers Had Become Pawns Of Korvac? 1.00 3.50
33 Dazzler Had Become The Herald Of Galactus?/Iron Man Was Trapped In The Time Of King Arthur? 1.00 3.50
34 Watcher cover. 1.00 3.50
35 Elektra Had Lived? 1.50 5.00
36 ...The Fantastic Four Had Not Gained Their Super-Powers? 1.00 3.50
37 The Beast And The Thing Continued To Mutate? 1.00 3.50
38 Featuring Daredevil and Captain America. 1.00 3.50
39 The Mighty Thor Battled Conan The Barbarian? 1.00 3.50
40 Dr. Strange Had Not Become Master Of The Mystic Arts? 1.00 3.50
41 Sub-Mariner Had Saved Atlantis From Its...Destiny? 1.00 3.50
42 The Invisible Girl Had Died? 1.00 3.50
43 Conan The Barbarian Were Stranded In The 20th Century? (Sequel to What If...? #12) 1.00 3.50
44 Captain America Were Revived Today? 1.00 3.50
45 The Hulk Went...Berserk? 1.00 3.00
46 Spider-Man's Uncle Ben Had Lived? 1.25 4.00
47 Loki Had Found The Hammer Of Thor? 1.00 3.00

WHAT IF...?
MARVEL (1989-CURRENT)

1 The Avengers Had Lost The Evolutionary War? 1.75 6.00
2-3 1.00 3.50
4 1.50 5.00
5 The Vision Had Destroyed The Avengers? 1.00 3.50
6 The X-Men Lost Inferno? 1.75 6.00
7 Wolverine Had Been An Agent Of S.H.I.E.L.D.? Art: Rob Liefeld. 2.00 7.00
8 Iron Man Lost The Armor Wars? 1.00 3.00
9 The X-Men Died On Their First Mission? 1.50 5.00
10 The Punisher's Family Hadn't Been Killed? 1.00 3.00
11 The Fantastic Four All Had The Same Power? 1.00 3.00
12 The X-Men Had Stayed In Asgard? 1.00 3.00
13 Professor X Of The X-Men Had Become The Juggernaut? 1.00 3.00
14 Captain Marvel Had Not Died? 1.00 3.00
15 The Fantastic Four Had Lost The Trial Of Galactus? 1.00 3.00
16 Wolerine Fought Conan? 1.75 6.00
17 1.00 3.00
18 The Fantastic Four Battled Doctor Doom Before They Got Their Powers? .75 2.50
19 Vision Of The Avengers Conquered The World? .75 2.50
20 The Amazing Spider-Man Had Not Married Mary Jane? .75 2.50
21 The Amazing Spider-Man Had Married The Black Cat? .75 2.50
22 The Silver Surfer Had Not Escaped Earth? 1.25 4.00
23 The New X-Men Had Never Existed? .75 2.00
24-31 .75 2.00
32 Phoenix Had Not Died? .75 2.00
33 The Phoenix Rose Again? .75 2.00
34 .75 2.00
35 The Fantastic Five Fought Doctor Doom & Annihilus? (Timequake, pt.1) .75 2.00
36 The Cosmic Avengers Battled The Guardians Of The Galaxy? (Timequake, pt.2) .50 1.50
37 Wolverine Had Been Lord Of The Vampires During Inferno? (Timequake, pt.3) .50 1.50
38 Thor Was A Thrall Of Seth!? (Timequake, pt.4) .50 1.50
39 The Watcher Saved The Universe? (Timequake, pt.5) .50 1.50
40 Storm Of The X-Men Had Remained A Thief? .50 1.50
41 The Avengers Had Fought Galactus? .75 2.50
42 Spider-Man Had Kept His Extra Arms? .50 1.25
43-44 .50 1.25
45 Barbara Ketch Had Become Ghost Rider? .50 1.25
46 Cable Destroyed The X-Men? .50 1.25
47 .50 1.25
48 Daredevil Had Saved Nuke? .50 1.25
49 The Silver Surfer Had Possessed The Infinity Gauntlet? .50 1.25
50 1.25 4.00
51-54 .50 1.50
55 The Avengers Lost Operation Galactic Storm? (pt.1) .50 1.50
56 The Avengers Lost Operation Galactic Storm? (pt.2) .50 1.50
57-60 .50 1.50
61 Spider-Man's Parents Destroyed His Family? .50 1.50
62 Wolverine Battled Weapon X? .50 1.50
63 War Machine Had Not Destroyed The Living Laser? .50 1.50
64 Iron Man Sold Out? .50 1.50
65-77 .50 1.50

WHAT IF? SPECIAL
MARVEL (1988)

1 ...Iron Man Had Been A Traitor? 1.00 3.00

WHAT IF THEY CALL ME CHICKEN?
DAIRY SELECT (1970)

NO# Anti-drug giveaway. 2.75 10.00

WHAT THE?!
MARVEL (1988-1992)

1 1.25 4.00
2 1.00 3.00
3-4 .75 2.00
5-8 .50 1.50
9-24 .50 1.25
FALL Special. (1993) .75 2.50
SUMMER Special. X-Men parody. (1993) .75 2.50

WHEATIES GIVEAWAYS
DISNEY (1950-1951)

A-1 Mickey Mouse And The Disappearing Island. 7.00 20.00
B-1 Mickey Mouse, The Pharoah's Curse. 7.00 20.00
C-1 Donald Duck And The Inca Idol. 7.00 20.00
D-1 Donald Duck In Indian Country. 7.00 20.00
A-2 Grandma Duck, Homespun Detective. 7.00 20.00
B-2 Pluto, Canine Cowpoke. 7.00 20.00
C-2 Mickey Mouse And The Magic Mountain. 7.00 20.00
D-2 Mickey Mouse And The Abandoned Mine. 7.00 20.00
A-3 Donald Duck And The Haunted Jewels. 7.00 20.00
B-3 Donald Duck And The Buccanneers. 7.00 20.00
C-3 Li'l Bad Wolf, Fire Fighter. 7.00 20.00
D-3 Pluto And The Mysterious Package. 7.00 20.00
A-4 Donald Duck And The Giant Ape. 7.00 20.00
B-4 Mickey Mouse And The Mystery Sea Monster. 7.00 20.00

WHAT IF? #35 (1ST SERIES)

WHAT IF? #6 (2ND SERIES)

WHAT IF? #23 (2ND SERIES)

WHAT IF? #68 (2ND SERIES)

WHEEL OF WORLDS #0

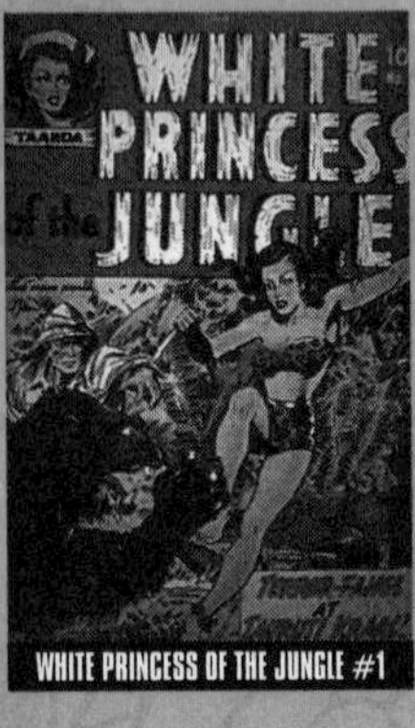

WHITE PRINCESS OF THE JUNGLE #1

WHIZ COMICS #154

WILDC.A.T.S #5

C-4 Gus And Jaq Save The Ship. 7.00 20.00
D-4 Bre'r Rabbit's Sunken Treasure. ... 7.00 20.00
A-5 Mickey Mouse, Roving Reporter. ... 7.00 20.00
B-5 Li'l Bad Wolf In The Hollow Tree Hideout.
.... 7.00 20.00
C-5 Donald Duck In The Lost Lakes. ... 7.00 20.00
D-5 Donald Duck, Mighty Mystic. 7.00 20.00
A-6 Li'l Bad Wolf, Forest Ranger. 7.00 20.00
B-6 Donald Duck, Trail Blazer. 7.00 20.00
C-6 Mickey Mouse And The Stagecoach Bandits.
.... 7.00 20.00
D-6 Mickey Mouse And The Medicine Man. 7.00 20.00
A-7 Goofy, Tightrope Acrobat. 7.00 20.00
B-7 Goofy And The Gangsters. 7.00 20.00
C-7 Goofy, Big Game Hunter. 7.00 20.00
D-7 Li'l Bad Wolf And The Secret Of The Woods.
.... 7.00 20.00
A-8 Pluto And The Bogus Money. 7.00 20.00
B-8 Donald Duck, Klondike Kid. 7.00 20.00
C-8 Donald Duck, Deep-Sea Diver. 7.00 20.00
D-8 Minnie Mouse, Girl Explorer. 7.00 20.00

WHEEL OF WORLDS
TEKNO-COMIX (1995)
0 .... .75 2.95
1 (Neil Gaiman's...) Cardstock cover. ... .75 2.95
1A Newsstand edition (regular cover). ... .50 1.95

WHEN KNIGHTHOOD WAS IN FLOWER
DELL FOUR COLOR SERIES (1956)
682 Disney movie tie-in. (2/56) ... 11.00 35.00

WHERE CREATURES ROAM
MARVEL (1970-1971)
1 .... 1.50 5.00
2-8 .... .75 2.50

WHERE MONSTERS DWELL
MARVEL (1970-1975)
1 .... 1.50 5.00
2-10 .... 1.00 3.00
11-38 .... .75 2.00

WHIP WILSON
MARVEL (1950)
9 Photo covers on all issues. Previous title: Rex Hart.
.... 70.00 220.00
10-11 .... 40.00 130.00

WHIRLWIND COMICS
NITA (1940)
1 1st & Origin: Cyclone. 145.00 480.00
2 "Cyclone Strikes Again!" 110.00 360.00
3 .... 110.00 360.00

WHIRLYBIRDS
DELL (1960-1961)
1124 TV photo cover. (8/60) 16.00 50.00
1216 TV photo cover. (8/61) 16.00 50.00

WHISPER
CAPITAL (1983-1984)
1-2 .... .75 2.00

WHISPER
FIRST (1986-1990)
1-37 .... .30 1.00

WHITE CHIEF OF THE PAWNEE INDIANS
AVON (1951)
NO# 16.00 50.00

WHITE INDIAN (A-1 SERIES)
ME (1954-1955)
11 (A-1 #94). 23.00 75.00
12 (A-1 #101). 23.00 75.00
13 (A-1 #104). 23.00 75.00
14 (A-1 #117). 13.00 40.00
15 (A-1 #135). 13.00 40.00

WHITE LIKE SHE
DARK HORSE (1994)
1-4 .... .75 2.95

WHITE PRINCESS OF THE JUNGLE
AVON (1951-1952)
1 Origin: White Princess. 31.00 100.00
2-5 .... 23.00 75.00

WHITE RIDER AND SUPER HORSE
STAR (1950-1951)
4-5 .... 11.00 35.00
6 Title changes to Indian Warriors with #7.
.... 11.00 35.00

WHITE WILDERNESS
DELL FOUR COLOR SERIES (1958)
943 Disney movie tie-in. (10/58) ... 11.00 35.00

WHIZ COMICS
FAWCETT (1940-1953)
2 1st & Origin: Captain Marvel. See Flash Comics Ashcan and Thrill Comics Ashcan. 13800.00 55000.00
NO#(3) No # on cover, #3 on inside. 1000.00 3900.00
3 (#4 in indicia) (4/40). 700.00 2600.00
4 "Captain Marvel Crashes Through" (5/40).
.... 500.00 1900.00
5 "Captain Marvel Scores Again!" ... 400.00 1500.00
6 "Captain Marvel And The Circus Of Death"
.... 400.00 1300.00
7 "Captain Marvel and the Squadron of Doom" Begin: Dr. Voodoo. 300.00 1100.00
8 "Saved By Captain Marvel!" 310.00 1000.00
9 "Captain Marvel On The Job!" ... 310.00 1000.00
10 "Captain Marvel Battles The Winged Death"
.... 310.00 1000.00
11 "Hurray For Captain Marvel!" ... 310.00 1000.00
12 "Captain Marvel Rides The Engine Of Doom!"
.... 310.00 1000.00
13 "Captain Marvel-World's Most Powerful Man!"
.... 280.00 900.00
14 "Captain Marvel Boomerangs The Torpedo!"
.... 280.00 900.00
15 Origin: Sivana, Dr. Voodoo. 280.00 925.00
16-18 ...vs. Spy Smasher. 250.00 825.00
19-20 .... 200.00 650.00
21 1st & Origin: Lt. Marvels. 220.00 700.00
22-24 .... 155.00 500.00
25 1st & Origin: Captain Marvel, Jr. ... 700.00 2600.00
26-30 .... 130.00 420.00
31-32 .... 110.00 350.00
33 App: Spy Smasher. 130.00 420.00
34 .... 110.00 350.00
35 App: Spy Smasher. 120.00 390.00
36-40 .... 80.00 260.00
41-42 .... 60.00 190.00
43 App: Spy Smasher, Ibis. 70.00 220.00
44-50 .... 60.00 190.00
51-60 .... 50.00 160.00
61-70 .... 40.00 130.00
71-90 .... 35.00 110.00
91-100 .... 31.00 100.00
101-130 .... 29.00 95.00
131-152 .... 28.00 90.00
153-155 Scarcer. 40.00 130.00

WHIZ COMICS WHEATIES GIVEAWAY
FAWCETT (1946)
NO# 6-1/2" x 8-1/4". Copies were taped to the Wheaties cereal box and are rarely found unused. 125.00 400.00

WHIZ KIDS
ARCHIE (1987)
NO# Tandy Computer (Radio Shack) giveaway.
.... 1.00 3.00

WHO IS NEXT?
STANDARD (1953)
5 .... 31.00 100.00

WHO LIVES ON THE FOREST FARM?
HOWARD (1954)
NO# International Paper Co. giveaway. 2.75 10.00

WHO'S MINDING THE MINT?
DELL (1967)
12-924-708 Movie photo cover. 13.00 40.00

WHO'S WHO
DC (1985-1987)
1-26 .... .30 1.00

WHODUNIT
D.S. (1948-1949)
1 Art: Matt Baker. 31.00 100.00
2-3 .... 19.00 60.00

WILBUR COMICS
MLJ/ARCHIE (1944-1965)
1 .... 70.00 220.00
2 .... 35.00 110.00
3-4 .... 23.00 75.00
5 1st: Katy Keene. 70.00 220.00
6 .... 17.00 55.00
7 Begin Archie publication. 17.00 55.00
8-12 .... 17.00 55.00
13-24 .... 14.00 44.00
25-30 .... 10.00 33.00
31-40 .... 7.00 22.00
41-50 .... 5.00 16.00
51-60 .... 4.00 11.00
61-70 .... 1.75 6.50
71-90 .... 1.50 5.50

WILD
MARVEL(ATLAS) (1954)
1 .... 17.00 55.00
2-5 .... 14.00 46.00

WILD ANGELS
MARVEL (1993)
1-2 .... .30 1.00

WILD BILL ELLIOTT
DELL (1950-1955)
2-10 .... 8.00 25.00
13-17 .... 7.00 20.00

WILD BILL ELLIOTT
DELL FOUR COLOR SERIES (1950-1955)
278 "...Comics". Photo cover. (5/50) 31.00 100.00
472 Photo cover. (6/53) 16.00 50.00
520 Photo cover. (12/53) 13.00 40.00
643 "Mystery Of Furnace Valley" Photo cover. (7/55)
.... 11.00 35.00

WILD BILL HICKOK
AVON (1949-1956)
1 .... 19.00 60.00
2 .... 10.00 30.00
3-6 .... 6.00 18.00
7-12 .... 5.00 15.00
13-28 .... 2.75 10.00

WILD BILL HICKOK AND JINGLES
CHARLTON (1958-1959)
68 Previous title: Cowboy Western. ... 13.00 40.00
69-70 .... 10.00 30.00
71-74 .... 7.00 20.00

WILD BOY
ZIFF-DAVIS/ST. JOHN (1951-1955)
1 (#10) Origin: Wild Boy. 19.00 60.00
2 (#11) 10.00 30.00
3 (#12) 7.00 20.00
4-8 .... 5.00 15.00
9 Begin St. John publication. 5.00 15.00
10-15 .... 5.00 15.00

WILD BOY OF THE CONGO
ST. JOHN (1954)
3 From Approved Comics series. (Same cover as Ziff-Davis series #1 (#10), story reprints #2 (#11)). ... 10.00 30.00

WILD FRONTIER
CHARLTON (1955-1957)
1 .... 8.00 25.00
2 .... 7.00 20.00
3-6 .... 5.00 15.00
7 Title changes to Cheyenne Kid with #8. 5.00 15.00

WILD THING
MARVEL (1993-1994)
1 Embossed cover. .... .75 2.50
2-13 .... .50 1.75

WILD WEST
MARVEL (1948)
1 .... 35.00 110.00
2 Title changes to Wild Western with #3. 22.00 70.00

WILD WESTERN
MARVEL(ATLAS) (1948-1957)
3 Previous title: Wild West. 35.00 110.00
4-5 .... 25.00 80.00
6-8 .... 20.00 65.00
9 Photo cover. 25.00 80.00
10 Movie photo cover (Charles Starrett in Horsemen Of The Sierras). 35.00 110.00
11-12 .... 20.00 65.00
13-18 .... 17.00 55.00
19-24 .... 13.00 41.00
25-30 .... 10.00 33.00
31-40 .... 9.00 27.00
41-57 .... 7.00 22.00

WILD WILD WEST
GOLD KEY (1966-1969)
1 TV tie-in. Photo covers on all issues. 13.00 40.00
2 .... 10.00 30.00
3-7 .... 7.00 20.00

WILDC.A.T.S ADVENTURES
IMAGE (1994-CURRENT)
1 Based on animated series. .... .50 1.95
2-3 .... .50 1.95
4-9 .... .75 2.50
SOURCEBOOK Guide to TV series. ...... .75 2.95

WILDC.A.T.S: COVERT ACTION TEAMS
IMAGE (1992-CURRENT)
1 1st: WildC.A.T.S. Art: Jim Lee. 2.00 7.00
1A Gold cover. 2.75 10.00
1B Gold cover, signed. 5.00 15.00
2 Direct sale copy (has holographic prism cover, newsstand copy doesn't). With coupon. 1st: WetWorks. 2.50 9.00
2A Coupon cut out. ...... .75 2.00
2B Newsstand edition (no prism). ...... .75 2.00
3 ...... 1.25 4.00
4 ...... 1.00 3.00
4A With red foil Wizard card. 2.75 10.00
5-6 ...... .75 2.25
7 ...... 1.00 3.50
8 ...... 1.25 4.50
9 ...... 1.00 3.50
10-11 ...... .75 2.50
11A Variant cover. 4.00 12.00
12-20 ...... .75 2.50
20A Newsstand edition (no cards). ...... .50 1.95
21-22 ...... .75 2.50
ASHCAN 1 Signed. 7.00 20.00
ASHCAN 1A Unsigned. 2.75 10.00
SB 1-SB 2 Sourcebook. ...... .75 2.50

WILDC.A.T.S. TRILOGY
IMAGE (1993)
1 ...... .75 2.50
2-3 ...... .50 1.95

WILDEST WESTERNS
WARREN (1960-1962)
1 ...... 95.00 300.00
2-6 ...... 23.00 75.00

WILDSTAR: SKY ZERO
IMAGE (1993)
1 1st: WildStar. ...... .75 2.50
1A Gold foil cover. 1.50 5.00
2-4 ...... .50 1.95
TPB Reprints issues #1-4. ...... 4.00 12.95

WILDSTORM RARITIES
IMAGE/WILDSTORM (1994-CURRENT)
1 Reprints. 1.25 4.95

WILDSTORM RISING
IMAGE/WILDSTORM (1995)
1 Comes with 2 cards. ...... .75 2.50
1A Newsstand edition (no cards). ...... .50 1.95
10 Comes with 2 cards. ...... .75 2.50
10A Newsstand edition (no cards). ...... .50 1.95
SOURCEBOOK ...... .75 2.50

WILDSTORM SWIMSUIT SPECIAL
IMAGE/WILDSTORM (1994-CURRENT)
1 (1994) ...... .75 2.95
2 (1995) ...... .75 2.50

WILL ROGERS
FOX (1950)
1 (#5) Photo cover. 31.00 100.00
2 Photo cover. 31.00 100.00

WILL TO POWER
DARK HORSE (1994)
1-12 ...... .30 1.00

WILLIAM SHATNER'S TEKWORLD
MARVEL(EPIC) (1992-1995)
1-17 ...... .50 1.75

WILLIE THE PENGUIN
STANDARD (1951-1952)
1 ...... 8.00 25.00
2-6 ...... 5.00 15.00

WILLIE THE WISE-GUY
MARVEL(ATLAS) (1957)
1 ...... 13.00 40.00

WILL-YUM!
DELL FOUR COLOR SERIES (1956-1958)
676 (2/56) 7.00 20.00
765 (2/57) 7.00 20.00
902 (5/58) 7.00 20.00

WIN A PRIZE COMICS
CHARLTON (1955)
1 Giveaway. Cover & art: Simon & Kirby. (2/55) 125.00 400.00
2 Cover & art: Simon & Kirby. (4/55) 95.00 300.00

WINDBLADE
WINSTON (1985)
1 Magazine-size black and white featuring early Elf Warrior by Barry Blair. ...... .30 1.00

WINGS COMICS
FICTION HOUSE (1940-1954)
1 ...... 310.00 1000.00
2 ...... 155.00 500.00
3-6 ...... 115.00 370.00
7-12 ...... 85.00 270.00
13-18 ...... 65.00 200.00
19-24 ...... 50.00 150.00
25-30 ...... 40.00 120.00
31-40 ...... 26.00 85.00
41-50 ...... 23.00 75.00
51-60 ...... 19.00 60.00
61-80 ...... 16.00 50.00
81-100 ...... 12.00 37.00
101-124 ...... 10.00 31.00

WINGS OF EAGLES, THE
DELL FOUR COLOR SERIES (1957)
790 Movie photo cover (John Wayne). (4/57) 40.00 125.00

WINKY DINK
DELL FOUR COLOR SERIES (1955)
663 (11/55) 16.00 50.00

WINNIE WINKLE
CUPPLES & LEON (1930-1933)
1 ...... 25.00 80.00
2-4 ...... 19.00 60.00

WINNIE WINKLE
DELL (1948-1949)
1 ...... 9.00 27.00
2 ...... 6.00 18.00
3-7 ...... 2.75 10.00

WINNIE WINKLE
DELL FOUR COLOR SERIES (1946-1947)
94 ...... 25.00 80.00
174 ...... 14.00 45.00

WINNIE WINKLE
SEE LARGE FEATURE COMICS (SERIES II) #2.

WITCHCRAFT
AVON (1952-1953)
1 "Heritage Of Horror" 95.00 300.00
2 ...... 70.00 220.00
3-6 ...... 50.00 160.00

WITCHCRAFT
DC (1994)
1 ...... 1.25 4.00
2-3 ...... 1.00 3.50

WITCHES TALES
HARVEY (1951-1954)
1 ...... 40.00 125.00
2 ...... 23.00 75.00
3-12 ...... 16.00 50.00
13-16 ...... 13.00 40.00
17 Art: Powell/Nostrand. 13.00 40.00
18-27 ...... 13.00 40.00
28 Title changes to Witches Western Tales with #29. ...... 13.00 40.00

WITCHES WESTERN TALES
HARVEY (1955)
29 Previous title: Witches Tales. 31.00 100.00
30 Title changes to Western Tales with #31. ...... 31.00 100.00

WITCHING HOUR
DC (1969-1978)
1 ...... 7.00 20.00
2 ...... 2.75 10.00
3 Art: Berni Wrightson. 2.25 8.00
4 ...... 1.50 5.00
5 Art: Berni Wrightson. 2.25 8.00
6-7 ...... 1.50 5.00
8 Art: Neal Adams. 1.75 6.00
9-12 ...... 1.25 4.00
13 Cover & art: Neal Adams. 1.50 5.00
14-24 ...... 1.00 3.00
25-37 ...... .75 2.00
38 100 pages. 1.25 4.00
39-85 ...... .30 1.00

WITCHING HOUR
MILLENNIUM (1992)
1 ...... .75 2.00

WITH THE MARINES ON THE BATTLEFRONTS OF THE WORLD!
TOBY (1953-1954)
1 Photo cover. (6/53) 31.00 100.00
2 Photo cover. (3/54) 16.00 50.00

WITNESS, THE
MARVEL (1948)
1 "The Witness Speaks!" 200.00 650.00

WITTY COMICS
RUBIN (1945)
1 ...... 25.00 80.00
2 ...... 16.00 50.00

WOLFF AND BYRD, COUNSELORS OF THE MACABRE
EXHIBIT A (1994-CURRENT)
1 ...... 1.50 5.00
2-6 ...... .75 2.50
TPB Reprints issues #1-4. ...... 2.25 8.95

WOLFMAN, THE
DELL (1963-1964)
12-922-308 Movie tie-in. 8.00 25.00
12-922-410 2nd printing. 5.00 15.00

WOLVERINE
MARVEL (1982) (MINI-SERIES)
1 Cover & art: Frank Miller (in all issues). 11.00 36.00
2-3 ...... 8.00 25.00
4 ...... 9.00 27.00

WOLVERINE
MARVEL (1988-1994)
1 ...... 11.00 36.00
2 ...... 5.00 16.00
3-5 ...... 4.00 12.00
6-9 ...... 2.50 10.00
10 1st: Wolverine/Sabretooth battle. 11.00 35.00
11-16 ...... 2.00 7.00
17 Begin: John Byrne cover & art. 2.00 7.00
18-19 ...... 2.00 7.00
20-22 ...... 1.50 5.00
23 End: Byrne cover & art. 1.50 5.00
24 ...... 1.50 5.00
25-36 ...... 1.25 4.00
37-40 ...... 1.00 3.00
41 ...... 4.00 12.00
41 (2ND) 2nd printing. ...... .75 2.00
42 ...... 1.75 6.00
42 (2ND) 2nd printing (Gold cover). ...... .75 2.00
43 ...... 1.25 4.00
44-49 ...... 1.00 3.00
50 Origin retold: Wolverine. Double size. 2.00 7.00
51-74 ...... 1.00 3.00
75 Hologram cover. Double size. 3.00 10.00
76-84 ...... .75 2.50
85 Final Sanction, pt.1. Foil stamped cover. 1.00 3.50
85A Regular cover. ...... .75 2.50
86 ...... .50 1.95
87 Deluxe edition. ...... .50 1.95
87A Regular edition. ...... .50 1.50
88 Deluxe edition. ...... .50 1.95
88A Regular edition. ...... .50 1.50
89 Deluxe edition. ...... .50 1.95
89A Regular edition. ...... .50 1.50
90 Deluxe edition. Title changes to Weapon X. ...... .50 1.95
90A Regular edition. ...... .50 1.50
91-92 ...... .50 1.95

WOLVERINE '95
MARVEL (1995)
1 Giant size. 1.00 3.95

WOLVERINE: ACTS OF VENGEANCE
MARVEL (1992)
NO# Reprints Marvel Comics Presents #64-71. ...... 1.75 6.95

WOLVERINE AND THE PUNISHER: DAMAGING EVIDENCE
MARVEL (1993)
1-3 ...... .75 2.00

WOLVERINE BATTLES THE INCREDIBLE HULK
MARVEL (1989)
NO# Reprints Incredible Hulk #180, 181. 1.25 4.95

WOLVERINE: BLOOD HUNGRY
MARVEL (1993)
NO# 1.75 6.95

WOLVERINE: BLOODLUST
MARVEL (1990)
1 One shot. 1.50 5.95

WILDSTAR #1

WITCHCRAFT #3 (DC)

WOLVERINE #69

WOLVERINE '95 #1

WOLVERINE VS. SPIDER-MAN #1

WONDER COMICS #1 (BETTER)

WONDER WOMAN #45 (1ST SERIES)

WONDER WOMAN #49 (2ND SERIES)

FAMOUS · FIRSTS

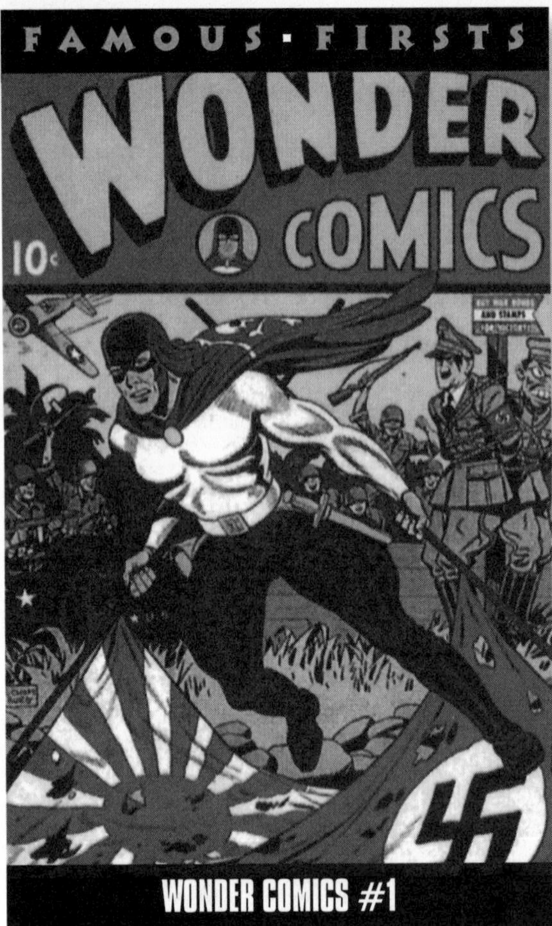

WONDER COMICS #1

This issue features the first appearance of WonderMan, the first Superman-like superhero. He was ultimately canned due to a copyright infringement lawsuit by DC, who claimed he was a rip-off of Superman.

WOLVERINE: BLOODY CHOICES
MARVEL (1993)
NO# 2.25 8.00

WOLVERINE: EVILUTION
MARVEL (1994)
1 Prestige format. 1.75 6.00

WOLVERINE: IN GLOBAL JEOPARDY
MARVEL (1993)
1 One shot. .... .75 2.95

WOLVERINE: INNER FURY
MARVEL (1992)
1 .... 1.50 5.95

WOLVERINE: JUNGLE ADVENTURE
MARVEL (1990)
1 Prestige format. 1.25 4.50

WOLVERINE: RAHNE FALL
MARVEL (1995)
1 .... 1.75 6.95

WOLVERINE: RAHNE OF TERROR
MARVEL (1991)
1 .... 1.50 5.95

WOLVERINE SAGA
MARVEL (1989)
1 History of Wolverine. 1.50 5.00
2-4 .... 1.50 5.00

WOLVERINE: SAVE THE TIGER
MARVEL (1992)
1 .... .75 2.95

WOLVERINE: TYPHOID'S KISS
MARVEL (1994)
NO# 1.75 6.95

WOLVERINE VS. SPIDER-MAN
MARVEL (1995)
1 Reprints Marvel Comics Presents #48-50. .75 2.50

WOLVERINE: WEAPON X
MARVEL
TPB Reprints Weapon-X stories. 4.00 12.95

WOLVERINE/GAMBIT: VICTIMS
MARVEL (1995)
1 .... .75 2.95

WOMEN IN LOVE
FOX (1949-1950)
1 .... 28.00 90.00
2 .... 20.00 65.00
3 .... 17.00 55.00
4 .... 25.00 80.00

WOMEN IN LOVE
ZIFF-DAVIS (1952)
NO# 85.00 270.00

WOMEN OUTLAWS
FOX (1948-1949)
1 SOTI 95.00 310.00
2 .... 80.00 250.00
3 .... 70.00 230.00
4-7 .... 55.00 180.00
8 Title changes to My Love Memoirs with #9.
.... 55.00 180.00

WOMEN TO LOVE
AVON (1953)
NO# Also see Complete Romance #1. 50.00 160.00

WONDER COMICS
BETTER (1944-1948)
1 Alex Schomburg covers on all issues. 105.00 340.00
2 .... 55.00 170.00
3-6 .... 45.00 140.00
7-19 .... 35.00 110.00
20 Art: Frank Frazetta. 65.00 200.00

WONDER COMICS
FOX (1939)
1 Wonder Man by Will Eisner. 1600.00 6000.00
2 1st Lou Fine cover. Becomes Wonderworld Comics #3.
.... 800.00 2800.00

WONDER DUCK
MARVEL (1949-1950)
1 .... 23.00 75.00
2-3 .... 14.00 44.00

WONDER WOMAN
DC (1942-1986)
1 "All New Never Before Published Adventures Of Wonder Woman!" (Summer/42) SeeAll Star Comics #8 for 1st appearance and origin. 2300.00 9000.00
2 1st & Origin: Mars. (Fall/42) 500.00 1900.00
3 (2-3/43) 300.00 1100.00
4 "The Adventure Of The Mole Men" 240.00 775.00
5 .... 240.00 775.00
6 (Fall/43) 240.00 775.00
7 "Wonder Woman 1000 Years In The Future!"
.... 200.00 650.00
8 "The Adventures Of The Undersea Amazons"
.... 200.00 650.00
9 "The Reversal Of Evolution" (Summer/44)
.... 200.00 650.00
10 "The Invasion From Saturn" 200.00 650.00
11 (Winter/44) 200.00 650.00
12 "The Winged Maidens Of Venus" 200.00 650.00
13 "Adventures In Bitterland" 155.00 500.00
14 "Shamrock Land" (Fall/45) 155.00 500.00
15 "The Tigeapes Of Neptunia" 155.00 500.00
16 "In Pluto's Kingdom" (3-4/46)" 155.00 500.00
17 "The Winds Of Time" 155.00 500.00
18 (7-8/46) 155.00 500.00
19 "The Tale Of The Witchdoctor's Cauldron"
.... 140.00 450.00
20 "Red Beard The Pirate!" (11-12/46) 140.00 450.00
21 "The Adventure Of The Atom Universe!" (1-2/47)
.... 140.00 450.00
22 "The Mad Thief!" 140.00 450.00
23 "A Story From Wonder Woman's Childhood"
.... 140.00 450.00
24 "The Challenge Of The Mask!" ... 140.00 450.00
25 (9-10/47) 120.00 390.00
26 "The Golden Women And The White Star!"
.... 120.00 390.00
27 (1-2/48) 120.00 390.00
28-29 .... 120.00 390.00
30 "The Secret Of The Limestone Caves" 120.00 390.00
31 "The Shrinking Formula!" 100.00 320.00
32 "The Amazing Global Thefts!" ... 100.00 320.00
33 "The Four Dooms!" (1-2/49) ... 100.00 320.00
34 "The Mystery Of The Rhyming Riddle!" (3-4/49)
.... 100.00 320.00
35 "The 9 Lives Club!" 100.00 320.00
36 "Paradise Island!" 100.00 320.00
37 "The Riddle Of The Chinese Mummy Case!"
.... 100.00 320.00
38 "The Girl From Yesterday!" 100.00 320.00
39 "The Trail Of Thrills!" (1-2/50) ... 100.00 320.00
40 "Hollywood Goes To Paradise Island!" 100.00 320.00
41 "Wonder Woman—Private Detective!"
.... 80.00 260.00
42 "Danger On The Speedway" 80.00 260.00
43 "The Amazing Spy Ring Mystery!" 80.00 260.00
44 "Monarch Of The Sargasso Sea!" 80.00 260.00
45 "The Wonder Woman Story!" (1-2/51) Origin retold: Wonder Woman. 130.00 420.00
46 "The Trail Of The Lost Hours!" ... 80.00 260.00
47 "The World Below The North Pole!" 80.00 260.00
48 "Wonder Woman Vs. Robot Woman!" 80.00 260.00
49 "Return Of The Phantom Empire!" 80.00 260.00
50 "The Menace Of The Master Spy!" 80.00 260.00
51 "The Amazing Impersonation!" (1-2/52)
.... 60.00 190.00
52 "Battle For Fairyland!" 60.00 190.00
53 "The Wonder Woman Nobody Knows!"
.... 60.00 190.00
54 "The Wizard Of Castle Sinister!" ... 60.00 190.00
55 "Ghost Train!" 60.00 190.00
56 "Homicide Highway!" 60.00 190.00
57 "The Man Who Shook The Earth!" (1-2/53)
.... 60.00 190.00
58 " 60.00 190.00
59 "Wonder Woman's Invisible Twin!" 60.00 190.00
60 "The War That Never Happened!" 60.00 190.00
61 "Wonder Woman—Hollywood Stunt Queen!"
.... 50.00 160.00

62 "Wonder Woman's Triple Identity!" 50.00 160.00
63 "The Secret Invasion!" (1-2/54) 50.00 160.00
64 "The 3-D Terror!" 50.00 160.00
65 "The Tornado Detective!" 50.00 160.00
66 "The Talking Tiara!" 50.00 160.00
67 "Confessions Of A Spy!" 50.00 160.00
68 "TNT Trap!" 50.00 160.00
69 "The Seeds Of Peril!" 50.00 160.00
70 "The Volcano Maker!" 50.00 160.00
71 "One-Woman Circus!" (1/55) 50.00 160.00
72 "The Golden Doom!" 50.00 160.00
73 "The Prairie Pirate!" 1st Code Approved issue. (4/55) 50.00 160.00
74 "One-Woman Rodeo!" 40.00 130.00
75 "The Winning Of Wonder Woman's Tiara!" 40.00 130.00
76 "The Bird Who Revealed Wonder Woman's Identity!" 40.00 130.00
77 "The Island That Wonder Woman Built!" 40.00 130.00
78 "Andy Gorilla—Prize Pupil!" 40.00 130.00
79 "The Amazon Flea Circus!" (1/56) 40.00 130.00
80 "The Mask Of Mystery!" 40.00 130.00
81 "The Dream Dooms!" 31.00 100.00
82 "Wonder Woman Meets Robin Hood!" 31.00 100.00
83 "The Flying Ambulance!" 31.00 100.00
84 "The Secret Wonder Woman!" (8/56) 1st "5000 Prizes" issue. 31.00 100.00
85 "The Woman In The Bottle!" 31.00 100.00
86 31.00 100.00
87 "Island Of The Giants!" (1/57) 31.00 100.00
88 31.00 100.00
89 "The Triple Heroine!" 31.00 100.00
90 31.00 100.00
91 "The Eagle Who Caged People!" 23.00 75.00
92 "The Circus Of Mystery!" 23.00 75.00
93 23.00 75.00
94 "The Channel Of Time!" 23.00 75.00
95 "The World's Most Dangerous Human!" (1/58) 23.00 75.00
96 "Diary Of An Amazon!" 23.00 75.00
97 "The Runaway Time Express!" 23.00 75.00
98 "The Million Dollar Penny!" 23.00 75.00
99 "Stampede Of The Comets!" 23.00 75.00
100 "The Forest Of Giants!" (8/58) 23.00 75.00
101 20.00 60.00
102 (10/58) 20.00 60.00
103-104 20.00 60.00
105 Wonder Woman's secret origin. (4/59) 80.00 280.00
106-110 15.00 50.00
111-120 10.00 40.00
121-126 7.00 25.00
127 1st 12 cent cover price. 5.00 20.00
128-130 5.00 15.00
131-155 5.00 15.00
156 Early comics history. (8/65) 5.00 15.00
157-158 5.00 15.00
159 Origin retold: Wonder Woman. 5.00 15.00
160-170 5.00 15.00
171-200 2.75 10.00
201-202 Catwoman appearance. 2.75 10.00
203-210 .75 2.00
211 100 pages. .75 3.00
212-213 .50 1.25
214 100 pages. .75 3.00
215-266 .50 1.25
267-268 Animal Man. 2.75 10.00
269-280 .50 1.25
281-283 Joker. .50 1.25
284-286 .50 1.25
287 New Teen Titans. .50 1.25
288-299 .50 1.25
300 Anniversary issue. 1.00 3.00
301-304 .50 1.25
305 1st: Circe. 1.50 5.00
306-326 .50 1.25
327-328 .50 1.50
329 Double size, final issue. .75 2.00

WONDER WOMAN

DC (1987-CURRENT)

0 (8/94) 2.25 8.00
1 .75 2.50
2-3 .50 1.50
4-48 .50 1.25
49 .50 1.50
50 Double size. .75 2.50
51-81 .50 1.25
82-84 .50 1.50
85 Mike Deodato's first work on Wonder Woman. 2.75 10.00
86-87 .50 1.50
88 Return: Circe. 2.25 8.00
89 Vs. Circe. 1.75 6.00
90 1st Artemis. 2.50 9.00
91 1.50 5.00
92 Artemis becomes the new Wonder Woman. 1.50 5.00
93 1.25 4.00
94-97 .50 1.50
98-99 .50 1.75
100 Double size, holographic foil-stamped cover. 1.50 5.00
100A Regular cover. .75 2.95
101 .50 1.95
ANNUAL 1 (1988) .75 2.25
ANNUAL 2 (1989) .75 2.25
ANNUAL 3 Eclipso. (1992) .75 2.50
ANNUAL 4 (1994) 1.00 3.50
SPECIAL 1 (1992) .50 1.75

WONDERFUL ADVENTURES OF PINOCCHIO, THE

GOLD KEY (1963)

10089-310 Disney movie tie-in. 8.00 25.00

WONDERFUL WORLD OF THE BROTHERS GRIMM

GOLD KEY (1962)

10008-210 Movie tie-in (photo insert). 7.00 20.00

WONDERLAND COMICS

PRIZE (1945-1947)

1 19.00 60.00
2 8.00 25.00
3-9 5.00 15.00

WONDERMAN

MARVEL (1991-1994)

1-24 .30 1.00
25 Double size. .30 1.00
26-33 .30 1.00
ANNUAL 1 .30 1.00
ANNUAL 2 Polybagged with card. .30 1.00

WONDERMAN SPECIAL

MARVEL (1986)

1 One shot. .30 1.00

WONDERS OF ALADDIN, THE

DELL FOUR COLOR SERIES (1962)

1255 Movie tie-in. 19.00 60.00

WONDERWORLD COMICS

FOX (1939-1942)

3 1st: Flame by Lou Fine. Previous title: Wonder Comics. 700.00 2600.00
4 310.00 1000.00
5-6 280.00 900.00
7-10 240.00 775.00
11 Origin: The Flame. 280.00 900.00
12 200.00 650.00
13 155.00 500.00
14-18 140.00 450.00
19-27 120.00 390.00
28 1st & Origin: U.S. Jones. 155.00 500.00
29 80.00 260.00
30 Origin: Flame Girl. 155.00 500.00
31-33 80.00 260.00

WOODSY OWL

GOLD KEY (1973-1976)

1 1.00 3.00
2-10 .75 2.00

WOODY WOODPECKER

DELL FOUR COLOR SERIES (1947-1952)

169 "Man Hunter Of The North" (10/47) 35.00 110.00
188 (5/48) 22.00 70.00
202 (11/48) 16.00 50.00
232 (6/49) 16.00 50.00
249 "The Globe Trotter" (10/49) 16.00 50.00
264 "The Magic Lantern" (2/50) 14.00 45.00
288 "Klondike Gold" (8/50) 14.00 45.00
305 (12/50) 8.00 25.00
336 (6/51) 8.00 25.00
350 (9/51) 8.00 25.00
364 (12/51) 8.00 25.00
374 (2/52) 8.00 25.00
390 (4/52) 8.00 25.00
405 (6/52) 8.00 25.00
416 (8/52) 8.00 25.00
431 (10/52) 8.00 25.00

WOODY WOODPECKER

DELL/GOLD KEY/WHITMAN (1952-1984)

16-20 2.75 10.00
21-40 2.25 8.00
41-72 1.75 6.00
73 Begin Gold Key publication. 80 pages. 10.00 30.00
74-75 80 pages. 10.00 30.00
76-90 1.50 5.00
91-120 1.25 4.00
121-150 .75 2.00
151-187 .30 1.00
188 Begin: Whitman publication. .30 1.00
189-200 .30 1.00

WOODY WOODPECKER BACK TO SCHOOL

DELL (1952-1957)

1 100 page Dell Giant. 25.00 80.00
2-6 100 page Dell Giant. 16.00 50.00

WOODY WOODPECKER CHRISTMAS PARADE

GOLD KEY (1968)

1 100 page Giant. 7.00 20.00

WOODY WOODPECKER COUNTY FAIR

DELL (1956-1958)

2-5 100 page Dell Giant. 16.00 50.00

WOODY WOODPECKER MEETS SCOTTY MACTAPE

SCOTCH TAPE GIVEAWAY (1953)

NO# 8.00 25.00

WORLD AROUND US, THE

GILBERTON (1958-1961)

1 "Dogs" 11.00 35.00
2 "Indians" 11.00 35.00
3 "Horses" 11.00 35.00
4 "Railroads" 11.00 35.00
5 "Space" 11.00 35.00
6 "The FBI" 11.00 35.00
7 "Pirates" 11.00 35.00
8 "Flight" 11.00 35.00
9 "The Army" 11.00 35.00
10 "The Navy" 11.00 35.00
11 "The Marines" 11.00 35.00
12 "The Coast Guard" 11.00 35.00
13 "The Air Force" 11.00 35.00
14 "The French Revolution" 11.00 35.00
15 "Prehistoric Animals" 11.00 35.00
16 "The Crusades" 11.00 35.00
17 "Festivals" 11.00 35.00
18 "Great Scientists" 11.00 35.00
19 "The Jungle" 11.00 35.00
20 "Through Time And Space...Communications" 11.00 35.00
21 "American Presidents" 11.00 35.00
22 "Boating" 11.00 35.00
23 "Great Explorers" 11.00 35.00
24 "Ghosts" 11.00 35.00
25 "Magic" 11.00 35.00
26 "The Civil War" 11.00 35.00
27 "High Adventure" 11.00 35.00
28 "Whaling" 11.00 35.00
29 "Vikings" 11.00 35.00
30 "Undersea Adventures" 11.00 35.00
31 "Hunting" 11.00 35.00
32 "For Gold And Glory" 11.00 35.00
33 "Famous Teens" 11.00 35.00
34 "Fishing" 11.00 35.00
35 "Spies" 11.00 35.00
36 "Fight For Life" 11.00 35.00

WORLD FAMOUS CREATURES

MAGSYN(WARREN) (1958-1959) MAGAZINE

1 65.00 200.00
2 Includes art by Severin. 50.00 150.00
3-4 50.00 150.00

WORLD FAMOUS HEROES MAGAZINE

CENTAUR (1941-1942)

1 190.00 600.00
2 125.00 400.00
3-4 110.00 350.00

WORLD FAMOUS STORIES COMICS

CROYDEN (1945)

1 Ali Baba and the Forty Thieves, Hansel and Gretel, Rip Van Winkle, A Midsummer Night's Dream. 23.00 75.00

WORLD IS HIS PARISH, THE

PFLAUM (1953)

NO# The story of Pope Pius XII. 10.00 30.00

WORLD OF ADVENTURE

GOLD KEY (1963)

1 Disney TV tie-in. 1.50 5.00
2-3 1.50 5.00

WORLD OF FANTASY

MARVEL(ATLAS) (1956-1959)

1 65.00 200.00
2 Art: Al Williamson. 35.00 110.00
3 26.00 85.00
4 22.00 70.00
5-6 20.00 65.00

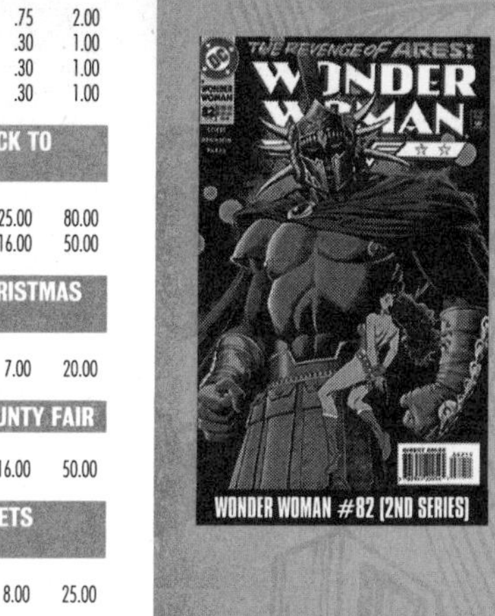

WONDER WOMAN #82 (2ND SERIES)

WONDER MAN #28

WORLD FAMOUS HEROES #3

WORLD OF FANTASY #2

WORLD OF FANTASY #16

WORLD'S BEST COMICS #1

WORLD'S FINEST COMICS #198

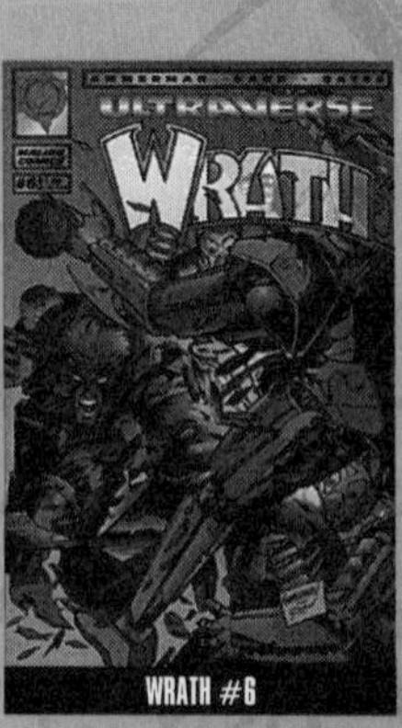

WRATH #6

7-12 .... 17.00 55.00
13-15 .... 16.00 50.00
16 Art: Steve Ditko, Jack Kirby, Al Williamson. 26.00 85.00
17-19 Art: Steve Ditko, Jack Kirby. ... 26.00 85.00

WORLD OF KRYPTON, THE
DC (1979)
1-3 .... .30 1.00

WORLD OF KRYPTON, THE
DC (1987-1988)
1-4 .... .30 1.00

WORLD OF MYSTERY
MARVEL(ATLAS) (1956-1957)
1 .... 65.00 200.00
2 .... 26.00 85.00
3 Art: Steve Ditko. 26.00 85.00
4-5 .... 20.00 65.00
6 Art: Steve Ditko. 26.00 85.00
7 .... 20.00 65.00

WORLD OF SUSPENSE
MARVEL(ATLAS) (1956-1957)
1 "A Stranger Among Us" (4/56) ... 65.00 200.00
2 Art: Steve Ditko. 26.00 85.00
3 "The Green Man!" by Al Williamson (4 pages). 20.00 65.00
4-8 .... 20.00 65.00

WORLD WAR III
ACE (1953)
1 .... 105.00 340.00
2 .... 85.00 280.00

WORLD WAR STORIES
DELL (1965)
1 .... 7.00 20.00
2-3 .... 4.00 12.00

WORLD'S BEST COMICS
DC (1941)
1 Superman, Batman and Robin, Red, White and Blue, Zatara. (Spring/41) "96 Thrilling Pages In Full Color!" Becomes World's Finest Comics #2. .... 1600.00 6000.00

WORLD'S FINEST
DC (1990)
1-3 .... 1.00 3.00

WORLD'S FINEST COMICS
DC (1941-1986)
2 Previous title: World's Best Comics. 900.00 3200.00
3 Begin: Sandman. 1st & Origin: Scarecrow. 700.00 2600.00
4 .... 500.00 1900.00
5 .... 400.00 1500.00
6 Begin: Star Spangled Kid. 400.00 1300.00
7 Begin: Green Arrow. "The Eight Doomed Men!" (Fall/42) 400.00 1300.00
8 Begin: Boy Commandos. 300.00 1100.00
9 End: 96 page issues. 310.00 1000.00
10 Art: Simon & Kirby. 300.00 975.00
11-16 .... 250.00 825.00
17 End: Cardboard covers. 250.00 825.00
18 End: Star Spangled Kid. 240.00 775.00
19-24 .... 200.00 650.00
25-40 .... 155.00 500.00
41 .... 130.00 420.00
42 "Introducing The Wyoming Kid!" (9-10/49) 130.00 420.00
43-47 .... 130.00 420.00
48 End: Squarebound issues. 130.00 420.00
49 "Introducing Tom Sparks, Boy Inventor!" (11-12/50) 120.00 390.00
50-51 .... 120.00 390.00
52 "River Of Diamonds!" 120.00 390.00
53-64 .... 120.00 390.00
65 Origin retold: Superman. 140.00 450.00
66-70 .... 140.00 450.00
71 "Read What Happens When Superman and Batman Exchange Indentities!" (7-8/54) Begin: Superman/Batman teamups. 1st 10-cent cover price (all prior issues were 15-cent cover price). 190.00 600.00
72 "Superman and Batman in Fort Crime!" 110.00 350.00
73 "Swamis, Inc!" 110.00 350.00
74 "The Contest Of Heroes!" (1-2/55) 110.00 350.00
75 "The New Team Of Superman And Robin!" 1st Code Approved issue. (3-4/55) 95.00 300.00
76 "When Gotham City Challenged Metropolis!" 70.00 230.00
77 "The Super-Batman!" 70.00 230.00
78 "When Superman's Identity Is Exposed!" 70.00 230.00
79 "The Three Magicians Of Baghdad!" 70.00 230.00
80 (1-2/56) 70.00 230.00
81 "The True History Of Superman And Batman!" 70.00 230.00
82 "The Three Super-Musketeers!" ... 55.00 175.00
83 "The Code Of The Mother Goose Mystery!" 1st "5000 Prizes" issue. (8/56) 55.00 175.00
84 "The Super-Mystery Of Metropolis!" 55.00 175.00
85 "The Super-Rivals" 55.00 175.00
86 "The Super Show Of Gotham City!" (1-2/57) 55.00 175.00
87 "The Reversed Heroes!" 55.00 175.00
88 "Superman And Batman's Greatest Foes!" (6/57) 1st: Joker/Luthor teamup. 55.00 175.00
89 "The Club Of Heroes!" 55.00 175.00
90 "The Super-Batwoman!" (10/57) App: Batwoman. 55.00 175.00
91 "The Three Super-Sleepers!" 40.00 125.00
92 "The Boy From Outer Space!" (1-2/58) 40.00 125.00
93 "The Boss Of Batman and Superman!" 40.00 125.00
94 "The Origin Of The Superman-Batman Team!" (6/58) Origin retold: Superman/Batman team. 115.00 375.00
95 "Battle Of The Super-Heroes!" ... 40.00 125.00
96 "The Super-Foes From Planet X!" (10/58) 40.00 125.00
97 "The Day Superman Betrayed Batman!" 40.00 125.00
98 "Menace Of The Moon Man!" ... 40.00 125.00
99 "Batman's Super-Spending Spree!" (1-2/59) 40.00 125.00
100 "The Dictator Of Krypton City!" ... 70.00 225.00
101 "Menace Of The Atom Master!" 23.00 75.00
102 "The Caveman From Krypton!" ... 23.00 75.00
103 .... 23.00 75.00
104 "The Plot To Destroy Superman!" 23.00 75.00
105 "The Alien Superman" (11/59) 23.00 75.00
106 "Superman and Batman battle the Amazing Duplicate Man!" 23.00 75.00
107 "Secret Of The Time Creature!" (1-2/60) 23.00 75.00
108 "Superman and Batman Vs. the Star Creatures!" 23.00 75.00
109 "The Bewitched Batman!" 23.00 75.00
110 "The Alien Who Doomed Robin!" 23.00 75.00
111 "Superman's Secret Kingdom!" 19.00 60.00
112 "The Menace Of Superman's Pet!" 19.00 60.00
113 "Bat-Mite Meets Mr. Mxyzptlk!" (11/60) 1st Bat-Mite/Mr. Mxyzptlk team-up. 19.00 60.00
114 "Captives Of The Space Globes!" 19.00 60.00
115 "The Curse That Doomed Superman!" (1-2/61) 19.00 60.00
116 "The Creature From Beyond!" ... 19.00 60.00
117 "The Creature That Was Exchanged For Superman!" 19.00 60.00
118-121 .... 19.00 60.00
122 1st 12 cent cover price. 10.00 30.00
123-128 .... 8.00 25.00
129 .... 11.00 35.00
130-141 .... 7.00 22.00
142 .... 8.00 26.00
143-150 .... 5.00 15.00
151-155 .... 4.00 12.00
156 1st: Bizzaro Batman. 20.00 65.00
157-160 .... 2.75 10.00
161 80 page Giant #G-28. .... 6.00 18.00
162-165 .... 2.25 8.00
166 Versus Muto & Joker in "The Danger Of The Deadly Duo!"(future story). 5.00 15.00
167-169 .... 2.25 8.00
170 80 page Giant #G-40. .... 6.00 18.00
171-174 .... 2.00 7.50
175-176 Art: Neal Adams. 4.00 12.00
177 ...vs. Joker & Luthor in "Duel Of The Crime Kings!" 4.00 11.00
178 .... 1.50 5.00
179 80 page Giant #G-52. .... 2.75 10.00
180-187 .... 1.50 5.00
188 80 page Giant #G-64. .... 2.75 10.00
189-196 .... 1.25 4.50
197 80 page Giant #G-76. .... 2.75 10.00
198 3rd: Superman/Flash race. 17.00 55.00
199 Superman/Flash race (pt.2). ... 17.00 55.00
200 .... 2.00 7.00
201-204 .... 1.25 4.00
205 .... 1.00 3.00
206 80 page Giant #G-88. .... 2.00 7.00
207-222 .... 1.00 3.00
223 Begin: 100 page issues. 1.75 6.00
224-227 .... 1.75 6.00
228 End: 100 page issues. 1.75 6.00
229-248 .... 1.00 3.00
249 Begin: The Creeper by Steve Ditko. 1.50 5.00
250 Origin: The Creeper. 1.00 3.00
251-254 .... 1.00 3.00
255 End: The Creeper. 1.00 3.00
256-259 .... 1.00 3.00
260-283 .... .75 2.00
284-299 .... .50 1.75
300 .... 1.50 5.00
301-323 .... .50 1.50

WORLD'S GREATEST SONGS ILLUSTRATED
MARVEL(ATLAS) (1954)
1 Eddie Fisher cover & story. 50.00 150.00

WORLD'S GREATEST STORIES
JUBILEE (1949)
1 "Alice In Wonderland Through The Looking Glass." 23.00 75.00
2 "Pinocchio." 22.00 70.00

WORLDS BEYOND
FAWCETT (1951)
1 Title changes to Worlds Of Fear with #2. 50.00 160.00

WORLDS COLLIDE
DC (1994)
1 Worlds Collide, pt.7. Collector's edition. 1.00 3.95
1A Newsstand edition. .... .75 2.50

WORLDS OF FEAR
FAWCETT (1952-1953)
2 Previous title: Worlds Beyond. 45.00 140.00
3 .... 35.00 110.00
4-5 .... 28.00 90.00
6 "A Death For A Death!" 28.00 90.00
7-9 .... 25.00 80.00
10 Cover: Norman Saunders. 55.00 170.00

WORLDS UNKNOWN
MARVEL (1973-1974)
1 .... 1.25 4.00
2-8 .... .75 2.00

WORST FROM MAD, THE
EC (1958-1969)
1 With labels and stickers. (1958) ... 80.00 250.00
2 With record. (1959) 85.00 280.00
3 .... 55.00 180.00
4 Includes an 8 page color Sunday Comic Section. 55.00 180.00
5 With record. (1962) 85.00 280.00
6 With record. (1963) 85.00 280.00
7-8 .... 40.00 120.00
9 With record. (1966) 65.00 210.00
10-12 .... 23.00 75.00

WOTALIFE COMICS
FOX FEATURES (1946-1947)
3 .... 19.00 60.00
4-6 .... 13.00 40.00
7-12 .... 10.00 30.00

WOTALIFE COMICS
GREEN (1959)
1 .... 8.00 25.00

WOW COMICS
FAWCETT (1940-1948)
1 (NO#) 2600.00 10000.00
2 .... 400.00 1200.00
3 .... 230.00 750.00
4 .... 190.00 625.00
5 .... 155.00 500.00
6 1st: Commando Yank. Origin: Phantom Eagle. 155.00 500.00
7-8 .... 155.00 500.00
9 Begin: Captain Marvel, Captain Marvel J.r, Mary Marvel. 190.00 625.00
10 .... 130.00 430.00
11-12 .... 115.00 370.00
13-18 .... 95.00 310.00
19-24 .... 80.00 250.00
25-30 .... 50.00 150.00
31-40 .... 31.00 100.00
41-50 .... 23.00 75.00
51-60 .... 19.00 60.00
61-64 .... 16.00 50.00
65 Begin: Tom Mix. 16.00 50.00
66-68 .... 16.00 50.00
69 Title changes to Real Western Hero with #70. .... 16.00 50.00

WOW WHAT A MAGAZINE!
HENLE (1936)
1 Cover: Dick Briefer. 1st Art: Will Eisner. Buck Jones in "The Phantom Rider," Fu Manchu, Scott Dalton. 800.00 3000.00
2 Art: Will Eisner. 500.00 1800.00
3 Cover & art: Will Eisner. Popeye, Ripley's Believe It Or Not, Fu Manchu, Scott Dalton. (9/36) 400.00 1500.00
4 Mandrake, Flash Gordon, Tillie The Toiler, Popeye, Hiram Hicks by Bob Kane. Early Will Eisner art. ... 600.00 2200.00

WRATH
MALIBU (1994-1995)
1 .50 1.95
1A Silver foil cover. 1.75 6.00
2-8 .50 1.95
9 .75 2.25
GIANT 1 .75 2.50

WRATH OF THE SPECTRE, THE
DC (1988)
1-4 .30 1.00

WRINGLE WRANGLE
DELL FOUR COLOR SERIES (1957)
821 Movie photo cover (Fess Parker). (8/57)
16.00 50.00

WULF THE BARBARIAN
ATLAS(SEABOARD) (1975)
1-4 .50 1.50

WYATT EARP
DELL (1957-1961)
1 (#860) From the 4-Color Series. TV photo cover. (11/57)
28.00 90.00
2 (#890) From the 4-Color Series. TV photo cover. (2/58)
17.00 55.00
3 (#921) From the 4-Color Series. TV photo cover. (6/58)
17.00 55.00
4 TV photo covers on all issues. 10.00 30.00
5-13 10.00 30.00

WYATT EARP
MARVEL (1972-1973)
30 Reprints in all issues. .75 2.00
31-34 .75 2.00

WYATT EARP
MARVEL(ATLAS) (1955-1960)
1 23.00 75.00
2 13.00 40.00
3-6 10.00 30.00
7-12 8.00 25.00
13-18 7.00 20.00
19-29 5.00 15.00

WYATT EARP FRONTIER MARSHALL
CHARLTON (1956-1967)
12 Previous title: Range Busters. 8.00 25.00
13-19 4.00 12.00
20 Double size. 10.00 30.00
21-30 2.50 9.00
31-40 2.00 7.00
41-50 1.50 5.00
51-72 1.00 3.00

X
DARK HORSE (1994-CURRENT)
1 Foil logo. .75 2.50
2-17 .75 2.50

X: ONE SHOT TO THE HEAD
DARK HORSE (1994)
NO# Reprints early X appearances. .75 2.50

X, THE MAN WITH THE X-RAY EYES
GOLD KEY (1963)
10083-309 Movie tie-in (photo insert). 11.00 35.00

X-CALIBRE
MARVEL (1995)
1 Deluxe edition. Previous title: Excalibur. 1.25 4.50
1 (2ND) 2nd printing. .50 1.95
2-4 1.00 3.00
TPB Reprints issues #1-4. 2.25 8.95

XENOBROOD
DC (1994-1995)
0 (8/94) .50 1.50
1-6 .50 1.50

XENOTECH
MIRAGE (1993)
1 "Top Secret" file cover. .75 2.75

XENOZOIC TALES
KITCHEN SINK (1987-CURRENT)
1 4.00 12.00
1 (2ND) 2nd printing. .75 2.00
2 2.50 9.00
2 (2ND) 2nd printing. .75 2.00
3 2.00 7.50
4 1.75 6.00
5-7 1.25 4.00
8-13 1.00 3.00

XENYA
SANCTUARY (1994-CURRENT)
1 Art: The Bros. Hildebrandt. 1.50 5.00
2-4 .75 2.95

X-FACTOR
MARVEL (1986-CURRENT)
1 3rd app. X-Factor (see Avengers 263 and Fantastic Four 286).
2nd: Baby Nathan (see X-Men 201). 2.50 9.00
2 1st Artie, Tower. 1.50 5.00
3 1.50 5.00
4 1st Frenzy. 1.50 5.00
5 Cameo: Apocalypse. 1.75 6.00
6 1st:Apocalypse (full story). 2.75 10.00
7-9 1.50 5.00
10 Mutant Massacre. 1.50 5.00
11 1st Berzerker. 1.50 5.00
12-16 1.50 5.00
17 1st Rictor. 1.50 5.00
18 Origin:Archangel. 1.50 5.00
19 1.50 5.00
20 X-Terminators. 1.50 5.00
21-22 1.50 5.00
23 Cameo:Archangel. 2.75 10.00
24 1st: Archangel (full story). 5.00 15.00
25 Double size. Fall Of The Mutants. 1.25 4.00
26 Fall Of The Mutants. 1.25 4.00
27-33 1.00 3.00
34 Death: Candy Southern. 1.00 3.00
35-37 1.00 3.00
38 Double size. 1.00 3.00
39 1.00 3.00
40 Cover & art: Rob Liefeld. Origin: Nanny. 1.00 3.00
41 1st Alchemy. 1.00 3.00
42-49 1.00 3.00
50 Double size. 1.25 4.00
51-53 Sabretooth. 1.00 3.00
54-59 .75 2.00
60 X-Tinction Agenda, pt. 3. 1.00 3.00
60 (2ND) 2nd printing. .25 1.25
61 X-Tinction Agenda, pt. 6. 1.00 3.00
62 X-Tinction Agenda, pt. 9. 1.00 3.00
63 Begin: Whilce Portacio cover & art. 1.00 3.00
64-66 1.00 3.00
67 Death: Sebastian Shaw. 1.00 3.00
68 Baby Nathan taken to the future. 1.00 3.00
69 1.00 3.00
70 .75 2.00
71 Begin: new Team. 1.50 5.00
71 (2ND) 2nd printing. .50 1.25
72-74 .75 2.00
75 ($1.75-c) Double size. 1st Nasty Boys. 1.00 3.00
76-87 .75 2.00
88 1st: Random. 1.25 4.00
89-90 .75 2.00
91 .50 1.50
92 ($3.50-c). Anniversary issue. Begin: Return of Magneto story.
1.50 5.00
92 (2ND) 2nd printing. .75 2.50
93-94 .75 2.50
95-97 .50 1.50
98 Havok battles Random. .50 1.50
99 .50 1.50
100 ($3.50-c) Double size. Foil-embossed cover. Death: Jamie Madrox. .75 2.95
100A Newsstand edition. .50 1.50
101-105 .50 1.50
106 Foil stamped cover. Life Signs, pt. 1; Generation X tie-in.
.75 2.95
106A Regular cover. .50 1.50
107 .50 1.50
108 Deluxe edition. .50 1.95
108A Regular edition. .50 1.50
109 Deluxe edition. .50 1.95
109A Regular edition. .50 1.50
110 Deluxe edition. .50 1.95
110A Regular edition. .50 1.50
111 Deluxe edition (with card). .50 1.95
111A Regular edition (no card). .50 1.50
112-114 .50 1.95

X-FACTOR ANNUAL
MARVEL (1986-CURRENT)
1 (1986) 1.00 3.00
2 (1987) 1.25 4.00
3 (1988) 1.00 3.50
4 Atlantis Attacks. (1989) 1.00 3.00
5 (1990) 1.50 5.00
6 (1991) 1.00 3.00
7 (1992) 1.00 3.00
8 1st Charon. Includes trading card. (1993) .75 2.95
9 (1994) .75 2.95

X-FARCE
ECLIPSE (1992)
1 Parody. .75 2.50

X-FILES, THE
TOPPS (1995-CURRENT)
1 TV tie-in. 13.00 40.00
1A Newsstand edition. 8.00 25.00
2 5.00 15.00
3 2.00 8.00
4 1.75 7.00
4A Newsstand edition. .75 2.50
5-6 1.25 4.00
7 .75 2.95
SPECIAL Reprints issues #1-3. (1995) 1.00 3.95
TPB Reprints issues #1-6. 6.00 19.95

X-FORCE
MARVEL (1991-CURRENT)
1 w/ Cable card. 1st G. W. Bridge. 1.25 4.00
1 (2ND) .75 2.00
1A w/ Shatterstar card. 1.00 3.00
1B w/ Deadpool card. 1.00 3.00
1C w/ Sunspot card. 1.00 3.00
1D w/ Team card. 1.00 3.00
1E Unbagged, without card. .50 1.75
2 1st: new Weapon X. 1.25 4.00
3-7 1.00 3.00
8 Origin: Cable. 1.00 3.00
9 Death: Masque. 1.00 3.00
10-11 .75 2.00
12 1st Crule. .75 2.00
13-24 .50 1.50
25 ($3.50-c) Double size, wraparound cover with hologram. Cable returns. 1.50 5.00
26 Cable. 1.00 3.50
27-37 .50 1.50
38 Foil-stamped cover. Lead-in to Generation X.
.75 2.95
38A Regular cover. .50 1.50
39 .50 1.50
40 Deluxe edition. .50 1.95
40A Regular edition. .50 1.50
41 Deluxe edition. .50 1.95
41A Regular edition. .50 1.50
42 Deluxe edition. .50 1.95
42A Regular edition. .50 1.50
43 Deluxe edition (with card). .50 1.95
43A Regular edition (no card). .50 1.50
44-45 .50 1.95
ANNUAL 1 Origin: Shattershot. (1992) .75 2.25
ANNUAL 2 1st X-Treme. Bagged w/ trading card. (1993)
.75 2.95
ANNUAL 3 (1994) .75 2.95

X-MAN
MARVEL (1995-CURRENT)
1 Age of Apocalypse. 1.75 6.00
1 (2ND) 2nd printing. .50 1.95
2 1.00 3.50
3 Domino. 1.00 3.00
4 1.00 3.00
5-7 .50 1.95

XMAS COMICS
FAWCETT (1941-1947)
1 324 Pages. Contains Bulletman 2, Captain Marvel 3, Master 18, Whiz 21 and Wow 3. 700.00 2500.00
2 Bulletman, Captain Marvel, Spy Smasher.
270.00 875.00
3 Begin: Funny Animal stories. 80.00 250.00
4-7 80.00 250.00

XMAS COMICS
FAWCETT (1949-1952)
4 115.00 370.00
5-7 85.00 280.00

X-MEN
MARVEL (1991-CURRENT)
1 (DELUXE) (3.95-c) Prestige format. Double gatefold cover.
1.50 5.00
1A Storm and Beast cover. .75 2.50
1B Colossus and Gambit cover. .75 2.50
1C Wolverine and Cyclops cover. .75 2.50
1D Magneto cover. .75 2.50
2 Vs. Magneto. 1.25 4.00
3 1.25 4.00
4 1st: Omega Red. Wolverine returns to original costume.
1.50 5.00
5 1st: Maverick. Longshot returns. 1.75 6.00
6 Origin: Sabretooth. Identity revealed. 1.75 6.00
7 1.25 4.00
8 Gambit battles Bishop. 1.25 4.00
9-10 1.25 4.00
11-13 .75 2.00
14-15 X-Cutioner's Song. .75 2.00
16 X-Cutioner's Song. Polybagged w/ card. .75 2.00
17-18 Polybagged w/ card. .75 2.00
19-24 .75 2.00

X-FACTOR #71

X-FILES SPECIAL, THE

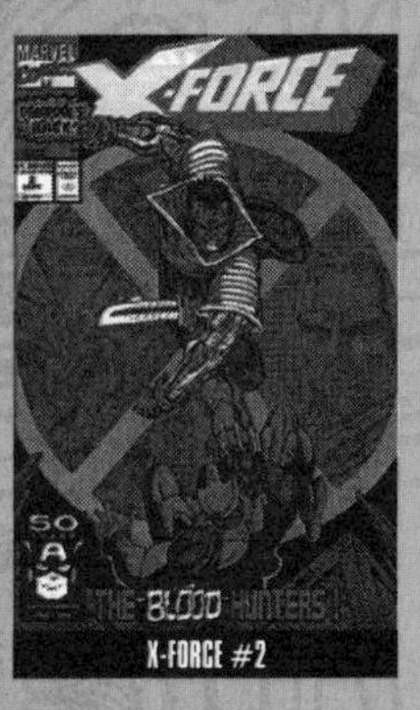

X-FORCE #2

X-MAN #4

a b c d e f g h i j k l m n o p q r s t u v w x y z

X-MEN #1 (1ST SERIES)

X-MEN #39 (1ST SERIES)

X-MEN #327 (1ST SERIES)

X-MEN #100 (1ST SERIES)

FAMOUS · FIRSTS

X-MEN #94

The X-Men's 1975 revival brought major changes to the title. Following the events of Giant-Size X-Men #1, this issue introduces the new line-up of Banshee, Colossus, Cyclops, Nightcrawler, Storm, Thunderbird and Wolverine.

25 ($3.50-c). 30th Anniversary issue w/ Gambit hologram. Magneto removes Wolverine's adamantium. Return of Cable. 2.50 9.00
25 (B&W) B&W cover version. 8.00 25.00
25 (GOLD) 7.00 20.00
26 Bloodties, pt. 2. .75 2.50
27-29 .75 2.50
30 Wedding issue (Scott & Jean), w/ trading cards. 1.50 5.50
31 .75 2.00
32-35 .50 1.75
36 Generation Next, pt. 2. Foil-stamped cover. 1.25 4.00
36A Regular cover. .50 1.50
37 Generation Next conclusion. Foil-stamped cover. 1.25 4.00
37A Regular cover edition. .50 1.50
38 Deluxe edition. .75 2.25
38A Regular edition. .50 1.50
39 Deluxe edition. .75 2.25
39A Regular edition. .50 1.50
40 Deluxe edition. .75 2.25
40A Regular edition. .50 1.50
41 Deluxe edition (with card). .75 2.50
41A Regular edition (no card). .50 1.50
42-44 .50 1.95
ANNUAL 1 Shattershot, pt.1, 1st: Mojo II. Polybagged with card. 1.00 3.00
ANNUAL 2 1st: Empyrean. Bagged w/ trading card. .75 2.95
ANNUAL 3 (1994) 1.00 3.25

X-MEN (UNCANNY X-MEN #143 ON)

MARVEL (1963-CURRENT)

1 1st & Origin: The X-Men (9/63). Story title: "X-Men." by Jack Kirby/Stan Lee. 1200.00 4800.00
2 1st Vanisher. "Nothing Can Stop The Vanisher!" by Kirby/Lee. 300.00 1150.00
3 1st: Blob. "Beware Of The Blob!" by Kirby/Lee. 140.00 460.00
4 1st Mastermind, Quicksilver, Scarlet Witch, Toad. "The Brotherhood Of Evil Mutants!" by Kirby/Lee. 160.00 525.00
5 "The Angel Is Trapped!" by Kirby/Lee. 95.00 300.00
6 Sub-Mariner app. 80.00 250.00
7 1st: Cerebro, 2nd: Blob. "The Return Of The Blob!" by Kirby/Lee. 65.00 210.00
8 1st: Unus in "The Uncanny Threat Of Unus The Untouchable!" by Kirby/Lee. 65.00 210.00
9 X-Men vs. The Avengers. 1st Lucifer. 55.00 180.00
10 1st: Ka-Zar (Silver Age), Zabu. "The Coming Of Ka-Zar!" by Kirby/Lee. 55.00 180.00
11 1st: Stranger. "The Triumph Of Magneto!" by Kirby/Lee. 40.00 130.00
12 Origin: Professor X, 1st & Origin: Juggernaut. 85.00 275.00
13 App:Juggernaut, Human Torch. "Where Walks The Juggernaut!" by Kirby/Lee. 40.00 130.00
14 1st: Sentinels. "Among Us Stalk...The Sentinels!" by Kirby/Lee. 40.00 130.00
15 1st: Master Mold, Origin: Beast. "Prisoners Of The Mysterious Master Mold!" by Kirby/Lee. 40.00 130.00
16 Death: Master Mold. "The Supreme Sacrifice!" by Kirby/Lee. 35.00 110.00
17 App: Magneto. "...And None Shall Survive!" by Kirby/Lee. 26.00 85.00
18 App: Magneto. "If Iceman Should Fail!" by Gavin/Lee. 26.00 85.00
19 1st & Origin: Mimic. "Lo! Now Shall Appear-The Mimic!" by Gavin/Lee. 23.00 75.00
20 Origin: Lucifer. "I, Lucifer!" by Gavin/Thomas. 23.00 75.00
21 Lucifer. 17.00 55.00
22 Count Nefaria. 17.00 55.00
23 Cameo: Locust. 17.00 55.00
24 1st Locust (full app.). 17.00 55.00
25-26 17.00 55.00
27 Mimic joins team. 17.00 55.00
28 1st: Banshee. 35.00 110.00
29 Mimic leaves team. 17.00 55.00
30 17.00 55.00
31-32 14.00 45.00
33 Dr. Strange app. 14.00 45.00
34 14.00 45.00
35 Spider-Man app. 22.00 70.00
36-37 14.00 45.00
38 Begin: X-Men origins series. 17.00 55.00
39-40 14.00 45.00
41 1st Grotesk. 14.00 45.00
42-43 14.00 45.00
44 1st Red Raven (Silver Age). 13.00 40.00
45-47 13.00 40.00
48 1st Computo. 13.00 40.00
49 1st Polaris. 14.00 45.00
50 Polaris. 14.00 45.00
51 13.00 40.00
52 10.00 30.00
53 Art: Barry Smith. 13.00 40.00
54 Art: Barry Smith. 1st&origin: Alex Summers. 16.00 50.00
55 Alex Summers. 13.00 40.00
56 Art: Neal Adams. 14.00 45.00
57 Art: Neal Adams. End: X-Men origins series. 14.00 45.00
58 Art: Neal Adams. 1st Alex Summers as Havok. 19.00 60.00
59 Art: Neal Adams. 14.00 45.00
60 Art: Neal Adams. 1st Sauron. 14.00 45.00
61-63 Art: Neal Adams. 14.00 45.00
64 1st Sunfire. 16.00 50.00
65 Art: Neal Adams. Return of Professor X. 14.00 45.00
66 Last new story: X-Men Battle The Hulk. 17.00 55.00
67 Begin: reprints of issues 12-45. 7.00 22.00
68-93 7.00 22.00
94 Begin: New X-Men series (8/75). New Team: Banshee, Colossus, Nightcrawler, Storm, Thunderbird, and Wolverine. 100.00 325.00
95 Death of Thunderbird. 20.00 75.00
96 16.00 55.00
97 11.00 40.00
98 13.00 45.00
99 15.00 50.00
100 15.00 55.00
101 1st Phoenix. 16.00 60.00
102 Origin: Storm. 7.00 25.00
103 1st time Wolverine is called Logan. 9.00 35.00
104-106 7.00 25.00
107 1st Gladiator, Starjammers. 9.00 35.00
108 Begin: John Byrne art. 19.00 65.00
109 1st Weapon Alpha. 12.00 40.00
110 No John Byrne art. 8.00 25.00
111 8.00 25.00
112-113 Magneto. 8.00 25.00
114-116 8.00 25.00
117 Origin retold: Professor X. 8.00 30.00
118-119 8.00 25.00
120 Cameo: Alpha Flight. 8.00 30.00
121 1st full Alpha Flight story. 13.00 40.00
122 Origin: Colossus, 1st Hellfire Club. 6.00 20.00
123 Spider-Man app. 6.00 20.00
124 6.00 20.00
125 1st Mutant X. 6.00 20.00
126 Mutant X becomes Proteus. 6.00 20.00
127-128 6.00 20.00
129 1st Kitty Pryde. 8.00 25.00
130 1st Dazzler. 6.00 20.00
131 6.00 20.00
132 6.00 20.00
133 Wolverine invades Hellfire Club. 6.00 20.00
134 Phoenix becomes Dark Phoenix. 6.00 20.00
135-136 6.00 20.00
137 Double size. Death: Dark Phoenix. 8.00 25.00
138 Cyclops quits. 6.00 20.00
139 1st Wolverine's new costume. 8.00 30.00
140 Alpha Flight disbands. 7.00 22.00
141 1st Rachel Summers (Phoenix II), Death: Frank Richards, 1st Future X-Men and Brotherhood Of Evil Mutants. 8.00 26.00
142 7.00 22.00
143 End: John Byrne art. 2.25 8.00
144-147 2.00 7.00
148 Magneto. 2.25 8.00
149 Magneto. 2.00 7.00
150 Double size. Magneto. 2.50 9.00
151-157 1.50 5.00
158 1st Rogue in X-Men, see Avengers Annual 10 for 1st app. 2.00 7.00
159 1.50 5.00
160 1.75 6.00
161 1.50 5.00
162 Wolverine solo story. 2.75 10.00
163 1.50 5.00
164 1st Binary. 2.00 7.00
165 Begin Paul Smith cover & art. 1.75 6.00
166 Double size. 1st Lockheed. 1.75 6.00

167 1st New Mutants in X-Men, released same month as New Mutants #1. 1.50 5.00
168-169 1.75 6.00
170 1.50 5.00
171 Cover&art: Walt Simonson. Rogue joins team. 2.50 9.00
172 Wolverine solo story, pt. 1. 1.75 6.00
173 Wolverine solo story, pt. 2. 1.50 5.00
174 1.50 5.00
175 End: Paul Smith art. Anniversary issue. Phoenix returns. 2.00 7.00
176-179 1.50 5.00
180 1st Cypher. Secret Wars tie-in. 1.50 5.00
181 Secret Wars. 1.50 5.00
182-183 1.50 5.00
184 1st Forge. 2.00 7.00
185 1.50 5.00
186 Art: Barry Smith/Terry Austin. 1.75 6.00
187 1st Naze. 1.50 5.00
188 Future Past. 1.50 5.00
189-190 1.50 5.00
191 1st Nimrod. Spider-Man app. 1.50 5.00
192 1.50 5.00
193 Double size. 100th New X-Men app. 1st Warpath (in costume), 1st Firestar. 2.25 8.00
194-199 1.50 5.00
200 Double size. 2.50 9.00
201 1st Cable (as baby Nathan-see X-Factor #1). 2.75 10.00
202-204 1.75 6.00
205 Wolverine solo story by Barry Smith. 5.00 15.00
206 1.75 6.00
207 Wolverine battles Phoenix. 1.75 6.00
208-209 1.75 6.00
210 Begin Mutant Massacre. 5.00 15.00
211 Mutant Massacre. 5.00 15.00
212 Mutant Massacre. Wolverine battles Sabretooth. 7.00 20.00
213 Mutant Massacre. Wolverine continues to battle Sabretooth. 7.00 20.00
214-218 1.50 5.00
219 Havok joins. 1.50 5.00
220 1.50 5.00
221 1st Mr. Sinister. 5.00 15.00
222 Wolverine battles Sabretooth. 5.00 15.00
223-224 1.50 5.00
225 Fall Of The Mutants. 1st: Roma. 2.00 7.00
226 Double size. Fall Of The Mutants. 2.00 7.00
227 Fall Of The Mutants. 2.00 7.00
228-243 1.50 5.00
244 1st: Jubilee. 7.00 20.00
245-247 1.50 5.00
248 1st Jim Lee art on X-Men (1989). 8.00 25.00
248 (2ND) .50 1.25
249-252 1.50 5.00
253 Storm, Forge, Magneto return to team. 1.50 5.00
254-255 1.50 5.00
256 Begin: Jim Lee cover&art. Acts of Vengeance. New Psylocke. 5.00 14.00
257 Wolverine battles Psylocke. 4.00 12.00
258 Wolverine solo story. 4.00 13.00
259 No Jim Lee art. 1.75 6.00
260-261 No Jim Lee art. 1.50 5.00
262 No Jim Lee art. Origin: Forge. 1.50 5.00
263 No Jim Lee art. 1.50 5.00
264-265 1.50 5.00
266 1st Gambit (full app.). No Jim Lee art. 11.00 36.00
267 Begin Jim Lee art. 2nd Gambit. 5.00 15.00
268 7.00 20.00
269 2.25 8.00
270 X-Tinction Agenda, pt 1. 4.00 10.50
270 2ND Gold ink. 1.00 3.00
271 X-Tinction Agenda, pt. 4. 2.25 8.00
272 X-Tinction Agenda, pt. 7. 2.25 8.00
273 2.00 7.00
274 1.75 6.50
275 Double size ($1.50-c). X-Men vs. Imperial Guard. 2.25 8.50
275 (2ND) Gold ink. .50 1.50
276 1.75 6.00
277 End: Jim Lee art. 1.75 6.00
278 1.00 3.50
279 1.25 4.50
280 1.00 3.50
281 Begin: Whilce Portacio cover&art; John Byrne scripts. Begin: new X-Men team (Archangel, Colossus, Iceman, Marvel Girl, and Storm). 4.00 11.00
281 (2ND) 2nd printing. .30 1.00
282 Cameo: Bishop. 5.00 14.00
282 (2ND) 2nd printing. .30 1.00
283 1st full app. Bishop. 4.00 12.00
284 Bishop. 1.25 4.00
285-286 1.00 3.00
287 Origin & join team: Bishop. 1.25 4.00
288 Bishop. 1.00 3.00
289-290 1.00 3.00
291-293 .75 2.00
294 Begin: X-Cutioner's Song. 1.00 3.00
295 1.00 3.00
296 End: X-Cutioner's Song. 1.00 3.00
297-299 .75 2.00
300 Holografix foil cover. Magneto. 1.50 5.00
301 1.00 3.00
302-303 .75 2.00
304 30th Anniversary issue. 1st Exodus. Wraparound cover w/ hologram. 1.75 6.00
305-306 .75 2.00
307 Bloodties part 4. .75 2.00
308-309 .75 2.00
310 With trading cards. 1.50 5.00
311 .75 2.00
312 Return: Yukio. .75 2.50
313 .75 2.50
314 .75 2.00
315 .75 2.50
316 Generation Next, part 1, lead-in to Generation X, foil-stamped cover. 1.25 4.50
316A Regular edition. .50 1.50
317 Prismatic foil-stamped cover. 1.25 4.50
317A Regular edition. .50 1.50
318 Deluxe edition. .75 2.25
318A Regular edition. .50 1.50
319 Deluxe edition. .75 2.25
319A Regular edition. .50 1.50
320 Deluxe edition. .75 2.25
320A Regular edition. .50 1.50
321 Deluxe edition (with card). .75 2.25
321A Regular edition (no card). .50 1.50
322-324 .50 1.95

X-MEN 2099

MARVEL (1993-CURRENT)

1 Foil-stamped cover. 1.25 4.00
2-3 .75 2.50
4-24 .75 2.00

X-MEN ADVENTURES

MARVEL (1992-1994)

1 1st: Morph. 1.75 6.00
2-5 1.25 4.00
6-10 1.00 3.00
11-12 .75 2.00
13 .50 1.50
14-15 .50 1.25

X-MEN ADVENTURES II

MARVEL (1994)

1 .75 2.50
2 .75 2.00
3-13 .50 1.75

X-MEN ADVENTURES III

MARVEL (1995-CURRENT)

1 .75 2.50
2-7 .50 1.50

X-MEN: ALPHA

MARVEL (1994-CURRENT)

1 Double size. 2.50 9.00
1 (GOLD) Gold edition. 16.00 50.00

X-MEN AND THE MICRONAUTS, THE

MARVEL (1984)

1-4 1.00 3.50

X-MEN ANNUAL

MARVEL (1970-CURRENT)

1 King-Size Special. Reprints X-Men #9, 11. (1970) 13.00 40.00
2 King-Size Special. Reprints X-Men #22, 23. (1971) 11.00 35.00
3 "A Fire In The Sky" (1980) 5.00 15.00
4 Joins: Kitty Pryde, Dr. Strange. (1980) 5.00 15.00
5 (1981). 4.00 12.00
6 Vs. Dracula. (1982) 4.00 12.00
7 (1983) 2.75 10.00
8 New Mutants. (1984) 2.75 10.00
9 Art: Art Adams. (1985) 4.00 12.00
10 Art: Art Adams. 1st: X-Babies. (1986) 4.00 12.00
11 1st: Horde. (1987) 1.50 5.50
12 Evolutionary War. (1988) 1.50 5.00
13 Atlantis Attacks. (1989) 1.50 5.50
14 Cover & art: Art Adams. 1st: Gambit (5 page cameo). (1990) 2.25 8.00
15 Origin retold. Wolverine story. (1991) 1.25 4.00
16 (1992) 1.00 3.00
17 1st: X-Cutioner. Polybagged with card. (1993) 1.00 3.25
18 (1994) .75 2.95

X-MEN ARCHIVES

MARVEL (1994)

1 Mini-series. .75 2.25
2-4 .75 2.25

X-MEN ARCHIVES: CAPTAIN BRITAIN

MARVEL (1995)

1 Reprints. .75 2.50
2-3 .75 2.95

X-MEN AT THE STATE FAIR

SEE UNCANNY X-MEN AT THE...

X-MEN CHRONICLES, THE

FANTACO (1981)

1 History of the X-Men. 2.75 10.00

X-MEN CHRONICLES

MARVEL (1995)

1-2 1.00 3.95

X-MEN CLASSIC

MARVEL (1990-1995)

46 Previous title: Classic X-Men. .50 1.50
47-73 .50 1.50
74-89 .50 1.25
90 Double size. .50 1.25
91-96 .50 1.25
97 Double size. .50 1.25
98-103 .50 1.25
104 .50 1.95
105-110 .50 1.50

X-MEN CLASSICS

MARVEL (1983-1984)

1-3 1.00 3.50

X-MEN: GOD LOVES, MAN KILLS

MARVEL (1994)

NO# 1.75 6.95

X-MEN: OMEGA

MARVEL (1995)

1 2.00 7.00
1 (GOLD) 14.00 45.00

X-MEN: PRIME

MARVEL (1995)

1 Chromium cover. 2.00 7.50

X-MEN RARITIES

MARVEL (1995)

1 Reprints. 1.50 5.95

X-MEN SPECIAL

SEE X-MEN ANNUAL #1 & 2

X-MEN SPECTACULAR

MARVEL (1994)

1 Reprints first Legion stories. .75 2.25
2-4 .75 2.25

X-MEN SPOTLIGHT ON STARJAMMERS

MARVEL (1990)

1-2 1.00 3.00

X-MEN: THE COMING OF BISHOP

MARVEL (1995)

TPB Reprints Bishop's origin. 4.00 12.95

X-MEN: THE EARLY YEARS

MARVEL (1994-1995)

1 Reprints. .50 1.50
2-16 .50 1.50
17 Double size. .75 2.50

X-MEN UNLIMITED

MARVEL (1993-1994)

1 2.00 7.00
2-3 1.75 6.00
4 1.50 5.00
5-7 1.25 4.00

X-MEN VS. DRACULA

MARVEL (1993)

1 Reprints X-Men annual #6. .50 1.75

X-MEN VS. THE AVENGERS

MARVEL (1987)

1 1.25 4.00
2-4 1.00 3.00

X-MEN/ALPHA FLIGHT

MARVEL (1985)

1 1.25 4.50
2 1.25 4.00

X-O MANOWAR

ACCLAIM/VALIANT (1992-CURRENT)

0 (GOLD) Gold edition. 2.25 8.00

X-MEN #142 (1ST SERIES)

X-MEN #268 (1ST SERIES)

X-MEN #319 (1ST SERIES)

X-MEN #41 (2ND SERIES)

X-O MANOWAR #11

X-O MANOWAR #14

YANKEE COMICS #2

YELLOW CLAW #4

0 Chromium double cover, prequel to regular series. 1.00 3.00
1 1st & Origin: Aric, 1st: Ken Clarkson, 1st: Spider Aliens. 2.50 9.00
2 Vs. Spider Aliens. 2.00 7.00
3 1st X-Caliber, Harada. 2.00 7.00
4 1st Jack Boniface (Shadowman). 2.25 8.00
5-6 1.50 5.00
7-8 1.25 4.00
9-11 1.00 3.00
12 Solar. 1.00 3.00
1/2 Wizard mail-away offer. 1.50 5.00
1/2A 5.00 15.00
13 .75 2.50
14-15 Turok. .75 2.50
15A Pink logo. 2.75 10.00
16-27 .75 2.25
28 Valiant Era II card. .75 2.25
29-50-X .75 2.25
TPB Polybagged with copy of X-O Database #1. 2.50 9.95
YEARBOOK 1 .75 2.95

XOMBI
DC (1994)
0 .75 2.00
1-13 .50 1.75
14-16 .75 2.50

X-TERMINATORS
MARVEL (1988-1989)
1 1.25 4.00
2-4 1.00 3.00

X-UNIVERSE
MARVEL (1995)
1 Age of Apocalypse. 1.25 4.50
2 1.00 3.50

X-VENTURE
VICTORY (1947)
1 Super-Heroes. 135.00 440.00
2 85.00 270.00

YAK YAK
DELL FOUR COLOR SERIES (1961-1962)
1186 Art: Jack Davis. 11.00 35.00
1348 Art: Jack Davis. 10.00 30.00

YANKEE COMICS
HARRY A. CHESLER (1941-1942)
1 Origin: The Echo, The Firebrand, and Yankee Doodle Jones. 155.00 500.00
2 95.00 310.00
3-4 70.00 220.00

YANKS IN BATTLE
QUALITY (1956)
1 10.00 30.00
2-4 7.00 20.00

YARDBIRDS, THE
ZIFF-DAVIS (1952)
1 16.00 50.00

YELLOW CLAW
MARVEL(ATLAS) (1956-1957)
1 Origin: Yellow Claw. 140.00 460.00
2 Art: Jack Kirby. 105.00 340.00
3 Art: Jack Kirby. 95.00 310.00
4 Art: Jack Kirby. 85.00 280.00

YELLOW KID
OUTCALT (1897)
1 1st comic book prototype. 5-cent cover price, comic book-like covers, all text inside. Rare. 1600.00 6000.00

YELLOW SUBMARINE
GOLD KEY (1969)
35000-902 Beatles movie tie-in. (2/69). Price is for issue with pull-out poster intact. Price is 1/2 without poster. 55.00 175.00

YELLOWJACKET COMICS
CHARLTON (1944-1946)
1 Origin: Yellowjacket (9/44). 85.00 270.00
2 50.00 160.00
3-9 35.00 110.00
10 Title changes to Jack In The Box Comics with #11. 35.00 110.00

YELLOWSTONE KELLY
DELL FOUR COLOR SERIES (1959)
1056 Movie photo cover. (10/59) 14.00 45.00

YOGI BEAR
DELL FOUR COLOR SERIES (1959-1962)
1067 TV tie-in. (12/59) 31.00 100.00
1104 "Goes To College" TV tie-in. (6/60) 19.00 60.00
1162 "Joins The Marines" TV tie-in. (4/61) 19.00 60.00
1271 "Birthday Party" TV tie-in. (11/61) 19.00 60.00
1349 "Visits The U.N." TV photo cover. (1/62) 26.00 85.00

YOGI BEAR
DELL/GOLD KEY (1961-1970)
4-9 11.00 35.00
10 Begin Gold Key publication. 10.00 30.00
11 80 Page Giant (1/63). 16.00 50.00
12 10.00 30.00
13 Double size. "Surprise Party!" 13.00 40.00
14-18 8.00 25.00
19-24 7.00 20.00
25-30 5.00 15.00
31-42 2.75 10.00

YOGI BEAR
MARVEL (1977-1979)
1-9 .30 1.00

YOGI BERRA BASEBALL HERO
FAWCETT (1951)
NO# Photo cover. 140.00 460.00

YOUNG ALLIES COMICS
MARVEL(TIMELY) (1941-1946)
1 1st & origin: The Young Allies. app: Captain America, Human Torch, Red Skull. Cover & art: Simon & Kirby. (Summer/41) 1600.00 6000.00
2 Cover: Simon & Kirby. (Winter/41) 400.00 1500.00
3 (Spring/42) 300.00 1100.00
4 (Summer/42) 300.00 1100.00
5 (Fall/42) 280.00 925.00
6 (1/43) 230.00 750.00
7 (4/43) 190.00 625.00
8 (7/43) 190.00 625.00
9 (Fall/43) 190.00 625.00
10 (12/43) 190.00 625.00
11 "The Spawn Of Death!" (3/44) 190.00 625.00
12 (Spring/44) 190.00 625.00
13 (Summer/44) 140.00 460.00
14 (Winter/44) 140.00 460.00
15 (Spring/45) 140.00 460.00
16 (Summer/45) 140.00 460.00
17 (Fall/45) 140.00 460.00
18 (Winter/45) 140.00 460.00
19 (Spring/46) 140.00 460.00
20 (10/46) 140.00 460.00

YOUNG ALL-STARS
DC (1987-1989)
1-31 .30 1.00

YOUNG BRIDES
PRIZE (1952-1956)
1 Art: Joe Simon & Jack Kirby. Photo cover. 31.00 100.00
2 Art: Joe Simon & Jack Kirby. Photo cover. 13.00 40.00
3-4 Art: Joe Simon & Jack Kirby. Photo cover. 10.00 30.00
5-7 Art: Joe Simon & Jack Kirby. 10.00 30.00
8 7.00 20.00
9-13 Art: Simon & Kirby. 10.00 30.00
14-25 7.00 20.00
26 All Simon & Kirby art. 13.00 40.00
27 7.00 20.00
28 Art: Simon & Kirby. 10.00 30.00
29-30 7.00 20.00

YOUNG EAGLE
CHARLTON (1956-1957)
3-5 2.75 10.00

YOUNG EAGLE
FAWCETT (1950-1952)
1 Photo covers on all issues. 16.00 50.00
2 10.00 30.00
3-10 7.00 20.00

YOUNG INDIANA JONES CHRONICLES, THE
DARK HORSE (1992-1993)
1-12 .75 2.50

YOUNG KING COLE
PREMIUM (1945-1948)
1 23.00 75.00
2 13.00 40.00
3-6 8.00 25.00
V2#1-V3#9 7.00 20.00

YOUNG LIFE
NEW AGE (1945)
1 10.00 30.00
2 Title changes to Teen Life with #3. 10.00 30.00

YOUNG LOVE
DC (1963-1977)
39 5.00 15.00
40-50 2.75 10.00
51-60 1.75 6.00
61-75 1.25 4.00
76-100 .75 2.00
101-126 .30 1.00

YOUNG LOVE
PRIZE (1949-1957)
1 Cover & art: Simon & Kirby. 65.00 200.00
2 Art: Simon & Kirby. 31.00 100.00
3 Art: Simon & Kirby. 23.00 75.00
4-6 8.00 25.00
7 Art: Simon & Kirby. 23.00 75.00
8-12 8.00 25.00
13 Cover & art: Simon & Kirby. 23.00 75.00
14 8.00 25.00
15-22 Cover & art: Simon & Kirby. 23.00 75.00
23-25 Art: Simon & Kirby. 16.00 50.00
26 7.00 20.00
27-31 Art: Simon & Kirby. 16.00 50.00
32-35 7.00 20.00
36 Art: Simon & Kirby. 16.00 50.00
37-42 7.00 20.00
43-50 5.00 15.00
51-60 2.75 10.00
61-73 1.75 6.00

YOUNG LOVE
PRIZE (1960-1963)
V3#5-V7#1 1.50 5.00

YOUNG LOVERS
CHARLTON (1956-1957)
16-17 2.75 10.00
18 Photo cover (Elvis Presley) and story. 95.00 300.00

YOUNG LUST (UNDERGROUND)
COMPANY & SONS (1970-1980)
1 7.00 20.00
2-4 2.75 10.00
5-6 1.50 5.00

YOUNG MARRIAGE
FAWCETT (1950)
1 Art: Bob Powell. Photo cover. 13.00 40.00

YOUNG MEN
MARVEL(ATLAS) (1950-1954)
4 Previous title: Cowboy Romances. 19.00 60.00
5-10 11.00 35.00
11-23 8.00 25.00
24 Origin retold: Captain America, Human Torch, & Sub-Mariner. (12/53) 220.00 700.00
25-28 Captain America, Human Torch, Sub-Mariner. 155.00 500.00

YOUNG ROMANCE
PRIZE (1947-1975)
1 Cover & art: Simon & Kirby. 65.00 200.00
2 Cover & art: Simon & Kirby. 40.00 125.00
3-12 Cover & art: Simon & Kirby. 31.00 100.00
13-36 Art: Simon & Kirby. 19.00 60.00
37-48 Art: Simon & Kirby. 16.00 50.00
49-51 7.00 20.00
52-71 Art: Simon & Kirby. 16.00 50.00
72-77 5.00 15.00
78-92 Art: Simon & Kirby. 16.00 50.00
93-94 2.75 10.00
95-97 Art: Simon & Kirby. 13.00 40.00
98 2.25 8.00
99 Art: Simon & Kirby. 13.00 40.00
100-101 2.25 8.00
102-103 Art: Simon & Kirby. 13.00 40.00
104-124 1.50 5.00
125-130 1.25 4.00
131-150 .75 2.00
151-208 .30 1.00

YOUNG ZEN
ENTITY (1993-1994)
1-3 .75 2.95

YOUNGBLOOD
IMAGE (1992-1993)
0 (GOLD) Gold foil cover. 2.75 10.00
0 Origin: Youngblood. With Image #0 coupon. 1.00 3.00
0A Coupon cut out. .30 1.00
1 With trading cards. 1.50 5.00

1 (2ND) 2nd printing. Gold border, without trading cards. ... .75 2.00
2 1st: ShadowHawk. 1st: Prophet. ... 1.50 5.00
3 ... 1.00 3.00
4 ... .75 2.00
5 Flip book with Brigade (mini) #4. ... .75 2.00
6-10 ... .75 2.00
ASHCAN 1 Limited (500). Signed. ... 2.75 10.00
ASHCAN 1A Limited (1000). Signed. ... 1.50 5.00
TPB Reprints issues 1-5 with additional material. ... 6.00 16.95

YOUNGBLOOD: BATTLE ZONE
IMAGE (1993-1994)
1-2 ... .75 2.50

YOUNGBLOOD: STRIKEFILE
IMAGE (1993)
1 1st: Glory ... .75 2.50
1 (GOLD) ... 1.50 5.00
2-11 ... .75 2.50
TPB Reprints issues 1-3. ... 4.00 12.95

YOUNGBLOOD: THE SILENT EDITION
IMAGE (1994)
1 Special edition of #1, without word balloons or sound effects. ... 4.00 12.95

YOUNGBLOOD: YEAR ONE
IMAGE (1994)
1-2 ... .75 2.50

YOUNGBLOOD YEARBOOK
IMAGE (1993)
1 ... .75 2.50

YOUR UNITED STATES
LLOYD JACQUET (1946)
NO# ... 25.00 80.00

YUMMY-FUR
VORTEX/DRAWN & QUARTERLY (1986-1994)
1 ... 8.00 25.00
2-14 ... 2.75 10.00
15-24 ... 1.50 5.00
25 Begin Drawn & Quarterly publication. 1.50 5.00
26-32 ... 1.00 3.00

Z-2 COMICS
HOLYOKE (1944-1945)
7 From the Holyoke One-Shot series. Reprints: Crash Comics 2. ... 16.00 50.00

ZAGO, JUNGLE PRINCE
FOX (1948-1949)
1 App: Blue Beetle. ... 70.00 230.00
2-3 ... 45.00 140.00
4 ... 35.00 110.00

ZANE GREY'S...
DELL FOUR COLOR SERIES (1948-1959)
197 "Spirit Of The Border" (9/48) ... 22.00 70.00
222 "West Of The Pecos" (3/49) ... 16.00 50.00
230 "Sunset Pass" (5/49) ... 16.00 50.00
236 "Heritage Of The Desert" (7/49) 16.00 50.00
246 "Thunder Mountain" (9/49) ... 11.00 35.00
255 "The Ranger" (11/49) ... 11.00 35.00
270 "Drift Fence" (3/50) ... 11.00 35.00
301 "The Mysterious Rider" (11/50) 11.00 35.00
314 "Ambush" (2/51) ... 11.00 35.00
333 "Wilderness Trek" (5/51) ... 11.00 35.00
346 "Hide-Out" (8/51) ... 11.00 35.00
357 "Comeback!" (11/51) ... 10.00 30.00
372 "Riders Of The Purple Sage" (2/52) 8.00 25.00
395 "Forlorn River" (5/52) ... 8.00 25.00
412 "Nevada" (8/52) ... 8.00 25.00
433 "Wildfire" (11/52) ... 8.00 25.00
449 "Tappan's Burro" (2/53) ... 8.00 25.00
467 "Desert Gold" (5/53) ... 8.00 25.00
484 "River Feud" (8/53) ... 8.00 25.00
511 "Outlaw Trail" (11/53) ... 8.00 25.00
532 "The Rustlers" (2/54) ... 8.00 25.00
555 "Range War" (4/54) ... 8.00 25.00
583 "The Lost Wagon Train". (9/54) 8.00 25.00
604 "Shadow On The Trail" (12/54) 8.00 25.00
616 "To The Last Man" (3/55) ... 8.00 25.00
632 "Fighting Caravans" (6/55) ... 8.00 25.00
996 "Nevada" (6/59) ... 8.00 25.00

ZANE GREY'S KING OF THE ROYAL MOUNTED
SEE KING OF THE ROYAL MOUNTED.

ZANE GREY'S STORIES
DELL (1955-1958)
27-39 ... 5.00 15.00

ZANY
CANDAR (1958-1959) MAGAZINE
1 Cover: Bill Everett. ... 11.00 35.00
2 ... 8.00 25.00
3 Cover: Bill Everett. ... 7.00 20.00
4 ... 7.00 20.00

ZAP (UNDERGROUND)
APEX/PRINT MINT/LAST GASP (1967-1980)
0 Art: Robert Crumb. Pages numbered in upper left-hand corner. 35 cent cover price. ... 125.00 400.00
0 (2ND) 2nd printing. 35 cent cover price. 25.00 80.00
0 (3RD) 3rd printing. 35 cent cover price (a diagonal scratch halfway down the drawing obscures some of Crumb's cross-hatching). ... 7.00 20.00
0 (4TH) 4th printing. 35 cent cover price (the cross-hatching has been corrected with thin lines). ... 2.75 10.00
0 (6TH) 6th printing. 50 cent cover price. 2.75 10.00
0 (7TH) 7th printing. 60 cent cover price. 2.75 10.00
0 (8TH) 8th printing. 75 cent cover price. 1.50 5.00
0 (9TH) 9th printing. $1.50 cover price. 1.50 5.00
1 Art: Robert Crumb in all issues. 25 cent cover price. 5000 copies printed. (11/67) ... 250.00 800.00
1 (2ND) 2nd printing. 35 cent cover price (states "Printed by Charles Plymell" on back cover). ... 65.00 200.00
1 (3RD) 3rd printing. 35 cent cover price (no mention of printer on back cover). ... 8.00 25.00
1 (4TH) 4th printing. 50 cent cover price. 2.75 10.00
1 (5TH) 5th printing. 60 cent cover price. 2.75 10.00
1 (6TH) 6th printing. 75 cent cover price. 2.75 10.00
1 (7TH) 7th printing. $1.50 cover price. 1.50 5.00
2 50 cent cover price. ... 8.00 25.00
2 (2ND) 2nd printing. ... 5.00 15.00
2 (3RD) 3rd printing. 75 cent cover price. 5.00 15.00
2 (4TH) 4th printing. $1.00 cover price. 1.50 5.00
3 50 cent cover price. ... 5.00 15.00
3 (2ND) 2nd printing. ... 1.50 5.00
3 (3RD) 3rd printing. 75 cent cover price. 1.50 5.00
3 (4TH) 4th printing. $1.00 cover price. 1.50 5.00
4 50 cent cover price. ... 5.00 15.00
4 (2ND) 2nd printing. Lighter cover stock. 1.50 5.00
4 (3RD) 3rd printing. 75 cent cover price. 1.50 5.00
4 (4TH) 4th printing. $1.00 cover price. 1.50 5.00
5 50 cent cover price. (5/70) ... 5.00 15.00
5 (2ND) 2nd printing. 75 cent cover price. 1.50 5.00
5 (3RD) 3rd printing. $1.00 cover price. 1.50 5.00
6 50 cent cover price. (1/73) ... 2.75 10.00
6 (2ND) 2nd printing. 75 cent cover price. 1.00 3.00
7 50 cent cover price. ... 2.75 10.00
7 (2ND) 2nd printing. 75 cent cover price. 1.00 3.00
7 (3RD) 3rd printing. $1.00 cover price. 1.00 3.00
8 75 cent cover price. (8/75) ... 1.50 5.00
8 (2ND) 2nd printing. $1.00 cover price. 1.00 3.00
9 75 cent cover price. (9/78) ... 1.50 5.00
9 (2ND) 2nd printing. $1.50 cover price. (1/80) ... 1.00 3.00

ZATANNA
DC (1993)
1-4 ... .50 1.95

ZATANNA SPECIAL
DC (1987)
1 ... .75 2.25

ZAZA THE MYSTIC
CHARLTON (1956)
10 Previous title: Charlie Chan. ... 19.00 60.00
11 Title changes to This Magazine Is Haunted with #12. ... 19.00 60.00

ZEGRA, JUNGLE EMPRESS
FOX (1948-1949)
2 Previous title: Tegra Jungle Empress. 80.00 250.00
3-5 ... 65.00 200.00

ZEN: ALTERNITY SAGA
ENTITY (1993)
0 Gold foil cover. ... 1.00 3.50
1-3 Gold foil logo. ... .75 2.95

ZEN, INTERGALACTIC NINJA
ARCHIE (1992)
1 "Defend The Earth" (pt.1). Both newsstand and direct market versions exist. ... .50 1.25
2 "Defend The Earth" (pt.2). ... .50 1.25
3 "Defend The Earth" (pt.3). ... .50 1.25

ZEN, INTERGALACTIC NINJA
ENTITY (1993-CURRENT)
0 Chromium cover. ... 1.00 3.50
0A Platinum hologram version. ... 5.00 15.00
1-4 ... .75 2.50

ZEN, INTERGALACTIC NINJA
STERN & COTE (1987-1993)
1-6 ... 1.00 3.00
V2#1 Reprint: Zen #1. ... 1.00 3.00
V2#2-V3#5 ... .75 2.00
ANNUAL 1 Earth Day. ... .75 2.95
SPECIAL 1 Christmas edition. ... .75 2.95

ZEN, INTERGALACTIC NINJA: MILESTONE
ENTITY (1994)
1 Reprint: Defend The Earth mini series. .75 2.95
2-3 ... .75 2.95

ZEN, INTERGALACTIC NINJA: STARQUEST
ENTITY (1994-CURRENT)
1 Gold foil cover. ... .75 2.95
2-4 ... .75 2.95

ZEN: NOVELLA
ETERNITY/EXPRESS (1994-1995)
1 Mistress Of Chaos. ... .75 2.95
2 Mercenary Blues. ... .75 2.95
3 Phaedra. ... .75 2.95
4 Scorpion Moon. ... .75 2.95
5 Immortal Combat. ... .75 2.95
6 Bubble Economy. ... .75 2.95
7 Zen City. ... .75 2.95
8 In A Blue Moon. ... .75 2.95

ZEN: THE HUNTED
ENTITY (1993-1994)
1 Silver foil logo, polybagged with card. .75 2.95
2-3 Silver foil logo. ... .75 2.95

ZEN: VIDEO WARRIOR
ENTITY (1994)
1 Summer Special. ... .75 2.95

ZERO HOUR: CRISIS IN TIME
DC (1994)
0 Part 5, ZERO HOUR concludes with the birth of a new universe; comes with time line and card. ... 1.00 3.50
1 Part 4. ... 1.00 3.00
2 Part 3. ... 1.00 3.00
3 Part 2. ... 1.00 3.00
4 Part 1. ... 1.00 3.00
TPB Reprints issues 0-4, and tie-ins from Showcase '94 issues 8-9. ... 2.50 9.95

ZERO PATROL
CONTINUITY (1984-1988)
1-8 ... .30 1.00

ZERO TOLERANCE
FIRST (1990-1991)
1-4 ... .75 2.25

ZIGGY PIG SILLY SEAL COMICS
MARVEL(TIMELY) (1944-1946)
1 ... 40.00 125.00
2 ... 20.00 65.00
3 ... 17.00 55.00
4-5 ... 16.00 50.00
6 ... 19.00 60.00

ZIP COMICS
MLJ (1940-1944)
1 Origin: Steel Sterling. ... 500.00 1800.00
2 ... 310.00 1000.00
3 ... 230.00 750.00
4-6 ... 190.00 625.00
7-9 ... 155.00 500.00
10-12 ... 125.00 400.00
13-17 ... 105.00 340.00
18 1st & begin: Wilbur. ... 130.00 430.00
19 ... 95.00 310.00
20 1st & origin: Black Jack. ... 155.00 500.00
21-26 ... 95.00 310.00
27 1st: Web. ... 155.00 500.00
28 Origin: Web. ... 155.00 500.00
29-30 ... 80.00 250.00
31-36 ... 55.00 180.00
37-47 ... 50.00 150.00

ZIP-JET
ST. JOHN (1953)
1 ... 85.00 270.00
2 "Assassin Of The Airlanes" ... 70.00 220.00

ZOO FUNNIES
CHARLTON (1945-1947)
1 (#101 on cover) ... 19.00 60.00
2 ... 10.00 30.00
3-14 ... 7.00 20.00
15 Title changes to Tim McCoy with #16. 7.00 20.00

ZOO FUNNIES
CHARLTON (1953-1955)
1 ... 10.00 30.00
2 ... 7.00 20.00

YOUNGBLOOD #1

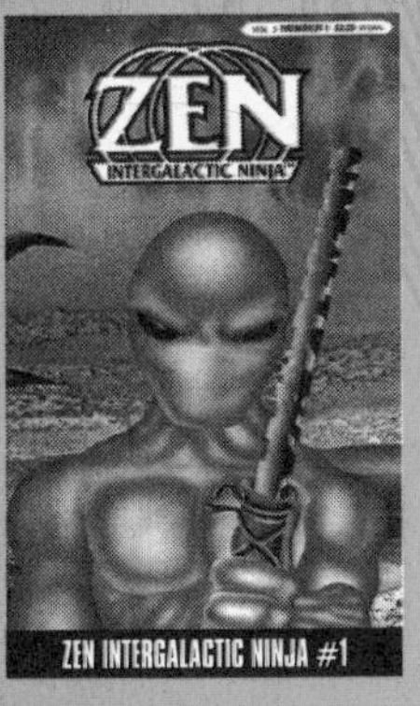

ZEN INTERGALACTIC NINJA #1

ZERO HOUR #4

ZIP COMICS #1

ZOO FUNNIES #2

ZOOT #9

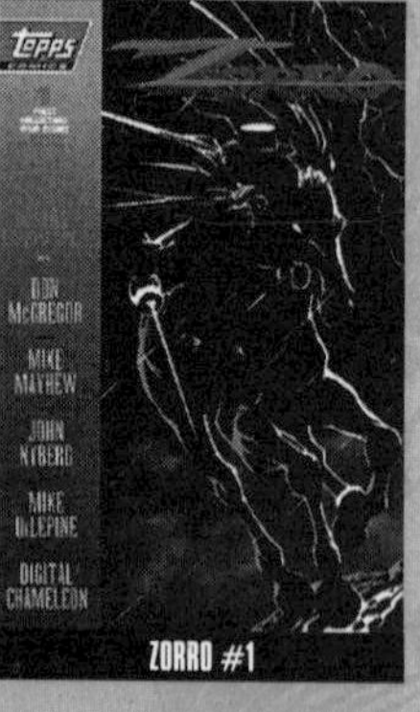

ZORRO #1

ZORRO #3

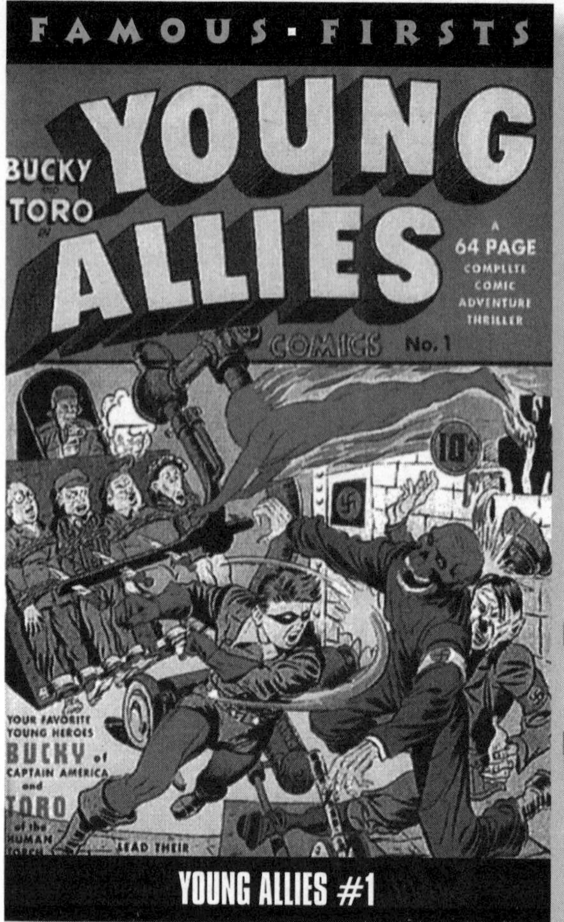

YOUNG ALLIES #1

The first of the popular "kid gang" books, this title featured Marvel's two major sidekicks, Cap's Bucky and the Human Torch's Toro, leading the kids in Cap's Sentinels of Liberty club.

3-7	5.00	15.00
8 Begin: Nyoka.	7.00	20.00
9-12	7.00	20.00
13 Title changes to Nyoka The Jungle Girl with #14.	7.00	20.00

ZOO FUNNIES
ECLIPSE (1984)

1	.30	1.00

ZOO PARADE
DELL FOUR COLOR SERIES (1955)

662 (11/55)	11.00	35.00

ZOOM COMICS
CARLTON (1945)

NO#	70.00	220.00

ZOOT
FOX (1946-1948)

NO#	28.00	90.00
2	22.00	70.00
3-6	15.00	48.00
7 1st & origin: Rulah. (6/47)	130.00	420.00
8-9	110.00	360.00
10-12	75.00	240.00
13 (2/48)	55.00	180.00
13A (4/48)	55.00	180.00
14 SOTI (3/48)	75.00	240.00
14A (5/48)	55.00	180.00
15	55.00	180.00
16 Title changes to Rulah Jungle Goddess with #17.	55.00	180.00

ZORRO
DELL (1959-1961)

8 TV photo covers on all issues.	16.00	50.00
9-15	16.00	50.00

ZORRO
DELL FOUR COLOR SERIES (1949-1959)

228 "The Mark Of..." (5/49)	55.00	175.00
425 "The Return Of..." (9/52)	40.00	120.00
497 "The Sword Of..." (9/53)	29.00	95.00
538 "The Mask Of..." (3/54)	31.00	100.00
574 "The Hand Of..." (8/54)	31.00	100.00
617 "The Quest Of..." (3/55)	31.00	100.00
732 "The Challenge Of..." (10/56)	28.00	90.00
882 Disney TV photo cover. (2/58)	40.00	125.00
920 "Ghost Of The Mission" Disney TV photo cover. (6/58)	31.00	100.00
933 "Garcia's Secret" Disney TV photo cover. (9/58)	31.00	100.00
960 "The Eagle's Brood" Disney TV photo cover. (12/58)	31.00	100.00
976 Disney TV photo cover. (3/59)	31.00	100.00
1003 "The Marauders Of Monterey" Disney TV photo cover. (6/59)	25.00	80.00
1037 "The Mystery Of The Spaniard's Secret" Disney TV photo cover (Annette Funicello). (9/59)	31.00	100.00

ZORRO
GOLD KEY (1966-1968)

1 TV photo covers on all issues.	10.00	30.00
2-9	7.00	20.00

ZORRO
MARVEL (1990-1991)

1 TV tie-in.	.30	1.00
2-12	.30	1.00

ZORRO
TOPPS (1993-CURRENT)

0	1.50	5.00
1 Cover: Frank Miller.	.75	2.50
2	1.25	4.00
3 1st: Lady Rawhide.	6.00	20.00
4 1st: Moonstalker.	.75	2.50
5	.75	2.50
6 Return: Lady Rawhide.	1.75	7.00
7 Lady Rawhide	1.50	6.00
8	.75	2.50
9-11	1.00	3.50

ZOT!
ECLIPSE (1984-1989)

1-36	.30	1.00

ZULU
DELL (1964)

12-950-410 Movie photo cover.	10.00	30.00

CONVENTION

CALENDAR

PACK THE PARTY VAN...TIME FOR A ROAD TRIP!

Thinking about planning that summer vacation? Why not plan it around this year's major comic conventions? Here is a list of what some of the major U.S. cities are hosting in 1996. And when you get there, please look us up. We here at *Wizard* would love to meet ya!

Motor City Comic Con
March 22-24, 1996
Novi Expo Center (Novi, Mich.)
(810) 350-2633

WonderCon
April 26-28, 1996
Oakland Convention Center (Oakland, Calif.)
(415) 731-1053

Dragon Con & Atlanta Comics Expo
June 19-23, 1996
Atlanta Hilton - Downtown
(404) 925-0115

Chicago Comic Con
June 21-23, 1996
Rosemont Convention Center
(708) 852-2514

San Diego Comic Con
July 2-7, 1996
San Diego Convention Center
(619) 544-9555

Gen Con
August 8-11, 1996
Milwaukee Convention Center
(414) 248-3625

There are, of course, hundreds of comic conventions from coast to coast each month. Check out our listings in monthly editions of *Wizard: The Guide to Comics* to get the scoop on what's going on near you.

a b c d e f g h i j k l m n o p q r s t u v w x y z

RESOURCE PAGE

HOW TO GET IN TOUCH WITH YOUR FAVORITE COMPANIES

COMIC BOOK PUBLISHERS

Aardvark-Vanaheim, Inc.
P.O. Box 1674 Station C
Kitchener, Ontario N2G 4R2
Canada

AC Comics
P.O. Box 521216
Longwood, FL 32752-1216

Acclaim Comics
275 7th Ave., 14th Floor
New York, NY 10001
[Valiant, Windjammer, Armada]

Adhesive Comics
101 West Sixth St., Suite 210
Austin, TX 78701

Alpha Productions
P.O. Box 1172
Rockland, ME 04841

Antarctic Press
7272 Wurzbach #204
San Antonio, TX 78240

Archie Comics
325 Fayette Ave.
Mamaroneck, NY 10543

Aria Press
12638-28 Jefferson Ave.
Suite 173
Newport News, VA 23602

Beanworld Press/Image
P.O. Box 25468
Anaheim, CA 92825

BIG Entertainment [Tekno • Comix]
2255 Glades Rd.
Suite 237 West
Boca Raton, FL 33431-7383

Blackout Comics
5 Highway 33
Freehold, NJ 07728

Blue Comet Press
1708 Magnolia Ave.
Manhattan Beach, CA 90266

Boneyard Press
17175 Simends St.
Granada Hills, CA 91344

Bongo Comics
1999 Avenue of the Stars
15th Floor
Los Angeles, CA 90067

Broadway Comics
736 W. Ingomar
Box 741
Ingomar, PA 15127

Caliber Comics
11918 Farmington Rd.
Livonia, MI 48150

Cartoon Books/Image
P.O. Box 16973
Columbus, OH 43216

Chaos! Comics
7349 Via Paso Del Sur
515-208
Scottsdale, AZ 85258

Claypool Comics
647 Grand Ave.
Leonia, NJ 07605

Comico
119 West Hubbard St., 4th Floor
Chicago, IL 60610

Continuity Comics
62 West 45th St.
New York, NY 10036

Coppervale Press
(formerly TALIESiN PRESS)
P.O. Box 40904
Mesa, AZ 85274-0904

Crusade Entertainment
65-27 Alderton St.
Rego Park, NY 11374

Cry for Dawn
360-A West Merrick Rd.
Suite #350
Valley Stream, NY 11580

DC Comics [including Paradox Press, Vertigo, MAD Magazine]
1700 Broadway
New York, NY 10019

Dark Horse Comics
10956 S.E. Main St.
Milwaukie, OR 97222

Double Diamond
P.O. Box 28157
Austin, TX 78755-2157

Drawn & Quarterly
5550 Jeanne Mance, Suite 16
Montreal, Quebec H2V 4K6
Canada

El Capitán Books
P.O. Box 487
Toms River, NJ 08754

Eternal Studios
15235 Rainhollow
Houston, TX 77070

Event Comics
3620 N. Lincoln Ave.
Chicago, IL 60613

Exhibit A Press
4657 Cajon Way
San Diego, CA 92115

Express Publications [Parody Press, Entity]
P.O. Box 1546
Chesapeake, VA 23327-1546

Extreme Studios/Image [Maximum Press]
2400 E. Katella
Suite 1040
Anaheim, CA 92806

Fantagraphics Books
7563 Lake City Way NE
Seattle, WA 98115

Fireman Press
2430 N. Humboldt
Milwaukee, WI 53212

Fleetway/Quality
P.O. Box 4569
Toms River, NJ 08754

Gladstone/Hamilton
P.O. Box 2079
Prescott, AZ 86302

Harris Comics
1115 Broadway, 8th Floor
New York, NY 10010

High Impact Studios
7100 Southwest 47th St.
Miami, FL 33155

Highbrow/Image
P.O. Box 20760
Oakland, CA 94620

Horse Press
P.O. Box 3112
Columbus, OH 43210-0112

Image Comics
P.O. Box 25468
Anaheim, CA 92825

King Hell Press
P.O. Box 1371
West Townshend, VT 05359

Kitchen Sink Press
320 Riverside Dr.
Northampton, MA 01060

Lightning Comics
31155 Portside Ste. #7109
Novi, MI 48377

London Night Studios
3906 Shakespeare Dr.
Hickory, NC 28601

Malibu Comics
26707 Agoura Rd.
Calabasas, CA 91302

Mars Media Group
7938 West 164th Place
Tinley Park, IL 60477

Marvel Entertainment Group
387 Park Ave. South
New York, NY 10016

Milestone Media
119 West 23rd St., Suite 406
New York, NY 10011

Mirage Studios
15 Market St.
Northampton, MA 01060

Motown Animation
5750 Wilshire Blvd. Suite 300
Los Angeles, CA 90036

MU Press
5014-D Roosevelt Way NE
Seattle, WA 98105

Mulehide Graphics
P.O. Box 5844
Bellingham, WA 98227-5844

Nightwolf Graphics
P.O. Box 5982
San Antonio, TX 76902

Patchwork Press
834 Hope St.
Providence, RI 02906

POP Entertainment
587 Post Rd. East
Suite 539
Westport, CT 06880

Rebel Studios
4716 Judy Ct.
Sacramento, CA 95841

Rival Productions
95 Robert Jemison Rd.
Birmingham, AL 35209

Sanctuary Press
P.O. Box 4144
Highland Park, NJ 08903

Shadowline, Ink/Image [Eyescream Graphics]
31878 Val Obispo
#118-312
San Juan Capistrano, CA 92675

Sirius Entertainment Inc.
P.O. Box 128
Stanhope, NJ 07874

Slave Labor Graphics
979 S. Bascom Ave.
San Jose, CA 95128

Spiderbaby Grafix
P.O. Box 335
Marlboro, VT 05344

Taliesin Press
(See COPPERVALE PRESS)

TMP Inc./Image
(Same as IMAGE COMICS)

Top Cow Productions/Image
1223 Wilshire Blvd.
#496
Santa Monica, CA 90401

Topps Comics [& Cards]
One Whitehall St.
New York, NY 10004

Viz Communications
P.O. Box 77010
San Francisco, CA 94107

Warp Graphics
43 Haight Ave.
Poughkeepsie, NY 12603

WildStorm Productions/Image [& Cards]
HOMAGE STUDIOS
7960 Ivanhoe Ave.
Suite #438
La Jolla, CA 93027

TRADING CARD MANUFACTURERS

Cardz
2505 N. Highway 360, 7th Fl
Grand Prairie, TX 75050

Collect-A-Card
P.O. Box 27129
Greenville, SC 29616

Collector's Edge
P.O. Box 9010
Denver, CO 80209

Comic Images
280 Midland Ave.
Saddle Brook, NJ 07663

Fleer Entertainment Group
1120 Route 73, Suite 300
Mt. Laurel, NJ 08054

Friedlander Publishing Group
2539 Washington Rd.
Bldg. 1000
Pittsburgh, PA 15241

SkyBox International I
P.O. Box 3009
Durham, NC 27702-3009

Upper Deck
5909 Sea Otter Place
Carlsbad, CA 92008

ORGANIZATIONS

Friends of Lulu
4657 Cajon Way
San Diego, CA 92115

Comic Book Legal Defense Fund
P.O. Box 693
Northhampton, MA 01060

If you are a publisher or manufacturer and would like your information listed in this section in *Wizard: The Guide Comics*, please send your company name and sample copies along with your compl address with contact name, phone number, fax number on-line address (if available) to:

Resource Page
c/o Wizard Press
151 Wells Ave.
Congers, NY 10920